SCRIBNER LIBRARY OF DAILY LIFE

ENCYCLOPEDIA OF CLOTHING AND FASHION

EDITORIAL BOARD

SCRIBNER LIBRARY OF DAILY LIFE

ENCYCLOPEDIA OF CLOTHING AND FASHION

VOLUME 1:
Academic Dress to Eyeglasses

Valerie Steele, Editor in Chief

CHARLES SCRIBNER'S SONS
An imprint of Thomson Gale, a part of The Thomson Corporation

For Reference

Not to be taken from this room

THOMSON
★
GALE

Detroit • New York • San Francisco • San Diego • New Haven, Conn. • Waterville, Maine • London • Munich

Encyclopedia of Clothing and Fashion
Valerie Steele, Editor in Chief

© 2005 Thomson Gale, a part of the Thomson Corporation.

Thomson and Star Logo are trademarks and Gale and Charles Scribner's Sons are registered trademarks used herein under license.

For more information, contact
Thomson Gale
27500 Drake Rd.
Farmington Hills, MI 48331-3535
Or you can visit our Internet site at
http://www.gale.com

For permission to use material from this product, submit your request via Web at http://www.gale-edit.com/permissions, or you may download our Permissions Request form and submit your request by fax or mail to:

Permissions Department
Thomson Gale
27500 Drake Road
Farmington Hills, MI 48331-3535
Permissions Hotline:
248-699-8006 or 800-877-4253 ext. 8006
Fax: 248-699-8074 or 800-762-4058

While every effort has been made to ensure the reliability of the information presented in this publication, Thomson Gale does not guarantee the accuracy of the data contained herein. Thomson Gale accepts no payment for listing; and inclusion in the publication of any organization, agency, institution, publication, service, or individual does not imply endorsement of the editors or publisher. Errors brought to the attention of the publisher and verified to the satisfaction of the publisher will be corrected in future editions.

Library of Congress Cataloging-in-Publication Data

Encyclopedia of clothing and fashion / Valerie Steele, editor in chief.
   p. cm. — (Scribner library of daily life)
Includes bibliographical references and index.
  ISBN 0-684-31394-4 (set: hardcover: alk. paper) — ISBN 0-684-31395-2 (v. 1) —
ISBN 0-684-31396-0 (v. 2) — ISBN 0-684-31397-9 (v. 3) — ISBN 0-684-31451-7 (e-book)
  1. Clothing and dress—History—Encyclopedias. I. Steele, Valerie II. Series.
GT507.E53 2005
391'.003—dc22
                                               2004010098

This title is also available as an e-book.
ISBN 0-684-31451-7
Contact your Thomson Gale Sales representative for ordering information.

Printed in the United States of America
10 9 8 7 6 5 4 3 2 1

EDITORIAL AND PRODUCTION STAFF

Project Editor
Nicole Watkins

Editorial Support
Dana Barnes   Sofia Begg   Deirdre Blanchfield   Mark Drouillard   Lynn Koch   Jeffrey Lehman
Nancy Matuszak   Mark Mikula   Kate Millson   Jenai Mynatt   Jamie Noce   Christine Slovey
Rachel Widawsky

Copy Editors
Richard Rothschild, Printmatters, Inc.   Neil Schlager, Schlager Group, Inc.

Proofreaders
Lisa Dixon   Margaret Haerens   Carol Holmes   Allison Leopold   Melodie Monahan   Anna Nesbitt
Eleanor Stanford   Shanna Weagle

Caption Writers
Sofia Begg   Andrew Claps   Shannon Kelly   Lynn Koch   Kimberly A. McCloud   John F. McCoy

Indexer
Laurie Androit

Design
Pamela A. E. Galbreath

Imaging
Dean Dauphinais   Randy Bassett   Leitha Etheridge-Sims   Lezlie Light   Michael Logusz   Robyn Young

Permissions
Margaret Abendroth   Ann Taylor

Compositor
GGS Information Services, York, Pennsylvania

Manufacturing
Wendy Blurton

Development Editor
Sarah Turner

Senior Development Editor
Nathalie Duval

Editorial Director
John Fitzpatrick

Publisher
Frank Menchaca

v

TABLE OF CONTENTS

PREFACE

The Encyclopedia of Clothing and Fashion is the product of a new, multidisciplinary field of inquiry and an extraordinary international collaboration. The emerging field of fashion studies, sometimes known as the "new" fashion history, differs significantly from traditional dress history, which tended to focus on the stylistic analysis of elite fashions. By contrast, contemporary fashion studies asks new questions, approaches a much wider range of topics, and draws on the expertise of scholars across the disciplines. Whereas traditional fashion reference books tend to be limited to an alphabetical survey of individual designers, this encyclopedia seeks to provide critical insights into the history and contemporary experience of clothing and fashion. By identifying the world's preeminent authorities, and by approaching the subject with a global focus and an interdisciplinary perspective, the editorial board of *The Encyclopedia of Clothing and Fashion* aims to provide the interested reader with an authoritative introduction to the wide range of issues that define the field. These issues include Eurocentrism vs. multiculturalism; gender and sexual identity; the relationship between fashion and other cultural manifestations, such as music; theories of fashion; clothing and material culture; and the fashion system, encompassing the design, manufacture, marketing, and representation of fashion. The editors of the encyclopedia, whose expertise spans a wide range of disciplines, subject matter, and geographical areas, have enlisted over 325 authors in an international survey of clothing, fashion, and related subjects from prehistoric times to the present.

The Encyclopedia of Clothing and Fashion contains 640 essays ranging from specific topics such as "African Textiles" and "Zoot Suit" to conceptual articles such as "Globalization" and "Music and Fashion," the latter cross-referenced to related entries such as "Hip-Hop Fashion." Naturally, we have tried to include all of the topics that readers would expect to find, including essays on specific fashion designers: Christian Dior, Coco Chanel, Yves St. Laurent, and dozens more. But these essays are neither hagiographies of great "artists" nor potted biographies of successful businesspeople. Of the hundreds of possible candidates for inclusion, we have concentrated on those who made a lasting contribution to the arts of fashion and to fashion culture; each designer's work is not only described in detail but also analyzed with reference to its social and cultural context. Readers interested in, say, Dior can also find related essays on topics such as the "New Look" and "Paris Fashion." Of course, fashion is a part of most people's lives, not only because they wear clothes, but also because they constantly consume images of fashion. This encyclopedia addresses the subject of fashion across the media, with essays on "Fashion Photography" (and on individual photographers such as Richard Avedon, Guy Bourdin, and Helmut Newton), "Caricature and Fashion," and "Film and Fashion." The encyclopedia also includes unexpected topics, such as "Cross-dressing," "Footbinding," and "Supermodels." There is even an essay on "The Future of Fashion." Because the production and marketing of textiles, clothing, and accessories is an integral part of the fashion system, the encyclopedia includes a wide range of essays on such topics as "Techno-textiles," "Sweatshops," "Fashion Magazines," and "Department Stores."

Typically, fashion refers to the phenomenon of a regular pattern of change in the prevailing mode of dress. Thus, for example, it could be said that miniskirts were in fashion during the 1960s. Most writers assumed that there existed a vast difference between modern Western fashion and traditional non-Western "costume." (For detailed analyses of "fashion" and other closely related terms, and a discussion of the important distinctions among them, please refer to the individual essays on "Fashion" and on "Clothing, Costume, and Dress.") Traditionally, most publications on fashion have focused almost exclusively on couture or designer fashions worn by elite Western women during the past 200 years. The clothing, adornment, and bodily practices of men, subcultural groups, working-class people, and non-Western and/or premodern peoples tended to be regarded as existing outside the realm of fashion; such topics were treated by scholars, if at all, as subfields of sociology, anthropology, folk arts, or decorative arts. This encyclopedia takes a very different approach. There are, for example, numerous entries on the clothing fashions of different historical periods and geographical areas. Fashion, in these pages, is not treated solely as a phenomenon of the modern Western world; full recognition is given to such fashion-oriented cultures as Tang dynasty China and Heian period Japan. (See, for example, the entries on "China, History of Dress," "Japanese Traditional Dress and Adornment," and "Japanese Fashion.") Survey essays in those fields are complemented by more specific topical entries ("Kimono"; "Qipao"), just as Phyllis Tortora's magisterial survey of "Europe and America, History of Dress (400–1900 C.E.)" sets the stage for numerous topical entries for the world of Western dress. And as Parminder Bhachu's essay on "Salwar-Kameez" demonstrates, the categories of "Western" and "non-Western," like those of "traditional" and "modern" dress, are highly permeable; similarly, disciplinary boundaries between history, sociology, anthropology, material culture, and other academic fields are transcended in the new field of fashion studies. It has been our explicit aim in this encyclopedia to create a work that is historical, cross-cultural, and multicultural in approach, and that will facilitate dichronic and comparative research.

The editorial team spent considerable time and effort identifying significant topics and commissioning articles from scholars who are among the world's leading authorities in their fields. Dorothy Ko, for example, is unquestionably the world's greatest expert on footbinding. A respected scholar of Chinese women's history, Professor Ko takes an unexpected, yet thoroughly documented, view of this 1,000-year practice. Readers of her essay may want to explore further by reading her book *Every Step a Lotus* (2001). Elizabeth Barber, author of our essay on "Prehistoric Clothing," is famous as the author of *Women's Work: The First 20,000 Years* (1994). Elizabeth Anne Coleman, whose 1982 exhibition *The Genius of Charles James* at the Brooklyn Museum was one of the first museum exhibitions to treat fashionable dresses unambiguously as works of art, has contributed a deeply insightful survey of James's work for this encyclopedia; her catalogue of that exhibition is *the* authoritative book on the subject. The list of highlights could go on and on. Walter Karcheski Jr., chief curator of the Frasier Historical Arms Foundation and a world-renowned historian of armor, has contributed an exemplary essay on armor with particular attention to its relationship with clothing. The essay on "Jewish Costume" by Orpa Slapak and Esther Juhasz of the Technical University of Israel is both wide-ranging and deeply learned. One of the greatest pleasures of being Editor-in-Chief of this book has been the opportunity to read hundreds of lucid and authoritative essays by a stellar team of expert contributors.

Since the nineteenth century there have been numerous descriptive and illustrated histories of dress, including classic works such as Auguste Racinet's six-volume *Le Costume Historique* (1888), Octave Uzanne's *Les Modes de Paris* (1898), and Elizabeth McClellan's *Historic Dress of America* (1906). There were also pioneering attempts to interpret the cultural significance of fashion, such as Thorstein Veblen's *Theory of the Leisure Class* (1899), George Simmel's *Philosophie der Mode* (1905), and J.C. Flügel's *The Psychology of Clothes* (1930). (The history of the study of fashion is also described and analyzed in this encyclopedia; see the essays on "Historical Studies of Fashion" and "Theories of Fashion," as well as individual essays on many of the most important fashion theorists from "Jean Baudrillard" and "Walter Benjamin" to "George Simmel" and "Thorstein Veblen.")

Among the most popular fashion histories published in the mid-twentieth century were those by James Laver, C. Willett Cunnington, and François Boucher, who amassed a wealth of information and developed a detailed chronology of styles, although Laver's and Cunnington's attempts to interpret these styles, often in terms of women's sexual psychology, were seriously flawed. More useful in the long run were detailed studies based on the interpretation of artifacts, often carried out by curators or collectors such as Doris Langley Moore. Their work laid an essential foundation for further advances in the study of clothing and fashion. There remains a division between object-oriented researchers (often curators) and university-based fashion theorists (some of whom lack detailed knowledge about the history and construction of dress). As with maritime and military history, dress history has become increasingly concerned with larger issues of social and cultural significance; as the field has moved on, some scholars have remained trapped in older, antiquarian approaches to the subject. Conversely, until very recently few scholars outside the narrow confines of costume history showed any interest in clothing as a subject of scholarly enquiry, probably in part because of the long association of fashion with "femininity" and "frivolity." Certainly, few academics thought of fashion as a subject to be taken seriously. (For example, scholarly studies of history very seldom include index entries for "clothing," "dress," "fashion," and related items.) The basic fact that virtually all humans wear clothes on a daily basis was perhaps too obvious to be noticed; it faded into the background of ordinary behavior.

In recent years, however, the study of fashion has been revolutionized, as scholars from other disciplines began exploring the intersections between dress, body, and the cultural construction of identity. Awareness began to spread in the academic world that clothing is not only a part of daily life, but that the ways people choose, acquire, wear, and vary their dress can say a great deal about such issues as class, gender, sexual preference, ethnicity, group identity and behavior, and aesthetics. Cultural, social, and economic historians, art historians open to new methodologies, anthropologists, semioticians, philosophers, students of material culture and design history, and scholars informed by feminist theory, critical theory, cultural studies, and studies in gender and sexuality all showed increasing interest in the hitherto despised subject of fashion. Pioneering works include Ellen Moers' *The Dandy* (1960), Anne Hollander's *Seeing Through Clothes* (1978), Dick Hebdige's *Subculture: The Meaning of Style* (1979), Philippe Perrot's *Les Dessus et les dessous de la bourgeoisie* (1981), Elizabeth Wilson's *Adorned in Dreams* (1985), my own first two books *Fashion and Eroticism* (1985) and *Paris Fashion* (1988), Rozsika Parker's *The Subversive Stitch* (1989), Daniel Roche's *La Culture des apparences* (1989), and Caroline Evans's and Minna Thornton's *Women and Fashion* (1989). By the 1990s, the field was rapidly expanding.

In 1997, when I founded *Fashion Theory: The Journal of Dress, Body & Culture*, the journal took as its starting point a definition of "fashion" as "the cultural construction of the embodied identity." By that definition, the term fashion embraced all forms of self-fashioning—from street styles like punk and hip-hop to body alterations such as tattooing and piercing. In many ways, this encyclopedia represents the flowering of a new generation of fashion scholars and curators, many of whom have published in *Fashion Theory*. Among them are Rebecca Arnold, Djurdja Bartlett, Christopher Breward, Caroline Evans, Amy de la Haye, Peter McNeil, Alexandra Palmer, and Claire Wilcox, to name only a few. Yet those wishing to study fashion still confront problems with professional training, since few universities offer advanced degrees in the subject. Nevertheless, the new approach to fashion studies has had a real and positive impact, not only in academe but in the museum world as well.

Just as the history of fashion was becoming richer and more theoretically sophisticated in the 1980s and 1990s, so also the exhibition of fashion in museums was moving away from static antiquarian displays to theatrical presentations of innovative themes. As fashion exhibitions proliferated, a much wider public began to take fashion seriously as a cultural phenomenon. The recent revolution in the study and display of fashion has contributed to the richness and depth of this encyclopedia and will also, I believe, make it a work that is interesting and useful to a very large and diverse readership. It will appeal, of course, to professionals and students in fashion design, museum studies, theatrical costume, textile arts, and other strongly clothing-related fields; but I hope it will also be extensively used by "mainstream" historians, anthropologists, literary scholars, journalists, and many others. Because all people wear clothes, there is almost no field of enquiry into human affairs that cannot be enriched by a consideration of clothing and fashion; I hope that this encyclopedia, the first of its kind, will assist its readers in making use of that insight.

I would like to thank the members of my editorial board—Associate Editors Christopher Breward, Joanne Eicher, and John Major, and Consulting Editor for Textiles Phyllis Tortora, for their inestimable contributions to this project. They suggested topics for entries, used their extensive professional networks to help me recruit potential authors, chased tardy authors when necessary, read and gave expert critical opinions on draft essays, and themselves each wrote several essays in their own areas of expertise. Throughout the process of creating this encyclopedia they were diligent, cheerful, supportive, and always ready to help. This book would hardly have been possible without their participation. My thanks also go to the professional staff of Charles Scribner's Sons, particularly Senior Development Editor Nathalie Duval, Development Editor Sarah Turner, and Project Editor Nicole Watkins. Their professionalism, hard work, and good humor were invaluable and very much appreciated by me, my Editorial Board colleagues, and the hundreds of contributors who participated in this great collaborative project. Finally, I would like to thank each of the hundreds of professionals who contributed essays to this encyclopedia and thus made it possible to present to the public this reference work of innovative scope and enduring worth.

Valerie Steele
New York, October 2004

SCRIBNER LIBRARY OF DAILY LIFE

ENCYCLOPEDIA OF CLOTHING AND FASHION

ACADEMIC DRESS Academic dress is the formal attire worn by students and officials at a commencement or graduation ceremony. The most common styles emulate the everyday clothing worn by scholars at the first universities in the eleventh and twelfth centuries. Typically, this included a flowing gown, a hood or cape, and some sort of head wear; the contemporary form of this ensemble depends on the rules dictated by the institution with which the student or official is associated.

Origin and History
The ancient universities were established in Italy and France in the late eleventh and early twelfth centuries, with the University of Oxford following in circa 1115 and Cambridge in circa 1209. It was these two English schools that set the tradition for academic dress by establishing strict decrees for their students and officials; the subsequent influence of the British Empire spread this tradition to many parts of the world.

Historically, schools of higher learning were referred to as *stadium generale* or *universitas*; titles conferred by the Pope of the day, with the latter being the higher honor. This early association with religion can still be seen in the similarities between academic dress and church robes. However, the early schools were not religious orders as a rule, but rather scholastic guilds made up of students and teachers organized around a cathedral or monastery. Not necessarily priests, the scholars wore clothes that were a sober reflection of lay fashions. In this respect, it was the degree that signified the scholar's full membership in the learned corporation, not the robe.

In medieval times the term "bachelor" was used to describe the assistant of a small landowner; the apprentice as opposed to the master who was already skilled, hence the academic use of the term "master" as well. Both of these titles were in widespread use in the universities during the thirteenth century. As such, there was a structure within these institutions related specifically to the degree of knowledge obtained by the scholar. This hierarchy, along with the medieval style of clothing, became the basis of academic dress.

The Cap and Gown
Medieval dress consisted of a flowing gown or *cappa clausa*, with a cape or cloak draped over the top. This often had a cowl-like appendage that could be pulled over the head, much like a hooded cape or *capitium*. By the second half of the fifteenth century, the fashion had progressed toward an open gown, said to be an expression of the new acceptance of academic learning and the arts. From 1490 onward this gown became standard academic dress, with the hooded cape becoming more ornamental than practical. Most commonly, bachelors and masters scholars wore black gowns made of "princes stuff" or "crape," with the senior man's garment having wider sleeves to allow for movement while teaching. The dress hood took the form of a drooping cape, lined with silk or fur to denote the scholar's faculty or social status. For example, in 1432 Oxford forbade the use of miniver for anyone except Masters of the Arts and those of great wealth or noble birth. Variations in sleeve style and lining continued to mirror fashionable dress, and by the sixteenth century academics followed professionals and the clergy in the wearing of caps.

It is difficult to pinpoint the origins of the academic cap, but it is thought to have evolved as a variation on the ecclesiastic *pileus* cap and the medieval head scarf. Most contemporary graduates wear the trencher form of the *pileus quadratus*—or the Oxford mortarboard. This consists of a small skullcap, shaped to fit the head, and a flat, square top, adorned with a silk tassel. This form of headwear became popular with the clergy after the Restoration, when it was thought that emphasizing "squareness" denoted greater dedication. However, the modern academic form was not popularized until the eighteenth century, when wood or card was used to stiffen the square. Some philosophical doctors or secular doctors may wear a variation of the Tudor Bonnet, a softer, fuller hat, or if of Scottish origin, the John Knox cap.

Contemporary Academic Dress
Most contemporary graduates wear a variation of the Oxford or Cambridge bachelor of arts gown. The Cambridge gown is knee-length, "princes stuff" and has pointed, open sleeves: the seam on the forearm is unsewn to the cuff, allowing a generous hole for the arm to pass through. The hood is partly lined with white fur or silk that is colored to denote the degree of the wearer. The sleeveless Oxford "commoners" gown sits a little below

1

French director Claude Autant Lara in academic dress. Flowing gowns and robes have been a major part of formal academic attire since medieval times. © ROBERT PATRICK/CORBIS SYGMA. REPRODUCED BY PERMISSION.

the knee and is expected to be worn with lay clothes that conform to a strict code. The lining of the hood is again appropriate to status. Hugh Smith's *Academic Dress and Insignia of the World* (1970) provides a thorough reference for those interested in all dress variations.

In the United States most universities accept the Inter-Collegiate Code (1895) of academic dress, a variation on the Cambridge style, but with an extensive system of color coding that denotes both the degree and the university. In many other countries students do not wear any academic dress: in Germany, it is seen as a sign of respect for the teachings of Martin Luther; in the former Soviet Union, students receive medallions; in Finland, doctors don swords for their commencement. And in many more countries, adaptations have been made to the English model, with Native Americans adding traditional jewelry and head wear, New Zealand Maoris wearing feathered capes, and Australian Aborigines adopting red, yellow, and black capes. Certainly, the fact that academic dress pays homage to establishment and tradition makes it the perfect dress for subversion.

Dress in American High Schools
The use of the cap and gown in American high schools originated in 1911 as a means of providing an economical and egalitarian code of dress. American educators joined with the academic dress companies to design an official ensemble for the high school graduate. It was gray, with long, pointed sleeves and the Oxford mortarboard cap. One of those who pushed for such dress in schools was the principal of Englewood High, Chicago, James Armstrong. He believed that the adoption of academic dress would ease the burden on parents to provide fashionable and expensive graduation outfits. By the early 2000s, traditional gray had been replaced by the official colors of the particular school, with religious or private girls' schools opting for white, grammar schools for maroon. Across America the cap and gown has been adopted by many institutions, with even nursery schools conferring honors on their infant graduates. This practice has not been widely emulated beyond the United States; however, some schools in Australia and Asia have adopted the practice.

As a means of historical record, academic dress encapsulates medieval fashion, preserving its character and form for what is an important modern occasion, both to the graduates and to those who have carried them through their time as a scholar. Hence, this form of dress is both steeped in tradition and very distinct from everyday clothes—such contrast clearly conveys significant achievement.

See also **Uniforms, School.**

BIBLIOGRAPHY

Goff, Philip. *University of London Academic Dress.* London: University of London, 1999.

Smith, Hugh. *Academic Dress and Insignia of the World.* 3 vols. Cape Town, South Africa: Balkema, 1970.

Walters, Helen. *The Story of Caps and Gowns.* Chicago and New York: E. R. Moore Publishing Company, 1939.

Internet Resources

Cox, Noel. "Academic Dress in New Zealand." Auckland: Private Monograph. Available from <http://www.geocities.com/noelcox/Introduction.htm>.

Joanne McCallum

ACETATE. *See* **Rayon.**

ACRYLIC AND MODACRYLIC FIBERS Acrylic and modacrylic fibers are produced from acrylonitrile, a petrochemical. The U.S. Federal Trade Commission defines fibers of 85 percent or more acrylonitrile units as acrylic fibers: for modacrylics the figure is 35–85 percent. Early fibers were based on 100 percent acrylonitrile, but more successful versions were produced by the inclusion of up to 15 percent of other chemical units that improved the ability of the resulting fiber to absorb dyes. In the 1950s, a golden age of new synthetic fibers, acrylic fibers became well known under trade names such as Orlon, Acrilan, Zefran, Creslan, and Courtelle: modacrylics included Dynel, Teklan, and Verel.

The variability of chemical composition, together with differences in fiber production methods, mean individual versions of acrylic fibers differ from each other more than other synthetic fibers. Likewise, many different modacrylic fibers have been produced, although they tend to contain considerable amounts of chlorine-based units. This chlorine component provides the flame-resistant properties of modacrylics. The market share of both acrylic and modacrylic fibers has declined somewhat since the 1980s, and although generically separate, it is appropriate to discuss them together.

Acrylic fibers have round or moderately irregular cross sections typically characterized as bean, dog-bone, or peanut shaped. A given volume of fiber is comparatively lightweight (fiber density is 1.17). Acrylic fibers are approximately half as strong as nylon or polyester (tenacity is 2–3.5 g/d), and they have limited use where strength is a major requirement. Like most synthetics, they absorb little water (moisture regain is 1–2 percent), and acrylic fiber materials are quick drying. Fibers recover well from small amounts of stretching. They have excellent resistance to sunlight and weathering and to a wide range of chemicals, particularly inorganic acids. They are thermoplastic, softening at 450–500°F (230–260°C), and can be heat set and texturized, although excessive heat will cause yellowing. Modacrylics have similar properties except a higher density (~1.35), softening temperatures that are 50–100°F lower, and the "self-extinguishing" flame response that comes from the chlorine content.

The variable chemical units in the fiber allowed for fibers of differing dyeing behavior, and some were produced to be dyeable with acid dyes, as wool is. In the early 2000s, most acrylic fiber variants are dyed with basic (cationic) dyes. Many early synthetic dyes (including Perkin's Mauve were basic dyes, and these were adopted for acrylics, but dyemakers later developed "modified" basic dyes specifically for use with these fibers. Disperse dyes may also be useful for pale shades. A considerable amount of acrylic and modacrylic fiber is colored during manufacture, either as "solution dyed" fiber or by applying dye to the fiber immediately after spinning in "gel-dyeing."

Most acrylic is produced as staple fiber, and bulky yarns are generated from blending fibers of different shrinkage properties. Fibers made from two different acrylic materials ("bicomponent fibers") produce especially bulky fibers and yarns. As the ease of creating bulky yarns suggests, and the suffix "-lan" or "-lon" implies, the fibers find favor in wool-like end uses: sweaters, blankets, socks, knitting yarn. In microfiber versions, acrylics make very soft scarves. Flammability issues and a lack of resilience has limited application of acrylic fibers in carpets. For many years, sweatshirts and pants were based on blends of cotton and acrylic fibers: polyester has now taken over the synthetic role in that end use. Modacrylic and acrylic fibers make the most successful fake furs and are widely used in hairpieces and doll hair. The superior sunlight resistance of both fibers makes them useful for outdoor applications such as awnings, with modacrylics providing additional flame resistance. The low flammability of modacrylics provides a measure of safety despite the low softening temperature: end uses based on this property have included airline blankets and military sweaters. Acrylic fibers are used as starting materials in the production of carbon (graphite) fibers.

Articles made of acrylic fibers are easy to care for: they dry easily and, if properly set during manufacture, maintain their dimensions. Excessive conditions may cause loss of bulk or shrinkage. Acrylic and modacrylic fibers are now mature: cheaper polyester has taken over several of their end uses.

See also **Dyeing; Fibers.**

BIBLIOGRAPHY

Adnaur, Sabit. *Wellington Sears Handbook of Industrial Textiles.* Lancaster, Pa.: Technomic, 1995.

Burkinshaw, S. M. *Chemical Principles of Synthetic Fibre Dyeing.* Glasgow, New York: Blackie Academic and Professional, 1995.

Cook, Gordon J. *Handbook of Textile Fibres, Part 2: Man-Made Fibers.* 5th ed. Durham, U.K.: Merrow, 1984.

Moncrieff, R. W. *Man-Made Fibres.* 6th ed. London: Newnes-Butterworth, 1975.

Martin Bide

ACTIVEWEAR The clothing known as activewear in the early 2000s traces its origins back to the high-performance sportswear designed for mountaineering, sailing, and hiking that became popular among urban youth during the 1970s. By the 1980s, such utilitarian styles swept through college campuses in North America, and, subsequently, sneakers were worn with suits, backpacks replaced briefcases, anoraks were paired with deck shoes, and sweatshirts were combined with khaki trousers or jeans. As the style began to characterize the sporty chic of city dwellers and coed campus life, activewear became a staple of the modern wardrobe.

While activewear is often regarded as a contemporary style, the combination of street clothes, travel accessories, and sportswear is nothing new. In the 1930s and 1940s, the American designers Bonnie Cashin, Claire McCardell, and Vera Maxwell updated garments produced for travel, leisure, and sport with vestiges of high fashion. The designers made functionality a statement of style by producing easy-fit, loosely constructed clothing in fabrics such as wool, denim, and calico. One of Cashin's signature garments was an overcoat with an integral purse, while Maxwell designed a jacket with built-in bags rather than pockets. Such garments were conceived as urban tools that expanded into wearable luggage, widening the appeal of apparel that could maximize the performance of clothing as well as the body's ability to transport necessities with ease.

For several decades, activewear was characterized by bulky, loose-fitting garments. As the body-conscious styles of the 1990s took hold, activewear gradually became more tailored and form-fitting, yet continued to suit the active leisure interests of urban dwellers. Dress codes became more fluid as Rollerbladers, inner-city cyclists, and speed-walking pedestrians dressed in smart basics that moved easily and provided protection from adverse weather. Mobility and versatility became key considerations for professionals, who started commuting to work in sneakers and multifunctional outer garments. Many were made with detachable hoods that transformed overcoats into raincoats as they were buttoned or zipped into place, or designed with removable collars and detachable sleeves that could be adapted to weather changes.

The hoods, zip-front seams, windproof jackets, pouch pockets, Velcro, and magnetic fastenings of activewear have become part of the everyday fashion vocabulary, along with drawstrings fitted at the neck, sleeve, and waist to make zippers and buttons redundant. Maharishi popularized these tailoring details on the catwalk as the 1990s drew to a close, updating them with elements of occupational uniforms to create a signature militaristic style. The rise of activewear's popularity throughout the 1990s indicated that the traditional compartmentalized wardrobe no longer sustained shifting social and cultural needs. As the style formed an essential part of the modern wardrobe, it encouraged the movement of materials and technologies across disciplines, moving high-tech fabrics into the collections of forward-thinking fashion designers. Activewear's multifunctional, dynamic features seemed to herald the dawn of twenty-first century fashion in garments that fused fashion with high-performance sportswear.

Labels such as CP Company, Mandarina Duck, Issey Miyake, Vexed Generation, and Final Home were among the first to use advanced textile technology to create an edgy, urban aesthetic in designs as durable as they were chic. CP Company led the pack with designs that transcended fashion altogether; their overcoats transformed into one-person tents or inflated into air mattresses, and their parkas puffed up into armchairs. The garments are transformed by the wearers themselves, introducing a notion of technical skill required beyond the point of purchase. Likewise, the "Jackpack," designed by Mandarina Duck in Italy, integrated a backpack's straps, fastenings, and compartments within the fabric of the jacket's back panel. By taking the jacket off, turning it inside out, and folding the sleeves, lapels, and fabric panels into an internal pouch, the structure of the garment was completely transformed. The pouch contains other zippered compartments for stowing away shopping or other items of clothing. Issey Miyake, for his "Transformer" series, also designed cotton jackets that concealed a nylon raincoat within.

The British fashion duo Vexed Generation countered the problems of modern life with clothing crafted from bullet-proof and slash-proof materials. Their designs combined high-performance fabrics with cutting-edge street style in garments incorporating many of the functions associated with protective clothing. Temperature-regulating materials manufactured for sportswear were incorporated into their winter coats, ending the need for bulky layering. By lining jackets and overcoats with phase-change materials such as Outlast, Vexed Generation created outer garments that could function as personal thermostats. Tiny paraffin capsules in the phase-change fabrics expand when body temperature climbs, absorbing the heat. Once body temperature drops below 98.6° F (37° C), they contract, releasing the heat they have stored. By maintaining a mean temperature within changing climatic environments, Vexed Generation created a comfort zone for the wearer.

The Japanese designer Kosuke Tsumura's signature garment, the Final Home jacket, expands the mobility of activewear into an expression of architecture as he claims that clothing constitutes the ultimate shelter. The multifunctional, transparent jacket is a nylon sheath equipped with forty-four zippered pockets that can be lined with warm materials for extra insulation, or cushion the wearer when sitting or reclining. Tsumura sees the jacket as a protective shell that enables the wearer to withstand harsh weather conditions. Along with personal items and accessories, Tsumura suggests that some of the pockets be filled with survival rations and practical supplies, eliminating the need for backpacks, shopping bags, luggage, and even tool kits.

As fashion consumers continue looking to activewear to reconcile the demands of the modern lifestyle, the boundaries between street clothes, office attire, and sportswear are blurring even further. High-performance designs and technologically advanced textiles are common to all three, as comfort, flexibility, and protection become central to all parts of the modern wardrobe. As the garments are updated with innovations that transcend conventional clothing, activewear is proving to be one of the fastest moving areas of fashion in the early 2000s. New tailoring techniques radically streamline the designs each season, and future styles of activewear portend such sophistication that the gym is probably the last place one can expect to see them.

See also **Outerwear; Sportswear.**

BIBLIOGRAPHY

Barnard, Malcolm. *Fashion as Communication.* London: Routledge, 1996.

Bolton, Andrew. *The Supermodern Wardrobe.* London: V & A Publications, 2001.

Jones, Terry, and Avril Mair. *Fashion Now.* Cologne, Germany: Taschen, 2003.

McDowell, Colin. *The Fashion Book.* London: Phaidon Press, Ltd., 2000.

Quinn, Bradley. *Techno Fashion.* Oxford: Berg, 2002.

Bradley Quinn

ACTORS AND ACTRESSES, IMPACT ON FASHION Professional actors and actresses have long fascinated their audiences, but until the twentieth century, they were often associated with licentious sexual behavior, making them problematic role models. Perhaps the first true stage professionals, in the modern sense, were the men and women who made up the repertory companies of the Italian commedia dell'arte in the sixteenth and seventeenth centuries. The stock characters they impersonated, such as Harlequin, Columbine, and Pierrot, left

A tailor makes adjustments to a gown for actress Betty Grable. Hollywood stars of the 1930s and 1940s had a great impact on style, setting many fashion trends both onscreen and off. © JERRY COOKE/CORBIS. REPRODUCED BY PERMISSION.

their mark on fashion. Shirts for women in the twentieth century have sported an extravagantly ruffled collar like that of Pierrot, while the diamond-patterned fabric of Harlequin's costume is now part of the fashion lexicon.

In England, theaters were established in London during the Elizabethan Age, but the first thing the Puritans did upon taking control of the city of London in 1620 was to close them. After the Royalist defeat in the English Civil War, Charles II, the future king of England, had to flee to Paris. He remained in exile there for a decade at the court of Louis XIV, where he saw actresses, whose costumes reflected current trends in fashion, on stage both at court and in the fashionable playhouses. When he returned to London in 1660, theater flourished; his most famous mistress was the actress Nell Gwyn. It was during his reign that the "first night" of a new play became both a social event and a dress parade, as it has remained ever since.

In the eighteenth century, the English actress Mrs. Sheridan (1754–1792), wife of the playwright Richard Brinsley Sheridan, was painted by Sir Joshua Reynolds and Thomas Gainsborough. Other actresses sat for fashionable portraitists, and their dress and hairstyles were widely copied. Caroline Abington, who married into the aristocracy, was perhaps the first fashion consultant; she was driven around London to advise her wealthy, titled friends on sartorial matters, particularly if a ball or marriage was imminent.

Many French actresses also had an influence on fashion. Sarah Bernhardt (1844–1923), in particular, was famed for her stylish clothes. She toured the world and was the first actress to be dressed for the screens of the new cinema by a couturier. In 1913, when her play *Elizabeth I* was filmed, she asked Paul Poiret to create her wardrobe, setting a trend that other couturiers would follow, from Coco Chanel and Hubert de Givenchy to the more recent long-term collaboration on- and off-screen between Yves St. Laurent and Catherine Deneuve.

The actor, writer, and director Noel Coward (1899–1973) made a polka-dotted silk Sulka dressing-gown part of every well-dressed man's wardrobe. His favored actress, Gertrude Lawrence, wore a backless dress on stage in *Private Lives* in 1930 and the style instantly became fashionable. Jean Harlow set trends in hair and makeup—the "silver screen" succeeded where the stage had always failed: it made the wearing of makeup not only respectable but a fashionable necessity.

In the early twenty-first century, the stage has less impact than film in fashion terms. The fashionable theatrical couples of the 1930s and 1940s—the Oliviers and the Lunts, for example—were eclipsed by the cinematic duos of the second half of the twentieth century and beginning of the twenty-first century. However, the stage door still has its appeal: its glittering first nights, its gala evenings, and its award ceremonies—all of which, like the Academy Awards, demand "occasion dressing," and act

as yet another showcase for designers and stylists canny enough to offer up their services.

See also **Animal Prints; Film and Fashion; Theatrical Costume; Theatrical Makeup.**

BIBLIOGRAPHY

Bruzzi, Stella. *Undressing Cinema: Clothing and Identity in the Movies.* London: Routledge, 1997.

Hartnoll, Phyllis. *The Theatre: A Concise History.* Rev. ed. London: Thames and Hudson, Inc., 1985.

Laver, James. *Costume in the Theatre.* New York: Hill and Wang, 1965.

Pointon, Marcia. *Hanging the Head: Portraiture and Social Formation in Eighteenth-Century England.* New Haven, Conn.: Yale University Press, 1993.

Ribeiro, Aileen. *The Art of Dress: Fashion in England and France, 1750 to 1820.* New Haven, Conn.: Yale University Press, 1995.

Pamela Church Gibson

ADINKRA Adinkra cloth is the traditional funerary dress of the Asante peoples of Ghana as well as many of their neighbors. Funerals are among the most lavish of all Asante ritual occasions and are clearly part of their still strong commitment to venerating their ancestors. The scholar J. B. Danquah defines the meaning of adinkra as, "to part, be separated, to leave one another, to say good-bye." Adinkra cloths are distinguished by designs applied with carved gourd stamps and a black dye placed within a rectilinear grid whose divisions are created by a three or four tine comb brushed in measured segments across the length and width of the cloth. Some cloths may feature a single stamped design while others may have over twenty different motifs applied to the surface.

For a cloth to be called adinkra, it must have these stamped designs. If the cloth is to serve as mourning dress, it must be dyed one of three colors—red, russet brown, or a dark blue-black. The latter is not typically stamped. Some sources state that the red adinkra is reserved for the closest members of the family and others assert that this is the role of the brown cloths. Clearly practices vary. Adinkra cloths that remain white or are printed on a brightly colored fabric are designated "Sunday adinkra," and are not used during funerals, but rather as festive dress for a variety of special occasions much like kente cloth.

The earliest known adinkra cloth (now in the British Museum) dates from 1817 and consists of twenty-four handwoven strips of undyed cotton cloth, each about three inches wide and woven on the same type of narrow strip horizontal treadle loom as Asante kente. The strips are sewn selvage to selvage (finished edges of a fabric) to produce a large men's cloth draped over the body toga style with the left shoulder covered and the right exposed. Women wear two pieces, one as a skirt and one as an up-

Asante boys going to a dance in adinkra robes, 1973, Accra. Color is important in adinkra garments; darker hues are reserved for funerary dress, while white or brightly colored garments are used for festive occasions. © OWEN FRANKEN/CORBIS. REPRODUCED BY PERMISSION.

per wrapper or shawl. In the early 2000s the latter piece is more frequently fashioned into a blouse.

The use of pieced-together narrow strips of a fixed width undoubtedly influenced the compositional divisions of the cloth as well as the size of the earliest stamps. By the end of the nineteenth century, however, imported industrially produced mill-woven cloth had largely replaced the handwoven strip weaves. Also about this time, the British were producing mill-woven cloth with roller-printed adinkra patterns for the West African market.

An additional design feature on many adinkra cloths is a further division of the men's cloths along their lengths with bands of multicolored whip-stitched embroidery in combinations of yellow, red, green, and blue. As seen in an 1896 photograph of the then king of Asante, Agye-man Prempeh I, this practice dates to at least the end of the nineteenth century. The embroidery is usually straightedged along the length of the cloth, but an important variant has serrated edges in a design called "centipede" or "zigzag." Although not necessarily referring to adinkra, the Englishman Thomas Bowdich observed this

practice in 1817. On some cloths multicolored handwoven strips about one and a half inches in width are substituted for the embroidery.

It is generally accepted that the adinkra genre was heavily influenced from the very beginning by Islam and in particular by Arabic inscribed cloths that are still produced by the northern neighbors of the Asante. These share a similar gridlike division of space and a number of hand-drawn motifs that are readily recognizable as adinkra patterns. Some of the same design principles and motifs are also found on Islamic inspired cast brass ritual containers called *kuduo*. The Asante attraction to the spiritual efficacy of Islam and to literacy in Arabic has been well documented since the early part of the nineteenth century. Significantly, an Arabic-inscribed cloth is still part of the wardrobe of the current king of Asante. The argument here is that the stamped adinkra cloth was developed as a shorthand for the more labor intensive and explicitly literate Muslim cloths.

Of particular interest in the study and appreciation of adinkra is the rich design vocabulary found on the

Man preparing adinkra cloth, 1995, near Kumasi, Ghana. The gridlike patterns and hand-drawn motifs of adinkra dress are similar to those found on many Arabic-inscribed fabrics and artifacts. © MARGARET COURTNEY-CLARKE/CORBIS. REPRODUCED BY PERMISSION.

stamps. Until the middle of the twentieth century, there were about fifty frequently repeated motifs. As with most Asante arts, there is a highly conventionalized verbal component to the visual images. The meaning of many motifs is elucidated by generally well-known proverbs. A design with four spiraling forms projecting from the center represents the maxim: "A ram fights with his heart and not his horns," suggesting that strength of character is more important than the weapons one uses. A fleur-de-lis-shaped stamp is identified as a hen's foot and is associated with the saying: "The hen's foot may step on its chicks, but it does not kill them," that is a mother provides protection and guidance and not harm. A stamp depicting a ladder depicts the inevitable, "The ladder of death is not climbed by one man alone." Perhaps the most common motif is an abstract form that represents what is generally translated as: "Except God," but its sense is better conveyed by "Only God." As with most of their arts, the worldview of the Ashanti is wonderfully articulated in this funerary fabric.

In the twenty-first century, the corpus of stamp designs has expanded to well over five hundred. These include numerous references to the modern world, including automobiles, hydroelectric power, and cell phones. A number of motifs depict the logos of an assortment of Ghanaian political parties that have contended for power since independence (hand, cock, elephant, and cocoa tree). Another trend is a series of stamps that literally spell out their messages. For example, "EKAA NSEE NKOA" carved into a gourd stamp references a longer proverb that translates as: "The woodpecker celebrates the death of the *onyina* tree." Since the bird nests and feeds in the dead tree, this is a kind of cycle-of-life statement. This practice recalls the origin of adinkra in script-filled, handwritten (albeit Arabic) inscribed cloths.

As with Asante kente, the verbal component of adinkra imagery is an important factor in its popularity in African American communities. Roller printed mill-woven adinkra is nearly as commercially successful as machine-made kente and appears in many of the same clothing forms, including hats, bags, scarves, and shawls. Individual adinkra motifs have even transcended clothing forms to become an important element in graphic design, fine arts, and even architecture.

See also **Africa, North: History of Dress; Africa, Sub-Saharan: History of Dress; Kente.**

BIBLIOGRAPHY

Glover, Ablade. *Adinkra Symbolism.* Accra: Liberty Press, 1971. This one sheet chart/poster, reprinted many times, remains the most accessible reference for adinkra. It can be found in many African American bookstores and museums.

Mato, Daniel. *Clothed in Symbol: The Art of Adinkra Among the Akan of Ghana.* Ann Arbor, Mich.: UMI Dissertation Services, 1987. Ph.D. dissertation is still the most comprehensive study of adinkra to date.

Rattray, Robert S. *Religion and Art in Ashanti.* Oxford: Clarendon Press, 1927. Chapter 25 is the first substantial reference to adinkra and is still worthwhile.

Willis, W. Bruce. *The Adinkra Dictionary: A Visual Primer on the Language of Adinkra.* Washington, D.C.: The Pyramid Complex, 1998.

Doran H. Ross

ADIRE *Adire* is a resist-dyed cloth produced and worn by the Yoruba people of southwestern Nigeria in West Africa. The Yoruba label *adire*, which means "tied and dyed," was first applied to indigo-dyed cloth decorated with resist patterns around the turn of the twentieth century. With the introduction of a broader color palette of imported synthetic dyes in the second half of the twentieth century, the label "adire" was expanded to include a variety of hand-dyed textiles using wax resist batik methods to produce patterned cloth in a dazzling array of dye tints and hues.

The Art of Making Adire

The traditional production of indigo-dyed adire involves the input of two female specialists—dyers (*alaro*), who control production and marketing of adire, and decorators (*aladire*), who create the resist patterns. In the oldest forms of adire, two basic resist techniques are used to create soft blue or white designs to contrast with a deeply saturated indigo blue background. *Adire oniko* is tied or wrapped with raffia to resist the dye. *Adire eleko* has starchy maize or cassava paste hand-painted onto the surface of the cloth as a resist agent. Further experimentation led to two additional techniques. *Adire alabere* involves stitching the cloth with thread prior to dyeing to produce fine-lined motifs. *Adire batani* is produced with the aid of zinc stencils to control the application of the resist starch.

The decorator works with a 1 x 2-yard fabric rectangle as a design field, making two identical pieces to sew together to make a square cloth most commonly used for a woman's wrapper. Most wrappers have repeated all-over patterns created with one or more resist techniques with no one focal point of interest. The motifs used in adire and the labels attached to them reflect the concerns of indigenous and contemporary Yoruba life: the world of nature, religion, philosophy, everyday life and notable events (Wolff 2001). Decorators, when not working with stencils, have a mental template in mind based on prototypes where particular motifs are combined together to identify a wrapper type, such as *Ibadandun*. Some motifs are pictographic, but often bear little resemblance to the thing signified by labels. For example, tie-dyed motifs such as "moon and fruits" have only a passing semblance to what they portray, while some motifs used in adire eleko like *ejo* (snake) or *ewe* (leaf) are recognizable.

The History of Adire

As a distinctive textile type, adire first emerged in the city of Abeokuta, a center for cotton production, weaving, and indigo-dyeing in the nineteenth century. The prototype was tie-dyed *kijipa*, a handwoven cloth dyed with indigo for use as wrappers and covering cloths. Female specialists dyed yarns and cloth and also refurbished faded clothing by re-dyeing the cloth with tie-dyed patterns. When British trading firms introduced cheap imported cloth and flooded the market with colorful inexpensive printed textiles, the adire industry emerged to meet the challenge. The women discovered that the imported white cotton shirting was cheaper than handwoven cloth and could be decorated and dyed to meet local tastes. The soft, smooth texture of the import cloth, in contrast to the rough surface of kijipa cloth, provided a new impetus for decoration. The soft shirting encouraged the decorators to create smaller more precise patterns with tie-dye methods and to use raffia thread to produce finely patterned stitch-resist adire alabere. The smooth surface of shirting led to the development of hand-painted starch-resist adire eleko. Abeokuta remained the major producer and

trade center for adire, but Ibadan, a larger city to the north, developed a nucleus of women artists who specialized in hand-painted adire eleko. The wrapper design Ibadandun ("Ibadandun" meaning "the city of Ibadan is sweet") is popular to this day.

In the early decades of the twentieth century, a vast trade network for adire spread across West Africa. Adire wrappers were sold as far away as Ghana, Senegal, and the Congo (Byfield 2002; Eades 1993). At the height of adire production in the 1920s, Senegalese merchants came to Abeokuta to buy as many as 2,000 wrappers in one day from the female traders (Byfield 2002, p. 114). In the 1930s, two technological innovations to decorate adire were developed that provided an avenue for men to gain entrance into the female-controlled industry. Women retained the dyeing specialty and continued to do tying, hand-painting, and hand-sewing to prepare the cloth for dyeing, but decorating techniques involving sewing machine stitching and applying starch through zinc stencils were taken up by men, because West Africans believe that men have an affinity for machines and metal that women do not. A regional and international economic decline at the end of the 1930s led to a decline in the craft, so that in the 1940s no major innovations in production occurred (Byfield 2002; Keyes-Adenaike 1993). The European restriction placed against exporting cloth to West Africa during World War II (1939–1945) also had negative effects. Following the war, the adire industry was dealt a further blow when the markets were flooded with low-priced printed cloth from European, Asian, and African textile mills. By the 1950s adire production had significantly slowed, and few young people were being trained in the craft.

In the 1960s, while rural women were still wearing the indigo-dyed wrappers, urban dwellers considered it "a poor people's cloth" (Byfield 2002, pp. 212–218). However, the 1960s marked a new period of innovation in handcrafted cloth production in Yorubaland. With the growing availability of chemical dyes from Europe, there was a revolution in color and techniques (Keyes-Adenaike 1993, p. 38). Adire patterns caught the eye of Nigerian fashion designers who adapted the designs to print high-quality cloth using imported color-fast dyes in colors other than indigo. Sold by the yard the "new adire" was used for clothing, tablecloths, bedspreads, and draperies (Eicher 1976, pp. 76–77). One expatriate woman, Betty Okuboyejo who lived in Abeokuta, is credited with introducing high-quality adire-inspired cloth using a full range of commercial color-fast dyes to expatriates and Nigerian elites (Eicher 1976, p. 76). New multicolored adire utilized a simple technology and became a backyard industry so that the markets filled with the new adire. This modern form of cheaply produced adire, dubbed "kampala" (because it became popular at the time of the Kampala Peace Conference to settle the Biafra War in Nigeria) was manufactured by individuals with no prior knowledge of dyeing—farmers, clerks, petty traders, and the jobless (Picton 1995, p. 17). Hot wax or paraffin was substituted for the indigenous cassava paste as a resist agent, and designs were created by simple techniques including tie-dye, folding, crumpling, and randomly sprinkling or splashing the hot wax onto a cloth prior to dyeing. As demand grew and the new adire makers began to professionalize, a block printing technique to apply the hot wax developed and largely supplanted stenciling (Picton 1995, p. 17).

In the twenty-first century, the new colorful adire continues to meet fashion challenges and to be an alternative to machine prints. In continually changing patterns, new adire appeals to the fashion-conscious Yoruba in the urban and rural areas. In Nigeria one can still buy indigo-dyed adire oniko and eleko made by older women in Abeokuta and Ibadan and by artisans at the Nike Center for the Arts and Culture in Oshogbo where the artist Nike Davies-Okundaye trains students in traditional adire techniques. But, increasingly, the lover of indigo-dyed adire must turn to collecting pieces from the cloth markets such as Oje Market in Ibadan or from traders who specialize in the old cloth. Soon those also will be gone from the Yoruba scene.

See also **Africa, North: History of Dress; Dyeing; Indigo; Tie-Dyeing.**

BIBLIOGRAPHY

Barbour, Jane, and Doug Simmonds, eds. *Adire Cloth in Nigeria*. Ibadan: The Institute of African Studies, University of Ibadan, 1971. Excellent source on dyeing technology, history, and motifs.

Beier, Ulli, ed. *A Sea of Indigo: Yoruba Textile Art*. Enugu, Nigeria: Fourth Dimension Publishing, 1997. Social history of adire, particularly contemporary conditions.

Byfield, Judith. *The Bluest Hands: A Social and Economic History of Women Dyers in Abeokuta (Nigeria), 1890–1940*. Portsmouth, N.H.: Heinemann, 2002. A definitive history of the peak years of adire production.

Eades, J. S. *Strangers and Traders: Yoruba Migrants, Markets, and the State in Northern Ghana*. Edinburgh, London: Edinburgh University Press for the International African Institute, 1993.

Eicher, Joanne Bubolz. *Nigerian Handcrafted Textiles*. Ile-Ife: University of Ife Press, 1976.

Keyes-Adenaike, Carolyn. *Adire: Cloth, Gender, and Social Change in Southwestern Nigeria, 1841–1991*. Ph.d. diss., University of Wisconsin, 1993.

Oyelola, Pat. "The Beautiful and the Useful: The Contribution of Yoruba Women to Indigo Dyed Textiles." *The Nigerian Field* 57 (1992): 61–66.

Picton, John. *The Art of African Textiles: Technology, Tradition and Lurex*. London: Barbican Art Gallery, Lund Humphries Publishers, 1995.

Picton, John, and John Mack. *African Textiles*. London: British Museum Publications Ltd., 1979.

Wolff, Norma H. "Leave Velvet Alone: The *Adire* Tradition of the Yoruba." In *Cloth Is the Center of the World: Nigerian Textiles, Global Perspectives*. Edited by Susan J. Torntore, 51–65. St. Paul, Minn.: Goldstein Museum of Design, Dept. of Design, Housing, and Apparel, 2001. An anthropological approach to production and cultural importance of adire.

Norma H. Wolff

ADRIAN Adrian, the great American film and fashion designer, was born Adrian Adolph Greenberg in Connecticut in 1903. Stage-struck at an early age, he had worked in summer stock and sold costume sketches to the producers of a Broadway show by the time he was eighteen. In 1921 he entered the New York School of Fine and Applied Arts (now the Parsons School of Design) to study stage design. He transferred to the Paris branch of the school in 1922.

Adrian returned to New York after three months to design costumes for Irving Berlin's *Music Box Revue*. He had designed costumes for his first movie and a number of Broadway shows by 1924, when he accepted a job designing costumes for Rudolph Valentino. Relocating to Los Angeles with Valentino, Adrian created costumes for three more of his films. He freelanced on *Her Sister from Paris*, starring Constance Talmadge, in 1925 and on Howard Hawks's *Fig Leaves* for Fox in 1926, a film that featured a two-color Technicolor fashion show sequence. Adrian signed a contract with Cecil B. DeMille the same year, moved with DeMille to Metro-Goldwyn-Mayer (MGM) in 1928, and subsequently signed with MGM. He stayed there until 1941, when he terminated his contract and left the movie business. In 1939 Adrian married Janet Gaynor, winner of the first Academy Award for best actress, and they had one son.

As MGM's chief designer, Adrian designed costumes for all the major stars in every important movie. Greta Garbo, Norma Shearer, Joan Crawford, Jean Harlow, Jeanette MacDonald, and Katharine Hepburn all wore his designs. Adrian was so important to the stars that Joan Crawford once said he should have been given cobilling on her movies. Film costumes had to make the stars look their best, be suitable for the character, and conform to the technical dictates of lighting, film stock, and sound recording. Period costumes had to be reasonably authentic but also accessible to the audience's eye. Modern wardrobes had to be of their time but independent of any specific fashion, for several reasons. First, the time lag between the production of a movie and its release meant that using current styles on a star would make her look out of fashion when the film was released months later. More important, each star's screen persona was carefully developed by the studio, and her roles never varied widely from it. For example, Norma Shearer represented the conservative-young-woman type; Garbo was always the unpredictable, mysterious exotic; and Joan Crawford typified sophisticated young America.

Film styles had influenced fashion since the silent movie era, but their impact was intensified by the advent of sound. With the "talkies," films became more realistic, and film costuming became less focused on theatrical effects. The European fashion world watched to see what Adrian put on Garbo, Shearer, and Crawford. Designs that Adrian introduced on individual stars frequently returned to America as "the latest from Paris."

The studios allowed manufacturers to market garments based on a star's film wardrobe, and thousands of dresses, blouses, and coats named for *Letty Lynton* (Joan Crawford, 1932) or *Queen Christina* (Greta Garbo, 1933) were sold. A number of Garbo's hats—the cloche from *A Woman of Affairs*, the plumed cap from *Romance*, and the pillbox and turban from *Painted Veil*—created new trends.

In 1930 the Modern Merchandising Bureau was established to organize the manufacture of styles introduced in a film before the picture's release, in order to have copies available in stores as soon as audiences saw the movie. Macy's in New York was the first store to open a Cinema Fashions shop, and crowds would gather on the sidewalk to see the new styles in the display windows. During the Great Depression, Hollywood further capitalized on film fashions by licensing patterns for home sewing based on them. The success of Condé Nast's *Hollywood Pattern Book* led to its becoming a whole new magazine, *Glamour of Hollywood*, in 1939; the title was subsequently shortened to *Glamour*. Movies exerted an enormous influence on world fashion, and Adrian was the leading Hollywood designer of his era.

After retiring from films, Adrian opened a couture and ready-to-wear business in Beverly Hills, which manufactured his designs and sold them to specialty stores throughout the United States. He showed his first collection in February 1942. Having designed suit variations for years in his movies on stars from Garbo to Hedy Lamarr—but most famously on Joan Crawford—he now produced the classic, square-shouldered, 1940s suit for which he is best known. Antecedents of this "V" silhouette throughout the 1930s had included such devices as the pagoda shoulder and the horizontal extension of the sleeve cap through pleating. To avoid both the faddish effect of the pagoda shoulder and the boxiness of the widened sleeve cap, Adrian squared the shoulder with pads of his own design, narrowing and neatening the silhouette to give it a classic line. As well as suits, he included a wide variety of day dresses, cocktail and evening wear, and coats in his collections.

In 1947 Adrian refused to follow the example of Paris when the New Look was introduced by Christian Dior. He found sloping shoulders, a cinched waist, padded hips, and long, full skirts unattractive on the average woman as well as cumbersome and impractical. Although he never significantly varied the "V" cut of his suits, he reduced the shoulder pads in his suits—never removing them altogether—and lengthened and slimmed the skirt. For evening wear, as opposed to daytime, Adrian had no quarrel with the New Look and encouraged women to

go "all out." His wartime evening silhouette—a neoclassic column of rayon crepe with the same slim, squared shoulders as his suits—mutated into a softer silk sheath. Adrian's evening collections expanded to include everything from voluminous ball gowns to variations on the sari to dinner dresses draped with bustle variations.

Throughout the collections of Adrian's fashion career, certain themes reappeared. He frequently designed prints of animals, such as the famous "Roan Stallion" evening gown or *The Egg and I* at-home dress with its furious barnyard chickens. After Adrian's trip to Africa in 1949, animal and reptile prints appeared in a ball gown of tiger-skin taffeta and a hooded evening suit made from heavy silk that looked like an iridescent python skin. His "Americana" theme included a quilted silk hostess gown appliquéd with cotton gingham motifs and a long gingham evening coat with a matching skirt and sequined bodice. He referenced modern art movements such as futurism with inset streamers that emerged from the gown's surface to drape and flutter and cubism in the extraordinary "Modern Museum" series of rayon crepe gowns executed in pieced, multicolor, biomorphic shapes. In 1952 Adrian suffered a heart attack that forced him to close his business. He died in 1959.

Adrian's career was unique among designers in that he conquered both the film and fashion worlds. He worked entirely in California, far off the beaten track for couture or ready-to-wear. In film he worked as a couturier, designing costumes to highlight a star's individuality and conceal her figure flaws. These singular creations in turn engendered worldwide fashion trends. After leaving films his greatest achievement lay in his mastery of the ready-to-wear market. As a film designer Adrian gave fashion inspiration and hours of entertainment to millions of people all over the world. As a fashion designer he set a standard both for originality of design and quality of workmanship.

See also **Actors and Actresses, Impact on Fashion; Costume Designer; Film and Fashion; Hollywood Style; Ready-to-Wear.**

BIBLIOGRAPHY

Gutner, Howard. *Gowns by Adrian.* New York: Harry N. Abrams, 2001.

Lee, Sarah Tomerlin, ed. *American Fashion: The Life and Lines of Adrian, Mainbocher, McCardell, Norell, and Trigère.* New York: Quadrangle/New York Times Book Company, 1975.

Jane Trapnell

AESTHETIC DRESS In 1851, London celebrated the Great Exhibition, showcasing the latest innovations in manufacture and design. Its warm reception by the public and the media confirmed, in many people's eyes, the triumph of increased industrialization and mass production. However, some, who found this way of life increasingly abhorrent, sought an alternative lifestyle by looking to the past.

Three years earlier, in 1848, the young artists William Holman Hunt, John Everett Millais, and Dante Gabriel Rosetti established the Pre-Raphaelite Brotherhood, taking inspiration from the art of the late medieval and early renaissance periods, which they felt produced a purer and more naturalistic style. As such, dress played an important role in the depiction of the subjects, but with no extant examples, references came from tomb effigies, illustrated manuscripts, and the artist's own inventions. The type of dress that emerged was worn by female members of the artists' circle.

Early styles of aesthetic dress took the form of flowing fabric with soft pleating falling from the neckline. The folds then gently gathered in at the natural, uncorseted waistline and fell into a small train at the back. The sleeves were a defining feature; unlike those of fashionable dress, they were set at the natural shoulder line and often decorated with puffs of fabric at the sleeve head, or gathered down the length of the arm. This enabled freedom of movement, as did the abandonment of the corset, which was felt to offer a more natural figure along the lines of the Venus de Milo, although critics noted "had Venus herself been compelled by a cold climate to drape herself, we have little doubt she would have worn stays, to give her clothes the shape they lacked" (Douglas, pp. 123–124). As such, the style found favor with dress reformers who spoke out against the damaging effects of tightly laced corseting. The two movements became closely allied and by 1890 the Healthy and Artistic Dress Union was established, publishing their ideas in their journal *Aglaia*.

Color was an all important element of the style, with soft browns, reds, blues, and—a popular choice and most recognizable of them all—a sage green, which was often referred to as "greenery yallery." Aesthetic dress was relatively unadorned, the only decoration appearing in the form of smocking or floral and organically inspired embroidery, with the sunflower and the lily being popular motifs. Accessories were kept to a minimum, with amber beads seen as the most appropriate choice, along with eastern or oriental-inspired pieces. The aesthetic woman herself was epitomized by the red-haired, pale-skinned beauties with their defined jawlines and sorrowful eyes as seen in Rosetti's *La Ghirlandata* (1877). A photograph of Jane Morris, the wife of the designer William Morris, taken in 1865, depicts her as the perfect embodiment of this ideal. Her untamed hair is loosely tied back, her dress draping in heavy folds.

By the 1870s, the style had really come to the attention of the public. In 1877, Mrs. Eliza Haweis published her book *The Art of Beauty* in which she outlined the drawbacks of contemporary fashion and commended the lines of historical dress. She was approached in 1878 by the ladies magazine *The Queen* to write some articles on the subject of Pre-Raphaelite dress. *The Queen* reported: "A great change has come over the style of English dressing within the last, say, five years. . . . The world of artists first started the idea of their wives and daughters dressing in harmony with . . . [their] surroundings, and thence the grandes dames of fashion were influenced" (pp. 139–140).

As fashion conscripted artistic dress, historic periods were plundered with a myriad of styles indiscriminately thrown together under the term "aesthetic"; Greek tunics, medieval sleeves, and Elizabethan ruffs became popular adornments for fashionable dress. The Watteau-back dress, a partly fashionable style, was characterized by a large pleat of fabric falling loosely from the shoulders and caught up above the hem; it was inspired by eighteenth-century sacque dresses, depicted in the works of Watteau. These styles were a feature of the tea gown, a loose informal garment that could be worn at home or while receiving guests for afternoon tea.

The year 1877 also saw the opening of the Grosvenor Gallery and the first of the satirist George Du Maurier's series of cartoons, published in *Punch*, and based around a family known as the Cimabue Browns. The images portrayed the wearers of aesthetic dress as lank and languid men and women—the men in velvet jackets and long hair, the ladies with frizzed hair in long drooping garments—who always seemed to be contemplating the emotional impact of art on life.

The International Exhibition held in London in 1862 had stimulated the growing interest in oriental and exotic foreign goods. Arthur Lasenby Liberty, a young employee of Farmer and Roger's Shawl Emporium in Regent Street, persuaded his employers to open an oriental department. Owing to its huge success, Liberty left to set up his own department store in 1875. His imported fabrics and unusual artifacts were extremely popular with many artists, such as George Frederick Watts, James Whistler, and Frederick Leighton, who frequented the shop. Liberty soon began to produce his own fabrics suitable to the English climate yet with the qualities and colors of imported Eastern examples. In 1884, he opened a dressmaking department, overseen by E. W. Godwin, an architect and honorable secretary of the Costume Society. Godwin had designed many of the costumes for his partner, the famous actress Ellen Terry, whose choice of aesthetic dress was well known.

In 1881, the aesthetic craze was at its height with the production of Gilbert and Sullivan's *Patience* and the start of Oscar Wilde's lecture tours in America. His lectures included the importance of Liberty to the aesthetic movement and, as Alison Adburgham notes, this could "be said to have sown the first seeds that germinated into the long love affair between the Americans and Liberty's of London" (pp. 32–33).

***May Morning, Jane Morris,* taken by J. Robert Parsons.** The heavily draped, unadorned dress, minimal accessories, and sorrowful expression are all typical of aesthetic fashion. © Stapleton Collection/Corbis. Reproduced by permission.

The aesthetic movement had a popular following in America, the most noted proponent being Annie Jenness Miller who published *Dress: The Jenness Miller Magazine*. The society painter W. P. Frith captured the aesthetic scene in his painting *Private View* (1881), which depicted many of the leading proponents of the movement, such as Wilde and Ellen Terry. In his memoirs of 1887, Frith recalled,

> Seven years ago certain ladies delighted to display themselves at public gatherings in what are called aesthetic dresses; in some cases the costumes were pretty enough, in others they seemed to rival each other in ugliness of form and oddity of color (p. 256).

This telling quote also illustrates how aesthetic dress was now somewhat passé. Many of its elements had entered the mainstream, with the popularity of the tea gown and the ready availability of "artistic dress" in most department stores. A guide to London of 1889 recommends Hamilton's of Regent Street for "those triumphs of needlework: smocked frocks and smocked tea gowns. But it is by no means only in so-called artistic dress that they excel" (Pascoe, p. 351). By the turn of the century, aesthetic dress was no longer seen as radical or revolutionary. While its themes may have lingered in the work of early twentieth-century designers, such as Mariano Fortuny, whose pleated fabrics seem directly inspired by the dress worn in Rosetti's painting *A Vision of Fiametta* (1878), or the draped velvets of Maria Monaci Gallenga, the sumptuous sophisticated style of art nouveau had captured the artistic imagination, and the soft muted colors and trailing drapery of aesthetic dress were considered démodé.

See also **Art and Fashion; Fortuny, Mariano; Wilde, Oscar.**

BIBLIOGRAPHY

Adburgham, Alison. *Shops and Shopping.* London: George Allen and Unwin Ltd., 1964.

———. *Liberty: A Biography of a Shop.* London: George Allen and Unwin Ltd., 1975.

Costume: The Journal of the Costume Society 1 (1967), 2 (1968), 13 (1979), 21 (1987).

Douglas, Mrs. J. *The Gentlewoman's Book of Dress.* London: Henry and Company, 1895.

Frith, W. P. *My Autobiography and Reminiscences.* Vol. 2. London: Richard Bentley and Son, 1887.

Haweis, Eliza. *The Art of Beauty and The Art of Dress.* New York and London: Garland, 1978.

MacDonald, Margaret F., et al. *Whistler, Women and Fashion.* New Haven, Conn.: Yale University Press, 2003.

Newton, Stella Mary. *Health, Art and Reason: Dress Reformers of the 19th Century.* London: John Murray, 1974.

Pascoe, Charles Eyre. *London of Today: An Illustrated Handbook for the Season.* London: Hamilton Adams and Company, 1889.

Punch. 14 September 1878, 9 April 1881, 30 April 1881.

The Queen. 24 August 1878.

Squire, Geo. *Dress, Art and Society.* London: Macmillan, 1974.

Thieme, Otto Charles, E. A. Coleman, M. Oberly, and P. Cunningham. *With Grace and Favour: Victorian and Edwardian Fashion in America.* Cincinnati, Ohio: Cincinnati Art Museum, 1993.

Oriole Cullen

AFRICAN AMERICAN DRESS African American dress intertwines with the history of Africans, who arrived in the Virginia colony in 1619. Within that century, southern codes forced the children of any enslaved woman to remain enslaved for life. West Africans continued to come unwillingly until the 1830s. President Abraham Lincoln proclaimed the emancipation of all enslaved peoples in 1863; but after the Civil War, African Americans lived on the margins of American society with poor jobs, substandard living and educational conditions, disenfranchisement, and public segregation. Nearly one hundred years later, in 1954, a Supreme Court decision began the desegregation process and in the 1960s, Federal legislation gave equal rights to African Americans.

Under enslavement, white owners demanded a certain form of dress for those in bondage: better dress for house servants and managers; poorer attire for field hands, children, and those too old to continue working. In spite of these constrictions, the nineteenth-century autobiographies and narratives, collected in the 1930s from formerly enslaved people, relate that African Americans put a great deal of thought into their dress. The narrators emphasized what clothing they had and did not have and described the clothing styles they desired and how they obtained them. "Correct" dress was especially important when "stepping out" for social occasions with community members, a habit that continues in the early 2000s. Narrators offered vivid depictions of dressing well for church, dances, and marriage.

Evidence shows that some retained West African forms of bodily adornment, particularly in the form of jewelry. From the African Burial Ground (1712–1795) in New York City, the remains of an adult female and an infant wore waistbeads as do West African women. Archaeological evidence from known slave sites sometimes includes cowries, seashells of economic importance before currencies became available in Africa and apparently worn as jewelry by the enslaved. The beads most often found at these sites consist of blue glass beads, worn as amulets in much of Africa and the Middle East. Former slaves provided testimony of wearing jewelry for both adornment and protection. Several Sea Islands narrators, for instance, describe single gold, loop earrings worn to protect the eyesight, retention of an African belief.

More outstanding as an African holdover than specific items of jewelry or clothing has been the interest in hairstyle and headwear by African American men and women. Documentation for West Africans' concern for well-groomed hair and ornamented heads is long-

Headwraps. Beginning in the 1960s, African American women began wearing traditional headwraps as an acknowledgment of their West African ancestral roots. This fashion trend, among others, became popular with white Americans as well. © BJ FORMENTO/CORBIS. REPRODUCED BY PERMISSION.

standing and survives among African Americans. Black men continue to sport ever-changing styles of facial hair and hairdos; the "conk" (straightened hair that is flattened down or slightly waved) of the 1930s remains a primary example. And, into the early twenty-first century, African American men consistently wear some type of headgear.

African American women also show a marked interest in their hairstyles and headwear. The slave narratives explain various ways of styling hair even under the most adverse conditions. Photographs of prominent women after the Civil War show them wearing the elegant, long, straight hairstyles in general fashion at the time. In 1906, this processing of the natural hair texture into straight hair spread across the country when Madame C. J. Walker began to market her highly profitable hair formula for managing African American women's hair. Black

women also choose to wear hats, especially prevalent for church attendance.

With one exception, portraits from the eighteenth and nineteenth centuries, and nineteenth-century photographs, of African Americans show them wearing dress appropriate in general society. The exception is the African American woman's headwrap, the oldest extant specific dress item of any immigrant group worn in the early 2000s. But over time, its meaning changed.

In the antebellum South, several states legally enforced the code that ordered black women to wear a cloth head covering in public and not the hats and feathers worn by white women. These codes thus marked certain females as a subservient class. During enslavement, women working in onerous conditions wore the head wrap to keep the hair cleaner and to absorb perspiration. Use of the head wrap at home continued after the Civil

War, but for public wear it was discarded. Beginning with the civil rights movement of the 1960s and 1970s, the head wrap took on other meanings. Young African American women again tied elaborate head wraps around their heads and publicly wore them in acknowledgment of their enslaved ancestors and as a reference to Africa and the way West African women adorn their heads.

During the civil rights movement, along with the head wrap, other young black revolutionaries adopted what they perceived to be West African attire, such as caftans and male head caps. Men and women grew their hair into enormous styles called "Afros," allowing for the natural texture to be emphasized in direct reaction against conks and Walker's straightening products that attempted to simulate European hair. Since the 1960s, some black men have continued to look back to Africa by wearing Rasta locks while black women have their hair intricately braided into elaborate African styles, often adding hairpieces.

African Americans generally have dressed in the prevailing fashions along with other Americans. Portraits of early black clergymen offer examples. Slave narrative frontispieces, however, illustrate the author in either slave clothing or formally dressed as a freed person, the choice obviously expressed what the author wanted to portray about his or her place in society. After the invention of photography, the images of eminent leaders such as Frederick Douglass and Booker T. Washington always show them dressed in formal, gentleman's clothing. Between 1895 and 1925, black intellectuals, literati, and artists strove to present themselves as quite different from the racist stereotypical cartoon illustrations of "Mammys" and "Sambos" drawn by whites. Many illustrations show these "New Negroes" groomed and adorned in conservative, mainstream dress.

Although African Americans adopted the prevailing cultural dress of each period, their style often sets them apart. For instance, travelers' accounts about the South prior to emancipation describe African Americans' dress as more flamboyant and colorful than that of whites. Contemporary African Americans similarly prefer to be well dressed for most occasions and have not adopted the white population's sartorial trends to casual and even sloppy dress.

In general, American fashions came from Europe until about 1950. But at the same time, black styles began to influence white American dress, particularly men's; for example, the zoot suit of the 1940s, highlighted by the popular singers Billy Eckstein and Frank Sinatra. In the 1960s, expensive, stylized brands of tennis shoes, first worn by professional African American athletes, notably basketball players, were adopted by the larger, adolescent community. In the 1990s, white, suburban youth began wearing the hip-hop clothing first worn by young, urban, black males. And in the early twenty-first century, white males wear the doo rag, for decades the African American male's inner-city hair tamer.

Since the mid-1950s, African Americans have become part of the greater American cultural scene. And, in a very real sense, this larger society in the early 2000s adopts African American culture in many aspects of life, not the least in styles of dress.

See also **Afro Hairstyle; Afrocentric Fashion; Ethnic Dress; Zoot Suit.**

BIBLIOGRAPHY

Cunningham, Michael, and Craig Marberry. *Crowns: Portraits of Black Women in Church Hats.* New York: Algonquin Books of Chapel Hill, 2001.

Foster, Helen Bradley. *"New Raiments of Self": African American Clothing in the Antebellum South.* Oxford: Berg, 1997.

———. "African American Jewelry Before the Civil War." In *Beads and Bead Makers: Gender, Material Culture and Meaning.* Edited by Lidia D. Sciama and Joanne B. Eicher 177–192. Oxford: Berg, 1998.

Gates, Henry Louis, Jr. "The Trope of the New Negro and the Reconstruction of the Image of the Black." *Representations* 24 (Fall 1988): 129–155.

Genovese, Eugene. "Clothes Make the Man and the Woman." In *Roll, Jordan, Roll: The World the Slaves Made,* 550–561. New York: Pantheon Books, 1974.

Rawick, George P., ed. *The American Slave: A Composite Autobiography.* Westport, Conn.: Greenwood, 1972, 1977, 1979.

Starke, Barbara M., Lillian O. Holloman, and Barbara K. Nordquist, eds. *African American Dress and Adornment: A Cultural Perspective.* Dubuque, Iowa: Kendall/Hunt, 1990.

White, Shane, and Graham White. *Stylin': African American Expressive Culture.* Ithaca, N.Y.: Cornell University Press, 1998.

Helen Bradley Foster

AFRICA, NORTH: HISTORY OF DRESS North Africa comprises Egypt and the lands to its west, known in Arabic as al-Maghrib, literally "the place of sunset": Libya, Tunisia, Algeria, and Morocco. These political divisions were essentially established by the Ottomans in the sixteenth century, but throughout history this part of Africa has been affected by, and has had a profound effect upon, the regions that surround it: the Mediterranean, sub-Saharan Africa, and the Middle East. It is impossible to appreciate one region without knowing something of the history of all; the style and patterning of dress provides one means of reading that history.

History, Geography, and Climate
The climate and topography of North Africa is extraordinarily varied. The peaks of the High Atlas mountains of Morocco tower over 13,000 feet, whereas oases in the depressions of the Libyan Desert descend to sea level or below. The mild, temperate conditions of the Mediterranean and Atlantic coasts give way to the searing daytime heat and freezing nighttime temperatures of the

desert lands to the south. Crops and vegetation thrive on the fertile northern plains and along the Nile valley, whereas scarcely anything grows in the desert save in the lush oases where the water table is close to the surface.

Ancient Egyptian art gives us a fairly detailed picture of how people in this part of North Africa dressed, at least as far back as 5000 B.C.E. Elsewhere, the extraordinary rock paintings of the Sahara, the Atlas Mountains, and the Nile valley, dating from c. 12000 to 3000 B.C.E., give us an idea of how people might have dressed when the interior of North Africa had a much wetter climate, supporting animals such as hippos, elephants, giraffes, and rhinos.

In the ninth century B.C.E., Carthage was founded near the modern city of Tunis; the Carthaginians traded cloth and other luxury goods across the Sahara in exchange for slaves, gold, and ivory, a pattern continued by the Romans following the sacking of Carthage in 146 B.C.E., only declining when the Portuguese and other Europeans began to trade along the west coast of Africa in the fifteenth century. Roman mosaic pavements from Carthage show garments that bear a remarkable similarity to tunics worn in the early twenty-first century as part of a woman's wedding costume in the Tunisian town of Mahdia.

In the seventh century, Muslim armies invaded North Africa and began the process that, despite resistance from the indigenous Berber peoples, culminated in the establishment of the Hispano-Moresque civilization; this society flourished in the Maghrib countries and southern Spain until the fall of Granada to Christian armies in 1492. After that event, many Muslim and Jewish artisans, including weavers and embroiderers, sought refuge in the large towns of North Africa, and at this point, a particular pattern of production, use of materials, and division of labor, which has remained essentially unchanged, was established.

Town and Country

Walk through the marketplace in any North African town, from Cairo to Marrakech, and at first glance you will find people dressed no differently than city dwellers in any other part of the world. Many male professionals and office workers wear a suit and tie, or possibly some version of the "safari" suit. Many women wear an equally conventional two-piece top and skirt, though most wear the *Hijab*, the Islamic head covering. Younger people of both sexes wear jeans, T-shirts, or football shirts. Among these now ubiquitous "Western" garments, however, people wear more obviously local fashions. Many working men in Cairo wear *djellaba*, the long, loose-fitting gown, sometimes in combination with the kaffiyeh, a turbanlike head cloth or cotton skullcap; older women may wear *burqa* and *bedla*, a black headscarf and flowing dress. In Tunisian towns, the red felt *chechiya*, a cross between skullcap and beret, is still the single most distinctive item of male attire, while in much of the Maghrib the burnoose, a hooded cloak, is worn by many men.

In rural regions, the cut and sewn garments of the city tend to be replaced by single-piece draped or wrapped clothes for women, secured by a fibula, or cloak pin. Berber women of the Atlas Mountains of Morocco wear elaborate headdresses on certain occasions, whereas men may wear large woolen cloaks or knitted "long johns" while herding their flocks during the winter. So-called "granny" dresses—often featuring "foreign" elements such as cuffs, collars, pockets, and pleated hems—are commonly worn by women in rural communities of North Africa. Variations on this style, based on European dresses of the eighteenth and nineteenth centuries, may be found in many other parts of the world, including the islands of the Pacific Ocean. However, the costumes worn for special occasions, particularly marriage, emphasize the real differences between town and country styles.

Marriage Costume

In North Africa, as in all Muslim societies, marriage is seen as the ideal adult state. Clothing for both bride and groom reflects their new social status as well as concerns over modesty and fertility; perhaps most importantly, clothing is seen to ease transition from the unmarried to the married state. As elsewhere in postcolonial Africa, the popularity of "traditional" attire has fluctuated according to political, religious, and economic circumstances. The dictates of fashion and the desire to appear modern has made the white European wedding dress a popular choice, though often dress designers have come up with styles that incorporate something old and something new, thus satisfying the desire to be both fashionable and culturally aware.

The names of certain wedding garments in North Africa suggest one or more of the ceremonies marking the different days of the marriage festivities; for example, *mwashma* (painted), an elaborately embroidered dress from the village of Raf Raf in Tunisia, evokes the *laylat al-henna*, or "night of henna," when the bride and groom are tattooed with henna to bless their marriage and encourage the birth of children.

The simple, T-shaped cotton tunics worn by the bride in Siwa, Egypt; Ghadāmis, Libya; and Mahdia, Tunisia, probably share a common ancestry with certain garments that appear in the mosaics of Roman Carthage. These loose-fitting, yet elaborately decorated dresses are designed to show off the status and beauty of the bride while preserving her modesty; they can also accommodate up to seven more garments beneath them, which are revealed to the bride's and then to the groom's relatives during the *jilwa* ceremony.

The Significance of Pattern

Similar patterns are known by different names in different regions of North Africa and do not necessarily have the same significance. However, universal concerns regarding protection from harm—and, by extension, promoting good luck, health, and fertility—are preoccupations that inform the patterning of artifacts throughout the region.

Concerns about the harmful effects of envy, focused in beliefs surrounding the evil eye, are often manifest in the form of patterning applied to marriage costume in particular, though such designs may perform a host of additional functions. The *bakhnuq*, a marriage shawl from southern Tunisia, is woven in a combination of wool and cotton that, when dyed, reveals the white cotton motifs resistant to dye. These motifs suggest items of jewelry and the pattern of women's tattoos, but also snakes' vertebrae and sharp cloak pins to repel or pierce the evil eye. The different colors of the *bakhnuq* traditionally indicate women's status: young, unmarried girls wear white; married women of child-bearing age don red, while older women wear black or blue.

The wedding dresses of women from the oases in the Western Desert of Egypt, with the exception of the oasis of Siwa, display unmistakable similarities to the embroidered dresses of Palestine, reflecting a long historical connection between the two regions. In the 2000s these dresses are only worn by older women, but they still display the very distinctive patterning, color, and style of embroidery peculiar to each oasis, and sometimes even to individual villages within the same oasis. The embroidered bodices of these dresses, embellished with numerous sequins and sometimes small coins to deflect the evil eye, are a certain way of establishing the identity and affiliation of the wearer. For example, the bodices of dresses from Bahriya oasis are invariably made up of rectangular areas of embroidery with distinctive tassels on the shoulders and chest; the dresses of Daqahlīya oasis, by contrast, have a quite different pattern of embroidery on the bodice, with a central section tapering to a point.

The patterning applied to male clothing reflects similar concerns. The woolen tunics, *gandura*, woven by women for their sons in the remote M'zab region of southern Algeria include named motifs, such as "birds with their young" and "a table of guests," emphasizing fertility and harmony; other motifs, such as forks and weaving combs, have the added dimension of sharp implements with the ability to pierce the evil eye.

Dress as Historical Document

The patterning, color, style, and design of dress and textiles in North Africa suggest clues that, through painstaking research, can be pieced together to provide a more detailed and reliable picture of the past than any written record. Few, if any, of the distinctive features of dress happen by accident or whim; many tell of the movements of people through warfare, religious persecution, trade, economic necessity, or natural disaster. Often this story goes back many centuries, perhaps reaching outside both the region and even the African continent, each event being recorded in a series of details that have gradually evolved into the form of modern dress.

The machine-embroidered wedding dresses worn by women of the Jewish faith in urban Morocco are developments of the elaborate, hand-embroidered dresses of the nineteenth century. These in turn can be traced back to Spanish styles of the late Hispano-Moresque period, brought to Morocco by Jewish craftsmen expelled from Andalusia during Christian persecution of the fifteenth and sixteenth centuries. These craftsmen settled not just in Morocco, but in major urban centers throughout the Maghrib. From the sixteenth century, Ottoman influence began to spread throughout the region, and many of the floral motifs that appear on textiles, such as the *tanshifa* of Algeria, and the *'ajar* and *rida' ahmar* of Tunisia, are of Turkish inspiration. The first two are no longer worn, but the *rida' ahmar* remains the most prestigious item of clothing worn by women of the town of Mahdia. At each end of this silk wedding veil is a set of design bands woven in silk and gold thread. The central band known as *dar-al-wust* (literally "the house in the middle") represents a mosque in stylized form; at the other end of the cloth, the *dar-al-wust* features two motifs in the form of the Star of David, an element of the design that continues to be included by the Muslim weavers out of respect for the Jewish weavers who once produced this garment.

Female weavers in the old silk-weaving town of Naqâda, in the Nile valley of Egypt, produce a style of shawl that has a similarly complex history. Using a tapestry weave technique widely practiced in Damascus and elsewhere in the Levant, male weavers of the nineteenth century produced the aba, a man's gown, as well as other garments such as the cotton and silk modesty garment worn by women of Bahriya oasis in Egypt's Western Desert until it began to go out of fashion in the mid-twentieth century. In recent years a collective of female weavers, taking over what had previously been an exclusively male profession, began to weave this shawl, using the same looms and weaving techniques, but in gaudy, two-tone rayon, rather than in silk and cotton. Their new markets were initially in Libya and Sudan, but when these dried up following political differences between the three countries, the women found other outlets in the tourist trade in Cairo from where these textiles are today exported to various European countries.

Distinctive ceremonial costumes continue to be produced by weavers and embroiderers in different parts of North Africa, displaying the dynamism with which textile traditions throughout Africa have developed since antiquity. Despite the clear influences that have helped to shape North African cultures, an internal dynamic has molded these elements into the distinctive material culture characteristic of each region.

See also **Africa, Sub-Saharan: History of Dress; Burqa; Djellaba; Hijab; Kaffiyeh; Textiles, African.**

BIBLIOGRAPHY

Besancenot, Jean. *Costumes of Morocco*. London and New York: Kegan Paul, 1990. Detailed paintings and drawings made by French artists working in Morocco during the 1930s; text in English.

Cuenot, Joel, ed. *Noces tissées, noces brodées: Parures et costumes féminins de Tunisie.* Paris: Editions Joel Cuenot, 1995. Exhibition catalog (text in French) with useful essays and many color photographs of traditional Tunisian female costume and jewelry.

Reswick, Irmtraud. *Traditional Textiles of Tunisia.* Los Angeles: Craft and Folk Art Museum and University of Washington Press, 1985. Survey of Berber textiles from rural Tunisia, including many technical details of weaving.

Rugh, Andrea. *Reveal and Conceal: Dress in Contemporary Egypt.* Cairo: American University in Cairo Press, 1987. In-depth study of the social significance of costume, both male and female, in late twentieth-century Egypt; numerous black and white illustrations.

Spring, Christopher, and Julie Hudson. *North African Textiles.* London: British Museum Press, 1995. Survey of the region, with additional information on Sudan and Ethiopia, and with an emphasis on the symbolic and social significance of dress; draws on the British Museum's collections and the fieldwork of staff and colleagues.

———. "Urban Textile Traditions of Tunisia." *African Arts* (forthcoming). Fieldwork-based article detailing the production and use of urban costume in Tunisia, 1997–1998; many color photos of weavers and embroiderers and their products; also refers to Tunisian contemporary artists working in the medium of textiles.

Stone, Caroline. *The Embroideries of North Africa.* London: Longman, 1985. Separate sections on Tunisia, Algeria, and Morocco as well as Turkish embroideries and their influence on North Africa; useful technical information on stitches and applications.

Christopher Spring

AFRICA, SUB-SAHARAN: HISTORY OF DRESS

African dress, like dress everywhere, communicates age, gender, occupation, ethnicity, power, and religious commitment for everyday, celebratory, ceremonial, and ritual occasions. Along with fashionable Western dress, Africans wear Islamic and indigenous apparel. Dress involves totally or partially covering the body by supplementing it with apparel and accessories such as head wraps and jewelry and modifying the body itself with tattoos or piercing. Dressing well for Africans involves proper conduct and elegant style, which includes appropriate apparel, cosmetics, and coiffure along with magnificent carriage, graceful movement, fastidious toilette, and immaculate garments.

African dress worn every day indicates socially significant categories, but may also express personal idiosyncrasy. When Africans wear identical dress, such as uniforms or garments made from the same fabric, their garb emphasizes group affiliation and minimizes individuality. African dress is not the same as African costume. Actors and masqueraders temporarily conceal personal identity through costume, whereas in everyday life people communicate and reveal their personal identity through dress.

African dress is as varied and diverse as the historical antecedents and cultural backgrounds of the African people in fifty-five countries and more than eight hundred linguistic groups. A continent two-and-a-half times as large as the continental United States, the physical environment of Africa ranges from the deserts of the Sahara and the Kalahari, to the mountains of the Great Rift Valley, and the rain forests in West and Central Africa, as well as the arid region of the Sahel that borders the Sahara. What African people wear relates to these factors of physical environment, to external and internal trade and migration, to the influences of explorers, missionaries, and travelers and to their own creativity. Specific information about the dress of each ethnic group comes from social, religious, and political histories, as well as oral, archaeological, trade, and mercantile records. Early evidence of dress is depicted in the rock art of northern, southern, and eastern Africa, indicating items of dress that predate contact with European, Asian, and Middle Eastern peoples. Tellem caves in Mali provide cloth fragments that give evidence of hand woven apparel before Saharan trade or coastal contacts.

In the twenty-first century, dress in Africa includes items fashioned from local resources and tools, such as wrappers hand woven from handspun cotton threads on handmade looms in the West African countries of Sierra Leone, Mali, and Nigeria. In addition, combinations of local resources and imported materials are used, as seen in the kente wrappers woven from imported rayon or silk threads on locally made looms in Ghana. African dress also includes imported items from worldwide sources made by complex machines and techniques (British top hats and homburgs, French designer gowns, Italian shoes and handbags, and Swiss laces along with secondhand clothing from the United States) from commercially produced materials. In addition, Africans produce their own designer garments from both imported and locally made textiles and also transform imported secondhand clothing into locally admired fashions. Some African designers, like the Malian, Xuly Bët, left Africa to become successful in Paris, New York, and elsewhere.

Purely indigenous items are becoming less common and therefore less often worn. Borrowed items are often creatively used and juxtaposed with other items that result in a readily identifiable ethnic style. The Kalabari-Ijo people, from the delta area of the Niger River in Nigeria, combine a variety of textiles and other items of dress that are imported from elsewhere in Nigeria and abroad. Their dress illustrates the term "cultural authentication," which designates adopted articles that are selected, characterized by symbolic representation, incorporated, and transformed. For example, the Kalabari-Ijo man's ceremonial hat, called *ajibulu*, stems from the European military and naval officers' bicorne hat from the late eighteenth and early nineteenth centuries. The Kalabari decorate a hat of this shape with hair from a ram's beard along with tiny mirrors, small, shiny Christmas ball ornaments, brightly colored feathers, and plastic hair clasps, each glued or stitched onto the basic fabric, resulting in a head covering that is uniquely Kalabari.

African residents who come from European and Asian ancestry may choose not to wear African items of dress; instead, they maintain forms of dress fashionable in the countries of their ancestors. Indian women whose families have lived in East and West Africa for several generations continue to wear the sari as commonly worn on the Indian subcontinent. In South Africa, Afrikaaners wear European dress that continues their European heritage. In contrast to those who refrain from wearing African items, some non-Africans embrace them: Peace Corps volunteers from the United States in Nigeria found the Yoruba *dansiki* (more commonly known in the United States as "dashiki") a handsome and comfortable shirt to wear. Tourists, too, often buy and wear African beads, hats, cloth, garments, and fans while travelling and take them home as souvenirs.

Dressing the Torso
The torso is usually the focus when dressing the body, although headwear and footwear are also significant. Items of dress generally may be classified as enclosing, attached, or hand held. Enclosing dress can be subdivided into wraparound, preshaped, and suspended categories; all examples are found in Africa. Wraparound garments are formed from rectangular pieces of fabric that are folded, crushed, or twisted around the body. Preshaped items include cut and sewn garments along with other items, such as jewelry, that are molded or cast. Most attached and many suspended enclosing items of dress are also jewelry, such as earrings and necklaces. Handheld items usually consist of accessories such as a fan, purse, cane, or walking stick. Throughout Africa, both men and women wear variations of the wrapper (also called *kanga*, *futa*, *lappa*, or *pagne*). As a garment, the loose fit of wraparound apparel seems particularly appropriate and comfortable to wear because of prevalent high temperatures, both dry and humid. Wrappers are also easily made from available materials such as skins, bark (or bark cloth), or wool, cotton, silk, and raffia for handwoven cloth. Preshaped garments for men and women in general came from contact with Europeans and Middle Easterners, as women adopted dresses and gowns and men adopted jackets, shirts, and trousers as clothing styles. African women and girls rarely wore pants or other bifurcated garments until jeans and pants became fashionable for women in Europe, America, and Japan, thus beginning an influence on young African women especially to adopt these styles for many occasions.

The wrapper, however, is probably the most frequent and popular indigenous garment in sub-Saharan Africa. Women may wrap cloth from their waist to their knees, calves, or feet. Sometimes they wrap the cloth under the armpits to cover their breasts and lower body. Men ordinarily wrap a small length of cloth from their waist to their feet, with the chest either bare or covered. For both men and women in the twenty-first century, a bare chest is not frequently seen in public, but remains an option for dressing informally at home. Non-Muslim Africans were influenced by European ideas of modesty after many countries became independent in the 1960s, because they discovered that journalists and outsiders commented negatively on African "nudity," usually referring to bare-breasted women. In fact, some Nigerian municipalities passed laws at that time specifically forbidding women to enter the town if they were bare-breasted.

Examples of wraparound garments abound. In Ghana, Asante men wear handwoven *kente* togas; in Ethiopia, Amharic women don handwoven shawls of sheer, white cotton; in Nigeria, Yoruba women garb themselves in indigo resist-dyed wrappers; in Zaire, the Kuba dress in raffia skirts. Other examples include several from southern Africa: Ndebele and Xhosa women wrap commercially made blankets around themselves, and Zulu men wrap skin aprons. Both sexes among the Baganda in Uganda traditionally wore bark-cloth wrappers, as did the Masai of Kenya and Somalis from the Horn of Africa; some continue the practice today. Masai warriors, depending on their geographical location, wear a wrapper that is either below the knee or very short, sometimes wrapping it around the waist and at other times wrapping it across one shoulder. Those warriors wearing short wrappers are said to choose that style to show off their handsome bodies. Masai women wear a skirt or cloth wrapped around their waist as well as a blanket or cloth wrapped over their shoulders. Somali people wore leather garments of their own making before the 1800s, but imported cotton textiles quickly made inroads and included several options of wrapping the body for both men and women, depending on the occasion and the weather.

For festive, ritual, or ceremonial occasions, Ghanaian men wear a well-known example of an African wraparound garment similar to the Roman toga. They take a large rectangle of cloth, sometimes as large as six yards square, depending on the size of the man, and wrap it full-length around the body with one shoulder uncovered. This style became internationally visible in the 1960s when the first president of Ghana, Kwame Nkrumah, wore it and was photographed in it for ceremonial occasions, both at home and abroad.

Preshaped dress involves cutting and sewing lengths of cloth to make a garment fit the body. Common styles are shirts, blouses, robes, and pants, or the Hausa man's *baba riga* (big gown). Cross-cultural contacts influenced the design of many preshaped garments. The colonial impact and trade contacts of the late nineteenth and early twentieth centuries are seen in several women's gowns.

For example, the long gown (called *boubou*) made popular by Wolof women in Senegal indicates probable Muslim and Middle Eastern origins, whereas the gowns of Herero women in Namibia, Efik women in Nigeria, and the "granny" gown of women in Egypt show nineteenth-century European contact.

Men's trouser shapes vary considerably. Along with Western fashions found across the continent, indigenous fashions also abound. In Nigeria, Hausa men wear enormously large drawstring breeches with a "*baba riga*" over the top. Yoruba men wear both wide or narrow trousers, often as a three-piece outfit along with a robe (*agbada*) and shirt (*dansiki*). When the men's ensemble is tailored from colorful, wax-printed cotton, the Yoruba outfit is interpreted as being informal. If made from damask, lace, eyelet, brocade, or the handwoven textile of nubby, native silk that the Yoruba call *sanyan* (produced by a different silk worm than the Asian one), the ensemble is considered formal.

Throughout Africa, males wear preshaped shirts and hip-length or calf-length garments with trousers or wrappers. Finishing and decorating details distinguish many of the garments as being associated with one ethnic group or another. In the Republic of Benin, Fon men's ensembles include a heavily embroidered, sleeveless tunic pleated at the neckline and flared at the hipline that they combine with embroidered trousers and an embroidered cap. In Cote d'Ivoire and Ghana, Mandinka and Akan men wear garments known as war shirts and hunters' shirts. Amulets decorate these garments and are made of animal horns, claws, teeth, or packets that contain slips of paper with magical or mystical words written on them.

Enclosing garments include suspended and combination forms. Some hats are suspended by being perched on top of the head and many items of jewelry are suspended around the neck or wrist. Capes (often worn by Hausa and Fulani emirs and other royalty) are combination forms. Preshaped and stitched, they are also loosely suspended from the shoulders.

Items held by or for a person complete an African ensemble. As accessory items, these include umbrellas, canes, walking sticks, purses, handbags, fans, switches, handkerchiefs, linguist staffs, and tusks, as well as weapons such as daggers, swords, and spears. Many materials are used for these items. An individual carries an umbrella for protection from rain or as a substitute for a cane. Attendants for a ruler carry large, decorative, and colorful umbrellas to emphasize the ruler's position and significance, for a ruler should not be so encumbered. Canes and walking sticks are made of wood, ivory, or plastic; fans, of paper, leather, hide, or feathers. Fashionable handbags are commercially manufactured; some are produced domestically while others are imported. When wearing an indigenous ensemble, an individual often carries a bag crafted from indigenous materials, such as domestically produced leather that is also dyed,

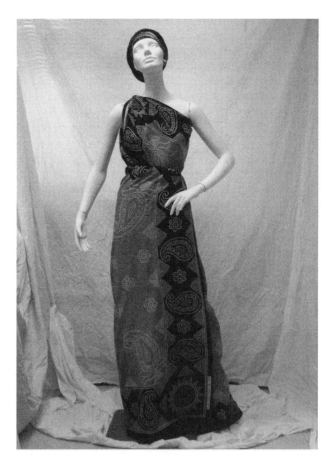

African wrapper. The wrapped garment is probably the most frequently worn by Africans of both sexes, as its comfortable, loose fit is the best suited to the humid environment. PHOTOGRAPH BY HEATHER MARIE AKOU, PERSONAL COLLECTION. REPRODUCED BY PERMISSION.

painted, or decorated with beads. An ivory elephant's tusk held by an important individual indicates high status and wealth.

Many types of body modifications and jewelry also dress the torso. Tattooing occurs among light-skinned people, like the North African Berbers, because tattoos do not show on dark skin. Instead, permanent markings in the form of scarification and cicatrization or temporary cosmetics (ochre, kaolin, indigo, henna, and chalk) decorate dark-skinned bodies. Many permanent-marking procedures began to die out in the twentieth century as Africans became exposed to Western cosmetic and body decoration practices, and interest grew in looking "modern." Cosmetics familiar to Westerners are easily available throughout Africa, although not always worn or used plentifully. Again, the issue relates to varieties of skin color, for lipstick and blush are not as visible on dark complexions as on light-colored ones. Similarly, henna—a common cosmetic in North Africa and the Middle East—is not used by Africans with darker skin, although it is sometimes used on the palms and bottom of the feet, which are lighter parts of the body. Both men and women wear scented products, but frequently, African men wear stronger scents than found among most European and American men. European perfumes and scents can be purchased throughout Africa, but prohibitive prices preclude wide usage. Instead, indigenous products are available and used, as in the case of Muslim women who stand over incense burners to scent their clothing with the fragrant smoke.

Africans display many kinds of jewelry. Items for the torso include necklaces, armlets, bracelets, and anklets of many types, along with items that circle the waist, such as "waist beads." Necklaces vary in size and style, from large to small, fashioned from metals, beads, shells, chains, and medallions. Some bracelets and anklets are modest in size, circling only the wrist and ankle with metal or beads. Others are massive, used to adorn the lower arm, upper arm, or lower leg with coils of copper or chunks of ivory. Materials used for body ornaments include gold, silver, brass, copper, ivory, natural stones like jasper, coral, and amber, and many cowrie shells (which often decorate garments as well). Both imported and locally produced glass beads exist throughout Africa. Italy, Austria, and Germany historically exported glass beads to all areas of Africa, and artisans in towns (Bida, Nigeria, for example) produce glass beads from recycled beverage bottles. Both Masai men and women wear necklaces of imported, colorful beads that that look like wide collars and rest on the back of the neck. Some Masai children wear miniature examples of these beaded necklaces as well as beaded bracelets and anklets. Small disk shapes cut from ostrich shells or celluloid are used for waist beads worn by women and girls in West Africa. These beads are decorative and also sexually attractive in intimate situations. Some make sounds that attract attention when the individual moves.

Color, texture, or fabric motif distinguishes the dress of different peoples. All types of textiles exist from imported natural and synthetic yarns along with domestic ones of cotton, wool, silk, and synthetics. Favorite fabrics include plain broadcloth, lace, eyelet, damask, brocade, and velvet. Suppliers are generally located in Africa, but import sources include the United Kingdom and such European countries as the Netherlands and Switzerland. Asian sources include Japan, China, and India, where manufacturers cater to African preferences for specific textile motifs and colors. Fashions in material, design, and color change over time, but preferences for muted and somber colors can often be found in some countries, bright and saturated colors in others, and dazzling whites or pastels in still others. A printed textile used for wrappers in Tanzania and Kenya known as *kanga*, domestically produced in the early 2000s, has a distinct pattern. Ordinarily, the colors are bright green, yellow, orange, and red. The cloth is printed in repeat motifs that include a motto or saying. These written messages communicate political or social points of view. Somali men

and women have used imported cloth for their wrappers for many years. Records from the nineteenth century indicate that one type, an inexpensive white cotton, was called *merikani* because it was imported from the United States. Another imported blue fabric worn during the same period, came from the Indian city of Surat to be used by married women as a head wrap.

Identical textiles worn for special events by a large number of people are popular in various locations. An entire community or special group may honor significant people (usually political) by having their portrait screen-printed on a commercially manufactured textile or T-shirt. Other times, members of the group select a special color or pattern of either handwoven or commercial cloth to wear. The custom of wearing identical cloth is known as *aso ebi* (family dress) and *aso egbi* (association dress) among the Yoruba of Nigeria, where it apparently began. Other groups, the Ibo of Nigeria, for example, have adopted the custom and call their identical dress "uniforms." Techniques to decorate garments include embroidery, beading, and appliqué. Various robes worn by men throughout West Africa are heavily embroidered; simpler embroidery is seen on some of the contemporary gowns worn by women, caftans or boubous, especially those being made for the tourist market in the early twenty-first century. Beading is found on robes of some royalty; sequins and beads decorate women's blouses, for example among the Yoruba and Kalabari-Ijo. Appliqué is often used for ceremonial attire, masquerade garb, and trappings for horses.

Hair Styles and Headwear

Stylish coiffure, headwear, and appropriate cosmetics often complete African ensembles of dress, and in addition provide information about gender, age, political position, or community standing. Hairstyles vary across the continent. Braiding (sometimes called plaiting or weaving) the hair and twisting are common as well as combing the hair in sections to produce a pattern on the scalp after the sections are braided or bound with thread. Wigs are worn, fashionable ones for every day, made from synthetic or human hair, as well as older types, made from indigenous fibers, for special ceremonies. Older customs also included adding oil, ochre, or mud to give textural and sculptural effects to the hair. Headwear is made from indigenous as well as imported materials including textiles, skins, feathers, straw, raffia, and beads. Children and youth wear headgear less often than adults do. Men's headwear includes caps, hats, and turbans and in some areas exhibits greater variety in type than the head wraps (often called head ties) and other headwear of women. This may be related to a wider range of available positions in political and religious systems for men than women, such as chieftaincies and priesthoods. Men's headwear includes many types of caps and hats from handwoven and hand-embroidered fabrics but, especially since the arrival of Europeans,

Kalabari chief. Beads, coral accessories, and elaborately ornamented headgear, such as the *ajibulu* crown shown here, are often worn by sub-Saharian Africans of elevated social or political status. © CAROLYN NGOZI EICHER. REPRODUCED BY PERMISSION.

men wear many styles of imported hats and caps. Opulent decorations for hats of high-status (often royal) men include embroidery with metallic threads of gold and silver or precious gems or metals. In some areas, men select an imported top hat, derby, or fedora as part of their dress ensemble, again indicating high status, whether born into the position or achieved by being granted a local honor or reaching a certain age. Veils and turbans may also be part of male dress. The wrapped white turban of a Hausa man shows that he has been to Mecca. The shiny, deep indigo-dyed veils worn by Tuareg males make them easily identifiable.

Adult females, particularly the Yoruba of Nigeria and Ndebele of Southern Africa, most often wear cloth head ties wrapped in numerous shapes and styles. Fashion changes as well as creativity and individual flair influence their head-tie arrangements. A highly desirable fabric for women's head ties in western Africa comes from a manufacturer in England, but women also select hand-woven cloth to match their wrapper set. An example of fashion change occurred among Herero women, who used skins for headwear in the 1800s, but use cloth in the early 2000s. Muslim women throughout Africa employ several methods to cover their hair. Some cut and sew cloth to preshape a head covering or suspend fabric to create a veil that reveals only their eyes. Others loosely wrap fabric over their heads and tie or pin it under their chins. Some veiling garments, such as the burqa, were once worn only by Arab women living in Africa but have spread to other Muslim populations. Jewelry also decorates the hair and head for men and women, including earrings, hair ornaments, and headbands using the same beads, metals, precious and semiprecious gems, ivory, stones, fibers, and many natural materials to fashion them. Imported items like buttons also provide decoration.

Footwear

Footwear is often desired to complete a person's dress ensemble. During colonial periods, some Europeans did not allow shoes to be worn by those subservient to them, whether in the house or at work in colonial offices. Many styles of leather sandals, boots, and shoes are worn; these may be handmade or commercially manufactured, locally or abroad. Inexpensive rubber and plastic thongs are widely available for people who want to protect their feet in a minimal fashion and for minimal cost. In contrast, men and women of special rank wear distinctive and expensive footwear decorated with beads, rare feathers, precious metals, or carefully worked designs in leather. For example, Hausa emirs in northern Nigeria display ostrich feathers on the insteps of their footwear to complement their royal gown and cape, and the horsemen in their royal entourage wear leather boots. In the south of Nigeria, rulers choose other footwear. The oba of Benin puts on slippers covered with coral beads as part of his ceremonial dress, and the royal ensemble of the Alake of Abeokuta includes colorful slippers covered with tiny imported glass beads.

Conclusion

African dress may consist of a single item or an ensemble and range from simple to complex. Single items such as a hat, necklace, or waist beads contrast with the total ensemble of an elaborate gown or robe worn with a head covering, jewelry, and accessories. A wrapper, body paint, and uncomplicated hairdo exemplify a simple ensemble whereas a complex one combines several richly decorated garments, an intricate coiffure, opulent jewelry, and other items. Either single items or total ensembles may have an additive, cumulative character created by clusters of beads or layers of cloth or jewelry. As an individual's body moves, such clusters and layers are necessary components of dress that provides ambient noise with the rustle of fibers or fabrics and jingle of jewelry. A bulky body often indicates power and the importance of the individual's position, but slenderness is gaining popularity as young people travel to the West or see Western media. Impressiveness through bulk can be achieved by layering garments and jewelry or using heavy fabric. Examples are the elaborate robes of a ruler, such as the Asantehene of the Asante people in Ghana. On top of his robes, he adds impressive amounts of gold jewelry and presents himself in an ensemble expected by his subjects. Similarly, the customers of a successful and powerful market woman expect her to wear an imposing wrapper set, blouse, and head wrap. In many cases, middle-class and wealthy African men and women enjoy a wardrobe of many types of dress, selecting from a variety of Western pieces of apparel or from indigenous items. Such a wardrobe allows selection of an outfit to attend an ethnic funeral or ceremonial event in their hometown as well as dress in current fashions from Europe and America when traveling, studying abroad, or living or visiting in African cosmopolitan cities.

The wide range of color and style in African dress, headdress, and footwear reflects the reality that covering and adorning the body is used to provide both aesthetic and social information about an individual or a group. Aesthetically, individuals can manipulate color, texture, shape, and proportion with great skill. An individual's dress may express an individual's personal aesthetic interest or it may indicate membership in an ethnic, occupational, or religious group. Similarly, an individual's dress conveys social information because specific expectations exist within groups for appropriate outfits for age, occupation, and group affiliation. Understanding the dress of the people who live on the large African continent means realizing that many complex factors contribute to choices that an African makes about what to wear at a particular time. To appreciate fully or depict accurately the dress of an individual African or of a specific African group of people, one needs to consult available social and historical records and contemporary scholarly information as well as African newspapers, magazines, television, and other media sources.

See also **Africa, North: History of Dress; Bogolan; Burqa; Dashiki; Indigo; Kanga; Kente; Pagne and Wrapper; Secondhand Clothes, Anthropology of; Textiles, African; Xuly Bët.**

BIBLIOGRAPHY

Allman, Jean. *Fashioning Africa: Power and the Politics of Dress.* Bloomington: Indiana University Press, 2004.

Arnoldi, Mary Jo, and Chris Mullen Kreamer. *Crowning Achievements: African Art of Dressing the Head.* Los Angeles: UCLA Fowler Museum of Cultural History, 1995.

Beckwith, Carol, and Saitoti Tepilit Ole. *Maasai.* New York: Harry N. Abrams, 1980.

Clarke, Duncan. *African Hats and Jewelry.* New York: Chartwell Books, 1998.

Daly, Catherine, Joanne Eicher, and Tonye Erekosima. "Male and Female Artistry in Kalabari Dress." *African Arts* 19 (3) (May 1986): 48–51.

Eicher, Joanne, ed. *African Dress: A Select and Annotated Bibliography of Sub-Saharan Countries.* East Lansing: African Studies Center, Michigan State University, 1970.

Fall, N'Goné, Jean Loup Pivin, Khady Diallo, Bruno Airaud, and Patrice Félix-Tchicaya. "Spécial Mode: African Fashion." *Revue Noire* 27 (December 1997, January–Feburary 1998).

Fisher, Angela. *Africa Adorned.* New York: Harry N. Abrams, 1984.

Hendrickson, Hilde, ed. *Clothing and Difference: Embodied Identities in Colonial and Post-Colonial Africa.* Durham, N.C.: Duke University Press, 1996.

Mertens, Alice, and Joan Broster. *African Elegance.* Cape Town, South Africa: Purnell and Sons, 1973.

Murphy, Robert. "Social Distance and the Veil." *American Anthropologist* 56, no. 6 (1965): 1257–74.

Perani, Judith, and Norma H. Wolff. *Cloth, Dress, and Art Patronage in Africa.* Oxford: Berg, 1999.

Picton, John. *The Art of African Textiles: Tradition, Technology, and Lurex.* London: Barbican Art Gallery, 1996.

Pokornowski, Ila, Joanne Eicher, Moira Harris, and Otto Thieme, eds. *African Dress: A Select and Annotated Bibliography.* Vol. 2. East Lansing: African Studies Center, Michigan State University, 1985.

Rabine, Leslie W. *The Global Circulation of African Fashion.* Oxford: Berg, 2002.

Sieber, Roy. *African Textiles and Decorative Arts.* New York: Museum of Modern Art, 1972.

van der Plas, Els, and Willemsen Marlous. *The Art of African Fashion*. Trenton, N.J.: Africa World Press, 1998.

Joanne B. Eicher

AFRO HAIRSTYLE At the end of the 1950s, a small number of young black female dancers and jazz singers broke with prevailing black community norms and wore unstraightened hair. The hairstyle they wore had no name and when noticed by the black press, was commonly referred to as wearing hair "close-cropped." These dancers and musicians were sympathetic to or involved with the civil rights movement and felt that unstraightened hair expressed their feelings of racial pride. Around 1960, similarly motivated female student civil rights activists at Howard University and other historically black colleges stopped straightening their hair, had it cut short, and generally suffered ridicule from fellow students. Over time the close-cropped style developed into a large round shape, worn by both sexes, and achieved by lifting longer unstraightened hair outward with a wide-toothed comb known as an Afro pick. At the peak of its popularity in the late 1960s and early 1970s the Afro epitomized the black is beautiful movement. In those years the style represented a celebration of black beauty and a repudiation of Eurocentric beauty standards. It also created a sense of commonality among its wearers who saw the style as the mark of a person who was willing to take a defiant stand against racial injustice. As the Afro increased in popularity its association with black political movements weakened and so its capacity to communicate the political commitments of its wearers declined.

Pre-Existing Norms

In the 1950s black women were expected to straighten their hair. An unstraightened black female hairstyle constituted a radical rejection of black community norms. Black women straightened their hair by coating it with protective pomade and combing it with a heated metal comb. This technique transformed the tight curls of African American hair into completely straight hair with a pomaded sheen. Straightened hair remained straight until it had contact with water. Black women made every effort to lengthen the time between touch-ups. They protected their hair from rain, did not go swimming, and washed their hair only immediately before straightening it again. If a woman could not straighten her hair, she covered it with a scarf.

The technology of hair straightening served prevailing gender norms that defined long wavy hair as beautifully feminine. While hair straightening could not lengthen hair and may have contributed to breakage, it transformed tightly curled hair into straight hair that could be set into waves. Tightly curled hair was disparaged as "nappy" or "bad hair," while straight hair was praised as "good hair." The Eurocentric underpinnings of these black community judgments have led many to characterize the practice of hair straightening as a black attempt to imitate whites. Cultural critics have countered by arguing that hair straightening represented much more than an imitation of whites. Black women modeled themselves after other black women who straightened their hair to present themselves as urban, modern, and well groomed.

In the post–World War II period, when the vast majority of black women straightened their hair, most black men wore short unstraightened hair. The male straightened hairstyle that was known as the conk was highly visible because it was the style favored by many black entertainers. The conk, however, was a rebellious style associated with entertainers and with men in criminal subcultures. Conventional black men and men with middle-class aspirations kept their hair short and did not straighten it.

Origins

In the late 1950s and early 1960s, awareness of newly independent African nations and the victories and setbacks of the civil rights movement encouraged feelings of hope and anger, as well as exploration of identity among young African Americans. The Afro originated in that political and emotional climate. The style fit with a broader generational rejection of artifice but more importantly, it expressed defiance of racist beauty norms, rejection of middle-class conventions, and pride in black beauty. The unstraightened hair of the Afro was simultaneously a way to celebrate the cultural and physical distinctiveness of the race and to reject practices associated with emulation of whites.

Dancers, jazz and folk musicians, and university students may have enjoyed greater freedom to defy conventional styles than ordinary working women and were the first to wear unstraightened styles. In the late 1950s a few black modern dancers who tired of continually touching-up straightened hair that perspiration had returned to kinkiness, decided to wear short unstraightened hair. Ruth Beckford, who performed with Katherine Dunham, recalled the confused reactions she received when she wore a short unstraightened haircut. Strangers offered her cures to help her hair grow and a young student asked the shapely Miss Beckford if she was a man.

Around 1960, in politically active circles on the campuses of historically black colleges and in civil rights movement organizations, a few young black women adopted natural hairstyles. As early as 1961 the jazz musicians Abbey Lincoln, Melba Liston, Miriam Makeba, Nina Simone and folk singer Odetta were performing wearing short unstraightened hair. Though these women are primarily known as performing artists, political commitments were integral to their work. They sang lyrics calling for racial justice and performed at civil rights movement rallies and fund-raisers. In 1962 and 1963

Activist Angela Davis, without and with an Afro. By the late 1960s, the Afro was less frequently associated with black political movements, but the notoriety of Davis caused many to refer to the Afro as the "Angela Davis look." © Bettmann/Corbis. Reproduced by permission.

Abbey Lincoln toured with Grandassa, a group of models and entertainers whose fashion shows promoted the link between black pride and what had begun to be called variously the "au naturel," "au naturelle," or "natural" look. When the mainstream black press took note of unstraightened hair, reporters generally insinuated that wearers of "au naturelle" styles had sacrificed their sex appeal for their politics. They could not yet see unstraightened hair as beautiful.

Early Reactions
Though they received support for the style among fellow activists, the first women who wore unstraightened styles experienced shocked stares, ridicule, and insults for wearing styles that were perceived as appalling rejections of community standards. Many of these women had conflicts with their elders who thought of hair straightening as essential good grooming. Ironically, a few black female students who were isolated at predominantly white colleges experienced acceptance from white radicals who were unfamiliar with black community norms. More mainstream whites, however, saw the style as shockingly unconventional and some employers banned Afros from the workplace. As more women abandoned hair straightening, the natural became a recognizable style and a fre-

quent topic of debate in the black press. Increasing numbers of women stopped straightening their hair as the practice became emblematic of racial shame. At a 1966 rally, the black leader Stokely Carmichael fused style, politics, and self-love when he told the crowd: "We have to stop being ashamed of being black. A broad nose, a thick lip, and nappy hair is us and we are going to call that beautiful whether they like it or not. We are not going to fry our hair anymore" (Bracey, Meier, and Rudwick 1970, p. 472). The phrase "black is beautiful" was everywhere and it summed up a new aesthetic ranking that valued the beauty of dark brown skin and the tight curls of unstraightened hair.

Increasing numbers of activists adopted the hairstyle and the media disseminated their images. By 1966 the Afro was firmly associated with political activism. Women who wore unstraightened hair could feel that their hair identified them with the emerging black power movement. Televised images of Black Panther Party members wearing black leather jackets, black berets, sunglasses, and Afros projected the embodiment of black radicalism. Some men and many women began to grow larger Afros. Eventually only hair that was cut in a large round shape was called an Afro, while other unstraightened haircuts were called naturals.

Popularization

As larger numbers of black men and women wore the Afro, workplace and intergenerational conflicts lessened. In 1968 Kent cigarettes and Pepsi-cola developed print advertisements featuring women with large Afros. Decorative Afro picks with black power fist-shaped handles or African motifs were popular fashion items. While continuing to market older products for straightening hair, manufacturers of black hair-care products formulated new products for Afro care. The electric "blow-out comb" combined a blow-dryer and an Afro pick for styling large Afros. Wig manufacturers introduced Afro wigs. Though the Afro's origins were in the United States, Johnson Products, longtime manufacturer of hair-straightening products, promoted its new line of Afro Sheen products with the Swahili words for "beautiful people" in radio and print advertisements that stated "Wantu Wazuri use Afro Sheen." In 1968 a large Afro was a crucial element of the style of Clarence Williams III, star of the popular television series, *The Mod Squad.* In 1969 British *Vogue* published Patrick Lichfield's photograph of Marsha Hunt, who posed nude except for arm and ankle bands and her grand round Afro. This widely celebrated image fit with an emerging fashion industry pattern of featuring black models associated with signifiers of the primitive, wildness, or exotica.

One wearer of a large Afro was the activist and scholar Angela Davis who wore the style in keeping with the practices of other politically active black women. When, in 1970, she was placed on the FBI's most wanted list, her image circulated internationally. During her time as a fugitive and prisoner she became a heroine for many black women as a wide campaign worked for her release. The large Afro became indelibly associated with Angela Davis and increasingly described as the "Angela Davis look." Ironically the popularization of her image contributed to the transformation of the Afro from a practice that expressed the political commitments of dedicated activists to a style that could be worn by the merely fashion-conscious.

The style that became the Afro originated with black women. Since most black men wore short unstraightened hair in the late 1950s, short unstraightened hair could only represent something noteworthy for black women. When, in the mid-1960s, the style evolved into a large round shape, it became a style for men as well as women. Since black men customarily wore unstraightened hair, an Afro was only an Afro when it was large. During the late 1960s and early 1970s, when men and women wore Afros, commercial advertising and politically inclined artwork generally reasserted gender distinctions that had been challenged by the first women who dared to wear short unstraightened hair. Countless images of the era showed the head and shoulders of a black man wearing a large Afro behind a black woman with a larger Afro. Typically, the woman's shoulders were bare and she wore large earrings.

Declining Popularity and Enduring Significance

In the late 1960s the black radical H. Rap Brown complained that underneath their natural hairstyles too many blacks had "processed minds." By the end of the decade many blacks would agree with his observation that the style said little about a wearer's political views. As fashion incorporated the formerly shocking style, it detached the Afro from its political origins. The hair-care industry worked to position the Afro as one option among many and to reassert hair straightening as the essential first step of black women's hair care. In 1970 a style known as the Curly Afro, which required straightening and then curling hair, became popular for black women. In 1972 Ron O'Neal revived pre-1960s subcultural images of black masculinity when he wore long wavy hair as the star of the film *Superfly.* Large Afros continued to be popular through the 1970s but their use in the era's blaxploitation films introduced new associations with Hollywood's parodic representations of black subcultures.

While the large round Afro is so strongly associated with the 1970s that it is most frequently revived in comical retro contexts, the Afro nonetheless had enduring consequences. It permanently expanded prevailing images of beauty. In 2003 the black singer Erykah Badu stepped onstage at Harlem's Apollo Theater wearing a large Afro wig. After a few songs she removed the wig to reveal her short unstraightened hair. Reporters described her hair using the language employed by those who had first attempted to describe the styles worn by singer Nina Simone, Abbey Lincoln, and Odetta at the beginning of the 1960s. They called it "close-cropped." Prior to the popularity of the Afro black women hid unstraightened hair under scarves. Through the Afro the public grew accustomed to seeing the texture of unstraightened hair as beautiful and the way was opened for a proliferation of unstraightened African American styles.

See also **African American Dress; Afrocentric Fashion; Barbers; Hair Accessories; Hairdressers; Hairstyles.**

BIBLIOGRAPHY

Bracey, John H., Jr., August Meier, and Elliott Rudwick, eds. *Black Nationalism in America.* New York: Bobbs-Merrill Company, 1970.

Craig, Maxine Leeds. *Ain't I a Beauty Queen: Black Women, Beauty, and the Politics of Race,* New York: Oxford University Press, 2002. Includes a detailed history of the emergence of the Afro.

Davis, Angela Y. "Afro Images: Politics, Fashion, and Nostalgia." *Critical Inquiry* 21 (Autumn 1994): 37–45. Davis reflects on the use of photographs of her Afro in fashion images devoid of political content.

Kelley, Robin D. G. "Nap Time: Historicizing the Afro." *Fashion Theory* 1, no. 4 (1997): 339–351. Kelley traces the black bohemian origins of the Afro and its transformation from a feminine to masculine style.

Mercer, Kobena. "Black Hair/Style Politics." In *Out There: Marginalization and Contemporary Cultures,* edited by Russell

Ferguson, Martha Gever, Trinh T. Minh-ha, and Cornel West, 247–264. Cambridge, Mass.: MIT Press, 1990. Mercer places the Afro in the context of earlier black hair care practices and challenges the widely held view that hair-straightening represented black self-hatred.

Maxine Leeds Craig

AFROCENTRIC FASHION An Afrocentric perspective references African history and applies it to all creative, social, and political activity.

Negritude and Afrocentricity

Afrocentricity was founded in the 1940s when Aimé Césaire and Léopold Sédar Senghor, president of Senegal and poet, used the term "negritude" to describe the effects of Western colonization upon black people without any reference to their culture, language, or place. The most significant example of colonization was the Atlantic slave trade that started in the fourteenth century and lasted for 400 years. However, the effects of colonization have arguably caused Africa to become economically underdeveloped and culturally bereft. For the descendants of slaves living in Western countries Atlantic slavery had resulted in them experiencing disadvantage and intolerance, which was based upon their physical dissimilarity from the indigenous population. These points are at the kernel of Aimé Césaire and Léopold Sédar Senghor's idea that negritude is defined by the physical state of the black person, which is blackness.

Afrocentrism gained gravitas when Cheikh Anta Diop (1974) argued that ancient Africans and modern Africans share similar physical appearances and other genetic similarities, as well as cultural patterns and language structures. Diop and others have used this insight to sponsor the idea of ancient Egypt (Kemet) as a black civilization and a reference point for modern Africans.

Frantz Fanon (1967) used the term "negritude" to illustrate the existence of black psychological pathologies that hindered black individuals from attaining liberation within Western modernism and the way all black people are affected by colonialism. An example of black psychological pathology in self-expression is found in the way fashion provides a visual backdrop to the engagement between mask and identity, image and identification. The purpose of fashion in the African setting is precise; it enables black individuals to attain status positions that are outside of their usual habitus. In doing so blacks use some of the visual tools of their oppression and liberation when creating their fashioned self image. Fanon provides a sketch of a black Caribbean man who arrives in the West after leaving his homeland. He leaves behind a way of life symbolized by the bandanna and the straw hat. Once in the West the man shifts into a position, which is manifest by his unease of existing in the West and perhaps from wearing Western clothes. Fanon's rather harsh indictment offers blacks in the West only two possibilities, either to stand with the white world or to reject it. This concept of negritude contributed to the conceptual basis of Afrocentrism.

Expression of Self

The way that black people use apparel in personal representations of *self* may differ and be dependent upon location and perspective. Afrocentric fashion is analogous to Western fashion. Both appropriate much from oppositional fashion expressions; consequently both expressions are fragmented and perennially incomplete. Avid Afrocentrists reject the idea that Afrocentricism might be influenced or contain traces of Western culture, though it is perceptible that Afrocentric fashion is less absolute than other expressive forms, such as music and art.

In Africa and in the African diaspora, disparate elements may be united by their adoption of Afrocentric apparel. Visualizations of Afrocentric clothing are made with reference to Kemet and are therefore mental constructions that are mimetic because they draw upon the idea of an ancient African self and its accompanied gestures, which are of course an aberration, occasioned by the pathology that Fanon alluded to. Around the time of the 1960s American civil rights movement, Afrocentricism became important and sometimes central to the fashion expressions of black people living in America, the Caribbean, and Britain.

Ordinarily, Afrocentric clothing does not feature fine linen dresses, kilts, collars, or the wearing of kohl on one's eyes; yet Afrocentric dressing does feature selected apparel motifs and long-established textiles, production, and cutting methods from the rest of Africa. Afrocentric fashion references the apparel traditions of multicultural Africa, including the traditions of both the colonizers and the colonized. The story of batik (which is Indonesian in origin) is an example of the former.

For Afrocentrists, Afrocentric dress is the norm; consequently Western dress is "ethnic" and therefore "exotic." For that reason, Afrocentric dress has become a virtuoso expression of African diaspora culture. Political and cultural activities like black cultural nationalism have adopted Afrocentric fashion for its visual symbolism. African and black identity and black nationalism are expressed by the wearing of African and African-inspired dress such as the dashiki, Abacos (Mao-styled suit), Kanga, caftan, wraps, and Buba. All of these items are cultural products of the black diaspora and are worn exclusively or integrated into Western dress.

These fashions connote a dissonance. The combination of Afrocentric and Western styles in a single garment or outfit is a direct confrontation of Western fashion, especially if the clothing does not simultaneously promote an Afrocentric leitmotiv or theme. Within its configuration, Afrocentric dress co-opts a number of textiles. Ghanaian kente cloth, batik, mud cloth, indigo cloth, and, to a lesser extent, bark cloth are used. Interestingly,

Trio modeling Afrocentric clothing. The women wear *bubas*, a type of floor-length West African garment, and the man wears a loose-fitting *dashiki* shirt and wooden jewelry. © BETTMANN/CORBIS. REPRODUCED BY PERMISSION.

dashikis, Abacos, Kangas, caftans, wraps, and Saki robes are all made in kente, batik, and mud cloth, but are also made in plain cottons, polyesters, and glittery novelty fabrics and tiger, leopard, and zebra prints.

Less popular are apparel items that do not assimilate well in everyday life; these are grand items such the West African Buba, which can be a voluminous floor-length robe that is often embroidered at the neckline and worn both by men and women. Various types of accessories such as skullcaps, kofis, turbans, and Egyptian- and Ghanaian-inspired jewelry are worn with other Afrocentric items or separately with Western items. Afrocentric fabrics that are made into ties, purses, graduation cowls, and pocket-handkerchiefs have special significance within the middle-class African diaspora.

Who Has Worn Afrocentric Fashion?
The most significant expression of Afrocentricity outside of Africa existed in America during the 1960s and 1970s. The Black Panthers and other black nationalist and civil rights groups used clothing as a synthesis of protest and self-affirmation. Prototype items consisted of men's berets, knitted tams, black leather jackets, black turtleneck sweaters, Converse sneakers, and Afrocentric items including dashikis, various versions of Afro hairstyles, and to a lesser extent Nehru jackets, caftans, and djellabas for men. Women adopted tight black turtleneck sweaters, leather trousers, dark shades, Yoruba-style head wraps, batik wrap skirts, and African inspired jewelry. For both men and women, the latter items were Afrocentric; the former were incorporated into Afrocentricity because the constituency wore them and popularized them, and they became idiomatic of black protest.

In 1962, Kwame Brathwaite and the African Jazz-Art Society and Studios in Harlem presented a fashion and cultural show that featured the Grandassa Models. The show became an annual event. The purpose was to explore the idea that "black is beautiful." It did so by using dark-skinned models with kinky hair wearing clothes that used African fabrics cut in shapes derivative of African dress. The impetus for the popularity of Afrocentric fashion in America arose from this event. The Grandassa Models explored the possibilities of kente, mud cloth, batik, tie-dye, and indigo cloths, and numerous possibilities of wrapping cloth, as opposed to cut-and-sewn apparel. Subsequently, such entertainers as Nina Simone, Aretha Franklin, the Voices of East Harlem, and Stevie Wonder on occasion wore part or full Afrocentric dress. In America, the Caribbean, and Britain, Afrocentric fashion was most popular during the 1960s and 1970s. Turbans, dashikis, large hooped earrings, and cowrie shell jewelry became the most popular Afrocentric fashion items.

Similar to the Black Panthers, Jamaican Rastafarians wear "essentialized" fashion items. However, spiritual, aesthetic, and cultural values of Rastafarianism are implied through various apparel items. The material culture of Rastafarianism is directly linked to cultural resistance, signified by military combat pants, battle jackets, and berets. These items were introduced in the 1970s and provided Rastafarians with a sense of identity that is further supported and symbolized by dreadlocks, the red, green, and gold Ethiopian flag, and the image of the Lion of Judah, which represents strength and dread.

Jamaican Dancehall, a music-led subculture that started with picnics and tea dances in the 1950s, features a wide repertoire of fashion themes. One widely used theme is African. African dress is omnipresent in Dancehall fashion; items such as the baggy "Click Suits," worn by men in the mid-1990s, were based on the African Buba top and Sokoto pants. Women's fashions—including baggy layered clothing made in vibrant and sometimes gaudy colors; transparent, plastic, or stretchable fabrics; and decorations, such as beading, fringing, or rickrack— were shaped into discordant Western silhouettes. Dancehall fashions of the 1990s symbolized sexuality, self-determination; and freedom. Wearers rejected apparel that was comfortable and practical in favor of clothing that celebrated hedonism.

Wearers of Afrocentric dress distinguish themselves and celebrate "Africanness" within the context of the West. Adoption of Afrocentric clothing is a way of casting aside the deep psychological rift of topographical past and modern present that the psychiatrist Frantz Fanon writes of in *Black Skin, White Masks* (1967). Afrocentric dress is also present in black music cultures of the Caribbean, United States, and the United Kingdom. In the early 2000s B-boys and girls, Flyboys and girls, Dancehall Kings and Queens, Daisy Agers, Rastafarians, neo-Panthers, Funki Dreds, and Junglist all include Afrocenticity in their fashion choices. Afrocentric fashion features combinations of commonplace apparel items that represent dissonance with selected preeminent pieces from Africa's primordial past and its present.

See also **African American Dress; Batik; Boubou; Dashiki; Kente.**

BIBLIOGRAPHY
Diop, Cheikh Anta. *The African Origin of Civilization: Myth or Reality.* New York: Lawrence Hill and Company, 1974.

Fanon, Frantz. *Black Skin, White Masks.* New York: Grove Press, 1967.

Vaillant, Janet G. *Black, French, and African: A Life of Leopold Sedar Senghor.* Cambridge, Mass.: Harvard University Press, 1990.

Van Dyk Lewis

AGBADA *Agbada* is a four-piece male attire found among the Yoruba of southwestern Nigeria and the Republic of Benin, West Africa. It consists of a large, free-flowing outer robe (*awosoke*), an undervest (*awotele*), a pair of long trousers (*sokoto*), and a hat (*fila*). The outer robe—

from which the entire outfit derives the name *agbada*, meaning "voluminous attire"—is a big, loose-fitting, ankle-length garment. It has three sections: a rectangular centerpiece, flanked by wide sleeves. The centerpiece—usually covered front and back with elaborate embroidery—has a neck hole (*orun*) and big pocket (*apo*) on the left side. The density and extent of the embroidery vary considerably, depending on how much a patron can afford. There are two types of undervest: the *buba*, a loose, round-neck shirt with elbow-length sleeves; and *dansiki*, a loose, round-neck, sleeveless smock. The Yoruba trousers, all of which have a drawstring for securing them around the waist, come in a variety of shapes and lengths. The two most popular trousers for the *agbada* are *sooro*, a close-fitting, ankle-length, and narrow-bottomed piece; and *kembe*, a loose, wide-bottomed one that reaches slightly below the knee, but not as far as the ankle. Different types of hats may be worn to complement the *agbada*; the most popular, *gobi*, is cylindrical in form, measuring between nine and ten inches long. When worn, it may be compressed and shaped forward, sideways, or backward. Literally meaning "the dog-eared one," the *abetiaja* has a crestlike shape and derives its name from its hanging flaps that may be used to cover the ears in cold weather. Otherwise, the two flaps are turned upward in normal wear. The *labankada* is a bigger version of the *abetiaja*, and is worn in such a way as to reveal the contrasting color of the cloth used as underlay for the flaps. Some fashionable men may add an accessory to the *agbada* outfit in the form of a wraparound (*ibora*). A shoe or sandal (*bata*) may be worn to complete the outfit.

It is worth mentioning that the *agbada* is not exclusive to the Yoruba, being found in other parts of Africa as well. It is known as *mbubb* (French, *boubou*) among the Wolof of Senegambia and as *riga* among the Hausa and Fulani of the West African savannah from whom the Yoruba adopted it. The general consensus among scholars is that the attire originated in the Middle East and was introduced to Africa by the Berber and Arab merchants from the Maghreb (the Mediterranean coast) and the desert Tuaregs during the trans-Saharan trade that began in the pre-Christian era and lasted until the late nineteenth century. While the exact date of its introduction to West Africa is uncertain, reports by visiting Arab geographers indicate that the attire was very popular in the area from the eleventh century onward, most especially in the ancient kingdoms of Ghana, Mali, Songhay, Bornu, and Kanem, as well as in the Hausa states of northern Nigeria. When worn with a turban, the *riga* or *mbubb* identified an individual as an Arab, Berber, desert Tuareg, or a Muslim. Because of its costly fabrics and elaborate embroidery, the attire was once symbolic of wealth and high status. Those ornamented with Arab calligraphy were believed to attract good fortune (*baraka*). Hence, by the early nineteenth century, the attire had been adopted by many non-Muslims in sub-Saharan

Africa, most especially kings, chiefs, and elites, who not only modified it to reflect local dress aesthetics, but also replaced the turban with indigenous headgears. The bigger the robe and the more elaborate its embroidery, the higher the prestige and authority associated with it.

There are two major types of *agbada* among the Yoruba, namely the casual (*agbada iwole*) and ceremonial (*agbada amurode*). Commonly called *Sulia* or *Sapara*, the casual *agbada* is smaller, less voluminous, and often made of light, plain cotton. The *Sapara* came into being in the 1920s and is named after a Yoruba medical practitioner, Dr. Oguntola Sapara, who felt uncomfortable in the traditional *agbada*. He therefore asked his tailor not only to reduce the volume and length of his *agbada*, but also to make it from imported, lightweight cotton. The ceremonial *agbada*, on the other hand, is bigger, more ornate, and frequently fashioned from expensive and heavier materials. The largest and most elaborately embroidered is called *agbada nla* or *girike*. The most valued fabric for the ceremonial *agbada* is the traditionally woven cloth popularly called *aso ofi* (narrow-band weave) or *aso oke* (northern weave). The term *aso oke* reflects the fact that the Oyo Yoruba of the grassland to the north introduced this type of fabric to the southern Yoruba. It also hints at the close cultural interaction between the Oyo and their northern neighbors, the Nupe, Hausa, and Fulani from whom the former adopted certain dresses and musical instruments. A typical narrow-band weave is produced on a horizontal loom in a strip between four and six inches wide and several yards long. The strip is later cut into the required lengths and sewn together into broad sheets before being cut again into dress shapes and then tailored. A fabric is called *alari* when woven from wild silk fiber dyed deep red; *sanyan* when woven from brown or beige silk; and *etu* when woven from indigo-dyed cotton. In any case, a quality fabric with elaborate embroidery is expected to enhance social visibility, conveying the wearer's taste, status, and rank, among other things. Yet to the Yoruba, it is not enough to wear an expensive *agbada*—the body must display it to full advantage. For instance, an oversize *agbada* may jokingly be likened to a sail (*aso igbokun*), implying that the wearer runs the risk of being blown off-course in a windstorm. An undersize *agbada*, on the other hand, may be compared to the body-tight plumage of a gray heron (*ako*) whose long legs make the feathers seem too small for the bird's height. Tall and well-built men are said to look more attractive in a well-tailored *agbada*. Yoruba women admiringly tease such men with nicknames such as *agunlejika* (the square-shouldered one) and *agunt'asoolo* (tall enough to display a robe to full advantage). That the Yoruba place as much of a premium on the quality of material as on how well a dress fits resonates in the popular saying, *Gele o dun, bii ka mo o we, ka mo o we, ko da bi ko yeni* (It is not enough to put on a headgear, it is appreciated only when it fits well).

Since the beginning of the twentieth century, new materials such as brocade, damask, and velvet have been used for the *agbada*. The traditional design, along with the embroidery, is being modernized. The *agbada* worn by the king of the Yoruba town of Akure, the late Oba Adesida, is made of imported European velvet and partly embroidered with glass beads. Instead of an ordinary hat, the king wears a beaded crown with a veil (*ade*) that partly conceals his face, signifying his role as a living representative of the ancestors—a role clearly reinforced by his colorful, highly ornate, and expensive *agbada*.

In spite of its voluminous appearance, the *agbada* is not as hot as it might seem to a non-Yoruba. Apart from the fact that some of the fabrics may have openwork patterns (*eya*), the looseness of an *agbada* and the frequent adjustment of its open sleeves ventilate the body. This is particularly so when the body is in motion, or during a dance, when the sleeves are manipulated to emphasize body movements.

See also **Africa, Sub-Saharan: History of Dress.**

BIBLIOGRAPHY

De Negri, Eve. *Nigerian Body Adornment.* Lagos, Nigeria: Nigeria Magazine Special Publication, 1976.

Drewal, Henry J., and John Mason. *Beads, Body and Soul: Art and Light in the Yoruba Universe.* Los Angeles: UCLA Fowler Museum of Cultural History, 1998.

Eicher, Joanne Bubolz. *Nigerian Handcrafted Textiles.* Ile-Ife, Nigeria: University of Ife Press, 1976.

Heathcote, David. *Art of the Hausa.* London: World of Islam Festival Publishing, 1976.

Johnson, Samuel. *The History of the Yorubas.* Lagos, Nigeria: CMS Bookshops, 1921.

Krieger, Colleen. "Robes of the Sokoto Caliphate." *African Arts* 21, no. 3 (May 1988): 52–57; 78–79; 85–86.

Lawal, Babatunde. "Some Aspects of Yoruba Aesthetics." *British Journal of Aesthetics* 14, no. 3 (1974): 239–249.

Perani, Judith. "Nupe Costume Crafts." *African Arts* 12, no. 3 (1979): 53–57.

Prussin, Labelle. *Hatumere: Islamic Design in West Africa.* Berkeley: University of California Press, 1986.

Babatunde Lawal

ALAÏA, AZZEDINE Azzedine Alaïa was born in southern Tunisia in about 1940 to a farming family descended from Spanish Arabic stock. He was brought up by his maternal grandparents in Tunis and, at the age of fifteen, enrolled at l'École des beaux-arts de Tunis to study sculpture. However, his interest in form soon diverted him toward fashion. Alaïa's career started with a part-time job finishing hems (assisted at first by his sister, who also studied fashion). He became a dressmaker's assistant, helping to copy couture gowns by such Parisian couturiers as Christian Dior, Pierre Balmain, and Cristóbal Balenciaga for wealthy Tunisian clients; these luxurious and refined creations set a standard for excellence that Alaïa has emulated ever since.

In 1957 Alaïa moved to Paris. His first job, for Christian Dior, lasted only five days; the Algerian war had just begun and Alaïa, being Arabic, was probably not welcome. He then worked on two collections at Guy Laroche, learning the essentials of dress construction. Introduced to the cream of Parisian society by a Paris-based compatriot (Simone Zehrfuss, wife of the architect Bernard Zehrfuss), Alaïa began to attract private commissions. Between 1960 and 1965 he lived as a housekeeper and dressmaker for the comtesse Nicole de Blégiers and then established a small salon on the Left Bank, where he built up a devoted private clientele. He remained there until 1984, fashioning elegant clothing for, among others, the French actress Arlette-Leonie Bathiat, the legendary cinema star Greta Garbo, and the socialite Cécile de Rothschild, a cousin of the famous French banking family. Alaïa also worked on commissions for other designers; for example, he created the prototype for Yves Saint Laurent's Mondrian-inspired shift dress.

Ready-to-Wear Collections

By the 1970s, in response to the changing climate in fashion, Alaïa's focus shifted from custom-made gowns to ready-to-wear for an emerging clientele of young, discerning customers. Toward the end of the decade he designed for Thierry Mugler and produced a group of leather garments for Charles Jourdan. Rejected for being too provocative, they have been kept ever since in Alaïa's extensive archive. In 1981 he launched his first collection; already favored by the French fashion press, he soon found international success. In 1982 he showed his prêt-à-porter, or ready-to-wear, line at Bergdorf Goodman in New York, and in 1983 he opened a boutique in Beverly Hills. The French Ministry of Culture honored him with the Designer of the Year award in 1985. He has dressed many famous women, such as the model Stephanie Seymour, the entertainer and model Grace Jones, and the 1950s Dior model Bettina. Moreover, Alaïa was the first to feature the supermodel Naomi Campbell on the catwalk.

In the early 1990s Alaïa relocated his Paris showroom to a large, nineteenth-century, glass-roofed, iron-frame building on the rue de Moussy. There he lives and works, accompanied by various dogs, and his staff, regardless of status, eat lunch together every day. Partly designed by Julian Schnabel and adorned with his artwork, the building's calm, pared-down interior, glass-roofed gallery, and intense workshops resemble a shrine to fashion. Alaïa has always been a nonconformist; since 1993 he has eschewed producing a new collection every season, preferring to show his creations at his atelier when they are ready, which is often months later than announced.

King of Cling

Alaïa's technique was formed through traditional couture practice, but his style is essentially modern. He is best known for his svelte, clinging garments that fit like a second skin. Although he is revered in the early 2000s, the

1980s were in many ways Alaïa's time; his use of stretch Lycra, silk jersey knits, and glove leather and suede suited the sports- and body-conscious decade. The singer Tina Turner said of his work, "He gives you the very best line you can get out of your body. . . . Take any garment he has made. You can't drop the hem, you can't let it out or take it in. It's a piece of sculpture" (Howell, p. 256).

Alaïa has described himself as a *bâtisseur*, or builder, and his tailoring is exceptional. He cuts the pattern and assembles the prototype for every single dress that he creates, sculpting and draping the fabric on a live model. As he explains, "I have to try my things on a living body because the clothes I make must respect the body" (Mendes, p. 113). Although his clothes appear simple, many contain numerous discrete components, all constructed with raised, corsetry stitching and curved seaming to achieve a perfect sculptural form. Georgina Howell wrote in *Vogue* in March 1990:

> He worked out dress in terms of touch. He abolished all underclothes and made one garment do the work. The technique is dazzling, for just as a woman's body is a network of surface tensions, hard here, soft there, so Azzedine Alaïa's clothes are a force field of give and resistance. (p. 258)

Utilizing fabric technology first designed for sportswear to skim the body in stretch fabric that made women's bodies look as smooth as possible, Alaïa produced a stunning variety of fashions. They included jersey sheath dresses with flesh-exposing zippers, dresses made of stretch Lycra bands, taut jackets and short skirts, stretch chenille and lace body suits, leggings, skinny jumper dresses with cutouts, and dresses with spiraling zippers. To this oeuvre he added bustiers and cinched, perforated leather belts; cowl-neck gowns; *broderie anglaise* or gold-mesh minidresses; and stiffened tulle wedding gowns. His palette favored muted colors, in particular, black, uncluttered and unadorned with jewelry.

Alaïa's Influence

Whether applied to his haute couture, tailoring, or ready-to-wear lines, Alaïa's work is typified by precision and control; these characteristics apply even to his designs for mail-order companies, such as Les 3 Suisses and La redoute. He survived the 1990s without glossy advertising campaigns and without compromise, and in 2001 Helmut Lang paid tribute to Alaïa's work in his spring and summer 2001 collection.

Alaïa is a perfectionist and has been known to sew women into their outfits in order to get the most perfect fit. Often accompanied by his friend, confidante, and muse, the model and actress Farida Khelfa, he is of small stature and invariably dresses in a black Chinese silk jacket and trousers and black cotton slippers, declaring that he would look far too macho in a suit. Alaïa's work has been shown in retrospectives at the Bordeaux Museum of Contemporary Art (1984–1985) and the Groninger Museum in the Netherlands (1998), and in the exhibition *Radical Fashion* at the Victoria and Albert Museum in London (2001). In 2000 Prada acquired a stake in Alaïa; the agreement contains the promise of creating a foundation in Paris for the Alaïa archive, which includes not only his own creations but also designs by many twentieth-century couturiers, such as Madeleine Vionnet and Cristóbal Balenciaga. Alaïa said, "When I see beautiful clothes I want to keep them, preserve them. . . . clothes, like architecture and art, reflect an era" (Wilcox, p. 56).

See also **Fashion Designer; Fashion Models; Jersey; Supermodels.**

BIBLIOGRAPHY

Alaïa, Azzedine, ed. *Alaïa.* Göttingen, Germany: Steidl, 1999.

Baudot, François. *Alaïa.* London: Thames and Hudson, Inc., 1996.

Howell, Georgina. "The Titan of Tight." *Vogue,* March 1990, pp. 456–459.

Mendes, Valerie. *Black in Fashion.* London: V & A Publications, 1999.

Wilcox, Claire, ed. *Radical Fashion.* London: V & A Publications, 2001.

Claire Wilcox

ALBINI, WALTER Walter Albini (1941–1983) was born Gualtiero Angleo Albini in Busto Arsizio, Lombardy, in northern Italy. In 1957 he interrupted his study of the classics, which his family had encouraged him to pursue, and enrolled in the Istituto d'Arte, Disegno e Moda in Turin, the only male student admitted to the all-girls school. A gifted student, Albini studied drawing and specialized in ink and tempera, at which he excelled. He took a degree in fashion design in 1960.

Fashion design remained an abiding interest for Albini. Even as an adolescent he worked as an artist for newspapers and magazines, to whom he sent sketches of the fashion shows held in Rome and Paris, a city for which he felt an intense and profound affinity. Paris was a fundamental step in his creative and emotional development, as evidenced by the many references to the French designers Paul Poiret and Coco Chanel in his work. In Paris, where he remained from 1961 to 1965, Albini met Chanel—a designer he admired throughout his life and to whom he dedicated his 1975 haute couture show in Rome. He was inspired by the importance Chanel gave to freeing the woman's body, to mixing and coordinating different pieces, and to accessorizing. While still in Paris he became friends with Mariucci Mandelli, who started the Krizia line and with whom he had a lifelong friendship. After Albini's return to Italy, he worked for three years (1965–1968) designing sweaters for Krizia. The designer, Karl Lagerfeld was also working for Krizia in this period. Mandelli once said of Albini, "I was never disappointed with Walter. He never gave in to vulgarity, pettiness, or mediocrity; he was a character straight out of (F. Scott) Fitzgerald, maybe the last. He gave us a lesson in style" (Bocca, p. 138).

Albini worked as a consultant for several companies and designed for Billy Ballo, Cadette, Trell, and Montedoro. He selected fabrics and designs for Etro and created several collections for Basile. In 1967 *Vogue Italia* published a six-page spread of his work for the Krizia collection, and by 1968 he was already well known to other designers. The next year he presented his own Mister Fox line, a name that had been suggested by his friend the journalist Anna Piaggi. The collection comprised sixteen elegant suits, eight of which (all black) were called "the widows" and the other eight (all flesh-colored), "the wives." The garments were made in collaboration with the industrialist, Luciano Papini.

Albini was the first to initiate a series of innovative reforms in Italian fashion that responded to a changing market. These innovations included freeing the designer from the anonymity of the world of production and treating him as a creator, as in the world of haute couture, and recognizing the need for the fashion industry to provide styles and images and not only clothing, so that it could reach new market segments in a rapidly changing world. Albini worked closely with fabric manufacturers and enhanced the presence of the designer in industrial production.

He also helped create specialized companies in different sections of industry, so that they could collaborate to produce a collection with a recognizable brand name. These companies included well-known names like Basile for coats, skirts, and jackets; Escargots for jersey; Callaghan for knitwear, Mister Fox for evening dress; Diamant's for shirts. An agreement with FTM (Ferrante, Tositti, Monti) gave rise to a new label—"Walter Albini for," followed by the name of the manufacturer. At the Circolo del Giardino in Milan (28 April 1971), a prêt-à-porter collection was presented for the first time. The collection, made of dresses, shirts, coats, trousers, evening dress, hats, shoes, and jewelry was designed by just one designer in coordination with producers from different industries, each of them specialized in its own field of production. The collection was then sold as a whole to shops, which sold them as they were conceived. It was the system of prêt-à-porter as we currently know it. The 7 June 1971 issue of *Women's Wear Daily*, entitled "Putting It Together," reported on this epochal change in fashion.

In 1971 Albini was the first designer to abandon the Sala Bianca at Palazzo Pitti in Florence—together with Caumont, Trell, Ken Scott, Missoni, Krizia—which was still associated with the older fashion tradition, in favor of Milan. That year, 1971, is considered the official birth of prêt-à-porter. Bianca was a place strictly connected to the name of Giovanni Battista Giorgini and to the offi-

cial birth of Italian fashion with the collective catwalk shows of January 1952. Sala Bianca continued its activities until 1982, when Milan, already the center of the emerging new design prêt-à-porter, took over.

The 1973 Venice catwalk show took place among the tables of the celebrated Caffè Florian, which had been closed for the day. It was a magical moment for Albini. "It had been a long time since so much tweed, velvet, silk, and lamé, worn by these elegant women, had grazed the exquisitely decorated woodwork of the Caffè Florian in Piazza san Marco" (Vercelloni 1984, p. 90).

There are a number of constants in Walter Albini's designs and inspiration: the deco style, Poiret interpretation of liberty, Bauhaus, futurism, constructivism, the art of the 1910s to 1930s when a new feminine representation emerged especially with the work of Chanel. Albini's constants in design are jackets with half belts, flat collars, wide pants, the famous shirt jacket that was to become a classic of Italian men's clothing, sandals, two-tone shoes, Bermuda shorts, sports jackets, knit caps worn low on the forehead, and the first waterproof boots. He invented the image of the woman in pants, jacket, and shirt and reintroduced the use of print designs, both abstract and figurative. His favorite themes were the zodiac, the ballerina, the Scottish terrier, and the Madonna.

Albini is considered the inventor of the "total look," derived from his single-minded emphasis on accessories and details that became almost more important than the garment itself. It was Albini who first developed the idea of using music in place of an announcer during fashion shows. He also conceived the idea of grouping advertising pages in fashion magazines. But Albini was even more tied to the past, to the historical roots that inspired him, to the perfect elegance that is never achieved without a fanatical attention to the search for perfection in the intelligent and ironic use of older styles.

When Albini's agreement with FTM terminated in 1973, he founded Albini Srl with Papini. The new company produced and distributed the WA label, with MISTERFOX as their commercial line of clothing. In this endeavor, too, Albini was ahead of his time. His love of fashion went hand in hand with his interest in research and traveling to Asia—India, in particular, and also Tunisia, where he found inspiration for his creations. He bought apartments in his favorite cities, one on the Grand Canal in Venice, another on Piazza Borromeo in Milan, and a third in Sidi-fu-Said in Tunisia. Each of them, in its own way, expressed the aesthetics of the surrounding environment.

In 1975 Albini presented his first fall collection for men—another area in which he was a precursor of later designers. But the fashion world was not quite ready for Albini's innovations. When Albini was at the height of his success, there was not sufficient financial support in a still immature clothing and textile market. Toward the end of his career, his manufacturers could not live up to their commitments; Paolo Rinaldi, his companion and press agent, remained his only supporter. Albini died in Milan at the age of forty-two.

Walter Albini cannot easily be categorized, because of the richness and variety of his designs, their intimacy and complexity, and the fact that the designs were ahead of their time. "A creative genius in the pure state," wrote Isa Vercelloni, Albini "is always somewhere else, at least one step ahead of what is predictable, and a thousand miles ahead of what we anticipate" (1984, p. 235). A key figure of Italian artistic culture, Albini still evokes deep admiration. His memory lingers on in the images taken by the many photographers who worked with him: Aldo Ballo, Maria Vittoria Corradi Backhaus, Giampaolo Barbieri, and Alfa Castaldi.

See also **Chanel, Gabrielle (Coco); Fashion Designer; Fashion Shows; Italian Fashion; Ready-to-Wear.**

BIBLIOGRAPHY

Bianchino, Gloria, and Arturo Quintavalle. *Moda: Dalla fiaba al design. Italia 1951–1989.* Novara, Italy: Istituto geografico De Agostini, 1989.

Bocca, N. "La coerenza dello stile." In *Walter Albini: Lo stile nella moda.* Edited by Paolo Rinaldi. Modena, Italy: Zanfi Editori, 1988.

Gastel, Minnie. *50 anni di moda italiana.* Milan: Vallardi, 1995.

Morini, E., and N. Bocca. *La moda italiana.* Volume 2: *Dall'antimoda allo stilismo.* Milan: Electa, 1987.

Vercelloni, Isa Tutino. "Walter Albini 1968." In *Il genio antipatico: Creatività e tecnologia della moda italiana 1951/1983.* Edited by Pia Soli. Milan: Mondadori, 1984.

———. "Albini Walter." In *Dizionario della moda.* Edited by Guido Vergani. Milan: Baldini and Castoldi, 1999.

Simona Segre Reinach

A-LINE DRESS The term "A-line" is used to describe a dress, skirt, or coat with a triangular silhouette, narrow and fitted at the top and widening out from the bust or waist in a straight line to the hem. More specifically, it is understood to mean a structured garment, which stands away from the body to form the sides of the *A.* The fronts of A-line garments are often cut in one piece, with darts for fitting, and the skirts often have no waistband.

The term first entered the vocabulary of fashion via the couturier Christian Dior's collection for Spring 1955, which he named the "A-Line." In the 1950s, the international fashion press looked to Paris, and Dior in particular, to set the direction fashion would take each season. Dior obliged by organizing each new collection around a specific idea, and giving each a name that described or evoked that idea. In 1954 and 1955, he designed three closely related collections, based on the shapes of the letters *H, A,* and *Y,* which marked a move away from the strongly emphasized, nipped-in waist that

A-line ensemble. Introduced by designer Christian Dior in the mid-1950s, A-line garments flared outwards toward the hem and de-emphasized the waist, creating a silhouette similar in appearance to the letter "A." © BETTMANN/CORBIS. REPRODUCED BY PERMISSION.

had been the dominant silhouette since his 1947 "Corolle Line" (or "New Look") collection. The most influential of these was the "A-Line" collection, characterized by narrow shoulders and a smooth, trumpetlike flare toward the hem; the elongated waistline, either high under the bust or dropped toward the hips, formed the crossbar of the *A.* The signature look of this collection (the "most wanted silhouette in Paris," according to *Vogue,* 1 March 1995, p. 95) was a fingertip-length flared jacket worn over a dress with a very full, pleated skirt; while it was clearly an A-shape, this silhouette was quite different from what was later meant by "A-line."

Though the example set by the A-Line collection was not immediately followed, and Christian Dior explored other ideas in subsequent collections, the idea of the A-shape was a success, and the term quickly entered common usage. The A-line was one of a series of controversial mid- to late-1950s looks that de-emphasized the waist and brought an easier, more casual look to fashion; chemise and sack dresses, loose tunics, and boxy suits were shown by Dior, but also by other couturiers, most notably Balenciaga and Chanel. The most dramatic of these, in which the A-line idea was given its ultimate expression, was the Spring 1958 "Trapeze Line" introduced by Dior's successor, Yves Saint Laurent, in his first collection for the house of Dior. The Trapeze silhouette, in which dresses flared out dramatically from a fitted shoulder line, was considered extreme by many, but it did establish the A-line dress, with its highly structured, clean lines, as a suitable look for modern times. A more subdued version of the A-line shape was introduced in the early 1960s, and A-line dresses and skirts remained a popular style choice through the mid-1970s.

By the early 1980s, however, A-line garments, and flared shapes in general, had almost completely disappeared. The new loose silhouette was an update of the sack shape, with dresses and tunics falling loosely from an exaggerated shoulder line. Some 1960s styles received a retro revival later in the decade, but as long as the shoulders remained padded and the tops loose-fitting, straight skirts were required to balance the look. A-line skirts and dresses were not revived until the late 1990s, when the retro trend embraced the styles of the 1970s, and closely fitted garments with narrow shoulders and fitted sleeves came back into fashion. By this time, following almost twenty years of straight skirts and dresses, the term had been out of use for so long that its earlier, more specific meanings had been forgotten. It is used loosely to describe any dress wider at the hips than at the bust or waist, and a variety of flared skirt styles. With the revival of true A-line shapes in the early 2000s, however, there are signs that the terms originally used to describe them are beginning to return as well.

See also **Chemise Dress; Dior, Christian; Saint Laurent, Yves.**

BIBLIOGRAPHY

Keenan, Brigid. *Dior in Vogue.* London: Octopus Books, 1981. Excellent chronological and thematic guide to the Dior collections and their influence.

Musheno, Elizabeth J., ed. *The Vogue Sewing Book.* Rev. ed. New York: Vogue Patterns, 1975. Contains helpful typology, with illustrations, of 1960s–1970s garments and style terms.

Susan Ward

ALPACA The alpaca is a domesticated member of the camel family and native to the high Andes Mountains of Peru, Bolivia, Chile, and northwestern Argentina. Alpacas are small animals raised primarily for their fleece. They were domesticated over 5,000 years ago, and it is thought that humans used their fiber for 4,000 years prior to domestication. Alpaca has been considered a luxury fiber for much of this time, for example the Incan Empire reserved alpaca fiber for royalty.

Alpacas are close relatives of the llama and vicuña (see sidebar). Llamas were used as beasts of burden, whereas alpacas were primarily used for their soft, luxurious fiber. Alpacas differ from llamas in that they are smaller and lack the coarse and brittle hair of the llama.

A Peruvian alpaca. Alpaca fleece is soft, luxurious, light weight, and free of many of the irritants found in sheep's wool. Alpacas are sheared in the spring and the fleece is spun to make yarn. © GEORGE D. LEPP/CORBIS. REPRODUCED BY PERMISSION.

Alpaca differs from sheep's wool in that it lacks the greasy lanolin coating on its fleece and wool fiber's prominent scales. Without the lanolin, the fiber hangs from the animal in glossy strands and can be processed into yarn without a complicated scouring process. In addition, people with sensitivities to wool generally find that they can wear alpaca without their skin being irritated. Its hypoallergenic nature is due to it being lanolin-free and having very fine scales on the surface of the fiber.

The fibers of the alpaca are hollow. This gives alpaca an excellent insulating ability and makes alpaca fiber products feel very light in weight.

The wool fiber is sheared from the alpaca in the spring of every year. The fiber ranges in length from eight to twelve inches, and sometimes longer. It is generally processed on the woolen spinning system to produce soft, airy yarns.

There are two types of alpacas, the *huacaya* and the *suri*. The *huacaya* alpacas have soft and crimpy (wavy) fiber. The *suri* alpacas have long, pencil-like locks of fiber, which are silky and lustrous. They both produce over twenty natural colors of alpaca, including white, light fawn (a light, grayish brown), light to dark brown, gray, black, and piebald (blotched with white and black). Like sheep's wool, alpaca fiber absorbs dyes very well.

Alpaca fiber is desirable because it is fine, soft, lustrous, and elastic. In the nineteenth century, Sir Titus Salt made use of alpaca's properties to create luxury fab-

VICUÑA

Vicuñas (vy-KOON-yuh) are the smallest member of the South American camel family. They live at an altitude of 12,000 to 16,000 feet near the snowline of the Andes Mountains. Adult vicuñas are 2½ to 3 feet (69 to 91 centimeters) high and weigh 75 to 140 pounds (34 to 64 kilograms).

Vicuña fiber's limited supply and luxurious qualities make it one of the most valuable luxury fibers. The vicuñas' wild nature made it easiest to obtain the fiber by killing the animals. In 1970, vicuñas were placed on the Endangered Species List. Over the last thirty years, the Andean countries protection efforts have allowed the vicuña population to increase. Efforts are under way to change its classification from an "endangered" to "threatened" species.

Each vicuña provides about 4 ounces (114 grams) of fine fiber and around 8 ounces (284 to 340 grams) of shorter, less choice fiber. Fine vicuña fibers measure 12 microns in diameter, which is finer than cashmere. Its color ranges from red-brown to light tan to yellow-red. The fiber's softness, luster, strength, and warmth without weight result in highly desirable fabrics. Raw vicuña fiber, which includes fine and less-choice fiber, has sold at auction for $200 per pound.

In 2004, the only vicuña wool that can be legally traded is that which is sheared from a live vicuña at an officially authorized facility. Since the vicuña is an endangered species, those wishing to import it must carefully examine and follow the regulations governing its trade.

BIBLIOGRAPHY

"Endangered and Threatened Wildlife and Plants: Proposed Reclassification of Certain Vicuña Populations from Endangered to Threatened and a Proposed Special Rule." *Federal Register*, Proposed Rules, 64, no. 173 (September 1999): 48743–48757.

Internet Resources

Alpaca Fiber Cooperative of North America, Inc. "About Alpaca." Available from http://www.americasalpaca.com.

"Species Profile for Vicuña." U.S. Fish and Wildlife Service. Available from http://endangered.fws.gov.

Ann W. Braaten

AMERICA, CENTRAL, AND MEXICO: HISTORY OF DRESS

Cultural artifacts such as clothing and cloth also serve as signs that communicate visually in a silent language. This communication is a kind of visual literacy: becoming familiar with the language of textiles is similar to learning how to read, only it means learning how to read cloth, clothing, and how it is worn. To the untrained eye, traditional clothing worn by indigenous people of Mexico and Central America may impress and startle. It may be embroidered or handwoven in rainbow colors with geometric, floral, animal, or human images, or elaborated with commercial trims. Clothing may convey categories relating to rank, class, status, region or town, religion, or age (Schevill 1986).

Geography

Mexico and Central America encompass cool temperate highlands and warm tropical lowlands and islands. The great northern desert is intersected by the Sierra Madre, which extends into Southern Mexico and Central America and forms the highlands and is inhabited predominantly by indigenous people. To the west is the Pacific Ocean, and the Gulf of Mexico and the Caribbean Sea lie to the east. Volcanoes, dense tropical jungles, long stretches of beaches, deep canyons, and fertile mountain valleys share a cultural history dating for over 3,000 years, from 1500 B.C.E. to C.E. 1519. Great ceremonial centers flourished in remote geographical areas connected by trade networks. Contrasting environmental conditions and a wide range of raw materials have influenced the evolution of clothing and have fostered the variety of styles in use in the early twenty-first century.

Persistence and Innovation

Why have typical clothing and cloth production persisted in parts of Mexico, Guatemala, and Panama, and not in Honduras, El Salvador, Nicaragua, and Costa Rica? Some factors to consider are: the geographic isolation of towns and regions; the continuance of markets and the fiesta cycle; the symbolization of town ideals in clothing; and the differentiation of civil-religious hierarchies through clothing. Closer to the urban areas, men's and

rics for the English market. Alpaca yarns were inserted into the weft (crosswise direction) of the fabric with yarns of cotton, silk, or wool in the warp (lengthwise direction). In the early 2000s, alpaca fiber is found in knit sweaters, hats, and scarves that are hand- or machine-made. Many handmade products are manufactured in the countries where alpaca first originated.

Alpacas have a gentle and docile disposition that has made them popular animals for hobby farms in the United States and Canada. In 2001 the Alpaca Breeders and Owners Association reported over 30,000 registered alpacas in North America. The products made from the fiber from these alpacas are being marketed through the Alpaca Fiber Cooperative of North America, Inc.

See also **Fibers; Wool; Yarns.**

TIMELINE

Mexico

  1519 Arrival of Cortés
  1521 Fall of Aztec Empire
  1528–1535 Mexico rules by Royal Audiencia,
      called New Spain
  1535–1810 Colonial Period
  1810–1821 Mexican Revolution
  1821 Independence from Spain

Guatemala

  1523 Invasion by Alvarado
  1524 Conquest of various Maya groups
  1523–1821 Colonial Period
  1821 Independence from Spain

children's Western-style dress has replaced typical clothing. The desire to dress like the rest of the world, encouraged by television and tourism, has created a market for jeans, T-shirts, and sport shoes. In the past, outsiders stereotyped indigenous communities as inherently conservative and resistant to change. Two conflicting principles, however, affect textile production: the artistic, creative impulse to innovate and the conservative constraint, which is tradition-bound. Artists of the loom and needle respond to new materials, techniques, and patrons—who are tourists, entrepreneurs, or advisers involved in marketing textiles abroad. The fashion impulse is part of innovation, and new clothing trends among certain age groups may be observed in the way a garment is worn, the colors and designs, and layout (Schevill 1997, pp. 129–143).

Dress Form Survivals
Present in contemporary indigenous dress are what some call pre-Columbian dress form survivals, such as the woman's *huipil*, or upper body garment, and the small shoulder *quechquémitl*, or shawl, as well as the man's *calzones*, or pants, and a sleeveless jacket, *xicolli*. Hispanic dress form survivals also exist. Women's blouses, head veils, gathered skirts, men's tailored pants and jackets, sombreros, and, of course, shoes for both men and women are only a few examples.

Western and Traditional Combinations
Urban and rural males still leave their homes seasonally to work on large coffee and cotton *fincas* (plantations) and wear Western-style clothing in order to avoid racial discrimination against them. But at fiesta time, people re-

turn to their communities and wear typical clothing and participate in traditional activities called *costumbre*. Women and men may use several elements of traditional clothing along with Western-style dress. The rebozo or *perraje*, a shawl, is a good example (Logan et al. 1994). Both ladinas and mestizas (persons of mixed Indian, African, and/or Spanish ancestry who do not belong to one of the indigenous cultural groups) include rebozos in their dress ensemble. Another fashion phenomenon relates to adaptations of other than Spanish foreign dress styles. The Tarahumaras (Raramuris) of Chichuahua's Sierra Madre, under the influence of the missionaries, adopted aspects of non-Indian culture, while retaining traditional arts, such as weaving. Their clothing is hand-sewn of commercial patterned cloth with full skirts and blouses, some with peplums. Women cover their heads with cloths in a bandanna style, while men continue to wear turbans and loincloths of white commercial cotton (Green 2003). The male Mam speakers of Todos Santos Cuchumatán, Huehuetenango (Guatemala), adapted black woolen tailored overpants, a style worn by the French Navy who visited Guatemala in the mid-nineteenth century and wear them over their own handwoven long pants. In southeastern Central America, off the northern coast of Panama, are the San Blas islands inhabited by the indigenous Kunas. The women's *molas*, or blouses, are made of commercial multicolored cotton. Two similar intricately hand-stitched appliquéd panels adorn a woman's blouse front and back. Some of the imagery reflects outside influences as seen in billboards, advertisements, and television.

The Art of the Weaver
Before the Conquest, a woman was expected to weave for herself and her family and to produce ceremonial clothes for use in temples and as offerings. A fine weaver had status in the community, as she does as late as the twenty-first century. Clothing and cloth also produced extra income when made for sale. Children learned by imitation, watching their mothers spin, prepare yarn, warp the loom, and weave. By the age of twelve, whether or not they like it, weaving must be taken seriously. Before that, it is like a game, but by the marrying age of sixteen, a woman must be an accomplished weaver.

Looms
The backstrap loom has been in use in Mexico and Central America since 1500 B.C.E. A Classic Maya ceramic figurine recovered from Jaina Island off the eastern coast of Mexico is of a weaver at her backstrap loom. This loom is sometimes called the hip-loom, or stick-loom (*telar de palitos*), and although both male and female indigenous weavers produce cloth on this simple apparatus, it is largely associated with women. When the cloth, often selvaged on both ends, is removed from the loom, only the sticks and ropes remain. Also in use are staked, horizontal looms and floor or treadle looms introduced by

Three Central American men in hats and shirts. Contemporary Central American dress draws from both native traditions and new styles, fusing the Old and New Worlds together. J.J. FOXX/NYC. REPRODUCED BY PERMISSION.

the Spanish after the Conquest. Weaving of this kind was taught to indigenous males, who soon learned how to produce yardage, a requisite for the cut-and-sew tailored fashions of the Spanish. In the early 2000s, Zapotec male weavers in Teotitlán del Valle, Oaxaca (Mexico), weave fine woolen rugs and blankets on treadle looms, and double-ikat cotton cloth for skirts is woven in Salcajá, Quezaltenango (Guatemala), by Maya men. Both male and female weavers in the Totonicapán (Guatemala) area use a unique loom that combines features of the backstrap and treadle loom to create headbands. In addition, both draw and jacquard loom weavers produce yardage of great complexity.

Materials

Cotton has been the most important fiber for weavers since pre-Columbian times. The two varieties are a long-staple white cotton and a short-staple, tawny colored cotton known as *ixcaq*, *ixcaco*, *coyuche*, or *cuyuscate*. Agave, yucca, and other vegetal fibers, as well as dyed rabbit hair and feathers are still in use. The feathered wedding dress continues to be worn by the Tzotzil women of Zinacantán, Chiapas (Mexico). After the Spanish introduced sheep, wool was readily adopted by native weavers for its warmth, its sturdy and thick texture, and its ability to take dyes. For ornamentation, colored imported silk, pearl cotton, assorted embroidery cottons, and synthetic yarn are employed.

Dyes

Because of the paucity of archaeological textile remains, it is not known with certainty what natural dyes were employed in pre-Columbian textiles. The painted codices, ceramics, and other visual material give some clues (Anawalt 1981). Indigo (blue), brazil wood, and cochineal (red), *palo de tinta* (black), cinnabar (red-brown), and *purpura patula* (lavender) may have been in use. The 1856 invention of chemical dyes in Europe expanded the color palette throughout the world. These dyes were quickly adopted and used along with some of the natural dyes. By early 2000s, natural dyes were reintroduced to many Mexican and Guatemalan weavers and embroiderers. Rainbow coloring is a predictable and enjoyable aspect of twenty-first-century clothing.

Techniques

Warp-predominant cloth with supplementary weft brocading is one of the most frequently represented combinations. It is a technique for decorating the cloth while still on the loom. There are three types of brocading: single-faced with a pattern recognizable on one side; two-faced with the decorative yarn floating on the reverse side

Oaxacan folk dancer. In Mexico and Central America, elaborate costumes consisting of embroidered cotton blouses and long ruffled skirts are frequently worn for special occasions and festivals. © BOB KRIST/CORBIS. REPRODUCED BY PERMISSION.

between pattern areas forming an inverse of the design; and double-faced brocading that creates a nearly identical pattern on both sides. Other techniques include, first and foremost, embroidery, then knitting, beading, crocheting, and more. As with the acceptance of chemical dyes, the advent of the sewing machine and availability of commercial cloth and trims have replaced in many areas what was formerly accomplished by hand.

Iconography
Iconography is varied. Geometric shapes, plants, animals, and human images are woven in a representational, stylized, or abstract fashion. The precise meaning of these designs to the weavers may never be known, as they are a part of the collective consciousness or mythical history and not actually discussed. Clothing is memory.

Garment Repertoire
There is a great variety of indigenous clothing worn throughout this vast geographic area. The individual garment styles, however, are a shared tradition.

Women. The upper garment or *huipil*, a Nahua word, is the most important component of a woman's clothing. Nahua was the language of the Aztecs and is still spoken in many Mexican communities. The *huipil* can be short or long, of two or three backstrap or floor-loomed pieces joined together, sometimes with a decorative stitching, and neck and arm openings. Designs are woven in as part of the weaving process, embroidered or commercial fabrics, such as ribbons or rickrack, can be added. Particularly fine, handwoven; or embroidered *huipiles* are worn by the Zapotecs of Oaxaca, Mexico, and by the Mayas of Chiapas, Yucatán, and Guatemala. Skirts are either wraparound and held in place by wide or narrow handwoven belts or gathered to a waistband. The fabric can be either solid colored, commonly dark blue, or patterned floor-loomed cotton. The tie-dyed or ikat (*jaspe*) multicolored skirts of the K'iche' and Cakchiquel Mayas (in Guatemala) are outstanding. Multipurpose backstrap-loomed cloths are essential for covering the head and to wrap food or objects. Aprons are cut-and-sew garments, a Hispanic dress form survival that serves decorative as well as functional purposes. The adornment of the head and hair is especially important. The Yalalags of Oaxaca use heavy yarn headdresses, while many Mayas wear tapestry woven headbands with elaborate tassels. The women of the northern Sierra of Puebla (Mexico) have perfected the art of the embroidered blouse with the sewing machine (Anawalt and Berdan 1994). In the early 2000s, young Maya women of Chiapas embroidered motifs on their blouses of commercial cloth, whereas in the past, the decoration was the result of supplementary weft brocading. The *quechquémitl*, or capelike shoulder garment, is still worn by older Nahua and Otomi women in Puebla, while large shoulder cloths are in general use throughout the area. Sandals and jewelry complete the woman's dress ensemble.

Men. Tailored pants, loose-fitting and held up with a wide belt, are of white manta or commercial cotton, as well as handwoven multicolored cloth. As with women's *huipiles*, the shirts may be loom-decorated. Shoulder bags are knitted or crocheted in cotton and wool. Often, men create their own bags. Others are made for sale, a popular tourist item. In colder areas, men need overgarments of black or multicolored wool and shoulder or hip blankets. Handwoven head cloths may be worn under the sombrero in a pirate fashion. Hatbands often adorn the sombreros. Tailored cotton or wool jackets, along with the sleeveless style, are worn over the shirt. Men also wear sandals or shoes.

Children. Children dress as their parents do when possible, in smaller versions of typical clothing.

Occasions for Special Clothing
Each region has distinctive styles of dress for special occasions; these styles are derived from family or area traditions and sometimes pay tribute to historical happenings.

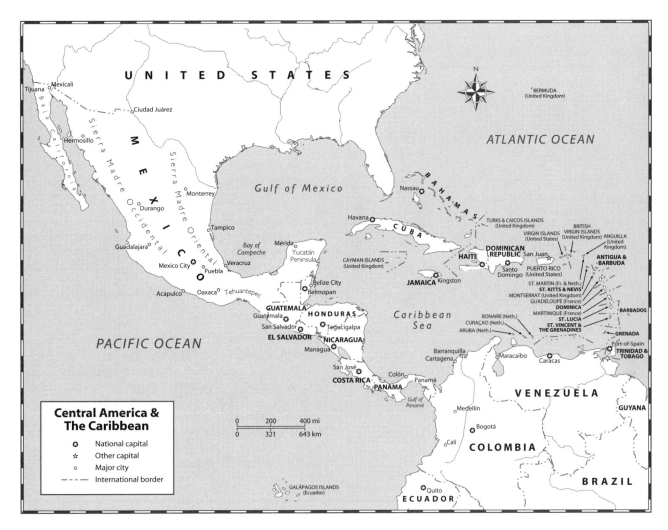

Map of Central America and Mexico. Similar clothing and cloth production can be found in parts of Mexico, Guatemala, and Panama, but are less apparent elsewhere in the region. THE GALE GROUP.

Cofradías. There are religious organizations associated with the Catholic Church for men and women called *cofradías*. Participants take care of the church, the statues of saints, and sponsor religious ceremonies often in their own homes. The women wear ceremonial *huipiles*, and men demonstrate their importance in the community with special head cloths, jackets, and hats.

Contests, Festivals, Fiestas. The indigenous population wears special clothing on festive occasions. For example, in El Salvador for fiestas, white ruffled cotton blouses with red embroidery and long white ruffled skirts replace Western-style dress (Valasquez 2003). In many regions of Guatemala and Mexico, there are beauty contests in which the indigenous and ladina contestants wear the most beautiful traditional clothing available. Fiestas celebrating the saints' days are the occasion for costumed dances that are often of Spanish origin, and special rented dance costumes are required on these occasions. The

quinceañera or fifteenth birthday party for a young woman is another occasion for special clothing.

Contemporary Mexican and Central American dress owes its richness and variety to the fusion of clothing styles and textiles from the Old and New Worlds.

See also **Embroidery; Handwoven Textiles.**

BIBLIOGRAPHY

Anawalt, Patricia Rieff. *Indian Clothing before Cortes.* Norman: University of Oklahoma Press, 1981. A pioneering research study that looks at a variety of visual materials to ascertain pre-Columbian indigenous dress.

Anawalt, Patricia Rieff, and Frances F. Berdan. "Mexican Textiles." In *National Geographic Society Research and Exploration* 10, no. 3(1994): 342–353. An exploration of acculturation, how changes are integrated into contemporary indigenous clothing.

Arriola de Geng, Olga. *Los tejedores in Guatemala y la influencia española en el traje indigena.* Guatemala City: Litografías

Modernas, S.A., 1991. A discussion of the Spanish influence on Guatemalan indigenous dress.

Asturias de Barrios, Linda, and Dina Fernández Garcia, eds. *La indumentaria y el tejido mayas a través del tiempo.* Guatemala City: Museo Ixchel del Traje Indígena, 1992. Available in Spanish and also in an English translation, scholars discuss the evolution of Maya dress and weaving from a historical perspective.

Asturias de Barrios, Linda, ed. *Nuestra nacionalidad tiene su propia identidad.* Guatemala City: Prensa Libre, occidente corporación, 1995. An overview in Spanish of language and clothing diversity among the Mayas of Guatemala.

Cordry, Donald, and Dorothy Cordry. *Mexican Indian Costumes.* Austin and London: University of Texas Press, 1968. The first complete study of Mexican Indian dress.

Green, Judith Strapp. Personal communication, 8 May, 15 May 2003.

Johnson, Grace, and Douglas Sharon. *Cloth and Curing: Continuity and Change in Oaxaca.* San Diego, Calif.: San Diego Museum of Man, San Diego Museum Papers No. 32, 1994. Johnson focuses on native clothing of Oaxaca and presents the Oaxacan textile collection at the San Diego Museum of Man. Schevill discusses the communicative nature of indigenous and mestizo clothing and cloth in Mexico and Guatemala.

Logan, Irene, Ruth Lechuga, Teresa Castello Yturbide, Irmgard Weitlaner Johnson, and Chloë Sayer. *Rebozos de la colección Robert Everts.* Mexico D.F.: Museo Franz Mayer-Artes de Mexico, 1994. In Spanish, scholars trace the history of the rebozo from the perspective of the Franz Mayer collection.

Morris, Walter F., Jr., and Jeffrey Jay Foxx. *Living Maya.* New York: Harry N. Abrams, 1987. A fine description of Maya life in Chiapas, Mexico, a landmark publication.

O'Neale, Lila M. *Textiles of Highland Guatemala.* Publication 567. Washington, D.C.: Carnegie Institution of Washington, 1945. The first complete study of Maya textiles of Guatemala. An outstanding piece of scholarship with great attention to detail.

Osborne, Lilly de Jongh. *Indian Crafts of Guatemala and El Salvador.* Norman: University of Oklahoma Press, 1965. The author combines folklore with her firsthand pioneering experiences in the field in the early part of the twentieth century.

Salvador, Mari Lyn. *The Art of Being Kuna.* Los Angeles: UCLA Fowler Museum of Cultural History, 1997. An exhibition catalog that fully documents all aspects of Kuna life.

Sayer, Chloë. *Costumes of Mexico.* Austin: University of Texas Press, 1985. An update of the Cordrys' book, including sections on pre-Conquest, post-Conquest, and twentieth-century textiles.

Schevill, Margot Blum. *Costume as Communication: Ethnographic Costumes and Textiles from Middle America and the Central Andes of South America.* Bristol, R.I.: Haffenreffer Museum of Anthropology, Brown University, 1986. A focus on the textiles from Mexico, Guatemala, Peru, and Bolivia in the Haffenreffer Museum collection and a theoretical discussion on the theme of costume as communication.

———. *Maya Textiles of Guatemala: The Gustavus A. Eisen Collection, 1902.* Austin: University of Texas Press, 1993. The Eisen collection is the earliest and best documented Maya textile collection extant. Included is an essay by Christopher H. Lutz that looks at late-nineteenth-century Guatemalan Mayas, and an essay comparing the Eisen collection with an overview of Maya textiles of the 1980s.

Schevill, Margot Blum, Janet Catherine Berlo, and Edward B. Dwyer, eds. *Textile Traditions of Mesoamerica and the Andes: An Anthology.* Austin: University of Texas Press, 1996. Twenty-one scholars write about specific features of Mesoamerican and Andean contemporary clothing, weaving and dyeing technology, and marketing practices.

Schevill, Margot Blum, ed., and Jeffrey Jay Foxx, photographer. *The Maya Textile Tradition.* New York: Harry N. Abrams, 1997. Four scholars, James D. Nations, Linda Asturias de Barrios, Margot Blum Schevill, and Robert S. Carlsen, write about Maya life in Mexico, Belize, and Guatemala from different perspectives.

Valesquez, Myra. Personal communication, 14 May 2003.

Margot Blum Schevill

AMERICA, NORTH: HISTORY OF INDIGENOUS PEOPLES' DRESS

The native peoples of North America are diverse in culture, language, and ecological adaptations to varied environments. This variation is expressed in their attire. The only major constant in their clothing prior to European contact was the use of the skins of animals—most notably the tanned skins of the variety of large North American mammals—buffalo or bison, antelope, mountain sheep, caribou, and others. Owing to its wide geographic distribution, deer was the most prevalent. Smaller animals such as mink, beaver, and rabbit were also used but mainly for decorative effects.

Native peoples in certain regional areas did create textile clothing technologies that mainly utilized fibers harvested from gathered plant products and sometimes used spun thread made from hair from both domesticated and killed or captured wild animals. From Alaska down through the gathering cultures of the Plateau, Great Basin, and California tribes as far to the southwest as the border of Mexico, woven products were worn literally from head to toe. Hats, capes, blouses, dresses, and even footwear were constructed of plant material. In the north, this practice reflected the deleterious effects of the constant dampness of the coastal temperate rain forest climate upon skin products, and in the south it was largely due to the scarcity or rarity of large animals for skins. For example, as a means to maximize available resources, several Great Basin tribes had developed a system of weaving strips of the skins of small animals (like rabbits) into blankets or shawls.

Before contact, the main decorative additions for clothing were paints and the quills of the porcupine and the shafts of stripped bird feathers. Entire feathers from a variety of birds were used as well, with the feathers from large raptors, especially the eagle, signifying prestige and sacred power among many tribes. Dyes and paints were

Hopi *Kachina* dolls. *Kachinas* were gods or spirits, and Hopi dancers often emulated them in their performances. Hopi mythology maintained that Kachina costumes gave magical powers to the wearer, and the masks in particular were considered sacred. © GEOFFREY CLEMENTS/CORBIS. REPRODUCED BY PERMISSION.

used to color both the additive elements and the main bodies of the clothes themselves. These coloring agents were derived from plant and mineral sources, and in some areas very sophisticated systems for obtaining different colors from the local flora were in place. These products, as well as paints derived from regional mineral outcroppings, became important trade items.

Bone and shell ornaments were used as jewelry—bracelets, earrings, combs, and hair ornaments—and to a lesser extent as clothing ornaments. Extensive precontact trade routes existed for the distribution of these items, with the coveted shimmering abalone shells and the tapering conical dentalia shells that resembled miniature elephant tusks being traded from California and the more northerly Pacific Coast to the Great Plains and beyond to the Great Lakes region. Similarly, shells found in the Gulf of Mexico and ornaments cut from them were traded up river trade routes to areas in the Northern Plains, Midwest, and Great Lakes regions. A wide network also existed for the disbursement of the beads cut from Atlantic shells, later known to early European settlers as "wampum."

The only evidences of metallurgy north of Mexico occurred among the so-called Mound Builders of the Mississippi and Ohio valleys, where copper mined largely in the islands of Lake Superior and traded south to be turned into jewelry and other ornaments existed. On the

Pacific Northwest Coast, exploitation of similar "native copper" deposits, allowed the nearly pure copper product to be exploited as jewelry, knives, and other implements. The unique metal shieldlike objects created were a pure demonstration of wealth, which represented prestige and status among the "Potlatch People" of the Northwest Coast.

The abundance of resources in the Pacific coastal region led to the extensive use of various vegetation sources for clothing; in the north from Alaska to Northern California people relied upon evergreen root and inner-bark fibers, together with sedges, grasses, and ferns. As the rain forest climate gives way to marshy environments and grassy savannas in the south, the material from grasses and other smaller plants predominates. Nevertheless, this general area created some of the finest basketry products ever made by humanity, and a great array of basket-woven products was used as apparel. Large rain hats, caps, various forms of capes and wraps, dresses, kilts, leggings, and even shoes met the varying needs of the people of the western coast.

Peoples of the arid Southwest and Great Basin areas also wove clothing, but to a lesser degree, incorporating more skin products. Some sedentary tribes raised cotton that had previously been domesticated in Mesoamerica and had been traded north together with chilies, corn, and squashes as part of an agricultural diffusion. The

Native American traditional dress. Plains Indian clothing was made from hides sewn together with sinew and decorated with quills, fringe, animal teeth, beads, and sometimes even the human hair of enemies. © CORBIS. REPRODUCED BY PERMISSION.

Hopi, for example, produced cotton mantas or women's dresses and sashes and kilts for men. Interestingly, the men wove their own apparel items in this culture.

In the Southwest in general, men tended to wear a belt and breechclout combination, while women wore either a skirt or kilt or a dress that covered the entire torso, depending upon the tribe. More warmth for the winter months was furnished by a robe of skin tanned with the hair on, of locally obtained deer, antelope, sheep, or of trade-obtained bison. Woven rabbit-skin robes were also used. Footwear appropriate to resist a rough, rocky environment and the often-thorned plants of the desert climate assumed increased importance.

In the far north, the Arctic culture area, the Inuit (formerly called Eskimo) often utilized skins processed especially with the fur retained in such a way as to combat the frigid weather. Fitted fur garments had hoods, which were bordered with specific species of fur to minimize the formation of frost around the edge due to the condensation of moisture from exhaled breath in extreme weather. Other areas of the clothing were specifically engineered as well, with some species' skins being used for specific traits in different areas of the garment. Seal was

used for water resistance, caribou for insulative ability. Sealskin-soled mukluks or boots with formed soles were stuffed with dried grasses or mosses to provide insulation and protect the feet. The different species' skins were used in decorative fashion as well, with different tailoring demarcating various culture groups and gender identification. In addition, coastal groups created waterproof clothing of finely stitched seal intestine that enabled sea-hunters to venture out on frigid Arctic waters, allowing them to fasten themselves into their one-man kayaks in a leak-proof manner, when the intrusion of frigid seawater might have meant death, both for the kayaker and for those he was providing for.

Referencing the next cultural area south in the interior of the continent, the Athapaskan and Northern Algonquin also designed their clothing to stave off the hazards of the northern winter. Ironically, hazards of the possibility of thawing ground occasionally posed more danger than cold itself and thus changed the clothing design needs as opposed to those of their neighbors to the north. Additional decoration possibilities were afforded by the existence of porcupine and moose in the arboreal forest, allowing the use of quills and moose-hair as overlay and embroidery elements.

Indians of the Eastern Woodlands also decorated their clothing with quill and hair, both in embroidery and appliqué. Even inland tribes could obtain trade beads and shaped objects made by the coastal tribes from the coverings of the abundant shellfish. Deer, being the most common large animal, provided the most common skins utilized for clothing. Breechclouts, deer-skin leggings worn with each end tucked into a belt, were the norm in male attire, with women generally wearing full dresses. Moccasins in the wooded areas tended to be soft-soled, of tanned deer, moose, or caribou hide, often smoked over a smoldering fire to aid in resisting moisture prior to being cut up for the shoe's construction. Deer-hide robes aided in warmth during the cooler months. Some tribes in the area did develop a textile culture using fibers from gathered plants such as the stinging nettle; however, it was largely limited to smaller objects such as pouches, bags, and sashes.

By contrast, the tribes of the Plains had virtually no textile cultural history. In addition, the environment of the Plains area necessitated a change in the footwear technology, with most tribes favoring a two-part moccasin, with a tanned-skin vamp or upper attached to a thicker rawhide sole. As in the Southwest, this was a response to the more barren ground surface and thorned plants.

With the majority of the buffalo or bison in North America residing in this area, they assumed a central position in the cultures of the Plains tribes. This importance is reflected in clothing as well, with buffalo hide becoming a major resource. In the northern tribes especially, robes of buffalo hide tanned with the hair on were highly prized as winter attire, and often highly decorated.

In order to counter the monolithic image of the Native American, one must consider, in the early 2000s, the estimated 565 viable native groups in their proper cultural contexts to truly comprehend their rich cultural diversity, linguistic variation, and clothing and design of attire.

The long utilized Culture Area concept still has pertinence in postcolonial life. Within these coalescing areas, indigenous nations were grouped, mainly along the lines of material culture items—as among the Iroquois in the Northeast where longhouses sheltered several families together based upon matrilineal clan affiliation. There, a mixed hunting and agricultural economy was fostered by matrilocal residence and inheritance through the female and allowed a focus on seasonal ceremonies such as the midwinter and harvest festivals. Ceremonial-plaited cornhusk and carved wood masks were used in these and other rituals, often in the context of healing. Stranded belts of cut-shell beads rose above mere decoration, often being created to commemorate specific events. These wampum belts served as historic record-keeping devices. Quite a number of existing belts document treaties between native and European groups, for example.

One can select any area and explicate the clothing and adornment of the groups interacting with the environmental opportunity. The Northwest Coast consisted of various peoples speaking unrelated languages, but largely sharing a vibrant cultural lifestyle based upon the possibility for economic surplus afforded by the rich maritime environment. The most dazzling and elegant designs were undoubtedly those of the Haida from the Queen Charlotte Islands off the coast of present-day British Columbia in Canada. Their totemic art was embodied in monumental totem poles and decorated house villages, masks for ceremonial use, and the beautification of virtually every object type in the culture, whether utilitarian or decorative. This urge to beautify transferred to clothing as well, with masterful painting incorporating the same curvilinear stylized totemic themes on the woven hats and mats made from cedar bark and on skin robes and tunics as well. Chilkat blankets woven of mountain-goat wool and cedar bark were important prestige items owned by powerful individuals.

All aboriginal people of North America have undergone coerced culture change by the colonizers. Although native beliefs, culture, and languages have been legally suppressed they have adapted and changed to new lifestyles. Many wear traditional styles adapted to new materials. In attire, they evidence modern styles in new fashions.

See also **America, Central, and Mexico: History of Dress; Beads; Fur; Leather and Suede.**

BIBLIOGRAPHY

Coe, Ralph T. *Sacred Circles: Two Thousand Years of American Indian Art.* London: Arts Council of Great Britain, 1972.

Howard, James H. "The Native American Image in Western Europe." *American Indian Quarterly* 4, no. 1 (1978).

Beatrice Medicine

AMERICA, SOUTH: HISTORY OF DRESS The vast South American continent is a study in geographic extremes, including the Amazon Basin, the world's largest tropical rain forest; the Andes, the second-highest mountain range in the world; and the coastal deserts of Peru and northern Chile, which are among the driest areas in the world. The ecology of these regions (and such areas as the hot, humid Atlantic coast and cold, wet Patagonia) naturally influenced the dress of the aboriginal South Americans. Dress includes clothing, footwear, hairstyles and headdresses, jewelry, and other bodily adornment (for example, piercing, tattooing, and painting).

Amazon Basin and the Coasts

Europeans landing on the coast of what is now Brazil in the early sixteenth century encountered such groups as the Tupinambás, who wore feathered headdresses, and early drawings of natives wearing feathers became shorthand for Native Americans. Feathered or porcupine quill

Men in a traditional Tarabuco dance. The Tarabucan dancers show off their Incan inspired tunics, worn over wide-legged cropped pants. The draped hats cover up long hair worn in a braid, an ethnic marker. Typical open-toed sandals are worn on the feet. © LYNN A. MEISCH. REPRODUCED BY PERMISSION.

Indigenous women in Saraguro, Ecuador. These Ecuadorian women display traditional, yet contemporary clothing that includes wide-brimmed woven hats with markings indicating ethnicity and pinned *anakus,* or wrap-around skirts and *Ilikllas,* or mantles. Decorative earrings and necklaces adorn them. © LYNN A. MEISCH. REPRODUCED BY PERMISSION.

headdresses are still worn by most Amazonian groups for daily or fiesta use. Clothing is often minimal, no more than a penis string for males and a *cache-sexe* (G-string) for females, along with body painting or tattoos, and/or earplugs or earrings, bead, fiber, animal bone or tooth necklaces, bandoleers, armbands, leg bands, and bracelets, nose and lip and hair ornaments—an infinite variety of ornamentation—and, among Kayapó and Botocudo males of Brazil, *ternbeiteras,* large circular wooden discs inserted in the lower lip.

Such groups as the Colombian and Ecuadorian Cofáns, Ecuadorian Záparos, and Ecuadorian and Peruvian Shuars and Achuars once wore bark-cloth tunics, wrap skirts or (for women) dresses tied over one shoulder. Cofán males now wear knee-length tunics of commercial cotton cloth.

Among such groups in the western Amazon as the Cashinahuas (Dwyer, 1975) and Shipibos in Peru, and the Kamsás in Colombia loom-woven cotton clothes are worn, usually long tunics (often called *kushma*) for men, and tubular skirts for women. Both male and female Ashaninkas (Campas), and Matsigenkas (Machiguengas) wear tunics, however.

Males among the Shuars and Achuars of Peru and Ecuador wear a woven cotton wrap skirt, while the women wear a body wrap that is tied over one shoulder. The male wrap is sometimes tied with a woven belt with dangling wefts of human hair (Bianchi et al. 1982). Contacted tribes in Amazonia may choose to wear traditional dress at times and Euro-American dress when visiting towns or if they have been Christianized.

Such groups as the now culturally extinct Onas of Tierra del Fuego, the cold, southern tip of South America near Antarctica, had no weaving, but wore fur robes, hats, and moccasins.

The Andean Countries

The countries that once constituted the Inca Empire (much of Ecuador, Peru, Bolivia, Chile, and part of northern Argentina) are significant for several reasons. The first is that the Pacific coastal deserts have resulted in the preservation of organic material including mummy bundles with cadavers completely dressed. Other archaeological artifacts, such as realistic ceramics portraying dressed humans, combined with the Spanish conquistadores' and other historical accounts allow us to reconstruct the dress of ancient peoples. It is possible to generalize about the myriad local and historical highland and coastal dress styles, which can be referred to overall as Andean. First, the main fibers, dyes, and many technical features of later dress were in use by the Common Era. Fibers, handspun and handwoven on simple stick or frame looms, included New World cotton and camelid (llama, alpaca, vicuña, and wanaku). Myriad dyes were used to great effect, including Relbunium and cochineal (red to purple), indigo (blue to black), and a number of plants that gave yellow. Garments for the wealthy or high ranking were often adorned with embroidery, feathers, beads, and gold or silver discs. Second, pre-Hispanic garments were variations of the square or rectangle, and they were woven to size using virtually every technique known to modern Euro-American weavers. Jewelry varied by sex, age, and rank.

Third, textiles were four selvage, meaning all four edges were finished before the piece came off the loom. It is rare to find a cut pre-Hispanic Andean garment; tailoring came with the Spanish. Fourth, cloth was highly valued and exchanged or sacrificed at major life-cycle events and religious rituals. Dress carried heavy symbolic weight and indicated age, gender, marital status, social, political, religious, economic rank, and ethnicity.

The Peruvian Coast

By the time of the Paracas culture (c. 600–175 B.C.E.) on the south coast of Peru, male ritual attire consisted of garments that were typical of the coast until the Spanish Conquest in 1532: headband or turban, waist-length tunic (sometimes with short, attached sleeves) or tabard, breechcloth or kiltlike wrap skirt, mantle, and sometimes sandals, and a small bag, usually used to hold coca leaves. Paracas dress was consistent in terms of size, shape, and patterning, but varied in terms of decoration. Many Paracas garments, for example, were elaborately embroidered and many garments had added fringes, tabs, or edgings (Paul 1990).

Coastal male tunics and tabards had vertical warps and neck slits, while women's tunics were worn with the warp horizontal, with stitches at the shoulders and a horizontal neck opening (Rowe and Cohen 2002, p. 114). Women also wore a mantle. Male garments from the Chimu culture (c. C.E. 850–1532) of the north coast were sometimes woven in matched sets with identical weave structures and motifs on the tunic, breechcloth, and turban (Rowe 1984, p. 28).

For all the coastal cultures, jewelry differed by gender and rank and could include neckpieces, pectorals, bracelets, crowns, nose rings, and earplugs of copper, silver, gold, Spondylus shell, turquoise, feathers, and combinations of these materials, including the magnificent jewelry excavated from the royal tombs of Sipán of the Moche culture (c. C.E.100–700).

Inca Dress

Before the Spanish arrived, the Incas, spreading from their center in Cuzco, Peru, between c. 1300 and 1532, reigned over a vast empire. Mandating that conquered groups maintain their traditional clothing, headdress, and hairstyle allowed the Incas to identify and control them.

Highland dress differed from that of the coast. Garments were generally woven of camelid hair because of the cold. Inca garments had a distinctive embroidered edging combining cross-knit loop stitch and overcasting, with striped edge bindings on finer textiles (called *qumpi*, often double-faced tapestry) and solid bindings on plainer ones (*awasqa*) (Rowe 1995–1996, p. 6). Cloth was important, even sacred, to the Incas, who burned fine clothing as sacrifices to the sun (Murra 1989 [1962]).

Inca women wore an ankle-length square or rectangular body wrap called an *aksu* in the southern part of the empire and *anaku* in the north. It was wrapped under the arms, then pulled up and pinned over each shoulder with a *tupu*, a stickpin made of wood, bone, copper, or—for higher status women—silver or gold. The *tupus* were connected with a cord with dangling Spondylus shell pendants. A *chumpia*, or wide belt with woven pattern, held the *aksu* shut at the waist.

Next came a *lliklla*, a mantle, held shut with another stickpin (*t'ipki;* later also called *tupu*), and an *istalla*, a small bag for coca leaves. Some females wore headbands known by *wincha*, their Spanish name, and some upper-class women wore *ñañaqas*, a type of head cloth (Rowe 1995–1996).

Male garments included the *unku*, a sacklike, sleeveless, knee-length tunic, a *yakolla*, a mantle, a *wara* (breechcloth), *ch'uspa* (coca leaf bag), and a *llautu* (headwrap). Inca noblemen wore large gold *paku*, earplugs that dis-

Peruvian couple in native dress. The man wears a cotton tunic, or *kushma*, and a traditional *chullo* hat. The woman wears a short jacket and a *pollera* skirt. © JEREMY HORNER/CORBIS. REPRODUCED BY PERMISSION.

tended their lower earlobes, inspiring the Spanish to call them *orejones* (big ears). Both sexes wore *usuta*, hide or plant-fiber sandals (Rowe 1995–1996).

The Aymara-speaking chiefdoms of the Peruvian and Bolivian altiplano deserve mention, as their region was known for extensive camelid herds and fine textiles (Adelson and Tracht 1983). Some pre-Hispanic-style garments are still worn by both Quechuas and Aymaras including belts, mantles, tunics, *ch'uspas*, and *aksus*, but for Aymara females on the altiplano, the emblematic gathered skirt, tailored blouse, shawl, and bowler hat are more recent.

The Spanish Conquest

The Spanish introduced new tools for cloth production (treadle looms, carders, spinning wheels), new fibers (sheep's wool and silk), and new fashions. Soon after the conquest, upper-class male natives were wearing combinations of Inca and Spanish clothes: an Inca *unku* with Spanish knee breeches, stockings, shoes, and hat (Guaman Poma). The Spanish first insisted that native people

with variations in the hats indicating the wearer's community. In Bolivia and Ecuador, a variety of hats indicate ethnicity and among three Ecuadorian groups (the Saraguros, Cañars, and Otavalos), and one Bolivian (the Tarabucos), one ethnic marker for males is long hair worn in a braid. The Tarabucos are also known for their unique helmet-like hat (Meisch 1986).

In several communities—for example Q'ero in Peru (Rowe and Cohen 2002), the Chipayas in Bolivia, and the Saraguros in Ecuador (Meisch 1980–1981)—males still wear versions of the Inca tunic, while the females of Otavalo, Ecuador, wear dress that is the closest in form to Inca women's dress worn anywhere in the Andes (Meisch 1987, p. 118). Throughout northern Ecuador, indigenous females of many ethnic groups still wear the *anaku*, now a wrap skirt, handwoven belt, *lliklla*, sometimes a *tupu*, and distinctive hat, while males wear ponchos and felt fedoras.

In the Cuzco, Peru, region, males wear the *chullu*, the poncho, and sometimes handwoven wool pants, or Euro-American style dress, while women are more conservative and wear short jackets and sometimes vests over manufactured blouses and sweaters, and *pollera* with *llikllas*, skirts with handwoven belts held shut with a *tupu*, or safety pin. In many communities, women still pride themselves on their ability to weave fine cloth using pre-Hispanic technology.

In the Ausangate region south Cuzco, such small differences in the women's dress as the length of their *pollera* and the presence of fringe on their *monteras* indicates residence (Heckman 2003, pp. 83–84).

In the Corporaque region (southern Peru), the women's dress (vests, hats, gathered skirts), while quite European in form except for their carrying cloths, is elaborately machine-embroidered in small workshops (Femenias 1980, p. 1). Although the technology is European, the importance of dress as an ethnic marker is Andean. Throughout the Bolivian, Peruvian, and Ecuadorian Andes, many indigenous people wear *usuta*, sandals made from truck tires, but in northern Ecuador, *alpargatas*, handmade cotton sandals, are worn.

Although Colombia has a small indigenous population, groups in two major highland regions maintain distinctive dress styles. The Kogis (Cágabas) and Incas of the Sierra Nevada de Santa Marta on the Atlantic coast wear long, cotton belted tunics over tight pants, and a small, round hat, cotton and pointed for the former, flat-topped fiber or cotton for the latter. Men also carry a *mochilas*, a cotton bag for their coca leaves and lime gourd. Women wear a garment that resembles the *aksu*, which is wrapped around the body, tied over one shoulder, and fastened at the waist with a belt.

After the Spanish conquest, the Páezes of southwestern Colombia developed a unique dress, abandoning simple cotton wraps. The most distinctive features of male dress are a short, wool, poncho-like garment, and a wool

Warrior tomb in Sipán, Peru. For coastal cultures in Peru, jewelry was an important indicator of rank, as indicated by the gold, silver, and copper ornamentation found in this lord's tomb. © KEVIN SCHAFER/CORBIS. REPRODUCED BY PERMISSION.

wear their own dress, but after the great indigenous rebellions of the 1780s, the government of Peru prohibited the wearing of the headband, tunic, mantle, and other insignia of the Incas including jewelry engraved with the image of the Inca, or sun. Fine Inca *qumpi unku*, however, continued to be made and worn well into the colonial period (Pillsbury 2002).

Although poncho-like garments were worn before the Spanish conquest, most males wore tunics sewn up the sides. The first reference to the open-sided poncho by that name came from a 1629 description of the Mapuches (Araucanians) of Chile (Montell 1929, p. 239).

Contemporary Andean Indigenous Clothing

Traditional Andean dress in the early twenty-first century is a mixture of pre-Hispanic and Spanish colonial styles. Dress still indicates ethnicity, and in Peru use of the *chullu* (knitted hat with earflaps) by males and *montera* (Spanish flat-brimmed hat) by females denotes indigenous identity,

wrap skirt. Throughout the Andes, children usually wear a wrap skirt until they are toilet trained; then they wear traditional dress like the adults. Native people continue to use indigenous dress to define themselves as ethnic communities, and to combine pre-Hispanic and European technologies in the manufacture of their clothing.

See also **Cache-Sexe; Homespun; Turban.**

BIBLIOGRAPHY

Adelson, Laurie, and Arthur Tracht. *Aymara Weavings: Ceremonial Textiles of Colonial and 19th Century Bolivia.* Washington, D.C.: Smithsonian Institution, 1983.

Bianchi César et al. *Artesanías y Técnicas Shuar.* Quito: Ediciones Mundo Shuar, 1982.

Dwyer, Jane Powell, ed. *The Cashinahua of Eastern Peru.* Providence, R.I.: The Haffenreffer Museum of Anthropology, Brown University, 1975.

Femenias, Blenda, with Mary Guaman. *El Primer nueva corónica y buen gobierno*, 3 vols. From the original *El Primer corónica y buen gobierno* by Felipe Poma de Ayala (1615). Jaime L. Urioste, trans., John Murra and Rolena Adorno, eds. Mexico City: Siglo Veintiuno, 1980.

Heckman, Andrea. *Woven Stories: Andean Textiles and Rituals.* Albuquerque: University of New Mexico Press, 2003.

Meisch, Lynn. "Costume and Weaving in Saraguro, Ecuador." *The Textile Museum Journal* 19/20 (1980–1981): 55–64.

———. *Otavalo: Weaving, Costume and the Market.* Quito: Libri Mundi, 1987.

———. "Weaving Styles in Tarabuco, Bolivia." In *The Junius B. Bird Conference on Andean Textiles.* Edited by Ann Pollard Rowe, 243–274. Washington, D.C.: The Textile Museum, 1986.

Montell, Gösta. *Dress and Ornament in Ancient Peru: Archaeological and Historical Studies.* Göteborg, Sweden: Elanders Boktryckeri Aktiebolag, 1929.

Murra, John. "Cloth and Its Function in the Inca State." In *Cloth and Human Experience*, edited by Annette B. Weiner and J. Schneider, 275–302. Washington, D.C., and London: Smithsonian Institution Press 1989 [1962].

Paul, Anne. *Paracas Ritual Attire: Symbols of Authority in Ancient Peru.* Norman and London: University of Oklahoma Press, 1990.

Pillsbury, Joanne. "Inka Unku: Strategy and Design in Colonial Peru." The Cleveland Museum of Art. *Cleveland Studies in the History of Art* 7(2002): 68–103.

Rowe, Ann Pollard. *Costumes and Featherwork of the Lords of Chimor: Textiles from Peru's North Coast.* Washington, D.C.: The Textile Museum, 1984.

———. "Inca Weaving and Costume." *The Textile Museum Journal* 34/35 (1995–1996): 4–53.

Rowe, Ann Pollard, and John Cohen. *Hidden Threads of Peru: Q'ero Textiles.* London and Washington, D.C.: Merrell Publishers and The Textile Museum, 2002.

Vanstan, Ina. *Textiles from Beneath the Temple of Pachacamac, Peru.* Philadelphia: The University Museum, University of Pennsylvania, 1967.

Lynn A. Meisch

AMERICAN INDIAN DRESS: *See* **America, North: History of Indigenous Peoples' Dress**

AMIES, HARDY The British couturier Hardy Amies is best known as Queen Elizabeth II's longest-serving dressmaker. Supported by a highly skilled team in the workrooms at Savile Row, Amies dressed the queen and a small clientele of aristocratic and wealthy women for half a century. His men's wear and international licensee business had a lower profile but were crucial to the financial viability of the company. The licensee business benefited from Amies's position as dressmaker to the queen and from his staff's expertise, but its success ensured the survival of the couture house.

Early Life

Edwin Hardy Amies was born in London on 17 July 1909. Although he had some knowledge of dressmaking through his mother's work as a saleswoman for Miss Gray, Ltd., a London court dressmaker, it was not his chosen career. He wanted to be a journalist and on the advice of the editor of the *Daily Express* went to work in Europe to learn French and German. Back in Britain in 1931 he joined W. and T. Avery, selling industrial weighing machines and hoping to be posted to Germany, but dressmaking

Woman modeling Hardy Amies evening gown. Prior to 1958, Amies concentrated on producing women's garments with a particularly feminine feel, such as this satin-bodiced dress comprised of many layers of tulle. © HULTON-DEUTCH COLLECTION/CORBIS. REPRODUCED BY PERMISSION.

was clearly his destiny. A chance letter describing a dress worn by Miss Gray led to the offer of a job as designer at Lachasse, a sportswear shop owned by Miss Gray's husband, Fred Shingleton. In late 1933, Amies was invited by Mr. and Mrs. Shingleton (Miss Gray) to join their party at a dance given in aid of the Middlesex Hospital. At Christmas 1933, Amies wrote a letter to Mlle. Louise Probet-Piolat (Aunt Louie), a friend of his mother, describing the dress worn by Mrs. Shingleton at the dance. Aunt Louie in turn wrote to Mrs. Shingleton, reporting "how vivid she found my description." Mrs Shingleton threw the letter across the table to her husband and said, "You ought to get that boy into the business in Digby Morton's place" (Amies 1954, pp. 52–53). Undeterred by his complete ignorance of practical dressmaking, Amies boldly grabbed the opportunity.

Lachasse and the War

Lachasse was set up in 1928 as an offshoot of Fred Shingleton's company Gray and Paulette, Ltd. The firm specialized in custom-made daywear designed for members of the British upper classes, who divided their time between London and the country. When Amies joined in 1934 he replaced the Irish designer Digby Morton, whom he credited with transforming the classic country tweed suit "into an intricately cut and carefully designed garment that was so fashionable that it could be worn with confidence at the Ritz" (Amies 1954, p. 54). Following Morton, Amies concentrated on producing stylish, feminine, tailored clothes. The year 1937 was a turning point. The April edition of British *Vogue* featured a Lachasse suit, and Amies made his first sales to U.S. buyers, in London for King George VI's coronation. *Vogue* praised Amies's facility with pattern and color but noted the comparatively static silhouette of his suits, which now incorporated the slightly low waist that became characteristic of his cut. This slowly evolving line was, in fact, exactly what Amies's customers wanted. They were looking for clothes that were in tune with fashion but that would blend with their existing wardrobe, that were smart but not ostentatious, and that were well cut, immaculately fitted, and hard wearing. Amies catered to this particularly English approach to dressing throughout his career. His customers at Lachasse included the society hostess Mrs. Ernest Guinness and the actress Virginia Cherrill.

By 1939 sales at Lachasse had doubled but Amies's appeals to design in his own name were rebuffed. Restless and frustrated, he saw World War II as an escape. He joined the Intelligence Corps, transferring in 1941 to the Belgian section of the Special Operations Executive, where he rose to the rank of lieutenant colonel. Amies designed throughout the war, contributing to government-backed export collections and, after resigning from Lachasse, selling through the London house of Worth. He was a founding member of the Incorporated Society of London Fashion Designers and served as the society's chairman from 1959 to 1960.

"I understand and admire the Englishwoman's attitude to dress . . . just as our great country houses always look lived in and not [like] museums, so do our ladies refuse to look like fashion plates" (Amies 1954, p. 239).

Savile Row

After demobilization, Amies set up his own house in November 1945 at 14 Savile Row, in the heart of London's tailoring district. Staff from Lachasse, Worth, and Miss Gray joined him, bringing their clients and skills and enabling Amies to establish a reputation for all-around excellence. Although nearly forty, he was considered young in couture terms. Amies played on this, promoting himself and his house as vigorous, youthful, and progressive. In 1950 he was among the first London couturiers to set up a boutique line aimed at export buyers, selected provincial retail buyers, and the general public. Within two years the new business was half the size of the couture business.

In 1950 Amies received his first order from the future Queen Elizabeth II. In 1955 he successfully applied for the coveted royal warrant, which he held until his death. Norman Hartnell was still the queen's premier dressmaker but Amies's position at the top of his profession was secure. Designing for the queen gave him international standing, attracted prestigious clients, and guaranteed his own personal acceptability in the highest echelons of society. He later designed for Princess Michael of Kent and Diana, Princess of Wales.

Men's Wear

Amies entered the men's wear market in 1959, when he designed a range of silk ties for Michelson's. During the 1950s the preference of young adult men for more informal, body-conscious clothes and the popularity of American and Italian styles persuaded British manufacturers to reformulate their image and product. Hepworths, a middle-market multiple tailoring group, approached Amies. His first collection for Hepworths in 1961 was designed "to make the customer feel younger and richer than they were, and more attractive" (Amies 1984, p. 68). His designs were never cutting edge but formulated to attract a broad customer base. By 1964 the annual sales of his men's wear was about £15 million, compared with £0.75 million for women's wear. His collaboration with Hepworths led to a string of licensee agreements selling men's wear and some women's wear across the globe from the United States and Canada to Australia, New Zealand, Japan, Taiwan, and Korea. As

50

Amies dedicated more time to the licensee business, the women's wear design was taken over by his codirector, Ken Fleetwood (d. 1996). Amies sold Hardy Amies, Ltd., to Debenhams in 1973 to develop a ready-to-wear business but bought the company back in 1980.

Hardy Amies was appointed a Commander of the Victorian Order (CVO) in 1977 and honored with a knighthood in 1989. He was elected a Royal Designer for Industry in 1964. He received the *Harper's Bazaar* Award in 1962, the *Sunday Times* Special Award in 1965, and the British Fashion Council Hall of Fame award in 1989. He sold Hardy Amies, Ltd., to the Luxury Brands Group in 2001. Amies died on 5 March 2003.

See also **Diana, Princess of Wales; Haute Couture; Savile Row; Travel Clothing; Tweed.**

BIBLIOGRAPHY
Amies, Hardy. *Just So Far.* London: Collins, 1954. Detailed account of the first ten years of the house of Hardy Amies, and considers London fashion in relation to Paris.

———. *Still Here: An Autobiography.* London: Weidenfeld and Nicolson, 1984. Covers Amies's involvement in menswear and the development of his licensee business and his work for Queen Elizabeth II.

———. *The Englishman's Suit: A Personal View of Its History, Its Place in the World Today, Its Future, and the Accessories Which Support It.* London: Quartet, 1994. Describes the evolution of the suit and Amies's taste in menswear.

Cohn, Nik. *Today There Are No Gentlemen: The Changes in Englishmen's Clothes since the War.* London: Weidenfeld and Nicolson, 1971.

Ehrman, Edwina. "The Spirit of English Style: Hardy Amies, Royal Dressmaker and International Businessman." In *The Englishness of English Dress.* Edited by Christopher Breward, Becky Conekin, and Caroline Cox. Oxford: Berg, 2002. Considers how Englishness informed Amies's style and how he used his association with Englishness as a marketing tool.

Edwina Ehrman

ANCIENT WORLD: HISTORY OF DRESS Evidence about dress becomes plentiful only after humans began to live together in greater numbers in discrete localities with well-defined social organizations, with refinements in art and culture, and with a written language. This happened first in the ancient world in Mesopotamia (home of the Sumerians, Babylonians, and Assyrians) and in Egypt. Later other parts of the Mediterranean region were home to the Minoans (on the island of Crete), the Greeks, the Etruscans, and the Romans (on the Italian peninsula).

The sociocultural phenomenon called "fashion," that is, styles being widely adopted for a limited period of time, was not part of dress in the ancient world. Specific styles differed from one culture to another. Within a culture some changes took place over time, but those changes usually occurred slowly, over hundreds of years. In these civilizations tradition, not novelty, was the norm.

Certain common forms, structure, and elements appear in the dress of the different civilizations of the ancient world. Costume historians differentiate between draped and tailored dress. Draped clothing is made from lengths of fabric that are wrapped around the body and require little or no sewing. Tailored costume is cut into shaped pieces and sewn together. Draped costume utilizes lengths of woven textiles and predominates in warm climates where a loose fit is more comfortable. Tailored costume is thought to have originated around the time when animal skins were used. Being smaller in size than woven textiles, skins had to be sewn together. Tailored garments, cut to fit the body more closely, are more common in cold climates where the closer fit keeps the wearer warm. With a few exceptions, ancient world garments of the Mediterranean region were draped.

Strengths and Weaknesses of Evidence about Dress
Most of the evidence about costume of the ancient world comes from depictions of people in the art of the time. Often this evidence is fragmentary and difficult to decipher because researchers may not know enough about the context from which items come or about the conventions to which artists had to conform.

The geography and climate of a particular civilization and its religious practices may enhance or detract from the quantity and quality of evidence. Fortunately, the dry desert climate of ancient Egypt coupled with the religious beliefs that caused Egyptians to bury many different items in tombs have yielded actual examples of textiles and some garments and accessories.

Written records from these ancient civilizations may also contribute to what is known about dress. Such records are often of limited usefulness because they use terminology that is unclear today. They may, however, shed light on cultural norms or attitudes and values individuals hold about aspects of dress such as its ability to show status or reveal personal idiosyncrasies.

Common Types of Garments
Although they were used in unique ways, certain basic garment types appeared in a number of the ancient civilizations. In describing these garments, which had different names in different locales, the modern term that most closely approximates the garment will be used here. Although local practices varied, both men and women often wore the same garment types. These were skirts of various lengths; shawls, or lengths of woven fabric of different sizes and shapes that could be draped or wrapped around the body; and tunics, T-shaped garments similar to a loose-fitting modern T-shirt, that were made of woven fabric in varying lengths. E. J. W. Barber (1994) suggests that the Latin word *tunica* derives from the Middle

Eastern word for linen and she believes that the tunic originated as a linen undergarment worn to protect the skin against the harsh, itchy feel of wool. Later tunics were also used as outerwear and were made from fabrics of any available fibers.

The primary undergarment was a loincloth. In one form or another this garment seems to have been worn in most ancient world cultures. It appears not only on men, but also is sometimes depicted as worn by women. It generally wrapped much like a baby's diaper, and if climate permitted workers often used it as their sole outdoor garment.

In most of the ancient world, the most common foot covering was the sandal. Occasionally closed shoes and protective boots are depicted on horsemen. A shoe with an upward curve of the toe appears in many ancient world cultures. This style seems to make its first appearance in Mesopotamia around 2600 B.C.E. and it is thought that it probably originated in mountainous regions where it provided more protection from the cold than sandals. Its depiction on kings indicates that it was associated with royalty in Mesopotamia. It probably came to be a mark of status elsewhere, as well (Born). Similar styles show up among the Minoans and Etruscans.

Mesopotamian Dress

The Sumerians, as the earliest settlers in the land around the Tigris and Euphrates Rivers in what is now modern Iraq, established the first cities in the region. Active from about 3500 B.C.E. to 2500 B.C.E., they were supplanted as the dominant culture by the Babylonians (2500 B.C.E. to 1000 B.C.E.) who in turn gave way to the Assyrians (1000 B.C.E. to 600 B.C.E.).

One of the chief products of Mesopotamia, wool, was used not only domestically but was also exported. Although flax was available, it was clearly less important than wool. The importance of sheep to clothing and the economy is reflected in representations of dress. Sumerian devotional or votive figures often depict men or women wearing skirts that appear to be made from sheepskin with the fleece still attached. When the length of material was sufficient, it was thrown up and over the left shoulder and the right shoulder was left bare.

Other figures seem to be wearing fabrics with tufts of wool attached, which were made to simulate sheepskin. The Greek word *kaunakes* has been applied to both sheepskin and woven garments of this type.

Additional evidence of the importance of wool fabric comes from archaeology. An excavation of the tomb of a queen from Ur (c. 2600 B.C.E.) included fragments of bright red wool fabric thought to be from the queen's garments.

Evidence about dress. Evidence for costume in this region comes from depictions of humans on engraved seals, devotional, or votive statuettes of worshipers, a few wall paintings, and statues and relief carvings of military and political leaders. Representations of women are few, and the writings from legal and other documents confirm the impression that women's roles were somewhat restricted.

Major costume forms. In addition to the aforementioned *kaunakes* garment, early Sumerian art also depicts cloaks (capelike coverings). Costumes of later periods appear to have grown more complex, with shawls covering the upper body. Skirts, loincloths, and tunics also appear. A draped garment, probably made from a square of fabric 118 inches wide and 56 inches long (Houston 2002), appears on noble and mythical male figures from Sumer and Babylonia. Because the garment is represented as smooth, without folds or drapery, most scholars believe that this unlikely perfection was an artistic convention, not a realistic view of clothing. With this garment men wore a close-fitting head covering with a small brim or padded roll.

Women's dress of this period covered the entire upper body. The most likely forms were a skirt worn with a cape that had an opening for the head or a tunic. Other wrapped and draped styles have also been suggested.

Transitions from Babylonian to Assyrian rule are not marked by clear changes in style. In time, the Assyrians came to prefer tunics to the skirts and cape styles that were more common in earlier periods. The length of tunics varied with the gender, status, and occupation of the wearer. Women's tunics were full-length, as were those of kings and highly placed courtiers. Common people and soldiers wore short tunics.

Fabrics ornamented with complex designs appeared in Assyria. Scholars are uncertain whether the designs on royal costumes are embroidered or woven. Elaborate shawls were wrapped over tunics, and the overall effect was complex and multilayered. Priests selected the most favorable colors and garments for the ruler to wear on any given day.

Hairstyles and headdress are important elements of dress and often convey status, occupation, or relate to other aspects of culture. Sumerian men are depicted both clean-shaven and bearded. Sometimes they are bald. In hot climates shaving the head may be a health measure and done for comfort. Both men and women are also shown with long, curly hair, which is probably an ethnic characteristic. Assyrian men are bearded and have such elaborately arranged curls that curling irons may have been used. In art women's hair is shown as either ornately curled or dressed simply at about shoulder length.

The status of women apparently changed over time. From laws it is clear that Sumerian and Babylonian women had more legal protections than did Assyrian women. Law codes make reference to veiling and it appears that in Sumerian and Babylonian periods, free married women wore veils, while slaves and concubines were permitted to wear veils only when accompanied by the

Nefertari's tomb, Valley of the Queens. Artistic representations such as in this mural painting, created circa 1290–1224 B.C.E., provide historians with much information on the clothing of the period. This tomb relief shows three different dress styles: a sheath dress, a pleated gown, and a man's skirt (*schenti*). © ARCHIVO ICONOGRAFICO, S.A./CORBIS. REPRODUCED BY PERMISSION.

principal wife. Specific practices as to how and when the veil was worn are not entirely clear; however, it is evident that traditions surrounding the wearing of veils by women have deep roots in the Middle East.

Egyptian Dress

The civilization of Ancient Egypt came into being in North Africa in the lands along the Nile River when two kingdoms united during a so-called Early Dynastic Period (c. 3200–2620 B.C.E.). Historians divide the history of Egypt into three major periods: Old Kingdom (c. 2620–2260 B.C.E.), the Middle Kingdom (c. 2134–1786 B.C.E.), and the New Kingdom (c.1575–1087 B.C.E.). Throughout this entire period Egyptian dress changed very little.

The structure of Egyptian society also seems to have changed little throughout its history. The pharaoh, a hereditary king, ruled the country. The next level of so-

ciety, deputies and priests, served the king, and an official class administered the royal court and governed other areas of the country. A host of lower level officials, scribes, and artisans provided needed services, along with servants and laborers, and, at the bottom, were slaves who were foreign captives.

The hot and dry climate of Egypt made elaborate clothing unnecessary. However, due to the hierarchical structure of society, clothing served an important function in the display of status. Furthermore, religious beliefs led to some uses of clothing to provide mystical protection.

Sources of evidence about dress. It is religious beliefs that have provided much of the evidence for dress of this period. Egyptians believed that by placing real objects, models of real objects, and paintings of daily activities in the tomb with the dead, the deceased would be provided with the necessities for a comfortable afterlife. Depictions and actual items of clothing and accessories were among the materials included. The hot, dry climate preserved these objects. Works of art from temples and surviving inscriptions and documents are additional sources of information.

Textile availability and production. Linen fiber, obtained from the stems of flax plants, was the primary textile used in Egypt. Wool was not worn by priests or for religious rituals and was considered "unclean" although the Greek historian Herodotus (c. 490 B.C.E.) reported that he saw wool fabrics in use. From samples of fabric that have been preserved, it is evident that the Egyptians were highly skilled in linen production. They made elaborately pleated fabrics, probably by pressing dampened fabrics on grooved boards. Tapestry woven fabrics appeared after 1500 B.C.E. Beaded fabrics are found in tombs, as are embroidered and appliquéd fabrics.

Major costume forms. Draped or wrapped clothing predominated in Egyptian dress. Lower status men wore the simplest of garments: a loincloth of linen or leather, or a leather network covering a loincloth. Men of all classes wore wrapped skirts, sometimes called *schenti, shent, skent,* or *schent* by costume historians. The precise shape of these skirts varied depending on whether the fabric was pleated or plain (more often plain in the Old Kingdom, more likely pleated in the New Kingdom), longer or shorter (growing longer for high status men in the Middle Kingdom and after), fuller (in the New Kingdom) or less full (in the Old Kingdom). Royalty and upper-class men often wore elaborate jeweled belts, decorative panels, or aprons over skirts.

Coverings for the upper body consisted of leopard or lion skins, short fabric capes, corselets that were either strapless or suspended from straps, and wide, decorative necklaces. Over time the use of animal skins diminished. These became symbols of power, worn only by kings and priests. Eventually cloth replicas with painted leopard spots replaced the actual skins and seemed to have had a purely ritual use.

Tunics appear in Egyptian dress during the New Kingdom, possibly as a result of cross-cultural contact with other parts of the region or the conquest and political dominance of Egypt for a time by foreigners called the Hyksos.

Long wrapped garments appear to have been worn by both men and women until the Middle Kingdom, after which they appear only on women, gods, and kings. Instead during the New Kingdom men were shown wearing long, loose, flowing pleated garments, the construction of which is not entirely clear. Shawls were worn as an outermost covering and were either wrapped or tied.

Slaves and dancing girls were sometimes shown as being naked or wearing only a pubic band. Laboring women wore skirts when at work. Women, especially those of lower socioeconomic status, wore long, loose tunics, similar to those worn by men. From the writings of Herodotus, it appears this garment was called a *kalasiris*. Some costume historians have mistakenly used this term to refer to a tightly fitted garment that appears on women of all classes. Although this garment has the appearance of a tightly fitted sheath dress, it is thought that this representation is probably an artistic convention, not a realistic view. The garment was more likely to have been a length of fabric wrapped around the body. Gillian Vogelsang-Eastwood (1993) in an extensive study of garments from Egyptian tombs has found no examples of sheath dresses, but has found lengths of cloth with patterns of wear that are consistent with such wrapped garments.

Sheathlike garments are often shown with elaborate patterns. Suggestions for how the patterns were made have included weaving, painting, appliqué, leatherwork, and feathers. The more likely answer is that beaded net dresses, found in a number of tombs, were placed over a wrapped dress.

Garments from tombs from the Old Kingdom and after also include simple V-necked linen dresses made without sleeves. A later, sleeved version has a more complex construction that required sewing a tubular skirt to a yoke.

Like men, high status women wore long, full, pleated gowns in the New Kingdom. Careful examination of representations of these gowns indicates that the method of draping these garments that was used by women was different from those of men. Like men, women used wrapped shawls to provide warmth or cover.

Egyptian jewelry often provided the main sources of color in costume. Wide jeweled collars, jeweled belts and aprons, amulets worn around the neck to ward off evil, diadems with real or jeweled flowers, armlets, bracelets, and, during the New Kingdom, earrings were all part of the repertoire of ornaments available to men and women.

Headdress and hair coverings were often used to communicate status. As a result works of art show a wide variety of symbolic styles. The pharaoh wore a crown, the *pschent*, that was made by combining the traditional crown of Lower Egypt with the traditional crown of Upper Egypt. This crown was a visible symbol of the king's authority over both Upper and Lower Egypt. Other symbolic crowns and headdresses also are seen: the *hemhemet* crown, worn on ceremonial occasions; the blue or war crown when going to war; the *uraeus*, a representation of a cobra worn by kings and queens as a symbol of royal power. The *nemes* headdress, a scarflike garment fitted across the forehead, hanging down to the shoulder behind the ears, and having a long tail (symbolic of a lion's tail) in back was worn by rulers. Queens or goddesses wore the falcon headdress, shaped like a bird with the wings hanging down at the side of the face.

Men, and sometimes women and children, shaved their heads. Although men were clean-shaven, beards were symbols of power and the pharaoh wore a false beard. When artists depict Hatshepsut, a female pharaoh, she, too, is shown with this false beard. The children of the pharaoh had a distinctive hairstyle, the lock of Horus or the lock of youth. The head was shaved, and one lock of hair was allowed to grow on the left side of the head where it was braided and hung over the ear.

Minoan Dress

While the Mesopotamian and Egyptian civilizations were flourishing in the Eastern Mediterranean, the island of Crete, farther to the west, was home to the Minoans. This people, named after a legendary king Minos, thrived from about 2900 to 1150 B.C.E. on the island of Crete. By 2100 B.C.E. the Minoans extended their influence to the mainland Greek city-state called Mycenae. After the Minoans went into decline in the period around 1400 B.C.E., the Mycenaeans gained control over Crete and the Minoans.

Archaeological evidence provides a glimpse of Minoan and Mycenaean dress. From wall paintings and statuettes scholars have reached some conclusions about clothing of these periods. Archaeologists have determined that both linen and wool were produced. Wall paintings show Minoan textiles with intricate patterns that required both simple and complex weaving processes, embroidery, or painting. Excavations reveal that dyestuffs were imported. And Egyptian wall paintings showing men dressed in Minoan styles lead to the conclusion that Minoan traders brought their textiles to Egypt.

Major costume forms. Minoan dress had some similarities to and some marked differences from other Mediterranean civilizations. Leaping over the horns of bulls was a sport or religious ritual in which both Minoan men and women participated. Wall paintings show that for this sport, both wore loincloths reinforced at the crotch for protection. Minoan men wore skirts that ranged in length from short thigh-length versions with a tassel in the front, to longer lengths that ended below the knee or at the ankle. Skirts that appear to be very similar to the Mesopotamian *kaunakes* garment are also seen in Minoan art.

Women, too, wore skirts, but the construction was quite different from those of men. Scholars propose three different skirt types. All are full length. One is a bell-shaped skirt fitted over the hips and flaring to the hem. Another appears to be made of a series of horizontal ruffles widening gradually until they reach the ground, and the third is shown with a line down the center that some have interpreted as depicting a culotte-like, bifurcated skirt. Others see that line as merely showing how the skirt fell. With these skirts women often wore an apronlike overgarment. Arthur Evans, an archaeologist who was one of the earliest to study Cretan sites, suggested that the apron garment was worn for religious rituals and was a vestige of a loincloth worn by men and women in earlier times.

With these skirts, the top women wore a garment unique to the Minoans: a smoothly fitted bodice that, if the art is being accurately interpreted, had to have been cut and sewn. Tightly fitted sleeves were sewn or otherwise fastened onto the bodice. It laced or fastened underneath the breasts, leaving the bosom exposed. Authorities do not agree on whether all women bared their breasts. Some believe this style was restricted to priestesses and that ordinary women covered their breasts with a layer of sheer fabric.

With skirts or loincloths both men and women wore wide, tight belts with rolled edges. They also wore tunics. Men's were short or long; women's were long. Most of the tunics, as well as bodices and skirts, seem to have had woven patterned braid trimmings covering what appear to be the seam lines or points where garments would have been sewn together.

Men and women are both depicted with long or short curly hair. A variety of headwear can be seen in Minoan art, much of which may have been used in religious rituals or to designate status. Women are often shown with their hair carefully arranged and held in place with decorative nets or fillets (bands).

Greek Dress

A "dark age" of which little is known separates the Minoan/Mycenaean period from the Archaic Period of Greek history on the mainland. The history of Ancient Greece is generally divided into the Archaic Period (800–500 B.C.E.), the Classical Age (500–323 B.C.E.), and the Hellenistic Period (after 323 B.C.E. to the absorption of Greece by the Romans).

Greek sculpture and vase paintings provide numerous illustrations of Greek costume as do some wall paintings. Some even show individuals putting on or taking off clothing; therefore, scholars believe they understand what was worn and how it was constructed. Color of clothing, however, can be problematic. When first created and displayed most sculpture had been painted with colors. Those colors have been bleached away over time. For many years people believed that Greeks wore white almost exclusively. Most vase paintings are not a good source for information about color because the traditions of vase painting showed either black figures on a red background or red figures on a black background. From the few white background vases on which figures were painted in color and from frescoes it is possible to see that Greeks wore a wide range of often vivid colors.

Married women in ancient Greece ran the household. They provided for the family's needs for textiles by spinning and weaving. Fibers used included wool, which was produced in Greece. Linen came to Greece by the sixth century B.C.E., probably making its way from Egypt to the Ionian region of Asia Minor, where some Greeks had settled, and from there to the Greek peninsula. Late in Greek history silk evidently came from China by way

Woman on urn. In ancient times, people in warmer climates wore draped clothing such as that depicted in this artwork. Garments of this nature were cooler and allowed freedom of movement. © THE CLEVELAND MUSEUM OF ART, THE ATALANTA LEKYTHOS, 1966.114. REPRODUCED BY PERMISSION.

of Persia, and the Greek island of Cos was known for its silk production. Imported woven silk fabrics were probably unraveled into yarns and then combined with linen yarns and woven into fabrics. In this way, less of the precious silk was needed to make a highly decorative fabric.

Dyes were made from plants and minerals. A particularly prized and valuable color was purple, which was obtained from shellfish. Dyeing, bleaching, and some other finishing processes were probably carried out in special facilities, not in the home, because of the noxious fumes they produced. Women were skilled in decorating fabric with embroidery and woven designs. Garments were draped and were most likely woven to the correct size and therefore required little cutting and sewing. Many garments appear to be pleated, so it is likely that there were devices for pressing pleats into fabric and for keeping textiles smooth and flat.

Major costume forms. The Greek name for the garment roughly equivalent to a tunic was *chiton*, which is what costume historians now call Greek tunics. Throughout Greek history one form or another of the chiton was the basic

garment for men, women, and children. Its size, shape, and methods of fastening varied over time. Even so, the chiton was constructed in much the same way throughout Greek history. A rectangular length of fabric was folded in half lengthwise and placed around the body under the arms with the fold on one side and the open edge on the other. The top of the fabric was pulled up over the shoulder in the front to meet the fabric in the back, and pinned. This was repeated over the other shoulder. This rudimentary garment was belted at the waist. Sometimes the open side was sewn or it may have been pinned or left open. By beginning with this simple garment, variations could be made easily. Often the top edge of the fabric was folded down to form a decorative overfold. The width of the folded section could vary. Belts could be placed at various locations or multiple belts could be used. The method of pinning the shoulder could also change.

The names used today for these different styles are not necessarily those given to them by the ancient Greeks, but have been assigned later by costume historians who sometimes differ about terminology. The terms employed here are those that appear to be most commonly accepted.

In the Archaic Period, the chiton type garments are known as the *chitoniskos* and the *Doric peplos*. Both had the same construction and were made with an overfold that came to about waist length. They appear to have been closely fitted and seem to have been made from patterned wool fabrics. Men wore the chitoniskos, which was usually short and ended between the hip and the thigh. Women wore the Doric peplos, similar in shape and fit but reaching to the floor. The Doric peplos was fastened with a long, sharp, daggerlike decorative pin.

Herodotus says that the transition from the Doric peplos to the Ionic chiton came about because the women of Athens were said to have used their dress pins to stab to death a messenger who brought them the news of the resounding defeat of the Athenians in a battle. Herodotus says that the use of these large pins was outlawed, and small fastenings mandated instead.

This story may be apocryphal, but it is true that the Ionic chiton did replace the Doric peplos for both men and women soon after 550 B.C.E. The Ionic chiton was made from a wider fabric and was pinned with many small fasteners part or all of the way down the length of the arm. With more fabric in the garment, overfolds were less likely to be used. Instead other shawls or small rectangular garments were placed over the chiton. Many of the wider Ionic chitons appear to be pleated and were most likely made of lighter weight wool or of linen. Styles could be varied by belting the fabric in different ways.

Around 400 B.C.E. the Ionic chiton gradually gave way to the Doric chiton. The Doric chiton was narrower and fastened at the shoulder with a single pin very much like a decorative safety pin. The Romans called such pins *fibulae* and this Latin term is now used for any such pin from ancient times. This garment was more likely than the Ionic chiton to have an overfold. Doric chitons could also be worn with the previously mentioned small draped garments and belted in various ways. They seem to have been made from wool, linen, or silk.

Some scholars see the transition from the large, ostentatious Ionic chiton to the simpler Doric chiton as reflecting changes in attitudes and values in Greek society. A. G. Geddes (1987) suggests that in the late fifth century B.C.E. emphasis was being placed on physical fitness (more obvious in the more fitted Doric chiton), equality, and less flaunting of wealth.

The Hellenistic chiton appears from around 300 to 100 B.C.E. It was a refinement of the Doric chiton that was narrower, belted just beneath the breasts, and made of lighter weight wool cloth, linen, or silk. It is this chiton that is closest in style to many of the later garment styles that were inspired by the Greek chiton.

In general, styles for men and women were very similar, with women's garments reaching to the floor and men's more likely to be short for daily use. A poor man's version of the chiton was the *exomis*, a simple rectangle of cloth that fastened over one shoulder, leaving the other arm free for easier action.

Several garments seem to have been used more by men than women. The *himation* was a large rectangle of fabric that wrapped around the body. In use from the late fifth century, the garment might be worn alone or over a chiton. It covered the left shoulder, wrapped across the back and under the right arm, then was thrown over the left shoulder or carried across the left arm. For protection against inclement weather and while traveling, men wore a rectangular cloak of leather or wool called the *chlamys*. It could also be used as a blanket. The *petasos*, a wide-brimmed hat that offered additional protection against sun or rain was often worn with this cloak.

The question of whether married, adult Greek women were required to be veiled when out-of-doors is still debated. Some statues do seem to show this. A respectable married woman's activities were limited; most of her time was spent in the home and she was excluded from men's social gatherings. The women shown socializing with men in Greek art are courtesans or entertainers, not wives. Some scholars believe that when a woman went outside the home, she pulled a mantle or veil over her head to obscure her face. C. Galt (1931) suggests that veiling came to Greece from Ionia in the Middle East about the time the Ionian chiton was adopted.

Etruscan Dress

A number of tribes occupied the Italian peninsula. By 800 B.C.E. one of these groups had occupied a fairly large area and had developed an advanced culture and economy. Their burial practices, which included tomb paintings showing daily life, provide good evidence for how they dressed.

Trade brought them into close contact with Greece, Greek art, and Greek styles. In some periods Etruscan costume shows more shaping in the sleeves, which flare out at the ends, and a fit that molds the body more closely. Other distinctively Etruscan garments included a tall peaked hat, called a *tutulus*; shoes with pointed, curved toes; and several different styles of mantles. One especially notable mantle was the *tebenna*, which was apparently made with curved edges and semicircular in shape. Scholars believe that this mantle was the forerunner of the Roman toga. Even though individual characteristics can be noted for some Etruscan styles, for the most part Etruscan and Greek costumes show so many similarities that Etruscan versions are virtually indistinguishable from the Greek.

As the Romans rose to power in Italy, the Etruscans were absorbed into Rome and by the first century B.C.E. no longer existed as a separate culture.

Roman Dress

A tribe occupying the hills near the present city of Rome, the Romans gradually came to dominate not only the Italian peninsula, but a vast region including present-day western Europe and large parts of the Middle East and North Africa. Because much of the Mediterranean region had been under the domination of Greece, Greek influences permeated much of Roman life. Dress was no exception. As with the Etruscans, it is often difficult to distinguish between Greek and Roman styles. However, Roman dress is far more likely than Greek to include elements that identify some aspect of the status of the wearer.

Not only are there ample works of art remaining from the Roman era, but also literary works and inscriptions in Latin that can be read and understood. Even so, some aspects of Roman dress are not clearly understood. The precise meaning of certain Latin words referring to clothing may not be clear. One example is a man's garment called the *synthesis*.

The *synthesis* was a special occasion garment, worn by men for dinner parties. The traditional Roman man's garment, the toga, was cumbersome. Romans reclined to eat, and apparently it was difficult to stretch out in a toga, so the synthesis was the solution to this awkwardness. Based on what Roman texts say about the garment, scholars have concluded that it was probably a tunic worn with a shoulder wrap. But there does not appear to be any depiction of the style in Roman art.

Wool, linen, and silk were used in Rome and apparently cotton was imported from India around 190 B.C.E. or before. Silk was available only to the wealthy; cotton might be blended with wool or linen. Textiles were not produced in the family home, as in Greece. Instead they were woven by women workers on large estates or by men and women in businesses located throughout the empire. While some clothing was made in the home, ready-to-wear clothing was also available in shops.

The Roman version of the *chiton* was called *tunica*, from which the word tunic derives. Roman men's tunics ended at about the knee and were worn by all classes of society. Bands of purple that extended vertically from one hem to the other across the shoulder designated rank. Tunics of the Emperor and senators had wider bands; those of knights had narrower bands. Precise placement and width of these bands, called *clavi*, changed somewhat at different time periods, and after the first century C.E. all male nobles wore these bands. At this time ordinary citizens and slaves had no such insignia, but later they became more common. All male citizens were expected to wear the toga over a tunic.

The toga was the symbol of Roman citizenship. It was draped from a semicircle of white wool and placed across the shoulder, around the back, under the right arm, and pulled across the chest and over the shoulder. As previously noted it probably derived from the Etruscan tebenna. Some officials wore special togas and throughout the history of Rome the size, shape, and details of draping did change somewhat.

Various types of cloaks and capes, with or without hoods, served to provide cover outdoors. Those worn by the military often identified their rank. The *sagum* was a red wool cape worn by ordinary soldiers. This term entered into the lexicon of symbols, and when people talked about "putting on the sagum" they meant "going to war."

Women's dress in Rome differed only a little from that of Greek women of the Hellenic period. They wore an under tunic, not seen in public, and an over tunic very much like a Greek chiton. A *palla*, rather similar to a Greek himation, was draped over this. The colors of these layers varied. Opinions differ as to just what the *stola* with the *instita* was. Many costume histories use the word *stola* interchangeably with outer tunic. However, literary works clearly indicate that the garment was associated only with free, married women. Some sources describe the *instita* as a ruffle at the bottom of the *stola* or outer tunic. But a careful analysis by Judith Sebesta (1994) leads her to conclude that it is a special type of outer tunic suspended from sewed-on straps.

Hairstyles show marked differences from one time period to another. Men are generally bearded during the years of the Republic, clean-shaven during the Empire until the time of the Emperor Hadrian who wore a beard. Each family celebrated the occasion of the first shave for a young boy with a festival at which they placed the hairs in a special container and sacrificed them to the gods.

Women's hairstyles were relatively simple during the first century C.E., but later grew so very complicated that they required the addition of artificial hair and special curls and braids arranged into towering structures.

Literary sources speak of extensive use of makeup by both men and women. Cleanliness was valued and public baths available to all levels of society.

The children of Roman citizens dressed like adults. Both boys and girls wore a toga with a purple band around the edge (*toga praetexta*). Boys wore it until age fourteen to sixteen, after which they wore the citizen's toga (*toga pura*), and girls gave it up after puberty. Initially this garment was only for the children of noble families, but eventually became part of the dress of all children of Roman citizens. Roman male children also wore a *bulla*, a ball-shaped neck ornament containing protective charms that was given to them at the time they were named.

Both brides and vestal virgins, women whose lives were dedicated to the goddess Vesta, seem to have worn a special headdress. It consisted of pads of artificial hair alternating with narrow bands. A veil was placed over this. For brides the veil was bright orange and a wreath made of orange blossoms and myrtle was set on top of it. This association of veils and orange blossoms with weddings continues until modern times and may have its origin in Roman custom.

See also **Textiles, Prehistoric; Toga.**

BIBLIOGRAPHY

General Works

Barber, E. J. W. *Prehistoric Textiles.* Princeton, N.J.: Princeton University Press, 1991.

———. *Women's Work: The First 20,000 Years.* New York: W. W. Norton and Company, 1994.

Born, W., III. "Footwear of the Ancient Orient." *CIBA Review* p. 1210.

Sichel, Marion. *Costume of the Classical World.* London: Batsford Academic and Education, 1980.

Tortora, Phyllis, and Keith Eubank. *Survey of Historic Costume.* New York: Fairchild Publications, 1998.

Mesopotamian and Egyptian Dress

"Herodotus on Egypt." Reprinted in *The World of the Past.* Vol. 1. Edited by J. Hawkes. New York: Alfred A. Knopf, 1963.

Houston, Mary G. *Ancient Egyptian, Mesopotamian, and Persian Costume.* New York: Dover Publications, Inc., 2002.

Vogelsang-Eastwood, Gillian. *Pharaonic Egyptian Clothing.* Leiden, Netherlands: E. J. Brill, 1993.

Minoan and Greek Dress

Evans, A. "Scenes from Minoan Life." In *The World of the Past.* Edited by J. Hawkes. New York: Alfred A. Knopf, 1963.

Evans, M. M. "Greek Dress." In *Ancient Greek Dress.* Edited by M. Johnson. Chicago, Illinois: Argonaut, Inc., 1964.

Faber, A. "Dress and Dress Materials in Greece and Rome." *CIBA Review* no. 1 (n.d.): 297.

Galt, C. "Veiled Ladies." *American Journal of Archeology* 35, no. 4 (1931): 373.

Geddes, A. G. "Rags and Riches: The Costume of Athenian Men in the Fifth Century." *Classical Quarterly* 37, no. 2 (1987): 307–331.

Houston, Mary G. *Ancient Greek, Roman, and Byzantine Costume.* Mineola, N.Y.: Dover Publications, Inc., 2003.

Etruscan and Roman Dress

Bonfante, Larissa. *Etruscan Dress.* 2nd ed. Baltimore, Md.: Johns Hopkins University Press, 2003.

Croom, Alexandra T. *Roman Clothing and Fashion.* Charleston, S.C.: Tempus Publishing Inc., 2000.

Goldman, N. "Reconstructing Roman Clothing." In *The World of Roman Costume.* Edited by J. L. Sebesta and L. Bonfante, 213–237. Madison: University of Wisconsin Press, 1994.

McDaniel, W. B. "Roman Dinner Garments." *Classical Philology* 20 (1925): 268

Rudd, Niall, trans. *The Satires of Horace and Persius.* Baltimore, Md.: Penguin Books, 1973.

Sebesta, Judith Lynn. "Symbolism in the Costume of the Roman Woman." In *The World of Roman Costume.* Edited by J. L. Sebesta and L. Bonfante, 46–53. Madison: University of Wisconsin Press, 1994.

———. "Tunica Ralla, Tunica Spissa." In *The World of Roman Costume.* Edited by J. L. Sebesta and L. Bonfante, 65–76. Madison: University of Wisconsin Press, 1994.

Sebesta, Judith Lynn, and Larissa Bonfante, eds. *The World of Roman Costume.* Madison: University of Wisconsin Press, 1994.

Stone, S. "The Toga: From National to Ceremonial Costume." In *The World of Roman Costume.* Edited by J. L. Sebesta and L. Bonfante, 13–45. Madison: University of Wisconsin Press, 1994.

Wilson, Lillian May. *The Roman Toga.* Baltimore, Md.: Johns Hopkins University Press. 1924.

———. *The Clothing of the Ancient Romans.* Baltimore, Md.: Johns Hopkins University Press, 1938.

Phyllis Tortora

ANGORA Though true angora fiber is from the hair of the Angora rabbit, because more than one animal bears the name "angora" some confusion exists regarding what really is angora fiber. Angora rabbits produce angora fiber, and Angora goats produce mohair fiber. Angora also differs from rabbit hair, which is the fiber obtained from the common rabbit, in that angora is longer and more flexible and better suited for luxury textiles.

Each rabbit produces ten to sixteen ounces of luxuriously soft fiber per year. The rabbits are clipped with a pair of scissors, sheared with electric clippers, or plucked by hand when the hair is three to five inches long. Plucking pulls the loose hair from the rabbit and produces the highest grade of angora wool because of the spiky fur-like quality it gives to the fabric. Some countries regard plucking as inhumane and have outlawed the practice.

Angora fiber differs from sheep's wool in several ways. Unlike wool, angora fibers do not have scales on their surface. This lowers the risk of shrinkage from felting (the permanent interlocking of the fibers) and makes the fibers slippery. Angora fiber's diameter is very fine, approximately 11 microns (1/25,000 of an inch). Only the finest wool is similar in diameter to angora. Angora fiber has a low density (weight) of 1.15 to 1.18 grams per cubic centimeter, compared to 1.33 for wool. Angora fibers have little elasticity, making them difficult to process into yarn. Wool, on the other hand, is very elastic because of its crimp and molecular structure. Blending angora with wool helps make spinning easier and helps to hold the angora in the yarn structure. During a garment's life, it is normal for short angora fibers to work their way out of the yarn and shed from the fabric.

Angora's small diameter fibers have air-filled chambers that give them warmth without weight. The fiber transmits moisture readily, so garments feel dry, warm, and comfortable. Angora's properties are of value not only for fashionable garments, but also for therapeutic garments designed for people with joint diseases. Garments featuring angora fiber include knitted sweaters, hats, gloves, and underwear for fall and winter-wear.

The highest quality commercial angora fiber is white, but the fiber is available in other beautiful colors including pure white, gray, fawn (a light grayish brown), brown, and black. Angora does not take dye well, so the dyed fiber usually has a lighter color than other fibers in the blend.

There are five grades of angora fiber. The first four require the fiber to be white, perfectly clean, and without tangles or mats. The lengths vary according to the grade: grade one, the top grade, is 2 to 3 inches long; grade two is 1.5 to 2 inches; grade three is 1 to 1.5 inches; and grade four is any length. Grade five is of any color and can be soiled and matted or unmatted. Naturally colored angora fiber is generally found in garments produced by small-scale manufacturers.

Angora rabbits were originally raised in North Africa and France. In the early twenty-first century, 90 percent of the world's production was from China. Other countries producing angora included Argentina, Chile, Hungary, France, and India.

See also **Felt; Fibers.**

BIBLIOGRAPHY

Spalding, K., and C. McLelland, eds., *Angora Handbook.* 2nd ed. Morgan Hill, Calif.: Northern California Angora Guild, 1991.

Ann W. Braaten

ANIMAL PRINTS Animal prints and skins are widely believed to convey power to the wearer. Fabrics with patterns and colors imitating the skins of animals were made into fashionable dress as early as the eighteenth century, when elaborate silk designs emulating exotic furs intertwined with expensive laces to evoke a sense of luxury and wealth.

Model wearing coat from Dolce & Gabbana collection. Leopard prints such as this are favorites of the fashion world, conveying a sense of boldness, independence, and power upon the wearer. © ASHBY DON/CORBIS SYGMA. REPRODUCED BY PERMISSION.

Characteristics associated with a particular animal, such as the fierceness of a tiger, are thought to be transferred to the wearer through animal-patterned clothing. Animal motifs are also widely regarded as erotic and thus tend to be utilized on clothing designed to attract others. For example, animal prints have a constant presence in overtly sexual lingerie. A person wearing an animal print makes a statement about confidence and expresses a desire to be noticed. These head-turning prints catch the viewer's attention with their multicolored patterns and irregular designs. Their reputation ranges from classic and sophisticated in high fashion to cheap and trashy in popular fashion. Mainstream fashion articles have suggested that wearers limit animal prints to accents to avoid sending an overly suggestive message.

From tiger stripes to cheetah spots, the patterns of the world's big cats have been constants in the fashion world. The rosette pattern of the leopard has been a favorite. Graceful and powerful hunters, they suggest "feminine" cunning and instinct. The movie *Tarzan the Apeman* was a huge success when it was released by MGM in 1932. The revealing, leopard-patterned clothing of stars Johnny Weissmuller as Tarzan and Maureen O'Sullivan as Jane, created a sensation for leopard and cheetah prints during the 1930s. Blouses, coats, and scarves were some of the popular items made in animal prints during that time. These items represented the excitement and adventure of the jungle and an independence of spirit especially unusual for depictions of women during that time.

The fashion designer Rudi Gernreich produced a collection of animal-patterned dresses with matching tights and underwear in 1968, documented in the movie *Basic Black* (1968) by the photographer William Claxton and the model Peggy Moffitt. Animal prints became very popular for dresses, leggings, and accessories in the 1970s and 1980s. Animal pelts and prints fit the free-spirited independence and heightened interest in world cultures in the 1970s. Animal motifs were perfectly suited to the combination of extravagance, bold patterns, and color in the 1980s. The fashion designers Dominico Dolce and Stefano Gabbana have made animal prints their signature. These prints enhance the diva persona of the celebrities they are known for dressing.

Political questions concerning the use of real leather and animal fur have affected the wearing of animal prints. International law prohibits the trade in endangered species. By raising the awareness of the treatment of animals that are killed for the use of their skins, animal rights activists and organizations have promoted wearing clothing made of fabric printed with animal motifs rather than actual pelts.

See also **Dolce & Gabbana; Film and Fashion; Fur; Gernreich, Rudi.**

BIBLIOGRAPHY

Dolce, Domenico, and Stefano Gabbana. *Dolce & Gabbana: Animal.* Photography by Steven Meisel and Bruce Weber New York: Abbeville Press, Inc., 1998.

Felderer, Brigitte, et al. *Rudi Gernreich: Fashion Will Go Out of Fashion.* Edited by Gerald Zeigerman. Philadelphia: Institute of Contemporary Art, University of Pennsylvania, 2001.

Dennita Sewell

AO DAI Vietnam's national dress, the *ao dai* (literally "long shirt"; pronounced "ow zai" in the north, "ow yai" in the south) consists of two elements: a long tunic with a close-fitting bodice, mandarin collar, raglan sleeves, and side slits that create front and back panels from the waist down; and wide-legged pants, often cut on the bias. While in the past both men and women wore ao dai, in the twenty-first century it is almost exclusively a women's garment. A popular uniform for civil servants, tour guides, hotel and restaurant staff, and high school students, the ao dai is also worn for weddings, religious rituals, and special occasions. Commonly seen as symbolizing traditional Vietnamese identity and femi-

Beauty pageant contestants in Vietnam. The *ao dai,* with its characteristic long shirt, mandarin collar, and loose-fitting trousers, enjoyed a revival in the 1990s, and is worn for special occasions, as well as by office workers and students. © STEVE RAYMER/CORBIS. REPRODUCED BY PERMISSION.

ninity, the ao dai in fact has a relatively brief history marked by foreign influence.

History

The ao dai provides a striking example of how Vietnamese have responded to both Chinese and French colonization by adopting elements of foreign cultures and modifying them to be uniquely Vietnamese. Prior to the fifteenth century, Vietnamese women typically wore a skirt (*vay*) and halter top (*yem*). These were sometimes covered by an open-necked tunic (*ao tu than*) with four long panels, the front two tied or belted at the waist. Women's garments were brown or black, accented by brightly colored tops or belts on special occasions. From 1407 to 1428, China's Ming Dynasty occupied Vietnam and forced women to wear Chinese-style pants. After regaining independence, Vietnam's Le Dynasty (1428–1788) likewise criticized women's clothing for violating Confucian standards of decorum. These policies were haphazardly enforced, and skirts and halter tops remained the norm. During the seventeenth and eighteenth centuries, Vietnam was divided into two regions, with the Nguyen family ruling the south. To distinguish their sub-

jects from northerners, Nguyen lords ordered southern men and women to wear Chinese-style trousers and long, front-buttoning tunics. After the Nguyen family gained control over the entire country in 1802, the conservative Confucian Emperor Minh Mang (r. 1820–1841) banned women's skirts (*vay*) on aesthetic and moral grounds.

Over the next century, precursors to the modern ao dai became popular in cities, at the royal court in Hue, and for holidays and festivals in the countryside. With some regional variations, the outfit consisted of pants and a loose-fitting shirt with a stand-up collar and a diagonal closure that ran along the right side from the neck to the armpit, both features inspired by Chinese and Manchu garments. Elites often layered several ao dai of different colors, with the neck left open to display the layers. Among peasants and laborers, however, the *vay* and *yem* remained popular for daily wear.

Under French colonialism (1858–1954), Vietnamese intelligentsia and an emerging urban bourgeoisie strove to adopt progressive elements of Western modernity while at the same time resisting colonialism and preserving select aspects of Vietnamese heritage. During the

1930s, as part of the efforts of Tu Luc Van Doan (Self-Reliance Literary Group) to fashion a modern "new woman," Hanoi artist Nguyen Cat Tuong, also known as Lemur, premiered ao dai styles inspired by French fashion. The light-colored, close-fitting tunics featured longer panels, puffy sleeves, asymmetrical lace collars, buttoned cuffs, scalloped hems, and darts at the waist and chest, thus requiring a brassiere or corset. Lemur's Europeanized flared pants were white with snugly tailored hips. Criticized by conservatives as scandalous, Lemur's designs nonetheless marked the emergence of a contemporary ao dai blending traditional Vietnamese elements with Western tailoring and bodily aesthetics, much like the Chinese cheongsam of the same period.

French colonialism ended in 1954 with the division of Vietnam into North and South. In North Vietnam, communist leaders criticized the ao dai as bourgeois, colonial, and impractical for manual labor, although women continued to wear it for special occasions. Meanwhile, in capitalist South Vietnam, experimentation with the garment continued. Madame Nhu (Tran Le Xuan), the sister-in-law of President Ngo Dinh Diem, became notorious in the 1950s and 1960s for the skin-baring open necklines of her ao dai. Also at this time, two Saigon tailors redesigned the ao dai to include raglan sleeves, thus reducing wrinkling around the shoulders and armpits.

Revival

In 1975, the Vietnam War ended with the reunification of North and South under communist rule. Leaders decried the southern ao dai as decadent and instead promoted simpler, utilitarian clothing styles. But austerity proved short-lived. By the 1990s, economic reforms and improved standards of living led to a revival of the ao dai within Vietnam and to growing international awareness of it as a symbol of Vietnamese identity. In 1989, the *Women's Newspaper* in Ho Chi Minh City (formerly Saigon) hosted the first Miss Ao Dai contest. Six years later, Miss Vietnam's blue brocade ao dai won the prize for best national costume at Tokyo's Miss International Pageant. Simple white ao dai have been reinstated in many cities and towns as uniforms for female high school students, while Vietnam Airlines flight attendants don red ao dai. Recent innovation has come in both decoration and form. The designers Si Hoang and Minh Hanh employ novel fabrics, abstract motifs, and ethnic minority patterns, while others alter the tunic by opening necklines, removing sleeves, or replacing the long panels with fringe. The once scandalous white pants now seem outmoded, and urban women instead favor pants the same color as the tunic. Although most Vietnamese women wear Western dress daily, the ao dai allows the fashion-conscious to be simultaneously trendy and traditional on special occasions.

International Influence

When the ao dai fell into disfavor in socialist Vietnam, Vietnamese who had immigrated to the United States, Canada, Australia, or France preserved it as a symbol of their ethnic heritage. Ao dai can be seen at fashion shows, Tet (Lunar New Year) celebrations, weddings, and musical performances throughout the diaspora, which numbered approximately 2.5 million in 2003. Like the Chinese cheongsam and the Japanese kimono, the ao dai has also inspired non-Asian designers. Following the 1992 films *Indochine* and *The Lover*, both set in the French colonial period, Ralph Lauren, Richard Tyler, Claude Montana, and Giorgio Armani debuted ao dai–inspired collections. While "Indo-Chic" fashions can be Orientalist in their celebration of a demure, sexy, and exotic Vietnamese femininity, they are typically welcomed in Vietnam as evidence that the ao dai has entered the canon of international fashion. The ao dai's twenty-first-century revival in Vietnam rests as much on this newly fashionable status as on its links to the past.

See also **Asia, Southeastern Mainland: History of Dress; Qipao; Shirt.**

BIBLIOGRAPHY

Doan Thi Tinh. *Tim Hieu Trang Phuc Viet Nam.* Hanoi, Vietnam: Nha Xuat Ban Ha Noi, 1987.

Leshkowich, Ann Marie. "The *Ao Dai* Goes Global: How International Influences and Female Entrepreneurs Have Shaped Vietnam's 'National Costume.'" In *Re-Orienting Fashion: The Globalization of Asian Dress.* Edited by Sandra Niessen, Ann Marie Leshkowich, and Carla Jones. Oxford and New York: Berg, 2003.

Ngo Duc Thinh. *Trang Phuc Co Truyen Cac Dan Toc Viet Nam.* Hanoi, Vietnam: Van Hoa Dan Toc, 1994.

Nguyen Ngac, and Nguyen Van Luan. *Un siècle d'histoire de la robe des Vietnamiennes.* Saigon, Vietnam: Direction des Affaires Culturelles, 1974.

Nguyen Thi Duc. *Van Hoa Trang Phuc tu Truyen Thong den Hien Dai.* Hanoi, Vietnam: Nha Xuat Ban Van Hoa Thong Tin, 1998.

Nguyen Van Ky. *La société Vietnamienne face à la modernité.* Paris: L'Harmattan, 1995.

Nhi T. Lieu "Remembering the Nation Through Pageantry: Femininity and the Politics of Vietnamese Womanhood in the *Hoa Hau* Ao Dai Contest." *Frontiers* 21, no. 1/2 (2000): 127–151.

Ann Marie Leshkowich

APPEARANCE The term "appearance" is commonly used in relation to the observable characteristics of a wide range of things in the environment such as human beings, plants and animals, geographical and atmospheric conditions, and buildings, to name only a few. However, this entry will be limited to a discussion of appearance in relation to the human body along with things placed on or about it in functioning as stimuli for communication.

Human beings have the capability of communicating in many different ways, often simultaneously. Appearance, because of visual characteristics and the versatility with which they can be structured to send various messages, is used frequently as a type of nonverbal communication as the primary focus of attention or in conjunction with other forms of communication.

The Body and Dress

For purposes of study and analysis, appearance can be considered according to two major components: the body and dress. Because the characteristics of each are complex, there is merit in considering them independently before examining their interrelatedness.

The body component. A wide range of observable characteristics of the body serve as stimuli during the process of communication. They fall into four main categories: body forms, body motions, body surfaces, and facial configurations. The category of body forms includes characteristics pertaining to the overall structure of the body in a fixed position as well as the structure of various units such as the head and limbs, each of which provides a different kind of stimuli in appearance. Because body forms include size, shape, and mass, they are among the most compelling aspects of appearance.

The category of body motions pertains to interrelationships between movement and the totality of the body as well as certain parts. Gait, hand gestures, shoulder shrugs, nods, and pelvic movements all fall into this category. Dynamic effects are often produced in appearance through the tempo and rhythm of body motions.

The category of body surfaces pertains to characteristics of coverings of the overall body and its parts such as the color and texture of skin and hair. Because body surfaces appeal to both the senses of touch and sight, they can be among the most sensuous qualities of appearance.

The category of facial configurations pertains to forms, motions, and surfaces that are unique to the face. Since the face is composed of various forms, has potential for movement, and has color and texture in skin and hair, this category is an integration of characteristics that are similar to those in the other categories but on a smaller scale. However, since the face is a particularly expressive part of the body and often serves as a major source of stimuli in appearance, there is merit in considering facial configurations as a category apart from its counterparts in the overall body composition.

Each of the four categories of the body component can be analyzed further on the basis of constituent parts referred to as elements. In addition to contributing to the totality of a major characteristic of the body, each has the potential of being a dominant aspect of appearance unto itself. For example, eye movements are among the mix of elements that constitute the overall characteristics of facial configurations, but they can also command special attention when they occur in such forms as unexpected winks or sudden blinks. In a similar way, skin color and texture are integrated characteristics of body surfaces, but

they can also be dominant features of appearance when they stand out for some reason.

In prehistoric times, appearance was based solely on the body since the concept of dress had not yet evolved. However, there is considerable documentation that even in the early years, the body was modified in various ways apart from donning items of clothing. Substances were discovered in nature that could be used to change the color and texture of both skin and hair and technological innovations were made that could change the size, shape, and contours of the body.

The dress component. As knowledge about materials expanded and skills concerning processes and techniques emerged, new ways of protecting and enhancing the body began to appear. Although scholars have referred to the classification of those innovations in various ways, they are referred to as dress in this entry.

Characteristics of dress fall into two main categories: articles of clothing and articles of adornment. The term "clothing" pertains to things that are placed over the body to bring about comfort or protection whereas the term "adornment" is used in reference to items that are placed on or about the body to enhance it. However, the dividing line is not always clear since clothing can serve as adornment and under certain circumstances, adornment functions as clothing.

Just as various categories of the body can be considered according to elements, so can the categories of clothing and articles of adornment. Materials, processes, and techniques function as elements in both the categories of clothing and adornment. New and compelling characteristics of both clothing and adornment are often the result of advancements in materials or innovations that have come about through processes and techniques.

In addition to serving different functions, clothing and adornments differ in other ways. Materials used for clothing are most likely to be softer and more pliable than those used for adornments. Since comfort and protection are often desirable qualities in clothing, characteristics of body forms, motions, and surfaces tend to be taken into greater consideration in clothing design than they are in that of adornment.

Interrelationships between the body and dress. Appearance is the result of various configurations of the body operating either independently or in conjunction with dress. As persons are born, raised, and socialized into a culture, they are introduced to prevailing standards of appearance, some of which pertain to the body, others to dress. They learn to assemble configurations of appearance from a wide assortment of elements pertaining to the body and dress. Some of those elements remain fixed for long periods whereas others are temporary.

A person's appearance undergoes considerable change throughout the life cycle; however, some influences account for more rapid changes than others. Physical characteristics, notions about beauty, and the influence of social and cultural norms about dress are more likely to evolve slowly whereas attitudes about material culture and lifestyle usually change more rapidly.

As cultures evolved in various parts of the world, appearance became increasingly important as a medium of self-expression and communication. Overall, body factors have tended to provide useful information about gender, age, race, ethnicity, physical conditions, and origins of human beings whereas dress has conveyed clues pertaining to individual and collective forms of expression, resourcefulness, technical expertise, attitudes about social class, and belief systems along with a wide range of other social and cultural factors.

In contemporary cultures of both the East and West, appearance has evolved into a rapidly changing complex interrelationship between components of the body and dress. In addition to being the result of ongoing cultural evolution that interrelationship has been nurtured by various economic-driven industries, such as print and electronic media, cosmetology, film, fashion, and more and more, cosmetic surgery. Participants of contemporary culture are exposed to a multitude of new images for changing appearance along with corresponding products for bringing them about. Once those images are adopted, persons are encouraged to both abandon and replace them with even more recent images, thereby maintaining an ongoing cycle of appearance change.

See also **Clothing, Costume, and Dress; Fashion and Identity.**

BIBLIOGRAPHY

Hillestad, Robert. "The Underlying Structure of Appearance." *Dress, The Journal of the Costume Society of America* 6 (1980): 117–125.

Robert Hillestad

APPLIQUÉ Appliqué is a decorative surface design technique that adds dimension and texture to the background fabric. The term derives from the French word *appliquer* (and the Latin *applicare*) that means to join or attach. While its early use was most likely to strengthen worn areas or serve as a patch over holes, appliqué developed into a creative art form used by many cultures over many centuries. Traditional appliqué is defined as laying pieces of fabric on top of the background fabric to form a pattern or picture. Intricate appliqués may have numerous colors and use many layers of fabrics. After each individual piece of fabric is cut out, the raw edges are turned under and hand-sewn to the background fabric using an invisible stitch. The invention of new materials (water dissolvable stabilizer, glue sticks, and fusible web), the development of new techniques, and acceptance of new standards (machine sewing vs. hand sewing) have made appliqué faster and easier to do and are responsible for its continued popularity.

A variation of traditional appliqué is *broderie perse* (Persian embroidery), or chintz appliqué. This technique involves cutting small motifs from printed fabrics and arranging them together into a design or pattern. The opposite of traditional appliqué is reverse appliqué. All of the fabrics that are going to be in the design are layered. Cutting down to expose the layers forms the pattern. The raw edges are turned under and sewn to the next fabric. The Kuna Indians who live on the San Blas Islands off the coast of Panama make their molas using this technique. The patterns range from modern graphics to traditional themes from their legends and culture. A variation on reverse appliqué is known as inlay appliqué. The desired shape is cut out from the background fabric. A second fabric is placed behind the opening and the turned under edges of the background opening are sewn to the new fabric. Any excess fabric is trimmed away. Appliqués can also be three-dimensional, extending above the surface of the background fabric.

Starting with the ancient Egyptians, examples of appliqué can be found on garments and household items in every part of the world. During the Middle Ages elaborate appliqué was used on heraldic and ecclesiastical banners and ceremonial clothing. Appliqué is a part of the decoration on national (festival) costumes (eighteenth and nineteenth centuries) and ethnic folk dress. Several appliquéd garments are associated with the twentieth century. The Irish dance competition dress, which was relatively unadorned in the 1950s, evolved into an elaborately appliquéd and embroidered garment by the end of the century. The poodle skirt, circa 1955, was a felt circle skirt with a poodle (or other design) appliqué. The hippies, or flower children, of the mid 1960s, decorated and customized their apparel with appliqués. Wearable artists use appliqués to create one-of-a-kind garments. Many fashion designers have used appliqué in their lines: Elsa Schiaparelli, Franco Moschino, Gianni Versace, Bob Mackie, and Christian Francis Roth are examples. Koos van den Akker's entire line is devoted to quilted, appliquéd collages.

See also **Embroidery; Moschino, Franco; Schiaparelli, Elsa; Versace, Gianni and Donatella.**

BIBLIOGRAPHY

Avery, Virginia. *The Big Book of Applique.* New York: Charles Scribner's Sons, 1978.

Teufel, Linda Chang. *Koos Couture Collage: Inspiration and Techniques.* Worthington, Ohio: Dragon Threads, 2002.

Nan H. Mutnick

APRONS "Apron" means an over-garment covering the front of the body (from the French *naperon*, a small tablecloth). For centuries, people worldwide have worn them as protective garments, as ceremonial indicators of marital and parental status, rank and group affiliation, and as decorations.

Cretan fertility goddesses and Assyrian priests wore sacred aprons. Egyptian rulers broadcast their status by wearing jewel-encrusted aprons. In Europe during the Middle Ages, women placed extra swaths of cloth in their laps to protect their skirts during rowdy communal meals, and tradesmen and artisans began wearing aprons to protect their clothing and their flesh. In fact, tradesmen in general were called "apron men," as aprons were so common that several trades boasted distinguishing styles. Gardeners, spinners, weavers, and garbagemen wore blue aprons; butlers wore green; butchers wore blue stripes; cobblers wore "black flag" aprons for protection from the black wax they used; and English barbers were known as "checkered apron men." Stonemasons wore white aprons as protection against the dust of their trade, and even in the twenty-first century, aprons survive as part of Masonic ceremonial attire. In contemporary South Africa, young women wear beaded aprons to celebrate their coming of age.

By 1500, decorative aprons had become fashion accessories for European women with lifestyles permitting such luxury and display. Their popularity waxed and waned over the centuries. By the time colonists settled in North America, aprons were firmly established in European women's wardrobes.

United States Aprons

Aprons were worn by some Native American women and men, for both practical and ceremonial reasons. Through the centuries, colonial immigrants and their descendants have worn functional aprons for work, while decorative aprons have fallen in and out of fashion.

Looking back just one century, from 1900 through the 1920s, well-heeled women wore ornate, heavily embroidered aprons. In the 1930s and 1940s, women working outside the home wore whatever protective garments their jobs required, including coveralls, smocks, or aprons. At home, they worked in full-length aprons with hefty pockets.

In the United States in the early 2000s, many people consider aprons 1950s kitsch, but aprons deserve more serious and thorough consideration than that. Many aprons are fine examples of textile craft; and most importantly, aprons are icons—symbols within popular culture. They conjure twin images: the mythology of motherhood and family in the cozy, homemade good old days; and the reality of the endless hard work those times required. Through a blend of individual and collective memory and fantasy, aprons have come to represent an idealized, apple-pie, June Cleaver–esque mom. Cartoonists adorn a stick figure with an apron to communicate that she's a mom and probably a housewife. Though this character is a manufactured stereotype, she has held great sway as a role model—often wearing an apron.

The heyday of this archetypal housewife—and U.S. women's aprons—was the post war era of the 1940s and

Aprons on display. Although the popularity of the apron has waned since the 1960s, they are still produced and worn, and can be both fun and functional, as illustrated by these whimsical gardening aprons. © ROBERT ERIC/CORBIS SYGMA. REPRODUCED BY PERMISSION.

1950s. Rosie the Riveter lost her well-paying job, and the media and government—thus the job market—encouraged her to be a housewife and mom. Sewing machines and cloth became available, and aprons—both commercial and homemade—became ubiquitous as the uniform of the professional housewife. Many 1950s aprons addressed housework and were decorated with sewing, cleaning, cooking, and "mom" themes.

This apron-wearing housewife served as family hostess and wore decorative serving aprons for holidays. She wore a more utilitarian model while in the kitchen getting things ready, but right before she entered the dining room, she donned her holiday froth. Commercial aprons were certainly available, but many holiday aprons were homemade. Not only were they made by the housewife herself, but they were also the stuff of church and neighborhood bazaars, often made of netting and festooned with ribbons, sequins, and felt. The at-the-ready hostess had at least one all-season party apron. In fact, if possible, she had several to match her outfits. They were flashy and flirtatious and often sheer. Aprons were common hostess gifts, as well.

The postwar archetypal housewife was practical and creative. She made aprons out of remnants, extra kitchen curtains, dish towels, handkerchiefs, and flour sacks. When she made her aprons, she considered design as well as function. Many handmade aprons from the 1950s have one-of-a kind designs and details.

The apron-wearing mom collected souvenir aprons—from maps of every state to "Indian aprons" that bore slight if any resemblance to authentic ethnic garb. At home, when she had "had enough," she donned her letting-off-steam apron that said, "The hell with housework," or the one that pictured a frazzled washerwoman and the caption, "Life can be beautiful." And in the 1950s, when "the man of the house" was back from the war, he was supposed to spend weekends at home, so "men's" aprons printed with barbecue and bartender themes became available.

By the early 1960s, the era of glorified housework was passing and with it the heyday of aprons. But aprons *are* still worn. At-home kitchen aprons have evolved into the unisex butcher/barbecue style. And aprons are filling a new at-work role as "the instant uniform." An apron tied over any assortment of clothes produces a consistent look for a fast food chain or discount store. Generic aprons are shipped in from Central Supply and stamped with corporate logos, and gone is the variety, the visual delight, and the individual expression that aprons once provided.

Aprons can reveal a lot about women's lives. Examining a store-bought apron found at an estate sale or antique shop may yield information about the time from which the garment came and the woman who bought and wore it; and besides meriting study as a handcrafted one-of-a-kind item, a homemade apron may also contain clues about the life and times of the woman who made and wore it.

See also **Protective Clothing.**

BIBLIOGRAPHY

Barber, Elizabeth Wayland. *Women's Work. The First 20,000 Years, Women, Cloth, and Society in Early Times.* New York: W. W. Norton and Company, 1994.

Cheney, Joyce. *Aprons: Icons of the American Home.* Philadelphia: Running Press, 2000.

———. *Aprons: A Celebration.* Philadelphia: Running Press, 2001.

Florence, Judy. *Aprons of the Mid-Twentieth Century, To Serve and Protect.* Atglen, Pa.: Schiffer Books, 2002.

McKissack, Patricia. *Ma Dear's Aprons.* New York: Alfred A. Knopf, 1997.

Joyce Cheney

HOW OLD IS THAT APRON?

If a woman gives you the aprons she's been saving all these years, talk with her about each one. When did she sew or acquire it? For what sorts of occasions did she wear it? For anonymous aprons, however, apron dating is both art and science.

Look through old magazines, catalogs, or patterns to find aprons like yours. Look at the apron's shape. What dress style is the apron designed to cover? Once you've determined dress shape, look for pictures of vintage clothing to identify your apron's decade. Check the fabric. How old is it? Study any decorations. What techniques and materials are used for embellishment and when were they in vogue? Note the colors. Colors pass in and out of fashion. If the fabric has a printed picture, check hairdos, clothes, appliances, furniture, or any other clues. If it's a commercially made apron, check the label for clues.

ARMANI, GIORGIO Giorgio Armani, one of the most authoritative names in Italian ready-to-wear design, was born in Piacenza, Italy, in 1934. He became interested in fashion in 1957, when he left the school of medicine at the University of Piacenza to become a buyer for the La Rinascete chain in Milan. In 1964 Armani met Nino Cerruti, owner of Hitman, the Italian men's clothing producer. After a brief period to see how Armani worked with materials, Cerruti asked him to restructure completely the company's approach to clothing. Armani worked with Cerruti for six years, developing a simplified form of menswear that could be reproduced in series.

In the late 1960s Armani met Sergio Galeotti, which was the beginning of a relationship that lasted for years. In 1973 Galeotti persuaded him to open a design office in Milan, at 37 corso Venezia. This led to a period of extensive collaboration, during which Armani worked as a freelance designer for a number of fashion houses, including Allegri, Bagutta, Hilton, Sicons, Gibò, Montedoro, and Tendresse. The international press was quick to acknowledge Armani's importance following the runway shows at the Sala Bianca in the Pitti Palace in Florence. The experience provided Armani with an opportunity to develop his own style in new ways. He was now ready to devote his energy to his own label, and in 1975 he founded Giorgio Armani Spa in Milan with his friend Galeotti. In October of that same year he presented his first collection of men's ready-to-wear for

Giorgio Armani with pieces from his collection. After freelancing for a number of fashion houses, Armani founded his own label in 1976, quickly capitalizing on a reputation for producing high-quality, distinctive clothing at affordable prices. AP/WIDE WORLD PHOTOS. REPRODUCED BY PERMISSION.

spring and summer 1976 under his own name. He also produced a women's line for the same season.

International Recognition

The secret of Armani's great success seems to derive from his having introduced, at the right moment, a new approach to clothing design that reflected the changes in post-1968 society, which was composed essentially of a middle class that could no longer afford to wear couture clothing but at the same time wanted to construct a distinctive image for itself. With this in mind, Armani established an innovative relationship with industry, characterized by the 1978 agreement with Gruppo finanzario Tessile (GFT), which made it possible to produce luxury ready-to-wear in a manufacturing environment under the attentive supervision of the company's designer. In 1979, after founding the Giorgio Armani Corporation, Armani began producing for the United States and in-

troduced the Mani line for men and women. The label became one of the leading names in international fashion with the introduction of several new product lines, including G. A. Le Collezioni, and Giorgio Armani Underwear and Swimwear, and Giorgio Armani Accessories.

In the early 1980s the company signed an important agreement with L'Oréal to create perfumes and introduced the Armani Junior, Armani Jeans, and Emporio Armani lines, followed in 1982 by the introduction of Emporio Underwear, Swimwear, and Accessories. A new store was opened in Milan for the Emporio line, followed by the first Giorgio Armani boutique. Armani's concern for the end user culminated in the development of a more youthful product with the same level of stylistic quality as his high-end line, but at a more accessible price.

Because of the democratic nature of the Emporio line, Armani felt that he had to make use of new and unconventional advertising methods. These included television spots and enormous street ads, together with a house magazine that was sent out by mail to consumers, faithful Armani eaglet wearers. Armani also felt that a relationship with the cinema was essential, both for promotional reasons and for the stimulus to creativity. He designed the costumes for *American Gigolo*, directed by Paul Schrader (1980), the success of which led to a long-term collaboration with the world of film. Armani designed costumes for more than one hundred films, one of the most important of which was *The Untouchables*, directed by Brian De Palma and released in 1987.

In 1983 the designer modified his agreement with GFT. They began to produce both the Mani line for the United States and his high-end ready-to-wear line, rechristened Borgonuovo 21, after the address of the company's headquarters. During the late 1980s, despite Galeotti's death (1985), Armani continued to expand commercial horizons and licensing agreements. He opened Armani Japan and introduced a line of eyeglasses (1988), socks (1987), a gift collection (1989), and a new "basic" men's and women's line for America known as A/X Armani Exchange (1991). After the frenetic expansion of the 1990s (sportswear, eyeglasses, cosmetics, home, and new accessories collections), the year 2000, the twenty-fifth anniversary of the brand, saw a flurry of investment activity, including stock sales and the acquisition of new manufacturing capacity intended to increase Armani's control over the quality and distribution of his products.

Style and Innovation

There is a common thread running through Armani's stylistic development that is closely associated with the change in contemporary society. It led to the creation of clothing and accessories that aimed at a clean, simple style, beyond fashion, designed to enhance the personality of the person who wore it. When, in 1976, the designer presented the first unstructured jackets for men, unlined and unironed, the product of years of experience in production design, they were intended to lower labor costs and simplify tailoring. But in introducing them Armani opened a third way in men's clothing, an alternative to the traditional approach of English tailoring and the expectations associated with Italian made-to-measure clothing, realizing an innovative synthesis between formal wear and loose, flexible sportswear. With the invention of the blazer worn as a pullover, Armani offered men a new identity that rejected rigid professional divisions and allowed them to present themselves as young, attractive, and vaguely feminine. Referred to as the "first postmodern designer," by several Italian newspapers, for his radically unstructured garments, Armani had simply softened men's wear and made women's wear more concise and modern, transforming changing social roles into an "Armani look," making the casual look authoritative.

Official recognition of his fame came in 1982 when he appeared on the cover of *Time* magazine, only the second fashion designer, after Christian Dior, to do so. Armani had freed women from their stiff suits, providing them with soft jackets without collars and with comfortable pants. Although initially somewhat severe, as if intended to assist women in their climb to professional credibility, these outfits greatly enhanced a type of femininity that, because it was not ostentatious, was ultimately more real. Armani sought to establish an image of a woman who was strong but not harsh (a mix of the film stars Greta Garbo and Marlene Dietrich in modern dress) and who could be practical and indispensable as well as glamorous. Over time the jacket has continued to remain the centerpiece of the Armani wardrobe, changing year by year through the use of new materials, new proportions, and new colors. For Armani the "greige" (somewhere between gray and beige) of 1997 remained the most typical element in a palette often centered on shades of white and black, soft earth tones, dusty blues, and occasional unexpected bursts of color.

The search for fabrics has always been one of the distinctive elements of Armani's collections for men and women, becoming a key design element in 1986, together with embroidery and the return to evening wear that he brought about. Here the look was precious and exclusive but always in a minimalist key, demystified through the use of low-heeled shoes or sneakers. An attentive analyst of past cultures and Eastern influences, Armani's clothing has never been a collage of banal ideas. Throughout his career he has always succeeded in providing new images of how men and women dress and in translating elegant, decorative patterns into a unique but accessible style.

See also **Film and Fashion; Italian Fashion; Jacket; Ready-to-Wear; Sports Jacket.**

BIBLIOGRAPHY

Bianchino, Gloria, and Arturo Carlo Quintavalle. *Moda: Dalla fiaba al design italia 1951–1989*. Novara, Italy: De Agostini, 1989.

Bucci, Ampelio. *Moda a Milano: Stile e impresa nella città che cambia*. Milan: Abitare Segesta, 2002.

Celant, Germano, and Harold Koda, eds. *Giorgio Armani*. New York: Guggenheim Museum Publications, 2000.

Sollazzo, Lucia. "Armani, Giorgio." In *Dizionario della moda*. Edited by Guido Vergani. Milan: Baldini and Castoldi, 1999.

White, Nicola. *Giorgio Armani*. London: Carlton, 2000.

Aurora Fiorentini

ARMOR Accommodating and enclosing the human form, body armor has a direct connection with costume. Over the centuries, and in cultures worldwide, armor has been made from virtually all natural and many man-made media. During the Middle Ages and the Renaissance, armor was an effective defense and became one of the most elaborate and complex bodily adornments. It both identified and concealed its wearer and made a definitive statement about personal fashion.

The Earliest Armor

Humans' earliest supplemental protection was probably skins and hides. However, the earliest purpose-built defense, found in Europe and western Asia, was a type of belly plate made originally of organic material and later in bronze or metal-reinforced fabric. The Sumerians employed metal helmets and a metal-reinforced cloak. In about 2000 B.C.E. textile coverings appeared with applied, overlapping metal scales, which continued in occasional use until the eighteenth century.

A rather similar defense was lamellar armor. This probably first appeared in eighth century B.C.E. Assyria, composed of interconnected plaques or hoops, all worn over an undergarment. The Roman legionary's metal lorica *segmentata* is an example, as is the lacquered leather armor of Japanese samurai. The remarkable terra-cotta tomb figures of emperor Qin Shih Huang (221–210 B.C.E.) demonstrate China's use of lamellar armor for various troops identified by rank via color-coding and tassels. Mycenaean warriors during the Trojan War, and Greek hoplite infantry who fought the Persians wore body armor of layered linen. The Greeks and the inhabitants of the Italian peninsula also made use of bronze cuirasses (torso armor) embossed with musculature. All types were worn over an undergarment resembling period male ensembles.

Mail also appeared in classical times. Probably a Celtic innovation of the fifth or sixth century B.C.E., this network of riveted metal rings spread throughout Europe and into the East, and was widely used by the Romans and their allies. Mail's use steadily increased in Europe, particularly after the collapse of the Roman military system in the fifth century C.E., and among those who experienced its use by invading Hunnish cavalry.

The Middle Ages

Leather and textile armor were used throughout the Middle Ages, and not surprisingly, their form and style conformed to prevailing civilian fashion. The most common metal armor in Europe until the thirteenth century was mail, the name derived from the French *maille*, or "mesh." Mail shirts, worn over a heavily padded undergarment, or *aketon*, eventually covered the thighs, and developed long sleeves with mittens. Mail hoods (*coifs*), leggings, a conical helmet or a barrel-shaped helm that covered all but the eyes, completed the defense. As extra protection against powerful weapons, a long, wooden shield was carried. Such warriors were expensive to maintain, and of great wealth—deriving this from lands given to them in return for military service. These armored men thus became the horse-mounted knights of popular imagination, and in many European languages, the words "knight" and "horseman" are identical. Each warrior was identified by a system of symbolism called heraldry. A

Those who wore armor recognized its importance and appreciated the expertise required in its manufacture. During a test-fitting of a new armor "his Majesty [Charles V] said that they [his armor parts] were more precious to him than a city . . . and they were so excellent that . . . if he [the armorer] had taken the measurement a thousand times they could not fit better" (Hayward, p.11).

knight's "coat of arms" appeared on his shield and, from the twelfth century, on a gownlike surcoat over his mail. The surcoat's length followed civilian fashion; some could actually trip up a warrior in combat.

However, better defenses were needed. By the early thirteenth century pieces of plate armor reappeared on a scale not seen since Classical Rome and became increasingly common on the torso and legs by mid to late century. Plate appeared in various forms—horn, bone, molded leather—but most often in iron. It offered rigidity and better resistance to weapons. It was shaped to the individual, thick where needed or thin to reduce weight, and its smooth, curving surfaces deflected weapons. It increasingly covered the body, although there seems to have been reluctance by some knights to be encased in rigid metal. Thus, there was a "transition" throughout the fourteenth century to mix mail and plate armor for the knight and his horse. This interim defense remained the primary form of protection in the armies of Islamic cultures and the Indian subcontinent until well into the nineteenth century.

Armor makers were divided into plate, mail, and textile (cloth armorers) specialists and tightly regulated. The transitional knight was a graceless, stout figure in layered textiles and iron, much of it cloth-covered. The plate edges had ribs to protect the armpits, elbows, and other

During the seventeenth century, a militia officer was struck by an arrow in the chest. His only defense was a hard piece of cheese inside his shirt. Almost unbelievably, the arrow hit the cheese. Informed of his subordinate's luck, his captain replied that this "may verify the old saying, *A little Armour would serve if a Man knew where to place it*" (Mason, p. 22).

vulnerable spots, with mail worn on the undergarment at these points.

By the beginning of the fifteenth century, the transition was complete. An individual wanting the latest in armor could have full plate—often without the textile covering, and with surfaces polished gleaming bright—virtually head to toe. The status of knights saw their clothing needs increasingly influencing male fashion, and vice versa. The change to all plate gradually produced a wasp-waisted appearance. This slim, hard-body look increasingly mirrored elegant male attire at the end of the century, and each complemented the other. For example, tubular arm defenses required slim sleeves on the undergarment, while shoulders broadened to accommodate extra padding for the load of a cuirass. Some armor elements were fastened to the aketon with laces called points. These also appeared on male apparel, to attach sleeves and hose. The aketon assimilated the new forms and was worn alone as knightly clothing. The surcoat became the short, form-fitting *jupon* (overgarment).

The Renaissance and Armor's Decline

The fifteenth through seventeenth centuries saw both armor's acme and nadir. Plate armor remained paramount, changing with the demands of war, sport, and ceremony, and the continuing influence of civilian fashion. Centers in Italy (the term "milliner" originally meant a Milanese armor vendor) and Germany grew wealthy from the production and sale of armor. Master armorers throughout Europe crafted spectacular suits through the tailorlike handwork of specialists, including locksmiths (for hinges and fasteners), artists (Holbein and Dürer provided themes for armor decoration), and cloth armorers (the cloth tabs of internal linings were called *pickadils*, inspiring the name of the London district where makers were centered). The slim, angular, and rippled form of fifteenth-century German "Gothic" armor is regarded as the peak moment, in which pure form blended perfectly with function. However, in the early part of the sixteenth century, this gave way in some areas to the rounded, "Maximilian" style whose fluted cuirass imitated a globose doublet cinched by a waistbelt. The average weight was about forty to sixty well-distributed, balanced pounds in which a trained individual could do the same as in everyday clothing, especially mounting a horse unaided. Aketons became arming doublets and hose, an affair of durable material, padded with grasses, wool waste, or cotton especially at the load-bearing shoulders and hips, with points and garters to secure components. Some clothing, such as the kiltlike "base" skirt, gave texture and color to plain metal. Fashions again changed with the times, as once-pointed foot defenses (that imitated the *poulaine* shoe) became broadly rounded, then narrower and more contemporary. Breastplates followed doublet changes, also placing acid-etched decorative bands to imitate embroidery, and by the end of the century developing the grotesquely dipped "peascod" shape. Mail continued as a

secondary defense, or primary for the less wealthy. Textiles and plate combined in the vestlike brigandine used by all classes, differing only in the quality of materials and finish. The jack was similar, but generally of cruder stuff, and both defenses mimicked the doublet lines. A wide range of helmets was worn, from visored types that enclosed the head, to hatlike open forms. Foot soldiers favored the latter, and wore pieces of munitions-grade armor, sometimes little more than helmet and breastplate, or as much as a half armor to the hips.

Armor was also made for jousts and tournaments. Formerly training for war, these equestrian events became pure sport during the fifteenth century and required highly protective equipment that could reach 100 pounds. These suits have fueled the erroneous stereotype of the heavy, awkward knight, unable to mount without aid, and helpless if unhorsed.

From about the 1530s into the second half of the century, "Roman" and "antique" style armor became popular for festivals and spectacles. Other types of ceremonial armors flourished, even for children, as armorers experimented in fantastic creations, using a range of precious or fragile media to embellish the products of wealthy clients. Some were so extravagant as to be moving examples of decorative art or metal costume and were built by goldsmiths rather than armorers. Most armor was embellished to some degree. The entire decorative arts vocabulary was employed, including plating, enameling, encrusting with gems, but most often acid-etching.

The armorer's craft culminated in the garniture, a set of various components together with a basic armor and creating a versatile ensemble for war, sport, and ceremony. While each element had a designated function, it had to harmonize structurally and artistically with dozens of others. Such sets were extremely expensive and available only to very wealthy individuals.

Armor was also used by bodyguards, representing the patron's importance, good taste, and artistic refinement. Guard armor was sometimes limited to helmets, but embellished body armor was worn by those like the Vatican's papal guard.

Throughout much of the sixteenth century developments in firearms and changing battlefield tactics had an impact on armor's use. Powerful handguns required bulletproof armor that could weigh some eighty pounds, but retained its fashion relevance of its form. The lines of certain armor elements, such as the form of breastplates, tended to follow those of male civilian fashion. Complete head-to-toe armor became rare, with protection concentrated on the head and torso. By the seventeenth century, half or three-quarter armor (to the knees) became typical for horsemen, who now carried firearms themselves. Some troops wore "buff" leather coats, or padded textiles, and by the end of the century it was rare to see armor in war.

The Enlightenment to the Present

Although most troops ceased wearing armor by the eighteenth century, military engineers (sappers) wore bulletproof helmets during sieges, and some horsemen wore breastplates and helmets against sword cuts and firearms. The knight's neck defense, or gorget, became a symbol of officer's rank, and many armors became theatrical props. The Napoleonic wars briefly revived the use of some cavalry armor, but by the middle of the nineteenth century, its military use was again largely ceremonial. There were some exceptions, such as the breastplates privately acquired by both sides in the American Civil War (1861–1865), and Australian outlaw Ned Kelly's crude 100-pound body armor worn during a shootout. World Wars I and II revived interest in protective armor on a large scale. Allied and Axis physicians and scientists worked with curators to develop helmets and body defenses for ground troops and "flak jackets" for aircrew, but they used media and technologies little different from those of centuries earlier. Armor developments late in World War II and the Korean Conflict benefited from new plastic polymers. Soldiers' needs in Vietnam led to better armor, but it remained rather heavy and hot. The invention of Kevlar in the 1980s provided a material five times stronger than steel. Produced in fabriclike sheets, then laminated and encased in textiles, this has produced a new range of highly protective and light armor and helmets for the military, sport, law enforcement, and individuals. However, even more remarkable systems are under development in commercial and governmental laboratories, striving to produce another breakthrough technology, one just as dramatic as the suit of knightly plate armor that continues to fascinate us.

See also **Military Style; Protective Clothing; Techno-Textiles; Uniforms, Military.**

BIBLIOGRAPHY

Blair, Claude. *European Armour.* New York: Crane, Russak, and Company, 1972; also published in 1958 by B. T. Batsford, Ltd., London. Remains the standard work.

Blair, Claude, and Leonid Tarassuk, eds. *The Complete Encyclopedia of Arms and Weapons.* New York: Simon and Schuster, 1982. Best one-volume source of information on a range of arms and armor terms.

Dean, Bashford. *Helmets and Body Armor in Modern Warfare.* Reprint of the 1920 edition, including the World War II Supplement. Tuckahoe, N.Y.: Carl J. Pugliese, 1977. Fascinating study of the development and use of personal armor in both World Wars.

Edge, David, and John Paddock. *Arms and Armour of the Medieval Knight.* Greenwich Conn.: Crescent Books, 1988. Well-illustrated and accessible to a general audience.

Ffoulkes, Charles. *The Armourer and His Craft.* Several printings available, the most recent by Dover Publications. Somewhat dated, but remains an important work on the topic.

Hayward, J. F. "Filippo Orsoni, Designer, and Caremolo Modrone, Armourer, of Mantua." *Waffen und Kostümkunde,* 3rd ser., 24, no.1 (1982): 11.

Mason, John. *A Brief History of the Pequot War.* Boston, 1736.

Pfaffenbichler, Matthias. *The Armourers.* Toronto: University of Toronto Press, 1992. Well-illustrated and excellent resource.

Pyhrr, Stuart W., and José-A. Godoy. *Heroic Armor of the Italian Renaissance.* New York: Metropolitan Museum of Art, 1998. Beautifully illustrated, premier study of Italian Renaissance parade armor.

Robinson, H. Russell. *The Armour of Imperial Rome.* New York: Charles Scribner's Sons, 1975. Excellent, and accessible to the general reader.

Snodgrass, A. M. *Arms and Armour of the Greeks.* Ithaca N.Y.: Cornell University Press, 1967. Scholarly and thorough.

Walter Karcheski Jr.

ART AND FASHION When one considers "fashion," as distinct from "clothing," "costume," or "dress," it is as a socially shared concept of what is to be worn at a particular point in time rather than an esoteric, ritualistic, or utilitarian cover or decoration of the body. The concept of fashion's point of origin in the mid-nineteenth century is contemporary with a fundamental change in the market for works of art. This was not accidental, since the institution of fashion, as clothing that adheres to particular modes of production, representation, and consumption, was connected to the emergence of similar structures in the creation and dissemination of works of art. Fashion came into being with the advent of the couture industry in Paris in the second half of the nineteenth century, when a bourgeois audience began to demand constant change as an intellectual, aesthetic, and, above all, economic stimulus for modern times. This is not to say that the notion of fashion did not exist previously. The timing qualifies the term as denoting clothing that is produced according to a certain seasonal rhythm, in quantities large enough to have an effect on sartorial appearances within a society, that can be exported as a "style," and that is consumed according to a prescribed agenda. Correspondingly, art as an autonomous production of subjective expression not bound directly to ecclesiastical or monarchist decrees emerged through the foundation of a bourgeois culture after the European revolutions between 1830 and 1848, when artistic education, independent structures of display, and expanded commercial possibilities allowed for a new creation and distribution of art. Thus, there exists a shared point of origin due to socioeconomic foundations in western Europe. Although fashion was produced elsewhere, too, it was this "Western" concept that eventually determined its global idiom and reception.

History I

The year 1868 saw "La Chambre syndicale de la confection de la couture pour dames et fillettes" establish the guidelines for the production and promotion of high fashion and the popularization of complex new fabrics through weavers such as Joseph Marie Jacquard and through the development of the sewing machine by men such as Thimonnier Barthélemy. It was also the time when the art market expanded significantly due to technical advances in the reproduction of artworks, the establishment of museums such as le Louvre (which became property of the French state in 1848), and the opening of commercial galleries by the Durand-Ruels and Bernheim-Jeune (late 1850s, early 1860s) in the French capital. Therefore, art and fashion together began to leave the confines of private spaces and made the consumption of commodities public. Paintings were no longer exclusive to collections in haute bourgeois drawing rooms, and clothing was no longer individually commissioned from the comfort of one's own home. To view art and to buy gowns one had to venture out into the public, into a commercial setting. Contrary to the social and political impetus of the bourgeois toward increased privacy, the consumption of fashion in particular ran as part of a wide social current—being *à la mode* became a highly publicized statement in art as well as in clothing.

History II

Art and fashion differ significantly in their respective attitudes to history. Art looks at its own historical tradition and, importantly, at the communication of history (historiography), as points of friction and contrast. History for artists consists of mythical or ideological narratives that can be illustrated, debated, and re-assessed in the context of artistic tradition. Styles or motifs are quoted, as in the historicism of academic painting, for example, but this process is consciously reflected upon. The costumes in European history paintings of the nineteenth century are often remodeled and redrawn to fit contemporary ideals of the past. Thus, for example, a subject wearing Roman toga is depicted with a contemporary hairstyle and contemporary makeup, and the face and body of the painterly subject follows modern perceptions rather than adhering to any archaeological evidence. The beholder of such artworks understands that historical authenticity is impossible but expects the painter or sculptor to communicate both the spirit of the past and its present interpretation. For fashion, too, authenticity is regarded as impossible; moreover, it is undesirable for the material impact of the design. Fashion's imperative, that is, its absolute contemporariness, has to be observed always. A costume for the stage might endeavor to evoke historical accuracy, but a piece of clothing created within the fashion industry has to transcend historical copy and be an absolute part of the present. In contrast to art, fashion is not expected to conform to ideals of reflection or visual truthfulness and integrity. Fashion is afforded a liberal view of history as a stylistic, pictorial sourcebook. The design of a dress or accessory can be a willful quotation that uses only one particular aspect of the history (such as the cut of a sleeve or waistline, or the setting for a jewel) while operating overall in a deliberately ahistor-

ical manner. In fashion the evocation of a historical period has to be immediate yet not necessarily correct in its aspects; visual impact and easy reading of the design take preference over historical accuracy in material or shape. History is filtered in fashion through the present; it is constantly updated and thus rewritten.

Inspiration

These diverging attitudes to history within art and fashion are not simply due to material reasoning, although the dress in fashion, as opposed to costume design, has to exist in the contemporary market and can thus not be seen as only retrospective or pedantic in its historical detail. The purported seriousness of art in its relation to history and its Platonic equation of truth with beauty renders art the established basis from which fluctuating fashions can draw inspiration. Fashion uses art, analogous to history, as a visual model for its contemporary interpretation. The elevated position that is given to the fine arts in occidental culture is employed by fashion to raise the cultural capital of its creations. When fashion design displays an overt reference to a painterly style or motif, or quotes a particular artwork, the standing and value that the artist or work has accrued in the course of history is also transferred to the fashion design. This transferral occurs in a number of ways: (1) the artist becomes fashion (not costume) designer. One example is Giacomo Balla's menswear of 1914, which cites his own paintings; (2) the designer employs artists for the decoration of the garment, as when Salvador Dalí worked for Elsa Schiaparelli in 1937; (3) fashion renders a contemporary style in painting a decorative motif on the dress, as in Yves Saint Laurent's Pop Art collection of 1966; (4) the presentation of the collection becomes an art-historical *tableaux vivant*, such as Vivienne Westwood's catwalk of 1994, which cited the works of Franz-Xaver Winterhalter and other artists of the Second Empire; (5) the rendition of fashion in a magazine or other promotional media inserts the design into an art environment, as in Karl Lagerfeld's photos of 1997 that deliberately copy Bauhaus motifs. Conversely, fashion—in dress, accessories, makeup, and so forth—provides the source of inspiration for artists, especially in portraiture. The depiction of women in couture clothing on the canvases of Henri Matisse or Pablo Picasso, for example, show how the extravagant shapes or colors of the designer's creation guide the pictorial representation by the painter. Here, the new perception of the body that fashion can instigate through vibrant textiles, constricting or revealing fabrics, elongation of members through extravagant sleeves or extensions or forms through bustles and padded hips, for example, inspires the artist to take a new look at corporeal representation.

Production I

Art and sartorial fashion have always shared terms to describe their procedure. Both the pictorial work of art as well as the couture dress are traditionally sketched out, and both are then transferred from a paper template to canvas (the *toile*). And while the painting exists as the final outcome of the artist's vision, the toile in couture subsequently needs a further transposition into fabrics in order to appear finished. These procedural similarities do not exclusively define the character of modern painting or contemporary couture, but they go some way to explain why fashion designers have traditionally felt a strong kinship with painters and sculptors in regard to the making of their garments. In the nineteenth century haute couturiers saw themselves as artists in the development of their designs and their frames of reference (shown, for example, in the titles of dresses that allude to pieces of music, histories, allegories, motifs, or styles in painting), but also in subjective perception of the body, which in turn prompted the challenge to sexual mores. By the early 2000s this challenge had become less important than the recourse to and structural engagement with the traditional kinship of couturier and artist, evidenced when the Maison Martin Margiela proposed the paper template or toile to be worn as dress proper.

Avants-gardes

The parallels in the development of art and fashion in the avants-gardes of the nineteenth and twentieth centuries thus became visible through shared patterns and methods and styles of production, but also in adopting moral reflection, oppositional expressions, and attitudes toward commodification. At first the comparatively small group of couturiers and couturières of the second half of the 1800s, styled themselves along the established lines of artistic bohemians. From Charles Frederick Worth and Émile Pingat in the 1870s to John Redfern in the 1880s, they occupied studios and received clients in salons—thus echoing the environment for working and exhibiting in the fine arts (for example, the Parisian Salon as seasonal event). The furnishing of these rooms with collections of portrait paintings and assorted wall hangings indicate the cross-references and quotations that underscore the relationship between art and fashion.

While fashion used from the outset painterly tradition as a culturally established frame of reference and stylistic sourcebook, art looked to fashion for decorative solution in three dimensions and for structural inspiration in regard to repeatedly coined styles and the constant propagating of "originality" as a commodity. With the subjectivism and professed decadence of the fin de siècle, the profusion of decoration was shared between artworks and clothes; expressive hyperbole was de rigueur for both fields, as seen in fashion by Jacques Doucet or the Callot Sisters.

The turn of the century saw an emancipation of the body and simultaneously that of fashion's female clientele. More couturières established economic independence within the fashion industry (for instance, Jeanne Lanvin or Jeanne Paquin), and this was reflected in the

cultural climate on the whole. An emerging performativity in art (for example, opera and ballet became much more dynamic), and the sense of physical experimentation that pervaded performances by, for example, the Ballets Russes, combined with the abolition of the corset through the commercial adaptation of non-Western costume, freed the body for new movements outside socially prescribed spaces. This led to a rapid succession of art movements that proclaimed the breaking up of corporeality (cubism), its progression in space (futurism), or the construction of a communal body politic (constructivism, Bauhaus)—efforts that were structurally inspired by and became visually reflected in contemporary couture. Fashion presented the body as a fluid concept that could be determined through a sartorial shell, not as mere social agency but as an aesthetic concept. Madeleine Vionnet, for instance, demonstrated how dress shapes the proportion of the body, and Gabrielle Chanel showed how to liberate its posture.

With political mass movements in the years between the wars the uniformity of dress became significant. Politically committed artists used the unifying potential of clothes to demonstrate equality, and nonobjective painting provided, literally, a pattern book for the abstraction in cut and decoration, which dispensed with societal signifiers. Postwar artistic reflections of consumer society and the culture industry caused an ambivalent intimacy between art and fashion, as the former looked at the latter for the expression of codified consumption that was to be critically assessed, while the latter viewed painterly solutions, for example in Pop Art, as affirmation of its structural significance. The art market in the 1950s, 1960s, and 1970s coined in quick succession a series of artistic styles that resembled seasonal proclamation in couture.

With the creative expansion of ready-to-wear, the need for stylistic inspirations multiplied, and the past and recent history of art was increasingly required to serve as source material. Now, the concept of using the fashion industry not for its structural and procedural differences but employing its tropes directly for the production and representation of art has become widespread. Contemporary art cites fashion not just as an aesthetic model, but also as a field of reference in which the challenges and perils of modern life are glamorously played out. The engagement with fashion in contemporary art is also curatorial, that is, in displaying—often experimental—clothing in museums and galleries, pairing dress and art in exhibitions about material objects or notions of beauty, or using the fashion industry to fund art projects. The curatorial awareness of fashion leads in some cases to the institutional support of collections; for example, the first catwalks of the Dutch duo Viktor and Rolf were made possible only through the support and acquisition policies of the Centraal Museum in Utrecht and the Groninger Museum in Groningen. This implies the positioning of fashion in contemporary culture as one of many interchangeable manifestations, rather than as a structurally distinct medium within a cultural hierarchy. The use of fashion's material basis (textiles, fabrics) and, significantly, its mode of representation through particular photographs, catwalk performances, and so forth, is used in contemporary art to play along with the late modernist staging of the culture industry.

Production II

The production of couture adopted the idea of the independent, subjective artist and developed this stance despite the growing commercial pressure and industrialization of the industry's progress toward ready-to-wear. In the fashion industry there exists a pronounced dialectic that is expressed in the need for stylistic, some would say artistic, innovation that cannot be catered for by the manufacturing process that had given rise to couture as the basis for the fashion market established in the early twenty-first century. Designers perceive themselves as removed from the production process in auxiliary industries like weaving in a way that is similar to the painter who professes to be removed from the maker of the canvas or paper. Thus, from the birth of haute couture onward, fashion has had to accommodate the problem of relying on a design process that contradicts its procedural basis. This is the reason for the oscillating parameters of art and fashion and for the curious hovering of the latter around the former. The dialectic of fashion found in an individualized creation that exists within mass manufacture (which establishes its social coinage in the first place) was recognized willingly by the art market itself. The dialectic does not necessarily show itself in creation, although there has been, at least since Marcel Duchamp and Andy Warhol, a profusion of objects that covet a "designed" look and that are alienated from the artists through their handing over of the actual production to others (such as craftsmen, designers, studio assistants), but it is evidenced in representation, promotion, and consumption, in which fashion's principle is increasingly approximated by art in its advertising, gallery openings, growth of multiples, or museum shops, and in the fact that more and more foundations for contemporary art, as well as for music, architecture, and so forth, are now run by fashion companies, who thus embrace the cultural credibility that rests on the consumption of "high" art.

Within the realm of fashion it is at times difficult to separate neatly the production process from reception and consumption because the interrelation of the three segments constitutes its methodological core. Fashion is largely conceived through trend prediction and marketing analyses that attempt to anticipate as correctly as possible its manner and level of consumption. Correspondingly, fashion coverage, even outside identifiable promotional vehicles, reflects directly the interests of the designer or manufacturer. This, of course, appears as very different from artistic creation that might be influenced by demands from gallerists or commissions—increasingly

so in late modernism—but still asserts subjectivism to guarantee itself creative autonomy and institutional independence.

Consumption I

The parallel consumption of art (in exhibitions) and fashion (in catwalk shows or shops) comes at the tail end of the change in modernity that moved from acquiring material goods for their functional purpose, through conspicuous consumption, in which objects are bought for their societal significance, to consuming the products as a spectacle, as entertainment within a saturated market. At the beginning art was consumed for "educational" purposes, to instruct the senses in what was understood to be morally just. It celebrated the dominant spirituality of the culture and favorably documented the established political system. Throughout the Enlightenment (as well as comparable tendencies outside occidental culture) the consumption of art began to operate along lines of individualized perception, and the communication of ideal beauty was understood to be based on temporal and spatial aspects and no longer as an unchangeable cogent. With the rise of a middle class that was socially mobile and less culturally dependent on one structure alone, art turned to the reflection and subsequent critique of its consumers. It no longer presented an unobtainable ideal of sentimental or spiritual perfection but introduced the vernacular, the popular, and the visceral into its discourse. The personal worldview of a particular consumer base took over from the universal understanding that had been propagated for the whole of a culture before. Western modernism challenged such particularity by looking again at quasi-scientific inquiries that should establish general principles for the aesthetic and social meaning of art. Yet such "empirical" principles were subject to change with every art movement that was usurping the one before and wiping the sociocultural slate clean for new individualized rules to be inscribed onto it. In the early 2000s, with the tropes of later modernism determining our understanding of art, its consumption has shifted from edification to entertainment.

Consumption II

In contrast, the consumption of fashion originates in the pragmatic triumvirate of protection, modesty, and decoration. Clothes were first acquired for their utilitarian value, providing warmth, pious cover of the body, and adornment. The latter quickly became the ubiquitous signifier of consumption in which social status was shown through the splendor and profusion of fabrics and accessories. However, sartorial aspirations were still constricted by sumptuary laws and customs. No matter how much money the consumer might spend, certain colors or materials remained the proviso of nobility or clergy. In the eighteenth and nineteenth centuries consumption became increasingly conspicuous; that is, fashion was consumed as the most obvious sign of material wealth. More than carriages or town houses, sumptuous garments acted as an immediate signpost of the social position that its wearer desired. Because fashion is a more direct but less expensive manifestation of wealth, compared with architecture or art collections, conspicuous consumption of clothes could be used by the nouveaux riches to present a façade of financial and social success that did not necessarily exist. Unlike art, the consumption of fashion is not based primarily on knowledge or education but functions through visual awareness, a type of sensuality and perception of the corporeal self. Obviously, couture, like fine art, was acquired originally by the most affluent parts of society, but fashion was still comparatively affordable for the aspiring middle classes, even if its constant change meant seasonal outlay rather than a one-off investment in a painting or sculpture.

Art can be consumed through beholding the object in a (more or less) public space without having to purchase it. The subsequent mental consumption, that is, its appreciation, possible interpretation, analysis or debate, occurs within the subjective personal domain. (This is apart from the art "professional"—artist, gallerist, critic, curator, for instance—who has to publicly communicate the result of such consumption.) In a reverse fashion, clothing is consumed by slipping on the dress or jacket and moving from personal confines, such as a changing room or bedroom, into a public space that is the shop, workplace, or social gathering. Modern media allows individuals to increasingly consume art in the privacy of their own homes. Concerts recorded on CD, films on DVD, and virtual museums on the Internet remove the necessity to withdraw from public space into one's own imagination. However, the principle of moving from the public to the private in art, and conversely from the private to the public in fashion, still separates the two fields. To consume clothes conspicuously and to consume art self-effacingly show a divide between materialist objective and subjective contemplation. Here, fashion's ontology marks it out as a public commodity, despite its very proximity to the individual, while the work of art ambiguously remains a more distant ideal (socially as well as physically) that is integrated into a wider cultural discourse and cannot readily be appropriated for personal consumption.

Consumption III

Consumption in the culture industry habitually operated between the poles of ephemeral following of fashion and the establishment of permanent structures in art. The distinction between understanding an object as "consumable," accepting its limited life span as characteristic, and the understanding object as a document or illustration of such consumption, separates fashion from art. When an object has become accepted *as fashion* it immediately ceases to exist. As sociologist Georg Simmel postulated at the beginning of the last century, fashion dies at the very moment it comes into being, in the instance when the cut of a dress or the shape of a coat is accepted into the cultural mainstream. In order to guarantee its survival in commodity culture, fashion has to constantly reinvent itself and proclaim a new style that supplants the previous one. Modern art, in contrast, is seen to come into being only when its progressive shapes are canonized. Even in its most fugitive performance it always claims its right to lasting values—whereas clothes cannot mean to be permanent; otherwise parts of the textile and fashion industries would have to cease production. The dialectic (not binary pairing) of ephemerality and permanence shape the respective reception of modern art and modern fashion. Art has to remain mobile to reflect and interpret the ever-increasing speed of changes in modernity, yet it must appear permanent, lest it would be regarded as insubstantial. Fashion intends to be lasting—the greatest achievement of a designer is to create a "classic"— in order to be accepted as a substantial cultural fact, yet simultaneously needs to be ephemeral for immanent material as well as conceptual reasons.

See also **Caricature and Fashion; Music and Fashion.**

BIBLIOGRAPHY

Anna, Susanne, and Markus Heinzelmann, eds. *Untragbar.* Ostfildern-Ruit, Germany: HatjeCantz, 2001.

Art/Fashion. New York: Guggenheim Soho, 1997.

Brandstätter, Christian. *Klimt und die Mode.* Vienna: Brandstätter, 1998.

Celant, Germanom, et al., eds. *Looking at Fashion.* Florence, Italy: Cantz/Skira, 1996.

De Givry, Valérie. *Art et mode.* Paris: Editions du Regard, 1998.

Evans, Caroline. *Fashion at the Edge.* New Haven, Conn.: Yale University Press, 2003.

Fausch, Deborah, et al., eds. *Architecture: In Fashion.* Princeton, N.J.: Princeton University Press, 1994.

Felshin, Nina, ed. *Empty Dress.* New York: Independent Curators Incorporated, 1993.

———. "Clothing as Subject." *Art Journal* 1 (1995).

Guillaume, Valérie, ed. *Europe 1910–1939.* Paris: Les Musées de la Ville de Paris, 1996.

Hollander, Anne. *Seeing through Clothes.* New York: Penguin Group, 1980.

Martin, Richard. *Fashion and Surrealism.* New York: Rizzoli, 1989.

———. *Cubism and Fashion.* New York: Abrams/Metropolitan Museum, 1998.

Mode et art 1960–1990. Brussels: Palais des Beaux-Arts, 1995.

Müller, Florence. *L'Art et la mode.* Paris: Assouline, 1999.

Ribeiro, Eileen. *Ingres in Fashion.* New Haven, Conn.: Yale University Press: 1999.

———. *The Gallery of Fashion.* Princeton, N.J.: Princeton University Press, 2000.

Simon, Marie. *Fashion in Art: The Second Empire and Impressionism.* London: Zwemmer, 2003.

Smulders, Caroline. *Sous le manteau.* Paris: Galerie Thaddeus Ropac, 1997.

Smulders, Caroline, and Catherine Millet, eds. *Art et Mode. Art Press* 18 (1997).

Steele, Valerie. *Paris Fashion.* New York: Oxford University Press, 1988.

Steele, Valerie, and John S. Mayor. *China Chic.* New Haven, Conn.: Yale University Press, 1999.

Stern, Radu. *Against Fashion.* Cambridge, Mass., and London: MIT Press, 2003.

Troy, Nancy. *Couture Culture.* Cambridge, Mass., and London: MIT Press, 2003.

Wollen, Peter, ed. *Addressing the Century.* London: South Bank, 1998.

Ulrich Lehmann

ART NOUVEAU AND ART DECO Art nouveau design penetrated into all types of modern, luxury European decorative arts in the period from 1895 to 1905. Its undulating vegetal curves and graceful floral swirls were also a design gift to the Parisian couturiers and until about 1908 or 1909 art nouveau style was energetically appropriated for seasonal, high-fashion use.

Evening garments were the most lavishly attuned to art nouveau. Couturiers swathed their evening wear with a profusion of silk brocade, appliqué, embroidery, and lace. From neckline to hem, the designers played art nouveau swirls around the voluptuousness of the fashionable figure, which itself was curvaceously shaped by "S"-bend corsets. Even tailored woolen walking costumes were trimmed with swirlings of appliqué. By 1907–1909, the style's popularity had waned, replaced by a more upright figure styled with a geometric simplicity drawn from the Vienna Werkstatte, a fashion drawing from *Les Modes* of August 1909 by Gaby, *Toilettes pour Le Casino.*

Prints by Aubrey Beardsley. Beardsley's distinctive works had an extensive influence on art nouveau and art deco clothing styles during the 1960s. TIME LIFE PICTURES/GETTY IMAGES. REPRODUCED BY PERMISSION.

Historical Content

This appropriation of art nouveau styling coincided with the moment in the history of couture when a united business structure was firmly established by the Chambre Syndicale de la Couture Parisienne. Unrivaled elsewhere in the Western world, Paris couturiers dressed the women of international royal courts and high society including in Japan and tsarist Russia, the wives of the wealthiest international plutocrats, and the great actresses of the Paris stage. Commercial clients already included the grandest department stores at an international level.

The art nouveau "look" was at the cutting edge of modern style. Only the most fashionable wore it in its fullest manifestation, while others preferred moderated versions. These styles were spread internationally through fashion journals, such as *Les Modes* and down through middle-class oriented magazines such as *The Ladies Field* and *La Mode illustrée. Les Modes* of July 1902 featured, for example, an art nouveau ball dress by Maggy Rouff with full-length swirls in silver and diamante, on a straw-colored silk ground trimmed with alençon lace.

Designers

From 1895 all the top twenty or so Paris salons were developing art nouveau fashions, from the House of Worth (whose designer was by then Jean-Philippe Worth) through the salons of Doucet, Maggy Rouff, Jeanne Paquin, and Laferriere to cite just a few. They launched season after season of art nouveau–styled garments on to the international fashion market. Examples survive in the great fashion collections of museums in Paris and the United States.

High Art and Popular Versions

Within middle-class levels of ready-to-wear manufacture (for department stores and top levels of wholesale manufacturers), the style was watered down but clearly visible, as in a tailored woolen walking costume featured in *La Mode illustrée, journal de la famille* in January 1901 for example. The swirl did not, however, penetrate the cheapest levels of mass manufacture of tailored clothing for women. At the level of John Noble's *Half Guinea Costume,* as seen in the *Lady's Companion* of 19 September 1896, there was no trimming or decoration at all. Described as "dainty and durable," consumers were concerned with little other than a vaguely stylish silhouette and issues of durability.

Art Deco Fashion

Following the demise of art nouveau as fashion inspiration, the appropriation of art deco design by Paris couturiers informed the next fashion look. This had two phases. The first ran from about 1910 to 1924 and was built around neoclassical/oriental/peasant styling. The second ran from 1924 to about 1930—a more minimalist style, with modernist design touches

Paul Poiret led the first art deco fashion phase. His life was absorbed by orientalism, even as the Ballets Russes arrived in Paris, in 1909. He launched his slim, simple, high-waisted line in 1908, with its less-structured cut and delicately layered exotic style. Poiret was a collector of fauve paintings, which inspired his use of purples, pinks, blues, greens, and golds. Poiret's passion for orientalism, chinoiserie, European peasant, and North African design introduced a fresh bold simplicity to the cut and decoration. His 1911 *One Thousand and One Night Ball* set off a lasting vogue for the exotic, with use of light silks, gold tassels, turbans, tunic dresses, and bold use embroidery. Poiret unwillingly shared his limelight with other couturiers such as Jeanne Lanvin, Lucile, and the Callot Soeurs, who all created versions of the slender, high waisted and often sumptuous exotic look.

Art Deco—Phase Two

From about 1924 Paris fashion crystalized into the hipless garçonne look, reflected in the new sportive couture client, with her flat chest, bobbed hair, and less socially restricted lifestyle. The new generation of key designers included Jean Patou and Chanel, who both borrowed elements from Sonia Delaunay's far more extreme Orphic cubist designs. Madeleine Vionnet developed her skillful bias cut while Lelong produced the first ready-to-wear to come from a couture salon These short-skirted, simple, art-deco garments were nevertheless always made from the finest wool or the most sophisticated gilded, flowered Lyon silks and embellished with complex beading or tucking to identify their couture provenance. Patou ended the look when he lowered the hemline in 1929.

Fashion Illustration

A group of young struggling fauve artists produced a generation of fashion illustration of lasting quality and celebrity. Under the original inspiration of Paul Poiret, and his pochoir printed *Les Choses de Paul Poiret of 1909 and 1911* this period launched the careers of Barbier, Lepape, Iribe, Dufy, Erté, Marty, Benito, and Bonfils.

Couture and popular versions. The short skirt and dropped waistline were copied at all levels of the fashion trade, this time right down to the cheapest ready-to-wear, as seen in Sears and Roebuck and English ready-to-wear wholesalers' catalogs. Fashion knowledge and consumption opportunities were spread to a mass audience through the movies, through new cheap fashion journals, through home dressmaking, and through the wide availability of artificial silk or rayon (albeit still an unreliable fashion fabric). All of this accelerated the demand for mass, machine-made ready-to-wear and thus "up and coming" working-class girls on both sides of the Atlantic embraced moderated forms of art deco fashion even though their financial means were limited.

Woman modeling Paul Poiret evening dress. Poiret introduced art deco fashions to the world in the early 1900s, and several other prominent designers soon followed his lead. HULTON ARCHIVE/GETTY IMAGES. REPRODUCED BY PERMISSION.

Retro Versions

While historical styling is never repeated in the same way, both art nouveau and art deco styles have been subject to fashion revivals. As the maxi hemline became accepted from the late 1960s, in Britain new psychedelic styles were linked to a subversive nostalgia for the imperial Edwardian period, for art nouveau, and for the work of Aubrey Beardsley. This is evident in the original art nouveau brand logo selected by Barbara Hulanicki for her fashion company Biba, founded in 1964. This is also clear in the art nouveau romanticism of her fashionable evening silhouette and use of feather boas, though she fused this with early 1930s style in her use of slinky satins and the bias cut. John Galliano presented several Edwardian-styled fashions in 1996–1997.

Art Deco

Art deco design is far more deeply etched on the public mind as epitomizing a mythical ideal of free, youthful gaiety, glamour, and sexuality. This image has been strengthened by a stream of popular movies set in the 1920s, including *Singin' in the Rain* (1952), *Some Like It*

Hot (1959), and *Thoroughly Modern Millie* (1967), brought to the stage in New York in 2002 and in London in 2003. A filmed version of F. Scott Fitzgerald's *The Great Gatsby* in 1974, while the *Chicago* of 2002 and the Art Deco exhibition at the Victoria and Albert Museum of the same year, further escalated public fascination. The mid-1960s revival was led by Yves Saint Laurent with his African art deco collection in 1967, which perfectly suited that period's young, androgynous style. At the turn of the second millennium, Galliano reworked the flapper style in 1994, while Diane von Furstenberg showed flapper dresses with dropped waists and beaded fringing in New York on 17 September 2003.

See also **Appliqué; Doucet, Jacques; Galliano, John; Orientalism; Poiret, Paul; Saint Laurent, Yves.**

BIBLIOGRAPHY

Benton, Charlotte, Tim Benton, and Gislaine Wood. *Art Deco, 1910–1939.* London: Victoria and Albert Museum, 2002.

Charles-Roux, Edmonde. *Chanel and Her World.* New York: Vendome Press, 1981.

Coleman, E. A. *The Opulent Era, the Work of Worth, Doucet and Pingat.* London and New York: Thames and Hudson, Inc., Brooklyn Museum, 1989.

Greenhalgh Paul, ed. *Art Nouveau: 1890–1914.* London: Victoria and Albert Museum, 2000.

Musée de la Mode et du Costume. *Paul Poiret et Nicole Groult: maîtres de la mode art deco.* Paris: Paris Musées, 1986.

Troy, Nancy J. *Modernism and the Decorative Arts in France: Art Nouveau to Le Corbusier.* New Haven, Conn.: Yale University Press, 1991.

———. *Couture Culture, A Study in Modern Art and Fashion.* Cambridge, Mass.: Massachusetts Institute of Technology, 2002.

White, Palmer. *Poiret.* London: Studio Vista, 1974.

Lou Taylor

ASIA, CENTRAL: HISTORY OF DRESS The styles of dress in Central Asia are as varied in appearance as are the ethnic origins of the people. Even in the early 2000s tribal groups living in remote valleys dress in a distinctive manner using their fabrics, their skills, and their accessories to accentuate their uniqueness.

The demarcation of territories with borders is a recent phenomenon in Central Asia. Earlier the people moved freely and intermingled. The nomadic peoples' yearly trek followed a designated path known as "The Way" and for special markets or meetings of different tribal groups they traveled across many territories. The land as a whole was known as Turkestan, and it was only under the Soviet regime that it was divided into Turkmenistan, Kazakistan, Kyrgyzstan, Uzbekistan, and Tajikistan. Uzbekistan, which has the largest population, has a large number of Tajiks, Kazaks, and Turkomans who are citizens of the country. The Ferghana Valley covers parts of Tajikistan and runs into Kyrgyzstan running right up to Osh and has a culture that is more akin to the Uzbek than the Kyrgyz traditions.

Despite the fact that the dress when seen worn by the people is distinctive, the basic structure of the main dress is very similar. This is perhaps true of all horse-riding nomadic cultures, qualities that molded the costume of the people of Central Asia. It is also interesting that the basic dress of men and women is also similar. A type of tunic or shirt, *kurta,* was worn by the men and women, with drawstring pantaloons, the *salwar,* which was very baggy at the top and tapered down to the cuffs, that were often decorated with embroidery or edged with woven tapes.

The tunic has a universal pattern. It is made of a narrow width of cotton or silk, which more or less matches the width of the shoulders and was folded over to cover the body, falling to about 4 inches (10 cm) from the ankles. A circular cut was made for the neck; the older pieces were open at the shoulders, while later ones had a cut from the center of the neck. The sleeves were also straight and sewn into the sides and the body piece, with the sleeve opening extending below the armpit. Diagonally cut pieces, narrow at the top and broader at the bottom, were attached to the side of the body of the tunic below the sleeves. They gave the shape to the tunic. The section joining the sleeve would have gussets attached between the sides and the sleeves giving a greater freedom of movement. A girdle, *futa,* or a length of cotton or silk either of one color, striped, or printed was worn wrapped around the waist, which supported the waist as men and women had an arduous life of walking through mountain areas often carrying heavy loads. Over this dress they wore an open coat, *chapan,* of cotton or silk material, which was either padded for winter or was plain, depending on the time of the year and the status of the user. The *khalat* was the more elaborate stylized silk coat of striped silk, cotton, or richly patterned *abr* (ikat) silk. These were invariably lined to preserve the cloth and the lining was often of hand-printed cotton material. Sheepskin coats embellished with embroidery were worn in winter.

Often men wore innumerable *khalat* one on top of the other to indicate their affluence. They began with the simplest at the bottom and worked their way up to the silk brocaded or velvet *khalat* given by the emir. Women normally wore an undershirt *munisak* and a tunic on top. In some cases women, too, wore more than one tunic and a shaped *chapan* on the top.

The dress worn next to the body was embellished at all the openings. This was not only for decoration, but also to protect the wearer. The neck carried elaborate embroidery around the collar and the sleeves as well as the side openings. The cuffs of the salwar were also embroidered or embellished with woven tapes, *zef.* These tapes were tablet woven and carried elaborate patterns. The finest were the tablet woven velvet tapes used for embellishing the *kahalats.*

The men's *chapans* or *khalats* were open in the front and had to be closed either with a shawl or with a leather belt with elaborate buckles. The belt was a sign of servitude and all the courtiers had to wear it when appearing before the emir.

The most elaborate part of the dress was the headdress. Men, women, and children used the headdress and they differed from region to region. By seeing the embroidery on the cap, the ethnic group and area could be identified. The most common were hand-stitched and embroidered skullcaps. Turbans were used by men and women. The bigger the turban the more important the person. Women in Kyrgyzstan wore elaborate turbans, which were decorated with silver and gold jewelry meant especially for the headdress.

Specialists wove the turban cloths, which could be of cotton or of silk. The indigo blue and white checks, *chashme bulbul*, the nightingale's eye pattern, was greatly appreciated. The skullcap worn by men was the base for the elaborate turban worn in public.

The most elaborate headdress was the one worn by young Kazak and Kyrgyzi women. The high conical hat, *Saukele*, was nearly 28 inches (70 cm) in height. It was made of felt, covered with velvet or silk and edged with fur along its rim. It was elaborately decorated with coral, turquoise, strings of pearls, and embellished with silver and gold pendants, as well as coins. The women of Karakalapak, a remote area near the Aral Sea, also used these headdresses, which were heirlooms and passed from one generation to the other. The use of such pointed caps is possibly an ancient tradition deriving from the clothing of the Scythian tribes of classical times, as it is linked with the famous Saka—*tigra khanda* Saka, that is to say, Scythian with pointed caps.

The Turkoman married woman wore an elaborate headdress covered with silver and gold work and over that she wore a richly embroidered mantle, which came over her head and covered her body. The mantle has mock sleeves at the back.

The children were dressed with great care to protect them from evil influences and the evil eye. Silken shirts of children would be covered with amulets of silver as protective devices.

A study of different ethnic styles of Central Asian dress reveals the importance of accessories in creating a distinctive dress. A remark made by an Uzbek woman "everyone knows how to put on a dress, but not everyone knows how to carry it off" is a very true indicator of a well-dressed woman among these tribal peoples.

Though the traditions of dress in the area have ancient linkages, they are subject to change. The influences that lead to a change of fashion vary according to what is important within their own group. The changes in the past were less extreme and are more or less a case of variations on the same scheme. Records of travelers, which

Uzbek man. In Uzbekistan, the traditional dress is the tunic-like *kurta*, often covered by a *pheran*, a long, loose, coat-like garment. An embroidered cap was also worn when leaving the house. © KEREN SU/CORBIS. REPRODUCED BY PERMISSION.

give descriptions of the dress of the people over the last couple of hundred years, indicate the changing fashions. The Soviet influence, especially in the urban areas, did introduce changes in style, but in the rural areas and among the older persons the style of dress remains to a great extent unchanged.

Uzbekistan

The basic dress of the men and women was the *kurta* and the *salwar*, but over that they wore a full *pheran*, generally made of *atlas*, a woven silk, satin, or the mixed cotton and silk cloth commonly used by the women. For special occasions they would wear a shirt of *abr*, the brilliantly colored ikat weave. These would be embroidered around the collar and the sleeves, as well as on the edges or edged with tablet woven tapes. A coat was worn when receiving visitors or if stepping out of the house and the head would be covered with an embroidered cap and a large shawl. The coat and even the overshirt would be padded for winter and the coat would be lined with

Kazak horseman. Basic dress for Central Asian nomadic cultures consists of a *kurta*, *salwar* (drawstring pants), and an overcoat, either a cotton *chapan* or the more elaborate silk *khalat*. © NEVADA WIER/CORBIS. REPRODUCED BY PERMISSION.

printed cotton and edged with silk. They also had the custom of wearing embroidered oversleeves, *ton janksh*, which were separate from the *kurta* and were taken off when washing the main garment. Over this an embroidered mantle, *kok koilek*, with mock sleeves was worn over the head. This was an essential part of their dress outside the home; the older women wore white while the young married women would wear a red mantle.

The *salwar* was also richly embroidered at the cuffs and peeped from below the *kurta*. Different types of scarves and shawls were used for wrapping around the waist. The headscarves would be either embroidered wool or the gossamer floating resist-printed silks of Bokhara.

Young brides wore elaborately embroidered clothes and they also wore an elaborately woven and decorated veil over the face. The dress of the bride was often blue and richly covered, as well as embellished with jeweled plaques. The area of Karakalpak, which is near the Aral Sea and quite remote, has very fine embroidered dresses and accessories as cover for the head and the nape of the neck, which was considered very vulnerable.

Bokhara was the main center for gold embroidery, which was prepared with a technique called couching to create a rich, raised effect. Couching is an embroidery technique in which threads are laid in a design on the surface of a base fabric and sewn to the fabric with small stitches that cross over the design threads. These outer robes were worn by women for special occasions, as well as by the men as *khilats* given to them by the emir.

It was a tradition for the emir to present a full "head to foot" set of clothes to the male head of a family who was employed by the emir or was a member of the court.

Men's dress was the *kurta*, *salwar*, with a cummerbund, a sash. Over this he wore a robe open in the front, which was held together either by a woven sash or a belt. Skullcaps were an essential part of Uzbek national dress and came in a range of shapes and sizes. Some are conical and formed the base of the turban; others may be four sided, round, or cupola-shaped. All the caps were embroidered whether it was the simple gray or black cap with white embroidery or rich multicolored embroideries. Until recently the cap would identify the ethnicity and the region of the wearer. For the young brides elaborate gold embroidered caps with tassels were specially made.

Turkmenistan

The Turkoman nomadic group came from the Altai Mountains. Their ancestors were the Oghuz and their traditions have been preserved in the "Book of Oghuz, *Oguz Nama*. Around the tenth century they were settled in the region east and south of the Aral Sea, when they came to be known as Turkoman. In the fifteenth century there were two confederations: *Qara-Qoyunlu*, "they of the black sheep", and *Aq-Qoyunlu*, "they of the white sheep". A number of the leaders entered Iran as shepherds and conquered it to remain as rulers; however, a large number of them remained in the area and evolved their own way of life with their swift horses, which were their pride and their lifeline; and their sheep, camels, and other cattle with which they migrated according to a seasonal cycle of available pastureland and water. However, their movement was not very far and it was confined to approximately within the radius of 31 miles (50 km). The round, felt-covered dwellings called *Oy*, yurts, were an essential part of the Turkoman way of life, and even the agricultural groups moved to the summer camps and lived in the yurts.

The Turkoman's women's costume is similar to the tunic. It is made out of silk because there is no prohibition to wearing that material. The silk is of narrow width because of the loom and is generally woven in red with a yellow stripe near the selvage. By joining the side panels and retaining the yellow line, a very well defined linear quality emerges in the garment. Ordinarily women in everyday life wear a tunic with an opening up to the breasts, held together with a silver button at the neck. For special occasions they wear an inner tunic that is embroidered at the edges. The embroidery stitches are limited, however, as they are a number of variations of looped stitches and create a rich texture. The main stitch is similar to the feather stitch. The chain stitch, *svyme*, is used by the Yomut, along with the stem stitch. The joining of two pieces in a dress is done with a raised decorative herringbone. Extra-embroidered sleeves are also worn. Over that they wear a jacket with short sleeves, *chabut*, which is covered with coins or silver plaques, which end with elaborate silver pendants. They also wear a long coat among some of the tribes, which had become common in the beginning of the twentieth century. The coat was held together with a checkered sash, which hangs in the front and is known as *sal qusak*. Silver belts may be used, but only rarely.

Turkoman women have an elaborate high cap, which has a base of a basketlike form made from coiled and stitched local grass and covered with silk. It is then decorated with silver coins, plaques, and chains and over that is worn a scarf, which is secured by chains studded with flat carnelian. On top of all this they drape the most dazzling piece of embroidery—a mantle with the *chyrpy*, carrying mock sleeves. The colors vary according to the age of the wearer. Young women wear blue or black, the middle-aged ones yellow, while the matriarch wears white.

Another simpler headdress composed of a long, folded scarf, *aldani*, is used along with a skullcap, which was worn like a turban with its ends hanging to the left shoulder. Often one edge of the scarf is kept loose to be used for veiling the face.

The pantaloons, *salwar*, have heavily embroidered cuffs worked in striped thick silk material. The baggy top is made from ordinary cloth to which the cuffs are attached. Only the embroidered part is visible from beneath the shirt. The pantaloons are tied at the hip.

The men wore silk tunics, which opened on the side. A woven sash was worn around the waist and a *salwar* tight at the base and loose above. Woolen puttees with decorated edges covered their legs from the ankle up to the calf and long leather boots were worn. They wore sheepskin jackets or long coats with the fleece inside, which were extremely warm. The fleece shows at the edges. The finest coat is that made of unweaned lambs having a curly fleece nearly 4 inches (10 cms) long. The shepherds used to wear a felted coat, *yapunca*, which protected them from the cold and from rain and snow. The most characteristic element is their bushy hat with a long fleece, which extended over the forehead and sheltered the eyes from the glare, as well as from snow and rain. The *abr* silk *khalat* was also used for celebrations. Mostly, these have remained in the family chests as heirlooms and hardly ever worn.

Kyrgyzstan

Kyrgyzstan is a mountainous country surrounded by deserts. The Tien Shan ("Heavenly Mountains") range

Man in Turkmenistan. The most distinctive item of clothing for the Turkman is a large hat made of drooping fleece, which serves to protect the face from the elements. © WAYMAN RICHARD/CORBIS. REPRODUCED BY PERMISSION.

separates it from the Ferghana Valley, part of which occupies the southwestern area of the country. The Kyrgyz's rich cultural traditions are seen in the mountainous areas of the northern part of the country, where they settled as they moved from the Altai Mountains in southern Siberia. The Chinese chronicles describe them as fair skinned, green eyed, and red haired. The Mongols arrived in the tenth century and the intermingling created a very sturdy, handsome people, whom even the Soviets could never change.

The Kyrgyz have traditionally been a nomadic people, living in yurts. Even in the early 2000s many Kyrgyz have a yurt in their compound, and the death ceremony even in the capital city, Bishkek, is performed in a yurt. Their 100-year-old epic Manas tells the story of the warrior king and the migrations, of his people. It is the world's longest epic and the Manaschi, who recite the story, keep the oral tradition alive.

The traditional dress worn by the men is often leather trousers, *terishym*, which are also used by women when they are migrating or helping with the animals. These are worn along with high leather boots for everyday, *chaitik*, or embroidered *massey*. Over that they wear a shirt and often a leather jacket with fur lining known as *ton*. For special occasions the older men wear a long coat, *chepken*, which may be held together by a sash or a leather belt with silver buckles, *kur*. Very fine suede long coats with extra-long sleeves were made with elaborate hook embroidery. The typical headgear is a conical embroidered felt cap with embroidery and a tassel at the top, *ak-kalpak*. For special occasions the urban men wore flat, gold embroidered caps with fur lining and fur edging the headdress.

The women wore a long shirt, which was often made out of striped red and black cotton known as *kalami* or it could be of *abr*, the ikat of cotton and silk. For everyday use they would wear a sleeveless jacket and a padded long coat along with leather shoes. They wore a bonnet with embroidered ear caps over which a turban would be worn or a decorated cap. Long, embroidered plait covers were worn to cover the nape of the neck, which was considered to be vulnerable to black magic. The women favored greatly the brightly colored ikat striped cotton of Kodzhent, which was given a glossy polished surface with the use of egg white. This was used as a sash, as well as a scarf. Elaborate dresses, *koinok*, were made from silken patterned cloth known as *kimkap*, probably derived from the name for woven gold brocade of India, the *kimkhab*. For special occasions they wore a wraparound skirt, *belde-mehi*. It was either made of velvet or silk with leather and fur lining, and rich embroidery. This could be worn easily on horseback and would cover them well, giving warmth as they rode their horses.

The *bishmant* was the elaborate dress worn by brides along with a long, conical headdress decorated with gold, silver, pearls, and precious stones and often with a highly decorative veil to cover only the front of the face, while a gossamer colorful veil floated beyond from the conical hat. Older women wore elaborate turbans made of fine cotton, *chosa*. The turban was held in place by an embroidered strap. From beneath the turban, a draped cloth covered the neck and the front of the neck giving great dignity to the matriarch. On special occasions even in the early 2000s one can see in the mountain villages the older married woman astride a horse with her elaborate dress and headdress, riding forth to accompany the men, who are dressed in their finest embroidered leather coats and caps and who carry hooded hawks on their wrists.

Jewelry is very much a part of the dress. Elaborate buttons were used on the dresses. Long silver and coral earrings, *iymek*, which extended nearly 9 inches in length, framed the face. Large pendants were worn on the breasts as protective shields and linked chains of pendants and corals were stitched to the jackets. Silver buckles were attached to the leather coats and belts of the men. The engraved symbols of the sun, the moon, the stars, the falcon (their totemic bird) and others, protected them from the evil eye. The magical skill of the silversmith associated with fire and molten metal imbued the wearer with strength to face the adversities of life.

See also **Cotton; Jewelry; Silk; Textiles, Central Asian; Traditional Dress.**

BIBLIOGRAPHY

Beresneva, L. *The Decorative and Applied Art of Turkmenia.* Leningrad: Aurora Art Publishers, 1976.

Burkett, Mary. *The Art of the Felt Maker.* Kendal, U.K.: Albert Hall Art Gallery, 1979.

Gafiar, Gulyam. *Folk Art of Uzbekistan.* Tashkent, Uzbekistan: Literature and Art Publishing House, 1979.

Geiger, Agnes. *A History of Textile Art.* London: Maney Publishing, 1979.

Harvery Janet. *Traditional Textiles of Central Asia.* London: Thames and Hudson, Inc., 1977.

Sidenvagen, Vid. *On the Silk Road.* Göteborg, Sweden: Historiska Museum, 1986.

Sumner, Christina, and Heleanor Fellham. *Beyond the Silk Road.* Sydney, Australia: Arts of Central Asia; Power House Publishing, 1999.

Jasleen Dhamija

ASIA, EAST: HISTORY OF DRESS East Asia includes the present countries of China, Korea, Japan, and Vietnam (the latter also can be considered part of Southeast Asia), along with adjacent areas of Inner Asia that have historically sometimes been part of the Chinese empire and often have been heavily culturally influenced by China. These regions include Manchuria (now the three northeastern provinces of China); Mongolia (including the Inner Mongolian Autonomous Region of China and the independent Republic of Mongolia); East Turkestan (now the Chinese province of Xinjiang); and Tibet (now the Tibet Autonomous Region of Chhia, plus adjacent areas of the provinces of Qinghai, Sichuan, and Yunnan).

China was historically the dominant presence in East Asia, by virtue of size, population, and wealth; China regarded itself as the center of the world, the fountainhead of culture, and a beacon of civilization to surrounding peoples. Surrounding peoples did not necessarily share that assessment, but they could not avoid, and often did not wish to avoid, the influence of Chinese culture. The importance of silk in the history of East Asian dress is both evidence and metaphor for China's cultural domination of the region.

Silk, produced in parts of China since at least the third millennium B.C.E., was the favored textile material of China's elite thereafter (commoners wore hempen cloth in ancient times, cotton increasingly after about 1200 C.E.). Both the technology of silk production and the cultural preference for wearing silk were exported from China to Korea, Japan, and Vietnam in the early centuries C.E. Silk cloth (but not, except by accident or industrial espionage, silk technology) was exported regularly and in large quantities from China to Central and Western Asia along the Silk Route beginning in the first century B.C.E.

The cultural frontier is a very old one. Around 1000 B.C.E., near the Tarim Basin in East Turkestan (now Xinjiang Province, China), the easternmost representatives of the Celtic people were weaving woolen twill cloth in plaid patterns indistinguishable from those made by Celts in Europe at the same time. A thousand miles to the east, the kings of China's Western Zhou Dynasty (1046–781 B.C.E.), in their capital city near present-day Xi'an, clothed themselves in richly patterned silks woven in royal workshops. The border between the Chinese culture and the Inner Asian culture areas may thus be thought of as the border between silk and wool, with Chinese silk serving to create trade connections between the two cultures.

China

The basic garment of China, for both sexes, was a robe-like or tunic-like wrapped garment. Elites wore robes, preferably of silk, that were wrapped around the body and tied closed with a waist sash. Such robes were either long enough to require no lower garments or somewhat shorter (e.g. thigh length) and worn over trousers or a skirt. Trousers and skirts were not closely tied to gender and were worn by both men and women. Both sexes considered it socially essential to wear their hair bound up in a topknot or other dressed style, and covered with a head cloth or hat of some kind. Elite women favored highly colorful patterned silk cloth for their clothing. Fashion in women's clothing went through an era of rapid change during the Tang Dynasty (618–907), when a wealthy and cosmopolitan imperial culture stimulated consumption and emulation, and novelty was supplied by cultural influences, via the Silk Route, of Persian and Turkic peoples.

Elite men's clothing in ancient times was also often quite colorful, but men's clothing tended to become more somber and plain-colored in later periods. This trend toward plainer clothing was offset, however, by the development, from the late Song Dynasty (twelfth century) onward, of the "dragon robe" for use as court dress.

Commoners generally wore short robes or jackets over trousers or leggings; women sometimes wore skirts, and men sometimes wore only a loincloth as a lower garment, particularly when doing heavy agricultural work. Cavalry became an important part of the Chinese military from the late first millennium B.C.E. onward, and cavalrymen typically wore short wrapped jackets or short robes over trousers.

The dragon robes of late imperial China conveyed, through color and design details, precise information about the rank of those who wore them. Similar information for lower-ranking officials was conveyed through

A Japanese woman in a *kimono,* ca. 1880. The T-shaped garments are often produced with richly embroidered fabrics. Following World War II, kimonos were usually worn only on special occasions. JOHN S. MAJOR. REPRODUCED BY PERMISSION.

Mandarin squares, embroidered cloth badges that showed a wearer's civil service rank and were worn on the front and back of official robes.

Chinese dress changed radically after the end of the imperial period in 1911. A new form of men's clothing, called the Sun Yat-sen suit, developed on the basis of European military uniforms and won widespread acceptance; this suit had a jacket with a high, stiff "mandarin" collar, four pockets, and a buttoned front, with trousers in matching cloth. A new women's dress, called the *qipao* or *cheongsam,* evolved in Shanghai and other Chinese cities in the 1920s and 1930s; it was based on a restyling of the Manchu long gown of China's last imperial era, the ethnically Manchu Qing Dynasty. After the Communist revolution of 1949, the Sun Yat-sen suit evolved into the ubiquitous blue cotton Mao suit worn by both sexes; the *qipao* fell into disfavor in Communist China. It has since had a modest revival as formal wear. In general, however, traditional dress has disappeared in China, except among China's ethnic minorities, some of whom retain traditional or quasi-traditional dress styles as markers of ethnic identity.

Many "national minority" groups exist in China, the majority of them concentrated in the southern and southwestern provinces of Guangxi, Guizhou, and Yunnan. Important minority groups include the Zhuang, Miao, Yao, and Dai, among many others. Some are ethnolinguistically akin to Austronesian-speaking populations of Southeast Asia, such as the Shan of Burma (Myanmar) and the Hmong of Vietnam and Laos. The dress of these minority peoples varies widely, but often (as in the case of the Miao) features black-dyed cotton tunics worn with skirts or trousers and ornamented with colorful embroidery and sewn-on silver coins or beads. Women of the Dai minority wear fitted blouses with wrapped skirts similar to the *lungyi* (sarongs) commonly worn by Burmese women.

Vietnam

Historically, Vietnam can be divided into three regions: from north to south, Tonkin, Annam, and Cochin China. The northern and central regions were strongly influenced by Chinese culture while vigorously resisting Chinese conquest or political domination over the course of many centuries. Elite dress for both sexes was based on Chinese models, with males of the ruling class wearing plain long robes for ordinary wear and dragon robes or robes with Mandarin squares for official use. Women's dress strongly reflected Chinese women's fashionable attire. Working people of both sexes wore dark, wrapped jackets with skirts for women or short trousers for either sex—the "black pajamas" of Vietnam peasants that became an iconic image for Americans during the Vietnam War.

Culturally, southern Vietnam—Cochin China—was more closely related to Southeast Asia, and especially Cambodia, than to China. That was reflected in local dress, which featured wrapped skirts (sarongs) for both men and women, with wrapped upper garments for women and light, shirtlike jackets (or no upper garment) for men.

Under French colonial rule, from the 1860s to the 1950s, some elite men wore variant or hybrid forms of European dress, and some women of the same classes wore fashionable Western dress. Partly in response to this Westernization of Vietnamese dress, a new women's ensemble, the *ao dai*, evolved in the early twentieth century. It features a blouse worn above loose silk trousers, the whole outfit topped with a long, loose tunic open to the hip at each side. Though a recent innovation, the *ao dai* was accepted as a "traditional" and national dress by the mid-twentieth century and had retained that role.

Korea

Korean national dress for both men and women is known as *hanbok*, which simply means "Korean robe." The traditional men's ensemble, which is related to clothing of Manchuria and the steppe lands beyond but has no close connections to Chinese men's clothing, consists of a wrapped short jacket worn over voluminously baggy trousers tucked into black felt boots, the whole outfit topped with a stiff silk gauze coat in some light color, such as pale green or pale blue. A stiff black horsehair or straw hat completes the outfit.

The woman's *hanbok*, in contrast, is probably derived from a Tang Dynasty women's fashion for high-waisted dresses worn with a short jacket (or from a later Chinese revival of that Tang style). It consists of a skirt or very wide trousers worn with a long-sleeved wrapped top tied with a ribbon just below the bustline, the whole outfit covered with a silk gauze overskirt. The woman's *hanbok* has undergone numerous changes in style over the course of time. A simplified version has been revived in Korea as a form of national dress that is considered beautiful, patriotic, and feminine.

Japan

Japan began to be influenced strongly by continental culture from Korea, and from China via Korea, by the end of the third century C.E., and increasingly with the introduction of Buddhism in the mid-sixth century. Soon domestically produced silk fabric competed with imported Chinese and Korean textiles, though the latter retained high prestige value. In the aristocratic culture of the Nara (710–785) and Heian (795–1185) periods, fashion was thoroughly assimilated to Japanese cultural norms and was expressed in details such as color, cut, and decorative motifs in clothing that retained always the basic theme of the wrapped long robe. Men wore long robes of patterned silk or, for riding and other activities, shorter wrapped jackets over wide, baggy trousers of matching or contrasting material. Women of that era wore multiple layers of wrapped robes, cut so as to reveal each layer beneath the last; the tasteful blending of colors of such layered ensembles was an admired feminine accomplishment.

During the era of rule by a warrior aristocracy (samurai) that began in 1185 and lasted for nearly 700 years, clothing for both men and women evolved toward the T-shaped wrapped garment known as the *kimono*, in which elements of taste were expressed more in textile elements than by the cut or style of the garment itself. Fashion and style found expression in dyed, woven, or embroidered fabrics of sumptuous quality and fantastic variety; the wearing of an embroidered family crest at the nape of the neck by families with the right to do so; the choice of fabric and tying technique of the wide *obi* sash used to fasten a woman's kimono, and so on. Kimonos were displaced for most purposes by ordinary western-style clothing in the post-World War II period, and afterward were largely worn only as formal wear and on special occasions.

Clothing of working-class Japanese in premodern times was made of hempen cloth or, from about the sixteenth century onward, of cotton, usually indigo-dyed using techniques that are now much admired by connoisseurs of folk textiles. Traditional working-class garb survives in some rural Japanese communities as a somewhat self-conscious expression of conservative values.

Inner Asia

The three northeastern provinces of China that formerly made up Manchuria, barely retain a separate ethnic tradition, and there are only a few thousand remaining native speakers of Manchu. Traditional clothing has largely disappeared.

Mongolia, in contrast, retains a vigorous national culture, both in the independent Republic of Mongolia and in the ethnically Mongol region of the Chinese Inner Mongolian Autonomous Region. The national dress of Mongolia for both sexes, called the *deel*, is a wrapped robe, preferably of colorfully patterned silk (imported from China), closed with a long sash at the waist, worn over trousers for riding, and sometimes worn with a silk sleeveless vest. For cold-weather wear the deel is padded with cotton or silk floss and sometimes lined with fur. In all seasons it is worn with heavy leather boots. Mongol women traditionally wore extremely elaborate headdresses set with silver ornaments, in styles that were identified with particular tribes and clans. Men, too, wore hats distinctive of clan affiliation, and the hat played a singular role as the repository of male honor; to knock off or even to touch a man's hat without permission was to invite violent retaliation.

An unusual and distinctive item of Mongolian dress is the costume worn by men for wrestling—one of the "three manly sports" (along with riding and archery) of Mongol tradition. It consists of very tight short shorts, ordinary heavy Mongolian leather boots, and a tight-fitting, vestlike top that covers the shoulders, upper back, and upper arms, but leaves the chest bare.

In East Turkestan (now Xinjiang Province, China), the non-Chinese indigenous population consists largely of Uighurs and Kazakhs, both Turkic peoples ethnically akin to other Turkic peoples of Central Asia. Traditional dress varied widely among specific groups but tended toward wrapped, coatlike outer garments worn over a shirt and trousers, for men; and blouses, voluminous skirts, and long vests for women. Many men of the region wear the small, round, embroidered caps found widely among Central Asian peoples. Today, because the Islamic belief of these groups is seen as a bulwark against Chinese cultural hegemony, there is an increasing trend among Uighur and Kazakh women to wear international Islamic *hijab* clothing, which consists of a shapeless outer garment and headscarf.

Tibet, now the Tibet Autonomous Region of the People's Republic of China, retains a strong indigenous dress tradition. The basic garment for both sexes is the *chupa*, a narrowly cut, long, side-closing wrapped garment bound at the waist with a sash. Men often wear a sheepskin coat over the *chupa*, leaving the right arm out of its sleeve and the right side of the coat pulled down off the shoulder—this is supposedly to facilitate knife- or sword-fighting should the need arise. An alternative women's ensemble consists of a loose, long-sleeved blouse, a dress, often of plain black cotton, with a sleeveless jumper top and a skirt that wraps in back and ties at the waist with cords, giving a trim line to the garment. It is worn with an apron sewn from several strips of multicolored, horizontally-striped cloth—a badge of married status for women. As in many cultures with a tradition of pastoral nomadism, Tibetan women often wear a wealth of jewelry, favoring in particular silver ornaments set with turquoise, coral, and lapis lazuli.

See also **Asia, Central: History of Dress; Asia, South: History of Dress; China: History of Dress; Hijab; Japanese Traditional Dress and Adornment; Kimono; Korean Dress and Adornment; Qipao.**

BIBLIOGRAPHY

Crihfield, Lisa Dalby. *Kimono: Fashioning Culture.* Rev. ed. New Haven, Conn.: Yale University Press, 1993.

Fairservis, Walter, Jr. *Costumes of the East.* New York: American Museum of Natural History, 1971.

Garrett, Valery M. *Chinese Clothing: An Illustrated Guide.* Hong Kong: Oxford University Press, 1994.

Kennedy, Alan. *Japanese Costume: History and Tradition.* New York: Rizzoli, 1990.

Roberts, Claire, ed. *Evolution and Revolution: Chinese Dress, 1700s–1990s.* Sydney: The Powerhouse Museum, 1997.

Vollmer, John E. *In the Presence of the Dragon Throne: Ch'ing Dynasty Costume (1644–1911) in the Royal Ontario Museum.* Toronto: Royal Ontario Museum, 1977.

Wilson, Verity. *Chinese Dress.* London: Bamboo Publishing Ltd. in association with the Victoria and Albert Museum, 1986.

Xun, Zhou, and Gao Chunming. *5000 Years of Chinese Costumes.* San Francisco: China Books & Periodicals, 1987.

Yang, Sunny. *Hanbok: The Art of Korean Clothing.* Elizabeth, N.J.: Hollym International, 1998.

John S. Major

ASIA, SOUTH: HISTORY OF DRESS

ASIA, SOUTH: HISTORY OF DRESS South Asia comprises India, Pakistan, Bangladesh, Sri Lanka, Nepal, and Bhutan. The geographical terrain varies from mountainous regions along the northern borders, to desert areas, arid and semiarid zones dependent on monsoon rains for agriculture, the uplands of the Deccan Plateau, tropical wetlands, and the rich valleys of the Indus and Ganges rivers, seats of ancient cultures.

Despite differences in physical appearance, language, and other ethnological features, the people of South Asia share to a considerable degree a common cultural heritage. Sanskrit and Prakrit, the languages of the region's most ancient texts, are still employed in religious rituals and classical learning. The *Mahabharata* and *Ramayana*, great epics dating from ca. 500–300 B.C.E., reinforce cultural links and a sense of shared tradition throughout the region.

Pakistani man in native clothing. The national dress of Pakistan is the long tunic, or *kamiz,* and loose-fitting pantaloons called *salwar.* © Corbis. Reproduced by permission.

Draped and wrapped garments are the most common form of clothing for both men and women in South Asia. The sari (also spelled *saree*), in many variant sizes and wrapping techniques, worn with a *choli* (blouse), is the most typical form of South Asian women's dress. An analogous wrapped garment for the lower torso and legs, the dhoti, is widely worn by men; it is usually wrapped and tucked to form a kind of unstitched pantaloon. In some areas both sexes wear the sarong (also known as a *lungi*), a wrapped skirt. Stitched garments are also widely worn in the region by both men and women; examples include the loose trousers called *payjamas,* and the ensemble of *salwar* (pantaloons) and *kamiz* (long tunic) that has become the national dress of Pakistan.

Wrapped and draped garments appear to be the oldest form of attire in South Asia. Nevertheless, awls found at archaeological sites of the Harappan civilization, in the Indus Valley (third millennium B.C.E.) indicate that leather stitching and embroidery were practiced there. Stitched garments entered the region with ancient migrations of people from Central Asia. The assumption made by some European scholars that Muslims introduced tailoring to South Asia is incorrect. Early literature preserves words for the needle (*suchi*), the thimble (*pratigraha*), scissors (*sathaka*), and even for the sewing-bag, showing that tailoring was practiced in ancient times.

Early Evidence

An early Harappan sculpture depicts a priest's draped garment with an embroidered trefoil motif. Women are shown wearing elaborate headgear and a scanty wrap around the hips and pubic area, a form of dress used even today by some tribal people of Central India.

The early Vedas (ca. 1200–1000 B.C.E.) mention shining raiments, indicating the use of gold thread. The *Mahabharata* and *Ramayana* describe elaborate garments, but their form is unclear. Draped garments continued to dominate in post-Vedic times and had evolved into an elaborate costume with distinctive names. *Antariya* was the lower garment, while the upper was *uttariya.* The lower wrapper was held in place by an elaborate sash or a girdle of jewelry and the upper wrapper was draped with innumerable folds. Embroidered wrap skirts, *pesas*, were also used; they are similar to skirts worn in Gujarat. Another garment of post-Vedic times was a breast cloth, *pratidi*, tied or wrapped even today by the hill tribes of Bangladesh.

Later stone sculptures show a form of pleated lower wrap formed into a pantaloon created by passing the lower pleats through the legs and tucking them in at the back. There were variations of this technique, with descriptive names such as "elephant's trunk" and "fish tail," a style of wearing which continues to be used even today. Men and women used a wrapped head covering called *usnisa*, which was quite distinct from the later turban.

Cotton was most commonly used for textiles, along with other plant fibers and wool. Silk was indigenous to Assam. Silk cloth had connotations of purity, as was also true of wool in mountainous areas.

Historical Survey

South Asia's first major empire flourished under Chandra Gupta Maurya (320–297 B.C.E.) and his grandson, Ashoka (274–237). They forged contacts with Central Asia, China, and the Greek world (which had expanded far into Asia under Alexander the Great). Chandra Gupta married a Greek princess and had Greek women bodyguards. The presence of Greek women at the Mauryan court possibly had significant consequences for the history of South Asian dress; the Greek women's single-piece draped *chiton*, pleated as a skirt and draped over the shoulder, may have been an ancestor of the sari. A Greek ambassador named Megastenes gave a detailed description of gold-embroidered garments, printed muslin, and a life of great luxury. The elaborate drapings of Greco-Asian Gandhara sculpture of the northern area reflect the local costume, while stitched garments are depicted as being worn by soldiers, possibly of Central Asian origin.

The Satavahana Empire in south India (200 B.C.E. to 200 C.E.) encouraged trade with the Roman Empire, Arabia, and Southeast Asia. Unstitched garments are shown in Satavahana sculptures, along with stitched garments such as a tunic with V-neck and sleeves. Soldiers wore sleeved tunics with tight trousers.

The Kushans, known to the Chinese as the Yueh-Chi, dominated Central Asia during the period from 130 B.C.E. to 185 C.E. They entered the Punjab, destroying the local rulers and consolidating their rule by defeating the Greeks and the Scythians (Sakas), who dominated Western India. The presence of Greeks, Kushans, and Sakas introduced varying cultural traditions. The monolithic statue of Kanishka at Mathura has a long coat worn over a tunic. The coat's open front flaps turn outward exactly in the same way as Turkoman coats worn in the twenty-first century. Women wore jackets over their sarongs held together with decorative buttons, and tunics with sleeves and rounded necks, probably opening at the back. A dancer wore a tunic, pajama pants, a floating scarf, and a cap, similar to later Central Asian dance costumes and also to the costume worn by the women dancers of Kathak, a classical dance of North India.

Stitched garments became common during the Gupta period (fourth to eighth century C.E.), for the Gupta rulers controlled territories from Central Asia to Gujarat. The Gupta-era murals at Ajanta, however, show royalty wearing flowing garments while the attendant, entertainers, and soldiers wore stitched clothes. Women wear a range of blouses, known by names similar to *choli*, the word for blouse today. The backless blouse with an apron worn by the dancer in the murals is still worn by some nomadic peoples.

The Sanskrit and Prakrit lexicons of the seventh century C.E. contain a wide range of terms for clothing, many of which are closely related to words that are in use today. This lexical continuity shows that upper wraps, veils, jackets, tunics, and various other types of garments have continued in use from that time to the present.

The conquest of most of Central Asia and northwestern India by Mahmud of Ghazni in the eleventh century played a major role in bringing Islam to South Asia. The Islamic influence exerted by the Ghaznavids and their successors had a notable effect on the clothing of South Asia. There was an extensive trade in textiles between India and the Middle East; records specifically mention fabrics for lining and edging, indicating a highly evolved style of stitched costumes. Mention is also made of costumes coming from Syria, Egypt, and Baghdad to be used by the Sultans and their court. Textiles were also produced locally under the patronage of Muslim rulers.

Robes decorated with woven or embroidered calligraphy were worn throughout the Islamic world. They originally were produced in textile workshops (*Dar-al-Tiraz*) set up by the Caliphate in Baghdad. They came up, however, throughout the Islamic world to serve the courts. Designs and techniques were exchanged from one area of the Islamic world to another and were incorporated into garments for royalty and robes of honor. The rulers of various sultanates of northern India set up their own royal textile workshops; one was described by the inveterate Arab traveler Ibn Batuta and thus the Indian courts began to follow the dictates of fashion set by the caliphate.

The consolidation of the Mogul Empire during the late sixteenth and early seventeenth centuries led to changes in governance and court life through the country. Lesser rulers followed the dictates of the ruling Mogul emperor. Humayun, who experienced the sophisticated life of Shah Abbas's court in Persia, evolved an urbane way of life. He returned with masters of many arts to set up royal ateliers in Agra and Lahore. He laid the foundation of the indigenous Mogul style, which Emperor Akbar (1556–1605) perfected. Abul Fazl, Akbar's chronicler, records that the Akbar's wardrobe contained dresses designed by the emperor himself to be suited to the Indian climate. He describes an unlined cotton coat in "the Indian form" tied on the left side, while Hindus tied theirs on the right. (The difference persists to this day.) He introduced the double shawl used by men, a style in keeping with the flowing garment of the Indian tradition. Foreign names for introduced garments were changed to indigenous or Sanskritized versions to enhance their acceptability.

Mogul miniature paintings demonstrate that fashions in clothing were dictated by the court. Men wore long coats over pantaloons, and turbans with jeweled plumes. In Akbar's court *chakdar jama*, a long coat with pointed corners was fashionable, while Jehangir introduced a fitting *Nadiri* coat. In the early Mogul period, the dress of men and women was similar, but during Jehangir's reign women's fashions changed. Miniatures show layers of fine muslin garments floating over rich brocaded tunics with gossamer tissue veils. Indigenous textiles and skills inspired a range of costumes influenced by local fashions.

The Mogul Empire's decline shifted patronage to regional courts and led to indigenous styles. A long, trailing coat was worn at the sophisticated court of Oudh. Women's pajamas evolved into elaborate slit skirts called *farshi payjama*. Only Hindu women wore skirts.

The impact of European clothing on India was gradual. In the seventeenth and eighteenth centuries, many European men adopted Indian dress and married or lived with Indian women. The arrival of substantial numbers of European women in the mid- to late nineteenth century brought about a change of lifestyles. The formation of a colonial government and the evolution of a formal social life led to a more formal dress code. The Indian civil servants, soldiers, and students were expected to dress accordingly. The Indian elite adopted the Western mode of dress, while the middle class blended it with their own. The Bengali *babu* wore his dhoti with a shirt, a coat, and an umbrella. In southern India, men wore the coat and shirt over the sarong. Women began wearing blouses imitating the neckline, collars, and puffed sleeves of Western fashion. The tunics of North India also followed some of the European fashions.

General Regional Styles
Despite the fact that South Asia preferred the use of draped garments, regional variations occur throughout the area. These are influenced by geo-climatic conditions, and sociocultural environment.

North India and Pakistan
In North India and Pakistan, stitched costumes similar to those of Central Asia are prevalent. Men and women wear a tunic called a *kamiz*, together with *salwar*, loose pantaloons, narrow at the ankles and tied at the waist. (The *salwar* is cut quite differently from the pajama.) The versions of *salwar kamiz* worn by men and women are similar but have a different cut and styling. In addition to the tunic and pantaloons, women wear a veil, *dupatta*, which is a head covering, and can envelop the body. Pakistan's women have adopted *salwar kamiz* as their national dress; for outdoors, many women wear a burqa over the *salwar kamiz* that covers them from head to toe.

In Greater Punjab (extending into both India and Pakistan), Sindh, and the North-West Frontier Province of Pakistan, people wear a longer style of tunic, called a *kurta*, as well as *salwar*. The embroidered tunic worn by women in Pakistan's Sindh and Baluchistan areas is similar to the one worn by the Baluchi women of Afghanistan and Iran.

The Hindu, Muslim, and Sikh peasants wore a long wide sarong known as *lacha* made of cotton, worn long at the back and knotted in the front, with the ends tucked into the side. Affluent landlords wore a silk *lacha* with broad borders. Men wore turbans with a crestlike fan rising from behind and a long, flowing end falling down the wearer's back. The Jats of East Punjab and Haryana in India wear a similar dress.

The men and women of Kashmir wear a long, loose tunic, *pheran*, with a *salwar* or a pajama; the Kashmir tunic is quite distinct from the kamiz. The women's tunic has embroidery at the neck and is worn with a headscarf.

Ladakh
Sometimes known as lesser Tibet, the small Himalayan territory of Ladakh maintains Buddhist lamaistic traditions. Men wear a long, woolen coat with side fastenings, with a shirt and a sash. Everyone wears a tall hat with an upturned rim, richly embroidered for special occasions. Women wear a long velvet dress, with a sheepskin, *lokp*, suspended from the shoulders at the back like a short cape, which is replaced by a brocade or richly embroidered version for festive occasions. Women also wear an elaborate headdress, *perak*, covered with large pieces of turquoise, which curves over the head like a cobra hood and hangs down the back.

Indian Regional Costumes
In northwestern India, the women of Gujarat and Rajasthan wear a wrapped skirt, *jimmi*, or a wide skirt, *ghagro*, with a fitting backless blouse, and a veil. The blouse has many variations, as described in the ancient literature. In Saurashtra and Kutch, men of the Kathiawari ethnic group, descendants of the Huns, wear a pleated blouse (*kedia*), tight pajamas, a large shawl around their waist, and a turban, a costume similar to some peasant costumes in the Balkans. People in the Tharparkar and Sindh areas of Pakistan dress in a similar manner. Hindu women wear a skirt, a backless blouse, and veil, while Muslim tribal women wear a thigh-length backless blouse, an embroidered salwar, and a veil. In the urban areas of Gujarat, men wear a *dhoti* with a shirt, while women wear a fourteen-and-a-half-foot sari with a cross border worn in the front.

In central India and the western coastal area, Hindu and tribal men and women wear unstitched garments. Urban men wear stitched upper garments during winter or for special occasions. Women of different groups wear saris of 137 inches to 312 inches in length (3½ meters to 8 meters in length). Tribal women wear shorter saris, while urban and more affluent women wear longer ones. They are wrapped so as to create unstitched pantaloons by taking the front pleats, passing them between the legs, and tucking them into the back. This style of sari wrapping is associated with women's chastity. Women in south India (including Karnataka and Tamil Nadu) wear the sari in a variety of styles, depending on geo-climatic conditions and cultural traditions.

Women in Kerala, in southwesternmost India, wear sarongs instead of saris, while men wear a white double-layered sarong, with an upper-body cloth along with a shirt.

Muslim men and women throughout India wear stitched garments. The common dress for men is a *kurta* (long tunic) and pajama. The affluent wear an embroidered coat, *angarkha*, and embroidered cap. For official occasions they wear a fitting long coat, *sherwani*, and tight pajama. The turban varies according to their vocation, the occasion, and their age. Women wear a tight pajama, a fitted shirt (often with a jacket), and an embroidered veil. For outdoors many women wear the burqa. Among the affluent, *farshi payjama*, a trailing, wide divided skirt, is worn for special occasions. Among non-Muslims, such as Hindus and Jains, stitched garments have to be removed by men and women for religious ceremonies or for entering a temple.

Sri Lanka
Sri Lanka, a large island lying at the southernmost tip of India, was an important maritime center from ancient times, linking the East with the West. The Greeks called

Refugees in Pakistan. In many South Asian countries, Muslim women wear *saris* inside the home, but are obliged to wear head-to-toe coverings called *burqas* outside the home. © Lynsey Addario/Corbis. Reproduced by permission.

it Taprobane, and the Arabs Serendib. Sri Lanka's recorded history dates from the mid-first millennium B.C.E. Around 400 B.C.E. King Pandukabhaya began developing the arts and established close contacts with Buddhist India. Theravada Buddhism remains the dominant religion of Sri Lanka's majority Sinhalese people today. Early sculptures show close linkages with Indian tradition and the figures are seen wearing flowing draped garments.

Sri Lanka has absorbed a great deal of external influence during its history. Arab traders drawn to the spice and textile trade visited the island from late Roman times onward. Colombo and Galle had colonies of Arab traders, who introduced Islam to Sri Lanka. Portuguese traders settled in coastal areas in the early sixteenth century. The Portuguese settlements were taken over by the Dutch in the mid-seventeenth century; the British, who established a colonial regime in 1833, in turn, expelled the Dutch. European influence on Sri Lankan culture can be seen in dress, especially among the so-called Burghers, who are of mixed Dutch and Sinhalese ancestry. Early drawings show Burghers mingling traditional dress with European elements. Men wore over the sarong a long coat with puffed sleeves and a sash, as well as a hat. Women dressed in a sarong and upper cloth combined with European

jackets. However, many people continued to wear clothing not affected by European influence.

The Sri Lankan population includes two major elements, the Sinhalese and, especially in the northeastern part of the island, the Tamils. The latter were migrants from southeastern India, many brought in by the British as plantation workers in the nineteenth century. The two communities have distinctive clothing traditions.

The traditional dress of the Sinhalese women is the sarong worn with a stitched blouse and a scarf over the shoulder. In some cases the sarong has a frill at the top. Some wear a blouse with lace inserts at the waist and the sleeves, with a silver belt. Men wear a sarong and a *kamiz* (tunic). The fact that two women heads of state have always worn the Sinhalese national dress has influenced even the Burghers to adopt the traditional costume. Tamil women wear the saris draped in the traditions of their community, while the men wear the *veshti*, a white sarong. Muslim men, who trace their roots to Arab settlers, wear a colorful sarong with a tunic and a cap. Muslim women traditionally wore local dress; however, in the early 2000s many have adopted Islamic dress, including wearing the headscarf.

A Sri Lankan Hindu in traditional attire. While some Sri Lankan attire has been influenced by Arab and Western styles, others have remained untouched by these outside elements. © BETTMANN/CORBIS. REPRODUCED BY PERMISSION.

Nepal

The Royal Kingdom of Nepal, a landlocked area with the highest mountains of the world, extends from the Gangetic plains to the Himalayas. The country's climate ranges from alpine cold, to hot and arid, to hot and humid. The country has many different ethnic groups, but they fall into two main divisions. In the mountains are found peoples of Tibetan origin, while people of Indo-Aryan origin live mostly at lower elevations.

Early references to clothing in ancient texts indicate that the various peoples of Nepal had diverse clothing traditions from ancient times and that some of those traditions persist to the present day. The earliest reference to Nepalese textiles is in Kautalya's *Arthashastra* (250 B.C.E.). It refers to black blankets stitched together from eight pieces. These continue to be used as a wrap by the people. Historic dress styles can be studied from sculptures, murals, and book illustrations. Draped and wrapped garments dominate, along with stitched jackets. In the early fifteenth century, the ruler classified the dress of sixty-five sub-castes; for instance, some were prohibited from wearing coats, caps, and shoes and others from having sleeves on their jackets.

Newari women of the central valleys and the lower mountain ranges wear a pleated wraparound skirt held together by a heavy shawl at the waist, while the men wear a long shirt, *nivasa*, pleated up to the waist and reaching to the ankles, which is worn with a waist cloth. A jacket and a *topi*, conical cap, completes the outfit. Gurkha men wear ordinary trousers with a blouse reaching below the hips and fastened by a heavy cummerbund with the *kukri* traditional dagger stuck into it.

The Kirant, one of the larger ethnic groups, wear an interesting blouse called *choubandi*, which means "four knots." The blouse crosses over, tying at the armpit and at the waist. Women wear it waist-length, while the men's comes to the hip. Women also wear a wraparound skirt with a sash. The Tharus of Terrai wore wrapped skirts made from multicolored panels and appliqué blouses.

Ethnic groups of Tibetan heritage, such as the Sherpas and Dolpos, generally wear clothing similar to that of Tibet. These include, for women, a silk blouse and a wrapped skirt, worn with a narrow apron of brightly colored stripes, stitched together from three pieces. Men wore woolen coats and trousers or left their legs bare. The Dolpo's woolen coat, *chuba*, came with multiple panels and had a distinctive style. Both groups use long sheepskin or goatskin fleece coats to ward off the high mountain cold.

The distinctive characteristic of Nepali dress was the more affluent the wearer the greater the length of cloth. Royal women used 80 to 90 yards of material for their gathered skirts. These thick and heavy skirts were worn with a thick sash to protect against back strain.

Bhutan

The Royal Kingdom of Bhutan is east of Nepal, between northeastern India and Tibet. The country is mostly mountainous. The majority of inhabitants, of Tibetan culture and ethnicity, live in the principal valleys among the high mountains. A hot and humid lowland area on the southern fringe of the country is home to many Nepalese immigrants. Finely woven woolen textiles are produced in the highlands, while cotton and silk is produced and woven in the lowlands.

Traditional dress is mandatory in Bhutan. Men wear Tibetan-style tunics, *gho*, with a belt; the style is, however, quite distinct. It is raised and tied at the waist with the legs left bare for greater mobility. Rich woven patterns give the tunic a distinctive character. Ceremonial scarves are essential for all rituals and ceremonies and the color denotes the status of the wearer. Even their raincoats woven out of yak wool and dyed with vegetable dyes, *char-khab*, are beautifully patterned.

Many men are monks and wear Tibetan Buddhist-style burgundy or orange woolen wrapped robes stitched together from separate pieces of cloth. Women wear a wraparound dress of wool or silk, *kiru*, with a sash. Silver brooches with a pin, *koma*, hold the wrapped dress in

Young Bengali women. Women of the Bengal region typically wear draped cotton *saris* over blouses (*cholis*), and those who practice the Hindu religion drape the end of the sari over the head to form a veil. © ROGER WOOD/CORBIS. REPRODUCED BY PERMISSION.

place. Over this they wear a jacket, *toego*, which gives the dress a very elegant style. A shoulder shawl, *rachu*, is essential for entry to the Dzong or in the presence of royalty or high officials. The finest *kiru*, known as *kushutharas*, is a highly elaborate weave and is worn mostly by royalty.

Bangladesh

The Vanga or Banga Kingdom is mentioned in early Sanskrit literature (1000 B.C.E.) and it was known as one of the earliest Indian kingdoms to embrace Buddhism. Bengal has a strong, local cultural tradition and has long had contact with Southeast Asia and with the West, via Arab

traders. Portugal was the first European state to have direct contact with Bengal. The region is ethnically diverse, with a Bengali-speaking majority in the broad river valleys and lowlands, and with hill tribes, especially in the east, that have connections with the peoples of Myanmar (Burma).

In 1576 C.E. the Moguls conquered Bengal, incorporating it into the Mogul Empire. The British East India Company established a trading settlement in 1651. Bengal was assimilated into the British Empire, and Calcutta became the seat of the empire, as well as the hub of the trade. The partition of India in 1947 saw East Bengal, which had a Muslim majority, become East Pakistan, while West Bengal, with a Hindu majority, remained part of India. In December 1971 East Pakistan became the sovereign state of Bangladesh.

Bengal was known from early times for its gossamer Dacca muslin, which was in demand throughout the world. Women spun cotton thread to the fineness of 400 count. The Roman senate bemoaned emptying their coffers to pay for this fine muslin. Caesar complained that his wife appeared naked in public and she responded that she wore seven layers of the Indian cloth.

The women of both West Bengal and Bangladesh wear cotton saris in the typical Bangla style of fold upon fold. Hindu women use the long end of the sari as a kind of veil by draping it over their head; Muslim women wear the sari at home in the same manner but cover it with a burqa outside the house. Muslim peasant men wear a colorful *lungi* (sarong), with short vest. Hindu men wear a *dhoti* (unstitched pantaloon), a vest, and a shoulder cloth. Urban Muslim men wear loose pajamas with a tunic known as a *Punjabi*. For formal occasions the men wear fitting, long coats, *sherwani*, with tight pajamas, while Hindus wear cotton or silk *dhotis* with *Punjabi* and a shawl. Tribal women wear sarongs and breast cloths with intricate patterns, woven on backstrap looms. Among some tribal women, the intricately woven sarong was formerly worn from the breast to the calf. The custom of wearing blouses with the sarong or sari was introduced much later. The younger generation has taken to wearing the *salwar kamiz*.

Conclusion

South Asia has the distinctive characteristic that women have maintained their traditional way of dress. The elite younger generation does wear Western dress and the universal jeans, but for special occasions and as they settle into domesticity, they wear their local dress. However, the different styles of wearing the sari in different regions dictated by the geo-climatic conditions and local culture is now disappearing. The eighteen-foot sari with the cross border thrown across the left shoulder has come to dominate throughout India, Bangladesh, and Sri Lanka; upper-class women of Nepal also wear the sari.

The freedom struggle and search for identity had led to the use of *khadi*, handspun handwoven cotton, and the Gandhi *topi* (cap), which became associated with the freedom struggle. After independence and the need for creating a national identity led to the introduction of the Jawahar jacket, a sleeveless fitting jacket worn with Indian clothes made fashionable by the first prime minister, Jawaharlal Nehru, as well as the Jodhpur coat, a close necked full-sleeved short coat worn with trousers as semiformal dress and the *sherwani* or *achkan*, a long coat worn with tight *churidar* pajama and formal dress.

Pakistan guards its separate identity and the women wear the *salwar kamiz*, which has also spread to Bangladesh and southern India. Women's magazines and Bollywood films have had an important influence in making the women innovative in enriching their costume. This began even before the advent of India's National Institute of Fashion Technology in the 1980s and the proliferation of boutique culture in the hands of young fashion designers, who are setting new trends in South Asian styles of dress.

See also **Colonialism and Imperialism; Cotton; Religion and Dress; Sari; Silk; Textiles, South Asian; Traditional Dress.**

BIBLIOGRAPHY

Abul-Fazl. *'Allami, The A'in-I-Akbari.* Translated by H. Blochmann. 3rd ed. New Delhi: South Asia books, 1977.

Agrawala, V. S. "References to Textiles in Bana's *Harshacharita.*" *Journal of Indian Textile History* (1959).

Ali, A. Yusuf. *Monograph on Silk Fabrics Produced in the North-Western Provinces and Oudh.* Allahabad, 1900; reprint Ahmedabad, 1974.

Alkazi, Roshen. *Ancient Indian Costume.* New Delhi: Art Heritage, 1983.

Askari, Nasreen, and Rosemary Crill. *Colours of the Indus.* London: Merrill Holberton and the Victoria and Albert Museum, 1997.

Baker, Patricia L. *Islamic Textiles.* London: British Museum Press, 1995.

Bartholomew, Mark. *Thunder Dragons Textiles from Bhutan.* Kyoto, Japan: Bartholomew Collection, 1985.

Beer, Alice Baldwin. *Trade Goods: A Study of Indian Chintz.* Washington, D.C.: Smithsonian Institution Press, 1970.

Bhushan, Jarmila Brij. *The Costumes and Textiles of India.* Taraporevala, Bombay, 1959.

Chandra, Moti. *Costumes, Textiles, Cosmetics and Coiffure in Ancient and Mediæval India.* Delhi: Oriental Publishers on behalf of the Indian Archaeological Society, 1973.

———. "Indian Costumes and Textiles from 8th to 12th Century." *Journal of Indian Textile History* 5 (November 1960): 1–41.

Chopra, P. N. "Dress, Textiles and Ornaments during the Mughal Period." *Proceedings of Indian History Congress,* 15th Session. Calcutta, 1954. Pp. 210–228.

Dar, S. N. *Costumes of India and Pakistan.* Bombay, India: D. B. Taraporevala Sons and Company, 1982.

———. "Survey of Embroidery Traditions." In *Textiles and Embroideries of India.* Bombay: Mark Publications, 1965.

———. *Folk Arts and Crafts of India.* New Delhi, India: NBT, 1970.

Dhamija, Jasleen. *Crafts of Gujarat.* New York: Mapin, 1985.

———. "Telia rumals, Asia rumal, Real Madras Handkerchief (RMH): Footnote to Global Textile Trade." Paper presented to the conference Cloth, the World Economy and the Artisan, Dartmouth, N.H., 1993.

———. *The Woven Silks of India.* Bombay, India: Mark Publications, 1995.

———. *Woven Magic.* Jakarta, Indonesia: Dian Rakyat, 2002.

Dhamija, Jasleen, and Jyotindra Jain. *Handwoven Fabrics of India.* New York: Mapin, 1981.

Elson, Vickie G. *Dowries from Kutch.* Los Angeles: UCLA Museum of Cultural History, 1979.

Frater, Judy. *Threads of Identity.* New York: Mapin Publishing, 1995.

Gajurela, Chavilala. *Traditional Arts and Crafts of Nepal.* New Delhi, India, 1984.

Gelfer, Agnes. *A History of Textile Art.* London, 1979.

———. "Some Evidence of Indo-European Cotton Trade in Pre-Mughal Times." *Journal of Indian Textile History* 1 (1955).

Guy, John. "Sarasa and Patola: Indian Textiles in Indonesia." *Orientations* 20, no. 1 (1989).

———. *Woven Cargoes: Indian Textiles in the East.* London and New York: Thames and Hudson, Inc., 1998.

Hitkari, S. S. *Phulkari: The Folk Art of Punjab.* New Delhi, India: Phulkari Publications, 1980.

Jain, Jyotindra, and Aarti Aggarwala. *National Handicrafts and Handlooms Museum.* New Delhi, India, 1989.

Krishna, Rai Anand. *Banaras Brocades.* New Delhi, India, 1966.

Maxwell, Robyn. *Textiles of South East Asia.* Melbourne, Australia: Australian National Gallery; Oxford University Press, 1990.

Mayors, Diana K. *From the Land of the Thunder Dragons: Textile Arts of Bhutan.* New Delhi, India: Timeless Books, 1994.

Nambiar, Balan, and Eberhard Fischer. "Patola/Viralu Pattu—from Gujarat to Kerala. New Information on Double Ikat Textiles in South India." *Asiasche Studien: Etudes Asiatiques* 41, no. 2 (1987).

Pavinskaya, Larisa R. "The Scythians and Sakians: Eighth to Third Centuries B.C." *Nomads of Eurasia.* Los Angeles: Natural History Museum of Los Angeles County, 1989.

Religious & Cultural Traditions of Bhutan. Catalog of Exhibition. Department of Culture. India & National Commission for Cultural Affairs. Bhutan. October 2001.

Scott, Philippa. *The Book of Silk.* London and New York: Thames and Hudson, Inc., 1993.

Tucci, Giuseppe. *Transhimalaya.* Translated by James Hogarth. London: Barrie and Jenkins, 1974.

Vogelsang-Eastwood, Gillian. *Resist Dyed Textiles from Quseir al-Qadim.* Egypt, Paris, 1990.

Wilson, Kax. *A History of Textiles.* Boulder, Colo.: Westview Press, 1979.

Jasleen Dhamija

ASIA, SOUTHEASTERN ISLANDS AND THE PACIFIC: HISTORY OF DRESS

Prior to Western contact that began as early as the sixteenth century, clothing in the islands of Southeast Asia and the Pacific was minimal due in part to the islands' tropical conditions. Bark cloth was produced on all of these islands and was made by felting fibers from the inner bark of the paper mulberry tree. Simple wrapped garments were worn primarily over the lower body, and some cultures occasionally wore unconstructed garments on the upper body as well. Dress included not only the wearing of bark cloth, but also involved tattooing for both sexes. As woven textiles were introduced into these islands, bark cloth pro-

Tattooed Polynesian man. Early Islanders used body art to express social and political standing. Clothing was minimal, and natural dyes were used to paint and tattoo the skin. © ROBERT HOLMES/CORBIS. REPRODUCED BY PERMISSION.

duction was reduced; where still produced it is used primarily for ritual purposes.

The islands of Southeast Asia (Malaysia, Indonesia and the Philippines) are the product of multicultural influences that began with trade along the sea lanes. Portuguese, British, Dutch and Spanish colonialism had an impact on the development of traditional dress. Although Western dress is worn in the islands today, traditional dress continues to be worn in villages and throughout these islands for ritual and ceremonial occasions. Brief details regarding the dress of the three major Southeast Asian islands (Malaysia, Indonesia and the Philippines) and the major Pacific Islands (Hawaii, Tonga, Samoa, Tahiti, the Marquesas and Cook Islands) will be provided here.

Malaysia is a Muslim country divided into West Malaysia, a peninsula of Southeast Asia, and East Malaysia, the northern portion of the island of Borneo, the rest of which belongs to Indonesia. The traditional textiles and dress of Malaysia and Indonesia are somewhat similar. Both island nations have developed highly

An Indonesian couple in everyday dress. The woman wears a traditional *kain,* while the man wears Western-style clothing. The variety of dress-styles in Indonesia is an indicator of local, Islamic, and Western influences on the country. JOHN S. MAJOR. REPRODUCED BY PERMISSION.

complex textiles, and the designs for these fabrics carry much symbolic meaning with regard to an individual's social status. Luckily, this traditional art is still considered to be important even in the face of westernization. Indonesia and Malaysia are known for textiles made with complex resist-dyed techniques; these include batik and ikat. Similarly, both Malaysia and Indonesia produce *songket,* a complicated fabric with a supplementary weft of gold, silver and other metallic threads.

In Malaysia, traditional clothing includes a lower body covering (sarong) worn by both sexes. Men's sarong are plaid, women's are designed with floral patterns. The upper body covering for men is a shirt referred to as a *baju.* For women, a sheer blouse referred to as a *kebaya* is worn in Malaysia. Sheerness is less acceptable today so a more accepted form of dress for women, especially in cities, is the *tudung*—an ensemble of a long-sleeved tunic and floor-length skirt accompanied by a head scarf.

Indonesian national dress derives from the Muslim inhabitants of Indonesia's main island, Java. Dress is an indicator of cultural change in Indonesia where history can

be divided into three eras categorized by dress terms: sarong (local dress), *jubbah* (Islamic influences) and trousers (Western influences). Although Western dress is most commonly worn in Indonesia's urban areas today, traditional textiles are used even in Western-styled clothing, and traditional dress styles continue to be important in Indonesia, where varied forms of traditional dress testify to the wide variety of subcultural groups in the nation.

Traditional dress is still commonly seen in rural areas and is especially important throughout Indonesia for national ceremonial occasions. For both sexes, traditional dress in Indonesia includes a wraparound lower-body cover (*kain,* a rectangular length of fabric, generally in batik), or a sarong (more often in ikat). Women in Java and Bali wear *sarongs* and *kain,* held in place with a *stagen.* The *kebaya* is a tight, often sheer, long-sleeved blouse worn on the upper body. It is often made of lace, and can be made of lightweight, sheer, elaborately embroidered cottons. In addition, women generally have a *selendang* (ikat or batik) draped over the shoulder (on less formal occasions a large *selendang* is used to carry babies or objects), or on Bali the *pelangi* is worn over the *kebaya* around the waist.

Indonesian men generally wear *kain* or sarongs only in the home or on informal occasions. A black felt cap or *peci,* is occasionally worn; though it was once associated with Islam it has acquired a more secular, national meaning in the post-independence period. These ensembles originated on Java and have become national dress in Indonesia because the vast majority of the population lives on Java and Bali. *Kebaya* and batik *kain* are considered Indonesia's national dress for women and *teluk beskap,* a combination of the Javanese jacket and *kain* are formal dress for Indonesian men. Shirts made with traditional batik and ikat designs are worn with trousers for less formal occasions.

Indonesians and Malays settled in the Philippines prior to the Spanish colonization during the sixteenth century. The dominant influence is Spanish Catholicism; priests were scandalized by the relative nudity of the Filipinos, who wore minimal lower body coverings. Spanish colonists brought Western notions of modesty and opulence in dress that influenced the styles of Filipino national dress. It retained features relevant to the environment; loose, light and long garments made of blended fibers of *pina* (pineapple fiber) and *jusi* (sheer raw silk) rather than the heavy silks and velvets brought by the Spaniards.

The early Filipino women wore the *baro't saya,* an ensemble of a loose, long-sleeved blouse over a wide skirt that fell to the floor. By the nineteenth century it evolved into the Maria Clara ensemble. The blouse (*camisa*) is a bell-sleeved blouse with a large, triangular, stiff shawl (*panuelo*) worn on top. From the Spanish, Filipinas learned to do embroidery, cutwork, drawn threadwork and other forms of surface design. *Camisas* and *panuelos* were heavily embroidered. In the early 2000s, the Maria Clara is worn for formal events. The Maria Clara is still a two-piece dress, with large, butterfly sleeves. In the twentieth century, another garment called the *mestiza*, a sheath dress with butterfly sleeves became popular. For Filipino men, the *barong tagalog* is national dress, and is worn for a wide variety of activities. It evolved from the *canga*, a loose cotton shirt worn outside the trousers. Over time, and due to Spanish influence, the shirt evolved into a sheer embroidered shirt. For all traditional Filipino dress, *pina* and *jusi* are favorite fabrics, but less expensive silks and fine polyesters are also used. All are heavily embroidered.

Pacific Islands

The islands in the Pacific Ocean were ruled by a hierarchy of hereditary tribal chiefs before European explorers visited in the eighteenth century. Visits by sailors had some impact, but the arrival of Europeans determined to stay in the islands was the key element leading to change in the dress of Pacific Islanders. The London Missionary Society saw it as their duty to convert the islanders to Christianity; to that end they sent missionaries in 1797 to the Society Islands, and with the support of the Pomares, the most powerful ruling family in the islands, by 1815 British missionaries had taken control of the islands. They did not just affect the islander's religious beliefs but had a significant impact on the culture by prohibiting traditional dance and music, while concurrently eliminating evidence of native religion.

Conflict between the French and British occurred on most islands as each nation tried to assert control. In the Marquesas, the French expelled the British and secured influence over the area, leaving the ruling Pomare family as token rulers. A French colony was proclaimed when King Pomare V was forced to abdicate in 1880 and within a few years it included the Marquesas, Society Islands, Austral Islands, Gambier Archipelago, and Tuamotu atolls. After World War II, Tahitians who had fought for France brought pressure against the government to extend French citizenship to all islanders; in 1957 the territory was officially renamed the Territory of French Polynesia.

Throughout all of the Pacific Islands, there has been a rebirth of indigenous culture since the 1970s. The Tahitian and Hawaiian languages are again taught in schools, and on some islands the indigenous language is even used in government meetings. Culture is being reclaimed from its near-death experience at the hands of missionaries, and in the islands the traditional arts, dance and music are now celebrated. The Pacific islands are now home to ethno-tourism, and the cultural displays of traditional arts are featured.

Pacific Island Dress: Pre-Contact

Prior to the arrival of missionaries in the Pacific Islands, dress was an important expression of social status, polit-

Traditional Javanese daily wear. Indonesian men and women generally wear this wrap-around lower-body cover in the home or on informal occasions. The dress originated on Java, Indonesia's main island. PHOTO BY JOHN. S. MAJOR. REPRODUCED BY PERMISSION.

ical standing and religious belief. Body art and clothing were key elements that helped people to socially locate themselves and others. The body was the main focus of material expression. The body was tattooed, painted, and decorated with natural materials, dyes, and paints. In Eastern Polynesia, feathers twined onto heavy backings, provided for rich cloaks and helmets for members of the noble classes. Clothing was made from bark cloth (*tapa*, or in Hawaii, *kapa*) that was then decorated with motifs that varied from one culture to the next. Generally, only the lower body was covered with loincloths for men and wrapped skirts of *tapa* for women. Throughout Polynesia, skirts made of various fibers and leaves were worn by both men and women. In Western Polynesia, fine mats (*toga* in Samoa) were made of pandanus leaves and were used to cover the lower body. Fine mats symbolized the interweaving of lineages and are still ritually significant.

Dress was not just symbolic of status, but was used to signal submission, dominance, and respect in the islands. It was believed that clothing allowed the wearer to capture and transmit *mana*, a spiritual force over life, health, and death. To produce *tapa* was a source of power for women. These cultures had a pre-exisiting system of cultural meaning for dress that facilitated conversion to Western-style dress after contact. Although missionaries perceived islanders' adoption of new forms of clothing as

Girl in traditional dress of Tonga Islands. While native Tongan clothing such as this woven mat and feather headdress are still worn occasionally, many of the younger generation in the early twenty-first century were adopting Western-style dress. © WOLFGANG KAEHLER/CORBIS. REPRODUCED BY PERMISSION.

proof of conversion to Christianity, they failed to understand the multi-dimensionality of dress in the Pacific Islands.

In Hawaii, the arrival of Western trade goods began with the sandalwood trade beginning in 1810. For Hawaiian rituals, the *ali'i* (royalty) wore the splendid feather capes and cloaks which they traded to foreigners (*haoles*) for high prices or Western garments.

Prior to the arrival of permanent residents from the Western world, the standard Hawaiian costume consisted of only a lower body covering for both sexes. Indigenous Hawaiians made and wore *kapa* garments. Men wore a loincloth called the *malo*, and women wore the *pa'u*, a wrapped garment of kapa that often had applied geometric designs. Occasionally cape called a *kikepa* might be worn. By the time the missionaries arrived in 1820, the *ali'i* had already come to appreciate Western textiles as a substitute for *kapa*, and preferred calico. Although *kapa* was the traditional fabric, it could not be cleaned, did not wear well, and even one layer was stiff.

The *pa'u* passed several times around the waist and extended from beneath the bust to below the knee. For commoners, the *pa'u* was short and might be composed of only one or two layers of *kapa*, with each layer about four yards long and three or four feet wide. *Ali'i* wore as many as ten layers.

Adoption of Western-Styled Dress: Post-Contact
The process of conversion to Christianity in the Pacific was a slow process during the early nineteenth century; as one might expect, during that time there were a variety of transitions in clothing. For the missionaries, covering the breasts was required for the sake of Christian notions of modesty. While much has been written about the missionaries' insistence that the indigenous groups must be clothed in a way considered morally decent to the Europeans, there was at the same time agency on the part of the indigenous groups. On many islands, where status was denoted by dress, the dominant social groups were anxious for new styles to continue to assert their elevated social status. Consequently, when the missionaries arrived in the islands, their new fashions were rapidly adopted by the *ali'i*.

In the Cook Islands and on Tahiti, bark cloth ponchos were worn until woven textiles became available midcentury. Expatriates wore clothing from their original homelands, but Europeans created garments that were Western-styled and made of woven textiles for indigenous groups, as a means of ethnic classification. The indigenous groups made European-styled garments of native *tapa*, as seen in ponchos from Tahiti and the Cook Islands, and the *kapa holoku* was made in Hawaii. Tongan and Hawaiian nobility wore European garments regularly, and often wore Western clothing covered waist or hip wrappings of *kapa* (Hawaii) or woven mats (Tonga and Samoa). Woven mats over skirts of leaves in Samoa gave way to the use of *tapa* as a substitute for woven cloth. Christian Samoans were identified by the use of *tapa* rather than mats in the nineteenth century.

When woven textiles became more readily available throughout the Islands in the mid-nineteenth century, they were readily adopted for a number of reasons; for comfort and durability, to engender good relations with the missionaries, and, yes, for fashion.

Missionaries brought Victorian notions of style to the Pacific islands; that legacy is seen in brightly colored floral prints throughout the islands. The contemporary dress of islanders is derived from what has come to be known as "traditional" dress. The high-necked, yoked, loose garments introduced by missionaries, and made in bright floral prints, continue to be worn. Their origin was in 1820 when the Hawaiian queens requested dresses like those worn by the missionary wives. As the American women were quite small and wore empire-waisted dresses in the style of 1819, they decided that because the Hawaiian women were quite large, the high waistline would not be attractive, and it was eliminated. The missionary wives designed the *holoku* as a long, loose dress with a high neckline and long sleeves. Until the 1930s they were made primarily in cotton calico prints and silk. The missionaries required the Hawaiian women to wear *holoku* when at the mission to signal ethnic differences. At the same time, they gave the Hawaiians chemises (knee-length slips), called *mu'umu'u*. The *holoku* was eagerly embraced by the upper-class women as a sign of their superior status. The *mu'umu'u* was not worn as a slip, as intended by the missionaries. Instead, it was used as a dress for sleeping in, or for swimming. It was not until the 1930s that the *holoku* became formal wear, and the *mu'umu'u* began to be made in bold cotton prints, and then became a common daytime dress.

As missionaries left Hawaii to convert other islanders, they took the *mu'umu'u* with them and introduced it to women on other islands. The *holoku* and *mu'umu'u* were the forerunners of the nightgown known in America as the Mother Hubbard, and that is the term for the floral print day dress worn in Vanatu. Similarly, this high necked, loose dress appears in many islands and now is considered traditional dress. Though they are quite similar throughout the islands, these garments have different names: they are referred to as Mother Hubbards (Vanatu); *vinivo* (Fiji); *pareau* (Tahiti), and *holoku* and *mu'umu'u* (Hawaii).

After Western contact, island men rapidly adopted Western dress, however on many islands wrap skirts of bright floral prints are worn (*lava lava*) while on some islands the wrap skirts are solid colors over which finely woven mats will be worn for special occasions. Aloha shirts developed on Hawaii in the early twentieth century, designed in the bold florals common to the islands. In twenty-first-century Hawaii, aloha shirts are daily wear for most men, and *mu'umu'u* are also common for women.

From the nineteenth-century beginnings of missionary activity in the islands, clothing has been and continues to be the focus of much debate. Missionaries wanted to do more than change the religious persuasion of islanders; they considered the adoption of Westernized dress as a symbolic manifestation of civilization.

Maintaining traditional island dress symbolizes reverence for the past and a preference for formality in the face of global change. Dress has become a focal point of conflicting values in the Pacific, as the older generation clings to old-fashioned standards of conveying modesty and respect through dress, while the youth wish to liberate themselves from the heavy legacy of the islands' missionary past.

In the Pacific, fashion activists and artists emerged in the 1990s; they use dress to illustrate issues of conflicts regarding ethnicity, globalization, and postcolonialism. In doing so, they use dress to critique their colonial pasts, and to overturn the status quo.

See also **Asia, East: History of Dress; Asia, South: History of Dress; Asia, Southeastern Mainland: History of Dress; Textiles, Southeast Asian Islands.**

BIBLIOGRAPHY

Acjhadi, Judy. "Traditional Costumes of Indonesia." *Arts of Asia* 6, no. 5 (1996): 74–79.

Arthur, Linda. "School Uniforms as Symbolic Metaphor for Competing Ideologies in Indonesia." In *Undressing Religion: Commitment and Conversion from a Cross-cultural Perspective*, pp. 201–216. Oxford: Berg, 2000.

———. *Aloha Attire: Hawaiian Dress in the Twentieth Century.* Atglen, Pa.: Schiffer Publications, 2000.

Arthur, Linda, ed. *Undressing Religion: Commitment and Conversion from a Cross-cultural Perspective.* Dress and Body Series, Oxford: Berg, 2000.

Colchester, Chloe, ed. *Clothing the Pacific.* Dress and Body Series, Oxford: Berg, 2003.

Linda B. Arthur

ASIA, SOUTHEASTERN MAINLAND: HISTORY OF DRESS Southeast Asia is recognized for its legendary aesthetic in traditional woven textiles (Gittinger and Lefferts 1992). The region of Southeast Asia includes eleven countries: Brunei, Cambodia (Khmer), Indonesia, Malaysia, Singapore, Vietnam, Myanmar (Burma), East Timor, Laos, the Philippines, and Thailand (Siam). Its geography is composed of both mainland and insular areas. In spite of the differences in language, culture, and religion, the forms of textiles and clothing are remarkably similar.

People of mainland Southeast Asia inhabit the countries of Thailand, Cambodia, Laos, Myanmar, and Vietnam. The origins and migration patterns of these people are still debated by historians and anthropologists. Minority ethnic people who settled along the border areas of the countries are referred to as hill tribes. These hill-tribe people migrated over 1,000 years ago from the southern part of China into Laos, Myanmar, Vietnam, and Thailand. Hill tribes in Southeast Asia include Karen, Hmong (Meo), Yao, Lisu, Lahu, Lawa, Palong, Khamu, Thins, Mlabri, and Akha. Each tribe has its own distinct culture, religion, language, and arts. They make their homes in the highlands, maintaining an agricultural lifestyle and preserving their way of living with only slight changes. Both lowland and highland Southeast Asian people have created rich textiles representing their unique aesthetic in fashion and clothing.

Traditional Mainland Southeast Asian Clothing

Clothing forms worn in Thailand, Laos, Myanmar, and Cambodia are quite similar. Influences from India and China, carried through trade and religious teachings, are evident in clothing styles. Archaeological evidence, mural paintings, and ancient sculpture indicate that the people

Member of Thai royal family. The traditional dress of southeastern Asia frequently reflects the influence of its early trading partners, China and India. © ALINARI ARCHIVES/CORBIS. REPRODUCED BY PERMISSION.

ment, and could also indicate social status. Typically women wore one wrapper as a covering cloth and one wrapper as decoration. The women's upper torso wrappers included breast cloths, called *pha taap*, and shoulder cloths or shawls, called *pha klum lai*. An upper torso wrapper for decoration made of pleated silk was called *sabai*.

Lower body wrappers were called *pha sin* or *pha sarong* in Thailand, and in Cambodia, *sampot*. Women usually used a piece of rectangular fabric to wrap the body, tucking in an end at the waist to form an ankle-length tube skirt. Knee-length skirts were worn for work activities such as harvesting rice. Men also wore wrapped textiles but the garment was called *pha khao ma*. Pants were also created by wrapping fabric around the body. Wrapped garments from India were the original influence for the wrapping pant. In the Sukhothai period (1238–1377 C.E.), wrapping pants, *pha chongkraben*, were adopted by Thai society from Cambodian costume.

The wrapping pant is formed with one long rectangular piece of fabric. The fabric is wrapped around the body, tied at the waist with excess fabric rolled or folded to pass between the legs from front to back where it is twisted and tucked in at the waist. A short style called *thok kamen*, typically worn by men, provided comfort and convenience when working. Women did not wear short wrappers, but typically wore garments that provided full coverage for the lower body.

Fabrics and garments symbolized social and organizational patterns that differed throughout the reign of the monarchs. A common person wore no shirt, or a shirt made of poor quality cotton with *pha chongkraben*. Fabric was plain or printed, with silk brocade worn by the wealthy. People of the upper social tiers wore elaborate, highly decorated fabrics, including brocades woven with gold or silver yarns. Special occasion fabrics—silks, satins, metallic brocades—were often imported from India and China.

High-ranking women, royalty, or nobility wore very large pieces of cloth gathered, pleated, and tucked in luxurious folds. The *pha sin* (skirt or tube skirt) was made of highly glazed cotton cloth made in India for the Thai market. The glazed finish was renewed after washing by polishing the starched cloth with a seashell (Prangwatthanakun and Neanna 1994). Children were often naked or wrapped in a length of cloth similar to adults. A child might wear a casual blouse made of woven cotton worn with a garment similar to *pha chongkraben*. Children from upper classes were adorned in elaborate, embroidered fabrics and wore ornaments such as bangles, bracelets, necklaces, ankle-lacings, and hairpins.

Cambodian men wore sarong and the women wore *sampot* with a shirt or blouse. Burmese men wore a head wrapper while wearing sarong. *Sampot* is approximately 40 inches (1 m) wide and as much as 120 inches (3 m) long. Special occasion *sampot* and sarong were woven of silk, and embroidered with gold or silver threads. *Sampot* and sarong can be worn with a long piece

in this region were weaving textiles more than 3,000 years ago, and these textiles were often used to wrap the body. Women are depicted in both mural paintings and ancient sculptures wearing ankle-length wrapped skirts. Men are depicted wearing loincloth-type garments. A wrapping cloth could also be used to form a shawl to protect and conceal the upper body (Prangwatthanakun and Neanna 1994). It appears that wrapping styles varied depending on the occasion of wear and the activity of the person.

Traditionally, Thais and Laotians most likely used cotton for everyday wear and silk for special occasions. Wrapping cloths and ties were used in different combinations to create garment ensembles. Wrapping cloths were worn extensively despite the fact that they required more fabric than tailored apparel. An advantage was that the uncut yardage was used for many purposes, including covering for warmth, repelling mosquitoes and other insects, and as a towel for bathing.

Thai and Laotian women wore upper body wrappers, while men did not cover the upper body. Women's wrappers for the upper body provided coverage or adorn-

of fabric gathered at the waist, passed between the legs, and tucked into the waistband in back like *pha chongkraben* worn in Thailand. Typically, Cambodian women wore dark colored (black, dark blue, or maroon) *sampot* with short-sleeved plain blouses. An essential part of Cambodian traditional clothing is the *karma*. It is a long scarf that can be worn around the neck and over the shoulders. It also can be wrapped turban-style around the head and loosely knotted. Cambodians living near the border of Vietnam adopted the Vietnamese conical hat style.

Vietnamese traditional clothing presents strong Chinese influence. The garment called *ao dai* (pronounced "*ao yai*" in the south and "*ao zai*" in the north) is a cut-and-sewn form of clothing instead of a wrapping cloth. *Ao dai* is a long body-hugging gown worn over trousers. The sheath is split at the sideseam hem to provide ease of movement and comfort. Girls wear pure white *ao dai* symbolizing their purity. Soft pastel shades are worn by young, unmarried women. Married women wear gowns in strong, rich colors, usually over white or black pants. Men wear *ao dai* less often, generally only for formal ceremonies such as weddings or funerals.

Southeast Asian mainland hill-tribe people live in the mountains of China, Vietnam, Myanmar, Laos, and northern Thailand. Women are skilled in weaving, using back-strap and foot-treadle looms. Some hill tribes, like Lahu, wear clothing that protects them from the cold mountain climate and fits their active lifestyle of hunting, trapping, and riding horses. Clothing forms include high-necked, long-sleeved jackets and long trousers that fit tightly at the ankles. They also produce delicate patchwork trims and unusual embroidery work and often wear plain, simple metal jewelry.

Other hill tribes, such as Hmong, embellish their clothing with detailed embroidery and silver jewelry. Women traditionally make clothing for their families from cotton or hemp. Hmong women wear pleated skirts with intricately embroidered bands of red, blue, and white. Black satin jackets provide a somber background for the embroidered motifs. Silver ornaments are worn during ceremonies devoted to the sky spirit.

Historical Influences on Southeast Asian Clothing

There are four major periods of Thai history: Sukhothai, Ayuthaya, Thonburi, and Rattanakosin. The Sukhothai period (1238–1377 C.E.) exhibited a very rich culture. The country was free from serious war, agriculture developed, and food was plentiful. In this prosperous climate, craftsmanship flourished and elaborate textile techniques and styles developed. However, garment fabrics for high-ranking people were imported from China, India, and Persia. The wrapping style, *pha chongkraben*, was adopted from Cambodia during this period.

The Ayuthaya period (1357–1767) is known as the golden period of textile trade. Ayuthaya, the ancient capital city, is located 50 miles (76 km) north of Bangkok.

Black Tai Vietnamese women. Elaborately embroidered headwraps such as these are worn by the Black Tai, an ethnic group that lives along the Red and Black Rivers in northern Vietnam. © CHRIS LISLE/CORBIS. REPRODUCED BY PERMISSION.

During this period Thailand was a major trading center. Agents from Holland, France, the Middle East, Persia, India, Japan, and insular Southeast Asia worked in the country to facilitate the textile trade. Fabrics were imported from many countries, including silk and satin from China, chintz from India, *pha poon* from Cambodia, and some fabrics from Europe. Fabrics used for high-ranking people were elaborate and often made to order. In contrast, textiles worn by common people were woven by villagers and exchanged in a barter system (Gittinger and Lefferts 1992).

During the Thonburi period (1767–1781), a short span of time between Ayuthaya and Rattanakosin, there was a decrease in the textile and fabric trade. Fashion and styles of the Thonburi period did not change substantially from the Ayuthaya period. The current period, Rattanakosin (1782 to present day), was established by King Rama I (1782–1809) in the royal house of the Chakri monarchy. King Rama V (1868–1910) initiated changes in clothing, and white, satin long-sleeved shirts became

Vietnamese family. While wrapped garments were the traditional clothing of choice on the Asian mainland for many centuries, by the early 2000s they were used primarily for special occasions, and pants, skirts, and shirts became the prevalent style. © Chris Lisle/Corbis. Reproduced by permission.

popular. Similar to other mainland Southeast Asian countries, westernization emerged as the prevalent style of clothing. Methods of making textiles and apparel gradually changed from handicraft to manufacturing. Plain, dark blue silk replaced traditional elaborate fabrics. Royalty dressed according to their position, with color indicating rank and status (1910–1925) (Gittinger and Lefferts 1992).

Southeast Asian Clothing of the Twenty-first Century

Globalization and advances in technology have affected Southeast Asian society and lifestyles. High-ranking people and nobility adopted Western, tailored garments that were seen as fashionable. Although Thailand was never colonized by a European power, Western styles of clothing were readily adopted and became fashionable. Tailored garments gradually replaced wrapping cloths as the form of everyday dress. Men adopted neckties, bowties, and suit jackets if they could afford them, even though these close fitting, restricting styles are not comfortable in the tropical climate of Southeast Asia. Women transitioned from wearing the breast cloth and *pha sin* or *pha chongkraben* to wearing blouses and skirts. The adaptation pace of Western clothing differs from country to country.

By the beginning of the twentieth century, tailored garments were prevalent. Traditional clothing gradually disappeared from metropolitan areas. In the twenty-first century traditional styles of clothing can be seen as special occasion dress or worn in rural areas as everyday wear. In urban areas men wear suit jackets, trousers, and shirts to the office and women wear pants, skirts, shirts, blouses, and dresses. As the popularity of traditional clothing forms decreased, efforts have been made to motivate people to wear traditional clothing. High quality textiles with traditional embroidered or printed motifs have been developed to be attractive and suitable for today's lifestyles and fashionable wrapping cloth styles are being developed to appeal to the modern consumer.

See also **Ao Dai; Textiles, Southeast Asian Mainland.**

BIBLIOGRAPHY

Gittinger, Mattiebelle, and Leedom Lefferts Jr. *Textiles and the Tai Experience in Southeast Asia.* Washington, D.C.: The Textile Museum, 1992.

Navikwimoon, Anak. *Ratanakosin Dress.* Bangkok, Thailand: Aksorn Sampan, 1982.

Prangwatthanakun, Songsak, and Patricia Neanna. *Thai Textiles: Threads of a Cultural Heritage.* Bangkok, Thailand: Amarin Printing, 1994.

Uraiwan Pitimaneeyakul and Karen L. LaBat

AUSTRALIAN DRESS Australia was first settled by the British in the late eighteenth century. Incoming officials, convicts, and later settlers brought with them dress practices and tastes at odds with customary attire of the indigenous inhabitants. Marking the nation's early history were confused cultural interpretations between newcomers and local indigenous peoples. Given the manner in which Australia was colonized, white Australians have persistently demonstrated strong reliance on Europe, the United Kingdom, India, the United States, and, later, China, for imported clothing, textiles, stylistic concepts, and manufacturing expertise. Somewhat surprisingly the most commanding influence on early Australian fashion was from France rather than Great Britain, with a continuing record of Parisian influence on dress and millinery from at least the 1820s until the late 1950s. At the same time the sleek, functional sports and leisure wear of the United States has been a significant source of inspiration for Australian ready-to-wear designers. It is a mistake, however, to regard Australian dress as a provincial version of other countries, although there is an element of truth to this view.

While one can point to no more than a few examples of recognizably Australian garments, the identity of Australians is expressed by clothing beyond this, in a complex mix of sometimes quite subtle elements and associated behaviors that challenge accepted understandings of class. Effects of climate certainly play a part, as does the early influence of life on the land and the goldfields. But even characteristically Australian garments, such as the all-weather Dryzabone coat, are not necessarily worn nationwide; there has always been a regional component to clothes in Australia, plus a distinctive metropolitan and rural divide. Close ties with Asia and migrants including

COMMENTARY ON THE DRESS OF MELBOURNE WOMEN

"I fancy that the French *modistes* manufacture a certain style of attire for the Australian taste. . . . It is a compound of the *cocotte* and the American" (Twopeny, p. 75).

Greeks and Muslims, with their own customary practices, add further dimensions to the picture of Australian dress. The attire of indigenous peoples, many who are disadvantaged and live in areas remote from cities, with limited capacity to purchase new clothing, add further layers of complexity to the overall picture of what people have worn, and do wear, in Australia.

Scholarship on Dress

Until the 1990s, the study of dress and fashion in Australia was marked by limited scholarship, one reason being the cultural disparagement of a practice traditionally associated with women's interests. Harsh environmental conditions in rural areas, especially dominated by men, meant fashionable dress was often given a low priority. Australian men have historically prided themselves on a lack of attention to the finer details of appearance, regarding this as incompatible with masculinity. While this conservatism shifted markedly with the expansion of urban living, and an increasingly materialistic social outlook after the 1980s, disparagement of clothing seems to have flowed on to a general unease about the subject of fashion itself. With some notable exceptions, such as the Powerhouse Museum in Sydney, museums and art galleries have shown little sustained interested in collecting Australian dress, especially everyday clothing. The collecting of penal clothing is one exception. All of this has lent a lack of legitimacy to the subject, something slowly being remedied as Australia gains confidence in the products of its own fashion industry and the showcasing of dress by its movie stars and sportspeople.

Dress and the First Australians

While colonial settlers regarded clothing as a means of displaying power and prestige, the same is not true of indigenous Australians. Variously accepting and disavowing the Western clothing system, their concerns have been and are focused on community affiliation, ceremonial adornment, or political resistance. In customary life, indigenous peoples went largely unclothed, apart from kangaroo and opossum skin cloaks, marking their bodies with earth pigments, and adorning them with accessories of local fibers, shells, bark, and leaves. However, government officials, missionaries, and pastoralists sought to impose Western dress on those with whom they came in contact, using it as a technique of acculturation and frequently as a reward system. Enforced use of European dress contributed to the decline in the techniques of indigenous people for making their own garments and almost certainly contributed to their early health problems. In the early 2000s, most indigenous people wear Western-style clothing, although in remote areas, regional patterns of T-shirt, dress, and scarf-wearing are evident. Some items of Western dress, such as the Akubra hat and the knitted cap (beanie), have been incorporated into indigenous cultural tradition.

From the 1960s, the Australian government encouraged indigenous peoples to make and market their own fabric, T-shirt, and jewelry designs as a way of achieving self-sufficiency. From the 1980s, some practitioners became fashion designers in their own right like Bronwyn Bancroft, Lenore Dembski, and Robyn Caughlan, the first indigenous designer to show a ready-to-wear line at the Mercedes Australian Fashion Week in 2003. The work of these designers, stressing bold textile designs, offers an interesting counterpoint to modern mainstream fashion. In other examples, the successful company Balarinji, and European designers like Jenny Kee, Linda Jackson, and Peter Morrissey, have and do cooperate cross-culturally, in the latter case using textiles designed by the indigenous artist Jacinta Numina Waugh.

Signaling Australian Identity

Since colonial times, Australian dress has been marked by strong regional differences. The dress of Sydney tends to be stylistically closer to American, with Melbourne more British and conservative, and subtropical cities like Brisbane and Perth favoring brighter, casual clothing affected mostly by the prevailing climate. Although these differences cannot be termed Australian per se, regionalism is one way that Australians define themselves. The other defining characteristic that emerged during colonial times was a supposed egalitarianism in men's dress. Associated with the dress of experienced rural "old hands," it consisted of rough rural and goldfields' attire quite different from conventional urban clothing. This comprised cabbage tree (palm-leaf) hats or slouch felt hats, later the Akubra hat, smock frocks, checked shirts, and hardwearing moleskin trousers and boots. A mythology has grown up around this masculine clothing, deeming it to be quintessentially Australian, though this has not been the case with women's dress. Companies, including RM Williams and Blundstone boots, continue to foster this mythology, and sell versions of their clothing worldwide, but nowadays to both sexes and not solely for rural wear.

A taste for Australian motifs and indigenous color schemes in dress and swimwear textiles was evident from the 1940s. But it was the 1970s that marked a particular watershed in the history of recognizably Australian fashions. Jenny Kee and partner Linda Jackson, who set up the Flamingo Park boutique in Sydney in 1973, initiated a novel style of art clothing that, among other romantic influences, later paid tribute to the native flora and fauna of Australia. It was in debt to the designs of indigenous peoples with whom they collaborated, or some would say exploited. The following decade saw a number of Australian companies achieve a degree of success in the international market. These included Coogi and Country Road, with its superior quality clothing in "natural" earthy colors, promoting so-called rural values, with outlets in the United States by 1985. The popularity of colorful, locally inspired Australiana designs, at their peak in the late 1980s, declined for everyday wear at the start of the next decade with the onset of more minimalist

tastes. Only vestiges of this linger on, mainly in garments destined for the tourist market.

Class and Social Position

From the early years of colonization, a noticeable tension was evident in the ways settler Australians expressed social position through dress. Colonial history is rich in accounts of mistaken social identity. Some of this tension arose from problems strangers had in decoding signs of class. It also stemmed from a prevailing myth of classlessness, coupled with a correspondingly intense awareness of social position characteristic of a small population. Some of the supposed lack of class differences related to informality in social interactivities and the dominance of the open-air lifestyle; other reasons pointed to the small, sometimes inward-looking population. Yet contemporary Australians of both sexes could be said to swing from a general disinterest in high fashion, to something more like pretentious investment in stylish, even vulgar visibility, originally the result of newfound money. For instance, Australians exhibit exuberance in clothes for special events, such as weddings and attendance at race meetings, even for leisure, but at the same time favor informality of clothing and dressing down. Some of the exuberance stems from a wayward form of "larrikinism" across both sexes. This is chiefly an Australian term meaning a kind of rowdy, non-conformism, complicated by a self-conscious disinterest in accepted routines of fashionable dress and behavior.

Clothing and Fashion Industries

Although always dependent on imported attire and fabrics, especially high-grade goods, a local clothing, footwear, and textile industry was set up in Eastern Australia soon after first settlement. These industries have been subject to a persistently troubled history, although until the mid-twentieth century, Australia sustained a sound reputation for manufacturing good-quality, comfortable clothing and textiles. Immediately after World War II, local wool fabrics were successfully promoted, initially by the Australian Wool Board and later the Australian Wool Corporation, but the situation has remained endemically volatile at the quality end of the fashion spectrum. While a fashion industry of sorts emerged by the early twentieth century, the real high point for the rag trade occurred in the decade immediately following World War II.

However, from the 1960s, Australia's textile and clothing industries started to lose what market share they had; coupled with protectionism, the mainstream industry, with some exceptions like the Prue Acton and Trent Nathan labels, began a serious decline. Chronic lack of capital, a small population, lack of ability to market high-volume goods and the steady lifting of tariffs from the late 1970s, made Australia's industries less and less competitive with imports, especially those from China. The latter became the country's main source of clothing by

Eugene Von Guerard, Black Hill. This 1984 watercolor is indicative of the clothing style of early Australians, where fashion was eclipsed by function. Until the late twentieth century, most Australian garments tended toward the masculine and unremarkable. LA TROBE PICTURE COLLECTION, THE STATE LIBRARY OF VICTORIA. REPRODUCED BY PERMISSION.

the 1980s. The decline in the local industry persisted. Following the worst clothing retail sales on record in 1996, the Mercedes Australian Fashion Week was inaugurated in Sydney, and the following year the first Melbourne Fashion Festival. Both were attempts to showcase Australian products and draw international buyers. While neither venture has had overwhelming success, a number of fresh, new Australian designers made a strong impact in Europe and the United States in the mid-1990s. These include Collette Dinnigan, Asian-born Akira Isogawa, who made his debut in 1996, the edgy clothing of Sass and Bide (launched in 1999), Easton Pearson, with its fusion designs combining traditional Indian and African cultures with contemporary ideas, and Morrissey (who launched solo in 1997). Despite these successes, Australian fashion remains somewhat marginalized, with its identity still under negotiation and overseas acceptance sporadic. In fact, competitive global marketing, the impression that the country is far removed from major centers of style, and its seasons out of step with the Northern Hemisphere has generally exacerbated rather than eased the industry's problems.

Leisurewear

Australia is not surprisingly at its most successful in the areas of leisure and beachwear. A local swimwear industry can be identified early in the twentieth century, soon reinforced by the presence of American swimwear manufacturers like Jantzen and Cole of California. In 1928, the Speedo label was created, and this company went on to be one of the most successful brands of Australian swimwear, exporting to the United States by the late 1950s. Many successful mainstream designers of swimwear became household names like Brian Rochford, the Gold Coast's Paula Stafford, and Nicole Zimmermann. Perhaps more significantly, innovative youth-oriented surf-wear companies who produce brightly colored, fun-loving designs like Rip Curl, Billabong, Mambo (with its bitingly satirical designs established in 1984 by Dare Jennings), and Quiksilver have gone on to represent Australian style most successfully in the international arena. Indeed, a major ingredient in the pervasive view of Australia as an outdoor nation, free from constraints, is a glowing tanned body, enhanced by attractive swimwear.

See also **Ethnic Dress; Swimwear.**

BIBLIOGRAPHY

Fletcher, Marion. *Costume in Australia, 1788–1901.* Melbourne, Australia: Oxford University Press, 1984. First serious account of colonial dress but with an emphasis on bourgeois fashions.

Joel, Alexandra. *Parade: The Story of Fashion in Australia*. Sydney, Australia: HarperCollins, 1998. Text focused on period styles in high fashion. Of limited theoretical use. Revised, augmented edition.

Maynard, Margaret. *Fashioned from Penury: Dress as Cultural Practice in Colonial Australia*. Cambridge, U.K.: Cambridge University Press, 1994. First academic study of colonial dress across all classes.

———. "Indigenous Dress." In *Oxford Companion to Aboriginal Art and Culture*. Edited by Sylvia Kleinert and Margo Neale. South Melbourne, Australia: Oxford University Press, 2000. First nonanthropological account of the dress of indigenous Australians.

———. *Out of Line: Australian Women and Style*. Sydney, Australia: University of New South Wales Press, 2001. First comprehensive text on twentieth-century women's dress and the fashion industry in Australia, including an account of indigenous designers.

Twopeny, R. E. N. *Town Life in Australia 1883*. Sydney, Australia: Sydney University Press, 1973.

Margaret Maynard

AVEDON, RICHARD Richard Avedon (b. 1923) was one of the most important and prolific photographers of the second half of the twentieth century, and in the eyes of many photography and fashion specialists, he was the most important fashion photographer of all time. In a career spanning sixty years he showed himself capable of almost constant stylistic reinvention, yet in retrospect his oeuvre also demonstrated a remarkable coherence and strength that far surpassed the narrow confines of fashion photography. He was acknowledged by his peers for his superb work as early as 1950, when he won the Highest Achievement Medal of the Art Directors Club in New York. Only eight years later he was named by *Popular Photography* magazine as one of the ten most important photographers in the world. By the end of the twentieth century, having garnered handfuls of honorary degrees, lifetime achievement awards, and other prestigious prizes, Avedon was identified by the *Photo District News* as "the most influential photographer of the past twenty years." These successes were due in no small measure to his acute sensitivity to the social and artistic revolutions in American culture. As the historian Nancy Hall-Duncan observed in 1979, "This sense of timing and flexibility—representing the desires of our society and reflecting its mood with uncanny sympathy—was Avedon's forte from the start of his career." This talent also helps to explain why he was never displaced by a younger pretender, as happened to so many of his rivals. John Durniak once reported in *Time* magazine that an admiring colleague considered Avedon "the white mechanical rabbit that all other photographers tried to catch" but never could. Even allowing for the hyperbolic language of the fashion industry itself, which anointed him the king of fashion photography, Avedon could claim a towering record of achievement.

Richard Avedon was born in New York City, the son of Russian Jewish immigrants who owned a department store in Manhattan. His school years revealed a marked literary aptitude: he was coeditor with James Baldwin of the De Witt Clinton High School literary magazine, and he was named poet laureate of the New York City high schools in 1941. A brief period of study in philosophy at Columbia University was followed by two years in the U.S. Merchant Marine (1942–1944), after which Avedon undertook intensive visual studies with Alexey Brodovitch at the Design Laboratory of the New School for Social Research. New York had everything the ambitious young man wanted: "theater, movies, music, dance." Part of Avedon's visual education had come from his love of photography. As a teenager he had decorated his room with the work of the masters; as a mature professional, he benefited from the lessons of his predecessors. This keen awareness of the accomplishments of previous artists in the field, and a philosophical bent that allowed him to consider the medium of photography in abstract as well as practical terms, encouraged him to explore the full gamut of the medium's possibilities. For example, switching to a large-format camera after he had started his career in fashion photography with the more flexible Rolleiflex made him realize that throwing the background of a shot out of focus reduced the sum of detail and created "an ambiguous narrative relationship between the knowable (what's sharp), and the unknowable (what's blurred)" (Thurman and Avedon).

Avedon's arrival on the scene coincided with the final years of the dominance of haute couture. In 1945 Carmel Snow invited him to join *Harper's Bazaar* as staff photographer, where his mentor Brodovitch was already working as art director. Avedon thus stepped into the shoes (but not the footsteps) of the great neoclassicist image-maker George Hoyningen-Huene, who was convinced high fashion was dead. Hoyningen-Huene greeted his young rival disdainfully with the phrase, "Too bad … Too late!" It was this atmosphere of ennui that Snow wished to dispel in and with her magazine. The visionary editor wanted to reinvigorate the Parisian luxury business by opening the vast American market to it, and she needed an interpreter of French taste who was less aloof than Hoyningen-Huene—someone who could temper the classicism of French couture with American zest.

It was not surprising that Avedon always acknowledged the Hungarian photojournalist-turned-fashion photographer Martin Munkacsi, rather than the patrician Hoyningen-Huene, as a key influence on his style. Munkacsi was a pioneer of the out-of-doors realistic fashion photograph, a major stimulus to Avedon's own approach, although the fact that Avedon skillfully combined the exuberance of outdoor photography with the static tradition of the studio showed that he had absorbed lessons from the Baron Adolf de Meyer, Edward Steichen, and George Hoyningen-Huene as well.

For the next four decades Avedon's name was synonymous with the best of fashion photography. Between 1947 and 1984 he photographed the Paris collections for either *Harper's Bazaar* or *Vogue*, and he worked exclusively for the latter from 1966 to 1990. Avedon preferred to work repeatedly with the same models, establishing a rapport that, in his words, was "built from sitting to sitting and from season to season." Whether the sitter was Suzy Parker wearing Gres, Dovima wearing Dior—"Dovima Among the Elephants" (1955) is arguably Avedon's most famous photograph—or Jean Shrimpton and Veruschka dressed in psychedelic whimsies, the models wore the clothes as if they were born to them. Avedon's earliest photographs showed women dancing, partying, skipping about from one lively *boîte* to another on the arm of debonair escorts, the images always striking a careful balance between factual information about the dresses and impressions of how the women looked—and more important, it was implied, felt—wearing them. Despite the seemingly spontaneous character of the images, however, the photographer carefully researched his outdoor and indoor settings before he undertook the sittings.

Avedon's intense early commitment inevitably took its toll. After twenty years in fashion photography, he decided that there was "too much narcissism and disenchantment" in the work. The outdoor images gave way to a harsher minimalist aesthetic that was even described as "cruel," the fabrication of which was possible only in the studio. "I've worked out a series of no's," Avedon wrote in 1994, " … no to exquisite light, no to apparent compositions, no to the seduction of poses or narrative. And all these no's force me to the yes. I have a white background. I have the person I am interested in and the thing that happens between us." If he continued to work in the arena of fashion, it was to support his family and his "art"—namely, portrait photography.

Avedon's sitters essentially comprised a gallery of the rich, the famous, and the powerful. All were treated equally, in such a way that fellow photographer Henri Cartier-Bresson could call them "inhabitants of an Avedon world." Avedon's twentieth-century gallery has been acknowledged as one of the greatest projects of its kind—in historian and curator Maria Hambourg's words, "a gallery of modern souls as intense and vivid as any ever achieved." Yet somehow, the portraits in the aggregate comprised Avedon's self-portrait, or as Thomas Hess wrote, Avedon seemed always to be "trying to climb into his image." After 1990, his portraits of the past and the present were regular features of the *New Yorker* magazine. Avedon's work was also exhibited in such prestigious institutions as the Metropolitan Museum of Art, the Smithsonian Institution, the Museum of Modern Art in New York, the Minneapolis Institute of Fine Arts, the Seibu Museum in Tokyo, the Museum "La Caixa" in Barcelona, and the University Art Museum in Berkeley, California.

Richard Avedon and model. Avedon's prestigious career spanned sixty years, during which he garnered numerous awards and was referred to by many as the "king of fashion photographers." THE LIBRARY OF CONGRESS. PUBLIC DOMAIN.

See also **Celebrities; Fashion Museums and Collections; Fashion Photography; Hoyningen-Huene, George; Vogue.**

BIBLIOGRAPHY

Avedon, Richard. "The Family." Special bicentennial issue of *Rolling Stone*, 21 October 1976.

———. *Photographs 1947–1977*. New York: Farrar, Straus and Giroux, 1978.

———. *In the American West 1979–1984*. New York: Harry N. Abrams, Inc., 1985.

———. *Evidence 1944–1994*. New York: Random House, 1994.

———. *Portraits*. New York: Metropolitan Museum of Art and Harry N. Abrams, Inc., 2002.

Avedon, Richard, and Truman Capote. *Observations*. New York: Simon and Schuster, 1959.

Avedon, Richard, and Arbus Doon. *The Sixties*. New York: Random House, 1999.

Baldwin, James, and Richard Avedon. *Nothing Personal*. New York: Dell Publishing Company, 1964.

Thurman, Judith, and Richard Avedon. *Richard Avedon: Made in France*. San Francisco: Fraenkel Gallery, 2001.

William Ewing

B

BALENCIAGA, CRISTÓBAL Born in 1895 in Guetaria (Getaria), a small fishing village on the tempestuous northern coast of Spain, Cristóbal Balenciaga Eisaguirre (1895–1972) was to become, in his own lifetime, the most famous Spanish fashion designer of his generation. He died in the mellower climate of Jávea, on the eastern coast of Spain, twelve years after receiving the Légion d'honneur for services to the French fashion industry and only four years after closing down his prestigious business in Paris. The contrast between Balenciaga's places of birth and death offers a touching analogy to his journey from rags to riches or, at the very least, from a relatively obscure, fairly modest, and extremely hardworking provincial background to the sunny prominence of an established position in international fashion. While he gained considerable material comfort, he did not lose his work ethic. He owned a flat in central Paris, an estate near Orléans (France), and a substantial house in Igueldo, near Guetaria. He was able to fill his homes with collections of decorative and fine arts and, from time to time, with friends from different walks of life.

Balenciaga evidently achieved this major change in circumstance, initially, through the patronage of a member of the Spanish aristocracy, the marquesa de Casa Torres, who recognized his talent at sewing—a skill learned from his seamstress mother—and apprenticed him to a tailor in fashionable San Sebastián (Donostia). From this training, he went on to become chief designer in a local dressmaking establishment, before opening his own house in Madrid. Armed with financial backing from a fellow Basque, he subsequently successfully established, directed, and designed for the Parisian couture house that bore his name. At the same time, he maintained three high-class dressmaking establishments in Spain, in San Sebastián, Barcelona, and Madrid. They functioned under the label Eisa, an abbreviated form of his mother's patronymic.

Balenciaga's formative experiences in Spain were fundamental to both his design practice and his ultimate move to Paris. His tailoring apprenticeship gave him a mastery of cut and construction and an obsession with perfection of fit. He was one of the few couturiers who was capable of "cutting material, assembling a creation and sewing it by hand," as even his archrival Coco Chanel acknowledged (Miller, p. 14). His fascination with certain simple forms (the manipulation of circles, semicircles, and tunics) may well have derived from familiarity with the cut of the ecclesiastical vestments and clerical dress so common in Spain. His use of certain colors (black, shades of gray, earth colors, brilliant reds, fuchsia, and purple), certain forms of decoration (heavy embroidery and braid), and certain fabrics (lace used voluptuously in flounces and heavy woolens or new synthetics "sculpted" into extraordinary shapes) owed much to the aesthetic of Spanish regional dress and to the drapery and costume depicted in Spanish painting and sculpture from 1500 to 1900. His early working experience in San Sebastián alerted him to the dominance of Paris in international women's fashion, as one of his responsibilities was to travel to the center of couture to the seasonal collections, to make drawings of models that might subsequently be translated into garments for Spanish clients. In this second, transitional, stage of his career, he was copyist or translator rather than originator of designs.

Historical Context

While the reasons for Balenciaga's departure from Spain in 1935 at the age of forty, and his subsequent establishment in Paris, are not clear, it is probable that the commercial and political situation in Europe contributed to his move. In the 1930s Paris was the fashion mecca not only for ambitious designers but also for the cosmopolitan women they dressed. The French government fostered couture and its ancillary trades because they were important national export industries. Subsidies encouraged the use of French textiles, and textile manufacturers supplied short runs of rare fabrics for couture collections. The trade organization Chambre Syndicale de la couture parisienne guided the regulation of conditions of employment, training for prospective couturiers, and the efficient coordination of the twice-yearly showings of all couturiers' collections. This arrangement made the trade desirable, as private clients and commercial buyers from department stores and wholesale companies from other parts of Europe, the United States, and Japan could plan their visits in advance and make the most of their time in Paris. Before World War II, no other country boasted such a highly organized and prestigious fashion system, a fact of which Balenciaga must have been aware as early as about 1920.

107

Woman modeling Balenciaga coat and dress. This ensemble smartly conveys several Balenciaga trademarks, such as elegance and grandeur, monochromatic colors, and a perfect fit. HENRY CLARKE/VOGUE © 1995 CONDÉ NAST PUBLICATIONS, INC. REPRODUCED BY PERMISSION.

That Balenciaga chose to "defect" some fifteen years later was probably linked to the increasingly difficult political situation in Spain, a state of affairs that did not bode well for those who made their living from fashion. In 1931 the Spanish monarchy fell, and a period of uncertainty preceded the Spanish Civil War (1936–1939). Balenciaga lost his main clientele of the 1920s, the Spanish royal family and the aristocracy who summered in San Sebastián and wintered in Madrid. Consequently, he

closed down his branch in the north of Spain just after it opened. The advent of war did not improve his prospects, so his move to Paris (via London) was timely. By 1939, when he reopened his houses in Spain, he had made a reputation in Paris, gaining an international clientele that far outstripped the captive following he had had in Spain.

During World War II, he moved back and forth between the two countries, keeping a connection with his familial and cultural roots and control of his modest fashion empire. At the end of the war he continued this practice. Even when he spent long periods in Paris, he did not lose contact with Spaniards, as both his business and home were in the district frequented by Spanish émigrés, many of his business associates or employees were Spanish, and his friends included his fellow countrymen the artists Pablo Picasso, Joan Miró, and Pablo Palazuelo.

The Businesses

Haute couture businesses are secretive about their internal workings, if not their ambitions, and often it is the design records rather than the accounts that survive. In the absence of financial or administrative archives for the house of Balenciaga, it is possible to reconstruct its organization and strategy only through its public registration, its rich design archive, and limited oral and written testimony from the salon, some of the more illustrious members of its clientele, and a few of the designer's colleagues or pupils. Tradition and continuity were particular characteristics of the house, in terms of its internal structure and workforce, its design output and quality of production, and its maintenance of a faithful and prestigious customer base. Gimmickry was avoided at all costs—even in the postwar period of consumerism, when many of Balenciaga's competitors engaged freely in a variety of new sales tactics, including the development of ranges of ready-to-wear clothing, accessories, and numerous fragrances and the use of advertising.

As was relatively common in Parisian couture, Balenciaga was a limited company, in the form of a partnership between Balenciaga himself, his hat designer and friend Vladzio Zawrorowski (d. 1946), and Nicolas Bizcarrondo, the Basque businessman who provided the initial capital. Balenciaga's previous success in Spain and the existence of three houses there (albeit that they were in limbo in 1937) might well account for Bizcarrondo's faith in Balenciaga and his willingness to support him. Established in 1937 on an initial investment of Fr 100,000, the value of Balenciaga's couture house rose to Fr 2 million in 1946 and to Fr 30 million in 1960. Injections of funding coincided with expansion in its activities. The investment reflected the size—large by couture standards but small relative to industrial enterprises before or after World War II.

The structure of the design house followed to the letter a traditional couture model, conforming without difficulty to the new haute couture regulations implemented in 1947. Throughout Balenciaga's reign, the seat of business was at 10 avenue Georges V—a suitable location in the golden triangle of Parisian luxury production. This six-story building served all functions—aesthetic, craft, commercial, and administrative. Discretion was the key to both the exterior and interior, with little overt reference to the house's sales function. On the outside, classical pillars flanked the shop windows, which never contained any hint of clothes for sale but rather pretended to a certain artistry.

On the ground floor the entrance was through the boutique (shop), which stocked accessories, such as gloves, foulards, and the perfumes Le Dix (1947), La Fuite des Heures (1948), and Quadrille (1955). This floor had the appearance of the hallway of a grand house, with a black-and-white tiled floor, rich carpets, and dark wooden and gilded furniture and fittings. On the first floor, reached by an elevator lined in red Cordoban leather and studded with brass pins, were the salon and fitting rooms, decorated in 1937 in the fashionable Parisian taste of the day, with upholstered settees, curvaceous free-standing ashtrays, and mirrored doors. Presided over by Madame Renée, this floor was home to the *vendeuses* (saleswomen), who greeted their own specially designated clients, consulted with them about their vestmental needs and social calendar, introduced them to the models that might suit them (specially paraded by a house mannequin), and then watched over their three fittings once they had placed their orders. Above the salons were the workshops where the clothes were cut and constructed; only occasionally were certain garments farmed out for special treatment, for example, to the embroidery firms of Bataille, Lesage, or Rébé for embellishment. Higher still in the building were the offices occupied by the administration.

Expansion and continuity. Workshop space expanded beyond the four workshops set up in 1937 (two for dresses, one for suits, and one for dresses and suits). During the war (1941) Balenciaga added two millinery ateliers; then, after the war (1947–1948), another two workshops for dresses and one for suits; and, finally, in 1955, another for dresses, bringing the total to ten. Just before the opening of the final workshop, Balenciaga's employees numbered 318. In the scheme of things, Balenciaga valued his cutters more highly than his workshop heads, paying the former 20–30 percent more than the latter between 1953 and 1954. Given the reputation of the house for high-quality tailoring, this prioritization is not surprising, nor is the fact that skilled employees in positions of trust remained with the firm over a prolonged period. In the case of the known workshop heads, the majority stayed for twenty to thirty years. Moreover, "new" senior staff members seem to have arrived from the Spanish houses, possibly because Balenciaga could rely on their standards and experience.

Client Base

Continuity was also an aspect of the client base, satisfying Balenciaga's firm belief that women should find and remain with the dressmaker who best served their needs and understood their personal styles. Many private and professional clients patronized the house for thirty years. At his height, Balenciaga showed his collections to two hundred wholesale buyers and made to measure about 2,325 garments per annum for private clients. Some of the latter bought as many as fifty to eighty items per year.

They made their choices from the four hundred models he created, a number in line with the output of other top couturiers of the time.

Major department stores bought Balenciaga models with particular customers in mind and then reproduced as closely as possible the couture experience in their salons, offering fashion shows, personal advice on customers' social and practical needs, and high standards of fitting and making. At different times these firms included Lydia Moss, Fortnum and Mason, and Harrods in London; Hattie Carnegie, Henri Bendel, Bloomingdale's, Saks Fifth Avenue, and Bergdorf Goodman in New York; I. Magnin in Los Angeles and San Francisco; and Holt Renfrew in Toronto. In contrast, wholesalers bought with batch production in mind, spreading Balenciaga styles through their adaptation of toiles from the house. The wholesalers who attended Balenciaga's shows included many members of the London Model House Group, the elite of ready-to-wear. For them, every model had about eight to ten derivatives, each of which was reproduced four hundred to five hundred times. Some Balenciaga models, however, were considered too complex for reproduction, whether in department stores or factories, and too outré for the tastes of more conservative clients.

Balenciaga's loyal band of private clients belonged to the wealthiest titled and untitled families across the globe and embraced both professional women and socialites. Some customers combined buying from him with purchases from other made-to-measure or ready-made sources or found his garments in special secondhand outlets. His true devotees developed a close relationship, even friendship, with "The Master," who provided for their every need: some daughters followed their mothers into the house, among them the future Queen Fabiola of Belgium, daughter of his patron, the marquesa de Casa Torres; Sonsoles, daughter of his most consistent client, the marquesa de Llanzol; and General Francisco Franco's wife and granddaughter, whose wedding dress was the last designed by Balenciaga. Others grew into Balenciaga through familiarity with his house in Paris, for example, Mona Bismarck, widow of Harrison Williams, one of the wealthiest men in America, who consistently acquired her wardrobe from him every season for twenty years, even the shorts she wore for yachting or gardening. Perhaps, like Barbara "Bobo" Rockefeller, she believed that a Balenciaga dress gave its wearer a sense of security. A cheaper way of buying made-to-measure Balenciaga fashions was open to those who knew his Spanish operations, where labor costs were lower and local fabrics sometimes were substituted for those used in Paris (and a favorable exchange rate prevailed for most foreign visitors). The film star Ava Gardner, a regular visitor to Spain in the 1950s, patronized Eisa, for example, as well as the Parisian house.

Balenciaga's final—and perhaps most intriguing—client was Air France. In 1966 the world's biggest airline asked him to design air stewardesses' summer and winter uniforms to a brief that probably appealed to him: "elegance, freedom of movement, adaptability to sudden changes of climate, and maintenance of a smart appearance even after a long journey" (Miller pp. 57–59). His experience of dealing with the soigné jet set and his fashion philosophy of practicality prepared him well for this request.

Fashion Philosophy and Signature Designs
Balenciaga was reticent in talking about himself and his craft, so the nature of his business, the identity of his clients, and actual surviving garments and designs are necessary to supplement his occasional observations about his fashion philosophy. Evolution rather than revolution, elegance and decorum rather than novelty and flash-in-the-pan fashion, practicality, wearability, and "breathability" were guiding principles in his design and, no doubt, suited a discerning, largely mature clientele. At his apogee in the 1950s and 1960s Balenciaga created designs that bear witness to his keen attention to the effects achieved by combining different colors and textures. Often the intrinsic qualities of fabrics, whether traditional woolens and silks or innovative synthetics, led the design process, as Balenciaga pondered their potential in tailored, draped, or sculpted forms. He was prepared to forgo the French government subsidy, granted to couturiers whose collections comprised 90 percent French-made textiles, in order to acquire the best-quality and most groundbreaking textiles from whichever part of Europe they came.

Balenciaga gradually honed his design in daywear, building out from the base of apparently traditional tailored suits with neat, fitted bodies and sleeves that sat perfectly at the shoulder into experimentation that led to the minimalist "no-seam coat" (1961), crafted from a single piece of fabric by the artful use of darts and tucks. This garment hung loose on the body and embodied the culmination of a range of loose or semifitted lines in various garments that probably constituted Balenciaga's most important contribution to fashion. These designs emerged gradually during the 1950s, flattering different female figures (mature and youthful) and allowing the wearer to move easily. The tunic (1955), chemise or sack (1957), and Empire styles (1958) drew attention away from the natural waist through the creation of a tubular line or the emphasis that a bloused back laid on the hip line or that a high waist laid on the bust. Suit jackets were judiciously cut, and their matching skirts were often gathered slightly into the waistband at the front to accommodate middle-age spread. Three-quarter- and seven-eighth-length sleeves and necklines set away from the neck sought to flatter the wrists and the neck, both graceful at any age. They also proved practical for busy lifestyles. In the 1960s a range of different lengths and fits of jackets and coats featured in Balenciaga's collections, from the very fitted to the loose.

Similar paring down is evident in Balenciaga's cocktail and evening wear; so, too, is a taste for the grandeur and elaboration appropriate to the purpose. For these gowns he drew on historical and non-European sources and sought his own version of modernism. Initially, for all their apparent ease, these dresses were often built on a corset base with boning, an understructure that was not obvious under the complex confections of drapery, puffs, and flounces popular in the 1950s. By the 1960s, however, shapes simplified and did not cling to or mold the body. The contrast between the slim black sheaths of the late 1940s and early 1950s and the outstanding models of gazar, zibeline, faille, and matelassé of the 1960s is absolute. The former took their drama from the swathes of contrasting satin in jewel colors that were attached at waist or neckline and could be draped to the wearer's fancy. The latter relied for their éclat on the sculptural simplicity of their lines and the substance of the fabric rather than on artificial flowers, feathers, or polychrome embroidery. While three-dimensional decoration was not obsolete, the shapes to which it adhered became tunic-like. The frills, ballooning skirts, and sack backs had given way to a more austere, almost monastic aesthetic.

Importance and Legacy

The fashion cognoscenti, from couturiers to journalists, still accord Balenciaga the laurel of the "designers' designer." They use his name to evoke certain standards in fashion—evolution in style, ease of dress, and meticulous attention to detail (visible or otherwise). Balenciaga's former apprentices (André Courrèges and Emanuel Ungaro), colleagues (Hubert de Givenchy), and aficionados (Oscar de la Renta and Paco Rabanne) have inherited and propagated certain elements of his philosophy and style. In the last quarter of the twentieth century approximately eight major exhibitions worldwide perpetuated his fame, many facilitated by the archivist of the house of Balenciaga, owned by Bogart perfumes from 1987 to 2001 and since then by the Gucci Group (91 percent) and the in-house designer, Nicolas Ghesquière (9 percent). Ghesquière's widely acknowledged talent and vitality revived the fortunes of Balenciaga in the late 1990s, and by the early 2000s the designer himself had begun to explore the riches of the archives and appreciate more fully the shadow in which he labored. He was quick to draw parallels between his own work and that of the "The Master," although couture represents a tiny element of his output.

In Spain, Balenciaga's reputation contributed to initiatives to encourage the Spanish fashion industry: in 1987 the Spanish Ministry of Industry and Energy named the first (and only) national prize for fashion design after him and in 2000 injected $3.2 million into the charitable foundation set up in Guetaria in his name. The overall objective of this trust is "to foster, spread and emphasize the transcendence, importance, and prominence that Don Cristóbal Balenciaga has had in the world of fashion," (www.fundacionbalenciaga.com) an objective that is meant to be achieved through the construction and development of a museum in Guetaria, the establishment of an international center for design training, the foundation of a research and documentation center, the publication of a fashion periodical, and the development of touring exhibitions about Balenciaga, fashion design, and haute couture.

With such sustained efforts at maintaining Balenciaga's reputation and values, his impact on fashion is bound to survive, disseminated through a range of techniques from which the reserved and publicity-shy Balenciaga himself might well have recoiled. The ramifications of his dedication to fashion for that once small fishing town of Guetaria are likely to be impressive.

See also **Chanel, Gabrielle (Coco); Courrèges, André; Ecclesiastical Dress; Haute Couture; Paris Fashion; Spanish Dress.**

BIBLIOGRAPHY

Ballard, Bettina. *In My Fashion*. New York: D. McKay Company, 1960. A contemporary fashion editor's autobiography, which incorporates substantial portraits of many Parisian couturiers, including Balenciaga, whom the author knew well.

Beaton, Cecil. *The Glass of Fashion*. Garden City, N.Y.: Doubleday, 1954. The fashion world seen through the eyes of the society fashion photographer Cecil Beaton, a friend of Balenciaga's.

Bertin, Célia. *Paris à la Mode: A Voyage of Discovery*. Translated by Marjorie Deans. London: V. Gollancz, 1956. A contemporary view of haute couture and its main protagonists.

De Marly, Diana. *The History of Haute Couture, 1850–1950*. New York: Holmes and Meier, 1980. Classic overview of the development of French haute couture.

Jouve, Marie-Andrée. *Balenciaga*. Text by Jacqueline Demornex. New York: Rizzoli International, 1989. The first major account of Balenciaga from the archivist of the house, with superb illustrations.

———. *Balenciaga*. New York: Universal/Vendome, 1997. A brief and useful introduction to Balenciaga, largely through images but also containing new data on clients.

Latour, Anny. *Kings of Fashion*. Translated by Mervyn Savill. New York: Coward-McCann, 1958. A contemporary fashion journalist's investigation of haute couture and its main protagonists.

Menkes, Suzy. "Temple to a Monk of Fashion: Museum to Open in Basque Designer's Birthplace." *International Herald Tribune*, 23 May 2000. An overview of the Fundación Balenciaga in Guetaria.

Miller, Lesley Ellis. *Cristóbal Balenciaga*. New York: Holmes and Meier, 1993. A historically contextualized account of the man and his background, clothes, clients, business, and legacy.

Palmer, Alexandra. *Couture and Commerce: The Transatlantic Fashion Trade in the 1950s*. Vancouver, Canada: University of British Columbia Press, 2001. A multidisciplinary approach to haute couture that unpacks many of its myths by delving into the dissemination of haute couture through transatlantic (especially Torontonian) outlets, the uses and meanings of couture clothing to clients (achieved through oral history), and the examination of objects in the Royal Ontario Museum's textile collection. Useful references to the reception of Balenciaga's designs.

Spindler, Amy M. "Keys to the Kingdom: A Fashion Fairy Tale Wherein Nicolas Ghesquière Finally Inherits the Throne." *New Yorker*, 14 April 2002, pp. 53–58. Ghesquière encounters the Balenciaga archives at last.

Exhibition Catalogs

Cristóbal Balenciaga. Tokyo: Fondation de la Mode, 1987.

de Petri Stephen, and Melissa Leventon, eds. *New Look to Now: French Haute Couture 1947–1987*. New York: Rizzoli International, 1989. A case study of haute couture and its San Francisco customers, with an excellent essay explaining how department stores adapted garments for their clients.

Ginsburg, Madeleine, comp. *Fashion: An Anthology by Cecil Beaton*. London: Victoria and Albert Museum, 1971. A short section of catalog entries on the Balenciaga clothes lent to the exhibition.

Healy, Robyn. *Balenciaga: Masterpieces of Fashion Design*. Melbourne, Australia: National Gallery of Victoria, 1992. An overview of Balenciaga and his oeuvre and its importance.

Jouve, Marie-Andrée. *Homage à Balenciaga*. Lyons, France: Musée Historique des Tissus, 1985. Emphasis on Balenciaga's relationship to the textile industry.

———. *Mona Bismarck, Cristobal Balenciaga, Cecil Beaton*. Paris: Mona Bismarck Foundation, 1994. An intriguing glimpse into the relationship of a major client, her couturier, and their mutual friend. Well-documented record of designs chosen and worn by Bismarck.

El mundo de Balenciaga. Madrid: Palacio de Bellas Artes, 1974.

Vreeland, Diana, curator. *The World of Balenciaga*. New York: Metropolitan Museum of Art, 1973.

Internet Resources

Cristóbal Balenciaga Fundazioa-Fundación. Available from <http://www.fundacionbalenciaga.com>. General information on the aims and objectives of the trust and the temporary displays of clothes.

Lesley Ellis Miller

BALL DRESS Ball dress is simply defined as a gown worn to a ball or formal dance. Beyond this fundamental description, there are remarkably intricate conventions related to appropriateness of ball dress. The most extravagant within the category of evening dress, a ball gown functions to dazzle the viewer and augment a woman's femininity. Ball gowns typically incorporate a low décolletage, a constricted bodice, bared arms, and long bouffant skirts. Ball gowns are visually distinguishable from other evening gowns by their lavishly designed surfaces—with layers of swags and puffs and such trim details as artificial flowers, ribbons, rosettes, and lace.

Additionally, ball gowns permit a woman to inhabit more space, as the especially billowing and expansive skirts extend the dimensions of her body. Fabric surfaces vary from reflective to matte, textured to smooth, and soft to rigid. Through the decades, undergarments have played a vital role in reshaping the natural structure of the body into the desired silhouette, from the corsets and petticoats of the nineteenth century to the control-top panty hose and padded bras of the twenty-first century.

Historical Significance

Balls have existed for centuries among royalty and the social elite, dating back to the Middle Ages. During the mid-1800s, the ball re-emerged as a desirable manner of entertainment among the upper and middle classes. Through the 1800s, the ball served as a means to bring together people of similar social backgrounds, often for purposes of introducing young women and men of marriageable age. Coming-out balls, debutante balls, or cotillion balls became standard events by the mid-1800s, and have continued in some form or another into the twenty-first century, with the high school prom added as a more middle-class and democratized version of a coming-out ball.

As popularity of the ball increased, ball gowns materialized and developed as a category of evening dress. Fashions during the first half of the nineteenth century included expansive skirts and tiny waistlines, and these characteristics were incorporated into the ball dress. Bouffant skirts functioned beautifully in the ballroom, as women skimmed across the floor as if they were floating on air. At all social levels and through the decades competition for the most opulent gown has remained a central ingredient of the event, as the finest ball gown may possibly result in the attentions of the most eligible suitor.

Contemporary Use

As the most splendid among evening dresses, ball gowns represent the romantic dreams of young women. *Cinderella* and *Beauty and the Beast* are recognizable fairy tales that instill in children the magnificence and fantasy of the ball, complete with appropriate full-skirted gown and a handsome prince. These ideas are reinforced and incorporated into our cultural consciousness. The profile of the traditional ball gown is evident in gowns for such modern-day events as weddings (bride and bride's attendants), high school proms, and the most elegant of evening occasions. Not surprisingly, designers of contemporary ball gowns continue to emphasize feminine curves while at the same time drawing from the nostalgic styles of expansive and lavishly decorated skirts, thereby establishing the wearer as a work of art.

See also **Evening Dress.**

Designer Madame Lucille fitting ball gown. Lavish works of fashion art, ball gowns are designed to emphasize femininity by drawing attention to the wearer's décolletage, bare arms, and small waist. © HULTON-DEUTSCH COLLECTION/CORBIS. REPRODUCED BY PERMISSION.

BIBLIOGRAPHY

Boucher, François. *20,000 Years of Fashion: The History of Costume and Personal Adornment.* New York: Harry N. Abrams, 1987.

Laver, James. *Costume and Fashion: A Concise History.* London: Thames and Hudson, 1982.

Milbank, Caroline Rennolds. *New York Fashion: The Evolution of American Style.* New York: Harry N. Abrams, 1989.

Payne, Blanche, Geitel Winakor, and Jane Farrell-Beck. *The History of Costume.* 2nd ed. New York: HarperCollins, 1992.

Russell, Douglas A. *Costume History and Style.* New Jersey: Prentice-Hall, 1983.

Steele, Valerie. *Women of Fashion: Twentieth-Century Designers.* New York: Rizzoli International, 1991.

——. *Fifty Years of Fashion.* New Haven, Conn., and London: Yale University Press, 2000.

——. *The Corset.* New Haven, Conn., and London: Yale University Press, 2001.

Watson, Linda. *Vogue: Twentieth Century Fashion.* London: Carlton Books Ltd., 1999.

Jane E. Hegland

BALLET COSTUME

BALLET COSTUME Ballet costumes constitute an essential part of stage design and can be considered as a visual record of a performance. They are often the only survival of a production, representing a living imaginary picture of the scene.

Renaissance and Baroque

The origins of ballet lie in the court spectacles of the Renaissance in France and Italy, and evidence of costumes specifically for ballet can be dated to the early fifteenth century. Illustrations from this period show the importance of masks and clothing for spectacles. Splendor at court was strongly reflected in luxuriously designed ballet costumes. Cotton and silk were mixed with flax woven into semitransparent gauze.

From the beginning of the sixteenth century, public theaters were being built in Venice (1637), Rome (1652), Paris (1660), Hamburg (1678), and other important cities. Ballet spectacles were combined in these venues with processional festivities and masquerades, as stage costumes became highly decorated and made from expensive materials. The basic costume for a male dancer was a tight-fitting, often brocaded cuirass, a short draped skirt and feather-decorated helmets. Female dancers wore opulently embroidered silk tunics in several layers with fringes. Important components of the ballet dress were tightly laced, high-heeled and wedged boots for both dancers, which constituted characteristic footwear for this period.

From 1550, classical Roman dress had a strong influence on costume design: silk skirts were voluminous; positioning of necklines and waistlines and the design of hairstyles were based on the components of everyday dress, although on the stage key details were often exaggerated. Male dancers' dresses were influenced by Roman armor. Typical colors of ballet costumes ranged from dark copper to maroon and purple. A more detailed description of the theatrical dress in the Renaissance and Baroque periods may be found in Lincoln Kirstein's *Four Centuries of Ballet* (1984, p. 34).

Prima ballerina Anna Pavlova. Early ballerina skirts were heavy, voluminous affairs that severely restricted the dancer's movements. Fortunately, by the early twentieth century, skirts were raised to the knees to showcase pointe work. © ARCHIVO ICONOGRAFICO, S.A./CORBIS. REPRODUCED BY PERMISSION.

Seventeenth Century

From the seventeenth century onward, silks, satins, and fabrics embroidered with real gold and precious stones increased the level of spectacular decoration associated with ballet costumes. Court dress remained the standard costume for female performers while male dancers' costumes had developed into a kind of uniform embellished with symbolic decoration to denote character or occupation; for example, scissors represented a tailor.

The first Russian ballet performance was staged in 1675, and the Russians adopted European ballet designs. Although costumes for male performers permitted complete freedom of movement, heavy garments and supporting structures for female dancers did not allow graceful gestures. However, male dancers *en travesti*, often wore knee-long skirts. The luxuriously decorated costumes of this period reflected the glory of the court;

details of dresses and silhouettes were exaggerated to be visible and identifiable to spectators viewing from a distance.

Eighteenth Century

From the early eighteenth century, European ballet was centered in the Paris Opéra. Stage costumes were still very similar in outline to the ones in ordinary use at Court, but more elaborate. Around 1720, the *panier*, a hooped petticoat, appeared, raising skirts a few inches off the ground. During the reign of Louis XVI, court dress, ballet costumes, and fashionable architectural design incorporated decorative rococo prints and ornamental garlands. Flowers, flounces, ribbons, and lace emphasized this opulent feminine style, as soft pastel tones in citron, peach, pink, azure, and pistachio dominated the color range of stage costumes. Female dancers in male roles became popular, and, after the French Revolution in 1789 in particular, male costumes reflected the more conservative and sober Neoclassical style, which dominated the design of everyday fashionable dress. However, massive wigs and headdresses still restricted the mobility of dancers. In the eighteenth and nineteenth centuries, Russian ballet and European ballet developed similarly and were often considered an integral part of the opera.

Nineteenth Century

From the early nineteenth century, the ideals of Romanticism were reflected in female stage costumes through the introduction of close-fitting bodices, floral crowns, corsages, and pearls on fabrics, as well as necklace and bracelets; Neoclassical style still dominated the design of male costumes. Moreover, the role of the ballerina as star dancer became more important and was emphasized with tight-fitting corsets, bejeweled bodices, and opulent headdresses. In 1832, Marie Taglioni's gauze-layered white tutu in *La Sylphide* set a new trend in ballet costumes, in which silhouettes became tighter, revealing the legs and the permanently toe-shoed feet. From this point on, the silhouette of ballet costumes became more tight fitting. The choreography required that ballerinas to wear pointe shoes all the time. The Russian ballet continued to develop in the nineteenth century and such writers and composers as Tolstoy, Dostoevsky, and Tchaikovsky changed the meaning of ballet through the composition of narrative productions. Choreographers of classical ballet, such as Marius Petipa, created fairy-tale ballets, including *The Sleeping Beauty* (1890), *Swan Lake* (1895), and *Raymonde* (1898), making fantasy costumes very popular.

Twentieth Century

At the turn of the twentieth century, ballet costumes reformed again under the more liberal influence of the Russian choreographer Michel Fokine. Ballerina skirts changed gradually to become knee-length tutus designed to show off the point work and multiple turns, which

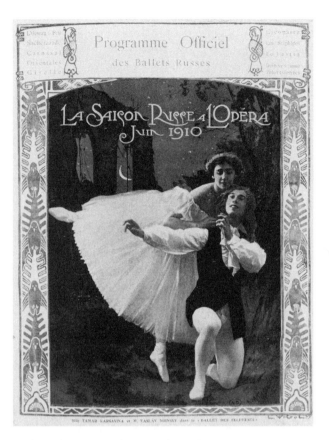

Program featuring Vaslav Nijinsky and Tamara Karsavina. By the end of the nineteenth century, tights were a standard part of the male dancer's ensemble due to the great range of motion they offered. © GIANNI DAGLI ORTI/CORBIS. REPRODUCED BY PERMISSION.

formed the focus of dance practice. The dancer Isadora Duncan freed ballerinas from corsets and introduced a revolutionary natural silhouette. The Russian impresario and producer Serge Diaghilev marked this era with his creative innovations, and professional costumers like Alexandre Benois and Léon Bakst demonstrated, in performances such as *Schéhérezade* (1910), that the influence of Orientalism had spread from fashion to the stage and vice versa. Indeed, fashion designers like Jean Poiret had already used the tunic shape taken up by dancers in the prewar era, and, in the 1920s, costume designers updated classical Russian story ballets with exotic tunics and veils wrapped around the body. Ballet dancers were dressed in loose tunics, harem pants, and turbans, rather than in the established tutu and feather headdress. Instead of discreet pastel colors vibrant shades, such as yellow, orange, or red, often in wild patterns, gave an unprecedented visual impression of exciting exoticism to the spectator.

Modernism and Postmodernism

Modernism liberalized the rules of ballet costumes, and, after Diaghilev's death in 1929, costume design was no longer impeded by restrictions imposed by traditionalists. Nowadays ballet dancers perform in various costumes, which can still include traditional Diaghilev designs. In postmodern productions like Matthew Bourne's *Swan Lake*, the costume designer Lez Brotherston turned the traditional gracile female cygnets into topless, feather-legged male swans. However, fashion designers of the 1990s have picked up the theme of ballerina shoes. The house of Chanel designed elegant, heelless slippers tied up with ribbons and brought the ballerina shoe from the stage to the street.

See also **Dance and Fashion; Dance Costume; Theatrical Costume.**

BIBLIOGRAPHY

André, Paul. *The Great History of Russian Ballet.* Bournemouth, U.K.: Parkstone Publishers, 1998.

Chazin-Bennahum, Judith. *A Longing for Perfection: Neoclassic Fashion and Ballet.* Oxford: *Fashion Theory* 6, no. 4 (2002): 369–386.

Clarke, Mary, and Clement Crisp. *Design for Ballet.* London: Cassell and Collier, Macmillan Publishers, Ltd., 1978.

Kirstein, Lincoln. *Four Centuries of Ballet.* New York: Dover Publications, Inc., 1984.

Morrison, Kirsty. *From Russia with Love.* Canberra: National Gallery of Australia, 1998.

Reade, Brian. *Ballet Designs and Illustrations 1581–1940.* London: Her Majesty's Stationery Office, 1967.

Schouvaloff, Alexander. *The Art of Ballet Russes.* New Haven, Conn., and London: Yale University Press, 1997.

Williams, Peter. *Masterpieces of Ballet Design.* Oxford: Phaidon Press, Ltd, 1981.

Wulf, Helena. *Ballet Across Borders.* Oxford and New York: Berg Publishers, 1998.

Thomas Hecht

BALMAIN, PIERRE Pierre Balmain (1914–1982) was born in the Savoie region of France in 1914. He studied architecture for a year in Paris before taking a position as a sketch artist with the fashion house of Robert Piguet in 1934. He worked at the House of Molyneux as an assistant designer from 1934 to 1938, and as a designer with Lucien Lelong in Paris in 1939 and from 1941 to 1945. During this time he worked alongside another young designer at Lelong, Christian Dior. In 1945 Balmain founded the Maison Balmain as a couture house with a lucrative sideline in fragrances. He expanded into the American market in 1953, showing his collections under the brand name Jolie Madame. The Balmain perfume business was sold to Revlon in 1960, but Pierre Balmain continued as the proprietor and chief designer of the Maison Balmain until his death in 1982.

The fashion historian Farid Chenoune described Pierre Balmain as one of "the supreme practitioners of the New Look generation," along with Christian Dior and Jacques Fath. During the 1950s and 1960s, Balmain's clients included some of the world's most elegant and best-dressed women, such as Katharine Hepburn, Vivien Leigh, Marlene Dietrich, and Queen Sirikit of Thailand.

Pierre Balmain fitting a dress. A devotee of the basic principals of fashion, Balmain opened Maison Balmain in 1945, and began producing elegant creations that yielded him several famous clients. © CORBIS. REPRODUCED BY PERMISSION.

Pierre Balmain, 1956. The woman models an elegant, strapless sheath dress made of embroidered French lace. A greige taffeta sash adds to the sleek line of the look, and the mink stole, lined with the lace, gives a flare of luxury. © BETTMANN/ CORBIS. REPRODUCED BY PERMISSION.

Balmain's work was characterized by an emphasis on impeccable construction and simple elegance. He is credited with popularizing the stole as an accessory. He once said, "Keep to the basic principles of fashion and you will always be in harmony with the latest trends without falling prey to them."

The Maison Balmain continued in business after Pierre Balmain's death, with several designers and under shifting ownership throughout the 1980s. A ready-to-wear line was added in 1982. The company reacquired its perfume business from Revlon but unwisely entered into extensive licensing agreements that put the Balmain name on a wide range of products, diluting the company's image. In 1993 Oscar de la Renta took on the position of chief designer for the Maison Balmain—the first American to become head designer for a Paris couture house. De la Renta's first collection for the company, which appeared on the runway in February 1994, was a critical and commercial success. Critics generally agree that de la Renta, who spent nearly a decade at Balmain, succeeded not only in reviving the company's fortunes, but also in restoring the house's old reputation for elegance. Oscar de la Renta presented his final collection for Balmain in July 2002. He was succeeded by Laurent

Mercier, who was artistic director from 2002 to 2003, and Christophe Lebourg, who was appointed in 2003.

See also **De la Renta, Oscar; Dior, Christian; Fath, Jacques; New Look; Paris Fashion; Perfume.**

BIBLIOGRAPHY

Benbow-Pfalzgraf, Taryn, ed. *Contemporary Fashion.* 2nd ed. Farmington Hills, Mich.: St. James Press, 2002.

Buxbaum, Gerda, ed. *Icons of Fashion: The 20th Century.* Munich, London, and New York: Prestel Verlag, 1999.

Milbank, Caroline Rennolds. *Couture: The Great Designers.* New York: Stewart, Tabori and Chang, 1985.

Pierre Balmain: 40 années de création. Paris: Musée de la Mode et du Costume, 1985.

John S. Major

BALZAC, HONORÉ DE Honoré Balzac was born to an aspiring bourgeois family in Tours, France in 1799. The family later attributed itself an aristocratic particle, making him Honoré de Balzac. The famous writer died in Paris in 1850, having authored over ninety novels and numerous plays, articles, and short stories.

Balzac avoided the word "dandy" in his writings. In France in the 1830s and 1840s it had negative connotations of foppishness and English eccentricity. In his *Traité de la vie élégante* (*Treatise on the Elegant Life*) of 1830, he wrote: "In making himself a dandy, a man becomes a piece of boudoir furniture, an extremely ingenious mannequin, who can sit upon a horse or a sofa … but a thinking being … never." Despite his critiques of the dandy's intellect, he greatly admired masculine elegance and British tailoring. One of his most famous literary dandies, Henry de Marsay, epitomizes the sexual appeal and ambiguity of Balzac's version of the dandy. De Marsay was "[…] famous for the passions he inspired, especially remarkable because of his beauty, like that of a young girl, a soft, effeminate beauty, but counterbalanced by his steady, calm, wild and fixed gaze, like that of a tiger: he was loved and he caused fear" (*Lost Illusions*). Balzac's writings emphasized the contrast between the dandy's leisured cultivation of elegance and the dull soulless drudgery of the workingman's life. His philosophy stands at the cusp between a British model of dandyism as a phenomenon embedded in a specific social context and later nineteenth-century French and British ideas of the decadent dandy. He influenced writers such as Charles Baudelaire and Joris-Karl Huysmans, for whom the dandy was a heroic outsider rebelling against increasing industrialization and social uniformity.

Balzac cultivated his personal style and public image. At the end of 1830, he owed his tailor 904 francs, which was more than his entire yearly budget for food and lodging in Paris. As a young, upwardly mobile writer he described his extraordinary dress as a *réclame* or advertisement and claimed that his cane caused all of Paris

Honoré de Balzac. Known for his own somewhat flamboyant fashion style, Balzac paid particular attention to dress and clothing in his writings, even using famous tailors as characters in his books. PUBLIC DOMAIN.

to chatter. Indeed, Balzac's accessories seem to have been particularly remarkable: he carried a monstrous cane studded with turquoise, wore coat buttons of elaborately carved gold, and modeled an astonishing variety of waistcoats and gloves. Despite his efforts at elegance, he did not always cut a fine figure and his flamboyant style was not always favorably received. Physically, he was short and squat, and he sacrificed attempts at personal hygiene when deeply involved in his work. Captain Gronow remarked that he wore sparkling jewels on dirty shirtfronts and diamond rings on unwashed fingers.

He patronized several famous tailors and these men, along with haberdashers, glovemakers, and other tradesmen, feature prominently in his novels. It is rumored that he had his clothing paid for by advertising certain tailors—including their names, addresses, and eulogies of their products—in his writing. For example, in the novel *Lost Illusions* (*Illusions Perdues*, 1837–1843) the young provincial poet Lucien de Rubempré is shamed when he pays cash for an ill-fitting, bright green readymade suit and wears it to the Paris Opéra. The mature dandy Henry de Marsay insults Lucien, comparing him with a clothed tailor's mannequin. The next day he goes

to Staub, who was one of Balzac's own tailors, and spends most of his yearly income on a new outfit. When he returns to his native Angoulême, he turns his new appearance to his advantage. In his skin-tight black trousers he attracts all of the noblewomen of the city. They flock to see him in his new role as a handsome *lion* or man of fashion. Balzac observes that the styles of the day were best suited to sculptural physiques: "Men still showed off their bodies, to the great despair of the thin or badly-built, and Lucien's form was Apollonian." The Staub suit transforms Lucien's existence in Paris, catapults him to instant notoriety and helps him launch his literary career. This novel celebrates the social power of dress and demeanor.

Honoré de Balzac's early journalistic writing pays particular attention to men's fashion. The most important publication related directly to dandyism is the *Traité de la vie élégante* (*Treatise on the Elegant Life*), which was published in Émile de Girardin's royalist review *La Mode* between 2 October and 6 November 1830. This text fictionalizes the British dandy George Brummell, whom he calls the "patriarch of fashion." Balzac uses him as a mouthpiece to expound his own principles on elegant dress and lifestyle. In the *Treatise*, he pioneered the concept of *vestignomonie* (vestignomony), a pun on the pseudoscience of physiognomy. While physiognomists claimed to be able to read human character from facial types and expressions, Balzac affirmed that clothing could be read and deciphered in the same way. Despite the seemingly increasing uniformity of dress in democratic, post-revolutionary France, Balzac claimed that it was easy for the observer to distinguish between men from various social strata and professions. He claimed that clothes revealed the Parisian doctor, aristocrat, or student from the neighborhoods of the Marais, the Faubourg Saint-Germain, the Latin Quarter or the Chaussée d'Antin.

While much of Balzac's early work was published in fashionable journals like *La Mode*, *Le Voleur* and *La Silhouette*, his later writings demonstrate a sustained interest in vestimentary style. Dress and clothing play a central role in the ninety-odd volumes of *La Comédie Humaine* (*The Human Comedy*) named as a pun on Dante's *Divine Comedy*. These novels constitute a panorama of French social life from the Revolution (1789) to the end of the July Monarchy (1848). The most important dandy figures in his novels include Eugène de Rastignac, Lucien de Rubempré, Maxime de Trailles, Charles Grandet, Georges Marest, Amédée Soulas, Lousteau, Raphael Valentin and Henry de Marsay. Some of his most important novels were *Old Goriot*, *Eugénie Grandet*, *Lost Illusions*, and *Cousin Bette*.

Balzac's detailed observations and extensive descriptions paint a vivid picture of the nuances of dress in his period and herald the importance given to fashion in realist literature. While Balzac's importance to the study of fashion is taken for granted in French literary criticism, many of his important journalistic texts have not yet been translated into English. Nonetheless, his novels contain some of the most engaging and sophisticated verbal descriptions of fashion in the history of literature.

See also **Fashion, Historical Studies of.**

BIBLIOGRAPHY

Balzac, Honoré de. *Lost Illusions* (*Illusions perdues*). Translated by Herbert J. Hunt. Harmondsworth, U.K.: Penguin, 1971.

———. *Traité de la vie élégante, suivi de théorie de la démarche.* Paris: Arléa, 1998.

Boucher, François, and Philippe Bruneau. *Le vêtement chez Balzac,* Paris: extraits de la Comédie humaine l'Institut Français de la Mode, 2001.

Fortassier, Rose. *Les ecrivains français et la mode.* Paris: Puf, 1988.

Moers, Ellen. *The Dandy: Brummell to Beerbohm.* London: Secker and Warburg, 1960.

Alison Matthews David

BARBERS The word "barber" is derived from the Latin *barba* meaning "beard," and the profession of barber has been in existence since the earliest recorded period. In Ezekiel 5:1, for instance, "the son of man" is urged to "take thee a barber's razor and cause it to pass upon thy head and upon thy beard." The professional status of the barber has changed dramatically over the centuries. The medieval barber was a "barber-surgeon" responsible for not only shaving and trimming hair, but also for dental treatment and minor surgery, especially *phlebotomy* or bleeding. Barber-surgeons were organized into guilds as early as the twelfth century in Europe, and one of the most famous, the Worshipful Company of Barbers, was created in London in 1308. Barber-surgeons could be recognized in the seventeenth century by their uniform, a "checque parti-coloured apron; neither can he be termed a barber, or poler, or shaver till the apron is about him" (Randle Holme, 1688; in Stevens-Cox, p. 220). The apron had a large front pocket that held the tools of the trade. A white or gray coat had supplanted this traditional outfit by the early twentieth century.

The barber's premises were marked out by a standard sign—a blue, red, and white striped pole. This symbol was derived from the pole gripped during bleeding when the vein in the bend of the elbow was opened. As this operation was performed without anesthetic, it was often painful. When not in use, the pole stood outside the barbershop as sign of service, and the image was incorporated into the characteristic sign that developed. The red and blue on the sign represented the blood of the veins and arteries, and the white symbolized the bandages used after bleeding. The seventeenth-century fashion for a smooth-shaven face led to a boom in trade. The barber would soften the client's bristles with a mixture of soap and water, oil, or fat using a hog bristle brush and then shave him using a well-stropped razor. Demand for bar-

bers' services continued with the increasing complexity of men's hairstyles in the late eighteenth century and the popularity of beards in the nineteenth century.

Barbers had declined in prestige by this time, however, as a result of the trades of barber and surgeon being made independent of one another in 1745. Surgery became a well-respected profession, and barbering began to be viewed as a lowly occupation (as had been true all along in many other cultures). The barbershop of the nineteenth century gained a reputation as a rather insalubrious place, a gathering place of idle and sometimes rowdy men. In Europe, barbers had a reputation as procurers of prostitutes and cigars, and by the mid-twentieth century, contraceptives, leading to the popular English phrase, "A little something for the weekend, Sir?"

The practice of barbering was also regarded as unsanitary. In the nineteenth century, a client could be the recipient of a "foul shave" from infected razors and hot towels passed from customer to customer without being cleaned, which caused infections commonly referred to as "barbers' itch." A contemporary description of a barber ran: "The Average Barber is in a state of perspiration and is greasy; his fingers pudgy and his nails in mourning; he snips and snips away, pinching your ears, nipping your eyelashes and your jaw... he draws his fingers in a pot of axle grease, scented with musk and age, and before you can define his fearful intent, smears it all over your head" (*Hairdressers' Weekly Journal*, p. 73). The British trade publication *Hairdressers' Weekly Journal* chose this description of 1882 to begin a concerted campaign calling for better education and standards of hygiene among barbers, designed to improve their image and status.

In America, a tradition had developed in the late eighteenth century of black-owned barbershops that catered to a white clientele; prosperous black barbers often became leading members of their communities. After the Civil War, however, the laws of racial segregation in many states prohibited black barbers from tending to white customers, and barbering declined in importance as an African American trade. By 1899–1900 Italian men made up sixty percent of immigrant barbers. In Italy, Spain, and France, haircutting was regarded as a profession of skill and dexterity. The contrast in public image was striking: Spain's Barber of Seville versus England's Sweeney Todd, the demon-barber of Fleet Street.

The practice of self-shaving also transformed the role of the barbershop. Jean Jacques Perret invented the first safety razor with a wooden guard along the blade in 1770, but the self-shaving revolution really began with the invention of the Gillette safety razor in 1895. Throughout the twentieth century, barbershops increasingly relied on haircutting rather than shaving as the basis of their trade.

By the 1920s some brave women were prepared to enter the masculine arena of the barbershop to get their

Nineteenth-century British illustration. Barbershops of the nineteenth century often had rather unsavory reputations, due partly to the clientele, which was regarded as uncouth, and partly to the perceived unsanitary practices of the barbers themselves. © HISTORICAL PICTURE ARCHIVE/CORBIS. REPRODUCED BY PERMISSION.

hair bobbed. One of these women remembers "walking through the barbershop and being very conscious that we were somehow transgressing male space. The barbershop was filled with groups of men chewing tobacco and engaged in conversations about weather, politics, rodeo, and wrestling" (Willett, p. 1). The vogue for short haircuts was so prevalent that the few hairdressers who could actually cut rather than dress hair were fully booked, and in any case many women preferred to give their hair up to the skill of the barber rather than the hairdresser. Women's hairdressers quickly fought back with formal education and the introduction of lush salons where female clients could be pampered.

With the more elaborate hairstyles of the 1950s, in particular the variations of the pompadour, men began to spend more time and money at the barbers', who began to use the term "men's stylists" to distinguish themselves from the old-fashioned barbershops. By the late 1960s, the longer hair trends for men, which had developed out of counterculture styles, meant fewer and fewer visits to the barber. In the United States, the census figures reported that between 1972 and 1982 the number of barbershops fell by more than 28 percent. This necessitated a change in tonsorial skills and marketing and by 1970 journalist Rodney Bennett-England, who specialized in male grooming, declared, "The old barber, trained in the use of electric clippers, was a technician. Today's barbers are stylists, even artists" (p. 104). He described salons for men that "resemble gentlemen's clubs with deep, comfortable armchairs, wood panelled walls and pictures or prints....you can easily while away a complete half-day having your hair heightened, lightened and brightened, your hands manicured and your tired face cleansed and patted back into new vigour" (p. 105). The old barbershop still existed by the early 2000s with a dwindling clientele, but many men with an interest in fashionable haircuts go to "unisex" hairdressers who no longer bother to specialize in either male or female clients.

See also **Hair Accessories; Hairdressers; Hairstyles.**

BIBLIOGRAPHY

Bennett-England, Rodney. *As Young as You Look: Male Grooming and Rejuvenation.* London: Peter Owen, 1970.

Byrd, Ayana D., and Lori L. Tharps. *Hair Story: Untangling the Roots of Black Hair in America.* New York: St. Martin's Press, 2001.

Cox, Caroline. *Good Hair Days: A History of British Hairstyling.* London: Quartet Books, 1999.

Hairdressers' Weekly Journal 3 (June 1882): 73.

Stevens-Cox, James. *An Illustrated Dictionary of Hairdressing and Wigmaking.* London: B. T. Batsford Ltd., 1989.

Willett, Julie A. *Permanent Waves: The Making of the American Beauty Shop.* New York: New York University Press, 2000.

Caroline Cox

BARBIE Since the Mattel corporation introduced Barbie in 1959, the doll's relation to fashion, sex, femininity, and cultural values has been a subject of spin control, change, and controversy.

Early official accounts of Barbie's beginnings emphasized the desire of Ruth Handler, Mattel's co-founder, to produce a three-dimensional version of the paper fashion dolls her daughter, Barbara, loved. But Barbie's body actually originated elsewhere: with a German character named Lilli, who appeared in cartoon and doll form primarily as a sexpot plaything for adult men. Mattel bought all the rights and patents required to remove Lilli from that context of meaning and turned her into Barbie, the "shapely teenage Fashion Model!" announced in early catalogs.

Changes followed soon after the doll's launch, as Mattel worked to gear Barbie's persona to sales and supplementary products. In a 1961 television ad, Barbie, although still described as a fashion model, had acquired a school life, a boyfriend, and outfits for activities ranging from school lunches to frat parties: "Think of the fun you'll have taking Barbie and Ken on dates, dressing each one just right." The ad's invitation to "see where the romance will lead" illustrated Barbie's dreamy future by showing her in a wedding dress, a costume that would recur in many subsequent versions. Other outfits to come included the latest in formal wear, casual attire, sports gear, and lingerie. Many fashions were modeled after the work of contemporary designers. Sometimes Mattel enlisted designers directly, especially for the high-end offerings later created to cash in on the ever-increasing traffic in Barbie collectibles. Like designer Bob Mackie's 1991 "Limited Edition Platinum Barbie," these sometimes sold for up to several hundred dollars each.

Careers and Colors

Over the years, too, Barbie saw expanding options in one type of costume that would generate praise, humor, doubt, and derision: the career outfit. In the early 1960s, Barbie's career identities were primarily traditionally female, like nurse; largely unattainable, like astronaut; or both, like ballerina. Barbie had less work, ironically, during the burgeoning of popular feminism in the 1970s.

Lettie Lane paper doll with clothes. Mattel co-founder Ruth Handler's desire to produce a three-dimensional version of paper dolls such as these was the genesis for Barbie. © Cynthia Hart Designer/Corbis. Reproduced by permission.

Her career life took off in the mid-1980s, however, with the Day-to-Night Barbie line. Its first incarnation presented Barbie as an executive, whose pink suit could be transformed into evening wear. She came with the slogan "We Girls Can Do Anything," a catchphrase relevant also to the range of careers that Barbie adopted into the 1990s, which included doctor, veterinarian, UNICEF ambassador, rock star, rap musician, teacher, chef, Marine Corps sergeant, and professional basketball player for the WNBA.

Besides addressing concerns about whether a girl with few apparent interests other than fashion, fun, and spending a vast amount of cash on clothes, cars (like the Barbie Ferrari), and real estate (like the famed Barbie Dream House) provided a good role model, career Barbies suited an important change in Mattel's marketing strategy. Initially, Mattel wanted consumers to supplement their first Barbie with outfits, accessories, and other characters such as Ken and Midge, Barbie's close yet dis-

Barbies on display. Since her introduction in 1959, Barbie has been marketed with many different looks to entice children to buy multiple dolls. This strategy appears to have paid off, as the average number of Barbies owned per child grew to ten in the 1990s. © BETTMANN/CORBIS. REPRODUCED BY PERMISSION.

tinctly unglamorous friend. In fact, the promotion for the 1967 Twist 'N Turn Barbie even offered a trade-in deal. Later, promotions became geared to the purchase of multiple Barbies. In 1992, for example, a Barbie owner interested in the rapper outfit had to buy Rappin' Rockin' Barbie, or four of them to get each of the different boom boxes. Another trend sponsored by Mattel that catered simultaneously to sales and social consciousness was the increase in Barbies of color and Barbies representing countries outside the United States. Changing statistics about how many Barbies the "average child" owns suggest Mattel's success at shifting multiple acquisitions to Barbie herself, with the number climbing from seven to ten over the course of the 1990s.

Controversies

With Barbie's popularity has come increasing controversy, both about Barbie's (unrecyclable) plastic body and about the flesh to which it does, or does not, refer. To a number of critics, Barbie represents shallow feminism, focused primarily on individual success and fulfillment, and Barbie's world looks like diversity lite, peopled by innumerable white, blond Barbies, unquestionably front

and center, and a much smaller number of Barbies who look like white Barbies with skin and hair dye jobs. Detractors have advanced other arguments as well: that Mattel's restriction of Barbie's dating life to boys adds yet another set of cultural narratives guiding young people to see heterosexuality as the desired, perhaps required, norm; that Barbie's impossible-to-attain proportions contribute to cultural ideals of beauty that invite self-loathing and unhealthy eating practices; and that Barbie promotes an undue focus on looks in general. Why give a girl Soccer Barbie (1999) instead of a soccer ball?

Yet as other commentators have noted, Barbie has generated a lot of play far from Mattel's official sponsorship. Mattel's WNBA Barbie may not emerge from the box with the characteristic butch flair displayed by many of her charming human counterparts, but in the hands and minds of many consumers, Barbie has been butched out, turned out, fixed up with diverse sex mates, and, of course, undressed; for a doll whose wardrobe forms the centerpiece of her reputation, she spends quite a lot of time naked. Then again, for some critics, this is Mattel's fault, too. People who like to imagine children as innocent of sexual desires have accused the company of turning their children's minds to sex with its big-breasted adult doll. Others, conversely, have mourned what Mattel couldn't do: inspire femininity in their daughters or distaste in insufficiently truck-minded sons.

Object of Attention

From all these diverse uses and assessments of Barbie, one certainty emerges. Barbie remains an object of attention, fascination, and, of course, purchase. Whatever her influence has been—and surely it has varied among individuals and over time—she has successfully convinced many of her importance as a symbol of femininity, as a catalyst for fantasy, and as a marker and agent of cultural values.

See also **Fashion and Identity; Fashion Dolls.**

BIBLIOGRAPHY

BillyBoy. *Barbie: Her Life and Times.* New York: Crown Publishers, 1987. Excellent source of fashion study and illustrations.

DuCille, Ann. *Skin Trade.* Cambridge, Mass.: Harvard University Press, 1996. Critical issues including race.

Lord, M. G. *Forever Barbie: The Unauthorized Biography of a Real Doll.* New York: Morrow and Company, 1994. History.

Rand, Erica. *Barbie's Queer Accessories.* Durham, N.C., and London: Duke University Press, 1995. History, consumers, subversions.

Erica Rand

***Rendez-vous* by Georges Barbier.** Barbier's illustrations employed strong colors and casual elegance to depict the 1920s fashionable ideal. Barbier's figures, with strong forms and dark-lidded, slightly exotic eyes, represented the concept of female beauty and grace. © STAPLETON COLLECTION/CORBIS. REPRODUCED BY PERMISSION.

BARBIER, GEORGES The French illustrator, painter, and theatrical designer Georges Barbier (1882–1932) was born in the seaport city of Nantes. The city's seventeenth- and eighteenth-century architecture, as well as its art museum collections, with works by Antoine Watteau and Jean-Auguste-Dominique Ingres, influenced Barbier's aesthetic sensibilities. As a young man he moved to Paris where, between 1908 and 1910, he studied at l'École des beaux-arts in the atelier of the academic history painter, Jean-Paul Laurens. Although Barbier's artistic style differed significantly from that of his teacher, his appreciation of the past as a source of inspiration was undoubtedly reinforced by Laurens's subjects.

In the galleries of the Louvre, Barbier discovered the art of classical antiquity. His enduring admiration for Greek and Etruscan vases, Tanagra figurines, and small Egyptian sculptures is evident in his depiction of the human body and resonates overall in the clarity and restraint of his graphic work. His refined color sense and use of strong colors, influenced by costumes of the Ballets Russes, which was founded in Paris in 1909, also characterize his work.

Barbier first exhibited at the Salon des humoristes in 1911, where his drawings were immediately acclaimed; subsequently, he was a regular contributor to the Salon des artistes décorateurs. Barbier was a prolific and skill-ful artist whose sophisticated style was in great demand. Over the course of his brief career, he contributed to most of the leading French fashion journals and almanacs; illustrated numerous publications of classic and contemporary French prose and poetry issued in limited, deluxe editions; and designed costumes for stage productions, including ballet, film, and revues, such as the Folies Bergère and the Casino de Paris. In addition, Barbier wrote essays on fashion that appeared in *La Gazette du bon ton* and other journals, and as a member of the Société des artistes décorateurs, he produced designs for jewelry, glass, and wallpaper. One of the most well-known and highly regarded artists working in the second and third decades of the twentieth century, Barbier died in Paris at the peak of his profession in 1932.

Barbier and Art Deco

In Michael Arlen's best-selling 1924 novel, *The Green Hat*, the heroine Iris March is compared to a figure in a Barbier fashion illustration: "She stood carelessly like the women in Georges Barbier's almanacs, *Falbalas et Fanfreluches*, who know how to stand carelessly. Her hands were thrust into the pockets of a light brown leather jacket—pour le sport" (Steele, p. 247). The casual elegance ascribed to Arlen's character, a quintessential element of the 1920s fashion ideal, epitomizes Barbier's

***The Judgement of Paris,* ca. 1915.** Painted by French artist Georges Barbier, three women display haute couture of the art deco period. Influences of classic antiquity show in the design of the head adornments, the jewelry, and the dresses. High-heeled shoes square off the modern look. © STAPLETON COLLECTION/CORBIS. REPRODUCED BY PERMISSION.

figures. With their strong yet lithe forms and dark-lidded, slightly exotic eyes, Barbier's women embody the notions of female beauty and grace of the time.

Beginning with the innovative and influential *Le Journal des dames et des modes* (1912–1914), launched by Lucien Vogel, Barbier's talents were sought after by the publishers and editors of avant-garde fashion magazines. Following the lead of the couturier Paul Poiret, whose collaboration with the artists Paul Iribe and Georges Lepape in 1908 and 1911, respectively, set the standard for a new, modernist presentation of fashion, these publications showcased the emerging art deco aesthetic. Rather than realistic, fussily detailed renderings of dress, Barbier and his fellow illustrators (Lepape, Iribe, Bernard Boutet de Monvel, Pierre Brissaud, and Charles Martin, among others) created bold, stylized images that conveyed mood and atmosphere. The laborious technique of *pochoir* printing used for these illustrations (a hand-stenciled process whereby layers of color are built up in gouache paint) enhanced their visual impact.

In addition to *Le Journal des dames*, Barbier contributed widely to other luxury fashion periodicals including *La Gazette du bon ton* (1912–1925), *Les Feuillets d'art* (1919–1922), and *Art goût beauté* (1920–1933), as well as *Vogue, Femina,* and *La Vie parisienne.* Barbier was also commissioned to illustrate more specialized fashion publications: couturiers' albums and almanacs, such as *Modes et manières d'aujourd'hui* (1912–1923), *La Guirlande des mois* (1917–1920), *Le Bonheur du jour* (1920–1924), and *Falbalas et fanfreluches* (1922–1926). Modeled after the early nineteenth-century publication *Le Bon genre* that chronicles the modes and lifestyle of the First Empire and the Bourbon restoration, Barbier's refined and often witty drawings for particular almanacs not only depict Parisian haute couture but also record the social scene and fashionable activities in charming vignettes.

Set Designs and Costumes

Although it is primarily through Barbier's fashion illustrations that one is familiar with his work, in his lifetime his book illustrations and theatrical costume designs contributed significantly to his artistic reputation and success. Both authors with whom he collaborated and critics agreed that Barbier was able to distill the essence of a literary text and give it visual form. His interpretations of historic dress and interiors for the stage (including *Casanova* and *La Dernière nuit de Don Juan* by Edmond Rostand, *Marion Delorme* by Victor Hugo, and *Lysistrata* by Maurice Donnay) were admired for their imaginative evocation of a particular time and place, rather than representing merely a scrupulous imitation or pastiche. Barbier's love of the exotic resulted in spectacular beribboned, furred, feathered, and jeweled fantasy costumes for revue performers at popular Paris nightclubs.

Legacy

In the preface to *Personnages de comédie* (1922), illustrated by Barbier, Albert Flament refers to him as "One of the most precious and significant artists of our era.... When our times are lost ... in the dust ... some of his watercolours and drawings will be all that is necessary to resurrect the taste and the spirit of the years in which we have lived" (Ginsburg, p. 3). Barbier was undoubtedly one of the preeminent fashion illustrators of the early twentieth century. Among the group of artists including Lepape, Iribe, and Monvel, dubbed "The Knights of the Bracelet" by *Vogue* in 1922 (a reference to their "dandyism ... and love of luxury" [Barbier, p. 6]), Barbier was in the forefront of the alliance between art and fashion. His superb draftsmanship, color sense, and ability to infuse freshness into historic influences combine to produce distinctive images that define the modernity of the art deco style.

See also **Art Nouveau and Art Deco; Fashion Illustrators; Fashion Magazines.**

BIBLIOGRAPHY

Barbier, Georges. *Art Deco Costumes.* New York: Crescent Books, 1988.

Mackrell, Alice. *An Illustrated History of Fashion: 500 Years of Fashion Illustration.* New York: Costume and Fashion Press, 1997.

Steele, Valerie. *Paris Fashion: A Cultural History.* New York: Oxford University Press, 1988.

Vaudoyer, Jean-Louis, and Henri de Régnier. *George Barbier: Étude Critique.* Paris: Henry Babou, 1929.

Weill, Alain. *Parisian Fashion: La Gazette du bon ton, 1912–1925.* Paris: Bibliothèque de l'Image, 2000.

Michele Majer

BARK CLOTH The term "bark cloth" has been known by various names in the Pacific Islands, including: tapa or *kapa* (Hawaii), *ngatu* (Tonga), *ahu* or *ka'u* (Tahiti), *masi* (Fiji), and *autea* (Cook Islands). "Tapa" is the popular word now used to describe bark cloth throughout the Pacific Islands. Bark cloth, or tapa, describes the fabric whose source material is the bark of a tree or similar plant material grown in tropical areas around the world and is, therefore, cellulosic. Like felting, bark cloth produces a nonwoven fabric. Like felting, bark cloth or tapa is produced in a warm, moist environment. While the bonding of fibers in felt is mechanical, the bonding in bark cloth is chemical.

One of the plants carried by exploring Polynesians was paper mulberry (*Broussonetia papyrifera*), called *wauke* by Hawaiians. In addition to paper mulberry, several other plants found in tropical locales have been used for making bark cloth.

Production
To start the bark-cloth–making process, the inner bark (bast) of a tree or plant was stripped or removed from its source, the outer bark of a tree or branch, and cleaned. The bast fibers were then placed in water, often seawater, causing the fibers to break down (ferment or ret) into a somewhat sticky substance resembling bread dough. The substance was spread on a specially carved flat wood surface called a *kua kuku* in Hawaiian and then beaten with grooved wooden beaters, called *hohoa*, of various thicknesses. As the substance was beaten, it became wider, longer, and thinner and began to dry. It was spread into a thin sheet and laid out to dry with stones holding the edges in place against the winds. The result, depending on thickness, was a fairly supple, somewhat paperlike sheet of fabric. The beating of a *hohoa* on a *kua kuku* was also reportedly sometimes used for sending messages. The special houses or sheds used for beating tapa were called *hale kuku*, and when people gathered for beating, it could be compared to a modern quilting group or party.

Bark-cloth–making was refined in many areas of Polynesia, especially Hawaii. Though pieces of tapa were most commonly beaten or pounded together to make larger pieces, tapa pieces were also sewn together with fiber and a wooden needle. Edges were turned under and fused, by beating or sewing, for evenness. Various thicknesses for different purposes could be achieved in the beating process. Fabric could be made so thin as to be gossamer, or thicker strips of the fabric were sometimes plaited.

Decorative Bark Cloth
Many sources agree that Hawaiians developed the most complex and greatest number of decorative prints for bark cloth. Some tapa was dyed first by soaking, or sometimes by brushing the dye onto the fabric, or even beating an already dyed piece of tapa into a larger piece. The Hawaiians carved designs into pieces of bamboo often shaped like thin paddles. These strips of carved wood were then used to stamp or print on the tapa with dyes from plants and soil and other sources. The Hawaiians were careful and precise printers, making sure that patterns were straight and continuous. Several patterns might be used on one length of tapa, creating unique patterns. Interesting patterns could also be obtained by plaiting or twisting pieces of tapa or other plant materials into a long strip and then pressing the length against the tapa. The most common colors used were brown, black, pink, red, green, pale to medium blue, and yellow.

Uses
Bark cloth was derived and used as fabric in other tropical areas well into the late twentieth century. South American Indian populations still living in the remote forests of Brazil, Panama, and Colombia used bark cloth, called *damajagua* (Colombia), as sleeping mats. Based on photographs and descriptions of researchers, the bark cloth of the South American Indians is crude compared with the bark cloth produced in the Pacific Islands. It appears that one of the biggest reasons South American bark cloth was coarser than that of Polynesia is that the retting time allowed for the bast fibers was considerably shorter, overnight, compared with the several days of retting by Polynesians.

Throughout the Pacific Islands, bark cloth was used as a household fabric for both bedding and clothing, and in making ceremonial objects. As clothing, the fabric was wrapped and tied onto the body. It could be gathered or pleated in various ways to create decorative effects for ceremonial occasions.

In everyday use, women commonly wrapped the bark-cloth fabric, called a *pa'u*, around their bodies and tied and tucked the ends in to keep it in place. Women commonly covered only the lower part of their bodies between the waist and knees with the *pa'u*.

Women fold bark cloth. Produced throughout the Pacific Islands, bark cloth is made from the bark of a tree or similar plant. The cloth was used for bedding and clothing, and in making ceremonial objects, but was rarely used by the early 2000s. © JACK FIELDS/CORBIS. REPRODUCED BY PERMISSION.

The *malo*, worn by men, was also wrapped around the body and between the legs to protect the genitalia. The *malo* might or might not have a flap in the front, which could be tucked away depending on tasks that needed to be performed on a given day. Originally only men performed the hula. When performing, additional pieces of tapa could be tied over the *malo*. Tapa was also tied around the shoulders by both men and women when a little extra warmth was needed. Such capes were called *kihei*.

The largest and most elaborate pieces of Hawaiian tapa were made into bedding. Five to eight sheets of plain white tapa were sewn along one edge and then topped with a dyed and watermarked piece. During cool nights the layers could be draped over the sleeper, or laid back, for desired warmth. Tapa was also scented on occasion. Sap, leaves, or flowers were mixed with oil and heated and then added to a dye.

Bark cloth is rarely used for clothing today. It lacks the pliability of woven fabrics, it tends to break down when wet, and processing is labor intensive. The fabric does, however, give important information about the tropical cultures in which it was developed. Hobbyists, historians, and others continue to make bark cloth to study and to keep the knowledge and skill of tapa-making alive. In the Pacific Islands, tapa was not found in common usage after the turn of the nineteenth century.

See also **Felt; Nonwoven Textiles.**

BIBLIOGRAPHY

Abbott, I. A. *La'au, Hawaii: Traditional Hawaiian Uses of Plants.* Honolulu, Hawaii: Bishop Museum Press, 1992. Abbott is a world-renowned psychologist and Hawaiian ethnobotanist of Hawaiian and Chinese extraction.

Hiroa, Te Rangi [Sir Peter H. Buck]. *Arts and Crafts of Hawaii: Clothing.* Honolulu: Bishop Museum Press, 1957. Buck was director of the Bishop Museum from 1936 to 1951. He was the son of a Maori chieftess and an Irish father. He served as physician and anthropologist and is noted for his substantial contributions to Pacific ethnology.

Kaeppler, A. L. *Artificial Curiosities.* Honolulu: Bishop Museum Press, 1978.

Kooijman, S. *Tapa in Polynesia.* Honolulu: Bishop Museum Press, 1972.

Carol A. Dickson and Isabella A. Abbott

BARTHES, ROLAND Better than anyone else, the author of *Roland Barthes par Roland Barthes* (1974) as well as of *Le Degré zéro de l'écriture* (1953) pointed out the illusory nature of the work of biography. Here, we will therefore merely recall a few fragments of a life whose intellectual twists and turns accompanied and helped to transform all facets of French, if not European, thought in the second half of the twentieth century. His publications easily demonstrate his role as developer—in the photographic sense of the term—of the founding questions of so-called postmodern thought. They reveal even more the qualities of a refined and elliptical writer haunted by *The Pleasure of the Text* (1973). Well known for works, alternately journalistic and scholarly, on the political use of myths, literary creation, mass culture, photography, semiological methods, and romantic desire, Barthes also wrote many diverse works on fashion. Often referred to but very little read for themselves, these works still call for a radically novel approach to the phenomena of fashion.

Fragments of Life
Following Jean-Baptiste Farges and Andy Stafford, one can try to distinguish three moments—but they are also three directions, closely connected but not successive—in the activities and the life of Barthes: the polemical journalist immediately after the war, the triumphant yet marginal university professor of the postwar boom, and the elusive "novelist" celebrated by the entire intelligentsia of the left in the 1970s.

More than the details of these moments, it is important to note the intellectual influences that guided Barthes. He himself, in the "Phases" section of his pseudo-autobiography, *Roland Barthes par Roland Barthes*, played with establishing a correspondence of these stages (he counted two more) with an "intertext" of those who inspired him: Gide gave him the wish to write ("the desire for a work"); the trio Sartre-Marx-Brecht drove him to deconstruct our social mythologies (*Mythologies* was published in 1957); Saussure guided him in his work in semiology; the dialogue with Sollers, Kristeva, Derrida, and Lacan led him to take intertextuality as a subject; as for Nietzsche, his influence corresponded to the pleasure of writing during and about his last years, when he produced books dedicated to the enigma of pleasure: *L'Empire des signes* (1970), *S/Z* (1970), *Sade, Fourier, Loyola* (1971), and *Fragments d'un discours amoureux* (1977). *La Chambre claire* (1980), written shortly after the death of his mother, offers a restrained emotional reading of the illusions of the resurrection of reality through photography and concludes with an alternative: accept the spectacle of the false, or "confront untreatable reality."

This represents a program of investigation, both political and aesthetic, that all the works and the very life of Barthes seem to have put into practice, even including the part of his work devoted to speaking about clothes and fashion, "stable ephemera."

Genealogy of an Interest
It has been little noticed how early Barthes developed a curiosity about clothing (at least the clothing of others), about its communicative functions, and about the problems of approach and reconstruction to which those functions give rise. His contribution was that of a student of sociology, considering a massive and poorly understood phenomenon that had been seldom studied in France. This contribution could be decoded on many levels, but it was also that of an aesthete, enamored with the feel of fabrics and the flaring of a white dress on the beach at Bayonne in the 1930s. This is the image—a blurry photograph of his mother—that opens (and closes on "a moment of pleasure") the introduction to *Roland Barthes par Roland Barthes*. Here, it is difficult to avoid noticing the trace of a nostalgic identification with the mother and a personal dandyism maintained with and by discreet and elegant companions. D. A. Miller (1992) may be right to regret that this genealogy, in part based on an unequivocal homosexuality ("L'adjectif," "La déesse H.," "Actif/Passif," and other vignettes in *Roland Barthes*), was never made explicit or "brought out."

However, attention to the body, to its costumes, and to the functions and imagery of those costumes, obsesses—literally—all aspects of the work of Barthes, and this is true beginning with his earliest theater criticism ("Les maladies du costume de théâtre" of 1955, reprinted in *Essais critiques* [1964]), and his various analyses of Brecht's staging of *Mother Courage* from 1957 to 1960. As late as 1980, some fashion details of the photographs illustrating his last book, *La Chambre claire*, become the focus of his reflective emotion and serve as a *punctum*.

In parallel, as early as 1957, he published in *Annales* the seminal article "Histoire et sociologie du vêtement," followed in 1960 by "Pour une sociologie du vêtement," and in 1959, *Critique*, under the title "Langage et vêtement," he published his review of books by J. C. Flügel, F. Kiener, H. H. Hansen, and N. Truman, writers then unknown to French specialists in the field. Other articles, such as "Le bleu est à la mode cette année" (*Revue française de sociologie*, 1960), "Des joyaux aux bijoux" (*Jardin des Arts*, 1961), and "Le dandysme et la mode" (*United States Lines Paris Review*, July 1962) exhibit the development of a semiological approach to clothing and the concern for a multifaceted way of writing able to adapt with virtuosity to diverse audiences. For example, he published in the women's magazine *Marie-Claire* (1967) "Le match Chanel-Courrèges," an article similar to one of the last of the *Mythologies*. Finally, although after that date, the language connected to fashion was no longer directly questioned, the last lines of *Roland Barthes* are still concerned with the weight of appearances: "Writing the body. Neither the skin, nor the muscles, nor the bones, nor the nerves, but the rest, a clumsy, stringy, fluffy, frayed thing, the cloak of a clown."

For a Systemic Approach to Fashion

Le Système de la mode (1967) is an austere and baroque book that came out of a planned thesis, in which a linguistic theory ("the dress code") develops, flourishes, and self-destructs. The book's luxurious jargon and absence of iconography has repelled many and led to various misunderstandings. Its author—famous and praised for other more "literary" publications—plays the role of the proponent of a hard and fast scientism, which he nevertheless declares in the preface is already outdated. He counters and even contradicts this by embellishing the text with precious formulations ("Le bleu est à la mode"), and with a second part (one fourth of the book) unexpected in a work with a methodological purpose: an essay on the rhetoric of fashion journalists along with caustic sociological commentary. "Fashion makes something out of nothing," and that "something" is first of all words, as Stéphane Mallarmé had shown. Hence, it is only the vocabulary and syntax of the captions for fashion pictures presented in the magazines of the 1960s that form the basis for the analyses—legitimately linguistic—offered by *Le Système*.

One should never forget that this was a practical exercise: the ingenious and inventive application of a new technique of reading (semiology) to a limited object but one requiring the creation of novel concepts. Those limits, explicitly set out by Barthes in his book and in contemporaneous interviews, were not understood by many readers who criticize the book for not speaking directly of the non-verbal communication carried out through clothing. Barthes is interested neither in clothing as artifact (clothing as made) nor in its figurative representations (iconic clothing), although those diverse subjects were part of the research program—too broad but more cautious on questions of linguistic analogy—proposed by the 1957 article. His aim is thus to find out "what happens when a real or imaginary object is converted into language" and thus becomes literature capable of being appropriated.

This lack of understanding—often unrecognized—and various ambiguities of expression making a faithful translation difficult, explain in part the delay of the book's publication in English (1985), and a limited reception (in quantity and quality), which needs, however, to be analyzed country by country and generation by generation. The book nevertheless remains an essential reference, at least in France, for sociologists and historians of clothing, but even, or perhaps especially, there, *Le Système* has not acquired a following, except among a few French ethnologists, like Yves Delaporte, Jeanne Martinet, and Marie-Thérèse Duflos-Priot, who do not restrict themselves to studying "spoken," that is, written clothing. It is a fashionable reference in a bibliography, but it has not really been assimilated, even though it has inspired several descriptive systems of clothing used by museums and it has provided a number of convenient metaphors for experts in fashion.

As Barthes wished, the book has to be read first of all as a historical monument, a dated polemic, focused on methodological questions. But it is also a book in which one may take pleasure in digressing, while acquiring expertise and understanding about the state of fashion rhetoric in the 1960s, the state of innovative practices linked to structuralism, and also the state of French backwardness in research on clothing and the still novel efforts to introduce into the field the indispensable theory required for any study of a cultural phenomenon. The phraseology of the fashion magazine signifies a "fashionable" representation of reality, the ideology of which is unveiled by breaking it down into subsets and elements and by the concomitant variations (combined or opposed) of signifier and signified: "A cardigan is sporty or formal depending on whether the collar is open or closed."

Barthes was a pioneer by rejecting the elitist linearity and the facile psychologism of "histories of costume," by engaging in contemporary, not nostalgic, analysis of consumerist ideologies, and by carrying out high-risk interdisciplinary work taking into account individual choices and collective tendencies, the *longue durée* and differential rhythms of transformation of forms and customs, as well as the ephemeral character of the analyses of those who produced them: all knowledge is by definition "Heraclitean." Even more, *Le Système de la mode* should be seen as an invitation to dissect (or possibly deconstruct) the discourse on other discourses that we fabricate with respect to all our objects of investigation. It should be done without illusions, but always with seriousness and irony.

See also **Fashion, Historical Studies of; Fashion, Theories of.**

BIBLIOGRAPHY

Barthes, Roland. *Œuvres complètes.* 3 vols. Paris: Seuil, 1993–1995.

———. *The Fashion System.* New York: Hill & Wang, 1983.

Boultwood, Anne, and Robert Jerrard. "Ambivalence, and Its Relation to Fashion and the Body." *Fashion Theory* 4, no. 3 (2000): 301–322.

Delaporte, Y. "Le signe vestimentaire." *L'Homme* 20, no. 3 (1980): 109–142.

Delaporte, Y., ed. "Vêtement et Sociétés 2." *L'Ethnographie* 130, nos. 92, 93, 94 (1984). Special issue.

Fages, Jean Baptiste. *Comprendre Roland Barthes.* Toulouse, France: Privat, 1979.

Harvey, John. *Men in Black.* Chicago: University of Chicago Press, 1995.

Hollander, Anne. *Seeing Through Clothes.* Berkeley: University of California Press, 1993.

Martinet, J. "Du sémiologique au sein des fonctions vestimentaires," *L'Ethnographie* 130, nos. 92, 93, 94 (1984): pp. 141–251.

Miller, D. A. *Bringing Out Roland Barthes.* Berkeley: University of California Press, 1992.

Stafford, Andy. *Roland Barthes, Phenomenon and Myth: An Intellectual Biography.* Edinburgh: Edinburgh University Press, 1998.

Wilson, Elizabeth. *Adorned in Dreams: Fashion and Modernity.* London: Virago, 1985. Rutgers University Press issued a revised edition in 2003.

Nicole Pellegrin

BATIK Batik is one form of a process known as resist dyeing, in which the surface design on cloth is applied with a semifluid substance (wax, in the case of batik) that resists dye. When the substance is removed the resulting "negative space" or motif contrasts with the dye. Repeated applications of resist and dye create a complex design. Resist dyeing has a broad geographic distribution, historically found on all continents except for the Pacific Islands and Australia. The resist substances include mud, pastes (rice, peanut, cassava, or bean), starch, hot resin, paraffin, and beeswax. Monochromatic palettes of white (cloth color) and dark brown such as the bogolan mud cloths of Mali, or white and indigo as in the batiks of the Blue Hmong are common, and motifs tend to be geometric such as those found in West Africa, Turkistan, the Middle East, mainland Southeast Asia, and south China. In Indonesia, particularly on Java, batik developed intricate styles not found elsewhere, and its sophistication is mirrored in the use of batik cloths in Indonesian dress.

Method

The rise of fine batik in Indonesia hinged on the availability of imported high thread count cotton fabric from Europe after the industrial revolution. Women create resist patterns on this cloth by gliding molten hot wax from a copper stylus called a *canting*, which just barely touches the cloth; coarse cloth would cause snags and wax drips. Both the surface and the underside of the cloth are waxed, so that the pattern is complete on both sides of the cloth. After each waxing, the cloth is dyed, and then boiled to remove the wax. Then another element of the design is waxed and the process repeats. The use of a stylus to create a hand-drawn batik pattern is called *tulis* ("writing"); the creation of tulis batik takes as much as two weeks for the waxing and a little over a month by the time the final dye bath is completed. Care must be taken to keep from cracking the wax, as this indicates poor craftsmanship.

Toward the middle or end of the nineteenth century, Chinese batik makers on the north coast of Java designed a type of copper stamp called *cap* (pronounced chop), a configuration of needles and sheet metal strips which was pressed into a hot wax stamp pad and used to transfer the wax to the cloth. *Caps* were paired as mirror images to wax the top and undersides of the cloth. *Cap* batik is a much faster process than *tulis*; a skilled worker can wax twenty cloths in a day.

Design Motifs

Classical batik designs from central Java can be grouped in four categories; three are strongly geometric and the fourth is more organic. The first is the *garis miring* of diagonally running designs such as *parang rusak* ("broken knife"). The second is *nitik*, consisting of small dots or scallops as filler in large designs; this pattern imitates the visual effect of woven cloth. The third is *ceplok* which has grid-formed designs inspired by rosettes and cross-sections of fruit. The fourth is the *semen* category of styled flora and fauna motifs.

In general, batik designs from the north coast tend to be more organic with mammal, sea creature, bird, insect, and floral themes. These batiks are also more colorful. Traditional batiks from central Java tend to have muted colors of indigo, browns, creams, and whites in geometric motifs. A few, such as the *parang rusak*, were restricted for use only in the royal palaces of Yogyakarta, Surakarta, and other central Javanese royal courts, but over time those sumptuary laws have fallen by the wayside.

Motif Placement and Dress

Batik on apparel involves strategic placement of multiple motifs, as can be seen from an examination of different garments: a head cloth (*iket kepala*), shawl (*slendang*), two kinds of wrapped skirts (*kain panjang* and *sarong*), and drawstring pants (*celana*). The head wrapper, worn by men, is about three feet long; it is a batik item that is produced in Java and worn throughout Indonesia. The inner area is a diamond shape, which may be solid or batiked. The outer part of the cloth is decorated with various motifs, with an ornate border that includes imitation fringe lines. It is possible for a head cloth to have different motifs in each quadrant, allowing for a high degree of decorative variety all in one head cloth.

Like the head cloth, the *slendang* or shoulder cloth can have borders and imitation fringe. There are many sizes; one for carrying children is about eighteen inches by seven and a half feet. Some may have one batik motif all over, or others might have each end specially decorated with *tumpal* (triangle) and other border motifs.

The *kain panjang*, a skirt wrapper about 250 centimeters long, may be covered with an all-over motif, or it may have narrow bands at the top and bottom. Sometimes *kain panjangs* are batiked with two contrasting patterns, called *pagi-sore* (morning-afternoon), an ingenious and efficient use of space because it allows a single length of cloth to serve as, in effect, two outfits. The cloth design is applied in the form of two triangles, so that as the cloth is wrapped about the body, only one design will show.

The sarong is shorter than the *kain panjang* (up to 220 centimeters in length) and sewn into a tube. Whereas the *kain panjang* was linked to central Java and the palaces there, the sarong was the regional dress of the north coast of Java, but eventually came to be used widely in Indonesia as informal dress. At the turn of the twentieth

A textile worker creates a batik in Malaysia. Classical batik designs were geometic and organic in nature. Diagonal lines, small dots, florals and fauna motifs were common in central Java. Batik designs from the north coast illustrated sea creatures, insects and floral themes. © CHARLES O'REAR/CORBIS. REPRODUCED BY PERMISSION.

century, Eurasian female entrepreneurs developed colorful Pekalongan-style batiks (named for a town on the northern coast of Java) with a tripartite layout. Floral borders (*pinggir*) lined the top and bottom of the textile, often with the lower border as the wider one. At one end was a wide panel (*kepala*) whose ground and motif contrasted with the body or rest of the textile (*badan*). The lower floral border framed the *kepala* on both sides. In general, the *badan* and *pinggir* were made with a *cap*, but the floral bouquet in the *kepala* would have been drawn by hand (*tulis*). As sewn into a sarong, the *kepala* worn in front would be shown to its fullest advantage.

That Pekalongan sarongs reflected Dutch floral and other themes was no accident. In the early years of Dutch colonization of Java, Dutch men married Javanese and Chinese women, who wore *kain-kebaya* (blouse-jacket with *kain panjang* or sarong). The women and children were Dutch citizens and at social events women wore *kain-kebaya*, showing off their prized Pekalongan batiks. In time the longish *kebaya* shortened to hip length to better display the *kepala* and *badan* of the batik wrappers. In the early twentieth century, more Dutch women joined husbands or married Dutch husbands in Java and also adopted the *kain-kebaya* as a practical alternative to the tailored European dress. Yet in the 1920s, as European racial attitudes hardened in the colonies, European women sought to differentiate themselves from Eurasian women and so tended increasingly to wear tropical-style European dress in public venues.

Batik drawstring pants (*celana*) were similarly tied to the dynamics of ruler and ruled. The origin of batik pants is not clear, but they seem to have been modeled after pants for little Chinese boys. Chinese and Dutch men found batik pants both exotic and comfortable, and the

pants were in use in the 1870s if not earlier. Dutch men favored them as loungewear in the privacy of their home, while their wives relaxed in *kain-kebaya*. Photographic evidence shows that the wearing of batik pants by adult men and children spread at least to Sumatra. The batik pants were made from a batik cloth or were made into pants from plain cloth first, then batiked. Batiks with border bands were incorporated in the batik pants by becoming the "cuff" of the pants. For taller individuals, an extension band of white fabric was sewn to the top of the batik pants; the band would be hidden under a shirt or jacket.

Batik and World Dress

In the 1970s the competition from cheaper screen-printed imitation batik led to two developments: the batik shirt and *tulis* batik as couture. The governor of Jakarta, Ali Sadikin, proposed that a collared, long-sleeved button shirt in batik would be an acceptable formal alternative to the three-piece suit and hoped this strategy would vitalize the batik industry. The batik shirt became the ubiquitous dress for the urban Indonesian male. In the second development, batik designer Iwan Tirta created couture lines in *tulis* by producing the textiles on silk (instead of cotton) and reworking traditional motifs through size, color, and gold enhancement. If Tirta began with a flat batik cloth with an overall pattern and border, the border might be seen at the hem or sleeve; Tirta made use of the whole cloth. Both Sadikin and Tirta helped to create new dress styles for Indonesians and to give Indonesian batik a place in world fashion.

See also **Dyeing, Resist.**

BIBLIOGRAPHY

Djumena, Nian S. *Batik dan Mitra, Batik and its Kind.* Jakarta: Djambatan, 1990.

Elliot, Inger McCabe. *Batik: Fabled Cloth of Java.* New York: Clarkson N. Potter, Inc., 1984.

Larsen, Jack Lenor. *The Dyer's Art: Ikat, Batik, Plangi.* New York: Van Nostrand Reinhold Company, 1976.

Schulte Nordholt, Henk. ed. *Outward Appearances: Dressing State and Society in Indonesia.* Leiden, The Netherlands: KITLV Press, 1997.

Heidi Boehlke

BATISTE. *See* **Cambric, Batiste, and Lawn.**

BAUDELAIRE, CHARLES Charles-Pierre Baudelaire (1821–1867) was perhaps the greatest French poet of the nineteenth century. He is most famous for a volume of poetry, *Les fleurs du mal* (Flowers of evil), published in 1857, which was prosecuted for blasphemy as well as obscenity. Baudelaire was also an important art critic and translator. He appears in an encyclopedia of fashion because he proved to be an influential theorist of fashion and dandyism.

In his youth, Baudelaire devoted considerable time and money to his appearance. At a time when the masculine wardrobe was becoming ever more sober, he adopted an austere form of dandyism that was neither foppish nor bohemian. Whereas many of his contemporaries deplored the trend toward dark, severe clothing for men, he embraced and even exaggerated the style by wearing all-black clothing. But dandyism involved more than clothing for Baudelaire; he would certainly not have agreed with Thomas Carlyle's definition of the dandy as "a clothes-wearing man." Although Baudelaire's poetry does not touch on dandyism per se, he explored the topic both in his intimate journals, under such headings as "The eternal superiority of the Dandy. What is the Dandy?", and in two of his most famous essays, "On the Heroism of Modern Life," a section of his *Salon of 1846*, and *The Painter of Modern Life* (1863).

The modernity of dandyism is central to Baudelaire's analysis. Dandyism, he wrote, "is a modern thing, resulting from causes entirely new." It appears "when democracy is not yet all-powerful, and aristocracy is just beginning to fall." Like many artists during the nineteenth century, Baudelaire was ambivalent about the rise of democracy and capitalism. He described contemporary middle-class masculine attire as "a uniform livery of affliction [that] bears witness to equality." It was, he suggested, "a symbol of perpetual mourning." On the other hand, Baudelaire insisted that one should be of one's own time. "But all the same, has not this much-abused garb its own beauty?" The modern man's frock coat had both a "political beauty, which is an expression of universal equality," and also a "poetic beauty."

In place of the equality which modern men's uniform attire seemed to proclaim, Baudelaire suggested that dandyism announced a new type of intellectual elitism. "In the disorder of these times, certain men . . . may conceive the idea of establishing a new kind of aristocracy . . . based . . . on the divine gifts which work and money are unable to bestow. Dandyism is the last spark of heroism amid decadence." Baudelaire's modern dandy eschewed not only the foppish paraphernalia of prerevolutionary aristocratic dress, but also denied the bourgeois capitalist dominance of wealth. The Baudelairean dandy was not just a wealthy man who wore fashionable and expensive dark suits.

"Dandyism does not . . . consist, as many thoughtless people seem to believe, in an immoderate taste for . . . material elegance," declared Baudelaire. "For the perfect dandy these things are no more than symbols of his aristocratic superiority of mind. Furthermore, to his eyes, which are in love with distinction above all things, the perfection of his toilet will consist in absolute simplicity." Part of Baudelaire's minimalist aesthetic involved the elimination of color in favor of black, a noncolor that remains strongly associated with both au-

French poet Charles Baudelaire. Baudelaire's essays emphasized the relationship between fashion, modern life, and art. He related the transitory nature, or constant change of fashion, as the hallmark of modernity. THE LIBRARY OF CONGRESS. PUBLIC DOMAIN.

thority and rebellion, as witnessed by the following lines from Quentin Tarantino's film *Reservoir Dogs*:

MR. PINK: Why can't we pick out our own color?
JOE: I tried that once. It don't work. You get four guys fighting over who's gonna be Mr. Black.

If modern men's clothing—and still more so the clothing of the dandy—was characterized by simplicity, the same could not be said of nineteenth-century women's fashion, which was highly complicated and decorative. It was only in the twentieth century that such women as Coco Chanel created a radically simplified style of female fashion epitomized by the little black dress. Indeed, it could be said that Chanel was one of the first female dandies. Yet Baudelaire's attitudes toward women are problematic for modern feminists. "Woman is the opposite of the dandy," declared Baudelaire, because she is "natural." Only to the extent that she creates an artificial persona through dress and cosmetics is she admirable, and, even then, Baudelaire describes her as "a kind of idol, stupid perhaps, but dazzling."

Putting aside his ambivalence towards women, Baudelaire analyzed fashion in ways that illuminate both modern life and modern art. In particular, his essay *The*

Painter of Modern Life was one of the first and most penetrating analyses of the relationship between *la mode* (fashion) and *la modernité* (modernity). For Baudelaire, fashion was the key to modernity, and one simply could not paint modern individuals if one did not understand their dress. Baudelaire argued that it was simply "laziness" that led so many artists to "dress all their subjects in the garments of the past." "The draperies of Rubens or Veronese will in no way teach you how to depict . . . fabric of modern manufacture," he wrote. "Furthermore, the cut of skirt and bodice is by no means similar. . . . Finally, the gesture and bearing of the woman of today gives her dress a life and a special character which are not those of the woman of the past."

According to Baudelaire, there were two aspects to beauty—the eternal and the ephemeral. The fact that fashion was so transitory, constantly changing into something new, made it the hallmark of modernity. The modern artist, whether painter or poet, had to be able "to distill the eternal from the transitory." As Baudelaire wrote, "What poet would dare, in depicting the pleasure caused by the appearance of a great beauty, separate the woman from her dress?"

As a theorist of fashion, Baudelaire moved far beyond such other dandies and writers of his era as George ("Beau") Brummell, Jules Barbey d'Aurevilly, and Théophile Gautier. He inspired such modernist poets as Stéphane Mallarmé and such philosophers as Georg Simmel and Walter Benjamin. Indeed, it is virtually impossible to imagine the modern study of fashion without taking account of Baudelaire's contribution.

See also **Benjamin, Walter; Brummell, George (Beau); Dandyism; Fashion, Theories of; Little Black Dress; Mallarmé, Stéphane; Simmel, Georg; Wilde, Oscar.**

BIBLIOGRAPHY

Baudelaire, Charles. *The Painter of Modern Life and Other Essays.* Edited and translated by Jonathan Mayne. London: Phaidon Press Ltd., 1964.

Lehmann, Ulrich. *Tigersprung: Fashion in Modernity.* Cambridge, Mass.: MIT Press, 2000.

Moers, Ellen. *The Dandy: Brummell to Beerbohm.* London: Secker and Warburg, 1960.

Steele, Valerie. *Paris Fashion: A Cultural History.* 2nd ed. New Haven, Conn.: Berg, 1999.

Valerie Steele

BAUDRILLARD, JEAN The French intellectual Jean Baudrillard (b. 1929) is widely acclaimed as one of the master visionary thinkers of postmodernism and poststructuralism. He was trained as a sociologist, and his early critique was influenced by a certain style of radicalism that appeared in France after 1968, which included critical challenge to the disciplines, methods, theories, styles, and discourses of the academic intellectual establishment. After the late 1960s Baudrillard's social theory witnessed major paradigm shifts. The theory of consumption that he began to articulate in the 1970s foresaw the development of consumer society, with its dual focus first on the visual culture (material objects) and, later, on the virtual (electronic and cyberspace) culture.

Baudrillard's fashion-relevant theorizing dates from his earlier writing: it forms part of his broader analysis of objects in consumer society. This scheme postulated a transition from "dress," in which sartorial meaning (of differentiation and distinction) resided in natural signs, through "fashion," in which meaning resided in oppositional (structuralist) signs, to "post-fashion," in which signs are freed from the link to referents and to meaning (poststructuralist). Baudrillard's early work is divided into three phases: (*a*) the reworking of Marxist social theory, as evident in *The System of Objects* (1968), *The Consumer Society* (1970), and *For a Critique of the Political Economy of the Sign* (1972) and with an emphasis on the "sign"; (*b*) a critique of Marxism, as seen in *The Mirror of Production* (1975) and *Symbolic Exchange and Death* (1976), where Baudrillard substitutes symbolic exchange for utilitarian exchange as an explanation of consumerism; (*c*) a break with Marxism, as manifest in *Seduction* (1979), *Simulations* (1983), *Fatal Strategies* (1983), and *The Transparency of Evil: Essays on Extreme Phenomena* (1993), which substitutes the carnival-esque principle (celebration, pleasure, excess, and waste) for the utility principle.

Signification

Initially, Baudrillard argued that when products move from the realm of function (reflecting use value and exchange value) to the realm of signification (reflecting sign value), they become carriers of social meaning. Specifically, they become "objects." Baudrillard's notion of sign value is based on an analogy between a system of objects (commodity) and a system of sign (language). He applied Ferdinand de Saussure's structural linguistics to the study of fashion, media, ideologies, and images. If consumption is a communication system (messages and images), commodities are no longer defined by their use but by what they signify—not individually but as "set" in a total configuration. The meaning of signs, according to de Saussure, is made up of two elements: *signifiers* (sound images), which index the *signifieds* (referent). Saussurian structural linguistics is based on two principles: a metaphysics of depth and a metaphysics of surface. The metaphysics of depth assumes that meaning links a signifier with an underlying signified. The metaphysics of surface implies that signs do not have inherent meaning but rather gain their meaning through their relation to other signs.

Using a linguistic (semiotic) analogy to analyze commodities, Baudrillard developed a genealogy of sign structures consisting of three orders. The first order, founded on *imitation*, presupposes a dualism where appearances mask reality. In the second order, founded on *production*, appearances create an illusion of reality. In the third order, founded on *simulation*, appearances invent re-

Signification

Order of Simulacra	Metaphor	Corresponding Stage of European Fashion	Metaphysical Analogy	Signification Order
Imitation	Counterfeit	Premodern stage	Metaphysics of depth	Direct signifier-signified links
Production	Illusion	Modern stage	Metaphysics of depth	Indirect signifier-signified links
Simulation	Fake	Postmodern stage	Metphysics of surface	Signifier-signifier links

Social meaning in products. Products that served as function, reflecting use and exchange value, but came to reflect sign value, Baudrillard believed, carried social meaning. He used Ferdinand de Saussure's structural linguistics to study fashion, media, ideologies, and images.

ality. No longer concerned with the real, images are reproduced from a model, and it is this lack of a reference point that threatens the distinction between true and false. There are parallels between Baudrillard's historical theory of sign structures and historical theorizing of European sartorial signification. The order of imitation corresponds to the premodern stage, the order of production corresponds to the modern stage, and the order of simulation corresponds to the postmodern stage.

Premodern stage. Throughout European fashion history the scarcity of resources symbolized rank in dress. Costly materials were owned and displayed by the privileged classes. Technological and social developments from the fourteenth century onward challenged the rigid hierarchy of feudal society. This challenge triggered the legislation of sumptuary laws that attempted to regulate clothing practices along status lines by defining precisely the type and quality of fabrics allowed to each class. Since styles were not sanctioned by law, toward the end of the fourteenth century clothes began to take on new forms. This tendency set in motion a process of differentiation (along the lines of Georg Simmel's "trickle-down theory" of fashion), whereby the aristocracy could distinguish itself by the speed with which it adopted new styles.

Modern stage. The technological developments that characterized industrial capitalism (among them, the invention of the sewing machine and wash-proof dyes), popularized fashion by reducing the price of materials. Mass production of clothes increased homogeneity of style and decreased their indexical function. The industrial revolution created the city and the mass society, improved mobility, and multiplied social roles. A new order was created in which work (achieved status) rather than lineage (ascribed status) determined social positioning. Uniforms were introduced to the workplace to denote rank, as dress no longer reflected rank order (but instead defined time of day, activities, occasions, or gender). As a result, a subtle expert system of status differentiation through appearance between the aristocracy and "new money" evolved. This system coded the minutiae of appearance and attributed symbolic meanings that reflected a person's character or social standing. It also anchored certain sartorial practices to moral values (for example, the notion of noblesse oblige).

Postmodern stage. Postmodernism denotes a radical break with the dominant culture and aesthetics. In architecture it represented plurality of forms, fragmentation of styles, and diffuse boundaries. It has substituted disunity, subjectivity, and ambiguity for the modernist unity, absolutism, and certainty. In the sciences it stands for a "crisis in representation." This challenge to the "correspondence theory of truth" resulted in totalizing theories of universal claims giving way to a plurality of "narrative truths" that reflect, instead, the conventions of discourse (for example, rules of grammar that construct gender, metaphors and expressions encode cultural assumptions and worldview, notions of what makes a "good" story). The postmodern cultural shift has left its mark on the fashion world through its rejection of tradition, relaxation of norms, emphasis on individual diversity, and variability of styles.

Baudrillard characterized postmodern fashion by a shift from the modern *order of production* (functionality and utility) to the aristocratic *order of seduction*. Seduction derives pleasure from excess (sumptuary useless consumption of surplus, such as is displayed by celebrities). Baudrillard posits seduction as a system that marks the end of the structuralist principle of opposition as a basis for meaning. His notion of seduction is that of a libido that is enigmatic and enchanted. It is not a passion for desire but a passion for games and ritual. Seduction takes place on the level of appearance, surface, and signs and negates the seriousness of reality, meaning, morality, and truth.

Analysis. Analysis of the three stages of sartorial representation in terms of Baudrillard's signification relations produces Figure 1. In the order of *imitation* that characterized the premodern stage, clothes refer unequivocally to status. They signify the natural order of things without ambiguity. The order of *production* characterized the modern stage, where mass-produced clothes ceased to be indexical of status. It became important to establish whether people were what they claimed to be or rather were just pretending. In the orders of imitation and production, the signifier indexes an underlying meaning, either inherent or constructed. In contrast, the order of *simulation* refers to the principle of the postmodern dress that is indifferent to any traditional social order and is completely self-referential, that is, fashion for its own sake. For Baudrillard, the effacing of real history as a referent leaves us nothing but empty signs and marks the end of signification itself. In sum, as simulation substitutes for production, it replaces the linear order with a cyclical order and frees the signifier from its link to the signified. Thus, fashion as a form of pleasure takes the place of fashion as a form of communication.

See also **Benjamin, Walter; Brummell, George (Beau); Fashion, Theories of; Mallarmé, Stéphane; Simmel, Georg; Wilde, Oscar.**

BIBLIOGRAPHY

Baudrillard, Jean. *The Mirror of Production.* Translated by Mark Poster. St. Louis, Mo.: Telos Press, 1975.

———. *For a Critique of the Political Economy of the Sign.* Translated by Charles Levin. St. Louis, Mo.: Telos Press, 1981.

———. *Simulations.* Translated by Paul Foss, Paul Patton, and Philip Beitchman. New York: Semiotext(e), 1983.

———. *Fatal Strategies.* Translated by Philip Beitchman and W. G. J. Niesluchowski. New York: Semiotext(e), 1990.

———. *Seduction.* Translated by Brian Singer. New York: St. Martin's Press, 1990.

———. *Symbolic Exchange and Death.* Translated by Iain Hamilton Grant. Thousand Oaks, Calif.: Sage Publications, 1993.

———. *The Transparency of Evil: Essays on Extreme Phenomena.* Translated by James Benedict. London and New York: Verso, 1993.

———. *The System of Objects.* Translated by James Benedict. New York: Verso, 1996.

———. *The Consumer Society: Myths and Structures.* Thousand Oaks, Calif.: Sage Publications, 1998.

Works about Jean Baudrillard

Gane, Mike, ed. *Jean Baudrillard.* 4 vols. Sage Masters of Modern Social Thought. Thousand Oaks, Calif.: Sage Publications, 2000.

Kellner, Douglas. "Baudrillard, Semiurgy and Death." *Theory, Culture, and Society* 4, no. 1 (1987): 125–146.

———. *Jean Baudrillard: From Marxism to Postmodernism and Beyond.* Stanford, Calif.: Stanford University Press, 1989.

Kellner, Douglas, ed. *Baudrillard: A Critical Reader.* Oxford and Cambridge, Mass.: Blackwell, 1989.

Poster, Mark, ed. *Jean Baudrillard: Selected Writings.* Stanford, Calif.: Stanford University Press, 1988.

Efrat Tseëlon

BEADS In their simplest form, beads are small, perforated spheres, usually strung to create necklaces. They can be made of metal, pottery, glass, or precious or semi-precious stones, such as ivory, coral, turquoise, amber, or rock crystal, or glass. The human desire for personal ornamentation and decoration is clearly evident from the frequent presence of beads in archaeological sites. The earliest beads, dating from the Paleolithic period, were made mainly with seeds, nuts, grains, animal teeth, bones, and, most especially, sea shells. Indeed, like sea cowries, beads

Rosary. Created centuries ago by Christian monks to count prayers, rosaries have become a symbol of a committed spiritual life and are a common element in modern Christianity. © ROYALTY-FREE/CORBIS. REPRODUCED BY PERMISSION.

were used in barter and in ceremonial exchanges; they thus contain precious information on early trade routes.

Beads found in early Egyptian tombs are thought to date from about 4000 B.C.E. Faience (glazed ceramic) beads appeared in Egypt's predynastic period and continued to be made in Roman times. The Phoenicians and Egyptians also made fancy beads with human and animal faces. What were probably the earliest gold beads, going back to 3000 B.C.E., were found in the Sumerian and Indus valleys; gold beads of later date have been found in Ashanteland (Ghana) and other parts of Africa. Mycenaean beads found in Crete, dating from the Late Bronze Age (c. 1100 B.C.E), were fashioned in original floral shapes, such as lilies and lotuses, as well as granulated surfaces. Stone and shell beads, and from the fifteenth century C.E. on, glass beads, were worn in large quantities by American Indians.

Among some populations, beads are worn as much for magical as for decorative purposes. For example, in Middle Eastern and southern European countries, coral beads are thought to encourage fertility and are frequently an essential part of a woman's trousseau. Turquoise and blue-colored beads are attached to the clothes of brides and children, as well as to the collars of domestic animals—or hung to cars' viewing mirrors—to avert bad luck and illness. Amulets thought to have the power to avert impotence, loss of breast milk, or the alienation of a husband's affection, often include "eye beads" strung together with cowries: thanks to a subtle resemblance of openings and curved lines, the latter are understood to symbolically represent the eye as well as the female genitalia.

The word "bead" comes from the Middle English word "bede," which means pray, and beads strung to make rosaries have been used since the Middle Ages to count prayers. But even as strings of beads took on well-defined religious significance in Europe, they rapidly took on new meanings, as they were exported to diverse cultures that had their own symbolic systems. Rosaries, which were among the earliest strings of crystal and glass beads exported from Venice in significant quantities by crusaders, soon became part of garments and ornaments related to entirely different belief systems and rituals. They were often used as counters in trade. Certain types of beads that acquired rarity value were removed from economic exchange cycles to become ancestral property, only changing hands as bride-wealth or used to validate claims to royal and aristocratic status.

European traders often exchanged beads for African or American Indian goods of very much greater value, such as gold or even slaves. According to traditional lore, the whole island of Manhattan was bought by Dutch settlers for the equivalent in beads of twenty-four dollars. The story—a foundation myth of the United States—is often told to show how the Indians were primitive and naive. But in reality, as research on different societies has shown, beads had been used in trade for centuries before the arrival of Europeans, and their value was determined by social consensus.

For many African populations, beads are important markers of identity. Beaded garments and hats are worn at all times, but most especially on ceremonial occasions. Young women make small bead jewels for their favorite boys. The contrast of different colors and shapes can give these jewels a variety of meanings and whites have described them as "love letters." For some South African Kwa-Zulu women, who have developed remarkable skill in creating beaded figures or dolls dressed in ethnic costume, to sell to tourists in the vicinity of Durban, beadwork has become a useful source of income.

The use of beads for personal adornment, as well as for decoration of a variety of objects, has continued uninterrupted through history. They can be stitched or woven into textiles, used in embroidery, or applied to hats, belts, handbags, or to household objects, such as boxes or lampshades. American Indians have long applied vividly colored glass beads in original geometrical designs to leather clothing, bags, and leather boots.

While Venetians dominated the manufacture and export of glass beads from the fifteenth to the mid-twentieth century, by the early 2000s beads were made in all parts of the world. Since the 1960s, interest in the cultures and customs of third-world countries has led to a keen search for old beads on the part of museum keepers and antique dealers. This in turn has led to a revival in large-scale production and use of beads by the general public. Fashion items such as handbags, ladies' waistcoats, and belts vividly decorated with beads are made in China and other parts of the Far East.

Venetian beads, while not produced on as large a scale as they were in the past, remain very high quality, and the city's association with glass beads helps it maintain a lively second-hand and antique trade, as well as a strong interest in experimentation and creativity in the search for new versions of the traditional craft of making glass beads and

Man working prayer beads. For centuries beads have been an instrument of prayer. In Middle Eastern countries, as well as other parts of the world, strung beads help one keep one's place in structured prayer. © DAVID H. WELLS/CORBIS. REPRODUCED BY PERMISSION.

their use in personal ornaments. Beadwork, in particular the stringing of necklaces and bracelets, has become a widespread pastime, and shops with lively displays of beads, fine metal, or cotton and silk thread are found in almost every city. The low cost of beads in relation to jewelry makes them a very versatile ornamental element, often specially created to enhance a particular outfit or occasion.

See also **Costume Jewelry; Jewelry; Necklaces and Pendants; Spangles.**

BIBLIOGRAPHY

Carey, Margaret. "Across the Atlantic: Beaded Garments Transformed." *Journal of Museum Ethnography* no. 14 (March 2002).

Dubin, Lois Sherr. *The History of Beads from 30,000 B.C.E. to the Present.* New York: Harry N. Abrams, 1987.

Eicher, Joanne B., and Barbara Sumberg. "World Fashion, Ethnic and National Dress." In *Dress and Ethnicity: Change across Space and Time.* Edited by Joanne B. Eicher. Washington, D.C.: Berg, 1995.

Hughes-Brock, Helen. "The Mycenaean Greeks: Master Bead-Makers. Major Results Since the Time of Horace Beck."

In *Ornaments from the Past: Bead Studies after Beck: A Book on Glass and Semi-Precious Stone Beads in History and Archaeology for Archaeologists, Jewelers, Historians and Collectors.* By Ian C. Glover, Helen Hughes-Brock, and Julian Henderson. London and Bangkok: Bead Study Trust, 2003.

Israel, Jonathan I. *Dutch Primacy in World Trade, 1585–1740.* New York: Oxford University Press, 1989.

Jones, Mark, ed. *Fake? The Art of Deception.* Berkeley: University of California Press, 1990.

Karklins, Karlis. *Glass Beads.* 2nd edition. Ottawa: National Historic Parks and Sites Branch, 1985.

Klump, D., and Corinne A. Kratz. "Aesthetics, Expertise, and Ethnicity: Okiek and Masai Perspectives on Personal Ornament." In *Being Maasai: Ethnicity and Identity in East Africa.* Edited by Thomas Spear and Robert Waller. Athens: Ohio University Press, 1993.

Orchard, William C. *Beads and Beadwork of the American Indians: A Study Based on Specimens in the Museum of the American Indian.* New York: Museum of the American Indian, Heye Foundation, 1929.

———. "Transport and Trade Routes." In *The Cambridge Economic History of Europe,* vol. 4. Cambridge, U.K.: Cambridge University Press, 1967.

Picard, John, ed. *Beads from the West African Trade.* 6 vols. Carmel, Calif.: Picard African Imports, 1986.

Sciama, Lidia D., and Joanne B. Eicher, eds. *Beads and Bead Makers: Gender, Material Culture, and Meaning.* Oxford: Berg, 1998.

Tomalin, Stefany. *Beads! Make Your Own Unique Jewelry.* New York: Sterling Publishing Company, 1988.

———. *The Bead Jewelry Book.* Chicago: Contemporary Books, 1998.

Tracey, James D., ed. *The Rise of Merchant Empires: Long-Distance Trade in the Early Modern World, 1350–1750.* New York: Cambridge University Press, 1990.

Lidia D. Sciama

BEARDS AND MUSTACHES Because facial hair is strongly associated with masculinity, beards and mustaches carry powerful and complex cultural meanings. Growing a beard or mustache, or being clean-shaven, can communicate information about religion, sexual identity, and orientation, and other important aspects of cultural heritage.

In many cultures, the wearing (or not) of facial hair has been a marker of membership in a tribe, ethnic group, or culture, implying acceptance of the group's cultural values and a rejection of the values of other groups. This distinction sometimes admitted a certain ambiguity; in ancient Greece, a neatly trimmed beard was a mark of a philosopher, but the Greeks also distinguished themselves from the *barbaroi* ("barbarians," literally "hairy ones") to their north and east. In early imperial China some powerful men (magistrates and military officers, for example) wore beards, but in general hairiness was associated with the "uncivilized" pastoral peoples of the northern frontier; by later imperial times, most Chinese men were clean-shaven. As Frank Dikotter puts it, "the hairy man was located beyond the limits of the cultivated field, in the wilderness, the mountains, and the forests: the border of human society, he hovered on the edge of bestiality. Body hair indicated physical regression, generated by the absence of cooked food, decent clothing and proper behaviour" (p. 52).

Conversely, in ancient Egypt beards were associated with high rank, and they were braided and cultivated to curl upward at the ends. False beards were worn by rulers, both male and female, and fashioned of gold. In the ancient Mesopotamian, Assyrian, Sumerian, and Hittite empires, curled and elaborately decorated beards were indicators of high social status while slaves were clean-shaven. In his book *Hair: The First Five Thousand Years,* Richard Corson analyzes the complexities of facial hair across history and points out that in the ancient world, "during shaven periods, beards were allowed to grow as a sign of mourning." Also, in a period of shaven faces such as early in the first century, "slaves were required to wear beards as a sign of their subjugation" but when free men wore beards in the second and third centuries slaves had to distinguish themselves free by shaving (p. 71). Long mustaches were the norm amongst Goths, Saxons, and Gauls and were worn "hanging down upon their breasts like wings" (p. 91) and by the Middle Ages again were a mark of noble birth.

Facial hair has been an issue for many religions. Pope Gregory VII issued a papal edict banning bearded clergymen in 1073. In Hasidic Jewish culture beards are worn as an emblem of obedience to religious law. Muslim men who shave their facial hair are, in some places, subject to intense criticism from more religiously conservative Muslims for whom growing a beard is an indication of cleanliness, obedience to God, and male gender. In some Muslim countries (such as Afghanistan under the Taliban), the wearing of untrimmed beards has been obligatory for men.

In Western culture in recent centuries, however, the wearing or shaving of facial hair has tended to become more a matter of fashion than of cultural identity. For most of history, the shaving of facial hair and the shaping of beards and mustaches has depended on the skills of barbers and personal servants who knew how to whet a razor and to use hot water and emollients to soften a beard. Jean-Jacques Perret created the first safety razor in 1770. It consisted of a blade with a wooden guard, which was sold together with a book of instruction in its use entitled *La Pogotomie* (The Art of Self-Shaving). In 1855 the Gillette razor was invented, the T-shape taking over from the cutthroat razor. Self-shaving became increasingly popular as the century progressed, especially after Gillette's further modification of his original design in 1895 with the introduction of the disposable razor blade.

The nineteenth and twentieth centuries have seen a myriad of different styles of beards and mustaches as facial hair took over as a focal point of male personal fashion, together with complementary hairstyles. Men might choose to wear their whiskers as muttonchops (so-called because of their shape), Piccadilly weepers (very long side-whiskers), Burnsides (that eventually evolved into sideburns), or the short and pointed Vandyke beard (alluding to a style popular in Renaissance Holland). Full mustaches that grew down over the top lip were dubbed soup strainers.

Many products, such as tonics, waxes, and pomades, were developed to help groom and style facial hair, and small industries grew up to manufacture and distribute them. Stylish mustaches and beards could be a point of personal pride. Charles Dickens wrote of his own facial ornamentation, "the moustaches are glorious, glorious. I have cut them shorter and trimmed them a little at the ends to improve their shape" (Corson 1965, p. 405).

In much of western Europe and America, facial hair was considered dashing and masculine because of its long associations with the military. By the mid-nineteenth century, doctors warned men that the clean-shaven look could be deleterious to their health; for example, it was said that bronchial problems could result if a mustache and beard were not worn to filter the air to the lungs. Thus to be clean-shaven was almost an act of rebellion, taken at the end of the century by bohemians and artists such as Aubrey Beardsley and the playwright Oscar Wilde. By the 1920s, however, the clean-shaven look had taken hold in mainstream fashion. Facial hair then became a mark of rebellion or artistic self-definition. Salvador Dali confirmed his artist status with an elaborate waxed mustache by the late 1920s. Mustaches continued to be worn by military men, and this is reflected in the names of styles such as Guardsman, Major, and Captain.

The beard had become rare by the mid-twentieth century, and was thus taken up by young bohemians in the 1950s as a gesture of nonconformity. Beards continued as a countercultural statement in the late 1960s with the hippie movement, when many young men saw facial hair as a sign of "naturalness," or a gesture of admiration for revolutionaries such as Che Guevara and the Cuban leader Fidel Castro. Hells Angels and bikers added a leather-clad hypermasculinity to the beard. Bearded hypermasculinity also was embraced within some subsets of gay culture. By the 1970s the clone look emanating from the streets of San Francisco included tight jeans, short hair, and mustaches. This look was adopted in mainstream fashion as seen on the actor Tom Selleck in *Magnum P.I.*, a popular television program.

By the mid-1980s, in place of full beards or mustaches designer stubble became de rigueur for actors and male models, as seen on the face of the pop star George Michael and the actor Bruce Willis, an effect achieved by going unshaven for a day or two. The 1990s witnessed a renaissance of beards and stubble as a result of the grunge movement emanating from Seattle and the New Age

Traveler alliance in Europe. Both groups, one associated with rock music and the other with environmental protest, advocated a return to "authenticity" and eschewed regular shaving. Stubble and short beards appeared on the singer Kurt Cobain, front man for the band Nirvana. Swampy, a well-known British environmental protester, sported a head of dreadlocks and a matching "natural" beard in protest against environmental destruction.

The most popular contemporary permutations of facial hair are the goatee or love bud (in which a small patch of beard is allowed to grow below the lower lip). The full beard with side-whiskers, now found mainly on the faces of men who were young in the 1950s and 1960s, has been generally rejected by men of later generations, most of whom are clean-shaven.

See also **Fashion and Identity; Hairstyles.**

BIBLIOGRAPHY

Corson, Richard. *Hair: The First Five Thousand Years.* London: Peter Owen, 1965.

Dikotter, Frank. "Hairy Barbarian, Furry Primates, and Wild Men: Medical Science and Cultural Representations of Hair in China." In *Hair: Its Power and Meaning in Asian Cultures.* Edited by Alf Hiltebeitel and Barbara D. Miller. Albany: State University of New York Press, 1998.

Peterkin, Allan. *One Thousand Beards: A Cultural History of Facial Hair.* Vancouver, Canada: Arsenal Pulp Press, 2001.

Caroline Cox

BEATON, CECIL Cecil Beaton (1904–1980) was one of the most original and prolific creative talents of the twentieth century. Born in London and educated at Harrow and Cambridge University, he worked not only as a fashion photographer but also as a writer, artist, and actor and in his primary field of interest as a stage and costume designer for ballet, opera, and theater. Beaton was a self-taught photographer: he was given a simple Kodak 3A camera for his twelfth birthday and soon was eagerly photographing his young sisters, Nancy and Barbara ("Baba"), in "period" costumes and sets he made from fish-scale tissues and pseudo-Florentine brocades, tinsel nets, and imitation leopard skins. His nanny developed his negatives in the bathtub. In 1927, at the age of twenty-three, he went to work for *Vogue* as a cartoonist, but he soon began freelancing as a photographer for Condé Nast Publications and *Harper's Bazaar*, taking fashion shots and portraits of royalty and personalities in the arts and literature.

Influences on Beaton

The most important influence on Beaton's fashion photography was his interest in stage design and theatrical production, in which he was extremely accomplished. He did costume design for the film *Gigi* and set and costume design for the play and the film *My Fair Lady*, receiving

Cecil Beaton. Beaton was a writer, artist, actor, and a costume and set designer for ballet and theatre, as well as a renowned self-taught fashion designer. He received two Oscars, one for costume design for the film *Gigi,* and the second for set and costume design for the play and film *My Fair Lady.* © JOHN SPRINGER COLLECTION/CORBIS. REPRODUCED BY PERMISSION.

Oscars for both. He also designed for the Metropolitan Opera, the Comédie Française, the Royal Ballet (London), and the American Ballet Theatre. "Completely stage struck" at an early age, he wrote in his *Photobiography* that he felt "a keen perverse enjoyment in scrutinizing photographs of stage scenery. The more blatantly these showed the tricks and artifices of the stage, which would never be obvious to a theatre audience, the greater my pleasure" (p. 16). This interest explains some of Beaton's most unusual fashion photographs, which include hanging wires and large sheets of pasted paper as backdrops for high-fashion outfits.

Beaton also had an extensive knowledge of Victorian and Edwardian photography and drew for inspiration on the costume depiction of such nineteenth-century portrait photographers as Camille Silvy and the collaborators D. O. Hill and Robert Adamson. He was also inspired by the soft-focus technique of the photographer E. O. Hoppé, the opalescent lighting of Baron Adolf de Meyer, and conventions of English portraiture and Renaissance painting. Beaton combined these influences with his innate taste for Victorian surface ornamentation and opulent effects, or what the critic Hilton Kramer has termed "extravagant and overripe artifice" (p. 28).

Beaton first traveled to Hollywood in 1931, and the world of tinsel as well as the influence of surrealism he encountered there were well suited to his insatiable taste for the theatrical and exotic. "My first impressions of a film studio were so strange and fantastic that I felt I could never drain their photographic possibilities," he wrote. "The vast sound stages, with the festoons of ropes, chains, and the haphazard impedimenta, were as lofty and awe-inspiring as cathedrals; the element of paradox and surprise was never-ending, and the juxtaposition of objects and people gave me my first glimpse of Surrealism" (*Photobiography*, p. 61).

Beaton began introducing strong shadows into his work, a motif he may well have borrowed from Hollywood productions. The use of such shadows was popular in movies and advertising photography of the 1930s, so much so that articles such as one entitled "Shadows in Commercial Photography" were devoted to it (Hall-Duncan, p. 61). A famous pair of pendant photographs taken by Beaton in 1935 each shows an elegant model attended by three debonair phantoms created by backlighting three tuxedoed male models against a white muslin screen (Hall-Duncan, pp. 114–115).

Beaton's Work at *Vogue*

Returning to New York for his *Vogue* assignments in 1934, Beaton took his always fussy sets to a new level of fantastic overindulgence. He combed the antique shops of Madison and Third Avenues for carved arabesques, gesticulating cupids, silver studio work, and ceilings in imitation of the Italian rococo painter Giovanni Battista Tiepolo. "His baroque is worse than his bite," was a comment heard around the Condé Nast studios.

At the same time, under the influence of surrealism, which advocated the surprising juxtaposition of objects as a way to release the subconscious, he began incorporating bizarre combinations that created some of the most unusual fashion photographs of the century. The commonest object became grist for Beaton's creative mill: expensive gowns were posed against backgrounds of eggbeaters and cutlet frills, wire bedsprings, and kitchen utensils. Models appeared wearing hats composed of eggshells or carrying baskets of tree twigs. Beaton was even accused of using toilet paper, though his background was actually made of what is called "cartridge" paper.

The most extreme example was one that would have profound implications for fashion photography decades later, particularly in the work of Guy Bourdin and Deborah Turbeville. In 1937 Beaton discovered an office building under construction on the Champs-Elysées in Paris that revealed a "fantastic décor" (*Photobiography*, p. 73) of cement sacks, mortar, bricks, and half-finished walls. The resulting prints, in which Beaton showed mannequins nonchalantly reading newspapers or idling elegantly in this debris, were published with much hesitation on the part of the magazine's editors. Yet even much later, as Beaton noted, "fashion photographers are still searching for corners of desolation and decay, for peeling walls, scabrous bill-boardings and rubble to serve as a background for the latest and most expensive dresses" (*Photobiography*, p. 73).

By the middle of the 1930s Beaton was starting to be disturbed by *Vogue*'s restrictions on his creativity. He was called into the *Vogue* offices for posing models in "unladylike" poses with their feet planted well apart. Then it was found that Beaton had incorporated anti-Semitic words into the border of a pen-and-ink sketch done for the February 1938 issue of *Vogue*. The offending line read, "Mr. R. Andrew's ball at the El Morocco brought out all the dirty kikes in town." The result, after 150,000 copies of *Vogue* were on newsstands, was catastrophic. Condé Nast recalled and reprinted 130,000 copies of the questionable issue and quickly issued a legal disclaimer. Walter Winchell wrote a snide review, as did many other columnists. As a result, Beaton "resigned." In time, the incident blew over and Beaton was reinstated at *Vogue*, where he continued to do fashion photography for several more decades. During World War II he was the official photographer to the British Ministry of Information, photographing the fronts in Africa and in the Near and Far East.

Beaton's Importance
Beaton had a long and extremely productive career in fashion photography, costume, and set design and writing and illustrating many books with his own witty drawings, based on the detailed diaries he kept all his life. Yet his work is of uneven quality. "When Cecil Beaton is good," the photography critic Gene Thornton said, "he is very, very good, but when he's bad, he's horrid. . . . It takes a kind of genius to be that bad" (p. 33). Indeed, the excesses of Beaton's style can be cloying, naive, and even trite, but few have questioned the inventive range of work or the important influence it would have on subsequent fashion photographers, particularly in the 1970s.

See also **Fashion Photography; Film and Fashion; Theatrical Costume; Vogue.**

BIBLIOGRAPHY
Beaton, Cecil. *Photobiography*. London: Odhams Press, 1951.

Danziger, James. *Beaton*. New York: Viking Press, 1980.

Garner, Philippe, and David Alan Mellor. *Cecil Beaton: Photographs 1920–1970*. New York: Stuart, Tabori, and Chang, 1995.

Hall-Duncan, Nancy. *The History of Fashion Photography*. New York: Alpine Book Company, 1979.

Kramer, Hilton. "The Dubious Art of Fashion Photography." *New York Times*, 28 December 1975.

Ross, Josephine. *Beaton in Vogue*. New York: Clarkson N. Potter, 1986.

Thornton, Gene. "It's Hard to Miss with a Show of the '30s." *New York Times*, 18 April 1976.

Nancy Hall-Duncan

BEENE, GEOFFREY Geoffrey Beene was born Samuel Albert Bozeman Jr. in Haynesville, Louisiana, on 30 August 1927, into a family of doctors. He dutifully enrolled in the premed program at Tulane University in New Orleans in 1943. Three years later he dropped out of Tulane and enrolled in the University of Southern California, Los Angeles, to pursue his lifelong interest in fashion design. However, he never attended classes as he decided to accept a job working in the display department of the I. Magnin department store, and then moved to New York to study at the Traphagen School of Fashion. By 1948 Beene had moved to Paris, where he attended the École de la Syndicale d'Haute Couture, the traditional training ground for European fashion designers. He then served a two-year apprenticeship with a tailor from the couture house of Molyneux. Beene returned to New York in 1951 and worked for a series of Seventh Avenue fashion houses before being hired by Teal Traina in 1954. He remained at Teal Traina until 1963, when he decided it was time to strike out on his own, opening Geoffrey Beene, Inc., offering high-quality ready-to-wear women's clothing. Beene's business partner was Leo Orlandi, who had been the production manager for Teal Traina.

An American Aesthetic
Beene started his career during the era when Parisian designers still dominated the fashion world and Americans were expected to look to them for inspiration. However, though Beene was trained in the traditional manner, educated in New York and Paris, he broke out of the mold after his training and apprenticeship working for other designers. His creativity and skill were soon rewarded with a Coty award in 1964, after just one year in business, thus beginning one of the most award-winning careers in American fashion. His first collection made the cover of *Vogue*, and he has been regarded as a dean of American design ever since. His high-profile clients have included several First Ladies, and he designed the wedding dress of President Lyndon B. Johnson's daughter, Lynda Bird Johnson, in 1967.

Beene's distinctive creative vision manifested itself fully in 1966 when he designed ballgowns using gray flannel and wool jersey. He went on to design a series of dresses inspired by athletic jerseys, most notably a sequined full-length football-jersey gown in 1968. Generally, his clothes did display a respect for traditional dress-making, which manifested itself in details such as delicate collars and cuffs, and minutely tucked blouses, applied to a paired-down silhouette.

By the mid-1970s Beene had a number of licensing agreements for products as diverse as eyeglasses and bed sheets. The Beene Bag line of women's wear, introduced in 1971, used the same silhouettes as his couture line, but he employed inexpensive fabrics such as mattress ticking and muslin. Everyday fabrics continued to make their way into his higher-priced line as they had since the late

Evening dresses on display at a Geoffrey Beene showing. Varied fabrics and colors are the hallmark of Geoffrey Beene's contemporary ball gown designs. Since his career began in the mid-1960s, the fashion designer experimented with common textures such as flannel, muslin and jersey to create sensual, comfortable evening wear. © REUTERS NEWMEDIA INC./CORBIS. REPRODUCED BY PERMISSION.

1960s, as he used sweatshirt fabric and denim for evening dresses in his 1970 collection.

Beene considers the years 1972–1973 as a turning point in his career. It was then that he set aside traditional Parisian tailoring methods and began to explore softer silhouettes. He commented on these years in the catalog to a 1988 retrospective of his work at the National Academy of Design:

> At that time there was so much construction in my clothes they could stand alone. I believed inner structure and weight were synonymous with form and shape. My sketches were dictating the design, not the fabric. When I became aware that my clothes lacked

modernity, I began to experiment more with fabric, working with textile mills abroad, commissioning new weights, textures and fiber mixes. (Beene 1988, p. 4)

By 1975 Beene had been awarded a fifth Coty and had launched Grey Flannel, one of the first and perennially most successful designer men's fragrances. He was able to buy out his partner and obtain complete control over his business by the early 1980s.

Influence Abroad

In 1976 Beene became the first American designer to show in Milan, Italy, set up manufacturing facilities there, and successfully compete in the European fashion market. This success led to his sixth Coty in 1977, which was awarded for giving impetus to American fashion abroad. It is the Coty award that he treasured most, as the challenge of success in Europe was significant to his development as an artist—he proved to himself that his designs and his unique American vision had validity in the international arena. The European success also brought the added benefit of prestige and significantly increased sales of the couture line in the United States. But by this point in his career, Geoffrey Beene Couture, Beene Bag, and two fragrances accounted for only one-third of Beene's sales; the remainder was from licensing royalties for Beene-designed men's clothes, sheets, furs, jewelry, and eyeglasses.

While Beene has always been regarded as a master of form silhouette, it has been his use of color and fabric mixtures that garner the most comment. In a 1977 article for *The New Yorker*, Kennedy Fraser stated: "The distinctive quality of Geoffrey Beene's work which at the same time reflects an immediate sensuous response to the color and texture of beautiful fabrics must be characterized as a variety of intellectualism" (Fraser, p. 181). His ability to push experiments with color and texture was remarked upon again by the *Cleveland Plain Dealer* in 1987: "In the hands of a less adept designer, a collection that encompasses everything from bedspread chenille and gold spattered faille or silver leather to monk's cloth would be a nightmare" (Cullerton, p. 181). Beene consistently revealed hidden characteristics of the fabrics that he chooses.

In 1982 Geoffrey Beene received his eighth Coty award—the most awarded to any one designer as of the early 2000s—and professional recognition continued through the 1980s as he was named Designer of the Year in 1986 by the Council of Fashion Designers of America.

The vocabulary of sportswear appeared consistently in Beene's work as he strove for a balance between comfort and style. During the 1980s, when jumpsuits began to appear frequently in his women's collection, he stated that "the jumpsuit is the ballgown of the next century." Neither hard-edged nor futuristic, Beene's jumpsuits emphasize the comfort and versatility of this form of garment. The same is true for his use of men's wear influences in women's wear—bow ties, vests, and suiting fabrics are used with whimsy.

Geoffrey Beene selecting shoes. Geoffrey Beene, a fashion designer whose career has spanned more than four decades, introduced an innovative mix of color and new fabrics to haute couture. His creations earned him eight prestigious Coty Awards. © DAVID LEES/CORBIS. REPRODUCED BY PERMISSION.

Later Career

In 1988 a retrospective at the National Academy of Design opened to coincide with the anniversary of Beene's twenty-five years in business. During this time, an article appeared in the *Village Voice* by Amy Fine Collins, who took on the role of Beene's muse through the 1990s. In analyzing Beene's work as an artist, she focused on his seemingly contradictory combinations of materials and influences, praising his courage to "regularly descend into the depths of taste in order to reemerge with his vision replenished" (Fine Collins, p. 34). In 1988 the Council of Fashion Designers of America gave Beene a newly created award, the Special Award for Fashion as Art.

Beene continued his innovations with fabric, treating humble textiles regally and using luxurious materials with throwaway ease. For example, a 1989 sheared mink coat for the furrier Goldin-Feldman in a bathrobe-like silhouette was created in fur dyed hot pink, edged with electric blue ribbon in a giant rickrack pattern, and lined with an abstract print in coordinating colors.

The year 1989 saw the opening of Geoffrey Beene on the Plaza, Beene's flagship retail shop on Fifth Avenue. He envisioned the shop as a design laboratory where he could "put in something new and in a few days have enough feedback to know if it's a success or if it has to go back to the drawing board" (Morris, p. B11).

Beene had shown a special interest in lace, for its combination of sheerness and strength along with its ability to stretch. In the late 1980s he began utilizing strategically placed sheer and cutout panels, especially in his evening clothes, culminating in the matte-wool-jersey-and-sequins lace-insertion gowns of 1991, which exemplify the exacting cut and technical intricacy of his work. His spiraling designs, which consider the body in the round rather than using flat pieces and treating the front and back as separate entities, reveal his admiration for and study of the work of the French couturier Madeleine Vionnet.

In 1994 Beene was honored again with an exhibition at the Fashion Institute of Technology to celebrate thirty years in business and was awarded the first-ever Award of Excellence by the Costume Council of the Los Angeles County Museum of Art. In 1997 and 1998 exhibitions of his work were featured at the Toledo Museum of Art, the Philadelphia Museum of Art, and the Rhode Island School of Design Museum.

Beene's clothes have consistently been praised for their individuality and wearability. In a 1994 interview with Grace Mirabella he explained his philosophy of design:

> The biggest change in fashion and the world has probably come in the past and present decade—the collapse of rules and their rigidity. This had to happen. There were too many illogical rules. I have never wished to impose or dictate with design. Its meaning for me is to affect people's lives with a certain joy, and not to impose questions of right and wrong. (Mirabella, p. 7)

Beene's lifetime achievement awards include the Smithsonian's Cooper-Hewitt National Design Museum's American Original award, presented in 2002. In 2003 he became the first recipient of the Gold Medal of Honor for Lifetime Achievement in Fashion from the National Arts Club. He received a career excellence award from the Rhode Island School of Design, which awarded him an honorary doctorate in 1992.

Beene weathered a famous seventeen-year feud with *Women's Wear Daily*, during which the publication refused to mention his name. By early 2002, Geoffrey Beene pulled his couture line out of retail stores; he continued to produce clothing for a select group of private clients.

See also **Fashion Designer; Paris Fashion; Vionnet, Madeleine; Women's Wear Daily.**

BIBLIOGRAPHY

Anderson, Susan Heller. "Geoffrey Beene Takes On Europe." *New York Times*, 20 November 1977.

Beene, Geoffrey. *Geoffrey Beene: The First Twenty-five Years: An Exhibition of the National Academy of Design, New York City, September 20 till October 9, 1988. Geoffrey Beene, Inc. Essay by Marylou Luther.* New York: National Academy of Design, 1988.

———. *Geoffrey Beene Unbound.* New York: Museum at the Fashion Institute of Technology, 1994. Interview by Grace Mirabella.

Cocks, Jay. "Geoffrey Beene's Amazing Grace." *Time*, 10 October 1988.

Cullerton, Brenda. *Geoffrey Beene.* New York: Harry N. Abrams, 1995.

Dennis, Harry. "Geoffrey Beene," *TWA Ambassador*, September 1989.

Fine Collins, Amy. "The Wearable Rightness of Beene." *Village Voice*, 10 January 1989.

Fraser, Kennedy. *The Fashionable Mind: Reflections on Fashion, 1970–1981.* New York: Alfred A. Knopf, 1981.

Martin, Richard. *American Ingenuity: Sportswear, 1930s–1970s.* New York: Metropolitan Museum of Art, 1998.

Milbank, Caroline Rennolds. *Couture, The Great Designers.* New York: Stewart, Tabori, and Chang, 1985.

Morris, Bernadine. "In New Retail Shop, Beene Envisions a Laboratory of Fashion." *New York Times*, 19 December 1989.

Schiro, Anne-Marie. "Geoffrey Beene Shows the Way." *New York Times*, 2 November 1996.

Melinda Watt

BELGIAN FASHION In October 2003, the American newspaper *Women's Wear Daily* asked, "Is Belgian Avant-Garde Out of Fashion?" Twenty years after Belgian fashion design, with Antwerp as its epicenter, had won its place on the world scene, it was time to ask how things now stood with the avant-garde character of the Belgians. The Belgian designers, who had instigated a small revolution in the early 1980s with their unexpected images and conceptual approaches, were by 2003 counted by critics among the classic designers in their field. During the intervening two decades, the perception of Belgian fashion evolved from avant-garde, edgy, and against-the-grain toward a generally accepted classic style. "Antwerp" and "Belgian" became prefixes laden with high symbolic—and in some cases financial—capital and had successfully earned themselves a secure place alongside "French," "Italian," "Japanese," and "American."

Writing about Belgian fashion in terms of nationality is, however, not without its problems. Where the first-generation designers were still quite literally "Belgian," younger generations have taken on an increasingly international character; consequently the word does not refer to nationality in the strict sense, but rather to a certain identity that manifests itself at different levels—varying from visual imagery and graphic design to training and corporate culture—and which is perceived as characteristically "Belgian."

Early History

Prior to the 1980s, there was in fact no Belgian fashion. One precursor of the 1980s generation, however, was Ann Salens, an Antwerp designer who for a short time in the 1960s generated international furor and is an important point of reference for Belgian designers. Her extravagant, brilliantly colored dresses and wigs in artificial silk, her flamboyant lifestyle, risqué fashion shows, and happenings at unusual locations earned her the title of "Belgian Fashion's Bird of Paradise."

During the first half of the twentieth century, fashion in Belgium had primarily reflected what was taking place on the Paris runways. Parisian chic also dominated the Belgian image of fashion. Until 1950, creativity was restricted to the realm of interpretation, which frequently amounted to all but literal copying of the creations from the great French houses, which were in fact geared to this form of commercial reproduction. Smaller and less resounding names outside France could select from among various formulas with associated price tags, beginning with attending the presentation of the collection—where it was strictly forbidden to take notes—up to the purchase of the patterns and original fabrics. If desired, the purchased design could be further sold under the new name. Even after the 1950s, however, it remained commercially uninteresting to advertise Belgian origins. In the early 1980s, established Belgian brands, such as Olivier Strelli, Cortina, and Scapa of Scotland, were choosing more exotic names that sooner disguised rather than emphasized their Belgian roots.

The Golden 1980s

At the beginning of the 1980s, the Belgian government launched a plan to give new incentives to the stagnating textiles industry. On 1 January 1981, the Instituut voor Textiel en Confectie van België (ITCB, Institute for Belgian Textiles and Fashion) was established to provide constructive guidance for the various economic, commercial, and creative initiatives of the government's *textiles plan*. On the one hand, the Belgian textiles and apparel industry could call on government support in order to modernize and introduce new technology. On the other hand, a wide-ranging commercial campaign was begun, under the motto, "Fashion: It's Belgian." Its purpose was to provide Belgian fashion with a new and convincing image. At the same time, there was growing awareness that such a campaign had to be supported by a creative substructure, in which young talent was given every possible opportunity. In 1982, this led to the establishment of the annual Golden Spindle competition, the first of which was won by Ann Demeulemeester. Other laureates of that first edition were Martin Margiela, Dries Van Noten, Walter Van Beirendonck, Marina Yee, Dirk Van Saene, and Dirk Bikkembergs. Along with the requisite attention from the press and an article in the *Fashion: It's Belgian* magazine, the laureates were given the opportunity to collaborate with manufacturers to produce their collections, resulting in the first important reciprocal overtures between Belgian manufacturers and the new avant-garde designers.

During the late 1970s and early 1980s, Paris reached an apex with spectacular shows by Jean-Paul Gaultier and Thierry Mugler, among others, and with creations by Comme des Garçons and Yohji Yamamoto, which were lauded as works of art. Italy also brought innovation, with Gianni Versace and Romeo Gigli. In both ladies' and men's apparel, Italy established itself as a trendsetter, and Italian men's collections presented a new, nonchalant man, designed by Romeo Gigli or Dolce & Gabbana. This passion for pushing fashion to its peak and the exuberance of these collections in turn stimulated academy graduates and young designers in Antwerp.

There was a growing sense that Belgians could also produce fashion, and do so without the show elements so dependent on extravagant budgets. *Les gens du Nord*, or "the folks from the North," presented an avant-garde reversal to fashion, or *l'Anvers de la mode*—as the journalist

Designer Véronique Branquinho. Branquinho was named designer of the year in 1998. Her creations presented a simple, unpretentious attitude that signified the young, fascinating, and pure woman. © CORBIS SYGMA. REPRODUCED BY PERMISSION.

Elisabeth Paillée aptly wrote in a wordplay on the French name for Antwerp. This was the backside, the recycled, throwaway fashion, an underground phenomenon, the underdog: not so extroverted as English fashion, not so sexy as Italian fashion, not so cerebral as Japanese fashion.

As the only member of this group to do so, Martin Margiela went to Paris to apprentice with Gaultier (1984–1987) and eventually established his own Maison Martin Margiela in 1988. Maison Margiela developed an impressive oeuvre comprising differing lines, with recurring focus on such themes as tailoring, haute couture, recycling, and deconstruction. Margiela's story is a tale about the system that underlies fashion, a journey to discover alternatives that remain economically alive and which, in the fashion world, give new substance to the supposedly unassailable notion of innovation.

The remaining six designers decided to pool their resources and in 1987, left together for London's *British Designer Show*, where they were quickly noticed by the

Veronique Branquinho Autumn/Winter 2004–2005 collection. In the mid-1990s, Branquinho introduced fashions that evoked an air of mystery. Her simple, yet refined collections are carried by her label *James*. VERONIQUE BRANQUINHO, AUTUMN/WINTER 2004–2005, PHOTO: ALEX SALINAS. REPRODUCED BY PERMISSION.

known for the ethnic or historic tone of his designs, with an almost naïve and at the same time touching exoticism. His flower motifs and the strong silhouette structure of his fashion shows are a trademark. In Ann Demeulemeester, there is a super-cooled romanticism, with a color palette reduced to the bare essentials: black and white. For her, the study of form is crucial, resulting in a union of such contrasts as masculine toughness and feminine elegance. Walter Van Beirendonck holds to an extreme eccentricity, with sources of inspiration ranging from science fiction to performance, comic books, and politics. From 1992 through 1999, he designed his W&LT line, followed by the introduction of his "Aestheticterrorists." Dirk Van Saene seems to harbor a love-hate relationship with couture. His image of women is fickle, even cynical, yet his apparel designs demonstrate great love and attention to craftsmanship. Finally, Dirk Bikkembergs initially created a sensation with heavy men's shoes with laces pulled through the heel. This subsequently evolved into an image that is sporty and sexy, perhaps most akin to Italian fashion.

What Is Belgian?

If Belgian fashion cannot be understood in terms of a single style and if nationality itself is not the determining factor, what do these different designers have in common that makes their work recognizably Belgian? It is not the intention here to formulate a definition as such, but rather to indicate a number of aspects that contribute to the specific identity of the Belgian designers. One important factor is undoubtedly their training at the Royal Academy in Antwerp, with "individuality" and "creativity" being the principle concepts. Personal growth and creative development of the student are fundamental at school, without this one loses sight of the link between professional life. The personal approach also extends to the various peripheral activities that come along with the presentation of a collection, ranging from exceptional attention to the graphic design for the invitations and catalogs and particular focus on the location and design of the fashion show to a warm welcome in the showroom. One need only think of the now historic presentations of Martin Margiela's collections in an abandoned Metro station or Salvation Army depots, Dries Van Noten's delight-to-behold, beautiful shows, or the art performance tone of the presentations by Bernhard Willhelm and Jurgi Persoons for illustrations of this approach.

Nonetheless, the collection and the love and passion for clothing always take first place. With the Belgians, there is no superstar allure, or coquetry, but a healthy mix of humility, sobriety, and daring, and this translates first and foremost in the apparel itself. There is no blinding haute couture for the Belgians, but there is attention to professional craftsmanship, the study of form and concept; no out-of-control profits in the wake of the luxury houses, but a self-sufficiently structured enterprise in which as many factors as possible are kept under the de-

press, who referred to them as the "The Antwerp Six"— purportedly because the difficult Flemish names were such tongue-twisters. Success was not long to follow. After London, they stormed Paris. By the late 1980s and early 1990s, most had their own fashion lines and retail outlets, as well as a permanent place on the Parisian fashion week calendar, with growing numbers of international selling points as a result.

Presenting these designers as a group, as the "Antwerp Six" or the "Belgians," indeed overlooks their individual styles and identities. Where content, form, and image are concerned, it can in fact be difficult to find something they share in common. Dries Van Noten is

signers' own control; no top models whose star status relegates the clothes to subservient status, but real girls with character.

The Next Generation

The generation following the "Belgian Six" found themselves faced with a very difficult challenge: how to create a profile and where to position oneself in the presence of such a strong avant-garde. Several responded by choosing not to present collections of their own. Perhaps the first to prove that there really was life after the Six was Raf Simons, who set his aims high with collections that indeed generated long-term changes in men's fashion. With images based on youth culture, the influence his work has had on the fashion field must not be underestimated.

In 1997, Véronique Branquinho presented a new woman: dreamy, young, mysterious, fascinating, and pure. Branquinho appeared on the scene as a young businesswoman with talent, and has been a pleasure to watch as her collections have grown together with their maker. Her collections are unpretentious and refined. Her label, James, refers to class—class without the glamour.

The A. F. Vandevorst designer team of An Vandevorst and Filip Arickx drew considerable press attention with the presentation of their second collection, in which girls slumbered and awoke in hospital beds. When the girls woke, their clothes still had the same pleats they had had when they lay down. It was an endearing and human image.

Bernhard Willhelm did not hesitate to begin by infusing his collection with humor. It was intended to provoke thought and balanced at the edge of cynicism, using new shapes and colors, and not be categorized in any single style. After only a few seasons, Willhelm was designing for the Italian house, Capucci, in addition to producing his own line.

Among the youngest designers, Haider Ackermann, of Colombian-French origins, has attracted particular attention. In 2002, he showed his first women's collection on the Paris catwalk. In 2003, he designed a collection for the Italian leather designers, Ruffo Research. His experiments with leather were astonishing, combining superb knowledge of material and form, along with the necessary dose of elegance and craftsmanship.

Brussels, too, is making itself heard. The super-talent Olivier Theyskens, who was designing for Rochas, prematurely broke off his training at the La Cambre School for Fashion in Brussels and almost immediately became a center of attention when the pop icon Madonna appeared in one of his creations. Theyskens achieved wonders in linking Parisian elegance to a certain Belgian conceptuality and sobriety. His designs are exquisitely beautiful, approaching perfection, yet at the same time possessing a dark underside, a gothic edge.

Dries Van Noten Spring/Summer 2002 Men's Ready-to-Wear Collection. Belgian fashion first arrived on the runway in the 1980s after the Belgian government gave incentives to revitalize the textile industry. Belgian designers created their own brand of individual, avant-garde apparel. © REUTERS NEWMEDIA. REPRODUCED BY PERMISSION.

The Fashion Nation

With the achievements of the 1980s generation in mind, Antwerp became increasingly conscious of the fact that a number of structures had to be brought into play if the unique position that the city enjoyed in the fashion world were to be maintained. The starting bell rang in 2001, during Antwerp's "Year of Fashion," with the hosting of a broad-ranged series of artistic events curated by Walter Van Beirendonck. At the same time, the "Fashion Nation" opened its doors in the heart of Antwerp. By way of three different organizations, the Fashion Nation unites three influences on fashion: education, culture, and economics. The fashion department of the Royal Academy is located on the top floor and also symbolically stands for "top floor" and creative input. The next story down is home to the MoMu Museum of Fashion and the Flanders Fashion Institute (FFI). The MoMu unites heritage and tradition with an innovative approach, while the FFI has the task of bridging a link with the financial world, by way of a production fund for starting designers and countless other activities to help Belgian designers achieve the aura they need at both national and international levels.

See also **Italian Fashion; Japanese Fashion; London Fashion; Margiela, Martin; Paris Fashion.**

BIBLIOGRAPHY

Coppens, Marguerite, ed. *Les Années 80: L'Essor d'une mode Belge* [The 1980s: The Rise of a Belgian Fashion]. Brussels, Belgium: Musées Royaux d'Art et Histoire, 1995.

Debo, Kaat, ed. *The Fashion Museum Backstage*. Ghent, Belgium, and Amsterdam: Ludion, 2002.

Derycke, Luc, and Sandra Van De Veire, eds. *Belgian Fashion Design*. Ghent, Belgium, and Amsterdam: Ludion, 1999.

Esch, Gerdi, and Agnes Goyvaerts. *Mode in de Lage Landen: België* [Fashion in the Low Countries: Belgium]. Antwerp, Belgium: Hadewijch, 1989.

Weekend Knack 20 Years Fashion It's Belgian. Issue 37. Roeselaere: Roularta Media Group, 2003. Jubilee issue with an excellent overview of who's who in Belgian fashion.

Windels, Veerle. *Jonge Belgische Mode* [Young Belgian Fashion]. Ghent, Belgium, and Amsterdam: Ludion, 2001.

Kaat Debo and Linda Loppa

BELTS AND BUCKLES A belt is any length of material that encircles and is secured around the waist. Popular materials include leather, fabric, and metal. Belts are worn by males and females to define the fashionable waist and for a variety of other functions in many world cultures.

Sometimes referred to as a girdle or sash, the belt was worn in the Bronze Age and in ancient Crete, Greece, and Rome and is mentioned in the Bible.

Belts accent the fashionable position of the waist as it travels from under the breast to its natural position to low on the hips. As shirtwaist and skirt ensembles became a popular option for women in the nineteenth century, they were often accessorized with contrasting belts. In the 1860s, the Swiss belt, a wide, back-laced, and usually black belt, defined a woman's waist. Belts held special importance again when the New Look dictated small waists for post–World War II women.

During the twentieth century, women's belts were often of the same fabric as their matching dress or coat. Belts of metal or plastic links have also been worn as trendy fashion accessories by women. Twentieth-century men almost exclusively wore leather belts to secure their trousers. Belts of webbing borrowed from military uniforms were another, more casual, option for males.

Functionally, belts relieve the wearer's shoulders of part of the weight of the garment. Another function of belts is for attaching items; during the Middle Ages and Renaissance, women hung chatelaines, cosmetics, mirrors, pomanders, and purses from their belts. Police officers in America continue to use belts to hold items such as their guns, clubs, and pepper spray, and carpenters and other tradesmen carry their tools in utility belts. In the twentieth century, garter belts, an undergarment, were used by women and children to hold up stockings before panty hose and tights became common.

Belts denote rank in the martial arts. Actually it is the color of the belt that denotes rank. Originally, there were three belt levels: white belt, brown belt, and black belt, with black belt as the highest rank. A common myth explaining this system states that all students started by wearing white belts and through use the white belts turned brown and then black over time. More likely the colored belt system was borrowed from the one used in Japanese school athletics, particularly in ranking swimmers. In the 1960s the white belt rank was divided into several different colored belt levels: yellow, orange, purple, blue, and green, as a way of showing progress toward the higher ranks. The ranking of the colors varies among each style of martial arts. Adding stripes to belts is another way of showing progress at the lower levels.

Belts can also reveal identity. In the military, opposing armies or regiments were identified by the color sash they wore (in the Thirty Years War), as well as different branches of the service (in the American Civil War for example, general officers: buff; cavalry officers: yellow; and medical officers: emerald). During the Middle Ages in some cities, belts were worn as a sign of respectability and position and women of questionable repute were prohibited from wearing them.

Infamous or mythical, chastity belts have endured in the popular imagination. Purportedly invented to ensure women's fidelity while their husbands were away during the Crusades, a woman locked into a chastity belt was effectively prevented from having sexual intercourse. Modern versions of the chastity belt are included in fetish gear.

Belts are also used to provide protection. Weightlifting belts provide stability to the spine and lower back thus reducing risk of injury to the lifter. Delivery people and others who do lifting in their occupations wear similar belts. Seat belts are often complained about for being uncomfortable or for crushing the wearer's clothing. Several decades after automobiles became common, a movement started to promote motor vehicle seat belts. In the 1960s seat belts became standard in new vehicles, and in the 1980s, many countries began passing laws that mandated seat belt use for drivers and passengers.

Another twentieth-century device is the sanitary belt. Similar to a garter belt, a sanitary belt secured a woman's menstrual pad. These belts were popular and available into the 1970s.

Some belts act as currency. Natives of the Solomon Islands used belts of shell money. American Indians used wampum, belts of shell beads, as well.

Buckles

Buckles are a common way to fasten belts. Often a metal-frame buckle may catch in holes punched into the belt. Sometimes the end of a belt is woven through the buckle to fasten it. And other belt buckles hook to fasten the belt.

Buckles can be very decorative—covered with fabric, studded with rhinestones, or elaborately carved or molded. In the early twentieth century, buckles of bone and shell were popular for females. Perhaps the most elaborate in design and size are western belt buckles. Ornate western buckles first appeared in the 1920s due to the popular western heroes in Hollywood films. Since then western buckles are sometimes given as trophies in rodeo competitions.

From the American cowboy's buckle to the Japanese woman's complex obi, belts and buckles are culturally and historically significant elements of fashion.

See also **Girdle; Hats, Women's; Leather and Suede; Veils.**

BIBLIOGRAPHY

Besancenot, Jean. *Costumes of Morocco.* London and New York: Kegan Paul International, 1990.

George-Warren, Holly, and Michelle, Freedman. *How the West Was Won.* New York: Harry N. Abrams, 2001.

Haines, Bruce A. *Karate's History and Traditions.* Rutland, Vt.: C.E. Tuttle, 1968.

Kybalova, Ludmila, Olga Herbenova, and Milena Lamarova. *The Pictorial Encyclopedia of Fashion.* Translated by Claudia Rosoux. New York: Crown Publishers, 1968.

Milbank, Caroline Rennolds. *The Couture Accessory.* New York: Harry N. Abrams, 2002.

Newman, Cathy. *Fashion.* New York: National Geographic, 2001.

Shep, R. L., W. S. Salisbury, and P. Dervis. *Civil War Gentlemen: 1860's Apparel Arts and Uniforms.* Mendocino, Calif.: R. L. Shep, 1994.

Mark Schultz

BENJAMIN, WALTER The German writer and cultural critic Walter Benjamin (1892–1940) was born in Berlin, one of three children of assimilated Jewish parents. In 1912 he began his studies in philosophy, German literature, and art history at the University of Freiburg and then moved back to Berlin, where he encountered the teachings of the philosopher Georg Simmel. In 1914 he continued his studies at the universities in Munich and Bern, Switzerland. Benjamin married Dora Kellner in 1917; they had one son, Stefan, in 1918, before the marriage ended in divorce in 1930. Benjamin's doctoral dissertation on German Romanticism was accepted by the University of Bern in 1919. In 1923 he met his closest intellectual friends, the philosopher Theodor Wiesengrund Adorno and the cultural historian Siegfried Kracauer. His attempts to submit another professional dissertation to the University of Frankfurt, on the origin of German tragic drama, were not successful. The work was published in 1928 under the title *Ursprung des deutschen Trauerspiels* (*The Origin of the German Tragic Drama*).

Benjamin eked out a precarious existence as writer, translator, and journalist. In 1925–1927 he journeyed to Moscow, to visit Asja Lascis, whom he had fallen in love with. In 1933, in the wake of the rise of Hitler and Nazism, he left Germany for Paris, where he stayed except for brief visits to the German dramatist Bertolt Brecht in Denmark. Before his exile to France, Benjamin had begun to formulate *Das Passagenwerk* (*The Arcades Project*), his work on Paris in the nineteenth century; he would devote the remainder of his life to this incomplete magnum opus.

In 1936 he wrote the famous essay "Das Kunstwerk im Zeitalter seiner technischen Reproduzierbarkeit" ("The Work of Art in the Age of Mechanical Reproduction"). The text is the first to postulate the loss of the work's aura, that is the demise of its multi-tiered authenticity in view of the cultural implications of art's reproducibility in modern media. The German occupation of Paris in 1939 drove Benjamin from the French capital, but his manuscripts remained hidden in the vaults of the Bibliothèque Nationale until after the war. Border police halted his attempt to escape to Spain across the Pyrenees in September of 1940. Mentally and physically exhausted, Benjamin committed suicide in Port Bou, Spain. He carried with him a black bag with what is rumored to have been a final version of *The Arcades Project*. It was never recovered.

Benjamin on Fashion

Benjamin's significance for the interpretation of fashion resides in his unfinished chef-d'œuvre, *Das Passagenwerk*. A vast array of fragments, excerpts, aphorisms, quotations, metaphysical musings, and sociopolitical observations constitute the material for this book on Paris in the nineteenth century, the "pre-history of modernity," as Adorno called it. Fashion, both as an economic force and a visual signifier, is one of the most important features of *The Arcades Project*. Benjamin collected some hundred entries that deal with couture, dress codes and the art, literature, philosophy, and sociology of clothing (including a wealth of quotations from Simmel). His works on French literature; translations of Charles Baudelaire and Marcel Proust, with whom he shared sensibilities in regard to fashion; and essays on visual art in France were preparatory to the project, and his collections *Thesen über den Begriff der Geschichte* (1942; *Theses on the Philosophy of History*) and *Zentralpark* (1955; *Central Park*) are methodological spin-offs. A number of abstracts that he produced over the course of a decade explain and modify his conceptual approach.

Common to all these writings is the centrality of fashion as a historical fact—not simply as a historicized element of the past but more as a force that through its constant self-reference and quotation breaks the historical continuum and activates, at times even revolutionizes, past occurrences for the present. It is Benjamin's principal achievement to use dialectical materialism—that is, the materialist philosophy that regards the process of development in thought, nature, and history as coined by the necessary contradiction of ideas (albeit rather unorthodoxically) in this context as a structuring device against historicism, which uses styles, ornamentation, and motifs from the past often in eclectic and not reflective combination, and also against the notion of history marked by linear progress toward constantly higher levels of technical proficiency and material satisfaction. The potency of Georg Friedrich Wilhelm Hegel's and Karl Marx's concept of history as turning from quantitative progression to qualitative change is used by Benjamin to create an analogy in fashion's willful quotations from its own source book, where a particular style or stylistic element is taken from costume history and brought into present fashion to create reference and friction simultaneously, along with new commodities. This method is seen as particular to fashion, not just as the result of the seasonal structure of haute couture but because fashion operates differently from the historicism inherent in other decorative or applied arts. Thus, for example, quotations in Empire furniture are different from citations of Greek dress in the Directoire fashion. Through the stylistic quote, the console or chair merely offers a consolidation of historical substance, while the high-waisted dress presents the direct impression of the democratic ideal on the body politic.

In his *Theses on the Philosophy of History* Benjamin finds a poetic definition of fashion in history, a definition that moves from metaphysical to material questions and perceives fashion as a structural device. Through the sartorial quotation, fashion fuses the thesis of the eternal or "classical" ideal with its antithesis, which is the openly contemporary. The apparent opposition between the eternal and the ephemeral is rendered obsolete by the leap that needs the past for any continuation of the present. Correspondingly, the transhistorical describes the position of fashion as detached both from the eternal, that is, an aesthetic ideal, and the continuous progression of history. Benjamin conjures up the image of the "*Tigersprung*" to explain how fashion is able to leap from the contemporary to the ancient and back again without coming to rest exclusively in one temporal or aesthetic configuration. This generates a novel view of historical development. Coupled with the dialectical image, the tiger's leap under the open skies of history marks a convergence that is revolutionary in its essence.

The text that contains the *Tigersprung* thesis indicates what *The Arcades Project* could have constituted in terms of a radical rethinking of fashion in modern culture, if Benjamin had finished it. Its excerpts demonstrate the leap from a sociological, art historical, or material observation of clothes to an understanding of fashion's unique character as a historical constituent, a structuring device, potentially even a revolutionary force. Benjamin tempts us in his unfinished work with glimpses of a new abstract perception of fashion viewed independently of its material basis (textile industry, haute couture, distribution, representation, and so forth), but retaining its materialism, that is, its sociopolitical significance. It is seen as part of intellectual culture, to be debated and interpreted simultaneously as sensuous and poetic, that is, as an expression of contemporary beauty, and on an abstract and metaphysical level, as an independent structure of modern existence and cognition.

See also **Fashion, Historical Studies of; Fashion, Theories of; Historicism and Historical Revival; Simmel, Georg.**

BIBLIOGRAPHY

Works by Walter Benjamin

"Theses on the Philosophy of History." *Illuminations.* London: Cape, 1970: 263.

The Correspondence of Walter Benjamin 1910–1940. Edited by Gershom Scholem and Theodor W. Adorno. Translated by Manfred R. Jacobson and Evelyn M. Jacobson. Chicago: University of Chicago Press, 1994.

The Arcades Project. Translated by Howard Eiland and Kevin McLaughlin. Cambridge, Mass.: Belknap Press, 1999.

Selected Writings of Walter Benjamin. 4 vols. Cambridge, Mass.: Belknap Press, 1996–2003.

Works about Walter Benjamin

Bolz, Norbert W., and Richard Faber, eds. *Antike und Moderne: Zu Walter Benjamins "Passagen."* Würzburg, Germany: Königshausen and Neumann, 1986.

Buck-Morss, Susan. *The Dialectics of Seeing: Walter Benjamin and the Arcades Project.* Cambridge, Mass.: MIT Press, 1989.

Bulthaupt, Peter, ed. *Materialien zu Benjamins Thesen "Über den Begriff der Geschichte": Text, Varianten, Briefstellen, Interpretationen.* Frankfurt, Germany: Suhrkamp, 1975.

Frisby, David. *Fragments of Modernity: Theories of Modernity in the Work of Simmel, Kracauer, and Benjamin.* Cambridge, U.K.: Polity, 1985.

Lehmann, Ulrich. *Tigersprung: Fashion in Modernity.* Cambridge, Mass.: MIT Press, 2000.

Smith, Gary, ed. *On Walter Benjamin: Critical Essays and Recollections.* Cambridge, Mass.: MIT Press, 1988.

———. *Benjamin: Philosophy, Aesthetics, History.* Chicago: University of Chicago Press, 1990.

Steinberg, Michael P. *Walter Benjamin and the Demands of History.* Ithaca, N.Y.: Cornell University Press, 1996.

Vinken, Barbara. "Eternity—A Frill on the Dress." *Fashion Theory* 1, no. 1 (1997): 59–67.

Wismann, Heinz, ed. *Walter Benjamin et Paris: Colloque international 27–29 Jun 1983.* Paris: Le Cerf, 1986.

Wolin, Richard. *Walter Benjamin: An Aesthetic of Redemption.* Berkeley: University of California Press, 1994.

Ulrich Lehmann

BERET A beret is a round, flat, visorless cap worn by both sexes over centuries. Berets are made from circular pieces of knitted, woven, or felted cloth, occasionally velvet, and drawn underneath by a string, thread band, or leather thong so as to fit around the head. They may be decorated with objects, such as ribbons, plumes, pins, tassels, jewelry, precious stones, fabrics, and cords.

Options for wearing the beret include set back on the head (halo style), flat on the head (pancake style), pulled down covering the ears (winter version), dipping diagonally to one side (fashion style), or pulling over the eyes for sleeping (oversized practical type).

Archaeological and art historical evidence indicates that variations of the beret have been worn by Bronze Age inhabitants of northern Europe, Ancient Cretans, Etruscans, English aristocrats such as Henry VIII, along with baroque and modern artists (Rembrandt to Picasso).

Basque Beret

The modern "Basque" beret originated with shepherds living on both sides of the Pyrenees in southern France and northern Spain. Little is known of Basque peoples' origins, and in the Spanish Provincias Vascongadas, different color berets were worn: red in Guipúzcoa, white in Ávala, blue in Vizcaya. Eventually, the Basques all adopted blue, while red berets were taken over as part of the provincial folk costume in neighboring Navarre. The wearing of black berets spread to villages throughout Spain, and by the 1920s they were associated with working classes in France.

Production

Basque beret production dates back to the seventeenth century in the non-Basque area of Oloron-Sainte-Marie, a small town in southern France, where sheep grazed on nearby mountainsides. Locals, like many other peoples, discovered that when wetted and rubbed together, small bits of wool became felted. While still moist, the felt could be hand manipulated by pulling it over the knee, thereby creating a rounded shape appropriate for covering the head.

Originally made by hand for male villagers, beret making became industrialized in the nineteenth century, with the first factory, Beatex-Laulhere, claiming production records dating back to 1810. Other factories followed and, by 1928, over twenty were producing millions of berets for international markets, stimulated by World

Polish Girl Scouts wear white berets as part of their uniform. Variations of the beret have been a popular head dress for centuries in Europe and other parts of the world. © PETER TURNLEY/ CORBIS. REPRODUCED BY PERMISSION.

War I military and civilian migrations. French sheep wool was originally used; later merino was imported from Australia and South Africa. By the mid-twentieth century, softer berets made of angora (molted rabbit fur) mixed with thermofibers attracted female wearers.

Basque berets are usually made during winter months and involve ten steps: knitting, sewing, felting, blocking, drying, checking, brushing, shaving, "confection" or finishing, and delivery. In 1996, a beret museum opened in the village of Nay, sponsored by the manufacturer Blancq-Olibet, which provides public educational tours on Basque beret manufacture.

Beret Usage

Over time, berets have been worn for political, military, religious, and aesthetic reasons. Symbolic meanings developed that were associated with color. The black beret became so popular with French urban workers that beret-wearing resistance movement fighters (Maquis) during World War II were able to blend into crowds without raising suspicion among German occupation forces. The dark beret became the trademark of Che Guevara, leader in the 1959 Cuban Revolution, and many of his later followers. A Che beret is preserved at the Museum of the Revolution in Havana.

A worker spins a Beighau beret. Originally, berets were made for male villagers from wet wool that was hand-shaped by pulling it over the knee creating a rounded shape that fit over the head. © PAVLOVSKY JACQUES/CORBIS SYGMA. REPRODUCED BY PERMISSION.

Because of its flexibility, the beret was ideal for low-ranking military uniforms. Originally worn by nineteenth-century French seamen, it was adopted during World War I for alpine troops. British Field Marshal Montgomery popularized the beret during World War II as a badge of honor for elite military units. Since the Korean Conflict, berets have identified Special Forces as the "Green Berets," paratroopers trained to drop behind enemy lines (maroon beret) and the U.S. Army Rangers (whose beret was changed from black to tan). During the 1960s Vietnam War, "The Ballad of the Green Berets" brought to public attention the exploits and heritage of these courageous units, symbolized through their caps and shoulder badges.

A controversy broke out in 2000 C.E. when black berets became standard issue to all incoming U.S. Army recruits in an effort to attract and boost morale for an all-volunteer army. Some traditionalists felt the beret as an elite symbol had become compromised. Additionally,

to meet the several million beret orders, manufacturers overseas were contracted, which required waiving a U.S. law requiring all clothing and textiles purchased by the military to be produced in the United States.

Over the past half century, United Nations troops have been identified by their baby-blue berets, and peacekeeping forces by orange ones. The beret is worn by modern armies worldwide, including Russia, Iraq, Pakistan, Venezuela, Democratic Republic of the Congo, and South Africa.

In an effort to combat urban crime during the 1990s, volunteer units known as Guardian Angels or "Red Berets" began patrolling city streets in the United States and Europe, later in urban centers in Africa, South America, and Japan. Their bright red berets serve as warnings to petty criminals and reassurance to community residents.

Jamaican Rastafari, and later followers in Central America and the United States, motivated by Black Religious Nationalism, follow biblical prescription by wearing long-uncut, uncombed, and matted hair (dreadlocks) covered by a knitted or crocheted black beret with red, gold, and green circles. Rastafari consider the beret and dreadlocks as an individual's crown, symbols of power representing the Biblical Covenant of God with His Chosen People, Black Israelites (Genesis 9:13).

As a Western fashion statement, the beret has been worn as "classic" sportswear by adults of both sexes and children since the 1920s and is especially popular during wartime and the winter olympics. As part of the U.S. Girl Scouts' required uniform, the beret was adopted in 1936 and only replaced in 1994 by the universally popular visor baseball cap.

Variations of the beret include the Scotch Bonnet, a flat, woven or knitted woolen cap with ribbon cockade and feathers that serve to identify the wearer's clan and rank. Worn at an angle and usually dark blue, called "Bluebonnet" for Scotland's national color, it has been a symbol of Scottish patriotism. The entire Highlander costume including the Bluebonnet was outlawed for many years by the British government. After construction of Balmoral Castle at Aberdeenshire, Scotland, in 1855, the Bonnet came to be called the "Balmoral" because of recognition given the Highlanders by Queen Victoria and Prince Albert.

Other Scottish types include the tam-o'-shanter, made of brushed wool with a large pompom in the center and named after a Robert Burns poem, and the striped woolen Kilmarnock Cap, also with pompom, named for a town in Strathclyde.

See also **Afrocentric Fashion; Felt; Hats, Men's; Hats, Women's; Military Style.**

BIBLIOGRAPHY

Denford, Carole. "Le Vrai Basque." *The Hat Magazine* (April/May/June 2001): 34–37.

Wilcox, R. Turner. *The Mode in Hats and Headdress.* New York and London: Charles Scribner's Sons, 1945.

Beverly Chico

BERTIN, ROSE Rose Bertin was born Marie-Jeanne Bertin (1747–1813) in Abbeville, a textile town in the Picardy region of France. Her family was not wealthy, and so she was apprenticed to a *marchande de modes* (fashion merchant) at a young age. By 1772 she had worked her way up to the exclusive rue Saint-Honoré in Paris, where she opened her own shop under the name of the *Grand Mogol.* She quickly won the patronage of several influential courtiers, including the duchess of Chartres, Louise Marie Adélaïde de Bourbon, who introduced Bertin to the newly crowned queen, Marie Antoinette, in the summer of 1774.

The queen of France quickly became Bertin's most famous customer. Sources of the day (including Bertin's surviving business records) document more than 1,500 clients; undoubtedly, there were many more of whom no credible record survives. In addition to Marie Antoinette, Bertin dressed the queens of Spain, Sweden, and Portugal; Grand-Duchess Maria-Fëdorovna of Russia; and many European aristocrats. The latter group included Marie Jeanne Bécu, the comtesse Du Barry; the duchess of Devonshire; Georgina Cavendish and the cross-dressing Charles Geneviève Louis D'Eon de Beaumont, Chevalier d'Eon. Bertin also dressed celebrities like the Vestris family of dancers and the actress Mademoiselle de Sainval of the Comédie-Française, who were fashion plates both onstage and off. Indeed, Bertin was the first "fashion designer" to become a celebrity in her own right.

In the twenty-first century, it is taken for granted that fashion designers can achieve international fame. But the ancien régime offered few avenues for social mobility, particularly for unmarried women of humble birth. Bertin overcame these obstacles with equal measures of talent and ambition, manipulating the young queen and the emerging fashion press to make her name and her creations known throughout the world.

Minister of Fashion
Marie Antoinette is remembered as a woman preoccupied with fashion. In fact, before she met Bertin, she was not considered particularly well dressed. Bertin was not Marie Antoinette's only *marchande de modes;* the task of clothing the queen was far too demanding for just one person, and Bertin had hundreds of other clients to accommodate. But no other *marchande de modes* enjoyed such easy access to the queen or to the royal purse. Thus, Rose Bertin and Marie Antoinette were inextricably linked in the public imagination.

When the *marchandes de modes* of Paris were incorporated in 1776, Bertin was elected as the guild's first mistress. In this post, she earned the right to dress the life-sized fashion doll that toured the mercantile centers of Europe and beyond, advertising French fashions. In 1777 Bertin had a staff of forty employees, not including dozens of subcontractors and suppliers. By 1778 Bertin had grown so powerful at court that the press dubbed her France's *ministre des modes,* or "minister of fashion." The unofficial title underlined Bertin's position as a trusted royal adviser as well as a representative of France to other nations.

Bertin's partnership with the queen ensured her success, but it would also prove to be her undoing. As Marie Antoinette's popularity waxed and waned, so did that of her favorite minister. Courtiers were outraged by Bertin's privileged place in the royal circle, unprecedented for a commoner. Furthermore, her success at court gave her an ego of princely proportions. Soon Bertin was as famous for her arrogance and astronomical prices as she was for her fashions and celebrity clients. Previously, labor had represented only a fraction of the cost of a garment. By demanding star status and a star's salary, Bertin helped elevate fashion from a trade to an art.

French Revolution
The outbreak of the French Revolution forced hundreds of fashion workers out of business or out of the country. Some left voluntarily, following their aristocratic clients; others feared that they would be persecuted if they remained in France. With her ties to queen and court, Bertin had every reason to fear for her life as well as her livelihood. While the aristocracy saw Bertin as an upstart and an interloper, to the revolutionaries she was no better than an aristocrat herself. Royalists and Republicans alike blamed Bertin for encouraging Marie Antoinette's excesses, which she continued to do right up until the queen's imprisonment.

Bertin fled Paris in 1792 and spent the next three years in such émigré havens as Brussels, Frankfurt, and London, where she continued to dress fashionable foreigners and French exiles. Unlike her royal muse, Bertin managed to survive the French Revolution unscathed. Although she was twice put on the government's émigré list, she managed to prove that she had left France on legitimate business both times. The émigré list was the official record of people who had emigrated, thus forfeiting their property and, in some cases, their lives. Effectively, Bertin was declared a fugitive.

By the time Bertin returned to Paris, she was out of danger but also out of fashion. Bertin could still count a few English, Russian, and Spanish aristocrats among her clients, but hardly any Frenchwomen. Indeed, many of her French clients had perished on the scaffold, leaving their bills unpaid. The Revolution cut Bertin's career short at the height of her power, and she never recovered financially or emotionally. She died at her country retreat in Épinay-sur-Seine just a few months too soon to see restoration of the monarchy in 1814. Even after her death Bertin remained a potent and provocative symbol of the elegance and excess of the ancien régime.

See also **Court Dress; Fashion Designer.**

BIBLIOGRAPHY

Chrisman, Kimberly. "Rose Bertin in London?" *Costume* 32 (1999): 45–51.

Langlade, Émile. *La marchande de modes de Marie-Antoinette: Rose Bertin.* Paris: Albin Michel, 1911. Entertaining but unreliable biography.

———. *Rose Bertin: The Creator of Fashion at the Court of Marie-Antoinette.* Translated by Dr. Angelo S. Rappoport. New York: Charles Scribner's Sons, 1913. An English-language biography adapted from the French version.

Nouvion, Pierre de, and Émile Liez. *Un Ministre des modes sous Louis XVI: Mademoiselle Bertin, marchande de modes de la reine, 1747–1813.* Paris: Henri Leclerc, 1911. Contains detailed information about Bertin's family history.

Sapori, Michelle. *Rose Bertin: Ministre des modes de Marie-Antoinette.* Paris: Regard/Institut Français de la Mode, 2004. Illustrated monograph incorporating recent research on Bertin's career, competitors, and clients.

Kimberly Chrisman-Campbell

PERENNIALLY BEST-DRESSED

Marella and Gianni Agnelli
Fred Astaire
Marisa Berenson
Tina Chow
Cary Grant
C. Z. Guest
Gloria Guinness
Audrey Hepburn
Slim Keith
Jackie Kennedy
Babe Paley
Millicent Rogers
John Hay "Jock" Whitney
The Duke and Duchess of Windsor

BEST-DRESSED LISTS Since their inception in the first half of the twentieth century, best-dressed lists have become a popular barometer of international style. By publishing best-dressed lists in the mainstream media, fashion editors and style arbiters have established a steady market for information about the wardrobes, grooming, and comportment of smartly dressed men and women.

Perhaps the most eminent best-dressed list was the "International Best-Dressed Poll," the brainchild of Eleanor Lambert (1903–2003), a New York City publicist considered the doyenne of fashion publicity. Lambert first penned the list in 1940 as a press release for the New York Dress Institute, a trade organization she helped establish to stimulate dress sales during World War II. Lambert claimed that her list was patterned after an anonymous poll of the world's ten best-dressed women issued by the Paris couture starting in the 1920s.

Lambert's annual list became a widely heralded tally of the world's most beautifully dressed people, derided as frivolous, yet eagerly anticipated. She coordinated the poll by canvassing a coterie of fashion insiders to nominate the contenders, and then revealed the winners in a press release to the media. Lambert elevated repeat winners to her own fashion Hall of Fame. Finally, at nearly 100 years old, she stopped coordinating her celebrated list in 2002.

Another important best-dressed list has been the domain of Richard Blackwell. In 1958, Blackwell established

a line of evening gowns under the label "Mr. Blackwell," which attracted high-profile buyers like Nancy Reagan and Zsa Zsa Gabor. In 1960, *American Weekly* magazine, a national Sunday newspaper supplement, hired him to compile a list of Hollywood's best- and worst-dressed stars. Mr. Blackwell's list became notorious for his willingness to criticize icons like Brigitte Bardot and Queen Elizabeth II. The lists established Blackwell as a popular arbiter of taste, and he continues to issue his controversial fashion pronouncements as of the early 2000s.

Given the visibility of Lambert's and Blackwell's lists, fashion editors were inspired to publish best-dressed lists of their own. Among the publications that have published, or continue to publish, best-dressed lists are *Vogue, Harper's Bazaar, Vanity Fair,* and *Prima. People* magazine publishes an annual special issue featuring best- and worst-dressed celebrities, while the annual Academy Awards show has spawned its own best-dressed subcategory. Other best-dressed lists have been printed by nonfashion publications like *Fortune* magazine and the *New York Post.*

Best-dressed lists allow readers to imagine that a winning profile is open to all, when in fact the top spots invariably go to wealthy people in the public eye: film stars and fashion industry or society figures. But the lists continue to fascinate as they impart lessons in style, self-presentation, and the ineffable quality of individual chic.

See also **Fashion.**

BIBLIOGRAPHY

Blackwell, Richard. *Mr. Blackwell's Worst: 30 Years of Fashion Fiascos.* New York: Pharos Books, 1991.

Haugland, H. Kristina, and Dilys E. Blum. *Best Dressed: Fashion from the Birth of Couture to Today.* Philadelphia: Philadelphia Museum of Art, 1997.

Nemy, Enid. "Eleanor Lambert, Empress of Fashion, Dies at 100." *The New York Times*, 8 October 2003.

Wilson, Eric. "Eleanor Lambert Celebrates an American Fashion Century." *WWD* 186, no. 26 (6 August 2003).

Kathleen Paton

BIBA Biba has become a potent legend quite out of proportion with its relatively brief life in the mid-twentieth century. It was a shop and a label—but it was more than either or both of these: it came to stand for the "swinging chick," the ideal, running, jumping and never-standing-still girl, the image that dominated fashion from the mid-1960s until about 1974. That one word, "Biba" calls up from memory the long-legged, zany, crop-haired Twiggy morphing into the druggy, Pre-Raphaelite hippie of 1970: from the futuristic to the retro in four short years.

Biba was the creation of Barbara Hulanicki and her husband, Stephen Fitz-Simon. It began as a mail-order firm, selling gamine gingham shifts with matching head scarf in the wake of Brigitte Bardot. In 1964 the couple followed the just emerging trend for the fashion boutique as opposed to the department store where most women bought their clothes in the 1950s. (Small dress shops, known in Britain as "madam shops," still existed, but were by this time considered very old-fashioned, and small dressmakers were also dying out.) Biba's first outlet opened in the smart Kensington district of London. The young couple rented what had been a chemist's shop, retained in the window the big period bottles of ruby- and topaz-colored liquids that traditionally decorated such shops at that time (suggestive of magical potions), and created a dark blue interior with William Morris curtains, more like an Aladdin's cave than an ordinary shop. This was a totally different shopping experience from the department store or the "madam shop." There were no assistants pressuring you to buy by peering into the claustrophobic changing room and commenting on the clothes; instead there was a communal changing room free for all, more reminiscent of the school locker room than of adult life—but in an exciting way. The message was always that these fashions were for the young and carefree.

Biba really began to make an impact just as the mood of the 1960s began to change. From 1966 on, a creeping sense of economic discontent and social unrest in Britain was beginning to supersede the optimism of the first half of the decade. One of the ways in which this was expressed stylistically was in the mutation from future to past. By 1967 the Courrèges look—flat white boots and a square-cut tunic, reminiscent of cinematic fashions of the future—was being displaced by much dreamier

Biba. From the mid-1960s until about 1974, Barbara Hulanicki and her husband, Stephen Fitz-Simon, capitalized on an emerging "old is new again" fashion trend with their London Biba boutique. The shop was furnished with Old World furniture and lamps while the clothing was reminiscent of the styles of the 1920s and 1930s. LARRY ELLIS/EXPRESS/GETTY IMAGES. REPRODUCED BY PERMISSION.

clothes. The two other most influential British fashion designers of the period, Mary Quant and Ozzie Clark, began to use such "old-fashioned" textiles as crêpe and satin in art deco colors of eau de nil, cream, rust, and even maroon. Biba was at the epicenter of this trend from the beginning. The shops had a distinctly period feel, with bentwood furniture, vases of ostrich feathers, Tiffany-style lamps, Victorian china pedestal jardinières, and even—in Biba's third shop—the Victorian gothic paneling from a recently relocated boys' school.

The clothes were subtly period, too. Minidresses looked like something out of Mabel Lucie Atwell, childishly high-waisted, with sleeves tight at the shoulder but ballooning out toward the cuff. Trousers flapped out at the hem, like men's "Oxford bags" of the 1920s; slithery satin evening dresses looked like gowns Jean Harlow might have worn in a 1930s' Hollywood melodrama. Then there were T-shirts, exaggeratedly long of hem and sleeve, and knee-high suede boots all in matching offbeat colors of dirty pink, brick dust, sage green, aubergine, and chocolate; and a makeup range that made the wearer look like the silent film star Theda Bara, with black lips and glistening eyes.

Biba was a way of life as much as a dress shop, and its greatest moment became its ultimate tragedy. From the original shop, it moved—still in Kensington—first to a grocer's shop, retaining all the period wooden shelving, then to a yet larger shop that had been a school outfitters, and finally to what had been Derry and Toms department store, a fabulous art deco building, complete with roof garden and all the original fittings, carpets, and staircases. On these five floors, Biba aimed to sell not just clothes but a whole lifestyle. As well as the dresses, there were to be aubergine refrigerators, Biba dinner services, art deco carpets, a food department complete with coffee, tea, flour, and sugar in Biba packaging, and—on the ground floor—all manner of trinkets, purses, scarves, accessories and, of course, the makeup range.

It was a magnificent vision. Unfortunately the hordes of young women who came to hang out among the satin bolsters on the tiger-print sofas of the ground floor, with its dark walls and druggy ambience, did not necessarily come to buy but simply to be Biba. By this time, Barbara Hulanicki and her husband had lost financial control of the enterprise to the multichain fashion company Dorothy Perkins, and the returns were not high enough to satisfy its board of directors. In 1975 Biba folded—and not only that; in an act of the utmost philistinism, the magnificent original Derry and Toms interiors were destroyed to make way for a utilitarian Marks & Spencer and British Home Stores.

Barbara Hulanicki and her husband moved to the United States, and Hulanicki made a second successful career designing interiors for the art deco mansions of Miami, Florida. In 1993, the Laing Art Gallery in Newcastle decided to hold a Biba exhibition. Many Biba aficionados previously donated the outfits they had treasured for thirty years. There were examples of the coffee—and even baked bean—tins, the cosmetics, and the soft furnishings, and the interiors of the shops were re-created. But what was extraordinary about the exhibition was the visitors' book. Visitors were invited to comment in any way they wished. Unlike other visitors' books, its pages were filled with loving reminiscences of how a Biba outfit had defined a major experience, a period, an identity, and although Biba the shop spanned only a decade, the memory gave promise of living on forever.

See also **Boutique; Clark, Ossie; Quant, Mary; Twiggy.**

BIBLIOGRAPHY

Fogg, Marnie. *Boutique: A '60s Cultural Icon.* London: Phaidon Press Ltd., 2003.

Hulanicki, Barbara. *From A to Biba.* London: Hutchinson, 1983.

Elizabeth Wilson

BICYCLE CLOTHING The bicycle was invented in Europe, but American ingenuity increased its usability and widespread use. Kirkpatrick Macmillan of Scotland is credited with inventing the first mechanical bicycle, while Pierre Michaux and son Ernest of Paris were the first to manufacture bicycles on a large scale in the mid-1860s. The aptly named "boneshaker" or velocipede was quickly followed by the high-wheeler and then the safety bicycle. In July 1865 Pierre Lallement brought the bicycle to America resulting in a wave of bicycle-related patents. The bicycle craze flourished through the end of the century. Clothing specifically designed for wear while bicycling has changed dramatically over the years.

Early bicycle riding was a man's activity due to the fact that in order to ride the velocipede, essentially two wheels connected by a frame and suspended seat, the rider had to wear bifurcated apparel to straddle the mechanism. With the introduction of the pneumatic tire in 1888, the popularity of the bicycle for transportation and leisure increased dramatically. In the same year the drop-frame bike was introduced in America. This new model made bicycle riding in a skirt much easier and more women participated in the activity. By the 1890s, clothing developed specifically for bicycling was being designed and produced. Racing clubs for men were formed and appropriate attire was required. Typical clothing included the "wheelman" or sleeveless vest with insignia worn over a shirt, long shorts (to the knee), and shoes without socks. In 1874 Charles Bennet, an avid bicyclist, decided to tackle "the delicate problem that men faced as they were jounced on their penny farthings" (Norcliffe, p. 128). He designed the "bike web," a knit and elastic garment to provide support and cushioning. Because the garment was worn by bicycle "jockeys" it was called the "jockey strap," soon shortened to "jock strap." Headgear and footwear were also designed specifically for bicyclists. Headgear varied from a small flat crown hat with visor brim to a pith helmet that might provide protection in a crash. Shoes were designed to prevent slipping on the bike pedals. One shoe model incorporated leather pleats on the sole that served this function.

Mid-Victorian society did not approve of women riding bicycles, but the activity became more accepted after 1881 when Queen Victoria ordered tricycles for her daughters. Besides the immodesty and physicality of women straddling a bicycle, the independence allowed the individual woman was unprecedented. By the late 1800s, women were becoming enthusiastic bicyclists. Soon many adventurous women started wearing shorter skirts to avoid catching them in the pedals. Barbara Schreier (1989, p. 112) declared "bicycling helped to smooth the way for future clothing changes and dramatically advanced the position of women in sports." Knickerbockers made bicycle riding even easier for women, but the style was ridiculed as being unfeminine and unattractive. More shocking was the association of bifurcated garments and immorality. P. Russell suggests, "the forked body astride a modern machine could be represented as an essentially sexual image" (p. 66).

By the 1920s, new trends in sportswear introduced new forms and fabrics that permeated all sports activities. The new casual lifestyle eliminated the need for specific bicycle wear. Practical, comfortable sportswear was now fashionable and accepted. From the 1920s to the 1960s bicyclists wore all varieties of readily available sportswear with the exception of professional bike racers who wore close-fitting knit tops and pants to facilitate speed.

Bicycle clothing in the early 2000s combines elements of function, fashion, and advertising. Function centers on the most aerodynamic ensemble while providing comfort for the rider. Fashion is evident in color choices while professional and leisure riders sport clothing with company names and logos. The avid bicyclist wears form-fitting shorts and jerseys with appropriate accessories. Bicycle shorts rely on properties of nylon and spandex fibers to provide the closest fit possible. A major functional feature of bicycle shorts is the pad sewn into the crotch of the shorts, providing cushioning between body and bike seat. Chamois leather was originally used for the pad, but synthetic chamois or gel inserts are used in the twenty-first century. The bicycle shirt or jersey is also body-conforming for the all-important aerodynamic form. Shirts are typically brightly colored making the rider highly visible. The well-known yellow jersey worn by the leader in the Tour de France bicycle race was introduced in 1919. The Tour de France uses other signifier color jerseys including the green "points" jersey for the race's most consistent sprinter or points winner, the red polka-dot jersey for the most consistent climber, and the re-introduced white jersey distinguishes the best young rider.

Bicycle helmets, when properly worn, prevent head injuries and are becoming more accepted as the "look" for riders. Indeed, bicycle helmets are required wear for child bicyclists in some states. Helmets vary in cost and design, but most are aerodynamic in shape. Cycling shoes are designed with a rigid sole to efficiently transfer energy from the downward push of the leg to the ball of the foot and so to the pedal. Shoes worn by professional racers can be almost impossible to walk in as the sole of the shoe is contoured to mesh with the pedal of the bicycle. Gloves and eyewear often provide the finishing touch to the cyclist's look. Gloves facilitate grip on the handlebars and may prevent injury in a fall. Eyewear provides protection from sun, wind, and insects.

Since the introduction of the bicycle to the general public, bicycle clothing has influenced everyday fashion. Bifurcated garments for bicycle wear in the late 1800s assisted in liberating women from cumbersome full-length skirts. The body-conforming look provided by modern materials, especially nylon and spandex knits, is evident in bicycle wear and fashion forms worn in the twenty-first century.

See also **Activewear; Elastomers; Nylon.**

Bifurcated riding ensemble, 1895. Women cast off long gowns in favor of more practical knickerbockers when riding bicycles. © Corbis. Reproduced by permission.

BIBLIOGRAPHY

Norcliffe, Glen. *The Ride to Modernity: The Bicycle in Canada, 1869–1900.* Toronto: University of Toronto Press, 2001.

Russell, P. "Recycling Femininity: Old Ladies and New Women." *Australian Cultural History* 13 (1994): 31.

Schreier, Barbara. "Sporting Wear." In *Men and Women: Dressing the Part.* Edited by Claudia Kidwell and Valerie Steele, 93–123. Washington D.C.: Smithsonian Institution Press, 1989.

Simpson, Claire. "Respectable Identities: New Zealand Nineteenth Century—'New Women'—on Bicycles." *The International Journal of the History of Sport* 18, no. 2 (2001): 54–77.

Karen L. LaBat

BIKINI The bikini, a two-piece bathing suit of diminutive proportions, first appeared on the fashion scene in the summer of 1946. Its impact was compared to that of the atomic bomb tests conducted that same summer by the United States at Bikini Atoll in the Pacific Islands,

Bikini worn by actress Ursula Andress. Made famous in the 1962 James Bond film *Dr. No,* this bikini was auctioned at Christie's auction house in London. The first bikini was worn at a Paris fashion show in 1946 but did not gain widespread acceptance until the 1960s. © AFP/Corbis. Reproduced by permission.

which was arguably the source of its name. Both the French couturier Jacques Heim and the Swiss engineer Louis Reard are credited with launching the skimpy two-piece, which they dubbed the *atome* and bikini, respectively. The French model Michele Bernardini wore the first bikini at a fashion show in Paris. Her suit consisted of little more than two triangles of fabric for the bra, with strings that tied around the neck and back, and two triangles of fabric for the bottom, connected by strings at the hips.

The legendary fashion editor Diana Vreeland dubbed the bikini the "swoonsuit," and declared that it was the most important thing since the A-bomb, revealing "everything about a girl except her mother's maiden name." Vreeland worked at the time for *Harper's Bazaar,* which was the first magazine to showcase the bikini in America. The May 1947 issue featured a Toni Frissell photograph of a model wearing a rayon green-and-white-polka-dot bikini by the American sportswear designer Carolyn Schnurer.

Vreeland's comments about the bikini speak to the controversy that erupted when it first appeared. Unlike its two-piece counterparts, first seen on beaches in the late 1920s and 1930s, which exposed only a small section of midriff, the bikini bared a number of erogenous zones—the back, upper thigh, and for the first time, the navel—all at once. It was almost immediately banned, for religious reasons, in such countries as Spain, Portugal, and Italy and was shunned by American women as lacking in decency. Many public parks and beaches prohibited bikinis, and wearing them in private clubs and resorts was looked upon with disfavor.

The bikini remained a taboo novelty throughout the 1950s. Made even of such unusual fabrics as mink, grass, and porcupine quills, bikinis were worn mostly by screen sirens and pin-up girls like Brigitte Bardot, Jayne Mansfield, and Diana Dors, along with sophisticates on the beaches of resorts along the Riviera. They were also showcased in bathing suit beauty contests in vacation spots like Florida and California. One-piece and more modest two-piece suits, resembling the highly structured undergarments of the period, held favor with the majority of women until the end of the decade, when bikini sales started to rise.

An increased number of private pools in suburban backyards and a growing awareness of health and fitness were cited as possible causes for increased acceptance of bikini-wearing, at least within the privacy of one's own home. *Harper's Bazaar* touted the bikini as putting one close to the elements. American retailers, however, who reportedly sold more sleepwear resembling bikinis than actual bikini swimsuits, were ambivalent about the extent to which they should promote the sale of bikinis.

It was not until the 1960s that the bikini gained more widespread acceptance. Youth culture, celebrity endorsements, and innovations in textile technology such as the manufacture of spandex, helped establish the bikini, and its variations, as a mainstay in swimwear fashion. In 1960, the singer Brian Hyland immortalized the bikini with his hit song, "Itsy Bitsy Teenie Weenie Yellow Polka Dot Bikini." A crop of beach movies with bikini-clad teenagers, including the former Mouseketeer Annette Funicello, appeared. Ursula Andress wore one of the most famous bikinis, with a hip holster, in the 1962 James Bond film *Dr. No*—a variation of which was worn by Halle Berry in the 2002 Bond movie *Die Another Day. Sports Illustrated* published its first swimsuit issue in 1964, with Babette March wearing a bikini on the cover; appearing on the cover of *Sports Illustrated's* much-anticipated, annual swimsuit issue is now a coveted rite of passage for fashion models. The prevailing form of the early 1960s bikini was a structured bra top and low-slung, hip-hugging briefs, often embellished with ruffles and fringe.

Relaxing sexual mores and shifting views on modesty brought about more daring variations of the bikini in the late 1960s and early 1970s. In 1964, the American fashion designer Rudi Gernreich, whose progressive, androgynous clothing pushed fashion's boundaries, debuted his "monokini" or topless bathing suit. The black wool knit suit consisted of briefs with suspenders that extended between bared breasts and around the neck, reminiscent of a bathing suit illustrated in 1940 by the Italian designer Umberto Brunescelli. Gernreich sold 3,000 of the monokinis by the end of the season. He again shocked the public when he unveiled his unisex thong bathing suits in 1974, and the "pubikini" in the mid 1980s. The thong bikini, which revealed the buttocks, has since become the unofficial uniform of professional bodybuilders, boxing ring girls who announce the rounds, and female dancers in music videos.

In 1974, the string bikini, or "tanga," consisting of little more than tiny triangles of cloth held together with ties at the hip and around the neck and back, emerged from Rio de Janeiro. Topless bathing, which had been accepted for some time in exotic beach locales such as Rio and Saint Tropez, started to gain popularity on public beaches in the 1970s, particularly in the United States.

By the late 1970s, the bikini, which had been pushed to extremely minimal proportions, had lost some of its shock value and allure, and in response the one-piece suit came into favor again. However, new one-piece styles were strongly influenced by the bikini phenomenon. A year after Gernreich's monokini was unveiled, "scandal suits" by Cole of California, also known as net bikinis, were popular, at once playfully revealing and concealing the body with solid patches of fabric connected with patches of net. The thong was also a clear antecedent of figure revealing one-pieces of the late 1970s and 1980s, which were cut high on the thigh, low at the neck and down the back, and open at the sides.

The trend toward less-structured, more figure-revealing suits such as the bikini corresponded with the sports and fitness craze that emerged in the 1970s and 1980s. Sport bikinis with racer-back tops and high-cut briefs appeared in the 1980s and were popular into the 1990s, worn, for example, as the official uniform for women's volleyball teams in the 1996 Olympics. In the twenty-first century, the bikini has regained popularity through new incarnations, many of which are, paradoxically, made with more fabric.

The "tankini," a two-piece that can provide as much coverage as a one-piece, has appeared, along with the "boy short" bottoms and surfer styles reminiscent of 1960s bikinis. High-end fashion houses such as Chanel, which debuted its minimal "eye-patch" bikini in 1995, contributed to the surfer craze with logo-emblazoned bikinis and surfboards in their Spring/Summer 2002 collection.

Despite the initial controversy, the bikini has become a perennial in swimwear fashion, particularly among the young. Youth-oriented culture, sexual emancipation, innovation in textile technology, an emphasis on sports and fitness, and the overarching societal shift to a more relaxed style of dress have all contributed to the bikini's success.

See also **Swimwear; Teenage Fashions; Vreeland, Diana.**

BIBLIOGRAPHY

Esten, John. *Diana Vreeland Bazaar Years.* New York: Universe Books, 2001.

Lencek, Lena, and Gideon Bosker. *Making Waves: Swimsuits and the Undressing of America.* San Francisco: Chronicle Books, 1988.

Martin, Richard, and Harold Koda. *Splash!: A History of Swimwear.* New York: Rizzoli International, 1990.

Poli, Doretta Davanzo. *Beachwear and Bathing-Costume.* Modena, Italy: Zanfi Editori, 1995.

Probert, Christina. *Swimwear in Vogue Since 1910.* New York: Abbeville Press, 1981.

Tiffany Webber-Hanchett

BLAHNIK, MANOLO Manolo Blahnik (b. 1942) was a designer and manufacturer of what were called "the sexiest shoes in the world"—beautiful, expensive, and highly coveted by many of the world's most fashionable women. Heir to a tradition of luxury shoemaking epitomized by André Perugia, Salvatore Ferragamo, and Roger Vivier, Blahnik produced shoes—"Manolos," to the cognoscenti—that became icons of the fashion culture at the turn of the

Manolo Blahnik with actress Sarah Jessica Parker. Manolo Blahnik's shoe designs are popular with celebrities. © GREGORY PACE/CORBIS. REPRODUCED BY PERMISSION.

CEO of Neiman Marcus Direct, Karen Katz. Katz sits near a display of Manolo Blahnik shoes that are now available for purchase online. Manolo Blahnik's shoes are universally recognized. © AP/WORLD WIDE PHOTOS. REPRODUCED BY PERMISSION.

twenty-first century. In the words of retailer Jeffrey Kalinsky, "There's never been a shoe designer whose reign as No. 1 shoe designer has lasted so long. His hold on the throne has no sign of doing anything but growing" (Larson, p. 6).

Manolo Blahnik was born on 27 November 1942 in the small village of Santa Cruz de la Palma in the Canary Islands, where his family—his Spanish mother, Manuela, his Czechoslovakian father, Enan, and his younger sister, Evangelina—had a banana plantation. Manuela, a voracious consumer of fashion magazines, bought clothes on shopping trips to Paris and Madrid and had the island's dressmaker copy styles from fashion magazines. She designed her own shoes with the help of the local cobbler.

Manolo Blahnik moved to Geneva at the age of fifteen to live with his father's cousin. Here he had his first experiences of the theater, opera, and fine restaurants. He studied law for a short period but soon switched to literature and art history. Blahnik left Geneva for Paris in 1965 to study art and theater design. He worked at the trendy Left Bank shop GO, where he met the actress Anouk Aimée and the jewelry designer Paloma Picasso.

With Picasso's encouragement, Blahnik soon moved to London. While working at Feathers, a trendy boutique, he continued to cultivate his connections to the worlds of fashion and culture and was known for his unique style. But Blahnik was still searching for a specific vocation; the search then took him to New York City.

Blahnik arrived in New York City in 1969. Hired by the store Zapata, he began designing men's saddle shoes. In 1972 Blahnik was introduced to Ossie Clark, then one of London's most fashionable designers, who asked him to design the shoes for his women's collection. While the shoes were not commercially successful, the press noticed their originality of design. Blahnik had no formal training as a shoe maker and in¡tally his designs were structually weak. He consulted with a London shoe manufacture in order to correct his lack of technical skills. Also during this time Blahnik met Diana Vreeland, who declared, "Young man, do things, do accessories. Do shoes" (McDowell, p. 84). This endorsement was seconded by China Machado, the fashion editor of *Harper's Bazaar. Women's Wear Daily* proclaimed Blahnik "one of the most exotic spirits in London" in 1973, and *Footwear News* described the Manolo Blahnik shoe on its front

EXCELLENCE IN DESIGN

Manolo Blahnik won three awards from the Council of Fashion Designers of America in the 1980s and 1990s. The first special award was given in 1987; the second, for outstanding excellence in accessory design, in 1990. The third award came with the following tribute in 1997: "Blahnik has done for footwear what Worth did for the couture, making slippers into objects of desire, collectibles for women for whom Barbies are too girlish and Ferraris not girlish enough .... an incredible piston in the engine of fashion, there is almost no designer he has not collaborated with, no designer who has not turned to him to transform a collection into a concert."

page as "the most talked about shoe in London." Blahnik purchased Zapata from its owner in 1973. In 1978 he introduced a line exclusive to Bloomingdale's, a well-known American retailer. Blahnik opened a second free-standing store a year later on New York's Madison Avenue.

Blahnik's creations received considerable publicity in the early 1980s, but his business was not running smoothly. Searching for alternatives, he was introduced by Dawn Mello, the vice president of Bergdorf Goodman, to an advertising copywriter named George Malkemus. Malkemus and his partner, Anthony Yurgaitis, went into business with Blahnik in 1982. They closed the Madison Avenue shop, opened a store on West Fifty-Fourth Street, and limited the distribution of Blahnik's shoes to such prestigious retailers as Barneys, Bergdorf Goodman, and Neiman Marcus. By 1984 the newspaper *USA Today* projected earnings of a million dollars for the New York shop alone. Manolo Blahnik shoes began to appear on the runways of designers from Yves Saint Laurent, Bill Blass, and Geoffrey Beene to Perry Ellis, Calvin Klein, Isaac Mizrahi, and John Galliano.

Manolo Blahnik's shoes became more popular than ever in the early twenty-first century. They appealed to an increasingly broad audience, in part because of their star billing on the television show *Sex and the City*. With production of "Manolos" limited to 10,000 to 15,000 pairs per month by four factories outside of Milan, the demand for these shoes exceeded the supply.

The December 2003 issue of *Footwear News* quoted Alice Rawsthorn, the director of London's Design Museum, which had been the site of a recent Blahnik retrospective: "Technically, aesthetically and conceptually, he is one of the most accomplished designers of our time in

any field, and is undeniably the world's most influential footwear designer" (Anniss, p. 16).

See also **Clark, Ossie; Ferragamo, Salvatore; London Fashion; Shoes, Women's; Vreeland, Diana.**

BIBLIOGRAPHY
Anniss, Elisa. "Prince Charming." *Footwear News*, 8 December 2003.
Larson, Kirsten. "Blahnik Holds Reins Tight on His Manolos." *Footwear News*, 10 November 2003.
McDowell, Colin. *Manolo Blahnik*. New York: HarperCollins, 2000.
Reed, Julia. "Walk This Way." *Vogue*, November 2003.

Liz Gessner

BLASS, BILL William Ralph (Bill) Blass (1922–2002) was born in Fort Wayne, Indiana, in 1922. At the age of nineteen he left the Midwest and moved to New York City, where he studied briefly at Parsons School of Design. He worked as a sketch artist for a sportswear firm in 1940–1941, but his budding career was interrupted for military service in a counterintelligence unit in World

Bill Blass. Blass's classic use of pinstripes and houndstooth checks, along with his tailored designs, drew attention from fashionable celebrities like Nancy Reagan and Barbara Walters. In the 1980s, Bill Blass Ltd. expanded to included sales of eyeglasses, fragrances and other fashion-related merchandise. © BETTMANN/CORBIS. REPRODUCED BY PERMISSION.

War II. After the war Blass began working as a fashion designer, mainly for the firm of Maurice Rentner, Ltd. In 1970 he purchased the Rentner firm, renamed it Bill Blass Ltd., and saw the company take off as one of the most successful American fashion houses of the late twentieth century.

Blass created a glamorous but restrained look that won him a faithful following among women of style, including Nancy Reagan, Barbara Bush, Candice Bergen, and Barbara Walters. His day outfits drew heavily on tailoring and fabrics usually associated with menswear, including pinstriped gabardines, worsteds, and houndstooth checks. His eveningwear referenced Hollywood glamour. One of his most famous evening gowns consisted of a cashmere sweater top and a bouffant satin skirt.

Blass showed great business acumen in making Bill Blass Ltd. one of the leaders of the licensing boom that took off in the fashion industry in the 1980s. In rapid succession the firm concluded lucrative licensing deals for eyeglasses, executive gifts, fragrances, and a wide range of other fashion-related products. Blass retired from his business after suffering a stroke in 1998, and the company was sold to its backers in 1999. Blass died in 2002, but Bill Blass Ltd. continued to thrive, with Lars Nilsson as the founder's first successor. Michael Vollbracht replaced Nilsson as the firm's chief designer in 2003.

See also **Celebrities; Fashion Marketing and Merchandising; First Ladies' Gowns; Perfume; Twentieth-Century Fashion.**

BIBLIOGRAPHY

Blass, Bill. *Bare Blass.* New York: HarperCollins, 2002.

Daria, Irene. *The Fashion Cycle: A Behind-the-Scenes Look at a Year with Bill Blass, Liz Claiborne, Donna Karan, Arnold Scaasi, and Adrienne Vittadini.* New York: Simon and Schuster, 1990.

O'Hagen, Helen, Kathleen Rowald, and Michael Vollbracht. *Bill Blass: An American Designer.* New York: Harry N. Abrams, 2002.

Wilson, Eric. "Bill Blass Receives a Retrospective." *Women's Wear Daily,* 16 May 2000.

John S. Major

BLAZER Possibly a development of the nautical reefer jacket, a blazer is a loose-fitting and lightweight flannel sports jacket. Coming in both double- or single-breasted styles, although most are double-breasted, a blazer is generally tailored in either plain navy or black, has brass buttons, two side vents, is thigh length and in many cases has a breast-pocket badge. A well-constructed blazer can make even a pair of jeans appear smart. The blazer is generally considered to be a vital component of the "preppy" or "British look."

History

The familiar navy blazer traces its origins back to the captain of the frigate HMS *Blazer*, who had short double-breasted jackets cut in navy blue serge for his scruffy-looking crew when Queen Victoria visited his ship in 1837. The crew's "blazers" with their shining brass Royal Navy buttons impressed the Queen and soon became part of their dress uniform.

It is believed that the heavier double-breasted reefer jacket was the inspiration for the captain's original blazer design. What is less clear is how and why the naval blazer came to be worn by civilians. One likely explantion, and probably why so many owners of yachts and other sailing vessels wear blazers, is that many people who had no obvious association with the sea or indeed the navy could still have blazer jackets made originally for maritime experiences. With traditional outfitters such as Gieves and Hawkes, on London's Savile Row, cutting blazers for Royal Naval officers it is likely that many civilians would get their own tailors to copy a version for them. If buttons with emblems were not used then simple flat brass buttons were, although it would then become difficult to distinguish the blazer from the other sports jackets.

Divorced from any military background, the single-breasted blazer was the favored style of club jacket worn by rowing clubs in the nineteenth century. These would be made up in college, school, or club colors to be worn at special outdoor sporting events, such as the Henley Royal Regatta. Crests and other insignia were often embroidered in heavy gold thread on the left breast pocket, and the buttons were similar to those used by the navy. Men who were not in a sporting club might still wear a blazer but, as with the naval-inspired version, more likely using enamel buttons instead of brass.

Worn by many Europeans for both work and leisure and popularized by Brooks Brothers for the American market in the early twentieth century (and later in bright colors, such as bottle green or yellow, for golf attire), the authentic British blazer (and its imitations) have held a minor but consistent place in the male wardrobe for decades. The blazer's most recent revival was as essential executive dress in the 1980s, often worn with open shirt and cravat. Its popularity is limited somewhat by its reputation as being too formal for the young, and too stuffy for the "casual dress" office.

See also **Jacket; Sports Jacket.**

BIBLIOGRAPHY

Amies, Hardy. *A,B,C of Men's Fashion.* London: Cahill and Company Ltd., 1964.

Byrde, Penelope. *The Male Image:—Men's Fashion in England 1300–1970.* London: B. T. Batsford Ltd., 1979.

Chenoune, Farid. *A History of Men's Fashion.* Paris: Flammarion, 1993.

De Marley, Diana. *Fashion for Men: An Illustrated History.* London: B. T. Batsford Ltd., 1985.

Keers, Paul. *A Gentleman's Wardrobe.* London: Weidenfeld and Nicolson, 1987.

Roetzel, Bernhard. *Gentleman: A Timeless Fashion.* Cologne, Germany: Konemann, 1999.

Schoeffler, O. E., and William Gale. *Esquire's Encyclopedia of 20th Century Fashions.* New York: McGraw-Hill, 1973.

Wilkins, Christobel. *The Story of Occupational Costume.* Poole: Blandford Press, 1982.

Tom Greatrex

BLOOMER COSTUME In the spring of 1851, three leading women's rights activists, Elizabeth Cady Stanton (1815–1902), Cady's cousin, Elizabeth Smith Miller (1822–1911), and Amelia Jenks Bloomer (1818–1894), editor of the *Lily, a Ladies' Journal Devoted to Temperance and Literature*, wore similar outfits on the streets of Seneca Falls, New York—ensembles consisting of knee-length dresses over full trousers. In nineteenth-century America, trousers were an exclusively male garment and women wearing trousers in public caused a sensation. The national press quickly linked this dress reform style to Amelia Bloomer, who had been writing articles about it. Soon both the costume and its wearers were popularly identified as "Bloomers."

Amelia Bloomer's strong association with the freedom dress, as it was known by women's rights advocates, began with an article in the *Lily* in February 1851. Bloomer wrote more pieces about the outfit over the next several months, particularly emphasizing its advantages as a healthful, convenient alternative to the many petticoats, long skirts, and tight corsets of current fashionable dress. In response to readers' inquiries, Bloomer described the costume in detail in the *Lily's* May issue, and when it sold out, repeated the description the following month, stating:

> Our skirts have been robbed of about a foot of their former length, and a pair of loose trousers of the same material as the dress, substituted. These latter extend from the waist to the ankle, and may be gathered into a band . . . We make our *dress* the same as usual, except that we wear no bodice, or a very slight one, the waist is loose and easy, and without whalebones . . . Our skirt is full, and falls a little below the knee.

But however closely she was connected with the Bloomer costume by the press and the public, Amelia Bloomer did not invent the style. Bloomer's full trousers gathered in at the ankle were called "Turkish trousers" and patterned after those worn by women in the Middle East. Since the eighteenth century, European and American women had also worn such trousers for fancy dress. French fashion plates of the 1810s show similar full trousers, called pantalets or pantaloons, peeking under calf-length fashionable dresses. Although this style was far too daring for American women, by the 1820s children of both sexes were wearing short dresses over narrow, straight-legged trousers, also called pantalets. Boys exchanged pantalets for regular trousers when they grew too old for dresses (typically at five or six), while girls wore them throughout childhood. In their late teens, girls graduated to long dresses and continued to wear pantalets as underwear beneath their skirts.

Amelia Bloomer credited Elizabeth Smith Miller with introducing the freedom dress. There are differing accounts of how Miller came to design her outfit, but it is likely that Miller was aware of similar attire worn by women in utopian communities or sanatoriums. Beginning in 1827 with Community of Equality in New Harmony, Indiana, women in several American religious and utopian groups wore straight-legged trousers like children's pantalets under knee-length loose-fitting dresses. Variously styled similar outfits were also promoted for women performing calisthenic exercises and patients at water cure sanatoriums. These early instances of women wearing short dresses over trousers did cause occasional comment in the press, but because the garments were worn in closed societies or in women-only situations, they did not challenge the basic social order, unlike the public displays of the Bloomer costume in the 1850s.

The initial press coverage of Bloomer wearers during the summer of 1851 was not completely negative but before long the reality of women publicly wearing trousers brought out underlying fears of gender role reversals. In a society based on male dominance and female submission, men saw the Bloomer costume as a threat to the status quo and male leaders from newspaper editors to ministers decried the fashion. Satirical cartoons depicted Bloomer-clad women as crude louts indulging in the worst male vices or bossy wives holding sway over their husbands.

Although women's rights activists generally favored dress reform, they came to view the Bloomer costume as a counterproductive force. When activists lectured wearing the Bloomer costume, audiences focused on the controversial trousers instead of radical change in women's education, employment, and suffrage. Consequently, by the mid-1850s, most women's rights advocates had stopped wearing the Bloomer costume in public. Amelia Bloomer herself continued to wear it until 1858, when she cited a move to a new community and the newly introduced cage crinoline, which eliminated the need for heavy petticoats, as the reasons she abandoned the freedom dress and returned to long skirts.

The Bloomer costume and a similar outfit called the American costume, which featured mannish, straight-legged trousers, were viable alternatives to constrictive fashionable dress during the second half of the nineteenth century. Although the number of women who wore such attire in public was very small, there are accounts of

The Bloomer Quick Step. The "Bloomer" described in the *Daily Richmond Times* account wore an outfit similar to the one seen on the girl illustrating the "Bloomer Quick Step." A publisher of dance scores apparently mistook the Bloomer costume as a fashion fad and released a series of illustrated "Bloomer" dances late in 1851. LIBRARY OF CONGRESS. REPRODUCED BY PERMISSION.

Yesterday afternoon, Main street was thrown into intense commotion by the sudden appearance . . . of a pretty young woman, rigged out in the Bloomer costume—her dress being composed of a pink silk cap, pink skirt reaching to the knees and large white silk trousers, fitting compactly around the ankle, and pink coloured gaiters. . . . Old and young, grave and gay, descended into the street to catch a glimpse of the Bloomer as she passed leisurely and gracefully down the street, smiling at the sensation which her appearance had created. The boys shouted, the men laughed and the ladies smiled at the singular spectacle. . . . Few inquired the name of the Bloomer, because all who visited the Theatre during the last season, recognized in her a third or fourth rate actress, whose real or assumed name appeared in the bills as "Miss O'Neil." During the Season, however, we learn she severed her connexion with Mr. Potter's corps of Super numeraries and entered a less respectable establishment in this city.

Richmond Dispatch, Tuesday, 8 July 1851, p.2, c.6.

women wearing it in private when doing housework, farming, or traveling, especially in the west. In 1858 *Godey's Lady's Book* promoted a Bloomer-style costume for calisthenics and similar clothing was worn as bathing costume. Physical training educators used the Bloomer costume as a prototype in developing garments for increasingly active women's sports programs. The full trousers themselves became known as bloomers and, by the 1880s, were an essential element of the gymnasium or gym suit; short bloomers continued to be worn as part of gym suits into the 1970s. Bloomers reappeared in public during the bicycling craze of the 1890s, now worn as part of a suit with a jacket instead of a short dress. Women wearing bicycling bloomers in the 1890s were less controversial than when Amelia Bloomer and her friends donned their famous outfits in the 1850s, but not until the mid-twentieth century did women routinely wear trousers in public without criticism.

See also **Dress Reform; Gender, Dress, and Fashion; Trousers.**

BIBLIOGRAPHY

Bloomer, Amelia. *The Lily, a Ladies' Journal Devoted to Temperance and Literature.* The February, March, April, May, and June 1851 issues of *The Lily* have articles by Amelia Bloomer related to female dress reform.

Cunningham, Patricia A. *Reforming Women's Fashion, 1850–1920: Politics, Health, and Art.* Kent, Ohio, and London: Kent State University Press, 2003. Comprehensive social history of women's dress reform with an excellent overview of the role of the Bloomer costume.

Fischer, Gayle V. *Pantaloons and Power: A Nineteenth-Century Dress Reform in the United States.* Kent, Ohio, and London: Kent State University Press, 2001. Detailed analysis of the cultural role of trousers in nineteenth-century American society.

Sims, Sally. "The Bicycle, the Bloomer and Dress Reform in the 1890s." In *Dress and Popular Culture.* Edited by Patricia A. Cunningham and Susan Vosco Lab, 125–145. Bowling Green, Ohio: Bowling Green State University Popular Press, 1991. Article about women wearing bloomers during the bicycle craze of the 1890s.

Colleen R. Callahan

BLOUSE Although the term "blouse" now refers to a woman's separate bodice of a different material than the skirt, the word derives from the French name for a workman's loose smock and was first used in English for men's and boy's shirts. The feminine blouse has its antecedents in the undergarment known as a smock, shift, or chemise, which served the same purposes as the male shirt: worn next to the skin, it absorbed bodily soil and protected outer garments.

In the early 1860s full-sleeved loose bodices came into vogue, called Garibaldi shirts since they were modeled on the famous red shirt of the Italian nationalist and freedom fighter. *Peterson's Magazine* in May 1862 (p. 421) thought these blouses, often made in red or black wool or white or striped cotton, were warm, comfortable, inexpensive, and practical, extending the life of a silk skirt which outlived its matching bodice. Puffed "in bag fashion" at the waist, Garibaldi shirts sometimes created an ungainly silhouette with a hooped skirt, but a boned waistband called a Swiss belt could be worn to gracefully ease the transition between top and bottom. The idea of fashionable separates for women had emerged. In January 1862 *Godey's Lady's Magazine* (p. 21) predicted that the advent of the feminine shirt was "destined to produce a change amounting to a revolution in ladies' costume."

By the 1890s, these bodices, now called shirtwaists or waists, had indeed dramatically increased the average woman's clothing options. Shirtwaists could be severely tailored with masculine-style detachable starched collars and cuffs, or very feminine in lightweight fabrics trimmed with lace, insertion, and other lavish decoration. Shirtwaists were suitable with tailored suits, with a skirt for housework and sportswear, and with bloomers for cycling or as gym costumes, while dressier versions were worn for afternoon receptions, the theater, and evening wear. In 1895, Montgomery Ward's spring and summer catalog (p. 37) told customers, "Your old dress skirt worn with a neat laundered waist provides you with a cool, comfortable and up-to-date costume that will quite astonish you." They commended the shirtwaist as "by far the most becoming and sensible article of woman's attire to receive fashion's universal approval."

Although they could be made at home and commercial patterns were widely available, shirtwaists, with their loose fit, were the first women's garment to be successfully mass-produced. Ready-made waists could be purchased at incredibly low prices—as little as twenty-five cents from Sears, Roebuck and Company in 1897. The burgeoning apparel industry utilized economies of scale and power machinery, but cheap garments were also the result of sweatshop production by unskilled and often exploited labor. Workers could toil seventy hours a week for as little as thirty cents a day, frequently in egregious conditions.

One of the many sweatshops in Manhattan churning out these popular garments was the Triangle Shirtwaist Company, which occupied the top three floors of a ten-story building and ensured maximum production by locking the exit doors. When fire broke out on 25 March 1911, many of the 500 workers, mainly Jewish immigrants aged thirteen to twenty-three, were trapped; 146 women died in less than fifteen minutes. While this tragedy helped crystallize calls for reform, led by organizations such as the International Ladies Garment Workers Union founded in 1900, mass production continued to create victims as well as affordable clothing.

Many sweatshop workers no doubt wore shirtwaists, for these practical, inexpensive, and unobtrusive garments were a boon to women in factories, offices, and those who would later be dubbed "pink collar" workers. Yet at the turn of the century, the well-to-do, imperiously handsome women immortalized by illustrator Charles Dana Gibson were often depicted wearing immaculate starched shirtwaists during vigorous walks or rounds of golf. The "Gibson girl" soon became such an American icon that she gave her name to styles of waists and the preferred high stand collars. As fashion evolved, shirtwaists gradually became more relaxed; by the 1910s the "middy blouse," modeled on the loose sailor-collared shirts of seamen, was especially popular with girls and for general sport and utility wear.

The shirtwaist, now also called a blouse, proved remarkably accommodating in style and price. By 1915 Gimbel's catalog (p. 44) could state, "The shirtwaist has become an American institution. The women of other lands occasionally wear a shirtwaist—the American woman occasionally wears something else." Mass-produced or custom-made, serviceable or dainty, the versatile blouse played an essential role in the democratization of fashion. *Suiting Everyone* (Kidwell and Christman, p. 145) states, "For the first time in America, women dressed with a uniformity of look which blurred economic and social distinctions."

While not as universally worn, the feminine blouse adapted itself to almost every occasion through the mid-twentieth century. The haute couture ensembles of elegant matrons often featured blouses to match suit jacket linings, while college girls coordinated Peter-Pan collared permanent-press blouses with casual skirts or slacks. As more women joined the labor force—nearly a third of the American labor force was female by 1960—the blouse continued to be the workhorse of clerical workers, teachers, and those in service industries. In 1977 John T. Molloy in *The Woman's Dress for Success Book* (pp. 54, 55) famously advocated a "uniform" for the executive woman consisting of a skirted suit and blouse—but warned that removing the jacket would make her look like a secretary. He argued that since the blouse made a measurable difference in the psychological impact of the suit, it should not be selected for emotional or aesthetic reasons, but for its message. Molloy claimed his research showed a white blouse gave high authority and status, and his recommended styles included man-tailored shirts with one button open and the "acceptable nonfrilly style" with a built-in bow tie at the neck—the so-called floppy bow that soon became a "dress for success" cliché.

While blouses were important in reflecting the wearer's personal style, this message was sometimes oversimplified. Toby Fischer-Mirkin's 1995 book *Dress Code* (p. 94), for example, definitively states that an unbuttoned shirt collar indicates an open-minded, flexible woman, a loose collar reflects a casual woman who may be slack in her work, while an angular or oddly shaped collar proclaims a highly creative and unconventional individual.

In the late twentieth and early twenty-first century, the blouse—like the earlier Garibaldi shirt and shirtwaist—has been overshadowed by trendier permutations of feminine tops, from T-shirts and turtlenecks to sweaters and man-tailored shirts. Introduced less than one hundred and fifty years ago, the concept of women's separates has become a democratic sartorial style.

See also **Shirtwaist; T-Shirt.**

BIBLIOGRAPHY

1897 Sears Roebuck Catalogue. Reprint edited by Fred L. Israel. New York: Chelsea House Publisher, 1968.

Fischer-Mirkin, Toby. *Dress Code.* New York: Clarkson Potter, 1995.

Gimbel's Illustrated 1915 Fashion Catalog. Reprint, New York: Dover Publications, Inc., 1994.

Kidwell, Claudia B., and Margaret C. Christman. *Suiting Everyone: The Democratization of Clothing in America.* Washington, D.C.: Smithsonian Institution Press, 1974.

Molloy, John T. *The Woman's Dress for Success Book.* New York: Warner Books, 1977.

Montgomery Ward & Company's Spring and Summer 1895 Catalogue. Reprint, New York: Dover Publications, Inc., 1969.

Schreier, Barbara A. *Becoming American Women: Clothing and the Jewish Immigrant Experience, 1880–1920.* Chicago: Chicago Historical Society, 1994.

H. Kristina Haugland

BODYBUILDING AND SCULPTING

BODYBUILDING AND SCULPTING The twenty-first century body, like those of preceding centuries, is still engaged in the eternal quest for an ideal shape. The modernist body of fashion has made it possible for both women and men to reconstruct themselves by a variety of means, resisting the body's unruly nature in order to achieve a firm, toned physique that conforms to sexual stereotypes and concepts of beauty. While women in earlier centuries relied mainly on dieting and corsetry to achieve the perfect shape, today's alternatives include muscular development through weight-lifting, strenuous exercise, and perpetual dieting. Cosmetic surgery has become an accepted method of transforming the body's natural shape. Many contemporary men rely on strenuous weight training, other forms of exercise, dieting, and cosmetic surgery to achieve bodies that conform to social ideals of masculine appearance.

During the latter half of the twentieth century, women in the developed world came to rely on medical science for regular health screening and routine medical procedures. The medicalization of the female body continued, and by the beginning of the 1990s plastic surgery was widespread and surgery became a "normal" means of fashioning the body. Whereas body-shaping fashions had merely manipulated the body into an ideal shape temporarily, the surgeon's scalpel could achieve enduring transformations intended to boost both the patient's self-esteem and her social desirability. Whereas during the early years of cosmetic surgery many women would be at pains to conceal the fact that they had undergone a face-lift or other procedure, toward the end of the twentieth century such surgery was socially acceptable and even regarded as glamorous.

That such radical procedures have nevertheless become commonplace is explained by a combination of the ever-increasing technical ability to perform them and the continually evolving notion of the ideal female body. Prior to the 1960s, changes in the ideal female form were more likely to have been achieved by clothing than by physical transformations of various sorts. The emergence of the "New Woman" in the late nineteenth century introduced an element of athleticism into the feminine ideal, even as corsets continued to be worn on the sports field. The ideal of the 1920s was youthful and trim, but women of the 1930s through the 1950s were shaped by elastic undergarments.

By the 1960s, perceptions of femininity were aligned to ideals of youth, and a fixation with the adolescent figure resulted in a very thin, androgynous physique often achieved by extremes of dieting. Dieting prevailed throughout the 1970s as the principal means of body modification, augmented by exercise regimes of jogging, tennis, and roller-skating, which gave way to aerobics, dancercise, and fitness classes in the 1980s. The lithe but shapely physiques of Jane Fonda and Cindy Crawford represented the sought-after ideal, which fashion augmented with shoulder pads and bulky "box" jackets that produced the appearance of a voluptuous, powerful physique. In the 1990s, the use of exercise and diet to achieve an ideal shape was increasingly supplemented by medical and surgical procedures. One group of women, however, took exercise itself to extreme levels.

The phenomenon of female bodybuilding, which had existed since the mid-twentieth century but only emerged from its subcultural milieu in the 1980s, introduced a rippling range of hyper-muscular bodies to the wider context of visual culture. Women with bulging thighs, enormous calves, rock-hard biceps, Herculean shoulders, and washboard abs introduced a new form of physicality that previously had only been associated with male bodybuilders or with the female superheroes of comic strips. Female mesomorphs, as women bodybuilders became known, inspired some women to strive for bodies with exceptional strength and definition.

Such physiques moved beyond the traditional stereotypes of the female body and in feminist circles were received as avatars of a future body image. While the female mesomorph was rarely seen on fashion runways, she gained ground in film and television. Programs such as *Xena: Warrior Princess* popularized the erotic appeal of muscular women and provided a role model for those striving for a similar body ideal.

Although fashion magazines typically promote weight loss and body conditioning to reinforce the image of women as being lean and toned, mesomorph bodies blur gender boundaries. This female body type reads as an emulation of masculinity, male power, and privilege. The feminist scholars Susan Bordo and Christine Battersby cite the female mesomorph as an example of the cultural difficulties over issues surrounding the body, gender, sexuality, and power. Robert Mapplethorpe photographed the bodybuilder Lisa Lyons as the AIDS epidemic grew, confronting the anxieties of a society riddled with fears of sickness and death with a representation of power and vitality.

But body modification is practiced by men as well as by women. In the Western tradition, elite male clothing has typically been body concealing, emphasizing attributes of wealth and status rather than physical form. Only in a few instances, such as the uniforms of cavalry officers, did men wear body-enhancing clothing; tellingly, the shoulder pads and corsets worn to shape their figures mirrored the dress of the early nineteenth-century dandy. By the end of the nineteenth century, however, an athletic physique, implying proficiency at such upper-class pursuits as tennis and college team sports, had begun to be considered a desirable attribute of young men. Sheer muscularity, however, remained the province of circus strongmen and manual laborers. Weight lifting, though a part of the modern Olympics since its inception, was in its infancy as a sport.

Following World War I, the gradual acceptance of men going bare-chested or nearly so while swimming in mixed company, helped to focus attention on the muscular torso as an attribute of masculinity. Bodybuilding as a defined set of techniques soon followed. For example, Charles Atlas, who billed himself as "the world's most perfectly developed man," began in 1929 to market his system for turning "97-pound weaklings" into muscular giants. The first "Mr. America" contest was held a decade later, won by the bodybuilding legend Bert Goodrich.

The invention of weight-training machines, such as the Nautilus in the late 1960s and early 1970s, transformed the nature of physical exercise and made strength training readily available to men of all ages and ability levels. By the mid-1970s, men and women alike were putting in more and more time at the gym in pursuit of the ideal body. Meanwhile, bodybuilding as a sport was popularized by specialized magazines, by famous gathering spots like southern California's "Muscle Beach," and by a network of professional and amateur contests.

Bodybuilding is a special subculture, in which extremely massive musculature, the hypertrophic development of all of the body's muscles (often relying in part on steroids and other metabolic enhancements), and the taking of sculptural poses tend to go far beyond mainstream society's criteria for the masculine ideal. In some gay subcultures, bodybuilding to a lesser extreme is the norm, and having a "cut" body (one with sharply defined musculature) is highly sought after. Within those communities, implants, liposuction, and other surgical enhancements have become commonplace. Most broadly, a toned, muscular body has become a widely accepted ideal for young men in Western cultures, to the extent that not to possess such a body is as much cause for self-conscious concern as it has become for a woman not to be toned, shapely, and firm.

As these body ideals are considered, new functions and new perspectives of the fashioned body unfold. The body's role as a site of resistance, empowerment, and emancipation reveals that the body ideals of fashion are not necessarily satisfied by the pursuit of beauty alone.

See also **Plastic and Cosmetic Surgery.**

BIBLIOGRAPHY

Arnold, Rebecca. *Fashion, Desire and Anxiety*, London: IB Tauris, 2001.

Balsamo, Annen. *Technologies of the Gendered Body*. Durham, N.C.: Duke University Press, 1977.

Bordo, Susan. "The Body and the Reproduction of Femininity: A Feminist Approach to Foucault." In *Gender/Body/Knowledge*. Edited by A. Jaggar and S. Bordo. New Brunswick, N.J.: Rutgers University Press, 1989.

Frueh, Joanna, et al., eds. *Picturing the Modern Amazon*. New York: New Museum Books; Rizzoli International, 1999.

Gaines, Charles. *Pumping Iron: The Art and Sport of Bodybuilding*. New York: Simon and Schuster, 1982.

Ince, Kate. *Orlan: Millennial Female (Dress, Body, Culture)*. Oxford: Berg, 2000.

Nettleton, Sarah, and Jonathan Watson. *The Body in Everyday Life*. London: Routledge, 1998.

Quinn, Bradley. *Techno Fashion*. Oxford: 2002.

Steele, Valerie. *The Corset*. New Haven, Conn.: Yale University Press, 2001.

Webster, David Pirie. *Bodybuilding: An Illustrated History*. New York: Arco Publishing, 1982.

Bradley Quinn

BODY PIERCING Body piercing is the practice of inserting jewelry (usually metal, though wood, glass, bone, or ivory, and certain plastics are used as well) completely through a hole in the body. Piercing is often combined with other forms of body art, such as tattooing or branding, and many studios offer more than one of these services. While virtually any part of the body can be, and has been, pierced and bejeweled (for evidence, see the well-known Web site http://www.bmezine.com) widely pierced sites include ear, eyebrow, nose, lip, tongue, nipple, navel, and genitals.

Much of what popularly passes for the history of body piercing is in fact fictitious. In the 1970s, the Los Angeles resident Doug Malloy, an eccentric and wealthy proponent of piercing, set forth with charismatic authority a set of historical references connecting contemporary Western body piercing to numerous ancient practices. He declared, for example, that ancient Egyptian royalty pierced their navels (consequently valuing deep navels), Roman soldiers hung their capes from rings through their nipples, the *hafada* (a piercing through the skin of the scrotum) was a puberty rite brought back from the Middle East by French legionnaires, and that the *guiche* (a male piercing of the perineum) was a Tahitian puberty rite performed by respected transvestite priests. No anthropological accounts bear out these claims.

What facts can be sorted from the fiction nonetheless attest to the remarkable antiquity of piercing. The oldest fully preserved human being found, the 5,300-year-old "ice-man" of the Alps, shows evidence of earlobe piercing. Like many with a serious interest in piercing in the twenty-first century, the ice-man has stretched his lobes, in his case to a diameter of about seven millimeters. Artifacts as well as bodies offer evidence of ancient single and multiple ear piercings from as early as the ninth century B.C.E.

While Malloy's claims are largely imaginative, there are geographically diverse cultures in which piercing has been continually practiced for quite some time. Ear and nose piercing seem to be, and seem to have been, the most popular; indeed, there are far too many examples to list here, and the following instances should be taken as representative rather than anything close to exhaustive. Many Native American peoples practiced ear or nose—generally septum—piercing (the latter most famously among the Nez Percé of the American Northwest). Multiple ear piercing was practiced by both men and women in the ancient Middle East, and a mummy believed to be that of Queen Nefertiti of Egypt, sports two piercings in each ear. The Maoris of New Zealand, though better known for their intricate and elegant tattoo designs, have also long practiced ear piercing, which along with nose piercing is widespread among native peoples of both New Zealand and Australia. Ear piercing for girls forms part of traditional rites in Thai and Polynesian cultures. Ear piercing among the Alaskan Tlingits could be an indication of social status, as could nose piercing.

Stretched ear piercings—in which the hole is gradually enlarged by the use of weights or by the insertion of successively larger pieces of jewelry—appear in diverse cultures as well. In Africa, the Masai and Fulani are known for ear-cartilage piercings, which may be stretched (a much slower and more difficult process than stretching earlobe piercings). Images and artifacts from native Central American cultures show stretched lobes with jewelry much like that used by contemporary enthusiasts. East Asian images and sculptures, some many centuries old, show long stretched lobes as well; these are emblematic especially of Buddhist saints. The Dayaks of Borneo traditionally pierce and dramatically stretch the earlobe; other piercings—including the *ampallang*, a horizontal piercing through the penis—have also been attributed to them.

Nostril piercing may have originated in the Middle East, and has been practiced in India for thousands of years, particularly among women. It may be through their interest in Eastern cultures that the hippies of North America took to nostril piercing around the 1970s.

While not as prevalent as the piercing of the ears or nose, lip piercing is also geographically widespread. Women in many regions of East Africa have traditionally worn lip piercings with plugs, while Dogon women may pierce their lips with rings. The men among some native Alaskan peoples also pierced the lower lip, either doubly or singly.

Other piercings are much less attested to in older or more traditional contexts. There is some indication of Central American tongue piercing, for example among the Mayas, but this may have been temporary, intended to draw blood for ceremonial purposes rather than for the lasting insertion of jewelry. More reliable is the evidence of the Indian Kama Sutra (written by the sixth century C.E.) where penis piercings resembling the contemporary *apadravya*—a vertical piercing through the penis—are described as enhancing the pleasure of both the penis-bearer and his partner.

There may also have been temporary upsurges of interest prior to contemporary versions—some sources, for example, report a fad for nipple piercings among women in the late nineteenth century in both London and Paris. (See both Kern and Harwood.) Here, as in its contem-

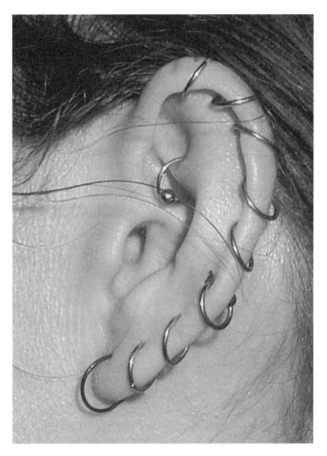

Ear with multiple piercings. Ear piercing is an ancient tradition dating back to prehistoric times that continues to be practiced by many traditional, as well as contemporary, cultures in the early twenty-first century. Multiple ear-piercing became popular in Western culture during the late-twentieth century among members of the punk, goth, and rave youth subcultures. COURTESY OF KARMEN MACKENDRICK. REPRODUCED BY PERMISSION.

porary form, piercing is removed from its more traditional social functions, such as marking one as a member of a community or as being of a particular status, and more specifically erotic as well as decorative functions are noted.

Recent History and Subcultures

"Body piercing" is generally distinguished from (unstretched) earlobe piercing, and is more recent in popularity. In its late-twentieth-century version, the interest in such piercing can be traced largely to a handful of figures, particularly Doug Malloy along with Jim Ward and Fakir Musafar (Roland Loomis) in the United States and Mr. Sebastian (Alan Oversby) in the United Kingdom.

With Malloy serving as patron and in some respects teacher, Ward began making specialized piercing jewelry in the early 1970s (Ward is credited with the design of the ubiquitous captive-bead ring, also called the ball-closure ring). He and Musafar opened the Gauntlet, a piercing shop that seemed a natural outgrowth of the jewelry business, in Los Angeles in 1975. Gauntlet shops in other major cities opened in succeeding years. Later he began the journal *PFIQ* (*Piercing Fans International Quarterly*), an important source of both information and community for those interested in body piercing. Mr. Sebastian, likewise taught at first by Malloy, was more secretive with his techniques, but was widely known as a piercer. For both, the initial clientele was largely gay men from the sadomasochistic (s/m) community.

In the 1980s, Elayne Binnnie (known as Elayne Angel in the early 2000s) joined the staff of the Gauntlet, attracting many more women clients. Angel, who was the first person to obtain the "Master Piercer" certificate from the Gauntlet, is also widely credited with popularizing the tongue piercing (having five herself). Along with the navel, the tongue is one of the most popular piercings in the early twenty-first century.

Musafar, who later fell out with his former partner, is responsible for the term "modern primitive," with which a number of highly pierced people have identified. Musafar emphasizes commonalities between contemporary and older, particularly tribal, traditions; he also emphasizes the psychological and spiritual elements of all sorts of body modifications, including piercing. Many serious piercers in the early 2000s are trained in his seminars. Modern primitives may ritualize the processes and meaning of their body art and often draw on traditional cultures for design in both piercing jewelry and other arts, such as tattooing.

From its start among gay leathermen, piercing grew in popularity to include a number of communities. Among the most influential in the spread of piercing's popularity was punk. The punks in both the United States and the United Kingdom were fond of non-ear piercings, particularly on the face (lip, nostril, and cheek piercings attained popularity early in this group). The punk emphasis is on rebellion and unconventionality; the modern primitive emphasis on cross-cultural connection and spirituality is quite absent here, replaced by punk's interesting combination of outrage and playfulness.

Music and cultural styles that emerged out of punk often have a place for piercing as well. The straightedge movement, generally dated to the early 1980s, though it attained more popularity later on, provides today a large subset of the heavily pierced. Along with tattoos (often of straightedge symbols such as XXX or sXe) piercings show both the punk influence on straightedge music and the subculture's deep interest in the body (most who identify as straightedge are vegetarian or vegan and abstain from the use of alcohol and other recreational drugs). Straightedge thinking may emphasize the slightly mind-altering sensation of the piercing experience, incorporating elements of the modern primitive emphasis on ecstasies (overcoming the limits of time and selfhood in experience) alongside punk unconventionality. The Goth scene emergent in the early 1980s and again in the 1990s has a religious sensibility very different from modern primitive spirituality, tending toward highly stylized and cultivated artifice in its use of religious, particularly Catholic and Wiccan, imagery. As these associations suggest, Goth style tends toward intense theatricality, and visually striking piercings are widespread; the "dark" emphasis of much Goth culture also meets up with an acceptance of s/m imagery and the pain that may be inherent in body piercing.

The rave scene emergent in the 1990s also includes an interest in visually compelling piercings, particularly facial and navel piercings. Often glow-in-the-dark or battery-powered flashing jewelry is used, giving the piercings a hypnotic effect in dimly lit spaces and playing off the more rapid pulse of the very high beats-per-minute music generally favored.

Not all highly pierced groups or scenes are connected to particular species of music, of course. S/m communities remain strongholds of piercing. Here both the physicality of the piercing experience (and the enhanced sensation often provided by healed piercings) and the symbolism of the jewelry are significant—with the significance ranging from pain-tolerance to community affiliation to ownership. Piercing is also popular, though not so much as tattooing, in biker culture. Here large-gauge (thickness) piercings are often favored, complimenting the traditional bold lines of biker tattooing. Finally, many people also simply understand themselves as members of a body-modification or body-art community, with a respect for body modification and an interest in its being practiced well—as well as in having their own bodies modified.

The Move to the Mainstream

Most piercers, however, will emphasize that the people who get pierced do not often fit into any of these groups, and may indeed be, for example, corporate or grandparental types whose under-the-clothes piercings almost certainly go unsuspected. The more fashionable piercings—particularly tongue, navel, nostril, and eyebrow—tend to attract a younger and more specifically (or overtly) fashion-oriented clientele. A significant influence on the entry of body piercing into mainstream fashion has been popular music, as formerly "edgy" or marginal looks were assimilated into pop and made widely visible in music videos. The most famous instance here is undoubtedly the inspirationally pierced navel of the singer Britney Spears, which has taken thousands if not millions of young women into piercing shops they might not otherwise have frequented.

In general, "mainstream" body piercing involves relatively small-gauge jewelry, often (particularly for navel piercings) with ornamental, even jeweled, beads. Gold, while expensive, may be used as well as more commonly used nonreactive metals including stainless steel and titanium. Perhaps in response, those who identify as more marginal or as members of the body-art community tend to prize piercings that are unusual in location or style, such as surface piercings (piercings that go under the skin rather than through a protruding part of the body—the eyebrow is a surface piercing, but less common versions include the nape or front of the neck, the back along the spine, and the wrists), multiple piercings in a single location (even the navel offers top, bottom, left, and right options), or very large-gauge piercings.

As body piercing has grown in popularity, it has come to be increasingly regulated, though it is still much less so than tattooing. In most of the United States, and in parts of Canada and Australia, local legislation sets hygienic standards via departments of health, and limits the piercing permitted to minors, either banning it outright or requiring parental permission. Interestingly, earlobe piercing is almost invariably excluded from this legislation, a reflection of its well-established and unthreatening presence. The Association of Professional Piercers, a voluntary organization, promotes self-regulation regarding cleanliness standards and piercing practices, and many piercers are members.

Legislation in the United Kingdom is somewhat ambiguous, although piercing seems in general to be legal so long as its purpose is solely cosmetic. In 1991, Mr. Sebastian was found guilty of "gross bodily harm" to thirteen of his clients (they had not complained, but their names were located in his records), on the principle that one cannot assent to assault or mutilation. Cosmetic piercing is regulated in London, and ear piercing elsewhere in the United Kingdom, but it is not quite clear how or whether laws on injury, surgery, or female circumcision might apply (see Tameside Metropolitan Borough Council).

Despite occasional suggestions that the proper legislation regarding body piercing is to ban it outright, the phenomenon seems unlikely to disappear altogether. Undoubtedly its popularity will wane, perhaps to wax again at some point, but the longevity of the practice among human beings suggests that it has an enduring, as well as cross-cultural, appeal.

See also **Plastic and Cosmetic Surgery; Punk; Scarification; Tattoos.**

BIBLIOGRAPHY

Camphausen, Rufus C. *Return of the Tribal.* Rochester, Vt.: Inner Traditions Ltd., 1997.

Harwood, Bernhardt. *The Golden Age of Erotica.* New York: Paperback Library, 1968.

Kern, Stephen. *Anatomy and Destiny.* Indianapolis, Ind.: Bobbs-Merrill Company, 1974.

Larratt, Shannon. *ModCon: The Secret World of Extreme Body Modification.* Toronto: BME Books, 2002.

Vale, V., and Andrea Juno. *Modern Primitives.* San Francisco: V/Search, 1989.

Internet Resource

Tameside Metropolitan Borough Council. 2000. "Guidelines for the Practice of Body Piercing." Available from <http://www.tameside.gov.uk/licensing/bodypiercingguidelines.html>.

Karmen MacKendrick

BOGOLAN *Bogolan,* also known as *bogolanfini,* is an African textile whose distinctive technique and iconography have been adapted to diverse markets and materials. The textile is indigenous to Mali, where it has been made and worn for generations. The cloth's bold geometric patterns and rich earth tones make it distinctive and readily adaptable to new contexts. In the past, bogolan was made exclusively by women, who created it for use in specific ritual contexts. During the past two decades, new techniques, forms, and meanings have brought bogolan to international markets even as the cloth continues to be made and used in its original contexts. In North America, where the cloth's patterns have been adapted to a wide range of products, this textile is marketed as "mud cloth."

Although bogolan is associated with a number of Malian ethnic groups, it is the Bamana version that has become best known outside of Mali. *Bogolanfini* is a Bamana word that describes this textile dyeing technique; *bogo* means "earth" or "mud," *lan* means "with" or "by means of," and *fini* means "cloth." Bogolan is unique both in technique and style, which makes the cloth particularly appealing to contemporary artists and designers. Many are also drawn to the fact that bogolan is uniquely Malian, made nowhere else in the world.

The Cultural Role of Bogolan

Until its recent revival in urban Mali, bogolan was made only by women, who learned techniques and patterns from their mothers and other older female relatives. The making of bogolan requires both technical knowledge and mastery of the cloth's many symbols. Some bogolan artists become well-known in their communities and beyond. The recent rise in bogolan's popularity has changed the lives of some of these women, who now sell cloth to art collectors and teach aspiring bogolan artists, who are primarily young men from Bamako, the capital of Mali.

The cloth's traditional uses reflect important aspects of Bamana social organization. Bogolan tunics are worn by hunters, a highly respected and powerful group for whom bogolan's earth tones serve as camouflage, ritual protection, as well as an immediately recognizable emblem of their occupation. The cloth is also present at important events in a woman's life. Bogolan wrappers are worn by girls following their initiation into adulthood, a process which includes female circumcision, and by women immediately following childbirth. The cloth is believed to have the power to absorb the dangerous forces released at these significant moments.

Making Bogolan

Bogolan cloth is woven on narrow looms by men to create long strips of cotton fabric approximately six inches wide, which are stitched together to create wrapper-sized cloths (approximately a yard by five feet [1 by 1.5 m]). Production of dyes and decoration of the cloths is the work of women, who develop their skills over years of apprenticeship to their elders. The first and most essential step in the dyeing process is, paradoxically, invisible in the final product. Leaves from a tree called *n'gallama* are mashed and boiled or soaked to create a dye bath. After immersion in the dye bath, the now-yellow cloth is dried in the sun. Using a piece of metal or a stick, women paint designs in special mud that has been collected from riverbeds and fermented in clay jars for up to a year. A chemical reaction occurs between the mud and the *n'gallama*-dyed cloth, so that after the mud is washed off, the black or brown design remains. The yellow tone of the *n'gallama* dye is then removed from the unpainted portions of the cloth: the undecorated parts of the fabric are treated with soap or bleach, restoring the white of the undyed cotton.

The patterns that adorn the cloth are created by applying the dark mud *around* the motifs. This work is very difficult; every line, dot, and circle must be carefully outlined not once but several times in order to create a deep, rich color. The designs that adorn bogolan often carry a great deal of cultural significance. The symbols may refer to inanimate objects, to historical events, to mythological subjects, or to proverbs. One popular pattern refers to a famous nineteenth-century battle between a Malian warrior and the French colonial forces. Other patterns depict crocodiles, a significant animal in Bamana mythology, and talking drums used to spur Bamana warriors into battle. Artists may select from a wide variety of motifs, which they employ in various combinations to produce a single piece of cloth.

Bogolan as a Contemporary Symbol

Over the course of the past two decades, bogolan has become a symbol of Malian identity, appearing at government-sponsored events and in official publications. Outside Mali, bogolan is made into a variety of products that represent Mali or, more broadly, Africa. The cloth is particularly well suited to serve as a symbol; in addition to being uniquely Malian, bogolan's bold colors and patterns are readily recognizable. In addition, its important uses in traditional contexts appeal to Malian national pride and to foreigners interested in Malian culture. Today, the cloth is familiar to nearly all Malians; it is made and worn by people of all ethnicities and ages. In Mali, bogolan is associated with local cultures, part of the heritage of the artists who make it and the merchants who sell it. In the United States, where bogolan is also popular, the cloth is foreign, exotic. While in some contexts bogolan is marketed as a symbol of African American culture, in others the cloth is presented as vaguely "ethnic."

BOGOLAN AND FASHION

Bogolan clothing, worn by Malians and non-Malians alike, is a common sight in urban streets, classrooms, and nightclubs. The cloth is prominent in Malian cinema and it is often worn by the country's musicians, many of whom tour internationally. Bogolan is used to make clothing in a wide range of styles, from miniskirts and fitted jackets to flowing robes in traditional styles. The designer Chris Seydou is credited with adapting the cloth to fashion in international styles, cultivating interest in this indigenous art form both in Mali and abroad. For some who wear it, bogolan clothing is an expression of national or ethnic identity. For others, the cloth is simply chic, a fashion statement rather than a political stance. Bogolan clothing is particularly popular among young people, who are often in the forefront of shifting fashions.

See also **Textiles, African; Traditional Dress.**

BIBLIOGRAPHY

ADEIAO. *Bogolan et Arts Graphiques du Mali.* Paris: ADEIAO et Musée des Arts Africains et Oceaniens, 1990. An introduction to the work of a cooperative group of artists who have adapted bogolan to contemporary studio art.

Aherne, Tavy. *Nakunte Diarra: A Bógólanfini Artist of the Beledougou.* Bloomington: Indiana University Art Museum, 1992. A small but excellent exhibition catalog on the work of an important rural bogolan artist.

Brett-Smith, Sarah. "Symbolic Blood: Cloth for Excised Women." *RES* 3 (Spring 1982): 15–31. An analysis of the role of bogolan in women's initiations.

Imperato, Pascal James, and Marli Shamir. "Bokolanfini: Mud Cloth of the Bamana of Mali." *African Arts* 3, no. 4 (Summer 1970): 32–41, 80. An excellent and well-illustrated overview of bogolan in the Bamana heartland.

Rovine, Victoria L. *Bogolan: Shaping Culture Through Cloth in Contemporary Mali.* Washington, D.C.: Smithsonian Institution Press, 2001. An exploration of bogolan's many contemporary forms and meanings in rural and urban Mali, as well as the cloth's international manifestations.

Victoria L. Rovine

BOHEMIAN DRESS "Bohemian" was the label attached to artists, writers, students, and intellectuals in early nineteenth-century France after the turbulent years of the Revolution. The reason for the name was that these artists were likened to wandering gypsies, and it was be-

Greenwich Village café. The Gaslight coffee house in New York's Greenwich Village in the late 1950s, and others like it, provided the setting for the Bohemian movement throughout the years. Artists, writers and students used their dress to illustrate both their poverty and their originality. © Bettmann/Corbis. Reproduced by permission.

lieved (incorrectly) that gypsies came from Bohemia in central Europe. With rapid economic and social change, the artist's status became financially insecure as the market replaced the old system of patronage. At the same time the Romantic Movement introduced the seductive notion of the "Artist as Genius." An artist was no longer someone with a particular talent, but became a special kind of person. In earlier times dress had signified social status, a trade, membership of a princely retinue, or a profession. Now for the first time, dress became part of the performance of an individual personality, as the young bohemians used costume to signify their poverty and originality.

There was no single chronological line of development in bohemian dress; rather, there were several different strategies. In the 1830s the styles of dress favored by French bohemians had echoes of the Romantics' love of the medieval and of orientalism. Influenced by the fevered poetry of Byron, they favored rich materials and colors, wide-brimmed hats, and long flowing curls.

A second style, described by the novelist Henri Murger (1822–1861), whose bohemian tales are best-known today as the basis for Giacomo Puccini's opera, *La Bohème*, was simply the uniform of abject poverty, threadbare coats and trousers, leaking shoes, and general dishevelment. A third influential style was the restrained black and white of the male dandy. Dandyism originated in Regency England and, although distinct from bohemian dress, was influential in that dandies, such as George Bryan "Beau" Brummell (1778–1840), developed a cult of the self. They went to such lengths that their appearances became almost works of art in their own right, blurring the dividing line between life and art. This was significant for the bohemian way of life, since for many bohemians this line was blurred in any case, and style, surroundings, and dress became as stylized and carefully wrought as any more conventional artwork.

Then there were those who were influenced by the nineteenth-century movements for dress reform. Dress reformers advocated an end to the distortions and restrictions of fashion, especially women's fashions, and searched for a permanently beautiful form of clothing that would put an end to the fashion cycle. The English Pre-Raphaelites were the best known such group. One of their members, William Morris (1834–1896), who built a successful business on the design and sale of alternative textiles, wallpapers, and embroidery, designed robes for his wife, Jane, that were far removed from the crinolines and corsets of the mid-Victorian period. These innovators were part of the Arts and Crafts movement that spread throughout Europe during the second half of the nineteenth century and by the 1890s had reached Germany, where the styles were combined with art nouveau motifs. The painter Vasily Kandinsky (1866–1944), for example, designed dresses for his lover, the artist Gabriele Munter (1877–1962), which had the natural Pre-Raphaelite line, with full sleeves and loose waists for ease of movement.

Kandinsky and Munter belonged to the artistic and bohemian culture that flourished in and around Munich during this time, where bohemianism was taken to extremes seldom seen before or since. Some of these eccentrics and revolutionaries expressed themselves by adopting what amounted to fancy dress, in imitation of ancient Greece and Rome, or sometimes borrowing from peasant culture.

Bohemian dress, like the whole bohemian counterculture, underwent many vicissitudes during the course of the twentieth century. Between World War I and II, bohemianism became for many young people little more than a phase during which they would dress in a picturesquely rebellious manner, live in artists' studios, and go to bohemian parties—a way of life not so different from that of students in the twenty-first century. The link between genuine creativity and a style of life became attenuated. The idea of "lifestyle" was developing, even if the word did not come into use until after World War II. Yet the idea of bohemia as a privileged and special place—or even just an idea—remained as a kind of umbrella concept beneath which society's dissidents, geniuses, misfits, and eccentrics still gathered to encourage and support one another. For example, lesbians in the 1930s often regarded themselves as bohemians rather than as belonging to a distinct "lesbian subculture."

After 1945 this changed. Bohemia had always effectively been a land of youth, but it was only with the development of the mass media and popular music that the existence and costuming of the generational divide became explicit. Jazz, swing, and rock and roll came with their own uniforms of rebellion. Then came beatniks with, for young women, white lips, black kohl-ringed eyes, peasant skirts, black stockings, and "arty" jewelry—but now for the first time such styles were quickly broadcast via the mass media to a much wider circle of bohemian wanna-bes. The 1957 Audrey Hepburn film, *Funny Face*, for example, satirized Greenwich Village style—at the beginning of the film the star is shown working in a bookshop, dressed in a tweed jumper, black turtleneck sweater, horn-rimmed-glasses, and flat ballerina shoes.

Artists and writers that were displaced as minority groups took center stage in the creation of countercultural dress. Alongside the huge influence of black American style, beginning with the zoot suit of the 1940s, the emergent lesbian and gay culture began to make an impact. Although the most familiar form of alternative dress in the 1960s and 1970s was the hippie style, which boasted bricolage, secondhand clothes, and ethnic items to create a statement about an alternative lifestyle opposed to the consumer society.

Yet at the dawn of the third millennium, it hardly seems as if rebellion can any longer be expressed in the wearing of outrageous garments. Bohemian dress was always a provocation, but in Western, or westernized urban settings, at least, there hardly exists a style of dress that can shock anymore. Grunge, and the styles of Nirvana in the early 1990s, was the last form of dress that aimed to express dissent of the traditional kind. But, like every style, it was no sooner seen on stage than it appeared in every mass-market fashion store in the Western world.

Some have suggested that rebellion of the old bohemian sort is no longer possible, since there no longer exists a single mainstream or dominant form of society against which to rebel. Instead we have what one French sociologist terms "neo-tribes,"—groups with fluid membership of young people who are no longer confrontational, but have an allegiance to certain styles of music, dress, and clubbing. There are exceptions: Goth style and the accoutrements of the anti-globalization movement single out participants fairly definitively. Yet what was once the casual originality of bohemian dress has become the height of celebrity fashion and of high-street style. It therefore follows that in the twenty-first century, when everyone is bohemian, no one can any longer be.

See also **Brummell, George (Beau); Subcultures.**

BIBLIOGRAPHY

Beard, Rick, and Leslie Cohen Berlowitz, eds. *Greenwich Village: Culture and Counter Culture.* Camden, N.J.: Rutgers University Press, 1993.

David, Hugh. *The Fitzrovians: A Portrait of Bohemian Society, 1900–1955.* London: Michael Joseph, 1988.

Siegel, Jerrold. *Bohemian Paris: Culture, Politics and the Boundaries of Bourgeois Life, 1830-1890.* New York: Viking Press, 1986.

Wilson, Elizabeth. *Bohemians: The Glamorous Outcasts.* Camden, N.J.: Rutgers University Press, 2001.

Elizabeth Wilson

BOOTS The modern definition of the term "boots" is a loose one; footwear covering the entire foot and lower leg. This is believed to have developed from one of the earliest forms of footwear—a two-piece unit covering the foot and lower leg. This wrapping of the leg formed the building block on which all modern forms of the boot have derived.

Throughout history the essential form of the boot has been adapted to fit the needs of the wearer and the culture. Materials vary as does form—but the essential purpose of the boot remains the same throughout most cultures; to provide protection from the elements. Boots are usually made of leather, but have been made of many other materials, including silk, cotton, wool, felt, and furs. A perfect example of this is the *kamiks* of the Inuits. The Inuits pride themselves on their efficient use of their resources and their traditional boots, called *kamiks*, are no exception. Crafted of caribou hide or sealskin (their two main food sources), these boots are warm and waterproof thanks to an ingenious raised band of stitching with sinews that ensures a waterproof join at the sole and upper.

The oldest known depiction of boots is in a cave painting from Spain, which has been dated between 12,000 and 15,000 B.C.E. This painting seems to depict man in boots of skin and a woman in boots of fur. Persian funerary jars have been found which date from around 3000 B.C.E. and are made in the shape of boots. Boots were also found in the tomb of Khnumhotep (2140–1785 B.C.E.) in Egypt. The Scythians of about 1000 B.C.E. were reported by the Greeks to have worn simple boots of untanned leather with the fur turned in against the leg. These simple baglike boots were then lashed to the leg by a thong of leather. This basic form can be found in the traditional dress of many Asiatic and Artic cultures as well.

In the ancient world, boots represented ruling power and military might. Emperors and kings wore ornate and colorful examples; this was a significant distinction when the majority of the population went barefoot. Leather was expensive, and roman emperors were cited as wearing colorful jeweled and embroidered examples—even with gold soles. Boots were also already associated with the

Frank and Nancy Sinatra, 1966. Nancy Sinatra's song *These Boots Are Made for Walking* came at a time when the footwear was enjoying particular popularity. © BETTMANN/CORBIS. REPRODUCED BY PERMISSION.

military—the *campagnus* was worn by the highest-ranking officers and some senators in ancient Rome, the height of the boot denoting rank. Other styles, such as the high, white leather *phaecasim*, were worn as ceremonial garb.

During the Middle Ages, the styles shoes and boots established by the ancient world continued. Courtiers of the Carolingian period were depicted wearing high boots laced halfway up the leg. Under Charlemagne the term *brodequin* is first used for these laced boots and roman terms rejected. The *huese*, a high, soft leather shoe and forerunner to the boot appeared toward the ninth century. During the twelfth through fourteenth centuries, a short, soft boot called the *estivaux* was popular. Toward the middle of the fourteenth century, people often wore soled hose, which precluded the need for shoes and boots.

In the fifteenth century, men wore long boots that reached the thighs and were usually of brown leather. This style was prevalent among all of the classes. Despite this widespread popularity, this was emphatically not an appropriate style for women; in fact this was one of the chief criminal charges against Joan of Arc in 1431. It was more common for women of the fourteenth century to wear laced ankle boots, which were often lined in fur.

By the sixteenth century, high boots of soft perfumed leather were worn to meet upper stocks and would soon develop into the wide, floppy cavalier styles of the first half of the seventeenth century. Soft boots folded down—and slouchy boots worn with boot hose elaborately trimmed with lace flaring out into wide funnel shapes to fold down over the boots—characterized these fashions. Boot hose was worn both for its decorative qualities and to protect the costly silk stockings. These high boots featured a leather strap on the instep (the *surpied*), and a strap under the foot, which anchored the spur in place (the *soulette*). They had funnel tops, which covered the knee for riding and could be turned down for town wear. Under Louis XIII a shorter, lighter model of boot emerged, the *ladrine* (Boucher, p. 266). In the early years of the eighteenth century, under the influence of the French court, boots disappeared except for those worn by laborers, soldiers, and devotees of active sports, such as hunting and riding.

The seventeenth century had seen the emergence of the first military uniforms, and the boot had played an essential role in this standardization. The high-legged cavalier boot of the previous century was transformed by a highly polished and rigid leg—the prototypical military jackboot. The high top and rigid finish was supremely practical and successful at protecting legs while on horseback. This style was seen as early as 1688 and continued to be worn into the 1760s. Other popular styles were essentially military in origin. One notable example was the Hessian or Souvaroff, which was brought to England by German soldiers circa 1776. This style featured a trademark center front dip and was trimmed with tassels and braid.

For the more gentlemanly pursuit of sport riding, the high cavalier boot of the seventeenth century developed into a softer and closer fitting "jockey" style boot with the top folded down under the knee for mobility which showed the brown leather or cotton lining. This style originated in 1727 and became increasingly fashionable into the 1770s. The popularity of the English style riding boot was a part of the greater Anglomania of the eighteenth century and foreshadows the "Great Masculine Renunciation" that would follow in the wake of the French Revolution and the early years of the nineteenth century.

The vogue for democratic, English style dress had made the boot more popular than ever. Beau Brummel epitomized the radical simplicity of the dandy. His typical morning dress was reported as "Hessians and pantaloons or top boots and buckskins" (Swann, p. 35). Despite this endorsement, the shape and design of the boot inevitably shifted with fashion. The Wellington supplanted the Hessian since the tassels and braid of the Hessian were difficult to wear with the newly fashionable trousers. The Wellington boot was essentially a Hessian that had had its curved top cut straight across with a simple binding. This style was reputedly developed by the Duke of Wellington in 1817 and dominated menswear in the first quarter of the nineteenth century. The success of the Wellington was

so pronounced that it was said in 1830, "the Hessian is a boot only worn with tight pantaloons. The top boot is almost entirely a sporting fashion…although they are worn by gentlemen in hunting, they are in general use among the lower orders, such as jockeys, grooms, and butlers. The Wellington…the only boot in general wear" (*The Whole Art of Dress* as quoted in Swann, p. 43).

The Blucher was another important style of the early nineteenth century named for a popular war hero. The Blucher was a practical, front-laced ankle boot worn by laborers in the eighteenth century, which had popularly been known as the "high-low." After 1817 this style was known as the Blucher and was worn for casual and sport wear. This basic laced-front style would prove to be popular in modified forms to this day, and has served as the basis of the modern high-top sneaker, hiking boot, and combat boot.

The popularity of boots began to influence women's fashions during the early years of the nineteenth century. Women had been wearing masculine-style boots for riding and driving during the eighteenth century, and by the 1790s their styles had become distinctly feminine with tight lacing, high heels, and pointed toes. By 1815 fashion periodicals begin to suggest boots for walking and daywear; boots were widespread by 1830. The most common style was the Adelaide, a flat, heelless ankle boot with side lacing. This style would remain in use for more than fifty years.

During the Victorian period boots of all kinds reached the peak of their popularity. The trend was for greater comfort and practicality in footwear for both men and women and was aided by technological advances like the sewing machine and vulcanized rubber. In 1837 the British inventor J. Sparkes Hall presented Queen Victoria with the first pair of boots with an elasticized side boot gusset. This easy to wear slip on style would be popular throughout the rest of the century with both men and women. By mid-century the two most popular styles were the elastic side—also known as the congress, side-spring, Chelsea, or garibaldi—and the front-lacing boot. The two most popular styles for front lace were the Derby and the Balmoral. The latter boot was designed for Prince Albert and was similar in style to the modern wrestling or boxing shoe. By the late Victorian period, balmorals or "bals" were most popular and frequently featured contrasting cloth tops and pearl button closures.

Although the Wellington had been almost entirely abandoned in England in favor of the short ankle boot by the 1860s, the style survived in United States and contributed to the development of the cowboy boot. The cowboy boot is believed to have originated in Kansas, and is considered to be a combination of the Wellington and the high heeled boots of the Mexican *vaqueros*. In the United States the Hessian continued to be worn as well and can be seen in photographs of the outlaw "Billy the Kid" from the 1870s.

For women in the mid-century, the majority of footwear was in boot form. The elastic side was a popular choice for daywear, but by the 1860s was replaced by front lace balmorals in satin or colored leather for dressy occasions. Tightly laced boots gave the impression of modesty but also accentuated the curves of the ankle and calf. Increasingly boot styles emphasized this aspect. By 1870 the principal styles worn were side springs, balmorals, and high-button boots. A new development was the barrette boot, which can be viewed as an extension of the shoe since so much of the stocking could be seen through the delicate straps.

In the early years of the twentieth century, boots were still prevalent but soon abandoned by fashionable dress in the 1920s. In this period boots returned to their functional role, and traditional forms remained in use for specific military and sport activities. The exception to this was the vogue among women for knee-high leather Russian boots which featured relatively high heels and a side zipper for a close fit. In the second half of the twentieth century, boots reemerged as an important element in the counterculture fashions favored by the young. Early rebels adopted the sturdy Engineer or Motorcycle boot as a visible sign of their rebellion inspired by films such as *The Wild One* and *Rebel Without a Cause*. In the late 1950s a trend developed for elastic side boots copied from the nineteenth-century originals, but with the addition of a high heel and a pointed toe which were worn with the new slim-fitting tapered trouser. These were the Chelsea boots and would later become known as "Beatle boots."

Women saw an explosion of fashion boots after 1960. While the flat-heeled, white kid leather boots launched by Parisian couturier André Courrèges was the ubiquitous boot of the decade, many styles of boot were popular. Go-Go boots could be ankle, knee, or thigh high and with or without heels, they all served as the perfect accompaniment to the miniskirt. By the end of the decade, retro styles became popular, and the front lacing granny boot became an essential part of the hippie style.

Styles were increasingly unisex in the 1970s, with both genders wearing suede chukka boots, cowboy boots, and high zip-up platform boots. The Dr. Martens boot, originally designed as an orthopedic shoe in the 1940s, was adopted by the punk counter-culture in the 1970s, but by the 1990s had been assimilated into popular fashion. Masculine-styled boots worn by women have been considered extremely provocative, especially when paired with more conventional symbols of femininity.

While traditional forms of boots continue to be worn throughout the world for specific functions, they have also played an important role in fashion throughout history.

See also **Inuit and Arctic Footwear; Sandals; Shoes.**

BIBLIOGRAPHY

Cunnington, C. Willett. *English Women's Clothing in the Nineteenth Century*. New York: Dover Publications, Inc., 1990.

McDowell, Colin. *Shoes: Fashion and Fantasy*. New York: Thames and Hudson, 1989.

Pratt, Lucy, and Linda Woolley. *Shoes*. London: V & A Publications, 1999.

Swann, Julie. *Shoes*. London: Butler and Tanner Ltd., 1982.

Wilcox, R. Turner. *The Mode in Footwear*. New York: Charles Scribner's Sons, 1948.

Clare Sauro

BOUBOU The boubou is the classic Senegalese robe, worn by both men and women all over West Africa and in West African diasporic communities of Europe and the United States. Sewn from a single piece of fabric, the boubou is usually 59 inches (150 cm) wide and of varying lengths. The most elegant style, the *grand boubou*, usually employs a piece of fabric 117 inches (300 cm) long and reaches to the ankles. Traditionally, custom-made in workshops by tailors, the boubou is made by folding the fabric in half, fashioning a neck opening, and sewing the sides halfway up to make flowing sleeves. For women the neck is large and rounded; for men it forms a long V-shape, usually with a large five-sided pocket cutting off the tip of the "V."

When stiffly starched and draped over the body, the boubou creates for its wearer the appearance of a stately, elegant carriage with majestic height and presence. Men wear the classic boubou with a matching shirt and trousers underneath. Women wear it with a matching wrapper or *pagne* and head-tie.

Fabric, Embroidery, and Dyeing

Tailors who specialize in making boubous invest their skills in the art of embroidery. The fabric for these embroidered boubous is cotton damask, called *basin* in the francophone West African countries. Although the fabric can be bought in colors, connoisseurs prefer to buy white cloth and have it hand dyed in rich hues by women dyers working out of their homes. Available in market stalls in several grades of quality, the damask at its most expensive comes from Europe, while cheaper imitations come from Asia or Nigeria.

After the fabric is dyed, the tailor creates the embroidery design with a small sewing machine, either electric or pedal driven. Traditionally, the embroidery was white or beige, but in the 1970s, tailors in Dakar, Senegal, introduced colored embroidery, and in the early 2000s they vie with each other to create intricate, multicolored designs in vibrant hues for women. Men continue to wear white or beige embroidery, or else use threads the same color as the damask, often dyed deep purple or green. The exception for men is a white voluminous boubou with gold embroidery. This is the special costume of *El Hage*, the Muslim who has made the pilgrimage to Mecca. It thus connotes wealth, prestige,

Senegalese women wear the Senegalese robe, or *boubou*. The garment is sewn from a single piece of embroidered cotton damask fabric. The boubou is the most basic garment in the Senegalese culture, much like blue jeans in the United States. © PRAT/CORBIS SYGMA. REPRODUCED BY PERMISSION.

and piety. As with the fabric, the high prestige embroidery threads are silk and come from France. Polyester imitations are imported from Asia.

Non-embroidered fabrications include *basin* resist-dyed in striking designs. For stitch-resist or tie-dyes, designs can be large enough to use one motif for the whole boubou, or small enough to demand thousands of tiny stitches in a fine repeated motif. It takes a group of women three months to sew the stitches before dyeing and three months to cut them out with a razor afterward. Techniques also include starch resist or wax resist. One technique, called *indigo palmann*, uses indigo in such a way as to dye the fabric a rich, deep bronze hue. Although a solid color, the *indigo palmann* boubou is so resplendent in its simplicity that it forgoes embroidery. For less elegant occasions, women have boubous made of Holland wax print or of imitation wax print called *légos*.

Historical and Geographical Changes

The word "boubou" comes from the Wolof *mbubbe*. (Wolof is the principal African language of Senegal.) This linguistic origin suggests that in contrast to borrowed dress styles, like the Arab caftan and the European suit, the boubou, as Senegalese people say, has always been Senegalese. In Anglophone West African countries, the cognate, *buba*, has a somewhat different meaning. Especially in Nigeria and Ghana, the *buba* is a hip-length shirt, with sleeves made of separate pieces of fabric and sewn to the body. It is worn under the long boubou, which in these countries is called the *Agbada*. The men's *buba* is also worn alone with matching trousers called *sokoto*. Women wear the *buba* with a wrapper.

This linguistic link suggests the historical changes in style that the boubou has undergone. In the nineteenth century, the Senegalese boubou, made of bulky, handwoven strip cloth, was often as short as the modern Nigerian *buba*, although without the sleeves (see P. David Boilat's sketches in Boilat 1853). In the course of the nineteenth century, the expanded use of imported factory-woven cloth and the expansion of Islam combined to bring into fashion for Muslim men the longer, more voluminous *grand boubou*, which resembled an Arab caftan. By the early twentieth century, as urban Christian men started wearing suits, and urban middle-class men had to wear suits for work, Muslim men adopted the *grand boubou* for leisure and for ceremonial or religious occasions. Peasant and working-class women wore a *grand boubou* of plain, imported factory-woven cloth. But wealthier urban Muslim women wore a hip-length boubou that showed off their *pagnes* (wrappers) of rich hand-woven strip cloth or fine imported French fabric. Young Christian women adopted a loose, high-waisted dress, called *boubou à la française* (in Wolof *ndoket*).

The elegant *grand boubou* for women did not come into fashion until after World War II. By the end of the twentieth century, young women would sometimes adopt a hip- or knee-length boubou as a fashion alternative and for more casual wear. The *boubou à la française* also returned as a high-fashion item, newly named the *mame boye* (Wolof for "darling grandmother").

Cultural Meanings

As the centerpiece of classic dress in Senegal and neighboring Francophone countries, the boubou occupies the symbolic position of the most basic garment in other cultures, comparable in this respect to blue jeans in American culture. Like blue jeans, the Senegalese *grand boubou* accrues to itself a multiplicity of contradictory uses and meanings. It can connote sexiness or modesty. It can attain the height of elegance or serve a utilitarian purpose. A stiffly starched, embroidered boubou, falling alluringly off one shoulder and perfumed with incense, can be worn with high heels, gold jewelry, a starched matching head scarf tied in a rakish knot, and dramatic makeup. This is the outfit young women wear for weddings, baby-naming ceremonies, and Muslim feast days. This is also the outfit of the *Dirriankhe*, a woman who fulfills the Senegalese ideal of seductive beauty. She is large, sensuous, and conveys the mystique of independence and wealth. She has mastered the art of wearing the boubou. Yet the boubou is also the obligatory dress of respectable Muslim matrons, considered too old and too modest to wear the form-fitting trousers and leg-baring skirts sported by slender young women. For Muslim men, an embroidered, damask boubou can be the height of elegant prestige, but it is also the dress required for praying at the mosque.

See also **Africa, North; History of Dress; Africa, Sub-Saharan: History of Dress; Pagne and Wrapper.**

BIBLIOGRAPHY

Bastian, Misty. "Female 'Alhajis'" and Entrepreneurial Fashions: Flexible Identities in Southeastern Nigerian Clothing Practice." In *Clothing and Difference: Embodied Identities in Colonial and Post-Colonial Africa.* Edited by Hildi Hendrickson. Durham, N.C.: Duke University Press, 1996.

Boilat, P. David. *Esquisses sénégalaises; physionomie du pays, peuplades, commerce, religions, passé et avenir, récits et légendes.* Paris: P. Bertrand, 1853.

Eicher, Joanne Bubolz. *Nigerian Handcrafted Textiles.* Ile-Ife, Nigeria: University of Ife Press, 1976.

Heath, Deborah. "Fashion, Anti-fashion, and Heteroglossia in Urban Senegal." *American Ethnologist* 19, no. 2 (1992): 19–33.

Mustafa, Huda Nura. "Sartorial Ecumenes: African Styles in a Social and Economic Context." In *The Art of African Fashion.* Edited by Els van der Plas and Marlous Willemsen. Eritrea: Africa World Press, 1998.

Perani, Judith, and Norma H. Wolff. *Cloth, Dress and Art Patronage in Africa.* New York: Berg, 1999.

Picton, John, Rayda Becker, et al. *The Art of African Textiles: Technology, Tradition, and Lurex.* London: Barbican Art Gallery; Lund Humphries Publishers, 1995.

Rabine, Leslie W. "Dressing up in Dakar." *L'Esprit créateur* 37, no. 1 (1997): 84–107.

———. *The Global Circulation of African Fashion.* Oxford: Berg, 2002.

Leslie W. Rabine

BOURDIN, GUY Guy Bourdin (1928–1991) has an extraordinary cult following within the field of fashion photography, expanded by the 2003 retrospective of his work at London's Victoria and Albert Museum. Critical, autocratic, dictatorial, and quirky, he had a personal life that was chaotic and probably sadistic, pushed his models to the point of tears and passing out, and even undermined his reputation during his lifetime and his legacy upon his death. Yet despite—or possibly because of—the morbidity and violence of his personal and professional life, Bourdin has had a profound influence on photographic and artistic currents of the late twentieth century.

Bourdin's Background
Guy Bourdin was born in Paris. His mother abandoned him when he was still an infant, and he was alternately raised by his grandparents in Normandy and Paris and placed in a boarding school. Bourdin was the only child to the age of fifteen, when his brother, Michael, was born, and he spent much time in the solitary pursuits of reading and drawing.

At age twenty Bourdin joined the French air force for his mandatory two years of military service, working as an aerial photographer in Dakar, Senegal. After he completed his service, he wanted to buy a small wedding photography business in Magny-en-Vexin, near the family home in Normandy. Refused a loan by his father, Bourdin worked at Bon Marché, the Paris department store, selling lenses and at a variety of odd jobs, including cleaning floors, acting as a messenger at the U.S. Embassy, and washing dishes at the Brasserie Lipp. During this period, he continued to draw, photograph, and produce paintings inspired by Balthus, Francis Bacon, and Stanley Spencer.

In the late 1940s Edward Weston's photograph of a pepper showed Bourdin that photography could be art. He was also inspired by the monumental landscapes of Ansel Adams and developed a friendship with the dada painter and photographer Man Ray, who wrote the gallery announcement for Bourdin's 1952 exhibition at Galerie 29 on the rue de Seine in Paris. It was undoubtedly through Man Ray that Bourdin became acquainted with surrealism, which was to infuse his photography throughout his life.

Bourdin's Editorial and Advertising Photography
In 1954 Bourdin took his work to French *Vogue*, where he was given a fashion assignment on hats. It included a shot, which has become one of Bourdin's early classics, showing a model walking by a butcher shop, three skinned and bloodied calves' heads swinging just above her impeccably turned head. Bourdin continued his exclusive editorial work for French *Vogue* from 1955 through 1987. Bourdin's advertising work for Charles Jourdan shoes from 1967 to 1981 was extremely important. He also did advertising work for the designer Grès and in 1976 photographed the controversial Bloomingdale's "Sighs and Whispers" lingerie brochure, which has become a collector's item.

The Charles Jourdan shoe campaign was groundbreaking in its approach, originality, and daring. In Bourdin's hands, the shoe was presented as a fetishistic object, both as an object of desire and the focal point of scenarios of violence. Bourdin's infamous 1975 photograph depicting the scene of a bloody automobile fatality, the body marked in chalk on the pavement next to the featured shoes, was a benchmark in the history of attraction by shock. The power and perversity of this image were legendary: that an image of death and tragedy (though fictitious) would be used to sell shoes was unthinkable, yet unforgettable. The image itself possessed the same power of attraction that causes a crowd to gather at the scene of a gory accident. In other shots Bourdin juxtaposed gigantic shoes and tiny shoes, which had been made especially for this purpose by the Jourdan company. In this way, Bourdin played on the type of size discrepancies often used in surrealist works, such as the paintings of René Magritte.

Background of Bourdin's Style

Bourdin clearly transformed his personal obsessions into a body of work that was stunningly daring and visually unforgettable. "What Guy did," his stylist Serge Lutens has said, "was conduct his own psychoanalysis in *Vogue* " (Hayden-Guest, p. 143). Abandoned as an infant by an unloving woman, he obsessively depicted women tied up, in compromising situations, or dead. He was said to favor models with pale red hair, because they reminded him of his mother, and he was renowned for making bizarre, macabre, and sometimes cruel demands on them. Stories abound about models being made to balance on a rock during an electrical storm, being subjected to props that cut into their flesh, and passing out after being suspended to appear as if they were flying.

One model, Louise Despointes, was said to have been kept waiting in a freezing studio, then wrapped in plastic and lowered into a bathtub of extremely cold water on which black enamel paint had been floated. She emerged from the tub "enameled" in black paint, uncomfortable and unable to work for days. Bourdin even reputedly placed models in life-threatening positions and delighted in the idea of their deaths. In another famous story, Bourdin initially smeared the faces of Despointes and another model with a thin layer of glue as a way to stick dozens of pearls to their faces. When he decided to cover their entire bodies with pearls, they passed out because they were not getting enough oxygen to their skin and could not breathe, and the editor stopped the shoot, thinking the models would die. Bourdin was reputed to have said, "Oh, it would be beautiful—to have them dead in bed!" (Hayden-Guest, p. 136).

Eroticism and Violence in Bourdin's Photography

Eroticism—and the link between sex and violence—is a major component of Bourdin's photography. The foundation had been laid by the imagery of the preceding decade, particularly the sexual emancipation of Richard Avedon's work of the 1960s. Yet the brilliant and sensitive use of nudity and sexual innuendo that Avedon and Bob Richardson had introduced into fashion depiction in those years—confronting lesbianism and the ménage à trois, for instance—was tame by 1970s' standards. The time was ripe for Bourdin's stylized violence and the darker realities of voyeurism, death, and rape.

Bourdin's photographic violence is thematically akin to the bloody climax of the film *Bonnie and Clyde*, the dental torture in *Marathon Man*, or the orgiastic violence of *The Wild Bunch*. This brand of violent depiction plays with the audience's attraction to the escalating brutality and demands that the viewer consider violence glamorous. The new brand of violent fashion photography and film supplies the viewer with a fantasy fulfillment unavailable in everyday life. As Stephen Farber explains in his *New Yorker* article "The Bloody Movies: Why Film Violence Sells":

> One of the functions of popular art has always been to give people some notion of experiences denied them in reality—a taste of romance, glamour, adventure, danger. But perhaps as everyday life becomes more smoothly homogenized, people need splashier, more grotesque vicarious thrills. Today, . . . [we only experience violence] at professional hockey and football games, at high-powered rock concerts, or at the movies. (p. 44)

Or, one might add, in fashion photography.

Guy Bourdin's violence against women—both actual and photographic—played on their vulnerability, which is a leitmotif in his work. Shadows are an effective device often used for creating an air of mystery, implied physical threat, and even frenzy. Bourdin used such shadows as early as 1966 to suggest the presence of Batman—normally a hero figure and protector—chasing a confused, worried woman through the streets. The thrown shadows, used repeatedly in Bourdin's oeuvre, represent the woman's living nightmare of vulnerability, of being threatened by indistinguishable forms and unseen presences.

Influence of Bourdin's Personal Life on His Work

Bourdin even materialized the reality of violence toward women into his personal life: his first wife is thought to have committed suicide, his second hanged herself, one girlfriend lived after slashing her wrists, and another died after falling out of a tree. As Tim Blanks suggested in his *New York Times Magazine* article, "Both masochism and sadism were bedfellows." Bourdin also seemed bent on undermining himself and his own reputation. He was infamous for not allowing his work to be used in books and exhibitions and for refusing to grant interviews. In 1985 he rejected the $9,000 Grand prix national de la photographie, given by the French Ministry of Culture.

In his article "The Return of Guy Bourdin," Anthony Hayden-Guest explained how Bourdin, when he died of cancer at age sixty-two, left his estate in disarray, compounding a horrendous tax situation and further paralyzing his legacy (p. 137). He had deeded his pictures to Martine Victoire, his common-law wife of seven years, in a signed and witnessed (but not notarized) contract; Samuel Bourdin, the photographer's estranged only child, contested the action. The legal decision gave Victoire possession of the archives but allowed Samuel to exercise his discretion in their use. Without his consent, Victoire could not publish, sell, or exhibit the photographs she owned. Subsequently, the reproduction rights were contested in court.

Bourdin's Influence

The vast influence Bourdin had on subsequent art and photography is only now becoming clear. Like it or not, Bourdin broke taboos and reflected the escalating violence in society, blazing the path for contemporary artists like Paul McCarthy and Matthew Barney in combining the disgusting with the exalted. He pioneered the narrative approach to photography that has become one of its dominant strains, from the work of Gregory Crewdson to that of David Leventhal. Bourdin created pictures filled with what seemed to be clues in a mystery, hinting at meanings rather than articulating them. We are often unsure of what is going on; we know only that we are dealing with a specific moment in which something has happened or is about to happen. Bourdin scatters clues in his pictures, such as water spurting from a pool with a shoe by its edge, a girl "talking" to a shark, or two girls dressed only in lingerie watching as items fall from a purse, frozen in midair.

Bourdin was also one of only a handful of photographers who had almost complete creative freedom within the field of editorial and advertising fashion photography. In both realms Bourdin was a technical virtuoso. His brilliance in producing a wide range of ideas with a continually fresh vision was equaled by his mastery of technique and execution. His background as a painter influenced his approach, particularly the way he built his compositions. Each shape and color was painstakingly and thoughtfully composed to contribute to the whole.

Bourdin's concern for the final effect of his work, including the exact placement on the printed page, is evidence of his commitment to fashion photography. With respect to the photograph itself as a compositional element, he created some of the most unusual and visually exciting layouts ever published in fashion periodicals. Particularly effective was his frequent grouping of photographs in multiples or sequences, repeating sections of the picture or making unexpected juxtapositions to heighten interest.

See also **Art and Fashion; Avedon, Richard; Fashion Advertising; Fashion Magazines; Fashion Photography; Vogue.**

BIBLIOGRAPHY

Blanks, Tim. "Beauty and the Beast." *New York Times Magazine*, 23 February 2003.

DeLano, Sharon. "Dead Girls." *New Yorker*, 3 September 2001, 58.

Farber, Stephen. "The Bloody Movies, Why Film Violence Sells." *New Yorker*, 29 November 1976, 39–45.

Hall-Duncan, Nancy. *The History of Fashion Photography.* New York: Alpine Book Company, 1979.

Hayden-Guest, Anthony. "The Return of Guy Bourdin." *New Yorker*, 7 November 1994, 136–146.

Nancy Hall-Duncan

BOUTIQUE Synonymous with the youth movement and counterculture fashions of the "Swinging Sixties," the boutique radically changed ways of making, marketing, displaying, and buying clothing. Names and places such as Mary Quant, Biba, Paraphernalia, the King's Road, and Carnaby Street evoke the spirit of freedom, individuality, and rebellion that characterized the social upheaval of that decade, and defined a style of dressing. As a retailing concept, the boutique is associated with a distinct identity that reflects the taste of the designer or owner; small-scale production with rapid turnover of merchandise; fashion novelty and experimentation; innovative displays and interiors; and an informality among owner, salespeople, and clientele. Although the boutique phenomenon of the 1960s played itself out by the mid-1970s, boutiques remain a vital part of the commercial world of fashion—whether as an individual enterprise or incorporated into a larger setting, such as a department store.

Origins

Small retailing establishments were not new to the post-World War II period. In the first half of the twentieth century, Paris, London, and New York all had specialty shops. Usually owned by a single designer or proprietor, these operated between the highly exclusive couture houses and the large department stores, and catered to a well-to-do clientele with an emphasis on personal attention to the customer.

As early as the 1920s, Parisian designers began to open small shops within the premises of their *maisons de couture* where they sold a variety of (often less expensive) merchandise including accessories. In 1925 Jean Patou, for example, opened *Le Coin des Sports* (The Sports Corner), a series of rooms on the ground floor of his couture house that offered specialized sports clothing. From its opening in 1935, Elsa Schiaparelli's boutique featured unorthodox and whimsical window arrangements that anticipated the eye-catching, frankly outré displays and interior decor of 1960s boutiques. By the 1950s, boutiques were well-established venues for selling designer clothes and accessories.

New Consumers, New Producers

The coming of age of the baby boomers in the late 1950s and early 1960s created a new consumer market that significantly affected the boutique explosion. The economic hardships of the war years had ended and a period of prosperity began in both Europe and America. Young men and women not only had money to spend but also sought to distinguish—and distance—themselves sartorially from their parents. Dissatisfied with what they saw as outmoded, irrelevant, and conformist styles promoted by the Parisian haute couture, emerging young designers, particularly in Britain, began to create clothing that reflected a new aesthetic and attitude toward dressing. Equally significant was their determination to produce clothing that was affordable to their peers. Rather than

A novel window display in the "Lady Jane" boutique on London's Carnaby Street, 1966. Boutiques in the 1960s changed the way merchandise was displayed and sold. The shops reflected an informality between the owner and clientele and included novelty fashions, smaller retail volumes, and innovative displays and interiors. © HULTON-DEUTCH COLLECTION/CORBIS. REPRODUCED BY PERMISSION.

work within the restrictions imposed by a couture house or a large manufacturing company, these designers often began by sewing garments in their homes and opening boutiques in out-of-the-way locations.

Dubbed the "Swinging City" by *Time* magazine in 1966, London was the undisputed capital of the youth movement in the early and mid-1960s, and young British designers were in the vanguard of the boutique scene. Of this group, Mary Quant was the highly influential pioneer. Her boutique, Bazaar, which she opened on King's Road in 1955 in partnership with her publicist husband, Alexander Plunkett-Green, and business manager Archie McNair, was the first of its kind. Bazaar offered clothing and accessories aimed at a youthful audience ready for fashion that emphasized informality, irreverence, and playfulness.

Quant's Bazaar set the standard for the many boutiques that opened in London and New York in the following decade, including Barbara Hulanicki's Biba; Alice

Pollock's Quorum, which featured clothes by the celebrated husband-and-wife team of Ozzie Clark and Celia Birtwell; the entrepreneur John Stephen's numerous emporia on Carnaby Street; and Paraphernalia, where Betsey Johnson's exhibitionist designs were modeled by Warhol "superstar" Edie Sedgwick.

Boutique Shopping

Inventive window displays and interior decor not only formed a particular boutique's image and identity, they also added a sense of fun and discovery to the shopping experience. Unconventional windows were designed to engage—even shock—passersby. At Bazaar, Quant created whimsical vignettes using attenuated, stylized mannequins in awkward poses, props, large-scale photographs, and banners. Historicism was the hallmark at Biba that would become famous for its art nouveau and art deco inspired interiors (and fashions). Paraphernalia was characterized by a space-age minimalism in which white and silver predominated. In these varied settings, clothes and accessories might be hung on walls or old-fashioned coat stands (as at Biba), or tucked away in dimly lit corners. The unexpected juxtaposition of different types of merchandise also encouraged the boutique shopper to linger and explore.

Although Biba's clientele was primarily working-class while Quorum was patronized by the Rolling Stones lead singer Mick Jagger, Marianne Faithfull, and other pop stars, boutique shopping in the 1960s was a shared social experience among young men and women. Strolling down King's Road or Carnaby Street and frequenting the "in" shops were part of the hip lifestyle. Boutiques were first and foremost places to see and purchase the most up-to-the-minute styles, but they were also "happening" places where one went to meet friends and listen to the latest rock music. Their generally small, often dark interiors and casual atmosphere fostered an intimate ambience. Some boutiques (such as Paraphernalia) stayed open late at night; music and live models dancing on platforms further blurred the distinction between store and party scene.

Boutiques and Fashion in the Early 2000s

By the late 1960s and early 1970s, the success and popularity of boutiques resulted in their being co-opted by mainstream fashion and big business. In New York, large department stores such as Bloomingdale's opened designer boutiques aimed at attracting a share of the enormous youth market. Geraldine Stutz, president of Henri Bendel, transformed the staid specialty shop into a highly visible showcase for the work of young British, American, and French designers, each with their own boutique space. By the time it closed in 1976, Biba had moved twice from its original, small location in Abingdon Road to occupy the former premises of Derry and Toms, a 1930s multistoried department store in Kensington High Street.

In the "Swinging Sixties," fashion was a defining aspect of the counterculture movement, and boutiques were the matrix in the creation and dissemination of those fashions. The boutique scene introduced a new set of expectations regarding fashion and shopping that is still a factor in the early twenty-first century. Boutiques expanded the concept of fashion as catering to more individualized—and adventurous—tastes. Along with the multiplicity of styles available was the possibility for creative self-expression through clothing, while the shopping experience became part of fashionable behavior. Boutiques continue to offer alternative fashions to elitist haute couture and mass-produced, mass-distributed ready-to-wear.

See also **Biba; Quant, Mary.**

BIBLIOGRAPHY

Bernard, Barbara. *Fashions in the 60s.* London: Academy Editions, 1978.

Fogg, Marnie. *Boutique: A '60s Cultural Phenomenon.* London: Mitchell Beazley, 2003.

Fraser, Kennedy. *The Fashionable Mind: Reflections on Fashion 1970–1982.* Boston: David R. Godine, Publisher, 1985.

Lobenthal, Joel. *Radical Rags: Fashions of the Sixties.* New York: Abbeville Press, 1990.

Mendes, Valerie, and Amy de la Haye. *20th Century Fashion.* London: Thames and Hudson, Inc., 1999.

Steele, Valerie. *Fifty Years of Fashion: New Look to Now.* New Haven, Conn.: Yale University Press, 1997.

Michele Majer

BOXER SHORTS Derived from the loose, full-cut shorts worn by professional boxers in the ring, boxer shorts are cotton or silk underdrawers with an elastic waistband, back panels, and buttoned front closure. The only form of underwear that can still be made to measure, many versions have vents at their sides to allow for ease of motion and to be unobtrusive beneath a well-tailored suit. The term is more often than not, shortened simply to "boxers."

History

Boxer shorts trace their heritage back to the long woolen drawers worn by boxers in the nineteenth century. But it was when the heavyweight fighters Jim Corbett and Bob Fitzsimmons both abandoned traditional boxers' tights in favor of loose-fitting trunks, at the turn of the twentieth century, that an icon was born. Shorts of similar cut, made of lightweight fabrics, were soon being produced as underwear. Prior to the twentieth century, most men wore undergarments that were akin to those worn as far back as the Middle Ages. They consisted of tight-fitting linen under-trousers of varying length that, rather than having a fly front, had a buttoned opening at the rear.

Boxers gained popularity when they were issued to United States infantrymen for summer wear during World War I. As with many pieces of functional military clothing issued during both World Wars (the parka, duffle coat, trench coat, and T-shirt) soldiers retained their boxer shorts during peacetime and became instrumental in accelerating their adoption by the general population. Soldiers found their baggy undershorts to be comfortable both because of their loose fit and because they allowed air to circulate in warmer temperatures. The association with military men (as well as with professional prizefighters) may also have helped to make boxer shorts a symbol of manliness. Many men prefer boxer shorts to the more restrictive briefs for those reasons.

Although the underwear market has changed dramatically since the 1940s, with many men opting for tighter-fitting styles such as briefs and bikini shorts, men's boxer shorts cut loosely and made of cotton or silk (or a mixture of the two) have remained standard men's wear items. Once made only in white fabrics, boxers are

Champion boxer Henry Armstrong wearing boxer shorts. Not long after boxers began wearing the looser shorts in the ring, they were produced in lighter fabrics as mens' underwear. AP/WIDE WORLD PHOTOS. REPRODUCED BY PERMISSION.

available in every color as well as in novelty prints. Winston Churchill was said to be partial to pink boxer shorts, and Union-Jack boxer shorts were popular at the coronation of George V (they have since been adopted by British football hooligans). Like many other leisure garments, boxer shorts are often heavily branded with conspicuous designer names. Name brand designer versions by Calvin Klein, Ralph Lauren, Armani, Tommy Hilfiger, and many others, of both boxers and briefs have turned the men's underwear trade into a multimillion-dollar industry. Men's underwear is no longer just a functional afterthought to completing a wardrobe, but an element in the creation of a casual-wear image. In the mid-1980s Jean Paul Gautier paraded a pair of men's trousers down the catwalk with a pair of boxer shorts visibly built in, symbolizing their importance to the new male look.

In the twenty-first century, boxer shorts are still as relevant to men's wear consumers as they have ever been. They have had an entirely new incarnation in hip-hop fashion, which established a trend for wearing them with very low-riding jeans or other trousers, with several inches of cloth (often including a brand-emblazoned waistband) of the boxers clearly visible.

Boxers or Briefs?

Although few custom tailors will take orders for bespoke boxer shorts any longer, neither will be they be impressed with a customer who prefers to wear briefs instead of boxers. Not only have briefs and thongs brought about the tightening of men's trousers, to the dismay of tailors, they may have had adverse health consequences as well. Medical research points to evidence that tight underwear can lead to a low sperm count brought on by increased temperatures. Boxer shorts on the other hand offer the wearer greater movement of air, which keeps the temperature lower. Thus for medical as well as sartorial reasons, boxer shorts seem likely to remain a staple item of male dress. But ultimately the choice between boxers and briefs is an individual one, subject to the essential goals of cleanliness and comfort.

See also **Underwear.**

BIBLIOGRAPHY

Byrde, Penelope. *The Male Image: Men's Fashion in England 1300–1970.* London: B.T. Batsford Ltd., 1979.

Chenoune, Farid. *A History of Men's Fashion.* Paris: Flammarion, 1993.

De Marley, Diana. *Fashion for Men: An Illustrated History.* London: B. T. Batsford Ltd., 1985.

Schoeffler, O. E., and William Gale. *Esquire's Encyclopedia of 20th Century Fashions.* New York: McGraw-Hill, 1973.

Tom Greatrex

BRACELETS Bracelets, cylindrical-shaped ornaments worn encircling the wrist or upper arm, have been one of the most popular forms of ornamentation since prehistoric times. Incredibly varied, bracelets are a universal form of jewelry. Historically and culturally, they have been worn singly or in multiples by both genders. Bracelets have been used for protective and decorative purposes, in rituals, and to indicate one's social status.

Materials

Materials for bracelets are innumerable. Peoples from all cultures across the globe have used indigenous or imported materials, man-made, and natural materials to make them. While the majority are made from metals, they also have been made from insect secretions (such as lac), rattan, wood, feathers, tortoiseshell, horn, teeth, tusks, feathers, leather, and stone. Man-made materials include glass, faience, enamel, ceramic, and plastic. Ancient Egyptians used bone and pebbles, adorned with finely worked beads and pendants of jasper, turquoise, alabaster, lapis lazuli, cornelian, and feldspar. In Eastern cultures, folk jewelry was often made of horn, brass, beads, and copper, while more expensive and finer quality bracelets were designed of mother-of-pearl, gold, and silver. Skillful jewelers in China were able to make bracelets cut from a single piece of jade. In India, the *patwa* (jewelry maker) often creates bracelets from braiding, knotting, twisting, or wrapping yarns made of cotton, silk, wool, or metallic fibers.

In the early 2000s bracelets are being made of soft or hard glass (such as borosilicate). While these glass bracelets can be made from molds or be free-formed, the latter process is slower and not nearly as precise. Microelectronics used in some modern bracelets can now produce movement, light, and sound.

Styles

There are many different styles of bracelets and where they are worn on the body determines what they are called. For instance, bracelets worn above the elbow are called "armlets," but "anklets" when worn around the ankle. The main design consideration for a bracelet is sizing; it must be neither so large that it slips off the hand when it is relaxed, nor so small that it cannot be slid over the hand or fit around the wrist. In general, there are three different types of bracelets: link, slip-on, and hinged. *Link* styles are sized to fit the wrist comfortably and to allow the links to drape flexibly. *Slip-on* styles are rigid shapes, and may be either open-ended or a closed circle or other shape. According to one source, solid circle or oval bracelets should be from 8½ to 9¼ inches in circumference. In the early twenty-first century, this is the most common style of the three types. *Hinged* styles require a hinge and locking catch to allow the bracelet to be opened and yet fit the wrist snugly at a recommended 6½ to 7 inches around with an opening of 1 to 1½ inches for the wrist. The bracelet should have rounded ends in order to fit the wrist comfortably. Solid hinged bracelets should be made from a thick gauge of metal (from 12 to 14 gauge) to maintain the necessary springiness of the form. Stones inserted in bracelets should rank at least 5 or 6 on the Mohs' scale, to prevent their damage.

Every period in history has had an impact on bracelet styles. Styles can range in complexity—from simply sawing off part of a mollusk shell to the intricate designs evident in East Asian metalworking. During the twentieth century, bangles, charm bracelets, and identification bracelets were some of the most popular styles.

Bangles are rigid bracelets with no closures, and may be worn singly or in multiples. Most bangles are made from bold colors or are decorated with numerous types of repeating motifs.

Charm bracelets are a special and unique type of jewelry with a long history dating back to Ancient Egypt. Charms were meant to ward off evil or to endow the wearer with special powers. The original charm bracelet was the Egyptian eye bead, attached to a circlet, used to charm, fascinate, or reflect the malevolent intention of others. Its spiritual function became so popular, it was adopted by neighboring cultures, and it is still worn today in many Middle Eastern countries. In the United States, charm bracelets gained popularity during World War II. Made of silver, gold, or silver-plated metals, enamel, plastic, and shell, most were inexpensive and mass-produced. The charms included military insignia, flags, planes, and wings worn by women in recognition of those serving in the armed forces. Postwar prosperity turned the inexpensive charm bracelets into fine quality jewelry made of medium to heavy gold links on which charms could be attached.

In the late 1950s, charms representing one's travel experiences became fashionable, and there is still a wide range of charms available. Like quilts, letters, and journals, these types of bracelets have a narrative quality that define some of the more important moments in a woman's life, or share information about her values, beliefs, interests, and personality.

Identification, or ID, bracelets are twentieth-century link bracelets with text engraved onto a flat metal plate. The text could be one's name or nickname, or it could contain important information about an individual's medical condition. One fashion trend in the United States has been stylish medical-alert bracelets, which have the primary function of alerting medical professionals to special medical considerations like diabetes or an allergy to penicillin. In the early 2000s, they also have an aesthetic appeal, as some of these bracelets are made with crystal, sterling silver, and 14-karat gold-filled beads, hooked onto a stainless steel medical-alert tag.

History

After neck ornaments, bracelets for the wrist, arm, or ankle are perhaps the oldest form of jewelry. One of the first written records of humans wearing bracelets is in the Hebrew Scriptures. The Bible mentions that there are three types of bracelets: one worn exclusively by men, one worn only by women, and one that may be worn by either sex. Although bracelets are mentioned frequently in the Hebrew Scriptures, their distinctive characteristics are not described. Some of the oldest bracelet artifacts were constructed of bronze and gold and date back to the Bronze Age. Most were penannular, or oval, with expanding, trumpet-shaped ends. The gold bracelets were typically unadorned, and hammered and bent into shape, while bronze bracelets were decorated with patterns and designs. At about this same time, German and Scandinavian warriors often wore spiral armlets for decorative and protective purposes. These armlets covered the entire forearm. In pre-Columbian America, indigenous artisans made bracelets from gold, precious minerals, and rock crystal.

In Ancient Egyptian tombs, strings of gold beads, hoops, and single, hinged bracelets have been discovered. Many of the bracelets made from plain or enameled metals were unadorned by stones. During the First Dynasty, bracelets worn by royalty were made of rectangular beads called *serekhs*, with turquoise, gold, and blue-glazed compositions. In Ancient Minoan and Mycenaean periods,

183

bracelets were made of sheet metal and had elaborate loop-in-loop chains. Ancient Assyrians and Greeks often had two types of bracelets: coiled spirals in the form of interlocking snakes and stiff penannular hoops with enameled sphinxes, lions' heads, or rams' heads. In the Iron Age these spiral forms were common in Europe as well. Scythian nobles wore rigid gold bracelets with animal motifs around the eighth century B.C.E. The Scythians, a group of powerful, nomadic tribes of southeastern Europe and Asia, were known for their fine metalworking and artistic style.

The Etruscans were among the first to create bracelets with separate, hinged panels, a style still popular in the early twenty-first century. Ancient Roman soldiers often were given gold bracelets to indicate their valor in battle. In Great Britain during the Celtic period, men often wore massive protective armlets and serpent-shaped bracelets. These may have been an adaptation of German and Scandinavian bracelets worn during the Bronze Age and used to protect against sword attacks. Toward the end of the pagan period in Europe, plaited silver bracelets and intertwisted strands of silver wire became popular. A decline in interest in bracelets occurred during the Middle Ages in Europe, probably due to the fact that Christian beliefs discouraged adornments, as they suggested an "unhealthy regard for personal vanity" (Trasko, p. 27). The Renaissance focus on humanism prompted a renewed interest in bracelets and other types of jewelry.

Cultural Examples

Bracelets have been worn by cultures all over the world since ancient times. Bracelets and other forms of jewelry were considered especially important in warm geographic regions, such as India and Africa, where few items of clothing were worn. Although both genders historically have worn bracelets, they seem more typically associated with women, especially in contemporary times. Cultural variations may be seen in the wearing of bracelets, for example, in the number of bracelets worn. In the United States, wearing one bracelet is common; however many Eastern cultures favor wearing several bracelets on one wrist. Some cultures in India wear anklets and armlets, as well as bracelets, while this is not as common in Western nations. In addition, Westerners often view bracelets as transitory, removing them at the end of the day. Married women in India, however, wear conch and glass bangles for life. They are broken only if the women becomes a widow.

While many cultural examples of bracelets abound, the intricacy of meanings behind bracelets are found among the people of Timor, a remote island in Indonesia. In Timor, bracelets are natural, stylized, or abstract. Using the lost-wax process, which requires a new mold for each bracelet, ensures a one-of-a-kind result. Timorese bracelets, as family heirlooms or household treasures, may indicate a marriage alliance, social status, and serve as protective amulets or as important artifacts for ritual dances and other ceremonies. In premodern times, bracelets also were badges awarded for the taking of heads. The Timorese have special bracelets for fertility, life cycle and life crisis ceremonies, and other important cultural rituals. Timorese men wear the most spectacular bracelets; the women's are similar in style, but smaller in size. Many bracelets display a traditional symbol indicating one's relationship to a specific Timorese house or family, called an *uma*.

See also **Costume Jewelry; Jewelry.**

BIBLIOGRAPHY

Evans, C. *Jewelry: Contemporary Design and Technique.* Worcester, Mass.: Davis Publications, Inc., 1983.

Ferris, M., and Y. Markowitz. "Charm Bracelets: Portable Autobiographies." *Ornament* 21, no. 4 (Summer 1998): 54–57.

Gill, B. "Jewelry from Yarn: The Indian Patwa." *Fiberarts* 28, no. 1 (Summer 2001) 21.

Goldberg, N. *Jewelry.* New York: Hart Publishing Company, 1977.

Kennard, S. J., III. "Timorese Tribal Bracelets: A Cultural Perspective." *Arts of Asia* 25: 62–69.

Liu, R. K. "Adorning the Wrist." *Ornament* 23, no. 2 (Winter 1999): 62–63.

———. "Kevin O'Grady: Borosilicate Glass Art." *Ornament* 25, no. 3 (Spring 2002): 60–63.

Morton, P. *Contemporary Jewelry.* New York: Holt, Rinehart, and Winston, 1970.

Strote, M. E. "Stylish Safety Bracelets." *Shape* 22, no. 6 (February 2003): 62.

Tait, H., ed. *Jewelry 7,000 Years: An International History and Illustrated Survey from the Collections of the British Museum.* New York: Harry N. Abrams, 1986.

Trasko, M. *Daring Do's: A History of Extraordinary Hair.* New York: Flammarion, 1994.

Von Neumann, R. *The Design and Creation of Contemporary Jewelry.* Rev. ed. Radnor, Pa.: Chilton Book Company, 1961.

Internet Resource

"Beautiful Bangles" (2000–2003). Available from <http://www.glamourdome.com/home.asp>.

Julianne Trautmann

BRAIDING The word "braid" has many different meanings that change over time and between social groups. For example, a braided fabric once meant material that had faded, but this definition is obsolete now. In the United States, the common use of the word "braid" would be called a plait in the United Kingdom. With global communication becoming commonplace, the problem of terminology increases in importance, as agreed definitions create a common understanding of terms.

International authorities still differ in their opinions. In *The Manual of Braiding*, Noemi Speiser defines "braiding" as "interworking a set of elements by crossing, interlacing, interlinking, twining, intertwining" (p. 146). On the other hand, Irene Emery in *The Primary Structure of Fabrics* sees braiding only as oblique interlacing (p. 68). This leaves a problem of classifying such braid techniques as card weaving, making inkles, cords, knotting, knitting, or lucet work. All these techniques as well as structures made using stand and bobbin equipment, free-end braiding, ply-split, and loop manipulated pieces are part of the costume world, though only some would be defined strictly as "braids."

Some of these techniques used to be domestic skills while others were more specialized methods, made in workshops after long training. In the domestic range come lucet work and loop-manipulated braids. Loop manipulation has a very long history and can be simple as the braids used as ties for clothing or to assemble samurai armor, or it can be very complex and decorative. We know from seventeenth-century household pattern books that these braids were in common use for all manner of things from purse strings to ties for clothing, and by the end of the eighteenth century a lucet was a common tool in most households, making ties for stays and other lacings. Reference has been found in the seventeenth and eighteenth centuries to the inkle loom, which was developed for the making of garters, sashes, and other necessary ties.

While not always considered braiding, card weaving, which dates far back into European history, is a weaving technique in which the warp threads, running the length of the work, are held by cards with holes at the corners. The textile is made by turning the cards to change the shed, the space between the warp threads, for the insertion of the weft, the threads running across the piece. It makes highly complex and decorative wares that have been found on early garments worn by the nobility and senior clerics. A medieval tomb opened during the restoration of York Minster contained card-woven edgings on vestments. Older pieces have been found in excavations in Verucchio, Italy, where they were used as edging for cloaks. Some of these were used as the starting edge of the garment while others were skillfully woven using the ends of the cloak warp as the weft to incorporate the edging into the garment.

Pieces made on stands with the threads on bobbins are chiefly associated with countries in the Middle and Far East, although they are not unknown in Europe. In Japan, braids made on equipment such as the circular warp loom, or *marudai*, were used as braids for ties (*obi-jime*) worn with kimonos. In Europe, a method for making a braid using bobbins is described by Lady Bindloss in the seventeenth century while *Diderot's Encyclopedia of Trades and Industry*, first published in 1751, illustrates two types of stand and bobbin equipment. In the early 2000s, the main use is in Sweden where the craft of hair braiding continues in the making of jewelry, and in many places, in the use of equipment to make decorative pieces traditionally associated with Japan. A technique such as free-end braiding, where the work is attached to a fixed point at one end and then worked in the hand, is still in use. Notable among these are the Dida skirts made from many hundreds of threads, attached to the worker's toe and then braided in the weaver's hands into a tubular garment.

Braids have been used for ties such as stay lacing, shoelaces, and points; to secure clothing as braces, belts, and garters; for ceremonial pieces and those with specific meanings such as military braids, and for decoration as in the Miao silk work from China and Khajuja work from the Middle East, while in Peru very old and varied patterns are used to make slings. North American First Nations produced long, wide sashes and belts, often with beads and cross-fertilized with European techniques and ideas. Braids are still being used for some of these things; although in the early twenty-first century, braids for costumes in the Western world are either mass produced or made as individual pieces by skilled makers. Ply-split, a technique originally used mainly, but not exclusively, for animal regalia in India, is being developed for highly decorative accessories, such as belts and bags, for neck pieces, bracelets, and even whole garments. There are also many developments in making jewelry pieces on stand and bobbin equipment.

See also **Homespun; Knitting; Knotting; Loom; Weaving.**

BIBLIOGRAPHY
Cahlander, Adele. *Sling Braids of the Andes.* Weavers Journal Monograph IV, 1980.
Campbell, Mark. *The Art of Hairwork* [1867]. Petaluma, Calif.: Unicorn Books, 1989.
Collingwood, Peter. *The Technique of Ply-Split Braiding.* Petaluma, Calif.: Unicorn Books, 1998.
Dendel, E. W. *The Basic Book of Finger Weaving.* New York: Simon and Schuster, 1974.
Dyer, Anne. *Purse Strings Unravelled.* London: Dyer, 1997.
Emery, Irene. *The Primary Structure of Fabrics.* London: Thames and Hudson, 1966.
Fuller, Elaine. *Lucet Braiding.* Berkley, Calif.: Lacis Publications, 1998.
Owen, Roderick. *The Big Book of Slings and Braids.* London: Cassell, 1995.
Speiser, Noemi. *The Manual of Braiding.* Basel, Switzerland: Speiser, 1983.
——. *Old English Pattern Books for Loop Braiding.* Basel, Switzerland: Speiser, 2000.
Sutton, Ann, and Pat Holtom. *Tablet Weaving.* Newton Center, Mass.: Charles T. Branford Company, 1975.
Tada, Makiko. *Comprehensive Treatise of Braids I.* Japan: Texere Inc., 1997.
——. *Comprehensive Treatise of Braids III.* Japan: Texere Inc., 1999.

Jan Rawdon Smith

BRANDING Branding is a body modification that permanently transforms the surface of the skin by causing a visible scar. The process of branding involves extreme heat or cold applied by a variety of methods. The branding burns and destroys the surface tissue of the skin and stunts or permanently changes the color of hairs growing from the resulting scars.

Historic Branding

Historically, branding has been used on the skin of animals and slaves, as a proof of ownership, and on the skin of criminals as proof of guilt. In Greece, Rome, and many parts of Europe convicted criminals were branded with specific marks that indicated their crime. French, English, Dutch, Spanish, and Portuguese slave traders branded their initials on slaves each time the slaves changed owners.

Contemporary Branding

In the twentieth and twenty-first centuries, microcultures, such as the modern primitives and punks, utilize branding as body modifications. These brandings visually indicate group identity, personal identity, rites of passage, spiritual beliefs, and body decoration. Fraternity members, such as Michael Jordan and the Reverend Jesse Jackson, also have brandings of their Greek fraternity letters. These brandings indicate lifelong membership and commitment to their fraternity's ideals and bylaws.

Strike Branding

Strike branding is the most common form of branding. A strike refers to an individual branding "hit" to the skin. Brandings can be created with either one strike or multiple strikes. The one-strike brand is pressed to the skin long enough to burn through all of the surface skin. The multiple-strikes brand divides the design into many smaller sections about an inch long, shorter if the branding has smaller details. Strikes will overlap and some areas may be re-branded for consistency. A uniform branding requires that all of the strikes be evenly distributed in relation to the surface of the skin.

The strike iron should be hot enough to cause third-degree burns to skin tissue, in order to form a permanent scar. Sources of heat can be anything from a propane torch to an open fire. Strike brand instruments are fabricated from metal, either as complete tools or as small, shaped designs held by a gripping tool. Metal retains and transfers heat effectively, quickly, and predictably to the skin.

Most strike branding tools are made from thin, high-grade stainless steel sheet metal. Other materials used as branding tools include the following: silver, copper, random metal findings, and ceramics. Thin materials are preferred for branding irons, because they are easy to heat and form, and decrease the risk of unwanted damage.

Cautery Branding

Cautery branding uses modern tools and technology, such as soldering irons and lasers, to apply the branding. An electrocautery unit, invented by Steve Haworth, has been called laser branding. This branding technology is similar to an arc welder, but designed for the skin. The body is negatively grounded while the positively charged electric spark jolts from the branding electrode to the skin, searing the skin tissue it touches. An electrocautery unit provides precise control over the depth of the brand and intricate nature of the designs. Cautery branding, regardless of the tools and technology utilized, is considered to be the most painful form of branding.

Chemical or Freeze Branding

Freeze branding is similar to strike branding. Instead of putting the branding iron into a fire to heat it, it is immersed into liquid nitrogen or another cooling solution. The iron is then pressed into the skin. If the hair grows back it will be white. Freeze branding takes longer to do than fire branding and may take days to become visible, while fire branding shows results immediately. This branding method is extremely rare and not often used among body modification enthusiasts, but ranchers consider it as an extremely effective method for branding their livestock, because it does only minor damage to the hide and leaves distinctive branding marks of white hair.

Branding Health Hazards

Branding fumes contain dangerous biological substances from the skin of the person being branded. While some of these airborne viruses and bacteria are dangerous to humans, the heat of the branding destroys most of these germs that can affect humans. Still, branders use HEPA air filters, ventilation systems, and respiratory masks while branding to prevent the transfer of airborne viruses and bacteria.

Branding Aftercare and Healing Process

There are two schools of thought regarding the aftercare of brandings—LITA or "leave it alone," or irritation. Leaving the branding alone will allow the body to heal consistently; however, if a person is not genetically disposed to keloiding, the raised area of the scar will be minimal. Irritating a healing branding wound increases the height of the resulting scar; however, it also produces unpredictable healing and scarring. Picking or rubbing the healing area with steel wool or a toothbrush, or using exfoliating agents can successfully irritate the healing branding.

The healing process for brandings usually lasts at least a year. Separate from the pain of the branding procedure, during the healing process the branded area will be extremely sensitive and sore. If the branding is on a body part that flexes, it may cause the wound to tear open during movement. Healing brandings undergo a few phases, which vary in length and extremes from person to person. A branding will first scab over, which can last from a few weeks to just over a month. At this phase, the appearance of the branding is a bright red raised scar, which slowly becomes lighter than the normal skin tone. This phase lasts about twelve months, and the scar tissue may rise slightly more during this time.

The appearance of a healed strike branding ideally is a design of thick raised lines, lighter than the skin's natural tone. The height of the branding varies significantly on a large number of variables, such as the method of branding, body part and area branded, and skin texture. Strike brandings produce thicker, raised scars, whereas cautery brandings produce thinner lines. Brandings typically heal three or four times the width of the branding tool used to make it.

Branding Removal

Cosmetic surgery claims the ability to remove a branding by using lasers or other advanced techniques; however, it is expensive and not always successful. Currently it is not possible to completely remove a branding without leaving some type of scar.

See also **Punk; Scarification; Tattoos.**

BIBLIOGRAPHY

Beck, Peggy, Nia Francisco, and Anna Lee Walters, eds. *The Sacred: Ways of Knowledge, Sources of Life.* Tsaile, Ariz.: Navajo Community College Press, 1995.

Camphausen, Rufus C. *Return to the Tribal: A Celebration of Body Adornment.* Rochester, Vt.: Park Street Press, 1997.

Mercury, Maureen. *Pagan Fleshworks: The Alchemy of Body Modification.* Rochester, Vt.: Park Street Press, 2000.

Theresa M. Winge

BRANDS AND LABELS Brands developed as a means of commercial distinction within the marketplace in the mid- to late-nineteenth century. The process of branding begins with the attachment of a name to a business, product, or a family of products, and involves the creation of an image for that business which sets it apart from its competitors. Brand image is usually disseminated through advertising, but the value of a brand generally resides in its reputation and the level of loyalty or desirability it can generate amongst consumers. In the fashion industry, a desirable brand name allows companies to bridge the gap between expensive, high-fashion garments and affordable mass-market goods such as perfumes, accessories, and ready-to-wear diffusion lines.

The emergence of brands is closely linked to the establishment of copyright, patent, and trademark legislation in the nineteenth century, as this allowed companies to legally protect their names, and seek redress from their imitators. Many other factors affected the emergence of modern brands, such as the growth of new distribution and retail networks; the increased dominance of fixed-pricing, the concomitant growth of the advertising and packaging trades, and the shift from local to national (and international) markets for consumer goods.

The fashion industry can seek legal protection for designs through patents legislation, which protects the unauthorized use of original designs for manufacture. It also benefits from complex trademark legislation, which protects the words, names, symbols, sounds, or colors that are used to distinguish goods and services. Effectively, this covers the use of a company's logo and brand identity from both counterfeit and "look-alike" goods, where the visual identity of brand is suggested rather than exactly copied.

One celebrated early example of branded clothing is Levi Strauss and Co., who incorporated many trademarked features into their garments (such as rivets and stitching) and gave proof of authenticity in the form of a patent and trademark "certificate" with each garment (later to be sewn on as a label). Authenticity is a central promise of branded goods, and the fashion industry has used it to generate high cultural value in a world of rapid turnover, fluctuating consumer loyalties, and the seemingly incessant demand for novelty. Fashion branding has become synonymous with a late-capitalist consumerist culture where it is the experience rather than the product that drives demand.

Many fashion houses developed as brands through the practice of franchising and licensed copying. In the period 1880–1914, couture businesses such as Worth and Paquin sold through an international network of department stores. In their attempts to cut down on illegal copying, they also sold reproduction rights to private dressmaking salons. The copying of models was a fundamental part of the nineteenth century fashion trade, and designer "names" such as Worth would produce models specifically for copy by retailers in both Europe and America, in order to gain some financial benefit from this practice. By the 1860s it was necessary for Worth to incorporate a house label into products, carrying the Worth name and address either stamped or woven into garments (labels were in turn copied by counterfeit producers).

This two-tier system of couture models and more accessible ready-to-wear lines bearing the same label was exploited by successive generations of designers, including Paul Poiret and Coco Chanel, who used it to build their international reputations. The "signature label" became a defining characteristic of twentieth-century fashion, allowing fashion houses and named designers to attach their names to goods including fashion, perfume, cosmetics, and even household products in order to give these goods distinction. In this way, fashion branding moved beyond the "naming" of a product into the creation of desirable lifestyle scenarios, which could supposedly be replicated by consumers purchasing even the smallest named item. During the 1930s, most of the major couture labels including Elsa Schiaparelli, Coco Chanel, and Jean Patou successfully marketed their signature perfumes well beyond the market for couture.

Franchising became a more widespread activity in the postwar period. Designers such as Dior used the success of franchise agreements in the1940s to underpin the more risky business of couture. In the 1970s and 1980s designers such as Paco Rabanne, Pierre Cardin, Calvin Klein, and Ralph Lauren capitalized on the value of their brands by franchising their names to the producers of housewares, accessories, and beauty lines. Some labels quickly became debased by the lack of quality control, and crossed the fine line from exclusivity to down-market ubiquity. Now that the practice is more commonplace, it is also more heavily controlled by the presence of major global conglomerates such as LVMH and the Gucci Group. Many brands, such as Donna Karan, have successfully created a family of brands or diffusion lines, each of which has a specific character and target market (Donna Karan and the various DKNY lines including Kids, City, Sport, and Pure).

Aside from the diversification of fashion houses, brand culture has also been driven by the expansion of the sports and leisure sectors into fashion. Despite its claim to be motivated only by the needs of athletes, the global sportswear brand Nike has become synonymous with street fashion since its diversification in the mid-1980s. Nike's phenomenal expansion was also due to its direct appeal to a sense of personal achievement through its "Just Do It" slogan and highly emotive advertising. It also fueled overt brand loyalty on the part of its wearers. The popularity of branded goods amongst closely defined "style tribes" has resulted in a profusion of goods where the logo is prominently displayed.

By the twenty-first century, investment in brand building has reached unprecedented levels, with many familiar brand names reinventing themselves by the hire of celebrity designers and radical company overhauls. Fashion and luxury brands have been most affected, as brands known for a particular product category (such as leather goods) launch couture and ready-to-wear collections. With a combination of business acumen and designer credentials, brand "auteurs" such as Tom Ford have transformed the fortunes of a company such as Gucci in a few short years. Many individual designers now work in several capacities at once: creating their own couture and ready-to-wear collections, producing a collection for another fashion house (John Galliano and Alexander McQueen have both held this post at Givenchy) and perhaps acting as consultant to a department store's own label (Betty Jackson for Marks & Spencer, Jasper Conran for Debenhams in the United Kingdom). These designers

may risk their individual reputations on the success of named collections, but the companies behind them are now multinational conglomerates, each with a huge portfolio of brands.

See also **Logos.**

BIBLIOGRAPHY

Clifton, Rita, and John Simmons, eds. *Brands and Branding.* Princeton, N.J.: Bloomberg Press, 2004.

Mendes, Valerie, and Amy de la Haye. *20th Century Fashion.* London: Thames and Hudson, 1999.

Pavitt, Jane, ed. *Brand New.* London: V & A Publications, 2000.

Troy, Nancy J. *Couture Culture: A Study in Modern Art and Fashion.* Cambridge, Mass.: MIT Press, 2003.

White, Nicola, and Ian Griffiths, eds. *The Fashion Business: Theory, Practice, Image.* Oxford: Berg, 2000.

Jane M. Pavitt

BRASSIERE A brassiere is a garment worn next to the skin with two shaped cups or pockets to hold female breast tissue; it is supported by a chest bandeau and generally two over-the-shoulder straps. It may have elastic, wire, padding, lace trim, and a variety of other parts. Strapless versions are also used on occasions where the shoulders are exposed. Specialized brassieres are made for holding breast prostheses of those with surgical removal of one or both breasts, in addition to the particular needs of maternity and nursing mothers. Brassiere styles are often dependent on the fashionable silhouette of the time: breast-flattening bands of the early 1920s, softly curved bias-cut styles of the 1930s, structured and circular stitched "torpedo" shapes of the 1940s and 1950s, unstructured and naturally shaped bras of the 1960s and 1970s, until the introduction of the Lycra-based knitted fabric sports bras of the 1980s. Any of those could be found in lingerie wardrobes, along with the ultimate in uplift and underwire by Wonderbra, Victoria's Secret, Warnaco, and others. It is not anatomically or physiologically necessary to support the breasts, but is strictly a fashionable or socially demanded item.

Breast coverings, in the form of tight bandeaus, have been worn throughout history and by many different ethnic groups of women, but the particularly designed and shoulder-supported garment we know today was a product of the nineteenth-century Dress Reform. United States patent #40,907 issued to Luman L. Chapman in 1863 may be the first recorded design in America, but is almost certainly not the first such garment produced for women wishing to substitute a more comfortable garment for their fashionable tight-laced corsets.

A Norman French word for a child's undershirt, the term "brassiere" was adopted in America about 1904 when it appeared in New York advertising copy of the DeBevoise Company to describe their latest bust supporter, thus giving it French cachet. Prior to that time,

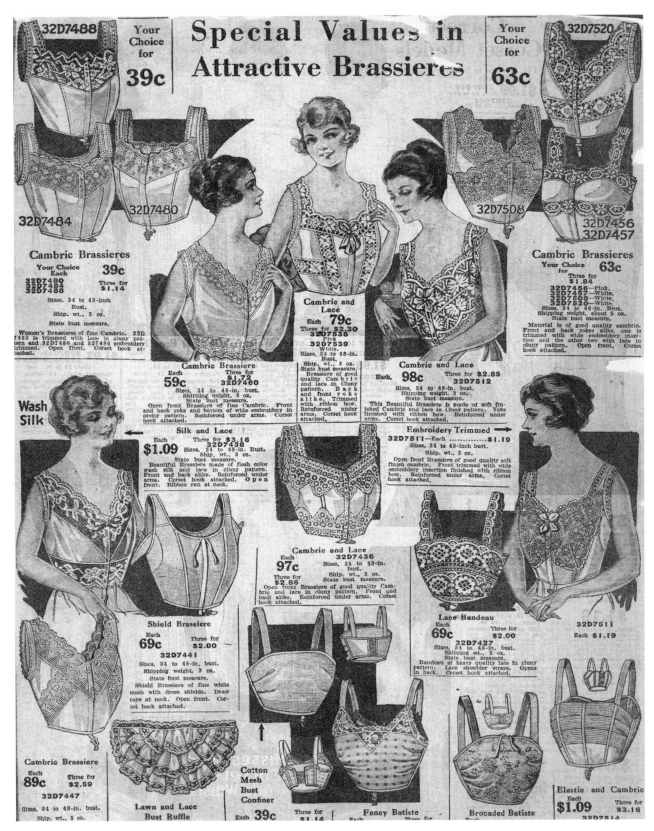

Brassiere advertisement. This advertisement shows the soft, curved bias-cut styles popular in the 1930s. The French word *brassiere*, adopted in the United States about 1904 when it appeared in an advertisement in New York, gave the garment a French quality. They were previously known as "bust, bosom, or breast supporters/corsets." © BETTMANN/CORBIS. REPRODUCED BY PERMISSION.

Maiden Form advertisement. This advertisement was part of an exhibit at the "Enterprising Women: 250 Years of American Business" at the National Heritage Museum in Lexington, Massachusetts, in 2002. The design shows a brassiere, boxing gloves, and athletic trunks. AP/WIDE WORLD PHOTOS. REPRODUCED BY PERMISSION.

strings, and commonly held by shoulder straps, may have inspired the dressmakers and reformers who attempted to produce garments later in the nineteenth century. One function that corsets provided was to help disperse from the waist, the weight of the crinolines, petticoats, and skirts, which may have been as much as thirty-five pounds. A garment with shoulder straps could transfer this weight to the shoulders by hitching lower garments to hooks and tapes. Dress Reformers, including about half of the doctors in a survey of the mid-nineteenth-century medical literature, encouraged women to wear garments that would not impede their digestion, lung capacity, or reproductive system; the new designs maintained the fashionable shape without harming the physique.

Several dozen American entrepreneurs patented breast-supporting garments in the decades up to World War I; about half were women. Olivia Flynt, Marie Tucek, Caroline Newell, and Gabrielle Poix Yerkes were early patentees and producers, with dozens following in the twentieth century. In the undergarment industry, enterprising women found opportunities in design, production, and management not readily available to them in other clothing manufacture. Dr. Jeanne Walters patented rubber brassiere designs with weight-loss claims; and Herma Dozier, R.N., patented three maternity and nursing bras for her company Fancee Free. The latter employed adjustable flaps to allow nipple access without removing the supporting garment. By the end of World War II, the vast majority of fashion-conscious women in America and Europe were wearing brassieres. Western fashions introduced the brassiere to Asia, Africa, and Latin America.

There have been many attributions about the invention of the brassiere. One oft-repeated story concerns Mary Phelps Jacob (a.k.a. Caresse Crosby), a self-described New York socialite who patented a bias-cut brassiere in 1914; it was neither first nor successful. Frenchwoman Herminie (Hermoinie) Cadolle set up a lingerie business in Argentina just as rubber fabric became available and parlayed her elastic insert brassieres (not unlike L. L. Chapman's 1863 design) into a fortune and eventually moved back to Paris, where her business survives in the early 2000s. Claims to her invention of the shoulder strap are misplaced. The Warner Corset Company of Bridgeport, Connecticut, also professed invention, but can only declare innovation and patents for several excellent designs, mostly after 1890. The Gossard Company dominated the English market for many years, with many unique adaptations in brassieres. In fact, there were hundreds of innovators. Not all patented designs, but many found success in the marketplace as women demanded more comfort in their clothing and fashion moved away from the rigid silhouettes of the nineteenth century. In a changing society, women entered universities and work places in great numbers, they took part in sports like hiking, tennis and bicycling, and they drove

the garments specifically designed for breast covering and support were designated variously as bust, bosom, or breast supporters or corsets. Occasionally they were patented as braces, waists, foundation garments, halters, or simply covers. The term "brassiere" became widespread in English-speaking nations within a few years, but the French have maintained their designation of *soutien-gorge* (literally "bosom supporter"). In the 1930s, when slang shortened words like pajamas to "pj's," brassieres became "bras." Custom-made in the nineteenth century, the brassiere made its entrance into mass production in the early twentieth century in the United States, England, western Europe, and other countries influenced by Western lifestyles.

The brassiere had early prototypes in undergarments worn by late eighteenth-century Western European women with the lightweight columnar fashions that emphasized the breasts and deemphasized the natural waist. Those unstructured pouchlike garments, fitted by draw-

cars, activities that demanded greater freedom of movement and lung capacity than allowed by restrictive corsets.

As the idea of the brassiere became popular, patterns for the home seamstress were available, but the intricacy of stitching required skills practiced by specialists. Dozens of small entrepreneurial firms entered the market to supply the growing demands for brassieres. Production could be mastered and as assembly lines using readily available components were set up in small quarters, the industry flourished. Designs were patented by the hundreds, along with specialized machinery for cutting, sewing, making fasteners, and even packaging as sales of brassieres increased. Special industries produced the rust-proof wires, hooks, fasteners, and straps in addition to the fabrics, elastics, lace trims, stitching machines, and molding units. Brassiere construction involves up to forty components per garment, using specialized machines for cutting and sewing. In early designs, chromium wire fasteners were the norm; these have been largely replaced by plastic components, which like straps are produced by specialized firms. Improvements in rubber and synthetic elastics have resulted in their almost universal use in brassieres. Fabric selection for brassieres has evolved from the firm coutil and twill weaves used in the nineteenth century to the fine cottons, embroidered polyester blends, delicate silks, fiberfill, and soft knits of the twenty-first century. The brassiere business gave opportunity to women in ownership, administration, design, and manufacturing not readily available in other fields. There were some self-regulatory aspects within the industry, particularly regarding nomenclature. What differentiated a bandeau from a brassiere was more than two inches of length below the breasts. Until war shortages created problems with supplies, there were few government regulations for work standards or for wages.

By the 1910s, retailers featured specialist "fitters" in departments devoted to corsets and brassieres, which did not have universal cup sizing until the early 1930s. Brassieres, like other items of clothing, were sewn in small production companies, often by sweated labor. Despite demands of complicated designs, sewers were expected to produce items of uniform style and size. The term "cup" was not used until 1916, and letter designation for cup size was first used about 1933 by S. H. Camp and Company to imply progression in volume of breast tissue to be replaced with their prostheses. The underbreast circumference or band dimension is one part of early twenty-first-century brassiere size, with the cup volume designated in letters AA thru I available in retail outlets. Introduction of the minimally shaped "training bra" in the 1950s opened the fashion door for countless adolescents.

Fabrics that could be sewn with flat-felled or bias-tape covered seams were used to ensure comfort to the wearer. In pre-1900 brassieres, linen, cotton broadcloth, and twill weaves were favored. "Whirlpool," or concentric, stitching shaped the bra structure of some designs after 1940. As man-made fibers were introduced, these were quickly adopted by the industry because of their properties of easy care. Since a brassiere must be laundered frequently, this was of great importance. Zippers were used in some designs, as well as Velcro, but these fasteners caused discomfort or caught on clothing and complicated laundering.

Small, medium, and large companies were making brassieres in America during the 1930s and 1940s. Some fell prey to shortages of material during World War II, others to changes in business practices in the drive for export markets. There were union problems, and in later decades challenges switching to computer-aided design. The need to supply and advertise to a nationwide market stretched some firms to the breaking point. Offshore production was initiated to save labor costs following the war, eroding influence of garment workers' unions. Introduction of self-service in lingerie departments was another cost-cutting measure, but did not stem the loss of declining brands. Individual brand-name manufacturers have been taken over by conglomerates, which resulted in fewer available designs and less attention paid to quality, in part due to manufacturing processes being moved offshore. Brassiere manufacturing companies like Kabo of Chicago and Kops of New York were in business from the 1890s until the mid-1960s. Many like G. M. Poix, Treo, Model, Dorothy Bickum, Van Raalte, and Lovable lasted fifty or more years, often run by successive family generations. Maiden Form (until 1948, when it changed to Maidenform) began production in 1922 as a direct competitor to the New York–based Boyshform Company, who made bandeau flatteners for the slim styles of the times. After being a leader in the industry and developing through their advertising campaigns one of the best recognized brand names in history, Maidenform continues eighty years later with a smaller market share. Familiar names like Olga, Bali, Exquisite Form, and Playtex played important roles in the brassiere industry but are now owned by conglomerates.

Eroticism is associated with breasts and brassieres, and brassieres do play a role in the fetish and transvestite dressing by males; however, the garment was designed with the female shape in mind. One prominent promoter of eroticism with a twist of humor was Frederick's of Hollywood, who has been almost eclipsed in the early 2000s by the very market-savvy Victoria's Secret Company. The latter has parlayed lingerie into an art form, taking eroticism from the boudoir to the front parlor in an upward thrust of lace. Décolletage, whether natural or enhanced by padding, is emphasized with the underwired push-up brassiere and by silicone gel in the cups. The metallic wire in many brassieres has been replaced by flexible plastic, perhaps in an attempt to increase comfort and durability. Brassiere designs have been adapted over the decades to fashions of backless dresses, open to the waist in center front, or completely strapless. The Bleumette brassiere and other brands featured gummed cup-shaped supports to the breasts directly when both bandeaus and straps were eschewed.

In 1969, a planned demonstration by a group of feminists who protested the proceedings at the Miss America pageant in Atlantic City, to call attention to their cause resulted in the myth of bra-burning; however, no fire was ever lit, and participants claimed that the bra, high heels, cosmetics, and girdles thrown into the "freedom trash can" were to be a non-pyrotechnic display. The assembled press reported the incident in ambiguous terms, leading many to believe the fire had consumed the offending brassieres. A few more aggressive feminists urged the disposal of all bras; however the majority of American women clung to their familiar fashions, if not their personal comfort.

The elasticized knitted fabric bras introduced in the 1970s and 1980s are now widely worn by athletes and nonathletes alike as comfortable substitutes for the underwired wonders of this age. As female athletes doff their jerseys to reveal brand-name sports bras, few eyebrows are lifted. In the later decades of the twentieth century, the structured brassiere continued its popularity with the majority of women in the middle of the age spectrum, but the youngest and oldest have often either resisted or refused to wear them. Whether for reasons of comfort or personal choice, many women in the twenty-first century are choosing not to wear brassieres.

See also **Fasteners; Lingerie; Underwear.**

BIBLIOGRAPHY

Banner, Lois W. *American Beauty: A Social History Through Two Centuries of the American Ideal, and the Image of Beautiful Women.* Chicago: University of Chicago Press, 1983.

Boucher, Françoise, and Yvonne Deslandres. *20,000 Years of Fashion: The History of Costume and Personal Adornment.* New York: Harry N. Abrams, 1987.

Cunnington, Cecil Willette. *The Perfect Lady.* London: Max Parrish and Company, 1948.

———. *Feminine Attitudes in the Nineteenth Century.* London: Heinemann, 1955.

Cunnington, Cecil Willette, and Phillis Cunnington. *The History of Underclothes.* New York: Dover Publications, Inc., 1992.

Ecob, Helen Gilbert. *The Well-Dressed Woman.* New York: Fowler, 1982.

Ewing, Elizabeth. *Underwear: A History.* New York: Theater Arts Books, 1972.

———. *Dress and Undress: A History of Women's Underwear.* New York: Drama Book Specialists, 1978.

Farrell-Beck, Jane, and Colleen R. Grace. *Uplift: The Bra in America.* Philadelphia: University of Pennsylvania Press, 2002.

Flower, B. O. "The Next Step Forward; or Thoughts on the Movement for Rational Dress." *The Arena* 6 (1892): 635–644.

Flynt, Olivia. *Manual of Underdressing for Women and Children.* Boston: C. M. S. Twitchell, 1882.

Gersheim, Alison. *Victorian and Edwardian Fashions.* New York: Dover Publications, Inc., 1981.

Lane-Claypon, Janet E. *Hygiene of Women and Children.* London: Henry Frowde and Hodder and Stoughton, 1921.

Newton, S. M. Health. *Art and Reason: Dress Reformers of the Nineteenth Century.* London: John Murray, 1974.

Payne, Blanche, Geitel Winakor, and Jane Farrell-Beck. *The History of Costume: From Ancient Mesopotamia through the Twentieth Century.* 2nd ed. New York: HarperCollins, 1992.

Steele, Valerie Fahnestock. *Fashion and Eroticism: Ideals of Feminine Beauty from the Victorian Era to the Jazz Age.* New York: Oxford University Press, 1985.

———. *The Corset: A Cultural History.* New Haven, Conn.: Yale University Press, 2001.

Treves, Frederick. *Dress of the Period and Its Relations to Health.* London: Hillman and Son, 1882.

Verbrugge, M. H. *Able-Bodied Women: Personal and Social Change in Nineteenth Century Boston.* Oxford: Oxford University Press, 1988.

Vicinus, M., ed. *Suffer and Be Still: Women in the Victorian Age.* Bloomington: University of Indiana Press, 1973.

Woolson, Anna G., and C. Hastings, eds. *Five Essays on Women's Health: Dress Reform,* 1874. New York: Arno Press., Reprint, 1984.

Colleen Gau

BREECHES Breeches are a man's bifurcated outer garment, covering the lower body from waist to knees or just below the knees. The term "breeches" is synonymous with any form of short pants or trousers and has been used to describe several types of men's lower-body undergarments and outer garments from classical Roman dress through the twentieth century. However, breeches as a fashion garment were standard everyday attire for European and American men from the sixteenth through eighteenth centuries (American men after 1565). The term comes from Middle English "breech," which was originally the Old English word "brēc" or "bre'c,"—the plural of "brōc," a leg covering. The term "breech" also refers to the lower rear part—the haunches or the buttocks—of the human body. Related clothing concepts include breech-cloth or breech-clout, a short cloth covering the loins, also called a loincloth; and breeching, the archaic English term used to refer to the rite of passage in which young boys wearing skirts were dressed in breeches to signify reaching the end of childhood. The term "drawers" is also used synonymously with breeches when referring to a man's knee-length, loosely fitted undergarment of separate legs covering the lower body. However, "drawers" also refers to various women's undergarments that are constructed of separate legs attached to a waistband, especially after the eighteenth century. In common usage today, breeches are essentially distinguished from trousers and pants by length.

Origin and Early Types

Various lower-body undergarments made of linen for men have been referred to as breeches in the history of Western dress. These garments ranged from knee to ankle length and were made of diverse fabrics and by diverse construction techniques. For example, the *bracchae*, or long, shapeless trousers worn by northern European ethnic groups contrasted with the shorter, knee-length, and more-fitted leg coverings called *feminalia* worn by Roman soldiers and horsemen through the fifth century. By the end of the twelfth century, the masculine wardrobe included some form of knee-length, loosely fitted, natural-colored linen breeches or drawers called *braies* that were worn under tunics of varying length. The lower legs were left bare, covered by hose or long stockings of woven cloth, or wrapped with crisscrossed lengths of narrow bands like bandages (sometimes referred to as *chausses*, from the French, a type of lower-leg chain mail armor). Images throughout the Middle Ages show peasants and laborers working in fields or on building sites dressed only in baggy, natural-colored linen braies, sometimes tucked into brightly colored hose worn with short leather boots or shoes. Higher-status men wore longer tunics that completely covered the linen braies. Braies were held up at the waist or hips by wrapping with a cord or belt and images show them to have been thickly rolled over at the top. They appear to be simply cut and sewn to shape around the legs but open and widely overlapped down the front. The prevalent style appears to have been constructed of a wide, gathered width of fabric draped from front to back between the legs but left open down both sides and tied around the waist or hips or rolled over the top at the waist.

Fifteenth and Sixteenth Centuries

As hose became longer and more fitted to the shape of the leg, braies also became shorter and more fitted, and by the fifteenth century they were no longer seen as part of the outer wardrobe. By the early fifteenth century, the two separate legs of a pair of hose were joined at the crotch by a tied overlap or a codpiece and attached for support to the bottom of the doublet (a short, close-fitting jacket) with laces called points. This body-dominant style became the primary form of men's lower-body covering through most of the fifteenth century, providing the under layer for a variety of outer garment styles and the expression of regional and decorative design features. In the first half of the sixteenth century, by the 1540s, the full-length style of men's hose was broken up into two or three different sections called stocks (upper and lower, or nether, stocks) and trunk hose. Nether stocks were tightly fitted, knitted stockings covering the lower legs, ending just below or just above the knees, and sometimes fitted with garters under the knees. They were tied into the leg band at the bottom of the upper stocks. Images show peasants and laborers working with points untied between the upper and lower hose, their lower hose rolled over and falling below the calf. The upper stocks, also called canions, covered the thighs and upper legs and were sewn into or tied onto the bottoms of the trunk hose, which covered the lower torso from waist to hips or mid-thigh. Although trunk hose were short and sometimes barely covered the buttocks in back or upper thighs in front, they were full and appeared puffy. Many were padded and constructed with an elaborate codpiece in front, but the codpiece gradually diminished and disappeared after the mid-sixteenth century. Compared with the lower hose, trunk hose were a more substantial garment designed to match the doublet with all of the fashionable and complex slashings (patterns of deliberate cuts in garments, allowing contrasting linings to show through), panes (narrow strips of fabric sewn over a contrasting lining), and parti-colorings of each period. It is a variation of the trunk hose that became the man's outer garment most commonly known as breeches, which also varied in cut and fit. Like hose, trunk hose and early breeches were constructed with pairs of hand-sewn eyelets along the upper edge and were laced or tied to the doublet for support. It was not until the seventeenth century that breeches became a separate, "stand-alone" garment constructed on a waistband, no longer worn suspended from the doublet.

Through the remainder of the sixteenth century, trunk hose expanded, and numerous variations in length and shape were common. Styles called round hose included paned and heavily padded shapes that resembled a ripe melon or pumpkin, ending at or just below the hip. Round hose were shaped and padded with horsehair, wool fleece, cotton, or linen tow. One extreme style of trunk hose rarely seen outside Elizabethan court circles was so abbreviated they resembled a wide pad around the hips, worn with very tightly fitted lower hose. Pluderhose (or *pluderhosen*, from the German) were another variation of trunk hose that resembled a pair of open breeches. Cut full and long, to below the knee, they were constructed of an under layer of contrasting fabric that spilled out between wide bands or panes of heavier fabric.

Trunk hose were at their most exaggerated in the last two decades of the sixteenth century. Different styles of longer, fuller upper hose called breeches were also fashionable in the late sixteenth century. Variations of breeches included Venetians, which were a baggy garment that were quite wide at the waist and tapered to the knee or just below. They were slightly padded to hold their shape and were constructed with seams on both inner and outer sides of the legs. The fullness at the waist was controlled with wide, deep gathers or cartridge pleats. Voluminous breeches called galligaskins, gally hose, *gascoynes* (from the French), or slops (also *slopp* or *sloppe*, from the Dutch) were cut with extra width at the knees, maintaining a bulky appearance without padding.

They had a softer and more informal appearance, drooping slightly over the knees with the extra fullness gathered or pleated into a band just below the knee.

Seventeenth Century

In the first quarter of the seventeenth century, the extreme and rigid shapes of trunk hose softened, and the full, longer breeches like Venetians and galligaskins were the predominant fashion. Many breeches were embellished with a row of ribbon loops or lace "ruffles" below the knees, called boot hose, to span the area between lower edge and boot top. Shorter styles of breeches were constructed with a wide fitted band over the knees or lower thighs also called canions. After mid-century, a shorter style called petticoat breeches or rhinegraves was most fashionable. There were two types, one bifurcated and one open, but both resembled a full wide skirt and many were heavily embellished with rows of ribbons at waist, hem, and side seam. Wide "flounces" of lace or ribbons over the knees were worn with some petticoat breeches. A flounce is a strip of fabric gathered along one edge and attached to the bottom of a garment, such as a skirt, that creates a ruffled effect.

As breeches became longer with varying degrees of fullness in the seventeenth century, the methods for attaching them to the doublet also changed. Earlier trunk hose and breeches were still tied to the doublet lining or waist with laces called points. Ribbon points tied in a bow through the outer waist of the doublet provided an important decorative feature in the early seventeenth century. By the 1620s, however, when breeches replaced trunk hose, they were suspended from the doublet by hooks-and-eyes. Large metal hooks sewn into the waistband of breeches were attached to hand sewn or metal eyelets on the inside of the doublet waist. By the early 1660s, breeches were no longer tied to the doublet at all, but were fastened instead at the waist with a button or strap and held up on their own by suspending them from a waistband around the body's waist or tying them tightly around the waist with a cord gathered through a sewn channel. Breeches were constructed with a lining, and the center front opening was buttoned up or tied closed. Linen breeches or drawers were also worn as an undergarment with breeches.

Eighteenth Century

By the end of the seventeenth century, breeches were quite simplified in shape and trim, slimmer and more fitted to the shape of the legs, but still cut with fullness in the seat, or over the hips and abdomen. They had a cuff or band that fastened just under the knee and were worn with separate stockings that rolled up over the knee. Throughout the eighteenth century, the fit and details of breeches changed as the style of coat and waistcoat changed. During the first two decades, breeches were virtually hidden under the knee-length vest and coat of the three-piece suit, and a somewhat baggy fit did not mat-

ter. As coats were cut away after mid-century, breeches became very slim and fit closely over the thigh and knee. As breeches became slimmer, they were cut on the bias to give movement to tightly-fitted thigh and seat areas. Knee-band closures included narrow cuffs with buckles, buttons, or ties. After 1730, as waistcoats shortened, the front of the breeches over the abdomen was more visible. For a smoother appearance, the buttoned-fly front changed. Breeches were closed down center front with a "fall," a large square flap five to eight inches wide, that buttoned to the waistband to cover an open fly. The center-front buttoned fly remained a less fashionable alternative to falls.

Breeches reached the end of their fashionability as standard men's garments by the early 1790s. Two other alternatives were gaining prominence, and the term "knee breeches" was used to distinguish them from pantaloons and trousers. Trousers were practical, ankle-length, loosely fitted bifurcated garments closely identified with the working class. In France, the combination of knee breeches and silk stockings was called *culottes*, and it was this elite style seen in such sharp contrast to the working class trousers that identified the French revolutionaries as *sans culottes*. Pantaloons were a type of longer, closely fitted men's day-wear breeches that fit into the top of riding boots. They became a very fashionable alternative to trousers and were worn with a strap under the sole of a shoe to increase the effect of the clingingly tight fit.

Nineteenth and Twentieth Centuries

During the first decade of the nineteenth century, fashionable young men preferred pantaloons or trousers while older generations continued to wear knee breeches. After trousers became standard everyday attire for men, breeches with a square front fall and diagonal side pockets were worn as riding breeches. By the 1890s, however, a specialized type of breeches was worn instead for horseback riding. The inside of each leg in these full-cut breeches was made with leather or suede, and tightly fitted wrappings for the lower leg were eventually constructed as part of this garment, creating the shape of the twentieth-century "winged" jodhpurs still used as riding dress. These late-nineteenth-century riding breeches were also worn by women, constructed with a detachable apron worn for modesty when astride a horse. Knee breeches were worn as the correct form of evening dress through the first decade of the nineteenth century and were worn with tailcoats as day-wear through the first quarter of the century. By the 1840s, the use of knee breeches was limited to British full ceremonial court dress. From the 1860s, the term "knickerbockers" was used to describe men's knee breeches with loose, baggy knees and a knee-band fastened by a strap just under the knee. Knickerbockers were worn as informal country dress, with a sweater or Norfolk-style jacket, and for certain sports such as shooting or golf. An early-twentieth-century style of knickerbockers known as "plus fours" were worn when hiking, biking, or playing golf. The name referred to the four inches added to their length to create an exaggerated overhang at the knee. Breeches were also used as livery for household servants such as footmen and chauffeurs in Britain and North America through the early twentieth century. In the twentieth century, a type of knee breeches was worn with leg wraps called puttees by some officers and troops fighting in World War I.

See also **Doublet; Hosiery, Men's.**

BIBLIOGRAPHY

Arnold, Janet. *Patterns of Fashion: The Cut and Construction of Clothes for Men and Women c. 1560–1620.* London: Macmillan, 1985.

Byrde, Penelope. *The Male Image: Men's Fashion in Britain, 1300–1970.* London: B. T. Batsford, Ltd., 1979.

Chenoune, Farid. *A History of Men's Fashion.* Translated by Deke Dusinberre. Paris: Flammarion, 1993.

De Marly, Diana. *Fashion for Men: An Illustrated History.* London: B. T. Batsford, Ltd., 1985.

Payne, Blanche, Geitel Winakor, and Jane Farrell-Beck. *The History of Costume: From Ancient Mesopotamia through the Twentieth Century.* 2nd ed. New York: HarperCollins Publishers Inc., 1992.

Tortora, Phyllis G., and Keith Eubank. *Survey of Historic Costume: A History of Western Dress.* 3rd ed. New York: Fairchild Publications, 1998.

Waugh, Norah. *The Cut of Men's Clothes, 1600–1900.* New York: Routledge Theatre Arts Books, 1964.

Susan J. Torntore

BROCADE. *See* **Weave, Jacquard.**

BROOCHES AND PINS Brooches, pins, and fibulas can be defined within two overlapping categories of dress, as both functional and decorative items. Historically, they are primarily defined as utilitarian, as clasps and fasteners for use in closing garments on the body or in holding pieces of a garment together. They were also designed or used as personal adornment with ornamental features that communicate ideas about the wearer, and the wearer's period and milieu. The word "pin" carries the most broad and general usage that includes brooches and fibulas. However, fibula is most sharply defined within its historical usage while the meanings of pins and brooches have a much wider scope over time. The common element among all three is the more general fastening function of the pin. Historically, these fasteners did not have gendered associations, but in contemporary usage women wear brooches as purely decorative pieces of jewelry. In the early 2000s, while the word "brooch" could be used synonymously with "pin" as jewelry, pins were more commonly understood to be small, sharp, metal-wire fasteners called "straight pins" and used in sewing and tailoring processes, unless modified by a descriptive prefix such as in "hatpin."

Pins

A pin is broadly defined as a straight, cylindrical piece of metal with a sharp point on one end and a blunt head on the other, used for fastening by piercing a piece of fabric twice. Throughout history and around the world, in their most simple shape and function, pins have been made in various sizes and from such diverse materials as bone, thorns, bronze, iron, brass, silver, and gold. The heads of larger, specialized pins used as elements of dress, such as hatpins, tiepins, and hairpins, have been elaborately decorated with gemstones and other jewelry techniques to create designs appropriate to their period. For example, long and elaborate hatpins secured European and American women's hats to their hair in the seventeenth and eighteenth centuries, and in the Victorian period through the 1930s. Combining materials such as glass, beading, gemstones, pearls, or various metals, these hatpins may be described as small, precious sculptures. In contrast, smaller straight pins with a flat head have been important as fasteners for women's dress. In the Renaissance, for example, a woman might have been pinned into her bodice, rather than laced or buttoned, for a tight, smooth fit.

In several periods of dress history, items such as aprons were pinned to a woman's outer garment. In the nineteenth century, in fact, the word "pinafore" was coined to describe the washable aprons pinned to the front of women's and girls' clothing to protect them from stains while working or playing. The kilt pin is a contemporary example of old-style pins worn to display one's ethnic identity. Plaid kilts from Scotland, Ireland, and Wales are fastened with a large, sword-shaped pin made from metal, horn, or wood and embellished with Celtic-inspired motifs or cultural icons such as the thistle. Kilt pins might also be decorated with a clan badge to display the wearer's ancestry.

Fibula

The fibula is defined as an ancient or classical period clasp for fastening garments with a simple pin, spring, and catch-plate mechanism. The structural design of a fibula resembles that of a modern safety pin in that the wire pin is extended from a small coil of wire on one end that acts as a spring or hinge. This allows the pin to be opened and closed numerous times without breaking. The coiled spring also puts the pin under tension and secures it in the catch-plate on the other end. This integrally hinged pin structure is technically called an acus. Because of their resemblance, the safety pin is often said to have developed from the fibula. However, it is a simple, functional, and very common mechanism that has been used for millennia in many forms.

A Tibetan woman wears a large metal brooch on her shawl. Brooches have long been worn as ornamental and functional pieces of jewelry. The designs, materials, and workmanship indicate the wearers culture, religion, and social or economic position. © CHRISTINE KOLISCH/CORBIS. REPRODUCED BY PERMISSION.

The most recognizable forms of ancient fibulae are the elaborately decorated, bow-shaped clasps of Greek, Etruscan, or Roman periods, with long thin sheaths covering the pin. Archaeological examples show they were made of gold, silver, and bronze and variously worked with filigree, enamel, repoussé, and granulation techniques, or embellished with gemstones. Several fibulae were required for Greek women to fasten the style of tunic called an Ionic chiton across her shoulders and upper arms.

A number of varieties of Byzantine, Anglo-Saxon, and Romano-British fibulae have been found. The use of fibulae declined as the rectangular, draped styles of clothing gave way to the cut-and-sewn tunics of the early medieval periods. Fibulae are seen in use again as translations of the Classical styles during the Renaissance in the fifteenth and sixteenth centuries. Small, jeweled clasps or the gold points called aglets or aiguillettes were pinned to hold paned or slashed fabrics together on the sleeves, bodices, and doublets of fashionable upper-class garments.

In the early twenty-first century, pairs of large, worked-silver clasps are used by women of nomadic groups in North Africa to close their cloaks and wrapped garments. While the European word "fibula" is used to describe them, they are not called such in indigenous use. For example, in Morocco they are called *tizerzai*. These clasps do not resemble ancient fibulae in appearance or structure. One style is made with a long pin hinged onto an open circle so that it slides. As the pin is pushed through the fabric, the circle is turned and one end is caught under the pin to hold it firmly in place. These fibulae, as a form of jewelry, are important elements of women's dress and reflect the wearer's social status and wealth in terms of their size, weight, and amount of silver used, and in how elaborately they are worked.

If safety pins are seen as a direct descendant of the fibula, one example of their use from contemporary dress should be mentioned, specifically, the use of safety pins in body-art piercings by punk youth subcultures in the 1970s and 1980s. Safety pins, as common, inexpensive, throwaway items, brought vernacular antifashion statements into play. In the 1990s, these ideas were extended to embellishing torn garments with patterns of multiple safety pins in both street dress and popular fashion. High-fashion designers such as Gianni Versace and John Galliano, referenced these street styles and embellished many designs with safety pins.

Brooches

A brooch is broadly defined as a large decorative clasp or pin, but it may be more specifically defined as a clasp with either a fixed pin attached to the back or a hinged pin and catch-plate on the back. The brooch has a long history as a functional clasp with great ornamental importance as a piece of jewelry. The body of a brooch can take many sizes and forms, and types of brooches can be based on specific shapes, such as bars, closed circles, rings, open or penannular circles, bows, knots, hearts, or crosses, or designed with more abstract forms. As with any piece of jewelry, the design, materials, workmanship, and forms of embellishment communicate many ideas about the wearer, and the wearer's period as well as culture, religious, fraternal, or guild affiliations and social or economic position.

The style of brooches and design changes with cultural and fashion changes and trends. The ancient brooch was often the focal point of an ensemble. Early brooches were large and made from sturdy metals such as bronze or silver to secure heavy wool or leather cloaks. As such, they also represented one of the most important and valuable objects of material culture and were buried with their wearer. In the early Middle Ages, brooches were the most widely used form of jewelry for European ethnic groups such as Germans, Lombards, Franks, and Anglo-Saxons.

For all of these reasons, many ancient brooches have survived. European men and women in the tenth through thirteenth centuries wore a round brooch called a *fermail* or *afiche* to fasten their outer mantle or surcote.

Religious uses include the medieval pilgrim badges sold or given to visitors at a shrine. Made to meet different levels of expense, they were worn as evidence of a successful pilgrimage and as a protective charm. In the sixteenth century, these badges inspired a type of round brooch called the *enseigne*, pinned by Italian men on the upturned brim of their hats. By mid-century they were worn throughout Europe by both men and women. Enseigne were upper-class brooches made from gold, encircled by gemstones, with enameled designs or carved cameos in the center representing a biblical or patron saint's theme. Other specialized types of brooches include mourning brooches worn from the time of the Middle Ages in memory of a deceased loved one. In the nineteenth century, these preserved a lock of the beloved's hair behind a crystal or glass cover.

After the early twentieth century, brooches were primarily categorized as costume jewelry worn by women for decorative reasons. Late-twentieth-century trends included wearing brooches from folk or ethnic dress to denote ethnic identity or to display cultural heritage. For instance, a large, round brooch called the *sølje* is considered the national jewelry of Norway. Its lacy filigree style is worked in silver, pewter, or gold and embellished with small, movable, concave metal disks that resemble a spoon bowl. It was originally worn in Norway, through the nineteenth century, as part of folk-dress ensemble by a bride, but by the early 2000s was worn by European and American women to show Norwegian heritage. Replicas of ancient Celtic brooches are also worn by men and women with plaid kilts and sashes from Scotland, Ireland, and Wales.

See also **Costume Jewelry; Jewelry; Safety Pins.**

BIBLIOGRAPHY

Borel, France. *The Splendor of Ethnic Jewelry: From the Colette and Jean-Pierre Ghysels Collection.* Translated by I. Mark Paris. New York: Harry N. Abrams, 1994.

Evans, Joan. *A History of Jewellery, 1100–1870.* London: Faber and Faber, 1970.

Gregorietti, Guido. *Jewelry through the Ages.* Translated by Helen Lawrence. New York: American Heritage Press, 1969.

Hackens, Tony. *Classical Jewelry: Catalog of the Classical Collection.* Providence: Museum of Art, Rhode Island School of Design, 1976.

Heaton, Harriet A. *The Brooches of Many Nations.* Nottingham, U.K.: Murray's Nottingham Book Co., 1904.

Jereb, James J. *Arts and Crafts of Morocco.* San Francisco: Chronicle Books, 1996.

Newman, Harold. *An Illustrated Dictionary of Jewelry.* London: Thames and Hudson Inc., 1981.

Tait, Hugh, ed. *Seven Thousand Years of Jewellery.* London: British Museum, 1986.

Susan J. Torntore

BROOKS BROTHERS The United States led a clothing revolution in the nineteenth and early twentieth centuries in which clothes went from being individually made to being mass produced and from class display to democratic dress. Brooks Brothers played a major role in this revolution.

Henry Sands Brooks was forty-five years old and a provisioner to seafarers and traders when he bought a property on the corner of Catherine and Cherry Streets in the thriving business district of lower Manhattan in 1818. Calling his business H. Brooks and Company, he was intent on a new career selling quality clothing to the gentry and prosperous businessmen. It was his innovative plan, according to an advertisement he ran in the local newspaper, the *Morning Courier*, that same year, "to have on hand a very large stock of ready-made clothing just manufactured with a due regard to fashion, and embracing all the various styles of the day." "Ready-made" heralded the appearance of reasonably priced, mass-produced clothing that was one of the United States' greatest achievements of the nineteenth century.

Through his readily attainable, mass-produced clothing, Henry Brooks became a great innovator and marketer for the democratization of society. "Ready-to-wear placed gentlemanliness within the reach of men who once inhabited the outer reaches of society, enabling them to subscribe to its tenets and tout its virtues" (Joselit, p. 79). It was the beginning of a great cultural shift.

After Henry S. Brooks's death in 1833, the store was refurbished and enlarged by his sons—Henry Jr., Daniel, John, Elisha, and Edward—"Brooks Brothers" for the business in 1850. Manufacturing trends in mid-nineteenth-century America had begun to seriously encroach on the preindustrial world of made-to-measure clothing. The invention of the inch tape measure early in the century allowed for standardized patterns. The Wilson and Wheeler factory sewing machine, invented in 1852, was the first to be used in the clothing industry and marks the beginning of industrial methods in U.S. clothing manufacturing. As Brooks Brothers was both maker and merchant, it was able to take advantage of these inventions. The firm noted in the 1860s that an overcoat required six days of hand-sewing to make, but could be done with the help of machines in half the time (Kidwell and Christman p. 77).

Along with industrialization, population rose to 20 million by mid-century, and westward expansion increased rapidly after gold was discovered at Sutter's Mill in 1848. Brooks Brothers advertised its ready-wear clothing to the "California trade" and reaped profits for its own expansion.

As Manhattan's business district began to move northward along Broadway, Brooks opened a new store, a large four-story building at Broadway and Grand Street in 1858, which moved to South Union Square in 1869. The Broadway store became the principal place of business for the firm during the Civil War, and it was from this store that many Northern generals—including Grant, Hooker, Sherman, and Sheridan—were outfitted. Brooks Brothers also made frock coats for President Lincoln, one of which he was wearing on the fateful evening he was assassinated at Ford's Theatre in April 1865. The Brooks label on the inside of the coat was embellished with an embroidered design of an American bald eagle holding in its beak a flowing pennant inscribed "One Country, One Destiny."

By the turn into the twentieth century, Brooks Brothers was on the verge of a golden age, the period from roughly 1900 to 1970. By 1900, the modern corporation, with a new managerial class emerged, and a third of the population was urban. The firm became the clothier to this new "white collar" businessman who embodied the corporate ideal in a tailored dark suit, white shirt (or at least collar), and discreet necktie, a standard civil uniform that "served to obliterate ethnic origins and blur social distinctions" (Kidwell and Christman p. 15).

Around this time, Brooks introduced its "natural" look suit for the modern businessman. Known as Sack Suit Model #1 from that day to this, the coat had a four-button, single-breasted front, narrow lapels, center vent, and little padding in chest and shoulders, and was accompanied by narrow, flat-front trousers. It was a decidedly understated silhouette and quickly became the look of choice for the Eastern establishment. Another innovation was to incorporate a Boys' Department" (a "University Shop came later), so that parents could educate their sons in the proper appearance.

Other introductions of the early 1900s, which anglophile John Brooks (grandson of Henry) brought back from vacations in Britain, included the button-down collar, the polo overcoat, Shetland sweaters, Harris Tweed sports jackets, Argyle and Fair Isle knits, and oxford cloth shirting. It was this relaxed, country house approach to fashion that endeared Brooks to so many young men of the period and paved the way for the "Ivy League" styling that commanded the lion's share of American men's wear design from the Roaring 1920s to the revolutionary 1960s. This youthful, slim, stylish, and collegially casual image is Brooks's contribution to the United States' sartorial canon.

In 1915, Brooks moved north again with other business firms and built a handsome new flagship store at 44th Street and Madison Avenue, in noticeable proximity to the Harvard and Yale clubs and the New York Yacht Club. In a few short years, the elegant Italianate ten-story building became a mecca of discreet finery for the commercial and professional world. When the troops came home from the Great War in Europe in 1918, Brooks Brothers entered its second hundred years with a roster of customers that included politicians and generals, old guard bankers, nouveaux riches manufacturing barons, and film stars. Literary voices such as Hemingway, F. Scott Fitzgerald, and John O'Hara sang Brooks's praises in print.

The Brooks Brothers catalog now contained a wide variety of dress, casual, evening, military, and livery clothing. About 1920, a three-button sack suit was introduced and soon became the standard model. Other introductions, such as white buckskin oxfords and canvas tennis shoes with rubber soles, Panama hats, and corduroy sports jackets also became classics, renowned in prose and poetry, such as Jimmy Rushing's vibrant "Harvard Blues":

> I wear Brooks clothes and white shoes all the time,
> I wear Brooks clothes and white shoes all the time.
> Get 3 "C"s, a "D," and think checks from home
>   sublime.

In the 1930s and 1940s, several warm-weather fabrics were introduced into its tailored clothing line, each weighing considerably less than the typical twelve- to fourteen-ounce woolens men were accustomed to wearing in the summer. Cotton seersucker, madras, tropical worsteds, and rayon at a mere nine ounces or less, reduced the weight of a summer suit from over four pounds to less than three.

With the end of World War II, the United States assumed the mantle of leadership in the West, and significant advances in automated manufacturing technology began to provide a host of consumer goods to the public.

Brooks placed its imprimatur on the gray flannel suit as the democratic uniform of choice for America's businessmen, an image soon familiarly known by several names: the "Madison Avenue Look," the "Ivy League Look," and, of course, the "Brooks Brothers Look." Casual conservative clothing with a campus flair rose to major fashion importance, as demobilized soldiers went to college with government loans on the G.I. Bill. Bermuda shorts, colorful plaid sports shirts, odd trousers, argyle hose, and penny loafers, all endorsed by Brooks, began to appear in men's closets. Modern jazz musicians such as Miles Davis, Gerry Mulligan, and Dave Brubeck helped spread the word that Ivy League styles were "the coolest."

Ironically, just as Brooks Brothers was about to reach the epitome of its popularity, the company passed out of the Brooks family's hands. In 1946, Winthrop Brooks, the "president who had piloted Brooks through a depression and a world war" (Cooke p. 67), sold the firm to Julius Garfinkel and Company of Washington, D.C. Garfinkel's was the first of many owners to acquire it (Allied Stores Corporation in 1981, Campeau in 1986, Marks & Spencer in 1988, and Retail Brand Alliance in 2001).

In 1952, the chemical firm Du Pont chose Brooks to develop and market a wrinkle-resistant shirt fabric utilizing its Dacron polyester fiber, reasoning that Brooks had the reputation, prestige, and credibility to popularize the concept. The following year, Brooks introduced the "wash-and-wear" shirt, and a polyester-and-cotton blended poplin fabric suit in 1958. The era of Brooks influence reached something of an apogee when, in 1961, the very Eastern establishment–looking senator John Fitzgerald Kennedy of Boston—where there had been a Brooks Brothers store since 1928—was elected President. In 1960, the *New York Times* referred to Kennedy as "a model of Brooks Brothers perfection," and his chosen cabinet comprised members of the Ivy League who favored Brooks-styled tweed sports jackets, club ties, and button-down shirts.

Perhaps the greatest clothing and sociological innovation of the postwar years for Brooks was the introduction of a Woman's Department in 1976, to cater to the newly emerging professional woman. At the same time, a program of accelerated expansion increased the number of Brooks stores to twenty-six and aimed at putting a store in every major shopping mall in the United States. By 1979, the firm became a recognized international retailer with the opening of a branch store in Tokyo. The Brooks Brothers style of business dress—propriety, understated elegance, and comfort—now became a global fashion statement. European designers and manufacturers began to copy the look.

In 1992, the firm initiated a "Wardrobe Concept" program of manufacturing and marketing suits as separate pieces, a technique that gained favor with other manufacturers. It also instituted a new "Digital Tailoring" approach to custom-made garments, using an automatic scanner to enter the customer's measurements into a pattern-producing computer. And, just a few years short of entering its third century, Brooks opened a large, new, more futuristic-looking store on Fifth Avenue in 1999.

However, the tide of popularity had been turning against Brooks for some time. First, the various owners of the firm seemed to be getting farther and farther away from Brooks's sense of quality and style, and "Brooks regulars must have felt increasingly unwelcome at the front door" (Cooke p. 134). Many thought that the integrity was gone from the label and the company was doomed to a drifting mediocrity. Designers like Ralph Lauren, a former Brooks salesman, made heavy inroads. In 2001 the company was bought yet again, this time by Retail Brand Alliance. But RBA had the aim and goal of putting the "golden" back into the famous "Golden Fleece" Brooks logo. Guided by Claudio Del Vecchio, son of a successful Italian eyewear manufacturer, the firm has made cautious progress since 2001 toward regaining its prestige.

See also **Polo Shirt; Ready-to-Wear; Sports Jacket; Suit, Business.**

BIBLIOGRAPHY

Boyer, G. Bruce. *Elegance.* New York: W. W. Norton and Company, 1985.

Cooke, John William. *Generations of Style.* New York: Brooks Brothers, 2003.

Hall, Lee. *Common Threads.* New York: Bulfinch, 1992.

Joselit, Jenna Weissman. *A Perfect Fit.* New York: Owl Books, 2001.

Kidwell, Claudia B., and Margaret C. Christman. *Suiting Everyone.* Washington, D.C.: Smithsonian Institution Press, 1974.

Martin, Richard, and Harold Koda. *Jocks and Nerds.* New York: Rizzoli International, 1989.

Zakim, Michael. *Ready-Made Democracy: A History of Men's Dress in the American Republic, 1760–1860.* Chicago: University of Chicago Press, 2003.

G. Bruce Boyer

BRUMMELL, GEORGE (BEAU) George Bryan Brummell (or Brummel), most famously known as "Beau" Brummell, was born in Britain in 1778 and died in 1840 in France. His dress and demeanor established many of the canons of dandyism. Although he was not an aristocrat by birth, he rose in the ranks of Regency society (1795–1820) and belonged to the circle of the Prince of Wales, known as the Prince Regent, who became King George IV. His father was a civil servant and secretary to Lord North, though his grandfather was probably a valet. Brummell was educated at Eton and left Oxford at the age of sixteen when he inherited a sum from his father estimated to have been 15,000 to 65,000 pounds. He became a cornet in the Tenth Hussars, the Prince's regiment, known as "the Elegant Extracts," and was a captain by the time of his retirement from the military in 1798. He then began his life as a stylish gentleman in his houses in Chesterfield and Chapel Streets in London and was a member of Brooks's and White's on St. James's Street, the most exclusive gentlemen's clubs of his day in an elite founded on the principle of exclusivity.

Brummell lived above his means, but his association with the Prince of Wales and his personal sense of style and cutting wit assured him a privileged place among the fashionable set. Many anecdotes mythologize his life, and though there is speculation as to his possible homosexuality, he was never linked specifically with a man or a woman, which the writer Jules Barbey d'Aurevilly took as a sign of his narcissism. In the second decade of the nineteenth century he fell out with the Prince Regent, and his creditors became more insistent. On 16 May 1816 he left Britain for Calais, France, because of his mounting debts and spent his last twenty-four years as an impoverished exile in Calais and then in Caen, Normandy, where he finished his life in a sanatorium.

Brummell's dress was austere and elegant. It was not flamboyant or extravagant but consisted of impeccably clean linen and finely tailored clothes. As Captain William Jesse (who published his biography in 1886) noted and Robert Dighton's portrait of 1805 illustrates, "His morning dress was similar to that of every other gentleman—top boots and buckskins, with a blue coat and a light or buff coloured waistcoat. . . . His dress of an evening was a blue coat and white waistcoat, black pantaloons which buttoned tight to the ankle, striped silk stockings and opera hat." Although this description suggests that his attire was not extraordinary in the context of Regency society, Brummell's personal attention to detail, function, and cleanliness as well as the fine materials, rare craftsmanship, dignified bearing, and mastery of social etiquette required to maintain such a wardrobe set him apart. The casual equestrian origins of his dress challenged courtly protocol and heralded the pared-down simplicity of masculine attire in the later nineteenth and early twentieth centuries.

Even in his lifetime Brummell was becoming a figure of fiction. A wide range of anecdotes and sayings were attributed to him. Sir Edward Bulwer-Lytton satirized him in his 1828 novel *Pelham; or, The Adventures of a Gentleman*. Mr. Russelton, a thinly disguised Brummell figure, boasts that he employs three tradesmen to make his gloves: "one for the hand, a second for the fingers, and a third for the thumb!"

Brummell's reputation spread to France, where Honoré de Balzac fictionalized him in his *Traité de la vie élégante* (Treatise on the Elegant Life), first published as a serial in *La mode* in 1830. The most important French writing on Brummell is Jules Amédée Barbey d'Aurevilly's short tract of 1845 entitled *Du Dandysme et de Georges Brummell* (On Dandyism and George Brummell). It celebrates Brummell's dandyism as a spiritual achievement of the highest order and raises the dandy's status to that of the poet or artist. This text shifts the terrain of dandyism to a superior intellectual and philosophical ground. Later nineteenth-century texts highlighted the artistic nature of the dandy and his cultivation of both his environment and his dress as works of art. These literary interpretations preserved the heritage of Brummell through the nineteenth century and brought him, transformed, to twentieth-century audiences.

In the first half of the twentieth century, his life would be reenacted in new venues, in the theater and on the silver screen. The playwright Clyde Fitch was commissioned by the matinee idol Richard Mansfield to write a play based on Brummell's legend. *Beau Brummell* premiered on 17 May 1890 at the Madison Square Theatre in New York City, starring Richard Mansfield and Beatrice Cameron. An illustrated version of the play was published in 1908 and remained popular into the second decade of the century.

Three Hollywood films loosely based on Fitch's play were made in the first half of the twentieth century. The first, just sixteen minutes long and directed by and starring James Young, was released in 1913. The second film,

produced by Warner Brothers in 1924, was a star vehicle for John Barrymore. This lavish costume movie was released worldwide and was on the *New York Times* top-ten list of films in 1924. In 1954 MGM studios came out with an even more extravagant production. This version cast the swashbuckling hero Stewart Granger in the starring role, alongside Elizabeth Taylor and Peter Ustinov, who is wonderfully petulant as the Prince Regent. Although it was produced in America, it featured both British and American actors and drew on the talents of the celebrated British costume designer Elizabeth Haffenden, who worked in collaboration with Walter Plunkett on this film. Despite the British cast and costumes, this Americanized Brummell is presented as a social and sartorial reformer who leads Britain from outdated, luxurious aristocratic mores into the more democratic, industrial, and progressive era of the nineteenth century. This was the final cinematic version of the Brummell legend, which has found new currency in literary accounts, such as George Walden's essay and translation of Barbey d'Aurevilly's text, entitled *Who Is a Dandy?*

William Jesse referred to Brummel as "cool and impertinent." Brummell's self-mastery and calculated sense of cool, his rise to fame in Regency society, and his sartorial perfection are his hallmarks. His name has become synonymous with dandyism, and the plaque marking his house in Chesterfield Street reads simply and appropriately, "A Man of Fashion."

See also **Art and Fashion; Dandyism; Fancy Dress; Fashion, Theories of.**

BIBLIOGRAPHY

Barbey d'Aurevilly, Jules. *Who Is a Dandy?* Translated by George Walden. London: Gibson Square Books, 2002.

Bulwer-Lytton, Edward. *Pelham; or, The Adventures of a Gentleman.* 3 vols. London: Colburn, 1828.

Fitch, Clyde. *Beau Brummel: A Play in Four Acts.* New York: John Lane, 1908.

Jesse, Captain William. *The Life of George Brummell, Esq., Commonly Called Beau Brummell.* London: John Nimmo, 1886.

Moers, Ellen. *The Dandy: Brummell to Beerbohm.* London: Secker and Warburg, 1960.

Alison Matthews David

BURBERRY Although overtly recognized by its trademark check of red, black, white, and camel, Burberry is principally renowned for its innovation in waterproof clothing, rather than for the design of the lining material that traditionally lies beneath the outer gabardine cloth. Yet such is the power of reinvention, that to many the reverse is true. Burberry as a company is a rare thing—a British brand of clothing and goods that has successfully held on to its traditions while being able to remold itself into a covetable luxury brand that competes in a worldwide market. Thomas Burberry's invention of waterproof gabardine cloth has ensured that the form of

Burberry's chief executive officer Rosemary Bravo. Bravo transformed the financially ailing company in 1997. Her decision to use the company's trademark check on the outer fabric of their famous raincoats, instead of on the lining material, marked the turning point for the company's bottom line. © REUTERS NEWMEDIA INC./CORBIS. REPRODUCED BY PERMISSION.

apparel his company sold became bound to his name, so that the definition of Burberry in the Oxford English Dictionary reads "a distinguished type of raincoat."

Born in 1835, Thomas Burberry opened an outfitters shop in Basingstoke in 1856 at the relatively young age of twenty-one. As an ambitious country draper, Burberry was inspired by metropolitan ideas of fashionable dress, but drew upon local examples of work clothing to develop his ideas. His starting point was a loose-fitting linen smock that farmers and shepherds wore all year-round. Noticing that it kept the workers cool in summer yet warm in winter, he found on closer inspection that the close weave of the fabric helped to keep out the wet, while the looseness of the garment allowed for the circulation of air without inhibiting movement. By 1879 Burberry had refined his prototype fabric from his own mill to a cloth woven from long-staple Egyptian cotton. It created a fabric that was waterproof, breathable, rip-resistant and crease-proof. Burberry termed it gabardine cloth, reviving an old

term for a loose coat or cloak. It soon came to the attention of motorists, travelers, and explorers who used the weatherproof overcoat, often referred to as a "slip-on," in all weather conditions. When supported on four sticks, many an intrepid Colonial knew its additional use as an impromptu bathtub.

With a London store opening on Haymarket in 1890 (it remains the company headquarters to this day), the company grew to include a wholesale division and shops in Paris and New York by the turn of the century. Ever ready to protect the interests of his business and its products, Burberry registered the logo in 1904 and the eponymous check in 1920 (it did not appear on the lining of the raincoat until 1924). Further, in 1932 the company pioneered the department-store concession devoted exclusively to the sale of Burberry's goods.

The British War Office in 1900 commissioned Burberry to design an overcoat to replace the heavily rubberized mackintoshes that were then standard issue.

The lightweight cotton raincoat designed incorporated D-ring belt clasps, straps, and epaulettes for better function in combat and it soon gained popularity when endorsed by Lord Kitchener. As the most suitable protection from the appalling conditions of trench warfare, it is the origin of what we now refer to as the trench coat.

In 1970, Burberry opened a New York flagship store on east Fifty-Seventh Street. With the resurgence of the luxury goods market in the last decade of the twentieth century, the financially flailing company appointed Rose Marie Bravo in 1997 from Saks, New York as Chief Executive whose responsibility was to revive the brand. According to a story in the *Daily Telegraph*, her American friends dismissed her new job as "selling raincoats in London," but within five years the value of the company rose from £200 million to £1.5 billion ($350 million to $2.67 billion). The linchpin of this transformation was the decision to use the check of the lining on the outer gabardine cloth of the raincoat in the first collection shown at London Fashion Week for A/W 1999/2000. When the model Kate Moss was caught by the paparazzi wearing the raincoat in the street rather than on the catwalk, demand for the item was unparalleled. In being worn in such a casual way, the raincoat signaled a metropolitan savvy that claimed as much an understanding of the visual heritage of British clothing, as an understanding of fashionable taste.

Although credited to Roberto Menichetti, the first appointed fashion designer for the company, the fashionability of the item was influenced by the subversive ideas of American fashion designer Miguel Androver and British fashion designer Russell Sage, who had both flaunted the inside-out Burberry raincoat in their catwalk collections for A/W 2000/1. While Androver mined the cachet of the checked lining in terms of the selling of vintage goods and their reuse, Sage questioned the legal permissibility of appropriating registered goods, sardonically titling his collection "So Sue Me." Later in the same year, Burberry commissioned Mario Testino to photograph their campaigns, astutely hiring Kate Moss as the chief model.

The allure of the check reached unprecedented heights: young mothers dressed their babies in checked bibs, hooligans wore Burberry scarves in tribute to the Casuals who wore them on football terraces in the 1980s, and even Cherie Blair, prime minister Tony Blair's wife, once sported a handbag. Menichetti's response to this popular exposure was to make the high-end Prosorum range showcased in Milan even more directional, causing him to be replaced by Christopher Bailey in 2000, who brought a more commercial and digestible level of reinvention to the product range. To this end, the variation on a raincoat remains core to the company's design repertoire.

From the water-logged trenches of military warfare at the beginning of the twentieth century to the swimming-pool terraces of the twenty-first century, the insatiable demand for the Burberry bikini in 2001 indicates that the kind of water protection the company is now investing in may have diversified considerably, but it remains curiously consistent with Thomas Burberry's sense of reinvention.

See also **London Fashion; Raincoat; Rainwear.**

BIBLIOGRAPHY

Barrow, Becky. "£10m Ride from Bronx to Burberry's." *Daily Telegraph*, 24 June 2002.

Ewing, Elizabeth. *History of Twentieth Century Fashion*. London: Batsford, 1974.

Sudjic, Deyan. *Cult Objects: The Complete Guide to Having It All*. London: Paladin, 1985.

Thornton, Phil. *Casuals: The Story of Terrace Fashion*. Lytham, U.K.: Milo Books, 2003.

Alistair O'Neill

BURQA The seclusion and veiling of women in the Near East apparently long antecedes the emergence of Islam in the seventh century C.E. Islam, however, gives it religious sanction and enforcement. The Qu'ran (Sura XXIV.31) directs women to "be modest, draw their veils over their bosoms, and not reveal their adornments" except to certain specified male relatives, slaves, eunuchs, women, and children. In practice, this has resulted in the system of *purdah* (literally, "curtain")—the enforced seclusion of Muslim women and their concealment under special outer garments in any situation where they might encounter non-familial men. These garments have taken different forms in various parts of the Islamic world.

In Afghanistan, Pakistan, and other parts of the Indian subcontinent, they take the form of the *burqa* (in Afghanistan, called a *chadri*), a voluminous, tentlike outergarment worn by women and girls from earliest puberty on, covering the entire figure from head to foot. Worn whenever a woman leaves her home or may otherwise be in the presence of proscribed males, it makes her totally anonymous and effectively invisible, also concealing and restricting her movements and activities. Its origins are uncertain, but may be pre-Islamic Persian.

The burqa is held in place by a quilted, fitted cap, elaborately embroidered in the same color as the fabric; from this cap flow many yards of fabric, gathered with masses of pleating at the sides and back, creating a hunched look. A small panel of openwork crochet over the eyes permits limited frontal vision. The unpleated front panel is only waist length, allowing the woman to use her hands. In permitted circumstances, this section can be thrown back over her head, exposing her face; otherwise, she holds the long side panels together for complete, stifling concealment. The fabric may be lightweight cotton, rayon, nylon, or silk, in a subdued color—gray, brown, white, pale blue, or green (but unlike the *chador* in Iran and coverings in many Arab countries, not black);

with the goal being anonymity, no bright colors, patterned fabrics, or individualized ornamentation are used.

The burqa is primarily urban, a symbol of nonlaboring status, and may conceal fashionable modern apparel. (Instead of the burqa, village women, whose farm and household work would be hindered, wear long, loose, baggy shirts and trousers and a large head scarf that they pull across the face in the presence of men outside the specified family circle. Some nomad women do not cover their faces.)

Efforts to eliminate or at least modify the rules of purdah, including the wearing of the burqa, have historically had mixed success. In Afghanistan in 1929, a modernizing king attempted to ban the *chadri* by fiat, triggering his overthrow. Wearing a burqa remained mandatory until 1959, when it was quietly made optional and was rapidly discarded by many urban Afghan women, particularly educated women, who adopted simple head scarves, long sleeves, and below-knee-length skirts to meet the requirement of modesty.

No such organized reform effort occurred in Pakistan or among Indian Muslims, where the burqa remains customary, though some modern educated women have abandon it. The rise of radical political Islamism in the 1980s revived its universal use, voluntarily or under duress, in Islamist-dominated areas, such as Pakistan's North West Frontier Province and Baluchistan, and Afghanistan under the Taliban regime from 1996 to 2002.

See also **Islamic Dress, Contemporary; Middle East: History of Islamic Dress; Religion and Dress.**

BIBLIOGRAPHY

Clifford, Mary Louise. *The Land and People of Afghanistan.* New York: J. B. Lippincott, 1989. Several black-and-white photos; text on women discusses the *chadri.*

Klass, Rosanne. *Land of the High Flags.* New York: Random House, 1964. Black-and-white photos and text regarding the psychology of living under the chadri.

Michaud, Roland, and Sabrina Michaud. *Afghanistan: Paradise Lost.* London: Thames & Hudson, 1980. Several fine color photographs show details of the burqa and chadri.

Rosanne Klass

BURROWS, STEPHEN Stephen Gerald Burrows was born on 15 September 1943 in Newark, New Jersey. He studied at the Philadelphia Museum College of Art from 1961 to 1963 and at the Fashion Institute of Technology in New York from 1964 to 1966. Perhaps most influential to the future career of this original American designer was his seamstress grandmother, Beatrice Simmons, who taught him to sew when he was eight years old. At an early age he discovered and delighted in the zigzag stitch that would become a signature. As a designer, instead of hiding stitching, Burrows celebrated and exaggerated it by using contrasting thread colors. He used a close, narrow zigzag stitch to create his trademark fluted "lettuce hem." In an endless range of shapes and combinations Burrows placed bright contrasting colors of chiffon or knit fabrics in a single ensemble.

After having success selling pieces to friends, Burrows cofounded the O Boutique at Nineteenth Street and Park Avenue South in 1968. Attracting the countercultural luminaries that hung out at Max's Kansas City across the street, the shop and its proprietor gained a following, but Burrow's lack of business experience resulted in O Boutique's eventual closure. In 1970 Geraldine Stutz, president of Henri Bendel, gave Burrows a space in the workroom of Bendel's Studio, the small manufacturing part of the store, and Pat Tennant, the manager of the design studio, became an important mentor to the designer. Stephen Burrows World opened in the summer of 1970 on the third floor of the store, as a packed audience watched a fashion show set to disco music. Leather garments with nail-studded embellishments, midiskirts, skin-tight sweaters, suede bags dripping with fringe, and Burrows's famous super bright jersey knits shown on ethnically diverse male and female models impressed audience and press alike.

Burrows's fluid, sexy separates are iconic of the individualist, confident woman of the 1970s. The "black is beautiful" philosophy of the 1970s was showcased through Burrows's use of African American models and his success as an African American fashion designer. More than any other designer of the 1970s, Burrows captures in his designs the vivacious energy of the disco scene. By 1973 he was at the top of the field, winning the prestigious Coty award, the highest honor in American fashion, which he was honored with again in 1974 and 1977. He was one of five American designers invited to show their clothes along with five French designers at a fashion spectacle at the Palace of Versailles in 1973. Influenced by his success and the lure of Seventh Avenue, Burrows moved out on his own that same year. With this move he lost the guidance and protection of Bendel's staff, however, and his business suffered due to poor management. Used to overseeing the details of his clothing line's production, he was unable to achieve the same quality utilizing mass-manufacturing processes.

From 1977 to 1982 Burrows relaunched a successful collection with Henri Bendel. He stepped out of the New York fashion world in 1982 when the mood in fashion was changing and the disco era was coming to a close. He relaunched a third time with Henri Bendel in 2002, when his now-retro fashions were once again in demand.

See also **Fashion Designer; Jersey; Leather and Suede.**

BIBLIOGRAPHY

Bellafante, G. "A Fallen Star of the 70's Is Back in the Business." *New York Times,* 1 January 2002.

Butler, J. "Burrows Is Back—With a Little Help from His Friends." *New York Times Magazine*, 5 June 1977.

Morris, Bernadine. "The Look of Fashions for the Seventies—In Colours That Can Dazzle." *New York Times*, 12 August 1970.

Dennita Sewell

BUSINESS CASUAL. *See* **Casual Business Dress.**

BUSTLE Exaggeration of the feminine posterior has been a periodic theme in Western fashion for several hundred years. The pulled-back overskirts of late-seventeenth- and early-eighteenth-century mantuas (loose-fitting gowns) emphasized this area, and pads or "cork rumps" sometimes supported the swagged-up styles of the late 1770s and 1780s. Even early-nineteenth-century neoclassical dresses often featured a small back pad—a so-called artificial hump—to give the high-waisted line a graceful flow. As waists lowered and skirts widened, the pad was retained, and by the late 1820s it was called a bustle. Throughout the mid-nineteenth century full skirts were enhanced by a small bustle made of padding, whalebone, or even inflatable rubber. In the 1870s and 1880s, however, both the skirt support and the silhouette created by the bustle became the focus of fashion.

In an age when men and women were considered to have distinct social roles, the late nineteenth century assumed the natural forms of the two genders also diverged. One arbiter of etiquette and aesthetics, "Professor" Thomas E. Hill, explained that, in contrast to the broad-shouldered male, the female figure is characterized by narrow, sloped shoulders but width across "the lower portion of the form." He stated that to avoid looking "masculine and unnatural," women's dresses should be tight on top while dressmakers are "permitted to arrange tuck and bow and flounce without stint below the waist." These enhanced derrieres proportionately lessened women's small waists, produced by corseting. The idea that women are naturally steatopygous or fat-buttocked is no more aberrant than the late-twentieth-century idea that all women should have "buns of steel."

The bustle, also known as a tournure, pannier, or dress improver, could be made in a wide variety of materials and shapes. Some types were full length, such as sprung steel half hoopskirts called crinolettes and petticoats with adjustable inset steels. Many bustles, however, were made to pad only the rump area, secured to the wearer by a buckled waistband. These could be simple rectangular- or crescent-shaped pads filled with horsehair or other stuffing, but more intricate forms included down-filled devices and puffed or ruffled constructions of crinoline or stiff fabric such as tampico hemp. Woven wire mesh bustles were advertised as not only cooler than padding, but uncrushable, eliminating the need for furtive rearrangement after sitting. Other structures featured several metal springs arranged vertically, placed a large crescent-shaped spring horizontally below the waist, or had projecting steel half hoops that adjusted with lacing and claimed to cleverly fold up when the wearer sat down.

The material used to create bustles was seemingly endless: M. V. Hughes in her memoir *A London Child of the Seventies* (Oxford University Press, p. 84) recalls that an acquaintance used *The Times* newspaper to achieve her effective bustle, saying, "I find its paper so good, far more satisfactory than the *Daily News*." Petticoats, often with layers of ruffles down the back, helped smooth the line of the bustle pad and support bustled skirts.

By 1868, the fullness of women's skirts had moved to the back, and a bustle was needed to support fashionable puffed overskirts and large sashes. The high back interest continued in the early 1870s as the bustle gradually swelled in size. Although the back of the skirt remained the dominant feature, the silhouette slimmed down after about 1875, when the skirt and petticoats, drawn back low and close to the figure and usually flowing into a long train, were often unsupported by a bustle. In the early 1880s, the bustle returned in dramatic proportions, often forming a shelflike protuberance at right angles to the wearer's body. An examination of images of fashionable women in extreme bustle dresses would lead an impartial observer to conclude—as Bernard Rudofsky proposed in the 1940s—that skirts shaped in this peculiar way must contain a second pair of legs behind the women's normal ones.

The wardrobe of a woman of the time included a chemise, drawers, corset, corset cover, stockings, and several petticoats, as well as a bustle. The bustle's size was accentuated by all the features of fashionable dresses, including tight sleeves, tight-fitting bodices with back tails, and elaborately constructed skirts with back poufs, swags, gathering, pleating, draperies, and asymmetrical effects. While a few called for reform of feminine dress for artistic and health reasons, most accepted women's convoluted clothing as in accord with High Victorian taste, with its love of the ornate, ostentatious, and overdone. A fashionable woman, dressed in a horsehair or spring bustle, layers of undergarments, and rich, heavy fabrics trimmed with fringe, did present an upholstered effect, similar to an overstuffed sofa of the time, both expensive, decorative objects. In 1899, Thorstein Veblen's *The Theory of the Leisure Class* introduced ideas, such as the conferring of status by "conspicuous consumption," reflecting the bustle period's excesses. Yet to most contemporaries, highly contrived feminine clothing was not seen as contradictory to the spirit of this "age of progress," but rather as a concomitant of civilization, showing commercial enterprise and mechanical ingenuity and firmly establishing the "civilized" division of the sexes. Throughout the period, although ridiculed, the bustle silhouette was widely accepted and worn by women

Women wearing bustles. Bustles have been an element of Western fashion intermittently since the seventeenth century. Women's dresses were form-fitting on top and created with a tuck and flounce in the back, below the waist, to avoid appearing masculine. © BETTMAN/CORBIS. REPRODUCED BY PERMISSION.

from all classes, as well as by little girls with their short skirts. As *The Delineator* noted in February 1886 (p. 99), some women did not wear a bustle pad, "except when such an adjunct if necessitated by a ceremonious toilette," relying instead on a flounced petticoat to support the drapery of simpler dresses.

After about 1887 the bustle reduced in size and skirts began to slim. The skirts of the early 1890s featured some back fullness, but emphasis had shifted to flared skirt hems and enormous leg-of-mutton sleeves, and bustle supports were not as fashionable. With skirts fitting snugly to the hips and derriere in the late 1890s, however, some women relied on skirt supports to achieve a gracefully rounded hipline that set off a small waist. While not as extreme as examples from the mid-1880s, the woven wire or quilted hip pads worn beyond the turn of century show the tenacity of the full-hipped female ideal.

Despite some historians' view that bustle fashions were surely the most hideous ever conceived, this very feminine silhouette has continued to fascinate. In the late 1930s,

Elsa Schiaparelli made playful homage to the bustle in some of her sleek evening dresses, while late-twentieth-century bustle interpretations by avant-garde designers, such as Yohji Yamamoto and Vivienne Westwood, have utilized the form with historically informed irony.

See also **Mantua; Skirt Supports.**

BIBLIOGRAPHY

Blum, Stella. *Victorian Fashions and Costumes from Harper's Bazar 1867–1898.* New York: Dover Publications, Inc., 1974.

Cunnington, C. Willett. *English Women's Clothing in the Nineteenth Century.* London: Faber and Faber, 1937. Reprint, New York: Dover Publications, Inc., 1990.

Gernsheim, Alison. *Fashion and Reality: 1840–1914.* London: Faber and Faber, 1963. Reprint as *Victorian and Edwardian Fashion: A Photographic Survey.* New York: Dover Publications, Inc., 1981.

Hill, Thomas E. *Never Give a Lady a Restive Horse.* From *Manual of Social and Business Forms: Selections.* 1873. Also from *Album of Biography and Art.* 1881. Reprint, Berkeley, Calif.: Diablo Press, 1967.

Hughes, Mary Vivian. *A London Child of the Seventies*. London: Oxford University Press, 1934.

Rudofsky, Bernard. *The Unfashionable Human Body*. New York: Doubleday and Company, 1971.

Severa, Joan. *Dressed for the Photographer: Ordinary Americans and Fashion, 1840–1900*. Kent, Ohio: Kent State University Press, 1995.

Waugh, Norah. *Corsets and Crinolines*. New York: Theatre Arts Books, 1954.

H. Kristina Haugland

BUTTONS Button-like objects of stone, glass, bone, ceramic, and gold have been found at archaeological sites dating as early as 2000 B.C.E., but evidence suggests that these objects were used as decoration on cloth or strung like beads. Nevertheless, they have the familiar holes through which to pass a thread, which gives them the appearance of the button currently known as a fastener.

Buttons can be divided into two types according to the way they are attached to a garment. Shank buttons have a pierced knob or shaft on the back through which passes the sewing thread. The majority of buttons are this type. The shank can be a separate piece that is attached to the button or part of the button material itself, as in a molded button. Pierced buttons have a hole from front to back of the button so that the thread used to attach the button is visible on the face.

Almost every material that has been used in the fine and decorative arts has been used historically in the production of buttons. Buttons exist in a variety of materials: metals (precious or otherwise), gemstones, ivory, horn, wood, bone, mother-of-pearl, glass, porcelain, paper, and silk. In the late nineteenth and twentieth centuries, celluloid and other artificial materials have been used to imitate natural materials.

Early History
The precursor to the button fastener was the fibula, a brooch or pin used to hold two pieces of clothing on the shoulder or chest. The button began to replace the fibula at least by the early Middle Ages, if not sooner.

Buttons functioned as primary fastenings for men's dress earlier than for women's. This may be due to the fact that the women's, from the late Middle Ages into the twentieth century, was required to be tight and smoothly fitted. Lacings and hooks are better suited to providing the strong hold and smooth appearance necessary for tight-fitting garments.

One of the earliest extant pieces of clothing to show the use of buttons as fastenings is the pourpoint of Charles of Blois (c. 1319–1364). This new outer garment was fitted in the body and sleeves, with buttons used to close the front and the sleeves from the elbow. At this point, however, men's lower garments (hose, and, later, breeches) were still fastened to their upper garments, or to an interior belt, by points (laces of ribbon or cord decorated with metal tips). These points with metal tips were often attached as purely decorative pieces to both male and female apparel.

There are records of buttons in documents relating to nobility during the late Middle Ages and the Renaissance. For example, Philip the Good, Duke of Burgundy (1396–1497) ordered Venetian glass buttons decorated with pearls, and Francis I of France (1494–1547) is said to have ordered a set of black enamel buttons mounted on gold from a Parisian goldsmith. These were obviously special buttons of the same quality as contemporary jewelry. Buttons of any material were generally round in shape and made of decorated metal or covered with needlework in silk or metal threads on a wooden core. The ball-shaped toggle button is probably the type of button that replaced the fibula as a fastening for cloaks, capes, and other outer garments. A sixteenth-century example exists in Nuremberg hallmarked silver, attached to a thin bar by a flexible chain link.

The Eighteenth Century
The eighteenth century is considered the Golden Age of buttons by collectors, as the variety of styles, as well as the physical size of buttons increase dramatically. Men's coats required buttons at the front opening, sleeves, pockets, and back vents. Waistcoats and breeches were also fastened with buttons. The size of the button grows and the shape generally flattens during the course of the century, ending in the flat disk as large as 1.38 inch (3.5 cm) in diameter. The value of decorations on a man's ensemble during this period, composed of metal thread embroidery and jeweled buttons, could account for as much as 80 percent of the cost of the suit of clothes. Thus, luxurious buttons became an increasingly essential part of the expression of status in upper-class men's dress. In Denis Diderot's *Encyclopédie* (c. 1746) the creativity of button-makers is exalted, though for moralists costly buttons became one sign of excess in fashion.

The newly fashionable paste jewels (imitation gemstones) appeared in the 1730s and were used to create some of the most highly prized buttons of the nineteenth century. Georges Frédéric Strass, a Parisian jeweler, perfected techniques of making these glass jewels.

As the button evolved from a ball to a flat disk, another notable change in decorative technique was the use of the button as a palette for painting. Representational images became immensely popular in the second half of the eighteenth century and are related to the miniature portraits that were worn as pendants or pins during the period. Portraits and subjects like rococo genre scenes, historical events, tourist views, and architectural monuments were produced. An extraordinary set of French

Women shop for buttons in London, 1953. Buttons have been a mainstay of fashion since 2000 B.C.E. and continue to hold their place as an object of function and style. Buttons are created in a variety of materials, including metals, plastics, gem stones, ivory, horn, wood, bone, mother-of-pearl, glass, porcelain, paper, and silk. © Hulton-Deutsch Collection/Corbis. Reproduced by permission.

portrait miniature buttons was made about 1790 and included portraits of personalities from the French Revolutionary period; each portrait was set in silver with paste-diamond border and the name of the sitter engraved on the back. Artists of note participated in the production of portrait buttons; Jean-Baptiste Isabey (1767–1855), a miniature painter and pupil of Jacques-Louis David, records that he painted decorative buttons at the beginning of his career.

By the second half of the eighteenth century, button making in Europe fell into two categories: French button production remained a craft tradition allied with other high-quality decorative arts, while the English button industry developed mass-production techniques. Probably the most influential of the new English technologies was the development of cut-steel buttons and accessories by the steel manufacturer Matthew Bolton (1728–1809) of Birmingham in the 1760s. Bolton's cut-steel or faceted

Button dyer at work. Buttons exist in a variety of colors and motifs and are a critical element in modern dress, as suit jackets and shirts are worn by white collar workers. © HULTON-DEUTSCH COLLECTION/CORBIS. REPRODUCED BY PERMISSION.

steel buttons were one of the most prevalent styles of the last three decades of the eighteenth century. The polished and faceted surface was created to imitate that of faceted gems or glass and the effect was quite successful.

The ceramic manufacturer Josiah Wedgwood began producing buttons made of his popular jasperware in 1773 as part of a collaboration with Matthew Bolton, who created cut-steel settings for the ceramic buttons. Jasperware ceramics, with their neoclassical motifs derived from cameos, had become the trademark product of the Wedgwood factory and the buttons were available in five colors and a variety of shapes. Another innovation in the ceramic industry, that of transfer printing, created a new type of ceramic button decorated with designs derived from copperplate engravings. At the end of the eighteenth century, buttons made from mother-of-pearl began to rival in popularity those of steel.

The eighteenth-century Enlightenment sensibility manifested itself in several unique types of buttons. Faithfully depicted insects and animals became the subject of button sets, as did buttons created from semiprecious materials such as agate, in which the natural patterns of the stones were the only decoration. The highlight of this natural history trend is probably the so-called Habitat buttons, which contain actual specimens of insects, plants, or pieces of minerals encased under glass domes.

Nineteenth and Twentieth Century

The standardization of military uniforms in eighteenth-century Europe led to the production of specialized buttons that continues to be a major portion of the button industry today. The number of buttons required for a soldier's coat could be as many as twenty to thirty. Each country, region, and specialization within the armed services required their own individual designs. Uniform buttons carried over into civilian life, as modern businesses, such as airlines, and local law enforcement agencies required special buttons for their uniforms.

Beginning in the early nineteenth century men's dress became much plainer and less ostentatious. Portraits by Jean-Auguste-Dominique Ingres (1780–1867) show men's fashion in the first half of the nineteenth century with plain gold metal or fabric buttons of the same color as the garment on which they are sewn. Women's bodices and outerwear became the outlet for the display of decorative buttons by the mid-nineteenth century. Women's buttons followed trends in jewelry: colored enamel, porcelain, pearl, silver, and jewels were used. Jet and black glass, introduced during Queen Victoria's mourning for Prince Albert, remained popular to the end of the century.

The nineteenth-century button industry continued along the two lines that had been established in the eighteenth century; industrial progress continued concurrently with handcraft techniques, which generally followed the historical revival styles of nineteenth-century decorative arts.

In 1812, Aaron Benedict established a metal button-making factory in Waterbury, Connecticut, to supply metal buttons for the military. Until that time many metal buttons were still coming from England, but the War of 1812 brought trade between the United States and Britain to a halt. As of 2003, Benedict's company, which became known as Waterbury Buttons, had been in business for 191 years. It is the oldest and largest producer of stamped metal buttons in the United States. Statistics from 1996 show that they produced 100 million buttons—about one-half for fashion trade and the remainder for military and commercial clients. Metal remains the main type of mass-produced button because the material lends itself to mass-production techniques.

The French firm Albert Parent et Cie, founded in 1825, exemplifies the brilliance of French manufacturers who combined mass-production techniques with the hand-finished details to produce luxury buttons in the manner of the eighteenth century. The company left an archive of sample books showing over 80,000 examples of buttons in every available technique of the time.

While more buttons were mass-produced in the nineteenth century that did not mean that fewer materials were employed in the creation of buttons. Natural materials like horn and shells, which had been used for centuries, were rediscovered as mass-produced items. New materials such as celluloid, the first plastic, were used as early as the 1870s to imitate other materials.

Representational picture buttons, first introduced in the late eighteenth century, reached their peak between 1870 and 1914. The nineteenth-century scenes were generally mass-produced stamped metal designs depicting any motif imaginable, but contemporary marvels like the Eiffel Tower were especially popular.

The late nineteenth and early twentieth centuries saw more and more men and women wearing suits with linen or cotton shirts underneath, the new uniform for the emerging white-collar working class. Both suit jackets and shirts required buttons as fastenings and they created the need for large numbers of inexpensive buttons. Thus, the four-holed pierced button was introduced to both men's and women's fashions. However, fine jewelry quality buttons were still produced by some of the best-known retailers of the day such as Cartier, Liberty's of London, and Georg Jensen.

Buttons received competition in the form of the new zipper that was patented in 1903 but did not come into general use until the 1930s. The zipper was considered a novelty at first and played a prominent role as decoration in the designs of top designers.

Bakelite was invented in 1907 and by the 1930s had replaced almost all other synthetics for accessories. Durable and versatile, Bakelite was the medium for some of the most extravagant buttons of the twentieth century, but other plastics eventually replaced it. Three-dimensional accessories, such as fruit shapes, were created in the 1930s and 1940s when small accessories like buttons were especially popular. The designer Elsa Schiaparelli (1890–1973), who was allied with surrealist artists in the 1930s, is notable for her use of extraordinary custom-made buttons.

Plastics replaced most inexpensive glass and pearl buttons by the 1960s. That coupled with the fact that natural materials such as ivory and tortoiseshell are now banned in the United States and other countries has led to the dominance of plastic buttons made to imitate these materials. Mother-of-pearl is still used but in much smaller quantities than in the past. American-made pearl buttons can cost from twenty-five cents to three dollars apiece, as some of the work must still be done by hand and the best shells are imported from the Pacific Ocean coastlines.

The use of stretch fabrics and increasingly informal dressing have led to a decrease in the demand for button fasteners. They have become a symbol of nostalgia and anachronistic tradition, as evidenced by retro button-fly jeans introduced by denim manufacturers in the 1990s and the continued use of rows of tiny buttons on the back of bridal gowns.

Buttons have become extremely collectible. The National Button Society exists for collectors and publishes a quarterly bulletin and holds an annual meeting and show. There are similar societies in Britain and Australia and elsewhere in the world. Military buttons represent a specialty among collectors, as the challenge of identifying the insignias of segments of the armed services adds to the interest of these items.

See also **Fasteners; Zipper.**

BIBLIOGRAPHY

Boucher, Francois. *20,000. Years of Fashion: The History of Costume and Personal Adornment.* New York: Harry N. Abrams, 1987.

DeMasters, Karen. "New Jersey & Co. Out of the Dust Emerge Lustrous Buttons." *New York Times,* 4 April 1999.

Epstein, Diana, and Millicent Safro. *Buttons.* New York: Harry N. Abrams, 1991.

Houart, Victor. *Buttons: A Collector's Guide.* London: Souvenir Press Ltd., 1977.

Pearsall, Susan. "In Waterbury, Buttons Are Serious Business." *New York Times,* 3 August 1997.

Roche, Daniel. *The Culture of Clothing: Dress and Fashion in the Ancient Régime.* New York: Cambridge University Press, 1996.

Melinda Watt

CACHE-SEXE The term "cache-sexe" refers to a covering for the female genitals. The term is derived from the French *cacher*, which means to hide, and *sexe*, which means genitals. Other terms used synonymously are modesty apron, marriage apron, modesty skirt, loincloth, string skirt, and girdle. The choice of term appears to be related to the country of origin or discipline of the observer. In this case, "cache-sexe" appears to be the term used in those areas of the African continent that were colonized by the French, such as the region from western Mali to southern Cameroon. Cache-sexe are used throughout much of West Africa and parts of East Asia, where the term modesty apron is more commonly used. In short, a wide variety of terms are employed to describe an article of dress that offers insight into the life ways of women in some small-scale societies.

Cache-sexe are constructed of a variety of materials including woven fabric, leather, beads, leaves, and metals. For example, cache-sexe created by the Kirdi (Fulani) women in northern Cameroon are skirts beaded with a fantastic range of colors. Cowry shells and brass beads ornament and give weight to the fringe. Cowry shells originate in the Maldive Islands, off the western coast of India, indicating Kirdi linkages to long distance trade. Cache-sexe are worn low on the hip and tied with a cord. Regardless of materials, the skirts measure approximately twelve to eighteen inches in length and twenty to twenty-two inches in width, excluding the cord.

The cache-sexe can be traced to the Paleolithic period, where stone carvings of fecund women, such as the Venus of Lespugue, depict panels of string fore and aft. String skirts dating from the fourteenth century B.C.E. have been uncovered in burial sites in Denmark. These skirts are wool, also ride low on the hip, fall to just above the knees, and wrap around the body twice. The cords of the skirt are thickly plied and knotted at the bottom, so that the skirt "must have had quite a swing to it" (Barber, p. 57). One of the oldest African examples of cache-sexe is described as a girdle from twelfth-century Mali. It can be described as a three-layer belt with very long fringes. The inner bark of the baobab tree is believed to be the source of the strands of fiber, which are plaited and twined into a solid chevron pattern. Its manufacture is closely related to the techniques used to produce snares,

nets, and baskets. This specific article of dress is significant because it was once believed that dress was introduced to sub-Saharan Africa by the spread of Islam. However, this object predates the expansion of Islam and is made of local, not imported, materials.

Cache-sexe appear to be exclusive to females. When and how a woman wears a cache-sexe varies from society to society. In some, a girl begins to wear the skirt after menarche; in others menarche is recognized by a change from a small leather panel skirt to a fringed skirt that wraps all the way around the body. In visual sources of information, cache-sex are part of an ensemble that includes necklaces or supplements to the nose. In parts of New Guinea and Irian Jaya, women use knitted net bags that hang from a strap across the forehead. In twentieth-century images women can be seen wearing brassieres, T-shirts, and blouses.

Female informants report that protection from the environment is the main reason they wear cache-sexe. However, because of the open styling of the of the skirt, either as panels hanging in front and back or as fringes, it may be less effective as physical protection than as spiritual protection. For example, in Papua New Guinea, the Doni believe that ghosts can attack vulnerable areas like the anal opening. Articles of dress with ritual power, such as the cache-sexe, are used to protect, if not actually conceal, the lower body against evil.

Like the penis sheath, one function of the cache-sexe was thought to be modesty. A more likely interpretation of this act of dressing has more to do with fulfilling a group aesthetic about standards of public appearance. Not wearing a cache-sexe is a visible statement of a woman's inability or unwillingness to participate in social interaction, as when ill or in mourning.

Indeed, the main function of the cache sexe, like the penis sheath, appears to be one of drawing attention to the female secondary sex characteristics by intermittently concealing them. In her contemplation of Paleolithic string skirts, Barber states:

> To solve the mystery of why they were [worn], I think we must follow our eyes. Not only do the skirts hide nothing of importance, but also if anything, they attract the eye precisely to the specifically female sexual

areas by framing them, presenting them, or playing peekaboo with them. . . . Our best guess, then is that string skirts indicated something about the childbearing ability or readiness of a woman, ... that she was in some sense "available" as a bride. (p. 59)

Thus, the cache sexe, by any other name, is exclusively a female symbol. Like the penis sheath, it is more than a covering or a display. It is a unique form of material culture that draws one in to an understanding of the physical, social, and aesthetic life of women in some small-scale cultures.

See also **Penis Sheath.**

BIBLIOGRAPHY

Barber, Elizabeth Wayland. *Women's Work: The First 20,000 Years.* New York: W. W. Norton and Company, 1994.

Heider, Karl G. "Attributes and Categories in the Study of Material Culture: New Guinea Dani Attire." *Man* 4, no. 3 (1969): 379–391.

Hersey, Irwin. "The Beaded Cache-Sexe of Northern Cameroon." *African Arts* 8, no. 2 (winter 1975): 64.

O'Neill, Thomas. "Irian Jaya: Indonesia's Wild Side." *National Geographic* 189, no. 2 (February 1996): 2–34.

Steinmetz, George. "Irian Jaya's People of the Trees." *National Geographic* 189, no. 2 (February 1996): 35–43.

Symonds, Patricia V. *Calling the Soul: Gender and the Cycle of Life in a Hmong Village.* Seattle: University of Washington Press, 2003.

Sandra Lee Evenson

CAFTAN The term "caftan" (from Ottoman Turkish *qaftan*) is used to refer to a full-length, loosely-fitted garment with long or short sleeves worn by both men and women, primarily in the Levant and North Africa. The garment may be worn with a sash or belt. Some caftans open to the front or side and are tied or fastened with looped buttons running from neck to waist. Depending on use, caftans vary from hip to floor length. The caftan is similar to the more voluminous *djellaba* gown of the Middle East. Contemporary use of the label "caftan" broadens the term to encompass a number of similarly styled ancient and modern garment types.

The origin of the caftan is usually tied to Asia Minor and Mesopotamia. Caftan-like robes are depicted in the palace reliefs of ancient Persia dating to 600 B.C.E. By the thirteenth century C.E., the style had spread into Eastern Europe and Russia, where caftan styles provided the model for a number of different basic garments well into the nineteenth century (Yarwood 1986, p. 321, 62). The caftan tradition was particularly elaborate in the imperial wardrobes of the sixteenth-century Ottoman Empire in Anatolian Turkey. Caftans of varying lengths constructed from rich Ottoman satins and velvets of silk and metallic threads were worn by courtiers to indicate status, pre-

served in court treasuries, used as tribute, and given as "robes of honor" to visiting ambassadors, heads of state, important government officials, and master artisans working for the court (Atil 1987, p. 177, pp. 179–180.) Men's caftans often had gores added, causing the caftan to flare at the bottom, while women's garments were more closely fitted. Women were more likely to add sashes or belts. A sultan and his courtiers might layer two or three caftans with varying length sleeves for ceremonial functions. An inner short-sleeved caftan (*entari*), was usually secured with an embroidered sash or jeweled belt, while the outer caftan could have slits at the shoulder through which the wearer's arms were thrust to display the sleeves (sometimes with detachable expansions) of the inner caftan to show off the contrasting fabrics of the garments (1987, pp. 182–198; p. 348). Loose pants gathered at the ankle or skirts were worn under the entari.

Caftan-style robes are worn in many parts of the world where Islam has spread, particularly in North and West Africa. In parts of West Africa, the practice of layering robes to express the aesthetic principle of "bigness" in leadership dress (Perani and Wolff 1999, pp. 90–95) and the giving of "robes of honor" is shared with the Ottoman tradition (Kriger 1988).

In Western culture, caftans became part of the international fashion scene in the mid-twentieth century. In the 1950s, French designer Christian Dior adapted the caftan style to design women's floor-length evening coats (O'Hara 1986, p. 60). In the 1960s, the caftan as a unisex garment gained visibility as hippie trendsetters adopted ethnic dress. Largely through the influence of fashion maven Diana Vreeland, the editor of *Vogue* magazine, the caftan entered into the haute couture fashion scene. After a visit to Morocco in the early 1960s, Vreeland published a series of articles in *Vogue* championing the caftan as fashionable for "The Beautiful People" (Harrity 2003). Yves Saint Laurent and Halston were designers who included caftan-styled clothing in their lines (O'Hara 1986, p. 60). Since that time, caftans continue to have a market for evening and at-home wear for women and a more limited market with homosexual males (Harrity 2003). The caftan is now marketed globally as "fashion." Contemporary designers draw their inspiration from a number of different historic traditions. For example, Hubert Givenchy draws upon the Middle Eastern tradition. African designers present the "dashiki caftan" based on West African prototypes. The J. Peterman Company markets a "Shang Dynasty Caftan" for women, copied from a Chinese silk ceremonial robe dated to 2640 B.C.E. In this globalization of the caftan, top Italian designers began marketing costly "designer caftans" in materials as diverse as silk and sheared mink to elite women of the Arab Middle East nations (*Time International*, Dec. 9, 2002).

See also **Djellaba; Iran: History of Dress; Middle East: History of Islamic Dress.**

BIBLIOGRAPHY

Atil, Esin. *The Age of Sultan Suleyman the Magnificent.* Washington, D.C.: National Gallery of Art; New York: Harry N. Abrams, Inc., 1987. Includes an excellent discussion of sixteenth-century imperial Ottoman caftans in the collection of the Topkapi Palace in Turkey.

Kriger, Coleen. "Robes of the Sokoto Caliphate." *African Arts* 21, no. 3 (1988): 52–57, 78–79.

O'Hara, Georgina. *The Encyclopaedia of Fashion.* New York: Harry N. Abrams, 1986.

Perani, Judith, and Norma H. Wolff. *Cloth, Dress, and Art Patronage in Africa.* Oxford and New York: Berg Press, 1999.

Stillman, Yedida Kalfon. *Arab Dress: A Short History from the Dawn of Islam to Modern Times.* Boston: Brill, 2000.

Yarwood, Doreen. *The Encyclopedia of World Costume.* New York: Bonanza Books, 1986.

Internet Resources

Calderwood, Mark. "Ottoman Costume: An Overview of Sixteenth Century Turkish Dress." 2000. Available from <http://www.geocities.com/kaganate>.

Harrity, Christopher. "Will You Know When It's Caftan Time?" July 25, 2003. Available from <http://www.advocate.com>

Norma H. Wolff

GLOSSARY OF TECHNICAL TERMS

Madder: Natural red dye obtained from the root of a Eurasian plant, *Rubia tinctoria*.

Mordant: A substance used in dyeing that helps to make the dye color more stable and permanent.

Resist dyeing: Any of a number of dyeing techniques in which part of the yarn or fabric is covered with some material that prevents the penetration of the dyestuff.

CALICO In the United States, the word "calico" refers to cotton cloth printed with tiny, tightly spaced, colorful motifs on a colored background. Because many people perceive it as pleasantly old-fashioned, calico has long found favor with quilt makers and it occasionally appears in children's wear. In the early twentieth century, instead of jeans or knits, women typically wore calico dresses and aprons to do housework.

Calico of the late 1500s was another matter. The Portuguese, intent upon being the first Europeans to trade for spices directly in the Malay archipelago, had arrived in Calicut, India. There they encountered colored and uncolored cotton cloths of all descriptions, which they designated generally as "calicoes." Perhaps by default, "calico" very gradually acquired a secondary meaning in reference to basic, unelaborated cottons lacking the distinctive characteristics of other ones like "dungaree" or "gingham."

Calico in Early Commerce

Centuries before European traders disembarked in India, a wide range of Indian calicos, including painted or printed ones called *chintes*, were carried by Arab traders to Turkey, the Levant, and North Africa as well as Southeast Asia. Through their Mediterranean trade connections, wealthy Europeans had enjoyed imported spices and Indian quilted silks. They knew—or desired—little of the cottons, although Armenian entrepreneurs managed a calico trade along with spices and silks.

Early in their enterprise, Portuguese, Dutch, and English spice traders learned to appreciate cotton because the spice islanders would not sell their merchandise reasonably for anything other than their preferred Indian cloths—or opium. Thus enmeshed in calico trading, the traders sent quantities of the cheapest—probably leftovers—and some of the most luxurious kinds back home on private speculation or as curiosities. These generated a voracious European market; by the 1660s calico imports had become big business. Fine and heavy linens both could be replaced by the more affordable cottons; the *chintes* or prints were like nothing else.

English traders further expanded their operations by selling calicos to other companies that profitably exported them to Europe and the old-established Mediterranean and Levantine markets. They discovered lucrative markets in West Africa where, in the 1630s, they began selling special checked and striped calico as barter for slaves. The unsold remainders were sold in the West Indies for slave clothing and returned in the form of tobacco and sugar.

Indian *Chintes*

The processes of indigo resist dyeing and of applying mordants to selected areas of a cloth prior to dyeing in chay (madder) are thought to have originated in ancient times in India. The colored designs were not only brilliant, but fast, or laundry-proof—traits which riveted European imaginations and dollars. Common qualities looked crude because they were produced by the shortcut method of block printing, which also compromised the purity of the colors; printed calicos were inexpensive or downright cheap, and not cherished. The best goods, *kalamkari*, commanded a much higher price than printed ones, for they were hand painted—a time-consuming, laborious method that moved one exasperated entrepreneur to make remarks about creeping snails. These are the treasures that came to rest in museum collections.

A designer arranges a calico dress on a model. Calicos became so popular in France and England in the 1700s that both countries prohibited importing, printing, wearing, and using cottons in an effort to protect their own textile industry. © Hulton-Deutsch Collection/Corbis. Reproduced by permission.

Europeans and *Chintes*

European textiles had woven designs, manipulated surfaces, or applied decorations, and, apart from humble stripes and checks, these added significantly to the expense. They were difficult to maintain. Some handkerchiefs were printed with ink—not dye—to make handy city maps or other novelties that were not laundry-proof.

Dutch gentlewomen were pleased to wear India *chintes* but English ladies at first disdained them because the "meaner sort" already had embraced the cheap piece goods that first came along. By the 1660s, however, the upper classes in Europe and America were eagerly augmenting their wardrobes with washable banyans and other informal attire made of calicos custom-painted to their taste. Everyone wanted *chintes* for the irresistible combination of eye-appeal, comfort, and launderability.

European Printed Calico

When Europeans decided to try their own hands at printing in the 1600s, they printed on Indian calico. To eliminate the problems of dependence upon imported cloth, over the next century England led in developing machinery for cotton spinning and weaving. By 1800, Eli Whitney's American cotton gin enabled a steady supply of American raw cotton to busy mills. All the while, printing processes were becoming highly mechanized.

Because European designs were necessarily block printed—painting was too slow and tedious—the mordants required thickening. The trick was to concoct thickeners that gave clean imprints with minimal dulling of the colors. The development of better colors concerned all; mineral dyes and steaming were explored. Dye chemistry became a new field of research. In all aspects of calico manufacture, competition was fierce and industrial espionage rampant; production exploded.

European Resistance to Calico

The path to commercial success was not straightforward. To protect its own textile manufacturers, France enacted a complex succession of prohibitions against importing, printing, wearing, and using *chintes* and cottons, effectively destroying its own opportunities from 1686 to 1759. In 1701, established English manufacturers got similar satisfaction, notably in the form of prohibitions against using, wearing, and importing calicos except for re-export. This was augmented twenty years later by prohibitions against using or wearing painted, printed, or dyed cottons made at home, with the exception of printed linens or fustians (linen warp with cotton weft) which were taxed. From 1774 to 1811, cottons woven with three blue selvage threads could be printed for export and a tax drawback obtained. Smuggling and subterfuge ensured that the market remained supplied; legal attempts to foil calico consumption were eventually abandoned.

Cotton and prints became accepted as facts of life. America gradually joined England, France, Holland, Germany, and Switzerland in the business of printing cottons. England surpassed its own reputation as the world's source of fine wools to become the world's source of plain and printed cotton cloth, exporting cheap cotton even to India by the 1840s.

Calicos are often made at least partly of polyester in the twenty-first century, and it may be safe to say that anyone who wears clothes has worn calico—a phenomenon founded on the ambitions of European spice traders to get to the pepper first. It could be argued that the industrial revolution happened in order to generate and supply a global appetite for calico. Machinery, chemistry, and transportation all tumbled into place seemingly to accomplish this purpose.

An engraver puts a design onto a printing roller. Hand-painted calico was very time-consuming and expensive to produce, and processes for printing and dyeing calico fabric were developed during the eighteenth and nineteenth centuries. © BETTMAN/CORBIS. REPRODUCED BY PERMISSION.

See also **Chintz.**

BIBLIOGRAPHY

Brédif, Josette *Toiles de Jouy.* London: Thames and Hudson, Inc., 1989.

Irwin, John, and P. R. Schwartz. *Studies in Indo-European Textile History.* Ahmedabad, India: Calico Museum of Textiles, 1966.

Irwin, John, and Katharine B. Brett. *Origins of Chintz.* London: Her Majesty's Stationer's Office, 1970.

Susan W. Greene

CALLOT SISTERS The Paris couture house Callot Sisters was founded in 1895 by four sisters, Marie Gerber, Marthe Bertrand, Régine Tennyson-Chantrelle, and Joséphine Crimont, at 24, rue Taitbout. The sisters came from an artistic family; their mother was a talented lace maker and embroiderer, and their father, Jean-Baptiste Callot, was an artist who came from a family of lace makers and engravers (including the esteemed seventeenth-century artist Jacques Callot) and taught at the École nationale supérieure des beaux-arts. Before opening the couture salon, the sisters owned a shop that sold antique laces, ribbons, and lingerie. Madame Gerber was generally acknowledged as the head designer and had worked as a *modéliste* (a designer who works under the house name but is not credited) with the firm Raudnitz et cie. By 1900 Callot Sisters was employing six hundred workers and had clientele in Europe and America. The house's inclusion in the 1900 Paris Exposition Universelle, where it displayed dresses alongside such venerable couture firms as Doucet, Paquin, Redfern, Rouff, and Worth, demonstrates the sisters' respected place within the industry.

A number of designers, including Madeleine Vionnet and Georgette Renal, began their careers at Callot Sisters before launching their own couture houses. According to Vionnet, who worked at the house from 1901 to 1907, Madame Gerber was a friend of the art collector and critic Edmond de Goncourt, with whom she shared an interest in the Orient and eighteenth-century rococo design. The decor of the sisters' salon reflected these two influences, and they received their clients in a Chinese-style room adorned with Coromandel lacquer, Song dynasty silks, and Louis XV furniture. The house's design repertoire encompassed daywear, tailored suits, and evening dresses, but it was best known for its ethereal, eighteenth-century-inspired dishabille and exotic evening dress influenced by the East.

The sisters' luxurious tea gowns, produced in the early part of the century, were made of silk, chiffon, and organdy and often incorporated costly antique laces into their designs. Their penchant for such delicate materials prompted Marcel Proust to write, in *Remembrance of Things Past*, that the sisters "go in rather too freely for lace" (p. 675). Their layered, filmy, pastel-toned garments were very fashionable; such contemporaries as Jacques Doucet and Lucile also created such "confections," as they were often described.

In the 1910s and early 1920s the house's garments also drew upon the brilliant fauvist colors and Eastern-inspired design that were a vital part of the visual culture of the period. While this exotic mode is commonly associated with the designer Paul Poiret, the sisters also created clothing that incorporated embellishment and construction techniques derived from Asia and Africa. Some of these dresses (sometimes referred to as *robes phéniciennes*) integrated design elements from the two continents into one garment. For example, a kimono sleeve might be used with an Algerian burnoose form. Madeleine Vionnet recalls that the adoption of the kimono sleeve was Madame Gerber's innovation and that she was incorporating the cylindrical sleeve into art nouveau dresses in the early part of the century.

The year 1914 was significant for the design house, in that it marked both a move to 9–11, avenue Matignon and the sisters' involvement in Le syndicat de défense de la grande couture française. Through this organization, Callot Sisters, along with the designers Paul Poiret, Jacques Worth, Jeanne Paquin, Madeleine Cheruit, Paul Rodier, and Bianchini and Ferier, put in place controls to protect their original designs from copy houses that sold them to ready-to-wear manufacturers without their permission. This is the period when the Callot Sisters, and many other designers, began to date their labels. While fashion activity in Paris subsided somewhat during World

"There are very few firms at present, one or two only, Callot—although they go in rather too freely for lace—Doucet, Cheruit, Paquin sometimes. The others are all horrible. . . . . Then is there a vast difference between a Callot dress and one from any ordinary shop?" Albertine responds that there is a great difference because what one could buy for three hundred francs in an ordinary shop will cost two thousand at Callot soeurs (Proust, p. 675).

War I, the house of Callot remained open, and the sisters continued to promote their clothing in America by exhibiting at the 1915 Pacific Panama International Exposition in San Francisco, California. By the 1920s the house also expanded its operations to include branches in Nice, Biarritz, Buenos Aires, and London, further extending the international recognition of their label.

Callot Sisters remained active throughout the 1920s and participated in the 1925 Exposition internationale des arts décoratifs et industriels modernes in Paris, along with Jeanne Lanvin, the house of Worth, and the jeweler Cartier in the Pavilion of Elegance. By 1926, however, the fashionability of the house was on the wane. The American designer Elizabeth Hawes, who was working as a copyist in Paris in 1926, writes of dressing herself at Callot for some time and "getting some beautiful bargains in stylish clothes which lasted me for years. I had an extra fondness for Callot because the American buyers found her out of date and unfashionable. She was. She just made simple clothes with wonderful embroidery. Embroidery wasn't chic" (Hawes p. 66). The sisters retained their interest in fashionable detail and luxurious materials even when the more graphic lines of the art deco silhouette were in ascendance.

In 1928 Madame Gerber's son Pierre took over the firm and moved it to 41, avenue Montaigne, where it remained until Madame Gerber retired in 1937. At that time the company was absorbed into the house of Calvet, although labels with the Callot Sisters name appeared until the closing of Calvet in 1948.

See also **Art and Fashion; Haute Couture; Orientalism; Paris Fashion; Proust, Marcel; Vionnet, Madeleine.**

BIBLIOGRAPHY

Chantrell, Maria Lyding. *Les Moires-Mesdames Callot Soeurs.* Paris: Paris Presses du Palais-Royal, 1978.

Hawes, Elizabeth. *Fashion Is Spinach.* New York: Random House, 1938.

Kirke, Betty. *Madeleine Vionnet.* San Francisco: Chronicle Books, 1998.

Milbank, Caroline Rennolds. *Couture: The Great Designers.* New York: Stewart, Tabori and Chang, Inc., 1985.

Proust, Marcel. *Remembrance of Things Past.* Vol. 2: *Within a Budding Grove.* Translated by C. K. Scott Moncrieff and Frederick A. Blossom. New York: Random House, 1927–1932.

Steele, Valerie. *Paris Fashion: A Cultural History.* New York and Oxford: Oxford University Press, 1988.

Michelle Tolini Finamore

CAMBRIC, BATISTE, AND LAWN From the early Middle Ages, the Low Countries had supplied Europe with superb linen fabrics. Among these was a thin, soft, notably white, closely woven, plain weave cloth called cambric after the Flemish city of its origin, Kambryk, now a French city called Cambrai. The French name for cambric, "batiste," reputedly honors the first cambric weaver, John Baptiste. This specialty item was preferred for ecclesiastical wear, fine shirts, underwear, shirt frills, cravats, collars and cuffs, handkerchiefs, and infant wear.

At the same time, India had been exporting cottons to neighboring countries in the Near East, Africa, and to southeast Asia. Although trade between Europe and the Levant brought Indian quilted silks and Indonesian spices into northern homes, cotton apparently held little appeal. In the early seventeenth century, as a spin-off of their spice trade, the English and Dutch East India Companies gradually began importing into Europe various India cottons, from sheer *mulmulls* to brilliantly colored, painted *chintes*. The finer muslins presented increasingly stiff competition to cambric weavers because they were more affordable; the traders obliged, assisting the idea by grafting familiar linen names like "cambric" onto the Indian product.

Struggling to survive efforts to stymie their competition with domestic textile manufacturers, European calico printers undertook to produce their own calico (plain cotton) for printing, rather than depend upon Indian trade goods. The English had learned to make fustian, originally a worsted fabric, from linen and cotton. To comply with and transcend prohibitions against importing India cottons, some manufacturers succeeded in producing fustians that closely resembled the Indian original. This accomplished, manufacturers went on to master the skills of spinning and weaving very fine cotton yarns in imitation of the Indian muslins. Consequently, linen and cotton cambrics existed side by side in the nineteenth century along with "percales" and "jaconet" muslins, which were a bit denser. Flimsy, heavily sized cotton "lining cambric" came into use by the nineteenth century for lining lightweight clothes. It was too sleazy for outerwear, except for such things as masquerade costumes, and became limper still if dampened.

By the early twentieth century, cambric was known as a fine cotton characterized by a smooth, lustrous fin-

Portrait of a Lady, **by Rogier van der Weyden, circa 1435.** A thin, soft, closely woven linen, known as cambric and batiste, was produced in France. The cloth was used for religious apparel, fine shirts, and underwear. © BILDARCHIV PREUSSISCHER KULTURBESTZ/ART RESOURCE, NY. REPRODUCED BY PERMISSION.

ish. In the twenty-first century its original distinction of fineness has been all but lost, and polyester often displaces cotton. Modern uses for polyester cambric are much the same as the earliest ones. Blouses, thin shirts, summer dresses, infant clothing, pajamas, robes, and underwear are still made of cambric; sometimes it is possible to find items made of fine cotton, but ironically the fabric may well have been woven in India.

Another fine linen known as lawn after the French city of its origin—Laon—had characteristics very similar to those of cambric. Of the two, lawn was the most likely to be sheer. The earliest lawns often were woven with stripes, figures, or openwork in them, while cambric was not. Cambric, lawn, and batiste now are made virtually alike, of cotton or polyester in varying degrees of fineness. They are easily confused because they differ mainly in points of finish.

See also **Cotton; Linen; Muslin.**

BIBLIOGRAPHY

Carmichael, W. L., George E. Linton, and Isaac Price. *Callaway Textile Dictionary*. La Grange, Fla.: Callaway Mills, 1947.

Irwin, John, and P. R. Schwartz. *Studies in Indo-European Textile History*. Ahmedabad, India: Calico Museum of Textiles, 1966.

Montgomery, Florence. *Textiles in America*. New York: W. W. Norton and Company, 1984.

Susan W. Greene

CAMEL HAIR The two-humped Bactrian camel furnishes the world with camel hair. Domestic Bactrian camels are an ancient crossbreed of the one-humped *Camelus dromedarius* of Syria and the two-humped, *Camelus bactranus* of Asia. The two camels were crossbred long ago to combine the heat resistance of the one-humped camel's fiber with the superior resistance to cold of the two-humped camel's fiber.

China produces the majority of the world's supply of camel hair, with the provinces of Xinjian and Inner Mongolia providing the most. The country of Mongolia is also a major supplier.

Each camel produces about five pounds of hair fiber per year. The fiber is double coated, meaning that it has one layer of long, coarse guard hairs, and an undercoat of soft, fine, downy fiber.

Camel hair is harvested in the spring of each year by shearing or by collecting the hair as it sheds naturally from the animals during their six- to eight-week molting season in the spring. In nomadic societies of years' past, a person called a "trailer" followed the camel caravan, collecting hair tufts as they dropped on the trail during the day and from the area where the camels had bedded down for the night. By the early 2000s shearing was done to increase the efficiency of harvest. The hair over the humps is generally left unshorn to increase the camel's disease resistance over the summer months.

The camel hair is roughly graded after it is shorn, then it is brought to herdsmen's cooperatives and central distribution facilities for further sorting and grading. Only about 30 percent of the raw fiber is suitable for apparel products.

Camel hair's three grades are determined by the color and fineness of the fiber. The highest grade is reserved for camel hair that is light tan in color and is fine and soft. This top grade fiber is obtained from the camel's undercoat and is woven into the highest quality fabrics with the softest feel and most supple drape.

The second grade of camel hair fiber is longer and coarser than the first. The consumer can recognize fabric using the second grade of camel hair by its rougher feel and by the fact that it is usually blended with sheep's wool that has been dyed to match the camel color.

A third grade is for hair fibers that are quite coarse and long, and are tan to brownish-black in color. This lowest grade of fibers is used within interlinings and interfacing in apparel where the fabrics are not seen, but help to add stiffness to the garments. It is also found in carpets and other textiles where lightness, strength, and stiffness are desired.

Under a microscope, camel's hair appears similar to wool fiber in that it is covered with fine scales. The fibers have a medulla, a hollow, air-filled matrix in the center of the fiber that makes the fiber an excellent insulator.

Camel hair fabric is most often seen in its natural tan color. When the fiber is dyed, it is generally navy blue, red, or black. Camel hair fabric is most often used in coats and jackets for fall and winter garments that have a brushed surface. Camel hair gives fabric warmth without weight and is especially soft and luxurious when the finest of fibers are used.

See also **Mohair.**

BIBLIOGRAPHY

Sclomm, Boris. "Gaining an Insight into Camel-Hair Production." *Wool Record* (November 1985): 25, 29.

Internet Resources

Petrie, O. J. *Harvesting of Textile Animal Fibers: FAO Agricultural Service Bulletin No. 122*. Food and Agricultural Organization of the United Nations, Rome, 1995. Available from <http://www.fao.org/docrep/v93843/v9384e00.htm>.

Ann W. Braaten

CAMOUFLAGE CLOTH Camouflage cloth was developed during the twentieth century to make military personnel less visible to enemy forces. The word "camouflage" (from a French expression meaning "puffing smoke") refers to a process of evading visual detection through some combination of blend-in coloration, cryptic patterning, and blurring of the silhouette. Camouflage is widespread in the natural world, from the barklike coloration and patterning of many moths to the stripes of tigers and zebras. Used by predators and prey alike, camouflage is all about gaining a survival edge in situations of conflict.

Human beings have no natural camouflage features, but it is likely that some forms of camouflage have been used by humans for thousands of years. Prehistoric hunters would readily have learned to attach pieces of brush or clumps of grass to their clothing in order to approach prey undetected. In historic times, Indian hunters of the American Great Plains practiced a related technique, mimicry, by draping themselves in bison skins to approach herds of bison without alarming them.

The same techniques of camouflage that were employed by early hunters were applicable to small-scale tribal warfare and raiding. However, the development of large-scale military operations, which accompanied the rise of civilization and the invention of metal weapons, made camouflage less important. Warfare for many centuries consisted largely of combat between forces in plain view of each other; camouflage has no role in an army of massed swordsmen or spearmen. Well into the nineteenth century, many armies wore brightly colored uniforms (such as the British redcoats) to aid in maintaining formations and to boost morale.

Armies fighting colonial and frontier wars, however, found such uniforms a disadvantage when dealing with irregular forces who fought from hidden places and employed time-honored camouflage techniques used in hunting and raiding. The development of improved firearms capable of accurate long-distance fire at individual targets also made it important for troops to make themselves less conspicuous.

During the nineteenth century, British military forces in India encountered khaki (Urdu for "dust-colored") cloth, which they began to adopt for field use. Khaki uniforms were standard-issue for British troops in the South African Boer War in the 1890s, which featured widespread use of guerrilla tactics by the Boer forces.

Camouflage paint in various colors and cryptic patterns was used by German, French, and other forces during World War I to decrease the visibility of bunkers, tanks, and even ships, but camouflage was not widely used to protect troops during that war. In the 1920s, the French military conducted extensive research into camouflage, and other armed forces soon followed suit; camouflage cloth as such dates to the period between the two World Wars. During World War II, camouflage paint and netting were extensively used to disguise combat vehicles and forward bases, and troops on all sides used camouflage-cloth combat uniforms or tunics in some situations (including white outfits for winter, arctic, and mountain operations). A problem arose in that camouflage cloth made it difficult for troops to distinguish friend from foe under combat conditions. Partly for that reason, American soldiers in WWII largely abandoned camouflage gear except for their helmets, with netting covers into which twigs, grass, and leaves could be inserted.

American troops continued to avoid camouflage cloth in the Korean War, but camouflage gear became ubiquitous in military forces worldwide during the 1950s. Camouflage outfits were widely used by American troops during the Vietnam War, the Gulf War, and other operations. Patterns and color schemes have been continually refined to produce better results in different environments, including jungle, grasslands, and desert.

Camouflage cloth entered the civilian wardrobe in the late 1960s as part of the counterculture appropriation of military surplus clothing for street wear—an ironic response to the Vietnam War. The trend faded but then resumed in the street styles of the 1980s. In the 1990s, in the wake of the Gulf War, camouflage cloth (including some pseudo-military patterns and colors developed especially for the civilian market) again entered civilian wardrobes. It was occasionally used even for such non-military clothing styles as sports jackets for men and dresses and skirts for women. In the second half of the decade, camouflage cloth was incorporated into the collections of several prominent designers, including John Galliano, Anna Sui, and Rei Kawakubo.

In the twenty-first century, camouflage cloth is firmly entrenched in the military wardrobe and continues to appear in civilian clothing from time to time. Though its military connotations are never absent, in some respects camouflage has become just another type of patterned cloth, like animal prints or plaid, available for optional use.

See also **Galliano, John; Protective Clothing; Uniforms, Military.**

BIBLIOGRAPHY

Newark, Tim, Quentin Newark, and J. F. Borsarello. *Brassey's Book of Camouflage.* London: Brassey's (U.K.) Ltd., 1996.

John S. Major

CANES AND WALKING STICKS

CANES AND WALKING STICKS A cane is a rod fabricated from wood, metal, plastic, or glass, used by individuals as walking aids, ceremonial or professional batons, or fashionable accessories. Some historians and collectors distinguish canes from walking sticks by materials, with the former constructed from bamboo and reed plants, and the latter from wood, ivory, or bone. Others distinguish on the basis of geographic linguistics—a cane in America is a walking stick in Europe.

Components and Materials

Most walking sticks and canes consist of a handle, shaft, and ferrules, one between the handle and the shaft to support the cane and conceal the juncture where the two meet, and one, at the bottom of the stick, to prevent wear of the shaft and to prevent splitting.

Wood is the most popular material for the shaft, and almost any kind of wood can be used—for example, chestnut, ebony, or beech. Naturally, the more expensive the wood, the more valuable the cane, and choice of material has historically helped to convey the status of the owner. For example, malacca wood, found only in the Malacca district of Malaysia, must be specially cultivated, and Irish blackthorn is a slow-growing wood that must be cut in parts and set aside for years to harden before it can be fashioned into a walking stick. Both types of canes are considered to be highly desirable for collectors. Other materials include ivory, bone, horn, and even glass. Metal and synthetic materials are also frequently used as orthopedic aids.

A cane's handle is traditionally decorative. Tops can be constructed from silver, gold, ivory, horn, or wood. They may also be fitted with precious gems.

The Many Uses of Canes

Early canes probably originated as weapons of defense or as implements used for journeys over rough terrain. Pilgrims in the Middle Ages used them, as did bishops who traveled with sticks called crosiers. Less self-evident is the history and use of the walking stick for its alternative purposes of ceremony, fashion, or a badge of professional rank or membership.

Modern items such as ski poles, pogo sticks, and white sticks for the blind are based on prototypes of canes.

Ceremony

Although in the early 2000s the cane is considered primarily an orthopedic aid, the ceremonial staff was present as early as Egyptian times.

In a historical context, ceremonial walking sticks and staffs have traditionally conveyed a sense of law and order to others. For example, in the fifteenth century, canes were important royal accessories. Henry VIII used a cane to symbolize British royal power. The cane has also functioned as a ceremonial token of military might. A short stick or baton was a favorite accessory for military officers in Europe between the eighteenth and early twentieth centuries. Canes were not only used in formal military dress but were also sometimes given to commemorate honorable service. It was thought that these canes bestowed confidence upon their owners, and British swagger sticks take their name from this thought. Ceremonial canes may also function as a badge of office or membership, and universities, political parties, and trade guilds adopted their usage for these purposes. The walking stick figures heavily into the official insignia of the medical profession. In the caduceus motif, a snake entwines around a walking stick, and this was modeled on the staff of Aesculapius. In Greek myth, Aesculapius's staff had the power to heal and thus symbolizes the godlike power attributed to the medical profession in modern times.

Fashion

In addition to symbolic ceremonial usage, canes and walking sticks were also indispensable fashion accessories for men and women between the seventeenth and nineteenth centuries, used to display a sense of gentility and social propriety. During this period, canes could be distinguished by day and evening use, and it was assumed that an individual of good social standing would have a cane for every occasion, much in the way that women had an array of daily toilettes. Day canes were wide-ranging in their styles, and rare and expensive materials, ornamentation, and intricate decoration helped to express wealth and taste to others. While men's sticks were stately, women's sticks were often delicately accentuated with ribbons or gilding. Evening sticks were more homogeneous in style. Traditional evening canes were usually made from ebony and were narrower and sometimes shorter than day sticks. Silver knobs or gold bands decorated ferrules and handles. These types of canes are those of popular imagination, featuring heavily into early twentieth-century Hollywood films.

Gadget Canes and Sword Sticks

The gadget stick of the nineteenth and twentieth centuries emerged out of the fashionability of walking sticks. These were canes with an additional purpose; they contained secret items, such as snuffboxes, cosmetic compacts, picnic silverware, and later, radios; or the handle could convert into a seat, or the shaft was actually carved out as a flute. As their name conveys, people tried to top each other's canes of ingenuity and these walking sticks were a great fad.

Sword sticks, a popular item for military officials and dignitaries in the eighteenth century, operated in a similar way to the later gadget canes, although sword sticks were closer to the cane's original historic usage as a defense weapon, rather than for an adherence to fashion. These canes hid swords within their shafts and replaced the prevailing fashion for men to carry both swords and canes on their person. This trend lasted into the 1800s and spawned the development of other weapon sticks and gadget sticks for hunting and sport.

During their heyday, fashion canes, whether decorative or purposeful, were governed by specific rules and etiquette. One was not supposed to carry a walking stick under the arm, nor lean on it. Canes were also not to be used on Sundays or holidays, nor brought on a visit to a dignitary or member of the royal family, given the cane's connotation of authority and rank and its capacity to conceal a weapon.

Manufacturing and Retailing

Canes and walking sticks have traditionally been sold through specialist retailers, such as mountaineering outlets and medical suppliers. Fashion canes were historically found at jewelers or shops that also sold umbrellas and sun parasols and still can be found there in the twenty-first century, although there are far fewer retailers than there were in earlier centuries. Many canes are also purchased through antique dealers, auction houses, or directly from the artisans.

The Decline of the Walking Stick

Until the 1800s, specialist carvers, metal workers, and artisans produced canes and walking sticks by hand. However, the popularity of fashion and gadget canes fueled a market for their mass manufacture and subsequently helped lead to their demise. By the late nineteenth century, materials could be sourced globally and produced in volume for public demand. Canes became less artistic

Moroccan slippers for sale. In the sixteenth century, Moroccan clothing styles began to be influenced by the Ottoman Empire, and some clothing has retained a Turkish flair. (*See* Africa, North: History of Dress) © Jeremy Horner/Corbis.

Left top: **Kapayo Indian tribe.** Due to the hot, humid climates found in many South American countries, some natives wear very little clothing, distinguishing themselves instead with ornamentation such as body paint, jewelry, and headdresses. (*See* America, South: History of Dress) © Whitemore Hank/Corbis Sygma.

Right top: **Indigenous men in Tarabuco, Bolivia.** The men carrying goods here exhibit colorful, wrap-around ponchos over wide-legged, short pants. Felt fedoras as well as helmet-like hats covering the ears, unique to Tarabuco, are also featured. (*See* America, South: History of Dress) © Lynn A. Meisch.

Bottom: **Kuna woman holding a *mola*.** The cotton molas (blouses) worn by the women of the Kuna tribe are brightly colored and often feature images pulled from advertisements or popular entertainment. (*See* America, Central, and Mexico: History of Dress) © Peter Guttman/Corbis.

Veil designed by Elsa Schiaparelli. Italian designer Elsa Schiaparelli often collaborated with artists such as Salvador Dalí to add distinctive accents to her clothing designs. (*See* Art and Fashion) © Philadelphia Museum of Art/Corbis.

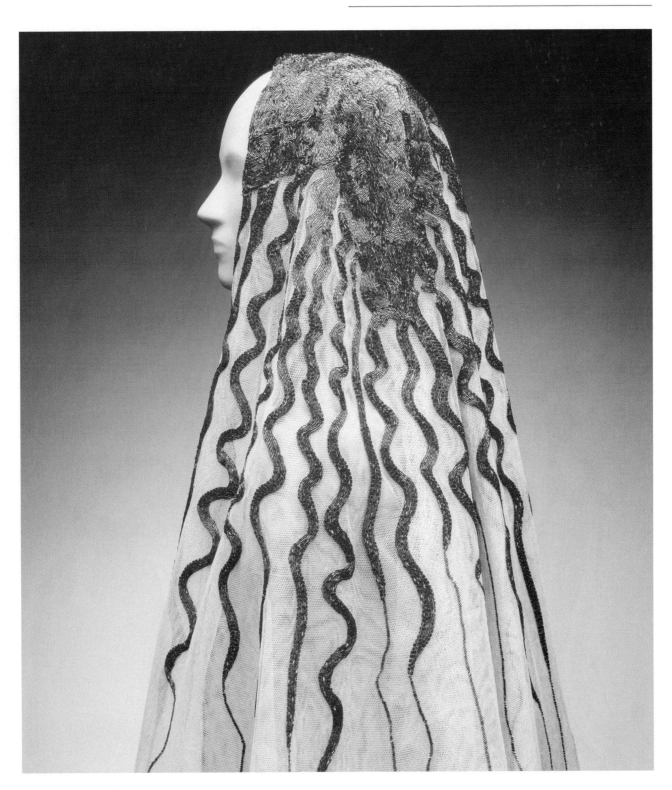

Top: **Gauguin's** *Tahitian Women on the Beach.* The long, flowing dress seen on the right-hand figure is found on many of the Pacific Islands. Tahitians call it a *pareau,* but Americans know it better as the muumuu or the Mother Hubbard. (*See* Asia, Southeastern Islands and Pacific: History of Dress) © Bettmann/Corbis.

Bottom: Dancers in Evening Wear, **1914, by Georges Barbier.** A prolific and skillful artist, Barbier contributed widely to fashion magazines, albums, almanacs, and other publications. (*See* Barbier, Georges) © Historical Picture Archive/Corbis.

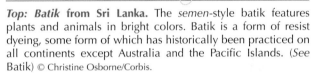

Top: Batik **from Sri Lanka.** The *semen*-style batik features plants and animals in bright colors. Batik is a form of resist dyeing, some form of which has historically been practiced on all continents except Australia and the Pacific Islands. (*See* Batik) © Christine Osborne/Corbis.

Bottom: **1925 Lesage embroidery.** François Lesage, a Parisian designer, has been creating garments with embroidered beadwork since 1924. The Lesage design house spends 16,000 hours a year making samples for its twice-annual collections. (*See* Beads) © Julio Donoso/Corbis Sygma.

Dries van Noten autumn/winter 2002–2003 collection. Belgian designer Dries van Noten's fashions are known for their ethnic or historic tones and often evoke a sense of exoticism. (*See* Belgian Fashion) Dries van Noten; Autumn/Winter 2002–2003. Photo: Yelena Yemchuk.

Woman in carnival costume and makeup. Carnivals have been found in many countries and cultures throughout the centuries, and outrageous dress appears to have always been a key element. (*See* Carnival Dress) © Bob Krist/Corbis.

Below: **Woman in colorful *chador*.** Worn by many Muslim women for reasons of modesty, the Islamic *chador* first developed during the Abbasid Era (750–1258), when the dynastic color was black. Most women continue to wear a black chador, though some choose color. (*See* Chador) © Keren Su/Corbis.

Right top: **Corset worn by Madonna.** Jean-Paul Gaultier designed this famous corset for Madonna's 1991 Blonde Ambition tour. Thanks to Gaultier, Vivienne Westwood, and other designers, corsets saw a resurgence of popularity in the late twentieth century. (*See* Corset) AP/Wide World Photos.

Right bottom: **Russian formal court dress.** During the nineteenth century, distinctive court dress began to evolve in many countries. Russian court dress incorporated traditional design elements, while other nations based their designs on military patterns. (*See* Court Dress) © Reproduced by permission of The State Hermitage Museum, St. Petersburg, Russia/Corbis.

and reflective of current fashions, and the modern crook-handled wood cane became the standard walking stick. By the turn of the century, walking sticks had become either novelty items or orthopedic aids. A London newspaper reported in 1875 how the usefulness of canes for many individuals had declined: "he needs not a help—he has no one to hit, and there is no one who will hit him; he needs not a support—for if he is fatigued, is there not the ponderous bus, the dashing Hansom, or the stealthy subterranean?" (Thornberry 1875).

Indeed, the visibility of canes and walking sticks as fashionable or ceremonial items declined more rapidly during the interwar period. The emergence of the automobile and public transportation and the fashionable popularity of briefcases and attachés rendered the cane less useful as a physical aid or storage device. It lost its traditional association with gentility, power, and authority, instead becoming a symbol primarily associated with the elderly or infirm.

See also **Europe and America: History of Dress (400–1900 C.E.).**

BIBLIOGRAPHY

Boothroyd, A. E. *Fascinating Walking Sticks.* London and New York: White Lion Publishers, 1973.

Dike, Catherine. *Cane Curiosa: From Gun to Gadget.* Paris: Les Editions de l'Amateur; Geneva: Dike Publications, 1983. Good for gadget canes and the many purposes of walking sticks.

Klever, Ulrich. *Walking Sticks, Accessory, Tool and Symbol.* Atglen, Pa.: Schiffer Publishing Ltd., 1984. Good for cultural history.

Stein, Kurt. *Canes and Walking Sticks.* York, Pa.: Liberty Cap Books, 1974. A good overview of the accessory and its many uses.

Thornberry, Walter. "My Walking Stick Shop." In *The Pictorial World.* 3rd edition. July, 1875. In Gilham, F. Excerpts on fashion and fashion accessories 1705–1915, Volume VI: Umbrella and Walking Sticks 1766–1915, 1705–1915. This volume contains an extensive range of primary news cuttings and advertisements for walking sticks. Available from the art library at the Victoria and Albert Museum in London.

Leslie Harris

CAPUCCI, ROBERTO Roberto Capucci was born in Rome on 2 December 1930. He attended the Liceo artistico and the Accademia di Belle Arti di Roma, undecided as to whether to become an architect or a film director. He began designing clothing when he was still quite young and soon turned to fashion as his primary activity.

Early Career
In 1950 Capucci opened his first atelier on the via Sistina in Rome; in 1951 he presented his designs in a fashion show organized by Marchese Giovan Battista Giorgini in Florence. On this occasion, Capucci showed overcoats lined with ermine and leopard, capes edged in dyed fox fur, garments of violet wool with brown and silver brocade—clothing that immediately won for him a loyal following. In reality, Capucci was still too young in 1951 to put together his own shows. The English-speaking fashion press referred to Capucci at this time as the "boy wonder" because he was not yet twenty when he opened his first atelier. Giorgini came up with a plan in which his wife and daughter modeled Capucci's clothes during the show; the buyers literally went wild for the talented young designer. By 1956 Capucci was acclaimed as the best Italian fashion designer by the international press; that same year, he was publicly complimented by Christian Dior. In 1958 he was awarded the Filene's of Boston "Fashion Oscar," given for the first time to an Italian. Capucci was given the American award for his collection of angular clothing, which was part of his *linea "ascatola"* or "white boxes" project. The so-called box look was invented at the end of the 1950s by Capucci, to introduce the concept of architecture, volume, and project; an idea of tailoring related to the dress only. Consuelo Crespi was named the world's most elegant woman wearing one of Capucci's dresses.

In 1962 Capucci opened a workshop on the rue Cambon in Paris, a city he loved and where he was well received. He lived at the Hotel Ritz and was on friendly terms with Coco Chanel. Capucci was the first Italian designer asked to launch a perfume in France. After six years in Paris, Capucci returned to Italy permanently in 1968 and opened an atelier on the via Gregoriana in Rome, which became his headquarters.

Capucci's Work in Costume Design
Capucci designed costumes for films and theatrical productions from the late 1960s through the 1970s. He believed that this experience was fundamental to his later artistic development. In 1968 Capucci designed the costumes for Silvana Mangano—in his opinion the most elegant woman he ever met—and Terence Stamp in Pier Paolo Pasolini's film *Teorema* (1970). In 1986 he designed the priestess's costumes for a production of Vincenzo Bellini's opera *Norma* in the Arena di Verona, in "Omaggio a Maria Callas." In 1995 Capucci was invited to China as a visiting lecturer in fashion design at the Universities of Beijing, Xi'an, and Shanghai.

Capucci's Significance
Capucci is most often associated with haute couture, one-of-a-kind garments, and experimentation with structure. His garments are studies in volume, three dimensional in conception. His research followed both the abstract shape of geometry and the shape inspired by nature. He searched for an individual solution, a style, but he was primarily interested in the shape of the finished garment. He worked with meticulous attention to detail when designing a collection, preparing sometimes as many as a

thousand sketches, always in black and white to better evaluate forms and their metamorphoses and avoid being directly influenced by color. The preparation of a garment could require several months of work. Capucci used yards and yards of fabric, seeking out the most precious materials: taffeta, the softest satin, raw silk, mikado, georgette, and dyed silk from Lyon. It was not so much the rarity of the materials that interested him as the infinite possibilities for their use.

During the 1960s Capucci experimented with commonplace materials like raffia, plastic, straw, sacking, and Plexiglas. But throughout his career Capucci remained faithful to his primary interests—geometry, form, naturalism, and botany. The art critic Germano Celant wrote that his designs might be described by a historian as "soft medieval armor" (Bauzano 2003). Capucci traveled often and drew inspiration from his frequent travels. This influence was reflected in his designs or, as he described it, "the transposition to paper of emotions, ideas, and forms that I see around me when I travel" (Bauzano and Sozzani, p. 40). One of his favorite countries was India.

When ready-to-wear clothing and consumer fashion took hold in Italy during the 1980s in response to the demands of the marketplace, Capucci decided to withdraw from a system he considered unsuited to his way of working. In the beginning of the 1980s he resigned from the Camera Nazionale Della Moda Italiana, translated as the No Profit Association, which was founded in 1958 to discipline, coordinate, and protect the image of Italian fashion. Among other activities the Camera Della Moda is in charge of the organization of four events a year concerning prêt-à-porter: Milano Collezioni Donna (February–March and September–October) and Milano Collezioni Uomo (January and June–July). He decided to show his work no more than once a year, at a time and at a rhythm that suited him, often in museums, and always in a different city—the one that most inspired him at the moment. Clearly, Capucci was not part of Italian ready-to-wear design, a field from which he quickly distanced himself because he felt its logic of mass production was foreign to his creative needs.

Capucci was opposed to the "supermodel" phenomenon, which, in his opinion, obscured the garment, as did all other aspects of contemporary fashion. He preferred to make use instead of opera singers, princesses, the wives of Italy's presidents, and debutantes from the Roman aristocracy. These women were called "capuccine" by the journalist Irene Brin. However, for more solemn occasions, he often turned to the famous and the beautiful: Gloria Swanson, Marilyn Monroe, Jacqueline Kennedy, Silvana Mangano, and the scientist Rita Levi Montalcini, whom he dressed for the Nobel Prize ceremony in 1986.

Capucci's designs are often based on twentieth-century artistic movements: futurism, rationalism (the focus on pure shape for which he searched), and pop art. Referred to as the "Michelangelo of cloth," Capucci claimed, "I don't consider myself a tailor or a designer but an artisan looking for ways of creating, looking for ways to express a fabric, to use it as a sculptor uses clay" (Bianchino and Quintavalle, p. 111). He considered himself a researcher more than a designer. His designs rarely seem to have dressing as their immediate goal. In this sense his creations can be appreciated for their intrinsic beauty and uniqueness. His designs are sculptural and architectural, which the body does not wear but inhabits; they are objects that blur the boundaries between art and fashion.

Capucci's designs have been shown in the world's leading museums, including the Galleria del costume in the Palazzo Pitti in Florence, the Museo Fortuny in Venice, the Victoria and Albert Museum in London, and the Kunsthistorisches Museum in Vienna. He has had many exhibitions of his work in Italy and around the world. In May 2003 the FAI (Fondo Italiano per L'ambiente) at Varese Villa Panza held an exhibition of Capucci's work. Giuseppe Panza di Biumo wrote in the introduction to the exhibition's catalog: "Capucci expresses his personality in a way that distinguishes him from everyone else. He is an artist in the fullest sense of the word, just as the painters who adorned their models with splendid garments." In 2003 Capucci's name became a brand, with a ready-to-wear line designed by Bernhard Willhelm, Sybilla, and Tara Subkoff, who have access to an archive of nearly 30,000 of Capucci's designs.

See also **Dior, Christian; Italian Fashion; Paris Fashion; Perfume; Theatrical Costume.**

BIBLIOGRAPHY

Bauzano, Gianluca, and F. Sozzani, eds. *Roberto Capucci: Lo stupore della forma, Ottanta abiti-scultura a Villa Panza*. Milan: Skira, 2003.

Bianchino, Gloria, and Arturo Carlo Quintavalle. *Moda, dalla fiaba al design*. Novara, Italy: De Agostini, 1989.

Gastel, Minnie. *50 anni di moda italiana*. Milan: Vallardi, 1995.

Laurenzi, L. "Capucci." In *Dizionario della moda*. Edited by Guido Vergani. Milan: Baldini and Castoldi, 1999.

Simona Segre Reinach

CARDIN, PIERRE During the last half of the twentieth century, Pierre Cardin (1922–) became a prominent and widely admired designer as well as a highly successful businessman. Cardin is known for his acute intuition, which often made him a trendsetter and design leader. Cardin has expanded his design operations far beyond fashions for both men and women to encompass all aspects of modern living. The name Cardin has become synonymous with his brand as he has expanded his commercial operations through timely licensing. As of the early 2000s, Cardin's corporate empire held 900 licenses for production in 140 countries.

Pierre Cardin displays his designs. Cardin's fashion empire is known the world over. He is one of the first designers to "brand" his products, which include accessories and handbags, home interiors, luxury cars, and luggage. © REUTERS/CORBIS. REPRODUCED BY PERMISSION.

Early Training

Born in Italy of French parents on 2 July 1922, the designer was originally named Pietro Cardini. After several years in Venice, however, his family relocated to France. As a young man Cardin briefly studied architecture before joining the house of Paquin in 1945. His tenure there gave him the opportunity of working with Christian Bérard and Jean Cocteau on the 1946 film *La Belle et la bête*, for which he created the velvet costume for the Beast, played by Jean Marais. After a brief stint with Elsa Schiaparelli, Cardin worked under the auspices of Christian Dior from 1946 until he went out on his own in 1950. Cardin honed his superb tailoring skills heading up Dior's

coat and suit workroom. Cardin's own business was first located on the rue Richepanse (renamed rue du Chevalier de Saint-George), but later moved to the famed rue du Faubourg Saint-Honoré, where the designer launched his first couture collection in 1953. In 1954 Cardin opened a boutique called Eve, followed by Adam for men in 1957.

From the beginning, Cardin showed himself to be an innovator and a rebel. He was quoted as saying, "For me, the fabric is nearly secondary. I believe first in shape, architecture, the geometry of a dress" (Lobenthal, p. 151). His experimentation with fabrics embraced geometric abstraction without losing sight of the human figure.

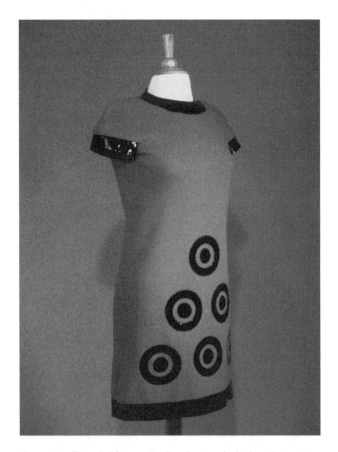

Pierre Cardin minidress. Cardin designed clothes that epitomized the mod look of the early 1960s, creating fashions with a minimalist look that featured clean lines and geometric shapes. This dress features the Cardin trademark bullseye. BULLS-EYE MINIDRESS BY PIERRE CARDIN (C. 1965). GIFT OF LOIS WATSON. COURTESY OF THE TEXAS FASHION COLLECTION, UNIVERSITY OF NORTH TEXAS. PHOTO BY ABRAHAM BENCID, COPYRIGHT 1995.

Cardin's ability to sculpt fabric with an architectural sensibility became his signature. Making garments with impeccable craftsmanship, Cardin possessed the skills and vision to make his dreams a wearable reality. Even during the 1970s, when his dresses shifted from a sculpted look to a more draped silhouette, the fluidity of his work remained formal. Cardin was highly successful as a couturier, but he also sought to redefine the field of fashion design commercially. For his efforts in launching a ready-to-wear line alongside his couture collection, however, Cardin's membership in the prestigious Chambre Syndicale was revoked in 1959. Cardin was soon reinstated, but voluntarily resigned from the Chambre in 1966.

Cardin's Men's Wear

Cardin's early training as a tailor's apprentice shaped his approach to fashion design for men as he matured throughout the 1950s. Cardin deconstructed the traditional business suit. He subtracted collars, cuffs, and lapels, creating one of the most compelling images of the early 1960s. This look became instantly famous when Dougie Millings, the master tailor who made stage outfits for numerous British rock musicians, dressed the Beatles in his version of matching collarless suits.

Cardin's men's wear line was housed in a separate building on the Place Beauvau by 1962. He was inspired by his travels; after seeing the traditional high-collared jacket of India and Pakistan, he distilled its form into another popular innovation in men's fashions of the 1960s, the so-called Nehru jacket. Cardin further disrupted men's customary suiting by heralding the wearing of neck scarves in place of ties, and turtlenecks instead of button-down shirts. Yet he also was capable of designing men's clothing in the classic tradition, such as the costumes worn by the character John Steed in the British television series *The Avengers*.

Space Age and Unisex Styles

Advances in fabric production and technology during the 1960s coincided with a widespread fascination with space exploration. Cardin's Space Age or Cosmocorps collection of 1964 synthesized his streamlined, minimal dressing for both men and women. This body-skimming apparel resembling uniforms featured cutouts inspired by op art. Cardin was innovative in his use of vinyl and metal in combination with wool fabric. Not just unisex, Cardin's clothing often seemed asexual. Unlike such other fashion minimalists as Rudi Gernreich and André Courrèges, Cardin did not promote pants for women. He often used monotone-colored stockings or white patterned tights to compliment his minidresses. The "Long Longuette," which was dubbed the maxidress, was Cardin's 1970 response to the miniskirt. In 1971, Cardin obtained an exclusive agreement with a German firm to use its stretch fabric, declaring that "stretch fabrics would revolutionize fashion" (Weir, p. 5). Continuing his reputation as a trendsetter, he showed white cotton T-shirts paired with couture gowns on the runway in 1974 and introduced exaggerated shoulders in 1979.

Licensing and Global Marketing

Cardin learned much about the business side of fashion from his mentor Christian Dior. Dior had been very successful in trading on his name to license his designs internationally. Cardin took this approach further when he sought and found a global acceptance of his designs in countries as diverse as the Soviet Union, India, and Japan. Cardin was an exponent of what is now called branding long before other fashion designers followed suit. He was the first designer to sell ready-to-wear clothing in the Soviet Union as early as 1971. While Cardin's men's wear lines were ultimately more successful than his women's fashions in the United States during the 1970s, he still owned more than two hundred American retail outlets. Cardin was embraced by the Japanese market with special enthusiasm. At the peak of his expansion in 1969, Cardin boasted of having 192 factories throughout the world.

> "The job of fashion is not just to make pretty suits or dresses, it is to change the face of the world by cut and line. It is to make another aspect of men evident."
>
> Pierre Cardin (in Lobenthal, p. 153)

Cardin's fashion empire spanned the globe with his trademark licensing as of the early 2000s. Products identified by the Cardin brand ranged from accessories and handbags to home interiors, luxury cars, and luggage, as well as to such personal items as Fashion Tress wigs, introduced in 1973. The ubiquitous brand name was recognized around the world. As Caroline Milbank stated, "It is difficult to name something that Pierre Cardin has yet to design or transform with his imprint" (Milbank, p. 338). In 1971, Cardin transformed the former Théâtre des Ambassadeurs into L'Espace Cardin to promote new talent in performance art and fashion design. Cardin capitalized again on his fame in 1981 by purchasing Maxim's, the famous Paris restaurant, and using its name to build a worldwide chain of restaurants in the mid-1980s.

Brand Identity and Logos

During the early 1960s, Cardin was a pioneer in designing clothing conspicuously adorned with his company's logo. This trend was picked up by many other designers from the 1970s onward. Cardin's logos, consisting of his initials or a circular bull's eye, were often three-dimensional vinyl appliqués or quilted directly into the garment. Cardin's unrestrained licensing, while symbolic of his success, may have resulted in untimely diluting his name brand image.

Many fashion writers criticized Cardin for overexposure, especially given the very rapid expansion of his product lines during the 1980s and 1990s. Nevertheless, Cardin's name was known throughout the world, and identified by the public with quality and high standards. Cardin stood out as one of the most complex designers of the twentieth century because he was one of a handful who understood that fashion is above all a business. His skills as an entrepreneur, and especially his creative licensing, made Pierre Cardin one of the richest people in the fashion world.

See also **Brands and Labels; Dior, Christian; Fashion Marketing and Merchandising; Logos; Nehru Jacket; Paquin, Jeanne; Paris Fashion; Schiaparelli, Elsa; Space Age Styles; Unisex Clothing; Vinyl as Fashion Fabric.**

BIBLIOGRAPHY

Lobenthal, Joel. *Radical Rags: Fashions of the Sixties.* New York: Abbeville Press, 1990.

Lynam, Ruth, ed. *Couture: An Illustrated History of the Great Paris Designers and Their Creations.* Garden City, N.Y.: Doubleday, 1972.

Mendes, Valerie. *Pierre Cardin: Past, Present, Future.* London and Berlin: Dirk Nishen Publishing, 1990.

Milbank, Caroline Rennolds. *Couture: The Great Designers.* New York: Stewart, Tabori, and Chang, Inc., 1985.

Weir, June. "Cardin Today . . . A New Freedom." *Women's Wear Daily* (26 January 1971): 5.

Myra Walker

CARICATURE AND FASHION From the Italian for "charge" or "loaded," the caricature print emerged in large numbers in the eighteenth century in industrializing western Europe. It was in the second half of the twentieth century that the caricature that concerned itself primarily with the subject of fashion and manners, rather than political or portrait themes, developed. The origins and conventions of the fashion caricature include overlapping literary, theatrical, and popular religious and artistic traditions. Greco-Roman theorizations, performances, and artistic depictions of the cosmic world turned upside down, and late medieval woodcuts, in which memento mori themes of the dance of death and the bonfire of the vanities established the tropes of the veneer of civilization and the futility of dress and cosmetics in arresting earthly time. The European carnival tradition, commedia dell'arte and puppetry, which highlight human foibles, and the figure of the hag who deploys fashion and makeup in an act of sartorial and spiritual delusion provided subjects for major artists working in the etching media such as Giambattista Tiepolo (1696–1770), Domenico Tiepolo (1727–1804), and Francisco de Goya (1746–1828). Not fashion caricatures as such, nor were these images widely available, but their themes recur in the eighteenth-century caricature print.

Caricature fashion prints also exist in a relationship to respectful engravings of the cries or occupations of the town, plates depicting national dress, and "costume plates" depicting courtier men and "women of quality" by seventeenth-century artists including Abraham Bosse and J. D. de Saint-Jean in France and the Bohemian Wenceslaus Hollar (1607–1677) working in England. The work of Jacques Callot (1592–1635) in France crosses the boundary between observation and satire. Etched images take on new meanings when pointed titles or moralizing verse are appended; the caricature generally makes use of a combination of word and image. Although censorship restricted production in France, prints were produced in neighboring Holland, and an early eighteenth-century fashion caricature entitled "The Powdered Poodle" survives in which the high-heeled shoes, forward posture, and long blond wig popularized by the court of Louis XIV is mocked in both image and appended verse (Paris, Bibliothèque Nationale).

Man tight-lacing a woman's corset. Caricatures began in Europe in the eighteenth century to depict social, political, national, geographic, and ethnic identity. New developments on the social, economic, and technological fronts were shown through exaggerated illustrations of clothing, dress, and mannerisms. © BETTMANN/CORBIS. REPRODUCED BY PERMISSION.

Eighteenth-Century Caricature

Drawing on Renaissance physiognomic studies or "caprices" by Leonardo da Vinci, Giuseppe Arcimboldo, and Albrecht Dürer, and the baroque caricatures of Annibale and Agostoni Carracci (*Heads*, c. 1590) and Gianlorenzo Bernini, eighteenth-century Italy saw a rise in the production of recognizable portrait caricatures. They included carefully delineated costumes etched by Pier Leone Ghezzi (1674–1755) and Pietro Longhi (1702–1785), and painted in Rome by the English artists Sir Joshua Reynolds (1723–1792) and Thomas Patch (1725–1782). These works did not circulate widely in the public realm but were designed for the amusement of aristocratic circles participating in the Grand Tour who understood the dialectic of the ideal and the debased explored in this work. Furnishing their sitters with hideous physiognomies and ill-formed bodies loaded with fine clothing and airs, the works depict the dress and demeanor of the aristocrat abroad when the mask of civility has slipped under the influence of alcohol and other vice. The paintings of Patch and Reynolds drew upon the

painted "modern moral subject" and subsequent etching cycles produced in England by William Hogarth (*The Harlot's Progress* 1731; *The Rake's Progress* 1733–1734; *Marriage à la Mode* 1743). Cinematic in its scenic narrative, Hogarth's finely produced work included satirical details of fashionable dress and deportment that were used to emphasize more general political, aesthetic, and moral questions.

As new and cheaper forms of reproduction and literate audiences for periodicals and prints arose in Enlightenment western Europe, there was a marked increase in the output of satirical printmaking from the 1760s in France, Germany, and the Dutch Republic, but notably England. England's freedom of the press and involvement of the public in political and cultural affairs through coffeehouse, print, and exhibition culture encouraged the production of thousands of caricatures. Fashion had two principal functions in these prints. In the first half of the century, the English political print included dress to indicate class, political party, geographic, ethnic, and national identity. In tandem with theatrical precedents, the shorthand device for a Frenchman was elaborate court dress and a simpering posture, for a Spaniard a ruff, and a Dutchman round breeches. Nationalist Tories and the English John Bull figure wore rustic frock coats and boots, in contrast to the rich court dress of Whigs which resembled that of continental court culture.

In the second half of the century, numerous English printmakers who were also printsellers switched their output from political caricatures to social ones in which fashion formed the principal and not the secondary subject. Matthew and Mary Darly, John Dawes, William Humphrey, William Holland, Samuel W. Fores, Carington and John Bowles, and John Raphael Smith exhibited their wares publicly in shop windows and printed single sheet caricatures that were sold in folio sets, reproducing the designs of others such as John Collett, Robert Dighton, Henry W. Bunbury, and Thomas Rowlandson. Themes include the speed of new fashionable items, textiles, patterns, and bodily silhouettes; the alleged spread of fashionability to the lower orders including the servant class; the concomitant difficulty of reading the social sphere; themes of metropolitan urbanity versus rustic simplicity; the role of the appearance trades, such as wigmaking and hairdressing, in promoting fashion; and alleged relationships between national fashions and character. The disjunction between the applied finery of fashion and the lumpen, deluded, or immoral physical body beneath continued older Christian themes.

The caricature print from 1760 extends the more general cultural association of women with extremes of fashion to that of men, as they scrutinize extensively the airs and dress of the macaroni (c. 1760–1780) and later the buck and the dandy (c. 1800–1820). Prints included both fictive and recognizable metropolitan individuals as well as referring to stock theatrical types such as the fop, the German friseur (an aged and ugly male hairdresser whose physiognomy was interchangeable with the Jew), the dancing-master (French and effete), the rustic, and the Scotsman, a "Billingsgate Moll" (a market woman), and a "Lady of the Town" (prostitute). In the etched prints of Matthew Darly, the more lowborn the person depicted, the more crude the illustrative style, suggesting a cruder imitation or performance of fashionability. These differences perpetuate the belief that the orders are inherently either vulgar or superior depending on rank, as well as highlighting the joke contained in the overstepping of sartorial boundaries from class to class. Just as the development of caricature demands its opposite, idealized aesthetics, so the convoluted forms, surprising gestures, and novel departures of caricature perfectly reflected contemporary notions of the chicanery of fashion.

Caricature prints appeared in the expanding number of English periodicals, such as *The London Museum*, *The Oxford Magazine*, and *The Town and Country Magazine*. Sometimes hand-colored, many such prints were also sold or hired out in suites. Etching and engraving were the dominant techniques until the 1770s, when the mezzotint was developed and during the 1780s aquatint and stipple engraving appeared. The latter techniques permitted longer print-runs of more than one thousand and conveyed detailed messages about the texture of clothing and the tone of complexion. Carington Bowles's and John Raphael Smith's figures were also set in backgrounds such as paved streetscapes and neoclassical dressing-rooms and masquerade venues which comment on the spread of consumption, comfort, and new design novelties, including dress.

Caricature prints were relatively expensive, sought out by the aristocracy, the gentry, and collected even by the king. If generally too expensive for the artisan, prints were available for viewing in print shops, on the walls of taverns, coffeehouses, and clubs, or in the 1790s, visited in exhibitions. Satirical prints were generally kept in folios, and it is unclear how often they were glazed and hung. Pasted on walls they made "print-rooms" (Calke Abbey, Derbyshire) and ladies' fans were occasionally composed of them. English prints were imported by French dealers and sent as far as St. Petersburg. Ambassadorial missions reported on their contents to rulers such as Louis XVI.

Although the circuits of exchange between English, French, Dutch, and German fashion caricature have not been clarified by scholars (most work has been done on revolutionary political imagery), it is apparent that the subject and style of English and continental work is interrelated. Hogarth derived much of his compositional virtuosity from a study of the French rococo fashion drawing and print by Boitard, Cochin, Coypel, Watteau, and Gravelot. The Matthew and Mary Darlys' calligraphic linear style set upon evacuated white backgrounds was copied around Europe. A group of crude French engravings on the topic of fops, fashion absurdities, and touristic interactions in the street are virtually indistinguishable in subject matter from English work, and the Darlys were copied in Germany. The French also produced caricature engravings of superb technical perfection and elegance in the 1770s, in which the style and format mocks both high fashion's perfection and the engravings of manners seen in Rétif de la Bretonne's *Monument du costume* (1789).

Meanings of Caricature Fashion Prints

In Germany, Daniel Nikolaus Chodowiecki's engravings for almanacs possess an elegant and animated line that epitomizes the ambiguity of some fashion caricatures. His paired contrasting images on the themes of artifice (court dress) and naturalism (neoclassical dressing) does not necessarily castigate the former: perhaps his suggestion is that pastoral dress is just as much an affectation for leisured peoples. His illustrations for Johann Kaspar Lavater's highly influential study of character and physiognomy (1775–1778) with a considerable focus on dress, do function as explicit attacks on ancien régime manners and morals and argue that the new man must reject the set of the courtier.

Eighteenth-century prints were often reproduced in the nineteenth century without the context of their original verbal text banners. This led to different interpretations that were frequently sentimental and nostalgic. Approaches to the caricature reflect shifts in twentieth-century art-historical and social analysis. A reflection model used exhaustively by British Museum cataloger and historian M. Dorothy George analyzed caricature prints as representations of real events such as the launch and spread of a new fashion. This approach is reductive in that prints had multiple meanings to different audiences and may have helped create the dynamic of an event. Whereas the art historian Ernst Gombrich argued that the aim of the printmaker and dealer was to sell the product and not unsettle the purchaser overly, the Hogarth historian Ronald Paulson argued that within graphic satire a range of explanations are true and not mutually exclusive. Paulson argued that Hogarth's work was designed for more than one audience and one reading. Like the theater, which assumed different reading positions from its multiple publics, the power of the caricature print is to function on several levels simultaneously. Although Brewer notes that there is almost no surviving evidence of how the common people viewed popular imagery, such as the caricature prints, there are many contemporary descriptions of the street and the theater, which emphasize that the fashionable and wealthy were often mocked or even abused for their pretension. Fashion caricatures participated in this dialogue.

Some men and women "of family and estate" such as W. H. Bunbury, Lady Diana Beauclerc, and the Marquis Townshend produced sketches which were engraved and distributed by professionals. Many of them laugh at the pretensions of the lower orders that emulate the manners and dress previously reserved for their social betters.

This is not the only meaning, however. As Maidment notes of the early-nineteenth-century "literary dustman" type, in form and technique such prints might simultaneously highlight the energy and ingenuity of laboring class subjects at the same time as mocking aspirational behavior. It partly explains the longevity of the caricature print in periodicals for all classes. Caricature fashion prints also provided information about the mood or set of a fashion such as the insouciance of the *Incroyable*, a fop of the Directoire period. As Anne Hollander noted of Renaissance art, forms such as engravings might teach people what it was to look fashionable. In the eighteenth century, high-art painting and caricature were both means through which fashion was read, experienced, and modulated.

Nineteenth-Century Caricature
Master illustrators in the nineteenth century continued the themes on fashion laid down in the 1760s, notably Thomas Rowlandson (1756–1827) who worked for publisher Ackermann, James Gillray (1757–1815), Robert Dighton (1752–1814) and son Richard; Isaac Cruikshank (1756–1811) and sons Robert (1789–1856) and George (1792–1878). In the Revolutionary and Napoleonic period, dress featured as part of the textual jokes in political caricature. Respectful fashion plates and caricatures issued from the same hand of experienced illustrators: Jean-Francois Bosio (1764–1827) and Philibert Louis Debucourt (1755–1832), who deployed an extremely elegant style and fine coloring as part of the joke. In Paris the famed series by Horace Vernet, *Le Supreme bon ton* from *Caricatures parisiennes* (c. 1800) used the figure types and linear illustrative style of the contemporary fashion periodical, but distorted the figures, poses, and situations to expose the ludicrous nature of contemporary manners. H. Vernet provided "serious" fashion plates for Pierre La Mésangère, who was both the publisher of *Le journal des dames et des modes* (c. 1810) as well as the famous caricature series *Incroyables et merveilleuses* (1810–1818), which continued the work of his father, Carle Vernet (1758–1836), from the 1790s. The paradox and collisions of exoticism and historicism of early-nineteenth-century dress is extremely well conveyed in these French images. The series *Le bon genre* (French periodical 1814–1816) set English and French fashions side by side, subject to some distortion, in order to have a ready-made caricature that also provides fashion information and comments on national identity. Louis-Léopold Boilly's exquisite painted genre scenes of fashionable life often verge on caricature with rather too much male and female buttock revealed through the chamois leather and muslin, and this interest was made explicit in his *Recueil de grimaces* (Paris, 1823–1828), caricature physiognomy lithographic studies.

Nineteenth-Century Journalism and the Caricature
In the nineteenth century, reading publics and leisure time increased and the costs of printing decreased, with a massive expansion of cheap periodicals and news-sheets including journals who now took the caricature as their very subject: in France *La caricature* (1830–1835) and its successor *Le charivari* (1832–1842) were run by Charles Philipon. Technical developments in lithographic, steel engraving, and wood-block reproductions meant that the caricature proliferated within these formats and ceased to be sold primarily within folio sets. When from 1835 political censorship was introduced in France, the caricature of Parisian manners became the screen through which other events might be filtered. Social, economic, and technological developments had major impacts upon fashion and there is no social topic in which the caricature did not participate. These included, but were not restricted to, male dandyism; the rise of the demimonde or courtesan class; sweatshops and the production of clothing; shopping and the department store; makeup and artifice; swells or dandies; middle-class hypocrisy and propriety; immodesty and the ball gown; women's participation in sport and education; feminism and the suffragette movement; dress reform; emancipation and embourgeoisement of slaves; issues of class and the "servant problem"; the aesethetic movement of the 1880s; and the general spread of consumer goods. Extremes and novelties of fashion, such as the women's crinoline and the bustle, the nature of fashionability and the *Parisienne*, and the interaction of the classes in the new public spaces of the metropoli of Paris, London, and New York, were delineated by highly accomplished artists working in lithography, notably Gustave Doré (1832–1883), J. J. Grandville (1803–1846), Joseph Traviès, Paul Gavarni (1804–1866), and Cham and J. L. Forain (1852–1931) Honoré Daumier (1808–1879) produced a massive output of 4,000 lithographs, many appearing in *Le charivari* and *Le Journal amusant*. His human comedy in which the same characters reappear relates to that of Balzac's literature. Nineteenth-century caricature employed novel compositional formats with overlapping vignettes and asymmetrical strip formats, as seen in the periodical *La Vie parisienne*.

In England Max Beerbohm and George du Maurier provided the journal *Punch*, or the *The London Charivari* (from 1841) with a constant stream of caricatures that contributed to the tenacious idea that fashions for both men and women represented an absurdity. Its illustrator John Leech termed the word "cartoon" within *Punch* in 1843. The German middle-class public had numerous journals in which fashion caricatures recurred—*Punsch* (1847), *Leipziger Charivari* (1858), *Berliner Charivari* (1847), and *Kladderadatsch* (1848); the generic term "Biedermeier" for the period referred to a middle-class everyman fictional figure. The journal *Simplizissimus* (from 1896) led to the milieu in which expressionists like Georg Grosz (1893–1959) produced stinging comments on the human condition, using dress to mark out issues of class, gender, and sexuality. In North America enormous amounts of fashion-related caricature were produced for journals after the 1820s such as *American Comic Almanach* (from

1841), *Punchinello, Harper's Weekly,* and *Vanity Fair.* At the turn of the century the work of Charles Dana Gibson blurred the distinction between satire and the exaggerated fashionability of the Gibson girl, a gentle caricature that might be emulated for the turn of a head or silhouette of a skirt. In that the cartoon strip, comic book, and Disney film rely on caricature for their conventions, North America generated several industries from this form.

Until the post-World War II period when photography eclipsed line and other drawing in the media, the fashion caricature continued to be prominent within twentieth-century periodicals for all classes. Many of the fashion images commissioned by French couturiers including Paul Poiret approach the mannerism of caricature. The work of Erté (Romain de Tirtoff) also blurs the division between the fashion plate and the caricature in order to express a mood. Caricature images constitute important documents of relatively submerged topics including lesbianism and mannish dressing for women in the 1920s and male dress within homosexual communities. The commodification of dress and the rise of the fashion parade as a theatrical spectacle are documented in caricatures by figures such as Sem (Georges Goursat). The ironies of modernist lifestyle were documented by the British caricaturist Osbert Lancaster (*Homes Sweet Homes,* London, 1939). Wartime Britain and America used the caricature as propaganda to castigate wasteful female consumers. The emergence of the New Look was mocked as absurd or extravagant and unsuitable to matronly women in the late 1940s. Illustrator-designers, such as Cecil Beaton, provided high-style magazines like *Vanity Fair* and *Vogue* with both drawn and composite photographic or collaged backdrop renditions of real society women (Elsa Maxwell, the Duchess of Windsor, Coco Chanel) which teetered upon caricature, as well as producing cutting versions for private consumption (Violet Trefusis).

Although caricatures continue to be included as cartoons in newspaper and periodicals, their power declined with the advent of television as an alternative form of entertainment in the 1950s. It could be argued, however, that the techniques of the caricature, related as they were to the theater and vaudeville stereotype, continued within popular culture forms of television and film. Many 1950s and 1960s situation comedies such as *Green Acres* and *I Love Lucy* feature absurd situations involving dress; the 1990s comedy series *Absolutely Fabulous,* written and acted by Dawn French and Jennifer Saunders, made the fashion industry and absurd fashions in dress and lifestyle its subject, as did the Robert Altman film *Pret-à-Porter.* Other popular situation comedies, such as *Designing Women* from the 1980s, *Seinfeld,* and the overdressed and shopping-addicted figure of Karen in the queer sitcom *Will and Grace,* deploy caricature-like exaggeration of dress, pose, and identity which is intertwined with both ancient tropes of theatrical farce and the caricature print of modern culture.

Much postmodern high-fashion illustration in the 1980s and 1990s used the form of the caricature to comment ironically on the place of fashion in contemporary life. The designers Moschino, Christian Lacroix (spring–summer 1994), and Karl Lagerfeld utilize a caricature-like irony in some of their illustration derived from Directoire imagery by the likes of Louis LeCoeur and Debucourt, as well as studying the genre for ideas; some fashion parades and styling by John Galliano and Vivienne Westwood resemble a caricature suite brought to life as a conscious strategy. Galliano's degree show (1984) and some subsequent collections (spring–summer 1986) were directly inspired by *Incroyables et merveilleuses.* Forms that are directly derived from the eighteenth-century caricature continue to be published in daily newspapers (the political cartoon in which prominent figures are characterized through their dress), journals such as *Country Life* (Annie Tempest's Tottering-by-Gently series) and *The New Yorker* (established 1925). Although amusing and trenchant, such caricatures now have an archaic air and may be replaced in the future by the three-dimensional and new temporal possibilities of digital technology. In that surrealism found fertile pickings in English Georgian and nineteenth-century French and German caricature, it could be said that surrealist-inspired contemporary digital fashion photography by Phil Poynter and Andrea Giacobbe continues the ludic project of the fashion caricature consumed in multidimensional ways.

See also **Fashion, Historical Studies of.**

BIBLIOGRAPHY

D'Oench, Ellen G. *"Copper into Gold." Prints by John Raphael Smith 1751–1812.* New Haven, Conn., and London: Yale University Press, 1999.

Donald, Diana. *The Age of Caricature: Satirical Prints in the Reign of George III.* New Haven, Conn., and London: Yale University Press, 1996.

———. *Followers of Fashion. Graphic Satires from the Georgian Period.* London: Hayward Gallery Publishing, 2002.

Duffy, Michael. *The Englishman and the Foreigner: The English Satirical Print 1600–1832.* Cambridge, Mass.: Chadwyck-Healey, 1986.

George, Mary Dorothy. *Hogarth to Cruikshank: Social Change in Graphical Satire.* London: Allen Lane; Penguin, 1967.

Hallett, Mark. *The Spectacle of Difference: Graphic Satire in the Age of Hogarth.* New Haven, Conn., and London: Yale University Press, 1999.

Maidment, B. E. *Reading Popular Prints, 1790–1870.* Manchester. U.K., and New York: Manchester University Press, 1996.

Paston, George [pseudonym for Miss E. M. Symonds]. *Social Caricature in the Eighteenth Century.* London: Methuen and Company, 1905.

Paulson, Ronald. *Hogarth: His Life, Art, and Times.* 2 vols. New Haven, Conn., and London: Yale University Press, 1971.

Perrot, Philippe. *Fashioning the Bourgeoisie: A History of Clothing in the Nineteenth Century.* Translated by Richard Bienvenu. Princeton, N.J.: Princeton University Press, 1994.

Sanders, Mark, et al. *The Impossible Image: Fashion Photography in the Digital Age.* London: Phaidon Press Ltd., 2000.

Peter McNeil

CARNIVAL DRESS In its broadest sense, "carnival" refers to a pageant, festival, or public celebration found all over the world. It originates in prehistoric times, varying in content, form, function, and significance from one culture to another. But in Europe and the Americas, "carnival" refers specifically to the period of feasting and revelry preceding Lent. The general consensus is that it began during the Middle Ages, evolving from the burlesque celebrations associated with Easter, Christmas, and other European festivities such as *Maypole, Quadrille Ball, Entrudo,* and *Hallowmas.* The word is said to derive from the Latin *carnem levare,* meaning abstention from meat or farewell to flesh, reflecting the self-denial such as fasting and penitence associated with Lent. Its synonyms are the French *carementrant* (approaching Lent), the German *fastnacht* (night of fasting) and the English

Women at carnival in Spain. Girls dress in traditional costumes during the carnival celebrations in Seville, Spain. © PATRICK WARD/CORBIS. REPRODUCED BY PERMISSION.

Shrovetide (referring to the three days set aside for confession before Lent).

Another school of thought links the word "carnival" to the Latin *carrus navalis,* a horse-drawn wagon for transporting revelers, arguing that its Christian aspects grew out of the seasonal Dionysian or Bacchanalian fertility rites of Greco-Roman times. These rites are noted for their emphasis on revelry, masquerading, satirical displays, and periods of symbolic inversion of the social order that provided an outlet for celebrants to let off steam.

In any event, while most of the principles underlying carnival remain more or less intact, its form, content, context, and dress modes have changed drastically over the centuries. This is particularly the case in the Americas where carnival was introduced after the fifteenth century following European colonization. Since then, it has absorbed new elements from the aboriginal populations, Africans and other ethnic groups. The emphasis here is on the carnival dress of the black diaspora in the Caribbean, United States, and Brazil where carnival is known by other names such as *Rara* in Haiti, Mardi Gras in New Orleans, and *Carnaval* in Cuba and Brazil.

The African contribution to carnival in the Americas began when the European slave masters allowed their African captives to display their ancestral heritage in the visual and performing arts on special occasions for recreational and therapeutic purposes. These occasions include the Day of the Kings in Cuba, the *Jonkonnu,* 'Lection Day and Pinkster celebrations in the United States and the Caribbean as well as the *Batuque* (recreational drumming) in Brazil. The various attempts by enslaved blacks to revive African festival costumes in the Americas are well documented. Early eyewitness accounts describe slaves as donning horned masks and feathered headdresses, wearing shredded strips of cloth or painting their faces and bodies in assorted colors, just as they had done in their homeland. Some of these elements survive in the modern carnival, though in new forms and materials. Several sketches of carnival masquerades in nineteenth-century Jamaica by Isaac Belisario document African carryovers. One of them done during the Christmas celebrations in Kingston in 1836, depicts a mask with a palm leaf costume similar to that of the *Sangbeto* mask of the Yoruba and Fon of Nigeria and Republic of Benin respectively. A painting of the Day of the Kings celebration in Cuba executed in the 1870s by the Spanish-born artist Victor Patricio de Landaluze shows not only black figures playing African drums, but also dancers wearing raffia skirts and animal skins. Near the drummers is a masquerade with a conical headdress introduced to Cuba by Ekoi, Abakpa, and Ejagham slaves from the Nigerian–Cameroon border where the masquerade is associated with the *Ekpe* leadership society. Now called *Abakua,* this masquerade is still a feature of the twenty-first-century carnival in Cuba. Another African retention in the modern carnival among blacks in the Americas and Europe is the *Moco Jumbie,* a masquerade on stilts. Apart from the fact that this masquerade type abounds all over Africa, it appears in the prehistoric rock art of the Sahara desert as early as the Round Head period, created about eight thousand years ago.

At first, the public celebrations by free and enslaved blacks in the Americas during the slavery era occurred on the fringes of the white space. However, by the beginning of the twentieth century, emancipation had brought about various degrees of racial integration, allowing blacks, whites, Creoles, Amerindians, and new immigrants from Europe, Middle East, Asia, and the South Pacific to perform the carnival together. Each group has since contributed significantly to the repertoire of carnival dress, while at the same time borrowing elements from one another. For instance, even though the emphasis on feathers in some masquerades has African precedents, influences from Amerindian costumes are apparent as well, most especially in the black Indian Mardi Gras costumes of New Orleans.

In the early 2000s a typical carnival is a public procession of musicians, lavishly attired dancers and colorful masquerades. Some are transported on decorated floats. The areas to be covered by the parade are usually closed to traffic. The costumes often combine assorted materials—fabrics, plastic beads, feathers, sequins, colorful ribbons, glass mirrors, horns, and shells—all aimed at creating a dazzling spectacle. In some areas, the parade lasts one, two, or three days; and in others, a whole week. There is usually a grand finale at a public square or sports stadium where all participants perform in turn before thousands of spectators. In Trinidad, Brazil, and other countries, a panel of judges selects and awards prizes to the most innovative groups and to the masquerades with the best costumes. As a result, carnival has turned into a tourist attraction—a big business, requiring elaborate preparations. In most cases, participants are expected to belong to established groups or specific clubs such as the Zulu of New Orleans, Hugga Bunch of St. Thomas (U.S. Virgin Islands), Ile Aye of Salvador (Brazil) and African Heritage of Notting Hill Gate (United Kingdom) whose members are expected to appear in identical costumes. Each group usually has a professional designer who is responsible not only for its costume themes, styles, colors, and forms, but also the group's dance movements. In Brazil, where African-derived festivals have been assimilated into the carnival, religious groups (*Candomble*) associated with the worship of Yoruba deities (*orixa*) may emphasize the sacred color of a particular deity in their carnival costumes. Thus, white honors *Obatala* (creation deity), blue, *Yemaja* (the Great Mother), red, *Xango* (thunder deity), and yellow, *Oxun* (fertility and beauty deity). Designers such as Fernando Pinto and Joaosinho Trinta of Brazil and Hilton Cox, Peter Minshall, Lionell Jagessar and Ken Morris—all of Trinidad—have become world-famous for their innovations. Some of Peter Minshall's costumes, for example, are monumental, modernistic puppetlike constructions whose articulated parts respond rhythmically to dance movements. Other cos-

tumes by him incorporate elements of traditional African art in an attempt to relate the black diaspora to its roots in Africa. This nationalism has led a number of black designers to seek inspiration from African costumes and headdresses, recalling the original contributions of African captives to carnival during the ancient *Jonkonnu*, Pinkster and Day of the Kings celebrations when they improvised with new materials.

In the recent past, grasses, leaves, raffia, flowers, beads, furs, animal skins, feathers, and cotton materials were used for the costumes. These materials are increasingly being replaced by synthetic substitutes, partly to reduce cost and partly to facilitate mass production. Some costumes or masquerades depict animals, birds, insects, sea creatures, or characters from myths and folklore. Others represent kings, Indians, celebrities, African or European culture heroes, historical figures, clowns, and other characters. Cross-dressing and masquerades with grotesque features are rampant. So too is seductive dancing. The loud music—calypso in the Caribbean and samba in Brazil—adds to the frenzy, allowing performers and spectators alike to release pent up emotion.

See also **America, South: History of Dress; Cross-Dressing; Masquerade and Masked Balls.**

BIBLIOGRAPHY

Besson, Gerard A., ed. *The Trinidad Festival.* Port of Spain, Trinidad and Tobago: Paria, 1988.

Cowley, John. *Carnival, Canboulay and Calypso: Traditions in the Making.* Cambridge, U.K.: Cambridge University Press, 1996.

Golby, J. M., and A. W. Purdue. *The Making of the Modern Christmas.* Athens: University of Georgia Press, 1986.

Harris, Max. *Carnival and Other Christian Festivals: Folk Theology and Folk Performance.* Austin: University of Texas Press, 2003.

Hill, Errol. *Trinidad Festival: Mandate for a National Theatre.* Austin: University of Texas Press, 1972.

Huet, Michel, and Claude Savary. *The Dances of Africa.* New York: Harry N. Abrams, 1996.

Humphrey, Chris. *The Politics of Carnival.* Manchester, U.K.: Manchester University Press, 2001.

Lawal, Babatunde. *The Gèlèdé Spectacle: Art, Gender, and Social Harmony in an African Culture.* Seattle: Washington University Press, 1996.

Mason, Peter. *Bacchanal! The Carnival Culture of Trinidad.* Philadelphia: Temple University Press, 1998.

Minshall, Peter. *Callaloo an de Crab: A Story.* Trinidad and Tobago: Peter Minshall, 1984.

Nettleford, Rex M. *Dance Jamaica: Cultural Definition and Artistic Discovery.* New York: Grove Press, 1986.

Nicholls, Robert W. *Old-Time Masquerading in the U.S. Virgin Islands.* St. Thomas, U.S. Virgin Islands: Virgin Islands Humanities Council, 1998.

Nunely, John W., and Judith Bettelheim. *Caribbean Festival Arts: Each and Every Bit of Difference.* Seattle: University of Washington Press, 1988.

Orloff, Alexander. *Carnival: Myth and Cult.* Wörgl, Austria: Perlinger, 1981.

Poppi, Cesare. "Carnival." In *The Dictionary of Art.* Edited by Jane Turner. Vol. 5. London: Macmillan Publishers, 1996.

Teissl, Helmut. *Carnival in Rio.* New York: Abbeville Press Publishers, 2000.

Turner, Victor, ed. *Celebration: Studies in Festivity and Ritual.* Washington, D.C.: Smithsonian Institution Press, 1982.

Babatunde Lawal

CASHIN, BONNIE One of America's foremost designers in the second half of the twentieth century, Bonnie Cashin (1908–2000) was a pioneer in the sportswear industry, specializing in modular wardrobes for the modern woman "on the go." Her lifelong interest in clothing design, however, encompassed a number of careers on both American coasts. Growing up in California, Cashin worked as an apprentice in a series of dressmaking shops owned and operated by her mother, Eunice. In her teens she worked as a fashion illustrator and dance costume designer. Between 1943 and 1949 she costumed more than sixty films at Twentieth Century–Fox. It was not until midcentury, when she was over forty years old, that she began designing the ready-to-wear for which she became best known.

Cashin favored timeless shapes from the history of clothing, such as ponchos, tunics, Noh coats, and kimonos, which allowed for ease of movement and manufacture. Approaching dress as a form of collage or kinetic art, she favored luxurious, organic materials that she could "sculpt" into shape, such as leather, suede, mohair, wool jersey, and cashmere, as well as nonfashion materials, including upholstery fabrics. Cashin's aim was to create "simple art forms for living in, to be re-arranged as mood and activity dictates" (Interview 1999).

Early Years
As a girl moving along the California coastline, Cashin developed a love for travel and a keen eye for the clothing of different cultures, which would underpin her later professional work. This interest in "why people looked the way they did" placed her in good stead to begin work in 1924, alongside Helen Rose, as a costume designer for the Los Angeles dance troupe Fanchon and Marco. In 1934 her producers took over performances at New York's Roxy Theater and asked Cashin to join them as costumer for the Roxyette dance line, the precursors and rivals to the Rockettes.

Fashion and Film
In 1937 the *Harper's Bazaar* editor Carmel Snow, an admirer of Cashin's costume designs, encouraged Bonnie to work in fashion and arranged for her to become the head designer for the prestigious coat and suit manufacturer Adler and Adler. Owing to the wartime focus on Ameri-

can fashion design, she became so well recognized that she was commissioned to design World War II civilian defense uniforms and was featured in a Coca-Cola advertisement. By 1942, however, Cashin felt boxed in by wartime restrictions. She returned to California to sign a six-year contract as a costume designer with Twentieth Century–Fox.

Cashin designed costumes for the female characters in more than sixty films. Her favorite projects, *Laura* (1944), *A Tree Grows in Brooklyn* (1945), and *Anna and the King of Siam* (1946), also became American cinematic classics. Designing for the lavish productions that typified Hollywood's golden age, she was expected to make innovative use of the day's finest materials to create historical, fantasy, and contemporary wardrobes. She used the resources at the Fox studios to experiment with designs for "real" clothing that she wore and made in custom versions for her leading ladies' offscreen wardrobes.

Return to Ready-to-Wear
Cashin returned to New York, and to Adler and Adler, in 1949. She received the unprecedented honor of earning both the Neiman Marcus Award and the Coty Fashion Critic's Award within the same year (1950). Displeased, however, with her manufacturer's control over her creativity, she decided to challenge the setup of the fashion industry. Working with multiple manufacturers, she designed a range of clothing at different price points, thereby specializing in complete wardrobes for "my kind of a girl for a certain kind of living."

In 1953 Cashin teamed with the leather importer and craftsman Philip Sills and initiated the use of leather for high fashion. She made her name through her unconventional choices in materials as well as her inexhaustible variations on her favorite theme of adapting the flat, graphic patterns of Asian and South American clothing to contemporary global living. Through her work for Sills and Company, she is credited with introducing "layering" into the fashion lexicon. In turn, she credited the Chinese tradition of dressing for, and interpreting the weather as, a "one-shirt day" or a "seven-shirt day." Her layered garments snugly nestled within one another and were easily converted to suit different temperatures and activities by donning or removing a layer. Cashin's objective was to create a flexible wardrobe for her own globe-trotting lifestyle, wherein seasonal changes were only a plane trip away. Frustrated by the categorization of sportswear designer, she declared that travel was her "favorite sport."

Coach and the Cashin Look
In 1962 Cashin became the first designer of Coach handbags and initiated the use of hardware on clothing and accessories, including the brass toggle that became Coach's hallmark. She revolutionized the handbag industry. Unlike contemporary rigid, hand-held bags, her vividly colored "Cashin-Carries" for Coach packed flat and had wide straps, attached coin purses, industrial zippers, and the famous sturdy brass toggles, the last inspired

by the hardware used to secure the top on her convertible sports car.

Without licensing her name, Cashin designed cashmere separates, gloves, canvas totes, at-home gowns and robes, raincoats, umbrellas, and furs. She also ran the Knittery, a consortium of British mills that produced one-of-a-kind sweaters knit to shape, rather than cut and sewn. Among many other industry awards, she received the Coty award five times and entered their hall of fame in 1972; in 2001 was honored with a plaque on the Fashion Walk of Fame on Seventh Avenue in New York City.

Cashin worked until 1985, when she decided to focus on painting and philanthropy. Among several scholarships and educational programs, she established the James Michelin Lecture Series at the California Institute of Technology. Cashin died in New York on 3 February 2000 from complications during heart surgery. In 2003 the Bonnie Cashin Collection, consisting of her entire design archive and endowments for design-related lecture series and symposia, was donated to the Department of Special Collections within the Charles E. Young Research Library at the University of California, Los Angeles.

See also **Costume Designer; Dance Costume; Film and Fashion; Ready-to-Wear; Sportswear.**

BIBLIOGRAPHY

Cashin, Bonnie. Interview by Stephanie Day Iverson. 12 September 1999.

Iverson, Stephanie Day. "'Early' Bonnie Cashin, before Bonnie Cashin Designs, Inc." *Studies in the Decorative Arts* 8, no. 1 (2001–2002): 108–124.

Steele, Valerie. *Women of Fashion: Twentieth-Century Designers.* New York: Rizzoli International, 1991.

Stephanie Day Iverson

CASHMERE AND PASHMINA On the windswept plateaus of Inner Asia, in a huge swathe encompassing Afghanistan, India's Ladakh, parts of Sinkiang, northern Tibet, and Mongolia, nomadic herdspeople raise great flocks of sheep, goats, and yak. The altitude, over 14,000 feet (4,300 meters), precludes cultivation; herding is the only possible economic use of a bleakly inhospitable environment. The bitter cold of winter, plummeting to minus 40 degrees Fahrenheit and below and aggravated by windchill, provokes the growth of a warm, soft undercoat of downy fibers in many of the region's mammals—goats, camels, yak, even dogs, as well as wild animals like the ibex and the Tibetan antelope or chiru. Known in the

Luxurious pashmina shawls are woven in Kashmir, India. Pashmina, a fabric woven from the downy fibers from goats, was an important part of the Indo-Iranian royal lifestyle in eighteenth and nineteenth centuries and was traded as far as Russia, Armenia, and Egypt. © EARL & NAZIMA KOWALL/CORBIS. REPRODUCED BY PERMISSION.

Cashmere yarn. Cashmere was produced painstakingly by hand until the twentieth century, when expanding demand for the fabric led to increased production. Now rolls of cashmere yarn are produced mechanically and are stored in clothing factories, like this one in the United Kingdom, ready for mass production. © HULTON-DEUTSCH COLLECTION/CORBIS. REPRODUCED BY PERMISSION.

Northern languages of urdu and Kashmiri as *pashm*, this fiber is collected in commercial quantities from the herds-people's goats. (Some authorities have identified the breed of *pashm*-producing goats as *Capra hircus*. This name, however, applies to all domesticated goats; scientific taxonomy makes no distinction between different breeds of domesticated animals.) The double-humped Bactrian camel also produces a less fine grade ("camel hair"). When the term *pashm* is used without qualification, it is goats' *pashm* that is meant.

Pashm was and is the raw material for the shawl industry of Kashmir. The fabric woven from *pashm* is properly called *pashmina*. When the British in India became aware of the Kashmir shawl, however, some of them, ignorant of the fiber's origin, adopted the term "cashmere" to refer to both fiber and fabric, and in the West this is the term that has stuck.

The Kashmir Shawl

The transformation of a mass of greasy, matted fibers into a patterned fabric of superlative softness and warmth involved a whole complex set of procedures. To begin with, the raw material had to be cleaned and the coarse hairs from the animal's outer coat removed. These processes and the spinning of the thread were (and continue to be) done by Kashmiri women in their homes, with the simplest of tools like combs, reels, and hand-operated spinning-wheels.

The classic means of decorating shawl-goods was by the twill-tapestry technique, unique to the manufacture of this fabric: a twill weave using, instead of a shuttle, a multiplicity of small bobbins laden with different colors of yarn to incorporate the design into the weave. Designers drew and colored the pattern, and a scribe translated it into a shorthand form called *talim*. Dyers tinted the yarn in the required colors with vegetable dyes, and other specialists made and dressed the warp and put it to the loom. Only then did the weaver put his hand to it. Two weavers sat at each loom, manipulating the bobbins in response to the instructions of the master weaver reading aloud from the *talim*. Shawls were woven in pairs, and an elaborate design could be months or even years in the making.

In the nineteenth century, as patterns became more complex, shawls were often woven in numerous small pieces, the skill of the darner who joined them together being such that the seams were practically invisible and the whole looked and felt like a single piece of material. Another development of the nineteenth century was the substitution of embroidery on plain pashmina fabric for tapestry work. At the start of the twenty-first century the skills of the twill-tapestry weaver have all but disappeared, but perhaps more embroidered pashmina shawls are being produced in Kashmir than ever before, in response to demand from the prosperous Indian middle class. Simultaneously, efforts are under way to revive the art of twill-tapestry, as well as to diversify the product, and a small number of superlative pieces are being created in both traditional and innovative techniques and designs.

From the mid-eighteenth century till about 1870, the shawl industry was heavily taxed and provided more revenue for successive governments of Kashmir than all other sources together. This burden of taxation fell most heavily on the weavers, the exploitation of whom reached an extent that could be described almost as serfdom.

The pashmina shawl of Kashmir has always been a luxury item; more than that, its beauty and fineness made it an integral part of the royal and aristocratic lifestyle of the Indo-Iranian world in the eighteenth and first half of the nineteenth centuries. It was exported as far afield as Russia, Armenia, Iran, Turkey, Egypt, and Yemen, long before it took the West by storm. The term "shawl" (originally *shal*) was not at that time confined to shoulder mantles, and the fabric often took the form of *jamawar*, or gown-pieces, designed to be made up into tailored clothes. There was indeed an extraordinary variety of "shawl-goods," including turbans, waist-girdles, saddlecloths for horses and elephants, curtains, carpets, and tomb-coverings. It was only in India that the long shawl was worn—by men, not women—as a shoulder-mantle. Elsewhere in Asia, men wore turbans or sashes of shawl fabric; or coats (*jama, qaba, choga*) tailored from *jamawar*. Shawls for women were square, and designed to be worn folded into a triangle around the shoulders or waist. It was only when they became a part of high fashion in Europe, especially France, and the United States of America, between approximately 1790 and 1870, that long shawls, as well as square ones, were appropriated to women's wear.

Cashmere Beyond Kashmir

Until about 150 years ago, the skills necessary to process *pashm* into a fabric that would realize its potential of delicacy as well as warmth existed only in Kashmir. The nineteenth century saw the beginning of a demand for *pashm*—under the appellation "cashmere"—from the West. Around 1850, European demand for luxury woolen-type fibers seems to have been met first of all by vicuña from South America; but as this grew scarce and

THE ORIGIN OF *TOOSH*

It is the chiru *(Pantholops hodgsoni)* that is the source of *toosh* (occasionally known as *tus,* also *shahtoosh),* a variety of *pashm* even more delicate than that from the goat, from which the famous "ring-shawls" were made. It is perhaps the finest animal material that has ever been put to the loom, the mean diameter of the fibers being in the region of 9 to 12 microns—about three-quarters that of cashmere. Sadly, no method has been found of harvesting the fiber from the living animal. Until about the middle of the twentieth century, the slaughter of chiru for *pashm* was on a sustainable basis, and herds numbering tens of thousands were reported by travelers in Tibet. The opening up of Tibet after about 1960 and the emergence of the shahtoosh shawl as a high-fashion

luxury item in the West, changed all that; and in the last 40 years there has been wholesale slaughter, an estimated 20,000 chiru being shot or trapped every year, while in 2000 the surviving population was estimated at a mere 75,000, down from perhaps a million in midcentury. In the twenty-first century, the chiru is recognized as being in imminent danger of extinction, and is classified under Appendix I of the Convention on International Trade in Endangered Species (CITES). Although trade in the animal and its products is accordingly banned everywhere in the world, it is believed that the slaughter continues, and that *toosh* is still being processed in Kashmir into shawls that are sold illegally in India and the West.

expensive, cashmere was increasingly used as a substitute, finally superseding vicuña completely. From as early as the 1860s commercial supplies were sourced from Mongolia rather than Tibet. Earlier it was only in the tracts convenient to Kashmir—that is southeastern Ladakh and western Tibet—that large-scale production actually took place, the amount reaching Kashmir annually in the 1820s being estimated at between 120,000 and 240,000 pounds. Expanding demand from the West through the twentieth century led to increased production, as nomadic herdspeople all over the potential *pashm*-producing area increased the proportion of goats in relation to sheep among their flocks. In the twenty-first century, total world production is in the region of 14,000 tons, the bulk of it from China (Tibet) and Mongolia.

Western companies have developed mechanical means of processing the fiber, even the finicky process of de-hairing (though in the twenty-first century almost all the Chinese and Mongolian *pashm* is exported already de-haired). They process it into both woven fabrics and yarn suitable for knitwear. The so-called "pashminas" that became so fashionable in the West in the 1990s were originally woven in Nepal from a mixture of *pashm* and silk. They are now also being produced in many different qualities in various centers in India and the term is frequently misapplied by retailers in the West to similar-looking fringed shawls woven from fine sheep's wools.

See also **Fur; India: Clothing and Adornment; Shawls.**

BIBLIOGRAPHY

Ahmed, Monisha. *Living Fabric, Weaving Among the Nomads of Ladakh Himalaya.* Bangkok: Orchid Press, 2002.

Ames, Frank. *The Kashmir Shawl and Its French Influence.* Woodbridge, U.K.: The Antiques Collectors, 1986.

Beardsley, Grace. "Piecing in Twill Tapestry Shawls of Persia and Kashmir." In *Textiles as Primary Sources: Proceedings of the First Symposium of the Textile Society of America.* St. Paul, Minn.: The Textile Society of America, 1988.

Goldstein, Melvyn C., and Cynthia M. Beall. *Nomads of Western Tibet: The Survival of a Way of Life.* Hong Kong: Odyssey Productions, 1990.

Harrison, E. P. *Scottish Estate Tweeds.* Elgin, Scotland: Johnstons of Elgin, 1995.

IFAW and Wildlife Trust of India. *Wrap Up the Trade: An International Campaign to Save the Tibetan Antelope.* New Delhi, 2001.

Internet Resource

Chiru Factsheet. Available from <http://www.earthisland.org/tpp/chirufacts.htm>.

Janet Rizvi

CASUAL BUSINESS DRESS During the 1990s in the United States a trend in dressing casually for work became more widespread in business offices. The trend soon spread to other countries such as Canada, England, Scotland, and Australia. Casual dress in the office may reflect a larger societal trend toward relaxation of manners and informal presentation of self in many aspects of life (Adler 1995) and may be symptomatic of a shift away from traditional ways of doing business (Janus, Kaiser, and Gray 1999; Weiser 1996).

Casual Business Dress Defined

Casual work dress has been identified by a number of terms, such as "dressing down," "business casual," and "Casual Day" dress. In a national U.S. study, Tootelian (2003) found that substantial uncertainty exists about what business casual means. The definition presented here is gleaned from a number of sources and can be offered only as a general and imprecise guideline.

Delineation of what is formal business dress is necessary to define categories of casual business dress. The sidebar contains a description of the standard for formal business dress at the turn of the twenty-first century. Women's formal business dress remains more varied than men's (Ogle and Damhorst 1999).

For men and women, "business casual" dress tends to include a reinterpretation of at least one formal power cue into a more casual ensemble (Rucker, Anderson, and Kangas 1999). A jacket (often a blazer or sports jacket) may be worn with more casual khaki pants and shirt, or a tie is worn without a jacket. Sweaters are permissible with a skirt or pants. Shoes are often more casual and comfortable. A great amount of variety is present, but includes more limits than does "casual dress."

Some offices allow highly casual dress, including jeans and shorts. Permissible styles vary greatly across firms, geographic areas, and occupations (Ogle and Damhorst 1999) and age and gender of workers (Tootelian 2003).

History of the Trend

The increase of casual dress among office workers began far earlier than the 1990s. Farrell-Beck (1999) offered evidence that components of men's casual dress have frequently been adapted into men's formal business wear throughout its history. King Charles II of England originally instituted the men's business suit in 1666 as an alternative to fancier styles popular in men's court dress throughout Europe (Kuchta 1990). The ensembles adopted by men of court and commerce to some extent reflected informal fashions worn by English country gentlemen (Kuchta 1990). The casual trend at the end of the twentieth century, however, did not entail a metamorphosis of casual into formal symbols. Casual Day and casual every day in essence have become a celebration of the right of office workers to legitimately wear casual clothing to work in the office.

The casual dress trend for business professionals may have begun during the 1970s as the computer industry blossomed. Silicon Valley computer "geeks" are often cited as the first to be given license to dress very casually at work (Weiser 1996). In certain areas of the country, some forms of casual dress were an option in many types of businesses by the late 1970s. In 1975 John Molloy railed against offices that were allowing men to wear the infamous leisure suit in place of a formal suit. A few managers in an early 1980s study of office workers in Austin, Texas, reported that they frequently went to work in somewhat casual attire, making them keep a jacket and tie at the office just in case a client might drop by (Damhorst 1984–1985). Saturn Corporation has encouraged casual work dress for employees at all levels in the organization since its inception in 1983 (Levi Strauss & Co. 1999).

A series of Levi Strauss & Co. surveys were quoted in the popular press during the 1990s to chronicle the rise of casual business dress. By 1992, 26 percent of businesses in the United States reported offering at least a casual attire day (Weiser 1996). Companies allowing casual dress every day rose to 33 percent in 1995 and 53 percent in 1997 (Maycumber 1998).

Reporters cite a new rash of surveys in the early twenty-first century to forewarn of the possible demise, or at least notable reduction, of the casual office dress trend. For example, the Men's Apparel Alliance found that 19 percent of over 200 firms with revenues greater than $500 million were returning to formal business attire (Egodigwe and Alleyne 2003). In 2000, only 87 percent of U.S. firms allowed casual dress, down 10 percent from 1998 (Kaplan-Leiserson 2000). The tough economy in the early 2000s was moving some companies to abandon a casual image to combat intense competition.

Functions of Casual Dress

Casual work dress has been imputed to have an array of symbolic powers (Biecher, Keaton, and Pollman 1999; Henricks 1996; Janus, Kaiser, and Gray 1999). Casual dress is believed to facilitate democratization through horizontal flattening of workplace hierarchies and to break down communication barriers posed by formal structures, thereby improving teamwork. Casual work dress may improve customer relations by implying mutual similarity. Many managers feel that casual dress improves employee morale and enhances worker productivity. Correspondingly, many firms instituted casual dress policies during the 1990s to reward workers and attract new recruits. In addition, communication technology used in many occupations increasingly allows people to do much business without ever coming face-to-face with clients or vendors, eliminating a need for constant expression of corporate image through dress.

Critics cite some negative outcomes of casual work dress, such as negative organizational image and confusion about how to define and enforce workplace dress policies (Egodigwe and Alleyne 2003). Confusion among employees about what to wear to work is not uncommon (Janus Kaiser, and Gray 1999; Tootelian 2003). Some critics assume that lack of control underlies the relaxation

CLASSIC FORMAL DRESS STANDARDS

For Men

> A two-piece suit;
> A jacket and pant with matching fabrics;
> Smooth wool or blend fabrics in solid colors or pinstripes;
> A jacket that has classic tailoring, a convertible collar, and welt pockets;
> A tie;
> A shirt;
> White or light colored stand-up collar; and
> Leather shoes in brown or black

For Women

> Pants, skirted suits, and dresses;
> A jacket worn closed with no blouse underneath;
> A jacket worn with a variety of blouses and knit tops;
> Jackets may be collarless, have varied pocket styles, and vary in length from upper to lower hip area;
> Neckline exposure is modest (no cleavage);
> Skirt length varies but not too far above the knee;
> Fabrics similar to men's suiting but in a greater variety of colors;
> Subdued tweeds or plaids;
> Jewelry is limited, one or two small pieces are permissible;
> Sheer hosiery, nude or in colors that blend with the skirt; and
> Shoes with closed-toe and one-inch or higher heels

to casual codes (Lillethun 1999), and many businesses in the early 2000s were concerned that casual work dress had resulted in increased tardiness, absenteeism, flirtatious behavior on the job, and an overall decrease in productivity (Egodigwe and Alleyne 2003). Powerful consequences of casual business dress have been attributed over time, but no research has been reported to verify any valid correlation of positive or negative outcomes for workplace behavior.

See also **Uniforms, Occupational.**

BIBLIOGRAPHY

Adler, Jerry. "Have We Become a Nation of Slobs?" *Newsweek* 25 (20 February 1995): 56–62.

Biecher, Elisa, Paul N. Keaton, and A. William Pollman. "Casual Dress at Work." *SAM Advanced Management Journal* 64 (Winter 1999): 17–20.

Damhorst, Mary Lynn. "Meanings of Clothing Cues in Social Context." *Clothing and Textiles Research Journal* 3, no. 2 (1984–1985): 39–48.

Damhorst, Mary Lynn, Kelly Jondle, and Christi Youngberg. "How Personnel Interviewers See Women's Job Interview Dress—A 2002 Update." In *The Meanings of Dress* 2nd ed. Edited by Mary Lynn Damhorst, Kimberly A. Miller, and Susan O. Michelman. New York: Fairchild Publications, 2004.

Egodigwe, Laura, and Sonia Alleyne. "Here Come the Suits." *Black Enterprise* 3, no. 8 (March 2003): 59.

Farrell-Beck, Jane. "Not So New: Casual Dress in the Office." In *The Meanings of Dress*. Edited by Mary Lynn Damhorst, Kimberly A. Miller, and Susan O. Michelman, 258–261. New York: Fairchild Publications, 1999.

Henricks, Mark. "Informal Wear: Does Dressing Down Send Productivity Up?" *Entrepreneur* 24, no. 1 (January 1996): 79–82.

Janus, Teresa, Susan B. Kaiser, and Gordon Gray. "Negotiations @ Work: The Casual Businesswear Trend." In *The Meanings of Dress*. Edited by Mary Lynn Damhorst, Kimberly A. Miller, and Susan O. Michelman, 264–268. New York: Fairchild Publications, 1999.

Kaplan-Leiserson, Eva. "Back-to-Business Attire." *Training and Development* 54 (November 2000): 39.

Kuchta, David. "'Graceful, Virile, and Useful'; The Origins of the Three-Piece Suit." *Dress* 17 (1990): 18–26.

Levi Strauss & Co. "Saturn Corporation: A Casual Businesswear Case Study." In *The Meanings of Dress*. Edited by Mary Lynn Damhorst, Kimberly A. Miller, and Susan O. Michelman, 257–258. New York: Fairchild Publications, 1999.

Lillethun, Abby. "An Interpretation of Negative Press Coverage of Casual Dress." In *The Meanings of Dress*. Edited by Mary Lynn Damhorst, Kimberly A. Miller, and Susan O. Michelman, 261–264. New York: Fairchild Publications, 1999.

Maycumber, S. G. "Young Men's Pants Preference Shifting." *Daily News Record* 28, no. 4 (9 January 1998): 8–9.

Molloy, John T. *Dress for Success*. New York: Warner Books, 1975.

Ogle, Jennifer P., and Mary Lynn Damhorst. "Dress for Success in the Popular Press." In *Appearance and Power*. Edited by Kim K. P. Johnson and Sharron J. Lennon, 79–101. Oxford, and New York: Berg, 1999.

Rucker, Margaret, Elizabeth Anderson, and April Kangas. "Clothing, Power, and the Workplace." In *Appearance and Power*. Edited by Kim K. P. Johnson and Sharron J. Lennon, 59–77. Oxford, and New York: Berg, 1999.

Weiser, Jay. "Denim Downsize." *The New Republic* 214, no. 9 (26 February 1996): 10–11.

Internet Resource

Tootelian, Dennis. "Mervyn's Career Casual Survey: Summary Report of Key Research Findings." Attachment to "CSUS Study Shows Workplace Fashion Confusion." Capital University News (10 February 2003). Available from <http://www.csus.edu/news/021003fashion.htm>.

Mary Lynn Damhorst

CELEBRITIES In November 2003, the Prince's Trust, an organization set up by Prince Charles to help disadvantaged young people, organized a charity event in the Albert Hall: "Fashion Rocks," a collaboration between the worlds of music and fashion. It was hosted by Elizabeth Hurley, the epitome of a new type of celebrity. She has been photographed constantly for nearly ten years, and used for countless magazine covers, including British *Vogue*. She has a multimillion-dollar contract with Estée Lauder, and her private life is constantly subject to close tabloid scrutiny. Everyone, it seems, knows who she is—she is often named in headlines as, simply, "Liz." If a job description is ever necessary, she is referred to as "model and actress." Yet apart from magazine covers where she is used because of her celebrity, and the Lauder campaign, she does no modeling. The films in which she has appeared—with the exception of *Austin Powers: The Spy Who Shagged Me* (1999) have done very badly at the box office. It would be more accurate to say that she is part of a new group of celebrities who have been instantly created by and perpetuated within the media. She is, quite simply, a construct—and, paradoxically, it is this that makes her a celebrity.

Her career in fact began in 1994, at the London premiere of *Four Weddings and a Funeral*. She accompanied her boyfriend, Hugh Grant, and borrowed a dress from the London offices of Versace. The black dress was short and revealing—held together by large, strategically placed safety pins. The following day she appeared on the front page of all tabloid and middle-market newspapers in Britain, while even the broadsheets saw fit to include the "story" on their inside pages. Since then, she has been continually photographed, and the dress has been retrospectively discussed as "That Dress." Indeed, when Grant was convicted of an indiscretion with a Hollywood prostitute, the English Sunday paper found the woman in question and photographed her wearing a red version of the Versace dress, which they put on their front page. Unsurprisingly, Versace has offered Hurley clothes for every subsequent photo opportunity, and she has repaid them by being photographed in all of them. One of the dresses was slit so high up the thigh that it revealed a pair of knickers in a leopard-print fabric to match the dress. Hurley is a perfect example of the new breed of fashion celebrity for, unlike fashion celebrities of the past, her taste is often deemed to be questionable. On this particular occasion, she was censured in the press for having worn this outfit, since it was to a "society wedding," and it was suggested that she had wished to divert attention away from the bride. This is in direct contrast to the former notion of a fashion celebrity who attained his or her status precisely because their taste in clothes was deemed to be excellent.

While there are still fashion celebrities who have been selected for their ability to look stylish—the model Kate Moss is a perfect example—the majority of today's celebrities are seen as legitimate targets for sartorial criticism. A weekly staple of journalism is now a roundup of the past week's fashion triumphs and disasters; if a celebrity wears a particularly unbecoming or unsuitable outfit, an appearance in the papers the very next morning is guaranteed.

A "celebrity," however, as opposed to an "icon," has always had a notoriety over and above the sum of their talent. But one of the many problems with today's culture of celebrity is a seeming disregard for the absence of any particular talent apart from the simple fact of being photogenic. Another is the disproportionate amount of media attention given over to celebrity stories. The past decade has seen an unprecedented growth in the cult of the celebrity—it is very different from the carefully controlled interest in "stars" that characterized the heyday of Hollywood.

Interestingly, it has meant huge shifts within the fashion industry, which seem to have gone at times unremarked. For instance, it was traditional within magazine journalism—from its infancy at the end of the last century until the late 1990s—for leading fashion journalists to have some effect on the success or failure of a particular collection, a particular look, and for the journalists themselves, if prestigious enough, to be able to assist the career of new designers. Some journalists are still sufficiently well known to be photographed as celebrities in their own right, known for their own particular style. Just as from the 1930s to the 1950s the characteristic "look" of Diana Vreeland was frequently discussed, so today Anna Piaggi of Italian *Vogue* is still photographed, as is Suzy Menkes of the *International Herald Tribune*. However, these are among a few exceptions—arguably the photographs from the collections are now of the celebrities in the front row—and it is their choice of designer or outfit which makes for success. Julien Macdonald owes his career as a designer to the fact that he was asked, early on, to design for Kylie Minogue. Donatella Versace has ensured the continued good fortunes of the house for which she designs not only through her shrewd use of different celebrities—she organized a wedding party for Jennifer Lopez, and always dresses singers for music award ceremonies—but through the fact that she has become a fashion celebrity in her own right. Her characteristic heavy makeup, long bleached-blonde hair, and year-round suntan are the constant focus of media comment.

Not only have journalists lost their power over designers, they have watched their employers make radical changes to cope with the new obsession with celebrity. The magazine *InStyle*, launched in America in 1998 by the publishers of *People*, has been extremely successful and has created a new template for fashion journalism both in America and the United Kingdom. Celebrities, rather than models, are now used for many cover shots, while the fashion and beauty pages tell their readers how to emulate particular star "looks."

Journalism has gone through extraordinary changes over the last century. A hundred years ago, "celebrity photographs" were rare within magazine journalism, and tended to involve the aristocracy or royalty. There was still some use of sketches; the British magazine *Queen* was specifically set up to portray the weekly activities of Queen Victoria and her companions and to depict the lifestyle of the very uppermost echelons of British society, and these scenes could not be photographed. But the development of the cinema brought the royal family onto the screen in newsreels, and they became the subject of special short films on ceremonial occasions. Princess Alexandra—later Queen herself—was of great interest because of her elegance in dress—royalty and aristocracy continued to be of interest as the new media forms developed. In the period between the two World Wars, Pond's ran a famous advertising campaign which used "society ladies," invariably titled, to endorse their range of skin-care products. But tastes gradually changed—celebrity endorsement for cosmetics and beauty products was more likely, by 1939, to involve a Hollywood star.

As advertising has become more sophisticated, so it has cast its net more widely. Not only has it used celebrities from every sphere of activity—the first sportsman to appear in a fashion-related advertisement was Henry Cooper, the British boxing champion, who advertised the aftershave, Brut, in the 1970s—but it has also created its own minor, usually transient, celebrities through its campaigns. A perfect example within the fashion sphere was the Calvin Klein men's underwear campaign, which ran during 2002–2003 and used an obscure young surfer, Travis, rather than a well-known model or a famous figure. Research showed that although women responded very positively to his image, men found his long hair and soft features off-putting. He was replaced in the Autumn 2003 campaign by the Arsenal soccer star, Fredrik Ljungberg, who has a more macho image—his hair is shaved, he wears a medallion, and the pictures all show clearly the large black panther tattooed on his lower abdomen.

Interestingly, despite the growing popularity of sports over the past century, fashion advertising was relatively slow to involve sportsmen and women. Things changed during the 1980s and 1990s—arguably Nike owes its global dominance to its use of the basketball star Michael Jordan, and more recently they have used international footballers such as Edgar Davits. The tennis stars Venus and Serena Williams have appeared on magazine covers and lent their names to sportswear, while the Russian Anna Kournikova was used for a Berlei bra campaign with the tag line "Only the balls should bounce."

The most notable development within the 1990s, however, has been the link forged between fashion and soccer. Eric Cantona appeared on the catwalk for John Paul Gaultier, while younger stars have modeled in men's fashion magazines. David Beckham's enormous popularity has meant that he has moved from fashion-related advertising—sunglasses, watches, children's clothes—and magazine shoots to becoming a global brand in himself.

He and his wife, the former Posh Spice, went on a tour of America in 2003 when their agents advised them that it was necessary, given the fact that many Americans are unfamiliar with soccer stars. He and his wife are important because they are among the new "celebrity couples" whose activities the media can chronicle and whose image is of interest. Their American counterparts are perhaps Brad Pitt and Jennifer Aniston—she was voted "The Most Popular Person in America" in the *Forbes* poll of July 2003. However, apart from Aniston's early contract with L'Oreal, neither she nor Pitt has taken part in direct advertising. Nevertheless, they can "endorse" products simply by wearing them when snapped on the street—they have popularized Maharishi trousers and Birkenstock sandals.

Celebrities within the music industry have been courted, too, both in the 1960s and more recently. In the past singers were used in fashion spreads or asked to lend their name to a range of merchandise—now they are directly approached by leading fashion brands to join film stars in rendering "luxury brands" more democratic. Donna Karan used Bruce Willis, action-man hero, in the 1990s, while Madonna modeled Tom Ford's early designs for Gucci. She also appeared in a Versace campaign photographed by Herb Ritts—but recently she has lent her celebrity to the high street, in a Gap television commercial with Missy Elliott. The high-fashion brands have tried to widen their appeal through the use of singers such as Christina Aguilera, in the Versace campaign for Autumn 2003, and Jennifer Lopez, used by Louis Vuitton in the same season. At the same moment, Tommy Hilfiger announced that he wanted to create a new image for his sportswear and had recruited the musician David Bowie and his wife, the ex-model Iman, currently working for Bulgari. Hilfiger sportswear is currently popular among the young and has some "street credibility"—this latest celebrity appointment suggests an attempt to interest forty-somethings in his sportswear, based perhaps on the success of Juicy Couture tracksuits after Madonna and Jennifer Lopez were photographed wearing them. Rap stars have been courted assiduously in an attempt to gain the kind of appeal Hilfiger's range possesses; the singer P. Diddy has launched a collection of casual wear, Sean Jean—while in another attempt to give expensive brands a broader appeal, Missy Elliott has been used as the face of Garrards, the royal jewelers.

This new reliance on celebrities for high-fashion endorsement is not worrying in itself—what is problematic, both within the industry and, more importantly, in a wider sociological context, are the sociological and psychological implications of celebrity obsession. It is tempting and not too far-fetched to suggest that the current climate owes much to the life—and unfortunate death—of Diana, Princess of Wales. In the early 1980s, she was far from being a glamorous fashion icon—and it was this perceived "ordinariness" that made her so appealing to the press at first. She had a haircut and a taste for frilly blouses that set trends precisely because this Earl's daughter seemed to the public to be "one of them," however false that assumption was. Her experiments with different hairstyles and her fashion education—she received guidance from the staff of British *Vogue*—were avidly followed. So too was the developing drama within her personal life. She featured in newspapers worldwide, and magazine editors found that her face on a cover guaranteed sales. Her battles with her weight—and her admission of her bulimia—were chronicled as carefully as the problems within her private life. When she died, the scenes in England were both extraordinary and unprecedented.

Arguably, the public had developed over two decades a need, even a craving, for celebrity worship—and the press has responded. The current pathological interest in body image, with its accounts of the different diets and fitness regimes followed by particular celebrities, seems to be spiraling out of control. And certainly in Britain, there is concern about the size of individual credit-card debt. A recent survey showed that the average woman now spends far more on shoes than in the past, and this is possibly linked to the fact that "Manolos" have become a household name through the television program "Sex and the City." They were worn not only on-screen by the heroine, Carrie Bradshaw, but by the actress Sarah Jessica Parker, who herself became a style icon. The new attempts to copy star images, decor, and lifestyle, the hours spent scouring celebrity websites, can only make for a stifling of individuality in dress, a feeling of discontent, and, more disturbingly, an unhappiness with faces or bodies that are not perfect.

See also **Actors and Actresses, Impact on Fashion; Fashion Icons; Models; Supermodels.**

BIBLIOGRAPHY

Berger, Maurice, Brian Wallis, and Simon Watson, eds. *Constructing Masculinity*. London and New York: Routledge, 1995.

Bruzzi, Stella. "Football, Fashion and That Sarong." In *Fashion Cultures: Theories, Explorations, and Analysis*. Edited by Stella Bruzzi and Church Gibson. London: Routledge, 2000.

Dyer, Richard. *Stars*. London: BFI Publishing, 1986/1998.

Gritten, David. *Fame*. London: Allen Lane, 2002.

Hilfiger, Tommy. *Rock Style*. London: Barbican Centre, 2000.

Macdonald, Paul. *The Star System*. London: Wallflower Press, 2000.

Rojek, Chris. *Celebrity*. London: Reaktion Books, 2002.

Thesander, Marianne. *The Feminine Ideal*. London: Reaktion, 1997.

Pamela Church Gibson

CEREMONIAL AND FESTIVAL COSTUMES

Ceremonies, festivals, and other rituals provide a structure for an individual or a group to reaffirm social values and ties. They tend to be public events, seen as different from everyday, which spotlight an important personal or cultural happening. Ritual helps to give meaning to the world in part by linking the past to the present and the present to the future. Ritual works through the senses to structure our perception of reality and the world around us; it is often when a society's deepest values emerge in the form of activity, objects, and dress. Ceremonies often combine religious belief with social and political concerns. Although rituals tend to evolve very slowly, cultures do change over time, and possible disjunctures may develop between a ceremony and the attitudes of the society, resulting in the modification or even elimination of the ceremony. The costumes worn at these times are frequently special to the occasion and dramatically symbolic; they can reflect historical or cultural preferences that are no longer in vogue. Different stages or events characterize some celebrations, requiring many changes of costume or dress. Dress is an inclusive concept that involves modifying the body by the use of textiles, cosmetics, scars, coiffures, apparel, jewelry, and accessories held by or for a person. Although in general dress can range from temporary acts of covering and adorning to permanent acts of modification, such as scarification, ceremonial dress is usually of a temporary nature.

Unlike masquerading, dress is not meant to transform an individual into something else but to enhance the identity of the individual. In many cultures, costumes have been used in a wide range of festivals stressing community solidarity or declaring the right of a person or group to a particular status, office, or possession. Since the nineteenth century, the Zulu of South Africa have used clothing and jewelry made from imported beads to demarcate changes in status associated with different life-cycle stages. Children and married women usually wear less beadwork. Young girls attire themselves in square or rectangular beaded loincloth panels attached to a bead string; pregnant women dress in leather aprons decorated with beadwork; and married women wear a knee-length skirt made of pleated goat skin or ox hide, hoop-like circular necklaces, and a flared headdress in the shape of a crown covered with red ocher or red beads and a beaded band around its base. The color schemes of beaded necklaces convey social messages about stages of physical and social development. Small rectangles, zigzag or vertical bands, diamonds, triangles, and lozenges are the most widespread motifs.

Rites of Passage

A rite of passage is a common ceremony that involves a transition from one status or condition to another. For an individual, these include birth, puberty, marriage, and death. Scholars usually divide this type of ritual into three stages: separation, a transitional or liminal one, and reincorporation; the latter two are most often associated with distinctive dress. For a community, annual rites of passage mark seasonal changes or cycles of renewal and regeneration. Individual and community rites of passage

serve to enhance social solidarity, confirm membership in a group, and channel any anxiety resulting from the potential dangers of the transition. Societies throughout the world institutionalize the physical and social transformation that boys and girls undergo at the time of puberty by marking their passage from childhood to adulthood. There is, however, considerable variation in the timing of the ritual, length of ritual, and age of initiate.

As part of the puberty ceremony carried out among Sepik River peoples in New Guinea, newly initiated boys enter a men's meetinghouse, the political and religious center of the community; after passing across the threshold, the boys encounter sacred cult objects that play a role in their introduction to appropriate beliefs and behavior. The young men are also given body paint in the course of initiation. After residing in the cult house for months, the boys return to their village as adults when all male members of the house elaborately decorate their bodies as a statement of their own attractiveness, to display characteristics identified with being a successful male and to identify themselves as sacred beings from the world of the ancestors. The men—dressed in fiber skirts—paint their bodies with yellow, black, red, and white curvilinear patterns. Paint is believed to be sacred and clearly adds to the seriousness of the occasion. Red and white are especially favored because these colors are associated with brightness and are viewed as auspicious. A wicker headdress adorned with flowers and feathers as well as large shells worn on the chest and forehead enhance the brilliance of the costume. In addition, other accessories of shell, bone, boar-tusk, seeds, and feathers are worn. Feathers are noteworthy for symbolizing growth and power.

In the early 2000s, the most important Apache ceremony is the girl's four-day puberty rite—sometimes referred to as the Sunrise Dance—that was taught to the Apache by White Painted Woman, an important deity in the American Southwest. A similar ritual is held by the Navajo, but the Apache put greater stress on the benefit of the ritual to the community. The ceremony is organized by a shaman hired by the girl's family who also select godparents to assist the young girl during the ceremony and throughout her life. On the second night, male masqueraders called Gan, wearing plank headdresses made of slats of agave stalk, impersonate Mountain Spirits who bless the area and help protect the community from dangers and disease. During the Apache puberty ceremony, the young girl is dressed in either a buckskin skirt or a long cotton skirt and a buckskin smock or cape painted yellow, the color of sacred pollen said to symbolize fertility. These garments are decorated with symbols of the moon, sun, and stars. Both skirt and smock utilize fringes that could represent sunbeams. An abalone shell is worn on the forehead along with shell necklaces, shell earrings, and feathers for the hair. Metal bells, buttons, and decorative metal cones cut from cans dangling from the dress have been used since the early nineteenth century. Buckskin moccasins and leggings might be added to the ensemble. The various items of dress must be put on in a prescribed sequence and draped in a particular way. The outfit of the girl, based on traditional female dress, is now specific to this ceremony; in the past, the Apache wore various items of dress made only from animal skins. The use of an older material or clothing style for ceremonies is not uncommon.

At the time of puberty in the West African country of Sierra Leone, Mende girls begin an initiation process into the female Sande association where they learn traditional songs and dances and are educated about their future roles as wives and mothers. During seclusion, the girls are covered with a white pigment of crushed shell and chalk and wear ornaments that define their status as novice and indicate that they are under the protection of the association. Formerly, this period lasted for several months, but in recent decades, the period has been reduced to a few weeks. After successfully completing all initiation obligations, the girls with similar hairstyles and dressed in fine clothing form a procession and parade back to town accompanied by masked dancers. Sande is the only documented African association in which women both own and perform masquerades. The masks—characterized by a shiny black surface, fleshy neck rolls, delicately carved features, a smooth, high forehead, and an elaborate coiffure—are seen as expressing a Mende feminine ideal. The coiffures of the mask are actually based on popular types of Mende hairstyles, especially those worn on special occasions by women of high status. The arrangement of the hair into a series of longitudinal ridges is a common coiffure and has been documented on women at the turn of the fifteenth century; it indicates the role of women as cultivators and bearers of culture.

Elaborately painted body decoration and scarification are customarily associated with initiation ceremonies in many parts of the world. Among the We of the Ivory Coast, the faces of young female initiates are painted when they leave the excision camp by initiated women, skilled in body painting. They paint the faces of the young girls with schematic designs in black, blue, red, and white. The girls' torsos are sprinkled with oil and rubbed with snail shell or porcelain to make their bodies shine; they will also wear a woven wrapper, necklaces, and bracelets. The purpose of such embellishment is to make the girls look attractive. After emerging from the camp, the initiated girls sit in state, displaying their newly acquired social status as marriageable women. Changes in role and status have been correlated with irreversible forms of body art to emphasize the accumulative and unalterable nature of the transition. Among the Ga'anda of Nigeria, girls are given facial and body scarification to mark different stages of their transition into adulthood. This procedure begins when a girl is five or six and at each stage consists of rows of slightly raised dots that form linear and geometric patterns. The scarification is displayed at each stage and when completed expresses the permanent nature of the transition as well as a visual identification with the group. At these times, the girls wear only a simple woven cloth apron allowing for maximum visibility of the body designs.

For centuries, the Kalabari people of southeastern Nigeria have worn an assortment of both foreign and indigenous items of dress. These they assemble into a distinctive ensemble that for women consists of an imported lace or eyelet blouse and a combination of wrappers embellished with bead, gold, or coral jewelry. The Kalabari do not produce textiles themselves, but purchase handwoven textiles made in Nigeria and Ghana along with imported, factory-made textiles. This type of composite dress is especially apparent during *iria*, a series of ceremonies that mark several stages of a woman's life. When women reach both physical and social maturity, they are allowed to tie and layer a series of short cloth wrappers around their waist to increase the bulk of their midsection, symbolizing their role as society's procreators. Textiles signify a family's wealth and are stored in special cloth boxes that are passed down from one generation to the next. The Kalabari also make use of these textiles by decorating funerary chambers of socially prominent elders with rich displays of heirloom textiles. The degree of a chamber's elaboration is directly related to the deceased's success in life. A group of elderly women, skilled in selecting and arranging textiles, completely drape the ceiling and walls with cloth. The bed, where the corpse is laid in state, is the visual focus of the chamber. Personal accessories that belonged to the deceased, such as beads, fans, canes, and textiles are folded and layered on the bed to reveal a variety of patterns, textures, and colors. The display of the family's textile collection in the funerary chambers is believed to facilitate an elder's transition from the human community to the realm of the ancestors.

Many societies or cultures associate a particular color or type of costume with mourning appropriate for wearing at funerary or memorial ceremonies. The Frafra of northern Ghana have elaborate funerary rituals that emphasize dress. The ordinary male funerary costume consists of a smock, quiver, bow, flute, and headdress. This costume, which is based on the dress worn by both hunters and warriors, symbolizes the origins of Frafra society and its early history. The most common funerary headdress, worn by any male old enough to be a hunter or warrior, is a wicker cap with a hole in the top for inserting a stick or bundle of reeds covered with the hair from the neck of a sheep. The use of sheep hair reflects the importance of domesticated animals, especially for sacrifices. Such a helmet may be made by the owner or purchased in the market. On the other hand, the wicker helmet with horns can be worn only by a hunter. The female funerary costume is based on traditional female dress. In much of northeastern Ghana, women in the past wore woven grass waistbands with small forked leafy branches attached to the front and rear. This leaf form has been replaced almost entirely by a tail made of dyed grass or leather strands. Women would receive such elaborate "tails" during courtship as signs of admiration and intent. The grass or leather "tails" are viewed as proper dress for special occasions. Today, a commercially printed cloth for the upper torso or head tie is often added. In addition, a woman may wear stone or ivory armlets to reflect pride in her family and household.

A wedding ritual not only unites two individuals, but provides a permanent linkage between families and kin groups. Ceremonies marking marriage put considerable emphasis on elaborate and often colorful dress. In Central Asia, special garments tailored from silk cloth were worn at marriage by high-status, wealthy women during the nineteenth century. Because Central Asians viewed silk attire as accumulated wealth, dresses and robes were seen as important components of a woman's dowry. For the marriage ceremony, women attired themselves in a series of dresses, worn in a layered manner so that the richly patterned sleeves of each dress were visibly displayed; an outer robe completed the bride's dress ensemble. This collarless robe, which was close-fitting in the torso with a flaring outward toward the hem, was worn open in the front to reveal the bride's brightly colored dresses; outer robes, considered the most sumptuous of all of the bride's garments, were held in such high esteem, that one or two of them were even draped over the owner's body during her funeral ceremony. The garments were fashioned from hand-loomed silk cloth, decorated with designs made using the ikat-dying technique in which the thread is tie-dyed prior to being woven. The designs were usually created through a process of tie-dying the lengthwise or warp threads before plain colored crosswise or weft threads were woven into them. In the finished textile, the edges where the warp threads had been bound together for dyeing, show a blurred, irregular outline.

The traditional dress for a Tunisian woman consists of a silk, cotton, or wool wrapper draped around the body and attached on the chest with one or two fibulae and gathered at the waist with a sash. The wrapper is covered by a loose-fitting tunic with seams on either side and, for some, sleeves made from another more exquisite material. This type of outfit is now used only for weddings with each region having its own specific patterns and colors. Women are allowed to express their own individual taste and preference. Tunisian wedding tunics are decorated with elaborate embroidery, sequins, and gold-covered wire thread. There is an increasing emphasis on such gold work, especially in the urban areas. Embroidered designs may represent popular symbols of luck such as a star, birds, fish, and crescents. Similar tunics are found in other parts of North Africa. The wedding costumes and jewelry, which have become increasingly expensive, may be borrowed from neighboring families or rented from a fe-

male specialist who helps plan wedding ceremonies. For jewelry, silver is preferred because it is believed to be pure and propitious. Women wear a variety of tunics with different types of decoration and design at distinct ceremonies during the wedding ritual. In Tunisia an important part of the wedding ceremony is for a bride to be displayed formally to the groom, her relatives, and the relatives of the groom. At these times she is dressed in several different tunics that she removes one by one until she is in the last one, the richest of all. For North Africans, marriages represent a significant change of status and require considerable expense and attention; they last for several days and most people of the village will turn out for the event.

Identity, Status, and Leadership
Costumes may also express cultural identity or membership in a group. For the Yoruba of Nigeria there are a number of secular occasions where dress plays a prominent role in affirming a person's Yoruba identity. Both family and community ceremonies, including funerals, childbirth, and child-naming occasions, weddings, chieftaincy celebrations, and house-opening feasts are important social events where members of different extended families come together and dress in their finest clothing. Men wear a gown ensemble consisting of tailored gowns, trousers, and hats made from strip-woven cloth while women wear a wrapper ensemble, blouse, and a head tie. The Yoruba have a custom called *aso-ebi*, where male and female members of families and social clubs appear together in dress made of the same type of cloth. *Aso-ebi* cloth may be special-ordered or purchased at the market and when worn, it visually reinforces the group's cohesion.

In the northwest coast of America, the confirmation of an inherited privilege or the authentication of a new rank or status occurs during a special type of public ceremony called a potlatch, which is especially well developed among the Kwakiutl, Haida, and Tlingit. A potlatch is often held over a period of days and accompanied by the display of objects and the giving of gifts to the guests. The acceptance of these gifts and the acknowledgment of their purpose are critical components of a potlatch. Although the ordinary dress of the northwest coast in the eighteenth century consisted of fairly plain cedar bark capes and blankets, when attending potlatch events, people dressed in their best clothing and seated themselves according to rank. Ceremonial garments in this area are colorful, elaborately decorated, and spectacular. A wealthy man might wear a Chilkat or button blanket, a waist robe or apron, a shirt, leggings, and a headdress, often made of woven spruce root or cedar bark. To the headdress, a carved frontlet, ermine strips, or basketry rings could be added. Trousers are currently worn under the garments. The costume of wealthy women is similar to that of men except for the substitution of a plain dress for the trousers or robe. Shredded cedar bark and mountain goat wool are used for weaving the Chilkat blanket, considered as a family heirloom. This garment is rectangular at the top and the sides and from the bottom edge in the shape of a shallow V, there extends a long warp fringe about one-quarter the length of the blanket. The surface design is clearly a transfer from another medium (painting) and has the effect of a low relief. In addition, the curvilinear forms, characteristic of northwest coast art, is successfully achieved. Black, blue, white, and yellow are the colors that establish the patterns. A newer ceremonial covering is the button blanket consisting of a dark blue blanket—usually Hudson's Bay blanket—decorated with red flannel border and appliqué outlined in small iridescent pearl buttons. Buttons are used as well for creating the details of an image. Dentalium shells—a symbol of wealth—could also ornament a button blanket. The images are normally crest animals, such as a raven, whale, beaver, or eagle, which connect to clan myths.

Ceremonial dress associated with identity and renewal can also reflect social and political points of view or be used for other functions such as protection. Although metal armor was worn by warriors and rulers in Europe as far back as ancient times, in the fourteenth century, overlapping plates of steel were developed to produce a more effective way for covering the entire body. Since plate armor was quite expensive to make, it was limited to warriors of noble birth and became an indicator of status. During the following two centuries, knights and kings who rode into battle on horseback both protected and defined themselves with full suits of plate combat armor while providing a festive element to the occasion. For tournaments or jousting events, knights needed to wear armor made of even heavier metal and often more elaborately decorated. Armor served to protect an individual as well as to enhance appearance. Therefore, decoration, based on a variety of metalworking techniques such as embossing, engraving, and etching, expressed the wealth and status of the wearer. The most commonly used technique in decorating armor was etching.

The Great Plains of North America consisted of many tribes sharing a dependence on the buffalo as a source of food and raw materials. The standard ceremonial regalia for a Plains' warrior included a painted buffalo robe, quill shirt, leggings, moccasins, and some kind of feathered headdress. Plains ritual, which encompassed songs and special dress including body and face painting, were performed for a war campaign, a major buffalo hunt, and a community ceremony such as the sun dance, which focused on renewal. All clothing was made by women who were responsible for tanning animal skins and tailoring the various garments. For the American Plains, the buffalo robe was a distinctive type of dress, which could be painted by men with figurative designs illustrating historical events—especially military exploits—hunting scenes or, in some cases, supernatural visions. Plains cultures attached great importance to these visions and animals were frequently involved, especially buffalo, elk,

bears, eagles, and sparrow hawks. The designs, which can symbolize less visually obvious ideas, were usually arranged horizontally without any overall composition. The actual painting of a buffalo robe was the responsibility of the owner. Originally the colors, each applied with a separate brush, were made from mineral or vegetable material. Quillwork and beadwork embroidery were also employed to adorn a robe. For the people of the Plains, robes served as an expression of both individual and community exploits. A men's robe is similar in form and construction to a woman's dress except it is shorter and has full sleeves.

The symbolic power of traditional Plains clothing was acknowledged again in the late nineteenth century with the Ghost Dance movement, a revitalization movement based on a belief that the Great Spirit would clear away the wreckage of the white man, bring back the buffalo herds, and reunite the Native American people—both living and dead—in a regenerated Earth. The ceremony, which originated among the Paiutes but quickly spread north and east to other Plains groups, began either late in the afternoon or after sundown and involved a circular dance, from East to West, following the movement of the sun. Preliminary activities included painting and dressing the body that took about two hours. The painted designs were an inspiration from a trance vision and consisted of elaborate designs in red, yellow, green, or blue upon the face or a yellow line along the parting of the hair. Suns, crescents, stars, crosses, and birds (especially crows) were the designs usually associated with both painting and clothing. Stars were the most common motif and consisted of a variety of forms such as the traditional four-pointed star, the five-pointed star of the American flag, dashes of paint representing falling stars or the many stars in the heaven. It was by wearing Ghost Dance shirts and dresses that the Great Spirit would recognize his people. Both shirts and dresses were usually made of muslin or cotton but garments of elk, deer, or antelope skins were also produced. These garments were decorated with painted designs, cones, bone, quillwork, and feathers. An eagle feather was also worn on the head.

Social status in most societies is usually expressed through the display of ornaments on the body; yet for a number of cultures, the permanent modification of the skin can exhibit societal membership or high status through scar and tattoo designs. For the Maori of New Zealand, tattooing was characterized by a dense, overall, and interrelated series of motifs organized into spiral and curvilinear patterns. In general, a tattoo results from pricking or piercing the skin and then pigmenting the punctured spots with a coloring substance. Pigment made from soot mixed with spring water, light fish oil, or plant sap, was rubbed into the cut skin. The entire process usually took months or even years to complete. Facial tattooing identified a man as belonging to a particular group and indicated the magnitude of his mana or spiritual power. Although permanent, tattooing was seen as a necessary item of dress for ceremonial occasions: each design had a specific name, and every tattooed individual was marked differently. People of high status had the right to be tattooed while those of lesser status had to earn that right. Wealth, position in the community, and the level of a person's courage would determine the extent and nature of the tattoos. The facial tattooing of a chief were considered so distinctive and varied that the chief would draw them at the bottom of European documents as his signature.

Frequently, leaders of the community will dress in a distinctive fashion, especially during ceremonial occasions. An individual's political power, social position, and wealth can be made visible by dress expressing prominent status or indicating particular social roles such as warrior, judge, and police officer. We must not forget that ordinary people also wear special dress for important events, including weddings, funerals, high school proms, or even gallery openings. Usually it is the entire ensemble of clothing and accessories that project authority and status. But at times, a single item of dress may announce social position and political power. For example, among the Yoruba of Nigeria, a conical, beaded crown with fringe veil is the primary symbol of kingship and must be worn by the ruler on all ceremonial occasions. The veil obscures the face of the living king while a face motif on the crown reveals the dynastic ancestors. In this way, the crown represents the spiritual and political force of the dynasty. Crowns also reference royal power in European cultures.

Royal dress and regalia has characterized the Asante people of Ghana since the seventeenth century. The two most spectacular elements of Asante dress are kente cloth and elaborate gold jewelry. Kente is a brightly colored, hand-loomed, narrow band cloth woven by men on a four-heddle horizontal loom. The weavers use silk or rayon thread to create bright color in a predominantly cotton textile. The names and meanings of kente designs can allude to proverbs, historical events, or important characteristics of leadership. During their reigns, Asante kings were expected to invent new kente designs. Kente is a good example of how a dress form that is adopted by another culture can shift meaning. In the United States, kente has become identified with African American culture and has been used in multiple forms and ceremonial contexts. The Asante have used gold extensively to adorn and glorify rulers as well as to validate their positions. The Asante king and various categories of chiefs wear many items of gold, such as necklaces, anklets, large armlets, and rings. Magnificently attired rulers, encumbered with as many gold ornaments as they can wear or carry while participating in religious or state ceremonies can be identified with the proverb "Great men move slowly." Gold objects are produced by the lost wax process or repoussé technique.

In Polynesia the spiritual power of rulers and other high-ranking people was often expressed by wearing apparel made of feathers, which associated it with the gods. In Hawaii, one of the most centralized and status-conscious societies in Polynesia, feather cloaks, sashes, and helmets were important components of ceremonial dress, enhancing the authority and divine status of a ruler. Cloaks, worn on state occasions and during battle, provided spiritual, and to some extent physical, protection to the wearer. Capturing an enemy's feathered cloak was a particularly powerful symbol of defeat. The size of a cloak was directly related to the amount of power a noble person possessed. Because so many feathers were required to produce a cloak, only individuals of great wealth could afford them. Feathers were in part collected as tribute paid by commoners to the chiefs each year. Although ordinary clothing was made by women, the cloaks were made by high-ranking men. Passing a cloak to a descendant involved a transfer of mana (power) from one generation to the next. Feathered cloaks were worn wrapped around the body so that the edges come together unifying the motifs that flank each edge. Many cloaks were decorated with four yellow, bladelike motifs set against a red background. With the imposition of American rule in the late nineteenth century, feathered cloaks were no longer used for warfare but continued to be indicative of chiefly rank. Also, red feathers, associated with the god of war, were used less and yellow became more common as yellow feathers were rarer and more valuable.

A complete clothing ensemble, consisting of cloak, robe, and turban, expresses religious identity as well as high social status for the Muslim Hausa-Fulani rulers of northern Nigeria and is worn for religious celebrations and major political events. On such occasions, the lavishly dressed ruler and officials of high rank appear in a public procession, mounted on richly adorned horses, to symbolically establish superiority over those they rule. Their dress not only sets the ruling aristocracy apart from the rest of the population, but also identifies the wearer with the larger Muslim world both within Africa and beyond. Robes, the most distinct part of the dress ensemble, are often worn layered, creating an imposing image of physical bulk and majesty. The visual focus of the robe, tailored from hand-woven or factory-made cloth, is a large pocket densely embroidered with geometric designs that are loosely inspired by Islamic calligraphy and believed to offer spiritual protection to the wearer. A turban is wrapped numerous times around the wearer's head and chin, creating an aesthetic effect that visually complements the bulky robe. The turban signifies that the man has completed the most important obligation of Islam—a pilgrimage to the sacred city of Mecca. Items in a ruler's dress ensemble are valued heirlooms that belong to the state; like the feathered cloaks of Hawaiian leaders, they can be passed on to descendants in the royal line or given as gifts to other rulers and officials to seal political alliances.

Symbolic dress is not limited to other times and cultures. The dress of modern political leaders and their families shapes the public image as well. A case in point is the wardrobe of Jacqueline Kennedy during the campaign and presidency of her husband, John F. Kennedy. Kennedy was criticized for her extravagant wardrobe and use of foreign designers—especially when compared to the plain style of the Republican candidate's wife, Pat Nixon. Soon after the election, Kennedy worked with the American designer Oleg Cassini to re-create her image. As First Lady, Kennedy established a unique style that was dignified and elegant but also photogenic and recognizable. For her husband's swearing-in ceremony in January 1961, Jacqueline Kennedy wore a Cassini-designed beige wool crepe dress. She also wore a pillbox hat from Bergdorf Goodman's millinery salon, in what was to become her trademark style—on the back of her head rather than straight and high, as was the fashion. Jacqueline Kennedy's style became widely popular and helped define the image of the Kennedy presidency as innovative, dynamic, and glamorous.

Viewed globally, ceremonial dress involves many acts of body modification that reflect both indigenous development and outside influences. As cultural artifacts, the specific elements of apparel and body adornment have many aspects of meaning; they serve as vehicles for the expression of values, symbols of identity and social status, and statements of aesthetic preference. Each item of a costume has its own history and sociocultural significance and must be considered along with the total ensemble. By looking at ceremonial costumes in other cultures, it becomes possible to understand better the form and function of similar types of dress in one's own culture.

See also **Carnival Dress; Kente; Masks; Masquerade and Masked Balls.**

BIBLIOGRAPHY

Adams, Monni. "Women's Art as a Gender Strategy among the Wé of Canton Boo." *African Arts* 26, no. 4 (1993): 32–43.

D'Alleva, Anne. *Art of the Pacific.* London: Calmann and King Ltd., 1998.

Eicher, Joanne B., and Tonye V. Erekosima. "Final Farewells: The Fine Art of Kalabari Funerals." In *Ways of the River: Arts and Environment of the Niger Delta.* Edited by Martha G. Anderson and Philip M. Peek, 307–329. Los Angeles: UCLA Fowler Museum of Cultural History, 2002.

Jonaitis, Aldona, ed. *Chiefly Feasts: The Enduring Kwakiutl Potlatch.* New York: American Museum of Natural History, 1991.

Mack, John, ed. *African Arts and Cultures.* London: British Museum Press, 2000.

Perani, Judith, and Fred T. Smith. *The Visual Arts of Africa: Gender Power and Life Cycle Rituals.* Upper Saddle River, N.J.: Prentice Hall, 1998.

Rose, Roger G., and Adrienne L. Kaeppler. *Hawai'i: The Royal Islands.* Honolulu, Hawaii: Bishop Museum Press, 1980.

Ross, Doran. *Wrapped in Pride: Ghanaian Kente and African American Identity.* Los Angeles: UCLA Fowler Museum of Cultural History, 1998.

Rubin, Arnold, ed. *Marks of Civilization.* Los Angeles: UCLA Fowler Museum of Cultural History, 1988.

Spring, Christopher, and Julie Hudson. *North African Textiles.* London: British Museum Press, 1995.

Turner, Victor, ed. *Celebration: Studies in Festivity and Ritual.* Washington, D.C.: Smithsonian Institution Press, 1982.

Fred T. Smith

CHADOR Chador, meaning "large cloth" or "sheet" in modern Persian, refers to a semicircular cloak, usually black, enveloping the head, body, and sometimes the face (like a tent), held in place by the wearer's hands. It is worn by Muslim women outside or inside the home in front of *namahram*, men ineligible to be their husbands, in Iran and with modifications elsewhere, including parts of Afghanistan, Iraq, and Pakistan. The chador is closely associated with the Islamic practice of *hijab*, which comes from the verbal Arabic word "hajaba," meaning to hide from view or conceal. *Hijab* stresses modesty based on Koranic passages (Surahs XXXIII:59 and XXIV:13) indicating that believing women should cover their hair and cast outer garments over themselves when in public.

Hijab and Politics

The Islamic chador, introduced during the Abbasid Era (750–1258) when black was the dynastic color, has been worn by Persian women with slight variations over many centuries. Western sartorial changes began in Iran during the reign of Shah Nasir al-Din (1848–1896) who, after visiting Paris in 1873, introduced European-style clothing to his country. The chador, however, was still worn by most Persian women. After World War I, with the government takeover in 1925 by Reza Khan Pahlavi, legislative and social reforms were introduced, including using the modern national state name "Iran." Influenced by Ataturk's Westernization clothing programs in the new Republic of Turkey, Reza Shah hoped his people would be treated as equals by Europeans if they wore Western clothing. His Dress Reform Law mandated that Persian men wear coats, suits, and Pahlavi hats, which resulted in compliance by some and protesting riots by others with encouragement from ulema, the group of Islamic clerics known as mullahs. Gradually, the traditional *Shari'a*, or Islamic Law, was being replaced by French secular codes. Because of emotional and religious opposition to unveiling women, the shah moved slower regarding female dress reforms, but by February 1936, a government ban outlawed the chador throughout Iran. Police were ordered to fine women wearing chadors; doctors could not treat them, and they were not allowed in public places such as movies, baths, or on buses. As modern role models, the shah's wife and daughters appeared in public unveiled.

In 1941, fearing a Nazi takeover during World War II, British and Soviet troops occupied Iran, whereby Reza Shah abdicated in favor of Mohammed Reza, the crown prince, age twenty-two, who agreed to rule as a constitu-

A Muslim woman wears a black *chador*. The garment is a semicircular cloak covering the head, body and sometimes the face. Women are required to wear the chador outside and also inside the home in front of men other than their husbands. MARY FARAHNAKIAN. REPRODUCED BY PERMISSION.

tional monarch. Attempting to placate both pro- and anti-chador advocates, the young shah removed government restrictions prohibiting wearing chadors, but asked Muslim leaders to call for tolerance toward women who chose to appear publicly unveiled. The chador controversy continued over several decades: some pro-Marxist, anti-Western groups opposed the shah and advocated the chador; pro-Westerners wanted European-style clothing. Ultimately, the chador came to symbolize "rebellion" against the regime, until finally in March 1979, after the shah's forced departure, the opposition leader Ayatollah Khomeini returned from exile, taking over government control. His pro-Islamic revolutionary policies included urging women to resume wearing the chador for modesty reasons. Reacting to large protest marches, government officials clamped down, ordering all women in government employment to wear the chador. By May 1981, legal reforms based on Islamic *Shari'a* required all women over age nine to observe *hijab*, wearing either the chador or a long coat with sleeves and a large dark head cloth. These legal regulations were still in effect in the early 2000s.

See also **Islamic Dress, Contemporary; Middle East: History of Islamic Dress; Religion and Dress.**

BIBLIOGRAPHY

Baker, Patricia L. "Politics of Dress: The Dress Reform Laws of 1920/30s Iran." In *Languages of Dress in the Middle East.* Edited by Nancy Lindisfarne-Tapper and Bruce Ingham. Surrey, U.K.: Curzon Press, 1997.

El Guindi, Fadwa. *Veil: Modesty, Privacy and Resistance.* Oxford, U.K.: Berg, 1999.

Scarce, Jennifer M. "The Development of Women's Veils in Persia and Afghanistan." *Costume* 9 (1975): 4–14.

Shirazi, Faegheh. *The Veil, Unveiled: the Hijab in Modern Culture.* Gainsville: University Press of Florida, 2001.

Beverly Chico

CHALAYAN, HUSSEIN Hussein Chalayan's fascination with architecture, spatial dynamics, urban identity, and aerodynamics is expressed in garments based on concepts, technological systems, historical dress, and theories of the body. His clothes are minimal in look but maximal in thought.

Early Career
Chalayan was born in the Turkish community of Nicosia on the island of Cyprus in 1970. His parents separated when he was a child. At the age of eight, he joined his father, who had moved to the United Kingdom. Chalayan was sent to a private school in London when he was twelve, but returned to Cyprus to study for his A-level examinations. He went back to London and attended Central Saint Martin's College at the age of nineteen to study fashion. Chalayan rose to fashion fame soon after he received his B.A. degree from Central Saint Martin's in 1993. His graduating collection, titled The Tangent Flows, was the now infamous series of buried garments that were exhumed just before the show and presented with a text that explained the process.

The rituals of burial and resurrection gave the garments a dimension of reference to life, death, and urban decay in a process that transported the garments from the world of fashion to the kingdom of nature. Since then, Chalayan has collaborated with architects, artists, textile technologists and aerospace engineers; has won awards; and has been recognized as an artist in numerous museum presentations of his work.

The genius of Chalayan's work lies in his ability to explore visual and intellectual principles that chart the spectral orientations of urban societies through such tangibles as clothing, buildings, vehicles, and furniture and through such abstractions as beauty, philosophy and feeling. Chalayan's Aeroplane and Kite dresses (autumn–winter 1995) used the spatial relationship between the fabric and the body to reflect the relative meanings of speed and gravity. The dresses became dynamic interfaces between the human body and its surroundings; the

A model steps into a Hussein Chalayan skirt. Chalayan incorporated a relation to architecture, geometry, and urban life into his designs. He launched his career in 1993 with a collection titled "The Tangent Flows," in which the garments had been buried and exhumed before the show, which depicted the process of life and death. AP/WIDE WORLD PHOTOS. REPRODUCED BY PERMISSION.

Kite dress actually flew and was reunited with its wearer when it returned to earth.

In Chalayan's eyes, all garments are externalizations of the body in the same way that vehicles and buildings are proportioned to contain the human form. "Everything around us either relates to the body or to the environment," Chalayan explained. "I think of modular systems where clothes are like small parts of an interior, the interiors are part of architecture, which is then a part of an urban environment. I think of fluid space where they are all a part of each other, just in different scales and proportions" (Quinn, p. 120). These sentiments were amplified in the Echoform collection (autumn–winter 1999) in dresses that mimicked airplane interiors. Chalayan attached padded headrests to the shoulders of the garments, evoking thoughts on the role of clothing as a component of a larger spatial system.

Likewise, the Geotrophics collection (spring–summer 1999) made chairs into wearable extensions of the human form. The chair dresses represented the idea of a nomadic existence facilitated by living within completely transportable environments. Determined to express "how the meaning of a nation evolves through conflict or natural boundaries," Chalayan explored the body's role as a locus for the construction of identity, highlighting the ways in which its appropriation by national regimes would orient and indoctrinate it according to the space in which it "belongs."

The relationship between space and identity was further explored in the groundbreaking After Words (autumn–winter 2000) collection. Chalayan based the collection on the necessity of evacuating one's home during wartime and having to hide possessions when a raid was impending. The theme evoked the 1974 Turkish military intervention that displaced both Turkish and Greek Cypriots from their homes and led indirectly to Chalayan's emigration to Britain several years later. The collection introduced the idea of urban camouflage through clothing, whereby fashion functions as a means of hiding objects in obvious places. After Words featured dresses-cum-chair covers that disguised their role as fashionable garments while simultaneously concealing the furniture beneath them. The collection included a table designed to be worn as a skirt, with chairs that were transformed into suitcases and carried away by the models.

For his before minus now collection (spring–summer 2000), Chalayan returned to the architectural theme expressed in Echoform and Geotrophics, designing a series of dresses in collaboration with an architectural firm. The dresses featured wire-frame architectural prints against static white backgrounds generated by a computer program designed to draw three-dimensional perspectives within an architectural landscape. The renderings' geometric dimensions suppress the depiction of real space and create a reality independent of the shapes and textures found in the organic world. Such absolute symmetry and concise angles create the illusion of a realm that is carefully ordered and controlled, yet the architectonic expressions correspond to physical registrations of surfaces and programmatic mappings.

The Remote Control Dress, which was commissioned in 2000 by Judith Clark Costume in London, was designed by means of the composite technology used by aircraft engineers, mirroring the systems that enable airplanes to fly by remote control. Crafted from a combination of fiberglass and resin, the dress was molded into two smooth and glossy pink-colored front and back panels fastened together by metal clips. The facade-like structure of the dress forms an exoskeleton around the body, arcing dramatically inward at the waist and outward in the hip region, echoing the silhouette produced by a corset. This structure gives the dress a well-defined hourglass shape that incorporates principles of corsetry into its design, emphasizing a conventionally feminine shape while creating a solid structure that simultaneously masks undesirable body proportions.

Chalayan's Importance

While Chalayan's work continues to question traditional readings of dress and to generate exciting interdisciplinary collaborations, he also opens new frontiers for other designers to explore. As many of his groundbreaking ideas begin to influence wider trends, Chalayan's work is gaining recognition in the mainstream fashion market while continuing to receive acclaim in fashion circles. Since Chalayan signed a licensing agreement with the Italian manufacturing company Gibo in 2002, his label has grown into a strong retail brand. The designer's appointment as creative director of fashion for the classically inclined British luxury retailer Asprey brings his conceptual oeuvre to a wider public. But the garments still require an audience with the confidence to carry off clothes heavy with the thought processes behind them.

See also **Fashion Designer; Fashion and Identity; Fashion Shows; Haute Couture.**

BIBLIOGRAPHY

Frankel, Susannah. *Fashion Visionaries: Interviews with Fashion Designers.* London: V and A Publications, 2001.

Quinn, Bradley. *The Fashion of Architecture.* Oxford: Berg, 2003.

Bradley Quinn

CHANEL, GABRIELLE (COCO)

Gabrielle Chanel (1883–1971) was born out of wedlock in the French town of Saumur in the Loire Valley on 19 August 1883 to Albert Chanel, an itinerant salesman, and Jeanne Devolle. Her parents were finally married in July of 1884. Her mother died of asthma at the age of thirty-three. When Chanel was just twelve years old, she was sent along with her two sisters to an orphanage at Aubazine. During the holidays the girls stayed with their grandparents in Moulins. In 1900 Chanel moved there permanently and attended the local convent school with her aunt Adrienne, who was of a similar age. Having been taught to sew by the nuns, both girls found work as dressmakers, assisting Monsieur Henri Desboutin of the House of Grampayre.

Early Career

Chanel sang during evening concerts at a fashionable café called La Rotonde. It is believed that her rendition of the song "Qui qu'a vu Coco dans le Trocadéro" earned her the nickname "Coco." Chanel started to mix in fashionable circles when she went to live in 1908 with Étienne Balsan, who bred racehorses on his vast estate at La Croix-Saint-Ouen. Chanel's astute choice of clothing—her neat tailor-made suits and masculine riding dress—and modest demeanor served to mark her out from the other courtesans. Thus from an early age Chanel demonstrated great confidence in her own sense of style, a formula that proved irresistible to other women. Soon Balsan's friends asked her to make them copies of the boater hats that she trimmed and wore herself. Seizing upon this opportunity for financial independence, in 1908–1909 Chanel persuaded Balsan to let her use his Paris apartment at 160, boulevard Malesherbes to set up a millinery business. She employed a professional milliner and she engaged her sister Antoinette and two other assistants as the business grew.

While Chanel was in Paris, her friendship with the millionaire entrepreneur and polo player Arthur Capel, known as "Boy," developed into love. It was Boy who lent her the money to rent commercial premises on the rue Cambon—where the House of Chanel was still located in the early 2000s—in the heart of Paris's couture district. Chanel modes opened at 21, rue Cambon in 1910. From the outset, Chanel was the perfect model for her own designs, and she was photographed for the fall 1910 issue of the magazine *Le théâtre: Revue mensuelle illustrée.* By 1912 hats by Chanel appeared in the popular press, worn by such leading actresses of the day as Lucienne Roger and Gabrielle Dorziat. Chanel had achieved financial independence. The terms of her lease, however, prevented her from selling clothes, as there was a dressmaker already working in the building.

First Collections, 1913–1919

While on vacation in Deauville on the west coast of France in the summer of 1913, Boy Capel found a shop for Chanel to open on the fashionable rue Gontaut-Biron, and it was here that she presented her first fashion collections. With the outbreak of World War I in July 1914, many wealthy and fashionable Parisians decamped to Deauville and shopped at Chanel's boutique. It is believed that she sold only ready-to-wear clothing at this date. Chanel had cut her hair short during this period and many other women copied her bobbed hairstyle as well as bought her clothes. Chanel's time had come: radical in their understatement, her versatile and sporty designs were to prove perfect for the more active lives led by many wealthy women during wartime.

In 1916 Chanel purchased a stock of surplus jersey fabric from the manufacturer Rodier, which she made into unstructured three-quarter-length coats belted at the waist and embellished with luxurious fabrics or furs, worn with matching skirts. That fall Chanel presented her first complete couture collection. The March 1917 issue of *Les élégances parisiennes* illustrates a group of jersey suits by Chanel, some of which are delicately embroidered, while others are strictly plain and accessorized with a saddlery-style double belt. All are worn with open-neck blouses with deep sailor collars. A 1918 design consisted of a coat of tan jersey banded with brown rabbit fur, with a lining and blouse of white-dotted rose foulard: this matching of the coat lining to the dress or blouse was to become a Chanel trademark. Striking in their simplicity and modernity, Chanel's jersey fashions caused a sensation.

While Chanel's daywear was characterized by its stylish utility, her evening wear was unashamedly romantic. In 1919 she presented fragile gowns in black

Karl Lagerfeld. Lagerfeld appears with models at the presentation of Chanel's 2002 spring-summer haute couture collection. Lagerfeld became chief designer of Chanel in 1983 and was credited with making Chanel goods highly desirable again. AP/WIDE WORLD PHOTOS. REPRODUCED BY PERMISSION.

Chantilly lace with gold-spun net and jet tassels and other gowns in silver lace brocade. Capes of black velvet adorned with rows of ostrich fringe revealed a Spanish influence—the very height of fashion that winter. This was the year that Chanel would announce, "I woke up famous," but it was also the year that Boy Capel was killed in an automobile accident.

The 1920s

Fashions of the early 1920s. From 1920 to 1923 Chanel conducted a liaison with the grand duke Dmitri Pavlovitch, grandson of Russia's Tsar Alexander II, and her collections during these years were imbued with Russian influences. Particularly noteworthy were loose shift dresses, waistcoats, blouses, and evening coats made in dark and neutral colors with exquisite, brightly colored, folkloric Russian embroideries stitched by exiled aristocrats. In 1922 Chanel showed long, lean, belted blouses based on Russian peasant wear.

By 1923 she had further simplified the cut of her clothes and offered fewer brocaded fabrics, while her em-

broideries—red and beige were favorite colors that year—displayed more restrained and modernistic designs. Chanel led the international trend toward shorter hemlines. Her premises on the rue Cambon, which had already expanded in 1919, grew to include numbers 27, 29, and 31 during the early 1920s.

Perfumes. Chanel launched her first perfume, Chanel No. 5, in 1921. Reputedly named for the designer's lucky number, No. 5 was blended by Ernest Beaux, who used aldehydes (an organic compound which yields acids when oxidized and alcohols when reduced) to enhance the fragrance of such costly natural ingredients as jasmine, the perfume's base note. Chanel designed the modern pharmaceutical-style bottle and monochrome packaging herself. Chanel No. 5 was the first perfume to bear a designer's name. Building upon the success of No. 5, Chanel introduced Cuir de Russie (1924), Bois des Îles (1926), and Gardénia (1927) before the end of the decade.

La garçonne. Chanel's interpretation of masculine styles and sportswear—her blazers, waistcoats, and shirts with cufflinks, as well as her choice of fabrics—were greatly inspired by the garments worn by the duke of Westminster (an Englishman with whom she was involved between 1923 and 1930) and his aristocratic friends. Following a fishing holiday in Scotland, she introduced her customers to Fair Isle woolens and tweeds. The duke bought her a mill to secure exclusive fabrics for her new styles. Chanel was also inspired by humbler items of masculine apparel, including berets, reefer jackets, mechanics' dungarees, stonemasons' neckerchiefs, and sailor suits, which she rendered utterly luxurious for her wealthy clients. Chanel herself often wore loose sailor-style trousers, flouting the rules of sartorial etiquette that generally restricted women from wearing trousers to the beach or within the home as evening pajamas.

In 1927 *Vogue* recommended Chanel's jersey suit in soft tan wool, with collar, cuffs, blouse, and jacket lining in rose jersey, for the woman who wanted to look chic on board ship. The long-line jacket buttoned diagonally, while the skirt was box-pleated at the front. Throughout her career Chanel paid great attention to the cut of her sleeves, ensuring that they permitted the wearer to move with ease without distorting the lines of the garment. By the fall of 1929 her sports costumes were still slim but longer, with hemlines reaching below the calf.

The little black dress. Chanel had designed black dresses as early as 1913, when she made a black velvet dress with a white petal collar for Suzanne Orlandi. In April 1919 British *Vogue* reported that "Chanel takes into account the lack of motors and the general difficulty of living in Paris just now by her almost invariably black evening dresses" (p. 48). But it was not until American *Vogue* (1 October 1926) described a *garçonne*-style black day dress as "The Chanel 'Ford'—the frock that all the world will wear" (p. 69) that the little black dress took the fashion world by storm. And although the use of black in fashion has a long history, Chanel has been credited as its originator ever since.

Theatrical costume. The stage was a prominent showcase for fashion designers during the nineteenth and early twentieth centuries. Chanel always moved in artistic circles, and she often supported the work of her friends both financially and by working collaboratively with them. In 1922 she designed Grecian-style costumes in coarse wool for Jean Cocteau's adaptation of Sophocles's *Antigone;* the designs were featured in French *Vogue* (1 February 1923). The following year she dressed the dancers of the Ballets russes in jersey bathing costumes and sports clothes similar to those seen in her fashion collections for the modern-realist production *Le train bleu* (1924). And in 1926 the actresses in Cocteau's *Orphée* were dressed head to toe in Chanel's latest fashions.

Jewelry. Chanel believed the role of jewelry was to decorate an ensemble rather than to flaunt wealth, and she challenged convention by wearing heaps of jewelry, often precious, during the day—even for sailing—while for evening she sometimes wore no jewelry at all. The loose, straight-cut shapes of Chanel's fashions and her use of many plain fabrics provided the perfect foil for the lavish costume jewelry that she introduced in the early 1920s. Lacking any desire to replicate precious jewels, Chanel's designs, initially made by Maison Gripoix, defied nature in their bold use of color and size. In 1924 she opened her own jewelry workshop, which was managed by the comte Étienne de Beaumont. Beaumont designed the long chains with colored stones and cross-shaped pendants that became a classic of her house. Chanel was fond of Byzantine crosses, and she was also inspired by the buttons, chains, and tassels of military costumes.

Her oversized fake pearls, worn in multiple strands, were an instant success. In 1926 Chanel created a vogue for mismatched earrings by wearing a black pearl in one ear and a white one in the other. In 1928 she introduced diamond paste jewelry and in 1929 offered "gypsy" necklaces—triple strands of red, green, and yellow beads, as well as colored beads combined with chunky wooden chains.

Fashions of the later 1920s. By the late 1920s Chanel's fashions were adorned with geometric designs. For daywear she used stripes and checks as well as patterns inspired by Fair Isle knitwear; for evening many of her black lace fabrics were combined with metallic, embroidered, or beaded laces.

At the height of her fame and with the demand for Paris couture at its peak, Chanel employed between two and three thousand workers during the mid- to late 1920s. She was said, however, to be a hard taskmaster and to pay poor wages. In 1927 she opened her London house. British *Vogue* pointed out in early June 1927 that, while the conception and feel of Chanel's current collection was essentially French, the designer had adapted

Gabrielle Coco Chanel. Chanel began designing at the beginning of the twentieth century, quickly gaining the attention of the fashion world with her stylishly functional daywear and her elegant evening wear. © CONDÉ NAST ARCHIVE/CORBIS. REPRODUCED BY PERMISSION.

it for London social life. For the Royal Ascot racing meet she offered a long-sleeved black lace dress with trailing scarf detail and, for presentation at court, an understated white taffeta dress with a train that was cut in one piece with the skirt, complemented by a simple headdress based on the Prince of Wales feathers. In September 1929 *Vogue* wrote, "When Chanel, the sponsor of the straight, chemise dress and the boyish silhouette, uses little, rippling capes on her fur coats and a high waist-line and numerous ruffles on an evening gown, then you may be sure that the feminine mode is a fact and not a fancy" (p. 35).

In tune with her modernist fashion aesthetic, Chanel installed faceted glass mirrors in her Paris couture salon around 1928. These mirrors brought the advantage of allowing her to sit out of sight to watch her shows. In complete contrast to the salon, her private apartment on the third floor of 31, rue Cambon was lavish and ornate. It is now carefully preserved, decorated with Coromandel screens, Louis XIV furniture, Venetian mirrors, blackamoor sculptures, and smoked crystal and amethyst chandeliers. When designing clothes, Chanel would pare away the nonessentials for the sake of the wearer's comfort; when designing domestic interiors, on the other hand, she believed that clutter was a necessity—that it was essential to be surrounded by the objects one needed and loved.

The 1930s

Fashions of the early 1930s. Although Chanel's business may have suffered during the depression—she is said to have halved her prices in 1932—her workforce increased to around four thousand employees by 1935. Chanel's saleswomen as well as her seamstresses went on strike in June 1936 to protest their poor wages and working conditions. In April 1936 the French people voted in a left-wing coalition government headed by Leon Blum, which was followed by a number of strikes including the workers at Chanel. Chanel refused to implement the Matignon Agreement, which introduced wage increases of 7 to 15 percent, the right to collective bargaining and unionize, a 40-hour week and a 2-week paid annual holiday. Instead she fired 300 women who refused to leave the building and only later, in order to produce her next collection, agreed to introduce a workers co-operative on the understanding that she managed it (Madsen, p. 216).

From 1930 Chanel's hemlines became longer and were slightly flared; she emphasized her waists, and her jackets had soft, bloused bodices. Bows were to become a signature motif, used as decorative details on the shoulders and skirts of her garments. Cravat bows provided a feminine touch to her blouses, and crisp white frills were added around the collars and cuffs of her black suits and dresses. From 1934 Chanel used American elasticized fabrics made with a brand of yarn with a latex core called Lastex in her collections to create clothes with a crepe-like surface, and she frequently combined these with jersey.

During the 1930s she launched her cosmetics line and introduced a new perfume called Glamour. She further boosted her revenue by endorsing other manufacturers' products and designing for other companies. In 1931 she promoted Ferguson Brothers' cottons—her spring collection included cotton evening gowns—and she designed knitwear for Ellaness and raincoats for David Mosley and Sons. She also earned $2 million for her work in Hollywood that year.

Screen and stage. When hemlines dropped in 1929, Hollywood's movie studios were devastated, as thousands of reels of film were instantly rendered old-fashioned. Rather than continue to follow Parisian fashions slavishly, the studio magnate Samuel Goldwyn invited Chanel to design costumes directly for his leading female stars, including Greta Garbo, Gloria Swanson, and Marlene Dietrich. Chanel, however, produced designs for just three Metro-Goldwyn-Mayer productions: *Palmy Days* (1931), *Tonight or Never* (1931), and *The Greeks Had a Word for Them* (1932). Many actresses refused to have Chanel's style imposed on them, and her designs were either overlooked or criticized for being too understated for the screen.

In Paris, Chanel continued to design for progressive plays, providing costumes for Cocteau's *La machine infernale* (1934) as well as *Les chevaliers de la table ronde* and *Oedipe-Roi*, both of which appeared in 1937. In addition, despite her dislike of left-wing politics, she created the costumes for Jean Renoir's radical film *La marseillaise* and for *La règle du jeu*, both produced in 1938.

Jewelry. In 1932 the International Guild of Diamond Merchants commissioned Chanel to design a collection of diamonds set in platinum called Bijoux de Diamants. Having designed fake jewels during affluent times, Chanel now declared that diamonds were an investment. Along with her current lover, Paul Iribe, she presented a line of jewelry based on the themes of knots, stars, and feathers. The collection was exhibited in her own home in the rue du Faubourg-Saint-Honoré in Paris.

During the 1930s, Fulco di Santostefano della Cerda, duc di Verdura, started to design jewelry for Chanel. He had been designing textiles for her since 1927. Most significantly, di Verdura pioneered the revival of baked enamel jewelry: his chunky, baked enamel bracelets inset with jeweled Maltese crosses were particularly successful. Christian Bérard also designed occasional pieces for her, and Maison Gripoix continued to make up many of her designs—notably those in romantic floral and rococo-revival styles. From the mid- to late 1930s Chanel's heavy triangular bibs of colored stones and coins and her silk cord necklaces with tassels of brilliantly colored stones showed influences from India and Southeast Asia.

Fashions of the later 1930s. Chanel's daywear continued to be characterized by its simplicity, but—perhaps surprisingly—she participated in the vogue for Victorian-revival styles, presenting cinch-waisted, full-skirted, and bustle-backed evening gowns worn with shoulder-length lace gloves and floral accessories. Decidedly more modern was the trouser suit worn by the fashion editor Diana Vreeland in 1937–1938 that consisted of a black bolero-style jacket and high-waisted trousers entirely covered with overlapping sequins. The metallic sheen of the sequins contrasted with a soft cream silk chiffon and lace blouse with ruffled neckline and fastened with pearl buttons. Chanel's dramatic combinations of black with white or scarlet remained popular. In the late 1930s her evening wear revealed influences from gypsy and peasant sources: skirts in multicolored taffetas, sometimes striped or checked, and worn with puff-sleeved, embroidered blouses.

The war years. Chanel closed her fashion house during World War II but continued to sell her perfumes. For the duration of the war she lived in Paris at the Hotel Ritz with her German lover, an officer in the German army named Hans-Gunther von Dincklage. When Paris was liberated in 1944, Chanel fled to Switzerland and did not return to the rue Cambon for almost a decade.

The 1950s

Fashions of the 1950s. Chanel started working again at the age of seventy in 1953, partly to boost her flagging perfume sales. Her fashion philosophy remained unchanged: she extolled function and comfort in dress and declared her aim of making women look pretty and young. On 5 February 1954 she presented her first post-war collection, a line of understated suits and dresses. The general press response, however, was that Chanel was too old and out of touch with the modern market, and only a few models sold. On the other hand, American *Vogue* (15 February 1954) thought "the great revolution-ist" sufficiently important to justify a three-and-a-half-page article devoted to her career and fashion philosophy: "A dress isn't right if it is uncomfortable. . . . A dress must function; place the pockets accurately for use, never a button without a button-hole. A sleeve isn't right unless the arm moves easily. Elegance in clothes means freedom to move freely" (American *Vogue*, p. 84).

By modernizing the formulas that had brought her so much success earlier in her career, Chanel succeeded in reestablishing herself as a fashion designer of international stature. For spring–summer 1955 she presented a gray jersey suit consisting of a softly-fitted jacket complete with pockets and a full box-pleated skirt, worn with a bow-tied white blouse. Navy jersey suits had school-girl-style blazer jackets and were banded with white trim or worn with knitwear striped in navy and white. Buttons were often covered in fabrics that matched the suit, and sometimes meticulously trimmed with the contrasting fabric that was used to outline the pockets and form the attached shirt cuffs. Other buttons were molded in bold brass, sometimes featuring a lion's head—Chanel's birth sign was Leo—or made in more delicate gilt, perhaps with a cutwork floral motif.

In 1957 Chanel introduced braid trimmings to her cardigan-style jackets. For fall–winter 1957–1958 her suits had a wrap pleat that ran down the side of the skirt and concealed a trouser-style pocket. Unusually, she showed a hat with every model—these were upturned sailor-style hats made in soft fabrics that matched the suits with which they were worn. As always, she paid great attention to the linings of her coats and suits: this season, camel hair was lined with red guanaco, gray tweed with white squirrel, and red velour with fluffy gray goatskin. Her coats were cut in the same style as her suit jackets, simply lengthened to the same level as the skirt hem.

Chanel's modern suits in nubby wools, tweeds, or jersey fabrics with their multiple functional pockets, teamed with gilt chains and fake pearl jewelry; her distinctive handbags; and her sling-back shoes with contrasting toe caps, became fashion staples for the affluent. And as before, her designs were widely copied for the mass market: the company sold toiles to the British chain store Wallis so that it could legitimately reproduce Chanel's designs.

For evening Chanel offered variations on her suits in such lavish materials as gold-trimmed brocade, and she remained faithful to her love of black-and-white laces for dresses. A cocktail dress from the spring–summer 1958 collection had a bodice of navy-and-white-striped silk with a

"The maison Chanel might be called the 'Jersey House', for the creations of Mlle. Chanel have long been and long will be in jersey. Of late, a thin firm quality of cotton velvet has been used by Chanel for cloaks and certain frocks." (British *Vogue*, early October 1917, p. 30).

large bow at the neckline and a full skirt of white organdy, banded at the hem with the same striped fabric.

For spring–summer 1959 she presented a black lace dress, dipping low at the back and molded to the hipline, which was threaded with black ribbon and flared into a full skirt; it was accessorized with a long chain with linked pearls and chunky, colored stones. That season the collection was modeled by the designer's friends—stylish young women who were accustomed to wearing her clothes.

Perfumes and accessories. In 1954 Chanel introduced a man's fragrance, Pour Monsieur. The same year Pierre and Paul Wertheimer, who already owned Parfums Chanel, bought her entire business, and it remained within the Wertheimer family as of the early 2000s.

In 1955 Chanel introduced quilted handbags with shoulder straps of leather plaited with gilt chains with flattened links, similar to those used to weight her jackets. The bags were offered in leather or jersey and were initially available in beige, navy, brown, and black, lined with red grosgrain or leather—Chanel chose a lighter color for the interior to help women find small items in their bags. Updated each season, Chanel's distinctive handbags were still top sellers in the early 2000s.

The 1960s

By 1960 fashions by Chanel were no longer at the fore-front of style. She abhorred the miniskirt, believing that a woman's knees were always best concealed. But nonetheless she continued to clothe a faithful clientele in suits that were subtly reworked each season. One of her most high-profile and stylish clients from this period was Jacqueline Kennedy.

A suit that Chanel herself wore during the mid-1960s (model 37750) was purchased by London's Victoria and Albert Museum. It consists of a three-quarter-length jacket and a dress made of black worsted crepe that reaches just below the knee, accessorized with a black silk stockinette-brimmed hat. Pristine white collar and cuffs are integral to the jacket—some clients complained that these touches wore out long before the jacket itself. Neat, unadorned, monochrome, and entirely functional, the suit has echoes of a school uniform.

In 1962 Chanel was again invited to design for the cinema, this time to dress Romy Schneider in Luchino Visconti's film *Boccaccio '70* and Delphine Seyrig in Alain Resnais's film *Last Year at Marienbad*. In 1969 Chanel herself became the subject of a Broadway musical called *Coco*, written by Alan Jay Lerner. With Chanel's permission, the title role was played by Katharine Hepburn.

Chanel died on 10 January 1971 in the midst of preparing her spring–summer 1971 collection. Her personal clothing and jewelry was sold at auction in London in December 1978.

Postscript
Following Chanel's death, Gaston Berthelot was appointed to design classic garments in the Chanel tradition between 1971 and 1973. The perfume No. 19, named after Chanel's birthday, was launched in 1970. From 1974 Jean Cazaubon and Yvonne Dudel designed the couture line; in 1978 a ready-to-wear range was designed by Philippe Guibourgé; and in 1980 Ramon Esparza joined the couture team. But it was not until 1983, when Karl Lagerfeld was appointed chief designer, that the House of Chanel once again made fashion headlines: it remains the ultimate in desirability for a clientele of all ages in the early 2000s.

Since his appointment, Lagerfeld has continued to reference the Chanel style, sometimes offering classic interpretations and at other times making witty and ironic statements. Ultimately, he has developed the label to make it relevant to the contemporary market. Like its founder, he draws on sportswear for inspiration: surfing and cycling outfits inspired his fall–winter 1990–1991 collection; training shoes bearing the distinctive interlocked CC logo were shown for fall–winter 1993–1994; nautical styles were shown for spring–summer 1994; and skiwear styles were featured in fall–winter 2003–2004. While Chanel looked to the utilitarian dress of the working man, Lagerfeld derives his ideas from contemporary social subcultures. He has presented fetishistic PVC jeans, lace-up bustiers, dog collars, and plastic raincoats (fall–winter 1991–1992); biker-style leather jackets, trousers, and boots (fall–winter 1992–1993 and fall–winter 2002–2003); B-Boy- and Ragga-inspired styles (spring–summer 1994); and a more eclectic "rock chic" (fall–winter 2003–2004). The tweed suit continues to be a mainstay of the collections, satisfying classic tastes with cardigan styles and the more adventurous younger clients with tweed bra tops and micro-miniskirts. The classic cardigan-style suit has also been offered in terry cloth, while denim jackets are trimmed with Chanel's favorite camellia flowers (both for spring–summer 1991). Costume jewelry is used in abundance, and the little black dress is still inextricably associated with the name of Chanel.

To ensure the survival of the refined craft skills of the couture industry, the House of Chanel purchased five artisan workshops in 2002: the top embroiderer François Lesage, the expert shoemaker Raymond Massaro, the flamboyant milliner Maison Michel, the feather specialist André Lemarié, and the leading costume jeweler Desrues.

Chanel perfumes remain top sellers. Since the founder died, the company has launched Cristalle (1974), Coco (1984), No. 5 Eau de Parfum (1986), Allure (1996), Coco Mademoiselle (2001), and Chance (2002) for women and Antaeus pour Homme (1981), Egoïste (1990), Platinum Egoïste (1993), and Allure Homme (1999) for men.

See also **Costume Jewelry; Handbags and Purses; Lagerfeld, Karl; Little Black Dress; Paris Fashion; Perfume; Vreeland, Diana.**

BIBLIOGRAPHY

Charles-Roux, Edmonde. *Chanel and Her World*. London: Weidenfeld and Nicolson, 1979. Extensively illustrated in black and white, a standard text covering Chanel's major design achievements as well as her private and social life.

———. *Chanel*. London: Collins Harvill, 1989.

de la Haye, Amy, and Shelley Tobin. *Chanel: The Couturière at Work*. London: V and A Publications, 1994. Detailed analysis of Chanel's designs and working practice. Extensively illustrated in color, including many museum garments in detail.

Madsen, Axel. *Coco Chanel: A Biography*. London: Bloomsbury, 1990. Comprehensive account of Chanel's life.

Morand, Paul. *L'allure de Chanel*. London: Herman, 1976. An insight into Chanel's life written by an author friend.

Mauriès, Patrick. *Jewellery by CHANEL*. London: Thames and Hudson, Inc., 1993.

Amy de la Haye

CHEMISE DRESS The term "chemise dress" has traditionally been used to describe a dress cut straight at the sides and left unfitted at the waist, in the manner of the undergarment known as a chemise. This term has most often been used to describe outer garments during transitional periods in fashion (most notably during the 1780s and the 1950s), in order to distinguish new, unfitted styles from the prevailing, fitted silhouette.

In the eighteenth century, the primary female undergarment was the chemise, or shift, a knee-length, loose-fitting garment of white linen with a straight or slightly triangular silhouette. The term chemise was first used to describe an outer garment in the 1780s, when Queen Marie Antoinette of France popularized a kind of informal, loose-fitting gown of sheer white cotton, resembling a chemise in both cut and material, which became known as the *chemise à la reine*. After chemise dresses, cut straight and gathered to a high waist with a sash or drawstring, became the dominant fashion, around 1800, there was no longer a need to describe their silhouette, and the term "chemise" reverted almost exclusively to its former meaning.

Christian Dior chemise. Beltless sack dresses such as this were introduced in 1957, immediately spawning great debate. While many praised their comfort, others complained because they concealed the feminine figure. © HULTON ARCHIVE/GETTY IMAGES. REPRODUCED BY PERMISSION.

Dresses were next described as chemises around 1910, when loosely belted, columnar dresses recalling early-nineteenth-century styles became popular. (The chemise was still worn as lingerie, but by the 1920s, it evolved into a hip-length, tubular, camisole-like garment with narrow straps.) Though the straight, unbelted dresses of the 1920s were more like chemises than any previous dress style, and have since been called chemise dresses by historians, the term was only occasionally used at the time. After fashion returned to a more fitted silhouette in the 1930s, the chemise dress reappeared around 1940, this time in the form of a dress cut to fall straight from the shoulders, or gathered into a yoke, but always meant to be worn belted at the waist.

The most important decade of the twentieth century for the chemise dress, however, was the 1950s. Early in that decade, the Parisian couturiers Christian Dior and Cristóbal Balenciaga, along with other designers in Europe and the United States, began experimenting with unfitted sheath and tunic dresses, and belted chemise dresses continued to be popular. The major change, however, came in 1957, when both Dior and Balenciaga presented straight, unbelted chemise dresses that bypassed the waist entirely. Called chemises or sacks, these dresses were considered a revolutionary change of direction in fashion, and became the subject of heated debate in the American press; many commentators, particularly men, considered such figure-concealing styles ugly and unnatural, while proponents praised their ease and clean-lined, modern look. (The term "sack" may have been a reference to the eighteenth-century sacque, or sack-back gown, which Balenciaga revived in the form of chemises with back fullness, but it was also an apt description of the bag-like chemise silhouette.)

Waistless styles, both straight and A-line, continued to be controversial over the next several years, but they were gradually incorporated into most wardrobes, and became a staple of 1960s fashion. The term "chemise," however, faded from use early in the 1960s, possibly because the press uproar of 1957 and 1958 had given it negative connotations (or because the lingerie chemise was a distant memory, having last been worn in the 1920s). Straight-cut dresses were now called shifts; more voluminous variants were the muumuu and tent dress. After another period of more fitted garments in the 1970s, unfitted dresses were again revived in the 1980s. Since then, however, women have had the option of choosing from a variety of silhouettes, and unfitted styles have simply been described as straight, or loose-fitting.

See also **A-Line Dress; Dior, Christian.**

BIBLIOGRAPHY
Keenan, Brigid. *Dior in Vogue.* London: Octopus Books, 1981.
Miller, Lesley Ellis. *Cristóbal Balenciaga.* London: B. T. Batsford, Ltd., 1993.
"Topics of the Times." *New York Times* (28 May 1958). Good contemporary overview and summary of the chemise controversy.

Susan Ward

CHENILLE. *See* **Yarns.**

CHEONGSAM. *See* **Qipao.**

CHILDREN'S CLOTHING All societies define childhood within certain parameters. From infancy to adolescence, there are societal expectations throughout the various stages of children's development concerning their capabilities and limitations, as well as how they should act and look. Clothing plays an integral role of the "look" of childhood in every era. An overview history of children's clothing provides insights into changes

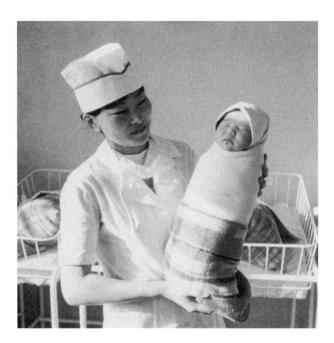

Nurse holding swaddled newborn in Mongolia. Although not practiced in Western cultures since the eighteenth century, swaddling infants continues to be practiced in many South American, eastern European, and Asian cultures. © DEAN CONGER/ CORBIS. REPRODUCED BY PERMISSION.

in child-rearing theory and practice, gender roles, the position of children in society, and similarities and differences between children's and adults' clothing.

Before the early-twentieth century, clothing worn by infants and young children shared a distinctive common feature—their clothing lacked sex distinction. The origins of this aspect of children's clothing stem from the sixteenth century, when European men and older boys began wearing doublets paired with breeches. Previously, both males and females of all ages (except for swaddled infants) had worn some type of gown, robe, or tunic. Once men began wearing bifurcated garments, however, male and female clothing became much more distinct. Breeches were reserved for men and older boys, while the members of society most subordinate to men—all females and the youngest boys—continued to wear skirted garments. To modern eyes, it may appear that when little boys of the past were attired in skirts or dresses, they were dressed "like girls," but to their contemporaries, boys and girls were simply dressed alike in clothing appropriate for small children.

New theories put forth in the late seventeenth and the eighteenth centuries about children and childhood greatly influenced children's clothing. The custom of swaddling—immobilizing newborn infants with linen wrappings over their diapers and shirts—had been in place for centuries. A traditional belief underlying swaddling was that babies' limbs needed to be straightened

and supported or they would grow bent and misshapen. In the eighteenth century, medical concerns that swaddling weakened rather than strengthened children's limbs merged with new ideas about the nature of children and how they should be raised to gradually reduce the use of swaddling. For example, in philosopher John Locke's influential 1693 publication, *Some Thoughts Concerning Education,* he advocated abandoning swaddling altogether in favor of loose, lightweight clothing that allowed children freedom of movement. Over the next century, various authors expanded on Locke's theories and by 1800, most English and American parents no longer swaddled their children.

When swaddling was still customary in the early years of the eighteenth century, babies were taken out of swaddling at between two and four months and put into "slips," long linen or cotton dresses with fitted bodices and full skirts that extended a foot or more beyond the children's feet; these long slip outfits were called "long clothes." Once children began crawling and later walking, they wore "short clothes"—ankle-length skirts, called petticoats, paired with fitted, back-opening bodices that were frequently boned or stiffened. Girls wore this style until thirteen or fourteen, when they put on the front-opening gowns of adult women. Little boys wore petticoat outfits until they reached at least age four through seven, when they were "breeched" or considered mature enough to wear miniature versions of adult male clothing—coats, vests, and the exclusively male breeches. The age of breeching varied, depending on parental choice and the boy's maturity, which was defined as how masculine he appeared and acted. Breeching was an important rite of passage for young boys because it symbolized they were leaving childhood behind and beginning to take on male roles and responsibilities.

As the practice of swaddling declined, babies wore the long slip dresses from birth to about five months old. For crawling infants and toddlers, "frocks," ankle-length versions of the slip dresses, replaced stiffened bodices and petticoats by the 1760s. The clothing worn by older children also became less constricting in the latter part of the eighteenth century. Until the 1770s, when little boys were breeched, they essentially went from the petticoats of childhood into the adult male clothing appropriate for their station in life. Although boys were still breeched by about six or seven during the 1770s, they now began to wear somewhat more relaxed versions of adult clothing—looser-cut coats and open-necked shirts with ruffled collars—until their early teen years. Also in the 1770s, instead of the more formal bodice and petticoat combinations, girls continued to wear frock-style dresses, usually accented with wide waist sashes, until they were old enough for adult clothing.

These modifications in children's clothing affected women's clothing—the fine muslin chemise dresses worn by fashionable women of the 1780s and 1790s look remarkably similar to the frocks young children had been wearing since mid-century. However, the development of women's chemise dresses is more complex than the garments simply being adult versions of children's frocks. Beginning in the 1770s, there was general movement away from stiff brocades to softer silk and cotton fabrics in women's clothing, a trend that converged with a strong interest in the dress of classical antiquity in the 1780s and 1790s. Children's sheer white cotton frocks, accented with waist sashes giving a high-waisted look, provided a convenient model for women in the development of neo-classical fashions. By 1800, women, girls, and toddler boys all wore similarly styled, high-waisted dresses made up in lightweight silks and cottons.

A new type of transitional attire, specifically designed for small boys between the ages of three and seven, began to be worn about 1780. These outfits, called "skeleton suits" because they fit close to the body, consisted of ankle-length trousers buttoned onto a short jacket worn over a shirt with a wide collar edged in ruffles. Trousers, which came from lower class and military clothing, identified skeleton suits as male clothing, but at the same time set them apart from the suits with knee-length breeches worn by older boys and men. In the early 1800s, even after trousers had supplanted breeches as the fashionable choice, the jumpsuit-like skeleton suits, so unlike men's suits in style, still continued as distinctive dress for young boys. Babies in slips and toddlers in frocks, little boys in skeleton suits, and older boys who wore frilled collar shirts until their early teens, signaled a new attitude that extended childhood for boys, dividing it into the three distinct stages of infancy, boyhood, and youth.

In the nineteenth century, infants' clothing continued trends in place at the end of the previous century. Newborn layettes consisted of the ubiquitous long dresses (long clothes) and numerous undershirts, day and night caps, napkins (diapers), petticoats, nightgowns, socks, plus one or two outerwear cloaks. These garments were made by mothers or commissioned from seamstresses, with ready-made layettes available by the late 1800s. While it is possible to date nineteenth-century baby dresses based on subtle variations in cut and the type and placement of trims, the basic dresses changed little over the century. Baby dresses were generally made in white cotton because it was easily washed and bleached and were styled with fitted bodices or yokes and long full skirts. Because many dresses were also ornately trimmed with embroidery and lace, today such garments are often mistaken as special occasion attire. Most of these dresses, however, were everyday outfits—the standard baby "uniforms" of the time. When infants became more active at between four and eight months, they went into calf-length white dresses (short clothes). By mid-century, colorful prints gained popularity for older toddlers' dresses.

The ritual of little boys leaving off dresses for male clothing continued to be called "breeching" in the nineteenth century, although now trousers, not breeches,

Brazilian men and boys in front of a church, 1942. While children's clothing was once more distinct from that of adults, by the twentieth century children's dress more often mimicked that of their elders. © GENEVIEVE NAYLOR/CORBIS. REPRODUCED BY PERMISSION.

were the symbolic male garments. The main factors determining breeching age were the time during the century when a boy was born, plus parental preference and the boy's maturity. At the beginning of the 1800s, little boys went into their skeleton suits at about age three, wearing these outfits until they were six or seven. Tunic suits with knee-length tunic dresses over long trousers began to replace skeleton suits in the late 1820s, staying in fashion until the early 1860s. During this period, boys were not considered officially breeched until they wore trousers without the tunic overdresses at about age six or seven. Once breeched, boys dressed in cropped, waist-length jackets until their early teens, when they donned cutaway frock coats with knee-length tails, signifying they had finally achieved full adult sartorial status.

From the 1860s to the 1880s, boys from four to seven wore skirted outfits that were usually simpler than girls' styles with more subdued colors and trim or "masculine"

Young girls in Brownie uniforms. Children, in a mimicry of adults, wear uniforms for certain occasions. © HULTON-DEUTSCH COLLECTION/CORBIS. REPRODUCED BY PERMISSION.

details such as a vest. Knickerbockers or knickers, knee-length pants for boys aged seven to fourteen, were introduced about 1860. Over the next thirty years, boys were breeched into the popular knickers outfits at younger and younger ages. The knickers worn by the youngest boys from three to six were paired with short jackets over lace-collared blouses, belted tunics, or sailor tops. These outfits contrasted sharply to the versions worn by their older brothers, whose knickers suits had tailored wool jackets, stiff-collared shirts, and four-in-hand ties. From the 1870s to the 1940s, the major difference between men's and schoolboys' clothing was that men wore long trousers and boys, short ones. By the end of the 1890s, when the breeching age had dropped from a mid century high of six or seven to between two and three, the point at which boys began wearing long trousers was frequently seen as a more significant event than breeching.

Unlike boys, as nineteenth-century girls grew older their clothing did not undergo a dramatic transformation. Females wore skirted outfits throughout their lives from infancy to old age; however, the garments' cut and style details did change with age. The most basic difference between girls' and women's dresses was that the children's dresses were shorter, gradually lengthening to floor length by the mid-teen years. When neoclassical

styles were in fashion in the early years of the century, females of all ages and toddler boys wore similarly styled, high-waisted dresses with narrow columnar skirts. At this time, the shorter length of the children's dresses was the main factor distinguishing them from adult clothing.

From about 1830 and into the mid-1860s, when women wore fitted waist-length bodices and full skirts in various styles, most dresses worn by toddler boys and preadolescent girls were more similar to each other than to women's fashions. The characteristic "child's" dress of this period featured a wide off-the-shoulder neckline, short puffed or cap sleeves, an unfitted bodice that usually gathered into an inset waistband, and a full skirt that varied in length from slightly-below-knee length for toddlers to calf length for the oldest girls. Dresses of this design, made up in printed cottons or wool challis, were typical daywear for girls until they went into adult women's clothing in their mid-teens. Both girls and boys wore white cotton ankle-length trousers, called pantaloons or pantalets, under their dresses. In the 1820s, when pantalets were first introduced, girls wearing them provoked controversy because bifurcated garments of any style represented masculinity. Gradually pantalets became accepted for both girls and women as underwear, and as "private" female dress did not pose a threat to male power. For little boys, pantalets' status as feminine underwear meant that, even though pantalets were technically trousers, they were not viewed as comparable to the trousers boys put on when they were breeched.

Some mid-nineteenth-century children's dresses, especially best dresses for girls over ten, were reflective of women's styles with currently fashionable sleeve, bodice, and trim details. This trend accelerated in the late 1860s when bustle styles came into fashion. Children's dresses echoed women's clothing with additional back fullness, more elaborate trims, and a new cut that used princess seaming for shaping. At the height of the bustle's popularity in the 1870s and 1880s, dresses for girls between nine and fourteen had fitted bodices with skirts that draped over small bustles, differing only in length from women's garments. In the 1890s, simpler, tailored outfits with pleated skirts and sailor blouses or dresses with full skirts gathered onto yoked bodices signaled that clothing was becoming more practical for increasingly active schoolgirls.

New concepts of child rearing emphasizing children's developmental stages had a significant impact on young children's clothing beginning in the late-nineteenth century. Contemporary research supported crawling as an important step in children's growth, and one-piece rompers with full bloomer-like pants, called "creeping aprons," were devised in the 1890s as cover-ups for the short white dresses worn by crawling infants. Soon, active babies of both sexes were wearing rompers without the dresses underneath. Despite earlier controversy about females wearing pants, rompers were accepted without debate as playwear for toddler girls, becoming the first unisex pants outfits.

Baby books into the 1910s had space for mothers to note when their babies first wore "short clothes," but this time-honored transition from long white dresses to short ones was quickly becoming a thing of the past. By the 1920s, infants wore short, white dresses from birth to about six months with long dresses relegated to ceremonial wear as christening gowns. New babies continued to wear short dresses into the 1950s, although by this time, boys only did so for the first few weeks of their lives.

As rompers styles for both day and night wear replaced dresses, they became the twentieth century's "uniforms" for babies and young children. The first rompers were made up in solid colors and gingham checks, providing a lively contrast to traditional baby white. In the 1920s, whimsical floral and animal motifs began to appear on children's clothing. At first these designs were as unisex as the rompers they decorated, but gradually certain motifs were associated more with one sex or the other—for example, dogs and drums with boys and kittens and flowers with girls. Once such sex-typed motifs appeared on clothing, they designated even styles that were identical in cut as either a "boy's" or a "girl's" garment. Today, there is an abundance of children's clothing on the market decorated with animals, flowers, sports paraphernalia, cartoon characters, or other icons of popular culture—most of these motifs have masculine or feminine connotations in our society and so do the garments on which they appear.

Colors used for children's clothing also have gender symbolism—today, this is most universally represented by blue for infant boys and pink for girls. Yet it took many years for this color code to be come standardized. Pink and blue were associated with gender by the 1910s, and there were early efforts to codify the colors for one sex or the other, as illustrated by this 1916 statement from the trade publication *Infants' and Children's Wear Review:* "[T]he generally accepted rule is pink for the boy and blue for the girl." As late as 1939, a *Parents Magazine* article rationalized that because pink was a pale shade of red, the color of the war god Mars, it was appropriate for boys, while blue's association with Venus and the Madonna made it the color for girls. In practice, the colors were used interchangeably for both young boys' and girls' clothing until after World War II, when a combination of public opinion and manufacturer's clout ordained pink for girls and blue for boys—a dictum that still holds true today.

Even with this mandate, however, blue continues to be permissible for girls' clothing while pink is rejected for boys' attire. The fact that girls can wear both pink (feminine) and blue (masculine) colors, while boys wear only blue, illustrates an important trend begun in the late 1800s: over time, garments, trims, or colors once worn by both young boys and girls, but traditionally associated with female clothing, have become unacceptable for boys' clothing. As boys' attire grew less "feminine" during the twentieth century, shedding trimmings and ornamental

A baby layette set. Parents in the late twentieth century could choose between gender-neutral and gender-specific clothing for their babies. Accents such as ribbons and flowers are designed for wear by a baby girl, wheareas sports- or automobile-related graphics are designed for boys. TIME LIFE PICTURES/GETTY IMAGES. REPRODUCED BY PERMISSION.

details such as lace and ruffles, girls' clothing grew ever more "masculine." A paradoxical example of this progression occurred in the 1970s, when parents involved in "nonsexist" child-rearing pressed manufacturers for "gender-free" children's clothes. Ironically, the resulting pants outfits were only gender-free in the sense that they used styles, colors, and trims currently acceptable for boys, eliminating any "feminine" decorations such as pink fabrics or ruffled trim.

Over the course of the twentieth century, those formerly male-only garments—trousers—became increasingly accepted attire for girls and women. As toddler girls outgrew their rompers in the 1920s, new play clothes for three- to five-year-olds, designed with full bloomer pants underneath short dresses, were the first outfits to extend the age at which girls could wear pants. By the 1940s, girls of all ages wore pants outfits at home and for casual public events, but they were still expected—if not required—to wear dresses and skirts for school, church, parties, and even for shopping. About 1970, trousers' strong masculine connection had eroded to the point that school and office dress codes finally sanctioned trousers for girls and women. Today, girls can wear pants outfits in nearly every social situation. Many of these pant styles, such as blue jeans, are essentially unisex in design and cut, but many others are strongly sex-typed through decoration and color.

Adolescence has always been a time of challenge and separation for children and parents but, before the twentieth century, teenagers did not routinely express their independence through appearance. Instead, with the exception of a few eccentrics, adolescents accepted current fashion dictates and ultimately dressed like their parents. Since the early twentieth century, however, children have regularly conveyed teenage rebellion through dress and appearance, often with styles quite at odds with conventional dress. The jazz generation of the 1920s was the first to create a special youth culture, with each succeeding generation concocting its own unique crazes. But teenage vogues such as bobby sox in the 1940s or poodle skirts in the 1950s did not exert much influence on contemporary adult clothing and, as teens moved into adulthood, they left behind such fads. It was not until the 1960s, when the baby-boom generation entered adolescence that styles favored by teenagers, like miniskirts, colorful male shirts, or "hippie" jeans and T-shirts, usurped more conservative adult styles and became an important part of mainstream fashion. Since that time, youth culture has continued to have an important impact on fashion, with many styles blurring the lines between children's and adult clothing.

See also **Shoes, Children's; Teenage Fashions.**

BIBLIOGRAPHY

Ashelford, Jane. *The Art of Dress: Clothes and Society, 1500–1914.* London: National Trust Enterprises Limited, 1996. General history of costume with a well-illustrated chapter on children's dress.

Buck, Anne. *Clothes and the Child: A Handbook of Children's Dress in England, 1500–1900.* New York: Holmes and Meier, 1996. Comprehensive look at English children's clothing, although the organization of the material is somewhat confusing.

Callahan, Colleen, and Jo B. Paoletti. *Is It a Girl or a Boy? Gender Identity and Children's Clothing.* Richmond, Va.: The Valentine Museum, 1999. Booklet published in conjunction with an exhibition of the same name.

Calvert, Karin. *Children in the House: The Material Culture of Early Childhood, 1600–1900.* Boston: Northeastern University Press, 1992. Excellent overview of child-rearing theory and practice as they relate to the objects of childhood, including clothing, toys, and furniture.

Rose, Clare. *Children's Clothes Since 1750.* New York: Drama Book Publilshers, 1989. Overview of children's clothing to 1985 that is well illustrated with images of children and actual garments.

Colleen R. Callahan

CHINA: HISTORY OF DRESS Chinese clothing changed considerably over the course of some 5,000 years of history, from the Bronze Age into the twentieth century, but also maintained elements of long-term continuity during that span of time. The story of dress in China is a story of wrapped garments in silk, hemp, or cotton, and of superb technical skills in weaving, dyeing, embroidery, and other textile arts as applied to clothing. After the Chinese Revolution of 1911, new styles arose to replace traditions of clothing that seemed inappropriate to the modern era.

Throughout their history, the Chinese used textiles and clothing, along with other cultural markers (such as cuisine and the distinctive Chinese written language) to distinguish themselves from peoples on their frontiers whom they regarded as "uncivilized." The Chinese regarded silk, hemp, and (later) cotton as "civilized" fabrics; they strongly disliked woolen cloth, because it was associated with the woven or felted woolen clothing of animal-herding nomads of the northern steppes.

Essential to the clothed look of all adults was a proper hairdo—the hair grown long and put up in a bun or topknot, or, for men during China's last imperial dynasty, worn in a braided queue—and some kind of hat or other headgear. The rite of passage of a boy to manhood was the "capping ceremony," described in early ritual texts. No respectable male adult would appear in public without some kind of head covering, whether a soft cloth cap for informal wear, or a stiff, black silk or horsehair hat with "wing" appendages for officials of the civil service. To appear "with hair unbound and with garments that wrap to the left," as Confucius put it, was to behave as an uncivilized person. Agricultural workers of both sexes have traditionally worn broad conical hats woven of bamboo, palm leaves, or other plant materials, in shapes and patterns that reflect local custom and, in some cases, ethnicity of minority populations.

The clothing of members of the elite was distinguished from that of commoners by cut and style as well as by fabric, but the basic garment for all classes and both sexes was a loosely cut robe with sleeves that varied from wide to narrow, worn with the left front panel lapped over the right panel, the whole garment fastened closed with a sash. Details of this garment changed greatly over time, but the basic idea endured. Upper-class men and women wore this garment in a long (ankle-length) version, often with wide, dangling sleeves; men's and women's garments were distinguished by details of cut and decoration. Sometimes a coat or jacket was worn over the robe itself. A variant for upper-class women was a shorter robe with tighter-fitting sleeves, worn over a skirt. Working-class men and women wore a shorter version of the robe—thigh-length or knee-length—with trousers or leggings, or a skirt; members of both sexes wore both skirts and trousers. In cold weather, people of all classes wore padded and quilted clothing of fabrics appropriate to their class. Silk floss—broken and tangled silk fibers left over from processing silk cocoons—made a light-weight, warm padding material for such winter garments.

Men's clothing was often made in solid, dark colors, except for clothing worn at court, which was often brightly ornamented with woven, dyed, or embroidered patterns. Women's clothing was generally more colorful than men's. The well-known "dragon robes" of Chinese emperors and high officials were a relatively late development, confined to the last few centuries of imperial history. With the fall of the last imperial dynasty in 1911, new styles of clothing were adopted, as people struggled to find ways of dressing that would be both "Chinese" and "modern."

Cloth and Clothing in Ancient China

The area that is now called "China" coalesced as a civilization from several centers of Neolithic culture, including among others Liaodong in the northeast; the North China Plain westward to the Wei River Valley; the foothills of Shandong in the east; the lower and middle reaches of the Yangtze River Valley; the Sichuan Basin; and several areas on the southeastern coast. These centers of Neolithic cultures almost certainly represent several distinct ethnolinguistic groups and can readily be differentiated on the basis of material culture. On the other hand, they were in contact with each other through trade, warfare, and other means, and over the long run all of them were subsumed into the political and cultural entity of China. Thus the term "ancient China" is a phrase of convenience that masks significant regional cultural variation. Nevertheless, some generalizations apply.

The domestication of silkworms, the production of silk fiber, and the weaving of silk cloth go back to at least the third millennium B.C.E. in northern China, and possibly even earlier in the Yangtze River Valley. Archaeological evidence for this survives tombs from that era; pottery objects sometimes preserve the imprint of silk cloth in damp clay, and in some cases layers of corrosion on bronze vessels show clear traces of the silk cloth in which the vessels had been wrapped. Silk was always the preferred fabric of China's elite from ancient times onward. As a proverbial phrase put it, the upper classes wore silk, the lower classes wore hempen cloth (though after about 1200 C.E. cotton became the principal cloth of the masses).

Depictions of clothed humans on bronze and pottery vessels contemporary with the Shang Dynasty (c. 1550–1046 B.C.E.) of the North China Plain show that men and women of the elite ranks of society wore long gowns of patterned cloth. Large bronze statues from the Sanxingdui Culture of Sichuan, dating to the late second millennium B.C.E., show what appears to be brocade or embroidery at the hemlines of the wearer's long gowns. Later depictions of commoners portray them in short jackets and trousers or loincloths for men, and jackets and skirts for women. Soldiers are shown in armored vests worn over long-sleeved jackets, with trousers and boots.

Ceramic statuette of a woman in empire-line dress. During the Tang Dynasty an empire-waisted dress tied below the bustline and a short jacket became a popular ensemble. JOHN S. MAJOR. REPRODUCED BY PERMISSION.

Chinese silk textiles of the later first millennium B.C.E. (the Warring States Period, 481–221 B.C.E.) testify to the possibility of making very colorful and elaborately decorated clothing at the time. Surviving textiles also demonstrate the widespread appeal of Chinese silk in other parts of Asia. Examples of cloth woven in the Yangtze River Valley during the Warring States Period have been discovered in archaeological sites as far away as Turkestan and southern Siberia. Painted wooden figurines found in tombs from the state of Chu, in the Yangtze River Valley, depict men and women in long gowns of white silk patterned with swirling figural motifs in red, brown, blue, and other colors; the gowns are cut in such a way that the left panel wraps over the right one in a spiral that goes completely around the body. The gowns of the women are closed with broad sashes in contrasting colors, while the men wear narrower sashes. Bronze sash-hooks are common in tombs from the second half of the first millennium B.C.E., showing that the style of narrow waist sashes lasted for a long time. Elite burials also demonstrate a long-enduring custom of the wearing of jade necklaces and other jewelry.

Chinese fashion magazine cover during the post-Mao period. Fashionable clothing returned to China in 1978, and by the 1980s the fashion industry surged with a re-establishment of fashion magazines, shows, and classes. JOHN S. MAJOR. REPRODUCED BY PERMISSION.

The Han Dynasty

Under the Qin (221–206 B.C.E.) and the Han (206 B.C.E.–7 C.E.; restored 25–220 C.E.), dynasties, China was unified under imperial rule for the first time, expanding to incorporate much of the territory within China's boundaries today. The famous underground terra-cotta army of the First Emperor of Qin gives vivid evidence of the clothing of soldiers and officers, again showing the basic theme of long gowns for elites, shorter jackets for commoners. One sees also that all of the soldiers are shown with elaborately dressed hair, worn with headgear ranging from simple head cloths to formal official caps. Cavalry warfare was of increasing significance in China during the Qin and Han periods; in funerary statuettes and murals, riders are often shown wearing long-sleeved, hip-length jackets and padded trousers.

The well-preserved tomb of the Lady of Dai at Mawangdui, near Changsha (Hunan Province, in south-central China) has yielded hundreds of silk dress items and textiles, from spiral-wrapped or right-side-fastening gowns, to mittens, socks, slippers, wrapped skirts, and

other garments, and bolts of uncut and unsewn silk. The textiles show a great range of dyed colors and weaving and decorating techniques, including tabby, twill, brocade, gauze, damask, and embroidery. Textual evidence from the Han period shows that government authorities attempted through sumptuary laws to restrict the use of such textiles to members of the elite landowning class, but that townsmen including merchants and artisans were finding ways to acquire and wear them also.

The period 220–589 C.E. (that is, from the fall of the Han to the rise of the Sui Dynasty), was one of disunity, when northern China was frequently ruled by dynasties of invaders from the northern frontier, while southern China remained under the control of a series of weak ethnically Chinese rulers. Depictions of dress from northern China thus show a predominance of styles suitable for horse-riding peoples. Elite men are sometimes shown wearing thigh-length wrapped jackets over skirts or voluminous skirtlike trousers. In southern China the traditions of colorful Yangtze River Valley silks predominated (though with a discernible trend toward plainer everyday clothing for elite men). Buddhism arrived in China via Central Asia during the late Han period, prompting the production of typical patchwork Buddhist monks' robes, as well as more formal embroidered or appliqué ecclesiastical garments.

The Tang Dynasty

Under the Sui (589–618) and Tang (618–907) dynasties, China was reunified and entered upon a period of unprecedented wealth and cultural brilliance. The capital city of Chang'an (now Xi'an) was, during the eighth century, the largest and most cosmopolitan city in the world. It supported a true fashion system, comparable to that of the modern West, in which rapidly-changing prevailing modes were adopted by fashion leaders and widely disseminated by emulation. Hairstyles (including the use of elaborate hairpins and other hair ornaments) and makeup also changed rapidly in fashion-driven patterns. Ceramic statuettes, produced in huge numbers during the Tang for placement in tombs, often depict people in contemporary dress, and thus give direct evidence for the rapid change of fashions at the time.

Under the Tang, trade along the Silk Route between China via Central Asia to the Mediterranean world flourished, and influence from Persian and Turkic culture areas had a strong impact on elite fashions in China. Chinese silk textiles of the Tang period show strong foreign influence, particularly in the use of roundel patterns. Young, upper-class women outraged conservative commentators by wearing "Turkish" hip-length, tight-sleeved jackets with trousers and boots; some women even played polo in such outfits. (Women more commonly went riding in long gowns, wearing wide-brimmed hats with veils to guard against sun and dust.) Another women's ensemble consisting of an empire-waisted dress tied just below the bustline with ribbons, and worn with

Chinese beauty pageant. The contestants wear *qipaos,* a colorful, tight-fitting garment, frequently slit up to the knee, which became the traditional dress of modern Chinese women by the mid-twentieth century. © CHINA PHOTO/REUTERS NEWMEDIA INC/CORBIS. REPRODUCED BY PERMISSION.

a very short, tight-sleeved jacket. This style would reappear several times in later ages, notably during the Ming Dynasty (1368–1644); it strongly influenced the development of the Korean national costume, the *hanbok.*

Dancers at court and in the entertainment districts of the capital and other cities were notable trendsetters. In the early eighth century, the fashionable ideal was for slender women wearing long gowns in soft fabrics that were cut with a pronounced décolletage and very wide sleeves, or a décolleté knee-length gown worn over a skirt; by mid century, the ideal had changed to favor distinctly plump women wearing empire-line gowns over which a shawl-like jacket in a contrasting color was worn. One remarkable later Tang fashion was for so-called "fairy dresses," which had sleeves cut to trail far beyond the wearer's hands, stiffened, wing-like appendages at the shoulders, long aprons trailing from the bustline almost to the floor, and triangular applied decorations on the

sleeves and down the sides of the skirt that would flutter with a dancer's every movement. "Sleeve dancing" has remained an important part of Chinese performative dance since Tang times. Near the end of the Tang period, dancers also inspired a fashion for small (or small-looking) feet that led to the later Chinese practice of footbinding.

The Tang Dynasty was an aristocratic society in which military prowess and good horsemanship were admired as male accomplishments. Depictions of foot soldiers and cavalrymen in scale armor and heavily padded jackets, and officers in elaborate breastplates and surcoats, are common in Tang sculptural and pictorial art.

The Song and Yuan Dynasties
In the Song Dynasty (960–1279), influenced by an increasingly conservative Confucian ideology and social changes that saw the gradual replacement of a basically

aristocratic society by one dominated by a class of scholar-gentry officeholders, clothing for both men and women at the elite level tended to become looser, more flowing, and more modest than the styles of the Tang. Women, who sometimes had bound feet, stayed home more, and sometimes wore broad hats and veils for excursions outside the home.

Portraits of emperors and high-court officials during the Song period show the first use of plain, round-necked robes worn either by themselves or as over-robes above more colorful clothing, and also the first appearance of the "dragon robes" embroidered with roundel figures of dragons as emblems of imperial authority.

The Yuan Dynasty (1279–1368) was the Chinese manifestation of the Mongol Empire conquered by Genghis Khan and ruled by his descendants. Mongol men in China, as well as men of Chinese ethnicity, wore loose robes similar to those of the Song period; horsemen wore shorter robes, trousers, and sturdy boots. Round, helmet-like hats were adopted for official use, replacing the earlier black horsehair or stiffened silk official cap. Women of the Yuan period sometimes wore two or more gowns at once, cut so as to show successive layers of cloth in harmonizing colors at the collars and sleeve-openings; Mongol women also wore high, elaborate headdresses like those of the Mongols' traditional homeland.

The Ming and Qing Dynasties

In Ming (1368–1644) times, both men and women wore voluminous clothing, a long robe with wide sleeves for men, a shorter robe worn over a wide skirt for women. In the early and middle Ming, there was a revival of the Tang style of empire-line dresses worn with short jackets, especially for young women. For much of its nearly three centuries of existence, the Ming was a time of prosperity and expanding production of goods of all kinds; there was a concomitant expansion of the type and variety of clothing available to all but the poorest members of society. Cotton, which had been introduced into China during the Song Dynasty, began to be raised extensively in several parts of the country. A short indigo-dyed cotton jacket worn over similar calf-length trousers (for men) or a skirt (for women) became and remained the characteristic dress of Chinese peasants and workers. Cotton batting substituted, in cheaper clothing, for silk floss in padded winter garments.

The dragon robe was adopted for standard court wear for emperors, members of the imperial clan, and high officials. The dragon robe evolved a standard vocabulary of motifs and symbols; typically such a robe was embroidered with large dragons, coiling in space and with the head shown frontally, on the chest and back; smaller dragon roundels on the shoulders and on the skirt of the robe; the space around the dragons embroidered with other auspicious symbols, and the bottom hem showing ocean waves and the peak of Mt. Kunlun, the mountain at the center of the world. The background color of the robe indicated rank and lineage, with bright yellow limited to use by the emperor himself. Official court robes for women were similar but decorated with phoenixes (mythical birds depicted as similar to pheasants or peacocks), the feminine *yin* to the male *yang* of the dragon. (Hangings, banners, and other decorative items showing both a dragon and a phoenix are wedding emblems.)

Associated with the dragon robe and the codification of court attire was the use of so-called "Mandarin squares," embroidered squares of cloth that were worn as badges of office for civil and military officials. These indicated rank in the official hierarchy by a set of sixteen animal or bird emblems—for example, a leopard for a military official of the third rank, a silver pheasant for a civil official of the fifth rank. These embroidered squares were made in pairs to be worn on the back and front of an official's plain over-robe, the front square split vertically to accommodate the robe's front-opening design.

The Qing Dynasty (1644–1911) brought new rulers to China—Manchus from the northeast, who overthrew the Ming Dynasty and preserved their hold on imperial power in part by being careful to preserve Manchu dress and other customs in order to keep the small population of conquerors from being submerged culturally by the much more numerous Chinese. The Manchus introduced new styles of clothing for official use; men were to wear short robes with trousers or wide skirts, cut more closely to the body than the flowing Ming styles, fastening at the right shoulder and with a high slit in front to accommodate horse-riding. A distinctive feature of the Manchu robe was its "horseshoe sleeves," designed to cover and protect the back of a rider's hands. Other Manchu styles were the "banner robe" (*qipao*), a straight-cut long robe worn by Manchu troops, and the "long gown" (*chang-shan*), a straight, ankle-length garment worn by Manchu women (who wore platform shoes on their unbound feet). Ethnic Chinese women wore loose-fitting jackets over wide skirts or trousers, often cut short enough to reveal the lavishly embroidered tiny shoes of their bound feet.

At court, the emperor, his kinsmen, and high officials wore dragon robes, the symbolic elements of which had been elaborately codified in the mid-eighteenth century; other officials wore plain robes with Mandarin squares. For all ranks, conical hats with narrow, upturned brims were worn for official occasions; buttons of precious or semiprecious stones at the hat's peak also indicated the wearer's rank.

Throughout China's history, the country's population has included many minority peoples whose language, dress, food, and other aspects of culture have been and remain quite different from those of the Han (Chinese) ethnic majority.

Chinese Dress in the Twentieth Century

After the Nationalist Revolution of 1911, it was widely felt in China that, after a century of foreign intrusion and

Chinese public official and family. During the Ming Dynasty, embroidered "Mandarin Squares" began appearing on the robes of court officials (third man from right). These squares indicated the wearer's rank in the government hierarchy. © Hulton-Deutsch Collection/Corbis. Reproduced by permission.

national decline, the country needed to rid itself of old customs in order to compete with the other nations of the modern world. Thus began a search for new styles of clothing that were both "modern" and "Chinese." The simple adoption of Western clothing was not a popular choice; foreign menswear was associated with Chinese employees of foreign companies, who were derided for being unpatriotic; fashionable Western women's clothing struck many Chinese as both immodest and odd. Loose, baggy Western dresses introduced at some missionary schools in China were modest but unattractive.

Many men continued to wear a form of traditional clothing until the mid-twentieth century—a plain, blue, long gown for scholars and older, urban men, jacket and trousers of indigo-dyed cotton for workers. But among urban elites, there emerged in the 1910s a new outfit, based on Prussian military dress and seen first in China

in school and military-cadet uniforms; this had a fitted jacket fastened with buttons in front, decorated with four pockets, and made "Chinese" by the use of a stiff, high "Mandarin" collar, worn over matching trousers. This suit was often made, Western-style, in woolen cloth, the first time that wool had ever been the basis of an important Chinese garment type. This outfit became known as the Sun Yat-sen suit, after the father of the Chinese revolution.

Several proposals for creating a modern women's dress for China met with little enthusiasm, but in China's cities, and especially in Shanghai, women and their dressmakers were trying out a modern variation of Manchu dress that was to have lasting consequences. The Manchu "banner robe" (*qipao*) and "long gown" (*changshan*, generally known in the West by its Cantonese pronunciation, *cheongsam*) were adapted by fashionable women to be somewhat more tightly fitting, with a closure folded left-over-right to the shoulder, then down the right seam, often fastened with decorative "frogs" (cloth buttons and loops), and sometimes with a slit to knee height. This new style, in colorful silk, rayon, or printed cotton, was widely publicized in "calendar girl" advertising prints of the1920s and 1930s, and soon became firmly entrenched as China's appropriately modern women's wear. The *qipao* (or *cheongsam*) continued to evolve to become more form fitting, and by the mid-twentieth century was widely accepted, both in China and the West, as China's "traditional" women's dress.

For a few years after the Communist revolution of 1949, older forms of dress, including the man's long "scholar's robe" and the women's *qipao*, continued to be worn in China. But by the late 1950s, there was strong political and social pressure for people to dress in "modest, revolutionary" styles—the Sun Yat-sen suit (usually in blue cotton, now beginning to be known as a "Mao suit"), or as an alternative, a modest blouse and calf-length skirt. By the time of the Cultural Revolution (1966–1976), the *qipao* had been denounced as "feudal," and the wearing of the blue Mao suit was nearly obligatory.

Fashion made a cautious return to China in 1978, with the promulgation of the post-Mao "Four Modernizations" program of economic reform. By the early 1980s, fashion magazines had resumed publication, fashion shows were held in major cities, and fashion design and related subjects were beginning to be taught once again at the high school and college level. The *qipao* also has had a revival, both in China and in overseas Chinese communities, as formal wear that conveys a sense of ethnic pride, and as "traditional" dress worn by women in the hospitality industry. But in general, Chinese dress today is a reflection of global fashion. By the turn of the twenty-first century, prestigious international brands were a common sight in the shopping districts of Shanghai, Guangzhou, Beijing, and other major cities, and Chinese consumers were participating fully in international fashion. Meanwhile China had become the world's largest manufacturer and exporter of garments.

See also **Asia, East History of Dress; Footbinding; Mao Suit; Qipao; Silk.**

BIBLIOGRAPHY

Cammann, Schuyler, R. *China's Dragon Robes.* New York: Ronald Press Company, 1952.

Finnane, Antonia. "What Should Chinese Women Wear? A National Problem." *Modern China* 22, no. 2 (1996): 99–131.

——, and Anne McLaren, eds. *Dress, Sex and Text in Chinese Culture.* Melbourne: Monash Asia Institute, 1998.

Garrett, Valery M. *Chinese Clothing: An Illustrated Guide.* Hong Kong: Oxford University Press, 1994.

Ng Chun Bong, *et al.*, eds. *Chinese Woman and Modernity: Calendar Posters of the 1910s–1930s.* Hong Kong: Commercial Press, 1995.

Roberts, Claire, ed. *Evolution and Revolution: Chinese Dress, 1700s–1990s.* Sydney: The Powerhouse Museum,1997.

Scott, A. C. *Chinese Costume in Transition.* Singapore: Donald Moore, 1958.

Steele, Valerie, and John S. Major. *China Chic: East Meets West.* New Haven and London: Yale University Press, 1999.

Szeto, Naomi Yin-yin. *Dress in Hong Kong: A Century of Change and Customs.* Hong Kong: Museum of History, 1992.

Vollmer, John E. *In the Presence of the Dragon Throne: Ch'ing Dynasty Costume (1644–1911) in the Royal Ontario Museum.* Toronto: Royal Ontario Museum, 1977.

Wilson, Verity. *Chinese Dress.* London: Bamboo Publishing Ltd. in association with the Victoria and Albert Museum, 1986.

Zhou Xun and Gao Chunming. *5000 Years of Chinese Costumes.* San Francisco: China Books and Periodicals, 1987.

John S. Major

CHINOS. *See* **Trousers.**

CHINTZ Originally, chintz was a brilliantly colored cotton calico from India. In the early 2000s, chintz, or glazed chintz, describes a firm, medium to heavyweight, balanced plain weave, spun-yarn fabric converted from print cloth or sheeting and finished with friction calendering. Chintz is usually all cotton or a cotton/polyester blend. Single carded and combed yarns are used in sizes ranging from 28 to 42 and counts ranging from 64 to 80 warp (lengthwise) yarns per inch and 60 to 80 filling (crosswise) yarns per inch. Chintz has a smooth, shiny glazed face and a dull back. Fully glazed chintz is finished with a compound that stiffens the fabric. A padding machine applies the finishing solution, then the fabric is partially dried, and friction calendered. One roll of the friction calender rotates faster than the other and polishes or glazes the fabric surface. If the solution is starch or wax, the effect is temporary. If the solution is resin based, the effect is permanent. Semi-glazed or half-glazed chintz has no stiffening agent and is friction calendered only. Similar fabrics are cretonne (not glazed) and polished cotton (glazed).

Chintz is usually printed in large, bright, colorful floral patterns. Sometimes it is dyed a solid color or printed with geometric patterns such as dots and stripes. It is made with fine, medium-twist warp yarns and slightly larger, lower-twist filling yarns. Chintz is used in draperies, curtains, slipcovers, and lightweight upholstery fabrics. Upholstery chintz usually has a soil- and stain-resistant finish. Chintz is sometimes used in women's dresses, skirts, and blouses, and children's wear. Permanently finished chintz can be machine washed and dried. Otherwise, dry cleaning is necessary to preserve the surface glaze. Chintz is a smooth, crisp fabric that drapes into stiff folds. The glaze may grow dull with use.

GLOSSARY OF TECHNICAL TERMS

Filling yarn: Crosswise yarn in a woven fabric.

Friction calendering: Passing woven fabric between heated rollers that oscillate. After this treatment fabric has an increased shine, which will be permanent only if either the fibers or a finishing material applied to the fabric and thermoplastic.

Warp yarns: Lengthwise yarns in a woven fabric.

Weft yarns: Crosswise yarns in a woven fabric.

History

The word "chintz" is from the Hindustani *chhint* or *chint*, derived from the Sanskrit *chitra* for spotted or bright. *Chints* was the original plural spelling of *chint*.

In the seventeenth century, plain weave cotton fabrics that had been hand-painted or block printed in India with brilliantly colored patterns of plants and animals were imported into Europe and America. The establishment of import/export companies in India by various European countries enhanced the trade of chintz as did the policy of sending sample patterns to India for craftsmen to copy. These novel fabrics were used for gowns, dresses, lounging jackets, robes, bed hangings and coverings, and household textiles. These fabrics quickly became popular because of their novel prints, texture, soft drape, and easy care. Because of their popularity, French craftsmen began to try to duplicate the patterns. This created competition problems for silk and wool goods produced by local weavers. Because of the potential loss of revenue and jobs, in 1686 the French government restricted production and importation of these fine quality, multicolored printed cotton fabrics (*Indiennes*) from India. England also restricted imports, even though India was an English possession.

In spite of various bans and prohibitions, the French, Dutch, Portuguese, and English imported chintz became the basis of European dress and furnishing designs throughout the rest of the seventeenth century and into the mid-eighteenth century. The imported fabrics combined indigo, madder, and an unknown yellow dye with a variety of mordants to achieve an amazing range of colors including blue, green, black, lilac, and crimson. The process of achieving this range of color with only a few natural dyes was not well understood in Europe at that time. The development of domestic printing facilities and the research needed to identify mordant and natural dye combinations and thickening agents for print pastes produced the European textile industry. Research by English, German, and French dyers led to advances in dye chemistry and ultimately the development of synthetic dyes.

By the 1740s, demand for white goods from India increased as European printing houses were established. By the early 1750s, a drop in the quality of Indian printed goods had occurred, probably due to pressure for increased production and lower costs. By 1753, the Indian chintz export trade to Europe had virtually ceased. Efforts to minimize the costs and time needed to produce the fabric and the demand for more printed fabric with better performance led to the development of new mechanized printing methods.

The influence of Indian chintz has not disappeared. Some contemporary floral elements related to early Indian chintz patterns include the use of sprigs and bouquets, trailing floral patterns, and large realistic, brightly colored flowers.

The Original Process

The cloth was flattened and burnished with buffalo milk and myrobolan (a dried fruit containing tannin) to give it a smooth surface. The protein in the milk probably provided bonding sites for the dyes. The pattern was drawn on paper. Holes were pierced through the paper along design lines. Powered charcoal was rubbed on the paper to transfer the pattern to the fabric. The design outlines were painted in. Then, the entire fabric surface was coated with wax except for those areas designed to be blue or green in the finished fabric. The fabric was immersed in an indigo vat, a requirement for fast blues and greens. After immersion in indigo, the dye was oxidized in the air and the fabric was dried. The fabric was scraped and washed to remove the wax. Most of the rest of the design was achieved by painting on a combination of mordants with thickening agents followed by dipping the fabric in a madder bath. Colors achieved in this manner include orange, brown, pink, crimson, lilac, purple, and black. Washing the fabric removed most of the madder in the non-mordanted areas. The fabric was aged in the sun to remove any residual color in the non-mordanted areas and to set the color in the mordanted areas. Finally, any areas requiring yellow (including any area dyed blue that was designed to be green in the finished fabric) were painted with saffron or another yellow dye. Unfortunately, since the yellow dye had poor light fastness, most historic chintz prints have lost that component of the design.

See also **Calico; Cotton; Dyeing.**

BIBLIOGRAPHY

Creekmore, Anna M., and Ila M. Pokornowski, eds. *Textile History Readings.* Washington, D.C.: University Press of America, 1982.

Storey, Joyce. *The Thames and Hudson Manual of Textile Printing.* London: Thames and Hudson, Inc., 1992.

Tortora, Phyllis G., and Robert S. Merkel. *Fairchild's Dictionary of Textiles.* 7th ed. New York: Fairchild Publications, 1996.

Wilson, Kax. *A History of Textiles.* Boulder, Colo.: Westview Press, 1979.

Sara J. Kadolph

CLARK, OSSIE British designer Raymond (Ossie) Clark (1942–1996) was born on 9 June 1942 in Liverpool, England. He was known by his nickname Ossie, after Oswaldtwistle, the Lancashire village to which the family was evacuated during World War II. Clark started making clothes at the age of ten for his niece and nephew. Although he was not regarded as academically promising—he went to a secondary modern school where he learned building skills—he began to draw and developed a love of glamour and beauty, encouraged by his art teacher and mentor, who lent him copies of *Vogue* and *Harper's Bazaar.* For Clark, Diana Vreeland was always "top dog."

Early Career
Clark's copies of fashion pictures and ballet dancers showed skill. In 1958 he enrolled at the Regional College of Art in Manchester, where he was the only male student in the fashion course. The college emphasized technical training, so that Clark learned pattern cutting, construction, tailoring, and glove making—skills in which he excelled and which formed the basis of his distinctive style. In 1959 he saw a Pierre Cardin collection in Paris; he was struck by chiffon "peacock" dresses cut in what he described as a "spiral line," which influenced his later work. In 1960 Clark became friends with Celia Birtwell, who was studying textile design at Salford College, and with the artist Mo McDermott, through whom he met David Hockney in 1961. Clark began a postgraduate course in fashion design at the Royal College of Art in London in 1962, under the aegis of Professor Janey Ironside.

The Royal College of Art produced not only such leading artists as Peter Blake and David Hockney, but also fashion designers who became well known in their own right: Janice Wainwright, Marian Foale, Sally Tuffin, Leslie Poole, Bill Gibb, Zandra Rhodes, and Anthony Price. Textile designer Bernard Nevill taught the students the history of fashion, taking them to the Victoria and Albert Museum, where they observed the collections, particularly those of clothing from the 1920s and 1930s. The students were introduced to the *Gazette du bon ton,* and Neville had them produce illustrations in the styles of George Barbier, Georges Lepape, and other artists of the period. Clark became an admirer of Madeleine Vionnet and Charles James; both designers influenced him, as did Adrian, who had designed the costumes for the film version of *The Women* (1939). "Bernard Nevill . . . opened all the students' eyes to the fact that fashion wasn't about rejecting what your parents stood for. . . . the glamour of the thirties and the satin bias; we thought, why can't people on the street wear them?"

Clark graduated from the Royal College in 1965, the only student in his class to complete the course with distinction. He was photographed by David Bailey for *Vogue,* with the model Chrissie Shrimpton wearing his Robert Indiana op art–print dress. His degree collection was sold at the Woollands 21 boutique; he also began designing for Alice Pollock, part owner of the boutique Quorum in Kensington, close to Barbara Hulanicki's Biba and the Kings Road. Quorum quickly became part of "the most exciting city in the world," as described by writer John Crosby in a 1965 article that discussed youth, talent, and sexual freedom in "swinging London." The new post-Profumo society had a Labour government; unemployment was low, exports were high, and young working women were wearing Mary Quant's miniskirts. Clark and Pollock articulated the new freedom through their clothes. In 1966 Clark's Hoopla dress, a short shift cut to fit without darts and influenced by John Kloss, was featured in *Vogue.*

Success
In 1967 Clark's Rocker jackets and culottes defined the look of "Chelsea Girls" like Patti Harrison, Anita Pallenberg, Marianne Faithfull, Amanda Lear, and Jane Rainey, who was married to Michael Rainey, the proprietor of the Kings Road boutique Hung On You. All were friends for whom Clark made clothes. At this time Alice Pollock suggested to Celia Birtwell that she should design fabrics for Quorum, especially for Clark's styles. Birtwell's floral patterns were influenced in color and design by the work of the Russian artist Leon Bakst as well as by flowers, naturalistic early imagery from manuscripts, and the textiles from collections at the Victoria and Albert Museum, consisting of printed silk chiffon, marrocain crepes, and velvets. Birtwell's fabrics were discharge-printed at Ivo Printers, and used to create such dresses as "Acapulco Gold" or "Ouidjita Banana." Clark cut chiffons and crepes on the straight and turned them to fit the body on the bias, to form the "spiral line" that he had seen at Cardin's show. He also experimented with alternatives to zippers, in particular ties or numerous covered buttons. His versatility in the period from 1967 to 1968 was best illustrated by his use of a range of materials as well as by the clothes themselves. Clark made use of snakeskin and leather as well as chiffon, satin, crepe, tweed, and furs. In 1967, the year in which the film *Bonnie and Clyde* was released and marked a return to nostalgia in fashion, Clark dropped his hemlines, shifting the focus to the wearer's bosom and shoulders, back, or waist to "find a new permutation and erogenous zones," he said. In 1968 *Vogue* featured his tailored redingote in a new "maxi" length. At the end of the same year he launched his "Nude Look," transparent chiffon dresses worn with little or no underwear. His couture pieces, made for such friends as Kari-Anne Jagger, had small hid-

den pockets, just big enough to hold a key and a five-pound note to pay the cab fare home. At the same time, a Clark menswear range was launched, which included ruffled shirts and printed chiffon scarves that were worn by the Rolling Stones, David Hockney, and Jimi Hendrix.

Both Quorum and the Ossie Clark name were sold to a middle-market company, Radley Gowns, in 1968. There were now three Clark lines: a couture line, Ossie Clark for Quorum, and Ossie Clark for Radley—which retailed at an accessible price not only at Quorum, which had relocated to the Kings Road, but also at other boutiques and department stores. In 1969 Clark and Birtwell were married when she became pregnant with their first child. Prudence Glyn, the fashion editor of *The Times*, chose a nude-look ruffled top and matching satin trousers made in Birtwell's trefoil print as the dress of the year for the Museum of Costume in Bath. "Ossie Clark is I believe in the world class for talent; in fact I think that we should build a completely modern idea of British high fashion around him," she wrote. Clark's contemporary Leslie Poole argued his importance at this point in his career: "He liberated women by constructing the low neckline with a bib front, tied at the back that could fit anybody. He borrowed lots of things like pointy sleeves and bias cut, but he effectively altered fashion through this new construction."

In 1970 Clark was invited to design a ready-to-wear collection by the French manufacturer Mendes, to be distributed in France and the United States. It was launched at the musée du Louvre on 22 April 1971 to high acclaim. Clark's collection featured top-quality chiffons, velvets, and silks, cut into frills and parachute pleats, 1940s-inspired panels and plunging necklines, floating shapes and tightly tailored wools. He produced one collection, for reasons still unclear, but continued to show and work in London, dressing Mick Jagger in jumpsuits based on anatomical drawings by Leonardo da Vinci, and making trouser suits for Bianca Jagger. David Hockney's portrait *Mr and Mrs Clark and Percy* (1970–1971) commemorated one of the most famous couples in fashionable London—and their pet cat.

Last Years

Clark's early success did not last. In 1974 he separated from business partner Alice Pollock, and was divorced by Birtwell, who had grown tired of his affairs with men. In October 1974, Clark was the featured speaker at a fashion forum at the Institute of Contemporary Arts in London; he discussed marketing opportunities for the future on that occasion while admitting that he was living the lifestyle of a rock star. Unfortunately his work became disjointed by depression and alcohol abuse in the mid-1970s and appeared in magazines only intermittently. A relaunch in 1977 was not a success because Clark's clothes were not in touch with the London of Vivienne Westwood and punk style. Clark had little business sense, and declared bankruptcy in 1981. Shortly before his death however, he

Ossie Clark ensemble. Clark utilized numerous different materials in his designs and showed a preference for garments that were tied or buttoned, rather than zipped. © HULTON-DEUTSCH COLLECTION/CORBIS. REPRODUCED BY PERMISSION.

had started to make clothes again. Clark was stabbed to death in October 1996 by a former lover, Diego Cogolato. Designers working today influenced by Clark include Anna Sui, John Galliano, Christian Lacroix, Dries van Noten, Marc Jacobs and Clements Ribeiro.

See also **Adrian; Biba; Cardin, Pierre; Celebrities; Galliano, John; Lacroix, Christian; London Fashion; Rhodes, Zandra; Vreeland, Diana.**

BIBLIOGRAPHY

Clark, Ossie. Recording of Ossie Clark at the Institute of Contemporary Arts, 16 October 1974, possession of this writer and with thanks to Ted Polhemus, host of the event.

———. Recording of Ossie Clark lecture at the Royal College of Art, 1996, courtesy of Dr. Susannah Handley and the RCA.

Green, Jonathon. *All Dressed Up: The Sixties and the Counterculture.* London: Jonathan Cape, 1998.

Vogue (British) August 1965.

Watson, Linda. *Ossie Clark*. Warrington, U.K.: Warrington Museum and Art Gallery, 2000.

Watt, Judith. *Ossie Clark 1965–1974*. London: Victoria and Albert Museum, 2003.

Judith Watt

CLASS. *See* **Social Class and Clothing.**

CLEAN-ROOM SUITS. *See* **Microfibers.**

CLOSURES, HOOK-AND-LOOP The hook-and-loop closure has been voted one of the best inventions of the twenty-first century by scientists. "Hooked" to numerous articles of our day-to-day life, hook-and-loop fasteners are used to secure footwear and clothing as well as to anchor equipment on NASA's space shuttles and simplify storage and fastening solutions.

The hook-and-loop closure was conceived in 1948 by the Swiss mountaineer George de Mestral who loved two things—inventing and the great outdoors; he went on to become an engineer. Confident that Mother Nature was the best engineer of all, George de Mestral was both intrigued and annoyed by the burrs that stuck to his wool hunting pants and his dog's fur. Determined to rid himself of the annoying and tedious task of their removal from clothing and fur, George de Mestral examined the burrs under a microscope. He discovered that each burr consisted of hundreds of tiny hooks that grabbed into the threads of fabric and animal fur. Convinced that nature had created something that could simplify fastening solutions, he discussed his idea of a hook-and-loop fastener that could compete with the zipper with textile experts in Lyon, France.

The first hook-and-loop closure was initially produced on a small handloom. The potential for mass production was not realized until de Mestral accidentally discovered that by sewing nylon under an infrared light, loops which were virtually indestructible could be formed in the same interlocking fashion as his cotton system.

In 1951 George de Mestral applied for a patent for this hook-and-loop invention in Switzerland and received additional patents in Germany, Great Britain, Sweden, Italy, Holland, Belgium, France, Canada, and the United States. Thus, de Mestral's company, Velcro S.A., was born.

Key Manufacturers
The name Velcro is derived from the French words "velour" (velvet), and "crochet" (hook). Although the patent expired in 1979, Velcro is a registered trademark of Velcro USA and the company is the largest manufacturer of apparel hook-and-loop fasteners. Over 251 trademark registrations are held in more than 100 countries. The 3M Company is its only significant competition in adhesive-back hook-and-loop closures. The 3M Company focuses on adhesive backed products instead of sew on, and therefore is not geared to the apparel industry. Hook-and-loop closures are integral components of outerwear garments, active sportswear, knee and elbow pads, as well as sports helmets. The elderly and handicapped greatly benefit from its versatility. The children's wear industry makes significant use of hook-and-loop closures in many aspects of apparel. Because of its child-friendly application, these closures are also used on a variety of notebooks, backpacks, and footwear.

The infant and newborn segment of the children's wear market takes full advantage of the benefits of hook-and-loop closures as the fastener of choice on diapers. Nike, who began the use of the Velcro brand fastener on infant sneakers in the late 1970s, continues in the twenty-first century with a sneaker that can be placed on the baby's foot with one hand. Children often wear shoes with Velcro brand fasteners before they learn to tie their shoes. Velcro brand products are manufactured in Canada, China, Mexico, Spain, and the United States.

See also **Children's Clothing; Shoes, Children's; Sport Shoes; Sportswear.**

BIBLIOGRAPHY
Tsuruoka, Doug. "Stick to the Fine Points." *Investor's Business Daily* (14 July 2003): A4.

Joanne Arbuckle

CLOTHING, COSTUME, AND DRESS
Clothing, costume, and dress indicate what people wear, along with related words like "apparel," "attire," "accessories" "garments," "garb," "outfits," and "ensembles." Many writers have tried to figure out why and when human beings began to decorate and cover their bodies; the reasons go beyond obvious considerations of temperature and climate, because some people dress skimpily in cold weather and others wear heavy garments in hot weather. Common reasons given are for protection, modesty, decoration, and display. One can only conjecture or speculate about origins, however, because no records exist detailing why early humans chose to dress their bodies.

Dress functions as a silent communication system that provides basic information about age, gender, marital status, occupation, religious affiliation, and ethnic background for everyday, special occasions and events, or participation in cinema, television, live theater, burlesque, circus, or dance productions. What people wear also can indicate personality characteristics and aesthetic preferences. People understand most clearly the significance and meaning of clothing, costume, and dress when the wearers and observers share the same cultural background. The words "clothing," "costume," and "dress" are sometimes used interchangeably to refer to what is being worn, but the words differ in several ways.

Clothing

"Clothing" as a noun refers generally to articles of dress that cover the body. "Clothing" as a verb refers to the act of putting on garments. Examples of clothing around the world include articles for the torso such as caftans, wrappers, sarongs, shirts, trousers, dresses, blouses, and skirts, as well as accessories for the head, hands, and feet such as turbans, hats, gloves, mittens, sandals, clogs, and shoes.

Costume

"Costume" as a noun describes garments of many types, particularly when worn as an ensemble. "Costume" as a verb often refers to designing an ensemble for an individual to wear. Frequently, "costume" refers to the clothing items, accessories, and makeup for actors, dancers, and people dressing up for special events such as Halloween, masquerade balls, Carnival, and Mardi Gras. A useful distinction between clothing and costume results when clothing refers to specific garments and costume refers to the ensemble that allows individuals to perform in dance, theater, or a masquerade, hiding or temporarily canceling an individual's everyday identity.

The words "costume" and "custom" are closely related, and the word "costume" can also refer to ensembles of clothing (folk costume) worn by members of an ethnic group for special occasions that serve as an affirmation of the group's traditions and solidarity.

Dress

As a noun, "dress" is used in several ways: to indicate a woman's one-piece garment, to indicate a category of garments such as "holiday dress" or "military dress," or as a general reference to an individual's overall appearance or various identities. As a verb, "dress" indicates the process of using various items to cover, adorn, and modify the body. The act of dress involves all five senses and encompasses more than wearing clothes. Getting dressed includes arranging hair, applying scent, lotion, and cosmetics, as well as putting on clothing of various textures and colors and jewelry, such as necklaces, earrings, and jangling bracelets. Dress ordinarily communicates aspects of a person's identity.

Distinctions among Clothing, Costume, and Dress

Items of clothing are components utilized in both costume and dress and designate specific garments and other apparel items such as footwear, headwear, and accessories. Costume is an ensemble created to allow an individual to present a performance identity for the theater, cinema, or masquerade, or to assert an identity as a member of an ethnic group on special occasions or for special events. Dress is the totality of body alterations and additions that help an individual establish credibility of identity in everyday life. In the United States, the term "costume history" ordinarily indicates the chronological study of dress, but in the United Kingdom, the term "dress history" is most frequently used.

Tutu and feathered headdress. Margot Fonteyn struts en pointe her lavishly decorated ballerina tutu and feathered headdress as the lead in the 1956 production of *Firebird*. Feathers and ruffles contribute to the creation of the *Firebird* costume look. © HULTON-DEUTSCH COLLECTION/CORBIS. REPRODUCED BY PERMISSION.

Requirements for Costume and Dress

Costume. Designers for theater, cinema, and dance carefully plan the array of costumes to represent and highlight various roles to be played; principal characters are set apart and highlighted by costume from the rest of the cast or dance troupe. Some costumes designed for single-time use also involve countless hours of fastidious design and construction for adults in high-visibility and prestige Halloween or Mardi Gras events. For example, members of organized groups such as the various Krewes (masking and parading clubs) celebrating a New Orleans Mardi Gras or the San Antonio debutantes selected to be the duchess or princesses in their special ball engage in advance planning and execute intricate costume designs. In contrast, some Halloween costumes for adults or children may be quickly, even carelessly, made and worn for a short evening of venturing out for "trick or treat" candy or a casual masquerade party.

Costumes for the theater, dance, Halloween, and Mardi Gras have special requirements in fit, color, and effect. Garments must allow the performer's body to

COAT

Man wearing African elephant mask. With some more extreme costumes, such as this one made mostly from palm fronds, much of the body is covered from view. © CAROLYN NGOZI EICHER. REPRODUCED BY PERMISSION.

body by allowing bare skin to be displayed; for example, shoulders, arms, legs, and feet in the case of the classic ballerina tutu or a swimsuit. In such examples as an ice-skater's bodysuit or dancer's leotard, the costume may cover but closely conform to and reveal the body shape. Sometimes aspects of a costume are exaggerated for ridicule and irony, as in the giant shoes seen on circus clowns or the padded bosoms of drag queens. In variations of Carnival and Mardi Gras costume, the body, including the head and face, is completely covered and the body is not easily discernible. Among the Kalabari people in the Niger delta of Nigeria one masquerade costume representing an elephant is made of massive palm fronds that eclipse the dancer's body. A small, carved sculpture of an elephant nestles among them, barely visible.

See also **Fashion.**

BIBLIOGRAPHY

Eicher, Joanne B. "Classification of Dress and Costume for African Dance." In *The Spirit's Dance in Africa.* Edited by E. Dagan. Montreal. Galerie Amrad African Art Publication, 1997.

———, and Mary E. Roach-Higgins. "Describing Dress: A System of Classifying and Defining." In *Dress and Gender: Making and Meaning in Cultural Context.* Edited by Ruth Barnes and Joanne B. Eicher. Oxford and Washington, D.C: Berg Publishers, 1992–1993.

Laver, James. *Costume in the Theatre.* London: George G. Harrap and Company, Ltd., 1964.

Joanne B. Eicher

move easily and be well made. For example, costumes of professional actors and dancers often receive hard wear. Constant use or vigorous movement for dancers, circus clowns, and acrobats can put a strain on garments, thus requiring sturdy fabrics and specific construction considerations like seam reinforcement. When many viewers see costumes from afar, colors or other aspects of design may be exaggerated for effect. Some colors, therefore, may be more bold or brilliant than choices for everyday dress. Others may be drab. Such choices depend on the interpretation of the costume designer in planning the garb for each performer's individual role and for the interaction among the performers.

Dress. In contrast to costume, dress establishes individual identity within a cultural context, emphasizing common social characteristics: age and gender, marital status, and occupation. Much information about identity is communicated through sensory cues provided by dress without the observer asking questions. Most individuals, especially in urban settings, have a variety of identities that are connected to dress, such as occupation, leisure-time activities (sports), and religious affiliation.

Costume, dress, and the body. Costumes and dress can reveal or conceal the body. Costumes or dress reveals the

COAT A very important item in any cold climate, a coat is an outerwear garment with sleeves and a center-front closure, and as such incorporates many variations of style and shape including the chesterfield, crombie, British warm, and loden. The garment is designed specifically to be worn outdoors to protect the wearer from the damp, cold, wind, and dust and is most commonly worn over the rest of the clothes, so is generally slightly longer and wider than normal pieces of the wardrobe. However, although designed with protection in mind, not all coats are waterproof. Coats that are used to provide the wearer with extra warmth may be cut from cashmere, tweed, or fur. Coats worn as protection from the rain or snow, such as the classic raincoat or cape, will be made from lighter materials like gabardine or cotton, since they might be used in warm or cold weather.

History

Although a man's wardrobe has always contained at least one piece of outerwear that can be worn as protection from the elements (such as a cloak, gambeson, gown, cote-hardie, or mantle), the overcoat has been a popular garment for both men and women since technical advances in the art of tailoring during the seventeenth century. The emphasis has been placed primarily on fit rather than on material and flamboyant style.

Many clothing styles throughout history either have filtered up from working dress or derive from garments worn by the military or for sporting activities. This was true of the functional long, loose coat worn by the military in the early seventeenth century for riding. Cut with two front panels and two at the back, cuffed sleeves and straight side seams to allow the wearer's sword to pass through, the coat had become fashionable among gentlemen by the last quarter of the century.

In much the same way, the frock—a loose overgarment worn by workingmen—was also given the tailor's treatment. Originally known as a justcoat, buttons were added, sleeves were shortened and trimmed with broad cuffs (which were matched to the color of the waistcoat), and it became known as a frock coat. By 1690, the frock coat was characterized by its collarless neck, narrow shoulders, and buttoned front. It also featured conspicuously large front pockets and an opening for a sword. By the 1730s it had become a fashionable piece of outerwear and would continue to be so, albeit with slightly altering shape, for many years to come.

Eighteenth Century to the Twentieth Century

With the riding coat firmly established as a fashionable staple garment, another form of overcoat known as the greatcoat would also become a functional style that inflluenced mainstream fashion. Available in either single-breasted or double-breasted options, with cape collar and center vent cut into the back, the greatcoat was considered essential for riding. By the latter part of the century, the greatcoat would feature overlapping collars similar to those on the coat worn by coachmen. By the early nineteenth century, greatcoats had become fashionable all-weather garments, worn both in the cities and the countryside. At this time some greatcoats would be lined or trimmed in velvet, have metal buttons, and the main body of the coat would be made from wool.

Taking the more practical or functional types of coats and turning them into fashionable garments remained a design and manufacturing trend that continued throughout the nineteenth century and is still noticeable today. A bewildering number of long or short coats, single- or double-breasted, would continue to be produced. Some coats were skirted, some would have pockets hidden in the pleats or otherwise flap pockets positioned on the skirt itself. The better-known styles from the period, coats still worn, would include the paletot (which was a shorter version of the greatcoat), inverness, covert, and the chesterfield that derived from a version of the earlier frock coat.

By the late 1850s coats were beginning to be cut with raglan sleeves which gave the wearer greater ease of movement, particularly if the coat was worn for riding.

The raglan or a shorter version of a single-breasted chesterfield, known as a covert coat, became "à la mode" for the growing trend for outdoor pursuits such as shooting and even country walking.

The biggest area of growth in the manufacturing of coats at the end of the nineteenth century and the turn of the twentieth century was the development of the raincoat. Effective waterproofing methods had been discovered by Charles Macintosh in the 1820s.

Aside from the move toward the development of the raincoat, overcoats remained much the same until the development of the driving coat in the first decade of the twentieth century. Once again a fully functional garment, the driving coat, produced by wardrobe companies such as Lewis Leathers (who would go on to produce iconic leather jackets during the 1950s) was designed to protect wearers from dust and water while keeping them warm in their open-top vehicles. Driving coats were often made from leather with a fur lining and worn with gauntlets and goggles.

Overcoats designed primarily for use in World War I made the transition to civilian use soon afterward. The British warm, as it is called in the United Kingdom, was a melton, double-breasted coat with shoulder tabs. It was developed for officers in the trenches and remains a popular style in the early 2000s. This was also true of the water-repellent and breathable Burberry trench coat made from fine-twilled cotton gabardine especially for trench warfare.

Coats changed very little during the interwar years. World War II again led to innovation, providing men's wear with the only classic coat to have a hood—the duffel coat. Worn principally by servicemen in the Royal Navy, and popularized by Field Marshal Montgomery, this style flooded the market when they were sold as surplus after the war.

Coats in the Twenty-first Century

Few coat styles have changed since the 1950s. Some may be shortened or lengthened, cut tighter to the waist, or even cut from a different cloth, but no classic new styles have been developed. Although the overcoat is still an essential item in the male and female wardrobe, heated offices and cars, central heating in the home, and the development of more technical fabrications have made it of much less importance than ever before.

See also **Jacket; Outerwear; Raincoat.**

BIBLIOGRAPHY

Amies, Hardy. *A,B,C of Men's Fashion*. London: Cahill and Company Ltd., 1964.

Byrde, Penelope. *The Male Image: Men's Fashion in England 1300–1970*. London: B. T. Batsford, Ltd., 1979.

Chenoune, Farid. *A History of Men's Fashion*. Paris: Flammarion, 1993.

De Marley, Diana. *Fashion for Men: An Illustrated History*. London: B. T. Batsford, Ltd., 1985.

Keers, Paul. *A Gentleman's Wardrobe*. London: Weidenfeld and Nicolson, 1987.

Roetzel, Bernhard. *Gentleman: A Timeless Fashion*. Cologne, Germany: Konemann, 1999.

Schoeffler, O. E., and William Gale. *Esquire's Encyclopedia of 20th Century Fashions*. New York: McGraw-Hill, 1973.

Wilkins, Christobel. *The Story of Occupational Costume*. Poole: Blandford Press, 1982.

Tom Greatrex

COCKTAIL DRESS During the 1920s, newfound concepts of individuality and a repudiation of the Edwardian matronly ideal of respectable womanhood gave rise to the new phenomenon of the "Drinking Woman," who dared to enjoy cocktails in mixed company (Clark, p. 212). She emerged at private cocktail soirées and lounges, and the cocktail dress, as a short evening sheath with matching hat, shoes, and gloves was designated to accompany her. The cocktail affair generally took place between six and eight P.M., yet by manipulating one's accessories, the cocktail ensemble could be converted to appropriate dress for every event from three o'clock until late in the evening. Cocktail garb, by virtue of its flexibility and functionality, became the 1920s uniform for the progressive fashionable elite.

Birth of the Cocktail Ensemble
By the end of World War I, the French couture depended rather heavily on American clientele and to an even greater extent on American department stores that copied and promoted the French *créateurs* (Steele, p. 253). As cocktailing had originated in the United States, the French paid less attention to the strict designations of line, cut, and length that American periodicals promoted for their *heure de l'aperitif*. Instead, the couturières Chanel and Vionnet created garments for the late afternoon, or "after five," including beach pajamas—silk top and palazzo pant outfits worn with a mid-calf-length wrap jacket. Louise Boulanger produced *les robes du studio*, chic but rather informal sheaths that suited the hostess of private or intimate cocktail gatherings.

As the popularity of travel grew, both in American resort cities like Palm Beach, "the Millionaire's Playground," and abroad with the luxury of the Riviera, these French cocktail garments gained favor in wealthy American circles. But while America's elite were promoting the exclusive designs of the French couture, the majority of the United States relied on the advertisements of *Vanity Fair* and American *Vogue*, as well as their patronage of American department stores to dress for the cocktail hour. Created by Chanel in 1926, the little black dress was translated to ready-to-wear as a staple of late afternoon and cocktail hours; American women at every level

of consumption knew the importance of a practical "Well-mannered Black" (*Vogue*, 1 May 1943, p. 75).

Mid-1920s skirt lengths were just below the knee for all hours and affairs. Though cocktail attire featured the longer sleeves, modest necklines, and sparse ornamentation of daytime clothing, it became distinguished by executions in evening silk failles or satins, rather than wool crepes or gabardines. Often the only difference between a day dress and a cocktail outfit was a fabric *noir* and a stylish cocktail hat. Hats in the 1920s varied little from the cloche shape, but cocktail and evening models were adorned with plumes, rhinestones, and beaded embroideries that indicated a more formal aesthetic. Short gloves were worn universally for cocktail attire during this period and could be found in many colors, though white and black were the most popular.

From Day to Evening
In the early 1930s, Hollywood sirens like Greta Garbo embodied a casual, sporty American chic that paired easily with the separates ensembles favored by the French. The more privatized cocktail party of the silver screen began to gain popularity, replacing the smoking rooms of Paris and the dance clubs of New York. The stock market crash of 1929 and the resulting economic depression dictated that it was no longer fashionable to display wealth by throwing ostentatious public affairs. Exclusive lounges emerged rapidly on the Paris scene; Bergère, the Blue Room, and Florence's were as popular for after-dinner cocktails as for the private affairs of the early evening. *Dames du Vogue* like Vicomtesse Marie-Laure de Noailles and Mrs. Reginald (Daisy) Fellowes, members of the elite international café society, became notorious for their exclusive soirées. Their patronage of Chanel, Patou, and Elsa Schiaparelli, all made famous by separates designs, helped popularize day-into-evening wear for upper-class Parisians and American socialites.

While Mademoiselle Cheruit had her *smoking*, a fitted jacket ensemble for early evening affairs, Schiaparelli was the most famous purveyor of the cocktail-appropriate dinner suit. Her suit consisted of a bolero or flared jacket that could be removed for the evening, revealing a sleeveless sheath dress. Unlike the previous decade, the 1930s dictated different skirt lengths for different hours: the silk, rayon, or wool crepe sheath of the dinner suit was steadfastly ankle or cocktail length.

In light of the economic hardships of the early 1930s, American designers like Muriel King designed "day-into-evening" clothes by championing a simple, streamlined silhouette and emphasizing the importance of accessories. Cartwheel hats, made of straw or silk and decorated with velvet ribbons or feathers, and slouchy fedoras of black felt were equally acceptable for the cocktail hour. Gloves were a bit longer than in the previous decade, but were still mandatory for late afternoon and evening. Costume jewelry, whether as a daytime pin or an evening parure, became the definitive cocktail accessory. Excessive jewelry was promoted as both daring and luxurious when clothing itself was regulated to be modest and unfettered.

During World War II, the hemline of the cocktail dress rose again to just below the knee, but the convenience and accessibility of the fashionable cocktail accessory sustained. Parisian milliners like Simone Naudet (Claude Saint-Cyr) produced elegant chapeaus with black silk net veils for the cocktail hour. In New York, Norman Norell attached rhinestone buttons to vodka gray or billiard green day suits to designate them cocktail ensembles. By the mid-1940s, cocktailing was made easy by the adaptability of cocktail clothing and the availability of the indispensable cocktail accessory.

A New Look for Cocktails

With his New Look collection of 1947, Christian Dior brought romanticism back to the catwalk. His cinched waists and full, mid-calf length frocks enforced a demure feminine aesthetic (Arnold, p. 102). The cocktail hour began to represent universal social identities for women: the matron, the wife, and the hostess. Cocktail parties rose to the height of sociability, and cocktail clothing was defined by strict rules of etiquette. While invitees were required to wear gloves, the hostess was forbidden the accessory. Guests were obligated to travel to an engagement in a cocktail hat (which had retained the veil made popular in the 1940s), but they were never to wear their hats indoors.

Parisian cocktail dresses were executed in black velvets and printed voiles alike, but they all retained the short-length of the original 1920s cocktail dress. American designers like Anne Fogarty and Ceil Chapman emulated the "New Look" line, but used less luxurious fabrics and trims. Dior, along with Jacques Fath and milliners Lilly Daché and John-Fredericks, quickly saw the advantages of promoting cocktail clothing in the American ready-to-wear market, designing specifically for their more inexpensive lines: Dior New York, Jacques Fath for Joseph Halpert, Dachettes, and John Fredericks Charmers.

Dior was the first to name the early evening frock a "cocktail" dress, and in doing so allowed periodicals, department stores, and rival Parisian and American designers to promote fashion with cocktail-specific terminology. *Vogue Paris* included articles entitled *"Pour le Coktail: L'Organdi,"* while advertisements in *Vogue* out of New York celebrated "cocktail cotton" textiles (*Vogue Paris*, April 1955, p. 77). Cocktail sets, martini-printed interiors fabrics, and cocktail advertisements all fostered an obsessively consumer-driven cocktail culture in America and, to some extent, abroad.

Though Pauline Trigère, Norman Norell, and countless Parisian couturiers continued to produce cocktail models well into the 1960s, the liberated lines of Gallitzine's palazzo pant ensembles and Emilio Pucci's

Chanel cocktail dress. In 1926, Coco Chanel originated the concept of the "little black dress," which, with the addition of certain accessories, could be worn for the evening cocktail hours. © Condé Nast Archive/Corbis. Reproduced by permission.

jumpsuits easily replaced formal cocktail garb in privatized European and American social circuits. Often direct appropriations of midcentury designs, the cocktail dress and its partner accessories exist today on runways and in trendy boutiques as reminders of the etiquette and formality of 1950s cocktail fashions.

See also **Chanel, Gabrielle (Coco); Dior, Christian; Little Black Dress.**

BIBLIOGRAPHY

Arnold, Rebecca. *Fashion, Desire, and Anxiety: Image and Morality in the Twentieth Century.* New Brunswick, N.J.: Rutgers University Press, 2001.

Clark, Norman H. *Deliver Us From Evil: An Interpretation of the American Prohibition.* New York: W. W. Norton and Company, 1976.

"Dior's Convertible Costumes." *Vogue* (1 September 1951): 183a.

Kirkham, Pat. *Women Designers in the USA 1900–2000.* New York: Yale University Press, 2000.

"Les Décolleté de sept heures." *Vogue Paris* (September 1948): 141.

"Les Pyjamas et les robes du studio." *Vogue Paris* (June 1930): 47.

Milbank, Caroline Rennolds. *New York Fashion: The Evolution of American Style.* New York: Harry N. Abrams, 1989.

Seeling, Charlotte. *Fashion: The Century of the Designer, 1900–1999.* Cologne, Germany: Konemann, 1999.

Steele, Valerie. *Paris Fashion: A Cultural History.* New York: Oxford University Press, 1988.

"The Well-Dressed Woman." *Vanity Fair* (June 1928): 87.

Elyssa Schram Da Cruz

CODPIECE The codpiece was a distinguishing feature of men's dress from 1408 to about 1575 C.E. Originally a triangle of cloth used to join the individual legs of men's hose, the codpiece emerged as a nonverbal statement of political and economic power.

The codpiece began as a solution to changing fashion. Throughout the Renaissance, various forms of the doublet-and-hose combination characterized men's dress. A doublet was a fitted, often quilted jacket that varied in length from above the knee to the natural waist. Hose were individually tailored legs of woven fabric cut on the bias grain. Each leg was stitched up the back and laced to the doublet, similar to the system of garter belts and stockings used by women in the middle twentieth century. An early version of underpants made of linen or

Henry VIII in codpiece. Often worn as a symbol of wealth or power, the codpiece had its heyday during the Renaissance period. © BETTMANN/CORBIS. REPRODUCED BY PERMISSION.

wool was worn underneath. As doublets shortened, hose were cut longer and wider to cover the underpants up to the waist. Across the genitals, a triangular gusset laced to the front of the hose between the legs. It satisfied decency requirements and calls of nature. By the sixteenth century, the codpiece was both shaped and padded. Squire and Baynes report that the term "cod" was both a Renaissance-era word for bag and a slang word for testicles. By the mid-1500s, the embellishment of the codpiece with jewels and embroidery exaggerated the genitals so that little was left to the imagination.

Once the codpiece achieved a pouch shape, it was used for a variety of purposes, including as a purse for small objects. When the fitted doublet/hose/codpiece combination is compared with the ankle-length, draped, and pleated robes of earlier periods, Renaissance men's dress appears slim and ready for action. However, the bias cut of woven hose, while more elastic than straight grain, does not allow for a full range of movement. The successful application of knitting to create fine, well-fitting hose contributed to the decline of the codpiece by the turn of the seventeenth century.

Clear examples of the codpiece can be seen in sixteenth-century court portraits by Clouet, Titian, and Holbein. During this period, men's dress extended the body into an overall horizontal silhouette. Codpiece, shoulders, and doublet were padded; luxury fabrics were slashed and their contrasting linings pulled out through the slits; and heavy gold chains were draped from shoulder to shoulder. Squire and Baynes describe the "aggressive solidity of appearance" and the "fantastic air of brutality" (1975, p. 66). Squire describes the fashionable man as, "broad-shouldered and barrel-chested, while a proudly displayed virility between his legs projected forcefully through the skirts of his jerkin" (1974, p. 52). In fact, the sixteenth century was a period of aggressive kingdom building in which more and more power was consolidated into the hands of fewer, very strong individuals. The codpiece contributed, in part, to the visible, and not at all subtle, expression of the power and the spirit of those times.

See also **Doublet; Penis Sheath.**

BIBLIOGRAPHY

Boucher, François. *20,000 Years of Fashion: The History of Costume and Personal Adornment.* New York: Harry N. Abrams, 1987.

Squire, Geoffrey. *Dress and Society: 1560–1970.* New York: Viking, 1974.

Squire, Geoffrey, and Pauline Baynes. *The Observer's Book of European Costume.* London: Frederick Warne and Company, Ltd., 1975.

Tortora, Phyllis, and Keith Eubank. *Survey of Historic Costume.* 3rd ed. New York: Fairchild Publications, 1998.

Sandra Lee Evenson

COLONIALISM AND IMPERIALISM

The term "empire" covers a range of ways of incorporating and managing different populations under the rule of a single dominant state or polity, as for example in the Roman Empire, the Carolingan Empire, and the British Empire. A more detailed categorization might distinguish between colonialism as the ruling by an external power over subject populations and imperialism as intervention in or dominating influence over another polity without actually governing it. The two processes differ largely in terms of the extent to which they transform the institutions and organization of life in the societies subject to their intrusion; the transformations of colonialism tend to be more direct than those of imperialism.

Many European nations, the United States, China, and Japan have at one time or another exerted colonial rule over subject populations as part of regionally shifting geopolitical strategies combined with economic motives for gain. Although they applied diverse approaches to governing local societies, most colonial powers considered the people they ruled to be alien and different. Entering into the affairs of other societies, differentiating between groups and individuals in racial, ethnic, and gender terms, colonial rule reorganized local life, affecting colonized people's access to land, property, and resources, authority structures and institutions, family life and marriage, among many others. These vast transformations of livelihoods had numerous cultural ramifications, including on dress.

Colonial powers have tended in recent centuries to be developed countries with strong agricultural and manufacturing economies and powerful urban centers. Their populations, and especially individuals directly involved in the colonial enterprise, have often regarded colonized indigenous peoples as "backward," both culturally and socioeconomically. Appearance was a strongly contested area in the relations between colonizers and colonized. Indigenous people in many colonized societies adorned their bodies with cosmetics, tattooing, or scarification, wore feathers and other forms of ornament, and habitually went naked or dressed in animal skins or other nonwoven materials. When they did wear woven cloth, it was often in the form of clothing that was draped, wrapped, or folded rather than cut, stitched, and shaped to the contours of the body. Dress and textiles conveyed information about gender and rank in terms different from those familar to the colonizers. Such vastly different dress practices, especially nakedness, struck colonizers as evidence of the inferiority of subject populations. Because colonizers considered their own norms and lifestyles to be proof of their superior status, dress became an important boundary-marking mechanism.

Clothing Encounters

The cultural norms that guided the West's colonial encounters were shaped importantly by Christian notions of morality and translated into action across the colonial world by missionary societies from numerous denominations. The colonial conquest by Spain and Portugal of today's Latin America developed caste-like socioeconomic and political systems in which indigenous people and African slaves were forced to convert to Christianity and to wear Western styles of dress. Yet the rich weaving traditions of the Maya and Andean regions did not disappear but developed creative designs combining local and Christian symbols. When the Dutch colonized Indonesia in the seventeenth century and introduced Christianity, Islam was already long established. Subsequent interactions encompassed three distinct cultural spheres: Dutch and European, Muslim, and non-Muslim indigenous. The Dutch initially reserved Western-style dress for Europeans and for Christian converts.

Clothing "the natives" was a central focus of the missionary project in the early encounters between the West and the non-West, for example in Africa. In Bechuanaland, a frontier region between colonial Botswana and South Africa, the struggle for souls entailed dressing African bodies in European clothes to cover their nakedness and managing those bodies through new hygiene regimes. Missionaries were pleased when indigenous peoples accepted their clothing proposals, seeing it as a sign of religious conversion in the new moral economy of mind and body. In the Pacific, the encounter between missionary and indigenous clothing preferences sometimes produced striking results, as in the cultural synthesis in Samoan Christians' bark cloth "ponchos" that not only expressed new ideas of modesty but also in fact made modesty possible by providing new ways to cover bodies. In a number of island societies, Pacific Islanders' innovations and transformations of clothing resulted in new styles and designs.

In Melanesia, missionaries saw the eager adoption of printed calico as an outward sign of conversion, or at least openness to conversion, while Melanesians interpreted these patterns with reference to ideas about empowered bodies. Native peoples in North America also found floral designs on European printed cloth to be very attractive, incorporating them in embroidery on garments and crafts objects in increasingly stylized and abstract forms. Throughout the colonial world, missionary-inspired dress, often with links to traditional dress, developed in many directions. European styles and fabrics were incorporated in many places, such as in the smocked *Sotho* dress and the *Herero* long dress that serve as visible markers for "traditional" dress in southern Africa. Following independence from colonial rule, many such dress practices have come close to being considered national dress and are associated with notions of proper womanhood.

Colonial Behavior

Western civilization set the standards of dress for colonizers in foreign outposts in a way that stereotyped the differences between colonizer and subject populations. For example, Westerners often made a point of dressing

British soldiers in naval uniforms attack Malay villagers. Indigenous peoples were often considered inferior by colonizers, in part because of their different dress practices, causing dress to become a status-defining mechanism. JOHN S. MAJOR. REPRODUCED BY PERMISSION.

in full European attire (woolen suits for men, corseted dresses for women) when touring up-country in the African bush or the jungles of Java; they wished their willingness to endure discomfort for the sake of dressing "properly" to be viewed as evidence of moral and cultural superiority. Although some Europeans in early encounter situations adopted local elements of dress, for example loose-stitched gowns of cotton and silk in India, colonial dress practice became increasingly rigid and formal. As time went by, colonial dress codes regarded cultural cross-dressing (a sign of "going native") to be an affront to the standards of the ruling group. Obsessions over dress extended to climate and disease. The British in India and Africa wore special underwear to guard themselves against sudden weather changes. They wore *sola*

topis, flannel-lined solar helmets, to protect themselves against the dangerous rays of the sun. The fears associated with the physical environment provoked a form of a sometimes suicidal depression that contemporary medical doctors in east and southern Africa decribed as tropical neurasthenia.

Oppression and Resistance

In cases where colonial rulers regarded indigenous dress as a potential focus of resistance to the occupying power, suppression of local dress might be rigidly enforced. For example, when Korea was a Japanese colony (1910–1945), all markers of Korean cultural identity, including the use of the spoken and written Korean language and the wearing of the national *hanbok* costume, were ruthlessly suppressed. In contrast, in the Japanese colony of Taiwan (ruled 1895–1945), there was no readily identifiable national dress, and so the Japanese authorities did not pay particular attention to what Taiwanese people wore.

Colonizers often could not fully control how subjected people dressed. Migrant labor, urban life, and education introduced new consumption practices and desires, among them factory-produced textiles and European-styled fashions. Local people sometimes wore the new garments as they saw fit. They were highly selective about which items of foreign dress they absorbed into their local dress repertoires. With new clothes also came new etiquettes that might be at variance with local ways, such as the practice in India and Indonesia of removing one's shoes when entering a building and covering one's head as signs of respect.

Indigenous persons of high rank, the new elite, and men were among the first to incorporate items of Western clothing into their wardrobes. Because the suit was a hallmark of colonial authority, jackets and trousers signified status, education, and colonial employment. In India, some men who adopted Western fabrics retained Indian dress styles while others had Indian garments tailored to take on a European look. New combination garments consisted of both Indian and European clothes—for example, shoes and trousers worn with coats in local styles and distinctive hats, a Western-style jacket on top of locally styled trousers or a sarong. In parts of Africa, highly decorated military uniforms were worn by kings and paramount chiefs on special occasions in combination with other styles of dress and accessories such as animal skins. The big robes, *boubous*, worn by Muslim men in West Africa, were not widely abandoned in favor of Western suits and are today worn with pride as evidence of a different dress aesthetic than the strong linear form of the Western suit.

Except for the elite, women in many parts of the colonial world were more resistant to adopt the new dress styles. Adopting European fabrics while retaining regional styles was popular among Indian women, who might add new accessories such as shoes, petticoats, and jackets to their Indian dress. Their saris might incorporate the latest trends in color and design from Europe. European suit jackets, often acquired in the used-clothing trade, are combined with indigenous garments in hybrid styles of men's clothing from Africa to Afghanistan. Across most of Africa, women eagerly appropriated factory-produced cloth, much of it manufactured in Europe incorporating "African" designs, into their everyday dress style of wrapper and headtie, tailored and highly constructed dresses, alongside a variety of Western-style garments.

Exoticizing Dress Practices

In early colonial encounters, the British in India and the Dutch in Indonesia mapped and organized the diversity of the peoples they ruled in terms of dress. In late nineteenth- and early-twentieth-century Paris, Brussels, Lon-

don, and Chicago, among other places, preoccupations with the racial attributes of dress were showcased at expositions displaying colonial subjects in "traditional" clothes. The contemporary desire to catalog the world by parading exotic people in "traditional" dress as ethnographic specimens helped to accentuate the difference between the familiar and exotic in highly stereotypical ways. Postcards, produced for example in Algeria and Indonesia, displaying women in erotic stances and exotic clothing, made women's dress central to the marking of cultural difference. With the West as voyeur, such postcards projected invidious images of the exotic onto women's dressed bodies.

Dress as Artifact and Cultural Revival

Not all segments of colonial society advocated the adoption of Western dress for their local subjects. Some, who were able to adopt an attitude of cultural pluralism, appreciated differences in dress without assuming the superiority of European styles, while others promoted the revival of local dress and adornment as a way of safeguarding threatened cultures and their aesthetics. In northeast Canada, French Ursuline nuns promoted pictorial and floral imagery among Native Americans in sewing and embroidery, stimulating a commodification of Indian curios. Over time, these depictions shifted from images of "noble savages" to colonial nostalgia scenes depicting the imminent disappearance of a way of life dependent on nature. Similar managed efforts in support of cultural survival were instituted in many places in Latin Americia, Africa, India, South and Southeast Asia, and the Pacific. Products of these cultural revival movements often did not remain within the societies that produced them, but were acquired for private and public collections and museums of textile arts. Although they all have given rise to interpretations about authenticity, such artifacts were everywhere the products of complex interactions and influences that demonstrate continuous incorporation of new developments and inspirations into "tradition."

The retention or revival of some of these clothing and textile traditions sometimes served to express rejection of colonialism, such as in Gandhi's call on Indians to wear homespun cloth. Some dress and textile traditions are used to make claims for political representation in states where indigenous people are subordinated or threatenend, for example in the Amazon region of Brazil. Another development of the cultural revival of textiles and dress practices has turned the process into fashion, in which newly developed styles that are considered ethnically chic attract consumers in former colonies and the world beyond.

The Seductions of Imperialism

Imperialism, which in the modern usage of the term usually involves influence on another country or culture but not direct colonial control, can have a powerful effect on the clothing of the subject culture. The effect is usually voluntary (as opposed to the actual imposition of new forms of dress by missionaries and colonial administrators), but it can be seen as a form of cultural coercion in which voluntarism is compromised. The effects can take a wide range of forms.

In Japan during the Meiji Period (1868–1912), the government energetically promoted modernization as a way of strengthening the country, with a twofold goal: to prevent Japan's being taken over as a colony by any European power, and to prepare Japan to compete on equal terms with Europe as a colonial power itself. The effort to emulate the strength of the West included a promotion of beef-eating (formerly nearly unknown in Japan) and a wholesale adoption of Western-style clothing, at least by urban elites.

In China at the end of the nineteenth century, a deliberate effort was made to design a new-style military and school uniform that would be "modern" but not too "Western." The result was an early version of the Sun Yat-sen suit (later to be known in the West as the Mao Zedong suit), based on the Prussian military uniform but with a collar derived from that of the traditional Chinese long gown.

A third example, one so ubiquitous as to be part of the common wisdom about the modern world, has been the worldwide spread of sartorial markers of Western popular culture: the T-shirt, jeans, and running shoes. No one has forced any teenager in the Third World to wear these garments; almost no one (short of fanatical religious dictatorships such as the Taliban in Afghanistan) has succeeded in preventing them from doing so. Denounced by nationalists and cultural conservatives as "cultural imperialism," the trend nevertheless seems irreversible.

Transformative Encounters and Contesting Clothes

Colonies and empires exerted a limited form of rule over subject populations both in relation to the exercise of power and the will and ability to transform society. The clothing practices colonialism inspired in many parts of the world demonstrate an important lesson about the relation between colonialism and dress. Colonialism was always a transformative encounter in which subject people were active participants rather then passive respondents to sartorial impositions from the outside. When dress served as a boundary-making mechanism, it did so in ways that were contested. Because the meanings of the dressed body everywhere are ambiguous, the colonial encounter enabled local people to take pride in long-held aesthetics expressed in new dress media and forms. It enabled the creation of styles of "national dress" that as invented traditions have served as cultural assertions for shifting claims to political voice and representation between the late colonial period and the present. Last but not least, colonial dress practices from Latin America, to India, to Japan have become part of everyday wardrobes everywhere, opening a world of dress for which everyone is the richer.

See also **Africa, North: History of Dress; Africa, Sub-Saharan: History of Dress; America, Central, and Mexico: History of Dress; America, North: History of Dress; Americas, South: History of Dress; Asia, East: History of Dress; Asia, South: History of Dress; Asia, Southeastern Islands and the Pacific: History of Dress; Asia, Southeastern Mainland: History of Dress.**

BIBLIOGRAPHY

Alloula, Malek. "The Colonial Harem." In *Theory and History of Literatures.* Manchester University Press, 1986.

Colchester, Cloe, ed. *Clothing the Pacific.* Oxford: Berg, 2003.

Nordholt, Henk Schulte, ed. *Outward Appearances: Dressing State and Society in Indonesia.* Leiden, Netherlands: KITLV Press, 1997.

Phillips, Ruth B. *Trading Identities: The Souvenir in Native North American Art from the Northeast, 1700–1900.* Hong Kong: University of Washington Press, 1998.

Steele, Valerie, and John Major, eds. *China Chic: East Meets West.* New Haven, Conn.: Yale University Press, 1999.

Tarlo, Emma. *Clothing Matters: Dress and Identity in India.* London: Hurst and Company, 1996.

Karen Tranberg Hansen

COLOR IN DRESS Color attracts attention, creates an emotional connection, and leads the consumer to the product (Brannon, p. 117). Color is often a primary reason why a person is attracted to and buys a particular item of clothing. A new T-shirt in a different color can help transform the look of a product year after year. Color captures a viewer's interest because it is both easily recognizable and distinctive. We often describe clothing in terms of color, such as "a blue suit."

The study of color is complex and involves light, vision, and pigment as well as science, technology, and art. In addition, colored pigment behaves differently than colored light. Although there are many models of color classification, the Munsell color system with its numeric notation for each color is widely used and accepted to describe color pigments and the color properties that relate to dress.

Color Dimensions

All pigment color systems recognize that three dimensions describe color—hue (the name), intensity (brightness/dullness), and value (lightness/darkness). All three dimensions are present in every color and every color starts with hue. Value and intensity are adjectives that describe variations of any hue (light bright green, or deep dull red, for instance).

Hue. The name of the color as designated on the color wheel is its hue—the visual sensation of blue, for example. Each hue has an individual physical character: pri-

COLOR FOR THE INDIVIDUAL

Packaging of colors for individual selection has been used to market color (Jackson 1981; Pinckney and Swenson 1981). Color selection for clothing is based upon colors that are grouped according to some easily remembered system, such as nature's seasons. Winter and spring colors are described as clear, vivid, and bright, while summer and fall are less intense. Winter and summer colors are cool; spring and fall colors are warm. Personal color analysis systems range from offering small pre-packaged color palettes, to specifically selected colors for each individual.

The Color Key system categorizes color according to warm or cool overtones that contain all basic hues, values, and intensities (Brannon 2000). Color Key 1 consists of cool, clear colors and Color Key 2 includes warm, earth tone colors; each has a corresponding color fan of paint chips that can be used to coordinate paint for interiors and apparel colors. This color key system implies that people will look and feel better when surrounded by colors that reflect their personal coloring.

mary pigment hues are red, yellow, and blue. No other colors combine to make them, but these colors combine to make all other hues. The secondary hues, orange, green, and violet are mixtures of the adjacent primary hues; orange is a mixture of red and yellow; violet is a mixture of red and blue. The hue spectrum runs from red to violet, and is usually depicted as a circle of hues with the primary hues separated by the secondary. Tertiary hues (sometimes called intermediate) result from mixing a primary and a secondary, that is, red-orange or blue-violet.

Groups or categories of colors that share common sensory effects are often called families. Related hues (sometimes called analogous) such as blue-violet, violet, and red-violet, are adjacent on the color wheel and constitute a color family. Contrasting colors are separated from each other on the color wheel. Contrasting color schemes include complementary and split-complementary. Hues opposite each other, such as yellow and purple-blue, are called complementary because they complete the spectrum; each contains primaries the other lacks. Complementary hues can produce an afterimage of each other. If you stare at one hue for several seconds, when you glance away to a neutral surface, you will see an image of its complement. In a split-complementary scheme

the color on either side of the complement is selected, green, red-orange, and red-violet, for example.

Value. Each hue has a specific normal or home value; the home value of yellow is close to white or light gray, and violet is as dark as very dark gray. Values have an effect upon colors in combination. For example, the complements red and green have similar values, offering hue contrast but not value contrast. However, the complementary hues of yellow and violet at normal value offer both hue and value contrast.

Contrasting values can affect the perception of edge in adjacent surfaces. A light value surface placed next to a dark one offers a strong visual pull to the difference between the two surfaces. Applications can be found in the value contrast between a white shirt and black trousers, light skin and dark hair, or dark hair and skin and pastel suit.

Intensity. The relative purity or saturation of a color is its intensity, sometimes referred to as chroma. This dimension describes the strength of a color. Saturated colors are primary and secondary hues at their purest and strongest on the color wheel. Each hue has a range of saturation from full intensity to neutral gray. Intensity provides hue with its vividness or neutrality. Intensity yields a variety of expressions. A saturated hue is intense and usually evokes a response of excitement or energy. Less saturated hues range from nearly bright to almost muted incorporating many moods. Hues in the lowest intensities are neutral colors and often are the foundation of a wardrobe. If used together at full strength, complementary colors can vibrate. The addition of a hue's complement lowers its saturation toward neutral gray and can increase its livability.

Intensity is influenced by surface texture. Even minor surface irregularities reflect minute areas of light that cast miniature shadows; this has the effect of dulling the intensity of a color. If a fabric with a distinct weave or surface were dipped into the same dye bath as a smooth material, it would appear duller in color because of the softening effect of the napped texture. Conversely, a smooth shiny surface will make a soft color appear stronger (Goldstein and Goldstein 1960, pp. 184–185).

Psychophysical Effects of Color

Psychophysical effects can be tied to hue characteristics. The temperature of a hue, the space from which it is viewed, and the color combinations used to create it can influence perception.

Warm and cool. Warm hues, light values, and strong intensities seem to advance while cool hues, dark values, and desaturated hues recede. Hues that advance also expand a shape. Warm colors and dark values are perceived as dense or solid and are often associated with muted earth tones such as brick or red-orange, ocher, or golden brown. Cool colors seem to reduce a shape. Cool hues and light values are associated with air, distant mountains, and water and may present an appearance of distance, depth, shadow, coolness, and lightness.

Warm hues, light values, and saturated colors such as bright orange or shocking pink can seem loud or noisy. Cool hues, dark values, and desaturated colors like deep taupe or dark violet are quiet by comparison.

Spatial position. Hues viewed singly can produce an afterimage and this affects colors on the body. When the viewer concentrates on a clothing surface and then glances at the face, the skin can appear to take on tinges of the complement to the hue of the clothing. Thus after looking intensely at a green sweater, a viewer who glances up at the face may find it tinged with the complement, red.

Whether a hue is directly surrounded by another hue or is separated in some way will influence its perceptual effect. When individual colors are separated by black or white, both their singleness of character and their interaction are suppressed somewhat. Black causes adjacent hues to seem lighter and more brilliant; a surround of white often appears to darken them.

Visual mixing. Colors combined in very small patterns or woven together appear to mix visually. When two or more colors are interwoven onto one surface the result can be more vibrant than a surface of just one color. Complementary hues or black and white threads woven together will create a surface that appears gray or neutral when viewed from a distance. If the size of the black and white threads is increased, a salt-and-pepper effect is created.

Color and the Body

Color and dress enter a relationship with color and the body. As a composite of colors, human coloration can be analyzed in the same way as other pigments to predict the effects of color in dress. Similarity of any of the attributes of colors placed upon the body can form a powerful visual relationship with the body.

A person's appearance is a combination of the surfaces placed upon the body and the individual's personal body coloring. Included in appearance are the body colors of skin, hair, and eyes. What surrounds a particular color affects how it appears. The pre-existing colors of the body are influenced by other colors placed upon it, so the body colors affect the surfaces placed upon it and the reverse is also true. In addition, the clothed body can be greatly influenced by colors of the surrounding environment and by lighting effects.

By matching, naming, and locating personal body colors, an individual can begin to understand color relationships. Intensity is a difficult dimension of color to describe when applied to body colors because the skin surface requires noting small and subtle differences. "Highlights" in one's personal coloring may include areas of the hair, skin, or eyes that seem more intense than other areas. "Undertone" is used to describe underlying colors of skin and hair. Identifying both highlights and undertones for an individual helps in placing colors on the body that are related by similarity or contrast.

Color as a source of association. Color is associated with many natural objects of similar color and therefore can acquire similar meaning according to that association. Sunshine is yellow and warm: yellow is warm. Blue is cool and distant as the mountains and water. Red is exciting like fire and in many cultures red signals danger. Mood is associated with color, too; we have the "blues," or we are "green" with envy.

Colors may be associated symbolically with specific peoples or historic periods. In the 1960s in the United States, psychedelic colors were symbolic of the decade and included combinations of intense hues of pink, yellow, blue, green, and purple. Koreans favor celadon green, a pastel blue-green, because of its traditional association with pottery and ceramics, and white is used for mourning dress in Korea (Geum and DeLong).

Color preferences. Human response to colors can be measured and identified both collectively and individually, and psychologists have studied the formation of and reaction to color preferences. Eysenck (Brannon 2000) published research in 1941 that showed a consistent order of color preferences in adults: blue, red, green, purple, yellow, orange. According to Itten (1973) people have subjective individual preferences that include dimensions of hue, value, and intensity. The Lüscher Color Test (1969) links personality to color preferences. Subjects are asked to arrange color chips in order of preference and the results are analyzed to take into consideration both the meaning and impact of the colors as selected.

Color Marketing

Color is rated as the most important aesthetic criterion in consumer preference (Eckman, Damhorst, and Kadolph 1990). Because color is a complex phenomenon, marketers can present merchandise in coordinated colors in an effort to help the consumer select purchases. When a line of clothing is color coordinated, wardrobe planning may seem less difficult to the consumer. Designers and manufacturers may coordinate colors within a season, or from one fashion season to another so that colors of a suit from the past season will coordinate with a shirt the next season. Selections of cosmetics are a part of color coordination of the body in a clothing ensemble and may be linked to personal coloring or to one's wardrobe colors.

Fashion in colors. Color has had a fashionable aspect historically. Editors of contemporary fashion often cite a color for a season as a means of marketing clothing. History is often recognized by the colors or color combinations fashionable at the time. Examples include the raspberry pink and lime green of mid-twentieth century, or the pastels and filmy light tints at the end of the nine-teenth century.

Forecasters take advantage of the importance attached to color by advancing a color palette for a given season. Color forecasting began in 1915 (Brannon 2000) and is based upon analysis of cultural demographics and color patterns. A cyclical pattern of color coordination occurs from High Chroma, Multicolored, Subdued, Earth Tones, Achromatic, Purple, and then back to High Chroma (Brannon 2000).

Target markets. Color is used for brand identification. Conceived broadly, this could include a designer's line of clothing or the introduction of a single color. Ralph Lauren tends to select middle value hues of low intensity for his depiction of "traditional" values. Elsa Schiaparelli introduced a single identifier, "shocking pink."

See also **Aesthetic Dress; Appearance; Dyeing.**

BIBLIOGRAPHY

Arnheim, Rudolf. *Art and Visual Perception.* Berkeley and Los Angeles: University of California Press, 1974.

Brannon, Evelyn. *Fashion Forecasting.* New York: Fairchild Publications, 2000.

Davis, Marian. *Visual Design in Dress.* 2nd ed. Englewood Cliffs, N.J.: Prentice-Hall, Inc., 1987.

DeLong, Marilyn Revell. *The Way We Look.* 2nd ed. New York: Fairchild Publications, 1998.

Eckman, Molly, Mary Lynn Damhorst, and Sara Kadolph. "Toward a Model of the In-store Purchase Decision Process: Consumer Use of Criteria for Evaluating Women's Apparel." *Clothing and Textiles Research Journal* 8, 2 (1990): 13–22.

Eiseman, Leatrice. *Alive With Color.* Washington, D.C.: Acropolis Books, Ltd., 1983.

Geum, Keysook, and Marilyn DeLong. "Korean Traditional Dress as an Expression of Heritage." *Dress* 19 (1992): 57–68.

Goldstein, Harriet, and Vetta Goldstein. *Art in Everyday Life.* 4th ed. New York: MacMillan, 1960.

Itten, Johannes. *The Art of Color.* New York: Van Nostrand Reinhold Company, 1973.

Jackson, Carole. *Color Me Beautiful.* New York: Ballantine Books, 1981.

Luke, Joy Turner. *The Munsell® Color System: A Language for Color.* New York: Fairchild Publications, 1996.

Lüscher, Max. *The Lüscher Color Test.* New York: Pocket Books, 1969.

Mathis, Carla Mason, and Helen VillaConnor. *The Triumph of Individual Style: A Guide to Dressing Your Body, Your Beauty, Your Self.* Cali, Colombia: Timeless Editions, 1993.

Meyers, Jack Fredrick. *The Language of Visual Art: Perception as a Basis for Design.* Chicago: Holt, Rinehart and Winston, Inc., 1989.

Munsell, A. *A Book of Color: Neighboring Hues Edition, Matte Finish Collection.* Newburgh, N.Y.: Kollmmorgen, 1973.

Pinckney, Gerrie. *Your New Image Through Color and Line.* Costa Mesa, Calif.: Crown Summit Books, 1981.

Pooser, Doris. *Always in Style with Color Me Beautiful.* Washington, D.C.: Acropolis Books, Ltd., 1985.

Marilyn Revell DeLong

COMME DES GARÇONS Rei Kawakubo was born in Tokyo in 1942, the daughter of a senior academic at Keio University. She studied fine art (both Japanese and Western) at Keio and, after graduating in 1964, joined the advertising department of the Japanese chemical company Asahi Kasei, which produced acrylic fabrics. From 1967 she worked as a freelance fashion stylist, but, critical of the selection of clothes available in Japan, she started designing them herself.

> I wanted to have some kind of job to earn money because at that time, having money meant being free. I never dreamt of being a fashion designer like other people. When I was young, it was just a way of earning a living by doing something I found I could do: making clothes and taking them around the shops to sell them. (Frankel, p. 8)

By 1969 she was producing clothing under the label Comme des Garçons, and in 1973 she formed a limited company. The moniker was typically enigmatic; named after the title of a French soldier's song meaning "Like the Boys," she designed clothes that eschewed conventional sexuality.

Distinctive Looks and Products

In 1975 Kawakubo showed her first collection in Tokyo, and in 1976, in a collaboration with the architect Takao Kawasaki, who has since designed most of Comme's typically calm and austere outlets, the first Comme des Garçons shop opened in the Minami-Aoyama district. The first shop did not even have mirrors, because Kawakubo wanted women to buy clothes because of how they felt rather than the way they looked. In 1978 Kawakubo introduced the Homme line; she followed it with Tricot and Robe de Chambre in 1981 and Noir in 1987. In 1981 Kawakubo launched her first women's collection in Paris at the same time as her compatriot Yohji Yamamoto, and soon afterward she joined the Chambre Syndicale du Pret-a-Porter.

Although the West was aware of other Japanese designers, such as Kenzo Takada and Issey Miyake, who had trained in Paris and New York, Kawakubo's vision was uncompromisingly severe and challenging. Her early shows made an indelible impression on the fashion world with their monochrome palette and distressed fabrics, with exposed seams and fraying edges influenced by Japanese work wear. Rather than echoing the contours of the body, she enclosed it in oversized swathes of fabric. The voluminous, layered, asymmetrical forms were accessorized with flat footwear, and the cosmetics and

Woman models Comme des Garçons dress. Japanese designer Rei Kawakubo's style is unconventional and cerebral, and she admits to favoring creations that are "difficult to wear." © COR-BIS SYGMA. REPRODUCED BY PERMISSION.

hair styles seemed apocalyptic to many, but the influence of her clothes soon spread, particularly for those who were prepared to be challenged by clothing, "I think that pieces that are difficult to wear are very interesting, because if people make the effort and wear them, then they can feel a new form of energy and a certain strength. I want to give people that chance" (Petronio, pp. 154–155).

Early supporters included Joan Burstein, proprietress of Browns, who stocked Comme des Garçons beginning in 1981, and more recent enthusiasts from the art and media world include contemporary art gallery owner and collector Charles Saatchi, furniture designer Tom Dixon, chef Ruth Rogers, Lucy Ferrry (rock-star Brian Ferry's wife), the actress Miranda Richardson, the rock star Sting, and Sting's wife, Trudi Styler. Kawakubo has explored color, and her silhouettes tend to be more fitted, but her work continues to be typified by complex patternmaking and experimentation with natural and man-made textiles. For those uncomfortable with overt sexuality in fashion and intrigued by her cerebral approach to material and form, Kawakubo's work offers an alternative aesthetic language to mainstream Western fashion. Kawakubo's clothes are architectonic, concentrating on structure rather than surface. A black pullover with holes in it in the Victoria and Albert Museum's collection of 1982 is an essay on deconstruction of form and the contained chaos that it inhabits.

Consistent Image

Kawakubo's aesthetic vision extends beyond clothes to embrace every facet of her company, giving consistency to her image all around the world. The controlled presentation of her clothes within the architecture of her shops includes photography, graphics, and packaging. She explains, "Everything that I do or that is seen as the result of Comme des Garçon's work is the same. They are all different ways of expressing the same shared values, from a collection to a museum, a shop or even a perfume" (Petronio, pp. 154–155). (Rather than having a name, each fragrance is simply numbered, based on its chemical components, and then vacuum packed like coffee in a plastic sachet.) Kawakubo's innovative graphics have been evident from early on in her career in a series of photographic catalogs of the collections and numerous brochures, posters, greetings, and announcement cards.

In 1988 she launched the biannual magazine *Six*, which is characterized by having little text, for Kawakubo prefers the images to speak for themselves. *Six* mixes images of clothes with portraits, photographic features, and shots of things that she finds beautiful, such as wildflowers growing beside a road or plastic sheeting flapping in the wind. This aesthetic was emulated in the photographic essay she designed for the exhibition catalog of the Victoria and Albert Museum's exhibition *Radical Fashion* (2001).

Creative Collaborations

Kawakubo's creativity has extended to many events and collaborations, from museum and gallery exhibitions to performances to collaborations with architects, photographers, graphic designers, and even a floral artist. She has worked with the artists Cindy Sherman and Jean-Pierre Raynaud, and in 1997 she designed the set and costumes for Merce Cunningham's work *Scenario*, performed at the Brooklyn Academy of Music and the Palais Garnier in Paris. Kawakubo said that fashion and modern dance are

> really the same. With a collection presentation, I think about the total concept, the environment, the lighting and the make-up as well as the clothes. And the pressure to create something new and beautiful is similarly the same. Of course, the added dimension is the dancers' movements which was the risk. When I saw the rehearsal for the first time, I was fascinated how the shapes changed and came alive with the movements of the dancers. (Johnson, p. 49)

The designs for *Scenario* derived from Kawakubo's spring 1997 collection, Body Becomes Dress, Dress Becomes Body, in which she used feather padding to produce bulges under the clothes, an effect that altered the natural silhouette of the body. Kawakubo said, "It is always stimulating to do new things. The goal of my work for 'Scenario' is the same as my goal for everything: to create something strong, and beautiful and new" (Johnson, pp. 48–53).

Distinctive Collections

Although Kawakubo's clothes are typified by an independence from mainstream fashion, the collections often obliquely reflect current styles. For example, she included strips of camouflage (which was fashionable at the time) in her Optical Shock collection of 2001. Her autumn–winter 2002 collection parodied overtly provocative clothing with large, tulle, 1950s skirts and bras with squashed-in cups worn on top of jackets or even slung around the posterior, while the back seams of billowing trousers gaped open to reveal an arc of flesh. This was really modern erotica. She remarked,

> What I would love to transmit and tell people isn't so much in my working method or creative approach, but more in the values in which I believe. It wouldn't be interesting if everyone wore the same clothes or worked the same ways. I would want to convince people to be courageous and try things differently. (Petronio, pp. 154–155)

Kawakubo's spring–summer 2004 collection featured skirt after skirt shaped like inverted flowers, teamed with a simple gauze top over bared breasts, radical because of its insistence on presenting only one form. The effect was to make the viewer focus on the variations on form and cloth, which varied from beige cotton to bright, bold patterns, completed with tricorn fabric headgear. Kawakubo described the collection as abstract excellence. Suzy Menkes described it as "an expression of artistry, imagination and a certain sweet elegance. And it represented the power of Paris to accommodate ideology in the industry."

Overview of Company

In the early twenty-first century Comme des Garçons is an extremely successful company. Its various lines are designed to appeal to audiences in both the West and the East, all overseen by Kawakubo herself. In 1982 and 1983 she opened her first shops in Paris and New York, and in 1984 the Comme des Garçons Homme plus collection was introduced. In 1986 an American subsidiary company was launched, and in 1988 the shirt line, which was manufactured in France and provided affordable garments to a European audience, was introduced. In 1989 the Comme des Garçons flagship store opened in Aoyama, Tokyo. Having first designed furniture pieces specifically for her stores, Kawakubo turned her attention to a retail line of furniture in the late 1980s. In 1987 Comme des Garçons's furniture showrooms opened in Tokyo and Paris, with the furniture manufactured by the Italian company Pallucco. In 1992 along with her protégé Junya Watanabe she launched the Junya Watanabe Comme des Garçons collection, and in 1993 the Comme des Garçons Comme des Garçons line was introduced. In 2000 a perfume boutique was opened in Paris.

Recognitions and Legacy

Kawakubo has received many honors in recognition of her achievements. They include the following: Night of the Stars award from the Fashion Group, New York (1986); the Mainichi Newspaper award (1988); the Business Woman of the Year award from Veuve Clicquot (1991); and Chevalier de l'Ordre des arts et des lettres, awarded by the French Ministry of Culture (1993). In 1997 she received an honorary doctorate from the Royal College of Art, London, and in 2000, the Excellence in Design Award from the Harvard University Graduate School of Design, Cambridge, Massachusetts. Her work has also been celebrated in many museum and gallery exhibitions, such as *Mode et photo*, an exhibition of Comme des Garçons photography at the Centre Georges Pompidou, Paris (1986), and *Three Voices: Franco Albini, Kris Ruhs, Rei Kawakubo*, Paris (1993). She has had a furniture exhibition at the Galleria Carla Sozzani, Milan, and the *Essence of Quality* exhibition of Comme des Garçons Noir with the Kyoto Costume Institute, Kyoto, Japan. In 1995 she participated in the *Mode and Art* exhibition in Brussels, Belgium. In 1996 she participated in the *Art and Fashion* exhibition at the Florence Biennale Internazionale dell'Arte Contemporanea in Italy. She featured in the *Three Women: Madeleine Vionnet, Claire McCardell and Rei Kawakubo* exhibition at the Fashion Institute of Technology, New York, and in *Radical Fashion* at the Victoria and Albert Museum in 2001.

Since Rei Kawakubo's first show in Paris, Comme des Garçons clothes have continued to be characterized by complex patternmaking and an unmistakable mix of the hand-crafted and technology. Her role in the history of twentieth- and twenty-first-century fashion is about the creative fusion of two cultures and two audiences. In her words, "If my ultimate goal was to achieve financial success, I would have done things differently, but I want to create something new. I want to suggest to people different aesthetics and values. I want to question their being" (Frankel, p. 158).

See also **Art and Fashion; Dance and Fashion; Fashion Designer; Fashion Magazines.**

BIBLIOGRAPHY

Fashion Institute of Technology. *Three Women: Madeleine Vionnet, Claire McCardell, and Rei Kawakubo*. New York: Fashion Institute of Technology, 1987. An exhibition catalog.

Frankel, Susannah. *Visionaries: Interviews with Fashion Designers*. London: V&A Publications, 2001.

———. "Quiet Storm." *The Independent Magazine* (2002): 8.

Grand, France. *Comme des Garçons*. London: Thames and Hudson, Inc., 1998.

Johnson, Robert. "The Bulges. Merce Cunningham's 'Scenario.'" In *Ballett International/Tanz Aktuell* (December 1997): 48–51.

Petronio, Ezra. *Self Service* 13 (Autumn/Winter 2000): 154.

Mendes, Valerie. *Black in Fashion*. London: V&A Publications, 1999.

Menkes, Suzy. "Abstract Artistry from Kawakubo." International Herald Tribune, October 10, 2003.

Sudjic, Deyan. *Rei Kawakubo and Comme des Garçons*. New York: Rizzoli International.

Claire Wilcox

COMMUNIST DRESS Communist dress appeared in diverse guises in Russia and East European countries during seventy-two years of communist rule, and both similarities and differences between them were informed by the political, economic, and social organization of society in the respective countries. The differences between those countries were twofold. The first group of differences is related to dogmatic implementation of communist orthodoxy, while the second refers to the fact that Soviet Russia turned to communism in 1917 and went through a series of very different communist practices, from Leninism through the NEP and its re-introduction of semicapitalism, to Stalinism, even before World War II. Soviet-style communism was imposed on other East European communist states, and after 1948 they were forced to reject their own fashion traditions and to officially accept the centralized Soviet model of clothes production and distribution. In that way, the periodization of communist dress codes from the 1950s onwards followed similar patterns in Soviet Russia and the East European countries. Still, practices of dress were diversified. Contrary to the prevailing image of communist dress as uniform and gray, three styles of clothing—official, everyday, and subversive—coexisted in communist societies, even though all communist regimes initially rejected the notion of fashion as decadent and bourgeois.

Bolshevik Rejection of Fashion
In 1917, Bolshevik Russia attempted to abolish Western-style dress. The sartorial eclecticism that nevertheless prevailed in everyday life was heavily attacked, first by the futurists and later by the constructivists, as part of petit-bourgeois culture.

The constructivist artists Varvara Stepanova, Liubov Popova, Aleksandr Rodchenko, and Vladimir Tatlin all proposed simple, hygienic and functional clothes. In 1923, Stepanova's programmatic article, "The Dress of Our Times: The Overall," with its insistence on functionality, anonymity, simplicity, efficiency, and a precise social role for clothes, was the most radical proposal. In practice, only Popova and Stepanova entered into real production when, in 1923, they became textile designers in the First State Textile Print Factory in Moscow. They abolished the traditional motives of flowers, but their minimalist geometric patterns never had a real chance compared with the old decorative florals, either inside the factory floor or among the traditionally oriented mass consumers.

Nadezhda Lamanova
After seizing power, the Bolsheviks nationalized both textile factories and retail establishments, and their activities centralized. The most prominent pre-revolutionary Russian fashion designer, Nadezhda Lamanova, who catered for both the aristocracy and the artistic elite, and had been officially recognized as a couturier to the court, embraced the political and social changes brought by the revolution. She lost her well-established high-class fashion salon, but subsequently either was in charge of, or actively involved in, the various state-initiated institutions dealing with clothes and fashion, and worked simultaneously as a costume designer for theater and film.

Westernized NEP Fashion
When the Bolsheviks finally won over their external and internal enemies in 1921, they had no resources left to implement their avant-garde social and cultural programs. In 1921, with the approval of Lenin, the New Economic Policy (the NEP) was established. By recognizing private ownership and entrepreneurship, the NEP signaled the return of capitalistic practices and a bourgeois way of life. In the NEP circles of newly-rich Russian capitalists, Western fashion experienced a true revival. The designer Alexandra Exter was instrumental in starting the Atelier of Fashion (Atel'e Mod) in Moscow, founded in 1923 by the Moskvochvey textile company. It was supposed to fulfill two tasks: supplying prototypes for mass production and catering to individual customers. In reality, Exter and her colleagues dressed the new NEP bourgeoisie in highly decorated, luxurious clothes. The aesthetics of the Atelier of Fashion was laid out in a fashion magazine *Atelier*, of which only one issue was published, in 1923. During the NEP period, the Western-style flapper dress found itself in the company of jazz and Hollywood movies, as attitudes toward the Western bourgeois urban culture shifted.

In 1924, Lamanova was put in charge of the artistic laboratory that supplied prototypes for the Kustexport, the craftsmen's association founded in 1920 in collaboration with the Ministry for Foreign Trade to export folk art. She and her collaborators (Vera Mukhina, Alexandra Exter, Evgeniia Pribylskaia, and Nadezhda Makarova) agreed on the approach of putting Russian folk motifs on current Western women's wear, and her folk-embroidered day dresses received the Grand Prix at the International Exhibition of Applied Arts in Paris in 1925.

Stalinist Representational Dress
Stalin's rise to power and the introduction of the First Five Year Plan in 1929 brought the NEP to its end. Dur-

Children walking to school. Political changes in Eastern Europe heavily influenced fashion, ranging from the austere, functional, classless communist dress during the post-World War II years to a more open attitude toward Western fashion influence in the 1950s. © BETTMANN/CORBIS. REPRODUCED BY PERMISSION.

ing the mid-1930s, the Stalinist regime encouraged social distinctions by creating huge disparities in wages and created a new socialist middle class, which received material goods, from housing to fashion, in exchange for supporting the system. For the first time, communism recognized the relation of fashion to femininity and adornment, allowing its incorporation into the new mass culture that was emerging.

In the mid-1930s, a huge official campaign of civilizing the new socialist middle class dictated, among other things, both good manners and appropriate dress. Stalinism abolished all previous socialist dress styles: the avant-garde, the westernized NEP, and the thematic textiles, which in the late 1920s featured the urgent issues of the day—construction, electrification, and agriculture. Stalinism needed a different, conservative fashion style.

Moscow House of Fashion

In 1934, fashion consciousness was officially confirmed as part of Stalin's mass culture with the opening of the House of Fashion in Moscow. The established fashion designer Nadezhda Makarova was its first director, while the doyenne of Russian fashion, Nadezhda Lamanova, was appointed artistic consultant. The main task of the designers and the sample-makers engaged by the House of Fashion was to impose genuine Soviet styles and to make prototypes for mass-production by huge textile companies.

Two luxurious fashion publications, the monthly *Fashion Journal* (*Zhurnal mod*) and the bi-annual *Fashions of the Seasons* (*Modeli sezona*), were designed in the House of Fashion and published under the auspices of the Ministry of Light Industry. In 1937, the same ministry advertised chic hats, fur coats, and perfumes, featuring fashionably dressed and made-up women, contrasting sharply with the poverty-stricken reality. Houses of Fashion were instituted in the other cities and capitals of the Soviet Republics, making clothes production highly controlled and centralized. But in the centrally organized system, which did not recognize the market, access to goods was the main privilege and determined hierarchically. Clothes and fashion accessories were either too expensive or unattainable for the masses.

Whereas the early Bolsheviks rejected even the very word "fashion" and insisted on functional clothing, Stalinism, in a sharp ideological turn, granted fashion a highly representational role. Stalinist dress featured a new Stalinist aesthetic, a blend of Russian folk tradition and Hollywood glamour, appropriate to Stalinist ideals of classical beauty and traditional femininity. The Bolshevik austere and undecorated "New Woman" became a "Super

Woman" during Stalinism, and dresses with accentuated waistlines and shoulders followed her curvy body.

East European Communist Dress
The Soviet system of centralized production and distribution of clothes was forced on East European countries after 1948, when the communists seized power, regardless of their previously higher levels of technical and stylistic skill in clothing design and production. The East European communist regimes embraced early Soviet ideology, officially rejecting Western fashion. East European communist dress was not only born inside a reality burdened with postwar material poverty, but also inside a reality stripped of all previous clothing references. Clothing was forbidden to evoke beauty or elegance. It was officially claimed that functional, simple, and classless communist dress, which would fulfill all the sartorial needs of working women, would result from serious scientific and technical research.

In the following decades, however, the East European communist regimes' attitudes toward clothes and fashion were influenced by political changes in the Soviet Union. A new ideological turn occurred when Khrushchev affirmed his rule in 1956 and declared war on excessive Stalinist aesthetics. Leaving the worst practices of Stalinist isolationism behind, Khrushchev opened the U.S.S.R. to the West. In the late 1950s, official attitudes toward Western fashion mellowed in the communist countries. Nonetheless, with neither tradition nor market, and aspiring to control fashion change within their centralized fashion systems, the communist regimes could not keep up with Western fashion trends. By the end of the 1950s, the official version of communist fashion returned to traditional sartorial expressions and practices of traditional femininity, bearing witness to the regimes' inability to create a genuine communist fashion.

Communist Fashion Congresses
From that period onward, the official fashions were exhibited in glamorous fashion drawings and photo shoots in state-owned women's magazines, representative fashion shows, and ambitious presentations at domestic and foreign trade fairs. However, clothing design, production, and distribution remained highly centralized throughout the communist world, leading eventually to serious shortages and dilution of quality. A glamorous official communist version of fashion existed as an ideological construct, despite the shortages and poor quality of clothes in everyday life. Annual fashion congresses between communist countries, at which new fashions were proposed and adopted, began in 1949 and continued through the end of the communist period.

As the need for an official communist fashion increased at the end of the 1950s, when the regimes rushed to clothe their emerging communist middle classes, the fashion congress became more ambitious and rotated among communist capitals, for which participant coun-

tries prepared collections of prototypes. The official communist fashions included orgies of luxurious fabrics and extravagant cuts for excessive evening wear and day wear of ensembles of overcoats and matching dresses or conservative suits, accompanied by ladylike handbags, shoes with high heels, hats, and gloves. This conservative style was diluted into anonymous and moderate dress codes through official womens' and fashion magazines. Media insistence on timeless and classical sartorial aesthetics conformed with socialist values of modesty and moderation and discomfort with individuality and unpredictability.

As the race between West and East to industrialize transformed into competition over standards of living and consumption, political and social shifts affected communist fashion trends. After decades of rejection of Western fashion, Christian Dior presented a prominent fashion show in Moscow in 1959, and in Prague in 1966. In 1967 an international fashion festival took place in Moscow, presenting both Western and East European collections. Coco Chanel's presentation was recognized as the best current trend, but the grand prix was awarded to the Russian designer Tatiana Osmerkina for a dress called "Russia." When mass culture and Western youthful dress and music trends could not be held back anymore, the communist regimes officially recognized a rationalized version of consumption, and the Five Year Plans in the 1960s and 1970s addressed fashion and appearance concerns. The fashions in the plans, however, did not materialize in the shops.

Everyday and Subversive Dress
Jeans provide the best examples of both the production inadequacies of the planned economies and the futility of their attempting to ignore fashion demands. Domestic production of jeans started in the Soviet Union, East Germany, and Poland only in 1975 but was marked by failures. In 1978, the Soviet media reported that manufacture of a new denim fabric, the fifty-sixth in a row, was officially promised to begin. The official ambivalence toward Western fashion continued throughout communist times, informed by isolationism, fear of uncontrollable fashion changes, and the rejection of the market.

In everyday reality, however, women in those societies found alternative ways of acquiring clothes, from doing it themselves (communist women's magazines regularly published paper patterns), to the black market, seamstresses, and private fashion salons, which catered to both the ousted prewar elite and the new ruling elite.

Scarcities in state shops and black market activity made Western fashion goods particularly attractive, and the immaculate and fashionable personal look became an ideal for millions of women in communist countries, who were prepared for many sacrifices in order to achieve it. From the end of the 1960s, unofficial channels, with the discreet approval of the regimes, became increasingly important, and dress and beautifying practices occupied an important position in second societies and economies. Small fashion salons, shoe repair shops, hair salons, and beauty parlors offered goods and services that the state did not provide.

In contrast to the official communist fashion, which suited the slow and over-controlled communist master narrative ideology, everyday dress reflected a wide range of influences, from bare necessity to high fashion. Fashionable street dress undermined the command economy by manifesting change, encouraging individual expression, and breaking through communist cultural isolationism.

But overtly subversive dress also existed in communist countries. Throughout the 1950s, the Soviet "Style Hunters" (*Stilyagi*) had their counterparts in other communist countries, such as *Pásek* in Czechoslovakia and the Bikini Boys (*Bikiniarze*) in Poland. Their rebellious dress codes produced the first elements of a Westernized youth subculture that became very important in the following decades. Western rock arrived in communist countries in the mid-1960s, and, by the 1970s, many domestic rock bands already existed. Youth subcultures, expressing themselves through distinct dress codes, continued to grow throughout the 1970s, and especially in the 1980s, throughout the communist world. Each Western youth trend had its Soviet counterpart, from *metallisti* (heavy metal fans) to *khippi* (hippies), *panki* (punks), *rokeri* (bikers), *modniki* (trendy people), and *breikery* (breakdancers).

In parallel, the communist regimes allowed the activities of groups who expressed their creativity through dress as an art medium. Because they catered to small numbers of like-minded people, they were believed to pose no threat to official ideology.

In Russia and East European communist countries, the official relationship with fashion was informed by ideological shifts inside the communist master narratives. It fluctuated between a total rejection of the phenomena of fashion in 1920s Russia and in the late 1940s in East European countries to a highly representational role of the official version of communist fashion from the 1950s onward. But the communist regimes failed to produce a genuine communist fashion. From the late 1950s, communist women's magazines started to promote classical, modest, and moderate styles, which suited the communist fear of change and its ideals of modesty. Throughout the communist times, design, production, and distribution of clothes and fashion accessories were centrally organized, which eventually led to serious shortages and a poor quality of goods. For communist officialdom, fashion could be art or science, but it was never recognized as a commodity. That is the reason why in the other two communist dress practices—everyday and subversive dress— fashionable items retained a large capacity for symbolic investment. While the official communist fashion was an ideological construct unaffected by poor offer of clothes in shops, everyday and subversive dress used a whole range of unofficial channels, from DIY (do-it-yourself) to black market, private fashion salons and networks of connections. From the 1960s to the end of communism, those unofficial channels grew in importance, and fashionable dress found place inside second societies and second economies in the respective communist countries.

See also **Fascist and Nazi Dress; Military Style.**

BIBLIOGRAPHY

Attwood, L. *Creating the New Soviet Woman: Women's Magazines as Engineers of Female Identity, 1922–53.* Houndsmill, Basingstoke, U.K., and London: Macmillan, 1999.

Azhgikhina, N., and H. Goscilo. "Getting under Their Skin: The Beauty Salon in Russian Womens Lives." In *Russia Women Culture.* Edited by H. Goscilo and B. Holmgren, 94–121. Bloomington: Indiana University Press, l996.

Bowlt, J. E. "Constructivism and Early Soviet Fashion Design." In *Bolshevik Culture: Experiment and Order in the Russian Revolution.* Edited by A. Gleason, P. Kenez, and R. Stites, Bloomington: Indiana University Press, pp 203–219, 1985.

Hlaváčková, K. *Czech Fashion 1940–1970: Mirror of the Times.* Prague, Czech Republic: u(p)m and Olympia Publishing, 2000.

Kopp, A. "Maroussia s'est empoisonnee, ou la socialisme et la mode." *Traverses La Mode* 3 (1976): 129–139.

Pilkington, H. "'The Future is Ours': Youth Culture in Russia, 1953 to the Present." In *Russian Cultural Studies: An Introduction.* Edited by C. Kelly and D. Sheperd, 368–386. Oxford: Oxford University Press, 1998.

Potocki, R. "The Life and Times of Poland's 'Bikini Boys'." *The Polish Review* 3 (1994): 259–290.

Ryback, T. *Rock Around the Block: A History of Rock Music in Eastern Europe and the Soviet Union.* New York and Oxford: Oxford University Press, 1990.

Strizhenova, T. *Soviet Costume and Textiles 1917–1945.* Paris: Flammarion, 1991.

Vainshtein, O. "Female Fashion: Soviet Style: Bodies of Ideology." In *Russia Women Culture.* H. Goscilo and B. Holmgren 64–93. Edited by H. Goscilo and B. Holmgren, 64–93. Bloomington: Indiana University Press, 1996.

Yasinskaya, I. *Soviet Textile Design of the Revolutionary Period.* London: Thames and Hudson, Inc., 1983.

Zaletova, L., F. Ciofi degli Atti, and F. Panzini. *Costume Revolution: Textiles, Clothing and Costume of the Soviet Union in the Twenties.* London: Trefoil Publications, 1989.

Djurdja Bartlett

CORDUROY Many sources claim the origin of the word is derived from the French *corde du roi* or "the king's cord." The fabric was supposedly used to clothe the servants of the king in medieval France. However, there are no written documents to credit this etymology. It is more likely that the term originated in England, from a fabric called "kings-cordes," which is documented in records in Sens, France, from 1807. Another possible origin of the name may be from the English surname Corderoy. This spelling was used in reference to the fabric as early as 1789 in America in a newspaper advertisement from a corduroy weaver in Providence, Rhode Island.

Corduroy is a durable fabric that is woven with three sets of yarns and has vertical ribs, or wales, that are formed by cut-pile yarn. The third set of yarns, which is generally loosely spun, is woven into a plain or twill weave backing in the filling direction to form floats that run over four or more warp yarns. A corduroy with a plain-weave backing may be referred to as "tabbyback," and a twill-backed corduroy can be called a "Genoa-back." Twill backing is more durable because the weave is denser and the pile tufts are held more tightly. The floats are cut after weaving to form ribs through the use of specialized machinery. The uncut fabric is run through the cutting machines once for ribs that are widely spaced apart and twice for closely-set ribs. The ribs are rounded with the longest floats in the center and the shorter floats on either side. After the pile is cut, the fabric is often singed and brushed to produce an even-ribbed finish.

Corduroy may be piece-dyed or printed in patterns and is named according to the number of wales per inch. Variations of corduroy include featherwale, pinwale, medium wale, thick-set corduroy, broad wale, wide wale, and novelty wale corduroys, in which different widths of wales are arranged in patterns.

Corduroy is used for trousers, shirts, jackets, skirts, dresses, and in home furnishings such as pillows and upholstery. Developments in the production of corduroy include the addition of spandex to provide more stretch in the fabric that is used for close-fitting garments.

See also **Napping.**

BIBLIOGRAPHY

American Fabrics Encyclopedia of Textiles. 2nd edition. Englewood Cliffs, N.J.: Prentice Hall, 1972.

Gioello, Debbie Ann. *Profiling Fabrics: Properties, Performance & Construction Techniques.* New York: Fairchild Publishing, 1981.

Kadolph, Sara J., and Anna L. Langford. *Textiles.* 9th edition. Englewood Cliffs, N.J.: Prentice Hall, 2002.

Linton, George E. *The Modern Textile and Apparel Dictionary.* 4th edition. Plainfield, N.J.: Textile book service, 1973.

Montgomery, Florence M. *Textiles in America 1650–1870.* New York: W.W. Norton and Company, 1984.

Wingate, Isabel, and June Mohler. *Textile Fabrics and Their Selection.* 8th edition. Englewood Cliffs, N.J.: Prentice Hall, 1984.

Marie Botkin

CORSET The corset is a garment with a long and controversial history. A rigid bodice, usually incorporating vertical and diagonal boning, and laced together, the corset was designed to shape the female torso to the fashionable silhouette of the period. Corsets have been worn by women in the Western world from the sixteenth century through the early twentieth century, at which point girdles and brassieres replaced them. Men, especially dandies and military officers, have also sometimes worn corsets. The primary significance of the corset, however, is its role as an essential element of women's fashionable dress for a period of about 400 years.

Throughout its history, the corset was frequently criticized as an "instrument of torture" and a cause of ill health and even death. Feminist historians have often argued that corsetry functioned as a coercive apparatus through which patriarchal society controlled women and exploited their sexuality. Recently, some historians have questioned this interpretation, arguing that corsetry was not one monolithic, unchanging experience that all women endured, but rather a situated practice that meant different things to different people at different times. Some women did experience the corset as an assault on the body. But for others, the corset also had positive connotations of social status, self-discipline, respectability, beauty, youth, and erotic allure. This revisionist view, which aims for a balanced and non-ideological history of corsetry based on carefully considered evidence, must not be confused with the uncritical defenses of corsetry that have been published by corset "enthusiasts." As for the long-standing claim that corsets were a source of disease and death, historians continue to disagree about the medical consequences of corsetry.

The word "corset" derives from the French *corse*, which simply designated a bodice. Early corsets were known as *corps à la baleine* (or in English, whalebone bodies), because strips of whalebone, or, more accurately, whale baleen, were inserted into the fabric (usually linen or canvas) to stiffen the cloth bodice. As whalebone became more expensive in the nineteenth century, lengths of steel increasingly replaced it. Traditionally, down the center front of the corset was inserted a *busk*, which, in shape and size, was not unlike a ruler. Busks were variously made of wood, horn, and whalebone; they were often elaborately carved and given as lovers' gifts. By 1850 the traditional, inflexible one-piece busk had been replaced by a steel, front-opening style, which made it much easier for women to put on and take off their corsets. Prior to this, women had usually relied on assistance to lace and unlace their corsets.

Corsets were also known as "stays," a term probably derived from the French *estayer* (to support), since they were thought to support the body. Because women were looked upon as the "weaker sex," it was commonly believed that their bodies habitually needed additional support. For similar reasons, children were also often placed in stiffened bodices, which were supposed to make them grow up straight. However, by the eighteenth century, many doctors argued that children's bodies were more likely to be deformed by corsets that were too tight. They also increasingly warned that women were endangering their health (and that of their unborn children) by wearing corsets. Over the course of the nineteenth century, medical journals published numerous articles criticizing corsetry. Yet the vast majority of middle- and upper-class women continued to wear corsets, and increasing numbers of working-class women also adopted corsets.

In her book, *Health and Beauty; or, Corsets and Clothing Constructed in Accordance with the Physiological Laws of the Human Body* (London, 1854), the English corsetière Madame Roxey A. Caplin defended corsets—at least if they were well-made: "It never seems to have occurred to the Doctors that ladies must and will wear stays, in spite of all the medical men of Europe." Because women "desire to retain as long as possible the charm of beauty and the appearance of youth," they wear corsets, which conceal "defects" (such as a thick waist or belly) and give support "where it is needed" (for example, in the absence of brassieres, corsets support "the fullness of the breasts"). Caplin even claimed that a French doctor had told her, "Madame, your corset is more like a new layer of muscles than an artificial extraneous article of dress!" It would be many years, however, before the majority of women stopped relying on corsets and started developing their own muscles.

The history of the corset is replete with myths and exaggerations. For example, the notorious "iron corsets" of the Renaissance were not fashion items worn by the ladies at the court of Catherine de Médicis, as is often claimed. Rather, they were orthopedic braces meant to correct spinal deformities. (Some of these metal corsets are also modern forgeries.) Accounts of extreme tight lacing are also problematic. During the second half of the nineteenth century, several English periodicals, most famously *The Englishwoman's Domestic Magazine*, published numerous letters purporting to describe how the authors had achieved waists of fifteen inches or even less. Although fashion historians and journalists have frequently quoted excerpts from this "corset correspondence," they cannot be taken at face value. Both internal and external evidence indicate that many of these letters represent sexual fantasies rather than descriptions of authentic experiences. Certainly the scenarios described, which often focused on coercive practices at anonymous boarding schools, were not typical of the average Victorian girl or woman, although they may reflect the role-playing practices of fetishistic subcultures.

Thorstein Veblen, author of *The Theory of the Leisure Class* (1899), famously described the corset as "a mutilation undergone for the purpose of lowering the subject's vitality and rendering her permanently and obviously unfit for work." In reality, however, ladies of the leisure class were not the only ones to wear corsets. By the mid-nineteenth century, with the development of cheap, mass-produced corsets, many urban working-class women also wore corsets. Clearly, the corset did not render them unfit for work, but did it lower their vitality?

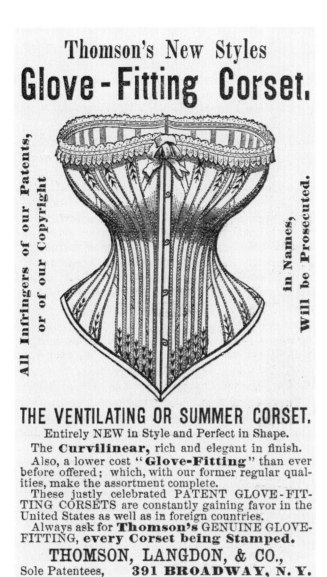

Nineteenth-century advertisement for corsets. Although many doctors warned of various health risks related to the wearing of corsets, the rigid bodices were a common clothing item for centuries. © CORBIS. REPRODUCED BY PERMISSION.

Certainly many eighteenth- and nineteenth-century doctors regarded the corset as a health hazard. They blamed the corset for causing dozens of diseases, including apoplexy, asthma, cancer, chlorosis (a type of anemia), curvature of the spine, deformities of the ribs, damage to internal organs such as the liver, digestive disorders, respiratory and circulatory diseases, and birth defects and miscarriages. Other doctors, however, approved of "moderate" corsetry, condemning only "tight lacing" (a notoriously imprecise term). In 1785, Dr. von Soemmering published comparative illustrations of corseted and uncorseted rib cages, which indicated that corsetry caused permanent deformity. Twentieth-century X-rays also show that a tightly laced corset compresses the ribs and moves the internal organs, although when the corset is removed, the body seems to revert to its normal appearance.

During the nineteenth century, relatively little was understood about the causes of various diseases, to say nothing of the treatments. One cannot, therefore, automatically accept the diagnoses of nineteenth-century doctors, many of which are patently absurd. This is not to say that corsets were totally harmless. Most authorities today agree that extremely tight corsets might risk various kinds of physical impairment or harm. There is no consensus among experts, however, on what risks were involved in ordinary corset wearing. Although contemporary scholars disagree about how dangerous corsets really were, corsets undoubtedly did contribute to some health problems. Spirometry (lung volume) testing conducted by Colleen Gau and her associates has demonstrated that corseted women suffered depleted lung volume, as well as changes in breathing (from normal diaphragmatic breathing to reliance on the accessory muscles of the chest wall). Lessened lung capacity would not necessarily contribute to respiratory disease, but it could certainly lower vitality and cause fainting. This would seem to lend credence to nineteenth-century accounts that associated corsetry with shallow breathing and fainting. In the 1880s, using an adaptation of the sphygmomanometer (blood pressure machine), the New York obstetrician Robert L. Dickinson measured corset pressure on several hundred women, recording pressures as high as eighty-two pounds per square inch. He believed that corset pressure caused digestive and breathing problems, as well as serious effects on the reproductive organs, such as prolapse of the uterus. It is sometimes alleged that some women underwent the dangerous surgical procedure of having their lower ribs removed in order to achieve a smaller corseted waist. There is, however, no evidence at all that any Victorian woman ever had her ribs removed; rib removal appears to be entirely mythical.

Some doctors and corsetieres tried (or claimed) to develop safer and more comfortable corsets. During the 1890s, for example, Dr. Inez Josephine Gaches-Sarraute designed the so-called straight-front corset, which she described as a "health" corset. However, recent physiologic testing using reenactors found the straight-front corset to be more uncomfortable and constraining than the hourglass styles of the mid-Victorian era.

The shape and construction of the corset changed dramatically over time, but there was no simple progression toward greater ease. Between about 1790 and 1810, the rigid cone-shaped stays of the eighteenth century were temporarily abandoned in favor of a shorter, lighter style, some variants of which resembled a brassiere. However, as high-waisted Empire dresses gave way to lowered waists and fuller skirts, the boned corset reemerged. Now, however, it was shaped more like an hourglass. Over the course of the nineteenth century, technological developments, such as steam molding, contributed to-

ward the fashion for long *cuirasse* corsets. At the turn of the century, the fashionable straight-front corset pushed the pelvis back and the bosom forward, creating the so-called S-silhouette. Yet as women engaged in more sporting activities, such as bicycling, they increasingly adopted flexible elasticized sports corsets. By the 1920s elastic girdles and brassieres had largely supplanted rigid corsets, particularly among the young. In 1939, and again after World War II, fashion showed renewed emphasis on femininity and the corset had a brief resurgence in the form of the "Merry Widow" or *guépière* (waspy).

By the 1960s and 1970s, however, a cultural focus on youth and body exposure resulted in greater reliance on diet and exercise, rather than foundation garments, to create a desirable figure. The corset was, thus, not so much abandoned as it was internalized through diet, exercise, and later, plastic surgery. A minority of corset enthusiasts, both male and female, continue to wear corsets and sometimes tight lace as part of fetishistic, cross-dressing, or sadomasochistic practices.

Beginning in the 1980s, inspired by subcultural fetish styles, avant-garde fashion designers, such as Vivienne Westwood and Jean Paul Gaultier, began to create corset fashions. Madonna famously wore a pink satin corset by Jean Paul Gaultier on her Blonde Ambition tour of 1991. Since then, every few years the fashion press reports on the reappearance of corsets by couturiers such as Christian Lacroix, Alexander McQueen, and Donatella Versace. Although some of these corsets incorporate lacing and (plastic or metal) boning, most are really more like zip-up bustiers than historic corsets. Cheaper versions are popular as club wear for both young men and women.

See also **Brassiere; Europe and America: History of Dress (400–1900 C.E); Gender, Dress, and Fashion; Girdle.**

BIBLIOGRAPHY

Steele, Valerie. *The Corset: A Cultural History.* New Haven, Conn., and London: Yale University Press, 2001.

Summers, Leigh. *Bound to Please.* Oxford: Berg; distributed by New York University Press, 2001.

Valerie Steele and Colleen Gau

COSMETICS, NON-WESTERN The earliest evidence of the role of cosmetics in human society was found in the remains of artifacts used for eye makeup in Egypt of the fourth millennium B.C.E. Anthropological research also shows that there are several ways used by humans to transform the physical and social appearance of their bodies into cultural manifestations. People use their bodies and faces as objects of aesthetic elaboration or as a medium through which they can project themselves in religious and social life. We can thus identify two distinct, though related, senses of the term "non-Western cosmetic." The first pertains to personal taste and is con-

Wahgi tribe members. In tribes such as this one in New Guinea, paints are used to portray the varying physical and emotional aspects of their community, both positive and negative. © CHARLES & JOSETTE LENARS/CORBIS. REPRODUCED BY PERMISSION.

cerned with the decorative/aesthetic aspect of non-Western cosmetic. The second is more general and is related to ritual and the symbolic essence of body decoration.

The ubiquitous interpretation of non-Western cosmetic in modern society is associated with the aesthetic or decorative. It is concerned with the visual and is related to personal style and denotes what is considered beautiful or fashionable. Non-Western cosmetic, in this case, is used in order to make a fashion statement. It is generally considered an exclusively feminine pursuit, used to aesthetically enhance the beauty of the person. Cosmetic and fashion industries make such physical appearances readily available under the rubric of the ethnic/tribal/oriental look. This look is epitomized by photographic studies of non-Western artistic practices and peoples confined to identifying what may be considered exotic and beautiful to the Western eye (Reifenstahl 1986; Ebin 1979; McCurry 1997).

Products originating from Africa, Asia, and South America and conceptualized in terms of respect for traditional beauty, natural or local ingredients, and non-animal tested products are sold in modern containers. This is meant to bring to mind ideas of purity, health, animal welfare, sunshine, adventure, travel, leisure, serenity, even exoticism and eroticism. Materials used include kaolin, henna, kohl, burnt cork, chalk, clay, and all sorts of vegetable, flower, and plant extracts. The growing demand for an exotic look in fashion has warranted their manufacture on a commercial scale. Production techniques, packaging, and advertising have helped to increase worldwide usage of such products. The best-known leader of this trend is the Body Shop.

The image industry created by advertising agencies mediates the changing aspect of the human body image through fashion and art in glossy magazines and books. This has privileged the aesthetic/decorative and attenuated the transcendent nature of the art of body painting (Baudrillard 1994). Conversely, in tribal and non-Western societies, the aesthetic aspect of body and face decoration often emphasizes the social aspect of the human body (Leach 1966). Non-Western cosmetic can thus be understood by looking into the interpretative properties of cosmetic in terms of rituals and symbols. This is especially helpful for clarifying the meaning of body adornment during festivities, ritual ceremonies, or even everyday occasions. For example, Tilaka is a vermilion

Henna tattoos. This reddish-orange dye is used by women in Africa and Asia to create elaborately beautiful tattoos, and by both women and men as a hair colorant. © CHARLES O'REAR/ CORBIS. REPRODUCED BY PERMISSION.

mark applied on the forehead by Indian women as a sign of being in wedlock. It is also used by both sexes as a culturally designed communication code, which embodies ritual and sacred symbols. Although red predominates, a variety of other pigments such as yellow, white, gray, saffron, and black are employed. In some cases these pigments are applied on the forearms and the abdomen as well. The origins of these practices are said to lie in a primitive tribal past. This is the case of followers of Shiva, a deity worshiped by proto-Aryan societies in the Indian subcontinent. Even today, the smearing of colors on arms, torso, or face is an essential aspect of the Hindu festival of Holi.

Women and men wear the Tilaka as a sign of belonging to the Hindu religion. Its versatile form, shape, and color also indicate adherence to the various Hindu sects and subsects. Worshipers of the Lord Vishnu apply a "U" sign made of a mixture of red ocher powder (*Sindhura*) and sandalwood paste (*Gandah*). Worshipers of the Lord Shiva prefer to draw three horizontal lines made of ash (*Abhira*). For men the application of Tilaka, made up of their own blood, is an indication of solemn commitment to an oath or a pledge being undertaken (Kelly 2002).

In tribal societies of tropical and equatorial regions the visual and interpretative value of body adornment is used as a schematic representation of values, beliefs, symbols, and myths. Differing pigments and patterns are used for instant recognition of group identity, social status, or age group, while still allowing for gender differences and personal idiosyncrasy. The most elaborate forms of decoration involve lengthy preparation, much care and expense, and hence are generally seen on ceremonial and ritual occasions. Men and women employ a combination of colors and designs in order to make a statement about the nature of a particular occasion. The adornment favored by individuals or group participants is intrinsic to the ceremony and is vital for conveying messages about the community's social and religious values.

The Melpa and Wahgi of Papua New Guinea use body decoration as an essential part of ritual performances and gift exchange ceremonies. During happy occasions men paint their bodies and weapons with white wavy lines intended to represent patterns reflected in water. They adorn their faces with white and red pigments and place similar feathers and flowers in their hair to evoke "brightness." Bright colors symbolize the physical and moral strength, vitality, and well-being of the community. Conversely, war paint is deliberately meant to transform the human body into a terrifying warrior. In times of war, bodies are covered with a deep black charcoal-based pigment, a color associated with poison. Faces and accessories are similarly decorated with dark hues to transmit the message of aggressive power and fierceness. Women in Papua New Guinea wear less brilliant body decoration emphasizing their primarily domestic and agricultural duties. Similarly Australian aborigines paint their body and faces with white clay dots and lines prior to going hunting or war as a protective measure. They also decorate their bodies during initiation ceremonies or when they re-enact stories of their mythical past through music and dancing (Ebin 1979; O'Hanlon 1989, 1992; Strathern and Strathern 1983; Groning, 1996).

In parts of Africa and South America, design and color are used to separate the sexes and invoke magical powers, which are believed to be inherent in nature and the spiritual world. Tchikrin men from Central Brazil paint their bodies white and black; women prefer yellow and red. The Kayapo Indians of Brazil make a connection between the color red and abstract qualities such as heightened sensory sensitivity, energy, and health. They smear red pigments on their faces, hands, and feet, because they associate these parts of the body with swiftness, agility, and sensory contact with the outside world. Black is applied to the torso and signifies the integration of the inner man into social life (Turner 1969). Turning to West Africa, shamans in the Ivory Coast paint their eyes with white clay mixed with herbs and water from "sacred rivers" in order to see into the spirit world. Ghanaian priestesses smear their faces with white clay and paint parallel lines across their foreheads and cheeks.

The color white represents the divine nature of the gods, while parallel lines are meant to deflect the attacks of evil mystical beings. Ashanti women from Ghana draw designs on their arms with white clay to invoke mythical protection for themselves and their babies after giving birth (Ebin 1979; Fisher 1984; Groning 1996).

People's preoccupation with rituals and symbols in social life often merges with their purely aesthetic impulses to decorate their bodies. Young Nuba men from the Sudan spend long hours applying elaborate designs all over their bodies to enhance the beauty, elegance, and well-being of their bodies. Their adorned bodies become a field upon which they demonstrate their physical beauty, sexual attractiveness, or personal status. Particular patterns or colors are used to portray in visible terms the individual's progress from infancy through puberty and adulthood or personal status within society. Deep yellow and jet black are only allowed to older age groups. Younger age groups are immediately recognizable by their use of red ocher and simpler hairstyles. The decline in physical strength and attractiveness in old age compels old men to cease to decorate their bodies, shave their heads, and start wearing cloth. Nuba women wear appropriate colors indicating their membership in a particular kinship group (Faris 1972; Brain 1979; Ebin 1979; Strathern and Strathern 1983; Riefenstahl 1986). The above examples of body and face decoration are not merely indicative of our tribal past. They are kept alive in the Western imagination through books on art and photography and their many fashion conscious modern imitators (Thevoz 1984; Vale and Juno 1989; Randall and Polhemus 2000)

See also **Cosmetics, Western.**

BIBLIOGRAPHY
Brain, Robert. *The Decorated Body.* London: Hutchinson, 1979.
Baudrillard, Jean. *Simulacra and Simulation. The Body in Theory: Histories of Cultural Materialism.* Ann Arbor: University of Michigan Press, 1994.
Ebin, Victoria. *The Body Decorated.* London: Thames and Hudson, Inc. 1979.
Faris, James. *Nuba Personal Art.* London: Duckworth, 1972.
Fisher, Angela. *Africa Adorned: A Panorama of Jewelry, Dress, Body Decoration and Hair Style.* New York: Harry N. Abrams, 1984.
Groning, Karl. *Body Decoration: A World Survey of Body Art.* New York: Vendome Press, 1996.
Kelly, Kevin. *Asia Grace.* Cologne, Germany: Taschen GmbH, 2002.
Leach, Edmund. "Ritualisation in Man." *Philosophical Transaction of the Royal Society* 251 (1966).
McCurry, Steve. *Portraits.* Bombay, India: Phaidon Press Ltd., 1997.
O'Hanlon, Michael. *Reading the Skin: Adornment, Display and Society Among the Wahgi.* London: Trustees of the British Museum by British Museum Publications, 1989.
———. "Unstable Images and Second Skins: Artifacts, Exegesis and Assessments in the New Guinea Highlands." *Man* 27, no. 3 (1992): 587–608.
Randall, Housk, and Ted Polhemus. *The Customized Body.* London: Serpent's Tail, 2000.
Riefenstahl, Leni. *The Last of the Nuba.* London: Collins Harvill, 1986.
Strathern, Andrew, and Marilyn Strathern. *Self-Decoration in Mt. Hagen.* Toronto: University of Toronto Press, 1983.
Thevoz, Michel. *The Painted Body.* New York: Skira/Rizzoli International, 1984.
Turner, Terence. "Tchikrin, A Central Brazilian Tribe and Its Symbolic Language of Bodily Adornment." *Natural History* 18, (1969).
Vale, V., and Andrea Juno, eds. *Modern Primitives: An Investigation of Contemporary Body Adornment and Ritual.* San Francisco: RE/Research Publications, 1989.

Paula Heinonen

COSMETICS, WESTERN In the twenty-first century, cosmetics include a full range of products to protect the skin and improve appearance, from moisturizers to makeup, manufactured by a multibillion-dollar, global cosmetics industry. Before the twentieth century, however, cosmetics were understood differently in Western cultures. In English, the word "cosmetic" referred to skin-improving substances, such as creams and lotions. Cosmetics to mask or color the skin were known as "paint" or, in a theatrical context, "makeup." This fundamental distinction was a legacy of the ancient world, and shaped the early use of cosmetics.

Cosmetics Before 1900
In the seventeenth and eighteenth centuries, European women prepared simple cosmetics from recipes appearing in household manuals and cookbooks or passed on orally from generation to generation. In that period, cosmetics were as much science as art, a branch of self-help therapeutics that women were expected to master. Recipes in early household manuals called for roots, wildflowers, and other plants to be mixed with water, beer, vinegar, and spices; these produced remedies to clear the complexion, improve color, and remove signs of smallpox. The principles governing these mixtures were based on Galen's theory of the humors, in which the correspondence between internal and external organs, and the balance between hot, cold, dry, and moist qualities, was the key to health and beauty. In addition, belief in the power of nature's cycles and astrology found their way into beauty preparations, in recipes using May dew, the first juice of spring plants, and "virgin milk."

Colonial Americans used similar cosmetic recipes, preparing cold cream, skin lotions, and lip salves from such common substances as wax, lard, nut oils, and sugar. They also incorporated the flowers and herbs of

Elizabeth Arden. The Canadian-born Arden opened a New York salon on Fifth Avenue in 1910, installing the trademark bright red door to make her shop distinctive. © HULTON-DEUTSCH COLLECTION/CORBIS. REPRODUCED BY PERMISSION.

the New World, such as puccoon-root or "Indian paint," prevalent in Algonquin therapeutics. Africans brought to the colonies as slaves similarly adapted native plants into traditional West African techniques of grooming and beautifying, using berries and roots to redden the skin, for example.

In addition to home preparations, a small but significant global trade made exotic herbs, extracts, dyes, and proprietary cosmetics available to the wealthy in the early modern period. French and English court society encouraged the use of enamels, white powder, rouges, and beauty marks to enhance appearance, serve fashion, and cover pockmarks and other disfigurements, and colonial elites followed suit. These paints, powders, and enamels to whiten the skin often contained dangerous substances, such as arsenic and lead, jeopardizing health while creating brilliant effects. Perfumers, hairdressers, and apothecaries in major cities offered fashionable cosmetics to both women and men. Until the early nineteenth century, cosmetics tended to mark rank as much as gender; they connoted gentility, social prestige, and political standing, and were as much a part of high culture as ornamental clothing and tea drinking.

Fashionable cosmetics became a source of controversy, however, in Europe and America. Puritans condemned painting as a mark of vanity and defiance of the divine order; masking the face falsified one's true identity. The American Revolution placed a political perspective on such cosmetics, valuing the plain appearance

of republican virtue over the foppery of aristocratic men. In the early nineteenth century, the religious sensibilities and domestic ideals of an emergent middle class in the North emphasized both natural beauty and women's duty to be beautiful, to be achieved through healthful regimens and a moral life. White southern women, especially those on plantations, held onto the earlier ideals of gentility that permitted powder and rouge. Still, the association of cosmetics with prostitution—the "painted woman"—remained a strong one through the 1800s, and women who dared to use cosmetics did so covertly and with a light touch.

Sales of skin creams and lotions grew through the middle of the nineteenth century, but they remained small in scale when compared with such commodities as patent medicines and soaps. According to an 1849 manufacturing census, thirty-nine toiletries firms produced only $355,000 in merchandise in the United States. Nevertheless, the expansion of the market in this period made formerly rare preparations more available and affordable. Typically pharmacists would use a range of chemicals, herbs, and oils to "put up" skin creams under a house label. Commercial agents also imported goods from around the world, including English patent preparations, French perfumes, Portuguese rouge dishes, and Chinese color boxes, containing color-saturated papers of rouge, pearl powder, and eyebrow blacking.

The most commonly used cosmetics of the nineteenth century, however, were skin whiteners and bleaches. Advertisements claimed they removed tan and freckles and made women look more refined and genteel. These were directed at white, middle-class women, playing on their social aspirations, as well as working-class, immigrant, and black women.

Cosmetics Use and the Beauty Industry

Cosmetics use began to increase in the late nineteenth century, a consequence of several key developments. Embracing photography and the theater, Americans became newly oriented to visual culture and social performances. In retailing, innovative department stores used mirrors, plate glass, and the latest fashions to encourage women to engage in self-scrutiny and display.

Many cosmetics businesses began as manufacturers of perfume, soap, and patent medicines and initially went into beauty aids as a sideline. Ponds, one of the leading sellers of skin-care products, started out making patent medicines; in an early instance of market research, it discovered a demand for skin-care products in the 1890s. By 1910, Ponds's advertising promoted cleansing cream at night and vanishing cream by day as a regular beauty treatment for women.

Most important, beauty salons and manicure parlors began to spring up in the nation's cities. These popularized a concept of "beauty culture," encouraging women to improve their looks systematically, using proper cos-

Cosmetic counter. Most major cosmetic lines have displays in department stores, complete with beauticians to demonstrate the products and make recommendations to customers. © GREG SMITH/CORBIS SABA. REPRODUCED BY PERMISSION.

metics and facial techniques. Emphasizing cleanliness, grooming, and skin care, they also sold tinted face powders, whitening creams, rouge, and lip pomades. Women entrepreneurs pioneered the new beauty culture and some became early leaders of the cosmetics industry. Helena Rubinstein and Elizabeth Arden created their New York salons in the 1910s; each developed a full line of cosmetics for facial treatments and home use. By World War I, each had expanded operations into manufacturing and distribution at the "class" end of the market, selling in exclusive stores, specialty shops, and a growing number of salons.

The Parisian fashion for maquillage was slow to be accepted in the United States, although by the 1910s style setters and socialites were purchasing French-made rouge and powder. Helena Rubinstein, Elizabeth Arden, and other women in the beauty business encouraged affluent American women to use makeup and quietly offered applications in their salons.

African American entrepreneurs also found a market for cosmetics within black communities. In the early twentieth century, Anthony Overton developed a "High Brown Face Powder" specifically for women with darker complexions. Although focusing on hair treatments, busi-

nesswoman Madam C. J. Walker also expanded her product line to include skin creams and powders for black women. Neither created products for the full range of African American skin tones at this time, but both sought to address black women's dignity and desire for good looks. In contrast, many of the cosmetics sold to African Americans manufactured by white-owned companies relied on blatantly racist appeals to bleach skin and look white. Such products were widely advertised in black newspapers and remained a subject of controversy through the twentieth century.

What is especially striking about cosmetics at this time, however, is the popularity of beauty preparations among workingwomen, including the daughters of immigrants. They embraced powder and paint, along with fashionable clothing, to assert a new sense of individuality. In the early twentieth century, when sexual mores were changing and young women had entered the workforce in large numbers, the "painted woman" could no longer be distinguished as a prostitute. Indeed, by the 1920s, women increasingly used the term "makeup" rather than "paint," thus indicating that cosmetics were not a means of covering up one's looks but rather an integral part of a public persona.

Beauty kit. In the early 1900s, cosmetics began being packaged for portability, increasing their popularity. © CONDÉ NAST ARCHIVE/CORBIS. REPRODUCED BY PERMISSION.

Growing through the 1910s, the cosmetics industry took off after World War I. From 1909 to 1929, the number of American perfume and cosmetics manufacturers nearly doubled; by 1929, Americans were spending $700 million annually for cosmetics and beauty services. The transformation of women's appearance in the 1920s—corsetless and revealing clothing, bobbed hair, a thin body image—went hand-in-hand with the increased consumption of beauty products and makeup.

Still, cosmetics use spread unevenly across the United States and Europe, more popular among the young, employed, and urban women than their mothers or small-town sisters. Surveys of nonurban women's daily regimens in the 1920s showed that most simply washed the face with soap and water, then perhaps applied cold cream or white powder. It was not until the end of the 1930s that farm women's use of cosmetics approximated that of city dwellers.

A number of innovations in cosmetics and packaging appeared in this time. French cosmetics firms had produced finely textured and tinted powders, and American firms followed suit, selling a wider range of shades. These included, in the mid-1920s, powders and rouges to complement suntanned skin, which had become a popular craze. Metal compacts and lipstick tubes emphasized the portability of cosmetics, so that women could touch

up throughout the day. Vanishing cream was typically used as a base for powder, but foundations began to appear in the 1930s. Among the most innovative and successful was Max Factor's Pan-Cake, a water-soluble foundation in cake form, invented for use by motion picture actors, then introduced to the general public in 1938.

In the first half of the twentieth century, however, most cosmetics manufacturers followed standard formulas, modifying basic creams, lotions, and other preparations. Firms selling lipstick, rouge, and eye makeup often depended on "private label" manufacturers, who offered similar products with small variations. Scientific discoveries led companies to make new claims for wrinkle removers, and small amounts of vitamins, hormones, and even radium were added to skin creams. By the 1930s, the public paid heightened attention to the composition of cosmetics and the exaggerated claims of advertisers. Consumer advocacy groups highlighted cases where women had been blinded by aniline dyes in mascara or burned by skin bleaches that contained a high percentage of ammoniated mercury, common in whiteners sold to African American women. Such concerns led to the increased regulation of cosmetics in the United States and passage of the Food, Drug, and Cosmetics Act in 1938.

It was advertising and marketing, more than product development, that spurred the expansion of the beauty industry and cosmetics use. Cosmetics and toiletries were heavily advertised in women's magazines, second only to food items, and appeared frequently in general interest magazines, in newspapers, and by the 1930s, on radio. These advertisements invoked aspirational images of beauty, youth, and romance, on the one hand, but also touched anxieties about social competition and failed romance, especially during the Great Depression. Hollywood also played an important role; motion picture actresses established new beauty ideals and endorsed a range of products, including mascara and eye shadow, cosmetics few women wore at the time. Whether sold in department stores or five-and-dimes, cosmetics were often an impulse purchase; retailers set up eye-catching displays in the central aisles of their stores and hired saleswomen to demonstrate beauty techniques and promote specific brands.

Postwar Expansion

By the 1940s, makeup had become accepted as an integral dimension of women's everyday appearance. Home economics courses taught how to use makeup in classes on good grooming; department stores held beauty days for schoolgirls; white-collar personnel offices looked favorably on job candidates with carefully applied lipstick and rouge. Psychologists and other professionals insisted that cosmetics were essential to women's mental health and a mature feminine identity.

During World War II, bright red lipstick became a sign of women's patriotism among the Allies. As women went into industry in record numbers, they continued to use cosmetics to affirm their femininity and boost their morale. When the American government tried to restrict cosmetics as a conservation measure in 1942, it found itself backpedaling six months later. Although discontinuing metal containers and limiting some ingredients, it nevertheless made a wide range of beauty preparations available.

Cosmetics use increased dramatically in the postwar world. Women purchased cosmetics to complement seasonal changes in fashion, buying wardrobes of lipstick and nail polish. As the market for cosmetics matured, the beauty business created distinctive brands intended to appeal to women according to demographics and lifestyle. Maybelline, Revlon, and Noxzema (Noxell)—small-scale firms that before the war had specialized in eye makeup, nail enamel, and skin cream, respectively—became large corporations with extensive product lines. New women entrepreneurs also emerged after World War II, including Estee Lauder and Mary Kay Ash. Home-based selling proved highly successful in this period. Avon, founded in 1886, used door-to-door sales to expand from rural communities and cities into the burgeoning postwar suburbs. Using the multilevel marketing strategy pioneered by earlier black businesswomen, Mary Kay organized home parties for women to learn about and purchase cosmetics.

Postwar youth culture spurred cosmetic firms to market cosmetics especially for teenage girls. Noxzema's Cover Girl offered sheer, medicated foundations and lighter tints as a "clean makeup" that would appeal to both teens and their parents. In the early 1960s, the sale of eye makeup—mascara, eyeliner, and colorful eye shadow—finally took off, an aesthetic trend among young women that coincided with the miniskirt and long hair of the time. Grooming aids, powder, and lip gloss for young girls appeared as early as the 1950s; by the 1970s, toy companies and major cosmetics firms competed for these juvenile consumers.

Market segmentation meant that advertising varied considerably in this period. Compared with their prewar counterparts, however, advertisements in the 1950s and 1960s more boldly accentuated women's sexuality and need to appeal physically to men. Revlon's Fire and Ice campaign in 1952 cast a playful yet erotic and charged aura around a medium-red lipstick. During the "British Invasion" of the 1960s, Mary Quant's Love Cosmetics used phallic packaging and Mod design to tie teen cosmetics to the sexual revolution.

Politics of Cosmetics

By the mid-1960s, the counterculture and a nascent feminist movement attacked these trends in advertising, the commercialization of beauty, and women's sexual objectification in the media. Embracing a "natural" look, some women gave up makeup entirely, while others began to compound their own creams and lotions using herbs, berries, and other organic ingredients. Major cosmetics firms were slow to respond to this challenge. Estee Lauder introduced Clinique in 1968, emphasizing a scientific and hygienic appeal. A number of cosmetics lines appeared that contained natural ingredients and were not tested on animals; these often sold in food coops or other alternative outlets. The Body Shop, founded by Anita Roddick, became highly successful marketing to women sensitive to the environment and influenced by the counterculture.

In the 1960s and 1970s, women of color also protested the narrow images of beauty that appeared in fashion magazines and limited cosmetics lines available to them. African American businesses like Fashion Fair and entrepreneurs from the post-1965 immigrant groups have created niche makeup lines for black, Latina, Asian-American, and other women. Increasingly attuned to American ethnic diversity and the global economy, corporations like Maybelline began to manufacture foundation and other cosmetics for the full range of human skin tones.

The feminist critique of cosmetics continued to be heard in the last decades of the twentieth century, notably in the 1991 best-seller *The Beauty Myth*. That critique, in turn, was challenged in the 1980s and 1990s by postfeminists, postmodernists, lipstick lesbians, and devotees of such subcultural styles as punk. They rejected the "natural" as a measure of authenticity, and held instead to the view that cosmetics use could be a source of play, pleasure, and self-expression. Again, cosmetics companies have picked up on that attitude, marketing lipstick, eye makeup, and nail polish in unusual and extreme colors and such provocative names as Vamp and Juicy.

Developments in the Early 2000s

Western cosmetics became widespread in the global economy in the second half of the twentieth century. Corporations like Unilever and Ponds established subsidiaries, contracted with local import firms, and sold beauty preparations in Latin America, the Middle East, Asia, and Africa. American manufacturers marketed cosmetics in a difficult balancing act, appealing to universal ideals of beauty, promoting the American style of actresses and models, and nodding to national and cultural differences. Avon's success in the international arena depended on native sales agents who understood local customs and concerns even as they projected the image of American beauty, lifestyles, and values. By the 1990s, "Avon calling" could be heard around the world, including post-communist and developing countries.

By the twenty-first century, cosmetics manufacturers had invested heavily in scientific research, working closely with chemists and dermatologists. These new "cosmeceuticals" went beyond the hypoallergenic products available since the 1930s and included creams and ointments containing such ingredients as Retin A, which appears to reduce the effects of aging and improves the skin. These products have increasingly blurred the lines between cosmetics, drugs, and medical specialties. The post-World War II baby-boom generation has fueled the growth of anti-aging research and product development, a trend that is expected to continue.

An important development in cosmetics is the partially successful effort to sell cosmetics to men, beyond the traditional grooming products like aftershave and cologne. Both mass manufacturers and some high-end firms, including Helena Rubinstein, tried unsuccessfully to sell cosmetics to men earlier in the twentieth century. Since 1980, however, a significant number of urban professional men and gay men have begun to use moisturizer, exfoliating liquids, and even bronzers to improve their appearance. Although often similar to women's cosmetics, these products are usually segregated in a separate men's counter in retail stores and appear with different brand names and packaging. Young men in such music and dance subcultures as heavy metal and goth will often wear colorful makeup as performers and audience members. Most makeup remains so deeply associated with femininity and effeminacy, however, that very few men choose to use it in everyday business and social life, and those who do seek a "natural" look.

See also **Appearance; Cosmetics, Non-Western.**

BIBLIOGRAPHY

Allen, Margaret. *Selling Dreams: Inside the Beauty Business*. New York: Simon and Schuster, 1981.

Banner, Lois. *American Beauty*. Chicago: University of Chicago Press, 1983.

De Castlebajac, Kate. *The Face of the Century: 100 Years of Makeup and Style*. New York: Rizzoli International, 1995.

Gunn, Fenja. *The Artificial Face: A History of Cosmetics*. London: David and Charles, 1973.

Koehn, Nancy. "Estee Lauder: Self-Definition and the Modern Cosmetics Market." In *Beauty and Business: Commerce, Gender, and Culture in Modern America*. Edited by Philip Scranton, 217–251. New York: Routledge, 2001.

Manko, Katina L. "A Depression-Proof Business Strategy: The California Perfume Company's Motivational Literature." In *Beauty and Business: Commerce, Gender, and Culture in Modern America*. Edited by Philip Scranton, 142–168. New York: Routledge, 2001.

Peiss, Kathy. *Hope in a Jar: The Making of America's Beauty Culture*. New York: Metropolitan Books, 1998.

Smith, Virginia. "The Popularisation of Medical Knowledge: The Case of Cosmetics." *Society for the Social History of Medicine Bulletin* 36 (1986): 12–15.

Vinikas, Vincent. *Soft Soap, Hard Sell: American Hygiene in an Age of Advertisement*. Ames: Iowa State University Press, 1992.

Wolf, Naomi. *The Beauty Myth*. New York: William Morrow, 1991.

Kathy Peiss

COSTUME DESIGNER Costume design as a profession is a twentieth-century phenomenon. Until the end of the nineteenth century, costumes for popular entertainments were assembled piecemeal, either by the director, the actor-manager or by the patron. Repertory companies were the norm in the nineteenth century, and it made sense for a company to maintain a stock of costumes that could be used in multiple productions. Individual actors, working with more than one company, might travel with their own costumes—a practice that continues in the twenty-first century among opera singers.

Exceptions to the piecemeal approach include entertainments devised by artists during the Renaissance and the court masques designed by Inigo Jones in seventeenth-century England, but both are rare examples of a unified vision.

The end of the nineteenth century saw a shift from companies of actors performing a rotating repertoire of plays to stand-alone productions with actors hired specifically for each role. With actors moving from show to show, it didn't make economic sense for producers to maintain a large wardrobe inventory. Simultaneously, a heightened interest in realism called for specialists with the ability to reproduce accurately clothing of the past. Enter the designer.

The First Designers
An article in the *New Idea Women's Magazine* says that by 1906 theatrical costume design firms flourished in most major cities. Some, like Eaves or Van Horn's, in New York and Philadelphia respectively, began as manufacturers of uniforms or regalia and expanded into the theatrical market. By contrast, Mrs. Caroline Siedle and Mrs. Castel-Bert, both in New York, established their ateliers specifically to cater to the growing theater industry.

Producers hired these pioneering designers at their discretion. They were under no obligation to commit to the services of a designer and many preferred to rent existing costumes. For a modern dress show, leading actresses might commission their dressmaker, while minor players raided their closets. Two events changed that.

The actor's strike of 1919 put an end to the practice of performers providing their own wardrobes. Thereafter, producers were required by contract to supply costumes for everyone. Then, in 1923, the stage designers unionized. As part of the collective bargaining agreement, producers of Broadway and touring productions had to hire a union designer. The first union members were set designers who might also design costumes. By 1936 the union recognized costume designers as a separate specialty.

Film designers also emerged in the 1920s. At first, actresses in contemporary films wore their own clothes, "so ladies with good wardrobes found they got more jobs" (Chierichetti 1976, p. 8). For period films, producers rented costumes.

Costumer designers at the Palais Garnier, Paris. Once the concept for a particular production has been agreed upon, the costume designer researches the script and creates sketches of possible garments for each character. © ANNEBICQUE BERNARD/CORBIS. REPRODUCED BY PERMISSION.

The industry moved from New York to California in the 1920s and the studio system replaced the independently shot films of the teens. Designers emerged partly because studio heads wanted their films to have a cohesive look but primarily because the shift from black and white to color film, and from silents to talkies, required costumes especially designed for the medium. The early film distorted colors. Blue, on film, appeared white. Red photographed as black. The early microphones were so sensitive to sounds that only soft fabrics could be used. Crisp fabrics rustled, drowning out the dialogue. By the end of the 1920s, every studio had at least one house designer, a support staff of sketch artists and costumers, and a research department and library.

The Process

The costume designer is responsible for the head-to-toe look of everyone who appears on stage or on screen. After reading the script, the designer meets with the director and others to debate their approach to the material. *Hamlet*, for example, has been set in medieval Denmark, in Vietnam, and in contemporary dress. All are valid approaches.

With the production concept agreed on, the designer has an interval for research. He or she develops color sketches for every costume worn in the show. Depending on the medium, a variety of people see and approve these sketches. In the theater, the director, producer, choreographer, and sometimes the star will have approval. For film, the costume designer works with the director, cinematographer, and art director in addition to the stars.

Once approved, the sketches go into the costume shop to be translated into three-dimensional garments. Many regional theater, opera, and ballet companies maintain their own costume shops. All university theater departments do so as well. For other venues, including Broadway and feature films, a range of independent theatrical costume shops submit bids for producing the costumes. Even when contemporary clothes are purchased or come from a rental house, fittings and alterations are performed by the costume shop.

In the Shop

With the sketches in the shop, the costume designer and assistants essentially move in for the length of the build time, which in theater equals the length of the rehearsal period, typically between three and five weeks. The practice differs for film and opera. In a university setting, the designers may do their own fabric and trim shopping. Elsewhere, costume shops have buyers whose job is to scour the market, bringing back swatches for the designer's consideration.

While the buyers are swatching, costume makers are creating custom-made patterns for each costume, which are then made up, usually in muslin. As each is completed, the actor who will wear it is called for the first of several fittings. An important function of the first fitting is to see that the actor can move well in a costume designed before rehearsals began. Once in rehearsal, the director or choreographer may decide that performing a somersault, despite the bustle gown, is integral to the show's concept. This is the designer's moment to learn that vital piece of information and to adapt the design to allow for the movement. For the 1972 Broadway production of *Pippin*, for example, director-choreographer Bob Fosse had insisted that the armor be rigid metal. When his designer, Patricia Zipprodt, saw what the dancers had to do, she realized that only something flexible would satisfy his needs.

At the first fitting, the designer also has a chance to see if the proportions of the garment suit the performer. At the second fitting, the costume has been made up in the actual fabric to be used. Custom underpinnings, shoes, and millinery are included so that both designer and performer can see the total look. At this fitting all the craftspeople have the opportunity to make adjustments that may increase the performer's comfort or that are requested by the designer.

The final fitting is in the completed costume with the expectation that no further work is necessary at this stage. The clothes move out of the shop and into the theater or onto location.

In Performance

Film designers view daily rushes to see how well their costumes work on screen, while a live performance will have one or more dress rehearsals and a series of preview performances before the opening night. The designer attends them all. This is the time when all of the production elements—scenery, lighting, movement, and costumes come together and occasionally what seemed like a good idea in the shop does not work in performance. With an original script, new scenes or musical numbers may be added, requiring new costumes. The designer has only a few days to produce new designs, get them into the shop, select the fabrics, attend fittings, and see the new costumes integrated into the production. The designer's job is finished only when the show opens to the public or when the last scene is filmed.

See also **Ballet Costume; Dance Costume; Theatrical Costume; Theatrical Makeup.**

BIBLIOGRAPHY

Anderson, Cletus, and Barbara Anderson. *Costume Design*. New York: Holt, Rhinehart and Winston, 1984. A good overview of the process.

Anderson, Norah. "Stage Dressmaking and Stage Dressmakers." *New Idea Women's Magazine* (November 1906): 12–16.

Bentley, Toni. *Costumes by Karinska*. New York: Harry N. Abrams, 1995. Especially chapter 5 on the design and construction of costumes for the ballet.

Chierichetti, David. *Hollywood Costume Design*. New York: Harmony Books, 1976. The introduction is good on the origins of film design.

Ingham, Rosemary, and Liz Covey. *The Costume Designer's Handbook: A Complete Guide for Amateur and Professional Costume Designers*. Portsmouth, N.H.: Heineman, 1992. Excellent overview of the profession.

Jones, Robert Edward. *The Dramatic Imagination*. New York: Theatre Arts, 1941. An inspirational classic, especially chapter 5, "Some Thoughts on Stage Costume."

Pecktal, Lynn. *Costume Design: Techniques of Modern Masters*. New York: Backstage Books, 1993. Interviews with Broadway and feature film designers including training and working methods.

Whitney Blausen

COSTUME JEWELRY The earliest costume jewelry was simply an imitation of precious jewelry and had little intrinsic value or original style of its own. However, once the French couturiers put their names to costume jewelry it became desirable, acceptable, and expensive. In the early 1910s, couturier Paul Poiret became a proponent of costume jewelry, accessorizing his models with necklaces of silk tassels and semiprecious stones designed by the artist Iribe.

Coco Chanel, Jean Patou, Drécoll, and Premet were also among the first famous couturiers to create costume jewelry along with clothing, which propelled its acceptance. By 1925, the Marshall Field's department store catalog described costume jewelry in positive terms, announcing, "The imitation is no longer a disgrace."

The most ubiquitous jewelry imitation in the 1920s was a pearl necklace. Strands of pearls or colored beads neatly circled the neck or swung to waist, hip, even knee-length, made to move with fast-paced dances like the Charleston. At the end of the period when the little black dress became a daytime standard, shorter strands of light-colored beads and pearls continued as the accessories of choice. Rhinestone jewelry also blazed into prominence, as it was the perfect foil for two fashion innovations: suntans and white evening gowns.

Beginning in the 1920s and continuing throughout the 1930s, fashion and jewelry shared a multitude of influences including Art Deco, the Far East, North Africa, and India. Egyptian motifs were inspired by the discovery of Tutankhamen's tomb in 1922. The Colonial Ex-

1960s costume jewelry. The versatility of plastic allowed costume jewelry designers of the 1960s to create jewelry in a wide variety of styles and colors. PHOTO COURTESY OF JOY SHIELDS. REPRODUCED BY PERMISSION.

hibition in Paris in 1931 and the New York World's Fair in 1939 expanded the vocabulary of foreign influences, and rough, raw, "barbaric" materials (real and imitation), including ivory (and faux versions), bone, amber, wood, and even cork, were used for over-scale jewelry. Chanel's signature necklace in 1939 was a massive East Indian–inspired bib of faux pearls, uncut emeralds, ruby beads, and dangling metal pieces with a cord tie.

In the mid-1930s, fashion's palette turned Technicolor, as plastic was produced in bright colors for the first time and metal jewelry was hand-enameled to add color. Toy-like novelty accessories (both costume and precious jewelry) were wildly popular, inspired by the Surrealists, couturier Elsa Schiaparelli, and Walt Disney's cartoons. The queen of whimsy, Schiaparelli put metal insects and caterpillars on necklaces, and her brooches ranged from

miniature musical instruments, roller skates, harlequins, blackamoors, and ostriches. Influenced by the lively antics of cartoons, jewelry also had movable parts: Brooches and necklaces were adorned with "trembler" flowers, hanging plastic fruit, or charms. Clips could be deconstructed into separate pieces. This silly jewelry lightened up the lapels of the fashionable severe and sober, fitted suits.

At the same time, the romantic rococo and Victorian styles flourished, lingering into the 1940s. Rococo jewelry, associated with the Empress Eugenie, was typically frivolous bow-knots, swags and ribbon curves, sparingly ornamented with large, faux-semiprecious cut stones. It was usually plated with real gold (pink, white, yellow) or sterling silver. Victorian styles were copied directly from the originals: lockets, cameos, chokers, even hat pins. Black plastic was the substitute for nineteenth-century jet.

During World War II, imports from Europe were cut off, and many jewelry materials were also restricted. Desperate costume jewelers bought beaded sweaters, evening dresses, and even stage costumes, and harvested their beads, rhinestones, and pearls. They also fashioned jewelry from humble materials that were readily available during wartime: pumpkin seeds, nuts, shells, olive pits, clay, leather, felt, yarn, and even upholstery fabrics. Women wore hand-carved wooden brooches, necklaces of multicolored painted shells, cork, and bits of driftwood. There was little difference between quirky, childish, commercially made jewelry and what the women made themselves following do-it-yourself instructions published in magazines.

Patriotic motifs flourished during wartime, ranging from red, white, and blue to all-American motifs related to California, Hawaii, Native American Indians, and cowboys. Costume jewelry also took on a militaristic theme, and miniature model tanks, airplanes, battleships, jeeps, soldiers, and even hand grenades were made up in metal or wood and worn as brooches, necklaces, and earrings. In the summer of 1940, "V" for victory was a popular design. As Mexico was America's wartime ally, jewelry imported from that country and its imitations was highly fashionable. Two notable Mexican artisans who worked in silver, Rebajes and Spratling, had their sophisticated jewelry featured at top department stores across the country. Patriotic jewelry completely vanished during peacetime.

Postwar fashion succumbed to couturier Christian Dior's highly structured New Look, followed by a series of equally severe styles: the chemise, sheathe, trapeze, and sack dress. The transformation was radical. Clothing concealed most of a woman's body, and only chokers, earrings, bracelets (notably charm bracelets), and brooches were visible. Dresses and suits in heavy, rough-textured fabrics were weighty enough to support the hunky, oversized circles, ovals, snowflake, or starburst-shaped brooches (associated with the atomic bomb), typically three-dimensional. Rhinestones were standard, produced in a rainbow of colors including white, black, pink, blue, yellow, and iridescent, which was an innovation.

Tailored jewelry was the most conservative accessory in the 1950s. Neat and small scale, it was made up in gold or silver metal with little ornamentation. Although clothing concealed their figures, women wore their hair upswept, in a ponytail, or cropped gamine short, to show off hoop, button, and neat pearl earrings. Later in the decade, metal jewelry was thicker, its surface scored, chiseled, or deeply etched, a treatment that lingered into the 1960s.

The distinction between accessories for day and night blurred as casual Italian sportswear became popular. For example, in 1959 actress Elizabeth Taylor was featured in *Life* magazine wearing Dior's black jet choker with a low-cut black sweater. Entertaining at home also created another new fashion category. Theatrical, over-sized chandelier and girandole earrings complemented lounging pajamas, caftans, and floor-length skirts, which remained stylish hostess garb into the 1960s.

Chanel plundered the Renaissance for jewelry inspiration. With her signature suits, in 1957 she showed pendants (notably the Maltese cross), brooches, and chain sautoirs in heavy gold set with baroque pearls, lumpy glass rubies, and emeralds. This style still continues to be identified with Chanel today.

In the 1960s, bold, pop-art graphic "flower power" motifs were fashion favorites. The ubiquitous daisy was produced in every material from plastic to enameled metal, and in a palette of neon bright colors. Daisies were linked into belts, pinned on hats and dresses, and suspended from chains around the neck. Even Chanel and Dior produced flower jewelry, although their brooches, necklaces, and earrings were petaled with fragile poured glass.

Hippies and the counterculture rejected this sophistication in favor of handmade and ethnic jewelry in humble materials: clay and glass beads, yarn, temple bells, papier-mâché, macramé, and feathers. Both men and women pierced their ears, crafted their own headbands, ornamented their clothing with beads and embroidery, strung love beads, or hung a peace sign, ankh, or zodiac symbol on a strip of rawhide around their necks. Singer Janis Joplin typically performed while weighed down with a massive assortment of new and vintage necklaces and bracelets.

Vogue and *Harper's Bazaar* also cultivated this theatrical style. Diana Vreeland, editor-in-chief of *Vogue*, commissioned wildly dramatic, oversized jewelry specifically for the magazine. Usually one of a kind, tenuously held together with wire, thread, and glue, these pieces were too fragile to be worn outside the photo studio. There were breastplates of rhinestones or tiny mirrors, golf-ball-size pearl rings, shoulder-sweeping feather earrings, wrist and armloads of painted papier-mâché bracelets.

Technology also contributed to this fantastical mode. In 1965, plastic pearls were produced for the first time in lightweight, gigantic sizes. They were strung together into multistrand necklaces, bibs, helmets, and even dresses.

Style-wise, costume jewelry was a match for fine jewelry. The so-called beautiful people gleefully mixed costume jeweler Kenneth Jay Lane's $30 rhinestone and enamel panther bracelets (inspired by the Duchess of Windsor's original Cartier models) with their real ones. Lane was well known for his weighty pendant necklaces, shoulder-length chandelier earrings set with gaudy, multicolored fake stones, and enormous cocktail rings. His clients ranged from Babe Paley to Greta Garbo and the Velvet Underground.

Chanel continued to produce Renaissance-style jewelry, notably Maltese crosses and cuff bracelets embellished with large stones, which morphed into a more exaggerated version. Diana Vreeland chose this style as her signature, sporting a pair of bejeweled enamel cuffs reportedly designed by Fulco di Verdura.

At the end of the 1960s and into the 1970s, "space age" style was an alternative to this ornate jewelry. Coolly modern, geometric, it was made up in industrial materials such as transparent plastic and metal hardware. This hard-edged jewelry was a match for clothing ornamented with oversized buckles, zippers, grommets, and nail heads.

Around the same time, punk ruled the streets. The devotees of this style favored leather jackets and jeans that were as aggressive and unisex as their accessories: dog collars and leather armbands bristling with nail heads and spikes, thick chains worn as chokers and around waists. The most notorious punk ornamentation was also the simplest: a safety pin stuck through an ear, nose, lip, or cheek.

Two designers, Elsa Peretti and Robert Lee Morris, heavily influenced costume jewelry during this period. Peretti began designing for Tiffany in 1974, and costume jewelers immediately copied her small-scale, streamlined "lima bean" and "teardrop" pendants, and "diamonds by the yard" of cut stones strung on slender chains.

In New York City, Robert Lee Morris set up his own boutique, Artwear, as a showcase for his handmade gold-bead necklaces, gladiator-size cuffs, metal breastplates, and hefty belt buckles. Fashion designer Donna Karan accessorized her line with Morris's bold and simple creations for several seasons.

In the 1980s, entertainers Cyndi Lauper and Madonna were the female forces that drove style through the new media of music videos, and both mixed lingerie with vintage clothing, and vintage jewelry with cheap new baubles. Madonna wore armloads of rubber bracelets with religious-cross pendants and rosaries. Hip hop and rap music stars sported jewelry in heavy gold or gold-plated look-alikes: nameplate pendants, knuckle rings, ID bracelets. A gold-covered front tooth was a more permanent and extreme ornament.

As the simplified styles of designers Giorgio Armani and Calvin Klein became popular, jewelry gradually shrank in scale until it disappeared. As minimalism ruled fashion, the jewelry business was abysmal. However, costume jewelry came back to glitzy glory in the early 1990s, propelled by the whimsical accessories of Christian Lacroix and Karl Lagerfeld at Chanel. Lagerfeld successfully revived and restyled many of Chanel's signatures, including multistrand pearl necklaces, and Renaissance-style jewelry. He used the "CC" logo as decoration on everything from earrings to pocketbooks.

Entertainers and movie stars steered fashion in 2000, and they wore the real thing, not costume jewelry. Pop music figures Jennifer Lopez and Lil' Kim flashed enormous precious stones on their fingers. Impresario Sean Combs (a.k.a Puff Daddy, P. Diddy) flaunted enormous diamond-stud earrings and monster diamond rings. A long line of movie stars, including Nicole Kidman and

Coco Chanel, late 1930s. By the 1930s, costume jewelry embraced bold designs and different influences of styles and cultures, becoming highly fashionable due in part to the influence of style icons such as Coco Chanel. Here Chanel models a sophisticated costume necklace. PHOTO COURTESY OF JODY SHIELDS. REPRODUCED BY PERMISSION.

Charlize Theron, borrowed jewelry, usually fine antique pieces, from established jewelers such as Harry Winston and Fred Leighton. It was a sign of the times when Chanel launched a line of precious jewelry, and Prada installed precious jewelry from Fred Leighton in their Soho store. Once again, the cycle had turned, and costume jewelry imitated precious jewelry, or "bling bling" as the blinding real thing was called in 2003.

See also **Bracelets; Brooches and Pins; Earrings; Jewelry; Necklaces and Pendants.**

BIBLIOGRAPHY
Becker, Vivienne. *Fabulous Fakes: The History of Fantasy and Fashion Jewellery*. London: Grafton, 1988.

Davidov, Corinne. *The Bakelite Jewelry Book*. New York: Abbeville Press, 1988.

Mulvah, Jane. *Costume Jewelry in Vogue*. London: Thames and Hudson, Inc., 1988.

Nadelhoffer, Hans. *Cartier Jewelers Extraordinary*. New York: Harry N. Abrams, 1984.

Shields, Jody. *All That Glitters: The Glory of Costume Jewelry.* New York: Rizzoli, 1987

Jody Shields

COTTON Cotton plants are native to several parts of the world, and the use of cotton fiber originated independently at least 7,000 years ago in both the India/Pakistan and the Mexico/Peru regions. One of the oldest extant cotton textiles dates to about 3000 B.C.E. Because cotton plants cannot be grown in cooler locales such as northern Europe, climate was an important limiting factor in the spread of cotton cultivation.

Cotton textiles were traded widely in Roman times, and the growing and production of cotton soon spread from India to Egypt and China. Cotton production did not begin in Greece until C.E. 200 or in Spain until tenth century C.E. By the thirteenth century, though, Barcelona was a thriving cotton industry center specializing in producing cotton canvas for sails. England began using imported cotton in the thirteenth century. Widespread use began in the seventeenth century when significant quantities of raw fiber began to be imported to Great Britain from the expanding British colonies for processing and weaving into cloth.

Cotton textiles were widely used in pre-Columbian Meso-American and Andean civilizations. With the beginning of European colonization of the Americas, cotton originating in Mexico and Peru began to be cultivated wherever climate and soil were suitable. Cotton became an established crop in many parts of the American South, and later spread into the regions now known as Texas, Arizona, and California.

Cotton also became an important global trade commodity. For example, England exchanged American cotton fiber for Indian and Egyptian cotton textiles. Among these trade goods, the finest cotton textiles were from long, fine staple cotton fiber. In fact, Indian prints and gauze cottons surpassed the popularity of fine woolens in the seventeenth century and played a role in greatly diminishing the demand for wool and tapestry textiles.

The cotton trade figured in the American War for Independence, as the British struggled to hold onto their source of raw fiber. Cotton production also played a controversial role in the slave trade; cotton, produced by slaves in America, was among the trade goods used to obtain other slaves in Africa. The emphasis on hand labor in cotton production increased the demand for slave labor at the same time that slave labor became ethically intolerable to many Americans (Parker 1998). The plantation system that was at the heart of cotton production thus was an issue in the controversies and regional disputes that led to the American Civil War.

With the invention of the cotton gin in 1793, cotton became a much higher volume commodity, as the machine took over one of the most laborious steps in cotton production, the separation of fibers from seeds. The cotton gin thus was a key component in the development of the U.S. textile and apparel industry. By 1859, two-thirds of the world production of cotton fiber came from the United States (Parker 1998).

Meanwhile, immigrants from Europe brought with them the knowledge and the technology to establish textile production in the United States. Using available water power to drive spinning and weaving machinery, New England became the center of the early textile industry. During the Civil War, a severe reduction in cotton fiber available from the American South led the British industry to seek other sources for cotton fiber and thus expanded cotton production globally. In the United States, both the production of cotton fiber and its processing into cloth continued to evolve according to changing economic circumstances. Between World Wars I and II, a majority of the U.S. textile mills relocated from the Northeast to the South and fiber production expanded in Texas and California.

At the beginning of the twentieth century, cotton production was led by China, the United States, Russia, India, Pakistan, Brazil, and Turkey. Cotton fiber had become an important economic force in as many as eighty countries worldwide. Cotton remains the most important fiber in apparel with nearly half of the world demand for apparel fibers traceable to cotton and cotton blends.

Processing Cotton Fiber

Cotton fiber is a seed hair removed from the boll (seed pod) of the cotton plant that bursts open when fully developed. Bolls emerge from blossoms that fall off to leave the exposed boll. One boll can produce more than 250,000 individual fibers. The cotton plant is a four- to six-foot tall shrubby annual in temperate climates, but a treelike perennial in tropical climates. The best qualities of cotton grow in climates with high rainfall in the growing season and a dry, warm picking season. Very warm, dry climates in which irrigation substitutes for rainfall, such as Arizona and Uzbekistan, are also well suited to cotton production. Rain or strong wind can cause damage to opened bolls. Cotton is subject to damage from the boll weevil, bollworm, and other insects as well as several diseases. Application of insecticides and development of disease-resistant varieties have helped achieve production goals for cotton. Recent innovations in organic cotton and genetically colored cottons continue the progression of putting science into the production process.

Processing cotton includes many stages. While *picking* mature cotton bolls by hand yields the highest quality, mechanized picking makes high production more feasible and affordable. In many countries where hand labor is more affordable than equipment, cotton continues to be hand-picked. *Ginning* is used to clean debris from cotton and prepare it for spinning into yarn. *Grading* separates cotton into quality levels in which short fibers tend

Genetically modified cotton in India. Recent scientific advancements have made it possible for genes to be injected into growing cotton. These genes target the main pests that feed on the plant without harming beneficial insects. © PALLAVA BAGLA/CORBIS. REPRODUCED BY PERMISSION.

to correspond to coarse and long fibers to make very fine quality textiles. *Carding* is the next step in all cotton fiber processing and is used to further clean and minimally align fibers. An additional processing called *combing* is used to further clean and align higher quality cottons. Yarn creation involves *drawing* fibers into a thinner strand that is then *spun* into a finished yarn ready for fabrication into the textile. So-called greige-good (unfinished) fabrics undergo final finishing, which typically involves s*inging* (burning off loose particles) and then *tentering* to align the grain of the fabric and adjust the width. Either at the fiber, yarn, fabric, or product stage, cotton may be subject to *bleaching* to remove natural colors (tan through gray) at which point fashionable colors can be added through *dyeing* and *printing* processes. Other final *finishing* processes might be used to obtain special features such as *sizing* for smoothness; durable press; a polished surface; or a puckered surface texture.

Characteristics of Cotton Textiles

Cotton fiber varies in length from as little as ⅛-inch linters that are not useable as fiber up to ultrafine long sta-

ple cottons of 2½ inches. Short staple fibers (¾–1 inch) are used for relatively coarse textiles like bagging; medium to long staple (1–1⅜ inches) are the Upland cottons used for a majority of cotton products; and extra long staple (1⅜–2½ inches) cottons labeled as *Egyptian, pima, Supima, sea island,* and *Peruvian* cottons are used for very high quality exclusive cotton goods. Many are hand picked to achieve top quality. Natural colors for cotton fibers include off-white, cream, and gray; selective breeding of naturally colored cottons has expanded the color range to include brown, rust, red, beige, and green. Higher quality, long staple cottons are closer to white than coarse shorter fibers. But regardless of natural color, bleaching is required to produce white or pure colors.

Cotton fiber is a flat, twisted, ribbon-like structure easily identified under the microscope. This characteristic can be somewhat modified by finishing fiber or fabric with sodium hydroxide (caustic soda) or liquid ammonia and thereby swelling the fiber. This rounder mercerized or ammoniated fiber is more lustrous and stronger than typical cotton. It also accepts dye better than untreated cotton. Applying this treatment in a pattern yields plissé,

Cotton gin. The 1793 invention of the cotton gin by Eli Whitney helped revolutionize the United States's textile industry and bolstered the value of cotton as a commodity. © UNDERWOOD & UNDERWOOD/CORBIS. REPRODUCED BY PERMISSION.

a puckered textured surface effect quite unlike the typical cotton fabric surface, which is flat, slightly wrinkled, and somewhat dull. Long-staple fine cottons exceed this standard and are often hard to differentiate from silk in surface smoothness. Cotton tends to be neutral on the skin, so is considered a comfortable fiber for everyday wear.

Cotton is cellulosic and thus has aesthetic, comfort, and performance characteristics reminiscent of linen and rayon textiles. These include high absorbency and low insulation and a tendency to be cool in hot temperatures. Cotton does not dry as quickly as linen and silk. As a relatively heavy textile, cotton is more useful for keeping cool or for dressing in layers than it is in providing warmth. Cotton is subject to linting, that is, the shedding of fibers that can result in bits of fiber lying on the surface of the textile. Cotton is also somewhat subject to abrasion and will become thin or develop holes in areas of recurring abrasion. Highly bleached cotton textiles have lower strength and durability than those that retain natural color. Cotton fibers resist absorbing dyes and fade easily in sunlight and from abrasion. Therefore the "faded" effect commonly found among fashionable cotton fabrics since the 1970s optimizes cotton's natural character.

Cotton is a medium strong fiber with a tendency to wrinkle. Wrinkling is diminished when fibers are long and fine and yarns are flexible. Wrinkle resistant finishes can help overcome lack of resiliency. Blending cotton with synthetic fibers such as polyester is the most common way to overcome wrinkling. This solution without careful attention to yarn quality can lead to pilling as short cotton fibers break off and synthetic fibers hold onto the broken fibers.

The twisted cotton fiber results naturally in a somewhat fuzzy spun yarn that holds onto dirt particles. Water- and oil-borne staining is also commonplace due to high absorbency. Cotton has high heat resistance, is stronger wet than dry, and withstands cleaning, pressing, and creasing very successfully. Cotton is resistant to most cleaning detergents but damaged by acid such as air pollutants. Cotton shrinks back to original dimensions when wet and thus experiences relaxation shrinkage. Because it can be sterilized by boiling, cotton is useful in clean room and medical applications. Cotton seldom irritates the skin or causes allergies. Cotton textiles are flammable and subject to damage by mildew, perspiration, bleach, and silverfish.

Cotton in Fashion across Time

Cotton holds a unique place in history, evolving from being more highly valued than silk and wool in the sixteenth and seventeenth centuries to becoming an everyday, comfort-oriented textile in contemporary apparel worldwide. Early Indian cottons were so ultra-fine that they were extremely valuable as trade goods and were highly competitive with fine woolen and silk textiles of the era. Cotton was originally available only to the wealthy due to the intensive hand labor needed to process fiber into yarns. In the early nineteenth century, wool held nearly 80 percent of world market share, with cotton and linen taking second and third place. However, by the early twentieth century, cotton became and remains in the early 2000s the leading apparel fiber worldwide. Liberty cottons are an example of the continued success of cotton as a prestige fabric; they have remained a trademark for the very finest Egyptian long staple cottons since 1875 when Liberty of London began copying Indian cotton prints onto ultra-fine long staple cottons. The advent of synthetic fibers proved strong competition for cotton in the 1970s, but cotton production rebounded as comfort became more important to many consumers than price. Faded cotton is an example of the power of the "comfort" aesthetic. Every decade since the 1970s has returned faded cotton to current fashion. While synthetic fibers can achieve the aesthetics of cotton, they only very recently came close to both the feel and the comfort of cotton with the advent of microfiber polyester. The widespread adoption of "casual Friday" dress codes by much of corporate America in the 1990s continued to make cotton an important element in the fashion aesthetic. Cotton has also achieved a good reputation as a "green" textile, because it is biodegradable.

Common Cotton Textile Uses

Cotton is highly valued for comfort and launderability. It is highly tolerant of heavy use. Wordwide, approximately 50 percent of apparel is made of cotton fiber, but pure cotton products are not as prevalent as cotton blends. In apparel, 100 percent cotton cloth is preferred for uses that demand being next to the skin or high physical activity. This includes a wide range of activewear that focuses on jersey, interlock, and sweatshirt knitwear for the upper body and woven textiles such as denim and khaki for the lower body. Apparel for situations where appearance is more important than comfort in physical activity is frequently made from cotton blends.

About 60 percent of all interior textiles (excluding floor coverings) are made of cotton or cotton blends; this category includes sheets, towels, blankets, draperies, curtains, upholstery, slipcovers, rugs, and wall coverings. In many of these applications, cotton's natural character is aesthetically pleasing, but performance characteristics such as high absorbency and tendency to soil are not advantageous. Manufacturers combat this tendency with stain-resistant finishes and often try to achieve the aesthetic qualities of cotton in cotton-synthetic blends.

Industrial uses account for less than 10 percent of cotton production, reflecting the advantages of synthetics for industrial applications requiring strength and durability. Cotton is preferred for many medical uses because it can easily be sterilized, is highly absorbent, and does not retain static electricity.

See also **Fibers; Textiles and International Trade.**

BIBLIOGRAPHY

Collier, B., and P. Tortora. *Understanding Textiles.* New York: Macmillan Publishing, 2000.

Hatch, K. *Textile Science.* Minneapolis, Minn.: West Publishing, 1993.

Kadolph, S., and A. Langford. *Textiles.* 9th ed. New York: Prentice-Hall, 2002.

Parker, J. *All about Cotton.* Seattle, Wash.: Rain City Publishing, 1998.

Carol J. Salusso

COURRÈGES, ANDRÉ

André Courrèges (1923–) was born in Pau, in the Basque part of France. He studied engineering before pursuing a career in fashion. Courrèges worked first under the illustrious couturier Cristóbal Balenciaga from 1950 until 1961, when he left to open his own house. Balenciaga, whose clients were primarily mature and conservative women of wealth, was paradoxically often years ahead of his time. He produced sculptured garments that served as architecture for the woman's body, and it was from Balenciaga that Courrèges learned a highly disciplined yet innovative approach to design.

Early Career

The London "youthquake" of the early 1960s produced experiments in fashion that glorified young people and sent shock waves all the way to Paris, the capital of haute couture. André Courrèges's success was based on his ability to revitalize and preserve high fashion by injecting elements of the youthquake into haute couture. Along with London-based Mary Quant, Courrèges was a leading figure in the introduction of the miniskirt—the article of clothing most closely associated with youthfulness in its disavowal of traditional social codes and the rules of fashion. The miniskirt offered minimal coverage of the lower body, the better to flaunt the young legs that became so visible in the 1960s. Gone were the days of ladylike propriety, now banished by the emphasis on youth.

Although opinion is divided as to who actually "invented" the miniskirt, Quant or Courrèges, it is generally accepted that Mary Quant was first, although only after "the girls on the street." Courrèges initially showed his miniskirts in the early 1960s, followed by futurist-inspired pantsuits, coats, hats, and his trademark white kid boots. *British Vogue* declared 1964 "the year of Courrèges" (Howell, p. 284). The spring–summer collection of 1964 represented a couture version of youth-oriented styles with the invention of the "moon girl" look; the collection ultimately secured for Courrèges the title the designer of the Space Age.

Courrèges's Space Age Design

Courrèges's 1964 Space Age collection unveiled, among other pieces, architecturally-sculpted, double-breasted coats with contrasting trim, well-tailored, sleeveless or short-sleeved minidresses with dropped waistlines and detailed welt seaming, and tunics worn with hipster pants. Vivid shades of pink, orange, green, and navy complemented the designer's bold repeated use of white and silver. Accessories for each ensemble included oversized, white, tennis-ball sunglasses or goggles with narrow eye slits, gloves, helmet-shaped hats and other hats recalling baby bonnets, and square-toed midcalf boots made of soft, white kid leather. Perhaps his most famous contribution to fashion after the miniskirt itself was the "Courrèges boot," originally designed in 1963. The entire 1964 spring collection was a phenomenal success and influenced other designers such as Pierre Cardin and Paco Rabanne to create their own versions of futuristic fashion. It also led ready-to-wear manufacturers, hoping to rake in huge profits, to copy and mass-produce similar designs.

Courrèges's visionary approach to fashion made use of clean geometrical lines and rejected superfluous material. He employed a minimal amount of decorative ornamentation; when he used it at all, it was most often his trademark daisy motif, chosen for its symbolic association with youth. The couturier's love of sharp lines and the angular crispness of his forms reflected his background in engineering. Courrèges's clothing not only

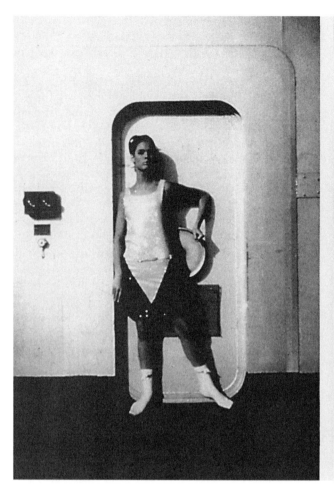 

Andre Courrèges designs. Two outfits illustrate Courrèges's preference for streamlined shapes and dramatic use of the color white. DESIGN BY ANDRÉ COURRÈGES, 1963, PHOTOGRAPH. COURRÈGES DESIGN.

emphasized technologically advanced synthetic materials that were evocative of the times, but also pushed fashion further into the future by situating it within modern life. This intellectual component, typical of Parisian design, carried over into Courrèges's work at his studio on the avenue Kléber, where he dressed luminaries from the duchess of Windsor to Jacqueline Kennedy, Lee Radziwill, and Jane Holzer. The "white" salon, as the studio was known, personified the designer's ideals of functionality and practicality with its modern minimalist decor. André Courrèges created modern clothes for modern women living in modern times.

Courrèges's first official couture collection made its debut in 1965; two years later Prototype, the made-to-order custom line, was introduced. The introduction of luxury prêt-à-porter with Couture Future at the end of the decade marked Courrèges's transition into the 1970s. The new decade saw the establishment of the designer's first fragrance, Empreinte, in 1970 along with a men's ready-to-wear line in 1973. The need to reach a mass-market audience brought with it the lower-priced Hy-

perbole line in the early 1980s, and the desire to solidify a world-renowned brand name through profitable licensing arrangements led to the sale of the company in 1985 to the Japanese firm Itokin.

Courrèges's Legacy
Along with his contemporaries Paco Rabanne and Pierre Cardin, André Courrèges helped to create an unmistakable style that defined an era. His lasting impact on fashion design was his astute recognition of the revolution launched by the younger generation. The explosion of the "youthquake" onto the scene fundamentally altered the direction of fashion in the 1960s. Fashion now not only celebrated the present but also looked forward to the future. The future was conceivably Courrèges's greatest muse, and the infinite possibilities of tomorrow stimulated his experiments with form.

The mod revival spearheaded in the early 1990s by Miuccia Prada recalled the design principles and iconic looks pioneered by Courrèges three decades earlier.

Andre Courrèges with model. Courrèges made his mark during the 1960s by capitalizing on his ability to inject high fashion with a dose of bold, youthful energy. © Richard Melloul/Corbis Sygma. Reproduced by permission.

From white, A-line minishift dresses to nylon microfiber accessories, Prada's continual search for innovation is influenced by Courrèges's designs from the 1960s. Furthermore, the fall 2003 collections represented a direct backward glance at youthquake fashion. Designs that evoked the Space Age appeared on catwalks from New York to Paris. White and metallic "lunar" shades with occasional splashes of bright color dominated the palette. Geometrical lines were everywhere. The miniskirt reappeared in full force at Chanel, Marc Jacobs, and Donna Karan, while midcalf leather boots accessorized mod ensembles at Moschino and Tommy Hilfiger. The focus on youth, the contemporary use of architecturally shaped minimalist designs in bold contrasting colors, and the deliberate application of detailing demonstrates the lasting impact of 1960s fashion. Henceforth, every retro mod fashion will forever be traced back to the work of André Courrèges.

See also **Balenciaga, Cristóbal; Cardin, Pierre; High-Tech Fashion; Miniskirt; Prada; Quant, Mary; Rabanne, Paco; Space Age Styles; Techno-Textiles; Youthquake Fashions.**

BIBLIOGRAPHY

"Balenciaga's Secret." *Women's Wear Daily*, 23 April 1961.

Braddock, Sarah E., and Marie O'Mahony. *Techno Textiles: Revolutionary Fabrics for Fashion and Design.* New York: Thames and Hudson, Inc., 1998.

"Eyeview." *Vogue* (October 1964): 87–89.

Giraud, Françoise. "After Courrèges, What Future for the Haute Couture?" *New York Times Magazine* (12 September 1965): 50–51.

Howell, Georgina. *In Vogue: Six Decades of Fashion.* London: Allen Lane, 1975.

Koski, Lorna. "Courrèges: 60s Encore." *Women's Wear Daily* (26 October 1984).

McDowell, Colin. *Fashion Today.* London: Phaidon Press Ltd., 2000.

Nonkin, Lesly. "Courrèges: Shops Stay in Touch with Customer." *Women's Wear Daily* (12 September 1979).

Sheppard, Eugenia. "Courrèges Back in Action." *World Journal Tribune* (19 March 1967): 8–11.

Steele, Valerie. *Fifty Years of Fashion: New Look to Now.* New Haven, Conn.: Yale University Press, 1997.

Jennifer Park

COURT DRESS In the increasingly informal society of the early 2000s, in which many social barriers have broken down, it is arresting to read of the rigid code of manners that once determined who was, and who was not, eligible to be received at court, and who was, or was not, therefore part of "Good Society." In Europe, by the seventeenth century, wearing the correct dress on this occasion was quite as important as having the right background.

Within a royal household, officers were appointed to supervise aspects of royal life. The officer, often called a lord chamberlain, who had charge of public and ceremonial events, would usually oversee the regulation of dress and matters of etiquette. By the nineteenth century, as the categories of people eligible for court presentation increased, and the styles of court dress became ever more various and complex, all earlier printed dress instructions were drawn together and published as formal regulations. In Great Britain, "Dress Worn at Court," first published in 1882, was updated and reissued at about five-yearly intervals until 1937. Subsequently, hand-lists have been provided to specific individuals within the Royal Household, Foreign Office, Parliament, and Law Courts where the wearing of court dress may survive.

Until the late eighteenth century, in many European countries, many offices and titles remained as the personal gift of the monarch and members of his family. Both politicians and merchants found it essential to demonstrate to potential supporters that they enjoyed the favor of the court, to see their projects succeed. Even as the political importance of the court began to wane, there was always social advantage to be gained and special efforts continued to be made within the royal household to regulate the numbers and social standing of those attending. It was necessary for any new aspiring attendee to locate someone who had already been presented, to serve as his or her sponsor. In seventeenth-century France, a set of rules called "les honneurs de la cour" were drawn up. A French lady craving admittance had to prove a title of nobility extending back to 1400. Since the eighteenth century, there is evidence that this system could be abused: court officials could be bribed to gain admittance, the services of a sponsor could be bought, and sometimes the monarch himself would override the rules allowing a person of humble birth to attend as "une faveur de choix."

The Spanish court was the earliest to actively promote a distinctive court dress from the sixteenth century. All courtiers, state officials, and those attending court had to wear a doublet and close-fitting knee breeches, made of silk or wool in a somber color, worn with the stiff "gorilla" collar of white linen. Eventually, the practice was adopted throughout the Spanish Empire, in Austria, and certain Catholic German states.

By the mid-seventeenth century, Louis XIV was concerned with promoting himself, the prestige of the French court, French fashion, and culture. In 1661 he devised a system whereby fifty of his closest friends and supporters were allocated by special warrant a specific court dress. It was composed of a blue coat called a "justaucorps a brevet," lined with red and trimmed with gold and silver galloon (braided trimming with scalloped edges), to a degree not allowed within earlier sumptuary legislation. The outfit was completed with a waistcoat, knee breeches, red-heeled shoes, and a sword. When the dauphin reached his majority, a brown coat similarly embellished was devised as the regulation dress for his household.

In about 1670, Louis XIV, perhaps with his brother, Philippe, duc d'Orleans and his wife, established the "grand habit" as a court dress for women. This dress had a stiff-boned bodice with a low, round neckline and cap sleeves trimmed with tiers of ruffles called "engageantes." The skirt was cut full, and pulled back to reveal the petticoat worn beneath. This was often richly decorated. For their first presentation to the French king the "grand habit" had to be black. Subsequently, colored dresses could be worn. By about 1730 the petticoat was worn supported on large side hoops. A train replaced the skirt.

French court dress was adopted with small variations as court dress throughout Europe. By 1700 it had even become the regulation dress at the Spanish court for all but the most formal occasions.

In Great Britain the "grand habit" or "stiff bodied gown" was worn by members of the royal family and their immediate circle for royal weddings and coronations. However, by about 1700, the mantua was the customary dress worn by ladies attending court. It had an unboned bodice and full skirt. The neckline was cut square, and the bodice was closed in front with a separate stomacher. The elbow-length sleeves were finished with tiers of ruffles. The skirt was lifted back to reveal a petticoat worn beneath and by about 1750 served as little more than a train. By 1730 the petticoat was supported with large side hoops.

Ladies attending court in 1750 were generally wearing ostrich feathers as a hair ornament, and in 1762 Horace Walpole notes that they were considered "de rigueur." Lace lappets had also emerged as the enduring trimming.

Men's court dress in Great Britain was also simpler than its French counterpart, comprising a coat, waistcoat, and knee breeches, often made of fine silks and velvet, and frequently lavishly embellished with embroidery.

The "grand habit" saw its demise in 1789 with the French Revolution. However, by 1804 a new official dress had been devised by Jean-Baptiste Isabey for French government officials, as well as Napoleon, his family, and inner circle. For ladies a court train alone was retained, worn over fashionable evening dress.

The second half of the eighteenth century had seen many European courts beginning to devise special uniform liveries to be worn by members of the royal family and royal circle. In France, Louis XV established a green and gold costume as "uniforme des petits chateaux." In 1734 Frederick, Prince of Wales in Great Britain, had devised a blue and buff uniform. His son George III in 1778 was responsible for the introduction of the Windsor uniform with its blue coat and distinctive red facings. It was also in 1778 that Gustavus III of Sweden put together a comprehensive order of court uniforms not only for his family and household, but also encompassing government officials, military officers, legal officials, and even university staff and students. They were of a consciously archaic style having its origin in seventeenth-century fashion, a period associated with Swedish greatness. Small variations in materials and ornament served to differentiate classes of officials. A court dress was also devised for Swedish ladies on similar lines. It was generally black and had a low round neckline trimmed with lace, and distinctive white puffed sleeves trimmed with a lattice of black ribbon.

Isabey's new system of official dress in France included uniforms for almost every office. By 1815 a similar program had been devised in Great Britain, the uniforms based on a pattern used by the French Army. This had a blue coat, embroidered with gold, worn with white knee breeches, silk stockings, flat pumps, a "chapeau bras" and a court sword. As the century progressed, more uniforms were added as new classes of officials were drawn into the system. Typically a uniform would be fashionable at the date of its introduction, but was rarely updated as the years passed. The embroidery would include motifs associated with the nation concerned or those, such as laurel or oak, traditionally associated with valor and steadfastness.

In early nineteenth-century Britain, the cloth court dress, worn by men for whom no uniform was prescribed, maintains the link with eighteenth-century custom. This was replaced in 1869 by "Velvet Court Dress" cut on very similar lines. While a more fashionable option was devised in the 1890s, this style of dress may still be seen worn in the early 2000s.

The French Revolution had comparatively little impact on women's court dress in Great Britain. The mantua continued to be worn, supported with an immense court hoop until 1820 when George IV suggested it should be abandoned. After this date court trains were worn over fashionable evening dress, with ostrich feather headdresses and lace lappets. By 1867 lace lappets were proving increasingly difficult to obtain, and the lord chamberlain permitted the wearing of two silk net streamers instead. In 1912, the lord chamberlain established that the streamers should be no more than forty-five inches long. The great profusion of ostrich feathers included in court headdresses of the early nineteenth century had been reduced to two or three by mid century. In the dress regulations published in 1912, it is noted that there should be three feathers worn after the manner of the Prince of Wales's crest toward the left side of the head. In 1922 the lord chamberlain ordained that the court train was restricted to eighteen inches from the heels of the wearer. The color of ladies' court dress was not prescribed, but it became the convention that the dresses were of a pale hue, particularly for those being presented to the monarch for the first time. Special permission had to be sought to wear black court dress, should the lady being presented be in mourning.

The nineteenth century saw the development in many nations of a distinctive court dress. Some countries such as Russia and Greece followed the Swedish lead and introduced elements of traditional dress into their design. Other countries, as diverse as Venezuela, Norway, and Japan, selected a system of uniforms based on European military patterns. Tailors, in London, Berlin, and Rome in particular, provided a comprehensive service designing as well as manufacturing the garments.

Many of the European courts, where the wearing of court dress had been so enthusiastically promoted, were swept away during World War I. The British court proved more resilient, and in London court dress continued to be worn until the outbreak of World War II in 1939. But Britain emerged from this conflict very changed. The social mores that had underpinned the court system had broken down. Even though court presentation continued until 1958, a special dress was not prescribed.

Court dress is rarely worn in the early 2000s. In most European countries a few particular officials working in the foreign office, parliament, and the law courts may be required to wear it on occasion. In Sweden, Denmark, and Norway since 1988 the wearing of a court dress within the royal family and its immediate circle has been reintroduced for the grandest ceremonial occasions. The new Swedish pattern is based in the eighteenth-century Swedish tradition. The styles in Norway and Denmark are modern creations.

See also **Royal and Aristocratic Dress.**

BIBLIOGRAPHY

Arch, Nigel, and Marschner, Joanna. *Splendour at Court: Dressing for Royal Occasions since 1700.* London: Unwin Hyman, 1987.

Delpierre, Madeleine. *Uniformes civiles ceremonial circonstances.* Paris: Ville de Paris, Musee de la Mode et du Costume, 1982.

de Marly, Diana. *Louis XIV and Versailles.* London: B. T. Batsford, Ltd.; New York: Holmes and Meier, 1987.

Mansfield, Alan. *Ceremonial Costume.* London: Adam and Charles Black, 1980.

Rangstrom, Lena, ed. *Hovets Drakter.* Stockholm: Livrustkammaren/Bra Bocker/Wiken, 1994.

Ribiero, Aileen. *Fashion in the French Revolution.* London: B. T. Batsford, Ltd.; New York: Holmes and Meier, 1988.

———. *Dress in Eighteenth Century Europe 1715–1789.* New Haven, Conn.: Yale University Press, 2002.

Joanna Marschner

COUTURE. *See* **Haute Couture.**

COWBOY CLOTHING "Cowboys," "vaqueros," "gauchos," each of these words conjures a different image, yet all these occupations originated in the Salamanca and Old Castile region of twelfth-century Spain where cattle herders wore low-crowned hats, bolero jackets, sashes, tight-fitting trousers, and spurred boots. The dress of gauchos, vaqueros, and cowboys may have originated in Spain but new articles of dress were added because of the various environments in which cattle herders

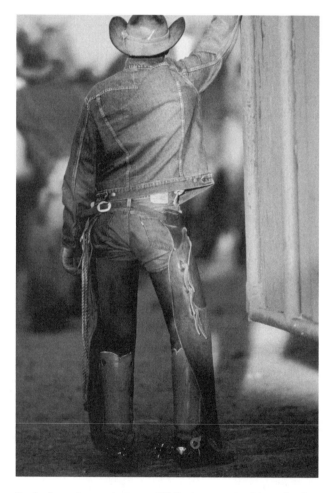

Typical cowboy outerwear. While low-crowned hats, leather chaps, and spurred boots have been major components of traditional cowboy garb for centuries, blue jeans are a more recent stylistic addition. © David Stoecklein/Corbis. Reproduced by permission.

performed their work. The dress of all three changed because of innovations in ranching culture and in technologies used for producing clothing; however, there is one characteristic that still remains among all three groups—their love of flamboyance in dress.

Gaucho Dress
The dress of gauchos reflected the influence of Spain while responding to environmental conditions found in South America. Nineteenth-century paintings show them wearing low-crowned hats, vests, and bolero jackets, all having Spanish influence. They also wore *calzoncillos* that bear a remarkable resemblance to petticoat breeches that were fashionable in sixteenth-century Europe. *Chiripá* that consisted of loose diaper-like pants were worn over the *calzoncillos.* The gauchos of Argentina and Chile added ponchos that originated among the native people of the region for protection from cold winds and rains generated by the Andes Mountains that rose above the pampas. During the colonial period, Argentinean gauchos wore *bota de potro,* boots made of the leg skins of colts. By the nineteenth century machine-made boots replaced the *bota de potro* since Argentineans enacted laws forbidding use of homemade boots to prevent the killing of colts. The most elaborate part of traditional gaucho's dress was a wide belt called a *cinturon,* trimmed with coins and fastened with a large plate buckle. By the mid-twentieth century, the *calzoncillos* and *chiripá* were replaced by wide-legged trousers called *bombachas* tucked into tall leather boots, but the *cinturon* remained a traditional part of gaucho dress. Gauchos in the twenty-first century still resemble their early-twentieth-century ancestors, since they are dressed in low-crowned, broad-brimmed hats, short jackets, *bombachas* tucked into tall boots, and, most important, *cinturons* decorated with coins and wide plate buckles. Some gauchos still use ponchos, both for decoration as well as for protection.

Vaquero Dress
Vaqueros of Mexico, the most direct ancestor of the American cowboy, also wore clothing that resembled the clothes worn in Spain, though there were differences. The low-crowned hat, bolero jacket, sash, and spurred boots remained, but a new form of dress developed in the North American Southwest. *Armas* were an early form of chaps made of slabs of cowhide hung from the saddle and folded back to protect a vaquero's legs from the thorny brush that was part of the New World environment. *Chaparejos* that fully enclosed a rider's legs were the next practical evolution of protective gear for Mexican vaqueros. By the late sixteenth century, vaquero dress included a leather *chaqueta* or jacket, a sash, knee breeches called *sotas* that were usually made of leather, long drawers visible under the *sotas,* leather leggings that wrapped to the knee, and spurs attached to buckskin shoes. Vaqueros, too, changed their dress to reflect changing technology and culture. By the mid-nineteenth century, their dress consisted of wide-brimmed, low-crowned hats, short

314

jackets, thigh-high *chaparreras* tied to a belt at the waist that were worn over trousers, boots and large rowelled spurs. The twenty-first century vaquero wears *chaparejos* that resemble those developed over 400 years ago but he wears a broad-brimmed hat with a higher crown trimmed with a fancy hatband and ready-made shirt and pants.

Cowboy Dress

Working cowboys. Woolie chaps, made of leather with the hair left on, originally developed in California, were introduced to northern cowboys by vaqueros who drove cattle from Oregon to Montana mining camps during the 1860s. They did not represent cowboy culture until the cattle industry had expanded to the northern plains during the 1880s when woolies, as they were called, were particularly useful for protecting cowboys from the cold that was a part of northern plains life.

Dude ranch dress. Eastern visitors to the West still sometimes buy flamboyant cowboy gear but they are more likely to do their horseback riding in running shoes and T-shirts instead of cowboy boots and satin shirts. One reason for this is that most dude ranch visitors no longer spend six to eight weeks on western ranches summer after summer, but visit a dude ranch for one or two weeks once in a lifetime.

Twenty-First-Century Western Dress

Cowboy dress is important in American culture, especially to those who live in the West. Often formal events are excuses for westerners to put on their best western outfits consisting of broad-brimmed Stetson hats, western-cut shirts with curved yokes and pearl snaps, tooled belts with fancy plate buckles (or trophy buckles if available), tight, boot-cut jeans, and high-heeled boots. Even ladies dress up in their best Native American jewelry, well-cut western shirts, full skirts, and high-heeled boots. Western style is hard to resist.

Gauchos, vaqueros, and cowboys are important in South and North American folk culture. All three repre-

Close-up of spur. Mexican *vaqueros* began attaching spurs to their shoes around the sixteenth century, and they have remained a traditional part of cowboy attire. © DAVID STOECKLEIN/ CORBIS. REPRODUCED BY PERMISSION.

sent fierce independence and self reliance but it is their clothing and gear that defines each group. Gauchos are recognized by their tall boots, wide-legged pants, coin-decorated belts, and wide-brimmed hats. Vaqueros wear sombreros that have decorated high crowns and very broad brims. They still wear *chaparreras* and boots and fancy spurs, but their pants and shirts are more formal than those worn by their ancestors. Cowboys often wear Stetson hats that have broad brims, bright-colored shirts, and blue jeans that are now part of the cowboy image. Slant-heeled cowboy boots, spurs, and tooled belts with fancy buckles are also part of the cowboy image. Rodeo cowboys now wear chaps made of leather embellished with Mylar in bright colors like shocking pink and turquoise that flash in the sun as the cowboys demonstrate their skills in the arena. Although gauchos, vaqueros, and cowboys can trace their origin to Spain, little in their appearance reflects the dress of twelfth-century Salamanca. Instead, each wears the clothing that developed because of changes in technology and culture.

See also **America, Central, and Mexico: History of Dress; America, North: History of Indigenous Peoples Dress; America, South: History of Dress; Boots; Fashion and Identity; Hats, Men's; Jeans; Protective Clothing.**

BIBLIOGRAPHY

Bisko, Charles. "The Peninsular Background of Latin American Cattle Ranching." *The Hispanic American Historical Review* 32, no. 4 (November 1952): 491–506.

Cisneros, Jose. *Riders Across the Centuries: Housemen of the Spanish Borderlands.* El Paso: University of Texas, 1984.

Dary, David. *Cowboy Culture.* Lawrence: Kansas University Press, 1989.

Slatta, Richard. *Cowboys of the Americas.* New Haven, Conn.: Yale University Press, 1990, p. 34.

"He was dressed like a Wild West Show cowboy, with such . . . extras as . . . a bandanna worn full in front like a lady's big bertha collar, instead of tied tight around the neck to keep dust out and sweat from running all the way down into your boots." Bronco Billy Anderson, a real cowboy who starred in *The Great Train Robbery.*

Cary, Dianna Serra. *The Hollywood Posse.* Boston: Houghton Mifflin, 1975, p. 17.

Taylor, Lonn, and Ingrid Marr. *The American Cowboy*. Washington, D.C.: Library of Congress, 1983.

Wilson, Laurel. "American Cowboy Dress: Function to Fashion." *Dress* 28 (2002): 40–52.

Laurel E. Wilson

CREPE "Crepe" is the name given to fabric having a crinkled or pebbled texture, often used for blouses and dresses with graceful drape. Almost any fiber may be used, and the fabric can be thin and sheer, fine and opaque, or even heavy. Crepe (alt. crape) fabric may be stretchy, requiring care to cut and sew accurately. Its distinctive surface may be achieved by taking advantage of yarn twist, by arranging a suitable weave structure, by employing uneven warp tension, or by applying a chemical treatment.

The first type utilizes the kinetic energy of two kinds of tightly-spun weft yarns (yarn that runs crosswise)—one

Crepe de chine wrap. Crepe de chine is a crepe made from silk or a similar thin, lightweight fabric. These crepes have a subtle luster and are frequently painted. © CONDÉ NAST ARCHIVE/ CORBIS. REPRODUCED BY PERMISSION.

S-twisted and the other Z-twisted—(spun so that the twists angle upward to the left or to the right, respectively), which are alternated singly or in pairs in a plain-weave cloth. Upon release from the loom's tension, the springy yarns attempt to unwind within the confines of the web, thus imparting the characteristic rippled surface of "flat crape" or *crêpe lisse*, as it was known in the nineteenth-century. Occasionally this technique is used in both warp (yarn that runs lengthwise) and weft, as in early nineteenth century Chinese export silk shawls. Georgette is a sheer, crisp, flat crepe; chiffon, a relatively modern fabric, is also sheer and crisp but has a smooth, uncraped surface. Since the terms "flat crepe" and *crêpe lisse* seem to have passed from common use, this fine crepe seems to have acquired the default name of "chiffon" as well.

The second type of crepe is made of yarns with ordinary twist in a weave having small, irregular floats that look fairly bumpy. This method is most effective in heavy fabrics whose larger threads produce an appreciable texture.

The third type of crepe, seersucker, has warpwise puckered stripes resulting from slack tension in the weaving. When the cloth is released from the loom's tension, it relaxes to a shorter length with closer-spaced wefts than the puckered stripes, which are forced to bulge from the fabric plane. It is usually an ideal choice for summer suiting, underwear, pajamas, and children's wear because it sheds wrinkles and needs no ironing.

The fourth crepe requires the application of a special finish that causes the fabric to shrink wherever it is applied. The method was first patented in England in 1822, when a plain, thin silk gauze stiffened with shellac was passed under a heated, engraved copper cylinder to receive embossed patterns. At this time, heavily textured crepes, particularly the printed varieties, were called "crepe." The term for flat crepes—*crêpe*—eventually came into use for all, no doubt because of the irresistible fashion cachet of anything French.

Heated, engraved rollers are still used to impress chemicals on cloth to make puckered "plissé" designs that may not be permanent. However, cottons printed with alkali are permanently altered by shrinkage. Synthetics, being heat sensitive, can be craped handily and permanently not only at the factory, but inadvertently at home by a mismanaged iron.

Well into the twentieth century, crisp, dull black, silk mourning "crepes" were woven in the gum and heat-treated with chemicals to produce the characteristic deeply grooved texture.

See also **Fibers; Mourning Dress.**

BIBLIOGRAPHY

Denny, Grace G. *Fabrics*. 4th ed. Chicago: J. B. Lippincott, 1936.

Montgomery, Florence. *Textiles in America*. New York: W. W. Norton and Company, 1984.

Susan W. Greene

CRINOLINE In the mid-nineteenth century, the ideal feminine figure was an hourglass above a broad base of full skirts. Wide skirts, which made the waist look smaller and were thought to give women dignity and grace, were supported by layers of petticoats, some made of crinoline, a stiff fabric woven from horsehair (the name derives from the French *crin*, horsehair, and *lin*, linen). Crinoline, however, was expensive, heavy, crushable, easily soiled, and could not be cleaned. To enable women's skirts to become as immense as fashion desired, a more effective skirt support was needed. Petticoats were distended with cane and whalebone—and even with inflated rubber tubes—but with limited success.

In 1856, a new support was introduced, made of graduated, flexible sprung-steel rings suspended from cloth tapes. The names for these structures included "hoopskirts," "steel skirts," and "skeleton skirts"; they were also called "crinolines," since, confusingly, this term was applied to all skirt expanders, and sometimes referred to as "cage crinolines" or "cages."

Indeed, some have perceived hoopskirts as cages imprisoning women. The hindrance of hoops reflected the ideal, cloistered social role of women of the time, who were, as a male commentator in *Godey's Lady's Book* of August 1865 (p. 265) put it, "unfitted by nature and constitution to move easily or feel in their place in the bustle of crowds and the stir of active out-door life." To many Victorian women, however, hoopskirts promoted "a free and graceful carriage" and were hailed as a blessing. In contrast to numerous hot and heavy petticoats, hoopskirts were lightweight, modest, healthful, economical, and comfortable.

Hoopskirts were a marvel of contemporary technology and manufacturing, with many possible variations in construction. Most hoopskirts were made using tempered sprung steel, which had an incredible ability to return to shape. This was rolled into thin sheets, cut into narrow widths, and then closely covered in cotton tubular braid finished with sizing to give a smooth surface. To make a hoop, a length was cut and the ends secured, usually with a small piece of crimped metal. Graduated hoops were then arranged on a frame in the desired shape and suspended from cotton tapes, secured either by metal studs or put through specially made double-woven pockets in the tapes. At the top, partial hoops left an opening over the stomach so the hoop could be put on and secured by a buckled waistband. The entire hoop weighed a mere eight ounces to less than two pounds.

The large skirt supports of earlier centuries, such as the Elizabethan farthingale and the eighteenth-century pannier, had been the preserve of the upper classes; by the mid-nineteenth century, however, more women could participate in fashion. Middle-class women and even maids and factory girls now sported hoopskirts, although their cheaper versions had twelve or fewer hoops while more expensive models with twenty to forty hoops gave a smoother line. The pretensions of the "lower orders" was one of the many aspects of hoops that inspired caricaturists. Also ridiculed—and exaggerated—was the balloon-like appearance of overdressed ladies in immense hoops and flounced skirts. (At the extreme, hoopskirts could be up to four yards in circumference, although three yards or less was more common.) More risqué cartoons highlighted the tendency of springy hoops to fly up revealingly; for modesty's sake, many respectable women now adopted long loose underpants or drawers.

The demand for hoopskirts was so great that factories flourished across the United States and Europe. *Harper's Weekly* of February 19, 1859 (p. 125) claimed that two New York factories each produced 3,000 to 4,000 hoopskirts per day. As production continued to increase throughout the 1860s, the hoopskirt industry employed thousands, consumed vast quantities of raw materials, and utilized the latest technologies. As numerous patent applications show, great ingenuity was applied to creating improved hoop machinery and specialized features. Advertisements touted the superiority of their products and gave them impressive names, such as "Champion," "Ne Plus Ultra," and one brand named after the fashion icon of the time, the French empress Eugénie.

During the era of the hoop, skirt silhouettes gradually evolved. The dome-shaped skirts of the 1850s gave way to tapered skirts that flared from waist to hem, so supports were correspondingly smaller on top and often had hoops only below the knee. Hoopskirts similarly responded to the fluctuations of fashionable skirt lengths. When the hoop was first introduced, women's skirts touched or nearly touched the ground, but shorter skirts increasingly became the rage in the 1860s, and skirts also began to be looped up over a shortened underskirt for walking, causing what some claimed was an "unseemly display of ankle." In the same period, trained skirts, dragging nine inches or more on the ground, also became increasingly fashionable; by the mid-1860s hoopskirts were specially designed with extra fullness at the bottom back to gracefully support and keep the train away from the feet.

The demise of the hoop skirt was forecast by fashion arbiters from the time of its introduction, yet hoops remained indispensable to most women throughout the 1860s. By the very late 1860s, attention shifted to the back of the skirt and emphasis was on the bustle which now augmented the hoop. As bustles became more pronounced, the hoop was definitively declared out of fashion by the early 1870s. However, even into the 1880s some women wore small hoops—as little as eighteen or even sixteen inches in diameter, which must have been a hindrance when walking—to keep their skirts clear of their legs.

Marvels of technology, industry, and ingenuity, hoopskirts perfectly suited the societal and aesthetic needs of their time. In the November 1861 issue of

Peterson's Magazine (p. 384), one writer went so far as to declare hoopskirts "a permanent institution, which no caprice of fashion will be likely to wholly destroy." While fashion soon belied this prediction, the hoop did enjoy a remarkably long reign, and stands as the defining garment of its era.

In the twentieth century, the hoop skirt was revived under full-skirted evening dresses, or *robes de style*, in the late 1910s and 1920s and, most famously, as nylon net "crinolines" and featherboned hoopskirts supporting bouffant New Look and 1950s fashions. The recurring popularity of hoopskirted looks for romantic occasions such as weddings continues to keep this extremely feminine fashion alive even into the twenty-first century.

See also **Petticoat.**

BIBLIOGRAPHY

Adburgham, Alison. *A Punch History of Manners and Modes, 1841–1940.* London: Hutchison & Co., 1961.

Calzaretta, Bridget. *Crinolineomania: Modern Women in Art.* Exhibition catalogue. Purchase, N.Y.: Neuberger Museum, 1991.

Cunnington, C. Willett. *English Women's Clothing in the Nineteenth Century.* London: Faber and Faber, 1937 (republished New York: Dover Publications, 1990).

Gernsheim, Alison. *Fashion and Reality: 1840–1914.* London: Faber and Faber, 1963 (republished as *Victorian and Edwardian Fashion: A Photographic Survey.* New York: Dover Publications, 1981).

Severa, Joan. *Dressed for the Photographer: Ordinary Americans and Fashion, 1840–1900.* Kent, Ohio: Kent State University Press, 1995.

Waugh, Norah. *Corsets and Crinolines.* New York: Theatre Arts Books, 1954.

H. Kristina Haugland

CROCHET Crochet, from the French for hook, is a form of needlework consisting of a doubly interlooped structure built from a chain foundation. The basic stitch is a simple slip loop yet a multitude of different stitches may be created by varying the number of loops on the hook and the ways in which they are integrated with the structure. Hooks of varying fineness are frequently made of metal, wood, or bone, and common threads used are cotton, wool, silk, or linen. This versatile and potentially rich and complex craft has been practiced by both men and women in many countries. Perhaps the most ubiquitous item of crocheted clothing today is the *kufi* cap, often worn by Muslim men.

Origins and History

Researchers have encountered considerable difficulty finding early examples of crochet, in contrast to woven or knitted artifacts. The textile scholar Lis Paludan has conducted extensive research into the origins of crochet in Europe but has been unable to document its practice before the early 1800s. Yet items of crocheted clothing from India, Pakistan, and Guatemala can be found in museum and private collections; non-European traditions of crochet would seem a promising area for future investigation.

Crochet in Europe seems to have developed independently in two quite different milieus. As with knitting, this technique was used to create insulating woolen clothing for use in inclement climates such as Scandinavia and Scotland, where an early-nineteenth-century version of crochet, known as shepherd's knitting, worked with homemade hooks improvised from spoons or bones. Through wear or design, these items became felted, offering further protection against the elements. Simultaneously, in the more leisured climate of the female drawing room, another form of the craft was developing out of a far older type of needlework called tambouring. Apparently originating in India, Turkey, and Persia, tambouring was executed with a very fine hooked needle inserted into fabric stretched over a frame. The transitional step was to discard the fabric and execute the looped chain stitch "in the air" as it was termed in France.

This latter form of crochet developed in Europe and the United States during the nineteenth century, primarily as a women's activity. Numerous crochet patterns appear in women's magazines of this period, ranging from conventional clothing applications such as collars, bonnets, scarves, blouses, slippers, and baby wear to such fantastical creations as birdcage covers. Museum collections contain a wealth of crocheted purses and bags from the second half of the nineteenth century. Some of the finest are miser's bags, worked with fine colored silks and tiny glass or steel beads. These bags were rounded at both ends or curved at one end and square at the other and had a small opening through which coins would fit.

By the middle of the nineteenth century, patterns for Tunisian crochet began to appear. This was a hybrid knitting/crochet technique capable of producing a firm, stable structure for clothing such as shawls, waistcoats, and children's dresses. The technique was also called Afghan stitch and is still practiced in southeastern Europe, suggesting other geographic avenues for further research into crochet's origins and dissemination.

While crochet was a pursuit of the leisured classes, it was also a cottage industry, providing economic relief in rural areas from the effects of industrialization and displacement. The most famous example of this industry, which produced some outstanding examples of crocheted clothing, was Irish crochet. This fine lacelike form (also called *guipure* lace) probably developed out of an economic imperative to find a cheaper alternative to needlepoint lace and bobbin lace. A variety of floral-like motifs were finely crocheted in cotton over thicker threads, and joined together with fine mesh to produce a lacelike structure often of great intricacy and delicacy. During the potato famine (1845–1850) Irish crochet provided a form of sustenance to hundreds of Irish peasant families. As with many cottage industries of this period, it was organized by upper-class philanthropic women who arranged classes and distribution (through agents) of inexpensive and widely fashionable Irish crochet collars, cuffs, and accessories. Irish crochet's success and dissemination through international exhibition led to its practice as an industry in several European countries such as France, Austria, and Italy, and clothing of Irish crochet was imported into the United States and Canada.

During the first part of the twentieth century interest in crochet waned; the ubiquitous crocheted plant holders and hot water bottle covers, often executed in heavy, coarse yarns, were indicative of a foundering creativity where repetition of form was matched by a decline in technical skill. As might be anticipated, though, the craft revival of the late 1960s and 1970s inspired renewed experimentation. Fiber artists realized that by crocheting in the round, crocheting free-form rather than by working in rows, and building up three-dimensional forms from the surface of the fabric, they could produce elaborate wearable sculpture. The increasing range of alternative yarns and the production of often imaginative and humorous garments led to an appreciation of the art form as a vehicle for self-expression.

At the same time, crochet's perceived status as an undervalued women's activity, and its accumulated associations with amateurism, were countered head-on by the conceptual art movement. Crochet became radicalized. Perhaps its best-known proponent in this field was Robert Kushner, who crocheted clothing to be used as performance art.

Ready-to-Wear and Couture
Unlike knitting, crochet has never become fully mechanized. Hence, it has not been a popular form of construction for ready-to-wear clothing. Discrete crocheted edging sometimes appears on the work of fashion designers best known for their knitwear, such as Adolpho. Otherwise, crochet has been used to great effect as part of the armory of couture techniques. The British design team Body Map has employed it in tongue-in-cheek homage to its "homemade" essence. The Irish designer Lainey Keogh uses knitting and crochet to celebrate a sensuous femininity. Vivienne Westwood has absorbed crochet into her stable of elaborate embellishment techniques and used it with aplomb on her reworkings of historical costume. Jean Paul Gaultier has combined knitting and crochet in ways that celebrate and subvert traditional patterns.

Crochet is an outstandingly versatile technique whose applications have ranged from the most basic utilitarian to haute couture. Over the past two centuries it has cycled in and out of fashion, but its potential for creative experimentation has regenerated attention from those who engage in it as a leisure pursuit, as well as professional designers. Regarding clothing and fashion, its potential for a mass market seems enormous if it were to become more mechanized.

See also **Knitting.**

BIBLIOGRAPHY
Helpful primary sources would include women's journals from the nineteenth century, which contain a wealth of crochet patterns. See, for example, *The Delineator, Harper's Bazaar, Ladies' Home Journal.*

Black, Sandy. *Knitwear in Fashion.* New York: Thames and Hudson, Inc., 2002. Although focusing on knitwear, illustrates application of crochet in contemporary designer fashion.

Boyle, Elizabeth. *The Irish Flowerers.* Belfast, Ireland: Ulster Folk Museum and Institute of Irish Studies and Queen's University, 1971.

Paludan, Lis. *Crochet: History and Technique.* Translated by Marya Zanders and Jean Olsen. Loveland, Colo.: Interweave Press, 1995. Comprehensive review of history of crochet in Europe, with section on technique and reproductions of patterns from the nineteenth century.

Lindsay Shen

CROSS-DRESSING Cross-dressing occurs for religious reasons, for burlesque, disguise, status gain, even for sexual excitement. It is as old as clothing itself. Mythology and history are full of cross-dressing incidents, mainly of men dressing or acting as women. Women cross-dressing and living as men began to appear in the early Christian Church where there are a number of women saints who were found to be women only upon their death. In fact, women living as men seemed to have been more successful at it in the past three centuries than men living as women, perhaps because their motivations were different. Many of them did so to overcome the barriers that women had to face in terms of economic opportunities and independence in the past.

Anthropologists, impressed by the variety of cultures where cross-dressing and gender change have been found, developed the term "supernumerary gender" to describe individuals who adopt the role and many of the customs of the opposite sex. In American Indian culture, for example, men who took on the roles of women were called berdaches. Berdaches took over special ceremonial rites and did some of the work attributed to women, mixing together much of the behavior, dress, and social roles of women with those of men. Often one can gain status by changing gender identification. Among one group of Blackfeet Indians, there are women known as "manly hearts," who have the character traits associated with men and often adopt the male role and clothing. Some groups such as the Navajo identify three, not two, sexes and designate the nonconformist to the third sex. Several identify more than three genders.

Hindu eunuchs. Members of the Sakhībhāva cult emulate women, often to the extent of being castrated, due to their belief that the god Krishnu is the only true male being in the world. © KARAN KAPOOR/CORBIS. REPRODUCED BY PERMISSION.

Male cross-dressing is part of religious worship in different Hindu sects. Sakti worshipers consider the godhead be essentially feminine, and men present themselves in women's costumes. In one Hindu cult, the Sakhībhāva, which holds that the god Krishna is the only true male while every other creature in the world was female, male followers dress like women and affect the behavior, movements, and habits of women, including imitating having a menstrual period. Many of them also emasculate themselves, and play the part of women during sexual intercourse, allowing themselves to be penetrated as an act of devotion. The technical term for these men is *hijra* (eunuch or transvestite). Some observers have called them homosexuals, although it is probably better to regard the role as asexual.

Such androgynous beliefs are not confined to Hinduism but exist in sects of other religions as well. In Islamic Oman, the Xanith are regarded by Oman society as neither male nor female but having the characteristics of both. Though they perform women's tasks, are classed as women, and are judged for beauty by women's standards, technically they do not cross-dress. Instead, they feminize their male costume in every way possible. A Xanith, however, can change her or his status in society by marrying and demonstrating his ability to penetrate a woman.

Because Islam is such a sex-segregated society, and public appearances by women limited, many Islamic areas have tolerated and institutionalized female impersonators. In Egypt one groups is called *khäal* ("dancers"). They perform at weddings and other ceremonial occasions, and though technically their costume is not quite like that of women, they do all they can to appear as women, including plucking out hairs on their face.

Though women's roles were not quite so restricted in the West, there were still strong prohibitions. They could not appear on the stage, for example, and women's roles were taken by female impersonators until the seventeenth century. This was also true in Japan, and in other countries as well, including ancient Greece.

The earliest recorded historical woman to dress and act like a man was Hatshepsut, an Egyptian from about the fifteenth century B.C.E. She is even portrayed in statues and carvings wearing a symbolic royal beard. After her death there was an attempt to obliterate her memory, but her record managed to survive. History, however, is less kind to male rulers who cross-dressed. A good example of this is the Assyrian king Sardanapulus (also known as Ashurbanipal) in the fifth century B.C.E., who is said to have spent much of his time in his palace dressed in women's clothing and surrounded by his concubines. When news of this behavior became widely known, some of his key nobles revolted. Although his cross-dressing was looked down upon because it showed feminine weakness, he fought long and bravely for two years, and before facing defeat, he committed suicide.

Greek literature is full of cross-dressing in both mythological tales and actual events. Greek writers reported that among the Scythians there were groups of individuals known as *Enarées*, who had been cursed with the feminine disease by the god Aphrodite for raiding her temple. Another Greek writer claimed that their cross-dressing was brought on by a temporary impotency caused by spending so much of their time on horseback. Cross-dressing was also part of religious rituals in Greece itself, usually as part of an initiation ceremony emphasizing the essential opposition between the male essence and the female one. Young men at such ceremonies appeared initially in women's clothing and after being initiated into manhood, tossed them aside. Cross-dressing figured prominently in the religious ceremonies associated with the god Dionysus, who according to some legends had been reared as a girl. Other gods and goddesses also required their worshipers to cross-dress at least some of the time. The ubiquity of such festivals might well indicate that the Greek who drew strict lines between sex roles and assigned a restricted role to women, needed periods during which the barriers were removed.

In Sparta, where marriage for men was delayed until they were thirty, men had to live in segregated barracks even after they were married. When they did marry, the young bride (probably a 14-year-old) was dressed in male clothing so that her husband could sneak away and come secretly to her in the night. She was not able to resume her traditional clothing until she had become pregnant, a true sign of womanhood.

Clearly temporary assumption of opposite gender by men was acceptable if the aim was laudable or if the alternatives to the impersonation were considered more socially undesirable than the disguise itself. Hymenaeus, a youth from Argive, disguised himself as a girl to follow the young Athenian maid he loved. Solon is said to have defeated the Megarians by disguising some of his troops as women to infiltrate the enemy forces. Achilles, in order to be protected from potential enemies, was said to have lived the early part of his life as a girl and was finally exposed by Odysseus. The legends are bountiful.

Latin literature, particularly of the imperial period, has a number of stories of cross-dressers. Julius Caesar found a man dressed as a woman at religious ceremonies held in his house who was there to arrange an assignation. The Emperor Nero cross-dressed, and so did the Emperor Elagabalus, who was proclaimed emperor as a fourteen-year-old boy in 218. In both of these cases, however, their cross-dressing was regarded as an indicator of their flawed character.

Christianity was hostile to cross-dressing, as was Judaism from which it derived. But as indicated above, a number of female cross-dressers are known, many of whom became saints. When their true sex was discovered, usually at their death, they were praised for their faithfulness and saintliness, and their ability to rise above female frailties. There were limits, however, on what was acceptable.

A recently discovered Medieval Romance, *Le Roman de Silence*, tells the story of a girl raised as boy in order to preserve the inheritance of her parents. Silence is told by her parents in her early teens that she is really a female; but, though torn by her "feminine desires," she maintains the male role until she is permitted to resume the woman's role by the king. There are other stories as well, but the easiest to document are the male actors who played feminine roles on the stage until they became too old to do so, up to the middle of the seventeenth century. Occasionally a legal case reports a cross-dresser, as did a London city record of a male prostitute who plied his trade as a woman. Even the woman's role in many operas was sung by castrati, a castrated male, until the nineteenth century.

Cross-dressing and impersonation was generally easier for a female to do than a male simply because of the beard problem. This meant that on the stage it was adolescents or young men who usually played the feminine role. Females, for their part, could pass as young men wearing loose clothing until fairly late in their life, and then with a false beard continue to do so. Some young enterprising Dutch girls served as seamen on ships bound for Indonesia, where they settled down. Many women fought as men in most wars and continued to do so until the twentieth century, when pre-induction physicals were established in the American and other armies.

Even the most dedicated transvestite, the Abbé de Choisy (1644–1724), whose memoirs of his life as a woman survive, more or less abandoned his public attempts to pass as a woman as he aged. He continued to cross-dress when the opportunity presented itself, but his identity was no longer a secret. To keep himself entertained he wrote fictional accounts of cross-dressing.

It was in eighteenth-century London where cross-dressing organizations appeared. A number of men's-only clubs were established and some of them became quite notorious. One group, known as the Mohocks, went out at nights regularly seeking lower-class women and girls whom they stood on their heads so that their skirts would fall down, exposing their bare bottoms. Not all clubs of this period, however, were quite so boisterous. One of the more subversive of the male tradition was the Molly club, whose members met in women's clothes to drink and party; Edward Ward, who in 1709 wrote *The Secret History of Clubs*, described their meeting where they dressed as women:

> They adopt all the small vanities natural to the feminine sex to such an extent that they try to speak, walk, chatter, shriek and scold as women do, aping them as well in other aspects. . . . As soon as they arrive, they begin to behave exactly as women do, carrying on light gossip, as is the custom of a merry company of real women. (p. 209)

Whether this club was an organization of homosexuals is not clear, but several historians believe that this was part of an attempt to establish a distinct gay identity.

Certainly there was a growing curiosity about cross-dressing and impersonation in public in both England and France in the eighteenth century. The most notorious cross-dresser was Charles d'Eon, known as the Chevalier d'Eon, who was a member of the personal secret service of the French King Louis XV. D'Eon apparently used his ability to pass as a woman to carry out his spying tasks, and later as he became involved in a struggle with the French government under King Louis XVI, he received a pardon from the King, providing he dressed as a woman that the king believed him to be and lived in exile. When gambling in England over his sex reached a peak, he apparently was involved in a bribery scheme in which two English physicians testified he was a woman, whereby his friends collected some money. For a time he became a sensation in Paris and in London, burlesquing the gestures and mannerisms of women, and when he ran into financial difficulties in England he supported himself by his expertise with the sword. He gave exhibitions and lessons while dressed in proper women's attire. He died in poverty in 1810; as his body was being prepared for burial, he was found to be a male. He might be called the first transvestite to become a media event.

It was not until the last part of the nineteenth century that cross-dressers appeared in ever-increasing numbers. That period in history is when distinctions between male and female domains were strongly entrenched in the upper and middle classes. It was also when there was an increasing emphasis on sports and manliness in these circles. Carried to an extreme, the demands of masculinity could turn to a kind of bullying, as it often did in the English public schools. In America, masculinity, at its worst, was a kind of anti-intellectualism in which music, literature, and all the "finer" things were feminine, and those boys who were interested or excelled in those pursuits were defined by the dominant male group as feminine. Terms such as *queer*, *fag*, *fairy*, or even *girlish* were applied to boys who outwardly seemed to express an interest in anything assigned to the women's sphere. This continued on until the rise of the new wave of feminism in the 1960s. In my own studies of cross-dressers carried out in the 1980s, I found that the male cross-dressers who identified themselves as heterosexual had adopted an almost dichotomized personality in their youth. They were well adjusted outwardly to the male world, but in order to express what they regarded as the feminine side of themselves, they felt a need to cross dress. In this way they could express, even temporarily, some of the feminine qualities they felt they had but then safely return to the masculine identity.

The separate-sphere concept tended to make women less understandable and more mysterious to men; the stricter the separation, the more defined the spheres, the more mysterious women were. One result of this was the fetishization of women's apparel. Women spent a good part of their time trying to better understand men's needs as mothers, caregivers, and teachers, but men, rather than attempting to understand women, objectified and eroticized objects identified with the female, such as underclothes or even outer clothing. In some ways clothing seemed to be the ultimate of being female.

At the same time female clothing was eroticized. The corset is a good example since it was not sold as a waist cincher or form maker but as a preserver of feminine virtue. Corsets also helped rearrange the female figure, emphasizing a narrow waist and resultant hourglass figure that gave prominence to the bust and buttocks. One of the more interesting results of this was the growth of what might be called "corset literature," aimed at a male audience. In this fictional literature adolescent boys are put into corsets to form their figures and to feminize them. In the late nineteenth and first part of the twentieth century, such literature was widespread. Eroticization of clothing was undoubtedly influenced by the fact that so many of the items of women's apparel were designed to emphasize or bring attention to certain aspects of the female figure, from bras to nylon stockings to high heels. High heels, for example, force the wearer to lean backward, thereby accentuating the buttocks and the breasts. Heels also force women to walk with smaller steps emphasizing their supposed helplessness. It was almost as if clothing made the woman. Men wearing it would often get an orgasm.

A number of plays were written in the last part of the century that included plots in which men had to get into women's clothes. Oscar Wilde's *The Importance of Being Earnest* is just one example. There were so many impersonator parts that some men made a career of playing them, including Ernest Boulton and Frederick William Park. They also dressed as women while offstage and were arrested for soliciting men.

Cross-dressing, in fact, had a significant role in the growing gay community. One way they could come together in public was in the masquerade or cross-dressing balls that began to be held in significant numbers in major urban centers in the late nineteenth century and continued through the twentieth. Not all cross-dressers, however, were homosexual and the phenomenon came under serious study by two pioneering sexologists, Havelock Ellis and Magnus Hirschfeld.

Advertisement for cross-dressing club. Though women still impersonate men, for them it is frequently more about the societal freedom than the clothing. With male cross dressers, wearing female clothing is usually an important part of the experience. © RYKOFF COLLECTION/CORBIS. REPRODUCED BY PERMISSION.

Ellis called the phenomenon *eonism*, after the Chevalier, while Hirschfeld coined the term "transvestism." Their pioneering studies were neglected by Americans, particularly Hirschfeld, who was not translated into English until the 1990s. The study of cross-dressing received renewed emphasis through the case of Christine Jorgensen, which received international publicity in 1952. Interestingly, the physician involved in the case called her a transvestite, and only gradually was the phenomenon of transvestism distinguished from transsexualism.

Organized transvestism began in the United States in 1959 through the efforts of Virginia Prince, a Los Angeles resident, who began meeting with a group of fellow transvestites she had met in a Hose and Heels club. She quickly emerged as a spokesperson for what she called heterosexual transvestites, to distinguish them from gay queens and transsexuals. The movement spread rapidly around the world so that there are clubs or groups with a variety of names in the majority of the countries of the world. In the United States there are competing national organizations and a lot of local groups that have no affiliation. Coinciding with this growth was the increase of merchants to supply clothes and accessories to would-be cross-dressers, whether gay, straight, or in between.

Interestingly, many of the cross-dressers in the organized groups dress in the style of clothes that were popular when they were young, almost as if there was an imprinting of what a woman should be. They seem to ignore the freedom that women have in clothing, and few of them for example, wear pants even if they lack a fly. One of the objectives of a significant number of transvestites is to appear in public as a woman without being read. This is the ultimate example of a cross-dresser. It is only the most daring of cross dressers who even belong to the organized groups, and it is estimated that there are hundreds of thousands of secret male cross-dressers who are closeted, keeping their clothes in a special suitcase or drawer, to be pulled out when the opportunity arrives. Often the only public indication of their secret life is in buying clothes, through catalogues or getting literature on the topic. Many have wives or significant others who do not know, although in organized transvestism there are wives and other female support groups to help them cope with the cross-dressing activities of the men in their lives.

Though women still impersonate men, it is not the clothing that interests most of them. With the clothing freedom women have, and the increasing breakdown of barriers to job and other economic opportunities for women, cross-dressing, in the sense that the men involved take part in, is almost nonexistent.

See also **Fashion and Homosexuality; Fashion, Gender and Dress; Politics and Fashion.**

BIBLIOGRAPHY

Allen, Mariette Pathy. *Transformations: Crossdressers and Those Who Love Them.* Boston: Dutton, 1990.

Boyd, Helen. *My Husband Betty.* New York: Thunder Mouth Press, 2003.

Bullough, Vern L., and Bonnie Bullough. *Cross Dressing, Sex, and Gender.* Philadelphia: University of Pennsylvania Press, 1993.

———. *Gender Blending: Transgender Issues in Today's World.* Buffalo, N.Y.: Prometheus Books, 1997.

Docter, Richard. *Transvestites and Transsexuals: Toward a Theory of Cross-Gender Behavior.* New York: Plenum, 1988.

Ellis, Havelock. "Eonism." *Studies in the Psychology of Sex*, vol. 2, part 2. Reprinted New York: Random House, [1906], 1936.

Garber, Marjorie. *Vested Interests: Cross Dressing and Sexual Anxiety.* New York: Routledge, 1997.

Hirschfeld, Magnus. *Transvestites.* Translated by Michael Lombardi-Nash, Preface by Vern L. Bullough. Buffalo: Prometheus Books, 1991.

Vera, Veronica. *Miss Vera's Finishing School for Boys Who Want to Be Girls.* New York: Bantam-Doubleday Dell, 1997.

Ward, Edward. *The Secret History of Clubs.* London: 1709, p. 290.

Vern L. Bullough

CROWNS AND TIARAS Throughout history, men and women of status have adorned their foreheads with various kinds of crowns and tiaras, which symbolized social superiority and power.

The ancient Egyptian pharaohs favored gold headbands that were sometimes decorated with tassels and other ornaments hanging over the forehead, temple, and down to the shoulders. A precious example was discovered in the tomb of Tutankhamun, King of Egypt in ca. 1339–1329 B.C.E. The excavation of his tomb in 1922 revealed the young king's mummy adorned with a gold diadem formed as a circlet. At the front was a detachable gold ornament with the head of a vulture and the body of a cobra, symbolizing the unification of Lower and Upper Egypt.

The origin of the term "diadem" is derived from the Ancient Greek "diadein," which means "to bind around." Diadems were made from all kinds of metal, and with only a limited amount of gold available, Greek craftsmen decorated them with embossed rosettes or other motifs, including the Heracles knot, a reef knot often found in Hellenistic jewelry. After Alexander the Great opened up the gold supply from the Persian Empire in 331 B.C.E., the styles became less austere and diversified into intricate garlands of leaves and flowers.

The Romans expanded on the fashion for gold headbands, adding precious stones to their designs. The first real diadem, a golden band with a raised point at the front, is attributed to the Roman Emperor Gaius Valerius Diocletianus (C.E. 245–313). According to the British historian Edward Gibbon, (1737–1794), "Diocletian's head was encircled by a white fillet set with pearls as a badge of royalty." "Fillet" is another word for a narrow decorated band encircling the hair.

The term tiara, in its original form, describes the high-peaked head decoration worn by Persian kings. It was later adapted as the Pope's headwear with a second and third crown added in the twelfth and thirteenth centuries, thus making up the Papal Triple Crown, which is used at the Vatican on ceremonial occasions.

To decorate the head with flowers or leaves was an ancient custom and signified honor, love, or victory. The Greeks celebrated victory in games by crowning the champions with a wreath made of natural laurel leaves. The Romans continued the tradition, but took it a step further by honoring their victorious generals with wreaths made of real gold, thus metaphorically turning perishable natural foliage into the eternal. While Roman conquerors were honored with golden wreaths of glory, Roman brides wore natural ones, made of flowers and leaves. Dressed in a white tunic and shrouded under a veil, the bride wore a bridal wreath symbolizing purity of body and soul. Lilies symbolized purity; wheat, fertility; rosemary, male virility; and myrtle, long life—metaphors followed by brides over the course of centuries thereafter. Symbolism was quintessential in the design of all ceremonial headwear. Emblems of victory, signs of virginity, or symbols of sufferance, like the crown of thorns placed on the head of Jesus Christ, were to play a part in the formation of religion, literature, and legends.

Tiaras were not popular during medieval times, as the demure fashion of the time dictated that a woman's head and hair should be covered by cone-shaped hats with soft or stiffened veils. The advent of the Renaissance changed social values again, and hair was allowed to assert its natural beauty with elaborate ringlets and waves framing the face. The tresses and curls could be tied back or flowing free and were adorned with a variety of natural or jeweled decorations, some of which came close to a diadem, but did not have the regal, stiff look of a tiara. Titian painted a sensual female lover in *The Three Ages of Men*, wearing a wreath of myrtle symbolic of everlasting love.

French society during Napoleon's reign (1799–1814) was inspired by a passion for classical aesthetics. With it, came a revival of the ancient fashion for diadems.

For his coronation in 1804, Napoleon wore a laurel wreath of golden leaves, each representing one of his victories. Made by the Parisian goldsmith Biennais after a design by the miniaturist Jean-Baptiste Isabay, it is alleged to have cost 8,000 francs. As Napoleon found the wreath too heavy to wear, six leaves were removed just before the coronation.

Napoleon's Roman wreath of victory was plagiarized by society ladies and a new fashion was born. Hairstyles had a new, swept-up classical look, which was perfectly complemented by the Spartan diadem, a high, flat tiara, pointed at the front, embossed in gold and decorated with jewels. Empress Josephine, Napoleon's consort until her divorce in 1809, was painted on several occasions, wearing different Spartan diadems, which were also known as bandeaux.

Napoleon bestowed an even more elaborate and costly diadem to his new Empress, Marie-Louise, Archduchess of Austria. In order to mark the birth of their only son, the King of Rome in 1811, Marie-Louise was presented with a parure of jewels. The most valuable piece was a magnificent Spartan diadem encrusted with 1,500 diamonds, surrounding four large crown-jewel diamonds. The most valuable one at the front was the "Fleur-du-Pecheur," a 25.53 carat stone from the collection of the Sun King's (Louis XIV) dynasty, ousted by the French Revolution. The diadem was designed and made by the Parisian jeweler F.R. Nitot, who charged the Emperor nearly one million francs.

The British Royal Court

While Napoleon was indulging in the purchase of illustrious jewels in France, a succession of Hanoverian Kings in England contented themselves with hiring the jewels for each coronation and leaving the crowns stripped and bare during their reigns. The young Queen Victoria, the niece of George IV, made a decisive change to this practice. She not only ordered a permanent crown to be made, but also started a collection of priceless tiaras, still owned by members of the British Royal Family today.

The nineteenth century also affirmed a trend of bridal purity expressed in dress. In Britain, Queen Victoria preferred a demure wreath of orange blossoms to a golden royal tiara when she married her German cousin, Prince Albert, in 1840. Countless brides followed the style of the romantic young Queen, which was accentuated by a white veil, symbol of virginity and chastity. Queen Victoria, crowned at the age of eighteen, appreciated floral symbolism. Her favorite diamond diadem had motifs of roses, shamrocks, and thistles, symbolizing her sovereignty over England, Ireland, and Scotland. This famous coronation circlet, made by Messr Rundell with hired diamonds in 1820, had belonged to her uncle, King George IV. Victoria had it restored and set permanently with her own diamonds, thus making it one of the most important heirlooms of the British Royal family. The present Queen Elizabeth II is portrayed wearing it on a series of British postage stamps.

The British Royal Collection of Precious Tiaras

The most splendid of all was the brilliant regal tiara especially made for Queen Victoria at the height of her

Hellenistic tiara. Herculean knots, or sailing knots, such as the one seen here, were often incorporated into the diadems of ancient Greece to save gold. © ARALDO DE LUCA/CORBIS. REPRODUCED BY PERMISSION.

reign in 1853. This diamond diadem, made by the royal jeweler Messr Garrard & Co, was to surpass all others in beauty and extravagance. Records in the company's ledger show that over 2,000 precious stones had been used to make this splendid tiara. The gems were set, forming a trellis framework around the central jewel, the most legendary of all diamonds, the Koh-i-noor or "Mountain of Light." This ancient, Indian diamond, weighing 186 carats, had been presented to the Queen by the Honorable East India Company after the Punjab fell under the rule of the British Crown in 1849. The five-thousand-year-old Koh-i-noor diamond was supposed to bring bad luck to all male rulers, but it had no such effect on Queen Victoria or on Queen Elizabeth, the Queen Mother, who had the stone reset into her own crown in 1938.

The regal Indian or opal tiara was also made for Queen Victoria in 1853. This oriental-style tiara was set with 2,600 diamonds surrounding seventeen large opals. Fifty years later, in 1902, Queen Victoria's daughter-in-law, Queen Alexandra, considered opals unlucky and had them replaced with eleven rubies, which had been a Maharajah's gift to her husband, the Prince of Wales, in 1875.

Another noteworthy diadem in the Royal Collection is the Scroll and Collet Spike Tiara, Queen Mary's wedding gift in 1911, affectionately known as "Granny's tiara." Made in 1893, this piece of jewelry has 27 graduating brilliants, all worked into a collet setting and topped by upstanding pearl spikes.

The Tear Drop Tiara is distinguished by its interlacing circles. Acquired by Queen Mary from the Russian

Imperial family in 1921, its large drop pearls, which can be exchanged with emeralds or other precious gems, are surrounded by circles set with diamonds. Queen Elizabeth II inherited this tiara when her grandmother died in 1953 and still wears it on state occasions.

The Hanoverian Fringe Tiara is dated 1830 and was a favorite of Elizabeth the Queen Mother. The brilliants are an heirloom from King George III and were mounted in a special way, so that the tiara could also be worn as a necklace. Princess Elizabeth wore it as a tiara on her wedding to Prince Philip in 1947.

Very similar in style is the Russian Fringe Tiara. Shaped like a Kokoshink (the stiff halo-shaped peasant's headdress of Sythian origin), the tiara was presented to Princess Alexandra by a subscription of ladies of society on her Silver Wedding Jubilee, in 1888.

Queen Elizabeth, the Queen Mother, adored diamonds and pearls as much as Queen Victoria once did. As the young Lady Elizabeth Bowes Lyon, she was often photographed wearing a Bandeau Tiara, worn deep down over her forehead, fitting the 1920s style and fashion. In later years, as Queen Elizabeth, she preferred wearing her tiaras high, embedded in her hairstyle. One of her favorites was the so-called "Modern Tiara," made for her from South African diamonds that had been presented to King Edward VII by de Beers in 1901. This diadem was designed in the form of a complete symmetrical circlet with a fleur-de-lis at the center front. Made by the French jeweler Cartier in 1953, the pattern, with three rows of interlocking diamonds, forming diamond-studded hexagons, is easily recognizable.

Tradition dictated that aristocratic ladies were married wearing their family tiara and Lady Diana, choosing her family's Spencer Tiara, was no exception when she married Prince Charles in 1981. The Queen presented her with another precious diadem as a wedding present, the Bow Knot Tiara, which had been designed for Queen Mary in 1914. Designed by the royal jeweler Garrards of London, it had nineteen drop pearls, each encircled by diamonds. The top edge is decorated with a row of delicate diamond bows, representing lover's knots, a motif first used on rings by the Romans.

Twentieth-Century Tiaras

During the twentieth century, Europe changed into a more egalitarian society, but, curiously, tiaras with their regal allure, survived. The turn of the century was a time of change and experimentation in all art forms, and jewelry was no exception. Art Nouveau and its parallel movement in Britain, called Arts and Crafts, evolved as a reaction to the Industrial Age of the previous century and aimed to restore the importance of individual craftsmanship. The Vienna Secession, founded by Gustav Klimt in 1897, was linked to the Wiener Werkstatten famous for art objects, including Jugendstil tiaras. The inspiration for many pieces of jewelry was based on a new discovery of nature,

expressed in a new, modern style. In Britain, Frederick Partridge (1877–1942), used cow's horn, rock crystals, and enamels for making his highly original and charming tiaras. René Lalique (1860–1945), a leading Parisian designer of jewelry of the same period, broke with traditional conventions of symmetry and designed charming tiaras inspired by trees, shrubs, and insects, using ivory, horn, and cast glass. He pioneered a new technique called *plique à jour*, a development from cloisonné enamel, which allowed transparency on leaves, petals, and insect wings.

Art Nouveau jewelry was prolific in Paris and contributed to the fashion for head ornaments in great diversity. Famous designers included Henri Vever, René Foy, and La Maison Boucheron, who all exhibited exquisite tiaras at the Exposition Universelle in Paris, in 1900. Fantasy was allowed to run wild and some headpieces were crafted in pierced gold lace and enameled peacock feathers. Jewelry and tiaras had attained the status of art rather than function, with many pieces too avant-garde and costly to find a buyer. Sadly, much was later taken apart and did not survive for posterity.

As fashion and couture established their power, many designers used tiaras to instill fantasy into their collections. Coco Chanel designed a whole range of tiaras in 1932 and adorned her models with comets and stars hung over their foreheads. The Duke of Westminster, who was a friend of Chanel, might have been inspired by her when he ordered a diamond tiara from the Maison Lacloche in Paris. It was to be a present to his forth wife, Loelia, who set a new fashion by wearing this precious piece of Art Deco jewelry straight, from ear to ear, framing her face. The design had a strong Chinese influence with a detachable rivière necklace built in at the outer border.

In Britain, the coronation of King George VI in 1937 was a perfect catalyst for the ordering of new tiaras, and Cartier in Paris is said to have created 27 different Art Deco tiaras for this high-society event. The war years and the following decades of youth culture resulted in a decline of regal headdresses, but silver-screen film stars, such as Audrey Hepburn, kept glamour alive. She looked ravishing as a runaway princess wearing a tiara in Billy Wyler's film *Roman Holiday*, filmed in 1953, and again, as Natasha in Tolstoy's epic story *War and Peace*, filmed in 1955.

Ironically, the 1970s Punk rebellion brought tiaras back as fashion designer statements, notably reinvented by Vivienne Westwood, who is said to have been seen wearing her Italian coral diadem, bicycling around London. Westwood used tiaras on her celebrated catwalk shows, recreating ancient Spartan diadems as well as designing brightly colored plastic ones. The most original design, created in 1997 was a diamond-encrusted dog's bone with a bow, which might have been inspired by the love knots of the Victorian era.

Gianni Versace was a designer who celebrated glamour, and tiaras had to be included in his collections. In

1996, he won a de Beers Award with a diamond tiara, which was consequently worn by pop-star Madonna, who like many modern brides, might live their lives in jeans and T-shirts, but chose a regal style of dress for their wedding day.

Philip Treacy, London's top millinery designer, has created a number of modern tiara headpieces using metal, crystals, and feathers in his extravagant creative designs. He seems to be leading a number of artists and craftsmen, who like to express their creativity in tiaras, including Wendy Ramshaw, Jan Mandel, Jan Yager, and Viscount Linley (who, being a high-class carpenter, designed a wooden one). Many spectacular new designs were on show in London's Victoria & Albert Museum, in a special exhibition marking the Golden Jubilee of Queen Elizabeth in 2002.

The fashion of wearing precious tiaras has fluctuated with history and gone in tandem with society's appetite for egalitarianism or elitism, but it has not vanished. The downfall of many European monarchies might have diminished its importance, but curiously, the notion of elitism and the dream of being a princess, even for one day, has continued to seduce generations and the tiara has remained in fashion, in its classical styles as well as in new art forms.

Outward Signs of Kingship

A crown is the most precious and important symbol of royalty. Usually made of solid gold and richly embellished with ornamental jewelry, a crown bestows power and status to kings, queens, and emperors. The basic circular design was derived from the earlier versions of fillets, circlets, and diadems. Some crowns are characterized by arches, which can be topped with a monde, a globular ornament under a "cross formée." Crowns, like diadems and tiaras, were often modified and redesigned for political or economic reasons, and so was the St. Edward's Crown, the oldest of all British crowns, that originated from the ancient Crown of England, dating back to the ninth century. Lined with a "Cap of State" of purple velvet, it weighs four pounds and is set with 440 gemstones. It is part of the collection of British Royal Crown Jewels kept in the Tower of London.

The "Reichskrone," or crown of the Holy Roman Empire, has an important political as well as a religious history. Also known as the Crown of Charlemagne, the legendary King of the Franks, crowned Roman emperor by the Pope in 752, it consists of eight gold plates decorated with precious gems and biblical images. As "Kaiserkrone des heiligen romischen Reiches deutscher Nation," it was in the possession of the Habsburgs from 1273 to 1806 and is still kept in the Imperial Schatzkammer in Vienna, Austria.

A more modern crown is the British Imperial State Crown, made in 1838 for Queen Victoria and worn by each British sovereign since. The gold, jeweled circlet with four arches and topped with a monde and a "cross formée," is encrusted with one of the most valuable diamonds in the world, the Cullinan or "The Second Star of Africa," weighing 309 carats. In her later years, Queen Victoria developed a very personal and less ostentatious style and favored a miniature design of the large Coronation Crown. Perched high on her head with a lace veil draped down over her back, this silhouette of the Queen is the one easily recognized by future generations.

Coronets are smaller crowns worn by the British nobility of lower ranks. The highest and most important coronet belongs to the Prince of Wales, followed by various circlets for different members of the aristocracy. Their shapes and decorations follow a strict hierarchy. A Duke's circlet is adorned with eight strawberry leaves, a Marquess's has four strawberries and four pearls, an Earl's has eight pearled rays, alternating with eight strawberry leaves, a Viscount has sixteen pearls and a Baron has just six pearls. They are only worn on the ceremonial occasion of the coronation of a new sovereign.

See also **Jewelry; Royal and Aristocratic Dress; Wedding Costume.**

BIBLIOGRAPHY

Bury, Shirley. *Jewellery, 1789–1910: The International Era*, Vols. 1 and 2. New York: Antique Collector's Club, 1991.

Menkes, Suzy. *The Royal Jewels*. London: Grafton Books, Collins Publishing Group, 1985.

Munn, Geoffrey. *Tiaras, Past and Present*. London: Victoria & Albert Museum Publications, 2002.

Newman, Harold. *An Illustrated Dictionary of Jewelry*. London: Thames and Hudson, Inc., 1981.

Stopford, Francis. *The Romance of the Jewel*. London: Hudson and Kearns, 1920.

Susie Hopkins

CUFF LINKS AND STUDS A cuff link is a piece of jewelry that inserts into a buttonhole to fasten a shirt cuff around the wrist. Most commonly, cuff links come in pairs and consist of an ornamental head connected to a backing plate by a maneuverable link.

Studs consist of an ornamental head fixed to a protruding pin or knob; front and back connect using a detachable clasp. Akin to buttons, studs can fix permanently to a collar or shirtfront, or can be detached when desired. There are various methods of fastening available. Harold Newman describes five basic forms: the chain link, fastened to each head by a jump ring; the lentoid form, a backing head joined by a fixer bar to the ornamental head; the dumbbell, with one or both heads screwed into a vertical bar; the extension cuff, which conceals a retractable coil, thus allowing the shirtsleeves to rise to the elbow; and the snap lock, a simple press stud. Peter Hinks, as well as Eve Eckstein and Gerald Firkins, provide illustrations of such mechanisms and information regarding original patents.

In the early nineteenth century, cuff links and studs became widely accepted accessories for any gentleman of taste. This emerging fashion paralleled the rise of the lounge suit (which appeared in the 1880s) and the white tailored shirt, which sported a turned-down collar and unfastened cuffs. Previously, men's shirts had stiff upright collars that required minimal fastening; extravagant bows or buttons fastened the cuffs. However, such ornate fashions did give way to uniform formality, this more somber attire required practical and discreet adornment. As such, men's jewelry became restricted to an ensemble of complementary pieces, made up of cuff links, studs, a tie or cravat pin, and buttons. These often came as a set—presented in a box or on a card—they tended to complement a gentleman's signet ring, fob watch, and chain. In essence, chromatic unity was the order of the day.

Initially, cuff links and studs were made of 15 to 18 karat gold; this indicated wealth and did not discolor the shirt. Round, square, or oval in shape, both pieces were often decorated with fine engraving, enamel work, or ivory. Sometimes small gems, pearls, or onyx were placed in the center of the head to add value. However, in the mid-to-latter part of the century, mass production revolutionized manufacture. Due to their simple design, cuff links and studs were perfect for bulk replication. As hand finishing was widely abandoned, 9 karat gold became the metal of choice. Consequently, compromised standards became the norm.

By the late 1800s, Birmingham was the center of all industrial enterprise. However, the production of cuff links and studs also occurred in the colonies, France, and the United States. Firms such as George West, Greaves' Patent, W. E. Riley and Sons, the French F. Moore, and the U.S.-based Baer and Wilde improved fastening technology and competed for a share of the lucrative accessory market. Accordingly, advertisements promoted function and style, longevity, and decorative appeal.

In the late nineteenth century, the Arts and Crafts movement advocated a return to handmade pieces, sparking a revival in the collection of quality items. However, mass production has prevailed and cuff links and studs remain popular unisex gifts. Their ability to convey affiliations and interests endures through the novelty of the ornamental head.

See also **Canes and Walking Sticks; Formal Wear, Men's; Jewelry; Neckties and Neckwear; Watches.**

BIBLIOGRAPHY

Eckstein, Eve, and Gerald Firkins. *Gentlemen's Dress Accessories.* Buckinghamshire, U.K.: Shire Productions Limited, 2000. The original edition was published in 1987.

Hinks, Peter. *Victorian Jewelry: An Illustrated Collection of Exquisite 19th Century Jewelry.* London: Portland House, 1991.

Marshall, Suzanne. *200 Years of American Manufactured Jewelry and Accessories.* Atglen, Pa.: Schiffer Publishing, 2003.

Newman, Harold. *An Illustrated Dictionary of Jewelry.* London: Thames and Hudson, 1981.

Joanne McCallum

CUNNINGTON, C. WILLETT AND PHILLIS

C. Willett (1878–1961) and Phillis (1887–1974) Cunnington were medical doctors with a general practice in North London in the 1930s; they were also major dress historians. C. W. Cunnington served in World War I as a captain in the Royal Army Medical Corps after graduating from Cambridge University. He married Phillis in 1918. The Cunningtons amassed a vast collection of English costume between the 1920s and the late 1940s, which they stored in a big shed in the garden of their house in North London.

Together they published on British dress history from the Middle Ages through the 1950s in their five *Handbooks of English Costume,* their *History of Underclothes,* and their *Dictionary of English Costume,* all published between 1951 and 1960. C. W. Cunnington also published his *English Women's Clothing in the Present Century* in 1952, while three of his earlier books, written between 1941 and 1948, elucidated his own theories about dress, fashion, and sexuality. He died in 1961.

The Cunningtons' famous handbooks mapped the development of styles of male and female dress. Each volume was illustrated with quotes from novels and newspapers of the period in question, and was illustrated by small line drawings as well as photographs of paintings. This approach paralleled and extended the work of German and French dress historians of the period as Oskar Fischel, Max von Boehn, and Maurice Leloir.

C. W. Cunnington's medical training influenced his primary interest, which was the psychological motives that he considered responsible for changes in women's dress styles in the late nineteenth century. Born in 1878, he would have been familiar with the bustles of the 1880s, the S-bend of the early 1900s, and the flat-chested boy-girl fashions of the 1920s. His interest in the psychosexual functions of women's dress had been enhanced by the 1930 publication of the psychiatrist John Carl Flügel's study, *The Psychology of Clothes.* James Laver, who was the Keeper of Prints and Drawings at the Victoria & Albert Museum as well as C. W. Cunnington's friendly rival for the leadership of British dress historiography, also took an erudite but more popular approach to similar themes in his book *Taste and Fashion* (1937).

C. W. Cunnington published five books on psychosexual themes in women's dress. His first was *Feminine Attitudes in the Nineteenth Century* (1935), followed by *English Women's Clothing in the Nineteenth Century* (1937),

Why Women Wear Clothes (1941), and *the Art of English Dress* and *The Perfect Lady* (both 1948). In *Feminine Attitudes* he used the fashionable middle-class Victorian garments he and his wife assiduously collected—which he called his "specimens"—as tools for studying "the psychological background of women," and specifically their sexuality (1935, p. 2). Cunnington added that "we were concerned with mass psychology, not with the psychology of the individual" (Tozer, p. 3).

Cunnington diagnosed "the feminine mind through analysis of a series of 'Attitudes,' ... That is to say those unconscious postures of mind and body which members of a social group will display as features in common." The attitudes that Cunnington listed included "the Conventional Attitude of those multitudes of mute, inglorious females ... who never did or said or thought anything that distinguished them from the mass of women of their day." The "Feminine Attitude," on the other hand, was influenced by the element of "sex attraction," while "the Herd Instinct" was defined as "the wish to imitate in appearance and conduct those in the same social group." Thus Cunnington showed that he shared Flügel's view of the centrality of sexuality as a driving motivation in fashion development among women. For example, he saw the development of the 1870s bustle as inspired by the "mating instinct," whereas that of the 1880s was inspired by the "maternal" instinct. He described the gait of Edwardian women, which he would have seen when he was in his mid-twenties, as "that provocative pelvic roll ... perhaps the most sensual Attitude of the century" (1935, pp. viii, 254, 306).

The first doubts about the accuracy of Cunnington's opinions surfaced among women dress historians in 1949, when Doris Langley Moore wrote that she "had the strongest doubt that fashion . . . is motivated by sex appeal" (p. 21). Nonetheless, C. W. Cunnington's reputation as a leading dress historian and theorist remained in place for a further thirty-seven years. In 1986, however, his work was subjected to a feminist reconsideration led by Jane Tozer, a curator at the Platt Hall, Manchester, Museum of Costume. While acknowledging the value of the Cunningtons' famous handbooks for their details of style chronology, etiquette, and specific nomenclature, Tozer specifically targeted Cunnington's "dated sexism," denouncing it as a "simplistic and now outdated appraisal of the origins of human sexuality." She also questioned Cunnington's anecdotal approach as well as "his notorious vagueness" in naming sources in his books (pp. 11–12). Cunnington's reputation was undoubtedly damaged.

Phillis Cunnington built on this critique, and later developed a more academic approach to dress history. She produced five meticulously researched specialist studies after her husband's death: *English Costume for Sports and Outdoor Recreation* (1969); *Occupational Costume in England* (1967); *Costume for Births, Marriages and Deaths* (1972); *Costume of Household Servants* (1974); and *Charity Costumes of Children, Scholars, Almsfolk, Pensioners*, published posthumously in 1978.

In addition to their published books, the Cunningtons made a major contribution to the study of fashion history through amassing their dress collection. Put together at a time when almost no one was collecting old garments, let alone late nineteenth- and early twentieth-century middle-class clothing, the Cunningtons' collection has since become one of the most renowned in Britain. They sold it to Manchester City Council in 1947 to form the basis of the Museum of Costume at Platt Hall. The museum's first curator was Anne Buck.

The Cunningtons were medical practitioners. They were not professional museum curators and undertook all their research unpaid if not unrewarded. They were interested in finding examples of "ordinary" people's dress to use as general representations of garment types, which C.W Cunnington then related to his typology of feminine attitudes. He had no interest in the owners of individual garments and felt no need to record their names or to provenance sources. Thus much of this information was lost or never recorded. It was left to Anne Buck and to later generations of curators to put this remarkable collection into order.

While C. W. Cunnington's more theoretical comments have not withstood the passage of time, the handbooks he co-authored with his wife as well as Phillis Cunnington's own work still offer a carefully compiled and useful introduction to the history of English costume. Publishing and collecting through the 1930s to the 1970s, at a time when fashion history still had no academic status and very little standing in museums, the Cunningtons educated the next generation of dress historians and curators who professionalized the field.

See also **Clothing, Costume, and Dress; Europe and America: History of Dress (400–1900 C.E.); Fashion, Theories of; Fashion Museums and Collections; Flügel, J. C.**

BIBLIOGRAPHY
Cunnington, C. W. *Feminine Attitudes in the Nineteenth Century.* London: W. Heinemann, Ltd., 1935.

——. *English Women's Clothing in the Nineteenth Century.* London: Faber and Faber, Ltd., 1937.

——. *Why Women Wear Clothes.* London: Faber and Faber, Ltd., 1941.

——. *The Art of English Dress.* London: Collins, 1948.

——. *The Perfect Lady.* London: Max Parrish, 1948.

——. *English Women's Clothing in the Present Century.* London: Faber and Faber, Ltd., 1952.

——. *Looking Over My Shoulder.* London: Faber and Faber, 1961.

Cunnington, C.W., and Phillis. *History of Underclothes.* London: Faber, 1951.

——. *Handbook of English Mediaeval Costume.* London: Faber and Faber, 1952 and 1973.

———. *Handbook of English Costume in the Sixteenth Century.* London: Faber and Faber, 1954 and 1970.

———. *Handbook of English Costume in the Seventeenth Century.* London: Faber and Faber, 1955.

———. *Handbook of English Costume in the Eighteenth Century.* London: Faber and Faber, 1957.

———. *Handbook of English Costume in the Nineteenth Century.* London: Faber and Faber, 1959.

———. *A Dictionary of English Costume: 900–1900.* London: Adam and Charles Black, 1960.

Cunnington, Phillis. *English Costume for Sports and Outdoor Recreation: From the Sixteenth to the Nineteenth Centuries.* London: Adam and Charles Black, 1967.

———. *Occupational Costume in England: From the Eleventh Century to 1914.* London: Adam and Charles Black, 1967.

———. *Costume for Births, Marriages and Deaths.* London: Adam and Charles Black, 1972.

———. *Costume of Household Servants: From the Middle Ages to 1900.* London: Adam and Charles Black, 1974.

———. *Charity Costumes of Children, Scholars, Almsfolk, Pensioners.* London: Adam and Charles Black, 1978.

Jarvis, Anthea. "An Agreeable Change from Ordinary Medical Diagnosis, the Costume Collection of Drs. C. Willett and Phillis Cunnington." *Costume* 33 (1999): 1–11.

Laver, James. *Taste and Fashion from the French Revolution Until Today.* London: George G. Harrap and Company, Ltd., 1937.

Moore, Doris Langley. *The Woman in Fashion.* London: Batsford, 1949.

Taylor, Lou. *Establishing Dress History.* Manchester, U. K.: Manchester University Press, 2004.

Tozer, Jane. "Cunnington's Interpretation of Dress." *Costume* 20: 1–17.

Lou Taylor

CUTTING The Oxford English Dictionary notes that the first recorded reference to the word "tailor" was made in 1297. By that date, guilds for tailoring, weaving, and cloth merchants were well established in Europe.

Boyer (1996) outlines that the Renaissance period saw a change from the loose robe, formed from one or two pieces of fabric draped around the body, to garments that were constructed by methods of cutting and sewing to follow the contour of the human form. This period also witnessed a shift from "homemade" to artisan and craftsman constructed garments. The division of labor in this latter professionalized sphere was divided into that of the cutter and the tailor. The cutter would make a paper pattern and cut the fabric while the tailor would construct the garment using sewing techniques. These craft skills were seen as both art and science and jealously guarded.

The Cutter

There have not been major changes in the process of cutting traditional tailored garments since the sixteenth century. The changes that have occurred have been more related to the mass-customization of tailored garments. There are still Master Tailors working today in Savile Row (London) and other major cities around the world who continue the traditional approach to tailoring methods and skills. It is in this world that the cutter may well advise the customer on their choice of cloth before taking the measurements, with a tape measure, writing down the figuration and style details that will form the worksheet for the finished product.

The cutter will meet the customer again when the garment is ready for the first fitting. The number of fittings can vary. Until relatively late in the twentieth century, it used to be as many as three, but today it is more often one fitting. The cutter "fits" the garment making adjustments using a series of chalk marks as instructions for recutting and for the tailor to follow to achieve a successful, well-fitting set of clothes. The cutter is responsible for producing the pattern, then marking and cutting the fabric. Sometimes an undercutter (striker) or apprentice will assist in this work.

The Process

First the client is measured to access the figure type. Then a pattern is cut in a card or paper. The fabric is laid onto the cutting table and inspected for any defects. The pattern pieces are positioned to ensure economic use of the fabric. The pattern is marked using a white cake of chalk, and then manipulated for any changes in the client's figure. Then the inlays are marked (extra fabric above the seam allowance to allow for future adjustments). The trousers may be drafted directly onto the fabric without using a pattern.

This process could include the use of block patterns. These are a set of patterns previously produced by the cutter for general use across all sizes and adjusted to each client's measurements.

When the marking is complete, the fabric is cut using traditional tailor's shears. When all the parts are cut they are passed to the "trimmer," who will thread mark the seam lines using cotton thread and cut the linings and interlinings. The cut parts are then rolled into a bundle ready for the tailor.

The cutter's tools include: shears, tape measure, chalk, set square (wooden), and a ruler (wooden). There have been some innovations which include a change from a clear-linen to a printed-linen tape measure.

The cut and style of tailored garments are usually unique to the "house" or the company. The cutter will build a reputation for a particular style of cut. Earlier cutting methods involved cutting shapes that were recut after the fitting of the garment and copied onto card or paper to establish a pattern. These patterns were developed into block patterns for future use. This helped to move the process forward without having to return to the start point with each new client and/or garment. A library of patterns would then be built up.

Training

The training of cutters usually followed a particular process: an apprentice would be assigned to a cutter. At first the apprentice would assist by learning to cut the canvases and pocket linings, working alongside the "trimmer." The apprentice would assist the cutter with spreading and checking the fabric prior to marking. This would include sharpening the chalk and having the tools ready for the cutter. Other elements would include the "fetching and carrying" to assist the cutter.

Gradually the apprentice would learn skills and become an undercutter. At this stage the apprentice would be present when the client was measured to learn this procedure. The apprentice would eventually acquire his own clients and develop his own cutting style This process would traditionally take approximately five years. Before the twelfth century until the mid-1800s, apprenticeships lasted seven years. Later on apprentice served five years followed by two years as an improver.

Cutting Systems

The taking and recording of measurements is still under the ownership of the cutter and is often closely guarded. Before the mid-1800s the cutter usually used a plain white linen tape onto which he would write using hieroglyphics to keep the exact nature of the measurements and figuration strictly to himself. It has been recorded that other methods of measuring using leather, parchment, and paper (Wampen 1863) was used by early cutters. The introduction of the printed tape measure was an important step forward, which, along with more accurate pattern cutting, allowed for the sharing of information.

The system of cutting from direct measurements and adding tolerances (for example, half chest measure plus 2½ inches) continued until the mid-1800s. Cutting became more scientific from the early 1800s with publications, which included *The True Principles of Scientific Cutting* (Good, 1842). In his book *Mathematical Instruction Constructing Modes and Draping the Human Figure*, Wampen (1863) uses "anthropometry" as the basis for his measuring system and makes references to "proportional measure" for the cutting instructions. The written instructions follow an alphabetic code identifying body points as A, B, C, etc., and uses formulas, such as $B'=3u+u=4u$, rather than direct measurements. Reference is made by Humphreys (*Coat Cutting*, 1881) to using scales based on half the chest measure. He refers to "Graduation Tapes," available from the "Tailor and Cutter" for cutting different sizes of garments. When the scale is used as a basis for cutting a jacket, it is based on half the chest measure—36 chest is an 18 scale. Differ-

ent body proportions are then calculated using the scale rather than taking a direct measurement.

The jacket as it is known today developed from the 1860s with the changes in lifestyle and transport. The lounge style of jacket developed in the early 1900s and an example is by the Tailor and Cutter Academy in the book by Vincent (*The Tailor and Cutter Academy Systems of Cutting Part 11*). The topics covered include the lounge jacket, use of the graduation square, figuration (shoulders, stance, etc.), riding jacket, and boy's lounge. The Tailor and Cutter Academy were prolific in publications for the subject areas. This included a series named *The Cutters' Practical Guide*, available in both full and pocket-sized editions.

Pattern Technology

Pattern and garment engineering developed in the 1960s and has had an impact on the made-to-measure tailoring sector. The cutting systems are focused on the made-to-measure and mass-customization sectors of the menswear industry rather than the traditional tailoring sector.

Numerical cutting systems exist to draft patterns and cut directly onto fabric using laser, water jet, and mechanical (vertical and circular) cutting heads. These cutting methods are used and combined with traditional tailoring methods by the larger tailoring manufacturers.

The use of body scanning for both size surveys and cutting made-to-measure garments has developed during the 1990s, and research is ongoing with a number of industrial and academic collaborators. The process includes full-body scanning, recording information that builds the basis for individualized pattern construction. The linkage through CAD/CAM systems extends into cutting systems and interfaces with sewing systems for the assembly of custom garments.

See also **Tailoring.**

BIBLIOGRAPHY

Aldrich, Winifred. *Metric Pattern Cutting for Menswear*. Oxford: Blackwell Science, 1980.

———. *Metric Pattern Cutting for Menswear: Including Unisex Clothes and Computer Aided Design*. 3rd ed. Oxford: Blackwell Science, 1997.

American Fashion Company, *American Garment Cutter*. 3d ed., 1914.

Good, T. *The True Principles of Scientific Cutting*, London 1842.

Humphreys, T. D. *Coat Cutting*. London: John Williamson, 1881.

Modern Tailor, The. *Outfitter and Clothier*, 1936.

Modern Tailor, The. *Outfitter and Clothier*. AA. Whife, London: Caxton, 1950.

Morris, F.R. *Pocket Edition of the Cutters' Practical Guide, Part One*. London: Tailor and Cutter, 1947.

The Tailor and Cutter, April 20th 1876.

Vincent, W.D.F. *The Tailor and Cutter Academy Systems of Cutting Part 11.* London: John Williamson, 1908.

Wampen, H. *Mathematical Instruction in Constructing Modes and Draping the Human Figure.* London: Messrs Boone, 1863.

The West End System of Cutting, 1895.

Internet Resource

Boyer, Bruce G. *The History of Tailoring: An Overview.* 1996. Available from <http://www.lone-star.net/mall/literature/tailor4.htm>.

Alan Cannon Jones

DAHL-WOLFE, LOUISE

Louise Dahl-Wolfe (1895–1989) was born in San Francisco. Aspiring to a career as a painter, she attended the California School of Design (now the San Francisco Art Institute), where she was greatly influenced by Rudolph Schaefer, known for his color expertise.

Dahl-Wolfe's Early Career

After completing her studies, Dahl-Wolfe designed electric signs from 1921 to 1923; in 1924 she began working for a leading decorator. In 1921 she was invited to the studio of photographer Anne Brigman; this meeting prompted her to buy her first camera, an Eastman bellows camera with a reflector made from a Ghirardelli chocolate box. She used her mother as the subject of her first pictures. Early photographic adventures included taking shots of herself and some friends nude on a beach, using the soft-focus style of her mentor. After Dahl-Wolfe befriended another San Francisco photographer, Consuela Kanaga, who taught her to use a 3¼-by-4¼-inch Thornton-Pickard English reflex camera with a Verito soft-focus lens, the two traveled together to Europe in 1927. While in Paris, Dahl-Wolfe bought a Pathé camera; in Germany she purchased a small film pack camera. On an excursion to Africa, she met Meyer (Mike) Wolfe, an artist from Tennessee, whom she subsequently married.

Dahl-Wolfe returned to San Francisco in 1928 and began taking commercial black-and-white photographs. Two years later, she and her husband spent a summer in a rented log cabin in the Great Smoky Mountains of Tennessee, where she began photographing still-life subjects and the local mountain people. She developed her film with a darkroom light powered by the battery of a Model A Ford. After moving with her husband to New York, Dahl-Wolfe was introduced to Frank Crowninshield, then editor of *Vanity Fair*, who decided to publish her work. The documentary pictures of her Tennessee subjects were a sensation when they first appeared in the November 1933 issue of *Vanity Fair*. This success led to the publication of her first black-and-white fashion work in *Harper's Bazaar* in 1936 and her first color work a year later.

Dahl-Wolfe's Work in Color

Dahl-Wolfe was one of the first and most important practitioners of fashion photography in color. Kodachrome film came on the market for the first time in 1935, although the product at that time could not reproduce colors reliably either in the studio or in natural light. A striking aspect of Dahl-Wolfe's work was her color sensibility—a flawless instinct for combinations of colors. This emphasis on the painterly values of tone, line, and color is not surprising, since she had been trained as a painter and strongly influenced by the philosopher of art Clive Bell's theory of significant form. Bell maintained that color is an inherent part of the expressive quality of form and that arrangements of colors carry emotional weight—particularly bright luminous colors, which have a pleasing effect. Dahl-Wolfe's early training in color theory with the painter Rudolph Schaefer also influenced her interest in color photography. In order to achieve the exact effects she desired, she worked with the new eight-inch by ten-inch sheets of Kodachrome because they gave the highest degree of resolution and detail. She often consulted with the printers of the magazines she worked for in order to retain her subtly beautiful effects on the printed page.

Many of Dahl-Wolfe's photographs seem to be built up of colored planes rather than objects. Many of her shots for *Harper's Bazaar* are masterly combinations of compositional lighting, varied textures, repeated patterns, and a broad variety of shades, particularly earth-tone colors. For example, a simple black-and-white suit is seen through a darkened archway leading into a room of exotic warmth; in the room the model is the focal point within the mix of textures, patterns, and colors. The same natural light, here bounced through various screened patterns, is seen in another picture, where it filters through the organdy curtains in a room of lovely femininity and charm. The setting of this photograph was Louise Dahl-Wolfe's own bedroom in her home in Frenchtown, New Jersey, one of her favorite shooting locations. In addition to her pioneering use of color, she was also one of the first fashion photographers to make use of location shots, using architectural backgrounds and exotic locales to add interest to the way the clothing was pictured.

Dahl-Wolfe's Importance

Dahl-Wolfe's style—elegant yet casual, sophisticated yet at ease—was ideally suited for depicting the independent American woman, wearing comfortable ready-to-wear styles by such American designers as Claire McCardell, Hattie Carnegie, and Norman Norell. Both the models and the clothes had a naturalness and authenticity that conveyed a cool and comfortable yet ineffably chic informality. This informality is perhaps the essence of Dahl-Wolfe's style: The models, the clothes, and the way she chose to portray them reflected the relaxed accessibility of a distinctly American fashion sense.

Dahl-Wolfe had a long and productive career as a fashion photographer. She worked for *Harper's Bazaar* for twenty-two years, from 1936 to 1958, leaving shortly after the magazine's editor Carmel Snow and its legendary art director Alexey Brodovitch resigned. Her career included eighty-six *Harper's* covers and over six thousand color photographs as well as thousands of black-and-white pictures. After leaving *Harper's Bazaar*, Dahl-Wolfe worked briefly for *Vogue* before finally retiring from professional photography in 1960.

See also **Fashion Magazines; Fashion Photography; McCardell, Claire; Norell, Norman; Vogue; Vreeland, Diana.**

BIBLIOGRAPHY

Bellafante, Ginia. "What Dahl-Wolfe's Eye Created in a Lens." *New York Times*, 6 June 2000.

Dahl-Wolfe, Louise. *Louise Dahl-Wolfe: A Photographer's Scrapbook.* Preface by Frances McFadden. New York: St. Martin's Press, 1984.

Goldberg, Vicki, and Nan Richardson. *Louise Dahl-Wolfe: A Retrospective.* Foreword by Dorothy Twining Globus. New York: Harry N. Abrams, 2000.

Hall-Duncan, Nancy. *The History of Fashion Photography.* New York: Alpine Book Company, 1979.

Nancy Hall-Duncan

Josephine Baker in banana costume. Baker's revealing dance costumes caused much scandal and controversy, but her style also served as an inspiration for designers of mainstream fashion. HULTON ARCHIVE/GETTY IMAGES. REPRODUCED BY PERMISSION.

DAMASK. *See* **Weave, Jacquard.**

DANCE AND FASHION The roots of the relationship between Western dance and fashion lay in the Renaissance period, where social dancing reflected the values of society. Dance as a channel of communication was as important as having the appropriate costume for socializing. After the French Revolution in 1789, professional ballet dancers left the Court spectacles in favor of the stage. From the beginning of the nineteenth century, the European ball culture emerged as a social activity and had an enormous impact on fashion and vice versa.

The Waltz Century

The nineteenth century was dedicated to the waltz, which had developed as a bourgeois activity in Europe and America. In *May I Have the Pleasure?*, Belinda Quirey argues that in the wake of political, romantic, and industrial revolutions, the waltz was a completely new dance

form that perfectly suited the new conditions of modern life—socially, psychologically, and materially. These nineteenth-century developments in dance were reflected in elaborate dance costumes for lower- and middle-class women, although upper-class ballroom-dance dresses were distinctively splendorous for women. The *danse à deux* activity reinforced the pleasure of watching other people: how they harmonized and what they wore. Ballroom fashion was therefore an enormously important component of acceptance by polite society.

Tango Craze

Modern ballroom dancing began just before World War I, when dance halls flourished in Europe. The Hammersmith Palais de Danse in London was among the first popular dance halls that provided an up-to-date program for modern ballroom dancing. Although the polka and the quadrille still remained very popular dance forms before the outbreak of World War I, the tango craze started and the fox-trot also became very fashionable. The origins of the tango lie in turn-of-the century Argentina and

ETIQUETTE HINTS FOR THE BALLROOM: DRESSED TO IMPRESS

Hillgrove's *Complete Practical Guide to the Art of Dancing* (1863) offers a vivid description of the importance of dress in the European ball culture:

> Ladies should remember that men look to the effect of dress in setting off the figure and countenance of a lady, rather than to its cost. Few men form estimates of the value of ladies' dress. This is subject for female criticism. Beauty of person and elegance of manners in woman will always command more admiration from the other sex than costliness of clothing.

In another chapter, Hillgrove recommends that on entering a ballroom, all thought of self should be dismissed: "The pretty ambition of endeavoring to create a sensation by either dress, loud talking, or unusual behavior, is to be condemned." Not only the dress was important; society ladies had to take care of a fashionable hairstyle as well. In 1860, Florence Hartley recommends in *The Ladies' Book of Etiquette, and Manual of Politeness* that "one has to be very careful, when dressing for a ball, that the hair is firmly fastened, and the coiffure properly adjusted. Nothing is more annoying that to have the hair loosen or the headdress fall off in a crowded ballroom." Accessories played a key role in fashionable dressing for social ballroom events. Henry P. Willis advises in *Etiquette, and the Usages of Society* (1860) that "ladies should draw on their gloves (white or yellow) in the dressing room, and they should not have them off for one moment in the dancing rooms. However, at supper the gloves can be taken off, because "nothing is more preposterous than to eat in gloves."

emerged among European and African immigrants. Since earlier dances did not have the close body contact of the tango, this new dance was considered very risqué at the time. With its sensual rhythm and intense body contact, the tango had a distinctly sexual connotation. In fact, the tango was at first deemed so illicit that it was thought suitable only for prostitutes and their pimps. However, when the tango was legitimized and came to Europe, it was soon taken up by Parisian high society, and ballroom fashion had to be adapted to this new "sexual" dance form. Dance costumes were designed to be more tight-fitting and embellished with shiny paillettes and stones. Soon the tango dress style spread from cabarets and theaters to evening fashion. At the beginning of the twenty-first century, the cinema industry has picked up the tango fashion in scenes of cult films such as *Moulin Rouge*.

Josephine Baker: A Black Pearl

In her 1920s' performances in "barely there" dresses, Josephine Baker shocked Parisian society with her display of naked skin. In the following decade, she became famous not only for her style of performing but also for her stage costumes: her elaborate headdresses and banana costume received standing ovations at the Folies Bergère. Although her look was considered vulgar, her dresses served as a source of inspiration for fashion in the 1920s and 1930s. Josephine Baker gave shape to a new culture, which liberalized fashion and dance to a new era of evening dresses.

Hollywood Screen Dancing

In the late 1920s, screen dancing became popular, and Hollywood style spread from the screen to day and evening fashion. The lightweight Charleston dress, with its long fringes, became part of the Roaring Twenties lifestyle. Anne Massey describes in *Hollywood Beyond the Screen* that the films *Our Dancing Daughters* in 1928, and *Our Modern Maidens* in 1929, represent the debut of the art deco style reflected in architecture and fashion. In the 1930s, Fred Astaire and Ginger Rogers were the source of inspiration for fashion-oriented cineastes in movies such as *Top Hat* (1935), and *Swing Time* (1936). The Hollywood culture and its concept of glamour advanced the Americanization of dance culture, which in turn influenced the fashion scene. During the harrowing Great Depression, dance marathons, with their emphasis on nonstop endurance for the entertainment of the masses, became popular in social dance clubs. Fashion companies advertised at these events to promote club fashion.

Lindy Hop: Swinging Parties

In 1926, the Lindy hop craze started at the Savoy ballroom in Harlem, New York. In the early 1930s, high society was interested in seeing Lindy hop performers entertain at parties. The resulting swing-dance fashion became popular: cotton blouses with fitted waists and puffed sleeves combined with an A-line skirt—sometimes with detachable suspenders to give maximum hold—for female Lindy hoppers, and high-waisted pants with matching fitted vests for their male counterparts. The Savoy style spread quickly over to Europe, and the Lindy hop and its fashions were adopted by the London and Parisian elites.

Broadway Dreams

In the 1940s, the evolution of dance on film had a crucial influence on the whole world of dance. The predominantly working-class audience was getting real Hollywood value for little money in the cinemas of the 1940s. Those who could afford musical theaters enjoyed the pleasure of live performances on Broadway. With the advent of television in the 1950s and movie theater attendance drastically down, financially strapped Hollywood studios turned to film adaptations of successful Broadway shows, as this was a more economical option than developing original screenplays. Film makeup and clothes of Broadway shows had a strong influence on everyday fashion. Department stores such as Bullocks in Los Angeles became the place where both Los Angeles inhabitants and foreign visitors bought their musical dance–inspired wardrobe. Later on, such Broadway shows as *West Side Story* (1957), a modern-day retelling of *Romeo & Juliet*, had a lasting influence on the American teenager, who copied the Broadway look.

From Rock and Roll to Saturday Night Fever

In the 1950s, the postwar generation brought a new form of dance into the nightclubs. Rock and roll—derived from African American rhythm and blues—and stars such as Elvis Presley and Bill Haley immortalized the image of the rebellious teenager and also influenced fashion and hairstyles well into the 1960s. Social dance moved away from couple dancing, and new freedom was expressed in checked shirts and tight-fitting denim jeans for young men, while teenage girls wore petticoats and backcombed their hair. By the end of the 1960s, a particular dance form no longer existed, and young people moved their bodies to the music in whatever way they wanted. The disco scene emerged and exerted a crucial influence on the fashion world. DJs combined records, encouraging dancers to stay on the floor for a long period. Fashion designers took advantage of the *en vogue* disco style and immortalized dance film stars such as John Travolta in *Saturday Night Fever* (1977). His white disco suit in the movie acquired iconic status, establishing disco as part of mainstream culture until the 1980s, when the public had lost its interest in it, and punk and new wave style challenged its dominance.

Street Style: Hip-hop, Break-Dancing, and Techno

In the early 1980s, hip-hop culture gained a mass appeal when black and Hispanic DJs evolved the use of backbeats in New York City and Los Angeles clubs. Break dancing and hip-hip were very athletic styles, often mimicking robotic movements, and therefore required a more casual clothing style. Sport brands such as Adidas, Nike, and Puma flourished among street-style dancers. During the following decade, the house music style developed from hip-hip and brought alive a new generation of club culture, and club fashion became less casual. In the late 1980s, the rave scene emerged. Rave represented more than a dance party; it illustrated a physical and mental state, unifying the club dancers. Melissa Harrison's *High Society: The Real Voices of Club Culture* offers a detailed description of the rave phenomena. Rave accessories such as glow-in-the dark-jewelery and clothing with utility bags became very important.

As Seen on Screen: Music Video Style

In the mid-1980s, music stars such as Michael Jackson and Madonna based their performances on dance, and revolutionized the power of music videos. In concept, music videos were based on song, choreography, special effects, and fashion, which was widely copied among club-goers. With the emergence of boy bands, girl bands, and teenage music groups at the beginning of the 1990s and their promotion through videos, a new generation was influenced by the music stars. Mainstream fashion was strongly influenced by performers such as Backstreet Boys, Spice Girls, Take That, Britney Spears, and Justin Timberlake, who pioneered and set up fashion trends, such as tank tops, low-cut jeans, very conspicuous and ostentatious gold jewelry for both male and female teenagers, and "visible" underwear for girls. At the start of the twenty-first century, music performers created a mixture between club style and contemporary dance while using the medium of fashion to create a celebrity style, which became an essential part of the music and dance industry.

See also **Dance Costume; Film and Fashion; Music and Fashion; Theatrical Costume.**

BIBLIOGRAPHY

Dodd, Craig. *The Performing World of the Dancer.* London: Breslich & Foss, 1981.

Driver, Ian. *A Century of Dance: A Hundred Years of Musical Movement, from Waltz to Hip Hop.* London: Hamlyn Octopus Publishing Group Ltd., 2000.

Jonas, Gerald. *Dancing—The Power of Dance Around the World.* BBC Books: London, 1992.

Harrison, Melissa. *High Society: The Real Voices of Club Culture.* London: Judy Piatkus Ltd., 1998.

Hartley, Florence. *The Ladies' Book of Etiquette, and Manual of Politeness.* Boston: 1860.

Hillgrove, Thomas. *A Complete Practical Guide to the Art of Dancing.* New York: Dick & Fitzgerald, 1863.

Massey, Anne. *Hollywood beyond the Screen: Design and Material Culture.* London and New York: Berg Publisher, 2001.

Silvester, Victor. *Modern Ballroom Dancing.* London: Stanley Paul & Co. Ltd., 1993.

Quirey, Belina. *May I Have the Pleasure?: The Story of Popular Dancing.* British Broadcasting Corporation: London, 1976.

Willis, Henry P. *Etiquette, and the Usages of Society.* New York: Dick & Fitzgerald, 1860.

Thomas Hecht

DANCE COSTUME The relationship between dance and dance costumes is complex and does not simply reflect dance practice in a specific period, but also social behavior and cultural values. Dance costumes can be divided into the following categories: historical, folk or traditional, ballroom, modern, and musical dance costumes. Influence has spread from fashion to dance and back again.

Historical Dance Costumes

From the fifteenth to the eighteenth century, festivities at European courts required highly elaborate dance costumes. The style of court dance costumes tended to be similar to everyday dress of the period, incorporating, for example, laced corsets, puffed and slashed sleeves, farthingales with skirts and applied decoration. In the early twenty-first century, the reproduction of historical dance costumes was evident in the activities of historical dance organizations, such as the Institute for Historical Dance Practice (IHDP) in Ghent, Belgium.

Folk-Dance Costumes

From the fifteenth century onward, folk dance developed steadily in Europe. The field of European folk-dance costumes is very complex, as each of the country's regions has its own dances, dress, and customs. Eastern European folk dances, such as czardas, mazurkas, and polkas, soon spread to England and France. Folk-dance costumes re-flected the East European look in the use of bright colors on dark backgrounds. Costumes were often highly decorated with beads, metal, and silk threads. The basic women's dress was a short, light-colored chemise and a petticoat, over which several layers of fabric were worn. A draped headdress indicated the marital status of the wearer (fancy headgear indicated that the girl was unmarried). European folk dance formed the basis for square-dance activities. European settlers who came to America introduced this special type of country dance and its costume first in New England, but before long, square dance started to spread across the country. Evening dress was the standard outfit for dancers: ankle-length hooped skirts for the women and formal jackets for men. During the following two centuries, the cultural mix of European settlers in America has led to a variety of national folk-dance costumes. Farmer and cowboy dance wear were mainly based on components of everyday clothing: shirts, cotton trousers, and cowboy boots for men, and ankle-long cotton gingham dresses for women. The minuet, polka, waltz, and quadrille via France and England brought more elaborated dance costumes to America: tailored long-sleeve shirts and trousers in a Western-cut style for male dancers and full floral-embroidered skirts

Dancers in unitards. These one-piece garments are typically made from spandex or a similar stretchy, pliable fabric, giving the dancer nearly unlimited range of motion. © Julie Lemberger/Corbis. Reproduced by permission.

and blouses for females. Accessories such as Western belts, string ties, or silk kerchiefs completed the square-dance outfit.

In the late 1990s, high-end designers such as Dolce & Gabbana, Roberto Cavalli, and Miu Miu had created an "urban cowboy look" with Western-inspired dress embellished with floral patterns on such articles of clothing as tuxedo shirts and jeans, as well as traditional pointed-toe cowboy boots.

In the early 2000s, amateur and professional female square dancers often wear double-swirl skirts with alternating ruffles in the fabric and wide white lace. The lace is used on bodice and sleeves, and an appliqué and bow are sewn on the fitted midriff. Male square dancers wear cowboy-style shirts with scarf tied around the collar, high-pocket jeans, and sometimes a cowboy hat. Pants cuffs are usually worn inside the cowboy boots. The United Square Dancers of America (USDA) booklet, *Square Dance Attire*, is probably the best resource for the history of square-dance costumes.

Belly-Dance Costumes

Oriental, or belly, dance originates from snakelike movements provided by the sisters of a woman giving birth as they tried to inspire her to deliver the baby. In 1893, belly dance was brought from the Arabic world to the United States on the occasion of the Chicago World's Fair. Exotic-colored fabrics embroidered with semiprecious stones, paillettes, and beads are characteristic of the style. Semitransparent tops with fringes reveal the stomach and navel while brassieres and wraparound skirts swing rhythmically to the beat of Middle Eastern music. Coin belts and hip scarves are an essential part of the belly-dance outfit. Sometimes belly dancers cover their face with a veil, especially when the dance is performed by a male dancer (cross-dressing). Alternatively, shoulder-to-floor-length beaded and sequinned tunics over harem pantaloons are worn. Historically, evidence points to the crucial influence of Islamic Orientalism in European fashion during the twentieth century, starting with the French designer Paul Poiret's use of the tunic shape and updating old-fashioned styles with exotic harem pants and veils wrapped around the body in the 1920s. In the 1990s, the prêt-à-porter and haute couture collections of Western European and American designers, such as Miguel Adrover, Jean Paul Gaultier, John Galliano, Alexander McQueen, and Rifat Ozbek, have been influenced by Oriental belly-dance costumes. Nancy Lindis-

Greek folk dancers. While traditional Greek costumes vary from island to island, some similarities can be found, such as basic construction, the use of certain fabrics, and head coverings such as those seen here. © GAIL MOONEY/CORBIS. REPRODUCED BY PERMISSION.

PROFESSIONAL AND AMATEUR BALLROOM DRESS

Tango dress:

Usually one piece with a tight-fitting top and a swinging bottom slit high to reveal the leg. Stretch materials are used to guarantee a tight silhouette. The dance dress is often highly decorated with rhinestones, beadings, glitter and paillettes.

Swing and Latin dress:

Very similar to tango dresses, but the much shorter hemline makes the dress more sexual and can reveal the complete leg. Animal prints such as tiger or leopard intensify the wild connotation of these dresses.

Waltz and fox-trot dress:

Elegant one-piece dress often made in expensive lightweight silks or satins. A wide-swinging, ankle-length style intensifies the soft movements of these dances.

Charleston dress:

The necessary freedom of movement was guaranteed by knee-length shirt-dresses embroidered with glass beads and paillettes. The light weight of the dress and long fringes made it swing rhythmically according to the movements of the dance, which was part of the lifestyle of the Roaring Twenties and became the most popular

American dance in Germany and Europe; thanks in great part to Josephine Baker, who gave performances in 1927 with her Charleston Jazz Band in Berlin.

Polka and mazurka dress:

Folkloric traditional dress with colorful print design and usually a peasant blouse and a wraparound skirt embellished with opulent frills and garlands. During the 1970s, peasant blouses became very fashionable in everyday clothing, and high-end designers such as Emilio Pucci designed ethnic-style garments with embroideries and frills. Floral peasant blouses with soft ruffled hems had a revival in the late 1990s when designer brands such as Yves Saint Laurent, Dolce & Gabbana, Moschino, and Christian Dior created a folkloric fashion theme.

Rumba and samba dress:

With contrasting ruffles on the skirt and sleeves, this dress is often designed in a Caribbean style with bright colors.

Cha-cha dress:

A two-piece dress with a tight-fitting top and a wide off-the-shoulder neckline, while the skirt is full and flounced at the bottom. Rhinestones are usually attached to the fabric to give a glamorous effect.

---

farne-Tapper's *Languages of Dress in the Middle East* is a detailed source about Middle Eastern dress in both the ancient and the modern world.

Ballroom-Dance Costumes

From the early nineteenth century, ballroom dances were taken up by a broad public, and special evening dresses were designed to fit these occasions. The waltz, fox-trot, polka, mazurka, and Viennese waltz required an elegant style. By the twentieth century, dance costumes for the tango, swing and Latin, Charleston, rumba, bolero, cha-cha, mambo, and samba were more erotic.

Modern-Dance Costumes

At the beginning of the twentieth century, Isadora Duncan's natural movements on stage characterized a new era for dance. Duncan's modern dance style has been influenced by Greek art, folk dances, social dances, and athleticism. Free-flowing costumes and loose hair permitted a great freedom of dance movement. After World War I, modern-dance groups emerged with predominantly female dancers. During the following decades, avant-garde choreographers, such as George Balanchine and Martha

Graham, and later Merce Cunningham, Paul Taylor, Alvin Ailey, and Pina Bausch, reformed and liberalized traditional dance and its costumes. Moving away from traditional ballet techniques, modern dance gave rise to a new era of costuming. Costumes and makeup took on a unisex look as choreographers felt it less relevant to differentiate female and male dancers. Theater designers experimented with seminude costumes: transparent T-shirts and short black trunks for men and simple bodices and plain tights for women were the standard outfits.

In 1934, neoclassical dance choreographer George Balanchine was the first to dress ballet dancers in rehearsal practice clothes for public performances. The use of noncolors characterized Balanchine's costumes, which were almost always black and white. His sense for minimalism on the stage developed through the revealing of nudity.

Martha Graham was one of the first to promote dance without pointe shoes on stage. In *Diversion of Angels* (1948), she dressed female dancers in draperies, and men were almost naked. Isamu Noguchi–inspired special crowns and hat pins by Graham became particularly famous as part of the modern-dance costume. Newly invented cuts made skirts and dance dress appear like trousers, permitting a great freedom of movement. At the beginning, Graham's dances were performed on a bare stage, which underlined the minimalism she demonstrated in the costumes. Later on, she also replaced the traditional ballet tunics of male dancers and the folk dress and tutus of female dancers with straight, often dark and long shirts or rehearsal leotards. Awarded the Medal of Freedom in October 1976, Martha Graham was the first dancer to receive that distinction.

In the 1950s, costumes of Balanchine- and Graham-oriented contemporary dance choreographers, such as Merce Cunningham and Paul Taylor, tended to continue an emphasis on the seminude style, though prints on leotards personalized the individual contemporary dance style and its costumes. In 1958, the artist Robert Rauschenberg created shiny silky tights speckled with rainbow dots for Cunningham's *Summerspace*. The designs of choreographer and costume designer Alwin Nikolais influenced the contemporary stage with performances such as *Noumenon Mobilus* (1953) and *Imago* (1963).

Musical-Dance Costumes

Evidence of musical theatres date to the eighteenth century when two forms of this song-and-dance performance emerged in Britain, France, and Germany: ballad operas, such as John Gay's *The Beggar's Opera* (1728), and later on comic operas, such as Michael Balfe's *The Bohemian Girl* (1843). At this time, many plays had short runs, and

MEN IN TIGHTS: THE MALE DANCER

In Russia, male dancers are highly regarded, and usually classical ballet training is the basis for a career in dance. Though a growing interest in dance exists among boys in other countries, many are too shy to take dance lessons and be obliged to wear tights, commonly considered a female article of clothing. Therefore, certain dance schools allow young male students to practice in T-shirts and short pants. Under the practice clothes, dancers usually wear suspensories, designed to isolate and support the testicles. Alternatively, a dance belt, specialized underwear, can be worn under tights. In both cases, the pouch in front is triangular, tight, and nearly flat to give support and form during dance moves. The subject of masculinity in dance has received popular treatment in such movies as *The Children of Theatre Street* (1977) and *Billy Elliot* (2000). Ramsay Burt's book *The Male Dancer* explores the subject of masculinity in dance in greater depth.

TAP-DANCE SHOES: FAMOUS SOUNDS

The origins of tap dance, a style of American theatrical dance with percussive footwork, lie in slave dances in the southern states that incorporated African movement and rhythm into European jigs and reels in the early nineteenth century. Tap dance was adopted in theaters from 1840, and clogging in leather-soled shoes became more and more popular. At the fin-de-siècle, turn of the century, two different styles of tap-dance shoes had been established: stiff wooden-sole shoes, also called buck-and-wing, made popular by the duo Jimmy Doyle and Harland Dixon, and soft leather-sole shoes popularized by George Primrose. In the 1920s, metal plates (taps) had been attached to leather-sole shoes, which made a loud sharp sound on the floor. In the 1940s and 1950s, dancers such as Fred Astaire, Paul Draper, and Gene Kelly popularized tap shoes to a wider audience through the medium of Hollywood films.

stage costumes were often based on everyday-dress design. In the late 1880s, comic operas conquered Broadway in New York, and plays, including *Robin Hood*, were designed for popular audiences. From the 1880s until the 1920s, the musical-comedy genre in London emerged, and designers such as Lady Duff-Gordon, known as Lucile, elaborated fashionable costumes for singers and dancers. In the early 1920s, tap-dance techniques were popularized and specially designed tap-dance shoes were available on the open market.

In the fifties, musicals such as *My Fair Lady* (1956) surprised the audiences with numerous costume changes. Costume designer Cecil Beaton had created costumes enhancing the transformation of Eliza, the main character, from a common flower vendor into a society lady. In 1975, Michael Bennett's *A Chorus Line* opened on Broadway, and aerobic and dance outfits became popular on stage and in everyday life. Bright neon shades in pink, green, and yellow dominated the range of colors. Dance tights, leggings, headbands, and wristlets spread from stage to fashion and vice versa. In 1988, the musical *Fame*, inspired by the movie and TV series, opened in London and reflected the fashion of the eighties, showing leotards and shorts. At the beginning of the twenty-first century, A. R. Rahman's Bollywood musical *Bombay Dreams* (2002) opened in London, and its Indian costumes demonstrated the ethnic influence on stage design.

See also **Dance and Fashion; Ballet Costume; Music and Fashion; Theatrical Costume.**

BIBLIOGRAPHY

Balasescu, Alexandre. "Tehran Chic: Islamic Head Scarves, Fashion Designers and New Geographies of Modernity." *Fashion Theory* 7 (2003): 1.

Buonaventura, Wendy, and Ibrahim Farrah. *Serpent of the Nile: Women and Dance in the Arab World.* Northampton, Mass.: Interlink Publishing Group, 1994.

Burt, Ramsay. *The Male Dancer: Bodies, Spectacle, Sexualities.* London and New York: Routledge, 1995.

Carter, Alexandra. *The Routledge Dance Studies Reader.* London and New York: Routledge, 1998.

Dodd, Craig. *The Performing World of the Dancer.* London: Breslich & Foss, 1981.

Lindisfarne-Tapper, Nancy, and Bruce Ingham. *Languages of Dress in the Middle East.* Surrey: Curzon, 1997.

Strong, Roy, Richard Buckle, and Ivor Guest. *Designing for the Dancer.* London: Elron Press Ltd., 1981.

Internet Resources

Education Committee of the United Square Dancers of America, Inc. *USDA Booklet B-018.* USDA Publications, 1997. Available from <http://www.usda.org>.

Institute for Historical Dance Practise (IHDP) 2004. Available from <http://www.historicaldance.com>.

Thomas Hecht

DANDYISM Walter Benjamin, in his treatise *Charles Baudelaire*, writes: "The dandy is a creation of the English" (p. 96). If dandyism, the style and the practice, is a uniquely English construct, it was the French who defined it in prose and poetry. The French author Jules Barbey D'Aurevilly, in his 1845 essay "Du dandysme et de George Brummell," described it as a nationally characteristic mode of vanity combined with "the force of [an] English originality . . . as profound as her national spirit." The dandy's dandy, George Bryan "Beau" Brummell, captured in the turn of his cuff and the knot of his cravat the studied irony and languor that defined his age. At the height of his popularity, from 1799 to 1810, Brummell, the son of a minor nobleman, held the entire British aristocracy in his sway. Attracted to no one particular feature of character (Brummell was neither great poet nor eminent thinker), his admirers were ostensibly captivated by his urbane sangfroid and impeccable dress, a clever and consummately constructed package that aimed to "astonish rather than to please" (Walden, p. 52). Essentially Brummell's philosophical stance was to stand for nothing in particular, a posturing that aptly crystallized the uncertainty of a period that witnessed the decline of aristocracy and the early rise of democratic politics. Sartorially, he refined a mode of dress that adopted English country style in a renunciation of the affectations of Francophile fashion (ironically so, if one considers that these very fripperies have become so linked to the dandyism of contemporary imagination). As the dress historian James Laver, writing in 1968,

points out, "whatever else it was, [dandyism] was the repudiation of fine feathers" (p. 10).

If Brummell was considered oppositional, it was in the privileging of this country clothing for wholly urban pursuits. Not an innovator (Thomas Coke of Norfolk was the first of the nobility to present himself in court in "sporting" attire over half a century previously), Brummell merely encapsulated and reflected back to society the sentiments of the times. In the early 1800s, the "sporting costume" of the English nobility reflected the increase in time spent supervising their estates; a top hat and tails in sober tones, linen cravats, breeches, and sturdy riding boots were a uniform of practicality and prudence. That Brummell appropriated this style for promenading through London's arcades and holding court at one of the many gentlemen's clubs of which he was a member served a dual purpose—suggesting the validity of entertainment as the "occupation" of the leisured classes while eradicating any immediate visible difference in status between himself and the "working" man.

In his recorded witticisms and his style, Brummell appeared to contemplate no distinction other than taste. His preoccupation with pose and appearance was derided as the last gasp of aristocratic decadence, but in many ways he anticipated the modern era—a world of social mobility in which taste was privileged above birth and wealth. Elevated as a style icon, he presaged the contemporary dominance of fashion and celebrity; clothing is as powerful a tool now as it was two hundred years ago for conveying new social and economic directions. Dedicated to perfection in dress (his lengthy toilette was legendary) and the immaculate presentation of his body, Brummell's total control over his image finds its legacy in twenty-first-century masculine dress styles.

Dandyism in France

Dandyism was a potent cocktail that swiftly endeared itself to England's European neighbor, France (and much later to Russia), privileging a love of beauty in material goods while appearing to nod to the revolutionary sentiment of the times. Most notable of France's dandies was the young Alfred Guillaume Gabriel, count d'Orsay. Only a teenager when dandyism first crossed the seas to Paris, d'Orsay's sartorial power had risen to Brummellian heights by 1845.

Unlike Brummell, however, d'Orsay's pursuit of dandyism was a search for personal fulfillment rather than social power. Already powerful by token of birth, d'Orsay's legacy was of dandyism as fashion plate, and he became known as the original "butterfly dandy." There was also none of Brummell's austerity; the French imagination had already mixed dandyism with English romanticism, as evidenced in d'Orsay's more sensual, lavish, and luxurious approach to dress—silk replaced linen, curves replaced stricter lines, gold for silver. That much of France's dandy traditions grew from literary interpretation

J. BARBEY D'AUREVILLY

Illustration of French author Jules Barbey d'Aureyville. D'Aureyville was a major force in defining dandyism in a positive way, placing more emphasis on the dandy's intellectual pursuits and bohemian spirit than on his clothing. © LEONARD DE SALVA/CORBIS. REPRODUCED BY PERMISSION.

is important in the context of the development of dandyism into a moral and artistic philosophy.

Dandy Philosophy

Defining dandyism is a complex task, and few writers have done so more successfully than Lord Edward Bulwer-Lytton in his treatise on the dandy of 1828, *Pelham; or, The Adventures of a Gentleman*. Considered at the time to be a manual for the practice of dandyism, it amply demonstrates the growing link between the promotion of the self and promotion through the social ranks. Notable maxims include: "III: Always remember that you dress to fascinate others, not yourself," and "XXIII: He who esteems trifles for themselves is a trifler—he who esteems them for the conclusions to be drawn from them, or the advantage to which they can be put, is a philosopher" (pp. 180–182).

That Bulwer-Lytton associates dandy practice with philosophy was concordant with later literary movements such as Barbey D'Aurevilly's toward enshrining dandyism as intellectual pose rather than fashionable consumption. More immediately, however, *Pelham* inspired a Victorian backlash against dandyism that was to define the 1830s. At around the same time as d'Orsay reached the peak of his influence, back in England William Makepeace Thackeray was releasing the serial of his novel *Vanity Fair*, at the venerable age of thirty-six. Thackeray had contributed significantly to the Victorian approbation of dandyism in the 1830s, epitomized by the views expressed in Thomas Carlyle's *Sartor Resartus* [The tailor retailored] (1838). Thackeray's regular columns and later novels, *Vanity Fair* and *The History of Pendennis*, were vivid representations of the moral and religiously driven belief that dandyism was a shallow and louche behavioral deficiency but they ironically were informed by his association with, and enjoyment of, the company of dandies such as d'Orsay.

It was the French, in particular D'Aurevilly, that were to define dandyism, through literature, as a positive practice and "robust moral philosophy" (Breward, p. 3). D'Aurevilly's *Du dandyisme et de Georges Brummell* had a profound influence on all the texts, British and French, that followed it. Although D'Aurevilly never met Brummell, he formed an intimate friendship with Guillaume-Stanislas Trébutien, a scholar and native of Caen, the provincial French town to which Brummell escaped following his indebtedness and ultimate disgrace in the English court. Trébutien met and befriended William Jesse, a young officer who had in turn met Brummell at a social event in Caen and was impressed with Brummell's "superlative taste." Jesse's accounts of Brummell, relayed to D'Aurevilly through Trébutien, were to form the basis of D'Aurevilly's text. Jesse was to broaden D'Aurevilly's already significant knowledge of dandyism, Regency literature, and the history of the Restoration, which formed the background to the practice by introducing him to more obscure texts that would never have

reached the shores of France. D'Aurevilly was a little known author and poet prior to *Dandyisme* and found it hard to find a journal willing to publish his text. Consequently he and Trébutien decided to publish it themselves, further driven by the notion that a book on dandyism should be, anyway, an "eccentric, rare and precious" (Moers, p. 261) object.

D'Aurevilly, for the first time, celebrated dandyism and dedication to pose as a distinction. Dress, while important, was relegated to second place behind D'Aurevilly's emphasis on the "*intellectual* quality" of Brummell's position. As Ellen Moers points out in her seminal text *The Dandy*, "Barbey's originality is to make dandyism available as an intellectual pose. The dandy is equated with the artist; society thus ought to pay him tribute. Brummell is indeed the archetype of all artists, for his art was one with his life" (p. 263).

The understanding of dandyism as an artistic presentation of the body related to the single-minded pursuit of bohemian individuality was developed thoroughly in the writings of Charles Baudelaire. Baudelaire was not that interested in Brummell, but more in the modernity, as he saw it, of the ideas that he expressed. Baudelaire saw in Brummell's dandyism the elevation of the trivial to a position of principle that perfectly mirrored, and offered an ideal framework for, his own beliefs. Baudelaire and D'Aurevilly maintained close contact through the 1850s and 1860s, exchanging letters, books and ideas about the practice. It was primarily through D'Aurevilly's writings that Baudelaire's bohemian dandy philosophy was made clear, although Baudelaire's one essay on the subject *Le peintre de la vie moderne* later came to define Baudelaire's approach to the subject. As Moers suggests, D'Aurevilly's text on Brummell was so definitive as to liberate Baudelaire to "reach for the Dandy whole, as a symbol in the poetic sense" (p. 276).

Baudelaire's view of dandyism as an "aristocracy superiority of [the] mind . . . [a] burning desire to create a personal form of originality" (Benjamin, p. 420), was taken up by the Aesthetic movement as a righteous crusade, a veneration of beauty and abhorrence of vulgarity that was defined by the Oxbridge scholar Walter Pater and, later, the decadent aestheticism of Oscar Wilde. Wilde's earlier interpretation of dandyism took little from Brummell's original aesthetic, influenced as his style was by the material tactility and medieval styling of the period (he later threw off the aesthetic-inspired costume in favor of a more somber style). What appealed to Wilde was the idea of beauty and perfection as expressed through the body and dress—the cultivation of the person as an art form that Baudelaire had crystallized in *La vie moderne*. Like Brummell (and Honoré Balzac, the Victorian-era dandy Benjamin Disraeli, and the Parisian aesthete Count Robert de Montesquiou-Fezensac), Wilde promoted himself and his work through the presentation of his public body and quickly rose to the top of Britain's social circle as a result. The era of decadence was the apogee of dandy performance in a world that was increasingly dominated by "advertising, publicity and showmanship," in front of a far greater audience than Brummell could ever or would have wished to envisage. Wilde's performed individuality and flamboyant costume were shackled to his desire for notoriety.

Like other notable dandies of the period, Aubrey Beardsley, Max Beerbohm, and James McNeill Whistler, Wilde also looked upon dandyism as a refuge from and bulwark against the burgeoning democracy of the times (although the dandyism of the fin de siècle was fueled by new money in a way that the Regency elitists would have decried). Although Wilde believed, hoped, that aestheticism would prevail, he was perhaps more accurate with his comment that London society was "made up of dowdies and dandies—The men are all dowdies and the women are all dandies."

The Female Dandy

The emergence of the female dandy was to coincide with the downfall of Oscar Wilde. In Joe Lucchesi's essay "The Dandy in Me," he cites the American artists Georgia O'Keeffe and Romaine Brooks as notable female dandies of the period along with Brooks's London-based circle of friends—in particular the aristocrat Lady Troubridge, the British artist "Peter" Gluck, and the writer Radclyffe Hall. By the 1900s, dandyism had reached New York, with O'Keeffe and her circle drawing on Baudelaire's dandy philosophy "to make of oneself something original" (Fillin-Yeh, p. 131). Certainly Brooks's adoption of the dandy code was conscious; she noted that "'They [her admirers in her London circle] like the dandy in me and are in no way interested in my inner self or value'" (Fillin-Yeh, p. 153).

Brooks's dandyism was bound up in her lesbian sexuality. The sartorial lexicon of dandy practice offered these women a model for negotiating a social position for themselves that shared signifiers with the dress of the modern woman. Joe Lucchesi writes that "lesbians adopted the signifying dress of the modern woman as a way of expressing their sexuality yet also linking it to a similar but less dangerous figure" (Fillin-Yeh, p. 173).

As Virginia Woolf was to note in *A Room of One's Own* (1929), the woman's position within the sphere of cultural production was still difficult to carve out in what was a male-dominated community. It seems to be no coincidence that Woolf's shape-shifting *Orlando* ultimately takes on masculine form in the character's twentieth-century incarnation. Baudelaire had suggested that lesbians were the "heroines of modernism . . . an erotic ideal . . . who bespeaks hardness and mannishness" (Benjamin, p. 90), and for Brooks and her circle, there was a direct link between the invisibility of the female artist and the invisibility of female homosexuality. The figure of the dandy, certainly following Wilde, united concerns of the self as art form, the feminized homosexual, and the position of the individual within the urban environment.

Inspired by her compatriot and friend James McNeill Whistler, Brooks's dress shared many similarities with his (and de Montesquiou-Fezensac's) gentlemanly elegance and refined creativity. Although the fashions of Brooks's portraits were already thirty years out of date for men, they emerged in parallel with the notion of the modern, heterosexual woman and the modernity of Gabrielle "Coco" Chanel. Masculine dress, within the fashion arena, served to emphasize the sexualized and idealized female physique in the same way that it had always done for the male body. In addition, it offered a means for women like Chanel, who went from country girl to courtesan to milliner to designer to affect a revolution in their social status and representation. Drawing inspiration from masculine, aristocratic sporting clothing, Chanel understood as deftly as Brummell its practical and social value. As Rhonda K. Garelick writes, "By casting off the complicated frill of women's clothing and replacing them with solid colours, simple stripes and straight lines, Chanel added great visual 'speed' to the female form, while granting an increased actual speed to women who could move about more easily than before" (Fillin-Yeh, p. 41).

Contemporary Dandies

The figure of the dandy provides an abundance of material for the subversive and frequently ironic interventions that have come to be associated with British cultural production. Throughout the twentieth century, periods of acute social upheaval have witnessed parallel and intense bursts of dandy behavior. Masculine consumption, and the relationship of material goods to class and status, have played an important role for social and cultural arrivistes from Noel Coward and Cecil Beaton in the 1920s and 1930s to the publisher Tyler Brûlé and the designer Ozwald Boateng in the 1990s. "And," as writer George Walden suggests, "English sensitivities are acutely alive to anything to do with social nuance, whether accent, posture, conduct or clothes" (Walden, p. 29).

The desires of Regency dandyism were amply catered for by a plethora of specialist boutiques that had grown up in and around the streets of London's Mayfair and Piccadilly. The tailors; breeches, boot, and glove makers; milliners; and perfumiers that vied to tend to the immaculate bodies of their dandy customers were sandwiched between numerous specialists catering to the refined tastes of their client's stomach, interior décor, and cultural entertainment and welfare. The consumerism of the Regency dandy makes him a particularly analogous figure to the contemporary British dandies of the late twentieth and twenty-first centuries. Moving beyond the golden triangle to Carnaby Street in the 1960s, and latterly Islington, Spitalfields, and Hoxton Square, the sites of dandy consumption are, for the most part, reassuringly familiar—small, select boutiques, elite tailors, exquisite restaurants and bars, exclusive members clubs, artisan publishers, and celebrity delicatessens still dominate the dandy landscape.

In the twenty-first century, the steady spread of globalization, of branded culture, is once again providing fertile ground for the emergence of the contemporary dandy. The figure of the dandy presents a sartorial and behavioral precedent that allows for the celebration of beauty in material culture while cultivating an aura of superiority to it, and the early twenty-first century has seen a resurgence of interest in the traditional purveyors of material status. London's Savile Row is increasingly populated by filmmakers, recording artists, visual artists, and designers, joining the existing ranks of the traditional British gentleman who is these tailors' staple client. At the same time, brands such as Burberry, Aquascutum, and Pringle, who have traded for decades on their status as suppliers of quality and standing, have seen their customer profile alter to include an international audience in search of distinction as well as a more specific sartorial subculture closer to home—the Terrace Casual.

The early 1980s Casual project was vehemently patriotic. Forays into Europe in the early 1980s showed Britain's football fans in stark contrast to their Italian and French counterparts whose immaculate dress prompted a revolution in British working-class style that saw the football fan become the principle consumer of mostly European luxury sporting brands. Today's Terrace Casual springs from similar terrain. What separates him from his forebears is that the garments he favors are principally British, the upper-class sporting pursuits which with they are associated redolent of the masculine camaraderie and corporeal engagement of club life favored by Brummell and his circle. As with Brummell, the Terrace Casual style is engaged in the positioning of traditional upper-class "country" style in the urban environment, coopting it for the pursuit of leisure rather than the management of rural estates. While adopting the trappings of aristocracy disrupts perceived social status, it acts as a celebration rather than rejection of all the mores and moralities that these garments imply.

Oscar Wilde once said, "One should either be a work of art, or wear a work of art," and Hoxton style is the ultimate expression of the "music/fashion/art" triumvirate that characterizes British street style in the twenty-first century. As Christopher Breward writes, "D'Aurevilly's dandy incorporated a spirit of aggressively bohemian individualism that first inspired Charles Baudelaire and then Joris-Karl Huysmans in their poetic celebrations of a sublime artificiality. . . . It is possible to see this trajectory leading forward through the decadent work of Walter Pater and Oscar Wilde to inform . . . . twentieth century notions of existential 'cool'" (Breward 2003 p. 3). While Wilde's bohemian decadence runs like a seam through the Bloomsbury set; the glam-rock outrage and rebelliousness of Jimi Hendrix, Mick Jagger, and David Bowie; the performativity of Leigh Bowery and Boy George; and the embodiment of life as art in Quentin Crisp, it is the Hoxton Dandy, as epitomized by the singer Jarvis Cocker, who presents an equally subversive contemporary figure. Originality is as crucial for the Hoxton Dandy as it was for Brummell and Hoxton Square, once a bleak, principally industrial quarter of East London, now at the heart of a trajectory of British bohemianism that began in Soho in Brummell's time. Hoxton has quickly become a hub of new media/graphic/furniture/fashion design style that embraces its gritty urban history of manufacturing. Artisan clothing has often drawn upon dress types more usually associated with the workingman in order to emphasize the masculinity of artistic pursuit, the physical labor involved in its production. This is no less true of the Hoxton style, which is rooted in a flamboyant urban camouflage—a mix of military iconography, "peasant" staples, and industrial work wear, made from high-performance fabrics whose functionality always far outweighs their purpose.

In his time, the modernity of Brummell's monochromatic style marked him out in opposition to more decadent European fashion and made him a hero to writers such as Baudelaire. Modernism in the twentieth century continued to struggle to establish itself as a positive choice in British design culture, yet the periods of flirtation with clean lines and somber formality were intense and passionate, a momentary reprieve from the ludic sensibilities British designers more commonly entertained. The early British Modernists of the 1950s sought to emulate the socially mobile elements of American society. Stylistically, they drew inspiration from the sleek, sharp, and minimal suit favored by the avant-garde musicians of the East Coast jazz movement. Philosophically, early mods saw themselves as "citizens of the world" (Polhemus 1994 p. 51), a world in which it only mattered where you were going, not from where you came. In 2003 clean lines and muted colors once more afforded relief from the riot and parody of postmodernism that had dominated British fashion since the emergence of Vivienne Westwood and, latterly, John Galliano. The Neo-Modernist style draws, as it did in Brummell's day, on established sartorial traditions but subverts them through materials (denim for suits, shirting fabrics for linings), form (tighter, sharper, and leaner than the norm) and, ultimately, function.

Brummell was, in fact, almost puritanical in his approach to style. Max Beerbohm wrote in the mid-twentieth century of "'the utter simplicity of [Brummell's] attire' and 'his fine scorn for accessories,'" which has led contemporary commentators such as Walden to note that "Brummell's idea of sartorial elegance, never showy, became increasingly conservative and restrained" (Walden, p. 28). Aesthetically, British gentlemanly style is the closest to Brummellian dandyism. As in previous centuries, the gentleman is defined by class and by his relationship to property (rural and urban). This easy, natural association reflects the apparent effortlessness of dress, manners, and social standing. Gentlemanly dress is loaded with expressive, but never ostentatious, clues; as Brummell suggested, "If [the common man] should turn . . . to look at you, you are not too well dressed; but neither too stiff, too tight or too fashionable." Brummell's refusal of finery for a more practical costume can be seen in the contemporary confinement of his own style of cravat, frock coat, and highly polished boots to special-occasion wear. In this, the early twenty-first-century gentlemanly uniform of gray or navy suit, black lace-up shoe, white shirt, and modestly colorful tie more than nods to Brummell's stylistic approach.

See also **Benjamin, Walter; Brummell, George (Beau); Europe and America: History of Dress (400–1900 C.E.); Fashion, Historical Studies of; Fashion and Identity; Wilde, Oscar.**

BIBLIOGRAPHY

Balzac, Honoré de. *Sur le dandysme. Traité de la vie élégante. Par Balzac. Du dandysme et de George Brummell par Barbey D'Aurevilly. La peinture de la vie moderne par Baudelaire. Précédé de Du délire et du rien par Roger Kempf.* Paris: Union générale d'Edition, 1971.

Barbey d'Aurevilly, Jules. In *Du dandysme et de George Brummell.* Edited by Marie-Christine Natta. France: Plein Chant, 1989.

Benjamin, Walter. *Charles Baudelaire: A Lyric Poet in the Era of High Capitalism.* Translated by Harry Zohn. New Left Books, 1973. Reprint, London: Verso, 1997.

Breward, Christopher. *The Hidden Consumer.* Manchester, U.K.: Manchester University Press, 1999.

———. "21st Century Dandy: The Legacy of Beau Brummell." In *21st Century Dandy.* Edited by Alice Cicolini. London: British Council, 2003.

Bruzzi, Stella, and Pamela Church Gibson, eds. *Fashion Cultures.* London: Routledge, 2000.

Evans, Caroline, and Mina Thornton, eds. *Women and Fashion.* London: Quartet, 1989.

Fillin-Yeh, Susan, ed. *Dandies: Fashion and Finesse in Art and Culture.* New York: New York University Press, 2001.

Garelick, Rhonda. *Rising Star: Dandyism, Gender, and Performance in the Fin de Siècle.* Princeton, N.J.: Princeton University Press, 1998.

Laver, James. *Dandies.* London: Weidenfeld and Nicolson, 1968.

Lucchesi, Joe. "The Dandy in Me." In *Dandies: Fashion and Finesse in Art and Culture.* Edited by Susan Fillin-Yeh. New York: New York University Press, 2001.

Lytton, Edward Bulwer. *Pelham; or, Adventures of a Gentleman.* London and New York: G. Routledge and Sons, 1828.

Mason, Phillip. *The English Gentleman: The Rise and Fall of an Ideal.* London: Deutsch, 1982.

Moers, Ellen. *The Dandy: Brummell to Beerbohm.* London: Secker and Warburg, 1960.

Polhemus, Ted. *Street Style.* London: Thames and Hudson, Inc., 1994.

Walden, George. *Who's a Dandy?* London: Gibson Square Press, 2002. Includes a translation of Jules Barbey D'Aurevilly's "Du dandysme et de George Brummell." 1845.

Alice Cicolini

DASHIKI A dashiki is a loose-fitting, pullover shirt usually sewn from colorful, African-inspired cotton prints or from solid color fabrics, often with patch pockets and embroidery at the neckline and cuffs. The dashiki appeared on the American fashion scene during the 1960s when embraced by the black pride and white counterculture movements. "Dashiki" is a loanword from the West African Yoruba term *danshiki*, which refers to a short, sleeveless tunic worn by men. The Yoruba borrowed the word from the Hausa *dan ciki* (literally "underneath"), which refers to a short tunic worn by males under larger robes. The Yoruba *danshiki*, a work garment, was originally sewn from hand-woven strip cloth. It has deep-cut armholes with pockets below and four gussets set to create a flare at the hem. Similar tunics found in Dogon burial caves in Mali date to the twelfth and thirteenth centuries (Bolland). In many parts of West Africa today such tunics of hand- or machine-woven textiles (with or without sleeves and gussets) are worn with matching trousers as street clothes. In the 1960s, the dashiki appeared in the American ethnic fashion inventory, along with other Afrocentric clothing styles, possibly from the example of African students and African diplomats at the United Nations in New York (Neves 1966). A unisex garment, the American dashiki varies from a sleeveless tunic to the more common pullover shirt or caftan with short or dangling bat sleeves. Both sexes wear the shirt, and women wear short or full-length dashiki dresses.

Dashiki as American Fashion

In the United States the term "dashiki" entered American English circa 1968 (*Merriam-Webster's Collegiate Dictionary* 2000). Following the Civil Rights Act of 1964, the popularity of Afrocentric clothing grew along with pride in racial and cultural heritage among Americans of African descent. First worn as an indicator of black unity and pride, the dashiki peaked in popularity when white counterculture hippies, who "set the tone for much of the fashion of the late sixties" (Connikie, p. 22), included the colorful shirts and dresses in their wardrobes. The aesthetics of mainstream male fashion shifted toward the ethnic, men began to "emulate the peacock," and the dashiki became trendy by the end of the 1960s. Worn by increasing numbers of young white Americans attracted to the bright colors and ornate embroidery, the dashiki lost much of its black political identity and epitomized the larger scene of changing American society. By the late 1960s, American retailers imported cheap dashikis manufactured in India, Bangladesh, and Thailand. Most of these loose-fitting shirts and caftans were sewn from cotton "kanga" prints, a bordered rectangle printed with symmetrical bold colorful designs, often with central motifs. Kanga prints were introduced in the nineteenth century by Indian and Portuguese traders to East Africa, where in the early twenty-first century women still wore them as wrappers (Hilger, p. 44). Contemporary kanga, manufactured in Kenya and Tanzania, was discovered by African American fashion designers in the 1960s (Neves

1966) and was ideal for the simply tailored dashikis. One kanga-patterned dashiki with chevron, geometric, and floral motifs became a "classic" and was still manufactured in the twenty-first century.

Dashiki as Symbol

Throughout its history in American fashion, the dashiki has functioned as a significant, but sometimes ambiguous, identity marker. In its earliest manifestation, with the Afro hairstyle, headgear, and African beads, it was associated with black power, the "Black Is Beautiful" movement, and the development of Afrocentrism. The historian Henry Louis Gates Jr. recalls, "I remember very painfully those days in the late sixties when if your Afro wasn't 2 feet high and your dashiki wasn't tri-colored, etc., etc., then you weren't colored enough" (Rowell, p. 445). Initially, the garment had strong political overtones when "dashiki-clad cultural nationalists . . . typified the antithesis of the suit-and-tie integrationists" (Cobb, p. 125). Political activists such as Huey P. Newton and Stokely Carmichael of the Black Panthers Party sometimes combined the dashiki with the black leather jacket, combat boots, and beret that identified the militant group (Boston, pp. 204–209). However, the dashiki never gained a clear militant identity in the African American community. Leaders of the more moderate wings of the Black Civil Rights movement, such as Jesse Jackson and Andrew Young, sometimes wore dashikis to project a distinctive Afrocentric look as they promoted the more peaceful goals of Martin Luther King Jr. (Boston, p. 67). As the dashiki grew popular with African Americans as a symbol of cultural pride, it gained metaphorical significance in black activist rhetoric. The educator Sterling Tucker stated, "Donning a dashiki and growing a bush is fine if it energizes the wearer for real action; but 'Black is beautiful' is dangerous if it amounts only to wrapping oneself up in one's own glory and magnificence" (Tucker, p. 303). The Black Panther Fred Hampton wore dashikis but declared, "we know that political power doesn't flow from the sleeve of a dashiki. We know that political power flows from the barrel of a gun" (Lee).

Dashiki in the Twenty-first Century

In the early days of the twenty-first century, the dashiki has retained meaning for the African American community and a historical marker of the 1960s counterculture. While seldom seen as street wear, the dashiki is worn at festive occasions such as Kwanzaa, the annual celebration to mark the unity of Americans of African descent and express pride in African heritage (Goss and Goss). A 2003 Internet search called up over 5,000 entries for "dashiki," largely from marketers who offer a range of vintage or contemporary African clothing. Vintage clothing retailers market dashikis as "a must for all hippie freaks" and for "wanna-be hippies." Costume companies offer "the dashiki boy" with a classic dashiki shirt, Afro wig, dark glasses, and a peace pendant necklace. Purveyors of African clothing have expanded the meaning of dashiki

Stevie Wonder wearing a *dashiki.* South African president Nelson Mandela escorts singers Kenny Latimore and Stevie Wonder at his Johannesburg home in 1998. Although the dashiki's popularity as everyday-wear waned after the 1960s, some African Americans continue to wear dashikis to festive occasions and as a symbol of pride in their African heritage. AP/WIDE WORLD PHOTOS. REPRODUCED BY PERMISSION.

beyond the distinctive shirt to include a variety of African robe ensembles and caftan styles. The dashiki's popularity as a street style has faded, but it continues as an integral part of the African American fashion scene for festive occasions and as a form of dress evocative of the lifestyle of 1960s America.

See also **African American Dress; Afrocentric Fashion.**

BIBLIOGRAPHY

Bolland, Rita. "Clothing from Burial Caves in Mali, 11th–18th Century." In *History, Design, and Craft in West African Strip-Woven Cloth.* Washington, D.C.: National Museum of African Art, 1966, pp. 53–82.

Boston, Lloyd. *Men of Color: Fashion, History, Fundamentals.* New York: Artisan, 1998.

Cobb, William, Jr. "Out of Africa: The Dilemmas of Afrocentricity." *The Journal of Negro History* 82, no. 1 (1997): 122–132.

Connikie, Yvonne. *Fashions of a Decade: The 1960s.* London: B. T. Batsford, Ltd., 1998.

De Negri, Eve. "Yoruba Men's Costume." *Nigeria Magazine* 73 (1962): 4–12.

Giddings, Valerie L. "African American Dress in the 1960's." In *African American Dress and Adornment: A Cultural Perspective.* Edited by Barbara M. Starke, Lillian O. Holloman, and Barbara K. Nordquist, pp. 152–155. Dubuque, Iowa: Kendall/Hunt Publishing Company, 1990.

Goss, Linda, and Clay Goss, eds. *It's Kwanzaa Time!* New York: G. P. Putnam's Sons, 1995.

Hilger, Julia. "The Kanga: An Example of East African Textile Design." In *The Art of African Textiles: Technology, Tradition and Lurex.* Edited by John Picton, pp. 44–45. London: Barbican Art Gallery/Lund Humphries Publishers, 1995.

Lee, Paul. "From Malcolm to Marx: The Political Journey of Fred Hampton." *Michigan Citizen*, 18 May 2002.

Neves, Irene. "The Cut-up Kanga Caper." *Life* (16 September 1966): 142–44, 147–8.

Rowell, Charles H. "An Interview with Henry Louis Gates, Jr." *Callaloo* 14, no. 2 (1997): 444–463.

Tucker, Sterling. "Black Strategies for Change in America." *The Journal of Negro Education* 40, no. 3 (1971): 297–311.

Norma H. Wolff

DEBUTANTE DRESS Once restricted to young women from wealthy families on the social register, the traditional long, white formal dress and opera-length kid gloves of the debutante are more and more frequently also worn by daughters of the middle class. Cultural variations, such as the Hispanic *quinceañera*, not only introduce a young woman into society but also reinforce ethnic identity. While making a debut no longer necessarily signifies that the deb is looking for a husband—the age of a debutante ranges from fifteen to the mid-twenties—it is still a rite of passage denoting adult status socially.

Development of Debuts

The term "debut," to enter into society, is French in origin but became familiar to English speakers during the reign of King George III (1760–1820) when Queen Charlotte began the practice of introducing young aristocratic women at court. From 1837 on, they were called "debutantes," later shortened to "debs." The Lord Chamberlain's Office developed strict regulations regarding proper dress for court presentations. From 1820 to 1900, ladies wore fashionable evening dresses, a mandatory headdress of veiling and feathers plus a train attached first at the waistline and, in later years, at the shoulders. Long, white kid gloves, bouquets, or fans were often added (Arch and Marschner 1987). In the United States of the early nineteenth century, elite families gave relatively small parties to introduce their marriageable-age daughters to their friends and to single men of appropriate age and status.

After the Civil War and the emergence of new wealth based on industry and railroads, the parties began to grow into lavish balls as old and new wealth vied with one another for status. One party featured an artificial lake with a large papier-mâché swan that exploded on cue, sending hundreds of roses into the air. American debutantes wore full evening dress but did not add the headdresses and trains of their English counterparts. White became standard for English debs by the end of the nineteenth century while American girls could also choose a color, as long as it was a very pale pastel. Male escorts wore formal evening wear, either tails or tuxedos, just as in the early twenty-first century. As an alternative to the private parties, exclusive social clubs, usually all male, were formed in the nineteenth and early twentieth centuries

Debutantes at a ball. Though variations exist, traditional dress for debutantes consists of a white formal gown, usually sleeveless, and long, white kid gloves. © SEATTLE POST-INTELLIGENCER COLLECTION; MUSEUM OF HISTORY & INDUSTRY/CORBIS. REPRODUCED BY PERMISSION.

to present a group of their daughters or granddaughters at a cotillion or ball. Social club cotillions are usually more formal than family balls with a master of ceremonies and a grand march or promenade before the dancing begins. All of the girls in the group must wear the same color, almost invariably white, but may choose their own style of dress. Long, white gloves are usually worn with strapless or sleeveless gowns (Post 1937, 1969, 1997). Individual parents may give an additional party sometime within the debutante social season, traditionally the period between Thanksgiving and New Year's when university students are home for the holidays (Mills 1959; Tuckerman and Dunnan 1995).

In the twentieth century, debutante balls, whether given by a family or by one of the exclusive social clubs, gained media attention, and the public began criticizing the lavishness of the events, particularly in the 1930s and 1940s. In the 1950s, subscription dances were organized to raise money for charity through debuts. For an entrance fee, debutantes could be introduced at an annual ball and the proceeds contributed to a charitable cause. One of the largest is the National Debutante Cotillion and Thanksgiving Ball, of Washington, D.C., benefiting the Children's Hospital National Medical Center. In addition to couching the social event within philanthropy, subscription debutante balls allow middle-class parents to give their daughters a debut, as long as they have a sponsor from the cotillion organization. Financial requirements for balls usually include a participation fee, the purchase of a table for eight, and sometimes the purchase or sale of space in a souvenir book, and, of course, the mandatory dress and gloves. Subscription balls or cotillions vary in prestige and exclusivity, and the costs reflect these differences.

Ethnic and Cultural Debuts

Every year thousands of fifteen-year-olds from a wide variety of Hispanic backgrounds celebrate their birthdays with a *quinceañera*, a unique combination of religion and debut that emphasizes cultural identity. Few young African American women make their debuts through the older social clubs, but many debut through African American organizations. The Van Courtlandt Society in San Antonio, Texas, was founded in 1915 and shortly thereafter began holding balls, and in Savannah, Georgia, the Alpha Phi Alpha fraternity has sponsored the Annual Debutante Presentation and Ball since 1944. Some African American debuts are as expensive and exclusive as those of the white balls, but others, like the Club Les Dames Cotillion of Waterloo, Iowa, are quite inexpensive and focus on the debutantes' social and academic accomplishments. The Chicago chapter of the Kosciuszko Foundation emphasizes scholastic achievement and community service in addition to the debs' Polish heritage. The San Marino Woman's Club of California requires that its debs perform a number of volunteer hours in community projects (Lynch 1999; Salcedo 1997). With the exception of the *quinceañera*, a fashionable white evening gown with long, white kid gloves is the standard dress for all of the above debuts.

Regional Variation

Debutante events vary ethnically and socioeconomically, but the biggest difference in dress is regional. Mardi Gras debutantes in New Orleans wear jeweled gowns and long trains with Medici collars as well as glittering crowns, while Texas debs stray the furthest from classic white formals. For instance, in Laredo, Texas, young women from the oldest families wear elaborate eighteenth-century-style ball gowns with panniers, and middle-class debs wear heavily beaded ultra suede "Native American" costumes in pageants held during the annual George Washington Birthday celebration. During Fiesta in San Antonio, Texas, twenty-four duchesses, a princess, and a queen wear elaborately bejeweled gowns and trains in a faux coronation. The trains are based upon the requirements for English court presentations. The earliest ones were usually of satin and lightly beaded, but soon became the background upon which motifs from such themes as "The Court of Olympus" (1931) or "Court of the Imperial House of Hapsburg" (1987) could be represented in rhinestones and beads. They may weigh up to seventy-five pounds, and up to thirty-five thousand dollars is spent

QUINCEAÑERAS: A HISPANIC RITE OF PASSAGE

Quinceañeras (from *quince* or fifteen) are traditional celebrations of a daughter's fifteenth birthday. Unlike Sweet Sixteen celebrations, they combine religious and social elements. A *quinceañera* begins with a full Catholic mass followed by a dinner and dance. Most parish priests require attendance at special religious classes before the event. The honoree wears a white or pastel dress with yards of ruffles and lace and is crowned with a tiara by her grandmother at the dance. Ten to fourteen of her closest friends and relatives, who with their escorts make up the court of honor, wear matching bridesmaid-like dresses. A boudoir-style "last doll" is dressed identically to the honoree and symbolizes the end of childhood (Salcedo 1997).

on the handwork. While wearing all of those rhinestones and beads, the young women must perform the royal bow in which they lower their bodies until they are essentially sitting on the floor and then bend forward from the waist until the head almost touches the floor. The bow has been copied all over Texas and is known as the "Texas dip" when it is performed by Texas debs at the International Debutante Ball in New York City (Haynes 1998).

Conclusion

Although many people feared that debuts would disappear in the 1960s when such elitist and ostentatious displays of wealth came under heavy social criticism, debuts have actually become more prevalent. The benefits of debuts have even extended to young men at times. A small number of *quinceañeros* have been given for fifteen-year-old boys in Hispanic communities, and in Dayton, Ohio, the Beautillion Militaire has been held annually since 1968 for African American males. The organizers felt that since debutante events seemed to enhance self-esteem and raise the aspirations of the young women who participated in them, similar benefits might accrue to their young men taking part in similar events. Now, thousands of daughters (and a few sons) from a wide socioeconomic range become Cinderellas (or Prince Charmings) for a night.

See also **Evening Dress; Fancy Dress**

BIBLIOGRAPHY

Arch, Nigel, and Joanna Marschner. *Splendour at Court.* London: Unwin Hyman, 1987.

Birmingham, Stephen. *America's Secret Aristocracy.* New York: Berkley, 1990.

Haynes, Michaele Thurgood. *Dressing Up Debutantes.* Oxford: Berg, 1998.

Lynch, Annette. *Dress, Gender and Cultural Change.* Oxford: Berg, 1999.

Mills, C. Wright. *The Power Elite.* New York: Oxford University Press, 1959.

Post, Emily. *Etiquette.* New York: Funk and Wagnalls, 1937.

———. *Emily Post's Etiquette.* New York: Funk and Wagnalls, 1969.

Post, Peggy. *Emily Post's Etiquette.* New York: HarperCollins, 1997.

Salcedo, Michele. *Quinceañera!* New York: Henry Holt, 1997.

Tuckerman, Nancy, and Nancy Dunnan. *The Amy Vanderbilt Complete Book of Etiquette.* New York: Doubleday, 1995.

Michaele Haynes

DE LA RENTA, OSCAR Born in Santo Domingo, in the Dominican Republic, on 22 July 1932, Oscar de la Renta traveled to Madrid when he was eighteen to study art at the Academia de San Fernando with the intention of becoming a painter. His career in fashion began when Cristóbal Balenciaga was shown some of his fashion illustrations, which led to a job sketching the collections at Eisa, Balenciaga's Madrid couture house. In 1961, eager to move to Paris, de la Renta went to work as an assistant to Antonio Castillo. Moving to New York in 1963, he was invited to design a couture collection for Elizabeth Arden. He later joined Jane Derby, Inc., as a partner in 1965 and founded his own company in 1967 to produce ready-to-wear.

Also in 1967, de la Renta married Françoise de Langlade, editor-in-chief of French *Vogue.* Together they became part of New York's fashionable social scene, often appearing in the society columns and giving valuable publicity to the label. His clothes initially showed the influence of his time at Balenciaga and Castillo: daywear of sculptural shapes in double-faced or textured wool that were cut to stand away from the body. It was also during his time at Lanvin that he developed his talent for creating feminine, romantic evening wear, which has remained his trademark.

In 1966 de la Renta became inspired by young avant-garde street fashions and produced minidresses with hot-pants and embroidered caftans. However, his love of the exotic and the dramatic soon surfaced, and by the 1970s he was one of the designers to tap into the desire for ethnic fashion, inspired by the hippie movement with its appropriation of other cultures. His embroidered peasant blouses, gathered skirts, fringed shawls, and boleros became part of mainstream fashion for the rich and the leisured. When in the 1970s the midiskirt was introduced, it was received with ambivalence and Oscar de la Renta was one of the designers to resolve the hemline quandary by incorporating trousers into his collections. The prevailing attitudes to women wearing trousers became much

Oscar de la Renta. Though probably best known for his romantic eveningwear, de la Renta dabbled in many styles of clothing, such as ethnic fashions and elegant casual wear. © OWEN FRANKEN/CORBIS. REPRODUCED BY PERMISSION.

more relaxed as he and other designers sought to give panache to what was then only associated with casualwear and informal occasions. His evening wear in many ways continued the tradition of the American "sweetheart" dress, full-skirted, with a fitted bodice and belted waist and big sleeves, very often in a paper taffeta, brocade, or chiffon, and embellished with ruffles.

In January 1981 the inauguration of President Reagan reintroduced the notion of formal dressing and entertaining to Washington, D.C., replacing the southern homespun style of the previous incumbents of the White House, the Carters. Charity balls and black-tie dinners gave society every opportunity to dress up in lavish ball gowns, following the lead of the impeccably groomed Nancy Reagan. There was a new appetite for the luxurious and the ornate. Oscar de la Renta anticipated the change, remarking, "The Reagans are going to bring back the kind of style the White House should have" (Kelly, p. 259).

As one of the First Lady's favorite designers, and alongside Adolfo Domínguez, James Galanos, and Bill

Blass, he was favored with invitations to state dinners. It was a period when designers became part of the social scene, invited as guests to the grand occasions for which their clients required clothes.

De la Renta's talents lay in designing and producing spectacular ball gowns and evening dresses, reflecting the 1980s' predilection for ostentatious display and conspicuous consumption that epitomized the Reagan years. From 1980 to 1985 the American dollar had never been stronger, and it was during this period that de la Renta was able to consolidate his business, becoming a multimillionaire with eighty international licenses from household goods to eyewear. Television soap operas, such as *Dynasty* and *Dallas*, made universal the desire to dress up in luxurious fabrics and expensive accessories. During the 1980s de la Renta particularly favored the use of black with a single bright color, such as black and bright pink or black and emerald green, with a somewhat narrower silhouette and lavish use of embroidery, passementerie, and beading. Following the ingenue 1960s and hippie 1970s, fashion once more became about glamour for grown-ups. These classic dresses appealed to the more mature, leisured socialites, rather than the working women who were "power-dressing" in Donna Karan.

De la Renta introduced his signature perfume Oscar in 1977, for which he received the Fragrance Foundation Perennial Success Award in 1991. It was his scent Ruffles, however, in a distinctive fluted glass bottle, and produced in 1983, that reflected the ultrafeminine aspect of his clothes. As the advertisement read, "When a woman thinks of Oscar de la Renta she thinks of Ruffles."

Twice winner of the Coty American Fashion Critics' Award, in 1967 and 1973, de la Renta was inducted into the Coty Hall of Fame in 1973 and received the Lifetime Achievement Award from the Council of Fashion Designers of America in 1990

In 2001 the designer was elected to the fashion walk of fame and honored with a commemorative plaque embedded into the sidewalk of New York's Seventh Avenue.

International acknowledgment came with his appointment as designer for the French couture house Pierre Balmain in 1993, the first American designer to be recognized in this way, and a reflection of the growing status of American designers worldwide.

The year 2001 saw the introduction of Oscar accessories—bags, belts, and jewelry, scarves and shoes—that reflect his passion for the ornate decoration of his native country. De la Renta has had a consistently high profile in fashion, from being the favorite designer of film star Dolores Del Rio in the early 1960s to receiving the Womenswear Designer of the Year Award from the Council of Fashion Designers of America in 2000, the honor that succeeded the Coty awards. His clothes reflect his passion for the romantic and the exotic resulting from a childhood and youth spent in the Dominican Republic and Spain. De la Renta's strength as a designer has always been his ability to combine his trademark love of the dramatic, with its roots in his Latin inheritance, with the American need for sophisticated elegance.

See also **Balenciaga, Cristóbal; Evening Dress; Fashion Designer; First Ladies' Gowns.**

BIBLIOGRAPHY
Coleridge, Nicholas. *The Fashion Conspiracy: A Remarkable Journey through the Empires of Fashion.* London: William Heinemann, 1988.
Kelly, Kitty. *Nancy Reagan: The Unauthorized Biography.* London: Transworld Publishers, 1991.
Milbank, Caroline Rennolds. *New York Fashion: The Evolution of American* Style. New York: Harry N. Abrams, 1989.

Marnie Fogg

DELAUNAY, SONIA The artist Sonia Delaunay sought ways to bring modern art out of the confines of traditional easel painting. She carried this out by refashioning everyday objects as tools to explore her theories of color and by infiltrating daily life with art in a way that traditional painting could not. While her involvement in the fashion business spanned less than a decade, her prolific career in textile designs and color studies continues to influence fashion designers.

Sonia Terk was born 14 November 1885 into a poor Jewish family in the Ukrainian village of Gradizhsk and adopted by her well-to-do aunt and uncle in Saint Petersburg at an early age. She studied art periodically in Karlsruhe, Germany, and continued her studies at the Académie de la Palette in Paris, where the intense color palette of artists of the fauvist movement influenced her early development as a painter.

In 1910 she married the painter Robert Delaunay, whose research into the theory of "simultaneity," or "Orphism," served as the basis for her lifelong experiments in color. This new style, which attempted an instantaneous visualization of the experience of modern life in all its complexity, conveyed rhythmic energy and dynamic movement through the creation of color contrasts on the painted surface. Sonia Delaunay's first "simultaneous" paintings include *Contrastes simultanés* (1912) and *Le Bal Bullier* (1913), and she created her first simultaneous dresses in 1913 to match the energy of the new foxtrot and tango at the popular Parisian dance hall Le Bal Bullier. She also collaborated with the poet Blaise Cendrars to design a simultaneous book, *La Prose du Transsibérien et de la Petite Jehanne de France* (1913). In the initial years of her marriage, she integrated the realms of home and art by fashioning her apartment in the simultaneous style, creating blankets, cushion covers, lampshades, goblets, and curtains.

The Russian Revolution of 1917 resulted in the cutting off of Delaunay's substantial family income, so she turned to her marketable designs as a new means of financial support. Living briefly in Spain, she quickly established her public reputation as an innovator in both costume and fashion there by designing costumes for Sergey Diaghilev's *Cléopâtre* (staged in 1918) and showcasing simultaneous dresses, coats, home furnishings, and accessories in her store, Casa Sonia. This exposure earned her interior-decorating commissions from wealthy patrons and the Petit Casino theater (opened 1919).

In 1921 Delaunay returned to Paris and developed a new genre, *robes-poèmes* (poem-dresses), by juxtaposing geometric blocks of color and lines of poetry by Tristan Tzara, Philippe Soupault, and Jacques Delteil onto draped garments. She received a commission for fifty fabric designs by a Lyons silk textiles manufacturer, and over the next thirty years, the Dutch department store Metz and Company purchased nearly two hundred of Delaunay's designs for fashion and home decoration. In 1923 she designed costumes for Tristan Tzara's theater production *La coeur à gaz* (The gas-operated heart) and her first exhibition-style presentation of her textiles and clothing took place at the Grand Bal Travesti-Transmental.

The following year, Delaunay established her own printing workshop, Atelier Simultané, so that she would be able to supervise the design process of her prints. Embroideries in wool and silk combinations, sometimes accented with dull metal and mixed furs, incorporated a new stitch she invented, *point du jour*, or *point populaire*. Delaunay's meticulously embroidered and appliquéd coats brought commissions from the wives of fashion designers, artists, and architects, and from film and theater actresses including Gloria Swanson, who brought the Atelier much publicity.

Delaunay approached her textile designs in the same manner as her paintings. She incorporated rigorous yet simple geometric shapes, stripes, spirals, zigzags, and disks, crossing and intermingling with the strict discipline typical of constructivism. Colors were limited to four, occasionally five or six, contrasting hues in the same design: deep blues, cherry reds, black, white, yellow, or green, or softer combinations of browns, beiges, greens, and pale yellows. The vibrant synergy of these colors exemplified Delaunay's concept of modernity and the rhythms of an electrified modern city.

At the 1925 Exposition des Arts Décoratifs, Delaunay collaborated with the furrier Jacques Heim in displaying female fashion, accessories, and interior furnishing in her Boutique Simultané. That same year, the Librairie des Arts Décoratifs responded to the positive reception of her work by publishing an album of her fashion plates titled *Sonia Delaunay, ses peintures, ses objets, ses tissus simultanés, ses modes*. Delaunay's success with fashion lay partly in the adoption of the liberating, contemporary silhouette for female clothing that developed during World War I. The stylish, unadorned tunic cuts of the mid-1920s, with straight necklines, no waistlines, and few structural details, served as a blank, two-dimensional canvas for her geometric forms. Shawls, scarves, and flowing wraps for evening gave her additional flat surfaces on which to explore, enabling her to expand her business. She also challenged traditional practices in the fashion industry. In a lecture at the Sorbonne, "The Influence of Painting on Fashion Design," she explained the *tissu patron* (fabric pattern), an inexpensive invention that allowed both the cutting outline for the dress and its corresponding textile design to be printed at the same time.

Financial pressures during the Great Depression, coupled with the 1930s trend toward fabric manipulation and construction details that did not accommodate her designs, led Delaunay to close her couture house in 1931. She foresaw that the future of fashion was in ready-to-wear, not the custom pieces she was creating. While she turned away from fashion design after this point, she continued to take private orders from the couturiers Chanel, Lanvin, and especially Jacques Heim.

Delaunay spent the rest of her life concentrating on painting and continued to apply her theories to a wide range of objects, including tapestries, bookbindings, playing cards, and a children's alphabet. She also became involved in projects with the poet Jacques Damase. Toward the end of her life, she exhibited frequently and was honored in 1967 with a major retrospective exhibition at the Musée National d'Art Moderne in Paris for her contribution to modern art. She died on 5 December 1979 at the age of ninety-four.

Textile and fashion design gave Delaunay the freedom of experimentation and spontaneity that she later transposed into her paintings. She brought art to the streets and made her wearable paintings an integral part of the everyday. Her artistry has had a profound influence on the work of contemporary fashion designers including Marc Bohan for Christian Dior, Perry Ellis, Yves Saint Laurent, and Jean Charles de Castelbajac, all of whom have referenced her work in their collections.

See also **Art and Fashion; Chanel, Gabrielle (Coco); Dior, Christian; Fashion Designer; Ellis, Perry; Lanvin, Jeanne; Saint Laurent, Yves.**

BIBLIOGRAPHY

Baron, Stanley, with Jacques Damase. *Sonia Delaunay: The Life of an Artist.* New York: Harry N. Abrams, 1995. A comprehensive biography of the artist's personal and professional endeavors.

Cohen, Arthur A. *Sonia Delaunay.* New York: Harry N. Abrams, 1975. Provides biographical and visual insight into the artist's overall career.

Damase, Jacques. *Sonia Delaunay, Fashion and Fabrics.* Translated by Shaun Whiteside and Stanley Baron. London and New York: Thames and Hudson, 1991. An extensive collection of the artist's fashion illustrations and textile designs of the 1920s.

Delaunay, Sonia. *Nous irons jusqu'au soleil.* Paris: Editions Robert Laffont, 1978. An autobiography based on journal entries starting from the early 1930s.

Morano, Elizabeth. *Sonia Delaunay: Art into Fashion*. New York: George Braziller, 1986. Explains the artist's impact on the development of modern fashion through a broad collection of fashion plates and textile designs.

Angel Chang

DEMEULEMEESTER, ANN

DEMEULEMEESTER, ANN Ann Demeulemeester (1959–) was born in Courtrai, Belgium. When she presented her first winter collection in Paris in 1987, six years after graduating in fashion design from the Royal Academy of Fine Arts in Antwerp, the press release described her work as "a collection for the conscious woman." The text went on to say, "[her] inspiration sources are neither directly definite nor visual; the clothes are brought about by personal impressions. A logical evolution, that is a result of a purification of ideas, which forms a specific style with its own atmosphere." These words seemed appropriate in the early twenty-first century, as Demeulemeester's work could be read as an interpretation of a very personal universe—one that was not immediately traceable, but could be felt in every article of apparel she designed. At their core lay the study of form and the development of a personal signature, rather than introductions of new trends or fashions or working around seasonal themes. For Demeulemeester, designing was a form of problem-solving. In a rational, almost scientific manner, she sought a solution for each "problem," often over several successive seasons. Cut and pattern were explored until the solution presented itself and perfection was achieved.

The experimental subject in this design laboratory was the designer's own body. Demeulemeester consistently tried out new creations on herself or on a select number of friends. The semiscientific aspect of Demeulemeester's creative process was in stark contrast with her ultimate silhouettes, which bore witness to intense emotion and extensive experience of life. However exhaustively thought out the cut may have been, the result was never sterile. The nonchalance that characterized her style was natural yet profoundly investigated; it was never just a matter of course. This dichotomy in Demeulemeester's creative process distinguished her entire oeuvre. Ann Demeulemeester sought out paradox; she seemed to go along with a certain duality or opposition in order to ultimately undermine it. Her investigation was in fact a study in search of balance, with the underlying thought that perfect balance is unattainable, just as the symmetrical body is in fact nonexistent—and for the designer, perhaps of no interest anyway. The shortcomings, the incompleteness, and the voids are what generate artistic creation. It was this continual search that lay at the root of Ann Demeulemeester's drive and passion—or as the text on a T-shirt and invitation suggested: *Aimer, c'est agir* ("to Love is to act").

Motion and Gravity

Motion was a leitmotif throughout Demeulemeester's work. The challenge of gravity, a force that allows ap-

Model wearing Demeulemeester ensemble. Demeulemeester liked to challenge gravity in her designs, creating garments that appeared to be in motion or were just barely held in check on the body. AFP/GETTY IMAGES. REPRODUCED BY PERMISSION.

parel to appear to be in motion even when its wearer is standing still, was technically explored in ever new applications, season after season. One symbol of this investigation was the feathers that reappeared in each new collection in the form of necklaces or jewelry, chosen for their beauty and natural perfection.

We are accustomed to the fact that gravity causes everything to fall, so how does one mislead a law of nature? How does one dislodge the balance of human form into balance, and how does one cut an article of clothing so that it looks as though it is being blown open? How does one summarize the beauty of a T-shirt that just happens to glide off the shoulder? Questions of this nature served as starting points for collections in which the different movements of Demeulemeester's models repeatedly accentuated and revealed different parts of the wearer's body—shoulders, stomach, or hips.

Unforgettable pieces in this context included Demeulemeester's asymmetrically-cut trousers that revealed part of the hips. Whether or not these garments were held up with a subtle ribbon, they looked as though they were just on the verge of sliding to the floor. The movement was subtle yet introduced a hint of danger. Such techniques as drapery and asymmetrical cut as well as ribbons and belts provided the technical tools. When gravity could not be conquered, Demeulemeester made use of ribbons or belts—which had evolved into fetish elements in her collections—to hold the fabric against the wearer's body.

The designer felt a need to find different ways to develop an article of clothing without traditional pattern techniques. Demeulemeester's 1998 winter collection began with a piece of cloth into which she cut holes for her arms. Careful observation of what subsequently happened to the fabric led her to develop a number of wrapping techniques, which in turn produced new forms. In her winter collection for 1999, she pushed this approach even further by applying the wrapping techniques to sheepskin. The result was a most unexpected interpretation of the *mouton-retourné*.

The feeling of motion and nonchalance in Demeulemeester's work found its counterweight in her elegant jackets and pantsuits of the 1990s, which exuded a certain discipline and masculinity. Perfect in cut and shoulder line, here too, it was such details as an asymmetrically-buttoned blouse or the selection of a subtly hanging fabric, for example, that softened the severity of the whole. In her 1997 winter collection, both aspects came together in a jacket that closely hugged the body on one side with the help of a belt, but fell loosely on the other side.

Materials

Alongside Demeulemeester's use of such supple fabrics as rayon, viscose, and silk, she had a passion for leather and fur, two hard-to-control materials that combine such opposites as aggression and tenderness. The tough character of the materials was undermined by the manner in which they were worked into the final pieces. One need think only of her elegantly draped wraparound jackets in fur (autumn–winter 2000–2001) or the jackets with large imposing capes that were produced in the finest leather for her 2002–2003 winter collection. The materials symbolized what the total silhouette demonstrated: the "wild warrior" versus the "fragile innocent girl."

A third noteworthy material was white painter's linen or canvas, which Demeulemeester initially used for invitations, catwalks, the interior of her shop in Antwerp, and a table she designed in 1995—for which she was awarded the first prize in design from the Flemish Community. Demeulemeester first worked this white canvas into her apparel collection in 1999. Since Demeulemeester studied art before going into fashion design, she was especially fascinated by the nude female body and its proportions—a factor that continued to play a central role in her fashion design. Beginning from nothing, from empty space or nudity, in order to then add only the es-

sentials without excess decoration, translated equally strongly into her emphatic choice of black and white, the two extremes of the color spectrum—a choice that is both hard and poetic. In the same way that a black-and-white photograph can embody the essence of an image, Demeulemeester was more interested in nuances, shadows, and forms than in decoration and color.

Gender Issues

Demeulemeester showed her first collection for men in 1996, which was presented together with her collection for women. For Demeulemeester, men and women are not opposites, but rather form a balance around the same extremes. The flow and interchange of masculine and feminine characteristics could be found in the mannequins who modeled her clothes, in the punk singer Patti Smith (her frequently mentioned and quoted muse), but above all in the apparel itself. It is worth noting here that tough-looking shoes or boots more than once formed a symbolic counterpoint within one of Demeulemeester's silhouettes, such as her 1998 shoe, which mounted a man's shoe form on a high heel.

See also **Belgian Fashion; Gender, Dress, and Fashion; Margiela, Martin; T-Shirt.**

BIBLIOGRAPHY

Derycke, Luc, and Sandra van de Veire, eds. *Belgian Fashion Design.* Ghent and Amsterdam: Ludion, 1999.

Kaat Debo and Linda Loppa

DEMIMONDE Nineteenth-century Paris was acknowledged by contemporaries as the "capital of pleasure" (Rearick, p. 40). Its reputation as a city of diversions and licentiousness was established following the Revolution and Reign of Terror during the period of the Directory (1795–1799), when a heterogeneous, parvenu society indulged itself in a hedonistic lifestyle. Returning émigrés, the newly distinguished, and the recently wealthy, as well as many visiting foreigners, enjoyed the city's luxury shops, restaurants, cafés, dance halls, public gardens, and boulevards. The pleasure-seeking atmosphere that characterized Paris in the Directory set the tone for the next hundred years.

The political upheaval of 1789 created a less rigidly stratified society than that of the *ancien régime*, a society in which birth and wealth no longer dictated access to power. Under Napoleon I and increasingly throughout the nineteenth century, a growing and affluent bourgeoisie claimed its right to the lifestyle and privileges formerly the prerogative of the elite. In this opportunistic culture of burgeoning capitalism and materialism, men and women were on the make. The social mobility, economic expansion, and, to a degree, the political uncertainty of nineteenth-century France gave birth to *le demimonde*.

Coined by Alexandre Dumas fils in 1852 for a title of his play *La dame aux camelias*, the inspiration for *La Traviata* and adapted as the film *Camille*, the term "demimonde" (literally, half-world) originally designated a class of fallen society women. But the definition came to be much broader, including all women of loose morals who lived at the edge of respectable society and, by extension, the men—royal, aristocratic, bourgeois, and bohemian—who frequented that ambiguous world. Although the demimonde certainly existed prior to the mid-nineteenth century, it was during the Second Empire (1852–1870) and the early Third Republic (1870–1914), that it flourished and that its supreme type, the courtesan, achieved spectacular notoriety.

The Courtesan

In an age of limited career possibilities for women, the courtesan took maximum advantage of one of the oldest professions open to her. Prostitution was widespread in nineteenth-century Paris, but the courtesan was set apart from the anonymous streetwalker by virtue of the wealth and status of her protectors and her own celebrity and visibility on the social scene. In addition to their physical beauty and sexual attractiveness, the most successful courtesans were also personages. In Colette's novella, *Gigi* (1944), Madame Alvarez, a former demimondaine and Gigi's grandmother, sums up a (real-life) leading courtesan: "She is extraordinary. Otherwise she would not be so famous. Successes and celebrity are not a matter of luck" (Colette, p. 24). Accomplished in the arts of gallantry, courtesans were strong-willed and independent women as well as cultivated, entertaining, and witty.

The *cocottes* (literally, hens) and "grand horizontals" of the latter half of the nineteenth and early twentieth century were the culmination in an evolution of women of dubious character. The *grisette* (a reference to her gray work dress) of the First Empire (1804–1814) and Bourbon Restoration (1814–1830) was a tenderhearted, good-natured young woman, toiling in the fashion trades, who formed a relationship—based on love and necessity—with a student, artist, or writer. The more venal *lorette* made her appearance during the July monarchy of the bourgeois king, Louis-Philippe (1830–1848), a time of rapid growth and industrialization in France. In 1841, the French writer Nestor Roqueplan applied the name *lorette* to the kept women who inhabited the newly developed area in the ninth arrondissement, around the parish church, Notre-Dame-de-Lorette. Unlike the *grisette*, the *lorette* did not work for a living; instead, she sold her favors and relied on liaisons (sometimes simultaneous) with men of substantial (though not lavish) means to support her.

The ostentatious lifestyle and moral corruption of the Second Empire produced *la garde*, as the group of about a dozen of the most flamboyant *grandes cocottes* was designated. In fact, the *fête impérial*, or imperial party, has been described both by those who lived through it as well as later historians as the heyday of the demimondaine.

Demimonde poster by Georges Redon, 1904. Liane de Pougy, a star of the Belle Epoque, strikes an uninhibited pose. De Pougy reigned at the top of the social structure of the "grand horizontals," leading an ostentatious and flamboyant lifestyle. © SWIM INK/CORBIS. REPRODUCED BY PERMISSION.

Napoleon III himself set the example; among his several mistresses were some of the era's most celebrated courtesans: Marguerite Bellanger, the Countess Castiglione, and Giulia Benini, known as la Barucci.

The Belle Epoque, too, contributed its stars to the demimonde firmament. Liane de Pougy, Caroline Otero ("la Belle Otero"), and Emilienne d'Alençon, known as *Les grandes trois*, were the undisputed trio at the apex of the coterié of grand horizontals.

In his essay "The Painter of Modern Life" (1863), the French poet Charles Baudelaire refers to the courtesan (and her alternate type, the actress) as "a creature of show, an object of public pleasure" (p. 36). And indeed the larger-than-life personae of these women not only inspired novels, plays, and paintings (themselves often controversial), but also provided regular fodder for gossip columns in the popular press. Their fabulous gowns, extravagant jewels, lavishly decorated mansions, superb horses and carriages, notable lovers, and outrageous ex-

Demimonde *cocotte,* ca. 1900. Dressed in a long, ruffled evening gown and matching headpiece, a Frenchwoman entertains three men. *Cocottes* were women of dubious character in the late nineteenth and early twentieth centuries. © BETTMANN/ CORBIS. REPRODUCED BY PERMISSION.

ploits riveted the public's attention. The avariciousness of the courtesans earned them the unflattering neologism of *mangeuses* (eaters—of men and fortunes). Throughout the period, social commentators and writers such as Honoré de Balzac, Emile Zola, and Walter Benjamin linked the courtesan (and prostitution in general) with the rise of capitalism, speculation, commodity exchange, and a culture of consumption, and deplored their degenerative influence on society.

The Courtesan and Fashion

As a signifier of modernity, fashion played an important part in nineteenth-century French society as a whole and for the courtesan in particular, for whom it was the primary vehicle by which she flaunted her power and challenged respectable women of the elite. The rules had changed since the eighteenth century when fashions were set by the court. Adopting a no-holds-barred attitude, the demimondaine used her enormous wealth and status as an outsider to wear the newest, most daring styles. Courtesans became the acknowledged leaders of fashion whose flashy ensembles were reported on, avidly studied, and often copied by upper- and middle-class women.

For the demimondaine, fashion operated on a number of levels. Many courtesans came from a background of poverty and obscurity. As the mistress of a wealthy man, having the means to dress in the height of fashion was surely a gratifying indulgence and a welcome source

of attention. But fashion was also a weapon in the battle between the *mondaine* (society lady) and the demimondaine. In the somewhat fluid society of nineteenth-century France, clothing was an all-important tool in the creation of persona. Fashion was unquestionably women's territory, and they were expected to take an active interest in its pursuit. Yet the society woman was confined by strictures of etiquette to maintain respectability in dress. The courtesan, on the other hand, was not bound by these same limitations. In fact, her conspicuous toilettes not only attested to her own originality in taste and sophisticated chic, they also reflected the wealth and generosity of her protector—in all likelihood, a married man. For the demimondaine, fashion was both socially and sexually empowering.

One of the most famous scenes in Emile Zola's novel *Nana* (published in 1880 but set in the Second Empire) illustrates this usurpation of sartorial prestige and supremacy by the courtesan. At the height of her success, Nana attends the Grand Prix de Paris at Longchamp dressed in a strikingly avant-garde and brazenly seductive ensemble. As a courtesan, Nana is prohibited from entering the weighing-in enclosure. However, on the arm of one of her aristocratic lovers, she gains admission to this exclusive preserve, where she walks slowly past the stands in full view of the empress and the wife of another noble lover whom she will eventually ruin. Zola's description of the dresses of the women in the enclosure is intentionally generalized; it is Nana's splendid costume that merits close observation in details of cut and color.

The blurred boundaries between the monde (high society) and the demimonde were nowhere more evident than in the patronage of leading couturiers by courtesans and society women alike. Charles Frederick Worth, considered the father of haute couture, created opulent toilettes for Empress Eugénie and women of the imperial circle. But his other, equally famous clients included Cora Pearl, who counted among her lovers the duc de Morny and Prince Napoleon (respectively half-brother and cousin to Emperor Napoleon III) la Païva, and other demimondaines of the era. At least on one occasion, a socialite and a demimondaine found themselves waiting for a fitting with Worth. Apparently, the couturier gave precedence to the courtesan. At the turn of the twentieth century, Maison Worth as well as more recently established designers such as Jacques Doucet and Jeanne Paquin continued to dress both women of the upper ranks and courtesans and actresses.

The Urban Landscape

Paris of the Second Empire and Third Republic provided the appropriate setting for the demimonde and the courtesan. Under the direction of Baron Georges-Eugène Haussmann, Napoleon III's prefect of the Seine, Paris was transformed from a still largely medieval city with insular neighborhoods of dark, winding streets to a modern metropolis with a more uniform architectural style, straight, broad boulevards, and public parks. In this new urban landscape, arenas of fashionable life multiplied. Already fixtures of the Parisian scene, theaters, restaurants, cafés, and dance halls proliferated, while newer venues such as the *café-concerts* (music halls) became popular toward the end of the century. In Montmartre, the Moulin Rouge and the Folies Bergère drew large audiences from both the moneyed and the plebeian public.

Within Paris itself, the haunts—and breeding ground—of the demimonde were located on the Right Bank. Certain areas such as the Faubourg Saint-Honoré had been known for their luxury shops and *hôtels particuliers* since the eighteenth century. In the first half of the nineteenth century, other fashionable neighborhoods developed north of this older quarter, and by the second half of the century, the epicenter of "le high life" encompassed the Rue de la Paix, the Place Vendôme, the Rue Royale, the Boulevard des Italiens, and the Opera. The most renowned couturiers, jewelers, and silk and lingerie merchants all had their premises here. The well-known Théâtre des Variétés, which figures in the opening scene of *Nana*, and legendary restaurants such as the Café Anglais, the Maison Dorée, and Maxim, the scenes of dazzling parties and amorous intrigue, were also located in this area.

Fashion was an integral part of the demimondaine's public lifestyle and one that required a different toilette for each occasion. Morning, afternoon, and evening dress varied depending on the season and the venue. Carriage dress, appropriate for the obligatory afternoon ride along the Champs-Elysées to the Bois de Boulogne, was deliberately showy. The scene in *Nana* referred to above depicts the fashion contest that took place at Longchamp amid the wide cross-section of society that attended the annual Grand Prix. At theaters catering to an upper-class audience, high fashion was on display both on the stage, as worn by leading actresses, and in the private boxes, where courtesans in décolleté gowns presided in the company of their admirers. Demimondaines of the Second Empire also made their mark at public dance halls such as the Jardin de Mabille, an open-air garden in the Avenue Montaigne patronized as well by Princess Metternich (a Worth client) and members of the exclusive Jockey Club. Since they were constantly on view, it was imperative for leading courtesans to make the most of fashion opportunities in their daily social schedule.

The Demimonde Legacy

World War I brought to an end the rarified lifestyle of the Belle Époque and with it the phenomenon of the demimonde and courtesan. The social, economic, and cultural conditions that permitted the excesses of debauchery and squandering of fortunes were irreversibly changed. The demimondaines who lived beyond the war years were no longer the idolized, public figures they had been. In their old age, many returned to a life of economic deprivation and obscurity.

Nonetheless, the demimonde has left its legacy in the wider world of twentieth-century fashion and celebrity culture. Actresses and performers such as Josephine Baker, Mae West, Marlene Dietrich, and Madonna have capitalized on their erotic appeal as a form of power and a significant aspect of their personae. Madonna in particular, in her collaboration with the French designer Jean Paul Gaultier, has explicitly challenged dress norms, exploiting the implications of both hyperfeminine and androgynous fashions. More than mere sex symbols, these women have an insolence and a flamboyance that derive from the example of the courtesan.

Popular culture of the past century has embraced different elements of the demimonde lifestyle, modes of behavior, and attitude toward fashion. Rock-and-roll musicians and their fans, for example, have carried on the tradition of social and sartorial rebellion and self-creation through clothing that defined the demimondaine. The discotheque and nightclub scene re-creates in a sense the ambiguous and socially mixed terrain of the demimonde with an undercurrent of dangerous glamour. The notoriously public lifestyle of celebrities in the early 2000s (film and sports stars, rock musicians, artists, socialites, and even royals), followed closely in the press, also mirrors that of the late nineteenth century. In these forms, the spirit of the demimonde continues to exert its influence.

See also **Balzac, Honoré de; Benjamin, Walter; Fashion and Identity.**

BIBLIOGRAPHY

Baudelaire, Charles. *The Painter of Modern Life and Other Essays.* Edited and translated by Jonathan Mayne. London: Phaidon Press Ltd., 1964.

Clayson, Hollis. *Painted Love: Prostitution in French Art in the Impressionist Era.* New Haven, Conn.: Yale University Press, 1991.

Colette. *Gigi; Julie de Carneilhan; Chance Acquaintances.* Translated by Roger Senhouse and Patrick Leigh Fermor. New York: Farrar, Straus and Giroux, 1980.

Griffin, Susan. *The Book of the Courtesans: A Catalogue of Their Virtues.* New York: Broadway Books, 2001.

Maneglier, Hervé. *Paris impérial: La vie quotidienne sous le Second Empire.* Paris: Armand Colin, 1990.

Rearick, Charles. *The Pleasures of the Belle Époque: Entertainment and Festivity in Turn-of-the-Century France.* New Haven, Conn.: Yale University Press, 1985.

Richardson, Joanna. *The Courtesans: The Demi-Monde in Nineteenth-Century France.* Cleveland, Ohio: World Publishing, 1967.

Steele, Valerie. *Paris Fashion: A Cultural History.* Oxford: Oxford University Press, 1985.

Zola, Emile. *Nana.* Translated by George Holden. New York: Penguin Books, 1972.

Michele Majer

DEMOREST, MME. Madame Demorest (1824–1898) created one of the most important and influential fashion empires in the late nineteenth century. She was born Ellen Louise Curtis in Schuylerville, New York, on 15 November 1824. After graduating from Schuylerville Academy at the age of eighteen, Ellen moved to Saratoga Springs, where she opened a millinery shop with the financial help of her father, a hat factory owner. She apparently achieved some success and decided to move to New York City with her business. There she met a widower, William Jennings Demorest, a dry goods merchant who had recently opened Madame Demorest's Emporium of Fashion on Broadway. Ellen Curtis and William Demorest married in 1858. A perfect embodiment of the new Madame Demorest's Emporium, Ellen was pivotal to the expansion and diversification of her husband's business and became one of the most influential arbiters of fashion of her era.

Fashion Innovations

Madame Demorest's entrepreneurial success can be attributed to her astute understanding of the American fashion business as a combination of creativity, marketing, distribution, and brand identity. She claimed a number of innovative products, including a line of comfortable corsets, an affordable hoopskirt, the Imperial Dress-elevators (loop fasteners enabling skirts to be raised), and a sewing machine that could sew backwards; moreover, she developed the Excelsior Dress Model drafting system, a tool for making dress patterns. However, her mass-produced and marketed paper dress patterns remain her most important contribution. Madame Demorest's foray into paper patterns came at a time of great social change, when a growing middle class was clamoring for access to affordable fashions and technical advances like the sewing machine were becoming increasingly common in the home, making these fashion ambitions possible. Madame Demorest's paper patterns reached women across America and Europe, bringing them up-to-date fashions, a feat of no little importance.

Evolution of Patternmaking

A Madame Demorest tissue-paper pattern for a boy's jacket was advertised in Frank Leslie's *Ladies Gazette* as early as March 1854. These early patterns were unsized and sold for twenty-five to fifty cents. Starting first with children's garments, Demorest moved to women's dress. The aim was to sell patterns for separate garments— bodices, sleeves, mantles, basques—that could be used in combination with others. Madame Demorest later made custom patterns by special order available. It was not until the early 1870s (nearly a decade after her archrival Ebenezer Butterick) that Madame Demorest was mass-producing sized patterns. The business burgeoned into an international enterprise within a few short years. In 1876 Madame Demorest sold over 3 million paper patterns throughout America and Europe.

Demorest Publications

Marketing played an enormous role in the success of Madame Demorest's fashion empire. By employing the title "Madame," Demorest imbued her products with the cachet and allure of French fashions, reinforced in the early advertising in fashion journals such as Frank Leslie's *Ladies Gazette* and *Godey's Lady's Book*. Madame Demorest also promoted her products, especially the paper patterns, in the Demorests' own publications, which were generally managed by her husband. In 1860 *Madame Demorest's Mirror of Fashions* began quarterly circulation. The magazine featured plates of their own dress patterns and included a paper pattern stapled to the inside as an enticement to the reader. In 1864 the magazine was expanded to be *Demorest's Illustrated Monthly Magazine and Madame Demorest's Mirror of Fashions*. In 1865 the name was changed to *Demorest's Monthly Magazine and Demorest's Mirror of Fashions* (commonly referred to as *Demorest's Monthly*) and reached over 100,000 readers. At the peak of her career, Madame Demorest also produced *Madame Demorest's What to Wear and How to Make It* (1877–1884) and quarterly catalogs. She also expanded the *Demorest's Monthly* to London circulation.

Merchandising

In addition to marketing through the magazines, the paper patterns were sold through a nationwide network of shops called "Madame Demorest's Magasins des Modes." In the mid-1870s there were 300 shops employing 1,500 (mainly women) sales agents. In addition to the paper patterns, the Excelsior drafting system was also showcased and sold at these satellite stores, which were located in major cities in the United States, Canada, Europe, and Cuba.

Madame Demorest continued to use the flagship Emporium store on Broadway to merchandise the full array of Demorest products. In the earliest years, Madame Demorest's Emporium of Fashion was located at 375 Broadway near Lord and Taylor and Brooks Brothers; then the business was moved to 473 Broadway in 1860. In 1874 the Emporium moved farther uptown, to 17 East Fourteenth Street, and catered to an increasingly fashionable set. The Emporium provided custom dressmaking services to wealthy clients, as well as ready-made accessories and undergarments; Demorest's unique line of cosmetics and perfumes; and, of course, the monthly magazines and paper patterns. Although it was only a small part of their overall business, the custom dressmaking service at the Emporium lent prestige and luxury to their name, a marketing tool that Madame Demorest was savvy enough to harness.

Madame Demorest's participation in numerous national and international exhibitions cemented her reputation as a fashion arbiter. A frequent exhibitor at London and Paris shows, she is noted as having created a large display at the Philadelphia Centennial Exhibition in 1876 in which she installed several women's and children's

MRS. STRATTON'S WEDDING TROUSSEAU

One of Madame Demorest's most newsworthy custom dressmaking projects was the wedding trousseau she designed for Mrs. Charles Stratton, née Miss Lavinia Warren, in 1863. The Strattons were better known at the time as General and Mrs. Tom Thumb, midgets who toured with P. T. Barnum's circus. After their wedding in New York City, which was attended by 2,000 people, Mr. and Mrs. Stratton headed to Europe on a world tour that included reception at several royal households. The Madame Demorest reception dresses, worn by Mrs. Stratton at these functions, were widely publicized.

fashions; her drafting tool, "Dress Model"; and a huge case filled with paper patterns.

Progressive Causes

In the 1880s Madame Demorest's fashion empire began to decline. Unlike her competitor Ebenezer Butterick, Madame Demorest had never filed patents for her paper patterns and eventually lost out in this arena. The paper pattern business was sold in 1887. In later years both Ellen and her husband, William, turned their attention to social causes that had always been of interest to them. William was deeply committed to the temperance cause, which often found expression in the pages of the *Demorest Monthly* magazine. Ellen increasingly supported women's causes. Both Demorests were strong advocates of abolition and deserve particular recognition for their unusually progressive business policy of hiring African American women agents who were treated equally with their white employees, sharing workplaces and receiving equal pay.

At the height of her career in the 1870s, Madame Demorest could rightly claim to be one of the most influential fashion disseminators of her era. Her paper patterns and fashion magazines reached millions of women in America and Europe, bringing sophisticated yet affordable fashions to the masses. At the same time, Madame Demorest created brand identity through her innovatively named lines of accessories and cosmetic products, while burnishing her reputation for quality through her luxury dressmaking establishment. While it could be said that she appeared at the right place at the right time when a population of women had the inclination and means, via the sewing machine, to make fashions at home, Madame Demorest was singularly astute in her comprehension of women's fashion needs and her ability to market to them through the widely read Demorest publications.

See also **Godey's Lady's Book; Patterns and Patternmaking; Sewing Machine.**

BIBLIOGRAPHY

Drachman, Virginia G. *Enterprising Women: 250 Years of American Business.* Chapel Hill: University of North Carolina Press, 2002.

Emery, Joy. "Development of the American Commercial Pattern Industry: The First Generation, 1850–1880." *Costume* 31 (1997): 78–91.

Gamber, Wendy. *The Female Economy: The Millinery and Dressmaking Trades, 1860–1930.* Urbana: University of Illinois Press, 1997.

Kidwell, Claudia Brush. *Cutting a Fashionable Fit: Dressmakers' Drafting Systems in the United States.* Washington, D.C.: Smithsonian Institution Press, 1979.

Milbank, Caroline Rennolds. *New York Fashion: The Evolution of American Style.* New York: Harry N. Abrams, 1989.

Mott, Frank Luther. *A History of American Magazines.* Cambridge, Mass.: Belknap Press of Harvard University Press, 1938.

Ross, Ishbel. *Crusades and Crinolines: The Life and Times of Ellen Curtis Demorest and William Jennings Demorest.* New York: Harper and Row, 1963.

Lauren Whitley

DENIM Twill patterns of weaving seem to have developed early in the first millennium B.C.E. Hallstatt culture in Europe. Technically speaking, denim is a warp-faced twill weave fabric. The most basic twill weave calls for passing the weft (crosswise) yarn over two and under two warp (lengthwise) yarns (2/2 twill), a pairing that gives the pattern its name, two-ing or twill. In warp-faced twills, warp yarns are predominant on the front or face of the fabric and because warp yarns have a higher twist, the resulting fabric is stronger than many other weaves. In denim, the warp-faced twill pattern calls for passing the weft yarn over one and under two (1/2), or over one and under three warp (1/3) yarns. Because there are fewer lacings in twills than in plain weaves, the yarns are freer to move when being worn resulting in a fabric that is both flexible and resilient. The fewer the lacings, as in twills compared to plain weaves, the closer together yarns may be packed, thus producing a higher number of yarns per inch, making the resulting fabric stronger yet.

Popularly speaking, denim has been associated with fabric coloring, garment style, and lifestyle. Whole books have been written about twentieth-century denim and its popularity with teenagers and celebrities. The word has become so popular and generic in its use that rock bands, stage troupes, and even bottled water, have taken the name denim. The name itself is derived from Nimes, a small city in southern France that had long been famous for its textile industry.

Levi Strauss is given the credit for the common use of denim in the rugged trousers first sold to gold miners

GOODBYE TO AN AMERICAN ICON

On 26 September 2003, the *San Francisco Chronicle* announced that in 2004 plant closings would mark the end of the Levi's U.S. jeans-making era. Levi Strauss & Co. was a reflection of more than 150 years of American history, from the rough days of the California Gold Rush and the opening of the wild west, through the Great Depression. The impact of Levis grew during two world wars and Vietnam resulting in fashions that emphasized casual dress and conspicuous consumption simultaneously. Through it all, Levi Strauss & Co. became an icon with undisputed class.

during the California gold rush of the 1850s and 1860s. While the twill weave used in those first trousers for gold miners was undeniably hardier than the plain weave that canvas miners had been wearing, it was the metal-riveted pockets that began to appear in the 1860s and 1870s that most interested the miners.

Jacob Davis, a tailor and wholesale customer of Levi Strauss, came up with the idea of putting metal rivets at the points of stress on denim trousers. Strauss hired Jacob Davis to oversee the manufacturing in San Francisco of the blue denim "waist overalls" as they were called. On 20 May 1873, Davis and Strauss received patent #139,121 from the U.S. Patent and Trademark Office for an "Improvement in Fastening Pocket-Openings." The riveted waist overalls were made from denim fabric furnished by the Amoskeag Mill in Manchester, New Hampshire. The waist overalls that are commonly called "jeans" or "blue jeans" were a hit with miners and other workers whose clothing had to be rugged. Cowboys who often spent days, and even nights, in the saddle herding cattle wore the trousers extensively.

In the 1900s, denim was most associated with rugged trousers dyed indigo blue. It is not known exactly when or why jeans or waist overalls yarns first began to be dyed blue. One of the best reasons given is that blue seems to hide dirt and stains better than the tan first associated with waist overalls. The uneven surface of twill weaves hides soil as well. Also, because the yarns can be more tightly packed in twills than in plain weaves, the fabric resists soiling by liquid spills.

Until the 1920s and 1930s denim waist overalls were scarcely known east of the Mississippi River. They were worn in the West as work pants.

From the mid-to-late 1950s and 1960s, blue denim ceased to be used mostly for work clothes. Indigo or blue denim became a hot fashion item. Men's and women's suits were made from denim, as well as evening dresses, which began to be studded with rhinestones instead of rivets. In the 1960s denim blue jeans became one of the signs of rebellion among teenagers and twenty-something young adults. The young rebels, known as hippies and flower children, embroidered their jeans and painted them with flowers, peace signs (in protest of the U.S. involvement in Vietnam), and psychedelic designs.

In the 1980s and 1990s, denim became associated with various shades of blue as much as with its twill weave. Sheets, pillowcases, upholstery, bathing suits, dresses, leather and cloth shoes, underwear, paper, and even pencils were called "denim." Wood furniture was stained to have a denim appearance.

Almost every well-known European and U.S. designer from Calvin Klein to Giorgio Armani has made denim part of their fashion lines. Denim was seen as an American lifestyle fabrication and style. Denim was no longer the fabric of choice for just the blue-collar worker. It became an upper-class classic, even "preppy" look. Casual denim skirts and trousers were often combined with cashmere jackets and mink or ermine coats on the runway and on the streets. Denim trousers became accepted in high profile, black-tie events, worn with a formal tuxedo shirt and jacket. Virtually the only place where the casual nature of blue jeans remained unacceptable was in the dress of attorneys in the courtroom.

Old or vintage blue denim was very popular in the 1980s and 1990s, particularly in Asia and the United States. In Japan, the demand for vintage denim blue jeans was so great in the 1990s that it outstripped supplies.

Blue denim jeans in the 1990s were decorated extensively with colorful braid and glass bead fringe at the waist and edges of trouser legs. Legs of denim jeans were often slashed from the mid-thigh to the trouser leg edge and then laced with cord. Cotton was combined with latex for a fabrication that could be worn skintight and yet remain comfortably elastic. Denim was produced in colors other than blue, including black, green, pink, and tan—but those colors never attained the popularity of blue denim. In the early 2000s, it appears that denim will never be seen as a fad. It is an international classic.

See also **Jeans; Levi Strauss & Co.**

BIBLIOGRAPHY

Barber, E. J. W. *Prehistoric Textiles: The Development of Cloth in the Neolithic and Bronze Ages with Special Reference to the Aegean.* Princeton, N.J.: Princeton University Press, 1991.

Kadolph, Sara J., and Langford, Anna L. *Textiles.* 8th ed. Upper Saddle River, N.J.: Prentice-Hall, 1998.

Internet Resource

Levi Strauss & Co. 2001. Available from <http://www.levistrauss.com>.

Carol Anne Dickson

DEPARTMENT STORE The birthplace of the department store was Paris. The Bon Marché opened in 1852, soon followed by Printemps (1865) and the Samaritaine (1869). Existing shops in the United States—Stewart in New York, Wanamaker in Philadelphia and Marshall Field in Chicago—adopted the format during the 1870s. The department store brought together a series of retail methods tested out in smaller European and American shops earlier in the century, for example, the proto-department stores in industrial cities in the north of Britain (Lancaster, chapter 1). The department store proper was distinctive from previous experiments in its scale, lavishness, and resonance with the society that spawned it. The early Parisian stores were hugely influential models for subsequent stores springing up all over the world. The history of the department store has been largely located in Western Europe and North America. The arrival of the format in East Asian cities such as Shanghai and Tokyo in the early twentieth century has been associated with westernization, but the stores were often locally owned and managed, creating complex issues surrounding their identity.

The conditions for the rise of the department store lay in late-eighteenth- and early-nineteenth-century industrialization and urbanization, which led to the growth of prosperous, urban, middle-class populations and the ready availability of mass-produced consumer goods, along with an increasingly sophisticated understanding of the pleasurable rather than merely utilitarian possibilities of consuming them. Important department stores were situated in urban centers, on principal shopping streets, working in conjunction with other shops, entertainment venues, and transport networks. However, well-heeled suburbs also had department stores in their high streets. By the late nineteenth century, considered the hey-day of the department store, these shops had become emblematic of metropolitan modernity and were famously made the backdrop of Émile Zola's novel *The Ladies' Paradise*.

The major department stores of each important city—for example, Harrods, Liberty's and Selfridges in London—quickly became urban landmarks and cultural institutions, cited in guide books as tourist attractions. During the early twentieth century, American stores took the lead as innovators, becoming increasingly influential on their European counterparts. During the interwar and early postwar periods, while alternative shopping sites were developing, fashion magazines such as *Vogue* show that the big department stores retained their central position within urban consumption practices in many cities. However, despite stores' attempts to address broader sections of the population, the opening of teen departments and the provision of new buildings, fundamental modernization of the format did not occur. The combined competition from the multiple store and alternative boutique in the urban high street and from the suburban shopping center and out-of-town mall led to a slow decline in the cultural and economic importance of the department

Moscow's GUM department store. Formerly known as the State Department Store, Gosudarstvenny Universalny Magazin (GUM) is located in Moscow's Red Square. Its three stories of shops boast some five kilometers of shelves. © DAVID H. WELLS/CORBIS. REPRODUCED BY PERMISSION.

store from the 1960s, accelerating during the 1980s. There were several factors that increased a store's chances of survival: possession of an international reputation, such as that of Harrods, London; absorption into a larger group, such as the House of Fraser or the John Lewis Partnership; positioning on a major metropolitan shopping thoroughfare or as the anchor in a shopping center. The early twenty-first century has witnessed a revival of the metropolitan department store, connected with a renewed focus on luxury goods and designer fashion, prime examples being Selfridges and Liberty in London. The department store has proved to be enduring.

Stock Diversity and New Selling Methods

An important innovation of department stores was their wide variety of merchandise, breaching the boundaries of previously largely trade-specific shop-keeping. Many of the early department stores actually developed from smaller existing shops, most commonly drapers. They grew department by department, taking over neighboring properties to house the expanding businesses, until it was necessary to provide a new building or reface the existing ones to provide coherence. Department store pioneer William Whiteley famously boasted that he sold "everything from a pin to an elephant." The system worked on a basis of low margins and high turnover. The stores were certainly a place for the sale of mass-produced goods and have been associated with the rise of ready-to-wear clothing. However, most stores continued to provide traditional tailoring and drapery well into the twentieth century. The diversity of stock was matched by an array of amenities and entertainments, including banks, restaurants, travel agents, fashion shows and live music, and services such as free delivery and alteration of garments.

Store histories are entwined with those of their owning dynasties, who usually gave their name to their stores, for example, the Wertheims and Schockens in Germany and the Lewises in England. Stores often merged with or were taken over by other stores, for example, the evolving nature of Britain's House of Fraser described by Moss and Turton. The business was organized in a hierarchical, rational, and paternalistic manner. Strict control of the workforce was balanced with benefits such as healthcare, pensions, and social clubs. Indeed during the early days many of the employees lived in the upper stories of the building. This practice faded out following several high profile, devastating fires caused by gas lighting and poor fire-proofing of buildings. The stores required vast staffs; for example, Harrods of London had 4,000 employees in 1914. For nineteenth- and early twentieth-century social commentators and novelists, the figure of the young female shop assistant symbolized the dubious respectability, moral ambiguity, and blurring of class boundaries they found so disturbing about the department store. However, until the interwar period, the majority of employees were actually male and lower middle class. Positions were sought after, although salaries were low.

Customers and a New Kind of Shopping

From the beginning, the department store was associated with bourgeois consumers. As Miller has argued, "The department store was . . . a bourgeois celebration, an expression of what its culture stood for and where it had come over the past century" (Miller, p. 3). It was also initially seen as the exclusive province of women. The stores' provision of basic amenities such as lavatories and refreshment rooms made a day trip to town newly accessible for suburban and provincial middle-class women, enabling them to take advantage of improved public transport networks. Early department store owners, such as William Whiteley of Bayswater in London, were vocal in their claims to make shopping in the city a safe and respectable activity for unchaperoned women (Rappaport). However, they also attempted to exploit feminine desires using new ideas about consumer psychology.

The distinctiveness of the department store model lay as much in the presentation of shopping as a pleasurable leisure activity as with the nature or number of goods available. Previously, shopping models had largely favored counter service and the acknowledgment of an obligation to buy once the shop was entered. In the new stores, the role of the retail staff was redefined and a different kind of shopping was encouraged, characterized by window shopping and browsing through displays of goods with fixed and ticketed prices. These practices drew on the cultures of the international exhibitions that followed London's Great Exhibition of 1851. All this, it was believed, would encourage impulse buying.

During the early twentieth century, department stores began to cater to men with dedicated departments. In 1936 Simpson Piccadilly opened in London's West End, claiming to be the first department store entirely for men. The lower ground floor alone was designed to house a barber's shop, soda fountain, gun shop, shoe shop, chemists, florist, fishing shop, wine and spirit shop, luggage shop, snack bar, dog shop, sports shop, cigar and tobacconists, gift shop, saddlery shop, theater agent, and travel agent. During the opening months the aviation department even exhibited full-sized airplanes. The opening of the store coincided with new ideas about masculinity, which allowed for the adoption of shopping methods previously labeled feminine. *The Lady* (7 May 1936) commented on this, "It is amusing to find that the man's shop is designed and set out with all the allure of one devoted to women's luxuries. Shopkeepers, evidently, do not share that masculine theory that a man always knows just what he wants and so is immune from display or advertisement."

Design, Display, and Advertising

Zola called the department stores "cathedrals of commerce" and they were certainly associated with lavish, striking, and fashionable architecture, acting as an advertisement for the goods inside. Famous and innovative architects were often employed: Victor Horta designed Innovation in Brussels (1901), Louis Sullivan designed Carson Pirie Scott in Chicago (1899–1904), and Erich Mendelsohn designed the Schocken store in Stuttgart (1926-1928). The *Scotsman* commented on the opening of Simpson Piccadilly in London designed by the modernist architect Joseph Emberton, "the building is an expression in every way of the modern spirit" (4 May 1936). But the buildings were not just fashionable shells. The latest technological advances were used to assist the retail process. Iron then steel frames created vast uninterrupted expanses of floor space and plate glass technology facilitated story-high bands of display windows flanking the shopping street. Inside, escalators and lifts were installed, helping to sustain a continuous flow of customers between the street and the upper echelons of the building. Pneumatic tube systems were provided for communication and placing orders. Tiers of galleries allowed light from the roof to penetrate the shop floor, assisted by the pioneering use of first gas then electric lighting. Lighting was also used on the facade of the building—floodlighting, lit signage, and window illumination—so that the stores had a nighttime presence in the city, catching the eye of revellers.

Department stores led the way with developments in retail display, with opulent displays of goods inside the stores, in the shop windows, and sometimes spilling onto the streets. Displays were often themed in relation with events being held in the stores or national celebrations. It was the shop window in particular that became emblematic of the department store's contribution to the urban spectacle and seduction of customers. The early department stores had a particularly sophisticated understanding of the power of advertising. To the consternation of traditional smaller-scale retailers, significant amounts were spent on newspaper and magazine advertisements, and on regular publishing of catalogs, the Bon Marché in Paris distributed 1.5 million catalogs. In 1894 (Crossick and Jaumain p. 12). This emphasis on design, display, and advertising was integral to the new kind of shopping promoted in the department store, encouraging consumption through the exploitation of visual pleasures.

See also **Boutique; Liberty & Co.; Retailing; Shopping; Window Displays.**

BIBLIOGRAPHY

Crossick, Geoffrey, and Serge Jaumain, eds. *Cathedrals of Consumption: The European Department Store.* Aldershot, U.K.: Ashgate, 1999. The key text in the field: an excellent and diverse edited collection of essays.

Lancaster, Bill. *The Department Store: A Social History.* London and New York: Leicester University Press, 1995. A comprehensive study of the British department store in social historical terms.

Leach, William. *Land of Desire: Merchants, Power and the Rise of a New American Culture.* New York: Vintage, 1993. A lively account of the American story from the 1890s to the 1930s.

MacPherson, Kerrie L., ed. *Asian Department Stores.* Richmond, Surrey U.K.: Curzon, 1998.

Miller, Michael *The Bon Marché: Bourgeois Culture and the Department Store, 1869–1920.* Princeton, N.J.: Princeton University Press, 1981. A case study of the first department store, highlighting issues of class and business methods.

Moss, Michael, and Alison Turton. *A Legend of Retailing: House of Fraser.* London: Weidenfeld and Nicolson, 1989. A detailed, well-illustrated account of one of Britain's most important department store groups.

Rappaport, Erika Diane. *Shopping for Pleasure: Women and the Making of London's West End.* Princeton, N.J.: Princeton University Press, 2000. A contextual study of the department store in its West End location in the Victorian and Edwardian eras, focusing on issues of gender.

Zola, Émile. *The Ladies' Paradise.* Oxford U.K.: Oxford University Press, 1998. This is a translation of Zola's novel *Au*

bonheur des dames, first published in 1883, reputedly based on the Bon Marché.

Bronwen Edwards

DIANA, PRINCESS OF WALES In 1997 the influential fashion photographer Mario Testino shot a series of seminal images of Princess Diana wearing Gianni Versace for *Vanity Fair* magazine. These photographs have come to define the look and glamour of a woman who became an important fashion icon of the twentieth century. In the early twenty-first century, media interest in her image remained undiminished.

Diana Frances Spencer (1961–1997) was born in Park House on the Queen's estate at Sandringham, the third child of Johnny, eldest son of the seventh earl of Spencer and a member of one of England's most important aristocratic families. In 1969 when Diana's parents were divorced, her father retained custody of the children, and in 1975 when Diana was fourteen, the seventh earl died, and the family moved to their ancestral home, Althorp in Northampton. When she was seventeen, her father bought her an apartment in Kensington, London, where Diana found work as a nanny until the day of her engagement to Prince Charles was announced.

The couple married on 29 July 1981, at St. Paul's Cathedral. Diana's wedding dress, designed by Elizabeth and David Emanuel, was a fairy-tale fantasy showcasing traditional English craftwork. It featured woven silk taffeta by Stephen Walters of Suffolk and historic lace from a flounce of Carrickmacross lace owned by Queen Mary and from the Nottingham Company, Roger Watson. The dress became one of the most famous outfits in the world, and the twenty-five-foot train added a touch of theatricality that would create an enduring image of the event, which was watched on live television by more than one billion people worldwide.

From that moment the princess became an international figure, photographed and documented wherever she went, and she became a global fashion icon. Diana loved clothes; they were a personal passion but also a requirement of her new public life. As one of the most important members of the British royal family, her wardrobe requirements were fixed in a world that required ball gowns and matching hats, shoes, and handbags, items that were not typical of mainstream fashion for young women in the early 1980s.

It is not surprising then that in the early years of her marriage she was steered toward established British fashion designers, including Murray Arbeid, Belville Sassoon, and Gini Fratini, whose traditions of classic tailoring for day and romantic evening wear dated back fifty years. Diana was, however, determined to stamp a modern and youthful personal style on this public and formal persona, and, more than any other British designer, Catherine

Dress worn by Princess Diana. Diana worked within the boundaries of royal tradition to create her own modern style, which was both elegant and youthful, quickly elevating her to fashion icon status. AP/WIDE WORLD PHOTOS. REPRODUCED BY PERMISSION.

Walker helped her to develop an elegant, tailored look that became her own.

From the 1980s Catherine Walker helped Diana create a streamlined modern version of clothes for her public life as the Princess of Wales. After her divorce from Prince Charles, Diana went on to develop a more individual style that reflected her new independence and freedom. Diana understood her role as a fashion icon and that everything she wore—every new accessory and change of hairstyle—would be scrutinized. In the 1990s, in search of a new look, she remained loyal to British designers, notably Jacques Azagury, who encouraged her to wear dresses cut revealingly low and to wear shorter skirts. Increasingly, however, she turned to European designers—the Italian designers Versace and Valentino and to the French couture houses of Dior, Lacroix, and Chanel. Her look became more international with a sophisticated and simple silhouette and an effect that was all in the details. Superb cut and luxurious materials worn with coordinated colored accessories, handbags, jewelry, and shoes became her hallmark. It is this image that defined an enduring fashion look of the late twentieth century.

See also **Royal and Aristocratic Dress.**

BIBLIOGRAPHY

Howell, Georgina. *Diana: Her Life in Fashion.* New York: Rizzoli International, 1998.

Tierney, Tom. *Diana, Princess of Wales, Paper Doll: The Charity Auction Dresses.* New York: Dover Publications, Inc., 1997.

Catherine McDermott

DIOR, CHRISTIAN The French couturier Christian Dior (1905–1957) was born in Granville, France. Descendant of a manufacturing family of the Norman bourgeoisie, Dior spent his early childhood in the comfortable surroundings of the family villa, Les Rhumbs, located on the Channel coast in Granville, which now houses a museum dedicated to his memory. At that time the little port was celebrated as a fashionable seaside resort, and in summertime it was transformed into "an elegant Paris neighborhood." The family moved to Paris in 1911, to the new bourgeois neighborhood of Passy, near the bois de Boulogne.

Following his father's wishes, Dior registered at the École de Sciences Politiques in Paris after passing his baccalaureate. He eagerly followed Parisian artistic developments and met various writers, painters, and musicians, befriending, among others, Pierre Gaxotte, Maurice Sachs, Jean Ozenne and his cousin Christian Bérard, Max Jacob, and Henri Sauguet. In 1927, after his military service and with his father's support, he opened an art gallery at 34, rue de la Boétie. Because his parents refused to have their name on a commercial sign, the establishment was given the name of his associate, Jacques Bonjean. The gallery exhibited the works of such contemporary artists as Giorgio de Chirico, Maurice Utrillo, Salvador Dalí, Raoul Dufy, Marie Laurencin, Fernand Léger, Jean Lurçat, Pablo Picasso, Ossip Zadkine, Georges Braque, and Aristide Maillol.

Christian Dior's carefree youth soon came to an end: in 1931 his brother was institutionalized, his mother died, and his father was completely ruined financially. "In the face of this accumulation of tragedies," Dior reacted by a "flight to the East." He was "naïvely impelled by a desperate search for a new solution to problems that this crisis of capitalism had made acute," embarking on a study trip to the Soviet Union with a group of architects, only to find on his return that his associate was also ruined. His impoverished family abandoned Paris, retreating first to Normandy and later taking refuge in the village of Callian, near Cannes. Dior stayed behind in Paris, closing his first gallery and later joining the gallery of Pierre Colle on the rue Cambacérès. He thus went from "losses to forced sales while continuing to organize surrealist or abstract exhibitions that drove away the last art lovers." In 1934 he had an attack of tuberculosis, and his friends took up a collection to send him for treatment. The following year he found himself in Paris with no income and no place to live. He survived on the sale of one of his last canvases, *Le plan de Paris* of Raoul Dufy, which the designer Paul Poiret had sold to Dior when he was in similar destitute circumstances.

Christian Dior. Christian Dior opened his first salon in Paris in 1946 and had expanded his network of shops to twenty-four countries before his death by a heart attack in 1957. THE LIBRARY OF CONGRESS. PUBLIC DOMAIN.

Couture and Costume

Jean Ozenne, who was designing for couture houses, introduced Dior to the fashion world and to his clientele. At the age of thirty, Dior devoted himself to studying fashion drawing, referring only to what he knew and appreciated of Edward Molyneux, Coco Chanel, Elsa Schiaparelli, and Jeanne Lanvin. He managed to sell his first sketches of hats and then of dresses. His clients were fashionable hat makers and couture houses but he "also sold ideas to foreign buyers." Publication of his drawings in *Le figaro* produced his first public recognition. In 1937 the couturier Robert Piguet selected four of his designs and asked him to produce them for his "half-collection" (midseason collection). Christian Dior was just thirty-two, and these were, he said, the "first dresses that I really created."

In June 1938 Robert Piguet offered him a position as a designer in his couture studio located at the Rond Point of the Champs Élysées. There he designed three collections in a row. The second contained his "first wide dresses," inspired by dresses worn by young heroines of the French second empire children's literature "les petites filles modèles" (well-behaved little girls). They were characterized by a "raised bust, round width starting from the waist, petticoat of English embroidery." As the creator of a successful design called "English coffee," he was introduced to Carmel Snow, editor of *Harper's Bazaar*. In 1939 his last prewar collection for Piguet launched the line of what came to be called "amphora dresses" marking the "beginning of rounded hips." In parallel with his work as a designer, Dior designed theater costumes for individual clients. He dressed, for example, the actress Odette Joyeux in *Captain Smith* by Jean Blanchon (at the théâtre des Mathurins, December 1939) and in *The School for Scandal* by Richard Sheridan (at the same theater, February 1940).

Dior was mobilized at the outbreak of war in 1939 and then joined his family in the unoccupied zone of France after the 1940 armistice. Piguet, still in Paris, asked him to resume his prewar position, but Dior was late in replying and found the position already taken by Antonio del Castillo in the fall of 1941. Dior then went to work for Lucien Lelong, together with another young designer, Pierre Balmain. The two shared design responsibilities throughout the war: "Balmain and I never forgot that Lelong taught us our profession in the midst of the worst restrictions," said Dior. The personality of Lucien Lelong, the clever president of the Chambre syndicate de la couture parisienne (association of haute couture) throughout the German occupation of France, deeply influenced the future couturier. After his study trip to the United States in 1935 and the launch of his Edition line, Dior had developed an interest in foreign markets and high-end ready-to-wear. In contrast, he saw fashion under the German occupation as "appalling" and exclaimed: "With what vengeful joy did I do the opposite later."

It was nonetheless a productive period for him: films (*Le Lit à colonne* by Roland Tual [1942], *Lettre d'amour* [1942] and *Sylvie et le fantôme* [1945] by Claude Autant-Lara, *Échec au roi* by Jean-Paul Paulin [1943], and *Paméla; ou, L'énigme du temple* by Pierre de Hérain [1945]) and Marcel L'Herbier's play *Au petit bonheur* (at the théâtre Gramont, December 1944) gave him the opportunity to escape from the textile rationing that governed ordinary clothing and to conceive, often for Odette Joyeux, historically inspired costumes full of long dresses and extravagant designs.

After the Liberation, Dior's colleague Pierre Balmain opened his own couture house in 1945 on rue François Ier and encouraged Dior to do the same. Marcel Boussac, a major French textile manufacturer and president of the cotton-marketing syndicate, offered Dior the artistic direction of the Gaston firm (formerly called Philippe et Gaston) on rue Saint-Florentin. Considering the business outmoded, Dior suggested instead that he start a couture house "where everything would be new, from the state of mind and the personnel to the furnishings and the premises," in view of the fact "that foreign markets, after the long stagnation of fashion due to the war, were bound to demand really new fashions." Marcel Boussac invested sixty million francs in the project.

The House of Dior
In 1946 Dior chose a private mansion located at 30, avenue Montaigne as the site of his own firm, which was established on 8 October 1946. The enterprise had four models and eighty-five employees, sixty of whom were seamstresses. The management team, in addition to the head couturier, included a financial director (Jacques Rouet), a studio head (Raymonde Zehnacker, who came from Lelong), a head of workshops (Marguerite Carré, who came from Patou), and an artistic adviser and head of high-fashion design (Mitzah Bricard, a designer from Molyneux). The couture house itself included two workshops for dresses and one for suits (whose head was Pierre

Cardin, then twenty years old). From the outset, it also had, on the ground floor, a shop selling articles and accessories not requiring fitting. Salons and shops were decorated by Victor Grampierre in tones of white and pearl gray and furnished in neo–Louis XVI style.

The opening was widely publicized: "When the summer 1946 collections came out, everyone was talking about Christian Dior, because an extraordinary rumor was spreading that the financial assistance of Marcel Boussac, the French king of cotton . . . would enable him to create his own house." Even before it was seen, Dior's first collection thus made news, and he won the support of the editors of *Vogue*, *Le figaro*, and *Elle*. The newcomer among couture houses, Christian Dior finally unveiled, at the conclusion of the winter shows, his first collection for spring 1947. Considered the opening shot for the New Look, it immediately gained notoriety for the couturier at the age of forty-two. "The first season was brilliant, even beyond my hopes," he said. The second, in which the couturier carried "the famous New Look line to its extreme," achieved "breathtaking" success and was accompanied by the launch of his first perfume, Miss Dior.

With this impetus, Dior spent the last ten years of his life developing his couture house and extending his influence on world fashion. (In 1955 the Dior firm had one thousand employees in twenty-eight workshops and accounted for half the exports of the French couture industry.) For his first collection, Dior received the Neiman Marcus Award in 1947. From his trip to the United States, he learned, as he put it, that "if I wanted to reach the large number of elegant American women . . . I had to open a luxury ready-to-wear shop in New York." The following year, he set up the subsidiary Christian Dior New York, Inc., at 745 Fifth Avenue. He repeated the process in Caracas in 1953 (Christian Dior Venezuela), in London in 1954 (Christian Dior, Ltd.), and later in Australia, Chile, Mexico, and Cuba. These companies custom-made styles from Paris and sold accessories. But it was not until 1967 that a real line of ready-to-wear was distributed, under the label Miss Dior.

In 1948 the Christian Dior perfume company was set up, and it launched the second fragrance, Diorama, in 1949, followed by Eau Fraîche (1953) and Diorissimo (1956); the first lipsticks came out in 1955. Dior opened a stocking and glove division in 1951 and established the Christian Dior Delman company, which made shoes designed by Roger Vivier; finally, the Paris shop added a gifts and tableware department in 1954. The range of products with the Dior label was enlarged thanks to a very innovative policy for licenses, the first of which was granted in 1949. By this means, the label was attached to all the accessories of female dress, from girdle to jewelry, but also, and very early on, to totally distinct articles, such as Christian Dior Ties (1950).

The growth of the house was fostered by a simple and effective public relations policy: little direct advertising but excellent relations with the press, which guaranteed great visibility for the fashions as well as for their creator (who was featured on the cover of *Time* on 4 March 1957). The couturier gave many interviews, designed disguises for memorable parties (among them, the Venetian ball of Carlos de Beistegui given at the Palazzo Labia on 3 September 1951), and continued to dress stars, such as Marlene Dietrich in Alfred Hitchcock's *Stage Fright* in 1950 and Henry Koster's *No Highway in the Sky* in 1951 and Ava Gardner in Mark Robson's *The Little Hut* in 1956. In *Christian Dior et moi* (1956), Dior described his career, strewn with Parisian celebrities, pitfalls, coups de théâtre, and palm readers' predictions. In passing, he reassured the reader about the motives for his long-ago trip to the Soviet Union and emphasized his admiration for the entrepreneurial spirit, thus helping to forge the paradoxical myth of the creator of scandals with a reassuring face.

The attention given to the collections was intensified each year by the expectation—followed by the announcement—of a new major change (affecting, notably, the length of skirts). The couturier himself issued descriptive communiqués adopted by the press that frequently took a peremptory tone, such as "No yellow" or "No hats with clean and tailored style," giving force to the new fashion tendency. The collections, each containing approximately two hundred items, unveiled in succession contradictory lines that imposed on fashion a rate of change never seen before: Corolle and 8 (1947), also known as the "New Look collection"; Zig-Zag and Envol, followed by Ailée (1948); Trompe-l'œil and Milieu de Siècle (1949); Verticale and Oblique (1951); Ovale ou Naturelle and Longue (1951); Sinueuse and Profilée (1952); Tulipe and Vivante (1953); Muguet and H (1954), A and Y (1955); Flèche and Aimant (1956); and Libre and Fuseau (1957).

La Belle Epoque Influences on the New Look

Differing in their lines, his creations were always related to one another through the constancy of certain characteristics. Structurally, the dresses came out of the intention to sculpt the silhouette along predefined lines. Whether it was the New Look, the Shock Look (the English name for the Vivante line), or the Flat Look (the H line), the body was always strongly stylized. The waist was displaced, cinched, or unbelted. The hips swelled or shrank thanks to the choice of materials able to express in shapes the energetic and tense designs of the couturier: shantung, ottoman silk, thick taffetas and satins, velvet, organza, woolen cloth, and cotton piqué generally replaced the customary use of fluid woolen and silk crepes. Originator of a style that used a large quantity of material, artifices, and ornaments, Christian Dior stimulated the growth of a number of parallel industries: corset makers, feather makers, embroiderers, makers of costume jewelry, flower designers, and also illustrators. Thus, the image of the creations of Christian Dior includes the shoes of Roger Vivier, the prints of Brossin de Méré, the tulles of Brivet, the fabrics of Rébé (René Bégué) and Georges Barbier, the jewels of Francis Winter, and the drawings of René Gruau. As for furs and hats, they were manufactured in specialized workshops of the couture house.

Stylistically, Dior's creations were frequently distinguished by ornaments that came directly from pre-1914 fashion. Simulated knots; false pockets; decorative buttons; play with cuffs, collars, basques, and tails; false belts; and bias cuts punctuated his collections with their trompe-l'oeil effects and, from the outset, erased any modernist intentions.

Dior did not specify the origin of his stylistic borrowings. In particular, he expressed only elliptical intentions to justify the inspiration for his New Look: "I have a reactionary temperament, a characteristic that is too often confused with the retrograde; we had barely come out of a deprived, parsimonious era, obsessed with tickets and textile rationing. My dream therefore naturally took on the form of a reaction against poverty." Hence, it is in the context of the presentation of his shows that we should look for an explicit expression of his historical inspiration. Speaking of the renovation of the mansion on the avenue Montaigne, the couturier asserted that he was striving "to prepare a cradle in the style and the colors of the years of [his] Paris childhood" and described "this neo-Louis XVI, white paneling, lacquered white furniture, gray hangings, glass doors with small beveled panes, bronze wall lamps, and small lamp shades that ruled from 1900 to 1914 in the 'new' houses of Passy." He displayed a "crystal chandelier and a proliferation of palms," while the shop, on the advice of Christian Bérard, was given a hanging of cloth of Jouy "in the tradition of notion shops of the eighteenth century."

In parallel with this nostalgic neo-neo-Louis XVI style, a veritable mirroring of pastiche, Christian Dior seemed throughout his career to draw the material artifice of his pleated, draped, corseted, and decorated effects from the clothing vocabulary of the Belle Époque. "I thank heaven that I lived in Paris during the last years of the belle époque . . . whatever life has granted me since then, nothing will ever be able to equal the sweet memory of those days," he wrote. But by choosing as his favorite period one in which taste was eclectic, the designer avoided the domination of a single style in order to free himself to adopt all possible reinterpretations of the past.

Neither the structural artifices nor the proliferation of appliquéd ornaments interfered with the readability of the line. Paradoxically, Dior's creations attracted primarily through their sobriety. As evidence of an eclectic sensibility, the ornamental resources derived from turn-of-the-century fashion were effectively deployed with a concern for modernity hostile to the composite. The conception of each model seemed to be guided only by emphasis on a single effect at a time. From one model to the next, one's attention was shifted, for example, from the emphasis of a cut to the shimmering of a pattern or to the luxurance of the embroidery. The directed gaze, channeled by the erasure of the superfluous—by the notorious choice of uniform and subdued colors when the cut was to be emphasized or, on the contrary, the choice of a simple cut to emphasize the fabric—guaranteed the visual impact of each model and pointed up its strong identity. It thus was beyond the individual model and only in the course of the show that the succession of appearances enabled the presentation of an aesthetic of the whole, both composite and romantic.

The constancy of stylistic borrowings from the past revealed a veritable postmodernist stance on the part of this man who was so admirably ensconced in his century. As Dior himself said:

It is strange that in 1956 people applied the names avant-garde and aesthetic of the future to the works and the masters that we had admired between the ages of fifteen and twenty and who had already been famous for ten years among the most aware of our elders, guided by Guillaume Apollinaire.

But for Dior, "the new at all costs, even to create the absurd, is no longer the essential area of exploration." Far from the aspirations of prewar surrealism, he confided the origin of his first collections: "After so many years of wandering, weary with consorting with only painters and poets, couture wished to return to the fold and rediscover its original function which is to adorn women and to beautify them." As a result, his haute couture, while remaining a privilege of the wealthy, appeared comprehensible to everyone. Christian Dior thereby gave his signature to the first democratization of taste, if not of fashion.

By conforming the feminine silhouette to design, by dictating the choice of accessories and the circumstances appropriate for every outfit, the couturier left little room for personal expression, risk, and feminine fantasy. On the other hand, the steadiness of his "total look" guaranteed his popularity. It enabled him to satisfy an enormous public, who saw in Christian Dior, whatever their national or individual clothing cultures, the label of a guaranteed elegance. In the end, Dior's conception of a wearable fashion was also that of an exportable fashion.

Christian Dior was, in succession, an avant-garde amateur, an artisan of a kind of return to order, and, finally, a manufacturer of elegance. The first superstar couturier, he died of a heart attack at the age of fifty-two in Bagni di Montecatini, Italy. The financier Marcel Boussac thought at the time of closing the house, but in the face of pressure from license holders, he appointed the young assistant Yves Saint Laurent as artistic director, and in this way the label survived its founder. When Yves Saint Laurent left in 1960, Marc Bohan took his place and held it until Gianfranco Ferré took over in 1989. Their designs upheld the image of a couture distanced from the multiple challenges and manifestos of contemporary fashion. The classicism of Christian Dior was not shaken until the arrival in 1997 of John Galliano, who revived the active media exposure established by Dior himself.

See also **Art and Fashion; Balmain, Pierre; Film and Fashion; Galliano, John; Haute Couture; New Look; Perfume; Ready-to-Wear; Saint Laurent, Yves; Theatrical Costume.**

BIBLIOGRAPHY

Cawthorne, Nigel. *The New Look: The Dior Revolution.* London: Hamlyn, 1996.

Dior, Christian. *Je suis couturier* [I am a dressmaker]. Paris: Éditions du Conquistador, 1951.

———. *Christian Dior et moi* [Christian Dior and me]. Paris: Amiot-Dumont, 1956.

Giroud, Françoise. *Dior.* Paris: Éditions du Regard, 1987.

Golbin, Paméla. *Créateurs de modes.* Paris: Éditions du Chêne, 1999.

Grumbach, Didier. *Histoires de la mode.* Paris: Éditions du Seuil, 1993.

Homage à Christian Dior 1947–1957. Paris: Musée des arts de la mode, Union centrale des arts décoratifs, 1986.

Martin, Richard, and Harold Koda. *Christian Dior.* New York: Metropolitan Museum of Art, 1996.

Milbank, Caroline Rennolds. *Couture: The Great Designers.* New York: Stewart, Tabori and Chang, 1985.

Pochna, Marie-France. *Christian Dior.* Paris: Flammarion, 1994.

———. *Dior.* Paris: Assouline, 1996.

Remaury, Bruno, ed. *Dictionnaire de la mode au XXème siècle.* Paris: Éditions du Regard, 1994.

Eric Pujalet-Plaà

DISTRESSING Distressing refers to a surface treatment of fabric that makes the material appear faded or wrinkled, as if from long, steady use. In order to obtain good results in distressing, it is important to have a good understanding of the fabric being treated. Necessary information includes the types of fibers that make up the fabric, how the fabric was made (for example, is it woven or knitted), the dyes used to color the fabric, and any other treatments or decorations that the fabric has undergone. Various sorts of fabrics can be distressed, and techniques for each may vary.

The most commonly encountered distressed fabric in modern times is denim. Almost everyone has a favorite pair of jeans whose fabric is worn in all the right places and washed out to the perfect color. Repeated wear may be the only natural way to get jeans just the way one wants them, but there are many ways to distress the denim to instantly create a pair of "worn" jeans. Fabric along the pocket tips may be distressed by using a sander or file to fray the denim until it has acquired the preferred look. The goal is to create wear in the fabric, but without tearing it, in any place where the jeans would normally show signs of wear. Jeans can also be distressed when laundering them by adding some pumice stones to the washer; the effect is enhanced by using cold water and a detergent that contains no brighteners.

Using such methods, it is possible to make a do-it-yourself project of distressing jeans, but most people in the early 2000s prefer to purchase pre-distressed denim. This trend has changed the jeans business, because the cost of worn-look jeans is almost double that of new jeans. This style started catching on in the early 1990s, according to the *New York Times*, when fashionable young Japanese consumers began to seek out used older jeans. The discovery of jeans as antiques quickly created a market for "antique-look" jeans, which manufacturers were happy to supply. Pre-distressed denim is processed with bleach and potassium permanganate, tumbled with pumice stones, and digested with enzymes.

Techniques of distressing fabric have existed long before the fad of distressed jeans, however. Theatrical costume designers have been using distressing techniques to make costumes more believable for many years. Distressed fabric is often used in costumes for movies, TV shows, and theatrical productions. Almost every movie wardrobe is likely to include at least one garment made from distressed fabric. Costume designers for westerns, horror films, and other film genres pioneered the techniques of fabric distressing that have come to be used in fashionable clothing in the early twenty-first century.

See also **Denim; Jeans.**

BIBLIOGRAPHY

Russell, Douglas. *Stage Costumes Design.* New York: Prentice-Hall, 1973.

Internet Resource

Family Education Network. 2004. "Distressed." Infoplease.com Dictionary. Available from <http://www.infoplease.com/ipd/A0411265.html>.

Aliecia R. McClain

DJELLABA Human clothing is about society and about culture. It communicates social standing, group identity, cultural values, gender, religion, cross-cultural influences, political resistance, and more. It can yield meaning at the material, the symbolic, and the sociocultural levels. Arab-Islamic clothing is no different. Not equally common among all cultures, however, is the fact that Arab culture has developed between a crossroads of cultures, empires, and civilizational developments since antiquity. Trade, contact, and conquest brought and spread diverse influences including clothing styles that enriched and diversified Arab dress forms and clothing vocabulary and their uses. Arab clothing serves in multiple ways, has various symbolic functions, and yields complex meanings in secular and religious settings. Despite cross-cultural and cross-ethnic similarities, certain symbolic and functional attributes and cultural nuances in usage and practices make Arab-Islamic clothing unique.

The word *djellaba*, or *jillaba*, refers to one of three related terms used in Arabic for a garment variably worn by men, by women, or by both. They are *jilbab*, *jillaba*, and *gallabiyya* (or *jallabiyya*)—the "g" consonant is characteristic of Egyptian Arabic and a few other spoken Arabic forms in different parts of the Arabic-speaking world. The verb derivative *jallaba or tajallaba* means to clothe or be clad in a garment, used in material or metaphoric terms. The *djellaba* connotes a mid-calf or (most commonly in the early 2000s) ankle-length, loose-fitting, shirtdress or garment worn in different Arab societies and among other Islamic groups. In most cases, it would be made of cotton, although less commonly of silk or wool fabrics. The garments referred to by the related terms *jilbab*, *jillaba*, and *gallabiyya* are similar in form and are worn as traditional secular garments throughout the region but acquire special meaning when applied to contemporary Islamic context.

In the contemporary Arabic usage, *jilbab* refers to a full-length, loose shirtdress and does not in itself connote head or face cover. In Morocco *jillaba* is the word used to refer to the long, hooded robe worn as an outer garment by both sexes. When hooded it is commonly referred to in Maghrebi societies (Arab societies of North Africa) as *burnus*. Neutral or dual-gendered dress among Arabs is not associated with unisex identity, behavior, or attitude. Even when similar or identical in form, dress items are "worn" differently by women and men, who carry themselves differently in ways that are culturally understood. Differences between culturally defined femininity and masculinity is seen in gait and body language evident even when both sexes wear identical garments.

It is significant to stress that men, not only women, in traditional Arab culture and in Islamic societies practice "veiling"—head and face covering. Islam and traditional Arab culture are concerned with clothing forms for both sexes, and that includes head and face covering for men and women. A systematic study (El Guindi) points to the importance of clothing, including veiling, for men and how, contrary to popular misconceptions, the Hadith sources point to the disproportional attention given by Prophet Muhammad during Islam's early days of community formation in the seventh century, to men's modesty in clothing and public behavior in comparison to women's. To fully understand Arab and Muslim dress, sartorial practices by both sexes must be examined.

Clothing is of special significance for Muslims because Islam prescribes a code about privacy-reserve-sanctity, which applies to cultural notions of body, dress, home, womanhood, and sacred space. In application, the code extends beyond body covering to general comportment and public behavior and applies to the notions of home, womanhood, and family (*bayt, harim*) and house of worship (*bayt al-haram*). Islam is specific about the extent of body coverage for Muslim men and women in times of worship and in sacred spaces. It is less specific when it comes to ordinary life. The phases in an individual Muslim's life cycle are clearly marked by specific rites, all of which involve a sociomoral code that translates through clothing forms in sacred time and space, such as during daily prayer and during the annual pilgrimage (the *hajj*). The latter consists of a complex set of rites during the individual's pilgrimage in Mecca, much of which involves the body and how it is clothed.

The term *jillaba* is henceforth used in a generalized way to refer to both a traditional (secular) garment worn by men and women, and also to women's and in some cases men's garment as part of the overall contemporary Islamic dress (*libas shar'i* or *ziyy Islami*) revived during the mid-1960s in the Islamic world. In its beginnings, Islam did not introduce new clothing forms. There was continuity in dress forms from the earlier period in Arabia that extended into the period of formation for the Umma (Islamic Community) in the seventh century. Clothing style was, however, influenced by new ideas emerging and new meanings rendered during Islam's early days.

Among these were concerns about marking group identity, distinguishing the status of the Prophet's wives, protecting the moral integrity of Muslim women, and establishing a sociomoral code for public behavior of Muslim men and women. References to clothing for both sexes reflected these concerns. There was a stress on a general comportment of reserve. Men's clothing was to be austere and modest, layered during worship and prayer to prevent body exposure when bending and prostrating.

With regard to women, the Qur'an mentions two clothing items: *khimar* and *jilbab*. Reference to these two is found in poetry and other literary forms as evidence of their use in pre-Islamic society. With the birth of Islam, special significance was given to them. References in the Qur'an regarding these two clothing items are specific. First, consider the reference to *khimar*. The most cited is Sura (chapter) 24 that refers to *khimar* (women's head cover) in the general context of public behavior and comportment by both sexes. This passage implies that women are singled out for "reserve" and "restraint." This selectivity also distorts Islam's intent by the Sura. Preceding this, is a sentence which addresses men first about "reserve" and "restraint" translating thus: *Tell the believing men to lower their gaze and conceal their genitals; for that is purer for them, God knoweth what they do.* The following sentence continues the same theme: *And tell the believing women to lower their gaze and conceal their genitals, and not reveal their beauty, except what does show, and to draw their khimar over their bosoms, and not to reveal their beauty except to ….* (emphasis added).

Jilbab is mentioned in Sura 33:59, which enjoins the Prophet's wives, daughters, and all Muslim women to don their *jilbab* so they are easily recognized and protected from molestation or harassment. It translates as follows:

O Prophet tell your wives, daughters and believing women to put on their jilbabs so they are recognized and thus not harmed (33:59).

Jilbab refers to a long, loose shirtdress. It does not in itself connote head or face cover. However, cross-cultural ethnography and Islamic references point to the practice by which these and similar outfits (referred to by different terms) can be physically manipulated in different social situations to cover head or face. Examples can be found among the Rashayda Bedouins of the Sudan, Muslim rural Indian women, and elsewhere. A systematic study on dress of women and men in Arab-Islamic culture (El Guindi) reveals a pattern of flexibility and fluidity in the manner by which women and men use clothing to cover face and head. Long, wide sleeves are often used to cover the head and face, and head covers to cover face. Some clothing items are inflexibly used in a single way, but other items are fluidly used in multiple ways, to cover and uncover, tighten or loosen. The face veiling by the men in the Berber group, the Tuareg, is only for face covering but is manipulated fluidly. Such complex, nuanced movements that communicate different messages about rank, gender, and identity characterize men's face-veiling behavior.

In the several-decades-old contemporary Islamic movement in Egypt and subsequently the rest of the Arab region, *hijab* is used to refer to women's Islamic head cover. However, it also referred to the general Islamic attire for women composed of at least two items, body cover and head cover. Similarly, in Indonesia *jilbab* became commonly used to refer to women's overall Islamic dress. Like the Arabic usage *hijab*, *jilbab* in Indonesia sometimes refers to head covering only and sometimes to the entire Islamic outfit that includes garment and head cover.

There is a language underlying dress usage and meaning derives from the social and cultural contexts of dress and movement and manipulation of dress items in particular situations. Often focusing analysis on the code underlying dress forms can prove more revealing than exploring a clothing item in material and functional terms. Other than its religious dimension, clothing for Arab and Muslim women and men cannot be reduced to a material element with utilitarian functions. It reflects a core code of privacy, functions to communicate status and identity, and even when identical in form for both sexes it communicates gender boundaries. It is intricately connected with historical situations of resistance to foreign occupation and against European ideals and Eurocentric images imposed through state or colonial sartorial rules and restrictions on people's choices of dress.

See also **Hijab; Iran: History of Pre-Islamic Dress; Islamic Dress, Contemporary; Middle East: History of Islamic Dress.**

BIBLIOGRAPHY

Brenner, Suzanne. "Reconstructing Self and Society: Javanese Muslim Women and 'The Veil.'" *American Ethnologist* 23, no. 4 (November 1996): 673–697.

El Guindi, Fadwa. *Veil: Modesty, Privacy, and Resistance*. Oxford and New York: Berg, 1999.

Young, William C. *The Rashaayda Bedouin: Arab Pastoralists of Eastern Sudan*. Fort Worth, Tex.: Harcourt Brace College Publishers, 1996.

Fadwa El Guindi

DOLCE & GABBANA Domenico Dolce was born in Polizzi Generosa (near Palermo, Sicily) on 13 September 1958. His family owned a small clothing business, where Domenico worked from childhood. Stefano Gabbana was born in Milan on 14 November 1962. He studied graphics but soon turned to fashion. After a brief period working as assistant designers, they founded the Dolce & Gabbana label, which had its first runway show as part of the New Talent group in Milan in 1985, upon the invitation of Italian fashion promoter Beppe Modenese.

In 1986 they produced their first collection, called "Real Women." In 1987 they launched their knitwear line and in 1989 their beachwear and lingerie lines. Beginning in 1988 they produced their ready-to-wear line in Domenico Dolce's family-owned atelier, located in Legnano, Milan. The first Dolce & Gabbana men's collection appeared in 1990. In 1994 they launched the D&G label, inspired by street style and a more youthful look. The clothes were produced and distributed by Ittierre.

The company launched several fragrances, including Dolce & Gabbana Perfume, By Dolce & Gabbana, and Dolce & Gabbana Men. One of their perfume ads was directed by the Italian film director Giuseppe Tornatore, with whom Dolce and Gabbana developed a close relationship, going on to act in his 1996 film *The Star Maker*. They introduced a line of eyewear under the Dolce & Gabbana and D&G labels and produced music CDs.

In 1996, for their tenth anniversary, they published *Ten Years of Dolce & Gabbana*, which included their most important advertising images and texts. In 1999 D&G Junior was created, their collection for children, which was presented at the children's fashion show Pitti Bimbo in Florence.

In 2003 their newest store, covering three floors, opened in Corso Venezia in Milan, in the former home of Brigatti, perhaps Milan's best-known luxury sportswear store. The store is designed in the round from a central piazza and includes a bar, a traditional barbershop, and an ultramodern spa. The individual stores are illuminated by lamps of Venini glass, made according to designs by Domenico Dolce.

In a 1995 interview Dolce and Gabbana recalled their first professional foray into fashion during the Milan collections as eliciting "one of the strongest emotions we have ever experienced" (Gastel, p. 238). The show marked the occasion of the birth of the Dolce & Gabbana label, which was destined to play a fundamental role in the history of Italian ready-to-wear. The designers

An advertisement for Dolce and Gabbana, circa 2001. Dolce and Gabbana's 2001 collection celebrated the exuberance of youth street style and rock and roll culture. THE ADVERTISING ARCHIVE LTD. REPRODUCED BY PERMISSION.

showed full-length garments of stretch jersey, silk jackets, and oversize shirts that could be worn with casual sandals. The collection, characterized by fluidity and difference, soon found an enthusiastic public.

Dolce and Gabbana are considered the inventors of a Mediterranean style that draws its inspiration from the Sicily of Luchino Visconti's 1963 film *The Leopard* and the women of Italian realism, sensual and austere like Anna Magnani, to whom they dedicated a collection whose key element was the 1940s slip. At the beginning of their career, the designers also turned to Sophia Loren, Claudia Cardinale, and Stefania Sandrelli for inspiration. The Dolce & Gabbana woman is unbiased and brazen, but fearful of God and devoted to church and family, an attitude typical of southern Italian Catholicism. A woman who simultaneously reveals and conceals brassieres and corsets, lace, lingerie, and veils, and who is disturbing in her impetuous sensuality—a provocative woman proud of her body. The designers' models are soft, round, and full-figured. "Dark girls with dark eyes evoke the women of the south—carnal, provocative, yet austere and proud at the same time" (Sozzani, p. 5). At a time when fashion saw women as executives in two-piece suits with padded shoulders, Dolce & Gabbana's first collection in-

Domenico Dolce and Stefano Gabbana. Dolce and Gabanna promote their fragrance "Sicily," at Saks Fifth Avenue in New York City in 2003. AP/WIDE WORLD PHOTOS. REPRODUCED BY PERMISSION.

The journalist Nicoletta Gasperini of *Donna*, the Italian fashion weekly that gave them their first cover—the model Marpessa photographed by Giovanni Gastel—helped define their image. "We convey to them how we feel and they give us back a mediated image of culture" (Gastel, p. 241).

The turning point in their international success began with their friendship with Madonna. The pop star ordered from their New York showroom a *guêpière* (corset) made of gemstones and a jacket to wear at Cannes to launch her film *Truth or Dare: In Bed with Madonna* by Alek Keshishian (1990). Madonna's participation in the 1992 D&G party and runway show publicized their friendship. Shortly after, the singer asked them to design the fifteen hundred costumes for her 1993 "Girlie Show" tour.

Dolce & Gabbana's Mediterranean style is not a rigid framework but the template of an imaginary world through which they draw inspiration. The collection changes for every season, ranging from the baroque to the plastic, from aristocratic to working class, brazen to bourgeois, from animal prints to a cardinal's cloak. In 1994, for example, after producing corsets, girdles, T-shirts, and styles emphasizing breasts and revealing cleavage, Dolce & Gabbana introduced a "Sapphic chic" masculine style for women characterized by short hair slicked down with brilliantine, which was exemplified by one of their earliest fans, Isabella Rossellini. In 2003 for their Milan men's show, they took their inspiration from contemporary soccer stars. The darlings of the Italian and international press, according to Suzy Menkes, a journalist for the *International Herald Tribune*, the two designers have the ability of being able to mix periods and countries, masculine and feminine looks, fabrics and styles.

Dolce & Gabbana is one of the best examples of the explosion in Italian ready-to-wear that occurred during the mid-1980s. Creativity and versatility, the union of the press and the star system, a range of products and clothing lines, and careful attention to distribution are all elements that contribute to the realization of an integrated system of communication.

See also **Italian Fashion; Madonna; Music and Fashion.**

BIBLIOGRAPHY

Asnaghi, Laura. "Dolce & Gabbana." In *Dizionario della Moda*. Edited by Guido Vergani. Milan: Baldini and Castoldi, 1999.

Gastel, Minnie. *50 anni di moda italiana*. Milan: Vallardi, 1995.

Sozzani, Franca. *Dolce & Gabbana*. Translated by Marguerite Shore. New York: Universe Publishing/Vendome Press, 1998.

Simona Segre Reinach

cluded tulle and angora, twin sets in jersey lace, and soft, wide, extravagant skirts. Their favorite materials were crocheted lace, wool, and silk.

They were not looking for a retro look; however, Dolce & Gabbana turned to the past for innovation. The designers remarked, "We want to use the past to project it into the future" (Sozzani, p. 11). And making it modern involved the creative use of fabrics and colors, and the ability to blend various sources of inspiration, primarily those whose origins could be traced to the heterogeneous world of the Mediterranean.

The elements of Italian culture are reinforced through their meticulous attention to their image, and their publicity campaigns have always been handled by the world's finest photographers. Every shot is organized as if it were a film set. Their first campaign was photographed by their friend, the Sicilian photographer Ferdinando Scianna, who, with Dolce and Gabbana, was just getting started in fashion. Besides Scianna, other photographers who have worked with the label include Fabrizio Ferri, Steven Meisel—famous for his pictures of the Italian film star Monica Bellucci and the supermodel Linda Evangelista—Peter Lindbergh, and Helmut Newton.

DOMESTIC PRODUCTION The idea of a Golden Age of self-sufficiency, before the advent of the factory system, when a household's skills and labor in domestic production could account for all its clothing and textile needs, is more nostalgia inspired by anti-industrial sentiment than a historical reality. In the modern period, working women and men formed a labor force that was interchangeable between small workshops and the home and domestic self-employment and outwork. Handicraft and mechanized mass production co-existed and developed differently in different regions and for different goods. For example, in the early nineteenth century some goods such as knitted hosiery were still commonly sent out to be made by hand on a cottage basis, while the spinning and weaving of cotton were already widely mechanized and centralized in factories. The history of home production of some kinds of clothing and textiles is evident in surviving architecture such as weavers' houses. The timetable of the move to factory production for all goods was complex and generally much debated by historians. In practice, before the domination of mass-production of clothing for men and women was completed in the early twentieth century, households were clothed by a combination of making, recycling, bartering, and buying new or secondhand from a variety of sources.

Sewing

Clothing for women and children, and some simple items for men such as shirts, were made in many homes across the social spectrum in modern times for private consumption. This has been concurrent with clothing made at home in poorer homes for wages in a regular or irregular way as self-employment or outwork. Both practices have existed alongside the increasing consumption of factory ready-mades, a situation that prevails in the early 2000s, although unwaged home dressmaking has substantially declined. Not all domestic production has been prompted by thrift or economic necessity: women have also sewn clothes for pleasure and as a creative act and in this same period skill with the needle has been prized for its association with leisure and femininity. In the eighteenth and nineteenth centuries, the domestic production of clothes also embraced the efforts of literate, middle-class women to teach their peers to make clothes for the deserving poor or to teach poor women to sew for themselves. The trend was reflected in a new genre of instructional literature, such as an 1838 publication called *The Workwoman's Guide*. Although philanthropic in some respects, this activity also served to provide a flow of skilled girls into domestic service. The introduction of reliable domestic sewing machines in the 1860s, for those who could afford them, accelerated home production of garments for both waged and unwaged purposes, as did the spread of well-illustrated mass part-works, books, magazines, and paper patterns that increased through the nineteenth century and helped to disseminate knowledge of home sewing, knitting, embroidery, and other handicrafts associated with clothing such as crochet. Home sewing included significant time spent on mending and renovation, in all

"[M]any women who have started home dressmaking as a means to economy have continued it as a[n] .... adventure in creative expression .... These days the only way to stamp one's individuality on a wardrobe is to make one's own .... "

"[Y]ou don't have to be an expert to make a chic dress" (Butterick Publishing Company, pp. 2–3).

classes of household. "Make-do and Mend," a campaign introduced by the British government during World War II, encouraged clothing economies in the home at a time of acute shortages. It promoted many ingenious solutions but was not universally popular; it may have unintentionally contributed to the postwar move away from thrift to more throwaway attitudes to clothing. Home sewing was regularly taught to girls in schools until the last quarter of the twentieth century when it was replaced by other courses that emphasized design and new technologies.

Knitting

Domestic hand knitting had been known for centuries as a convenient way of making shaped garments, especially smaller items such as hosiery and caps. Its precise origins are conjectural, though many believe otherwise. Historically, both men and women knitted, but it became a gentrified and fashionable pastime primarily for women during the first half of the nineteenth century in Britain and America. The craft was promoted by the publication of countless knitting books and helped by a ready supply of fancy wool yarns from Germany, from which also developed the hugely popular tapestry work known as "Berlin" work. Domestic knitting of this period produced a wide variety of small household objects such as pincushions, purses, and doilies, as well as shawls, baby clothes, cuffs, caps, scarves, gloves, and numerous other items of clothing. Domestic knitting was undertaken for items used in the household but also given as gifts and for charity. Knitting for the troops in both world wars was a continuation of this altruistic knitting practice, still seen in hand knitting for fund-raising or for distribution to developing countries. This strand of its history is distinct from the long history of small-scale commercial hosiery knitted by cottagers and the frame knitters, first incorporated in England as a worshipful company in 1657, whose mechanical knitting did not entirely replace commercial hand knitting for two hundred years. Mass-production of cheap knitwear has come to mean that "no one needs to knit in order to keep clothed" (Rutt p. 161). Hand knitting at home is a leisure activity and, since the

1970s, has become more glamorous due to innovative design and exciting yarns.

Embroidery

Embroidery has a long history and, despite male practitioners, and a substantial role in the decoration of ecclesiastical vestments and furnishings, it has been closely linked to the domestic lives of women. "To know the history of embroidery is to know the history of women" (Parker p. vi). It has been used on small and large scale furnishing fabrics and on male and female clothing to great impact since medieval times in Europe. Samplers have been a way to demonstrate skill and catalog the rich range of stitches and effects available to embroiderers; historic samplers have become much appreciated and command high prices. Some feminist historians have identified embroidery, even more than other needlework, as a repetitive and repressive task promoted historically to construct a submissive femininity within patriarchy. However, in the early 2000s it is also widely acknowledged as an important textile art, an expressive and satisfying medium in its own right. Embroidery was famously represented in the feminist artist Judy Chicago's 1979 project *The Dinner Party*. It sustains large numbers of specialist publications, courses, and suppliers of yarns, kits, and patterns, and has enjoyed popularity as a way to customize mass-produced clothes such as jeans. In some developing countries, embroidery for export can represent a crucial source of cash for families and has replaced much domestic embroidery formerly done in richer countries.

See also **Embroidery; Knitting; Seamstresses.**

BIBLIOGRAPHY

Buck, Anne. *Dress in Eighteenth Century England.* London: B. T. Batsford, Ltd., 1979.

Burman, Barbara, ed. *The Culture of Sewing: Gender, Consumption and Home Dressmaking.* Oxford and New York: Berg, 1999.

Butterick Publishing Company. *Making Smart Clothes: Modern Methods in Cutting Fitting and Finishing.* New York and London: Butterick Publishing Company, 1931.

Byrde, Penelope. *A Frivolous Distinction: Fashion and Needlework in the Works of Jane Austen.* Bath City Council, n.d.

MacDonald, Anne. *No Idle Hands: The Social History of American Knitting.* New York: Ballantine Books, 1990.

Parker, Rosika. *The Subversive Stitch: Embroidery and the Making of the Feminine.* London: The Women's Press, 1984.

Rutt, Richard. *A History of Hand Knitting.* London: B. T. Batsford, Ltd., 1987.

Ulrich, Laura. *The Age of Homespun: Objects and Stories in the Creation of an American Myth.* New York: Alfred A. Knopf, 2001.

Weissman, Judith, and Wendy Lavitt. *Labors of Love: America's Textiles and Needlework, 1650–1930.* New York: Wings Books, 1994.

Barbara Burman

DOUBLET The doublet is a man's upper body garment that was worn in Europe between the fourteenth and seventeenth centuries. In this time frame, it moved from undergarment to outer garment and from specialized military dress to fashionable civilian dress. The doublet's function as standard everyday attire was primarily to support men's hose, while providing warmth and shaping a man's upper torso. It was used to display appropriate decorative and stylistic features through each period, such as padding, paning (panes or narrow strips of fabric sewn over a contrasting lining), and slashing (pattern of deliberate cuts made in garments as a decorative feature), and it was one of the first garments to display highly technical construction and sophisticated cutting and tailoring skills after the Middle Ages.

Origins

The doublet originated in the late thirteenth and early fourteenth century as part of military dress, closely related to technological advancements in armor. By the end of the thirteenth century, as chain mail was replaced by plate armor, a layer of padding was needed to protect the body from abrasion by the tightly fitted, sharp-edged metal plates. Quilted undergarments and leather tunics were long used by soldiers as protection and under chain mail, but the early doublet, called a *pourpoint* or *gipon* (also *jupon*; and in Italian, *giubbetto*, *zuparello*, or *zuppone*), was a closely fitted undergarment heavily padded in front over the chest and quilted around the back. Worn over a loose linen undershirt and short linen drawers, the *pourpoint* was sleeveless, had a round neckline, and was closed down the center of the front using laces or numerous buttons. The padding gave extra definition to the silhouette of the upper torso and shaped outer garments. Length varied, but the French term *pourpoint* also explains an important functional aspect of this garment. Translated as *pour les points* or "for the points," laces held up a man's hose by tying them to the doublet through pairs of hand-sewn eyelets in the tops of the hose and in corresponding eyelets along the doublet's lower edge. The leather laces were capped with small metal tags or "points" at each end, giving the defining name to this garment.

Late Fourteenth Century

After the mid-fourteenth century, the doublet was worn as a belted outer garment, serving a more fashionable function in civilian dress. Doublets were sleeveless or worn as a type of sleeved jacket, some with skirts extending over the upper thighs, shaped with a tightly tapered fit through the waistline. The points were attached to the inner lining and tied to the hose at the hips. Doublets became increasingly shorter through the second half of the fourteenth century, barely covering the hips, and many had full-length sleeves, ending below the wrist in a point over the knuckles and tightly fitted with a row of buttons from elbow to wrist. The narrow, two-part sleeves were seamed at the elbow and set into wide, round-shaped armholes for full arm movement. Low, rounded necklines had short standing collars. By the end of the fourteenth century, as an outer layer of dress, the term "doublet" replaced *pourpoint* or *gipon* in general English usage, while *pourpoint* continued in French.

Fifteenth Century

By the beginning of the fifteenth century, images show young knights in public without their armor, dressed in short, waist-length, padded and fitted doublets with full hose laced to their lower edges. This look eventually inspired a new body-dominant fashionable silhouette for civilian men. As the doublet shortened and more of a man's upper leg was exposed, construction of hose changed by joining two separate stockings into one garment that closed or overlapped in front with laces or a codpiece. The look of the doublet as outerwear also makes a visual reference to the dress of rural and urban laborers who often removed their outer tunics to work in underwear and hose. Images show laborers with their hose loosened and unfastened in back to relieve strain on the doublet when bending over to work. The need for this feature was a sign of low status. The expression "in zuppone" was equivalent to our contemporary reference about the informality of taking off one's business suit jacket and working in one's shirt sleeves.

In the first half of the fifteenth century, the doublet remained a short, waist-length garment with sleeves worn over a linen undershirt and layered under a jacket or outer tunic-like garment. The sleeves and collars were often the only visible portions of the doublet. By mid-century, the silhouette was pared down, more slender and elegant, and the waist-length doublet was expertly constructed and tightly fitted with four seams—down the front, back, and sides. Collars were removed and necklines lowered and squared-off. The center front was often open or slightly unlaced, revealing the edges of the linen shirt underneath, a feature that became more prominent through the end of the fifteenth century. Doublets that showed no front openings may have been pulled on over the head. At the end of the fifteenth century, detachable sleeves appeared or tightly fitted sleeves were slit at the elbow and along the forearm to allow movement.

Sixteenth Century

In the sixteenth century, the doublet was a major men's garment covering the upper torso from neck to waist. It was tightly fitted with low, U- or V-shaped necklines and wide sleeves, and was constructed with panes or slashing of heavy velvet or satin fabrics. Doublets were worn under the man's jerkin or gown, but no longer served the function of supporting a man's hose. Instead, breeches and stockings were sewn together; the top of a man's breeches was held up with silk or linen laces at the doublet waist. Some doublets were cut with short, gored skirts, or worn with the separate military skirt called

***Saint Roch* by Carlo Crivelli.** The doublet originated in Europe as a component of military dress, but soon made the transition to the civilian fashion world. BY THE KIND PERMISSION OF THE TRUSTEES OF THE WALLACE COLLECTION, LONDON.

bases. By mid-century, necklines were higher on the throat, and by century-end doublets had a stiff, standing collar to support the ruff. Doublet waistlines were lowered in front, and the elongated wool, bran, horsehair, or short, waste linen fibers, V-shaped waistline was padded and stuffed with wool, bran, horsehair, or short linen fibers by the end of the century, imitating the exaggerated style called a peascod belly. Layers of stiff linen canvas were stitched together to create the doublet front, and extra layers of stiffened linen strengthened the front button closure. Doublet waistlines were further accentuated with a row of small square flaps called pecadils. Doublet sleeves were padded with felted woolen cloth at the shoulders, and shoulder seams were constructed with a narrow wing or padded roll over the top.

Seventeenth Century

The padding and exaggerated features of the doublet were gradually abandoned in the first quarter of the seventeenth century, but the narrow-waisted silhouette remained. Through the 1630s, ribbon points tied into bows at the waist were used as a decorative feature. In the second quarter, the overlapping pecadils, or short peplum, lengthened to cover the hips, and waistlines were set slightly above the natural waistline. Heavy fabrics richly embellished with silk and metallic embroidery lend a stiff, formal silhouette to portraits in the early to mid-seventeenth century. By 1620, breeches were suspended from the doublet by large metal hooks sewn into their waistband and attached to metal eyelets on a tape sewn into the doublet waist. By the early 1660s, doublets were straight, unfitted, and shortened to above the waist; breeches were no longer tied to the doublet at all. By 1670, the doublet had been replaced by the waistcoat and coat of the three-piece suit introduced by the British monarch Charles II.

See also **Breeches; Hosiery, Men's.**

BIBLIOGRAPHY

Arnold, Janet. *Patterns of Fashion: The Cut and Construction of Clothes for Men and Women, c. 1560–1620.* London: Macmillan, 1985.

Byrde, Penelope. *The Male Image: Men's Fashion in Britain, 1300–1970.* London: B. T. Batsford Ltd., 1979.

de Marly, Diana. *Fashion for Men: An Illustrated History.* London: B. T. Batsford Ltd., 1985.

Frick, Carole Collier. *Dressing Renaissance Florence: Families, Fortunes, and Fine Clothing.* Baltimore: John Hopkins University Press, 2002.

Herald, Jacqueline. *Renaissance Dress in Italy, 1400–1500.* Edited by Aileen Ribeiro. Atlantic Highlands, N.J.: Humanities Press, 1981.

Payne, Blanche, Geitel Winakor, and Jane Farrell-Beck. *The History of Costume: From Ancient Mesopotamia through the Twentieth Century.* 2nd ed. New York: HarperCollins Publishers, Inc. 1992.

Tortora, Phyllis G., and Keith Eubank. *Survey of Historic Costume: A History of Western Dress.* 3rd ed. New York: Fairchild Publications, 1998.

Waugh, Norah. *The Cut of Men's Clothes: 1600–1900.* New York: Routledge Theatre Arts Books, 1964.

Susan J. Torntore

DOUCET, JACQUES Claiming to have been established in Paris in 1817, the House of Doucet reached its greatest prominence under the design influence of the founder's grandson, Jacques Doucet (1853–1929). While many members of the Doucet family were involved in various aspects of the apparel and related trades, the fashion house of Doucet can be traced to Antoine Doucet (1795–1866) and his wife (née Adèle Girard, d. 1866), who began as vendors of items of lingerie, laces and embroideries, and related merchandise for customers of all ages and both sexes. In 1869 the haberdashery aspect of the business was sold. By 1840 the firm had been established on the rue de la Paix, an increasingly important shopping street, and the second of the couple's six offspring, Edouard (1822–1898), was taking an increasing role in the business. Edouard Doucet, Jacques's father, took the firm over in the early 1850s.

Surviving from the last third of the nineteenth century are a number of stylish garments carrying the label of Mme. Doucet, 21, rue de la Paix. (With the renumbering of streets, the old address number of 17 became the new 21.) What is unclear is who might be behind the courtesy title "Mme.," as Adèle was deceased, and there is no indication that either her daughters or daughters-in-law were involved in business at this address. Beginning in 1858 Maison Doucet is listed in a business directory under the category of "*nouveautés confectionnées,*" and by 1870 Edouard was supplying the queen of Wurtemberg with couture garments. Royal commissions, awards at numerous international exhibitions, actress modeling and patronage, and a long-established association with a highly desirable and valued material, lace, assured interest from a wide client base at Maison Doucet. During the house's peak, Jacques Doucet's personal friend, the well-known actress Réjane, became a one-woman advertising vehicle for the house.

Jacques, who was born on the rue de la Paix and died in Paris, grew up in the family business, which he appears to have joined in 1874. While Jacques Doucet is generally credited with being the house's designer, there is enough evidence to question the scale of such a role. As late as 1894 fashion correspondents do not give readers a clue as to whether they are dealing with the elder or younger Doucet, believing that readers are versed in the knowledge of who indeed is "Doucet, the famous dressmaker." Additionally, M. José de la Peña worked at the house as a fitter and designer from the 1870s into the 1920s. Another designer of the time, Paul Poiret, saw flashes of brilliance in de la Peña's fingers that were unmatched by the house's titular head.

There is no question that Jacques Doucet was interested in apparel and what visual message it could convey. He was a fastidious personal dresser, and he happily applied aesthetic judgments not only to the garments made by the house that bore his name but also to the historic garments he personally collected. Indeed, he was one of the greatest art connoisseurs of his day, first establishing an internationally recognized collection of eighteenth-century artifacts and then a second remarkable collection of modern art. Garments carrying the Doucet name frequently incorporate an historical fashion reference or two, particularly to the modes of the eighteenth century. For decades, the prevailing taste for festoons of lace was sympathetically incorporated by the house into a variety of creations. Embroideries, especially floral and insect interpretations, frequently were executed in prevailing styles, such as art nouveau. Moreover, many of the garments were executed in more fluid fabrics than is usually associated with applications in such decades as the 1880s or 1890s.

As a promoter of fashions Jacques Doucet is best recognized for endorsing delicate, feminine toilettes featuring laces and other fripperies, but the house has also been credited with creating one of the enduring staples of a woman's wardrobe, the tailored suit or *tailleur*. Another innovation accorded Doucet is that of working with furs as if they were fabric, specifically making fitted coats. Doucet garments were popular with American clients, and by 1895 American merchants were busily buying models to export and copy. By the end of the nineteenth century the couture house was one of the largest in Paris, with a yearly turnover in business of more than thirty million francs. Between 1896 and 1912 it was the training ground for two of the emerging and talented young designers who would go on to define fashion in the early twentieth century: Paul Poiret, who worked for Doucet from 1896 to 1900, and Madeleine Vionnet, who worked there from 1907 to 1912. Vionnet's first collection is said to have been revolutionary not only for the house but also the time. Interestingly, but for very different reasons, neither Poiret's nor Doucet's houses productively survived World War I. Initially Jacques Doucet had had the luck to land in a period of fashion that perfectly matched his own design sensibilities. The Great War changed not only what women wore, however, but also how they wore it, and the aging Doucet simply could not keep up with the times. In 1924 the house merged with the lesser firm of Doueillet, and the combined firms ceased business in 1932.

See also **Lace; Paris Fashion; Poiret, Paul; Vionnet, Madeleine.**

BIBLIOGRAPHY

Coleman, Elizabeth A. *The Opulent Era: Fashions of Worth, Doucet, and Pingat.* New York: Thames and Hudson, Inc., 1989.

Elizabeth Ann Coleman

DRESS CODES Dress codes may broadly be defined as rules that regulate an individual's appearance. Sociological variables—age, occupation, class, gender, religion, or ethnicity—stipulate what can and cannot be worn. However, most people probably have a narrower, more specifically modern understanding in mind of dress codes. This stricter definition is associated with a massive uniformization of populations that began in the early nineteenth century as workers and students were disciplined to meet the demands of capitalism, industrialization, and national state formation.

Dress codes, whether explicit or implicit, may apply to small groups (for example, school or company) or an entire nation (China's "Mao suit"). Besides mandating what should be worn, dress codes dictate what should not be worn, and they can be better appreciated by conceptualizing a continuum of uniformity, ranging from strict integration into a politico-economic order to being free from its constraints. Some of the variations are as follows:

- highly standardized, group-dominated, clear hierarchy (military uniforms);
- standardized, group-oriented, hierarchy (occupational dress);
- nonstandardized, displays individuality, no hierarchy (casual dress); and
- anti-standardized, overly individualistic, anti-hierarchy (avant-garde fashion).

As an example of how politico-economic institutions regulate daily dress codes, consider how the life cycle of most individuals in Japan is characterized by uniformization, de-uniformization, and re-uniformization. During the first phase (ages 3–18), individuals begin to don school-specific uniforms that have been inspired by European military uniforms. Boys are outfitted in a blue or black jacket with brass buttons and stand-up collar. Girls often wear the *sêrâ-fuku* ("sailor clothes"), modeled after the traditional English sailor suit. It consists of a sailor-type collar and a pleated skirt. During the second phase of de-uniformization (ages 18–22), the dress code is relaxed as students are allowed to dress casually while at university or other postsecondary schooling institutions. The final phase, re-uniformization (ages from 22), begins after leaving postsecondary schooling and entering the adult workforce.

Inducted into Japan's corporate culture, individuals are required to adopt dress codes that reflect socioeconomic class and gender variables. White-collar male workers, or *sararîman* ("salary man"), are expected to don a white cutter shirt, red necktie, dark blue or gray suit, and black leather shoes. Hair should be short, preferably in the "seven-three part." Facial hair is generally frowned upon. Accessories complete the picture: a briefcase (or shoulder bag or attaché case). Blue-collar workers are seen in uniforms with an open collar, large, functional pockets, and a tag with name or section on the breast pocket. Helmet, boots, work gloves, and safety belt complete the ensemble. Women, who are lower in the corporate pecking order, must adhere to more standardization. OLs ("office ladies") or secretarial staff typically wear a company uniform of white blouse, vest with name tag, skirt (usually 1.9 in, 5 cm, below the knees), and high heels.

At some companies, dress codes are enforced by military-like morning inspections. Besides company loyalty and dedication to work, adhering to dress codes indicates an individual's aspiration to work toward a middle-class lifestyle as well as commitment to Japan's collective project of economic nationalism.

See also **Mao Suit; Uniforms, Diplomatic; Uniforms, Military; Uniforms, Occupational; Uniforms, School; Uniforms, Sports.**

BIBLIOGRAPHY

Davis, Fred. *Fashion, Culture, and Identity.* Chicago: University of Chicago Press, 1992.

Lurie, Alison. *The Language of Clothes.* New York: Random House, 1981.

McVeigh, Brian J. *Wearing Ideology: State, Schooling, and Self-Presentation in Japan.* Oxford: Berg, 2000.

Rubinstein, Ruth P. *Dress Codes: Meanings and Messages in American Culture.* Boulder, Colo.: Westview Press, 1995.

Brian J. McVeigh

DRESS FOR SUCCESS "Dress for success" is the modern equivalent of "clothes maketh the man"—that is, it articulates the belief that what you wear matters in everyday life. However, in its modern guise, this is a discourse specifically on business dress that proclaims the importance of sartorial presentation in the workplace. Dress for success became popular during the mid-1970s and 1980s in the United States and Europe, but the principles that underpin it stem back much further. The idea that one can dress for success is closely aligned to the more general notion of "impression management," the origins of which go back to the work of sociologist Erving Goffman and his dramaturgical metaphor (the idea that the social world functions like a stage and we, its social actors, are performers). Goffman's work on "the presentation of self in everyday life" demonstrates how mundane features of body management are essential to the ongoing maintenance of a person's identity: Specifically, how our body looks and behaves is often the basis of how others read and judge us (1971). While Goffman's work was concerned with describing social order and interaction, his ideas were popularized outside sociology and have since achieved wide social application. Today "impression management" has become part of mainstream popular psychology and management and business studies, with dress for success a central plank of both. For evidence of the cultural significance of dress for success, one needs look no further than the huge market for books and services offering advice on how to dress ef-

fectively at work. Alongside popular "self-help" books, there is a huge industry in "image consultancy" offering all manner of "expert" advice on body presentation, from color analysis to wardrobe and shopping services. More recently, alongside such money-making ventures have sprung not-for-profit, dress-for-success shops offering services to the unemployed.

The Dress-for-Success Manual

The exposition of the "rules" of business dress are laid down in dress manuals, such as the now-classic John T. Molloy's two manuals, *Dress for Success* (first published in the United States in 1975) and *Women: Dress for Success* (published in the United States in 1979). These manuals describe his formula for "successful" dressing. What Molloy calls his "wardrobe engineering" is a (pseudo) "science of clothing" based on quantitative "testing" of the different meanings individuals give to individual garments. What kind of dress did Molloy find was the most "effective" at conveying "one means business"? The dress found to "succeed" is conservative, tailored, and always "smart." However, the way in which men and women should dress for the world of work differs. For men, this means black and gray suits, teamed with not-too-daring ties, and smart, polished shoes. However, while the traditional trousered suit works for men, it does not work for women. Indeed, by the very fact of his writing two manuals on work dress, Molloy points to the way in which dress at work is gendered, both reflecting and reproducing sexual difference. While both manuals have the same goal—the acquisition of status and power at work—men and women must attain it by different means, according to Molloy, and for a woman this means managing her sexuality. While an aspiring professional man need only worry about his dress (which suit to wear and in which color, which briefcase to carry, and so on), his female counterpart must also worry about her body, since her body is sexualized in a way that the male body is not.

The public world of work is a world that demands a clear separation from the erotic, and thus, women's potentially sexual bodies must be covered appropriately. Women, Molloy argues, have to dress for "authority" since their social position, as women, puts them at some disadvantage compared with men at work. The wearing of tailored clothing, namely a smart jacket with tailored knee-high skirt is, according to Molloy, the most "effective" dress. It would seem, therefore, that while suggestive clothes must be avoided, women should aim to look "feminine" at all costs: the wearing of a skirt and the deployment of decorative items, a necktie, brooch, or other accessory, help to soften the severity of the suit. Indeed, Molloy warns career women against trying to "ape" men and claims that his 1980 manual was, in part, a response to those women who had been adopting the garb he had outlined in his first manual. His second stated reason is captured by his story of how, in the mid-1970s, when meeting three businesswomen in a bar, he was unable to spot them. The businesswoman was literally not "visible" as such and was, according to Molloy, in need of a "uniform" that could be relied upon to connote the appropriate status.

The "uniform" that he subsequently helped inaugurate became known as the "power suit" and was a major phenomenon of the 1980s, defining a style of female professional dress that has now become something of a sartorial cliché: tailored skirt suit with shoulder pads, in gray, blue, or navy, accessorized with "token female garb such as bows and discreet jewelry" (Armstrong 1993: 278). These dress-for-success rules arose against the historical backdrop of the women's movement into more prestigious forms of paid employment and addressed the increasing problem of how to rise on the career ladder and break the so-called "glass ceiling." Note that in maintaining the suited torso, the tailored jacket and fitted skirt aimed to separate this female worker from her secretarial counterparts. Power dressing articulated the "career woman" and in doing so gave visible evidence of a new relationship of women to work that had once been the preserve of men (Entwistle 1997, 2001).

That fact that the "power suit" became a major fashion story for women in the 1980s is beside the point for "experts" such as Molloy. The aim of dress for success was to devise techniques that eliminate fashion from the daily process of dressing. The dress-for-success discourse is, in fact, an oblique and sometimes open critique of the fashion system. By virtue of its incessant momentum, fashion keeps the range of choices open, choices left to individuals who run the risk of making the "wrong" one. As individuals come to feel that more is at stake in how they look, especially at work, such a universe of choice is a problem. As a pseudoscience of clothing strategies, dress-for-success formulas, such as Molloy's "wardrobe engineering," offer clearly established guidelines to circumnavigate this precarious world of choice and provide a stable basis upon which to base decisions as to what to wear to work.

Historical Precursors

As it is primarily a "self-help" manual, the modern dress manual sets out to mold and shape the self, calling upon readers to think about themselves and act upon themselves in particular ways. Molloy's manual can therefore be examined as a "technology of the self," to draw on Foucault's concept (1988). "Technologies of the self permit individuals to effect . . . . a certain number of operations on their own bodies and souls, thoughts, conduct and way of being so as to transform themselves" (Foucault 1988, p. 18). In this way, dress-for-success strategies encourage particular ways of thinking and acting upon the self, producing the individual as a "reflexive subject" (Giddens 1991); that is, a person who thinks about and calculates body and self, in this case, developing skills and techniques for dressing and presenting the self as a committed career-minded person. The idea that one's dress conveys something of the "self" and that, specifi-

cally, one can dress for success at work may seem almost "common sense" today. However, these ideas have arisen out of particular historical circumstances and beliefs about the body and its relationship to personal identity. These are closely related to the emergence of particular forms of modern individualism.

One can trace the circumstances that gave rise to discourses on dress and appearance as far back as the eighteenth century, to the emphasis placed on the "self-made man" under conditions of industrial capitalism and the rise of Romanticism. The eighteenth and nineteenth centuries heralded an era of upward mobility: the new capitalist classes were achieving status and power through their own efforts, not through privileges of the old aristocracy. Individuals could, in other words, rise through the social hierarchy by virtue of their own efforts. This idea of the "enterprising" self reached its apotheosis with the ascendancy of neo-liberalism in the 1970s and 1980s under Reaganomics and Thatcherism; in other words, around the same time as dress-for-success ideas took hold. However, in the history of our modern self, another discourse at variance with capitalism is also important, namely Romanticism, and it underpins the idea of dress for success. Romantic poets, painters, and writers emphasized the idea of the "authentic" self and suggested that one's outward appearance unproblematically reflects the inner self. While up until the eighteenth century public life had allowed a distance between outward appearance and inner self—a clear separation between public and private—under conditions of modern life, according to Richard Sennett (1977), one's public appearance has to be a "true" reflection of the self. This Romantic notion of authenticity has become attached to the public sphere and is the dominant theme permeating discourse on the self at work, suggesting that how you look, from the first day of your job interview, signals your identity and commitment as a worker. Thus, in contemporary society, our bodies are bearers of status and distinction, as the sociologist Pierre Bourdieu (1984) has described in detail. This makes the body, its dress and manners, matters of great import in terms of the "envelope" of the self. As Joanne Finkelstein (1991) notes, increasingly over the nineteenth century appearance comes to stand as an important indicator of inner character and she suggests that the eighteenth-century socialite and "dandy" Beau Brummel exemplifies the wider social movement toward the self-styled or "fashioned" individual, concerned with promoting the self through the careful deployment of clothing. Finkelstein also analyzes the emergence of various "physiognomic" discourses over the nineteenth and twentieth centuries. Such discourses link outward appearance, from the shape of the face and overall body to dress, to inner "self." She points to how, in America over the course of the nineteenth century, there was a movement toward individual self-promotion through dress: "for upwardly mobile young men how they looked was important not only as a means of business advancement, but also as a measure of self-esteem" (Branner, in Finkelstein 1991, p. 114).

Important to the heightening self-consciousness of body and its outward appearance, and introducing the idea of dress for success, was the dress manual. It is important to note that such manuals are not, therefore, a recent phenomenon and can be seen as closely aligned with other kinds of "self-help" publications which have a longer history (Hilkey 1997). In the eighteenth and nineteenth centuries, as well as in the first half of the twentieth, one can find manuals on "how to dress like a lady" and how to put together a lady's wardrobe on a modest budget. What is different about the manuals on dress that emerged in the 1970s and 1980s was the type of self they addressed and the kind of success sought. A number of commentators (Giddens 1991; Featherstone 1991; Lasch 1979; Sennett 1977) have argued that a new type of self has emerged in the twentieth century and an examination of the dress manual can be seen to indicate this. Featherstone calls this new self "the performing self" which "places greater emphasis upon appearance, display, and the management of impressions" (Featherstone 1991, p. 187) while Lasch (1979) calls it the "narcissistic self." Featherstone (1991) argues that a comparison of self-help manuals of the nineteenth and twentieth centuries provides an insight into the development of this new self and conveys the movement from notions of "character" to "personality." In the earlier self-help manual the self is discussed in terms of character values and virtues—thrift, temperance, self-discipline, and so on—and dress is discussed in terms of such things as thrift and "ladylike" decorum. In the twentieth century we find how "personality" in the self-help manual depends upon how one *appears* as opposed to what one is or should *become;* how, for example, to look and be "magnetic" and "charm" others. In this way, appearance comes to be something malleable, something transmutable. The increasing significance of appearance from the eighteenth century onward meant that people began to be concerned with the control of appearance and clothing. Contemporary Western societies testify to the intensification of these processes with more and more aspects of outward appearance "correctable" through diet, exercise, makeup, and plastic surgery, as well as dress, and with these appearances increasingly linked to identity. All these physiognomic discourses proclaim the notion that achieving the "right" outward appearance will result in greater personal happiness and, of course, success.

Conclusion

It may well seem that the dress-for-success formulas of the 1980s have long since been replaced by more "individuality" and "creativity" in clothing. Indeed, the backlash to all these rules came in the 1990s with "dress down on Friday" introduced in offices both in the United States and United Kingdom. While we may like to think we are "individual" and while dress choice is welcomed by some,

the business and professional worlds remain conservative places, even today. Indeed, there has been a swing away from casual Fridays after some offices found that employees dressed far too casually to perform their duties effectively. Meeting a client in jeans or shorts is still taboo in most professions. Only in the "creative industries" are fashion and individuality openly welcomed, indeed, here one finds them essential. The body at work has to fit in with the overall business ethos of the office or sector. In young industries, like popular music, advertising and graphic design, for example, informality rules. However, older professions and industries still prefer the bodies at work to look suitable—that is, in a suit. The dress-for-success idea lives on and a lucrative industry of self-help advice and "experts" maintain the notion that what we wear to work really matters in our overall career "success."

See also **Casual Business Dress; Fashion and Identity; Suit, Business.**

BIBLIOGRAPHY

Armstrong, L. "Working Girls." *Vogue*, October 1993.

Carnegie, Dale. *How to Win Friends and Influence People: How to Stop Worrying and Start Living.* London: Chancellor, 1994.

Entwistle, Joanne. "Power Dressing and the Fashioning of the Career Woman." In *Buy This Book: Studies in Advertising and Consumption.* Edited by M. Nava, I. MacRury, A. Blake, and B. Richards. London: Routledge, 1997.

———. "Fashioning of the Career Woman: Power Dressing as a Strategy of Consumption." In *All the World and Her Husband: Women and Consumption in the Twentieth Century.* Edited by M. Talbot and M. Andrews. London: Cassell, 2001.

Featherstone, Mike. "The Body in Consumer Society." In *The Body: Social Process and Cultural Theory.* Edited by M. Featherstone, M. Hepworth and B. Turner. London: Sage, 1991.

Finkelstein, Joanne. *The Fashioned Self.* Philadelphia: Temple University Press, 1991.

Foucault, Michel. "Technologies of the Self." In *Technologies of the Self: A Seminar with Michel Foucault.* Edited by L. Martin, H. Gutman and P. Hutton. Amherst: University of Massachusetts Press, 1988.

Giddens, Anthony. *Modernity and Self-Identity: Self and Society in the Late Modern Age.* Stanford, Calif.: Stanford University Press, 1991.

Goffman, Erving. *The Presentation of Self in Everyday Life.* London: The Penguin Press, 1971.

Hilkey, J. *Character is Capital: Success Manuals and Manhood in Gilded Age America.* Chapel Hill: University of Carolina Press, 1997.

Lasch, Christopher. *The Culture of Narcissism.* London: Abacus, 1979.

Molloy, John T. *Dress for Success.* New York: Peter H. Wyden, 1975.

———. *Women: Dress for Success.* New York: Peter H. Wyden, 1980.

Sennett, Richard. *The Fall of Public Man.* New York: W. W. Norton and Company, 1977.

Joanne Entwistle

DRESS REFORM

DRESS REFORM Over the course of history the emergence of unorthodox clothing styles has revealed much about the social norms governing appearances. New ideologies concerning spirituality, health, hygiene, and gender have not only subverted existing social boundaries but also shaped the trajectory of fashion in the process. Quakerism, Bloomerism, aesthetic dress, and Jaeger dress may be examined as catalysts for both fashion and social change.

Nonconformist Quaker Dress

During the years following the English Civil War of 1642, various influential clothing-reform movements flourished. One of the nonconformist groups that emerged during this time was the Religious Society of Friends, commonly known as Quakers. The group's founder, George Fox, established a set of social practices that were based on Christian ideologies and utopianism. The main thesis proposed by Fox was simplicity of appearance and lifestyle. His favor of spirituality over what he considered to be the unholy virtues of fashion signaled a radical move within the history of fashion.

The alternative clothing choices embraced by George Fox and his followers were set in direct opposition to the fashionable styles of the time. Quakers believed that the focus on aesthetics within the fashion industry was immoral. Instead Quakers wore modest, unstructured, and natural-colored garments that better reflected their Christian values of humility, piety, and simplicity. The strict adherence to their faith led Quakers to eschew contemporary fashions and any decorative clothing.

Both male and female apparel was constructed of functional, utilitarian fabrics such as calico and flannel. The simple color palette for both sexes consisted of gray, brown, cream, and pale green tones. Women commonly wore loose-fitting, long-sleeved dresses, aprons, and bonnets. Men wore unstructured coats, plain hats, trousers, and buckled shoes. For both sexes, functional garment details were also kept simple. Pockets were often placed internally, the use of buttons was restricted, and small accessories or jewelry was forbidden. The commonality of dress between the sexes not only created group uniformity but also visually reinforced their detachment from the wider society.

Quaker dress maintained popularity within marginal groups until the 1920s. The Quaker adherence to plain dress styles was a nonverbal protest against the aesthetic focus of fashion. "Plain clothing" was adopted by other religious groups as well, such as some sects of German Pictists. Although the movement only achieved minority status, it nevertheless succeeded in challenging the ornamental nature of eighteenth-century dress.

Dr. Gustav Jaeger

Another revolutionary movement within the history of fashion involved the promotion of a healthy and rational approach to dress. During the eighteenth century, various medical professionals gradually began to question the irrational and unhealthy nature of the existing fashionable garments. Many argued that corsets and heavily layered undergarments restricted movement, crippled the spine, and harmed internal organs. As a consequence, certain medical professionals began to encourage men and women to turn their attention away from aesthetics and toward their health.

During the 1880s, Dr. Gustav Jaeger, a German Professor of Physiology and Zoology at the University of Stuttgart, promoted what he believed to be a healthy alternative to conventional dress. In 1884 Dr. Jaeger developed a unique system of dress based on the belief that wearing undyed sheep wool against the skin would enable skin to breathe freely and prevent perspiration. Dr. Jaeger recommended avoiding clothing made of silk, cotton, or linen—or any cloth which had been dyed. He was also highly critical of the corset.

The nonconformist apparel Dr. Jaeger introduced was designed to follow the contours of the body closely, so as to prevent exposure to drafts that he believed dangerous to the health. Jaeger was best known for undyed woolen undergarments for both sexes, including chemises, petticoats, and breeches. The range was later expanded to include other items of clothing such as jackets and trousers, as well as bedsheets.

The protective properties of woolen undergarments were widely promoted. Dr. Jaeger was an exhibitor at the *International Health Exhibition* of London in 1884. He also published widely and released a book in 1887 titled *Essays on Health Culture*. Although the Jaeger mode of dress was targeted to all, it initially only acquired a minority and predominately middle-class following.

As the system gained gradual acceptance however, London retailer Lewis Tomalin purchased the name and opened a store on London's Regent St. As public interest in health and comfort progressed, Lewis Tomalin gained popularity among male and female consumers alike. Competitive retailers gradually became aware of the changing social consciousness and began producing varied ranges that expanded upon Jaeger's original ideologies.

By the 1920s, however, the popularity of Dr. Jaeger's undergarment designs gradually began to wane as fashions became increasingly fitted. Nevertheless, the adoption and persistence of his health-reform movement illustrates that a portion of society was prepared to choose clothing primarily on the grounds of supposed health benefits rather than fashionability.

Bloomerism

In the nineteenth century, as male clothing became increasingly utilitarian, certain women began to feel constrained by the fashionable clothing styles available to them. The most famous dress-reform movement was called Bloomerism. The movement was named after New York resident, Amelia Jenks Bloomer. In 1851 Bloomer published an article in the feminist publication she edited called *The Lily*, stressing the importance of introducing reformed garments for women. The article was later reprinted in popular American press and gained a widespread readership. Later that year, along with her friends Elizabeth Smith Miller and Elizabeth Cady Stanton, she was seen in public dressed in a shortened skirt with Turkish trousers. Although Amelia was not the first woman to wear or invent the garment, the name evolved as a consequence of her association with *The Lily*.

The bloomer costume consisted of loosely fitting, Turkish-style trousers that gathered and frilled at the ankle with an elasticized cuff. The trousers were worn beneath a shortened skirt that fell below the knee, and a fitted bodice. In contrast to the prevailing fashions, the outfit was claimed to be comfortable, convenient, safe, and healthy. Bloomer dress focused not on the way one looked, but rather on the way one felt. The original intention of the garment was thus not to challenge established gender boundaries, but rather to increase mobility and function.

A majority of Victorian society was highly critical of the innovative style of dress. Since trousers were considered to be a traditional symbol of masculinity, female devotees of Bloomerism were subject to ridicule and abuse. For example, satirical caricatures of Bloomers appeared in magazines such as *Punch*. As a consequence, most abandoned the costume after only a few months.

Amelia Bloomer had herself discarded the costume by the mid-1850s. Although the movement was short lived, it exposed entrenched gender stereotypes and challenged the dominant ideals of femininity. As a consequence the innovative costume signaled an advance in the direction of female emancipation.

Rational Dress

The bloomer costume was revived through the establishment of the Rational Dress Society in London during the 1880s. The Society was chaired by Viscontess Haberton and sought to advocate the development of a rational system of clothing. During the late 1880s, the Society started publishing the *Rational Dress Society Gazette* that campaigned against restrictive fashions.

One of the main premises of the Society was the belief that women should forsake heavy undergarments and corsets, as such items restricted movement. In later years members adopted short jackets with bifurcated knee-length skirts, as it was believed such garments enhanced physical mobility. The introduction of new sports such as bicycling and lawn tennis greatly assisted the growing tendency toward functional clothing. In these arenas bifurcated garments became an acceptable mode of sports dress.

Aesthetic Dress

During the same period, the Aesthetic Movement began to emerge out of the field of decorative arts. Aesthetic devotees encouraged women to discard the restrictive garments in vogue and adopt loose-fitting, "artistic" apparel instead.

The style of dress was inspired by the work of Pre-Raphaelite painters such as Rossetti and consisted of loosely draped, medieval-styled robes. The style appealed to a significant number of middle-class women. Oscar Wilde was an avid supporter of the movement. In London, the Liberty Company produced aesthetic dresses.

In the early twentieth century, reform styles influenced the fashions created by avant-garde designers such as Paul Poiret and Mariano Fortuny.

See also **Aesthetic Dress; Bloomer Costume; Corset; Gender and Dress; Liberty & Co; Politics and Fashion; Religion and Dress.**

BIBLIOGRAPHY

Breward, Christopher. *Fashion*. Oxford: Oxford University Press, 2003.

Crane, Diana. *Fashion and its Social Agendas: Gender, Class and Identity in Clothing*. Chicago and London: University of Chicago Press, 2000.

Etten, Henry Van. *George Fox and the Quakers*. London: Longmans, 1959.

Fischer, Gayle V. *Pantaloons and Power: A Nineteenth-Century Dress Reform in the United States*. Kent, Ohio, and London: Kent State University Press, 2001.

Gattey, Charles Neilson. *The Bloomer Girls*. London: Femina Books, 1967.

Newton, Stella Mary. *Health, Art and Reason: Dress Reformers of the 19th Century*. London: John Murray, 1974.

Kristina Stankovski

DRESS SHIRT Interestingly, the term dress shirt has a different meaning on both sides of the Atlantic. In the United Kingdom, a dress shirt is known as a formal shirt. In the United States, the dress shirt makes up part of the standard ensemble required for evening dress for formal occasions. A man will be required to wear a dress shirt, which essentially must be white with double French cuffs and cuff links, with his tuxedo, cummerbund, and butterfly or bat-wing black tie.

History

Shirts appeared first in European dress in the seventeenth century as a kind of underwear, designed to protect expensive waistcoats and frock coats from sweat and soil. By the early nineteenth century, shirts had assumed importance as garments in their own right. The emphasis placed by Beau Brummell and other dandies on wearing clean, perfectly styled linen brought the shirt into increased prominence as an essential male garment.

Even up to the turn of the twentieth century, the white shirt was considered to be the symbol of a gentleman. But in order for shirts to look clean, particularly the collar, a man would have to have enough money for them to be washed frequently. According to popular legend, Mrs. Orlando Montague of New York City realized the collars on her husbands' shirts needed washing much more than the main body and set about removing all the collars and sewing on strings to reattach them once they had been washed. The trend soon caught on, even though many men struggled to piece their shirts back together again.

Detachable versions of both the turndown and wing collar were available with the added advantage of being able to alter the collar depending on circumstance. Victorian men were also known to buy celluloid or paper collars to save money. However, due to the laborious process of refitting the collars on the shirts, the development of the domestic washing machine, and developments in fabric technology, the detachable collar has all but disappeared from the male wardrobe.

The Twentieth Century

Shirts made to be worn with formal attire were traditionally cut with a stiff wing collar in the late nineteenth century, and that style remained standard into the period after World War I. The Duke of Windsor developed the move to a pleated front formal shirt with a turned-down collar in the 1920s. The Duke explained to his shirt maker that he wanted a softer alternative to the stiff-winged collar shirt. The pleated front of the dress shirt is designed not to extend below the waist, so that the front will not bulge forward when the wearer sits down.

The wing collar remains the more formal of the two styles and usually comes in reinforced pique and sometimes with a fly front to conceal the buttons. The wing-collared shirt remains the more flattering to those with long necks and the preferred choice for their partners by women.

By the late 1960s there was a trend in evening shirts toward more ornate styles. Almost-feminine dress shirts, with huge ruffles, horizontal pleats, embroidery, and lace all featured, were finished off with mandarin collars and a variety of new colors. This trend carried on until the 1970s, but such ostentation is considered a sartorial blunder in the early 2000s, and most men have reverted to the more traditional styles in white fabrics.

An interesting trend that developed during the 1980s was the adoption of the dress shirt by women, who wore it both formally to black tie events and as an item of casual wear. This trend has all but vanished. (The formal dress shirt had hitherto been an entirely masculine item of dress, though in the 1890s some women who adopted the tailored styles of the New Woman also wore blouses that somewhat resembled men's formal shirts.)

The American Dress Shirt

A dress shirt in the United States is considered to be any shirt with a collar (attachable or detachable) that is worn with a jacket and a tie. This includes both the wing-collared and turned-down collared shirts worn by men as evening wear, but these are referred to as formal shirts.

Styles of American dress shirts include pinned, button-down, Barrymore, plain, or tab-collared shirts.

See also **Shirt; Sport Shirt.**

BIBLIOGRAPHY

Amies, Hardy. *A,B,C of Men's Fashion*. London: Cahill and Company Ltd., 1964.

Barnes, Richard. *Mods!*. London: Plexus Publishing Ltd., 1979.

Byrde, Penelope. *The Male Image: Men's Fashion in England 1300–1970*. London: B. T. Batsford, Ltd., 1979.

Chenoune, Farid. *A History of Men's Fashion*. Paris: Flammarion, 1993.

De Marley, Diana. *Fashion for Men: An Illustrated History*. London: B. T. Batsford, Ltd., 1985.

Keers, Paul. *A Gentleman's Wardrobe*. London: Weidenfeld and Nicolson, 1987.

Roetzel, Bernhard. *Gentleman: A Timeless Fashion*. Cologne, Germany: Konemann, 1999.

Schoeffler, O. E., and William Gale. *Esquire's Encyclopedia of 20th Century Fashions*. New York: McGraw-Hill, 1973.

Tom Greatrex

DRY CLEANING Dry cleaning is the cleansing of a textile utilizing an organic solvent as opposed to water. The development of dry cleaning is predicated on the fact that as a solvent, water is ineffective in the removal of non–water soluble soils. These soils are primarily oil-based stains such as paint, grease, wax, tar, and body oils.

Early attempts at "dry cleaning" were uncovered within the ruins of Pompeii. Evidence suggests that clothing tradesmen used fuller's earth to absorb soils and grease from garments. Until the end of the seventeenth century, absorption by the means of fuller's earth, or (in later centuries) paper and a hot iron, were the only methods available for the removal of oily stains.

The first use of an organic solvent as a spot-removing agent occurred in Western Europe during the 1680s. Oil of turpentine is a by-product derived from the distillation of turpentine (pine pitch). Used in medicines and for the making of varnish, oil of turpentine was discovered to also be an effective solvent for removing grease stains from fabric. Fabric processors known as dyers and scourers began utilizing this new solvent to supplement the washing process.

By the early nineteenth century, two solvents—camphene (a mixture of oil of turpentine and naphtha) and benzine, a petroleum distillate—had replaced oil of turpentine for use in clothing care. Camphene, primarily sold as illuminating oil, was employed in an immersion bath process for cleansing satin goods, silk dresses, fancy waistcoats, and lace. Another major benefit derived from cleaning natural fibers in dry solvents had been realized.

Dry solvents are liquids that do not wet or swell textile fibers. The cleaning mechanisms of dry solvents are thus different from water, in which wetting and swelling play a significant role. In natural fibers (silk, wool, cotton, and linen), this swelling can lead to shrinkage, distortion, finish loss, or dye bleeding. Cleaning with dry solvents is a gentler process that requires less finishing, thus prolonging the life and feel of the textile.

There were two problems associated with the use of these early solvents. The solvents were extremely flammable, having flashpoints around 70° F. (21° C.), and a strong odor remained in the clothes without proper drying.

Commercial dry cleaning was first practiced in the Jolly Belin Dye Works in Paris in 1825. William Spindler of Berlin visited the Jolly Works in 1854 and brought the process to Germany. James Pullar, Spindler's son-in-law, introduced commercial cleaning to Scotland.

At the beginning of the twentieth century, mechanized improvements such as rotating cleaning drums, hydro extractors, solvent purification systems, and the first dry solvent soap increased both the safety and effectiveness of the dry-cleaning process. The solvent of choice was gasoline.

Modern dry cleaning was ushered in with the development of two new solvents. In 1926 came Stoddard solvent, a petroleum-based hydrocarbon with a flashpoint of 100° F. (38° C.), and in 1932, nonflammable perchloroethylene, or perc, was introduced. Equipment advances derived from the electric motor and pneumatics allowed for controlled rotation of the cleaning drum and high-speed solvent extraction. The steam boiler enabled controlled drying, utilizing moist heat as well as providing steam for the finishing irons and presses.

In the late 1980s, perchloroethylene was designated a possible carcinogen, and stricter controls monitoring usage were imposed. This led to the development of several alternative solvents: the silicone-based Green Earth process, liquid carbon dioxide, and synthetic hydrocarbons with flashpoints exceeding 145° F. (63° C.). These solvents are considerably less aggressive, meaning they have less degreasing power than perchloroethylene. The benefit is that they can safely clean any material from feathers to a heavily beaded gown. With proper application, the equipment and solvent options available in the early 2000s can effectively clean any fabric or design element used in the realization of haute couture fashions.

See also **Laundry.**

BIBLIOGRAPHY

Cambridge, E. M. "Benzene and Turpentine: The Pre-History of Dry-cleaning." *Ambix* 38 (2) (July 1991).

International Fabricare Institute. *Dry Cleaning Fundamentals.* Silver Spring, Md.: IFI, 2003.

Textile Conservation Center. "Dry-cleaning I: Solvents." *Technical Bibliographies.* North Andover, Mass.: Museum of American Textile History.

John Lappe

DUFFLE COAT Duffle is a coarse, heavy woolen fabric with a thick nap, traditionally worn by fishermen. Its name derives from the town in Belgium where it was originally manufactured beginning in the seventeenth century. The fabric is most commonly associated with a box-cut, loose-fitting, three-quarter-length coat with patch pockets and a square shoulder yoke, fastened with wooden or buffalo horn toggles and hemp loops. Sharing the name of its fabric, the duffle coat is the only classic overcoat to have a hood.

History

Although hoods of a similar shape to that of the modern duffle coat were indeed used as far back as the Bronze Age (some think a monk's habit was the forerunner of the duffle coat), the actual design of the duffle coat originated in Poland (known as the Polish-coat) in the first half of the nineteenth century. John Partridge, a British purveyor of outdoor clothing, began to design and sell the duffle in 1890.

The duffle actually came into its own when the Royal Navy adopted it early in the twentieth century. Sailors wore the coat, sometimes with a pair of matching drawstring trousers, as protection from the elements when assigned to deck watch. It was further popularized by Army Field-Marshal Bernard Montgomery during World War II, and indeed the beige desert version he sported at that time became known, in Europe at least, as the "Monty." Huge quantities of army surplus duffles flooded the market after the war ended and it soon become a warm winter favorite with British and American consumers alike. Mothers would dress their young children in them due to their warmth, but duffle coats also achieved cult status among college students and intellectuals, worn with an former naval sweater, college scarf, and corduroy trousers.

The Duffle in the Twenty-first Century

Little has changed with the duffle since its Polish origins. The classic version is generally tartan lined and has a hood and an extra layer of cloth around the shoulders for added protection against the elements. Genuine horn toggles and hemp-fiber loops add an element of authenticity.

Modern fabrication, fastenings, and styling have led to a new generation of duffle coats featuring zippers, reflective safety tape, Gore-Tex linings, and printed designs on the outer fabric.

The British designer Alexander McQueen produced a version of the duffle coat for his autumn 2002 collection. Jean-Charles de Castelbajac showed a duffle coat in 1990, cut in wool with leather trim. More interestingly, the Savile Row tailor Richard Anderson is the first tailor on the Row to create a bespoke option. Instead of the original classic beige and deep blue hues, consumers have a wide variety of colors to choose from, such as dark brown, yellow, red, racing green, and burgundy.

With fans spanning a spectrum from the actress Gwyneth Paltrow, to the rock band Oasis, the duffle continues to maintain a following that transcends class, wealth, or creed.

See also **Coat; Outerwear.**

BIBLIOGRAPHY

Amies, Hardy. *A,B,C of Men's Fashion.* London: Cahill and Company Ltd., 1964.

Byrde, Penelope, *The Male Image: Men's Fashion in England 1300–1970.* London: B. T. Batsford, Ltd., 1979.

Chenoune, Farid. *A History of Men's Fashion.* Paris: Flammarion, 1993.

De Marley, Diana. *Fashion for Men: An Illustrated History.* London: B. T. Batsford, Ltd., 1985.

Schoeffler, O. E., and William Gale. *Esquire's Encyclopedia of 20th Century Fashions.* New York: McGraw-Hill, 1973.

Tom Greatrex

DYEING A general term that describes many complex processes in which color is added in the form of a solution of synthetic or natural dyes to fibers, yarns, or fabrics. Dyes are organic chemicals that produce intense color, are water soluble or dispersible, and bond with fibers. When struck by energy in the form of light, the chemical absorbs, reflects, or transmits specific wavelengths of the energy. The wavelengths and concentrations of the reflected light determine the color seen. The composition and structure of the dye chemical determines its color and the fiber with which it forms a chemical attraction. This means that dyes are fiber specific. Dyes are incorporated into fibers by chemical reactions, absorption, or dispersion. Commercially important dyes must be relatively fast to resist environmental factors such as cleaning agents, light, air pollutants, and perspiration.

Dyeing is usually done by immersing and moving the textile in a heated, dilute dye solution in a bath or vat. Except for a few cases (for example, resist methods), the desired result is an even or level color. Dyeing includes some preparation steps, such as scouring, bleaching, and mordanting, as well as some after-treatment steps to improve the fastness of certain dyes. Dyeing can be classified based on the stage of processing of the textile when the dye is added, the process used in dyeing, or the type of dye used.

Dyeing Stage
In mass pigmentation, dope dyeing, or solution dyeing, colorant is added to manufactured and synthetic fibers before fiber formation. Mass pigmentation is permanent and relatively expensive. Fiber or stock dyeing adds dye to loose fibers, fiber top, or sliver (a yarn precursor in producing yarn from staple fiber). Stock dyeing creates heather effects in which adjacent fibers are different colors. In yarn and skein dyeing, yarns are dyed for fabrics, such as denim and chambray, in which only the warp yarns are dyed. Yarn dyeing produces better quality stripes, plaids, and structural designs with colored woven or knit designs. Piece dyeing is used to dye fabric lengths or yardages a solid uniform color. However, fiber blends, mixtures, and combinations present other options for piece dyeing. In cross dyeing, each fiber type absorbs a different color dye. Cross dyeing is one way of achieving a yarn-dyed appearance while skipping the yarn-dyeing step. In union dyeing, dyes from different classes are carefully selected to create a solid color on a fabric of two or more different fiber types. In product or garment dyeing, the textile is cut and sewn into the final product and then dyed. Careful preparation and selection of thread, closures, labels, and trims is necessary to ensure that all desired components are dyed the same color while other components (labels, for example) are not dyed or stained.

Dyeing Process
Many different dyeing processes exist. In batch processes, a predetermined quantity of fiber or length of yarn or fabric is dyed. In continuous methods, very long lengths of yarn or fabric are dyed. In skein dyeing, yarns are wrapped around poles and vat dyed. In package dyeing, yarn is wound onto perforated tubes through which dye is pumped. In beam dyeing, yarn or fabric is wrapped around a large perforated beam through which dye is pumped. In beck and jet dyeing, fabric is loosely twisted into a long loop and circulated around reels and guide rollers into and out of the dyebath. Jig dyeing is a batch process in which the fabric is under tension during dyeing as it passes through the dyebath and winds onto one roller, reverses direction, and passes back through the dyebath and onto the other roller. In continuous dyeing, the dye is padded onto the fabric, excess dye is removed by rollers, and steam heat sets the dye.

Dye Class
Dye classes can be organized by application method. Acid dyes require an acidic pH, are used on wool, silk, and some manufactured fibers, and produce strong clear colors. Metalized or mordant dyes incorporate metal in their molecular structure that dulls color but improves wash fastness. Direct dyes are applied directly to cellulosic fibers in a neutral or alkaline bath and give slightly dull shades. They exhibit poor wash fastness, unless after-treated with a metal salt solution. Disperse dyes are slightly water soluble and used to dye most synthetic fibers. Fiber reactive or reactive dyes are applied in an alkaline environment, react with the hydroxyl groups of cellulose, and produce bright shades on cellulose. Sulfur

Dyers working in a tannery. Though most dyeing today is done with the help of machinery, the centuries-old process of hand dyeing has not completely disappeared. © JOHN R. JONES; PAPILIO/CORBIS. REPRODUCED BY PERMISSION.

and vat dyes are solubility cycle dyes that are applied to cellulosic fibers in a reduced, colorless form and reoxidized to the insoluble, colored form on the fiber. They have good fastness to washing and sunlight. Basic or cationic dyes are applied to cellulosic, protein, and some synthetic fibers in slightly acidic or neutral solutions. Azoic dyes are formed on the fiber through a coupling reaction of two components. Natural dyes are complex mixtures of components derived from plants, animals, or minerals.

History of Dyeing

Dyeing was a hand process for thousands of years. Dyers used large containers or vats for coloring relatively short lengths of fabric or small quantities of fiber and yarn. Until the development of synthetic dyes, all dyes were natural compounds. Fastness varied widely among the natural dyes. The processes required to achieve certain colors were long and involved and carefully guarded by dyers. In the latter half of the nineteenth century, research into a better understanding of the chemistry of natural dyes led to the development of synthetic dyes. By approximately 1900, synthetic dyes had replaced natural dyes in almost all applications.

Developments during the industrial revolution increased the amount of fiber, yarn, or fabric dyed in a vat. Dye boxes, vats, and jigs were the primary pieces of equipment used to dye industrial quantities of fabric in batch methods. However, in the twentieth century, researchers developed continuous methods so that undyed fabric would enter and dyed fabric would exit the machine. Other twentieth-century developments increased production rates, improved dye quality, and lowered costs.

See also **Dyeing, Resist; Dyes, Chemical and Synthetic; Dyes, Natural.**

BIBLIOGRAPHY

Kulkarni, S. V., C. D. Blackwell, A. L. Blackard, C. W. Stackhouse, and M. W. Alexander. *Textile Dyeing Operations: Chemistry, Equipment, Procedures, and Environmental Aspects.* Par Ridge, N.J.: Noyes Publications, 1986.

Society of Dyers and Colourists and the American Association of Textile Chemists and Colorists. *Colour Index.* 3rd ed. London: Author, 1971.

Tortora, Phyllis G., and Robert S. Merkel. *Fairchild's Dictionary of Textiles.* 7th ed. New York: Fairchild Publications, 1996.

Trotman, E. R. *Dyeing and Chemical Technology of Textile Fibres,* 6th ed. New York: John Wiley and Sons, 1984.

Sara J. Kadolph

DYEING, RESIST Resist printing is a method used to apply a design on a fabric. It requires the covering of parts of the fabric in a way that will keep the dye from penetrating the open areas. The cover may be a variety of materials. Other than flat bed silk-screening and rotary silk-screening, resist-printing processes are hand methods. Wax is used in batik, while string or rubber bands are used in the tie-dye process. Similar to tie-dye is the ikat process, where the warp yarns are tied before dyeing. Another similar process to tie-dye is Shibori, where the fabric is given a three-dimensional form and folded, stitched, plaited, or twisted.

Also similar to tie-dye is the process called tritik. To prepare the fabric for dyeing, the fabric is stitched by hand or machine in the planned design. The thread is then pulled to draw the fabric. Where the fabric is close together it resists the dye.

Stencil printing is another form of resist printing. To make the stencil, designs are cut out of wood, paper, waxed paper, thin metal, or cardboard to cover the parts that will not be dyed. The open design areas need to be fastened to the adjacent areas; the attachments are usually noticeable in the print. A separate stencil is made for each color. The stencil is placed over the fabric. A color paste is applied to the open areas or the dye may be applied by an airbrush or spray gun. The stencil is removed and the next stencil is placed on the fabric.

Silk-screen printing is a process to apply designs either by hand or by automatic methods. The screen is coated with a material that is then removed in the design areas. Screens at one time were made from silk but in the early 2000s screens are either made from synthetic fibers or a metal mesh. A screen will be prepared for each color in the design. The screens are placed individually on top of the fabric by hand and the dye paste is forced onto the fabric through the open (design) areas of the screen by a squeegee. The screen is removed and moved to the next position on the fabric.

Flat bed silk-screening and rotary silk-screen printing are automatic methods. Flat silk-screening is similar to hand silk-screening but the fabric moves on a conveyor belt at regular intervals. The screens are placed above and are lowered automatically. Flat silk-screen printing is economically feasible for small runs and large designs.

Rotary silk-screen printing is a much faster system and used more often. Instead of flat screens, the screens are cylindrical and the dye paste is inside the roller. The squeegee forces the dye paste out of the roller on the fabric as it rotates. The design repeat is only as large as the circumference of the roller. Colorfastness of resist prints will be dependent on the dyestuff, the fiber, the pretreatment and absorbency of the fabric used, and the method of application.

See also **Batik; Ikat; Tie-Dyeing.**

BIBLIOGRAPHY

Bosence, Susan. *Hand Block Printing and Resist Dyeing.* London: David and Charles, 1985.

Wells, Kate. *Fabric Dyeing and Printing.* Loveland, Colo.: Interweave Press, 1997.

Robyne Williams

DYES, CHEMICAL AND SYNTHETIC Synthetic dyes are manufactured from organic molecules. Before synthetic dyes were discovered in 1856, dyestuffs were manufactured from natural products such as flowers, roots, vegetables, insects, minerals, wood, and mollusks. Batches of natural dye were never exactly alike in hue and intensity, whereas synthetic dyestuffs can be manufactured consistently. The use of computers and computer color matching (CCM) produces color that is identical from batch to batch.

William Henry Perkin, an eighteen-year-old English chemist, was searching for a cure for malaria, a synthetic quinine, and accidentally discovered the first synthetic dye. He found that the oxidation of aniline could color silk. From a coal tar derivative he made a reddish purple dye. The brilliant purple was called mauve. The dye was not stable to sunlight or water and faded easily to the color presently named mauve, a pale purple. This discovery resulted in additional research with coal tar derivatives and other organic compounds and an entire new industry of synthetic dyes was born. In the twenty-first century, synthetic dyes are less expensive, have better colorfastness, and completely dominate the industry as compared with natural dyes. Thousands of distinctly different synthetic dyes are manufactured in the world.

Dyes are classified by their chemical composition, the types of fibers to which they can be applied, by hue, or by the method of application. Dye molecules may attach to the surface of the fiber, be absorbed by the fiber, or interact with the fiber's molecules. Each fiber reacts differently to dyes. Fiber modifications will also react differently to the same dye. Within a dye classification, different hues will have different colorfastness.

The Society of Dyers and Colourists (SDC) and the American Association of Textile Chemists and Colorists (AATCC) classify dyes by their chemical composition. In the publication, *The Colour Index International*, dyes are listed by their generic name, which indicates the application class, and by a *Colour Index constitution number* (CI number) which indicates the chemical structure.

Classes of Dyes

Acid (anionic) dyes are water-soluble dyes applied to wool, silk, nylon, modified rayon, certain modified acrylic, and polyester fibers. Fibers that will be damaged by acids, such as cellulosics, cannot be dyed with this family of dyes. The dyes in this class vary in their chemical composition but all use an acid bath. These dyes produce bright colors and have a complete color range but colorfastness varies.

Azoic (naphthol) dyes are produced within the fiber of cellulose fibers. The fiber is impregnated with one component of the dye, followed by treatment with another component, thus forming the dye. When the two components are joined under suitable conditions (a low temperature water bath is employed) a large, insoluble, colored molecule forms within the fiber. Because the color is within the fiber, colorfastness is excellent. Excess color on the outside of the fiber will rub off (crock) if not removed.

Basic (cationic) dyes are very bright but have poor colorfastness; they have limited use on cellulosic and protein fibers. Wool and silk can be dyed by basic dyes in a dye bath containing acid. Cotton fibers can be dyed by basic dyes but only in the presence of a mordant, generally a metallic salt. The colored portion of the dye molecule carries a positive charge. Basic dyes are relatively colorfast on acrylic fibers. Nylon and polyester fibers that have been modified to accept basic dyes will exhibit excellent colorfastness. The first synthetic dye, mauveine, belongs in this class.

Direct (substantive) dyes are soluble and have an affinity for cellulose fibers. An electrolyte, salt, is added to the dye bath to control the absorption rate of the dye by the fiber. The dye is absorbed by the fiber; colorfastness to light is good but colorfastness to laundering is not. Direct dyes are best used when wet cleaning is restricted. Developed direct dyes are those that are developed on the fabric after dyeing. They produce an insoluble dye that forms a chemical bond with the fiber molecules. Developed direct dyes have better wash fastness but poorer light fastness as compared with direct dyes. Both are used on lower-cost fabrics.

Disperse dyes were first developed to dye acetate fibers. Hydrophobic fibers have little affinity for water-soluble dyes. A method to dye hydrophobic fibers by dispersing colored organic substances in water with a surfactant was developed. The finely colored particles are applied in aqueous dispersion and the color dissolves in the hydrophobic fiber. Disperse dyes are the best method for dyeing acetate and polyester. Acrylic, aramid, modacrylic, nylon, olefin, and polyester are dyed by dispersed dyes; colorfastness is good to excellent.

Pigment dyes are not dyes but insoluble coloring particles. Pigments are added to the spinning solution (the liquid fiber before extrusion) of synthetic fibers and become an integral part of the fiber. Colorfastness is excellent. Pigments are also printed on fabric using resin binders. The adhesive attaches the color to the fabric. Colorfastness is dependent on the binder or adhesive used rather than the pigment. Pigment printing is an economical and simple means of adding color to fabrics.

Reactive (fiber-reactive) dyes combine with fiber molecules either by addition or substitution. The color cannot be removed if properly applied. Colors are bright with very good colorfastness but are susceptible to damage by chlorine bleaches. Reactive dyes color cellulosics (cotton, flax, and viscose rayon), silk, wool, and nylon. Reactive dyes are used in conjunction with disperse dyes to dye polyester and cellulosic fiber blends. They were introduced to the industry in 1956.

Sulfur dyes are insoluble but become soluble in sodium polysulphide. They have excellent colorfastness to water. Another advantage is their low cost and ease of application. Dark shades—black, brown, navy blue—are typical of sulfur dyes. Newer sulfur dyes are available in brighter colors. They perform well if correctly applied. They are susceptible to damage by chlorine bleaches. Sulfur dyes color primarily cellulosics, such as heavyweight cotton and viscose rayon.

Vat dyes are insoluble in water but become soluble when reduced in the presence of an alkali. Oxidizing the dyed fabric produces a water insoluble dye. The term vat dyes is derived from the large vessels used to apply the dye. The first synthetic indigo dye, introduced to the industry in 1896, belongs to this class. Vat dyes have an incomplete color range but good to excellent colorfastness. They are primarily used to dye cotton work clothes, sportswear, prints, drapery fabrics, and cotton polyester blends. (1068)

See also **Dyeing; Dyes, Natural.**

BIBLIOGRAPHY

Aspland, J. R. *Textile Dyeing and Coloration.* Research Triangle Park, N.C.: American Association of Textile Chemists and Colorists, 1997.

Perkins, Warren S. *Textile Coloration and Finishing.* Durham, N.C.: Carolina Academic Press, 1996.

Society of Dyers and Colourists, and the American Association of Textile Chemists and Colorist. *The Colour Index International.* 9 vols. 3rd ed. West Yorkshire, England: Bradford, 1971–1992. Fourth edition (2004) available online through subscription <www.colour-index.org>.

Robyne Williams

DYES, NATURAL Natural dyes are obtained from natural sources. Most are of plant origin and extracted from roots, wood, bark, berries, lichens, leaves, flowers, nuts, and seeds. Others come from insects, shellfish, and mineral compounds. Natural dyes were the only source of color for textiles, leather, basketry, and other materials until synthetic dyes were developed in the latter half of the nineteenth century. Of the thousands of natural color substances, very few became significant commercially. Dyestuff refers to the plant or other material from which the dye is extracted. Complete palettes are achieved by dyeing in one bath and sequential dyeing in two or more baths.

There are two types of natural dyes. Adjective or additive dyes such as madder must use a mordant (a chemical that fixes a dye) to bond with fibers. These are the most common type and have been used for at least 2,000 years. Substantive dyes bond with a fiber without the use of a mordant or they contain tannin, a natural mordant. Examples of substantive dyes include safflower, cochineal, and black walnut. Mordants are chemical compounds that combine with the fiber and the dye forming a chemical bridge between the two. Madder, cochineal, and other commercially important natural dyes are polychromic, meaning that they yield different colors with different mordants. Common mordants are weak organic acids, such as acetic or tannic acid, and metal salts including aluminum ammonium or potassium sulfate, ferrous sulfate, and copper sulfate. Usually, the textile to be dyed is simmered in a mordant solution before dyeing (pre-mordanting). Other options include adding the mordant to the dyebath or treating with another mordant after dyeing to shift the color.

Current Use

Natural dyes are used in small quantities by artists and craftspeople. Some commercial use of natural dyes is a response to concerns about synthetic dyes and environmental pollution. Natural dyes are a renewable resource and contribute to rural economic development. However, in most commercial applications, natural dyes do not compete with synthetic dyes that are available in more colors, more uniform in composition facilitating color matching, and of known ratings to fading agents. Contrary to common assumptions, some natural dyes have excellent fastness to light, cleaning agents, water, and perspiration. Commercially available natural dye extracts facilitate color matching and make the dyeing process less involved.

Historic Natural Dyes

Evidence of well-developed dye works exists in many parts of the world. Ancient Egyptians, Phoenicians, and Peruvians were known for their excellent dyeing. Italian dyers were among the best from Roman times through the sixteenth century. Dyers from India were supreme in dyeing cotton. Dyers in China specialized in dyeing silk. Natural dyes were major trade items throughout history until the development of synthetic dyes. By the early years of the twentieth century, natural dyes had been replaced in most applications. However, most of these dyes remain important for artists, craftspeople, and niche producers.

Yellow dyes are the most numerous natural dyes, but most are weakly colored with poor lightfastness. The most important yellow dye in Europe was weld (*Reseda luteola*), which had better lightfastness than the dyes imported from Asia: saffron (*Crocus sativus*), safflower (*Carthamus tinctorius*), and quercitron (*Quercus tinctoria nigra*). Osage orange (*Maclura pomifera*) is a contemporary dye extracted from wood and sawdust from a native North American tree.

Red dyes included madder, cochineal, kermes, lac, cudbear, and brazil wood. Madder is a fast, rich-red dye obtained from the root of the Eurasian herbaceous perennial *Rubia tinctoria*. It was used in a long and complex process to produce Turkey Red on cotton and wool. With different mordants, madder produces a range of colors. Insect dyes include cochineal (*Dactylopius* sp.) from Central and South America, kermes (*Kermoccus vermilis*) of the Mediterranean region, and lac (*Lakshadia chinensis* and *communis*) of Asia. Cudbear (from *Ochrolechia*, *Lasallia*, and *Umbilicaria* spp.) is a lichen dye from northern Europe. Brazil wood (*Caesalpinia* spp.) from Asia and South America produces red, pink, and purple. Of these, madder and cochineal were the most important and the most readily available to contemporary dyers.

Indigo is extracted from the stems and leaves of plants of the *Indigofera* species from India, Central America, and Africa and from woad (*Isatis tinctoria*) from Europe. Indigo, originally from India, is used for cotton, wool, and silk. Woad was an important source of blue in Europe until it was replaced by imported indigo. Indigo from all sources was fermented to produce the dye. The dye must be reduced to be absorbed by the fiber and the fabric exposed to oxygen to develop the blue color.

Log wood (*Haematoxylon campechiancum L.*) from Central America was one of the most important black dyes. It also was used for blue and purple. Black walnut (*Juglans nigra*) is used in the twenty-first century to produce substantive black and brown dyes.

Purple dyes have been among the most difficult natural colors to achieve in large quantities. Shellfish (or Tyrian) purple was removed from shellfish of the species *Murex* found in the Mediterranean Sea and *Purpura* found along the coasts of Central America. Orchil, another important purple dye, was derived from lichens.

Mineral dyes include iron buff, iron black, manganese bistre, chrome yellow, and Prussian blue. They were used primarily on industrial fabrics.

Dyeing with Natural Dyes

Natural dyes are most often processed in this way. The dyestuff is harvested or collected, soaked in water for several hours, and heated to a low simmer for approximately an hour or more to extract the dye. The extract is poured into another pot and water is added to achieve the desired dyebath volume. Wet, pre-mordanted textile is added to the dyebath, which is heated to a low simmer for approximately an hour. After the dyebath is cool, the textile is removed. Some dyers rinse before letting the textile dry. Other dyers prefer to dry the textile for several days before rinsing.

Contact dyeing is an alternate method in which the dyestuff, a tiny volume of water or other liquid, sodium chloride or mordant, and found materials like rusty nails or copper wire are placed in and around the textile that is sealed in a plastic bag or glass jar for several days, weeks, or months. Contact dyed textiles have unusual, one-of-a-kind patterns.

See also **Dyeing; Dyes, Chemical and Synthetic.**

BIBLIOGRAPHY

Casselman, Karen Leigh. *Craft of the Dyer: Colour from Plants and Lichens of the Northeast.* Toronto: University of Toronto Press, 1980.

Gordon, P. F., and P. Gregory. *Organic Chemistry in Colour.* Berlin: Springer-Verlag, 1987.

Liles, J. N. *The Art and Craft of Natural Dyeing: Traditional Recipes for Modern Use.* Knoxville, Tenn.: University of Knoxville Press, 1990.

Sara J. Kadolph

EARRINGS Earrings, ornaments decorating the ears, have been one of the principal forms of jewelry throughout recorded history. The term usually refers to ornaments worn attached to the earlobes, though in the late twentieth century it expanded somewhat to include ornaments worn on other parts of the ear, such as ear cuffs, and is used to describe pieces of jewelry in earring form, even when they are worn through piercings in other parts of the body (for example, in the nose). The most common means of attaching earrings to the earlobes has been to pierce holes in the lobes, through which a loop or post may be passed. But a variety of other devices have also been used, including spring clips, tensioning devices such as screw backs, and, for particularly heavy earrings, loops passing over the top of the ear or attaching to the hair or headdress.

In many cultures and contexts, earrings have traditionally been worn as symbols of cultural or tribal identity, as markers of age, marital status, or rank, or because they are believed to have protective or medicinal powers. Even when they have served other purposes, however, the primary function of earrings has been a decorative one. As earrings are so prominently placed near the face, and at the juncture between costume and coiffure, they, perhaps more than any other element of jewelry, have been particularly responsive to changes in fashion; as hairstyles, hats, collars, and necklines have risen and fallen, earrings have correspondingly increased and decreased in size and prominence, and during many periods they have been instrumental in balancing and tying together the desired fashionable appearance.

The Ancient World
In antiquity, earrings were one of the most popular forms of jewelry. The crescent-shaped gold hoops worn by Sumerian women around 2500 B.C.E. are the earliest earrings for which there is archaeological evidence. By 1000 B.C.E., tapered hoop (also known as boat-shaped) earrings, most commonly of gold but also of silver and bronze, had spread throughout the Aegean world and Western Asia. In Crete and Cyprus, earrings were embellished with twisted gold wire, clusters of beads, and pendants stamped out of thin sheet gold.

In Egypt, earrings were introduced about 1500 B.C.E. and were later worn by both men and women. Many Egyptian earrings took the form of thick, mushroom-shaped studs or plugs, which required an enlarged hole to be stretched in the earlobe; these could be of gold, with a decorated front surface, or of humbler materials such as colored glass or carved jasper. Ear studs consisting of two capped tubes that screwed together could be worn alone, but some also had elaborate pendants of gold cornflowers, or falcons with flexible tail feathers inlaid with glass.

In the first millennium B.C.E., Etruscan and Greek goldsmiths brought new refinement and artistry to earrings, which were valued as both an adornment and a sign of wealth. Variations on the hoop were the so-called leech earring, a thick tube secured by a hidden wire, and the Etruscan box-type earring, which encased the earlobe in a wide horizontal cylinder. Disk earrings, with pendants in the form of amphorae (ancient Greek jars), figures of Eros, and decorative beads and chains, were another popular form, joined about 330 B.C.E. by twisted gold hoops with animal-head finials. All of these forms were stamped out of thin sheets of gold and decorated with fine palmettes, scrolls, and flowers in twisted wire and granulation; such earrings were fairly light in weight, but gave an extremely rich effect.

Roman earrings were similar to Etruscan styles until the first century C.E., when new styles with disks and pendants mounted on s-shaped ear hooks appeared. Colored stones and pearls were favored, and earring styles proliferated to satisfy the Roman taste for ostentatious display. At its height, the Roman Empire had the effect of standardizing styles of jewelry over much of the known world; after the center of influence shifted to Byzantium (Constantinople) in C.E. 330, and Roman influence began to decline, local variations once more emerged. Characteristic Byzantine earrings were plain gold hoops with multiple pearl pendants hung on chains, and crescent-shaped earrings of gold filigree.

The Sixteenth to Eighteenth Centuries
In Europe, earrings virtually disappeared between the eleventh and sixteenth centuries, as hairstyles and headdresses that completely covered the ears, and later high

Roman bust of woman wearing earrings. The Roman Empire's influence at its height of power resulted in the standardization of jewelry styles over much of the known world. © ARALDO DE LUCA/CORBIS. REPRODUCED BY PERMISSION.

ruff collars, made them impractical. Earrings finally began to revive in the late sixteenth century, as ruffs gave way to standing collars. At first, complex enameled designs were popular, but improved techniques of gem cutting soon shifted the emphasis to faceted diamonds. In the seventeenth century, large, pear-shaped pearl pendants were a favorite earring style, and those who could afford to do so wore two in each ear. It was also fashionable to wear pendant earrings on strings or ribbons threaded through the earlobes and tied in bows, and to tie ribbon bows at the tops of earrings to achieve the same effect. Similar earring styles were also worn by fashionable gentlemen, but usually in one ear only.

By the late seventeenth century, earrings had become an essential element of dress, and larger and more elaborate forms began to develop. Two of these became the dominant styles of the eighteenth century: the girandole, in which a single top cluster branches out like a chandelier to support three pear-shaped drops, and the pendeloque, a top cluster with a long single pendant. New sources of diamonds, along with new methods of cutting them, developed early in the eighteenth century, made them the material of choice for jewelry, and high-quality paste imitations were also available. Glittering girandoles

and pendeloques, visually tied to the ears by stylized ribbon bows of diamonds set in silver, effectively balanced the high, powdered hairstyles of the period. Despite their refined and delicate appearance, such large earrings were quite heavy; some had additional rings soldered to the tops, permitting the wearer to take some of the weight off of her ears by tying the earrings to her hair.

The Nineteenth Century

When the neoclassical style of dress and simpler hairstyles came into fashion at the end of the eighteenth century, earrings became lighter and simpler. Jewelry of cut steel, seed pearls, Berlin iron, and strongly colored materials such as coral and jet, harmonized well with neoclassical fashions, and classically inspired cameos and intaglios were set in all kinds of jewelry. Heavy girandoles gave way to pendant earrings composed of flat, geometric elements connected by light chains. "Top-and-drop" earrings, composed of a small top element attached to the ear wire, from which a larger, often teardrop-shaped element is suspended, also came to the fore around 1800, and remained the most popular earring style throughout the nineteenth century. Matched sets of jewelry, known as parures, assumed new importance in the nineteenth century, and they were available even to women of modest means. These sets usually included at least a matching necklace or brooch and earrings, but could also include bracelets, buckles, and a tiara or tiara-comb.

In the 1810s and 1820s, the trend toward lighter and more delicate jewelry continued, and settings of gold filigree or elaborate wirework (known as cannetille) were very popular. In the 1820s, a romantic interest in the past also inspired jewelry designers to revive historical styles from the ancient world to the eighteenth century, and a modified version of the girandole earring returned, along with elaborate gothic tracery and rococo-revival scrollwork. As hairstyles became more elaborate in the 1830s, earrings became more prominent, with small tops and long drops reaching nearly to the shoulders. In spite of their size, these earrings were fairly light in weight, owing to lightweight settings of gold cannetille or of *repoussé* (embossed relief raised from behind with a hammer), which had largely replaced cannetille by the 1840s. Earrings with long, torpedo-shaped drops of carved gemstones with applied gold filigree were also popular, many with detachable drops to allow the tops to be worn alone.

In the late 1840s and through the 1850s, a new hairstyle, with hair parted in the middle and gathered to the back of the head in loops that covered the ears, caused a virtual disappearance of earrings. Around 1860, once again owing to a return to upswept hairstyles, long pendant earrings made a comeback, and through the 1860s and 1870s they were produced in an astonishing variety of styles. One major theme was historical revival, with Egyptian and Classical styles particularly popular. Some revival earrings, such as those produced by the Castellani family in Rome, were fairly faithful reproductions of recent archaeological discoveries; others were fanciful pastiches of classical earring forms, architectural elements, and other motifs such as amphorae. Earrings with carved classical reliefs of coral or lava, or Roman glass micro-mosaics, were very fashionable, and were often brought back as souvenirs by travelers to Italy. Other popular styles were naturalistic renditions of leaves, flowers, insects, and birds' nests in gold, enamel, and semiprecious stones; enameled renaissance-revival styles; and, for more precious gems, floral sprays and cascades. A new style in the 1870s was the fringe or tassel earring, with a graduated fringe of pointed drops suspended from a large oval pendant.

In the last two decades of the nineteenth century, large pendant earrings went out of fashion, in part because they were incompatible with the newly fashionable high dress and blouse collars, and with the elaborate "dog collar" necklaces worn for evening, which almost completely covered the neck. Small single-stone and cluster earrings, either firmly mounted to the ear wire or mounted as pendants to move and catch the light, were the most commonly worn style through the early twentieth century. The most fashionable earrings of all were diamond solitaires, which became more available after the opening of the South African diamond fields in the late 1860s. New cutting machines and open-claw settings, both of which increased the amount of light reflected by diamonds and made solitaire earrings more appealing, were developed in the 1870s. To prevent valuable diamond earrings from being lost, catches were added to secure the bottoms of the ear wires. Another innovation, first patented in 1878, was the earring cover, a small hinged sphere of gold, sometimes finished in black enamel, which could be snapped over a diamond earring to protect it from loss or theft. By the end of the century diamond ear studs (also called screws), with a threaded post passing through the ear, and held securely in back by a nut screwed onto the post, were also popular.

The Twentieth Century

By 1900, as earrings declined in size and importance, many women stopped wearing them altogether. Some commentators denounced ear-piercing as barbaric, and women who pierced their ears were considered "fast," or not quite respectable. (In the United States, some of the reaction against pierced ears may be credited to the desire of "native" Americans to distinguish themselves from the large numbers of immigrant women, almost all with pierced ears, who were arriving from Europe at the time.) In spite of piercing's negative image, small screw earrings continued to be worn, and new screw-back fittings, which could be tightened onto unpierced earlobes, were available for those who did not wish to pierce their ears. Around 1908, pendant earrings were revived, but with light, articulated drops of smaller stones rather than single-stone drops; diamonds, pearls, and stones matching the color of the costume were the most popular materials.

The earring revival continued into the 1910s, aided considerably by a growing acceptance of costume jewelry. Jewelry could now be selected for its decorative value rather than its intrinsic value, and women could afford to own many pairs of earrings to match particular costumes; the rise of costume jewelry also made ear piercing less necessary, as women were less concerned about losing inexpensive earrings. (Many women, as was still true in the early 2000s, also had adverse reactions to the cheaper metals used in costume jewelry, which made pierced earrings seem less practical.) The fashion for the Oriental and exotic inspired by Paul Poiret and the Ballets Russes was reflected in bead necklaces and long drop earrings of Chinese amber, jade, black and red jet (glass), and carved tortoiseshell. Empire-revival fashions also inspired a revival of nineteenth-century jewelry styles and materials, including cut steel and cameos.

By the early 1920s, earrings were again almost universally worn, and the range of exotic styles had expanded to include hoop and pendant earrings of Spanish or Gypsy inspiration, Egyptian styles inspired by the discovery of King Tutankhamen's tomb in 1922, nineteenth-century antiques, and picturesque "peasant" styles from around the world. As reported by the *New York Times* in 1922, in the 1920s earrings could "no longer … be considered as an article of jewelry; they are *the* article of jewelry." With dress styles now comparatively simple, and many women bobbing their hair, earrings were considered an essential finishing touch—a means both of filling in the area between the ear and shoulder and of expressing the wearer's personality. Bold geometric pendant earrings, made of diamonds and platinum contrasted with strongly colored materials such as onyx and lapis lazuli, were displayed at the Exposition International des Arts Décoratifs in 1925, and this style, which became known as Art Deco, remained popular for both precious and costume earrings for the remainder of the decade.

In the early 1930s, although there was no sudden change in style, earrings began to move closer to the head again, partly in response to smaller, close-fitting hats and the return of high, tied and ruffled collars. Another major influence was the introduction, in 1931, of clip fastenings for earrings, which made it possible to concentrate ornamentation over the earlobe, and compact designs following the line of the ear soon became popular. Matching earrings, bracelets, and other jewelry made of brightly colored bakelite were another signature 1930s look. For evening, long earrings in Art Deco style were still popular, but earrings with white stones (diamonds or pastes) were now the most popular, and the pendants now added volume by branching out to the sides, in a modern version of the girandole, or "chandelier," style.

In the 1940s, compact clips or screw backs, often made with a matching brooch, were the dominant earring style. Gold, strongly colored stones, and bolder, more sculptural forms were now preferred, in keeping with the

Gold hoop earring. Hoops are the earliest known form of earrings, dating from about 2500 B.C.E., and they have been a popular style for most of the proceeding centuries. © IMAGES.COM/ CORBIS. REPRODUCED BY PERMISSION.

padded shoulders and highly structured coiffures of the period. Close-to-the-ear styles, with clip or screw backs, continued to be the most popular in the 1950s, but settings became more delicate, to harmonize with the more deliberately feminine fashions in the years following Christian Dior's 1947 "New Look" collection. An important look of the 1950s was the matched set of choker necklace and button earrings, and these were produced in a wide variety of styles and materials, including newly developed plastics. White and colored rhinestones were popular, as were beads and faux pearls of all kinds, colors, and finishes, often looped in multiple strands around the neck, and fastened with a clasp of clustered beads matching the earrings. Ear piercing, while still not common, began to revive in the early 1950s; in the United States, the trend began as a fad among college girls, and Queen Elizabeth II set an example for many in England when she had her ears pierced in order to be able to wear diamond earrings she received as a wedding present in 1947.

In the 1960s, as in the 1920s, clean-lined dresses and hairstyles, including the long, straight hair popular later in the decade, provided an ideal background for large and decorative earrings. Earrings were again among the most important of accessories, and were often designed to stand alone, rather than as part of a matched set. In both fine and costume jewelry, abstraction was popular, and creative design, visual impact, and wit were often considered more important than the intrinsic value of jewelry. Hoop earrings were one of the signature styles of the decade, and they appeared in designs inspired by tribal jewelry, enormous space-age styles of chrome and plastic, and kinetic designs of concentric, articulated rings. Ethnic styles, particularly from India and the Near East, were also popular, and delicate dangling earrings helped to propel handcrafted sterling silver jewelry, which had been growing in popularity since the 1940s, into the fashion mainstream.

By the early 1970s, the new fashionable ideal was the "natural look," and large costume earrings disappeared in favor of smaller and more delicate earrings, usually of silver or gold, and almost always worn in pierced ears. In terms of design, earrings remained fairly inconspicuous throughout the decade, though they were given new prominence by the fashion for multiple piercings in the same ear, which began as a teenage fashion around the middle of the decade, and continued into the twenty-first century to be a popular way to wear earrings. Earrings worn in the upper part of the ear, and ear cuffs, which grip the edge of the upper ear, were fashions introduced late in the decade. The 1970s was also when earrings for men returned to fashion after a 300-year absence; earrings had continued to be worn by sailors, by some homosexual men, and by members of groups such as motorcycle gangs, but many more men now began to wear single earrings largely for their decorative value.

Large and flashy earrings, both real and frankly fake, returned in the 1980s, to balance the bolder shapes and colors, padded shoulders, high-volume hairstyles, and dramatic makeup then in fashion. Chunky button earrings covering the lower half of the ear and large pendant hoops were popular styles, and common finishes were shiny gold, bright colors contrasted with black, and a variety of bronzed and iridescent metallic finishes. Even relatively understated earrings tended toward strong shapes, worn close to the earlobe; though most women still had pierced ears, clips were popular because they kept earrings close to the head, and because they distributed the weight of heavier styles.

In the early 1990s, silver, brushed finishes, and simple, elegant earrings began to succeed the shiny gold and jagged shapes of the 1980s, in keeping with the monochromatic and minimalist mood of fashion. At the same time, the trend toward simple, versatile clothes that could be dressed up or down inspired women to use elaborate or unusual earrings to vary the effect of an ensemble, and earring styles proliferated. Since the mid-1990s, there has not been a dominant style in earrings, although historical revivals have been an important trend; the popularity of glamorous "chandelier" earrings inspired the return of girandole and top-and-drop designs from the eighteenth and nineteenth centuries, along with the more familiar kinetic designs of the 1920s and 1960s. Earrings have become a popular form of personal expression, and how and when they are worn, along with their function within an ensemble, became largely a matter of personal choice.

See also **Bracelets; Brooches and Pins; Costume Jewelry; Jewelry; Necklaces and Pendants.**

BIBLIOGRAPHY

Andrews, Carol. *Ancient Egyptian Jewellery*. London: British Museum Publications, 1990.

Bury, Shirley. *Jewellery 1789–1910—The International Era*. 2 vols. Woodbridge, Suffolk, U.K.: Antique Collectors' Club, 1991.

Fales, Martha Gandy. *Jewelry in America 1600–1900*. Woodbridge, Suffolk, U.K.: Antique Collectors' Club, 1995.

"Fashions: Earrings Essential Now for Smart Dressing." *New York Times* (23 July 1922): 80.

Flowers, Margaret. *Victorian Jewellery*. New York: Duell, Sloan and Pearce, 1951.

Mascetti, Daniela, and Amanda Triossi. *Earrings from Antiquity to the Present*. London: Thames and Hudson, Inc., 1990.

Scarisbrick, Diana. *Jewellery*. London: B. T. Batsford, Ltd., 1984.

———. *Tudor and Jacobean Jewellery*. London: Tate Publishing, 1995.

Walters Art Gallery, Baltimore. *Jewelry, Ancient to Modern*. New York: Viking Press, 1979.

Susan Ward

ECCLESIASTICAL DRESS

ECCLESIASTICAL DRESS The term "ecclesiastical" derives from the Greek *ekklesiastikos*, from *ekklesia*, an assembly or meeting called out, which in turn derives from *ekkalein*, to call forth or convoke, *ek*, out, and *kalein*, to call. This assembly often referred to the Christian Church and its clergy. Ecclesiastical dress refers here to garments worn by Christian leaders, including members of monastic orders—as distinct from the laity—from the early Christian era until the present, not only in the West but also in all parts of the world where the Christian religion is practiced.

Historical and Cross-Cultural Examples

The origins of ecclesiastical dress have been debated, with some attributing early forms to garments worn by Jewish religious leaders, while others have argued that these vestments derived from everyday Roman dress worn during the early Christian era. In the early 2000s, the latter explanation prevails. Different forms of ecclesiastical dress have developed with the expansion and elaboration of the Western and Eastern Churches. The forms and meanings of ecclesiastical dress have changed over time and have variously been used to separate the mundane from the spiritual, to emphasize the glory of God through beautiful raiment, to express religious humility and piety, and to identify individuals within the church hierarchy.

Depictions of early Christians in the Catacombs of St. Domitilla in Rome include a painting of the Good Shepherd, wearing a white tunic or *tunica*, a rectangle of white material—made either from linen or wool—with a girdle holding it in place. The secular use of this garment was as an undergarment, covered by a toga. Church leaders adopted the dalmatic, also a tunic-like garment, worn in ancient Rome, by the eighth century as an upper-vestment worn by bishops, deacons, and sub-deacons. The *paenula*, which was worn as an outer garment, was the secular precursor of the chasuble, a term derived from the Latin, *casula*, little house or cottage—a circular piece of cloth with a head opening and sometimes a hood, which protected its wearer like a house. It was formally decreed as an outside garment for clergy in 742 by the Council of Ratisbon. One of the earliest examples of the wearing of these garments by church leaders come from depictions of the chasuble or *paenula*, dalmatic, and *pallium* (a long woven band of white wool, decorated with crosses) in the sixth century mosaic from the Church of St. Apollinaire, in Ravenna.

Ecclesiastical dress in the West and East developed along the same lines until the eleventh century; however, there were differences in the meanings and uses of these garments. In the West, vestments were worn to express Christian beliefs about the sacred and the mundane, as well as to distinguish the roles of clergy within the Church hierarchy. In the Eastern churches, these ideas were also present although the belief that ecclesiastical vestments literally represented the garments of Christ also existed. This belief was visually expressed, for example, in the vestment known as the *sticharion*, a tunic-like garment that had its counterpart in the alb, a white linen tunic used as a vestment in the West by the twelfth century. The *sticharion* had two bands of red ornamentation, known as *clavi*, which referred to the wounds made on Christ's body during the Crucifixion. Similarly, embroidery at the ends of the *sticharion*'s narrow sleeves was meant to represent the manacles with which Christ's wrists were bound. While embroidered pieces known as apparels were used on albs, dalmatics, and tunicles to represent Christ's stigmata when placed at the end of sleeves and at hems, the practice of incorporating this form of ornamentation on vestments was gradually replaced by the use of lace in Western vestments during the sixteenth century.

Vestments used in the Eastern Church include the *phelonion*; the *saccos* (a tunic with wide sleeves, worn by patriarchs); as well as the priestly insignia—the *omophorion*—the Western *pallium*—worn by bishops; two forms of stole—the *epitrachilion* and the *orarion*, worn by priests and deacons, respectively—and the square ceremonial cloth known as the *epigonation*, symbolically representing "the Sword of God," worn only in the Greek and Armenian churches by vested bishops. The *phelonion*, as depicted in medieval frescoes, was a round cloak sim-

Embroidered chasuble. Long a staple of the Roman Catholic Church, the chasuble has been worn by clergy members since at least the sixth century. © PHILADELPHIA MUSEUM OF ART/CORBIS. REPRODUCED BY PERMISSION.

ilar to the medieval bell-shaped chasuble. Initially, it was made from white or colored materials alone, but by the eleventh century it was embroidered with small crosses. The art of Byzantine embroidery of ecclesiastical dress flourished during the period of the Palaeologus Dynasty, from the mid-thirteenth to mid-fifteenth century. Byzantine embroiderers used gold, silver, and silk thread to depict a range of scenes and personages from the Old and New Testaments on silk vestments. Several extant embroidered *sacci* from the fourteenth and early fifteenth century illustrate this Byzantium style of vestment, including two *sacci* associated with the Metropolitan Photius of Moscow (1408–1432). One side of the Grand *Saccus* of Photius includes heavily embroidered portraits of the Grand Prince of Moscow, along with a depiction of the Crucifixion, the Prophets Isaiah and Jeremiah, and three Lithuanian martyrs, all on a blue silk background, with the embroidery outlined with pearls.

The Byzantine or Eastern Orthodox Church also includes the Syrian, Armenian, Nubian, Ethiopian, and the Coptic Churches, with their own traditions of ecclesiastical dress. There was considerable overlap in the vestments of the early Coptic Church with those of the other Byzantine churches. For example, the *sticharion* (tunic), *orarion* (strole), *epitrachelion* (stole), and *phelonion* (chasuble) were used by both. Later developments, particularly the introduction of the stole-like *ballin* that was worn by priests and bishops during church services, distinguished Coptic practice. Much of what is known of early ecclesiastical dress worn in these churches comes from texts, illuminated manuscripts, and wall paintings.

During the Medieval Period, ecclesiastic dress in the Roman Catholic Church included a range of vestments used in relation to church services: the alb, cassock (an ankle-length garment with sleeves), chasuble, cope (a capelike garment used as outerwear), dalmatic, hood (a hood attached to cope, often nonfunctional), maniple (a folded cloth or narrow strip worn over the left shoulder of bishops, priests, deacons, and sub-deacons during Mass), mitre (a cap worn by bishops often with two tabs—lappets—of cloth hanging from the back), stole (a long strip of cloth, worn in particular ways to identify members of priesthood), and surplice (a loose, white, outer ecclesiastical vestment usually of knee length with large open sleeves). It was also during the thirteenth century that the English embroidery of ecclesiastical dress flourished, referred to as Opus Anglicanum. In continental Europe, vestments made of patterned silk velvets with intricately embroidered orphreys, decorative woven bands (used in the forms of crosses, pillars, and simple selvage bands on copes, dalmatics, and chasubles) were also produced at this time. With the separation of the Church of England from Rome in 1534, the embroidery of vestments in England fell into decline, to be resumed there during the nineteenth century Gothic Revival.

Controversies Relating to Ecclesiastical Dress

During periods of religious reform and political change, ecclesiastical dress has often served as a symbol of the old regime, which must be replaced or denigrated by reformers, while those opposing the abandonment of older forms of ecclesiastical dress (and the church doctrine associated with them) have sought to maintain them. One famous example of a controversy was the debate over the white linen surplice, which became a symbol of Roman Catholicism during the Protestant Reformation in sixteenth-century England. With the separation from the Roman Catholic Church made final by an act of Parliament in 1534 and the subsequent establishment of the Church of England during the reign of Queen Elizabeth I (1558–1603), the surplice became the universal vestment of all Anglican clergy in 1563. Yet surplices, along with copes, albs, and chasubles, were seen as remnants of "popish dress" by Protestant religious reformers such as the Puritans, Methodists, and Baptists. Tracts with titles such as "A briefe discourse against the outvvarde apparell and ministring garmentes of the popishe church" written by Robert Crowley in 1578 were published and some Protestant leaders were imprisoned for refusing to wear a surplice during church services. These leaders preferred to wear simple, everyday dress, which did not distinguish them from the laity or from everyday affairs. Nonetheless, Anglican Church leaders preserved distinctive ecclesiastical garments, particularly those that continued to be used for royal services. During the seventeenth century, English Protestant ecclesiastical dress was modeled on contemporary dress fashions—specifically, a simple black suit, including a coast, waistcoat, and knee breeches, and a white neckcloth, while Anglican clergy wore cassocks and gowns. However, during the 1840s, those associated with the Gothic Revival in England sought to reinstate the practices of the Church of England during the reign of King Edward VI. In 1840, the Bishop of Exeter directed Anglican clergy to wear surplices, which led to the Surplice Riots when mobs in Exeter pelted those wearing surplices with rotten eggs and vegetables. The Bishop's order was rescinded, but by the second half of the nineteenth century, ecclesiastical dress—including surplices, copes, and albs—was incorporated into Anglican services, modeled after gothic vestments design, as interpreted by Victorian artists. This revival of the use of vestments coincided with the fluorescence of the Arts and Crafts movement during the nineteenth century in England. One prominent member of this movement, William Morris, who as an Anglo-Catholic, had supplied specially designed vestments to the Roman Catholic Church following the Catholic Emancipation of 1829. In 1854, the Ladies' Ecclesiastical Embroidery Society was organized to produce embroidered replicas of medieval designs (Johnstone 2002, p. 123). Along with these specialized workshops, ecclesiastical dress, which was mass-produced and mass-marketed through catalogs, also became available, in part, due to the increasing demand for such vestments from missionaries working in the British colonies during this period.

Another example in which ecclesiastical dress became the focus of controversy took place in Mexico. Prior to the Mexican Revolution, the wealth and political power of the Roman Catholic Church was evident in ornate cathedrals and ecclesiastical dress. During the second half of the eighteenth century, dalmatics, copes, chasubles, and stoles made with silver and gold threads and elaborately embroidered with the emblem of the Convent of Santa Rosa de Lima, were probably made in the Mexican city of Puebla. While the Church had considerable popular support, its extensive landholding and its association with the political elite contributed to the view that it was an impediment to economic progress and social justice. During the Mexican Revolution that began in 1910, a series of anticlerical measures were taken, culminating with the writing of the Constitution of 1917, which provided for the confiscation of church lands, the replacement of religious holidays with patriotic ones, and the banning of public worship outside of church buildings, including processionals (Purnell 1999, p. 60). While these laws were enacted, they were not always strictly enforced until 1926, when Government leaders sought to further restrict the power of the Church through the Calles Law. This law outlawed Catholic education, closed monasteries and convents, and in Article 130, restricted the wearing of ecclesiastical dress in public. When the Mexican Episcopate ordered the closing of churches in response to the Calles Law, a popular uprising known as the Cristero Rebellion resulted, primarily in central West Mexico, during the period from 1926 to 1929. With the state's agreement to stop its insistence on registering priests and with the restoration of religious services—including the wearing of ecclesiastical dress—the rebellion ceased.

Ecclesiastic dress has also served as a vehicle for expressing anticolonial sentiments in Africa, during the nineteenth and twentieth centuries. However, many early African Christian converts did not reject European styles of vestments, but rather incorporated indigenous elements into ecclesiastical dress as an expression of their discontent. In colonial Nigeria during the first half of the twentieth century, converts who occupied leadership positions in Roman Catholic and orthodox Protestant churches—primarily, Anglican, Methodist, and Baptist—generally wore the tailored garments (cassocks, chasubles, surplices, copes, and mitres) used by home church leaders. These garments distinguished Christian converts from those practicing various forms of indigenous religion, which had their own, often untailored, dress traditions. Yet some early Nigerian Christian leaders sought to assert independence from Orthodox churches over doctrinal disputes, often concerning polygynous marriage. Establishing their own churches, referred to generally as African Independent Churches, they did not entirely abandon tailored, Western-style vestments. Rather, these leaders developed distinctive ecclesiastical dress forms that identified these new churches and emphasized particular aspects of their doctrine. For example, Bishop J. K. Coker, the founder of the African Church, incorporated indigenous textiles, for example handwoven narrow strip cloths, into ecclesiastical dress. Leaders of the Independent African Churches such as Bishop Coker were the predecessors of nationalist independence leaders who supported secular independent states based on Euro-American models combined with African social and cultural elements.

The controversies surrounding freedom of religious expression have, at times, been moderated through gradual change in ecclesiastical dress, which reflected church leaders' responses to changing political and social contexts. For example, early members of the Marist Brothers apostolic movement, which was founded in France by Father Marcellin Champagnat (1789–1840), wore "a sort of blue coat, . . . black trousers, a cloak, and round hat" garments, which he believed were imbued with spiritual power that protected its wearers from anticlerical attacks. While these vestments helped to attract and visually to distinguish new members during the post-revolutionary period in France, they also gave followers a sense of special protection. However, with the incorporation of the Marist Brothers' Institute as a religious order of the Roman Catholic Church in 1863, Marist ecclesiastical dress came to lose its mystical aspects and shifted to a uniform prescribed by the Church authorities, including a black soutane, white rabat, and a black cloak. With the Second Vatican Council in 1962, Marist Brothers' ecclesiastical dress again changed as a loss in church membership suggested a simpler, less-clerical style—such as a suit—would be more appropriate to modern worship. However, by 1987, some Marist priests returned to wearing the soutane, while others continued to wear secular suits, depending on their preferences and those of their parishioners. This shift from distinctive ecclesiastical dress that identified Catholic orders according to particular configurations and types of garments to current secular dress styles, indistinguishable from contemporary clothing is also evident in Western nuns' garb. Western nuns or Women Religious, whose name as well as dress changed with Vatican II, as of the turn of the twenty-first century wore everyday garments as a way of emphasizing their role in modern society, rather than their separation from it.

Role in Contemporary Society

In the West, this shift back to simplicity in Roman Catholic and Anglican ecclesiastical dress is expressed in simple, fully-cut vestments made from materials using natural fibers, reminiscent of those of the early Christian era. A leading figure in this movement is Sister M. Augustina Fluëler, a Capuchin nun, associated with the Cloisters of St. Klara, in Switzerland. One chasuble that she designed was made of off-white, plain-weave wool, with a stole of plain-weave silk with two embroidered crosses in gold thread. In a simple and elegant wool and silk dalmatic, she used narrow bands of rose and purple as edging, with broader alternating bands of these colors incorporated into the sleeves.

Other expressions of this simplicity of vestment design may be seen in the embroidered works of Beryl Dean Phillips (England), in the handwoven chasubles of Barbara Markey Wallace (United States) and copes and mitres with lappets of Lennart Rodhe (Sweden), in the painted chasubles of Willam Justema (United States) and in the appliquéd chasubles of Henri Matisse (France). While utilizing different techniques—embroidery, handwoven twills, overshot, and tapestry, painting, and appliqué in their production, they share a spareness of patterning—often of crosses or of stylized floral patterns with little background ornamentation—and of natural materials—silk, wool, cotton, and linen. The design and production of these vestments by craftswomen and men underscores the belief that the careful and creative making of objects used in divine service is in itself a form of worship. These

vestments convey "a certain splendid sobriety," the essence of the reform of the Roman Catholic Church associated with the *General Instructions* of 1962 that emphasize that the beauty of ecclesiastical vestments derives from "the excellence of their material and the elegance of their cut" (Flannery, p. 197), rather than from their elaborate ornamentation or color. The concept of the simple yet distinctive beauty of vestments coincides with Anglican views of contemporary ecclesiastical dress, the use of which should mark special religious events, but without ostentation.

Ecclesiastical Dress and Globalization

The counterpart to simplicity of ecclesiastical dress produced by vestment makers in the West, which in the Roman Catholic Church was associated with the reforms instituted by Vatican II, is seen in the appearance of individual national churches, whose identities are expressed, in part, through use of local materials in vestments. The basis for the local development of ecclesiastical dress is found in the General Instruction on the Roman Missal:

> 304. Bishops' Conferences may determine and propose to the Holy See any adaptations in the shape or style of vestments, which they consider desirable by reason of local customs or needs.

> 305. Besides the materials traditionally used for making sacred vestments, natural fabrics from each region are admissible, as also artificial fabrics which accord with the dignity of the sacred action and of those who are to wear the vestments. It is for the Bishops' Conference to decide on these matters. (Flannery, p. 197)

The use of local materials may refer to particular techniques—types of weaving, embroidery, or drawnwork—and types of materials—cotton, wool, lurex, among others. In the Philippines, for example, locally made vestments are constructed from handwoven cloth of pineapple (*piña*) and *abaca* (commonly known as Manila hemp) fibers. Abaca fibers are processed from the long plant stalks and the finely spun threads are handwoven into plain-weave abaca cloth, with designs made through discontinuous supplementary weft patterning (*sinuksok*) and resist-dyed ikat techniques. Abaca cloth made into vestments may also be embellished with a range of decorative techniques including, embroidery, appliqué, beadwork, and cut-and drawn work. Chasubles, copes, stoles, and mitres with lappets made from cloth handwoven with *piña* fibers are similarly decorated. A new type of vestment was introduced in the Philippines in the 1970s, the chasuble-alb, known in the Philippines as the tunic. This vestment, worn with a stole, serves as both an alb and a chasuble, thus limiting the number of vestments needed by concelebrants and reducing the discomfort of wearing multiple layers of cloth in a tropical climate. However, not all liturgists have agreed with this change and in 1973, the Catholic Bishops of the Philippines restricted its use to particular circumstances.

In Nigeria, there has been a shift from the purchase of ecclesiastical dress, mainly from Great Britain to the production of vestments in Nigeria itself, using locally woven narrow-strip cloth and batik-dyed textiles. Chasubles, mitres, and stoles, machine-embroidered with depictions of scenes and texts from the Old and New Testament as well as with more abstract shapes and symbols, may be produced by individual specialists or by nuns working in convent workshops. One woman, Mrs. Anne Salubi of Ilorin, a university-trained artist, is renowned throughout Nigeria for her chasubles, which have been commissioned by bishops in various Nigerian cities as well as in Ireland. During the recent visit of Pope John Paul II to Nigeria, Mrs. Salubi was commissioned to make the chasuble given to the Pope during his visit. Anglican and Methodist church leaders in Nigeria have also begun to incorporate handwoven cloth strips into ecclesiastical dress, using them mainly as stoles in different colors used for particular church seasons, with simple machine-embroidered design such as crosses. Smaller workshops combine the production of church stoles and choir robes with academic gowns.

The mass-production and mass-marketing of ecclesiastical dress through catalogues reflect the accelerating interdependence of nations and communities in a world system linked through economics, mass media, and modern transportation systems. For example, Mexico-style ecclesiastical vestments are marketed on the website of the Mexican American Cultural Center, of San Antonio, Texas, which includes embroidered chasubles produced by the congregation of Sisters in Guadalajara, Mexico, as well as stoles made with locally handwoven *zarape* cloth strips. The web not only facilitates the marketing of vestments but also serves as a source of materials, such as metallic threads, which might not be available locally. Thus, globalization allows for specialization of local styles of ecclesiastical dress while also expanding the availability of supplies and the marketing of these national or ethnically identified vestment styles to communities outside the immediate homeland.

Conclusion: Main Themes

Several recurrent themes have emerged during the long history of ecclesiastic dress. Early church dress consisted of simple forms, using natural materials, in part due to the persecution of Christians and in part due to a lack of well-defined church doctrine on dress. By the third century, with the acceptance of Christianity by Constantine, there was a shift toward ecclesiastical dress, which both identified wearers as Church leaders and also indicated their rank within the church. These two tendencies—one, toward visually portraying church hierarchy with ever more elaborate ecclesiastical dress, exalting the worship of God and Christ through beautiful vestments; the other toward downplaying distinctions between church leadership and laity through simple, unadorned styles of dress and, in the case of the Protestant Reformation, aban-

Pope John Paul I wearing richly detailed epitrachelion. The epitrachelion is the second fundamental vestment in the Christian Church and is worn by both priests and bishops. AP/WIDE WORLD PHOTOS. REPRODUCED BY PERMISSION.

doning ecclesiastical dress entirely—have been expressed in various ways over the centuries. A related theme, uniformity and individualism, has also been expressed in ecclesiastical dress. For example, U.S. "women religious" have abandoned wearing habits, in order to address the contradiction between American social ideals of secular individualism and the religious uniformity that ecclesiastical dress represent, and to function more effectively in the secular world. These themes also reflect the relationship of changes in ecclesiastical dress and political, economic, and social changes, with reformers tending toward simplicity and contemporary secular garments, and with counter-reformers tending toward more elaborated vestments which reflect a nostalgia for past "traditions" in preference to secular "modernity." Contests between church and state have also been reflected in controversies over the wearing of ecclesiastical vestments.

The themes of worldliness and spirituality, unity and individualism, and simplicity and elaboration, have been concerns expressed largely in terms of vestment use in Western and Eastern Churches in Europe and in the United States. The use of ecclesiastical vestments as expressions of anticolonial sentiments and, more generally, to counter assumptions about Western cultural hegemony are themes that emerge in Christian communities in Africa, Asia, and Latin America, where conversion to Christianity has been more recent. European ecclesiastical dress has been viewed as a sign of modernity but also as a symbol of acquiescence to Western power. With national independence and with the later reforms of Vatican II introduced in 1962 and thereafter, African, Asian, and Latin American Roman Catholics began to incorporate locally produced vestments using indigenous materials into religious worship, supporting modern local and Roman Catholic identities simultaneously.

Ecclesiastical dress is especially appropriate for asserting different identities and distinctions among individuals and groups because of the range of materials, colors, embellishments, and styles into which this dress can be shaped. Ecclesiastical dress may also be used to construct new identities that acknowledge cultural distinctiveness, while at the same time emphasizing membership in a universal world church. The continually changing configurations of vestments used in Christian worship attest to this aspiration for unity and distinction. The attempts to find an acceptable balance of old and new ways, of simplicity and ornamentation, of indigenous and foreign ideas and practices, reflect a striving for the harmonious unity of humankind and at the same time, a need for distinctive identities and beliefs, both expressed through the use of ecclesiastical dress.

See also **Religion and Dress.**

BIBLIOGRAPHY

Innemée, Karel C. *Ecclesiastical Dress in the Medieval Near East.* Leiden, New York: E. J. Brill, 1992.

Mayo, Janet. *A History of Ecclesiastical Dress.* New York: Holmes and Meier Publishers, Inc., 1984.

Elisha P. Renne

ECONOMICS AND CLOTHING The economics of clothing involve three processes: production, making the clothing; distribution, getting the clothing from the maker to the consumer; and consumption, actually using the clothing. Although consumption drives production and distribution, the three processes are in many ways inseparable. The system is fiercely competitive at all stages, partly but not entirely because clothing is a fashion good. Although some plain utilitarian garments may seem to be little affected by fashion, their production and distribution are highly competitive as well.

In developed nations, fashions in clothing and other goods and services change so rapidly and in so many ways that it's difficult to keep track. People may assume that, in ancient cultures or isolated societies, styles of clothing, dwellings, tools, and customs remained static for generations. Yet scholars discern small incremental changes when they can find sufficient data. Major features of the economics of clothing today have roots in the distant past.

Perhaps in prehistoric times, or on the frontier of pioneer America, isolated family units produced all their own clothing. But in fact, most people probably hunted in groups for large, fur-bearing animals and specialized in doing certain tasks. Production of apparel has always been highly labor-intensive, and evidence of specialization appears early.

Twenty thousand to twenty-six thousand years ago, in the north of what is now Russia, a young man was buried in a shirt and trousers elaborately embroidered with ivory beads. At roughly the same time, in what is now France, craftsmen were carving delicate sewing needles from bone. To shape and drill beads or make needles with the materials and tools available then would require both inherent manual skill and considerable practice. Probably only one person in a settlement or a cluster of settlements mastered the skills for such work; others did tasks such as harvesting and processing fibers or skins and assembling garments. Presumably these specialists bartered what they made for goods and services of other group members. Specialization optimizes use of individuals' time and abilities and makes better quality clothing possible for all. Scientists who uncovered the grave of the youth in the beaded outfit concluded that he was a person of importance—he or his family possessed wealth or power to command a costume of such splendor. Clothing already expressed status, more than 200 centuries ago.

A Global Economy

The apparel economy is truly global. From earliest times, it has extended to the limits of human occupation. In each geographic area, people exploited native plants, animals, and minerals. The Chinese learned the secrets of the silkworm; linen grew in the Nile valley, cotton in the Indus River valley; Mesopotamians raised sheep for their wool. Shellfish found at the eastern end of the Mediterranean sea provided precious purple dye. Polar cultures relied upon the furs and skins of local creatures, both land and sea. Natives of what is now the Pacific coast of Canada used cedar bark garments to shed rain; some peoples made cloaks of grasses.

In time, precious textiles, furs, and ornaments moved by long, difficult overland trade routes or hazardous water voyages. Later, textile centers evolved where people demanded large quantities of luxury fabrics and were willing to pay well for them. Byzantium, as well as Sicily, produced fine silks during the Middle Ages, although they were far from the original sources of silk. Even so, proximity of raw materials gave some geographic areas advantages over others. Certain districts in Italy, Germany, Flanders, and England became textile centers, specializing in locally produced fibers and distinctive techniques. In medieval times, traveling merchants transported fine textiles from production centers to regional trade fairs on a regular basis.

The ramifications of trade in textiles and other apparel materials extended far beyond the obvious. In an-

THE CONCEPT OF FASHION

"Fashion" is a complex concept, but economic analyses require simple, operational definitions. Therefore this essay uses definitions based on those stated by Paul Nystrom in his 1928 book, *Economics of Fashion*. He defined "style" as "a characteristic or distinctive mode or method of expression in the field of some art" (p. 3) and "fashion" as "the prevailing style at any given time" (p. 4). A source of confusion is that the word "fashion" can be used to mean either "content" or "process."

In writing or speech, the word "fashion" is often misused as a synonym for women's clothing. Yet most consumer goods and services are subject to the fashion process. Fashion also affects noneconomic matters such as social customs. The economic structure of consumer goods industries reflects the role of fashion, which in turn indirectly affects basic industries. Because "fashion" can involve virtually all aspects of contemporary life, this essay concentrates on the economics of clothing.

---

cient Mesopotamia, the need to record exchanges of these and other goods stimulated development of counting systems and writing. Eventually, coinage evolved to expedite transactions. Still later, Italians pioneered bookkeeping, banking, and legal systems to facilitate and organize international commerce.

The great plague, the Black Death, which killed as many as one-third of the people in Europe, may have reached Europe from Asia in the middle 1300s, transported by infected fleas on furs carried by caravans along the ancient silk road. As the plague abated, fashion change accelerated because of greater concentration of population in cities, shifts in the distribution of wealth, and growing importance of commercial life. The demand for furs in the sixteenth century, including beaver skins to make fine felt hats, became a major force driving the exploration of North America. Remote Australia and New Zealand were settled largely because sheep could be raised profitably there.

Guilds

In the Middle Ages and Renaissance, members of guilds produced elegant and costly clothing to order for wealthy and high-ranking people on the European continent. Guilds were part civic associations, part trade associations, part labor unions. Guilds specialized in certain crafts ranging from hats to shoes. Membership was strictly controlled; new members served long apprenticeships and had to meet strict criteria for admission. Detailed rules served to uphold quality of production and limit competition. In general, men dominated the guilds; women did certain specialized tasks such as embroidery but had little role in governance. Not until the late 1600s, as guilds were ebbing in power, was the first guild controlled by women, the mantua makers, officially recognized in France.

National Pride and Profit

Nations have long promoted fashions to stimulate demand for their products. In the 1600s, King Louis XIV displayed the beauty of French silks and laces by wearing them and dictating that members of the French nobility also showcase French products. France sent dolls dressed in the latest fashions to other nations to create desire for French goods among the upper classes. According to Mr. Pepys' diary, Charles II of England introduced a subdued style of men's clothing in England in 1666, partly to promote English wool and linen fabrics.

The Origin of Ready-to-Wear

During the reign of Charles II, according to Beverly Lemire, the ready-to-wear clothing industry originated when shipowners or the British navy ordered plain, coarse garments in quantity to outfit crews of English ships heading to sea on voyages lasting months or years. There were as yet no garment or textile factories in the modern sense. Garment production was controlled by (mostly) men who contracted with the government or shipping companies, bought materials in quantity and then hired workers who

"Demand" is not a quantity; it is the relationship between prices and how much consumers are willing to buy at various prices. If demand for a commodity is great, people will generally buy larger amounts of it at various prices than they will buy if demand is small.

took the supplies home with them to make the garments by hand. Workers were paid by the unit, and the contractors often cheated them. The system of subcontracting clothing production continues today.

Mechanization of Production

Although production of ready-to-wear clothing began before sewing machines existed, an English clergyman had invented a hand-operated knitting frame near the end of the sixteenth century. Queen Elizabeth I refused to grant him a patent because she feared it would put English hand-knitters, using knitting needles and mostly working at home for contractors, out of work. But by the eighteenth century, England led the industrial revolution with a stream of inventions that eventually reduced prices of many goods and improved their quality so that ordinary people could afford them. By the later 1700s, English factories were turning out fabric on water- or steam-powered spinning and weaving equipment. Demand for inexpensive clothing gradually increased in England as lower-class people, some of them employed in the new factories, began to have a bit more money to spend, as well as a growing interest in fashionable clothing. London stores began to display appealing merchandise in lighted shop windows and encouraged shopping as recreation. Even low-income people could buy small ribbon ornaments and other accessories (See McKendrick, Brewer, and Plumb).

Meanwhile, clothing styles of English noblemen became simpler and more functional as they supervised agricultural activities on their estates rather than hanging around the royal court, as was the case in France. French noblemen copied English styles when the French Revolution made it dangerous to be seen in public wearing silks and laces.

By the early nineteenth century, workingmen's clothing was being cut and hand-sewn by workers who specialized in specific tasks rather than each making a garment from start to finish. In American coastal cities, workers constructed garments for sailors in lofts where sails were made, from the same sturdy materials. Inventors designed the first sewing machines, but handworkers, who feared losing their jobs, broke up the machines, which didn't work very well anyway. Improved versions soon followed; the 1800s brought numerous apparel-related inventions and discoveries, including shoemaking machinery, vulcanized rubber, artificial cellulosic fibers, and synthetic coal-tar dyes.

Wars such as the American Civil War created demand for large quantities of uniforms. Based on measurements of servicemen, standardized sizing of men's clothing evolved. By the later 1800s, men's factory-made clothing of reasonably good quality and fit was being produced in quantity. Although wealthy men still wore custom-made clothing, moderate-income men could dress better than ever before.

The situation for women's clothing differed from that for men's clothing. Styles were relatively simple in the later 1700s and early 1800s, but then outfits became increasingly ornate and complex and remained so for the rest of the nineteenth century. This complexity, plus lack of measurement data for women, delayed large-scale factory production of women's clothing. Late in the century, when separates—shirtwaist and skirt styles and tailored women's suits—became fashionable, it was easier for women to find ready-made clothing to fit. By the end of the 1800s, output of women's factory-made clothing was growing rapidly.

Paris Couture

Although wealthy people still wore custom-made clothing in the 1800s, the guilds were gone by the time Charles Worth, ironically an English immigrant to Paris, opened the first couture house in the mid-nineteenth century. The Paris couture, offering exclusive new styles for women to be made-to-order each season, reached its peak volume in the late 1800s and early 1900s. Only the richest women could afford couture apparel, and volume was never large, but the couturiers were masters of publicity. Actually, the practice of holding well-publicized "showings" of new fashions each season originated in England not with clothing designers but with such enterprising businessmen as Josiah Wedgwood, who in the late eighteenth century invited well-to-do customers to seasonal openings of his latest designs in tableware and decorative ceramics (See McKendrick, Brewer, and Plumb).

Fashion for Everyone

With the help of fashion magazines, which originated in the early 1800s, and paper dress patterns for home sewers, introduced later in the century, seamstresses copied or adapted couture designs for middle-class clientele far from fashion centers. In America, some dressmakers traveled from household to household twice a year, spending a couple of weeks making new clothes for all females in a family. Electric-powered sewing machines were installed in factories, but home sewers and dressmakers used machines with foot treadles so they were not dependent on electricity.

The first department stores opened in major cities in the United States and Europe in the mid-1800s, with clothing as a major category of merchandise. Instead of bargaining with customers over selling prices, as small shopkeepers did, department stores began putting price tags on their goods. Retail magnates such as B. Altman, John Wanamaker, and Marshall Field built palatial stores to dramatize shopping as recreation. Streetcar transportation, first horse-drawn and later electric-powered, brought customers downtown. Smaller stores specializing in men's or women's apparel, children's clothing, undergarments and lingerie, or shoes, profited from customer traffic attracted to city centers by big stores.

Catalog order firms such as Sears, Roebuck originated in the 1800s as postal service and railroads developed in the United States. Mail order made ready-to-wear clothing available to rural and small-town residents. The first outlying shopping centers opened in the second and third decades of the twentieth century, as automobiles multiplied; Sears, Roebuck opened its first retail store in an early shopping center. After World War II, building of suburban branches of large department stores and major regional shopping centers accelerated, leading to the decline of downtown shopping and the closing of many central city stores. Giant regional shopping centers capitalized on the entertainment aspect of shopping and consumers' seemingly limitless appetite for variety.

Competition for Consumers' Money

Accelerating competitive trends in the apparel business has been the gradual decline of clothing's share of total consumer spending. What limited records survive show that during the Middle Ages and Renaissance in Europe, in the heyday of the guilds, rich people spent huge proportions of their incomes on luxurious clothing for themselves. Furthermore, the nobility outfitted the various ranks in their households, even down to the lowest servant, in appropriate styles and the manor's heraldic colors for specific festivals or occasions.

Once, there were only limited ways to spend money to demonstrate one's wealth—what Thorstein Veblen named "conspicuous consumption." In the past 150 years, factory production has made clothing for ordinary people less expensive, while many appealing new products have become available: phonographs and parlor pianos, household appliances—including sewing machines—motor vehicles, and electronic goods, starting with telephones and radios. All of these impressed people's friends and rivals, competing with clothing for the consumer's money. Of every twenty dollars Americans now spend, only about one goes for clothing. Simultaneously, long-term fashion trends, dating back at least to Charles II of England in the 1600s, have moved toward ever-simpler, less-formal, more casual clothing even for people in the upper ranks of society. As more women work outside the home, fewer of them dress to showcase their husbands' wealth and prosperity, as they might have in Veblen's world. Demand for men's tailored clothing declined in the later twentieth century, as did the number of specialty stores selling men's clothing, as men chose more casual clothing and active sportswear.

Growing Ferocity of Competition

Couture was not profitable after World War I; its client base dwindled further during the Depression of the 1930s. Designers tried to control copying of their designs and sometimes produced lower-priced replicas of their own exclusive models. Design piracy has long been a plague for clothing manufacturers and designers, but no tactics seem to stop it, especially when consumers are ea-ger for the latest fashions at the lowest possible prices. The spending of fickle teenaged customers, anxious to look like popular entertainers, accelerates the pace of fashion change.

For a time after World War II, couture houses licensed their names to other firms to produce lower-priced clothing merchandise and accessories. Some ventured into men's wear, with limited success. In Europe and North America, the number of establishments producing fine custom-made clothing and the number of customers that bought it had declined. Demand continues to shrink for complex and costly custom-made apparel such as elaborately embroidered or beaded garments. To the extent that such clothing is still produced, production moves to India and other Asian countries.

By the late twentieth century, large European corporations, some outside the apparel business, competed to buy Paris couture houses and leading Italian design firms, while other high-end design houses gobbled up each other. Sales of expensive apparel and luxury accessories to wealthy people and entertainers all over the world burgeoned in the 1990s' economic boom. Designer-name firms outdid each other by opening showy retail stores, designed by avant-garde architects, in major cities around the world, but some of these stores attracted more lookers than purchasers and soon closed. Young design-school graduates from England, Belgium, New York, California, and elsewhere started their own small firms; only a lucky few achieved enough recognition or financial backing to stay in business.

A Low-Paid Workforce

Clothing workers have always been poorly paid. Clothing for serfs and servants on medieval estates was produced on-site, usually from materials grown, harvested, and processed by serfs—essentially, slave labor. Slaves made their own clothing on American cotton plantations. Clothing production prospers where cheap labor is plentiful. Although some operations require great skill, most construction tasks are divided into small steps that can be learned quickly. In the past 200 years, garment factories have been among the first large-scale manufacturing enterprises to open in developing nations. In nineteenth-century New York, manufacturers crowded hundreds of poorly paid immigrants into high-rise buildings, often in unsafe situations. Contracting and homework were widespread. One group of immigrants after another supplied the labor—German, Irish, Jewish, Italian; in the twentieth century, Puerto Ricans, Chinese, and Blacks joined the list. Even today, "sweatshops" owned by and employing immigrants from Asia flourish in New York City. During the second half of the twentieth century, garment manufacture spread to Hong Kong, then to China and other parts of southeast Asia, not to mention Latin America and African locations that have large numbers of people willing to work for low wages. Although machines facilitate clothing construction, much of the process resists automation. Reading clothing labels is a lesson in geography.

Factoring

A longtime practice in the fashion industry is "factoring," whereby a company takes out short-term loans to buy fabrics and other materials to produce garments for the season, then repays the loans as retailers purchase the goods. The specialized lenders are called "factors." Factoring is not limited to apparel production; it also exists in other industries where fashion changes quickly, such as toys. A plague of the fashion business is that retailers squeeze manufacturers by returning unsold goods or paying less than the agreed-upon price. Because the garment business is so competitive, profits are low and existence is risky.

The Used Clothing Trade

Trade in secondhand clothing has been important for many centuries. Once wealthy and high-ranking people gave their unwanted clothing to servants. Usually, servants sold the garments—they had no use for them and needed the money. Patrons of theatres such as Shakespeare's Globe donated clothing to actors who could not otherwise afford credible costumes when playing high-ranking characters. Used clothing, including stolen items, was sold by peddlers alongside crude, early ready-to-wear. In the nineteenth century, the first factory-made garments were sometimes introduced by secondhand clothing retailers. Stores selling both used and new clothing (including military surplus) existed until after World War II. Postwar, "yard" and "garage" sales became common, apparently inspired by such sales on military bases, especially when officers' families had to move to totally different climate zones. Consignment shops, operated by charitable organizations or private entrepreneurs, multiplied.

As the quantity of discarded clothing in Europe and North America exceeded the capacity of welfare agencies to distribute it to the poor, large quantities of used clothing have been shipped to developing nations. In Africa, inexpensive used clothing can displace traditional apparel and compete with local industries. At the other extreme, "vintage" clothing—used couture or high-fashion women's clothing—has become so popular and acceptable that leading Hollywood actresses may wear old designer gowns to the Academy Awards ceremonies. Exclusive auction houses sell vintage designer clothing for high prices; retail stores in New York and Los Angeles specialize in such clothing.

Continuing Change

The garment business consists of all sizes of firms from giant to tiny. Although the trend is giant companies, these are not assured of success. Large corporations manufacture clothing under many labels. Some famous brand names produce different qualities of clothing for different types of retailers, contracting out production of some merchandise lines to other corporations. Major producers can go bankrupt unexpectedly; failure lurks just around the corner due to shifting customer tastes and a variety of other uncertainties. International trade regulations, tariffs, and quota systems engage the services of a corps of lawyers and other specialists.

Everything changes quickly in the apparel world. Cities of developed nations are littered with abandoned factories, empty retail stores, defunct design houses, and wreckage of supporting industries. Once-famous department stores are now history; Montgomery Ward is nearly forgotten; Sears Roebuck slips in importance. Someday Wal-Mart may fade away. As more shopping centers and big-box stores open, downtowns and old shopping centers die. Everyone in the business knows that there is too much retail space, yet they keep building stores. Change is the only certainty.

The next phase in clothing distribution may be the Web, whether goods are sold by conventional retail stores, catalog retailers, Web-based retailers, or something completely different. Auction sites such as eBay offer vintage clothing and also help manufacturers and retailers trade large quantities of materials and clothing among themselves.

See also **Department Store; Fashion Industry; Globalization; Labor Unions; Mantua; Ready-to-Wear; Retailing; Secondhand Clothes, Anthropology of; Secondhand Clothes, History of; Sewing Machine; Sweatshops.**

BIBLIOGRAPHY

Benson, Susan Porter. *Counter Cultures: Saleswomen, Managers, and Customers in American Department Stores, 1890–1940.* Champaign: University of Illinois Press, 1988.

Cobrin, Harry A. *The Men's Clothing Industry: Colonial Through Modern Times.* New York: Fairchild Publications, 1970.

Cooper, Grace Rogers. *The Sewing Machine: Its Invention and Development,* 2nd ed. Washington, D.C.: Smithsonian Press for the National Museum of History and Technology, 1976.

Cray, Ed. *Levi's.* Boston: Houghton Mifflin, 1978.

Danish, Max D. *The World of David Dubinsky.* Cleveland: The World Publishing Co., 1957.

DeMarly, Diana. *The History of Haute Couture, 1850–1950.* New York: Holmes & Meier, 1980.

Frick, Carole Collier. *Dressing Renaissance Florence—Families, Fortunes, and Fine Clothing.* Baltimore: Johns Hopkins University Press, 2002.

Hansen, Karen Tranberg. *Salula: The World of Secondhand Clothing and Zambia.* Chicago: University of Chicago Press, 2000.

Helfgott, Roy B. "Women's and Children's Apparel." In *Made in New York: Case Studies in Metropolitan Manufacturing.* Edited by Max Hall. Cambridge: Harvard University Press, 1959.

Hendrickson, Robert. *The Grand Emporiums.* New York: Stein and Day, 1979.

Kirke, Betty. *Madeleine Vionnet.* San Francisco: Chronicle Books, 1998.

Lemire, Beverly. *Dress, Culture and Commerce: The English Clothing Trade Before the Factory, 1660–1800.* New York: St. Martin's Press, 1997.

Lockwood, Lisa. "Mega-Merger Mania: The New Blueprints of Five Ravenous Firms." *WWD* 186, no. 36 (2003): 1, 6–7.

McKendrick, Neil, John Brewer, and J. H. Plumb. *The Birth of a Consumer Society: The Commercialization of Eighteenth–Century England.* Bloomington: Indiana University Press, 1982.

Nystrom, Paul H. *Economics of Fashion.* New York: The Ronald Press Company, 1928.

Rexford, Nancy E. *Women's Shoes in America, 1795–1930.* Kent, Ohio: Kent State University Press, 2000.

Sandars, N. K. *Prehistoric Art in Europe,* 2nd ed. New York: Viking Penguin, 1985, pp. 49–50.

Spufford, Peter. *Power and Profit: The Merchant in Medieval Europe.* New York: Thames & Hudson, Inc., 2003.

Veblen, Thorstein. *The Theory of the Leisure Class.* New York: Macmillan, 1899. Reprint, New York: The Modern Library, 1934.

Walker, Richard. *Savile Row: An Illustrated History.* New York: Rizzoli International, 1989.

Winakor, Geitel. "The Decline in Expenditures for Clothing Relative to Total Consumer Spending, 1929–1986." *Home Economics Research Journal* 17 (1989): 195–215.

Geitel Winakor

EGYPTIAN COTTON. *See* Cotton.

ELASTOMERS

When most textile fibers are stretched more than around 10 percent of their length, they may recover a little of this distortion rapidly, some more slowly, but some permanent distortion remains. In contrast, an elastomeric fiber will typically recover rapidly and completely from elongations of 100 percent or more. They provide textiles with greater stretchiness and recovery than is possible by the use of texturized yarns and knitted structures and are used in waistbands, sock tops, foundation garments, and exercise wear.

The prototype elastomeric fiber is rubber. Natural rubber latex can be coagulated in many forms (balloons and rubber gloves, for example) and also in the form of fibers, although it is not possible to produce rubber as fine as most other textile fibers. Rubber fibers are difficult to dye, so when incorporated into a fabric that is stretched, the white rubber is visible. For that reason, most rubber is covered by another fiber spun or wrapped around it, such as cotton, which can be dyed. Fabrics containing covered rubber yarns are used in waistbands, sock tops, and foundation garments. Natural rubber is cheap, but suffers from degradation by chlorine bleach, and in the longer term by body oils, atmospheric contaminants, and metal salts.

Occasional shortages of natural rubber have led to a search for synthetic alternatives, and fibers have been produced from many synthetic rubbers. Anidex and Lastrile are two generic names assigned to such elastomeric fibers, although these are now obsolete.

Spandex dominates the synthetic elastomeric fiber market in the early 2000s. Originally developed by DuPont as "Lycra," it is produced by many manufacturers around the world. Chemically, spandex is a polyurethane, and in Europe such fibers have been simply called polyurethane, but more often are referred to as "elastane."

Spandex is a comparatively weak fiber (it has a tenacity of around 0.7g/d) but since it will stretch 3 to 7 times its length before breaking, its lack of strength is not cause for concern. It can be produced as fine as most other manufactured fibers, and it is dyeable. It can be incorporated directly into fabrics (knitted or laid in to knits), or like rubber, it may be covered or core spun with another fiber for weaving. Depending on the end use, spandex may comprise 2 to 20 percent of a blend. It shares many of rubber's end uses and is also incorporated in less-specialized fabrics such as those used for swimsuits, exercise wear, and regular fashion apparel. In low percentages, it improves the recovery of worsted and denim fabrics. Its dyeing properties are similar to those of nylon, and it is commonly found in blends with that fiber. Blends with polyester are cheaper, but the high temperatures useful for dyeing polyester are damaging to polyurethanes, and such blends are less common than expected. While spandex is less susceptible to chlorine than rubber, it is still damaged by chlorine: polyester-based spandex fibers are less prone than the polyether-based versions. It melts at around 450°F and one of its few drawbacks is a relatively high cost.

Research into new elastomeric fibers continues. Recently, Dow has introduced a metallocene-based, cross-linked olefin elaostomeric fiber, Dow XLA, that has been given the generic name "lastol." It is heat resistant, and maintains its stretch properties through processes such as dyeing and finishing, although the fiber itself is not dyeable. The FTC has also given the generic name "elasterell-p" to DuPont's fiber T400. Elasterell-p is based on a combination of polyester polymers.

See also Dyeing; Fibers.

BIBLIOGRAPHY

Adnaur, Sabit. *Wellington Sears Handbook of Industrial Textiles.* Lancaster, Pa.: Technomic, 1995.

Cook, J. Gordon. *Handbook of Textile Fibers. II: Man-Made Fibers,* 5th ed. Durham, U.K.: Merrow, 1984.

Moncrieff, R. W. *Man-Made Fibres.* 6th ed. London: Newnes-Butterworth, 1975.

Martin Bide

ELLIS, PERRY

Perry Ellis (1940–1986) was regarded as an outstanding designer of American sportswear in the 1970s and 1980s. In order to appreciate the far-reaching allure of his best-known invention, a deceptively simple homemade-looking sweater, one should understand the

Model in Perry Ellis design. Perry Ellis launched his sportswear collection in 1978, garnering instant acclaim for his concept of separates that could be mixed and matched. © REUTERS NEW-MEDIA, INC./CORBIS. REPRODUCED BY PERMISSION.

potent appeal that American sportswear held in the 1970s. Separates dressing at that time meant individual style—a radically new approach after more than a century of one dominant silhouette following another. And individual style was particularly relevant at a time when gender roles were being tossed in the air. What Perry Ellis did best was take elements of classic American style—stadium coats, tweed jackets, and culottes—and adapt them to suit changing times.

Perry Ellis was born on 3 March 1940. He grew up in Churchland, a small suburb of the Virginia coastal town of Portsmouth. Ellis earned a B.A. in business from the College of William and Mary, and went on to acquire a master's degree in retailing from New York University. He then went to work in Richmond at Miller and Rhoads, a Virginia department store that was similar in size and quality to such New York emporia as B. Altman or Bonwit Teller. During Ellis's tenure with Miller and Rhoads, his department, junior sportswear, had the highest sales in the store.

At Miller and Rhoads, Ellis worked closely with manufacturers, making design suggestions as he saw fit. His suggestions sold well, leading a favorite supplier, John Meyer of Norwich, to offer Ellis a job in 1968 as design director. This firm's preppy style was aimed at high school and college students, offering coordinated ensembles of cotton print blouses with Peter Pan collars, cable-knit cardigans, and corduroy skirts. In 1974 Ellis moved to Manhattan Industries, where he became vice president and merchandising manager for Vera Sportswear. Vera Neumann was an artist whose popular scarves and outfits were based on her signed paintings. Ellis was intrigued by the challenge of working with her designs, and came up with styles that attracted considerable positive attention in the fashion press. In 1975 he debuted his own line for Manhattan Industries, which was known as Perry Ellis for Portfolio. He then launched his own label, Perry Ellis Sportswear, in 1978. Acclaim was instant. A menswear line and various licensing arrangements soon followed, as did a number of professional honors. After winning two Coty awards each for women's wear and men's wear, Ellis was voted into the Coty Hall of Fame in 1981. He also received awards from the Council of Fashion Designers of America (CFDA) for women's wear in 1981 and men's wear in 1982.

The launch of Perry Ellis Sportswear for the fall–winter season of 1978 was memorable. The show opened with a group of Princeton University cheerleaders wearing little pleated skirts and sweaters emblazoned with a large "P." This collection firmly established what became the signature Perry Ellis look—what he coined the slouch look. It consisted of separates based on pieces that could work in different combinations: oversize jackets, thick yarn sweaters, lots of layers, ribbed socks worn rumpled like leg warmers, men's Oxford shoes for women. While the riffs on scale and silhouette were sophisticated, the casual fabrics seemed fresh. Although the references might have been collegiate, these were clothes for adults who were confident enough to thumb their noses at the rigid styles associated with dressing for success.

Further notable collections followed. The fall 1981 collection featured a mix of challis prints in deep jewel tones with duck and pheasant motifs, with all scales of prints and colors worn together in a single ensemble. Ellis's spring 1982 collection coincided with the release of the film *Chariots of Fire*, and featured relaxed flapper lines in pale linens. The fall–winter 1984 collection was an homage to French painter Sonia Delauney—bold geometric patterns in deep rich colors for men and women.

Much has been made of Ellis's perfectionism. What seemed mandatory for the visually oriented person in the early twenty-first century, such as insisting on a specific look for everything from the company's logo and store interiors to bouquets of flowers sent to fashion editors and the postage stamps used on invitations to shows, was noteworthy in the late 1970s for a Seventh Avenue designer—especially one working in the less glamorous area of sportswear. Ellis's perfectionism extended to every part of his collection; the models' hair and makeup had to look natural, and nail polish was forbidden. Manolo Blahnik designed shoes for Perry Ellis, usually ghillies, ankle boots, or spectator pumps in an Edwardian or prairie mood. Patricia Underwood designed strikingly simple hats, and Barry Kieselstein-Cord made jewelry, belts, and hair ornaments in precious metals.

At a time when fashion designers were becoming glamorous celebrities, Perry Ellis remained somewhat of an enigma. He was startlingly handsome, yet dressed in an antifashion uniform consisting of khaki pants, a dress shirt with the cuffs rolled up, and Topsider shoes left over from his college fraternity days. Famously shy, he exuded charisma. Although heralded as an overnight sensation, he had definitely paid his dues on the way up. A household name, he kept his personal life private. One minute he was at the top of his game, or so it seemed, and next came the shocking news of his death. After an appallingly rapid decline, witnessed silently by his staff, friends, and the fashion industry, he died of AIDS on 30 May 1986.

After Ellis's death, his long-time assistants Patricia Pastor and Jed Krascella designed for the company. The firm then hired a rising star, Marc Jacobs, in 1988. As a teenager, Jacobs had asked Perry Ellis for career advice, and was told to go to Parsons School of Design, where he won the Perry Ellis Golden Thimble Award in 1984.

At first Perry Ellis and Marc Jacobs seemed like a good combination. Jacobs's stretch gingham frocks, cheerful colors, and prints suited the mood of the firm and the late 1980s. Then came the infamous grunge collection, shown in 1993, which appalled the press and potential buyers alike. However, like most controversial fashions, the grunge look of layered vintage military surplus pieces was merely ahead of its time. After Jacobs left the company, Perry Ellis International decided against having a star designer, choosing for a time to have a team of people developing the brand. In 2003 Patrick Robinson was hired as designer. His fall–winter 2004 collection, based in part on a vintage Perry Ellis scarf found for sale on an Internet site, received good reviews. A particularly American touch from Robinson's spring 2004 collection—the models wore Converse sneakers—paid homage to both Perry Ellis and Marc Jacobs.

See also **Blahnik, Manolo; Dress for Success; Grunge; Seventh Avenue; Sportswear.**

BIBLIOGRAPHY

Brubach, Holly. "Camelot." *New Yorker* (25 July 1988): 83–86.

Diamonstein-Spielvogel, Barbaralee. *Fashion: The Inside Story.* New York: Rizzoli International, 1985.

Milbank, Caroline Rennolds. *New York Fashion: The Evolution of American Style.* New York: Harry N. Abrams, Inc., 1989.

Moor, Jonathan. *Perry Ellis: A Biography.* New York: St. Martin's Press, 1988.

Caroline Rennolds Milbank

EMBROIDERY Embroidery is an ancient form of needlework that has been used worldwide to embellish textiles for decorative and communicative purposes. In terms of form and aesthetics, embroidery may add color, texture, richness, and dimension. Used on clothing, it may reveal the wearer's wealth, social status, ethnic identity, or systems of belief. Typically, embroidery is executed in threads of cotton, wool, silk, or linen, but may also incorporate other materials such as beads, quills, metal, shells, or feathers. Some materials, techniques, and stitches occur across many cultures, while others are specific to region.

Historical Overview

The origins of this art form, mentioned in the Bible and in Greek mythology, are lost. Textile scholar Lanto Synge posits that it probably originated in China, and documents early surviving fragments that are estimated as being 4,500 years old. In South America embroideries from the fifth century B.C.E. have been recovered from tombs.

Throughout the history of embroidery, religious institutions have been among its greatest patrons. For example, the Medieval church in Europe fostered one of the greatest peaks in needlework history—*Opus Anglicanum* (English work). A type of needlework made in England during the Middles Ages, it was widely exported throughout Europe. Worked by highly skilled professionals in embroidery workshops, *Opus Anglicanum* was known for its artistry of ecclesiastical vestments. The sophisticated embroideries, made with the finest linens and velvets, were worked with silk threads in a split-stitch technique and also utilized an underside couching technique to secure the decorative gold and silver threads. Couching is an embroidery technique in which threads are laid in a design on the surface of a base fabric and sewn to the fabric with small stitches that cross over the design threads. The religious designs were well conceived and executed in a form of needlepainting, or *acupictura*. Figures of the Virgin Mary and the saints as well as religious scenes were executed in flowing circles and geometric patterns.

Opus Anglicanum illustrates the potential of embroidery as a conveyor of narrative and of ecclesiastical power; simultaneously, the courts of Europe applied embroidery to secular dress whose lavish decoration served to display secular power and prestige. During the Medieval period, the production and consumption of embroidery became increasing codified. Guilds regulated the training of professional embroiderers, while sumptuary laws attempted to restrict the wearing of embroidered garments to specific socioeconomic classes. Renaissance court costume was often elaborately embroidered with floral imagery. Inventories of Queen Elizabeth I's wardrobe list gowns embroidered with roses, oak leaves, and pomegranates. As with *Opus Anglicanum*, metal thread work was employed to connote the prestige of the subject—in this case human rather than divine.

For centuries, European court dress was often lavishly embroidered as a signifier of status. Catherine of Aragon, arriving in England in 1501 with embroidered blackwork as part of her trousseau, is credited with encouraging the use of Spanish-style embroidery, rich in blackwork. Blackwork, which originated in the thirteenth and fourteenth centuries in Islamic Egypt, is a type of embroidery stitched in monochrome on white or natural linen. Traditionally worked in black, it was also worked in red, blue, and dark green and often enriched with gold and silver threads. Geometric and scrolling patterns are executed in backstitch or double-running stitch, a reversible stitch used for edgings of collars and cuffs that could be seen on both sides. Little of this dress survives because it was worn out or recycled. It is through inventories and portraiture that much information about historic costume is gleaned. In portraits of Henry VIII and the royal family, Hans Holbein the Younger (1497–1543) so clearly defines the stitching technique used in their elaborate costumes that the double-running stitch is also known as the Holbein stitch. Eighteenth-century portraiture again reveals much about the elegance and refinement of embroidery on high society dress.

As has been the case across many time periods and cultures, embroidery was practiced in different settings, and by different levels of society. Both men and women worked in professional workshops, while women embroidered at home for domestic use and recreation. Additionally, producing embroidery at home for sale has been a means of economic sustenance for women in many cultures, as the following case illustrates.

Many countries have traditions of whitework embroidery, executed with white thread on a white ground.

Hardanger—a counted thread technique originating in the west of Norway and brought by emigrants to the United States—Madeira cutwork, Dresden whitework, and Isfahani whitework are a few examples. In terms of application to dress, some of the most widely consumed whitework was produced in Scotland and Ireland in the eighteenth and nineteenth centuries. The example of Ayrshire whitework provides a fascinating insight into the interaction of professional designers, workshops, individual women, and commercial and philanthropic interests within the fashion system.

This intricate whitework was characterized by floral motifs worked with fine cotton thread on a cotton ground, typically in satin stitch, stem stitch, and needlepoint in-filling. Labor-intensive and delicate in appearance, it was used to decorate babies' christening gowns, women's dress, and undergarments. Its production was highly organized by commercial firms and philanthropic organizations concerned with improving living standards in rural areas. A woodblock or lithograph design was printed on the cloth, which was then distributed to individual households, and executed by women and children. With agents as intermediaries, the finished cloths were sent to depots in large cities, made up into garments, and sold in Britain or exported to Europe and America. By the mid-nineteenth century, Ayrshire whitework was a significant industry, with an individual firm contracting with 20,000 to 30,000 workers.

Against this context another distinctive embroidery movement in Scotland evolved—that of the Glasgow School of the early twentieth century. Influential teachers such as Jessie Newberry and Ann Macbeth revolutionized the teaching of embroidery, stressing self-expression in design, and a more simplified approach to form, typically incorporating appliqué outlined in satin stitch.

Embroidery and Couture

Because of its decorative potential as well as its ability to connote status, hand embroidery was from the beginning included in the battery of haute couture's specialized techniques. The lavishly time-intensive, specialized nature of the art, and the costliness of the materials, made it the ultimate signifier of luxury. Embroidery houses, employing highly talented designers and technicians, became an integral part of the couture industry. The most famous of these was the House of Lesage.

It is fitting that Charles Frederick Worth, designer of the Empress Eugenie's court clothing, was a master in the incorporation of embroidery as a status confirming (or conferring) accoutrement. An early design that won a medal at the 1855 Exposition Universelle was of bead-embroidered moire. Jeanne Lanvin typically eschewed patterned fabrics for embroidery. She was one of the first designers to exploit the use of machine embroidery, incorporating parallel line machine stitching as a decorative motif.

Designers such as Mary McFadden and Zandra Rhodes have adopted embroidery, with a particular interest in the manipulation of textiles for artistic effect. When combined with other techniques such as stenciling, batik, quilting, or handpainting, embroidery draws attention to the textile as a rich surface, rather like a canvas. In other cases designers use embroidery to float over the surface fabric. Dior was a master of this illusionary approach to embroidery, which ignores seamlines and construction, creating its own field of vision.

Ethnic embroidery inspirations have long infused couture, from Lanvin's designs of the 1920s to Yves Saint Laurent's "peasant" blouses and skirts. Other designers have mined long-established associations between embroidery and femininity; the sensuous aesthetic of Nina Ricci and Chloé is often heightened by delicate embroidery.

World Traditions

All cultures have traditions of embroidery. Influences and cross-fertilizations can be traced across trade routes and patterns of migration. In other cases, techniques and stitches are unique to geographic area.

China has a long and rich tradition of embroidery centered on the ceremonial dress of the Imperial court. From the Tang dynasty (618–907) onward, silk ceremonial robes were heavily embroidered to communicate the status of the wearer within a strict hierarchy. Mythological creatures, birds, flowers, waves, and clouds were some of the panoply of forms used symbolically to situate the wearer, or allude to personal qualities or aspirations for longevity and good fortune.

The embroidery on eighteenth- and nineteenth-century robes reached an apogee of technical perfection. Motifs were meticulously rendered in satin stitch, chain stitch, and Chinese stitch—a form of backstitch interlaced with a second thread. Areas were intricately in-filled with tiny knots. As with Renaissance court dress in Europe and Medieval church vestments, liberal use of couched metal thread conveyed status and wealth.

Throughout the history of its production, the development of embroidery traditions has been fostered by imperial patronage. The Ottoman court in Istanbul was a major patron for embroidery. However, in the Ottoman Empire, embroidery was also highly integrated into everyday life. The court commissioned fine embroideries from workshops and professional women working at home, but the making of embroidered clothing and household items was part of most women's everyday activities. Within the Empire embroidery was an important commercial and domestic enterprise. The major Ottoman embroidery style is *dival*, in which metal threads are secured to the ground with couching threads.

Native American embroidery also has its own culturally expressive characteristics. The techniques of porcupine quillwork and beading predate European explorers to North America. Traditionally, this decorative art was embroidered on skins, but after the arrival of Europeans and the subsequent acquisition of new materials, it was worked on cloth. All items of dress were embellished with needlework—coats, jackets, shirts, hoods, leggings, moccasins, and accessories such as medicine bags.

Of various techniques employed in quillwork embroidery, sewing was the most common method. Bone bodkins were used to accomplish these designs until the white trader brought needles to America. The stitch methods are similar to modern sewing terms used today: backstitch, couching stitch, and chain stitch.

Beading was another long-held practice of the Native Americans who initially used crude beads that they made from natural materials. Later, Europeans introduced finer quality beads known as trade beads that proved to be highly desirable to the Indian tribes in their embroideries. Beads were strung on thread and sewn onto the skin or cloth according to the pattern by either massing the beads in little rows or working them in an outline formation.

On one level, Native American embroideries communicate systems of beliefs. This too has been an important function of embroidery worldwide. One example is *shishadur*, or mirror work, practiced by the Baluchi people of western Pakistan, southern Afghanistan, and eastern Iran. Fragments of silvered glass attached to a cotton ground were believed to deflect evil. In Eastern Europe a folk belief that embroidered designs on clothing protected the wearer from harm infused the development of embroidery. Items of clothing such as dresses, blouses, skirts, aprons, shirts, vests, and jackets, as well as ecclesiastical vestments, were embellished with beautiful embroideries.

The unique appearance of Eastern European needlework comes from the precise use of materials, designs, techniques, and colors that when combined can often indicate a specific region of the country. Embroidery stitches in the straight, satin, and cross-stitch families are employed; but, for example, among the specialty stitches in Ukrainian embroidery are the *Yavoriv* stitch, a diagonal satin stitch, and the *Yavoriv* plait stitch, a variation on the cross-stitch.

In the early 2000s, embroidery remained a vibrant component of dress. In a global marketplace, designers and consumers may choose from an infinite variety of world traditions. For example, mirror work was absorbed into western fashion trends of the 1970s, and has periodically resurfaced as a trend in clothing and home furnishings. Embroidery has remained a pervasive element of couture and has had an enormous influence on ready-to-wear. As sewing machines for the home sewer become increasingly sophisticated, the application of machine embroidery to home-sewn clothing has burgeoned. And, possibly as a reaction to mass-production, a thriving industry has grown around the provision of custom embroidery as a means of personalizing dress.

See also Beads; Feathers; Sewing Machine; Spangles; Trimmings.

BIBLIOGRAPHY

Embroidery. London: The Embroiderers' Guild. An informed periodical with articles on historic, ethnographic, and contemporary embroidery, exhibition, and book reviews.

The Essential Guide to Embroidery. London: Murdoch Books, 2002.

Gostelow, Mary. Embroidery: Traditional Designs, Techniques and Patterns from All Over the World. London: Marshall Cavendish Books Ltd., 1982. Useful for a cross-cultural perspective of embroidery.

Harbeson, Georgiana Brown. American Needlework: The History of Decorative Stitchery and Embroidery from the Late 16th to the 20th Century. New York: Coward McCann, Inc., 1938.

Krody, Sumru Belger. Flowers of Silk and Gold; Four Centuries of Ottoman Embroidery. London: Merrell Publishers Ltd., in association with The Textile Museum, Washington, D.C., 2000. Excellent discussion of a major embroidery tradition within its cultural context. Well-illustrated with close-up details, and glossary of stitches.

O'Neill, Tania Diakiw. Ukrainian Embroidery Techniques. Mountaintop, Pa.: STO Publications, 1984.

Parker, Rozsika. The Subversive Stitch: Embroidery and the Making of the Feminine. New York: Routledge, 1984. Insight into the sometimes overlooked role of women as professional embroiderers and discussion of embroidery and the construction of femininity.

Swain, Margaret. Scottish Embroidery: Medieval to Modern. London: B. T. Batsford, Ltd., 1986. Useful discussion on methods of production and the role of embroidery as a commercial and domestic activity.

Swan, Susan Burrows. Plain and Fancy: American Women and their Needlework, 1650–1850. Rev. ed. Austin, Tex.: Curious Works Press, 1995.

Swift, Gay. The Batsford Encyclopaedia of Embroidery Techniques. London: B. T. Batsford, Ltd., 1984. A comprehensive guide to techniques and their applications to historic clothing.

Synge, Lanto. Art of Embroidery: History of Style and Technique. Woodbridge, U.K.: Antique Collectors' Club, 2001.

Lindsay Shen and Marilee DesLauriers

EMPIRE STYLE In its broadest sense as a term in contemporary fashion, "empire style" (sometimes called simply "Empire" with the French pronunciation, "om-peer") refers to a woman's dress silhouette in which the waistline is considerably raised above the natural level, and the skirt is usually slim and columnar. The reference is to fashions of France's First Empire, which in political terms lasted from 1804 when Napoleon Bonaparte crowned himself Emperor, to his final defeat at the Battle of Waterloo in 1815. It should be noted that the styles of this period, when referring specifically to English or American fashions or examples, may be termed "Regency" (referring to the Regency of the Prince of Wales, 1811–1820) or "Federal" (referring to the decades immediately following the American Revolution).

None of these terms, whose boundaries are defined by political milestones, accurately encompasses the time frame in which "empire style" fashions are found, which date from the late 1790s to about 1820, after which skirts widened and the waistline lowered to an extent no longer identifiable as "empire style."

The Empire style in its purest form is characterized by: the columnar silhouette—without gathers in front, some fullness over the hips, and a concentration of gathers aligned with the 3–4" wide center back bodice panel; a raised waistline, which at its extreme could be at armpit-level, dependent on new forms of corsetry with small bust gussets, cording under the breasts, and shoulder straps to keep the bust high; soft materials, especially imported Indian white muslin (the softest, sheerest of which is called "mull"), often pre-embroidered with white cotton thread; and neoclassical influence in overall style (the silhouette imitating Classical statuary) and in accessories and trim.

Neoclassical references included sandals; bonnets, hairstyles, and headdresses copied from Greek statues and vases; and motifs found in ancient architecture and decorative arts, such as the Greek key, and oak and laurel leaves. The use of purely neoclassical references was at its peak from about 1798 to just after 1800; after that, they were succeeded by other influences.

The adoption of these references has been linked with France's Revolution and adoption of Greek and Roman democratic and republican principles, and certainly the French consciously sought to make these connections both at the height of their Revolution, and under Napoleon, who was eager to link himself to the great Roman emperors.

Applying this political reference to America is more problematic. The extremely revealing versions of the style were seldom seen in America, where conservatism and ambivalence about letting Europe dictate American fashions ran deep. However, Americans did adopt the general look of the period, and plenty of dresses survive to testify that fashionable young women did wear the sheer white muslin style. Moreover, there is ample evidence that women of every class, even on the frontiers, had some access to information on current fashions, and usually possessed, if not for everyday use, modified versions of them.

The origins of the neoclassical influence are visible in the later eighteenth century. White linen, and later, cotton, dresses were the standard uniform for infants, toddlers, and young girls, and entered adult fashion about 1780. During the 1780s and early 1790s, women's silhouettes gradually became slimmer, and the waistline crept up, the effect heightened by the addition of wide sashes, whose upper edge approached the level that waistlines would in another decade. After 1795, waistlines rose dramatically and the skirt circumference was further reduced, the fullness no longer equally distributed but confined to the sides and back. By 1798, fashion plates in England and France show the form-clinging high-waisted neoclassical style, with England lagging a little behind in its adoption of the extreme of the new look.

As England and France were at war for nearly all of this period, English styles sometimes took their own direction, showing a fluctuating waistline level (which should not be taken literally, as garments from this period show remarkably little deviation from a norm) and numerous decorative details borrowed from peasant or "cottage" styles, historic references, especially medieval and "Tudor," and regional references such as Russian, Polish, German, or Spanish. Often, contemporary events inspired fashions, such as the state visit of allies in the Napoleonic wars; military uniforms also inspired trim and accessories in women's fashions during these years.

Several myths persist about the styles of this period, including the idea that the style was invented by Josephine Bonaparte to conceal her pregnancy, and that ladies of fashion dampened their petticoats to achieve the clinging-muslin effects seen in classical statues. Fashions can rarely be attributed to one person (although a hundred years earlier, a pregnancy at the French court did inspire the invention of a style) and the most cursory glance at fashions of the 1780s and 1790s shows a clear progress of internal change in fashion.

The dampened petticoat myth may have arisen from some early historians', and historical novelists', misunderstanding of some comments on the new style. Compared to the heavier fabrics and stylized body shapes (created by heavily-boned, conical-shaped corsets and side-hoops) that immediately preceded them, the new sheer muslins, worn over one slip or even, by some European ladies, a knitted, tubular body stocking, would have revealed the contours of the natural body to an extent not seen in centuries. Several contemporaries and early fashion historians wrote that women looked *as if* they had dampened their skirts. However, no evidence, including scathing denunciations of the indecent new style, as well as gleeful social satirists' commentary and caricatures, exists to document that this was ever done.

The Empire style has seen numerous revivals, although modern eyes must sometimes look closely for the reference, as it is always used in tandem with the silhouette and body shape fashionable at the time. Tea gowns of the 1880s and 1890s are sometimes described as "empire style." Reform dress often borrowed the high waist and slender skirt of the Empire period, perhaps finding the relatively simple construction notably different from the styles it rejected, the high waist providing freedom from the era's constrictive corsets. By about 1908, "empire style" dresses were a large segment of fashionable offerings. The 1930s saw another minor revival, as did the 1970s. The release in the late 1990s of several film and television adaptations of Jane Austen's novels, all set during the Empire period, inspired another revival.

See also **Dress Reform; Maternity Dress; Tea Gown.**

BIBLIOGRAPHY

Ashelford, Jane. *The Art of Dress: Clothes and Society 1500–1914.* Great Britain: The National Trust. Distributed in the United States by Harry N. Abrams, New York, 1996.

Bourhis, Kate, ed. *The Age of Napoleon: Costume from Revolution to Empire, 1789–1815.* New York: Metropolitan Museum of Art and Harry N. Abrams, 1989.

Cunnington, C. Willet. *English Womens' Clothing in the Nineteenth Century.* London: Faber and Faber, Ltd., 1937. Reprint, New York: Dover Publications, 1990.

Ribeiero, Aileen. *Fashion in the French Revolution.* New York: Holmes and Meier, 1988.

——. *The Art of Dress: Fashion in England and France 1750–1820.* New Haven, Conn.: Yale University Press, 1995.

Alden O'Brien

EQUESTRIAN COSTUME

Comfort, practicality, and protection from the elements are central qualities of riding attire, though it has always been considered stylish. Distinctive accessories marked equestrian costume from streetwear: sturdy knee-high boots with a heel and sometimes spurs for both men and women, a crop, whip or cane, gloves to spare the wearer from the chafing of leather reins, and most importantly a hat for style and later a helmet for safety. Contemporary riding dress still emphasizes comfort and protection but modern materials are used in its construction, including cotton-lycra fabrics for breeches, polystyrene-filled helmets, and Gore-Tex jackets, bringing it in line with high-technology clothing used in other sports.

Construction and Materials

The materials worn for riding from the mid-seventeenth to the early twentieth centuries were easily distinguished from the silks, muslins, and velvets of fashionable evening dress. Equestrian activities required sturdy and often weatherproof fabrics such as woolen broadcloth, camlet (a silk and wool or hair mixture), melton wool, and gabardine for colder weather and linen or cotton twill for summer or the tropics. In the eighteenth and early nineteenth centuries, habits were frequently adorned with gold, silver, or later woolen braiding, often imitating the frogging on Hussar or other military uniforms.

For example, in Wright of Derby's double portrait of Mr. and Mrs. Coltman exhibited in 1771, both wear stylish riding dress. Thomas Coltman's dress consists of a deep blue waistcoat trimmed with silver braid, a loosely fitting frock coat, high boots, and buckskin breeches fitted so tight that the outline of a coin is visible in his right-hand pocket. British styles of equestrian dress strongly

Princess Anne of Great Britain in riding attire. Women's riding trousers, such as these, were introduced during the Victorian period, and gained in popularity after riding sidesaddle fell out of fashion. In the early twenty-first century, there was little difference between riding habits for men and women. © TIM GRAHAM/CORBIS. REPRODUCED BY PERMISSION.

influenced civilian fashions in other countries. In particular, French Anglophiles imitated British modes as early as the eighteenth century. The British frock coat became known as the *redingote* in France, a corruption of the word "riding-coat." Equestrian influence has subtly shaped men's dress to the present day, and vestiges of it remain in the single back vent of coats and suit jackets, which derive from the need to sit comfortably astride a horse and wick off the rain. Mary Coltman sits sidesaddle and wears a habit in one of the most fashionable colors for women in the eighteenth century when red, claret, and rose were in vogue. Her light waistcoat is trimmed with gold braid and she sports a jaunty plumed hat. Other portraits that feature eighteenth-century riding dress include Sir Joshua Reynolds's portrait of Lady Worsley and George Stubbs's double portrait of the Sheriff of Nottingham and his wife, Sophia Musters.

In the nineteenth century, riding dress became more subdued in style and hue for both sexes. The early nineteenth-century gentleman wore a single-breasted tail-coat, sloping in front with a single-breasted waistcoat and cravat or stock. On horseback, he wore the same garments on his upper body but his coat might have distinctive gilt buttons. His legs required more specialized garments: breeches made from buckskin were typically worn and for "dress" riding trousers or pantaloons with a strap to keep them from riding up. If he wore shoes rather than boots, he could use knee-gaiters to protect his legs.

Because of their practicality, lack of decorative detail, and allowance for mobility, women wore riding habits not only on horseback but also as visiting, travelling, and walking costumes during the day. For women, the upper half of riding habits often differed little from the clothing worn by their male counterparts, with the addition of darts and shaping for the bust. The bottom half of the horsewoman's costume expressed her femininity. Because ladies were expected to ride sidesaddle from the fifteenth to the early twentieth centuries, they wore skirts specially designed for the purpose. This contrast between the masculine upper half and feminine lower half led one early eighteenth-century writer to call it "the Hermaphroditical." While skirts tended to be relatively simple in cut and construction and quite voluminous in the early modern period, the Victorian habit-skirt was a masterwork of tailoring. Because the skirt could catch on the saddle in the event of a fall, injuring or killing the rider, many "safety skirts" were designed and patented by British firms like Harvey Nicholl and Busvine. These asymmetrical shorter skirts took many forms, including the apron-skirt, a false front that covered the legs when mounted and could be buttoned at the back when the rider dismounted.

Emerald green habits with short spencer jackets were popular in the early decades of the nineteenth century and during the 1830s followed the fashions for leg o'-mutton sleeves. During the Victorian period, as men's dress became more somber, so did women's riding habits. This is because riding habits were made by tailors rather than dressmakers and cut and fashioned with the same techniques from the same selection of fabrics. By the end of the century, black was the most appropriate color for women's riding dress. As riding became a popular leisure activity for the middle classes, etiquette and equitation manuals flourished for those who had no experience of riding flourished, and these often included strict advice about dress. As Mrs. Power O'Donoghue wrote in *Ladies on Horseback* (1889):

> A plainness, amounting even to severity, is to be preferred before any outward show. Ribbons, and coloured veils, and yellow gloves, and showy flowers are alike objectionable. A gaudy "get-up" (to make use of an expressive common-place) is highly to be condemned, and at once stamps the wearer as a person of inferior taste. Therefore avoid it.

The Victorian period introduced breeches and riding trousers for women. This garment prevented chafing and was concealed under the skirt. Tailors and breeches-makers often advertised a lady assistant to measure a woman's inseam, and the resulting breeches were made from dark wool to match the habit and remained invisible if the skirt should fly up.

Colonialism, female emancipation, and increased participation in a wide variety of sports, especially bicycling, changed women's relationship with the riding costume. On their travels, women used horses for practical transportation and exploration and these animals were not always broken to ride sidesaddle. For safety and comfort, women had to ride astride and new habits with breeches or "zouave" trousers and jackets with long skirts were devised. Jodhpurs, named after a district in Rajasthan, were based on a style of Indian trousers that ballooned over the thighs and were cut tightly below the knees. These became popular for both men and women on horseback. "Ride astride" habits began to become acceptable in the first decades of the twentieth century, though many women continued to ride sidesaddle until mid-century. A 1924 illustration in American *Vogue* shows both a more formal black sidesaddle habit worn with cutaway coat and top hat and a tweed ride-astride habit worn with jodhpurs and a floppy-brimmed hat. Tweeds were standard for informal riding wear such as "hacking jackets." In the second half of the twentieth century riding had evolved in the directions of both recreation and competitive sport and specialized clothing with higher safety standards had become the norm, and less expensive materials like rubber replaced leather boots while polar fleece, Gore-Tex, and down jackets were used for warmth and waterproofing.

Different types of equitation demanded variations in dress and etiquette. While horses were often the most practical means of transportation in the eighteenth century, the advent of rail travel increased the popularity of riding as a leisure activity. The degree of formality in dress depended on whether the activity was an informal country hack, an aristocratic foxhunt, or a ride in an urban park. The most fashionable urban sites for riding were Rotten Row in London and the Bois de Boulogne in the west of Paris.

Functional clothing worn for work with horses included the carrick or greatcoat of the coachman with triple capes to keep off rain and snow. Each equestrian profession, from the groom to the liveried postillion, had a distinctive form of dress. Those who worked in agricultural contexts around the world developed specialized attire, such as the leather or suede chaps worn by the American cowboy, the sheepskins worn by herders in the French marshes of the Camargue, or the poncho worn by gauchos in South America.

Hunting clothing was often regular riding clothing adapted for convenience and protection from the elements. In the eighteenth century some hunts adopted specific colors and emblems, though the red coat was by no means universal and green, dark blue, and brown were popular. Red woolen frock coats or "hunting pinks" with black velvet collars were the mark of the experienced fox-hunter.

Racing developed its own specialized clothing as well. In contrast with the thick and waterproof garments worn on the hunt, the jockey's clothing had to be light and streamlined, fitting the body very tightly. By the early eighteenth century, jockeys were wearing attire that is recognizable in the early-twenty-first century: tight jackets cut to the waist, white breeches, short top-boots, and peaked cap with a bow in front. At that time, the cap was black; but the bright and highly visible, often striped or checked "colored silk" livery of the jacket made the owner's identity clear. Satin weaves gave these silks their glossy sheen. Because of its sexual appeal and bright coloring, jockey suits were often copied in women's fashions by nineteenth-century couturiers like Charles Worth.

For example, in Zola's novel *Nana*, the eponymous heroine, a Parisian courtesan, goes to the races dressed in a jockey-inspired outfit:

> She wore the colours of the De Vandeuvres stable, blue and white, intermingled in a most extraordinary costume. The little body and the tunic, in blue silk, were very tight fitting, and raised behind in an enormous puff . . . the skirt and sleeves were in white satin, as well as a sash that passed over the shoulder, and the whole was trimmed with silver braid which sparkled in the sunshine. Whilst, the more to resemble a jockey, she had placed a flat blue cap, ornamented with a feather, on the top of her chignon, from which a long switch of her golden hair hung down in the middle of her back like an enormous tail. (pp. 289–290)

Manufacture and Retail

Because of its traditions of equestrian sport, Britain has led the Western world in making riding costumes. Men could go to their habitual tailors who specialized in sporting dress.

The fabric used for making women's habits could be very expensive and because of the amount of cloth needed, it often cost substantially more than an evening gown. Like men's suits, riding habits were expected to last several years and to stand up to intensive use. Despite its elite connotations, ready-made habits were available in the eighteenth century from mercers and haberdashers' shops, and in the nineteenth century from department stores and working-class men's clothiers and outfitting firms trying to move upmarket by advertising "ladies' habit rooms." At the upper end of the market, firms offered luxury services to their clientele. In the 1880s, British tailoring firms such as Creeds opened branches in Paris. The suites of the British women's tailor and couturier Redfern in Paris, situated on the rue de Rivoli, were celebrated as "the rendez-vous of all the sportswomen whom the foreign and Parisian aristocracy count among their number." Redfern proposed stuffed block horses of several colors so that his clients could choose their habits in a tone that matched the hide (*robe*) of their favorite mount. The word for the hue of a horses' hide and woman's dress were the same in French.

Riding attire has always symbolized grace and leisured elegance. It implied that its wearer belonged or aspired to belong to the horse-owning classes. Wearers often used it to challenge formal social mores in dress, deportment, and gender roles. Its rustic simplicity and informality connoted youth, ease, and sometimes impudence. For example, the dandy George Bryan Brummell made riding dress fashionable in the salons of Regency Britain, bringing "rural" modes into an urban setting. For horsewomen, etiquette was more stringent. Any woman who wore gaudy or overly ornate habits or who made a spectacle of herself was in danger of being branded a "pretty horsebreaker" or "fast woman" rather than a "fair equestrienne" in the Victorian period. Contemporary fashion designers continue to recycle traditional equestrian motifs and fabrics in haute couture and prêt-à-porter collections. In this context riding costume is most often used to connote country elegance and traditional elite English style.

See also **Boots; Breeches; Brummell, George (Beau); Protective Clothing.**

BIBLIOGRAPHY

Arnold, Janet. "Dashing Amazons: The Development of Women's Riding Dress, c.1500–1900." In *Defining Dress: Dress as Object, Meaning and Identity.* Edited by Amy de la Haye and Elizabeth Wilson, 10–29. Manchester U.K.: Manchester University Press, 1999.

Chenoune, Farid. *A History of Men's Fashion.* Paris: Flammarion, 1993.

Cunnington, Phillis, and A. Mansfield. *English Costume for Sports and Outdoor Recreation: From the Sixteenth to the Nineteenth Centuries.* London: Adam and Charles Black, 1969.

David, Alison Matthews. "Elegant Amazons: Victorian Riding Habits and the Fashionable Horsewoman." *Victorian Literature and Culture* 30, no.1 (2002): 179–210.

O'Donoghue, Power [Nannie]. *Ladies On Horseback: Learning, Park-Riding and Hunting, With Hints Upon Costume, and Numerous Anecdotes.* London: W. H. Allen, 1889.

Zola, Émile. *Nana.* London: Vizetelly and Company, 1884.

Alison Matthews David

ETHNIC DRESS Ethnic dress ranges from a single piece to a whole ensemble of items that identify an individual with a specific ethnic group. An ethnic group refers to people who share a cultural heritage or historical tradition, usually connected to a geographical location or a language background; it may sometimes overlap religious or occupational groups. Ethnicity refers to the common heritage of an ethnic group. Members of an ethnic group often distinguish themselves from others by using items of dress to symbolize their ethnicity and display group solidarity. The words "ethnic" and "ethnicity" come from the Greek word *ethnos*, meaning "people." Many anthropologists prefer to use the inclusive term "ethnic group" instead of "tribe," because the latter is often employed as shorthand for "other people" as opposed to "us." Sometimes the term "folk dress" is used instead of ethnic dress when discussing examples of ethnic dress in Europe and not elsewhere in the world. "Folk" and folk dress ordinarily distinguish European rural dwellers and peasants and their dress from wealthy landowners, nobility, or royalty and their apparel. Ethnic dress, however, is a neutral term that applies to distinctive cultural dress of people living anywhere in the world who share an ethnic background.

Ethnic Dress and Change

The readily identifiable aspect of ethnic dress arises from a garment characteristic (such as its silhouette), a garment part (such as a collar or sleeve), accessories, or a textile pattern, any of which stems from the group's cultural heritage. Many people believe that ethnic dress does not change. In point of fact, however, change in dress does occur, because as human beings come into contact with other human beings, they borrow, exchange, and modify many cultural items, including items of dress. In addition, human beings create and conceive of new ways of making or decorating garments or accessories, and modifying their bodies. Even though changes occur and are apparent when garments and ensembles are viewed over time, many aspects of ethnic dress do remain stable, allowing them to be identifiable. In many parts of the world, ethnic dress is not worn on a daily basis; instead items are brought out for specific occasions, particularly holiday or ritual events, when a display of ethnic identity is a priority and a source of pride. When worn only in this way, ethnic dress may easily be viewed as ethnic costume, since it is not an aspect of everyday identity.

Ethnic Dress and Gender

Across the contemporary world as well as historically, gender differences exist in all types of dress, including ethnic dress. Thus, ethnic dress and gender become intertwined. Sometimes women retain the items of dress identified as ethnic while men wear items of dress and accessories that come from the Western world, especially in urban areas. For example, in India, many women commonly wear a sari or *salwar* and *kameez*, but many men wear trousers and a shirt or a business suit. One explanation is that those who work in industrial and professional jobs connected with or stemming from Westernized occupations begin to wear types of tailored clothing that have arisen from Europe and the Americas.

Another explanation for the continued wearing of ethnic styles is that a widely shared cultural aesthetic in dress may influence preferences for particular garments. For example, the soft lines of the sari in India, and the shapely but body-covering sarong and blouse (*kain-kebaya*) in Indonesia, reflect the cultural ideal of femininity in those countries.

Selected Examples of Ethnic Dress

Garments and accessories for ethnic dress are fashioned from a wide variety of materials, often thought to be made by hand. In today's world, however, many are manufactured by machine. Textiles of many types are most frequently used for garments, although in some locations, people wear furs, skins, bark cloth, and other fibers. Particularly in tropical and subtropical areas in Africa, Asia, and the Pacific, examples of ethnic dress include wrapped garments, such as the wrapper, also called *lappa*, the sari, sarong, and pareo. In moderate and cold climates on all continents, tailored or preshaped clothing is cut and sewn to fit the body closely to provide warmth.

Asia and the Pacific

On the Asian continent, where the climate extends from tropical to Arctic, garment types range from wrapped to cut-and-sewn examples. Throughout India, women wrap six to nine yards of unstitched fabric in specific styles to fashion the wrapped garment called the sari, which is ordinarily worn with a blouse (called a *choli*). Many styles of wrapping the sari exist that distinguish different ethnic backgrounds within India. Indian men wrap from two to four yards of fabric to fashion garments called *lungi* and *dhoti* that they wear around their lower body. Among the Hill Tribes of Thailand, Hmong women wear a blouse and skirt with an elaborate silver necklace, an apron, a turban-type head covering, and wrapped leg coverings. In the steppe lands of Asia (for example, Mongolia), tailored garments of jacket and trousers are worn with caps and boots. In China, types of dress have changed over time, in relationship to contact with other peoples. Turks, Mongols, Manchus, and other peoples of China's Central Asian and northern borderlands sometimes influenced the cut and style of tailored garments in China itself. The fitted, one-piece women's garment with mandarin collar and side-slit skirt known as a cheongsam, or *qipao*, was invented in Shanghai in the 1920s as a garment that was acceptably both "Chinese" and "modern." Its use declined in the People's Republic of China after the late 1950s, but it continued to be worn in Chinese communities outside the mainland and is widely regarded as the "ethnic dress" of Chinese women. In Japan, variations of the garment known as kimono are cut and sewn, as well as wrapped. The kimono's body and sleeves are formed by stitching textiles together, but the body of the garment wraps around the human form and is secured by a sash known as the obi. The Korean ensemble called a *hanbok* includes a skirt for women and pants for men that are cut and sewn, but the top garment, a jacket for both men and women, is called *chogori* and wraps across the breast.

In Indonesia, cloth (*kain*) is wrapped around the lower body for both women and men, and is worn with a blouse (*kebaya*) or a shirt (*baju*). Another option for clothing the lower body is the sarong, cloth sewn to make a tubular garment. (This word was borrowed by Hollywood to refer to the wrapped garment worn by Hedy Lamarr and Dorothy Lamour that also covers the breasts. Among many of the peoples of Indonesia, the latter style is regarded as highly informal, worn for example by women on their way to the bathing pool.) Bare feet or various types of sandals and slippers are worn with these garments.

On many of the islands of the Pacific, such as Samoa and Hawaii, the wrapped garment is called a pareo. The long, shapeless dress called a muumuu, or *robe mission* ("mission dress"), introduced by missionaries to clothe women who traditionally were only lightly dressed, is now widely accepted as a form of ethnic dress throughout the Pacific islands. Elaborate feathered headdresses are worn in many parts of New Guinea with few other body coverings. At the time of European arrival in Australia, Aborigine dress consisted of animal skin cloaks, belts, and headbands along with body piercings, scarification, and body paint. Tattooing various parts of the body has been common among many groups in the Pacific, such as the Maori people of New Zealand and some groups of Japanese.

Because of extensive colonization in Asia and the Pacific, Europeans influenced garments and accessories of indigenous people. In return, the colonizers were influenced by exposure to Asian types of dress and borrowed or modified Asian garments, such as the cummerbund, the pajama, and bandannas, into both everyday and formal dress, thus culturally authenticating them.

Africa

The African continent extends from the Mediterranean Sea to the Cape of Good Hope and from the Atlantic Ocean to the Indian Ocean, providing a wide variation in climate, temperature, and terrain. A majority of indigenous garments include wrapped textiles. Both men and women in West Africa wear wrappers that cover the lower body and a shirt or blouse on the upper body. African women's head ties also exemplify a wrapped textile. In Ghana, some men's garments wrap the body with a large rectangle of cloth pulled over one shoulder that extends to the feet, similar to the Roman toga. Many indigenous people wrap blankets and skins around their bodies in South Africa, and in East Africa ethnic groups like the Maasai and Somali wear variations of garments wrapped around the torso and over one shoulder to below the knees, exposing bare legs and sandals. Distinctive printed textiles that evolved from Dutch influence in

Indonesia are highly visible in African ethnic dress, but the patterns and motifs are now specifically African and often manufactured on the African continent. In North Africa, Islamic influence in dress exists that ties some of this region of Africa to other countries that are primarily Islamic in the Middle East with such examples as the gowns called caftan, djellaba, and *jilbab*. Tailored fashions with European influence also prevail across the continent, particularly in cosmopolitan cities, where the frequency of Africans wearing ethnic dress is particularly diminished. Many Africans have traveled elsewhere in the world, are exposed to mass media such as television, cinema, magazines, and newspapers, and also share knowledge of fashions from Europe and the Americas based on their colonial past. Schoolchildren frequently wear Western-style school uniforms. The secondhand market of clothing from Europe and America has also affected what Africans wear in many countries. Alterations change the garments into local fashions. In comparison to the higher prices of ready-made or tailor-made garments, the lower cost makes secondhand clothing highly desirable. Europeans and Americans who have visited or lived in African countries borrowed items and styles of dress that became incorporated into their wardrobes. Examples are the dashiki, the Yoruba shirt adopted by returning Peace Corps volunteers who served in West Africa during the 1960s, African women's head ties and hairstyles (such as cornrowing) worn by African American women, and children, and garments made from the striped Ghanaian textile called *kente*.

Europe and Eurasia

Ethnic dress in Europe and Eurasia consists primarily of ensembles, often called folk dress that relate to garments generally from the eighteenth century on. Many such examples can be found in folk museums, such as the Benaki Museum in Athens or the Nordiskmuseet in Stockholm. Sometimes the distinctive aspect of ethnic dress appears minimally to be one item, such as the plaid or tartan kilt of men in Scotland or the elaborate lace headdress of women in Brittany that is known as the *coiffe*. Such items become romanticized as ethnic dress, worn for special events and holidays. A strong argument has arisen that indeed the tartan is a relatively recent invention that arose for clan distinction in Scotland. Among most European countries, from as far north as Norway and as far south as Greece, smaller geographic areas are often identified with a specific ethnic group that initially occupied the area. The members of these groups may vary their ensembles or particularly distinct dress items only minimally to set themselves apart from other groups within that country as in the examples of both Norwegian and Greek ethnic dress. The Saami (formerly known as Lapplanders) who live in northern Norway, Sweden, and Finland wear a distinctive tunic-suit, sedge-grass boots, and the "four-winds" hat with four corners that allow the storage of items. For those coming from the

ethnic backgrounds known as Czech and Slovak, a large linen shawl and a matron's cap surface as ethnic social indicators.

The Americas

The enslaved Africans arrived with few examples of garments or their traditions remaining from their past, except for the African women's tradition of wearing a wrapped piece of cloth on her head. In the northern part of North America, the Inuit people (formerly known as Eskimo) fashioned furs to keep their bodies snugly warm from frigid winter temperatures. The many examples of indigenous people across the two continents often called Indians (also known as Native Americans or Native Peoples, depending on government policy and idiomatic expressions) had traditions that stemmed from various weaving and embroidery practices in Central and South America. Many weaving traditions continue from earlier times that first set apart the garments of indigenous people from the Spaniards and Portuguese who encroached upon their land and wore European-types of clothing. In such cases, it is tempting to call only the indigenous examples "ethnic dress," yet the Argentine gaucho ensemble that arose from the work traditions of Argentinean cowboys can equally be called ethnic.

See also **Caftan; Clothing, Costume, and Dress; Dashiki; Jilbab; Kente; Qipao; Sari; Sarong.**

BIBLIOGRAPHY

Baizerman, S., J. B. Eicher, and C. Cerny. "Eurocentrism in the Study of Ethnic Dress." *Dress* 20 (1993): 19–32.

Barnes, R., and J. B. Eicher, eds. *Dress and Gender: Making and Meaning in Cultural Context.* Oxford and Providence, R.I.: Berg, 1992.

Boulanger, C. *Saris: An Illustrated Guide to the Indian Art of Draping.* New York: Shakti Press, 1997.

Chapman, Malcolm. "Freezing the Frame: Dress and Ethnicity in Brittany and Gaelic Scotland." In *Dress and Ethnicity: Change across Space and Time.* Edited by J. B. Eicher. Oxford and Washington, D.C.: Berg, 1995.

Eicher, J. B., ed. *Dress and Ethnicity: Change across Space and Time.* Oxford and Washington, D.C.: Berg, 1995.

Hansen, Karen Tranberg. *The World of Secondhand Clothing and Zambia.* Chicago: University of Chicago Press, 2000.

Hobsbawn, E., and T. Ranger, eds. *The Invention of Tradition.* Cambridge, U.K.: Cambridge University Press, 1983.

Kennet, F. *World Dress.* New York: Checkmark Books, 1995.

Tarlo, E. *Clothing Matters: Dress and Identity in India.* Chicago: University of Chicago Press, 1996.

Van der Plas, Els, and Marlous Willemsen, eds. *The Art of African Fashion.* Trenton, N.J., and Asmara, Eritrea: Africa World Press, 1998.

Welters, L., ed. *Folk Dress in Europe and Anatolia.* Oxford and New York: Berg, 1999.

Joanne B. Eicher

ETHNIC STYLE IN FASHION During the 1990s and the first years of the new millennium, ethnic style has been one of the strongest influences in fashion. Designers such as Christian Lacroix, Dries van Noten, John Galliano, Kenzo, Vivienne Tam, Yeohlee and many others have taken their inspiration from a variety of Asian, African, Arctic, Native American and several other dress forms and aesthetic styles and created colorful, syncretic styles evocative of the past or faraway lands. They have also found sources for ethnic fashion within the West, for example in the folk traditions of Northern and Eastern Europe. The fantasy element is strong in ethnic fashion; even when based on detailed research, designs are typically given a twist so they appear contemporary.

For many Western designers, non-Western aesthetics have provided a fertile subject matter, which has enabled them to develop creatively. This ability to break conventions is associated with a way of seeing, rather than faithful adherence to any particular ethnic style. The overall eclecticism of ethnic fashion is expressed, for example, by Dries van Noten, as noted in *Touches d'exotisme, xive–xxe siècles*:

> For me, exoticism is the elsewhere, the other, the difference. It is generally associated with distant countries. But for me, it is rather everything that reroutes us from the ordinary . . . from our habits, our certainties and from the everyday to plunge us into a world that is amazing, hospitable and warm. (p. 203)

Fashion theory has been informed by the distinction between fashion—modern, changeable, and emanating from Western urban centers—and ethnic clothing—stable, oriented toward tradition, and belonging in the periphery. This distinction has not always been precise; however, it has had a profound influence on how society thinks about fashion. Many accounts of ethnic fashion thus tend to overemphasize the original reworking of exotic designs on the part of Western creators, just as they exaggerate the fixity of non-Western dress. In this respect, the ongoing impact of ethnic styles on Western fashion has been marginalized.

Historically, luxury has been associated with foreign origins. It is therefore impossible to date the starting point of ethnic style in Western consumption modes; in ancient times, novel and sumptuous goods arrived through trade routes from Persia, Egypt, and Central Asia, and later from India, China, Japan, Colombia, Mexico, and elsewhere. Designs and production methods of these imports were imitated, and whole industries—such as Italian and French silk production—were founded to cater for what had initially been a demand for exoticism. The taste for the foreign was also evident in the initial popularity of the cashmere shawl as a fashion item among European and American women from 1800 to 1870. Materials such as silk and cashmere are now fully naturalized in Western fashion, but from time to time their foreign origins are rearticulated in the context of ethnic fashion, for example in the recent trend for *luxe povera*.

Looking at clothes design in a stricter sense, ethnic styles were an important element in the intense experimentation with female dress in the first decades of the twentieth century. Paul Poiret adapted the lines and silhouette of the Japanese kimono to contemporary dresses, and a few years later, he picked Middle Eastern inspiration to a sultan-and-harem mode of loose garments and bold color combinations. Mariano Fortuny combined inspiration from contemporary Middle Eastern clothing and European art, especially Italian renaissance, in pleated dresses that follow the lines of the body. His artistic dresses connote both timelessness—they are not made for special occasions or age brackets and are beyond the seasonal changes of fashion—and femininity that comes "from within," in the sense that it is less formal and less manifestly visible than the conventional gender code.

The second wave of ethnic fashion came in the late 1960s with such representatives in haute couture as Yves Saint Laurent, Kenzo, and Sonia Rykiel. Also in this period, ethnic style was associated with transcendence of conventions, thereby allowing perceived deeper sensual qualities to be expressed. The philosopher Hélène Cixous said about a jacket by Sonia Rykiel, and by implication about ethnic fashion as such: "A garment which is not a noisy manifestation of the street, but a fine manifestation of the world" (p. 97). She adds, "The dress doesn't separate the inside from the outside, it translates, sheltering" (p. 98).

In the 1960s and 1970s, ethnic style provided a rich field for fashion without designers: Palestinian scarves, Latin American skirts, Indonesian batik sarongs, Moroccan djellabas, Chinese jackets, rattan baskets, embroidered purses, leather sandals, and tribal jewelry, bought either in special third-world import stores or on long-distance travels, were worn in combination with ordinary clothes. Ethnic style thus became a highly personal as well as cosmopolitan way of dressing, sometimes associated with a political attitude.

An important issue is the position of non-Western fashion designers. When Japanese avant-garde designers, including Issey Miyake, Yohji Yamamoto, and Rei Kawakubo (of Comme des Garçons), presented the most sought-after collections in Paris in the 1980s, the international fashion press wrote them off as a mere exotic—in the pejorative sense of passing—influence. There was a tendency to interpret their designs in the light of traditional Japanese aesthetics, rather than acknowledge them as innovative designers working with a minimalism that self-consciously fused elements of East and West with very few overt ethnic references. In this respect, the Western fashion world has pushed non-Western designers towards self-exoticization. While some Asian fashion designers find it stimulating to apply their creative skills to their cultural backgrounds, others experience the demand for exoticization as devaluation of their talents and skills in the highly globalized fashion business.

In some markets, especially in the United States, there has been considerable recognition of non-Western designers; however, they have tended to remain identified with a particular ethnic style as aesthetic exponents of multiculturalism. A key example is Vivienne Tam: born in China, educated in Hong Kong, resident of New York City in the early 2000s. She incorporates Chinese motifs in her designs, but highly eclectically, so that her clothes have included both Buddhist and Maoist imagery. In contrast to Western designers, whose engagement with ethnic styles tends to be superficial, Tam's consistent work with Chinese aesthetics has led to a deep involvement with cultural tradition, including spiritualism, architecture, medicine, art, and performance.

There are also minority niche markets where diaspora women in the West find their *salwar-kameez*, the so-called Punjabi suit, or their Vietnamese *ao dai*. These markets are typically operated by women entrepreneurs without any formal training in fashion design. They tend to keep in touch with the styles current in the homeland; however, this does not stop them from influencing dynamics of fashion in the West, as was the case with the Punjabi suit in the late 1990s.

Ethnic style in fashion is an important, yet somewhat neglected, area of fashion studies. As fashion continues adjusting to the multicultural condition, both within each Western nation and at the transnational level, ethnic style provides a particularly rich and diverse field of study—one that is likely to produce major future developments in fashion theory.

See also **Fads; Folklore Look; Galliano, John; Miyake, Issey; Saint Laurent, Yves; Yamamoto, Yohji.**

BIBLIOGRAPHY

Bhachu, Parminder. "Designing Diasporic Markets: Asian Fashion Entrepreneurs in London." In *Re-Orientating Fashion: The Globalisation of Asian Dress*. Edited by Sandra Niessen, Ann Marie Leshkowich, and Carla Jones. London: Berg, 2003.

Cixous, Hélène. "Sonia Rykiel in Translation." In *On Fashion*. Edited by Shari Benstock and Suzanne Ferriss. New Brunswick, N.J.: Rutgers University Press, 1994.

Kondo, Dorinne. *About Face: Performing Race in Fashion and Theatre*. New York: Routledge, 1997.

Legrand-Rossi, Sylvie, et al. *Touches d'exotisme, xive–xxe siècles*. Union centrale des arts decoratifs. Paris: Musée de la mode et du textile, 1998.

Leshkowich, Ann Marie. "The *Ao Dai* Goes Global: How International Influences and Female Entrepreneurs Have Shaped Vietnam's 'National Costume.'" In *Re-Orientating Fashion*. Edited by Sandra Niessen, Ann Marie Leshkowich, and Carla Jones. London: Berg, 2003.

Skov, Lise. "Fashion-Nation: A Japanese Globalization Experience and a Hong Kong Dilemma." In *Re-Orientating Fashion*. Edited by Sandra Niessen, Ann Marie Leshkowich, and Carla Jones. London: Berg, 2003.

Steele, Valerie, and John Major. *China Chic: East Meets West*. New Haven, Conn.: Yale University Press, 1999.

Tam, Vivienne, with Martha Huang. *China Chic*. New York: Regan Books, 2000.

Lise Skov

EUROPE AND AMERICA: HISTORY OF DRESS (400–1900 C.E.) For historians, the naming in 395 C.E. of two consuls, or emperors—one for the Eastern and one for the Western parts of Europe—marks the end of the Roman Empire. As the Western empire gradually fell under barbarian control, the empire in the East (its capital in Constantinople) flourished. Dress in Byzantium was an amalgam of Roman and Eastern styles. From the East came elaborate ornaments, decorative motifs, and textiles—especially those of silk. The result was extensive use of embroidery, appliqué, precious stones, or woven designs added to the long or short tunics and some of the draped outer garments characteristic of Roman dress.

As the major cultural center, these styles of the Byzantine court influenced all the courts of Western Europe from about 400 to 900 C.E. It was not until after the tenth century that a European economic recovery began, making Byzantine influences somewhat less important.

Dress in the Early Middle Ages

The period from 400 to 900 C.E. in Western Europe is known as the Dark Ages. As the name implies, the picture of cultural developments over this period is somewhat obscure. Clear images of dress are few. Apparently dress in Europe combined Roman forms with those of the barbarians. Men wore long or short tunics with a sort of trousers that were gaitered (wrapped close to the leg) with strips of cloth or leather. Women wore an under tunic and an outer tunic covered by a cape, or mantle. Married women covered their hair with a veil. Among royalty and the upper classes, Byzantine influences were most evident in the use of silk fabrics, manufactured in Byzantium and imported, and in ornamental bands that trimmed sleeves, necklines, hemlines, and other areas of tunics.

The basics of dress remained fairly constant in the eleventh and twelfth centuries of the Middle Ages for both men and women. Next to his body a man typically wore *braies*, an undergarment similar to underpants, and a shirt. A woman wore a loose-fitting undergarment called a chemise. Undergarments were made of linen. Outer garments for both men and women consisted of an under tunic and an outer tunic. These were most likely made of wool. For important occasions, royalty might wear silk. Men of higher status who did not need to be physically active wore longer tunics. The under tunic often was of a contrasting color or fabric and showed at the hem, the neckline, and the end of the sleeves. Art shows both solid and figured fabrics, although solid colors predominate.

Medieval bridal procession. An illustration from the tale *L'histoire de Renaud de Montauban* depicts the types of clothing worn by the upper class in the late fifteenth century. © Bibliothèque Nationale de France. Reproduced by permission.

Twelfth-Century Changes in Dress

By the twelfth century, artistic and literary evidence indicates that significant changes in political, economic, technological, and social life had begun to affect clothing. After the Roman government of Europe broke down, local rulers administered smaller or larger areas. Charlemagne (768–814), one of the kings of a Germanic tribe called the Franks, came to exercise significant power over much of Western Europe and was crowned emperor by the pope in Rome in 800 C.E. This empire did not long survive Charlemagne.

A feudal society developed in which local lords granted land (fiefs) to subjects who, in turn, provided loyalty, payment, and military support to the lord. These lords or kings built castles where large numbers of people lived and worked. Such centers provided a stage for the display of status, which was often expressed through dress.

As the European economy prospered and courts expanded, the Christian church served as a unifying force with its central authority, the pope, in Rome and local bishops in important cities and towns. When the pope called on the many feudal lords and their soldiers to liberate the Holy Lands from the Muslims, who had taken control of that region, thousands responded. Their reasons for joining the Crusades ranged from genuine religious fervor to opportunities for looting and pillaging. The impact on dress was significant. The crusaders, who continued their warfare for almost 200 years, brought back new fabrics, design motifs, and clothing styles that were adapted for European dress. At the same time, civilian dress incorporated elements of military dress.

While the Crusades increased trade and communication with the Middle East, European traders were rekindling trade with the Far East as well. Marco Polo

(c. 1254–1324) wrote of his adventures as a trader in a book that helped to encourage commerce with the Far East.

In decline over the post-Roman period, urban centers once again became the hubs of production and trade after the feudal period. Technological advances in the production of textiles such as water-powered fulling (finishing) of wool, a horizontal loom at which the worker could sit and use foot treadles and a shuttle, and a spinning wheel that replaced the hand spindle all served to increase the capacity of the growing textile industry. Craftsmen formed guilds that set standards and pay rates. Trade opportunities expanded, and wealth extended beyond the courts and royalty to this newly affluent merchant class.

The Beginnings of Fashion

Though the precise origins of fashion change in dress are still debated by costume historians, it is generally agreed that the phenomenon of a large number of people accepting a style for a relatively short period of time began during the Middle Ages. The aforementioned social and economic changes established the necessary conditions for fashion. Textile manufacturing advances provided the raw materials needed for increased production and consumption of clothing. The courts provided a stage for display of fashions. Social stratification was becoming less rigid, making it possible for one social class to imitate another. Increased trade and travel spread information about styles from one area to another.

Evidence of the international spread of information about style change can be found in developments in the arts. Architectural styles changed radically after circa 1150 when buildings in the Romanesque style gave way throughout Europe to the newer Gothic forms. Both used carvings as ornamentation and to tell biblical stories. These, along with the images portrayed in stained-glass windows, have served as a major source for information about dress. Manuscript illumination also began to show more lay figures dressed in contemporary costume.

These statues and drawings of the twelfth century show alterations in fit that clearly resulted from changes in the cut of clothes. Instead of being loose tunics, garments followed the lines of the body closely from shoulder to below the waist where a fuller skirt was sewn to the upper bodice. Sleeve styles varied. Some outer tunic sleeves were shorter in order to show more of the under tunic sleeve. Some were wide, and some were so elongated that they had to be knotted to keep from dragging on the ground.

French writers of the period called elaborate versions of these fitted styles *bliauts*. The garment is described as being made of expensive silk fabrics. Its appearance indicates that the fabric was probably manipulated using bias (diagonal pieces with greater stretch) insets to assure a close fit and that elaborate pleats were used in the skirt. Clearly advances were being made in clothing construction.

Chainse, another French term, seems to refer to a pleated garment that was probably made from lightweight linen and may have been worn alone as a sort of housedress by women (Goddard 1927). Some versions of these garments seem to have closed by lacing, which allowed a closer fit.

Dress in the Middle Ages: 1200–1400

With the increased variety of dressing styles, terminology for items of clothing in these early periods grows more complicated and confusing. Names for garments often come directly from French. Frequently English-speaking costume historians adopt these French terms. This is especially evident when costume historians write about medieval styles of the thirteenth century and after. From this time on, the under tunic was usually called a *cote*; the outer tunic, a *surcote*, a word that has gained English usage.

The layering remained the same as in earlier centuries and undergarments did not change radically, but the cut and fit of outer garments has started to alter with greater frequency. Also, a number of new outdoor garments appeared. These included the *garnache*, "a long cloak with capelike sleeves," the *herigaut* or *gardecorps*, "a cloak with long, wide sleeves having a slit below the shoulder through which the arm could be slipped," and the chaperon, "a hood cut and sewn to a chape" [cape] (Tortora and Eubank 1998).

The influence of important individuals on style is evident. The reign (1226–1270) of the pious King Louis IX of France coincided with a turn toward looser fitting, more modest, and less ostentatious dress.

Around the middle of the fourteenth century, a wider range of types of dress appeared. At the same time, dress for men and women started to diverge, length of skirt being a major difference. Men of all classes now wore short skirts. One important short-skirted garment was the *cotehardie*. The exact features of this garment seem to have varied from country to country, and it was probably a variant of the surcote. The Cunningtons, writing about English costume, define the term as a garment with a front-buttoned, low-waisted, fitted bodice with fitted sleeves that ended at the elbow in front and had a hanging flap at the back, with the bodice attaching to a short skirt (1952).

Under this garment, men wore a garment variously called a pourpoint, *gipon*, or doublet. In commenting on problems of terminology, Newton observes, "It is doubtful whether at any one time the exact differences between an aketon, a pourpoint, a doublet, a courtpiece, and a jupon were absolutely defined. In France the cotehardie comes into this category, and in England, from the early 1360s, the paltok" (1980). Probably adopted for civilian wear from a padded military garment, the pourpoint (later more likely to be called a doublet) attached to hose with laces that had sharp metal tips known as "points."

***Maria Leczinska, Queen of France,* by Louis Tocque, oil on canvas, 1740.** Skirts worn by the upper echelons of French society in the eighteenth century were up to eight feet wide. The skirt's broadness was created by hoops near the hem or padding at the hip. REUNION DES MUSEES NATIONAUX/ART RESOURCE, NY. REPRODUCED BY PERMISSION.

This combination might be worn alone or under an outer garment. Hose were worn either with shoes or boots or had leather soles and required no shoes. Shoes often had very long, pointed toes and were called *poulaines* or *crack-owes*, which may testify to a possible origin in Poland. Upper-class men wore the most extreme of these styles and thereby showed that they did not need to do any hard labor.

The *houppelande* was another important garment that appeared about 1360. Made in either thigh or mid-calf length or long, it was fitted over the shoulders, then fell in deep, tubular folds and was belted at the waist. Sleeves could be quite elaborate, sometimes long and full and gathered in at the wrist or widening at the end and falling to the floor. Fur trim was common.

Although women were wearing *houppelandes* by the end of the fourteenth century, they were more common in the fifteenth century. Other styles for women included close-fitting gowns, sometimes with either sleeved or sleeveless surcotes. Certain garments were visual statements of status. French queens and princesses wore surcotes cut low at the neck, with enormous armhole openings through which a fitted gown could be seen, and a hip-length stiffened panel with a row of jeweled brooches down the front. A full skirt was attached to the panel.

The imposition of sumptuary laws (limits placed on spending for luxury goods) on dress indicate that the elite classes feared that the lower classes were attempting to usurp their status symbols. Fashionable dress had become affordable to more people, and legislators attempted to restrict by rank the types of fur used, the types and quantities of fabric, kinds of trimmings, and even the length of the points of shoes. These laws were not obeyed and rarely enforced.

During the fifteenth century, styles continually evolved. Men's doublets grew shorter and hose longer, looking much like modern tights. A new construction feature, the codpiece—a pouch of fabric closed with laces—allowed room for the genitals. *Houppelandes* underwent some changes in style and construction, becoming more elaborate in trimming and sleeve construction. A short, broad-shouldered garment, sometimes called a jacket, had an attached skirt that flared out from the waist.

Women wore *houppelandes* and fitted gowns. One style appears so often in art that it has become almost a stereotype for modern illustrators who want to show medieval princesses. This gown had fitted sleeves, a deep V-neck with a modesty piece filling in the V, a slightly high waistline with a wide belt, and a long, trained skirt. Another style seen in Northern European art is a loose-fitting gown with close-fitting sleeves, a round neckline, and fullness falling from gathers at the center front. Some sources call this gown a roc.

Accessories. In the earlier centuries, medieval head coverings were relatively simple: veils that covered their hair for adult women and hoods or small caps like modern baby bonnets, called coifs, that tied under the chin for men. By the fifteenth century, upper-class men and women were wearing many fanciful styles. Men's hoods were wrapped turbanlike around the head, sometimes made with wide, padded brims. The prevalence of turbans may reflect contacts with the Orient. Hats with high crowns and with small brims resembled a loaf of sugar and were called sugar loaf hats. Adult women's hair was still covered, but coverings were often of decorative net fabrics, padded rolls, or tall, flat or pointed, structures. Lightweight, sheer veils were often attached.

Other accessories included purses, belts, and jewelry. Belts were often a mark of status, being highly ornamented and jeweled.

Dress in the Italian Renaissance: 1400–1600

In Italy circa 1400, scholars turned to the literature and philosophy of ancient Greece and Rome as a source of ideas about their world. Historians examining this period assigned the name "Renaissance" (French for "rebirth") to this time when a new focus on humanism contrasted with the medieval emphasis on spirituality.

These ideas spread from Italy to Northern Europe, influencing scholars and creative artists. The artists created realistic portraits and scenes of daily life and showed clear views of dress even to the point of showing where the seams were located. They faithfully depicted the lush velvets, satins, and brocades worn by their sitters.

Royalty wore the most lavish garments, but the well-to-do merchant classes could easily imitate court styles. Intermarriage among the rulers of European countries provided one means of spreading fashions from one country to another as royal brides and grooms dressed themselves and their retinues in the latest styles from their home country.

By the sixteenth century, the recently developed printing press was turning out books that purported to show clothing styles in different parts of the world. Such books, which are of some use to costume historians, require careful evaluation because many of the styles depicted are imaginary and contain both realistic and inaccurate representations.

Predominant styles. Styles worn in Italy in the early fifteenth century showed some similarities to those of Northern Europe in the thirteenth through fifteenth centuries. At the same time, with the proximity of Italy to the Middle East, Asian influences are evident in fabrics with Eastern design motifs, in clothing showing some similarities to Turkish robes, and in headwear in turbanlike forms. Part of the differences in styles came from the Italian failure to adopt northern styles such as the extreme pointed-toed shoes and the V-necked, high-waisted women's gown. Silhouettes of women's gowns were wider than those in the north. Necklines were low.

Bodices were attached to gathered skirts. Many gowns and men's doublets or jackets were made of figured velvets, brocades, and damasks produced by skilled Italian weavers. Small puffs of fabric of contrasting color were pulled through the elbow, armhole, and some seam lines.

This decorative idea became a feature of men's styles all over Europe in the early years of the 1500s. The exterior fabric was slashed and puffs of contrasting color pulled through the slits to make elaborate decorations. The silhouette for men grew wide and full.

Italians styles remained somewhat different from those of the north until the later 1500s when Spain, France, and Austria came to dominate the Italian city-states. By the sixteenth century, international events helped to move Spanish styles to the center of the fashion stage. Christopher Columbus's voyage to America in 1492 made Spain, which had financed the trip, rich. When Charles V became not only king of Spain but also ruler of the Low Countries and what has become Germany, Spanish influences spread throughout Europe. Dark, rich textiles were made into women's garments with fairly rigid, hourglass-shaped silhouettes. A stiff, hooplike structure held out skirts. Handsome black-on-white embroideries ornamented collars and undergarments. By the latter years of the century, the conservative, narrower, more rigid lines of Spanish origin also predominated for men.

Portraits and inventories of clothing provide an excellent picture of the dress of the colorful monarchs of England, Henry VIII and Elizabeth I, as well as that of the rulers of France and Spain. The evolution of men's shoulder shapes from broad at the beginning of the century to narrower, and of women's skirts from inverted cone shapes to barrel-like forms (called farthingales) is clear evidence of fashion as an integral part of dress. Narrow white frills at the neck grew wider, rounder, and still wider to become huge, stiff, starched, lace ruffs, which in the sixteenth century eventually subsided into wide, flat collars.

Dress in the Baroque and Rococo Period: 1600–1700

The styles in the fine arts from about the end of the sixteenth century to the first several decades of the eighteenth century is called baroque. Elements characteristic of baroque styles include extensive ornamentation, curved forms, and freely flowing lines, all in relatively large scale. The dress of the period clearly reflected these tendencies. Those who could afford to wear fashionable dress did so. The courts remained the most important stage on which to display opulent clothing. It has been said that Louis XIV (king of France from 1643 to 1715) used fashionable dress as a political tool, keeping his courtiers so busy following court etiquette and style that they had neither the funds nor the time to plot against him.

Clothing also played a political role in England. The royalist supporters of the King opposed the Puritan fac-

Eighteenth-century suit. During the reign of King Charles II, the three-piece suit, which consisted of knee breeches, a vest, and a jacket, became the standard dress for men. THE METROPOLITAN MUSEUM OF ART, PURCHASE, IRENE LEWISOHN BEQUEST AND POLAIRE WEISSMAN FUND, 1996. (1996.117A-C) PHOTOGRAPH, ALL RIGHTS RESERVED, THE METROPOLITAN MUSEUM OF ART. REPRODUCED BY PERMISISON.

tion. The Puritans wanted to reform the Church of England and stress a simpler, more moralistic, and less lavish lifestyle. The resulting civil war led to the defeat and execution of King Charles I, after which a Commonwealth replaced the monarchy for about eighteen years. The Puritans dressed in more somber styles with little ornamentation. Their "Roundheads" nickname came from the short hairstyles they adopted. Portraits, inventories, and other written records show that although the Puritans stressed simplicity, their clothing followed fashionable lines. Among the affluent Puritans, high-quality, expensive fabrics were in use.

The Pilgrims who settled in Massachusetts in 1620 were Puritans. The dress styles of the American colonists of the seventeenth and eighteenth centuries lagged behind those of Europe, but were otherwise the same. Only the trappers and explorers appear to have adapted some of the more practical elements of Native American dress such as moccasins; almost nothing made its way back across the Atlantic. Native Americans were depicted by portrait painters in garb usually containing European elements, whereas the dress of early American colonists is virtually indistinguishable from dress in Europe.

By contrast, trade with the Far East had a significant impact on fashion. These influences can be seen in the fabrics imported from India, China, and Japan and in some specific garments. The vest adopted by Charles II of England is one example of Eastern influences. The prototype of the vest may have been Persian men's coats (Kuchta 1990).

When the English monarchy was restored, Charles II (son of the executed Charles I) returned from exile in France under the protection of Louis XIV, and Puritan dress modifications were eclipsed by French influences and the court once again became the arbiter of style. One noteworthy item of dress adopted by King Charles II was the vest, the forerunner of what became a virtual uniform for men in the eighteenth century and later: the three-piece suit. Its seventeenth-century style consisted of knee-length breeches, a long, buttoned vest that reached just below the knee and covered the breeches, and a jacket of the same length over this.

The Puritans were not the only seventeenth-century group to deviate from contemporary styles. The conservative nature of Spanish society was probably responsible for the preservation of older styles and a slower adoption of new ones. The wide-skirted farthingale of the sixteenth century disappeared in the rest of Europe in the early seventeenth century. Spanish upper-class women adopted this style in the mid-1600s. The Spanish *guardinfante* (literally, "infant guard") consisted of an oval farthingale, very wide from side to side, worn with a bodice that extended far below the waistline to cover the top of the skirt. As Reade noted, "Since exertion was difficult for anyone wearing it, the vogue emphasized social distinctions" (1951). Spanish men continued wearing the ruff and trunk hose longer than men elsewhere in Europe. By the eighteenth century, the Spanish dressed in mainstream fashion.

How individuals acquired clothing differed depending on social status. Less affluent families bought used clothing or produced their own clothing, mostly by having women of the family make the clothes. Those sufficiently affluent hired professional tailors. Although most professional tailors were men, women did the fine hand and ornamental sewing. In 1675, responding to a petition from a group of French women seamstresses that they be allowed to make women's clothes, Louis XIV permitted the formation of a guild of women tailors. Over time, using female dressmakers to make women's clothes and male tailors to make men's suits became customary.

Some economists consider the economic changes that took place in England in the late seventeenth and eighteenth centuries a consumer revolution. Consumer interest in less costly imported cottons from India led businesses to stimulate demand for fashionable goods in order to increase their profits. To accomplish this, they needed to provide information about current fashions to potential customers. Engraved, sometimes hand-colored, pictures of the latest fashions were sold. Dolls dressed in the latest styles were circulated, and by the late eighteenth century, paper dolls showing current styles were also available. Styles were given names, and fashion terminology increased exponentially.

As the demand for fashionable goods grew, more fibers, yarns, and fabrics were needed. Such requirements helped to fuel the industrial revolution and its mechanization of production. Consumer demand for cotton led to increased settlement in the colonies of the New World and to the use of slaves to cultivate and harvest the fiber. As supplies of cotton increased, invention of the cotton gin met the need to process more fiber. Inventors improved machines for spinning and weaving. Mass production of fabric made inexpensive fabrics available. As a result, by the end of the eighteenth century, following fashion was possible for all but the very poor and slaves.

The name "rococo" has been assigned to the subtle changes in the art and dress styles of the period from about 1720 to 1770. Rococo styles are characterized by smaller scale but still curvilinear lines; more delicate ornamentation; and Asian, Gothic, and floral motifs. After 1770, the arts and architecture experienced a classical revival. These neoclassical influences came into clothing styles gradually and were accepted as the prevailing mode only toward the close of the century.

The three-piece suit became the predominant component of men's clothing. Throughout the eighteenth century, men wore knee breeches, a vest, and an outer coat. When coat, vest, and breeches were made of the same fabric, the outfit was called a "ditto suit." The length of the vest, and the cut of both the vest and coat, varied over time. Early in the century, coats and vests were wide and full. When the coat was buttoned, it hid the vest. By midcentury, the coat was slimmer. So was the vest, which also shortened. The coat no longer buttoned shut, but remained open and the vest and breeches were visible. For formal wear, coats and vests were elaborately embroidered or made of very decorative fabric. A frock coat was looser and shorter than coats for more formal occasions. Early in the century, frock coats were worn in the country, but gradually they were also deemed proper for more formal wear.

The silhouettes and the ornate woven, embroidered, or printed designs of the fabrics from which upper-class women's dresses were made in the 1700s reflected the curvilinear forms of baroque and rococo arts. The shape of skirts changed gradually. After the early eighteenth century, when loose, full sacque gowns were popular, the silhouette altered and bodices fitted the front of the body closely. Necklines were low, square, or round. In back some dresses were fitted, while others had full pleats at center back that opened into a loose, flowing skirt. Costume historians of the nineteenth century called this style a "Watteau back" after Jean-Antoine Watteau, an eighteenth-century artist, who frequently painted women in this style of dress.

Skirts were held out by supporting hoops (called *paniers* in France) that were first cone-shaped, then dome-shaped, next narrow from front to back and wide from side-to-side. By the period from 1740 to 1760, skirts were enormously wide (as much as 2 ¾ yards). Double doors helped to accommodate the passage of women in these *panier*-supported dresses, and small tables often had raised edges to prevent objects from being swept from them by a passing skirt. After the 1760s, *paniers* were replaced by cushions or pads worn at the hip, and the fullness of skirts moved toward the back.

Hints of the classical revival in the arts could be seen in the dress of small girls, who wore high-waisted, slender white muslin dresses reminiscent of Greek Doric chitons. Women, too, began to wear white muslin dresses and moved away gradually from the full-skirted silhouette, but the adoption of styles closely modeled on Greek and Roman women's dresses came only after the French Revolution (1789–1795).

The French Revolution and the Empire Style

Costume is said to reflect the zeitgeist, or "spirit of the age," and fashions of the late eighteenth and early nineteenth centuries are frequently cited to illustrate this point. Political developments in France were to a considerable extent inspired by the examples of the ancient Greek and Roman republics. As previously noted, classical influences were already evident in architecture, and the fine and decorative arts. By the last decade of the eighteenth century, they permeated women's dress as well.

Because the marble statues of antiquity had been bleached white over time, it was believed that the Greeks and Romans had worn white garments. The high-waisted styles of Hellenic Greek Doric chitons served as the model for slender, white muslin dresses with high waistlines. Fashionable women wore classically inspired sandals. Men cut their hair in "Titus style" (named after a Roman emperor). Women dressed their hair *à la Greque*. Although specific details changed year-by-year, the high-waisted dresses were the basis of a fashionable silhouette that was to persist for more than two decades.

Dress in the Nineteenth Century

Many cultural forces contributed to the stylistic changes of the nineteenth century. These included the industrial revolution, the French Revolution, changes in women's roles, changes in the political climate, the expansion of the United States, and artistic movements.

The industrial revolution produced not only technological but also social and economic changes that affected dress. The ability to produce textiles rapidly and less expensively facilitated participation in fashion. As industrialization brought more women into the workforce, giving them less time to make clothing for their families, by the end of the century, some garments were being mass-produced. Rural workers who migrated to urban areas needed different kinds of clothes.

As the United States expanded, it gradually took on a more important role in the Western world as a producer of raw materials and manufacturer of goods. Technological innovations and refinements made in the United States such as the patenting and distribution of the first commercially successful sewing machine, the development of the sized-paper pattern, and the invention of machines that could cut multiple pattern pieces contributed to the growth of mass fashion. Immigration brought skilled workers to work in the mass production of clothing, and immigrant consumers expanded the market for inexpensive ready-to-wear.

Although ready-to-wear fashion came later to Europe than to the United States, Europe remained the center of innovation in fashions. British tailoring set the international standard for menswear. And the beginnings of the haute couture in Paris at midcentury confirmed the preeminent place of Paris in women's fashion.

Charles Worth is considered to have been the father of the haute couture. He first came to public notice around 1860 when the French empress Eugénie began wearing clothes he had designed. His atelier was soon known around the world, and women from Queen Victoria to Parisian courtesans were dressed by Worth. Worth was instrumental in founding an organization of French couturiers, the Chambre Syndicale de la Couture Parisienne, in 1868 that regulated the French high-fashion industry.

Political events on both sides of the Atlantic also influenced dress. For example, the restoration of the French monarchy spawned a host of fashions named after earlier royals and the Italian revolutionary leader Giuseppe Garibaldi inspired women to wear red blouses like those of his soldiers.

The nineteenth-century movement of Europe and America toward more egalitarian societies contributed to an overall revolution in men's dress. The lavishly decorated eighteenth-century suits with knee breeches worn by the nobility were, henceforth, replaced by dark, trousered, three-piece suits. The skill of its tailoring and quality of the fabric in these suits attested to the status of the wearer.

Through its ornamentation and obvious cost, women's clothing had to bear the burden of attesting to the wealth and social standing of the family. Thorsten Veblen (1857–1929) recognized this role for women in his classic study, *Theory of the Leisure Classes*. He noted that upper-class women's clothing showed that their husbands or fathers could afford to spend lavishly on elaborate clothing (conspicuous consumption) and, furthermore, these women could not do any menial labor when encumbered by such dresses (conspicuous leisure) (Veblen 1936).

At the same time, some women were beginning to question the roles assigned to them in nineteenth-century society. After the accession of Queen Victoria to the throne of England in 1837, the ideal Victorian matron was wife and mother of a large family who ran the household smoothly, supervised the servants, and led a sedate, scandal-free life. The example set by abolitionists working to free the slaves at the time of the American Civil War led some women to state that they, too, were held in a type of bondage. Some women active in the women's suffrage movement believed that women's clothing was a severe handicap to freedom of movement and physical activity. Attempts to reform dress and establish more rational styles for women such as the Bloomer costume were not especially successful at first. The Bloomer costume (named after women's-rights author and lecturer Amelia Bloomer, one of its more visible proponents) consisted of a shorter version of the full-skirted dress of the 1840s worn over a pair of full trousers gathered in to fit tightly at the ankle. The style was based on the dress worn by women in European health sanitariums (Foote 1980). Though abandoned by suffragettes after a few years, photographs show that the style was adopted by some American women settlers for the westward trek and the rigors of pioneer life. Variations of the style also showed up in gymnastics classes for young women, evidence of increased importance given to women's health and fitness.

By the 1890s, women were participating actively in many sports. Bicycling was especially popular and special dress, including bloomer suits called rationals and split skirts, had been adopted.

Throughout history, connections between the fine arts and dress can be found. In the nineteenth century, the pre-Raphaelites and participants in the aesthetic movement made conscious efforts to apply their philosophies to dress. In rejecting contemporary art forms, the pre-Raphaelites drew their inspiration from the art of the Middle Ages and the Renaissance. The artists painted women in idealized costumes from these earlier periods, and women of the group began to wear styles based on the paintings while rejecting the tight corseting and wide skirts of the 1840s and 1850s. In the 1880s and 1890s, the ideas of the small pre-Raphaelite group inspired followers of the more popular aesthetic movement. Women wore no corsets, few or no petticoats, and large

leg-of-mutton sleeves. Oscar Wilde, British writer, lectured about aestheticism in a softly-fitted velvet jacket and knee breeches worn with a wide, soft collar and loose necktie. While this costume was worn in protest, the protest was against the aesthetics of the time and not against the inconvenient and unhealthy aspects of dress to which feminists and health reformers objected.

Means of spreading information about current styles expanded. Magazines for women incorporated hand-colored, engraved fashion plates, making it possible for women of all socioeconomic levels to see styles from Paris and keep abreast of current fashion each month. Full-sized paper patterns were bound into some magazines in the late 1800s. The invention of photography in the 1840s provided another way of spreading style information.

Silhouette and style changes. The nineteenth century was marked by increasingly rapid style changes. Costume historians recognize this by dividing the century into a number of relatively short fashion periods that cover ten to twenty years. These periods were characterized by an incremental evolution of fashions year-by-year that eventually added up to a distinct new style.

The more somber styles worn by men throughout the 1800s showed only relatively subtle changes. One can see parallels in the cut of men's suits and the silhouette of women's dresses. When women's sleeves were large, men's tended to be enlarged; when women's waists were narrow, tailors made men's jackets with nipped-in waistlines. But it was in women's clothing that the more pronounced changes in style were evident.

The Empire period (1790–1820) is named after Napoleon Bonaparte, the first Emperor of France. For women, the high-waisted, relatively narrow silhouette first seen in the late 1700s continued to be the predominant line throughout this period. In fashion terminology, this high waistline placement is still known as an "empire waist."

The expanded trade with the Far East and the military campaigns of Napoleon in Egypt fueled fashions with Asian links. Imported cashmere shawls were all the rage. Napoleon tried to ban the importation of these shawls in order to protect the French textile industry. Soon European mills were copying them. The output of the mills in the town of Paisley, Scotland, was so prodigious that the shawls became known as paisley shawls.

Year by year, subtle changes appeared in the Empire styles until the high waistline had moved lower, approaching the anatomical waist, the skirt had flared out, and sleeves had grown larger, eventually becoming enormous. By the 1820s, that line was distinctive enough for costume historians to see this as a new period that they named after the art and literary movements of the same time: the Romantic period (1820–1850).

Differences in style between the late Romantic and the later Crinoline period (1850–1870) were subtle. In some costume histories, the period from circa 1838 to 1870 is known as the early Victorian period, Victoria having acceded to the British throne in 1837. The most distinctive aspect of the silhouette of this period was the increasing width of the skirt, the return of the waistline to its natural anatomical position, and a dropped shoulder line. Until the invention of the cage crinoline, or hoopskirt, in the mid-1800s, skirts were held out by heavy layers of starched petticoats that were often reinforced with fabric stiffened with horsehair (*crin* is French for "horsehair," and *lin*, "linen," hence the name of the fabric: crinoline). The originator of the nineteenth-century hoopskirt is unknown. The basic structure was a series of horizontal hoops of whalebone or steel of gradually increasing size that were fastened to vertical tapes. Far lighter than the many layers of petticoats, the hoop was an immediate success.

The hoopskirt itself went through numerous transitions, being first round, and then gradually swinging its fullest areas to the back. As the back fullness increased, the front flattened, and by 1870, the bustle had taken over as the preferred shape.

The silhouette of the Bustle period (1870–1890) might be divided into three distinct phases. In the first phase (1869–1877) the fullness at the back of the dress was supported by a bustle. Bustles were structures equipped with some device to hold skirts out in the back. The skirt shape was flat in front with a full, draped fall of fabric and ornamentation down the back. Most sleeves were three-quarters length or longer and were set in at the shoulder instead of being dropped below the shoulder on the arm, as in the Crinoline period. Bodices were tightly fitted. In the second phase (1878–1883), the bustle itself disappeared, garments were fitted closely from neck to hip in what was called a cuirass bodice, below which the skirt remained tight at the front. The decoration of the skirt dropped to below the hips in back. Many skirts had long, ornamental trains. In the third phase (1883–1890), the bustle structure returned with a vengeance, looking like a shelf at the back of the dress. Dresses had high, tightly fitted collars and very close-fitted bodices.

By the final decade of the nineteenth century, the back fullness of the Bustle period had diminished to a few pleats. The silhouette was hourglass-shaped, with enormous leg-of-mutton sleeves balancing a full, cone-shaped skirt that was wide at the bottom. The ubiquitous high-standing collar remained, however.

BIBLIOGRAPHY

Baines, V. B. *Fashion Revivals from the Elizabethan Age to the Present Day.* London: B. T. Batsford, Ltd., 1981.

Boucher, E. *20,000 Years of Fashion.* London: Thames and Hudson, Inc., 1987.

Breward, C. *The Culture of Fashion: A New History of Fashionable Dress.* New York: St. Martin's Press, 1995.

Byrde, P. *The Male Image: Men's Fashion in England 1300–1970.* London: B. T. Batsford, Ltd., 1979.

Chenoune, F. *A History of Men's Fashion.* Paris: Flammarion, 1993.

Cunnington, C. W., P. E. Cunnington, and C. Beard. *A Dictionary of English Costume 900–1900.* London: Adam and Charles Black, 1972.

Davenport, M. *The Book of Costume.* 2 vols. New York: Crown, 1948.

DeMarly, D. *Fashion for Men: An Illustrated History.* New York: Holmes and Meier, 1985.

———. *Dress in North America.* New York: Holmes and Meier, 1990.

Tortora, P., and K. Eubank. *Survey of Historic Costume.* New York: Fairchild Publications, 1998.

Waugh, N. *The Cut of Men's Clothes, 1600–1900.* London: Faber and Faber, 1964.

———. *The Cut of Women's Clothes, 1600–1930.* New York: Theatre Arts Books, 1968.

Medieval Dress

Cunnington, C., and P. Cunnington. *Handbook of English Medieval Costume.* Northampton, U.K.: John Dickens, 1973.

Evans, J. *Dress in Medieval France.* Oxford: Clarendon, 1952.

Goddard, E. R. *Women's Costume in French Texts of the 11th and 12th Centuries.* New York: Johnson Reprints, 1973.

Newton, S. M. *Fashion in the Age of the Black Prince.* Totowa, N.J.: Rowan and Littlefield, 1980.

Piponnier, F., and P. Mane. *Dress in the Middle Ages.* New Haven, Conn.: Yale University Press, 1997.

Scott, M. *The History of Dress: Late Gothic Europe, 1400–1500.* New York: Humanities Press, 1980.

———. *Visual History of Costume: 14th and 15th Centuries.* London: B. T. Batsford, Ltd., 1986.

Renaissance Dress

Arnold, J., ed. *Lost from Her Majesty's Back.* Birdle, Bury, England: Costume Society, 1980.

Ashelford, J. *The Visual History of Costume: The 16th Century.* New York: Drama Book, 1983.

———. *Dress in the Age of Elizabeth I.* New York: Holmes and Meier, 1988.

Birbari, E. *Dress in Italian Paintings, 1460–1500.* London: John Murray, 1975.

Cunnington, C. W. *Handbook of English Costume in the Sixteenth Century.* Boston: Plays, 1972.

Frick, C. *Dressing Renaissance Florence: Families, Fortunes, and Fine Clothing.* Baltimore, Md.: Johns Hopkins University Press, 2002.

Herald, J. *Renaissance Dress in Italy, 1400–1500.* New York: Humanities Press, 1981.

Vecellio, C. *Vecellio's Renaissance Costume Book.* Mineola, N.Y.: Dover Publications, Inc., 1977.

Seventeenth- and Eighteenth-Century Dress

Baumgarten, L. *What Clothes Reveal.* Williamsburg, Va.: The Colonial Williamsburg Collection, 2002.

Buck, A. *Dress in 18th Century England.* New York: Holmes and Meier, 1979.

Cumming, V. *A Visual History of Costume: The 17th Century.* New York: Drama Book, 1984.

Cunnington, C., and P. Cunnington. *Handbook of English Costume in the Eighteenth Century.* London: Faber and Faber, 1957.

———. *Handbook of English Costume in the Seventeenth Century.* London: Faber and Faber, 1972.

Delpierre, M. *Dress in France in the Eighteenth Century.* New Haven, Conn.: Yale University Press, 1998.

De Marly, D. *Louis XIV and Versailles.* New York: Holmes and Meier, 1988.

Hart, A., S. North, and R. Davis. *Fashion in Detail from the 17th and 18th Centuries.* New York: Rizzoli International, 1998.

Kuchta, D. M. "'Graceful, Virile and Useful': The Origins of the Three-Piece Suit." *Dress* 17 (1990): 118.

Reade, B. *Costume of the Western World: The Dominance of Spain.* London: Harrap, 1951.

Ribeiro, A. *A Visual History of Costume: The Eighteenth Century.* New York: Drama Book, 1983.

———. *Dress in Eighteenth Century Europe: 1715–1789.* New York: Holmes and Meier, 1985.

———. *Fashion in the French Revolution.* New York: Holmes and Meier, 1988.

———. *The Art of Dress: Fashion in England and France 1750–1820.* New Haven, Conn.: Yale University Press, 1995.

Roche, D. *The Culture of Clothing: Dress and Fashion in the Ancien Regime.* New York: Cambridge University Press, 1994.

Nineteenth-Century Dress

Bradfield, N. *Costume in Detail.* London: Harrap, 1975.

Buck, A. *Victorian Costume.* Carlton, Bedford, England: R. Bean, 1984.

Cunnington, C., and P. Cunnington. *A Handbook of English Costume in the 19th Century.* London: Faber and Faber, 1970.

Earle, A. M. *Costume of Colonial Times.* Detroit: Gale Research Company, 1974.

Foote, S. "Bloomers." *Dress* 5 (1980): 1.

Foster, V. *A Visual History of Costume: The 19th Century.* New York: Drama Book, 1983.

Hall, L. *Common Threads: A Parade of American Clothing.* Boston: Bulfinch Press, 1992.

Newton, S. M. *Health, Art, and Reason: Dress Reform of the 19th Century.* New York: Schram, 1976.

Severa, J. *Dressed for the Photographer. Ordinary Americans and Fashion 1840–1900.* Kent, Ohio: Kent State University Press, 1995.

Steele, V. *Paris Fashion: A Cultural History.* New York: Berg, 1998.

Veblen, T. *Theory of the Leisure Class.* New York: Viking Press, 1936.

Walkey, C., and V. Foster. *Crinolines and Crimping Irons: Victorian Clothes. How They Were Cleaned and Cared For.* London: P. Owen, 1978.

Phyllis Tortora

EVENING DRESS Simply put, evening dress is the prevailing style prescribed by fashion to be worn in the evening. Though straightforward in its basic definition, there are surprisingly complex expectations related to appropriateness of fashionable dress for evening. Regardless of the era, evening dress is intricately connected to fashions of the day, with specific characteristics that distinguishes it from everyday dress. An evening gown is a special form of dress that amplifies a woman's femininity and often proclaims her desirability. In general, necklines are low, bodices are tightly fitted, arms are bared, and skirts are extravagantly designed. Fabric surfaces vary from reflective to matte, textured to smooth, and soft to rigid. Gowns may be bouffant or hug the body, emphasizing every curve and swell. Regardless of these distinctions, there tends to be an overall emphasis on the woman's body and in many instances on the gown itself. Through the decades, undergarments have played a critical role in reshaping the body into the desired silhouette, from corsets and petticoats of the nineteenth century to control-top panty hose and padded Wonderbras of the twenty-first century.

Historical Overview

Although formal court dress has existed for centuries, there is consensus among dress historians that evening dress materialized as a discrete category in the mid-1820s. It is probably not coincidental that this form of dress emerged at roughly the same time the Romantic Movement in art and literature surfaced as an influence in European and American cultures. Romantics accentuated passion and sentiment, placing a greater emphasis on love rather than on duty. Other cultural factors such as increased fabric production, a thriving textile industry, and an expanding ready-made clothing industry resulted in greater access to resources. By the 1820s, fashion had been fairly democratized. Additionally, Parisian and American fashion magazines experienced a burgeoning popularity among women in the United States and Europe. Dresses of the 1820s were frequently identified in *Godey's Lady's Book* and *Peterson's Magazine* according to explicit activities or time of day. Women viewed fashion plates with captions like morning dress, day dress, walking dress, promenade dress, carriage dress, seaside dress, dinner dress, evening dress, or ball dress. From these labels, it seems the evening dress was born.

1820 to 1899

During the last eighty years of the nineteenth century, women's fashions evolved from an X-shaped silhouette (1820s) to the introduction of the cage crinoline (1850) through the bustle period (1870–1890) and ended with an hourglass silhouette (1890s), and in each era evening dress took its profile from current styles of the day. However, evening dress was discernible by its use of opulent and supple gauze and satin fabrics, the cut of the neckline—typically low or off-the-shoulder—short sleeves, and by the lavishness of surface embellishment. Skirts were especially complex in ornamentation—with layers of swags and puffs and such trim details as artificial flowers, ribbons, rosettes, and lace. During the bustle period and the 1890s, trains were frequently attached to full-length skirts.

1900 to 1945

The early years of the twentieth century included a progression in women's fashions from an S-shaped silhouette to a revival of Empire styles to the flapper style of the 1920s to the bias-cut fashions of the 1930s. With the exception of the latter part of this time-period, evening dress followed the conventions of daytime dress. Necklines tended to be deep and wide, sleeves were short or were mere straps on the shoulder, skirt lengths varied according to fashions and frequently involved complex floating panels, draping, or layers. Fabrics were extravagantly pliant chiffons and satins and luxuriant velvets and taffetas. Pleating, embroidery, lace, beading, fringe, braid, and ruffles decorated the surfaces.

During the 1930s, evening dress made an uncharacteristic split from daytime styles, remaining floor-length while daywear fluctuated in length from mid-calf to ankle. Evening gowns were designed in bias-cut styles and were usually constructed with an open back, with fabric skimming the body to the hips and flaring out and to the floor.

1945 to 2003

The late 1940s through the early 1960s saw the last of a singular identifiable fashion for evening. Dior's New Look—with a rounded shoulder line, a nipped waist, and either an exceptionally full skirt or a pencil-slim skirt—defined the style of the day. Evening dress generally paired strapless bodices with full rather than narrow skirts and it was not unusual for skirts to be floor-length.

By the 1960s, a plethora of options in evening wear emerged. Mini-skirted straight dresses were made from metallic fabrics or brilliantly patterned fabrics, and surfaces may have been trimmed with sequins, beads, or plastic bits. By the late 1960s, evening dresses had returned to floor length. Pantsuits with full-legged trousers and palazzo pants paired with a coordinating top also became viable options. In the mid-1970s, fashionable evening dress was typically long and made from fabrics that were soft, clinging, and often knitted. In the 1980s, the glamour of evening dress contrasted with professional dress for career women and integrated bright and vibrant colors with plenty of glitter, embroidery, sequins, and beading. Lacroix introduced a gown with a short wide puffy skirt, nicknamed *Le Pouf*, which was eagerly copied and made available to the masses. Wide-skirted, short styles called mini-crinolines were also popular. By the late 1980s, evening dresses made from elasticized fabrics hugged the body were short, and were strapless or had tiny shoulder straps. In the early 1990s, basic slip dresses made from soft crepe fabrics became popular. By the mid-1990s, full-skirted, short, strapless evening gowns re-

1913 advertisement for evening dress created by Georges Barbier. This dress, with its low neckline, tight bodice, draped skirt, and eye-catching fabrics, is a typical example of the style of early twentieth century evening wear. © HISTORICAL PICTURE ARCHIVE/CORBIS. REPRODUCED BY PERMISSION.

emerged. Also fashionable were lace or elaborately decorated bustiers and fitted evening gowns and black was the color of choice.

Contemporary Use of Evening Dress

Today, evening dress is limited to such formal or semi-formal events as balls, high school proms, gala fundraisers, pageants, and awards ceremonies. While men's dress tends to be quite typical (usually a standard dark-colored suit or tuxedo), women's gowns vary drastically from demure black garments to revealing objets d'art, as might be seen on celebrities at the Academy Awards. Despite the range of possibilities for contemporary evening

Nineteenth-century dresses. The evening dress on the left is a classic example of the X-shaped silhouette that was prevalent during the 1820s. © Bettmann/Corbis. Reproduced by permission.

dress for women, a gown will undoubtedly include a low-cut neckline, a constricting bodice, bared arms, and lavish skirts. Evening dress draws attention to a woman's body and serves to define her gender, establishing her as an object to be gazed upon by her audience.

See also **Ball Dress; Cocktail Dress.**

BIBLIOGRAPHY

Boucher, François. *20,000 Years of Fashion: The History of Costume and Personal Adornment.* New York: Harry N. Abrams, 1987.

Laver, James. *Costume and Fashion: A Concise History.* London: Thames and Hudson, Inc., 1982.

Lobenthal, Joel. *Radical Rags: Fashions of the Sixties.* New York: Abbeville Press, 1990.

Milbank, Caroline Rennolds. *New York Fashion: The Evolution of American Style.* New York: Harry N. Abrams, 1989.

Mulvey, Kate, and Melissa Richards. *Decades of Beauty: The Changing Image of Women 1890s–1990s.* New York: Octopus, 1998.

Payne, Blanche, Geitel Winakor, and Jane Farrell-Beck. *The History of Costume.* 2nd ed. New York: HarperCollins Publishers, Inc., 1992.

Russell, Douglas A. *Costume History and Style.* Englewood Cliffs, N.J.: Prentice-Hall, 1983.

Steele, Valerie. *Women of Fashion: Twentieth-Century Designers.* New York: Rizzoli International, 1991.

——. *Fifty Years of Fashion.* New Haven, Conn., and London: Yale University Press, 2000.

——. *The Corset.* New Haven, Conn., and London: Yale University Press, 2001.

Tortora, Phyllis, and Keith Eubank. *Survey of Historic Costume.* 3rd ed. New York: Fairchild Publications, 1998.

Watson, Linda. *Vogue: Twentieth Century Fashion.* London: Carlton Books Ltd., 1999.

Jane E. Hegland

EXTREME FASHIONS In any single culture, the definition of what constitutes an extreme fashion may be agreed upon; but extreme fashion, like beauty, is in the eye of the beholder. Particularly between Western and non-Western views there are very different ideas of what is excessive or outlandish, or verging on the unacceptable.

The most common denominator of fashion considered "extreme" is exaggerated broad shoulders and wide skirts, or small waists and small feet. It is possible to make the general statement that in Western Europe the body is usually amplified or reduced by the application of a garment or accessory, while in some African and Asian cultures, the body is permanently altered, and the alteration often augmented by accessories or garments.

As Harold Koda states, "There is no doubt that much of the material has a multitude of meanings and intentions: displays of status, wealth, power, gender, cultivation, ceremony, and group affiliations" (p. 11). An extreme fashion may, and most likely does, perform more than one function simultaneously. Ragnar Johnson points out that any type of body adornment is rarely, if ever, purely utilitarian, and the form that adornment takes depends on a variety of factors, from the resources available in a particular society to the relative social standing and aesthetic tastes of the individual.

Permanent body alteration, which is more common in African and Asian cultures, has traditionally held a negative connotation in the West, with the relatively recent exception of tattooing. The word "mutilation" is often used to describe any lasting modification to the natural body's appearance. To mutilate is defined in Webster's dictionary as: "to deprive . . . of a limb or other essential part, to disfigure, or make imperfect." Since the latter part of the twentieth century, however, publications have elucidated these traditions and have begun to erode the notion that dramatic permanent alterations are forms of deviant or perverse behavior.

The culture of study and criticism of extreme fashion is probably as old as extreme fashion itself. The European clergy were active in their criticism of fashions that distorted or exaggerated the human silhouette. A fifteenth-century source criticized stiffened skirts for their ability to deceive the viewer as to the fullness of a woman's hips, and therefore her suitability as a child-bearer. Travelers recorded non-Western fashions as soon as the Age of Exploration commenced by the late fifteenth century.

Western Fashions

For the Western fashion historian, the corset is perhaps the first example of extreme fashion that comes to mind. Stiffened underbodices were worn by women from the 1400s through the early twentieth century. The corset, or "stays" as they were also called, was condemned when incidents of "tight-lacing," to make the waist appear as small as possible, began to appear. In that form, it was seen as deforming and detrimental to women's health almost from its inception. However, not all societies value a diminished female waistline; in Japan the waist is emphasized but not minimized with the obi—a wide sash of contrasting fabric—wrapped over the kimono, and tied at the back with an elaborate knot of huge proportions.

The exaggerated skirt appeared in the form of the round sixteenth-century farthingale, the wide eighteenth-century pannier, and nineteenth-century hoopskirt or crinoline. All of these skirt shapes in their largest forms could prevent a woman from moving freely. In her classic study of undergarments, Norah Waugh surmises that upper-class women could afford to be more physically burdened by fashion, as they were not required to be active, as in battle. This premise has led to a situation where women's fashion is more often criticized for its extreme manifestations in Western society, but men have participated in extreme displays as well.

The pleated collar known as a ruff is one example of a style worn by both sexes in Western Europe, notably at the court of Elizabeth I. It developed from a simple embellishment of the collar and grew to the cartwheel proportions evident in portraits of the late sixteenth and early seventeenth centuries. The face-framing function of the ruff was appreciated by men and women alike.

Non-Western Fashions

The most commonly remarked upon body modification of Eastern cultures is certainly the practice of Chinese footbinding. Feminist theorist Andrea Dworkin suggests that footbinding and other body "mutilations" (quoted in MacKendrick, p. 3) may contain an element of romanticized tolerance of pain that signals the participant's character. In the case of footbinding, which is only performed on women, it may signal the willingness of women to endure the pain of childbirth and other forms of self-denial, as she is rendered unable to walk on her tiny feet.

While a long, slender neck has been valued in the West, the practice of elongation of the neck reached exaggerated proportions among the Paduang people of Burma. The wearing of metal neck rings, increasing in number over time, forces the collar bones down, giving

Paduang woman. Some women of the Paduang tribe begin wearing a brass coil around their necks at age six, adding a ring or two every year until the age of sixteen. © KEVIN R. MORRIS/CORBIS. REPRODUCED BY PERMISSION.

the illusion of a longer neck, and the rings are worn constantly to further decorate the exaggerated area.

Piercing of the ears has become entirely acceptable in Western society, but in numerous African cultures the pierced hole is manipulated to accept larger and larger accessories. This practice is notable in Ethiopia, where piercing is only the beginning of a long process of stretching either the earlobes or the lower lip in order to receive further decorations, known as labrets.

Twentieth-Century Fashions

The advent and acceptance of cosmetic surgery has brought permanent body modification to mainstream Western society. Generally the results are not meant to be extreme, or even noticeable, but the possibility of dramatic alteration has been explored. Bodybuilding can be pushed to the extreme as well.

Two genres of extreme fashions have developed in the twentieth century: fashions that are deliberately provocative or unattractive, and those that are intellectually challenging. In the 1970s, the punk movement, with Vivienne Westwood as its leading design creator, set out to provoke shock with its mix of overt sexual display and aggression. In the 1990s, the work of the Japanese avant garde was seen as unintelligible in the accepted fashion vocabulary. Rei Kawakubo's 1997 "Lumps" collection exemplifies the intellectual challenge to either renounce or alter traditional ideas of beauty.

"Although one zone may be the focus of a period or culture, any extreme intervention is often accompanied or balanced by other manipulations of the body's proportions," notes Koda (p. 11). No matter how outrageous or extreme a garment or accessory is, it does not function in a vacuum and is stabilized by the other zones of the fashionable body.

See also **Footbinding.**

BIBLIOGRAPHY

Johnson, Ragnar. "The Anthropological Study of Body Decoration as Art: Collective Representations and the Somatization of Affect." *Fashion Theory* 5, no. 4 (2001): 417–434.

Koda, Harold. *Extreme Beauty: The Body Transformed.* New York: Metropolitan Museum of New York, 2001.

MacKendrick, Karmen. "Technoflesh, or 'Didn't That Hurt?'" *Fashion Theory* 2, no. 1 (1998): 3–24.

Robinson, Julian. *The Quest for Human Beauty: An Illustrated History.* London, 1998.

Rubin, Arnold, ed. *Marks of Civilization: Artistic Transformations of the Human Body.* Los Angeles: University of California, 1988.

Rudofsky, Bernard. *The Unfashionable Human Body.* New York: Doubleday and Company, 1971.

Waugh, Nora. *Corsets and Crinolines.* London: B. T. Batsford, Ltd., 1954. Reprint, New York: Theatre Arts Books, 1970, 1991.

Wilcox, Claire. *Radical Fashion.* London: Harry N. Abrams, 2001.

Melinda Watt

EYEGLASSES The term "eyeglasses" is used to indicate lenses that are held up to or worn before the eyes, either as an aid to vision or as a fashion accessory. This term formerly encompassed a wide variety of single and double lenses and kinds of frames; in modern American usage, it is taken to mean spectacles (the term more commonly used in the United Kingdom). Originally a practical vision aid, eyeglasses have at various times in their history served as such fashionable symbols of status, learning, and other desirable qualities that they have even been worn by those with perfect vision. Although their form has been influenced by fashion throughout their history, not until the twentieth century did they truly evolve from a practical necessity into a fashion accessory in their own

right, becoming a vehicle for design, individual expression, and enhancement of personal appearance.

Early History
The earliest double eyeglasses, which appeared in Italy by the late thirteenth century, took the form of two magnifying lenses with the handles riveted together, and needed to be held in front of the eyes or balanced on the nose. The round lenses were ground from beryl, quartz (known as pebble), or glass, with frames of iron, brass, horn, bone, leather, gold, or silver. As eyeglasses were primarily used by monks, scholars, and those both learned enough to be able to read and wealthy enough to own them, they became associated with persons of importance. The demand for eyeglasses increased dramatically with the invention of printing in the fifteenth century, and mass-production methods evolved to produce inexpensive eyeglasses for the new reading public.

Once spectacles were available to everyone by the early seventeenth century, the wealthy and fashionable sought means of distinguishing themselves from the lower classes. Spectacles, therefore, dropped out of fashion, at least for public wear, and would remain so for the next three centuries. Since fashionable people did still need to see clearly, beautifully made hand-held lenses came into favor, in part because they provided an opportunity for elegant gesture and display. Variations included the so-called perspective glass, a small single lens with a handle, worn attached to a cord or ribbon around the neck; elaborate scissors glasses, a pair of lenses held up to the eyes with a long, Y-shaped handle; and small spyglasses (telescopes), which were incorporated into fans and walking sticks, or worn around the neck like charms.

The Eighteenth and Nineteenth Centuries
In the early eighteenth century, spectacle-makers introduced steel spring bridges and frames, and the first spectacles with temples (rigid side pieces). Improvements in the design of eyeglasses continued in the nineteenth century; rimless glasses became commonly available around the middle of the century, and the invention of fine steel wire riding bow and cable temples, with the end curved around the ear, greatly improved the fit and practicality of spectacles in the 1880s. Frames of tortoiseshell, steel, silver, and gold were the most commonly worn, joined later in the century by celluloid, hard rubber, gold-filled, and aluminum frames.

Although spectacles had become quite practical by the nineteenth century, it was still not considered attractive, especially for ladies, to wear them in public. The lorgnette, a pair of folding glasses held up to the eyes by a handle at the side, was introduced around 1780 and remained popular for women through the early twentieth century. A new eyeglass style for men, the monocle, a single lens held in the eye socket and attached to a ribbon or cord, experienced brief periods of popularity in the 1820s, 1880s, and 1910s. The most commonly worn form of eyeglasses from the mid-century on, however, for both sexes, was the pince-nez. These consisted of two small lenses (oval, rectangular, octagonal, or semicircular), attached by a bridge, with a variety of spring and nosepiece arrangements to keep them in place. Lacking temples, they were known at the time simply as eyeglasses (as distinct from spectacles). They were usually worn attached to a cord, chain, or ribbon, which was attached to the vest or dress, looped around the neck, or, for ladies, attached to a hairpin. An 1883 article in the *New York Times* declared that eyeglasses had "virtually driven spectacles off the field," and noted that they were considered so stylish that some young ladies and gentlemen were adopting them simply "because they think it gives them a distingué appearance" (p. 14).

The Twentieth Century

In the early twentieth century, though pince-nez continued to be worn, spectacles finally began to gain acceptance. Large, round spectacles, with heavy frames of real or imitation horn or tortoiseshell (referred to as hornrims) were at first affected by university students, and by the 1910s had become fashionable for both men and women. They were considered to give an air of wisdom, seriousness, and sincerity to the wearer, an association exploited by the silent film comedian Harold Lloyd, whose earnest and sympathetic screen persona owed a great deal to his trademark horn-rim glasses.

By the mid-1920s, horn-rims began to decline in popularity, as women's bobbed hair and close-fitting hats made heavy frames uncomfortable and too conspicuous, and as Harold Lloyd's popularity made men see them as a symbol of comedy. Smaller rimless spectacles and frames of white gold became the style, and through the 1930s more attention was paid to making eyeglasses more becoming, largely by making them as inconspicuous as possible. Glasses were still considered a necessary evil, as famously summed up by Dorothy Parker in her 1927 poem "News Item": "Men seldom make passes / At girls who wear glasses." In an attempt to change this state of affairs, Altina Sanders designed the harlequin frame, with solid dark rims and upswept sides based on the shape of a carnival mask, which was introduced in New York in 1939. These were considered the first glasses designed solely with the idea of improving a woman's appearance, and eyeglasses began to be taken seriously as a fashion accessory.

By the early 1940s, eyeglasses were available in a wide variety of colored plastic frames to harmonize with the wearer's complexion or costumes, and women were advised to have a spectacle wardrobe, with jeweled frames for evening and special frames for beach and sportswear. After World War II, variations on the harlequin shape (later known as cat-eye or cat's-eye) were the dominant style for women, and they were available in many new textures and finishes—opalescent pastels, laminates of glitter, or patterned fabric—and embellished with carving, gilding,

Marilyn Monroe wearing eyeglasses. After World War II, eyeglasses began to be fashionable and fun, and designers began marketing them in various colors, shapes, and styles. © Bettmann/Corbis. Reproduced by permission.

metal studs, and rhinestones. More conservative styles were also available, with solid eyebrow bars and clear plastic or light metal lower rims. With glasses so prominent, chic eyeglass wearers were advised to keep other accessories simple and subdued, advice that fit in well with the short coiffures, off-the-face hats, and button earrings of the 1950s. For men, the heavier metal-and-plastic brow-bar frame and thick black horn-rims such as those worn by the singer Buddy Holly were the most popular styles, and remained so well into the 1960s.

Fashion Eyewear: 1960s to the Early 2000s

In July 1965, just as the use of contact lenses was on the rise, *Vogue* magazine devoted its "Beauty" section to eyeglass fashions, and noted that women with no eye problems were now "writing their own prescriptions: '20/20, but plenty of frame'" (p. 108). Simple, solid-colored frames, whether small and rectangular or large and round or hexagonal, were offered by a newly formed industry group, the Fashion Eyewear Group of America.

By 1965, the first retro fad in eyewear had emerged from the boutique scene in London and New York, and early-twentieth-century-style granny glasses, as worn by such celebrities as John Lennon and the Byrds's Roger McGuinn, continued in vogue for the rest of the decade.

The fashion designers Elsa Schiaparelli and Claire McCardell, among others, had designed some eyewear lines as early as the 1950s, but the first high-profile line of designer eyeglasses was launched in 1969 by Christian Dior. The trend toward designer frames continued in the 1970s, with designers such as Yves Saint Laurent, Diane von Furstenberg, and Halston joining the field. The decade's signature look was oversized frames with rounded corners, in semitransparent pastels or faux tortoiseshell, with tinted or gradient lenses in colors to coordinate with the wearer's eye makeup. Bolder styles, often with shiny gold accents and curved or wavy temples, were balanced by the high-volume, blow-dried hairstyles of the time, and were well-suited to the glitz of disco fashions.

In the 1980s, many more designer frames were available, often with visible designer logos, in new eyewear boutiques carrying thousands of styles for men, women, and children. The same style trends continued, but there were also harder-edged styles, in brighter, solid colors, in response to the new boxy silhouette and large, bold costume jewelry. Some retro styles from the 1940s and 1950s were produced to complement the trendy preppy and nerd looks. Toward the end of decade, designers such as Ralph Lauren, Giorgio Armani, and Calvin Klein started a move toward smaller frames, with cleaner, refined styling. These were updated versions of the serious horn-rims of the 1910s and 1920s, and celebrities such as Richard Gere soon adopted the new look, inspiring

even contact-lens wearers and those with 20/20 vision to invest in new frames.

In the late 1980s, eyeglasses for sports, or performance eyewear, began to be reconsidered as an industrial design problem, and new materials such as titanium were employed to create stronger, lighter frames. In the 1990s, the high-tech, minimalist aesthetic carried over into fashion eyeglasses, and the quest for refinement continues to be an important theme in eyeglass design. At the same time, in synch with the decade's retro fashions, designers began to look more carefully at the past, and frame styles from every decade of the twentieth century are available in the twenty-first, either updated or faithfully reproduced, from a multitude of designer collections. Even deliberately unbecoming glasses have been embraced as nerd chic, a symbol of hipness and sophistication, and baby boomers have transformed humble drugstore reading glasses into a fun fashion accessory.

See also **Sunglasses.**

BIBLIOGRAPHY

Acerenza, Franca. *Eyewear Gli Occhiali.* San Francisco: Chronicle Books, 1997.

"All About Eye-Glasses." *New York Times* (6 May 1883): p. 14. Excellent contemporary account of nineteenth-century eyewear fashions.

Corson, Richard. *Fashions in Eyeglasses.* London: Peter Owen, 1967. Excellent and readable survey.

Schiffer, Nancy N. *Eyeglass Retrospective: Where Fashion Meets Science.* Atglen, Pa.: Schiffer Publishing, 2000. Short on documentation, but many examples are shown.

Susan Ward